Applied C: An Introduction and More

Alice E. Fischer
University of New Haven

David W. Eggert
University of New Haven

Stephen M. Ross
University of New Haven

Boston   Burr Ridge, IL   Dubuque, IA   Madison, WI   New York   San Francisco   St. Louis
Bangkok   Bogotá   Caracas   Lisbon   London   Madrid
Mexico City   Milan   New Delhi   Seoul   Singapore   Sydney   Taipei   Toronto

McGraw-Hill Higher Education

A Division of The **McGraw-Hill** *Companies*

APPLIED C: AN INTRODUCTION AND MORE
Published by McGraw-Hill, an imprint of The McGraw-Hill Companies, Inc. 1221 Avenue of the Americas, New York, NY 10020. Copyright ©2001 by The McGraw-Hill Companies, Inc. All rights reserved. No part of this publication may be reproduced or distributed in any form or by any means, or stored in a database or retrieval system, without the prior written consent of The McGraw-Hill Companies, Inc., including, but not limited to, in any network or other electronic storage or transmission, or broadcast for distance learning. Some ancillaries, including electronic and print components, may not be available to customers outside the United States.

This book is printed on acid-free paper.

1 2 3 4 5 6 7 8 9 0 FGR/FGR 0 9 8 7 6 5 4 3 2 1 0 9

ISBN 0-07-021748-3

Vice president/Editor-in-chief: *Kevin T. Kane*
Publisher: *Thomas Casson*
Executive editor: *Elizabeth A. Jones*
Developmental editor: *Emily J. Gray*
Senior marketing manager: *John T. Wannemacher*
Project manager: *Paula M. Krauza*
Production supervisor: *Michael McCormick*
Freelance design coordinator: *Pam Verros*
Cover photograph: *©Photodisc*
Compositor: *Techsetters, Inc.*
Typeface: *10.5/12 Times Roman*
Printer: *Quebecor Printing Book Group/Fairfield*

Library of Congress Cataloging-in-Publication Data

Fischer, Alice E., 1942–
    Applied C: An Introduction and More / Alice E. Fischer, David W. Eggert, Stephen M. Ross.
        p.   cm. – (McGraw-Hill series in computer science)
    ISBN 0-07-021748-3 (softcover: alk. paper)
    1. C (Computer program language) I. Eggert, David W., 1964– II. Ross, Stephen M. (Stephen Mark), 1945–
    III. Title. IV. Series.
    QA76.73.C15 F56 2001
    005.13′3–dc21

                                                                          00-020888

http://www.mhhe.com

We dedicate this massive effort to the people who really made it possible

Dr. Bertram Ross
mathematician, professor and author of several books and many journal articles
who died in 1993

Dr. Michael J. Fischer
professor, husband, helper, advisor, L^AT_EX expert, and system administrator

Clarence and Evelyn Eggert
who raised their son to aim for the best and never give up
(unless, of course, things really are too hard)

Judi, Noel and Kate McDermott
who introduced David to the richness of life
(even if he sometimes wishes he were a little less rich)

Contents

I INTRODUCTION

1 Computers and Systems   2

1.1 The Physical Computer   2
1.2 The Operating System   10
1.3 Languages   12
1.4 What You Should Remember   16
1.5 Exercises   17

2 Programs and Programming   20

2.1 What Is a Program?   20
2.2 Problem Specification and Analysis   23
2.3 The Development Environment   27
2.4 Program Construction   29
2.5 Program Execution and Testing   34
2.6 What You Should Remember   37
2.7 Exercises   38

3 Fundamental Concepts   42

3.1 Parts of a Program   42
3.2 The Simplest Program   44
3.3 Variables, Input, Output, and Sequencing   46
3.4 Simple Calculations   52
3.5 The Flow of Control   57

3.6   Asking Questions: Conditional Statements   60
3.7   Loops and Repetition   70
3.8   An Application   75
3.9   What You Should Remember   80
3.10 Exercises   84

II *COMPUTATION*

4 Objects, Types, and Expressions   94

4.1   Variables, Constants, and Literals   94
4.2   Expressions and Parse Trees   101
4.3   Arithmetic, Assignment, and Combination Operators   107
4.4   Increment and Decrement Operators   108
4.5   Relational Operators   114
4.6   Logic Operators   115
4.7   An Example: A Voltage Ramp   120
4.8   Case Study: Using a Parse Tree to Debug   123
4.9   What You Should Remember   128
4.10 Exercises   131

5 Using Functions and Libraries   138

5.1   Libraries   139
5.2   Using Libraries   141
5.3   Function Types   147
5.4   User-Defined Functions   148
5.5   Math Library Application: Roots of a Quadratic Equation 155
5.6   What You Should Remember   159
5.7   Exercises   162

6 More Repetition and Decision   170

6.1   New Loops   171
6.2   Applications of Loops   179
6.3   The `switch` Statement   196
6.4   Counted Loop Application: Integration by Simpson's Rule 202
6.5   Sentinel Loop Application: Interpolation (Optional Topic) 209
6.6   What You Should Remember   216
6.7   Exercises   220

III BASIC DATA TYPES

7 Using Numeric Types 228

7.1 Integer Types 228
7.2 Floating-Point Types in C 231
7.3 Reading and Writing Numbers 234
7.4 Integer Operations 240
7.5 Mixing Types in Computations (Advanced Topic) 246
7.6 Pseudo-Random Numbers 260
7.7 Application: A Guessing Game 264
7.8 What You Should Remember 269
7.9 Exercises 274

8 The Trouble with Numbers 282

8.1 Floating-Point Comparisons 282
8.2 Calculation Errors (Advanced Topic) 288
8.3 Optional Application: Finding the Real Roots of an Equation 294
8.4 What You Should Remember 302
8.5 Exercises 304

9 Program Design 312

9.1 Modular Programs 312
9.2 Communication Between Functions 316
9.3 Declaration-Call Correspondence 321
9.4 Data Modularity 331
9.5 Function Call Graphs 339
9.6 Program Design and Construction 340
9.7 What You Should Remember 353
9.8 Exercises 356

10 An Introduction to Arrays 366

10.1 Arrays 366
10.2 Using Arrays 374
10.3 Parallel Arrays 378
10.4 Array Arguments and Parameters 382
10.5 What You Should Remember 398
10.6 Exercises 400

11 **Character Data and Enumerations**   410

11.1   Representation of Characters   410
11.2   Input and Output with Characters   413
11.3   Operations on Characters (Advanced Topic)   419
11.4   Character Application: An Improved Processing Loop   423
11.5   Enumerated Types   425
11.6   What You Should Remember   432
11.7   Exercises   435

12 **An Introduction to Pointers**   442

12.1   A First Look at Pointers   442
12.2   Call by Address   448
12.3   Application: The Bisection Method (Advanced Topic)   459
12.4   What You Should Remember   471
12.5   Exercises   474

IV   *STRUCTURED DATA TYPES*

13 **Strings**   486

13.1   String Representation   486
13.2   String I/O   493
13.3   The String Library   501
13.4   Arrays of Strings   508
13.5   String Processing Applications (Optional Topic)   517
13.6   Application: A Gas Pressure Table   530
13.7   What You Should Remember   535
13.8   Exercises   539

14 **Structures Types**   552

14.1   Declarations   552
14.2   Operations on Structures   555
14.3   Application: Points in a Rectangle   565
14.4   Application: The Monte Carlo Method (Optional Topic)   578
14.5   What You Should Remember   585
14.6   Exercises   588

15 **Streams and Files**   598

15.1   Streams and Buffers   599
15.2   Programmer-Defined Streams   604

15.3   Stream Output   607
15.4   Stream Input   612
15.5   Errors and Exceptions   617
15.6   File Application: Random Selection Without Replacement   628
15.7   Application: Measuring Torque (Optional Topic)   638
15.8   What You Should Remember   643
15.9   Exercises   647

16 Simple Array Algorithms   656

16.1   Searching an Array Data Structure   656
16.2   Application: Screening out Faulty Data (Optional Topic)   663
16.3   Sorting by Selection   677
16.4   What You Should Remember   687
16.5   Exercises   691

17 Two-Dimensional Arrays   698

17.1   Nested Loops: Printing a Table   698
17.2   Introduction to Two-Dimensional Arrays   701
17.3   Application: Transformation of 2D Point Coordinates   711
17.4   Application: Image Processing   719
17.5   What You Should Remember   728
17.6   Exercises   730

18 Calculating with Bits   742

18.1   Unsigned Numbers and Hexadecimal Notation   743
18.2   Bitwise Operators   748
18.3   Application: Simple Encryption and Decryption   755
18.4   Bitfield Types   759
18.5   What You Should Remember   771
18.6   Exercises   774

V ADVANCED TECHNIQUES

19 Dynamic Arrays   786

19.1   Dynamic Memory Allocation   786
19.2   Using Dynamic Arrays: A Simulation   799
19.3   Dynamic Matrix: An Array of Pointers (Advanced Topic)   809
19.4   What You Should Remember   823
19.5   Exercises   827

20   Working with Pointers   834

20.1   Pointers—Old and New Ideas   834
20.2   Application: A Menu of Pointers to Functions (Advanced Topic)   842
20.3   Using Pointers with Arrays   846
20.4   Insertion Sort   852
20.5   What You Should Remember   859
20.6   Exercises   864

21   Recursion   874

21.1   Storage Classes   874
21.2   The Run-Time Stack (Advanced Topic)   878
21.3   Iteration and Recursion   881
21.4   A Simple Example of Recursion   883
21.5   A More Complex Example: Binary Search   886
21.6   Quicksort   896
21.7   What You Should Remember   908
21.8   Exercises   911

22   Making Programs General   918

22.1   Command-Line Arguments   918
22.2   Functions as Parameters   927
22.3   What You Should Remember   934
22.4   Exercises   937

23   Modular Organization   944

23.1   Constructing a Modular Program   944
23.2   Modular Application: Finding the Roots of an Equation   954
23.3   What You Should Remember   977
23.4   Exercises   979

APPENDIXES

A   The ASCII Code   984

B   The Precedence of Operators in C   986

C   Keywords   988

D Advanced Aspects of C Operators

D.1 Assignment Combination Operators   990
D.2 More on Lazy Evaluation and Skipping   992
D.3 The Conditional Operator   996
D.4 The Comma Operator   998
D.5 Summary   998

E Number Representation and Conversion

E.1 Number Systems and Number Representation   1000
E.2 Signed and Unsigned Integers   1001
E.3 Representation of Real Numbers   1002
E.4 Base Conversion   1004
E.5 Self-Test Exercises   1006

F The tools Library

F.1 Using the tools Library in a Program   1008
F.2 Portability Command   1013
F.3 Functions Declared in tools.h and Defined in tools.c 1014
F.4 Process and Stream Management   1015
F.5 Time and Date Functions   1020
F.6 Numeric Functions   1022
F.7 Strings and Menus   1023

G The Standard C Environment

G.1 Built-in Facilities   1026
G.2 Standard Files of Constants   1027
G.3 The Standard Libraries and main()   1028
G.4 Libraries Not Explored   1039

H Glossary   1042

I Answers to Self-Test Exercises   1058

Index   1096

Preface

How it all began.   This book arose from our need to teach C programming to beginners at the University of New Haven, and from what we perceived as the lack of any appropriate elementary text to do this. Applied C is the brainchild of Stephen Ross and Alice Fischer, the two original authors, who are professors of mechanical engineering and computer science, respectively. David Eggert, an assistant professor of computer science, joined them midway through the project.

The blending of our talents has produced a book that is technically correct (well, nobody is perfect) and comprehensive (due mostly to David's thoroughness). It contains explanations that can be understood by a beginner (Alice has taught a lot of new programmers), and at the same time reflects the soul of an engineer (Steve's that is), with its emphasis on precise specification, careful testing, complete examples, highly varied applications, diagrams and visual aids of all sorts.

This text takes a "hands-on" approach: students are encouraged to learn from example and to begin programming immediately in a subset of the language. Simple programming skills are presented both by exposition and through many complete examples from the fields of mathematics, science and engineering. Familiarity with the core of the C language is developed through reading and writing basic programs. Following this, each topic is revisited and information is presented in depth. This approach leads to greater understanding.

Why C and not C++?   Many universities are now teaching their first programming courses in C++, while we focus on C. There are many reasons why we believe C is more appropriate than C++ for an introduction to programming. One of these is evident in the names of the languages. C++ is C plus constructs for handling large-scale complexity. One problem beginning students have is how to handle the wealth of information that is being thrown at them. While it is true that C++ has several advantages over C, many of these do not become evident until a program becomes larger and more complex. Then the object-oriented paradigm functions as a powerful organizational tool.

Ultimately, most computer science and engineering students need to be fluent in both C and C++. It therefore seems more natural to teach them C first, and build upon this knowledge when introducing C++. By then, they will have a better foundation for understanding abstract data types. And yet, even though we are teaching in C, the programming style developed in the later chapters leads gradually but consistently into the object-oriented paradigm.

In addition to these larger issues, there are smaller advantages of beginning in C. While it is true that some of the I/O in C++ (e.g., integers) is simpler than in C, other data types such as strings and floating-point values can actually be formatted more easily in C. Another important factor for beginners is the set of error and warning messages provided by a compiler during program development. While most of today's systems compile both C and C++ code, the quality of the error comments is usually worse for C++. They are often vague or just not understandable without greater knowledge. (The error comments in C are not perfect, either, but they are simpler.)

Should you use this book?

Applied C is intended as an introduction to C programming for students who have not previously programmed. The text is also eminently suitable for those already familiar with other programming languages such as FORTRAN, Pascal, and Java. It has been in use at the University of New Haven since 1995 with students from the engineering, math and computer science fields, and the occasional student from other scientific disciplines.

While it is not necessary for a student to be familiar with computers before using this book, he or she should have a mind-set that is receptive to the programming process. (We have found that students who have strong math skills do best.) Many parallels can be drawn between the process of solving a word problem in a math text and devising a computer program to solve a problem. Since many of the examples used are drawn from the engineering and mathematics fields, having a background which includes algebra, geometry and trigonometry can be very helpful. Of course, instructors can choose to supplement this material with other less sophisticated examples for audiences with lesser math backgrounds.

Scope and a roadmap.

The text is quite comprehensive and contains enough material for two quarters of instruction. Topics in Parts 1 through 3 can be covered in one quarter or a trimester and are the most important for students entering technical careers. A semester course can also cover most of Part 4. A second quarter or trimester course would allow one to cover Parts 4 and 5 entirely. The nature of these parts is as follows.

- *Part 1: Introduction.*

  Chapters 1 and 2 cover computers, algorithms, program specifications, test plans, and the programming process. The first chapter on computers can be omitted easily if the instructor is pressed for time or the students already have this background. Chapter 3 is a progressive series of annotated programs that introduces variables, the types `double` and `int`, simple input and output, arithmetic, the `if...else` conditional statement and the `while` loop. Emphasis is on learning by doing. By the end of Chapter 3, the student should be able to write a simple program that takes interactive input, validates it, performs a computation, and produces output.

- *Part 2: Computation.*

   The next three chapters cover declarations, expressions, functions of zero and one parameter, using libraries, and the remaining control statements (`for`, `do...while`, `switch`, `break`, and `continue`). Emphasis is on safe programming practices and generating modular code. In Chapter 5, we introduce the `tools` library, a small package of functions we have found useful when teaching this material. It serves as a vehicle for demonstrating many different aspects of programming throughout the text. By the end of Chapter 6, the student should be able to write a program specification and a test plan, as well as write and debug a program that includes calls on library and programmer-defined functions.

- *Part 3: Basic Data Types.*

   Chapters 7, 8, and 11 complete the coverage of primitive data types in C. Types `float`, `short int`, `long int`, and `char` are introduced, along with their I/O formats, specialized operators, library functions, and examples of appropriate usage. Several important issues are discussed, including numeric overflow, approximate representation of real values, and type conversions.

   Chapter 9 extends the coverage of functions to include an arbitrary number of parameters of any combination of types. It introduces a method for modular program development that is designed to minimize the terror a student feels when confronted by a blank page and a "story problem". Stages of analysis are prescribed, starting with an informal specification and testing plan. Then the student is asked to write down the familiar and routine parts of a program, deferring parts that seem complicated at first. Gradually attention is focused on each deferred section, which is always simpler when considered in isolation. Important issues discussed include function call charts, stub testing, scope and lifetime of variables, the proper use of parameters and local declarations and the bad effects of global variables.

   Chapters 10 and 12 introduce the use of arrays, subscripts, and pointers. Issues include array parameters, simple array processing techniques, parallel arrays, walking on memory, and call-by-address parameters. These chapters complete the coverage of the fundamental aspects of the C language. At the end of this material, the student should be able to program fluently in a restricted subset of the language.

- *Part 4: Structured Data Types.*

   Chapters 13 through 18 cover simple data structures and algorithms that normally are of general interest and commonly covered at the end of a one-semester course: namely, files, strings, structures, multi-dimensional arrays and bit vectors. We stop short of introducing more complex data structures that typically are collections of various structures via pointers (i.e., linked lists, trees and graphs). Instead, several additional topics are presented that are rarely given good textbook coverage: ragged arrays, arrays of structures, bit-level computation, hardware interfacing, streams, and I/O exception handling. These topics provide a rich resource for a second quarter course or later self-study. By the end of this part, students will be transitioning from writing simple one page programs to those requiring the use of multiple functions to solve a problem properly.

- *Part 5: Advanced Techniques.*

  Chapters 19 through 23 develop more sophisticated topics and provide a transition to the higher level of skill and knowledge needed by a student who will continue in a computer science major. They present and carefully illustrate several standard algorithms for searching, sorting, finding roots of equations, and simulation.

  The topics and techniques presented in this section include some that are rarely covered in an accessible manner by textbooks. This includes dynamic memory allocation, the use of pointers to process arrays, recursion, command-line arguments, the use of generic library functions like `qsort()`, and the construction and linking of multi-module programs. By the end of the text, students should be able to write and debug a moderately long modular program and have the background and skills needed to begin a typical data structures course.

- *Appendices: Useful information.*

  The appendices include standard tables (ASCII, precedence, C keywords), a glossary, and a summary listing of the functions, data types, and constants found in the standard C libraries. We also describe the complete contents of a local library, `tools`, that accompanies this text. Two more appendices give information that we deem to be beyond the scope of the main line of this text, but necessary for completeness; these cover advanced aspects of some C operators and number representation and base conversion. Lastly, Appendix I gives the answers to the Self-Test exercises.

The spiral approach to teaching.   Unlike many programming books, this text is not organized as a reference manual. In the spirit of the newer methods of teaching engineering and science, several topics are introduced briefly, used in a restricted manner, and then considered in detail later. For example, arrays are introduced in Chapter 10 and used in simple ways. More details, simple sorting and searching algorithms and two-dimensional arrays are later explained in Chapters 16 and 17. Finally, dynamic array allocation and the use of pointers in array processing are presented in Chapters 19 and 20. This "as needed", or "just in time" approach has many advantages:

- It motivates the student, because programs of more interest can be shown in the early chapters of the book.

- It permits an early introduction of functions and arrays, but allows for a gradual development of their complexity in the programming examples and exercises.
- It eases the transition to the detailed explanations that occur in later chapters.
- It has an inductive quality that is very appropriate for the attitudes and skills needed by engineers and scientists: partial knowledge precedes full understanding, with much experimentation in between.
- The order in which major topics are presented has been tested in class and adjusted several times. The resulting order given here works; students are ready for each topic when it comes, and professors are able to work within the bounds of the gradually increasing subset of C.

In many of the early chapters, certain sections are labelled with the terms "Advanced" or "Optional". Those labelled as "Advanced" go into more depth on a topic than may really be necessary for basic understanding. However, the material is relevant to some later section of the book, and it would be best if the topic was covered prior to reaching that point. Similar detailed material has been included in certain appendices or may be found in footnotes. Those topics labelled as "Optional" are just that. They contain information which is relevant and should one day be learned by the student. Yet, these sections can be skipped without losing continuity in the text's material.

Teaching design to the beginner.   Modular design is stressed from the beginning, starting with the need for a complete and accurate program specification, and the importance of a test plan and careful program verification. The design process is dealt with at three levels. In Chapter 5 we focus on using libraries and writing simple functions. Chapter 9 extends and expands the basic principles of writing functions and deals with top-down design. Finally, Chapter 23 introduces multi-module applications and the facilities provided by the C language, as well as typical operating systems, to support them. In the intervening chapters, many examples of top-down design are presented.

One of the authors teaches advanced courses in C++ and object-oriented design. All of the material presented here is developed with the assumption that students will eventually be programming in an object-oriented language. The program design techniques that are taught here will carry over gracefully into the object-oriented environment. Stress is put on making everything highly modular and designing a program so that its functions correspond to the data structures that they process. In later chapters, the concepts of encapsulation, privacy, objects with state, and reusable code are introduced and integrated into every application. As mentioned earlier, we believe this is a more effective approach to teaching both C and C++ than beginning with the more complex language.

A host of useful features.   Topics are generally introduced by first providing some background and explaining the importance of the topic. We hope this will motivate the reader and help maintain interest. This is followed by a careful exposition of the principles involved, written in accessible language and illustrated liberally with diagrams, graphs, and short programs that exercise the principles and demonstrate proper syntax. In addition, each chapter has a full complement of pedagogic aids:

- Each major topic is illustrated by a complete program, with output and annotations that show the relevance of the program to the material at hand. These annotations refer to sections of the code which have been boxed and highlighted to further emphasize the use of the current topics.
- An application program or a case study is given that uses the techniques presented in the current chapter. Each is developed using the modular design steps that have been discussed in the text.
- A summary section at the end of each chapter gives perspective on the most important concepts introduced. It can be a valuable study guide for the student or an aid to lecture preparation for the instructor.
- Programming style hints and a list of frequent errors suggest a series of Do's and Don'ts for the developing programmer.
- A vocabulary list is also included in each chapter-end summary.
- A variety of self-test exercises are provided, with solutions that can be found in Appendix I. Similar exercises, without solutions, are given under the heading "Using Pencil and Paper". These exercises serve to test how well the student understands the theory of the material just presented.
- In addition, each chapter has a set of programming exercises that are highly varied in difficulty and complexity. Some problems present entirely new situations, while others ask the student to adapt or extend an existing program so that it uses a new technique.
- All code described or shown in the text is provided in electronic form on the web site www.mhhe.com//engcs//. Solutions to the Paper and Pencil exercises, as well as the programming problems, are available in electronic form for instructors.
- Lastly, the web site contains a set of hints for the instructor on how to present the material in each chapter.

Teaching responsible programming.   A computer is a powerful tool. When we teach students how to use such a tool, we have an obligation to teach them responsible use of it and to help them develop a professional attitude toward programming. This philosophy is integrated into every part of this book as follows:

- Part 1 stresses the importance of writing careful specifications before any coding begins, and doing adequate testing during the debugging process.

- Part 2 preaches and models an avoidance of techniques and language features that are prone to error. It demonstrates simple, safe, and effective methods that can be used instead. Fancier is not always better.
- Part 3 stresses that we must understand the limitations of computers and develop mechanisms to counteract them.
- Part 4 presents safe paradigms for using pointers and files, which can often be difficult topics for new programmers.
- Part 5 shows how to encapsulate a data type and provides the necessary background for participation in a team project.

Throughout, we are careful to avoid giving wrong information, or even misleading information in the guise of simplification. Similarly, we avoid solving problems by the use of poor designs or inappropriate techniques. Where more than one viable alternative exists, we note this and explain why the chosen method was presented. At all times, we attempt to show only code that the student should emulate. Footnotes and forward references are used to inform the reader when a topic has aspects which are not being covered for the time being, or maybe not at all.

Many Thanks.   We would first like to thank the many anonymous and not so anonymous reviewers whose careful critiques have helped to shape the material in this text:

Jeanne Douglas, University of Vermont
Glynis Hamel, Worcester Polytechnic Institute
Abhijit Pandya, Florida Atlantic University
Alexander Pelin, Florida International University
James Gips, Boston College.

We send our appreciation to the staff at McGraw-Hill, including the multiple project managers, who helped make this book a reality, when at times it seemed like it would never be finished.

Dr. Michael J. Fischer was instrumental in bringing this effort to completion. The authors have relied on him for system support, advice, and technical assistance of all sorts. In several instances, he designed and constructed application examples, for which the authors are grateful. We thank him, along with Trina Woo, Judi McDermott-Eggert, Noel, and Kate for their patience in putting up with missed meals and long work hours.

Similarly, we thank and applaud the people at Techsetters Inc. for handling an extremely difficult typesetting job with judgement and skill far beyond our expectations.

PART

I

Introduction

CHAPTER

1

Computers and Systems

1.1   The Physical Computer

It is not necessary to understand how a computer works in order to use one—but it helps. An elementary understanding of computer architecture helps demystify the nature and rules of programming languages and enables one to use these languages more wisely. It is essential for anyone who needs to attach devices to a computer or buy one wisely. The architecture of modern computers varies greatly from type to type, and new developments happen every year. Therefore, it is impossible to describe how all computers work. The following discussion is intended to give a general idea of the elements common or universal to personal computers and workstations today.

The main logical parts of a computer, diagrammed in Figure 1.1, can be roughly compared to parts of a human body:

- The **CPU** (central processing unit) is the brain of the computer.
- The computer's **RAM** (random access memory) chips are its memory.
- The **bus** is the nervous system; it carries information between the CPU and everything else in the computer.
- The **input** devices (e.g., keyboard) are the computer's senses.
- The **output** devices (e.g., monitor) are the computer's effectors (hands, voice).

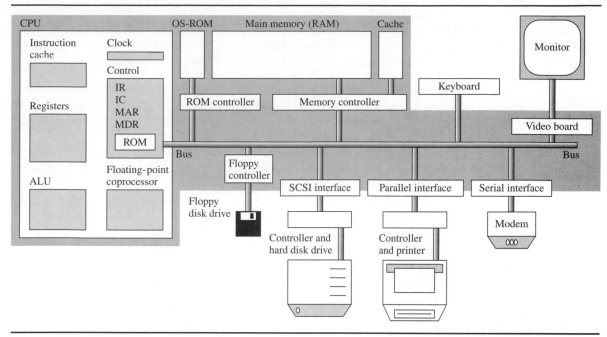

Figure 1.1.   Basic architecture of a modern computer.

1.1.1 The Processor

In a typical modern computer, the central processing unit (CPU) is the main element on the processor chip. The CPU controls and coordinates the whole machine. It contains a set of **registers**:

- The instruction register (IR) holds the current machine instruction.
- The instruction counter (IC) holds the address of the next machine instruction.
- The memory data register (MDR) holds the data currently in use.
- The memory address register (MAR) holds the address from which the data came.

One of its components is the **clock**, which ticks at a fixed rate and controls the fundamental speed at which all of the computer's operations work. The clock rate on a microprocessor chip is set as fast as is (conservatively) possible without causing processing errors. This setting is the megahertz (MHz) rating published by the manufacturer.

The ALU.   The *arithmetic and logic unit* (ALU) is the part of the processor containing the many circuits that actually perform computations. Typically, an ALU includes instructions for addition, negation, and multiplication of integers; comparison; logical operations; and other actions. Many computers also have a

floating-point coprocessor, for handling arithmetic operations on real (floating-point) numbers. Floating-point instructions are important for many scientific applications to achieve adequate accuracy at an acceptable speed. Taken together, this set of instructions forms the **machine language** for that particular processor.

Control ROM and the instruction cycle.   A small read-only memory inside the control unit contains instructions (called *microcode*) that control all parts of the CPU and define the actions of the instruction cycle, the ALU, and the instruction cache (discussed next).

To use a computer, we write a **program**, which is a series of instructions in some computer language. Before the program can be used or run, those instructions must be translated into machine language and the machine-language program must be loaded into the computer's main memory. Then, one at a time, the program's instructions are brought into the processor, decoded, and executed. A processor executes the program instructions in sequence until it comes to a "jump" instruction, which causes it to start executing the instructions in another part of the program. A typical instruction brings data into one of the registers, sends data out to the memory or to an output device, or executes some computation on the data in the registers.

1.1.2 The Memory

The memory of a computer consists of a very large number of storage locations called **bits**, which is short for "binary digits." Each bit can be turned either off (to store a 0) or on (to store a 1). All memory in a computer is made out of bits or groups of bits, and all computation is done on groups of bits. The bits in memory are organized into a series of locations, each with an address. In personal computers, each addressable location is eight bits long, called a **byte**. In larger computers and older computers, the smallest addressable unit often is larger than this; in a few machines, it is smaller. Figure 1.2 is a diagram of main memory, depicted as a sequence of boxes with addresses.

A byte could contain data of various types. It could contain one character, such as *'A'*, or a small number. The range of numbers that can be stored in one byte is from 0 to 255 or from -128 to $+127$, which is not large enough for most purposes. For this reason, bytes generally are grouped into longer units. Two bytes are long enough to contain any integer between 0 and 65,536, while four bytes can hold an integer as large as 2 billion.[1]

Traditionally, a **word** is the unit of data that can pass across the bus to or from main memory at one time.[2] Small computers usually have two-byte words; workstations and larger computers have words that are four bytes or longer.

---

[1] Number representation is covered in Chapters 7, 8, and 18.

[2] In machines where the bus transports only one byte, *word* means two bytes and *long word* means four bytes.

- Memory is a very long series of bytes; we show only the first few here.
- Every byte has an address (only the even addresses are shown here).
- In this picture, even-address bytes are white; odd-address bytes are gray.
- We diagram the addresses outside the boxes because they are part of the hardware. They are *not* stored in memory.
- The addresses in the diagram begin with the address 0 and continue through 43.

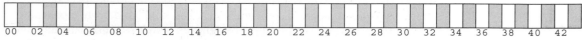

This amount of memory could store

- 44 characters (one byte each), or
- 22 short integers (two bytes each), or
- 11 long integers or single precision floating-point numbers (four bytes each).

Figure 1.2.   Main memory in a byte-addressable machine.

A computer might have several different types of **memory** to achieve different balances among capacity, cost, speed, and convenience. The major types are cache memory, main memory, secondary memory, and auxiliary memory. These are diagrammed in Figure 1.3 and discussed next.

Cache memory.   The fastest and most expensive kind of memory is a **cache**. Some machines have small caches to speed up access to frequently used data that are stored in the main memory. The first time an item is used, it is loaded into the cache. If it is used again soon, it is retrieved from the cache rather than from the main memory, reducing the access time. Cache memories are small because they are very expensive. Their small capacity limits the extent to which they can improve performance.

Main memory.   The computer's main memory (sometimes called *RAM*, for random access memory) is where the active program (or programs) is kept with

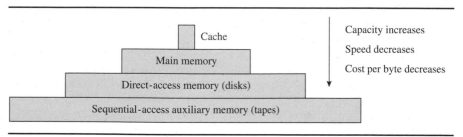

Figure 1.3.   The memory hierarchy.

its data. Sometimes the operating system, which controls the computer,[3] also is kept in RAM; otherwise it is in read-only memory.

OS-ROM memory.   **ROM** stands for "read-only memory." An operating system (OS) in ROM is a real convenience for the user for two reasons. First, it is installed in the computer and need not be brought in from a disk. This saves time when the system is turned on. Second, ROM is read-only memory, which means its contents can be read but not changed, either accidentally or on purpose. A partly debugged program sometimes can "run wild" and try to store things in memory locations allocated to some other process that is simultaneously loaded into the computer. With the operating system in ROM, most of the system is protected from this kind of random modification. The only remaining vulnerable part of the system is the area near memory address 0, which is called **low memory** and contains the locations used to communicate between the operating system and the input/output devices.

The disadvantage of using ROM for an operating system is that it is difficult and expensive to improve the system or correct errors in it. When a company wishes to release a new version of a ROM operating system, the code must be recorded on a set of ROM chips. The computer owner must buy a set, remove the old ROM chips, and install the new ones.

Direct-access memory.   Direct-access memory, also called *secondary memory*, is needed because even the largest main memory cannot store all the information we need. Data files and software packages are kept in secondary memory when not in use.[4]

A **CD-ROM** (compact disk, read-only memory) is an optical disk storage device, like an audio disc except that it is used to store various types of data, not just music data. A CD-ROM reader contains a laser that reads the minute marks etched into the surface of the disk. Once a CD-ROM has been used to record data, it cannot be reused to record different data. Large collections of data of interest to many people are recorded and distributed on CD-ROMs.

Hard disks and diskettes are the most common direct-access memory devices today. Through the years, the physical size of these devices has decreased steadily, and the amount of information they can hold has greatly increased. As technology has progressed, we have been able to store the bits closer and closer together, enabling us to simultaneously decrease size and increase capacity.

---

[3] Section 1.2 covers operating systems.

[4] As memory capacities have expanded, our desire to store information has kept pace, so that this statement is as true today as it was when direct-access memories were the size of today's main memories.

Auxiliary memory.   Today's disks can store large volumes of information: 2 gigabytes (2 billion bytes) now is a common disk capacity. However, most businesses and individuals find that 2 billion bytes of secondary memory is not enough to meet all of their needs. Larger, cheaper memory devices are needed to store backup (duplicate) copies of the files on the hard disk and infrequently used files. Magnetic tapes and tape drives meet this need for auxiliary storage. A tape has very large capacity but must be read or written sequentially. This makes retrieving a file from a tape that contains hundreds of files or recording a new file on the end of the tape very slow and inconvenient.

1.1.3   Input and Output Devices

Input and output devices permit communication between human beings and the CPU. The most common input devices include keyboards, mice, and track balls. Typically, output is displayed either on a video screen or via a printer. Since humans and the computer speak different languages, some translation is needed. Using a mouse allows the human to point or click at a portion of the screen to convey a screen position and an intent to the computer. Interactions with a keyboard, the screen, or a printer take place using the English language and some hardware-level translation.

In a simple view of the computer world, hitting the Z key on a keyboard causes a Z to go into the computer, after which that Z can be sent to the video screen or a printer and reappear as a Z. While this usually is true, it is very far from a direct or necessary connection.

Consider the keyboard. When you type the key in the lower left (usually marked with a Z), the information that goes into the keyboard controller is the coordinates of that key, not a Z. Somewhere a code table says "bottom row, first key means Z." When the same keyboard is used in Germany, the key in that position is marked with a Y, and the code table says "bottom row, first key means Y." Similarly, changing the wheel on a daisy-wheel printer changes the letter that prints on the paper.

Translation codes are arbitrary, and several codes are in common use. The most common character code for personal computers is named ASCII (American Standard Code for Information Interchange), a seven-bit code that supports upper- and lowercase alphabets, numerals, punctuation, and control characters. Each device has its own set of codes, but the codes built into one device are not necessarily the same as the codes built into the next device. Some characters, especially characters like tabs, formfeeds, and carriage returns, are handled differently by different devices and even by different pieces of system software running on the same device. For example, the character whose ASCII code is 12 is named *formfeed* in the ASCII code table. The idea of the code makers was that a printer would eject the paper when it received this code. The program in each printer's controller was supposed to look for this code and handle it, and most did. Today, also, some video controllers are programmed to respond to a formfeed character in an analogous way, by clearing the screen.

As a computer user, you need to be aware that equipment not designed to be used together might be incompatible in unexpected ways. You may find computer systems in which the label on the key that you type, the letter that shows on the screen, and the one that comes out of the printer are all different. This can happen because all three depend on software interpretation as well as hardware capabilities.

1.1.4   The Bus

The bus is the pathway between the processor and everything else. It consists of two sets of wires: one set has enough wires to transmit an address; the other set transmits data. When the processor needs a data item, it puts the address of the item in the memory address register (MAR) and issues a `fetch` command. The memory address register and the memory data register (MDR) sit at the end of the bus line (see Figure 1.1).

When a `fetch` command is given, the address goes from the MAR out over the bus's address lines and a copy of the required data comes back over the bus's data lines to the MDR. Similarly, to store information into the memory, the information and the target address are put into these two registers and a `store` command is given. The information goes out over the bus to the given address and replaces whatever used to be there.

Control of peripherals and interfaces.   The input and output devices are attached to the bus lines. Each device has its own address and handles the information in its own way. Each device, in fact, has a different set of instruction codes that it can handle and a controller to carry out those instructions. A **device controller** is a small processor connected between the bus and the device that is used to control the action of the device. For example, consider a hard disk. A disk has a controller that understands how to get addresses, disk instructions, and information off the bus and how to put information and signals back on the bus. It knows how to carry out and oversee all the disk operations.

Making all the highly varied devices respond to instructions in a uniform way is the job of **device drivers**. A device driver consists of software that knows about the specific quirks and capabilities of a specific device. It translates the uniform system commands into a form that the device can handle prior to putting the commands on the bus lines. A different driver may be needed for every combination of operating system and hardware. For example, a UNIX driver for a SCSI[5] disk would translate the UNIX `read-disk` command to the SCSI format.

---

[5]The small computer systems interface (SCSI) is a standard disk interface.

The user becomes aware that device drivers exist when he or she wants to install a new device and must also install the appropriate driver.

Between a device's driver and its controller is an interface, a doorway between the bus and the device. There are many kinds of interfaces, with varied transmission properties, which can be classified into two general groups: serial and parallel. A **serial interface** transmits and receives bits one at a time. A **parallel interface** can transmit or receive a byte (or more) at a time, in parallel, over several wires. Parallel interfaces commonly are used for printers; serial interfaces for modems, certain printers, mice, and other slow-speed devices. A MIDI (musical instrument digital interface) is a serial interface used to communicate with electronic musical instruments such as synthesizers and keyboards.

1.1.5 Networks

Inside the computer, the various hardware components communicate with each other using the internal bus. It now is common practice to have computers communicate with each other to share resources and information. This is made possible through the use of networks, physical wires (often phone lines) along which electrical transmissions can occur. The extent of these networks is varied. A **local area network** typically joins together tens of computers in a lab or throughout a small company. A **global network**, such as the Internet, spans much greater distances and connects hundreds of thousands of machines but is truly just a joining together of the smaller networks via a set of gateway computers. A **gateway** computer is a bridge between a network such as the Internet on one side and a local network on the other side. This computer also often acts as a **firewall**, whose purpose is to keep illegal, unwanted, or dangerous transmissions out of the local environment.

Sharing resources.   One use of networks is to let several computers share resources such as file systems, printers, and tape drives. The computers in such a network usually are connected in a **server-client** relationship, as illustrated in Figure 1.4. The server possesses the resource that is being shared. The clients, connected via a **hub** or **switched ethernet connection**, share the use of these resources. The user of a client machine may print out documents or access files as if the devices actually were physically connected to the local machine. This can provide the illusion of greater resources than actually exist, as well as present a uniform programming environment, independent of the actual machine used. This kind of sharing is less practical over larger networks due to delays caused by data transmissions through gateway machines.

Communication.   The other typical use of networks is communication. E-mail has become a popular way to send letters and short notes to friends and business associates. Chat rooms provide the opportunity for more direct, interactive communication. The World Wide Web makes a wealth of information

This is one way that a lab network might be set up. It is not drawn to scale; a hub is a small device that could fit on the corner of a table.

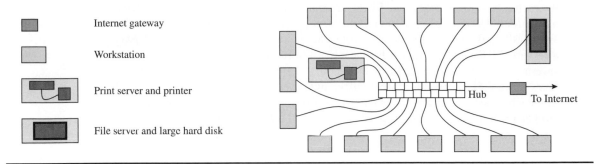

Figure 1.4.   A local network in a student lab.

available to the average user at home that used to be available only in distant libraries. It also provides new commercial opportunities; people now can shop for many items on the Web and are able to buy specialty items or get bargains that were previously unavailable to them.

Networks also have changed the workplace and work habits. Many professionals use network transmissions between home and office or between two office locations to gain access to essential information when they need it, wherever they are. This may include using a laptop computer that is connected to the network via a cellular phone.

Distributed computing.   Networks also are used to allow the computers to communicate between themselves. The complexity of many of today's problems requires the use of reserve computing power. This can be achieved by synchronizing the efforts of multiple computers, all working in parallel on separate components of a problem. A large distributed system may make use of thousands of computers. Synchronization and routing of information in such systems are major tasks, among the many performed by the operating system's software, as discussed next.

1.2   The Operating System

The **operating system** (OS) is the most important piece of system software and the first one you see when you turn on your machine. It is the master control program that enables you to use the hardware and communicate with the rest of the system software. The operating system has several major components, including the **system kernel**, which is the central control component; a **memory**

management system, which allocates an area of memory for each program that is running; the **file system manager**, which organizes and controls use of the disks; **device drivers**, which control the hardware devices attached to the computer; and the **system libraries**, which contain all sorts of useful utility programs that can be called by user programs. In addition, a multiprocessing system (described later) has a process scheduler, which keeps track of programs waiting to be run and determines when and how long to run each one.

Command shells and windows.   Operating systems can be divided into two categories: command-line interpreters and windowing systems. **Command shells**, or command-line interpreters, were invented first and can be used on small, simple machines. A command shell displays a system prompt at the left of the screen and waits for the user to type in a command. Then, the command is executed by calling up some piece of system or user software. When that program terminates, control goes back to the operating system and the system prompt again is displayed.

A newer idea is a **windowing system**. Window-based systems include the Apple Macintosh system, Microsoft Windows (which is an extension of DOS), and NextStep and X-Windows, which provide window interfaces for UNIX. Except for the Macintosh, these windowing systems can run side-by-side with a command shell and provide access to it. This is important because command-line interpreters generally provide capabilities that are not available within the window environment.

In a window environment, multiple windows can be displayed on the screen, including perhaps a command window. Windows can be used to display file directories, run programs, and so forth. The user accesses the contents of the windows using a mouse or some other point-and-click device. Seeing your files, moving and copying them, renaming them, and every other thing that you do is much easier in a window environment.

Multiprogramming systems.   Another way to categorize systems is by whether they can run several programs at the same time or are limited to one at a time. Ordinary personal computers are limited to one process at a time. However, modern personal workstations and large computers, often called *mainframes*, have **multiprogramming** operating systems. UNIX is one of the best known and most widely used multiprogramming systems.

Workstations are capable of running a few processes concurrently, and mainframes often can support 50 or 100 users, running the programs in a **time-shared** manner. In time sharing, each user process is given a short slice of CPU time, then it waits while all the other users get their turns. This works because users spend much more time thinking and typing than running their programs. Any request by a program for input or output (I/O) also ends a time slice; the OS initiates the input or output, then selects another process to be run while the I/O happens. The process scheduler is the system component that coordinates and directs all this complex activity.

Each kind of computer must have its own custom-tailored operating system. Some systems are proprietary and have been implemented for only one manufacturer's models. For example, Apple's system for the Macintosh is jealously guarded against copying. Other systems, such as UNIX and DOS, are widely implemented or imitated. Increasingly, the computer owner has a choice about what system will be installed on his or her hardware.

The choice of hardware is important because it determines what software you can run and what diskettes you can read. Software and file systems are constructed to be compatible with a particular system environment, and they do not work with the wrong system. For example, you cannot read a UNIX diskette in a DOS system, and a C **compiler** that works under UNIX must be modified to work under DOS. Windowing systems and multiprogramming are powerful aides to program development. However, both consume large amounts of main memory, disk space, and processing time. Trying to run them with a machine that is not big enough or fast enough is a mistake.

1.3   Languages

The purpose of a computer language is to allow a human being to communicate with a computer. Human language and machine language are vastly different because human capabilities and machine capabilities are different. Each kind of computer has its own machine language that reflects the particular capabilities of that machine. Computer languages allow human beings to write instructions in a language that is more appropriate for human capabilities and can be translated into the machine language of many different kinds of machines.

1.3.1 Machine Language

Built into the CPU of each computer is a set of instructions that the hardware knows how to execute. The behavior of each instruction and its binary code are documented in the hardware manual. Technically, it is possible to program a computer by making lists of these codes. That is how programming was done 45 years ago.

A machine language program is a sequence of instructions, each of which consists of an instruction code, often followed by one or two register codes or memory addresses. In a machine, these are all represented in binary.[6] In the early days of computers, when people still wrote programs in machine language, they did not write them in binary because people were (and are) abominably bad

---

[6]Binary is the base 2 number system. Information is represented as strings of bits (see Chapter 18).

at writing long strings of 1's and 0's without making errors. Instead, they used the octal number system,[7] in which information is represented as strings of digits between 0 and 7. Each octal digit translates directly into three binary bits. Thus, a machine language program was written as a long series of lines, where each line was a string of octal digits.

1.3.2   Assembly Languages

When people had to use machine language, it took a very long time to write and debug a program. The next development was symbolic assembly language. Instead of writing octal codes, the programmer wrote symbolic codes for instructions and defined a name for each data-storage location. The three lines that follow show how a simple action might look when expressed in assembly language; this code adds two numbers and stores them in a variable named **sum**. The same addition expressed in C would be **sum = n1 + n2;**

```
ldreg *n1, d1    / Load first number into register d1.
add   *n2, d1    / Add second number to the register.
sto   d1, sum    / Store result in the location for sum.
```

A translator, called an **assembler**, analyzed the symbolic codes and assembled machine-code instructions by translating each symbol into its code and assigning memory locations for the data objects used by the program.

Every name and quoted string used in a program must be stored at some address in the computer's memory. To write in machine language, you manually assign an address to each object. Happily, assembly languages and high-level languages such as C free you from concern over these addresses. The programmer declares the names to be used at the top and defines each name by giving it a data type or quoted string value. When the assembler translates this into machine language, it assigns memory locations for these objects.

Assembly languages still are very important for writing programs so closely related to the hardware that high-level languages like C simply have no commands to express them. Many large systems are written primarily in a high-level language but contain some parts coded in assembly language. These portions are part of the system kernel. They work directly with parts of the machine and must operate as efficiently as possible.

1.3.3   High-Level Languages

Programming in an assembly language is very tedious. Furthermore, an assembly language is specific to one type of machine and probably very different from assembly languages for machines of other manufacturers. Therefore, assembly

---

[7] Octal is base 8.

language programs are not portable—that is, they are not easily converted for use on other machines. In contrast, programs in languages like FORTRAN and C are highly portable, because compilers for these languages have been created for nearly every kind of computer.

Over the past 40 years many high-level languages have been developed, some of which have stood the test of time and some of which have not. Each instruction in a high-level language translates into several at the assembly or machine language level. Programs written in a high-level language appear much more like English and are more understandable to humans. In this section, we discuss a few widely used programming languages.

The C language.   C is a relatively old[8] language that recently became very popular. It has characteristics of both high-level languages such as Pascal[9] and FORTRAN[10] and low-level languages such as assembly language. You still might see several dialects of C in older programs or books. In 1988, however, the American National Standards Institute (ANSI) adopted a standard for the language, known as ANSI C. This standard was adopted with a few minor changes by the International Standards Organization (ISO) in 1990 and amended in 1994. This new standard is known as ISO C. The phrase *standard* C can be applied correctly to either version of the standard. The changeover to the standard language is nearly complete, so the beginning C student can safely focus all efforts on standard ISO C.

There are several reasons for the recent growth in the use of C:

- As the UNIX operating system has spread, so has C. C is the tool by which much of the power of UNIX is accessed. UNIX has spread because of the very large amount of valuable software that runs under it.
- From the beginning, C was a very powerful language and fun for the experienced programmer to use. However, it lacked certain important kinds of compile-time error checking and therefore was quite difficult for a beginner to use. ISO C incorporates important new error-checking features and has eliminated many hardware dependencies. It developed into a much better language and became suitable for both beginners and experienced programmers.
- C allows large programs to be written in separate modules. This makes it easier to manage large projects, greatly facilitates debugging, and makes it possible to reuse program modules that do common, useful jobs.

---

[8]Created originally in 1972, the language has been updated and expanded several times.

[9]Pascal has been used most extensively as an instructional language in universities.

[10]Short for "formula translator," this language was developed primarily for doing scientific calculations.

- The ISO C library is extensive and standardized. It contains functions for mathematical computation, input and output facilities, and various system utilities.

On the other hand, ISO C remains more error prone than languages of a similar age with similar features, such as Pascal and Ada.[11] It is popular among experienced programmers partly because of the features that cause this error-prone nature:

- C allows the programmer to write terse, compact code that can run very efficiently. Any programmer who is a slow typist appreciates this. Sometimes programmers even make a game of squeezing the unnecessary operations out of their code. On the negative side, compact code can be hard to read and understand unless comments are used liberally to explain it.
- The error-checking system in ISO C is less rigid and more permissive than in competing languages. Expert programmers claim that this permissiveness is an advantage and that the rigid mechanisms in other languages often "get in the way" when they want to do something unusual. However, these rigid systems are easier for the new programmer to understand and to use.
- C supports bit-manipulation operators that can select or change a single bit or group of bits in a number. These are very important in system programs that must interface to hardware devices that set and test values in specific memory locations. However, working with arbitrary machine addresses and bit patterns must be done with extreme care to avoid errors.
- No restrictions are placed on the use of pointers. (A **pointer** is a variable representing the location, as opposed to the value, of data.) This permits the use of some very efficient computational methods, at the potential cost of destroying information anywhere in memory when an error is made in setting a pointer value. Unfortunately, such errors are common, and many result in system crashes and the need to reboot the system.

C and FORTRAN.   FORTRAN is a very old language that has been used by engineers and scientists since the infancy of computers. Originally, it was a language for scientific computation, and it still serves that purpose. Over the years, the language has been updated, revised, and expanded, but its primary focus remains high-performance numerical computation. A massive amount of scientific programming now exists in the form of FORTRAN libraries and FORTRAN application programs that are used, and shared, by scientists worldwide. The FORTRAN libraries are extremely efficient, reliable, and trusted.

Because many engineering departments are acquiring UNIX workstations, C is beginning to supplant FORTRAN-77 in many engineering applications. This has

---

[11] Ada is a programming language developed in the 1970s to support large-scale, portable application systems.

some advantages. FORTRAN-77 still bears the burden of being an old language. It is full of unnecessary complications and nonuniform conventions. Much of the space in a FORTRAN textbook is spent explaining how to *write* the language correctly. In contrast, a C textbook has a much simpler language to present and can spend more time explaining how to *use* the language well.

On the other hand, FORTRAN-77 is a "safer" language. A program can get into trouble in very few ways that will cause a system crash or cause the result of a seemingly correct expression to be nonsense. C is prone to these problems, even when the programmer avoids using the advanced parts of the language. When a C programmer begins to use pointers, debugging becomes substantially more difficult than it ever could be in FORTRAN-77. Nonetheless, C is here, and thousands of former FORTRAN programmers are beginning to use it. FORTRAN-to-C conversion programs exist and are being used to make the transition less costly.

C and C++.   The C++ language extends C to eliminate more causes of error and provide software-engineering tools that are important for large projects. Also, C++ (but not C) is fully compatible with the FORTRAN libraries. This can be a very important consideration for a department switching from FORTRAN to C. C++ is a superset of C. The ordinary line-by-line code in a C++ program is written in C. The extensions involve the way code is organized into modules and the way these modules are used. The C++ extensions are a powerful tool for program organization and error prevention. However, since the entire C language is included as a subset of C++, any error that you can make in C also can be made in C++. The advantages of C++ are there only for those who know how to use them. For beginners, C++ is a more difficult and confusing language than C.

The differences between C and C++ become significant only for moderate to large programs, and only when C++ is used with proper object-oriented design techniques. All software-engineering techniques presented in this book are appropriate for use with both C and C++. The way in which C language elements are presented will lead toward an understanding of the design requirements for C++.

1.4   What You Should Remember

1.4.1   Major Concepts

- This chapter provides a brief description of computer hardware and software. It describes the parts of the machine a programmer must know to comprehend the operation of a program or buy a personal computer system wisely.
- Computer languages and the process of translation are discussed, and the C language is compared to FORTRAN and C++.

1.4.2 Vocabulary

The terms and concepts that follow have been introduced and described briefly. The first and second columns contain terms related to computer hardware and operating systems; the third column relates to the programming process.

CPU	device controller	program
register	device driver	machine language
memory	serial interface	operating system
cache	parallel interface	system kernel
ROM	local area network	system libraries
CD-ROM	global network	command shell
RAM	gateway	windowing system
bit	firewall	multiprogramming
byte	server	assembler
word	client	compiler
clock	memory management system	ANSI C
bus	file system manager	ISO C
hub	floating-point coprocessor	C++

1.5 Using Pencil and Paper

1.5.1 Self-Test Exercises

1. Which terms on the vocabulary list relate to the computer's processor?

2. Which terms on the vocabulary list relate to the memory of a computer?

3. Which terms on the vocabulary list relate to the peripherals of a computer?

4. Which terms on the vocabulary list relate to a computer network?

5. Which terms on the vocabulary list relate to system software?

6. For what does each of the following abbreviations stand?

    a. ALU

    b. bit

    c. CPU

    d. ISO

    e. ASCII

    f. ANSI

    g. I/O

    h. OS

    i. ROM

j. WAN

k. LAN

l. MIDI

m. SCSI

n. MHz

o. RAM

1.5.2   Using Pencil and Paper

1. Choose three terms from *each column* of the vocabulary list in Section 1.4.2. In your own words, give a brief definition for each (a total of nine definitions).

2. What computer will you use for the programming exercises in this course? What kind of processor chip does it have? How big is its main memory? What input and output devices are available for it? Is it attached to a computer network?

3. Have you used a local area network? Why? Have you used the Internet? For what purposes?

4. What operating system runs on the computer that you will use for the programming exercises in this course? Is this a multiprogramming system? What compiler will you use?

5. Explain the difference between

a. a byte and a word.

b. ROM and RAM.

c. cache memory and main memory.

d. a device controller and a device driver.

e. a compiler and an assembler.

f. a command shell and a windowing system.

g. a LAN and a WAN.

h. a gateway and a hub.

CHAPTER
2

Programs and Programming

What Is a Program?

A program is a set of instructions for a computer. Programs receive data, carry out the instructions, and produce useful results. More precisely, the computer **executes a program** by performing its instructions, one at a time, on the supplied data. The instructions a computer is capable of carrying out are very primitive—add two numbers, move a number from here to there in memory, and so forth. Large numbers of instructions are required to carry out even the simplest task, so some programs are thousands or even millions of instructions long.

Nowadays, programs are so big and complicated that they cannot be constructed without the help of a computer. A C **compiler** or C program development system is a computer program whose purpose is to take a description of a desired program coded in a programming language and generate the instructions for the computer from that code. This process is called *compilation*. The program description is called **source code** or C *code*. And the compiled program is called **object code** or **machine code**. One often blurs the distinction between source code and object code by using the word *program* to refer to either. Ideally, the intended meaning always is clear from context.

The C *programming language* is the notation used for writing C code. The purpose of this book is to help you learn how to write programs using the C programming language and to use a C compiler and program development system to generate the instructions that will allow the computer to carry out the actions specified by your program. A program written in C or a similar language has several defining characteristics:

1. Programs are written in a computer language and converted to machine code by a translator, called a *compiler.*

2. The language contains notations (called *commands*, *operations*, and *functions*) that correspond to instructions (or groups of instructions) built into a computer's hardware. It provides names for actions such as *add* and *compare* but not for complex activities like *solve this equation* or abstract activities such as *think.*

3. The programmer combines these elements into a series of sentencelike **statements** that describe the actions to be carried out and the order in which they must happen.

4. A program uses the computer's memory to create abstract models of real-world objects such as people, buildings, or numbers. Statements called **declarations** are used to create and name these objects.

5. A program is sequential; it has a beginning and an end. During translation, the program is analyzed and translated, in order, from beginning to end. When a program is executed, the instructions in the program are run in order. However, that order is modified by control instructions that allow for conditional execution and repetition of blocks of code.

6. Programs must conform exactly to the rules for spelling, grammar, and punctuation prescribed by the language. Not every piece of source code describes a valid program. To be valid, every word used in the source code must be defined and the words must be arranged according to strict syntactic rules. Invalid program descriptions result in **compilation errors** when fed to the compiler, and then no object code is generated.

7. A program, as a whole, has a *meaning.* The meaning of a machine-code program is its effect when executed. The meaning of a C program, likewise, is its effect when it is translated into machine code and the machine code version is executed.[1]

8. Ideally, the actual meaning of a program, when it is executed, is what the programmer intended. If not, we say that the program contains a bug, or **run-time error**. A program can contain two kinds of bugs: compilation errors and run-time errors.

---

[1] In some ways, the meaning of a C program depends on the hardware on which it is executed. Although it always will produce the same results when executed on the same machine with the same data, the results might be different when executed on a different kind of computer.

This is an algorithm for computing the average of the three numbers that are the inputs:

1. Read the first number. Let this number be your initial sum.
2. Read the second number and add it to the previous sum to get a new sum.
3. Read the third number and add it to the sum.
4. Divide the sum by 3.
5. Print the result.

Figure 2.1.   A simple algorithm: Find an average.

2.1.1   Algorithms

An **algorithm** is a method for solving a well-structured problem. The method must be completely defined, unambiguous, and effective; that is, it must be capable of being carried out in a mechanical way. An algorithm must terminate; it cannot go on forever.[2] As long as these criteria are met, the algorithm may be specified in English, graphically, or by any other form of communication. Figure 2.1 is an example of a very simple algorithm specified in English.

Thousands of years ago, mathematicians and scientists invented algorithms to solve important problems such as computing areas and multiplying integers. More recently, algorithms have been developed for solving engineering, mathematical, and scientific problems such as summing series, integrating functions, and computing trajectories. A major area of computer science focuses on the creation, analysis, and improvement of algorithms. Computer scientists have invented new algorithms for computing mathematical functions and organizing, sorting, and searching collections of data. The growing power and sophistication of computer software are due largely to recently invented algorithms that solve problems better and faster.

A large number of algorithms are known for solving many standard problems. A professional programmer or engineer should own one or several reference books that explain these standard algorithms, along with each one's advantages and limitations. These books sometimes explain the algorithms using a mixture of English and computer language called **pseudocode** (because it looks like computer code but is not). Other books present the algorithms in C, in a similar high-level language, or as flow diagrams that graphically depict the sequence of calculations and decisions that form the algorithm. For many problems, several

---

[2]Many programs are based on algorithms. Some programs, however, are designed to go on forever. These generally are called *systems programs*; their purpose is to help operate the computer.

possible algorithms are given. Some are more efficient than others, some are more tolerant of unexpected data than others, and some are easier to program or are less prone to programmer error.

2.2   Problem Specification and Analysis

You should read this section quickly now, to gain a general idea of the way a program is built and verified. Later, as you begin to write your own code, you will want to reread this material carefully and try to follow each step of the process.

2.2.1   Define the Problem

Before we can begin to solve a problem, we must understand exactly what the problem is. Suppose we need to calculate the numbers in a geometric series such as 1, 2, 4, 8, . . . or 1, 5, 25, 125, ... To begin, one might say, "I want a program to compute my series." This specifies the general goal but falls far short of being an adequate problem specification because it fails to give any detail at all about what is needed. We must answer such questions as, "Which series?", "How many terms?", and "With what precision?" Figure 2.2 gives a problem specification for this application; the parts of the specification are discussed in the paragraphs that follow.

Define the scope and generality of the solution needed.   To write a computer program, one must start by defining the nature of the answer needed. Do we want to know the terms of a particular series? Or should we write a program to handle any geometric series? Should the program handle all inputs or are we allowed to narrow our concern to inputs that make sense? Geometric series grow rapidly and the terms become too large to represent as integers. Can we ignore this fact or must we do something about it? It is easy to write a program that will compute the terms of a geometric progression, but handling extremely large numbers properly or avoiding them would complicate it substantially.

Define the input and output.   Let us assume that our goal is to write a program to compute any geometric series whose terms are all of a moderate size. To achieve this, we must limit both inputs to very small integers.

We also must decide how the output will be presented. First, all output should be labeled clearly with a word or phrase that explains its meaning. Also, it is a very good idea to "echo" every input as part of the output. This lets the user confirm that the input was typed and interpreted correctly and makes it clear

---

Definitions: A *geometric progression* is a series of numbers in which each term is a constant times the preceding term. The constant, R, is called the **common ratio**. If the first term in the series is a, then succeeding terms will be $a * R$, $a * R^2$, $a * R^3$, ... For instance, if $a = 1$ and $R = 2$, we get 1, 2, 4, 8, ... and if $a = 1$ and $R = 5$, we get 1, 5, 25, 125, ...

Goal: Compute and print out the terms of a geometric series.

Scope: The number of terms printed, as well the values of a and R, should be limited to small integers to ensure that all terms of the series produced are small enough to represent in the computer as integers.

Input: The user will enter the integers a and R interactively.

Output: The program will echo the inputs, then compute and print out the first five terms of the series defined by the inputs.

Constants and formulas: No constants are needed. The formula for the kth term of the series is $t_k = a * R^{k-1}$.

Computational requirements: Both a and R may be any nonzero positive or negative integer in the range $-7 \ldots 7$. No term computed will be larger than five digits.

Figure 2.2.   A problem specification: Geometric series.

which answer belongs with each input set. Spacing should be used to make the answers easy to find and easy to read.

Define constants and formulas.   Some applications require the use of one or more formulas and, possibly, some physical constants. This information is part of a complete specification.

Define basic computational needs.   The representations used for integers in a computer all have a very limited range. The representations for real numbers have a much wider (although still finite) range, but the number in the computer may be only an approximation of the actual real number. Before the specification of a program is complete, we must define the type, range, and precision of the numbers we will deal with. If we are using real numbers, we also must say how many decimal places of accuracy will be required in the answer. Is it enough to be within 0.5 of the actual answer, or must we ensure that any error is less than 0.00001? In general, computations must be carried out to a greater degree of accuracy than that required for the answer, since error tends to build up with repeated operations.

For this application, we must know the largest integer that our computer can store in order to limit the inputs to those that can be handled without chance of error. The values used in Figure 2.2 are based on limits that will be discussed in Chapter 7.

2.2.2   Design a Test Plan

Verification is an essential step in program development. When a program is first compiled and run, it generally contains errors due to mistakes in planning, unexpected circumstances, or simple carelessness. Although program testing and verification take place after a program is written and compiled, a **program verification** plan should be created much earlier in the development process, as soon as the program specifications are complete. Designing a test plan at this stage helps clarify the programmer's thoughts. It often uncovers special cases that must be handled and helps create an easily verified design for the solution.

A **test plan** consists of a list of input data sets and the correct program result for each, which often must be computed by hand. This list should test all the normal and abnormal conditions that the program could encounter. To develop a test plan, we start with the problem definition. The first few data sets (if possible) should have answers that are easy to compute in one's head. These test items often can be created by looking at the formulas and constants that are part of the problem definition and choosing values for the variables that make the calculations easy. Figure 2.3 shows a test plan for the geometric series problem.

Next, all special cases should be listed. The test designer identifies these by looking at the computational requirements and limitations given in the problem definition. Extreme data values at or just beyond the specified limits should be added to the plan. The next step is to analyze what could go wrong with the

Case	Inputs		Output expected
	a	R	
Easy to compute	1	2	1, 2, 4, 8, 16
Special cases	1	1	1, 1, 1, 1, 1
	7	−1	7, −7, 7, −7, 7
	−1	−7	−1, 7, −49, 343, −2401
	0	0	Bad data, zeros
	8	−1	Bad data, a too large
	1	−8	Bad data, R too small
Typical case	3	6	3, 18, 108, 648, 3888
	2	5	2, 10, 50, 250, 1250

Figure 2.3.   Test plan for geometric series program.

program and enter data sets that would be likely to cause failure. For example, some data values might result in a division by 0.

The last data sets should contain data that might be entered during normal use of the program. Since the answers to such problems generally are harder to compute by hand, we list only one or two of them. The results for these items allow the programmer to refine the appearance and readability of the output.

After the coding step is complete, the programmer should return once more to the test plan. If necessary, more test cases should be added to ensure that every line of code in the program is tested at least once.

These guidelines have been stated in general terms so that they are applicable to a wide range of program testing situations. Because of this, the guidelines are somewhat vague and abstract. Concrete examples of test plans are given as part of the case studies in later chapters of this text. These examples will help you gain understanding of verification techniques and learn to build test plans for your own programs.

2.2.3   Design a Solution

When designing a program solution to meet a specification, three things must be considered:

1. *The algorithm.* The program must use the input to calculate the correct output according to the specification.
2. *The driver.* The program must accept input, produce output, and keep the user informed of its progress. When inconsistent or illegal input is identified, the program should not attempt to process it. Rather, an appropriate error comment should be displayed for the user.
3. *Testing and debugging.* The program should provide a convenient way to carry out the test plan and an effective way to monitor the progress of the calculations.

Select or create an algorithm.   Some part of the program must implement the required calculation or process. The programmer must select or create an algorithm that fits the specification. This might be as simple as calculating a formula or as complex as sorting a set of data or choosing the next move in a chess game. In this text, we begin with very simple problem specifications that use formulas a beginner can code with little difficulty.

Many complex problems can be solved by borrowing code developed by others. (We sometimes call such programs *canned code.*) For example, many well-known algorithms exist for sorting data and performing common numerical computations; these may be found in books about computer algorithms or programming. Experienced programmers also are good sources of information.

If code for the algorithm you need is given in a book, what is left for you to do? Can you just copy it and be done? Actually, you cannot. You must adapt the given code to your own context by copying it, changing the variable names to fit your own needs, and adding essential constants.

Design the driver.   Whether you are computing a simple formula or using canned code, you also need a *driver*, a part of the program that forms the interface between the user and the computation. The driver takes care of user interaction. It queries the user for the input (or reads it from a file or some other device), puts the data into the form necessary for the computation, invokes the computation algorithm, and receives the results from it. Finally, the driver must format the results and produce usable output.

Design debugging printouts.   A good programmer usually writes code to produce extra output that will help monitor the progress of the program while it runs and verify that the intermediate results make sense at every stage. It is quite distressing (and quite common) to start a program running and have nothing at all happen. Sometimes the program is tangled in an infinitely repeating process. At other times, it simply is waiting for input. On a large, time-shared system, a lack of response can mean that the system is overly busy or that some process has caused it to crash and all running programs are lost.

Frequent output statements, called **debugging printouts**, scattered throughout your code, let you know what is happening. They seem like extra trouble to write in the first place but save much time and trouble in the long run. Debugging printouts are used to display the input values before computation starts and the results after each important computation. They are very helpful inside loops (introduced in Section 3.7) to show how data values change each time a portion of code is repeated. A little thought given to this issue at the design stage can save a lot of trouble later.

2.3   The Development Environment

A program **development environment** consists of a set of system programs that enable a programmer to create, translate, and maintain programs. Many modern commercially available compilers are part of an *integrated development environment*, which includes an editor, compiler, linker, and run-time support system including a symbolic debugger. These system programs are used through a menu-driven shell. The stages of program creation are illustrated in Figure 2.4 and described next.

2.3.1   The Text Editor

The **text editor** is a tool used to enter a program into a computer file. Text editors permit a typist to enter lines of code or data into a file and make changes and rearrange parts easily. They lack the font and style commands and control over page layout included in a word processor because these "bells and whistles" are

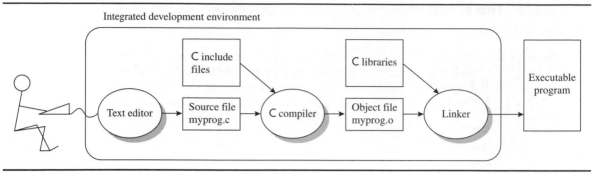

Figure 2.4.   The stages of program translation.

neither useful nor desirable in a program file. If you were to use a word processor and enter your program into a normal word-processor document file, the compiler would be unable to translate the program because of the embedded formatting commands.

When you enter a text editor to create a new program or data file, its screen will show a blank document. To type a program, just start at the top and type the lines of code. This is your source code. The first time you save the program file, you must give it a name that ends in *.c*. Be sure to save your file periodically and maintain a backup copy. When the program is complete, save it again. Data files are created similarly, except that they are given names ending in *.in* or *.dat*.

Text editors come in three general varieties. The very old editors, like the UNIX ed editor, are line editors. They operate on one line of a file at a time, by line number, and are slow and awkward to use. Somewhat newer are the full-screen editors, such as UNIX vi and older versions of emacs, which allow the programmer to move a cursor around the video screen and delete, insert, or change the text under the cursor. They also can delete, copy, or move large blocks of code. Some make periodic, automatic backup copies of your file, which is a tremendous help when the power unexpectedly goes off. To use one of these editors, the programmer enters a command into the operating system interpreter that contains the name of the program to be executed, the names of the files to be used, and sometimes other information regarding software options.

Modern text editors permit all the necessary text editing operations to be done using a mouse and a text window with scroll bars. They often display the text in color, using different colors for C's reserved words, user-defined words, and comments.

Use the most modern text editor you can find. Scroll bars and mice make a huge difference in the ease of use. A good editor encourages you to write good programs. You will be much more willing to make needed changes and reorganize program parts if it is not much work to do so.

2.3.2   The Translator

We use programming languages to communicate with computers. However, computers cannot understand our programming languages directly; they must be translated first. When we write source code in a symbolic computer language, a translator is used to analyze the code, find the declarations, assign memory addresses for the data objects, and determine the structure and meaning of each command.

There are two kinds of translators: compilers and interpreters. After analyzing the source code, a compiler generates machine instructions that will carry out the meaning of the program at a later time. At **compile time**, it plans what memory locations will be needed and creates an object file that contains machine-language instructions to allocate this memory and carry out the actions of the program. Later, the object code is linked with the library, loaded into memory, and run. At **run time**, memory is allocated and information is stored in it. Then, the machine instructions are executed using these data.

An interpreter performs the translation and execution as a single step. After determining the meaning of each command, the interpreter carries it out. Some languages, such as BASIC, normally are interpreted. Others, such as FORTRAN and C, normally are compiled. In general, compiled code is more efficient than interpreted code.

2.3.3   Linkers

An object file is not executable code. Before you can run your program, the linker (another system program) must be called to link it with the precompiled code in the C system libraries. Normally, linking is done automatically when compilation is successful. However, the two processes can be done separately. If you have a correct object file, the next step is to link. The result of linking is a **load module** or **executable file**; that is, a file that is ready to load into the computer's memory and execute. The programmer should give this file, which will be used to run the program, a convenient and meaningful name. In some systems, the name automatically will be the same as the name of the source file except that it ends in *.exe*. In UNIX, however, the name of the load module is *a.out* unless the user provides a better name as part of the compile command.

2.4   Program Construction

You have specified the whole project and selected an algorithm to do the computation. Now you are ready to write the actual code for your program. In the old days, when computers were scarce and expensive, programmers wrote out their code, in detail, on paper so that everything was complete before approaching the computer. This ensured a minimum amount of computer time was consumed.

Today, computer time is no longer scarce, so experienced programmers often skip the paper-copy phase; they approach the computer with a detailed sketch of the code but without actually writing it in longhand. Others, especially beginners, still prefer to write the entire program on paper before sitting down at the computer. This permits them to separate the process of writing the code from the difficulties of dealing with a computer and a text editor. It also is helpful in getting "the big picture"; that is, seeing how all the parts of the program fit together. However, whether you are a beginner or an expert, it is important to have at least a well-developed and well-specified program sketch when you begin entering code into the computer. Programming without one is difficult and failure prone, because without a good plan, it is hard to know what to do and what order to do it in.

This text presents two methods for coding a program: Start from scratch or adapt an existing program to meet the new specification. The first several chapters rely primarily on adapting the programs given as examples in the text. In Chapter 9, after the fundamental concepts of programming have been covered, we discuss the process of building a program from scratch, using a specification. In this section, we use a very simple problem as an example: finding the average of three numbers. An algorithm for this problem was given in Figure 2.1; a complete specification is given in Figure 2.5 and a test plan in Figure 2.6. From this, we create the detailed program sketch shown in Figure 2.7.

2.4.1   Create a Source File

You have been given an assignment and created a program specification and test plan for it. You have designed an algorithm and a driver. The next step is to create

---

Goal: Find the average of three numbers.

Input: The user will enter three numbers interactively, $n1$, $n2$, and $n3$.

Output: Echo the three inputs and print their average.

Formula:

$$Average = \frac{n1 + n2 + n3}{3.0}$$

Computational requirements: Real numbers will be used. The inputs and the output will be in the range $-1,000,000$ to $+1,000,000$. Answers must be accurate to at least two decimal places (a total of eight digits of precision).

Figure 2.5.   Problem specification: Find an average.

$n1$	$n2$	$n3$	Average
1	1	1	1
21	5	66	30.6667
−2	20.5	−6.5	4

Figure 2.6.   A test plan for the average program.

a source code file containing your C program statements. To begin, you should create a new subdirectory (folder) on your disk for use only with this program. By the time a program is finished, it will have several component files (source code, backup, error file, object code, executable version, data, and output). Your life will be much simpler if you keep all the parts of a program together and separate them from all other files.

Once you have made a directory for the new project, you are ready to create a new source code file in that directory. This can be done by copying and renaming an existing program you intend to modify or by starting with a blank document and storing it under your new program name. Then either type in your new source code or modify the existing code. When you are finished, print out a copy of your file and look carefully at what you have done. (If your printer is inconvenient or produces output of poor quality, you may find it easier to examine the code on the video screen.) Mark any errors you find and use the text editor to correct them. Figure 2.8 shows the program developed from the sketch in Figure 2.7.[3]

2.4.2   Translate the Program and Correct Errors

Before you can run your program, it must be compiled (translated into machine language) and linked with the previously compiled library code modules.

---

1. Define real numbers $n1$, $n2$, $n3$, and *Average*.
2. Print program titles.
3. Prompt the user to enter three numbers.
4. Read $n1$, $n2$, and $n3$ and print them out again so that the user can verify that they were entered and read correctly.
5. Add the three numbers and divide the sum by 3.0. Store the result in *Average*.
6. Print the result with two decimal places.

Figure 2.7.   Program sketch: Find an average.

---

[3] This example is presented to illustrate the program development, coding, and translation process. Do not try to understand the actual C code at this time.

This is the final version of the program, after correcting the errors.

```
/* -------------------------------------------------------------------- */
/* This program will compute and display the average of three numbers.  */

#include <stdio.h>
void main( void )
{
    double n1, n2, n3;                /* The three input numbers.       */
    double average;                   /* The average of the three numbers. */

    printf( "\n Compute the average of 3 numbers \n" );
    printf( "------------------------------\n" );
    printf( "Please input 3 numbers: " );
    scanf( "%lg%lg%lg", &n1, &n2, &n3 );          /* Read the numbers.  */
    printf( "Averaging %g, %g, %g;", n1, n2, n3 ); /* Echo inputs.      */

    average = (n1 + n2 + n3) / 3.0;               /* Average is sum / 3.*/
    printf( " the average is %g\n\n", average );  /* Print average.     */
}
```

Sample output:

```
Compute the average of 3 numbers
------------------------------
Please input 3 numbers: 21 5 66
Averaging 21, 5, 66; the average is 30.6667
```

Figure 2.8.   A C program for the average algorithm.

Compiling.   When we use the compiler, we tell it the name of a C source file to translate. It runs and produces various kinds of feedback. If the job was done perfectly, the compiler will display a `successful termination` comment and create a new object file, which contains the machine code instructions that correspond to the C code in the source file. However, it is rare that all the planning, design, coding, and typing are correct on the first try. Human beings are prone to making mistakes and compilers are completely intolerant of errors, even very small ones. Spelling, grammar, and punctuation must be perfect or the program cannot be translated. The result is that the compiler will stop in the middle of a translation with an error comment (or a list of them). The programmer must locate the error, fix it, and use the compiler again.

Correcting compile-time errors.   When we first entered the average program, we made typographical errors in the last two lines. The code typed in looked like this:

```
average = (n1 + n2 + n3) / 3.0
print( " the average is %g\n", average );
```

The compiler responded with this error comment:

```
f10_mean.c: In function 'main':
f10_mean.c:15: parse error before 'prinf'
```

We looked at the end of the line before `prinf` and noticed a missing semicolon after the 3.0. We edited in the semicolon and compiled again. This time, compilation was successful, and the program was passed on to the linker.

Error comments differ from system to system. Language designers try to make these comments clear and helpful. However, especially with C, identifying the source of the error is guesswork, at best. Sometimes the comments are quite misleading. For example, the comment `undefined symbol` might indicate a misspelling of a symbol that is defined, and `illegal symbol line 90` might mean that the semicolon at the end of line 89 is missing. Worse yet, a missing punctuation mark might not be detected for many lines, and an extra one might not be detected at all—the program just will not work right.

If there is a list of error comments, do not try to remember them all. Write them down or print them out, then fix the first several problems. Very often, one small error near the beginning of a program can cause the compiler to become confused and produce dozens of false error comments. After fixing a small number of errors, recompile and get a fresh error listing. Often, many of the errors will just go away.

It takes some practice to be able to interpret the meaning of error comments. Sometimes beginners interpret them literally and change the wrong thing. When this happens, a nearly correct program can get worse and worse until it becomes really hard to fix. Anyone who is not sure of the meaning of an error comment should seek advice from a more experienced person.

Correcting linking errors.   The linking process also may fail and generate an error comment. When a **linking error** happens, it usually means that the name of something in the library has been misspelled or that the linker cannot find the system libraries. The programmer should check the calls on the specified library function for correctness. If the compiler is newly installed, a knowledgable person should check that it was installed correctly. When we tried to link our program, the linker produced this error comment:

```
ld: Undefined symbols:
_prinf
```

We then noticed that `printf` was misspelled, corrected that error, and recompiled. This time, both compilation and linking were successful and we were ready to run the program.

2.5   Program Execution and Testing

2.5.1   Execute the Program

When a program has been successfully compiled and linked, the testing phase begins. To run the program, type its name on the command line or click the mouse on the program's icon. If you are using an integrated development environment such as Borland C/C++ or Microsoft Visual C++, go to the menu bar and click on **Run**. The operating system will respond by loading the executable program into the computer's memory. The memory will then contain the program instructions, any constants or quoted strings in the program, and space for the program's data. Figure 2.9 shows how the constants and data might be laid out in the memory for the program in Figure 2.8.

When loading is complete, the operating system transfers control to the first line of the program. At this time, you should begin to see the output produced by your program. If it needs input, type the input and hit the Enter key. When your program is finished, control will return to the system. When the program's instructions are executed, the computer's devices perform input and output and its logic circuits perform calculations. These actions produce data and results that are stored in the memory. In an integrated development environment, the system screen may disappear while your program is running and appear again when it is finished.

When a program is running, the contents of the memory cells change every time a **read** or **store** instruction is executed. In some systems, a program can be run with a debugger. A **debugger** is another program that runs the program for you. As shown in Figure 2.10, you communicate with the debugger, and it

---

This diagram shows how the constant values used in the program of Figure 2.8 might be stored in main memory. Later chapters will explain why.

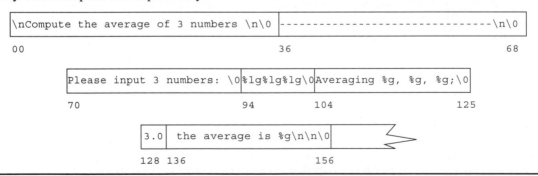

Figure 2.9.   Memory for constants.

A program can be tested by running it directly (left) or through an on-line debugger (right).

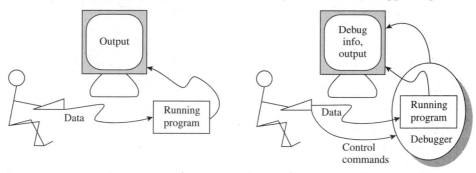

Figure 2.10.   Testing a program.

interprets your program instructions one at a time, step by step. You can ask to see the results of computations and the contents of selected parts of memory after each step and, thus, monitor how the process is proceeding. Figure 2.11 shows, step by step, how the values stored in the memory change when the program in Figure 2.8 is executed.

A debugger can be a powerful tool for figuring out why and how an error occurs. Even though the C language is fully standardized, C debuggers are not. Each one is different. Because of this, it is helpful to learn other ways to monitor the progress of a program. Such techniques are presented in the next section.

2.5.2 Test and Verify

Many errors are caught by the compiler, some by the linker. When a program finally does compile and link without warnings, though, the process of finding the **logical errors** begins. The primary method for detecting logical errors is to test the program on varied input data and look carefully at the answers it prints. They might or might not be correct. Sometimes a program operates correctly on some data sets and incorrectly on others. Sometimes an unusual data condition will cause a program to crash or begin running forever. In any case, *you must verify the correctness of your answers.*

You now are ready to use your testing plan. Run your program and enter each of the data sets in your plan, verifying each time that the computer got the same answer you got by hand calculation. Compare the correct answer on your test plan to the answer the computer has printed. Are they the same? We tested

This diagram shows how the values stored in main memory change when we run the program from Figure 2.8. A ? indicates that any garbage value might exist at that location.

When the program is ready to run, the memory area for variables might look like this:

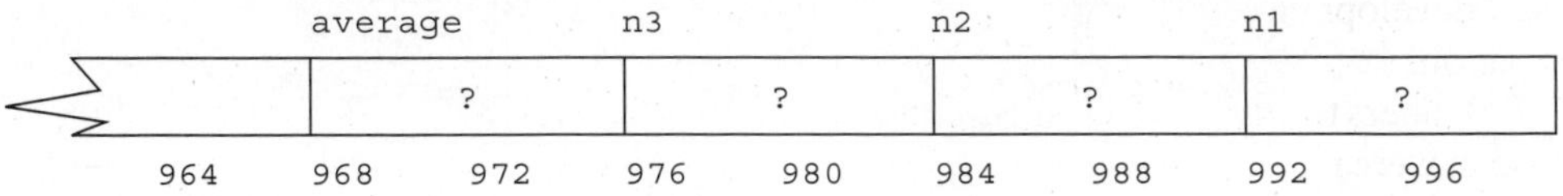

	average	n3	n2	n1
	?	?	?	?

964   968   972   976   980   984   988   992   996

After returning from `scanf()`, with inputs of 21, 5, and 66,

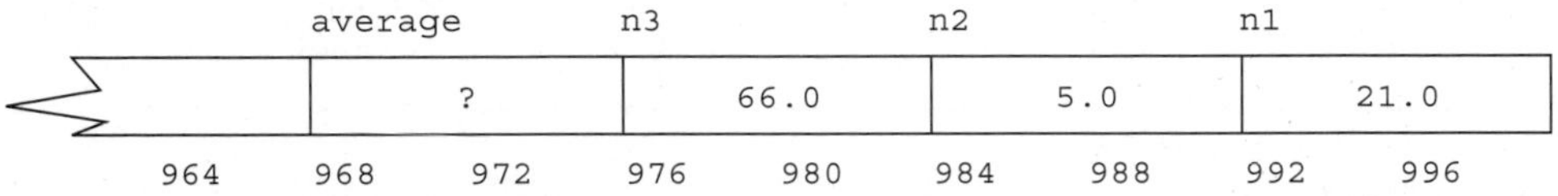

	average	n3	n2	n1
	?	66.0	5.0	21.0

964   968   972   976   980   984   988   992   996

After computing the formula and storing the answer,

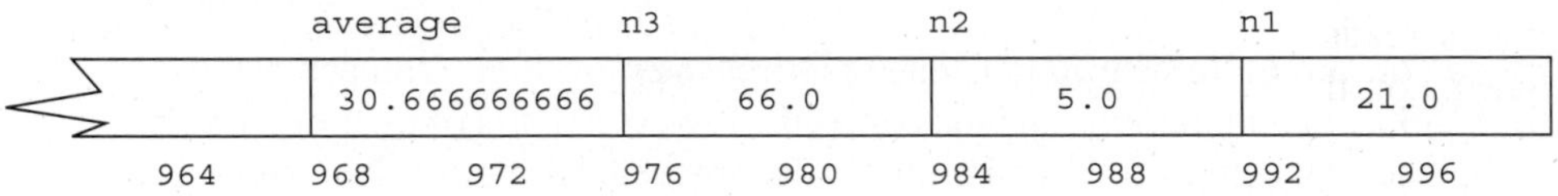

	average	n3	n2	n1
	30.666666666	66.0	5.0	21.0

964   968   972   976   980   984   988   992   996

Figure 2.11.   Memory during program execution.

our program using the plan in Figure 2.6; the output from our third test is shown here:

```
Compute the average of 3 numbers
---------------------------------
Please input 3 numbers: -2 20.5 -6.5
Averaging -2, 20.5, -6.5; the average is 4
```

This answer (and the other two) matched the expected answers, so we have some confidence that the program is correct. We now look at the output with a critical eye. Is it clear and easy to read? Should it be improved? If the answer is not correct, why not? Where is the error—in the test plan or in the program code? If the test plan has the correct answer, you must analyze the code and find the reason for the error; that is, you must find the logical error, better known as a *program bug*. The useful debugging method of using printouts is described next. Another technique (parse trees) is given in Section 4.8.

Debugging: locating and correcting errors.   As you start writing your own programs, you must learn how to find and eliminate programming errors. Debugging printouts are a powerful technique for locating a logical error in a program. When your program computes nonsense answers, add debugging print-outs until you discover the first point at which the intermediate results are wrong. This shows you where the problem is. With that information (and possibly some expert help), you can deduce why the code is wrong and how to fix it. In an integrated development environment, the debugger can be used to provide similar information.

Beginners tend to form wrong theories about the causes of errors and change things that were right. Sometimes this process continues for hours until a program that originally was close to correct becomes a random mess of damaging patches. The best defense against this is to be sure you understand the reason for the error before you change anything. If you do not understand it, ask for help. Be sure to save a backup copy of your program when you modify it. This can be helpful if you need to undo a "correction."

Finishing the test.   Whether you find an error or a needed improvement, the next step is to figure out how to fix it and start the edit–compile–link–test process all over again. Eventually the output for your first test case will be correct and acceptably readable. Then the whole testing cycle must begin again with the other items on the test plan: Enter a data set, inspect the results critically, and fix any problems that become evident. When the last test item produces correct, readable answers, you are done.

2.6   What You Should Remember

2.6.1 Major Concepts

The stages of program development.

1. Problem definition.
2. Design of a testing process.
3. Design of a solution.
4. Program construction.
5. Program translation.
6. Verification.

The moral of this story.   If you wish to avoid grief in your programming, you should take to heart these proverbs:

1. It is harder than it seems it ought to be.
2. The program itself is like the tip of an iceberg: It rests on top of a lot of invisible work and it will not float without that work.
3. Attention to detail pays off. Compilers expect perfection.
4. Debugging seldom is an easy process, and if a program is not well-structured, it can become a nightmare.

5. Every development step skipped is hours wasted. (Beginners rarely understand this.)

6. You cannot start a program the day before it is due and finish it on time.

2.6.2 Vocabulary

These are the most important terms and concepts presented or discussed in this chapter.

program	development environment	compile time
algorithm	text editor	compilation error
pseudocode	compiler	linking error
test plan	linker	execute a program
source code	debugger	run time
object code	debugging printouts	run-time error
executable file	statement	logical error
load module	declaration	program verification

2.7   Exercises

2.7.1 Self-Test Exercises

1. Explain why a beginner usually fails to finish a program on time when he or she starts it the day before it is due.

2. True or false: A program is ready to turn in when it compiles, runs, and produces results. Please explain your answer.

3. Explain the difference between

   a. an algorithm and a program.

   b. a command and a declaration.

   c. a compiler and an interpreter.

   d. a linking loader and a load module.

2.7.2 Using Pencil and Paper

1. A test plan is a list of data inputs and corresponding outputs that can be used to test a program. This list should start with input values that are easy to check in your head, then include input values that are special cases and values that might cause trouble, perhaps by being too big or too small.

   a. Following the example in Figure 2.2, create a problem specification for a program to convert Fahrenheit temperatures to Celsius using the formula

$$Celsius = (Fahrenheit - 32.0) * \frac{5.0}{9.0}$$

Specify the following aspects: scope, input or inputs required, output required, formulas, constants, computational requirements, and limits (if any are necessary) on the range of legal inputs.

b. Write a test plan for your algorithm. Include inputs that can be checked in your head, those that will test any limits or special cases for this problem, and typical input values. For each input, list the correct output.

c. Using English or pseudocode, write an algorithm for this problem. Attempt to verify the correctness of your algorithm using the test plan. (Do not attempt to actually write the program in C.)

2. Explain the difference between

a. pseudocode and source code.

b. a text editor and a word processor.

c. compile time and run time.

d. program verification and program execution.

3. Given the short C program that follows,

a. Make a list of the memory variables in this program.

b. Which lines of code contain operations that change the contents of memory? What are those operations?

```
void main( void )
{
    int square;
    int number;

    printf( "Enter a number:" );
    scanf( "%i", &number );
    square = number * number;
    printf( "The square is %i\n", square );
}
```

2.7.3   Using the Computer

1. Decide which computer system you will use for these exercises. If it is a shared system, find out how to create an account for yourself.

a. Create an account and a personal directory for your work.

b. Find out how to create a subdirectory on your system. Create one called **info**.

c. You will use a text editor to type in your programs and data files. Some C systems have a built-in text editor; others do not. Find out what text editor you will be using and how to access it. Create a text file (not a program) containing your name, address, and telephone number on separate lines. Next, write the brand of computer you are using and the name of the text editor. Then write a paragraph that describes your past experience with computers. Save this file in your **info** directory.

d. Find out how to print a file on your system. Print out and turn in the file you created in (c).

2. Given the short C program that follows,

   a. Make a list of the memory variables in this program.

   b. Which lines of code contain operations that change the contents of memory? What are those operations?

```c
void main( void )
{
    double base;
    double height;
    double area;

    printf( "Enter base and height of triangle: " );
    scanf( "%lg", &base );
    scanf( "%lg", &height );
    area = base * height / 2.0;
    printf( "The area of the triangle is %g\n", area );
}
```

3. Write a simple program that will output your name, phone number, E-mail address, and academic major on separate lines.

CHAPTER
3

Fundamental Concepts

The C language is a powerful language that has been used to implement some of the world's most complex programs. However, by learning a modest number of fundamental concepts, a newcomer to C can write simple programs that do useful things. As with any language, the beginner needs a considerable amount of basic information before it is possible to read or write anything meaningful. In this chapter, we introduce some of the capabilities of C by using them in simple, but practical, programs and explaining how those programs work. These examples introduce all the concepts necessary to read and write simple programs, providing an overview of the central parts of the language. Later chapters will return to all of the topics introduced here and explain them in greater detail.

3.1   Parts of a Program

A C program is a series of comments, preprocessor commands, declarations, and function definitions. The function definitions contain further comments, statements, and possibly more declarations. Each of these program units is composed of a series of words and symbols. We define these terms very broadly in the next several paragraphs; their meaning gradually should become clearer as you look at the first several sample programs.

- *Comments.* At the top of a program, there should be a few lines enclosed between the symbols /* and */ that supply information about the program's purpose and its author. These lines are comments. Their purpose is to inform the human reader, not the computer, and so they are ignored by the compiler. Comments also can and should appear throughout the program, wherever they could help a reader understand the form or function of the code.
- *Preprocessor commands.* Also, normally a series of commands at the top of a program tell the C compiler how to process the pieces of a program and where to look for essential definitions. These **preprocessor commands** all start with the symbol # and are handled by the C preprocessor before the compiler starts to translate the code itself, as indicated in Figure 3.1.
- *Words.* Many of the words used to write a program are defined by the C language standard; these are known as **keywords**. A list of keywords can be found in Appendix C. Other words are defined by the programmer. These words can be grouped into categories analogous to English parts of speech; the table in Figure 3.2 lists the kinds of words in C and their English analogs.
- *Declarations.* The purpose of a **declaration** is to introduce a new word, or **identifier,** into the program's vocabulary. In C, a declaration must be written in the program prior to any statement that uses the word it defines.

Stage	Purpose
1. Lexical analysis	Identify the words and symbols used in the code
2. Preprocessing	Carry out the preprocessor commands
3. Parsing	Analyze the structure of each declaration and statement, according to the official grammar of the language
4. Code generation	Select the appropriate machine operation codes and produce the actual machine instructions that will carry out the C-language program statements

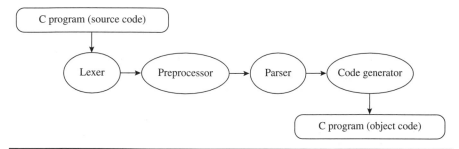

Figure 3.1.   The stages of compilation.

C Category	In English	Purpose
Identifiers	Nouns	Used to name objects
Data types	Adjectives	Used to describe the properties of an object
Operators	Verbs	Denote simple actions like add or multiply
Function calls	Verbs	Denote complex actions like finding a square root
Symbols	Punctuation	Symbols like a semicolon or # are used to mark the beginning or the end of a program unit
Symbols	Grouping	Pairs of parentheses, brackets, quotes, and the like are used to enclose a meaningful unit of code

Figure 3.2.   The parts of speech in C.

- *Statements.* A **statement** is like a sentence; it expresses a complete thought. Just as an English sentence has a verb and a subject, a typical C statement contains one or more words that denote actions and one or several names of objects to use while doing these actions. The objects we study in this chapter are called *variables* and *constants*; the action words are assignment statements, arithmetic operations, and function calls. Sometimes, C statements are grouped together by **control statements** and curly brackets into action units that resemble paragraphs. An entire program is like an essay, covering a topic from beginning to end.

This chapter shows how to use a subset of the C language we call the *beginner's toolbox*. It consists of the basic elements from each category: comments, preprocessor commands, declarations, objects, actions, and control statements. Each section will focus on one or a few elements and use them in a complete program. The accompanying program notes should draw your attention to the practical aspects of using each element in the given context.

The sample programs should help you gain a general familiarity with programming terminology and the C language and provide examples to guide the first few programming efforts. Each topic is revisited in more depth in later chapters. As you read this material, try to understand just the general purpose and form of each part. Then test your understanding by completing one of the skeletal programs given at the end of the chapter.

3.2   The Simplest Program

We start with the simplest possible complete program, shown in Figure 3.3. This example illustrates the overall form of a simple program and a first output statement. Although a program can be organized in many ways, most simple C programs are similar to this one; its parts are

```
/* -------------------------------------------------------------- */
/* This is the first easy program--it just prints a greeting. */
#include <stdio.h>
void main( void )
{
    puts( "Hail and farewell, friend!" );
}
```

Figure 3.3.   Hail and farewell.

- One or more lines of comments that draw the viewer's attention to the beginning and identify the purpose of the program. A C comment starts with /* and ends with the next */.
- One or more **#include** commands, which are needed to properly link a program to routines provided by the C system libraries (the standard I/O library in this case).
- The definition of a function called **main()**, which consists of

    A header line that says **void main(void)**.

    A block of code, which is a series of declarations (optional), followed by statements enclosed in curly brackets.

The program notes that follow explain more about each of these parts.

Notes on Figure 3.3: Hail and farewell.

1. The first two lines of "Hail and Farewell" are comments. Good programmers put comments at the top of a program and throughout the code to explain the purpose of each group of statements. The compiler does not use the comments—we write them for the benefit of the humans who will read the code.
2. Any line that starts with a **#**, called a *preprocessor command*, is handled by the preprocessor before the compiler translates the code. In this program, as in most, we ask the preprocessor to bring in the file **stdio.h** and include the contents of that file as part of the program. This is the header (basically, the table of contents) for the standard I/O library. We need the definitions in it to connect our program to the standard input and output facilities.
3. Every program must contain a function named **main()**. This is where execution will begin.
4. The keyword **void** appears twice, before and after the name **main()**. These two **void**s indicate that **main()** does not receive any information from or send any information back to the operating system. This is explained more fully in Chapter 5; until then, just write the first line of **main()** as shown.

5. The { and } (curly bracket) symbols may be read as "begin" and "end." The brackets and everything between them is called a **program block**. Every function has a program block that defines its actions. For simplicity, we usually use the shorter term **block**.

6. A program block contains a series of one or more statements that, like sentences, specify an action the computer should perform and the objects to use while performing that action. Every C statement ends with a semicolon. This **main()** function has only one statement, a call on the standard output function **puts()** (pronounced "put-ess," short for "put string").

7. A series of characters enclosed in double quotes is called a **string**. Each call on **puts()** has a pair of parentheses enclosing a string; it causes the characters in the string, but not the quotes, to be written to an output device (normally the user's screen).

8. If you load this program into your own C system, compile it, and run it, you should see the following message on your terminal screen:

```
Hail and farewell, friend!
```

3.3   Variables, Input, Output, and Sequencing

Before we can write a program that does anything useful, we need to know how to get information into and out of a program and how to store and refer to that information within the program.

3.3.1   Variables

A **variable** is an area of computer memory that has been given a name by the program and can be used to store, or remember, a value. The programmer may choose any name (there are certain rules to follow when picking a name) for a variable, so long as it is not a keyword[1] in the language. Good programmers try to choose meaningful names that are not too long.

Each variable can contain a specific **type** of value, such as a number or a letter. In this chapter, we introduce two types of numbers that are built into C: the types **double** and **int**. The amount of memory required for a variable depends on its type and the characteristics of the local computer system. Normally, simple variables are 1 to 8 bytes long.

A programmer creates variables by writing declarations. C has a somewhat arbitrary restriction that all of the declarations in a program block must come

---

[1] Keywords are words such as **main()** and **void** that have preset meanings to the translator and are reserved for specific uses. These are listed in Appendix C.

immediately after the { that follows `main( void )` and before any statements. (This restriction is relaxed in C++.)

The simplest declaration is a type name followed by a variable name, ending with a semicolon. The following declaration creates an **integer variable** named `minutes`:

```
int minutes;
```

For each name declared, the compiler will create a storage object by allocating the right amount of memory for the specified type of data. The address of this storage object becomes associated with or *bound* to the variable name. Thereafter, when the programmer refers to the name, the compiler will use the associated address. Sometimes we need to refer explicitly to the address of a variable; in those contexts, we write an ampersand (which means "address of") in front of the variable name. For example, `&minutes` means "the address of the variable `minutes`."

3.3.2   Input and Output

A call on an input function is one way to put a value in a variable; we call an output function when we want to see the value stored there. The input and output facilities in C are some of the most complex parts of the language, yet we need to use them as part of even the simplest programs. The best way to start is to learn to do input and output in a few simple ways. In this chapter, we focus on the elementary use of just three I/O functions:

Function name	Meaning of name	Purpose of function
`puts()`	Put string	To write messages on the output screen
`printf()`	Print output using a format	To write messages and data values
`scanf()`	Scan input using a format	To read data values from the keyboard

These functions (and many others) are in the standard input/output library (`stdio`), which is "added" to the program when you write `#include <stdio.h>`. Several examples given in this chapter use these functions with the hope that you can successfully imitate them.[2]

---

[2] A note about notation: In writing about C functions, we often use the name of a function separately, outside the context of program code. At these times, it is customary to write an empty pair of parentheses after the function name. The parentheses remind us that we are talking about a function rather than some other kind of entity.

Streams and buffers (advanced topic).   Input and output in C are handled using **streams**. An *input stream* is a device-independent connection between a program and a specified source of input data; an *output stream* connects a program to a destination for data. In this book, we use streams connected to data files or devices such as the computer's keyboard and monitor screen. Three streams are predefined in standard C: one for input (**stdin**), one for output (**stdout**), and one for error comments (**stderr**). The standard output stream is directed by default to the operator's video screen but can be redirected to a printer or a file. The standard input stream normally is connected to the keyboard but also can be redirected to get information from a file.

Input and output devices are designed to handle chunks of data. For example, a keyboard delivers an entire line of characters to the computer when you hit Enter, and a hard disk is organized into clusters that store 1,000 or more characters. When we read from or write to a disk, the entire cluster is read or written. On the other hand, programs typically read data only a few numbers at a time and write data one number or one line at a time. To bridge the gap between the needs of the program and the characteristics of the hardware, C uses buffers. Every stream has its own **buffer**, an area of main memory large enough to hold a quantity of input or output data appropriate for the stream's device.

When the program uses **scanf()** to read data, the input comes out of the buffer for the **stdin** stream. If that buffer is empty, the system will stop and wait for the user to enter more data. If a user types more data than are called for, the extra input remains in the input buffer until the next use of **scanf()**.

Similarly, when the program uses **printf()** to produce output, that output goes to the output buffer and stays there until the program prints a newline character (denoted by **\n**) or until the program stops sending output and switches to reading input. This permits a programmer to build an output line one number at a time, until it is complete, then display the entire line. However, the most common use of **printf()** is to print an entire line at one time.

Formats.   Some input and output functions, like **puts()**, read or write a single value of a fixed type. A call on **puts()**, which outputs a single string, is very simple: We write the message enclosed in double quotes inside the parentheses following the function name. For example, we might write these two lines as the first and last statements in a program that computes square roots:

```
puts( "Compute the square root of a number." );
...
puts( "Normal termination of square root program." );
```

Other input and output functions, including **scanf()** and **printf()**, can read or write a list of values of varying types. Using these functions is more complex than using **puts()** because two kinds of things may be written inside the parentheses. First comes a **format** string, which describes the form of the data. It describes how many items will be read or written and the type of each item. Following that is either an input data list (for `scanf()`) or an output list (for `printf()`). The complete set of rules for formats is long and detailed.[3] Fortunately it is not necessary to understand formats fully in order to use them. In this chapter, we show how to write simple formats for each type of data introduced.[4]

A format is a string (a series of characters enclosed in double quotes) that describes the form and quantity of the data to be processed. Input and output formats are quite different and will be described separately. Both, however, contain conversion specifiers. The **conversion specifiers** in the format tell the input or output function how many data items to process and what type of data is stored in each item. Each conversion specifier starts with a percent sign and ends with a code letter(s) that represents the type of the data. For example, to read data of type `int`, we write the conversion specifier `%i`.

Using input formats.   An input format is a series of conversion specifiers enclosed in quotes; for example, the format string `"%i"` could be used to read one integer value and `"%i%i"` could be used to read two integers that are separated by spaces on the input line. In a call on `scanf()`, the format is followed by a list of the addresses of the variables that will receive the data after they are read. Here are two complete calls on `scanf()`:

```
scanf( "%i", &minutes );
scanf( "%i%i", &age, &weight );
```

The first line tells `scanf()` to read one integer value and store it at the memory location allotted to the variable named `minutes`. The second line tells `scanf()` to read two integer values. The first will be stored at the address of the variable named `age` and the second in the variable named `weight`.

Using output formats.   Output formats contain both conversion specifiers and words that the programmer wishes to see interspersed within the data. Therefore, output formats are longer and more complex than input formats. An appropriate output format to print the two integers just read might look like this: `"Age: %i  Weight: %i\n"`. The two instances of `%i` tell `printf()` where to insert the data values in the sentence. The `\n` represents a newline character. We need it with `printf()` to cause the output cursor to go to a new line. (The `\n` is not needed with `puts()`.) Hence, most `printf()` formats end in a newline character. Make this a habit: *Use* `\n` *at the end of every format string to send the information to your screen immediately and prepare for the next line.*[5]

---

[3] These rules can be found in any standard reference manual, such as S. Harbison and G. Steele, *C: A Reference Manual*, 4th ed (Englewood Cliffs, NJ: Prentice-Hall, 1995).

[4] As other types of data are introduced in Chapters 7 through 18, more details about formats will be presented.

[5] The exception is a format string used to display a user prompt. These normally end in a colon and a space so that the screen cursor does not move to a new line and the user types the input on the same line as the prompt.

Following the format string in a call on **printf()** is the list of variables or expressions whose values we want to write (do not use the ampersand for output). Exactly one item should appear in this list for each **%** in the format. A complete call on **printf()** might look like this:

```
printf( "Age: %i   Weight: %i\n", age, weight );
```

This tells **printf()** to print the integer values stored in the variables age and weight. These values will appear in the output after labels that tell the meaning of each number. The output from this line might be

```
Age: 21   Weight: 178.
```

3.3.3   Read and Echo: Using the stdio Library in C

The second sample program, Echo (shown in Figure 3.4), incorporates a declaration and calls on one input and two output functions from the **stdio** library. This program will display a prompt and wait for the user to type in a number. The number will be read, stored in the variable **number**, and echoed back to the terminal screen, after which the program will stop.

Notes on Figure 3.4: Echo.

- *First box: the include command.* We must include the file **stdio.h** in every program that uses functions from the standard input/output library. This file, called a *header file*, supplies the compiler with the information it needs to translate our calls on the library functions. The actual code for the input and output functions is in a different file that the user normally does not see and need not be concerned with.

```
/* ------------------------------------------------------ */
/* This program reads and echoes a single number. --------- */
#include <stdio.h>

void main( void )
{
    int number;          /* To store the number. */

    puts( "Please type a single number and hit Enter: " );
    scanf( "%i", &number );
    printf( "You typed %i.\n", number );
}
```

Figure 3.4.   Echo.

- *Second box: the declaration.*

  1. Declarations are used to define the names of variables that will be used in statements later in the program.
  2. We declare one integer variable named **number**. This instructs the compiler to allocate enough space to store an integer value and use that specific location in memory every time we refer to **number**. On most common machines, either 2 or 4 bytes of memory will be allocated.
  3. We chose **number** as the name for our variable because we will be using it to store an arbitrary numeric value.

- *Third box: the statements.*

  1. This program has three statements. A statement denotes an action that must be executed at run time. Declarations are not statements, and, in C, they must precede all statements.
  2. The function **scanf()** is defined in the standard input library. It reads one item from the standard input stream, **stdin**. This stream normally is connected to the user's keyboard. The type of item to be read is specified by the format in the quoted string to the left in the parentheses. We use a **%i** here to read data into an integer variable.
  3. After the format we must give the address of the variable where **scanf()** can store the number it will read. The *ampersand* in front of the variable name means that **scanf()** will store the value you type into the given address in the computer's memory. Suppose the variable **number** was allocated at memory address 3068; then the phrase **&number** denotes memory location 3068 and that is where **scanf()** will store the number it reads.
  4. The *keyboard buffer* is an area of memory associated with the keyboard that holds one line of input, up to and including the newline character, which represents the Enter key. When entering input for a program, the characters you type stay in the keyboard buffer until you hit Enter. This gives you an opportunity to see and correct typing errors before the characters are sent from the keyboard to the program.
  5. Like **puts()**, the **printf()** statement writes output to the standard output stream. The difference is that **puts()** can write only strings and **printf()** can write any kind of data by using the proper format. Also, **puts()** moves the output cursor to the beginning of the next line automatically and **printf()** does not.
  6. We use a *format* to tell **printf()** what kind of data it needs to write. The format is the quoted string just after the left parenthesis. In this format, the **%i** tells us that we want to write an integer.
  7. We put a **\n** on the end of the format to send the information to the screen immediately and prepare for the next line (even though there is none in this simple program).

8. After the format string is the list of variables or expressions whose values we want to write. Here we ask to write the value of **number**.

- *Output.* After running this program, your screen might look like this:

```
Please type a single number and hit Enter:
121
You typed 121.
```

The first and third lines were printed by the program; the second was typed by the user.

3.4   Simple Calculations

Now that you know how to get integers into and out of the computer's memory, we are ready to do simple calculations. In this section, we introduce constant definitions and the data type **double**, which is used to represent real numbers. Then we will show how to write a computation statement using variables, constants, and operators.

3.4.1 Numbers

Type **int** is used in C to represent numbers that are integers such as 987 or -21. Integers come in three sizes on a typical computer: one, two, and four bytes long. The number of bytes determines the maximum value that the variable can hold. Many scientific applications of computers require numbers longer than the largest integer or numbers that have fractional parts such as 3.1416. For this reason, C supports the type **double** (which stands for "double-precision floating-point number").[6] **Double** variables are used in a computer to represent real numbers; that is, numbers with a fractional part. They can represent an immense range of numbers, but most are represented only approximately.

To read an input value of type **double**, we use a conversion specifier of **%lg**; to write a **double**, we can use the code **%g**. Note that we use an **l** (letter "ell") in the input format but not in the output format.[7] A complete **scanf()** statement and its corresponding **printf()** for a **double** value follow:

```
double radius;
puts( "Please enter a real number for the radius: " );
scanf( "%lg", &radius );
printf( "You entered %g.\n", radius );
```

---

[6]Types **float** and **long double** also are supported and will be explained in Chapter 7.

[7]The reasons for this nonuniform notation, however, are obscure and cannot be adequately explained at this point in the text.

The value of **radius** will be printed with between none and six digits of **precision**. We compiled and ran this code (using appropriate accompanying code as in Figure 3.4); the output was

```
Please enter a real number for the radius:
12.3456789
You entered 12.3458.
```

3.4.2 Assignment

A call on **scanf()** is one way to put a value into a variable; an assignment statement is another. The term *variable* is used because a program can change the value stored in a variable by assigning a new value to it. An **assignment** begins with the name of the variable that is to receive the value. This is followed by an = sign and a value to be stored (or an arithmetic expression that computes a value, see later). As an example,

```
minutes = 10;    /* Store value 10 in variable minutes. */
```

3.4.3 Constants

A **constant** is a value that, once defined, never changes. C allows us to write a constant such as 3.1 or −2 literally or to give a name to the constant and refer to it symbolically. Physical constants such as π often are given symbolic names. We can define the constant **PI** as

```
#define PI 3.1416
```

The **#define** commands usually are placed after the **#include** commands at the top of a program. It is sound programming practice to use **#define** to name constants rather than to write literal constants in a program, especially if they are used more than once in the code. This practice makes a program easier to debug because it is easier to locate and correct one constant definition than many occurrences of a literal number.

Note three important differences between **#define** commands and assignment statements: (1) the **#define** command does not end in a semicolon while the assignment statement does; (2) there is no = sign between the defined constant name and its value, whereas there always is an = sign between the variable and the value given to it; and (3) you cannot use the name of a constant on the left side of an assignment statement, only a variable.

3.4.4 Arithmetic and Formulas

Arithmetic formulas, which are called **expressions**, are written in C in a notation very much like standard mathematical notation, using the **operators**

+ (add), - (subtract), * (multiply), and / (divide). Normal mathematical operator **precedence** is supported; that is, multiplication and division will be performed before addition and subtraction. As in mathematics, parentheses may be used for grouping.[8] These operators are combined with variable names (such as **radius**), constants (such as **PI**), or **literal** values such as 3.14 or 10 to form expressions. The result of an expression can be used for output or it can be stored in memory by using assignment. For example, the following statement computes the area of a circle with radius **r** and stores the result in the variable **area**:

```
area = 3.1416 * r * r;
```

Using a constant definition permits us to rewrite the area formula thus:

```
area = PI * r * r;
```

3.4.5   A Program Prototype

The next program follows a simple form that is typical of many programs in the next few chapters. Briefly, it accepts input, performs calculations, and produces output. We describe its form more fully thus:

```
/* Comments that explain the purpose of the program.    */
#include and #define commands.

void main( void )
{
    Variable declarations,
        each with a comment that describes its purpose.

    An output statement that identifies the program.
    Prompts and statements that read the input data.
    Statements that perform calculations and store results.
    Statements that echo input and display results for user.
}
```

This simple format is extended as functions and arrays are introduced in later chapters.

3.4.6   A Program with Calculations

The problem.   A grapefruit is dropped from the top of the World Trade Center. It has no initial velocity since it is dropped, not thrown. The force of gravity accelerates the fruit. Determine the velocity of the fruit and the distance

---

[8]The details of operator precedence and associativity are given in Chapter 4.

it has fallen after t seconds. The time, t, is read as an input.[9] The program for this problem is shown in Figure 3.5.

Notes on Figure 3.5: Grapefruits and gravity.

- *First box: a constant.* We use a #define command to give a symbolic name to the constant for the acceleration of gravity at sea level.
- *Second box: declarations.*
  1. Floating-point types are used to represent real numbers. They can represent an immense range of numbers but do so with limited precision.
  2. The ISO C standard specifies that a double value must have at least 10 decimal digits of precision, while the IEEE hardware standard specifies 15 digits. Most implementations fall somewhere in this range.
  3. Note that t, y, and v all are variables of type double. When you have several variables of the same type, you also may declare them all on one line like this: double t, y, v;. However, in this problem, we declare one variable per line so that there is space for a comment that explains the meaning or purpose of each variable. This is good programming practice.

- *Third box: title.*
  1. Execution begins with the first box following the declarations, proceeding sequentially through the other boxes to the end of the code. This is studied more fully in the next section.
  2. A well-designed program displays a title and greeting message so that the user knows that execution has started.

- *Fourth box: user input.*
  1. A **prompt** is a message displayed on the video screen that tells the user what to do. Here we ask the user to type in the time. The user sees

     ```
     Welcome.
     Calculate the height from which a grapefruit fell
     given the number of seconds that it was falling.

     Input seconds:
     ```

  2. The first piece of information sent to scanf() is the format string; the second is the address of the variable to receive the input. This call on scanf() scans the stdin input stream to find and read a value for t (time, in seconds). This value may be entered with or without a decimal point.

---

[9]This problem will serve as the basis for a series of example programs in the next sections.

```
/* This program will determine the velocity and distance traveled by a */
/* grapefruit with no initial velocity, t seconds after being dropped  */
/* from a building.                                                     */

#include <stdio.h>

#define GRAVITY 9.81             /* gravitational acceleration (m/s^2)    */

void main( void )
{
    double t;    /* elapsed time during fall (s)                        */
    double y;    /* distance of fall (m)                                */
    double v;    /* final velocity (m/s)                                */


    printf( "\n\n Welcome.\n"
            " Calculate the height from which a grapefruit fell\n"
            " given the number of seconds that it was falling.\n\n" );


    printf( " Input seconds: " );   /* prompt for the time, in seconds. */
    scanf ( "%lg", &t );            /* keyboard input for time          */


    y = .5 * GRAVITY * t * t;       /* calculate distance of the fall   */
    v = GRAVITY * t;                /* velocity of grapefruit at impact */


    printf( "    Time of fall = %g seconds \n", t );
    printf( "    Distance of fall = %g meters \n", y );
    printf( "    Velocity of the object = %g m/s \n", v );


    puts( " Normal termination." );
}
```

The user might see this sample output:

```
Welcome.
Calculate the height from which a grapefruit fell
given the number of seconds that it was falling.

Input seconds:  1
   Time of fall = 1 seconds
   Distance of fall = 4.905 meters
   Velocity of the object = 9.81 m/s
Normal termination.
```

Figure 3.5.   Grapefruits and gravity.

3. Each **%** sign in the format is the beginning of a conversion specifier. It tells us to read one item and specifies the type of that item. We use **%lg**, for "long general-format **double**," to read a value of type **double**. (The letter between the **%** and the **g** is a lowercase *letter* **l**, not a numeral 1.)

4. After the format comes a list of addresses for storing the input data. In this case, we need only one item in the list because we have only one conversion specifier in the format. The data will be stored at **&t**, the address of **t**.

- *Fifth box: calculations.*

    1. The symbol **=** is used to store a value into a variable. Here we store the result of the calculation **.5 * GRAVITY * t * t**, which is the standard equation for distance traveled under the influence of a constant force after a given time, in the variable named **y**.
    2. The calculation for height, **y**, uses several ***** operators. The ***** means "multiply." When there is a series of ***** operators, they are executed left to right.
    3. The second formula is standard for computing the terminal velocity of an object with no initial velocity under the influence of a constant force.

- *Sixth box: the output.*

    1. First, the input value (time) is echoed onto the screen to convince the user that the calculations were done with the correct value.
    2. Two **printf()** statements write the answers to the video screen. We use a **%g** specifier to write a **double** value. Note that this is different from a **scanf()** format, where we need **%lg** for a **double**.
    3. The **printf()** function leaves the output cursor on the same output line unless you put a newline character, **\n**, in the format string. In this case, we use a **\n** to put the velocity value on a different line from the distance.

- *Last box: termination.* It is sound programming practice to display a termination comment. This leaves no doubt in the mind of the user that all program actions have been completed normally.

3.5 The Flow of Control

All the examples we have considered so far execute the code (instructions) line by line from beginning to end. However, in most practical programs, it is necessary to follow alternative paths of execution, depending on the data values and other conditions. For example, suppose you want to calculate the velocity of an object, as in Figure 3.5, but you want to prohibit cases that make no physical sense; that is, negative values of time. Two potential courses of action could be taken: (1) Do the calculation and display the answer or (2) comment on the illegal input data and skip the calculation. Another reason we need nonsequential execution is to enable a program to analyze many data values by repeating one block of code.

When a C program is executed, action starts at the first statement following the declarations. For example, in Figure 3.4, execution starts with the **puts()** statement. From there, execution proceeds to the next statement and the next, in order, until it reaches the end of the program, at which point control returns to the operating system. This is called **simple sequential execution**. *Control statements* are used to create conditional branching and repetitive paths of execution in a program. *Flow diagrams* are used as graphical illustrations of the execution paths that these control statements create.

A **flow diagram** is an unambiguous, complete diagram of all possible sequences in which the program statements might be executed. We use flow diagrams to illustrate the flow of control through the statements of a program or part of a program. This is not so necessary for simple sequential execution. However, a two-dimensional graphic representation can greatly aid comprehension when control statements are used to implement more complex sequencing. A few basic rules for flow diagrams follow and are illustrated in Figure 3.6:

1. A flow diagram for a complete program begins with an oval "start" box at the top and ends with an oval return box at the bottom.
2. Declarations need not be diagrammed unless they contain an initializer (used to give the variable a starting value and discussed more in the next chapter). It is probably clearer, though, if you include one round-cornered box below the start oval that lists the variables declared within the function.

This is a flow diagram of the program in Figure 3.4. It illustrates simple straight-line control and the way we begin and end the diagram of a function.

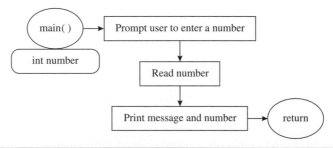

Figure 3.6.   A complete flow diagram of a simple program.

3. The purpose of each statement is written in the appropriate kind of box, each depending on the nature of the action. Since the purpose of the diagram is to clarify the logic of the function, we use English or pseudocode, not C, to describe the actions of the program. Such a diagram could be translated into languages other than C.

4. Simple assignment statements and function calls are written in rectangular boxes. Several of these may be written in the same box if they are sequential and relate to each other.

5. Arrows connect boxes in the sequence in which they will be executed, from start to finish. In the diagram of a complete function, no arrow is left dangling in space and no box is left unattached. All arrow heads must end at a box of some sort, except in the diagram of a program fragment, where the beginning and ending arrows might be left unattached.

6. The diagrams are laid out so that flow generally moves down or to the right. However, you may change this convention if it simplifies your layout or makes it clearer.

7. No arrow ever branches spontaneously. Every tail has exactly one head.

As another example, Figure 3.7 shows the diagram of the program in Figure 3.5. The graph consists of five nodes connected by arrows that indicate the flow of control during execution:

1. A start oval at the top, attached to a box listing the variable declarations.

2. A rectangular box listing statements that print a title and prompt for and read the input.

This is a flow diagram of the program in Figure 3.5.

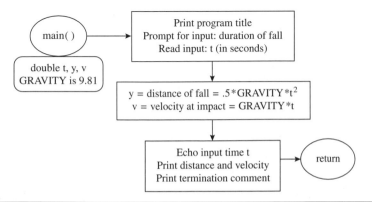

Figure 3.7.   Diagram of the grapefruits and gravity program.

3. A box that calculates the values for distance and velocity using appropriate formulas.
4. A box that echoes the input and outputs the answers.
5. A return oval at the bottom that terminates the program.

Note that these boxes correspond roughly to the boxed units of code in the program.

3.6   Asking Questions: Conditional Statements

A large part of the power of a computer is the ability to take different actions in different situations. For this purpose, all computers have instructions that do various kinds of conditional branching. These instructions are represented in C by the `if` and `if...else` statements.

3.6.1   The Simple `if` Statement

In a simple `if` statement, the keyword `if` is followed by an expression in parentheses, called the *condition*, followed by a single statement or a block of statements in curly brackets, called the *true clause*. At run time, the expression is evaluated and its result is interpreted as either true or false. If true, the block of statements following the condition is executed. If false, that block of statements is skipped. Execution continues with the rest of the program following the conditional.

This control pattern is illustrated by the program in Figure 3.8. We use a simple `if` statement here to test whether the input data make sense (the input is a valid time value). If so, we process the data; if not, we do nothing.

Notes on Figure 3.8. Asking a question.   The outer box contains the entire simple `if` statement, which is diagrammed following the code.

1. This simple `if` statement consists of

   The keyword `if`.

   The condition `(t > 0)`.

   A block (inner box) containing two assignment statements and three `printf()` statements.

   As shown in the flow diagram, there is only one control path into the `if` unit and one path out. Control branches at the `if` condition but rejoins immediately below the true clause.
2. We use an `if` statement here to test whether the input data makes sense (the time is positive). If so, we process the data; if not, we do nothing. On the flow diagram, this corresponds to taking the path marked *false*, which

This solves the same problem as Figure 3.5, except that we screen out invalid inputs.

```
/* --------------------------------------------------------------------- */
/* This program will determine the velocity and distance traveled by a */
/* grapefruit with no initial velocity, t seconds after being dropped  */
/* from a building.  Input time value is checked for being positive.   */
#include <stdio.h>
#define GRAVITY  9.81  /* gravitational acceleration (m/s^2) */

void main( void )
{
    double t;        /* elapsed time during fall (s) */
    double y;        /* distance of fall (m) */
    double v;        /* final velocity (m/s) */

    printf( " \n\n Welcome.\n"
            " Calculate the height from which a grapefruit fell\n"
            " given the number of seconds that it was falling.\n\n" );

    printf( " Input seconds: " );   /* prompt for the time, in seconds. */
    scanf( "%lg", &t );             /* keyboard input for time */

    if (t > 0) {                    /* check for valid data.  */

        y = .5 * GRAVITY * t * t;  /* calculate distance of the fall */
        v = GRAVITY * t;           /* velocity of grapefruit at impact */
        printf( "    Time of fall = %g seconds \n",  t );
        printf( "    Distance of fall = %g meters \n",  y );
        printf( "    Velocity of the object = %g m/s \n",  v );

    }

    puts( " Normal termination.\n" );
}
/* --------------------------------------------------------------------- */
```

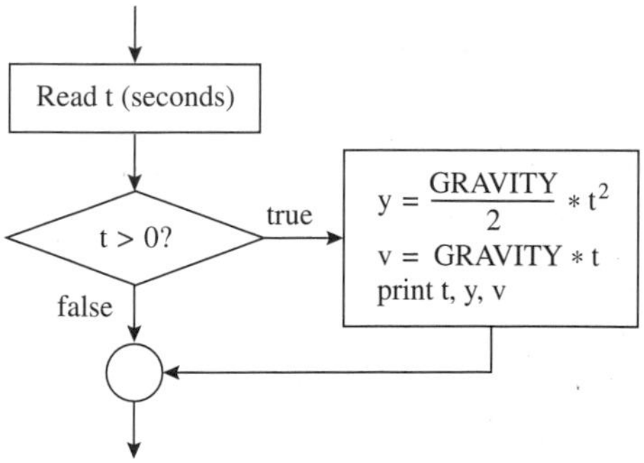

Figure 3.8.   Asking a question.

leaves from the bottom of the diamond. The next statement executed will be the final `puts()`. A sample output from this path follows. Note that the user gets no answers at all and no explanation of why. This is not a good human–machine interface; it will be improved in the next program example.

```
Welcome.
Calculate the height from which a grapefruit fell
given the number of seconds that it was falling.

Input seconds: -1
Normal termination.
```

3. The inner box (the true clause) shows what happens when `t` is positive. If the time is positive, we execute the statements that calculate and print the answers. On the flow diagram, this corresponds to taking the path marked *true*, which leaves from the right side of the diamond. A sample output from this path might be

```
Welcome.
Calculate the height from which a grapefruit fell
given the number of seconds that it was falling.

Input seconds: 10
    Time of fall = 10 seconds
    Distance of fall = 490.5 meters
    Velocity of the object = 98.1 m/s
Normal termination.
```

3.6.2   The `if...else` Statement

An `if...else` statement is like a simple `if` statement but more powerful because it lets us specify an alternative block of statements to execute when the condition is false. It consists of

The keyword `if`.

An expression in parentheses, called the *condition*.

A statement or block of statements, called the *true clause*.

The keyword `else`.

A statement or block of statements, called the *false clause*.

The syntactic difference between an `if...else` and a simple `if` statement is that the true clause of an `if...else` statement is followed immediately by the keyword `else`, while the true clause of a simple `if` statement is not.

At run time, the condition will be evaluated and either the true or the false clause will be executed (the other will be skipped), depending on the result.

The **if...else** statement is diagrammed as a diamond-shaped box containing the question, with one arrow going in and two coming out. These two arrows are labeled *true* and *false* to show which way to go based on the results of the test. The **true** and **false** actions hang from them like saddlebags. The small circle below the diamond is very important: It is the point at which the two control paths rejoin. The entire **if...else** unit has only one control path leading into it and one control path leading out.

In the next program example, we improve on the human–machine interface of the grapefruit and gravity program by adding an **else** clause to tell the user why no calculation was done. If the input is reasonable, the output from this program will be exactly like the output from Figure 3.8. If the input is negative (which is impossible in reality), the output will be an error comment. This is not the only way to handle such an error. Other methods will be discussed in future chapters. The logic for this program is illustrated by the flow diagram in Figure 3.9. As you work through the boxes in the program, note how they correspond to the boxes in the flow diagram.

Notes on Figure 3.9: An action with an alternative.

1. In this **if...else** statement, the condition is **t > 0**. The **true** clause (first inner box) contains actions appropriate for valid data. The keyword **else** follows the **true** clause, and the **false** clause (second inner box) is a single **puts()** statement.
2. As shown in the flow diagram, there is only one control path into the **if...else** unit and one path out. Two possible control paths flow out of the **if**, but they rejoin at the end of the statement.
3. If the time is positive, the calculations and print statements on the right will be executed. Otherwise, the error comment on the left will be printed. One clause always is skipped.
4. Here is a sample of the headings and output from the first inner box (**true** clause):

```
Welcome.
Calculate the height from which a grapefruit fell
given the number of seconds that it was falling.

Input seconds:  5.241
   Time of fall = 5.241 seconds
   Distance of fall = 134.731 meters
   Velocity of the object = 51.4142 m/s
Normal termination.
```

5. Here is a sample output from the second inner box (**false** clause):

```
Input seconds:   -1
Try again; input must be a positive number.
Normal termination.
```

We can improve the human–machine interface of the grapefruit program by adding an `else` clause to the `if` statement. This code should replace the box in Figure 3.8.

```
if (t > 0) {                          /* check for valid data. */

    y = .5 * GRAVITY * t * t; /* distance of the fall */
    v = GRAVITY * t;          /* velocity at impact */
    printf( "    Time of fall = %g seconds \n", t );
    printf( "    Distance of fall = %g meters \n", y );
    printf( "    Velocity of the object = %g m/s \n", v );

}
else {                                /* otherwise... */

    puts( " Try again; input must be a positive number." );

}
/* ------------------------------------------------------------ */
```

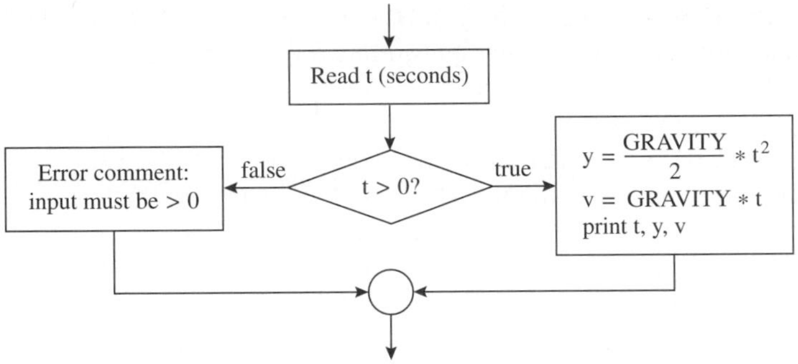

Figure 3.9.   An action with an alternative.

3.6.3 A Series of `if…else` Statements

To validate input data, it often is necessary to perform more than one test. For example, one might need to test two inputs or whether an input lies between minimum and maximum acceptable values. To do this, we can use two or more **if…else** statements, as demonstrated in Figure 3.10, which is an extension of the program in Figure 3.9. In this program, we make an additional test using two **if…else** statements in a row. We ensure that the input both is positive and does not exceed a reasonable limit, in this case 60 seconds.

This solves the same problem as Figure 3.9, except that we limit valid inputs to be less than 1 minute.

```
/* ------------------------------------------------------------------- */
/* This program will determine the velocity and distance traveled by a  */
/* grapefruit with no initial velocity, t seconds after being dropped   */
/* from a building. Input time value must be between 0 and MAX seconds. */
#include <stdio.h>
#define GRAVITY 9.81            /* Gravitational acceleration (m/s^2) */

#define MAX      60             /* Upper bound on time of fall. */

void main( void )
{
    double t;        /* elapsed time during fall (s) */
    double y;        /* distance of fall (m) */
    double v;        /* final velocity (m/s) */
    printf( " \n\n Welcome.\n"
            " Calculate the height from which a grapefruit fell\n"
            " given the number of seconds that it was falling.\n\n" );
    printf( " Input seconds: " );    /* prompt for the time, in seconds. */
    scanf( "%lg", &t );              /* keyboard input for time */

    if (t < 0) {                     /* check for negative input */
        printf( " Error: time must be positive.\n\n" );
    }

    else if (t > MAX) {              /* Is time value too big?  */
        printf( " Error: time must be <= %i seconds.\n\n", MAX );
    }

    else {  /* Input is valid; calculate distance and velocity */
        y = .5 * GRAVITY * t * t;   /* calculate distance of the fall */
        v = GRAVITY * t;             /* velocity of grapefruit at impact */
        printf( "    Time of fall = %g seconds \n", t );
        printf( "    Distance of fall = %g meters \n", y );
        printf( "    Velocity of the object = %g m/s \n", v );
    }

    puts( " Normal termination." );
}
```

Figure 3.10.   Asking more than one question.

The flow diagram corresponding to this new version of the program is given in Figure 3.11. In this diagram, you can see the column of diamond shapes typical of a chain of **if** statements. The **true** clause actions form another sequence to the right of the tests in the diamonds, and the final **false** clause terminates the diamond sequence. All the paths come together in the bubble before the termination message.

Notes on Figure 3.10: Asking more than one question.

- *First box: maximum time.*

    1. This program checks for inputs that are too large as well as those that are negative.
    2. Since the upper limit is an arbitrary number, it might be necessary to change it in the future. To make such changes easy, we define this limit, **MAX**, at the top of the program and use the symbolic name in the code.

This is a diagram of the program from Figure 3.10.

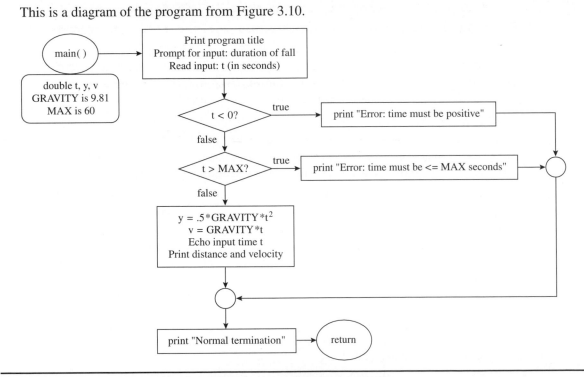

Figure 3.11.   Flow diagram for asking more than one question.

- *Large outer box: the* `if...else` *chain.*

  1. Before computations are made, we inspect the data for two errors (first two inner boxes). We skip the remaining tests and the calculations if either error is discovered. This method of error handling avoids doing a computation with meaningless data, such as the negative value in the previous version of the program.
  2. If no errors are found, we execute the code in the third inner box.

- *First inner box: negative input values.*

  1. As in the prior example, the input must be positive to correspond to physical reality. The first `if` statement handles this.
  2. The `true` clause of this `if` statement prints an error comment. Following that, control goes to the `puts()` statement at the bottom of the program, skipping over the `else if` test and the `else` clause.

- *Second inner box: input values that are too large.*

  1. The elapsed time also must be reasonable. We compare the input value to a maximum allowable value, as defined in the problem specification (60 seconds in this case). The second `if` statement handles this.
  2. The `true` clause of this `if` statement prints an error comment. Then control skips the `else` clause and goes to the `puts()` at the bottom of the program.
  3. Here is a sample of the program's error handling:

```
Welcome.
Calculate the height from which a grapefruit fell
given the number of seconds that it was falling.

Input seconds: 100
Error: time must be <= 60 seconds.

Normal termination.
```

- *Third inner box: the computation and output.*

  1. If the input seems valid, we calculate and print the distance and velocity using the given formulas. Then we echo the input and print the answers.
  2. Here is the output (without the titles) from a run with valid data:

```
Input seconds: 20
    Time of fall = 20 seconds
    Distance of fall = 1962 meters
    Velocity of the object = 196.2 m/s
Normal termination.
```

3.6.4   Which `if` Should Be Used?

We looked at three different ways to use `if` statements. These three control patterns are appropriate for different kinds of applications.

The simple `if` statement.   The primary uses of the simple `if` statement:

- *Processing a subset of the data items.* Sometimes a collection of data contains some items that are relevant to the current process and others that are not of interest. We need to process the relevant items and ignore the others. For example, suppose that a file contains data from a whole census but the programmer is interested only in people over the age of 18. The entire file would need to be read but only a subset of the data items would be selected and processed.
- *Handling data items that require extra work.* Sometimes a few items in a data set require extra processing. For instance, a cash register program must compute the sales tax on taxable items but not on every item. It must test whether each product is taxable and, if so, compute and add the tax. If not, nothing happens.
- *Testing for an error condition or goal condition within a loop and leaving the loop if that condition is found.* This use of `if` with `break` will be discussed in Chapter 6.

The `if...else` statement.   The primary applications of the `if...else` statement:

- *Processing one of two valid alternatives.* Consider a program that computes the roots of a quadratic equation: $ax^2 + bx + c = 0$. Such a program must first calculate the "discriminant" of the equation; namely, $d = b^2 - 4ac$. If this value is positive, the roots of the equation are real numbers; if it is negative, the roots are complex. Both cases are valid but require different processing and different output statements. An `if...else` statement would be used to test the discriminant. Then the `true` clause would execute the code for one kind of roots and the `false` clause would contain the code for the other.
- *Normal processing versus nonfatal error handling.* In this control pattern, an input value is read and tested for legality. If it would cause a run-time error, an error message is given and the input is not processed in the usual way. This control pattern is illustrated by the outer box and diagram in Figure 3.9.

The if...else series.   The applications of the if...else series:

- *Validating a series of inputs.* We can use a series of if...else statements to test a series of inputs. The **true** clause of each statement would print an error comment, and the **false** clause of the last statement would process the validated data. This decision pattern is incorporated into a program in Figure 3.10.
- *Choosing one from a series of alternatives.* Sometimes several alternative actions are possible and one must be selected. In this case, we often use a series of if...else statements to test a series of conditions and select the action corresponding to the first test whose result is **true**. This decision pattern will be incorporated into programs in later chapters; the first example starts in Figure 5.10.

3.6.5   Options for Syntax and Layout (Optional Topic)

Normally each part of an if statement is written on a separate line and all the lines are indented except the if, the else, and the closing curly bracket. However, a C compiler does not care how you lay out your code.

Indentation.   Inconsistent or missing indentation does not cause any trouble, it simply makes the program hard for a human being to read. Since the compiler determines the structure of the statement solely from the punctuation (semicolons and brackets), an extra or omitted semicolon can completely change the meaning of the statement. Therefore, consistent style is important, both to make programs easier to modify and to help avoid punctuation errors.

The condition.   The condition in parentheses after the keyword if can be any expression; it does not need to be a comparison. Whatever the expression, it will be evaluated. A zero result will be treated as false and a nonzero result will be treated as true. (Note, therefore, that any number except 0 is considered to be *true*.) The name of a variable, or even a call on an input function, is a legal (and commonly used) kind of condition.

Curly brackets.   A **true** or **false** clause can consist of either a single statement or a block of statements enclosed in curly brackets. If it consists of a single statement, the curly brackets { and } may be omitted. This can make the code shorter and clearer if the resulting clause fits entirely on the same line as the keyword if or else. Figure 3.12 illustrates this issue. In it, the same if statement is written with and without brackets. The first version is preferred by many experts, even though the brackets are not required. However, others feel that the second version, without brackets, is easier to read because it is written

With brackets the code is spread out:

```
if (age > 18) {
    adults = adults + 1;        /* Count the adults. */
}
else {
    kids = kids + 1;            /* Count the children. */
}
```

Without brackets the code is more compact:

```
if (age > 18)    adults = adults + 1;  /* Count the adults. */
else             kids = kids + 1;      /* Count the children. */
```

Figure 3.12.   The `if` statement with and without curly brackets.

on one line as a single, complete thought. In either case, consistency makes code easier to read; a program becomes visually confusing if one part of an `if` statement has { and } and the other does not.

| 3.7 | **Loops and Repetition** |

The `if` statement lets us make choices. We test a condition and execute one block of code or another based on the outcome. Another kind of control structure is the loop, which lets us execute a block of statements any number of times (zero or more). Conditionals and loops are two of the three fundamental control structures in a programming language.[10] Loops are important because they allow us to write code once and have a program execute it many times, each time with different data. The more times a computation must be done, the more we gain from writing a loop to do it, rather than doing it by hand or writing the same formula over and over in a program.

C provides three types of loop statements that repeatedly execute a block of code: `while`, `do`, and `for`. The `while` statement is the most basic and is introduced first, in Figure 3.13.[11]

3.7.1   A Counting Loop

Every loop has a set of actions to repeat, called the **loop body**, and a loop test to determine whether to repeat those actions again or end the repetition. In this

---

[10] The third control structure, functions, will be introduced in Chapter 5.

[11] The other two loop statements will be presented in Chapter 6.

This program demonstrates the concept of a counting loop.

```
/* ---------------------------------------------------- */
/* This program fills a screen with 20 numbered lines. */
#include <stdio.h>
#define ITERATIONS  20

void main( void )
{
    int m;                              /* The loop counter. */

    puts( " This is a heading line." );

    m = ITERATIONS;                     /* Initialize the loop counter. */
    while (m > 0) {                     /* Count downward from 20 to 1. */
        printf( " %i. \n", m );         /* Print the counter.          */
        m = m - 1;                      /* Decrement the counter.       */
    }

    puts( "\n This message should appear after a blank line." );

    puts( "Normal termination." );
}
/* ---------------------------------------------------------------- */
```

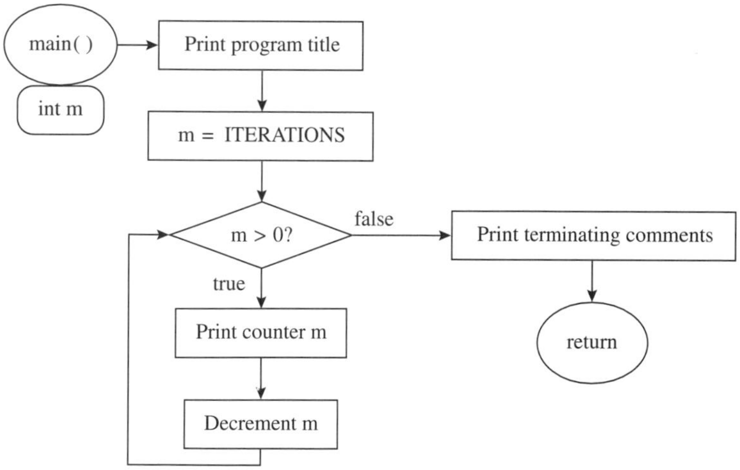

Figure 3.13.   Countdown.

chapter, we study loops based on counting. In these loops, a variable is set to an initial value, then increased or decreased each time around the loop until it reaches a goal value. We call this variable a **loop counter** because it counts the repetitions and ends the loop when we have repeated it enough times. Our next example, shown in Figure 3.13, introduces a counting loop implemented using a `while` statement. It is a very simple program whose purpose is to make the repetition visible. The corresponding flow diagram used for `while` loops follows the code in the figure.

Notes on Figure 3.13: Countdown.

- *First box: the loop variable.* A counter is an integer variable used to count some quantity such as the number of repetitions of a loop.
- *Second box: the loop.*

  1. Before entering a `while` loop, we must initialize the variable that will be used to control it. Here we give an initial value of 20 to `m`, the counter variable.
  2. A `while` statement has three parts, in the following order: the keyword `while`, a condition in parentheses, and a body. The loop body consists of either a single statement or a block of statements enclosed in curly brackets, as shown in the program.
  3. To execute a `while` loop, first evaluate the condition. If the result is true, the loop body will be executed once and the condition will be retested.
  4. This sequence of execution is illustrated by the flow diagram at the bottom of Figure 3.13. In the diagram, the `while` loop is an actual closed loop. Control will go around this loop until the condition becomes false, at which point control will pass on to the termination code. The same diamond shape used to represent a test in an `if` statement is used to represent the loop termination test. The presence of a closed cyclic path in the diagram shows that this is a loop, rather than a conditional control statement.
  5. The statement `m = m - 1` tells us to use the old value of `m` to compute a new one. Read this expression as "`m gets m minus 1`." (Do not call this assignment operation *equals*, or you are likely to become confused with a test for equality.) In detail, this statement means

     Fetch the current value of `m`.

     Subtract 1 from it.

     Store the result back into the variable `m`.

  6. Each time we execute the body of the loop, the value stored in `m` will decrease by 1.

7. This loop will use 20 lines on the screen to display numbers starting with 20, then 19, and continuing down to 1.

8. Control will leave the loop when the condition becomes false; that is, the first time that **m** is tested after its value reaches 0. This will happen before displaying the 0.

- *Third box: after the loop.* After leaving the loop, control goes to the statements that follow it. The call on **puts()** displays a message at the bottom of the output.

3.7.2 An Input Validation Loop

Interactive computer users are prone to errors; it is very difficult to hit the right keys all the time. It is common to lean on the keyboard or to hold a key down too long and type 991 instead of 91. A crash-proof program must be prepared for bad input, sometimes called *garbage input*. A much-repeated saying is "garbage in, garbage out" (GIGO); that is, the results of a program cannot be meaningful if the input was erroneous or illegal. Although it is impossible to identify all bad input, some kinds can be identified by comparing the data to the range of expected, legal data values. When an illegal data item is identified, the program can quit or ask for re-entry of the data.

A good interactive program uses input prompts to let the user know what specific inputs or what kinds of inputs are acceptable and what to do to end the process. If an input clearly is faulty, the program should (at a minimum) refuse to process it. Preferably, it should explain the error and give the user as many chances as needed to enter good data. One way to do this is the data validation loop.

A **data validation loop** (shown in Figure 3.14) prompts the user to enter a particular data item. It then reads the item and checks whether the input meets criteria for a reasonable or legal value. If so, the loop exits; if not, the user is informed of the error and reprompted. This continues until the user enters an acceptable value.

Notes on Figure 3.14: Input validation using `while`.

- *First box: A valid odometer reading.*

1. Before the beginning of a **while** data validation loop, the program must prompt the user for input and read it.

2. The **while** loop tests the input. If it is good, the loop body will be skipped; otherwise, control enters the loop. Numbers entered must be small enough to be stored in an integer variable.

3. The loop must print an error comment that indicates what is wrong with the input, reprompt the user, and read another input.

```
/* Compute the average speed of your car on a trip. --------------- */
#include <stdio.h>

void main( void )
{
    int begin_miles;        /* Odometer reading at beginning of trip. */
    int end_miles;          /* Odometer reading at end of trip.       */
    int miles;              /* Total miles traveled.                  */
    double hours;           /* Duration of trip (hours, minutes).     */
    double minutes;
    double speed;           /* Average miles per hour for trip.       */
    puts( "\n Miles Per Hour Computation \n" );

    printf( " Odometer reading at beginning of trip: " );
    scanf( "%i", &begin_miles );
    while (begin_miles < 0) {
        printf( " Re-enter; odometer reading must be positive: " );
        scanf( "%i", &begin_miles );
    }

    printf( " Odometer reading at end of trip: " );
    scanf( "%i", &end_miles );
    while (end_miles <= begin_miles) {
        printf( " Re-enter; input must be > previous reading: " );
        scanf( "%i", &end_miles );
    }

    printf( " Duration of trip in hours and minutes: " );
    scanf( "%lg%lg", &hours, &minutes );
    hours = hours + (minutes / 60);
    while (hours < 0.0) {
        printf( " Re-enter; hours and minutes must be >= 0.\n" );
        scanf( "%lg%lg", &hours, &minutes );
        hours = hours + (minutes / 60);
    }

    miles = end_miles - begin_miles;
    speed = miles / hours;
    printf( " Average speed was %g \n", speed );

    puts( " Normal termination.\n" );
}
```

Figure 3.14.   Input validation using while.

4. Note that we need two prompts and two `scanf()` statements for this control pattern: one before the loop and another inside the loop.

- *Second and third boxes: validating the other input.*

  1. Data validation loops all follow a pattern similar to the first loop. The major difference between the first two loops is that the mileage read by the first loop is used in the validation test of the second.
  2. In the third loop, a computation must be made before the data can be tested. Like the `scanf()` statement, this computation must be written twice, once before entering the loop and again at the end of the loop.

- *The fourth box: correct data.* The box produced this output when correct data were supplied:

```
Miles Per Hour Computation

Odometer reading at beginning of trip:  061234
Odometer reading at end of trip:  061475
Duration of trip in hours and minutes:  4 51
Average speed was 49.6907
Normal termination.
```

- **Faulty data.** Here are the results of supplying two kinds of invalid data (greeting and closing comments have been omitted):

```
Odometer reading at beginning of trip: -1
Re-enter; odometer reading must be positive: 061234
Odometer reading at end of trip: 061521
Duration of trip in hours and minutes: 5 28
Average speed was 52.5

Odometer reading at beginning of trip: 023498
Odometer reading at end of trip: 022222
Re-enter; input must be > previous reading: -32222
Re-enter; input must be > previous reading: 032222
Duration of trip in hours and minutes: 148 43
Average speed was 58.6618
```

3.8   An Application

We have analyzed several small programs; now it is time to show how to start with a problem and synthesize a program to solve it. We will create a program for Joe Smith, the owner of a gas station in Niagara Falls, New York. Joe advertises that his prices are cheaper than those of his competitor, Betty, across the border in Niagara Falls, Ontario. To be sure that his claim is true, he computes the U.S. equivalent of Betty's rates daily. Joe's employee reads Betty's pump prices on the way to work each day, and Joe uses his Internet connection to look up the current exchange rate (U.S. dollars per Canadian dollar). Canadian gas is priced in Canadian dollars per liter. U.S. gas is priced in U.S. dollars per gallon. The conversion is too complicated for Joe to do accurately in his head. Figure 3.15 defines the problem and specifies the scope and properties of the desired solution. We will write a solution step by step. As we go along, we will write a comment for every declaration and any part of the code we defer to a later step.

Step 1. Writing the specification.   Sometimes you will be given a specification, like that in Figure 3.15, and you can begin to plan your strategy based on it. Much of the time, though, you will be given only a general description, as in the previous paragraph. You can fill in many of the details of the specification directly, but you might need to look up in a reference book things like constants or formulas, and you may need to decide the level of accuracy to maintain in your calculations. Until you have completed this step, you will be wasting time by trying to jump into writing the program.

Problem scope: Write a short program for Joe that will compute the price per gallon in U.S. funds that is equivalent to Betty's price for one grade of gas.

Inputs: (1) The current exchange rate, in U.S. dollars per Canadian dollar. This rate varies daily. (2) The Canadian prices per liter for one grade of gasoline.

Constants: The number of liters in 1 gallon = 3.78544

Formula:

$$\frac{\$\_US}{gallon} = \frac{\$\_Canadian}{liter} * \frac{liters}{gallon} * \frac{\$\_US}{\$\_Canadian}$$

Output required: Echo the inputs and print the equivalent U.S. price.

Computational requirements: All the inputs will be real numbers.

Limitations: The exchange rate and the price for gas should be positive. If the user enters an incorrect input, an error message should be displayed and another opportunity given to enter correct input.

Figure 3.15.   Problem specification: Gas prices.

Step 2. Creating a test plan. Before beginning to write the program, we plan how we will test it. The first test case should be something that can be computed in one's head. We note that one of the simplest computations will occur when the exchange rate is 1.0. Then, if the price per liter is the same as the number of gallons per liter, the price per gallon should be $1.00. We enter this set of numbers as the first line of the test plan in Figure 3.16. We enter the inverse case as the second line of the table: For a price of $1.00 Canadian per liter, the U.S. price should be the same as the conversion factor for liters per gallon.

As a third test case, we enter an unacceptable conversion rate; we expect to see an error comment in response. We also must test the program's response to an invalid gas price, so we add a line with a negative price.

Finally, we enter a typical conversion rate and a typical price per liter, expecting to see an answer that is consistent with real prices. We use a hand calculator to compute the correct answer. We now have five lines in our test plan, which is enough for a simple program that tests for acceptable inputs.

Step 3. Starting the program. First, we write the parts that remain the same from program to program, that is, the **#include** command and the first and last lines of **main()** with the greeting and closing messages. The dots in the code represent the unfinished parts of the program that will be filled in by later coding steps.

```
#include <stdio.h>
...                      /* Space for #defines. */
void main( void )
{
    ...                  /* Space for declarations. */
    puts( "\n Gas Price Conversion Program \n" );
                         /* Input statements.   */
                         /* Computations.   */
                         /* Output statements.   */
    puts( "\n Normal termination.\n" );
}
```

Rate	Can.$/liter	U.S.$/gallon
1.0	$0.26417	$1.00
1.0	$1.00	$3.78544
−0.001	$1.00	Error
1.0	−$0.87	Error
0.7412	$0.55	$1.543173

Figure 3.16.   Test plan: Gas prices.

Step 4. Reading the data.   The exchange rate is a number with decimal places, so we declare a `double` variable to store it and put the declaration at the top of `main()`:

```
double US_per_Can;    /* Exchange rate, $_US / $_Canadian */
```

We decide to use a data validation loop to prompt for and read the current exchange rate, so we write down the parts of a `while` validation loop that always are the same, modifying the loop test, prompts, formats, and variable names, as appropriate, for our current application. This code goes into the `main()` program in the second spot marked by the dots.

```
printf( " Enter the exchange rate, $US per $Can: " );
scanf( "%lg", &US_per_Can );

while (US_per_Can < 0.0) {
    printf( " Re-enter; rate must be positive: " );
    scanf( "%lg", &US_per_Can );
}
```

When writing the calls on `scanf()`, remember to use `%lg` in the format for type `double` and put the ampersand before the variable name.

Next, we must read and validate the Canadian gas price. We declare a variable with a name that reminds us that the input is the price in Canadian dollars for a liter. We also remember to declare a variable for the price in U.S. dollars.

```
double C_liter;         /* Canadian dollars per liter */
double D_gallon;        /* US dollars per gallon */
```

Now we write another data validation loop, modifying the loop test, prompts, formats, and variable names, as needed. We write it in the program after the first loop.

```
printf( " Canadian price per liter: " );
scanf( "%lg", &C_liter );

while (C_liter < 0.0) {
    printf( " Re-enter; price must be positive: " );
    scanf( "%lg", &C_liter );
}
```

Step 5. Converting the gasoline price.   We defined a constant for liters per gallon at the very top of the program. Now we are ready to compute the price per gallon. Remember that we do not use an = sign or a semicolon in a `#define` command:

```
#define LITR_GAL    3.78544
```

```
/* -------------------------------------------------------------
** Compute the equivalent prices for Canadian gas and U.S. gas
** ------------------------------------------------------- */
#include <stdio.h>
#define LITR_GAL    3.78544

void main( void )
{
    double US_per_Can;            /* Exchange rate, $_US / $_Canadian */
    double C_liter;               /* Canadian dollars per liter */
    double D_gallon;              /* US dollars per gallon */

    puts( "\n Gas Price Conversion Program \n" );
    printf( " Enter the exchange rate, $US per $Can: " );
    scanf( "%lg", &US_per_Can );
    while (US_per_Can < 0.0 ) {
            printf( " Re-enter; rate must be positive.\n " );
            scanf( "%lg", &US_per_Can );
    }
    printf( " Canadian price per liter: " );
    scanf( "%lg", &C_liter );
    while (C_liter < 0.0 ) {
            printf( " Re-enter; price must be positive: " );
            scanf( "%lg", &C_liter );
    }
    D_gallon = C_liter * LITR_GAL * US_per_Can;
    printf( "\n Canada: $%g  USA: $%g \n", C_liter, D_gallon );

    puts( "\n Normal termination.\n" );
}
```

Figure 3.17.   Problem solution: Gas prices.

We check the conversion formula given in the specification, making sure that the units do cancel out and leave us with dollars per gallon. Then we write the code for it and a **printf()** statement to print the answers:

```
D_gallon = C_liter * LITR_GAL * US_per_Can;
printf( "\n Canada: $%g  USA: $%g \n", C_liter, D_gallon );
```

Step 6. Testing the completed program.   The finished program is shown in Figure 3.17. Now we run the program and enter the first data set from the test plan. The results are

```
Gas Price Conversion Program

Enter the exchange rate, $US per $Can: 1.0
Canadian price per liter: .26417
```

```
Canada: $0.26417    USA: $1
```

```
Normal termination.
```

We run the program twice again to test the error handling (greeting and closing messages have been omitted):

```
Enter the exchange rate, $US per $Can:  -0.001
Re-enter; rate must be positive:  1.001
Canadian price per liter:  1.00
```

```
Canada: $1   USA: $3.78923
------------------------------
```

```
Enter the exchange rate, $US per $Can: 1.0
Canadian price per liter: -.087
Re-enter; price must be positive: 2.30
```

```
Canada: $2.3   USA: $8.70651
```

Finally, here is a test run using ordinary data (the last line in the test plan):

```
Enter the exchange rate, $US per $Can: .7412
Canadian price per liter: .55
```

```
Canada: $0.55   USA: $1.54317
```

3.9   What You Should Remember

3.9.1 Major Concepts

The C language contains many facilities not mentioned yet, and those that have been introduced can be used in many more ways than demonstrated here. It can take years for a programmer to become truly expert in this language. In the face of this complexity, a beginner copes by starting with simple applications, mastering the basic concepts, and learning only the most important details. In this chapter, we have taken a preliminary look at the most basic and important elements of the C language and how they can be combined into a simple but complete program. These are grouped into related areas and summarized.

- Overall program structure:

  An `#include` command is needed at the top of your program to allow your program to use system library functions.

  A program must have a `main()` function.

The **main()** function starts with a series of declarations.

A series of statements follows the declarations.

A program should start with a statement that prints a greeting and gives instructions for the user.

A program should end with a statement that prints a **Normal termination** message.

- Types, objects, and declarations:

A **#define** command can be written at the top of a program to create a symbolic name for a constant.

Declarations are used to create variables and are grouped at the top of a program block.

Every object has a type. The two basic data types seen so far are **int** and **double**.

- Simple statements:

Each statement tells the computer what to do next and what variables and constants to use in the process.

The **scanf()** statements perform input. They let a human being communicate with a computer program. If a program requires the user to enter data, the input statement should be preceded by an output statement that displays a user prompt.

The **puts()** and **printf()** statements perform output. These statements let a computer program communicate with a human being.

An assignment statement can perform a calculation and store the result in a variable so that it can be used later. In general, calculations follow the basic rules of mathematics.

- Compound statements:

Statements can be grouped into blocks with curly brackets.

The simple **if** statement is a conditional control statement. It has a condition and one block of code that is executed when the condition is true.

The **if...else** statement is a conditional control statement that has a condition and two blocks of code, a true clause and a false clause. When an **if...else** statement is executed, the condition is tested first and this determines which block of code is executed.

The **while** statement is a looping control statement. It has a condition and one block of code. The condition is tested first, and if the condition is true, the block is executed. Then the condition is retested. Execution and testing are repeated as long as the condition remains true.

The counting loops seen so far require that a counter variable be initialized prior to the loop and updated in some manner each time through the loop.

3.9.2 Programming Style

- A comment should follow each variable declaration to explain the purpose of the variable.
- Input data should be checked for validity: Garbage input causes garbage output.
- When writing your own programs, it often helps to model your work after a sample program that does a similar task. This makes it easier to find a combination of input, calculation, output, and control statements that are consistent with each other and work gracefully together.
- Indentation is important for readability. A programmer should adopt a meaningful indentation style and follow it consistently.
- Line up the words `if` and `else` with the } brackets that close each clause in the same column. Indent all the statements in each clause. This assures a neat appearance and helps a reader find the end of the clause.[12]
- If the clause to be executed in one part of an `if` statement is short and the other part is long, put the short clause first. This helps the reader see the whole picture easily. For example, suppose the program must test an input value to determine whether it is in the legal range. If it is legal, several statements will be used to process it. If it is illegal, the program will print an error comment and terminate execution, which takes only two lines of code. This program should be written with the error clause first (immediately following the `if` test) and the normal processing following the `else`.
- Where possible, avoid writing the same statement twice. This makes the program clearer and easier to debug. For example, do not put the same statement in both clauses of an `if` statement; put it before the `if` or after it.
- If both the `true` clause and the `false` clause are single statements, the entire `if` statement can be written on two lines without curly brackets ({ and }) to begin and end the clauses. If either clause is longer than one line, both clauses should be written with curly brackets.

---

[12] This layout scheme is advocated by *Recommended C Style and Coding Standards*, guidelines published in 1994 by experts at Bell Laboratories.

3.9.3 Sticky Points and Common Errors

- When you compile a program and get compile-time error comments, look at the first one first. One small error early in the program can produce dozens of error comments; fixing that single error often will make many comments go away.
- If you misspell a word, it becomes a different word in the eyes of the compiler. This is the first thing to check when you do not understand a compile-time or link-time error comment.
- An extra semicolon after the condition in an `if` or `while` statement will end the statement, and the code that should be within the `if` or `while` statement will be outside it. For example, suppose the `while` statement in the countdown program (Figure 3.13) were written incorrectly:

```
m = ITERATIONS;
while (m > 0);
{   printf( " %i.  \n", m );
    m = m - 1;
}
```

The programmer will expect to see 20 lines printed on the page, with the first line numbered 20 and the last numbered 1. Instead, the semicolon ends the loop, which therefore has no body at all. The update line `m = m - 1;` is outside the loop and cannot be reached. The program will become an infinite loop because nothing *within the loop* will decrement the loop variable, `m`.
- A missing semicolon will not be discovered until the compiler begins working on the next line. It will tell you that there is an error, but give the wrong line number. Always check the line before if you get a puzzling error comment about syntax.
- Quotation marks, curly brackets, and comment-begin and -end marks come in pairs. If the second mark of a pair is omitted, the compiler will interpret all of the program up to the next closing mark as part of the comment or quote. It will produce odd and unpredictable error comments.
- If the output seems to make no sense, the first thing to check is whether the declared type of each variable on the output list matches the conversion specification used to print it. An error anywhere in an output format can affect everything after that on the line. If this does not correct the problem, add more diagnostic printouts to your program to display every data item calculated or read as input. If the input values are correct and the calculated values are wrong, check your formulas for precedence errors and check your function calls for errors.
- If the input values are wrong when you echo them, make sure you have ampersands before the names of the variables in the `scanf()` statement. Check also for type errors in the conversion specifiers in the format.

3.9.4   New and Revisited Vocabulary

These are the most important terms and concepts that were presented in this chapter:

preprocessor command	string	garbage
program block	prompt	undefined value
declaration	stream	sequential execution
statement	buffer	control statement
keyword	format	condition
literal	conversion specifier	loop test
constant	assignment	loop body
variable	expression	loop counter
type	operators $(+, -, *, /)$	data validation loop
precision	precedence	flow diagram

The following C keywords and functions were presented in this chapter:

`#include`	`\n` (newline character)	`double`
`#define`	`&` (address of)	`int`
`{...}` (block)	`<stdio.h>`	`main()`
`/*...*/` (comment)	`stdin`	`scanf()`
`if...else` statement	`stdout`	`puts()`
`while` loop	`stderr`	`printf()`

3.10   Exercises

3.10.1   Self-Test Exercises

1. What is wrong with each of the following `if` statements? They are supposed to identify and print out the middle value of three `double` values, **x**, **y**, and **z**.

   a.
   ```c
   if (x < y < z) printf( "y=%g", y );
   else if (y < x < z) printf( "x=%g", x );
   else printf( "z=%g", z );
   ```

   b.
   ```c
   if (x < y)
        if (y < z) printf( "y=%g", y );
        if (z < y) printf( "z=%g", z );
   else
        if (x < z) printf( "x=%g", x );
        if (z < x) printf( "z=%g", z );
   ```

   c.
   ```c
   if (x > y)
   {   if (x < z);
       printf( "x=%g", x );
       else printf( "z=%g", z );
   }
   else
   {   if (y < z);
   ```

```
      printf( "y=%g", y );
      else printf( "z=%g", z );
}
```

2. What conversion specifier do you use in an output format for an **int** variable? For a **double** variable?

3. What happens when you omit the ampersand (address of) before a variable name in a **scanf()** statement? To find out, delete an ampersand in one of the sample programs. Compile and run the resulting program.

4. What happens when you type an ampersand before a variable name in a **printf()** statement? Try it.

5. What happens when you type a comment-begin mark but forget to type (or mistype) the matching comment-end mark? To find out, delete a comment-end mark in one of the sample programs and try to compile the result.

6. What happens when you type a semicolon after the closing parenthesis in a simple **if** statement? Try it.

7. Four code fragments and four flow diagrams follow. Note that each diagram has two action boxes and one or two question boxes. All four represent distinct patterns of logic. Match each code fragment to the corresponding flow diagram and show how the code fits into the boxes.

(1)
```
if (radius < 0) {
    volume = 0;
}
if (height < 0) {
    volume = 0;
}
```

(2)
```
if (radius < 0) {
    volume = 0;
}
else if (height < 0) {
    volume = 0;
}
```

(3)
```
if (t < 1) {
    v = t;
}
else {
    v = 1;
}
```

(4)
```
if (rad > 100)
    puts( "Too big" );
area = PI * rad * rad;
```

8. Find the error in each of the following declarations.

   a. `integer count;`

   b. `double weight = 1,024.5;`

   c. `int k; count;`

   d. `int k==10;`

   e. `duble age;`

3.10.2   Using Pencil and Paper

1. What does your compiler do when you misspell a keyword such as **while** or **else**? What happens when you misspell a function name such as **main()** or **scanf()**? Try it.

2. What happens when you type a semicolon after the closing parenthesis in a **while** statement? Try it.

3. What conversion specifier do you use in an input format for an **int** variable? For a **double** variable?

4. Find the error in each of the following preprocessor commands.

   a. `#include <stdio>`

   b. `#define NORMAL = 98.6`

   c. `#include stdio.h`

   d. `#define TOP 1,000`

   e. `#define LOOPS 10;`

   f. `#include <studio.h>`

5. Given the declarations on the first two lines that follow, find the error in each of the following statements:

   ```
   int age, count;
   double price, weight;
   ```

   a. `scanf( "%g", &price );`

   b. `scanf( "%lg", &weihgt );`

   c. `printf( "%i", &count );`

   d. `scanf( "%i", age );`

   e. `printf( "%i", weight );`

6. Draw a flow diagram for each set of statements, then trace their execution and show the output. Use these values for the variables: `w=3, x=1, y=2, z=0`.

   a. `if (x < y) z=1; if (x > w) z=2;`
      `printf(" %i\n", z);`

b. ```
if (x < y) z=1; else if (x > w) z=2;
   printf(" %i\n", z);
```

c. ```
if (w < x) z=1; else if (w > y) z=2; else z=3;
   printf(" %i \n", z);
```

7. What is the output from the following program?

```c
#include <stdio.h>
void main( void )
{
    int k, m;
    k = 0;
    m = 1;
    while (k <= 3) {
        k = k + 1;
        m = m * 3;
    }
    printf( "k = %i m = %i \n", k, m );
}
```

3.10.3 Using the Computer

1. Weight conversion.
   Write a program that will read a weight in pounds and convert it to grams. Print both the original weight and the converted value. There are 454 grams in a pound. Design and carry out a test plan for this program.

2. Distance conversion.
   Convert a distance from miles to kilometers. There are 5,280 feet per mile, 12 inches per foot, 2.54 centimeters per inch, and 100,000 centimeters per kilometer.

3. Heat transfer.
   Complete the following program for heat transfer that already has been designed and partially coded. The program analyzes the results from a heat transfer experiment in which hot water flows through a pipe and cold water flows in the opposite direction through a surrounding, concentric pipe. Thermocouples are placed at the beginning and end of both pipes to measure the temperature of the water coming in and going out, as diagrammed here.

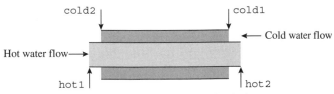

Thermocouples are at both ends of both pipes

To calculate the heat transfer, we need the average hot temperature, the average cold temperature, and the change in temperature from input to output for both hot and cold pipes. This is a standard engineering calculation.

```
/* This program will compute heat characteristics of a concentric-pipe */
/* heat exchanger, including mean hot and cold temperatures, and the    */
/* differences in temperatures of the ends of the pipes.               */
#include <stdio.h>
void main( void )
{
    double hot1;          /* hot inlet temperature */
    double hot2;          /* hot outlet temperature */
    double cold1;         /* cold inlet temperature */
    double cold2;         /* cold outlet temperature */
    double mean_hot;      /* average of hot temperatures */
    double mean_cold;     /* average of cold temperatures */
    double dthot;         /* difference in hot temperatures */
    double dtcold;        /* difference in cold temperatures */

    puts( "Heat Transfer Experiment" );
```

```
    Prompt user to enter four inlet and outlet temperatures.
    Use a separate prompt for each temperature you read.
    Use scanf() to read each and store in the appropriate variable.
```

```
    Calculate the mean of the hot temperatures (their sum divided by 2)
        and the mean of the cold temperatures.  Save each value in an
        appropriate variable.
    Calculate dthot (difference in hot temperatures = the hot outlet
        temperature minus the hot inlet temperature) and dtcold.
        Again save these in the appropriate variables.
    Put comments on these lines describing the calculations.
```

```
    Write printf() statements to echo the four input temperatures.
    Write printf() statements to print the four calculated numbers.
    Label each output clearly, so we can tell what it means.
    Use \n and spaces in your formats to make the output easy to read.
```

```
    puts( " Normal termination." );
}
```

Figure 3.18.   Sketch for the heat transfer program.

Test Objective	Data				Answers			
	Inlets		Outlets		Means		Differences	
	Hot	Cold	Hot	Cold	Hot	Cold	Hot	Cold
Easy to calculate	100	0	50	50	75	25	−50	50
Another legal input	120	35	100	50	110	42.5	−20	15

Figure 3.19.   A test plan for the heat flow program.

Your job is to start with the incomplete program in Figure 3.18, fill in the boxes according to the instructions that follow in each box, and make the program work.

a. Get a copy of the file **fex_heat.c**, which contains the partially completed program in Figure 3.18. Write program statements to implement the actions described in each of the comment boxes. Delete the existing comments and add informative ones of your own.

b. Compile your code and test it using the test plan in Figure 3.19. Prepare proper documentation for the project including the source code, output from running the program on the test data, and hand calculations that prove the output is correct.

4. Gasket area.

A specification for a program that computes the area of a ring gasket is given in Figure 3.20. From this, the flow diagram in Figure 3.21 was constructed.

a. Develop a test plan for this program based on the problem specification in Figure 3.20.

Problem scope: Write a program that will calculate the surface area of a ring gasket.

Inputs: The outer diameter of the gasket, **d_gasket**, and the diameter of the hole in the center of the gasket, **d_hole**. Both diameters should be given in centimeters.

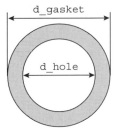

Formula:

$$\text{area} = \frac{\pi \times (\text{d\_gasket}^2 - \text{d\_hole}^2)}{4}$$

Limitations: The value of **d_gasket** must be nonnegative. The ratio of **d_hole** to **d_gasket** must be greater than 0.3 and less than 0.9.

Constant: $\pi = 3.14159265$

Output required: The surface area of the gasket. (Echo the inputs also.)

Computational requirements: All the inputs will be real numbers.

Figure 3.20.   Problem specification: Gasket area.

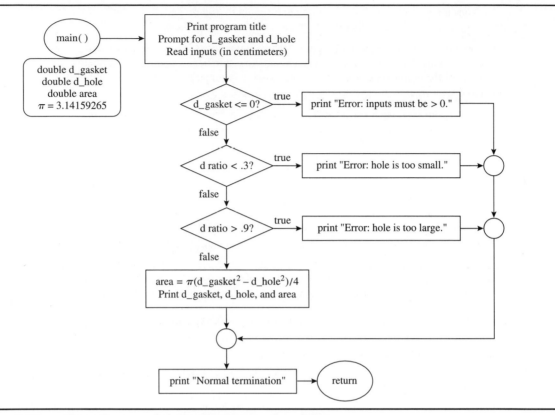

Figure 3.21.   Flow diagram for the gasket area program.

    b. Write a program based on the algorithm in Figure 3.21.

    c. Make sure all of your prompts and output labels are clear and easy to read.

    d. Test your program using the test plan you devised.

    e. Turn in the source code and output results from your test.

5. Temperature Conversion.
   Complete a program for temperature conversion that has been designed and partially coded. The program will read in a temperature in degrees Fahrenheit, convert it into the equivalent temperature in degrees Celsius, and display this result. Your job is to start with the incomplete program in Figure 3.22, fill in the boxes according to the instructions given below in each box, and make the program work.

    a. Make an appropriate test plan for your program following the layout scheme below.

```
/* ------------------------------------------------------------------ */
/* This program will convert temperatures from degrees Fahrenheit into  */
/* degrees Celsius.  Input temperature must be above absolute zero*/

#include <stdio.h>
```

```
Define a constant for absolute zero in Fahrenheit (-459.67).
```

```
void main( void )
{
    double fahr;          /* Temperature in Fahrenheit degrees */
    double cels;          /* Temperature in Celsius degrees    */

    puts( "\n Temperature Conversion Program" );
```

```
Prompt the user to enter a temperature in degrees Fahrenheit.
Use scanf() to read it and store it in the appropriate variable.
Write a printf() statement that will echo the input.
```

```
Test whether the input temperature is less than absolute zero.
If so, print an error comment.
If not, calculate the temperature in degrees Celsius according
to the formula C = 5.0/9.0 * (F - 32.0) and print the answer.

Label the output clearly.
Use newlines and spaces in your formats to make the output
easy to read.
```

```
    puts( " Normal termination." );
}
```

Figure 3.22.   Sketch for the temperature conversion program.

Test objective	Input Fahrenheit	Output Celsius
Easy-to-calculate input		
Another legal input		
Minimum legal input		
Out-of-range input		

b. Start coding with a copy of the file **fex_temp.c**, which contains the partially completed program in Figure 3.22. Following the instructions given in each comment box, write program statements to implement the actions described. Delete the existing comments and add informative ones of your own. Compile and run your code, testing it according to the first line of your plan. Check the answer. If it is correct, print it out and go on to the rest of your test plan. If it is incorrect, fix it and test it again until it is correct. When the answers are correct, print out the program and its output on these tests, and hand them in with the test plan.

6. Skyscraper.
   Assume that the ground floor of a skyscraper has 12-foot ceilings, while other floors of the building have 8-foot ceilings. Also, the thickness in between every floor is 1 foot. On top of the building is an 8-foot flagpole. If the building has N stories altogether, and N is given as an input to your program, calculate the height of a blinking red light at the top of the flagpole and print out this height.

7. Meaningful change.
   Write a program that will input the cost of an item from the user and output the amount of change due if the customer pays for the purchase with a $20 bill. What kinds of problems might this program have? (Think about unexpected inputs.) Design a test plan to detect these problems. Use an **if** statement to validate your data to prevent meaningless outputs.

8. A snow job.
   Your snow blower clears a swath 2 feet wide. Given the length and width of your rectangular driveway, calculate how many feet you will need to walk to clear away all the snow. Be sure to include the steps you take when you turn the snow blower around. Write a program that contains validation loops for the two input dimensions, echoes the input, and prints out the calculated distance.

9. Plusses and minuses.
   Your program will be used as part of a quality control system in a factory that makes metal rods of precise lengths. The current batch of rods is supposed to be 10 cm long. An automated measuring device measures the length of each rod as it comes off the production line. These measurements are automatically sent to a computer as input. Some rods are slightly shorter and some slightly longer than the target length. Your program must read the measurements (use **scanf()**). If the rod is too short, add it to a **short_total**; otherwise, add it to a **long_total**. Also, count it with either the **short_counter** or the **long_counter**. After each batch of 20 rods, print out your totals, counters, and the average length of the rods in the batch.

Computation

CHAPTER

4

Objects, Types, and Expressions

This chapter focuses on how a program can define and name objects and how those objects can be used in computations. New ways are introduced to write variable declarations and constant definitions. Formal rules and informal guidelines for naming these objects are discussed. Informal rules for diagramming objects are presented.

Computation is central to computer programming. We discuss how the usual mathematical operations can be applied to variables and introduce the concepts of precedence and associativity that govern the meaning of an expression in both mathematical notation and in C. Parse trees are introduced to help explain the structure and meaning of expressions.

Finally, declarations, expressions, and parse trees are brought together in a discussion of program design and testing methodology. We propose a problem, develop a program for it, analyze how we should test the program, and show how to use data type rules and parse trees to find and correct an error in the coding.

4.1 Variables, Constants, and Literals

A **data value** is one piece of information. Data values come in several types; the most basic of these are numbers, letters, and strings of letters. When a program is running in a computer, it reads and writes data values, computes them, and sends them through its circuits. A computed data value might stay for a while in a CPU register, be stored into a variable in memory, or be sent to an output device. C keeps track of where data values are when they are being moved around within the computer, but you must decide when to output or store a value (assign it to a variable).

4.1.1 Variables

A **variable** is a storage object. You can visualize it as a box that can hold one data value at a time; the information in the box is a data value. For each type of data value, such as an integer or a real number, there is a corresponding type of variable. Some types of variables require more bytes of memory than others. For example, an `int` (in many machines) uses four bytes of memory while a `double` occupies eight.

A variable is created by a **declaration**. (Unlike some languages, C requires every variable name to be declared explicitly.) The declaration specifies the type of object that is needed, supplies a name for it, and directs the compiler to allocate space for it in memory. Declarations can appear at the beginning of any block of code, just after the opening `{`. Only the statements within a block can use the names declared at its beginning. We call them **local names** because they are not "visible" to other blocks. Technically, we could declare variables inside a block that is part of an `if` statement or a loop. However, this is considered poor style in C. We normally write our declarations at the top of `main()`. In this section, we explore some declaration options.

Syntax for declarations.   The general form of a declaration, shown in Figure 4.1, contains four parts: zero or more modifiers,[1] a type name, an object

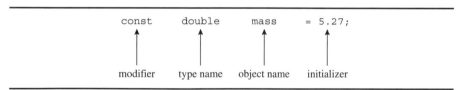

Figure 4.1.   Syntax for declarations.

---

[1] In the C standard, the properties `const` and `volatile` are called *type qualifiers* and `extern`, `static`, `register`, and `auto` are called *storage class specifiers*. For simplicity, and because the distinctions are not important here, we refer to both as *modifiers*. The modifiers are optional and, with the exception of `const`, you need not understand or use them for the time being. We use `volatile` in Chapter 18. We discuss `static` in Chapter 16 and all storage classes, in general, in Chapter 21. Additionally, the modifier `extern` is important in complex, multimodule programs and is demonstrated in Chapter 23.

name or names, and an optional initializer for each name. The parts are written in the order given, followed by a terminating semicolon, as diagrammed in Figure 4.1. The various different data types will be explored in the next few chapters. Object naming conventions are discussed shortly. An **initializer** gives a variable an initial value. This is done by using an = sign, followed by a value of the appropriate type.[2]

If multiple objects are declared, and possibly initialized, using a single statement, the objects are separated by commas. We have adopted a style in which most declaration lines declare one variable and have a comment explaining the use of that variable. This is a good way to write a program and make it self-documenting.

Declaration examples.　Many examples of variable declarations were given in Chapter 3; for example, the program in Figure 3.17 declares one **int** variable, **m**, and three **double** variables; **US_per_Can**, **C_liter**, and **D_gallon**.

Figure 4.2 illustrates more variations on the basic declaration syntax and shows how to draw diagrams of variables. The first line declares one variable of type **double**, as we have done many times already. This line tells C to allocate enough memory to store a **double** value and use that storage location whenever the name **length** is mentioned. The declaration does not put a value into the variable; it will contain whatever was left in that storage location by the program that previously ran on the computer. This value is unpredictable and meaningless in the present context. Formally, we say that it is an **undefined value**; informally, we call it **garbage**. The garbage stays there until a value is read into the variable (perhaps by **scanf()**) or stored in the variable by an assignment statement.

A variable is diagrammed, as in Figure 4.2, by drawing a box with the variable name just above the box and the current value inside it. The size of each

---

Four variables are declared here and diagrammed below.

```
void main( void )
{
    double length;              /* Length, in meters. */
    double weight = 1.5;        /* Weight, in kilograms. */
    int k, m = 0;               /* Two integer variables. */
    ...                         /* Rest of program goes here. */
}
```

length	weight	k	m
?	1.5	?	0

Figure 4.2.　Simple declarations.

---

[2]The rules for initializers will be given as each type is considered.

box is proportional to the number of bytes of storage required on a representative C system. In the diagram of `length`, its undefined value is represented by a question mark. Variable diagrams, or **object diagrams**, are a concrete and visual representation of the abstractions that the program manipulates. We use them to visualize relationships among objects and to perform step-by-step traces of program execution. Object diagrams become increasingly important when we introduce compound data objects such as arrays, pointers, and data structures.

The second line in Figure 4.2 declares the variable `weight` and gives it an initial value. This shorthand notation combines the effect of a declaration and an assignment:

```
double weight;        /* Weight, in kg.  Contains garbage. */
...
weight = 1.5;         /* Now weight contains value 1.5 */
```

As we progress to more complex programs, the ability to declare and initialize a variable in one step will become increasingly important.

The third line in Figure 4.2 declares two variables, `k` and `m`, and it initializes `m`. It does not initialize `k`. To do that, another = sign and value would be needed prior to the comma. This omission is a common mistake of beginning programmers. Combining two declarations in this manner on one line saves space and writing effort. However, it does not provide a place to put separate comments explaining the purpose of the variables and so should be done only when the meaning of the variables is the same or they are logically related.

4.1.2   Constants and Literals

In addition to variables, most programs contain **constants**, which represent values that do not change. A **literal constant** is one that is written, literally, in your code; in the assignment statement `radius = diameter/2.0;` `2.0` is a literal `double`. For each type of value in C, there is a way to write a literal constant. These will be explained as we go through the various types. A **symbolic constant** is a constant to which we have given a name. There are two ways in C to create a symbolic constant: a `#define` command and a `const` declaration.

Often, using symbolic names rather than literal constants saves trouble and prevents errors. This is true especially if the literal constant has many digits of precision, like a value for π, or if the constant might be changed in the future. Well-chosen descriptive names also make the program easier to read. For example, we might wish to use the temperature constant, `-273.15`, which is absolute zero in degrees Celsius. A name like `ABS0_C` is more meaningful than a string of digits.

Using `#define`.   The `#define` command was introduced in Chapter 3. These commands generally are placed at the top of a file. They are used to define physical constants, such as `PI`, `GRAVITY` (see Figure 3.5) or `LITR_GAL` (see Figure 3.17), and give names to arbitrarily defined values, such as the loop limit **N** in Figure 6.9, that are used throughout a program but might have to be changed at some future time. We use a **#define** at the top of the program for an arbitrary constant so that changing the constant is easy, if change becomes necessary. Changing one **#define** is easier than changing several references to the constant value, and finding the **#define** at the top of the file is easier than searching throughout the code for copies of a literal constant.

When you use a name that was defined with **#define**, you actually are putting a literal into your program. Commands that start with **#** in C are handled as a separate part of the language by a part of the compiler, called the *preprocessor*, that looks at (and possibly modifies) every line of source code before the main part of the compiler gets it. The preprocessor identifies the **#define** commands and uses them to build a table of defined terms, with their meanings. Thereafter, each time you refer to a defined symbol, the preprocessor removes it from your source code and replaces it by its meaning. The result is the same as if you wrote the meaning, not the symbol in your source code. For example, suppose a program contained these two lines of source code before preprocessing:

```
#define PI   3.1415927
area = PI * radius * radius;
```

After preprocessing, the **#define** is gone. In some compilers, you can instruct the compiler to stop after preprocessing and write out the resulting code. If you were to look at the preceding assignment statement in that code, it would look like this:

```
area = 3.1415927 * radius * radius;
```

Note the following things about a **#define** command:

- *No* = sign appears between the constant's name and its value.
- The line does *not* end in a semicolon, and you do *not* write the type of the name. (The C translator will deduce the type from the literal.)
- In this example, **PI** is a **double** constant because it has a decimal point.

The C preprocessor always has been a source of confusion and program errors. However, these difficulties are caused by advanced features of the preprocessor, not by simple constant definitions like those shown here. A beginning programmer can use **#define** to name constants with no difficulty. The programmer usually is unaware of the substitutions made by the preprocessor and does not see the version with the literal constants.

The const qualifier (advanced topic).   You also can create a constant by writing the **const** *modifier* at the beginning of a variable declaration. This creates an object that is like a variable in every way except that you cannot change its value (so it is not really like a variable at all). A **const** declaration is like a variable declaration except that it starts with the keyword **const** and it must have an initializer.

A symbolic name is one way to clarify the purpose of a constant and the meaning of the statement that uses the constant. That C provides two different ways to give a symbolic name to a constant value (**#define** and **const**) might seem strange. C does so because each kind of constant can be used to do some advanced things that the other cannot. We recommend the following guidelines for defining constants:[3]

- Use **#define** to name constants of simple built-in types.
- Use **const** to define anything that depends on another constant.

This usage is illustrated in Figure 4.3. The lines in this figure are excerpted from a program that computes a payment table for a loan. The program uses **#define** for the annual interest rate, because while it is constant for this particular loan, it is likely to change for future loans. By placing the **#define** at the top of the program, we make it easy to locate and edit the interest rate at that future time. The monthly rate is one-twelfth of the annual rate; we declare it as a **const double** initialized to **RATE/12**. We use **const** rather than **#define** because the definition involves a computation.

The loan amount and the monthly interest are defined as variables, because they decrease each month. The monthly payment normally will be $100 but we do not define it as a constant because the loan payment on the final month will be smaller.

```
#define RATE .125          /* Annual interest rate. */
const double mrate = RATE/12;  /* Monthly interest rate. */
double payment = 100.00;   /* Monthly payment. */
double loan = 1000.00;     /* Remaining unpaid principle amount. */
double interest;           /* Current month's interest. */
```

Constants:	mrate		Initial values of variables:	payment	loan	interest
RATE: .125	0.01042			100.00	1000.00	?

```
interest = mrate * loan ;
loan = loan + interest - payment;
```

	payment	loan	interest
Variables after assignments:	100.00	910.4166	10.4166

Figure 4.3.   Using constants.

---

[3] These guidelines are consistent with the advanced uses of constants and with usage in C++.

Following the declarations in the figure are diagrams for the objects declared. The variables **payment**, **loan**, and **interest** are diagrammed as variable boxes. The striped box indicates that **mrate** is a constant variable and cannot be changed. No box is drawn for **RATE** because it is implemented as a literal. The lower line in the diagram shows the changes in the variables produced by the two assignment statements.

4.1.3 Names and Identifiers

As a programmer works on the problem specification and begins writing code to solve a problem, he or she must analyze what variables are needed and invent names for them. No two programmers will do this in exactly the same way. They probably will choose different names, since naming is wholly arbitrary. They might even use different types of variables or a different number of variables, since the same goals can often be accomplished in many ways. In this section, we introduce guidelines and formal syntactic rules for naming objects.

The technical term for a name is an **identifier**. You can use almost any name for an object, subject to the following constraints.

These are absolute rules about names:

1. It must begin with a letter or underscore.
2. The rest of the name must be made of letters, digits, and underscores.
3. You cannot use C keywords such as **double** and **while** to name your own objects. You also should avoid the names of functions and constants in the C library, such as **sin()** and **scanf()**.
4. C is case sensitive, so **Volume** and **volume** are different names.
5. Some compilers limit names to 31 characters. Very old C compilers use only the first eight characters of a name.

These are guidelines for names:

1. Use one-letter names such as **x, t**, or **v** to conform to standard engineering and scientific notation. Writing **d = r * t** is better for our purposes than writing the lengthier **distance = rate * time**. Otherwise, avoid single-letter names.
2. When you have two similar quantities, such as two time instances, you might call them **t1** and **t2**. Otherwise, avoid using such similar names.
3. Use names of moderate length. Most names should be between 2 and 12 letters long.
4. Avoid names that look like numbers; **O**, **l**, and **I** are very bad names.
5. Use underscores to make compound names easier to read: **tot_vol** or **total_volume** is clearer than **totalvolume**.
6. Try to invent meaningful names; **x_coord** and **y_coord** are better names than **var1** and **var2**.

7. Do not use names that are very similar, such as `metric_distance` and `meter_distance` or `my_var` and `my_varr`.

4.1.4 Types

When we declare an object, we say what type it will be. Types (sometimes called **data types**) are like adjectives in English: The type of an object describes its size (number of bytes in memory) and how it may be used. It tells the compiler how much storage to allocate for it and whether to use integer operations, floating-point operations, or some other kind of operations on it.

Many types are built into the C language standard; each has its own computational properties and memory requirements. Each type has different advantages and drawbacks, which will be examined in the next few chapters. Later, we will see how to define new types to describe objects that are more complex than simple letters and numbers.

The current popularity of C is based largely on its power and portability. However, the same data type can be different sizes on different machines, which adversely affects portability. For example, the type `int` commonly is two bytes on small personal computers and four bytes on larger machines. Also, some computer memories are built out of words not bytes.

The actual size of a variable, in bytes, becomes very important when you take a program debugged on one kind of system and try to use it on another; the variability in the size of a type can cause the program to fail. To address this problem, C provides the `sizeof` operator, which can be applied to any variable or any type to find out how big that type is in the local implementation. This is an important tool professional programmers use to make their programs portable. Figure 4.4 shows how to use `sizeof`. The output from this program will be different on different machines. It depends partly on the hardware and partly on the compiler itself. You should know what the answers are for any system you use. One of the exercises asks you to use `sizeof` to learn about your own compiler's types. The results from the program in Figure 4.4 are shown following the code. From this we can deduce that the workstation is using four bytes for an `int` and eight bytes for a `double`, which is usual. The literal constant e is represented as a `double`.

4.2

Expressions and Parse Trees

An **expression** is like an entire sentence in English. It specifies how verbs (operators and functions) should be applied to nouns (variables and constants) to produce a result. In this section, we consider the rules for building expressions out of names, operators, and grouping symbols and how to interpret the meanings

This short program demonstrates the proper syntax for using `sizeof`. Note that the parentheses are not needed for variables but they *are* needed for type names.

```
/* ---------------------------------------------------------------------
** Demonstrate the use of sizeof to determine memory usage of data types
*/
#include <stdio.h>
#define e 2.7182818284590452353602874713530   /* Mathematical constant e. */

void main( void )                       /* how to use sizeof */
{
    int s_int, s_double, s_unknown, k;

    s_double = sizeof (double) ;   /* use parentheses with a type name */
    s_int = sizeof k ;             /* no parentheses needed with a variable */
    printf( " sizeof int = %i \n sizeof double = %i \n", s_int, s_double );

    s_unknown = sizeof e ;
    printf( " sizeof e = %i \n", s_unknown );
}
```

Results when run on our workstation:

```
    sizeof int = 4
    sizeof double = 8
    sizeof e = 8
```

Figure 4.4.   The size of things.

of those expressions. We use a kind of diagram called a *parse tree* to see the structure of an expression and to help us understand its meaning.

4.2.1 Operators and Arity

C has several classes of operators in addition to those that perform arithmetic on numbers. These include comparison and logical operators, bit-manipulation operators, and a variety of operators that are found in C but not in other languages. Each group of operators is intended for use on a particular type of object. Many will be introduced in this chapter; others will be discussed in detail in the chapters that introduce the relevant data types. For example, operators that work specifically with integers are explained in Chapter 7. Operators that deal with pointers, arrays, and structured types are left for later chapters. Issues to be considered with each class of operator include the type of data on which it operates, its precedence and associativity, any unusual rules for evaluation order, and any unexpected aspects of the meaning of an operator.

An **operand** is an expression whose value is an input to an operation. *Operators* are classed as unary, binary, or ternary according to the number of operands each takes. A **binary operator** has two operands and is written between those operands. For example, in the expression `(z/4)`, the `/` sign is a binary operator and `z` and `4` are its operands. We also say that a binary operator has arity $= 2$. The **arity** of an operator is the number of operands it requires.

A unary operator (arity $= 1$), such as `-` (negate), has one operand. Most unary operators are **prefix operators**; that is, they are written before their operand. Two unary operators, though, also may be written after the operand, as **postfix operators**. There is only one ternary operator (arity $= 3$), the conditional expression. The two parts of this operator are written between its three operands.

4.2.2   Precedence and Parentheses

Many expressions contain more than one operator. In such expressions, we need to know which operands go with which operators. For example, if we write

$$13/5 + 2$$

it is important to know whether this means

$$(13/5) + 2 \quad \text{or} \quad 13/(5 + 2)$$

because the two expressions have different answers.

Using parentheses.   Parentheses are neither operators nor operands; called *grouping symbols*, they can be used to control which operands are associated with each operator. Parentheses can be used to specify whatever meaning we want; a fully parenthesized expression has only one interpretation. If we do not write parentheses, C uses a default interpretation based on the rules for precedence and associativity. This default is one of the most common sources for errors in writing expressions.

The precedence table and the default rules.   Experienced programmers use parentheses only to emphasize the meaning of an expression or achieve a meaning different from the default one. They find it a great convenience to be able to omit parentheses most of the time. Further, using parentheses selectively makes expressions more readable. However, if you use the default precedence, anyone reading or writing your program must be familiar with the rules to understand the meaning of the code.

The precedence and associativity of each operator are defined by the C precedence table, given in Appendix B. The rules in this table describe the meaning of any unparenthesized part of an expression. **Precedence** defines the grouping order when different operators are involved, and **associativity** defines the order of grouping among adjacent operators that have the same precedence. The concepts and rules for precedence and associativity are simple and mechanical. They can be mastered even if you do not understand the meaning or use of a particular operator. The portion of the **precedence table** that covers the arithmetic operators is repeated in Figure 4.5, with a column of examples added on the right. We use it in the following discussion to illustrate the general principles.

Precedence.   In the precedence table, the C operators are listed in order of precedence; the ones at the top are said to have *high precedence*; those at the bottom have *low precedence*.[4] As a convenience, the precedence classes in C also have been numbered. There are 17 different classes. (The higher the number, the higher is the precedence.) Operators that have the same precedence number are said to have *equal precedence*. You will want to mark Appendix B so that you can refer to the precedence table easily; until all the operators are familiar, you will need to consult it often.

Associativity.   The rule for associativity governs consecutive operators of equal precedence, such as those in the expression (3 * z / 10). All these operators with the same precedence will have the same associativity, which is either left to right or right to left.[5] With left-to-right associativity, the leftmost operator is parsed before the ones to its right. (The process of parsing is explained next.) With right-to-left associativity, the rightmost operator is parsed first. In the expression (3 / z * 10 % 3), the three operators have the same precedence and all have left-to-right associativity. We therefore parse the / first and the * second, giving this result: (((3 / z) * 10) % 3). The parse of this expression is diagrammed in Figure 4.7.

Almost all the unary operators have the same precedence (15) and are written before the operand (that is, in prefix position). The chart shows that they

Arity	Symbol	Meaning	Precedence	Associativity	Examples
Unary	-	Negation	15	right to left	-1, -temp
	+	No action	15	"	+1, +x
Binary	*	Multiplication	13	left to right	3 * x
	/	Division	13	"	x / 3.0
	%	Integer remainder (modulus)	13	"	k % 3
	+	Addition	12	"	x + 1, x + y
	-	Subtraction	12	"	x - 1, 3 - y

Figure 4.5.   Arithmetic operators.

---

[4]Most of the C operators will be described in the next four chapters; others will be explained in later chapters.

[5]The term *left-to-right associativity* is often shortened to *left associativity* and *right-to-left* to *right*.

associate right to left. Therefore, in the expression (- - x), the second negation operation is parsed first and the leftmost negation operation second, giving this result: (- (- x)). Restated simply, this rule states "the prefix operator written closest to the operand is parsed first."

4.2.3   Parsing and Parse Trees

Parsing is the process of analyzing the structure of a statement. The compiler does this when it translates the code, and human beings do it when reading the code. One way to parse an expression is to write parentheses where the precedence and associativity rules would place them by default. This process is easy enough to carry out but can become visually confusing.

An easier way to parse is to draw a *parse tree*. The **parse tree** shows the structure of the expression and is closely related to what the C compiler does when it translates the expression. A parse tree helps us visualize the structure of an expression. It also can be used to understand the order in which operators will be executed by C, which, unfortunately, is not the same as their order of precedence.[6]

To parse an operator, either write parentheses around it and its operands or draw a tree bracket with one branch under each operand and the stem under the operator. A simple, two-pronged bracket is used for most binary operators. The bracketed or parenthesized unit becomes a single operand for the next operator, as shown in Figures 4.6 and 4.7. Brackets or parenthesized units never collide or cross each other. Figure 4.6 shows a parse tree that uses the precedence rules, and Figure 4.7 shows an expression where all operators have equal precedence and the rule for associativity is used. The steps in parsing an arbitrary expression are these:

1. Write the expression at the top, leaving some space between each operand and operator.

The * operator has highest precedence so it was parsed first and it "captured" the middle operand. The assignment has lowest precedence so it was parsed last. The arrowhead on the assignment operator bracket indicates that the value of **x** is updated with the right operand value.

```
x = m + k*y
x = m + (k*y)
x = (m + (k*y))
(x = (m + (k*y)))
```

Figure 4.6.   Applying precedence.

---

[6]Complications of evaluation order are covered in Sections 4.4 and 4.6.3 and Appendix D.

In the diagram, three brackets are used to show which operands go with each of the operators in the expression `(3 / z * 10 % 3)`. These operators have equal precedence, so they are parsed according to the associativity rule for this group of operators, which is left to right.

```
3 / z * 10 % 3                    3 / z * 10 % 3
(3 / z) * 10 % 3
((3 / z) * 10) % 3
(((3 / z) * 10) % 3)
```

Figure 4.7.   Applying associativity.

2. Parse parenthesized subexpressions fully before looking at the surrounding expression.
3. If there are postfix unary operators (`--` or `++`), do them first. These are mentioned here for completeness and will be explained later in the chapter.
4. Next, find the prefix unary operators, all of which associate right to left. Start at the rightmost and bracket each one with the following operand, drawing a stem under the operator. (An operand may be a variable, a literal, or a previously parsed unit.)
5. Now look at the unparsed operators in the expression and look up the precedence of each one in the table. Parse the operators of highest precedence first, grouping each with its neighboring operands. Then go on to those of lower precedence. For neighboring operators of the same precedence, find their associativity in the table. Proceeding in the direction specified by associativity, bracket each operator with the two adjacent operands.
6. Repeat this process until you finish all of the operators.

Figure 4.8 shows an example of parsing an expression where all the rules are applied: grouping, associativity, and precedence.

Notes on Figure 4.8.   Applying the parsing rules.   The steps in drawing this parse tree are as follows:

1. Subexpressions in parentheses must be parsed first. Within the parentheses, the prefix operator - is parsed first. Then the lower precedence

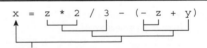

Figure 4.8.   Applying the parsing rules.

operator, +, uses this result as its left operand to complete the parsing in the parentheses.

2. The * and / are the operators with the next highest precedence; we parse them left to right, according to their associativity rule.

3. The - is next; its left operand is the result of / and its right operand is the result of the parentheses grouping.

4. The = is last; it stores the answer into x and returns the value as the result of the expression (this is explained in the next section).

4.3   Arithmetic, Assignment, and Combination Operators

The **arithmetic operators** supported by C are listed in Figure 4.5. All these operators can be used on any pair of numeric operands. The **assignment operator** was described and its uses discussed in Chapter 3. These operators can be combined to give a shorthand notation for doing both actions. For example, the expression (k += 3.5) has the same meaning as (k = k + 3.5). It means "fetch the current value of k, add 3.5, and store the result back into k." The symbol for a **combination operator** is formed by writing the desired operator symbol followed by an assignment sign, as in += or *=. The arithmetic combinations are listed in Figure 4.9, and a parse tree for assignment combinations in Figure 4.10. All combination operators have the same very low precedence, which means that other operators in the expression will be parsed first. If more than one assignment or combination operator is in an expression, these operators will be parsed and executed right to left.

Side effects.   The assignment combinations, along with ordinary assignment and the increment and decrement operators (described in the next section), are different from all other operators: They have the **side effect** of changing the value

---

All these operators associate right to left. The left operand of each must be a variable or storage location. The parse diagram for a combination operator is shown in Figure 4.10.

Symbol	Example	Meaning	Precedence
=	x = 2.5	Store value in variable	2
+=	x += 3.1	Same as (x = x + 3.1); add value to variable and store back into variable	2
-=	x -= 1.5	Same as (x = x - 1.5); subtract value from variable and store back into variable	2
*=	x *= 5	Same as (x = x * 5); multiply and store back	2
/=	x /= 2	Same as (x = x / 2); divide by and store back	2

Figure 4.9.   Assignment and arithmetic combinations.

This is the parse tree and evaluation for the expression **k += m**. Note that the combined operator is diagrammed with two brackets. The upper bracket is for **+**, which adds the initial value of **k** to the value of **m**. The lower bracket shows that the sum is stored back into **k**.

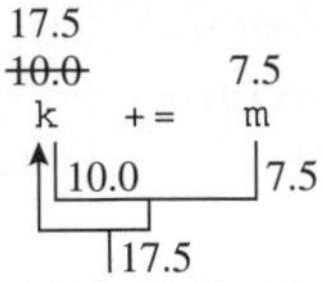

Figure 4.10.   Parse tree for an assignment combination.

of a memory variable. Assignment discards the old value and replaces it with a new value. The combination operators perform a calculation using the value of a memory variable then store the answer back into the variable. When using a combination operator, the right operand may be a variable or an expression, but the left operand must be a variable, since the answer will be stored in it.

Using combination operators.   Figure 4.11 shows how two of the arithmetic combinations can be used in a loop. It is a preliminary version of an algorithm for expressing a number in any selected number base; the complete version is shown in Chapter 7, Figure 7.17.

Notes on Figure 4.11. Arithmetic combinations.

- *Outer box.* This loop is slightly different from the counting loops and validation loops seen so far. It simply continues a process that decreases **n** until the terminal condition, **n** equals 0, occurs. More loop types are discussed in Chapter 6.
- *First inner box: halving the number.* The statement **n /= 2;** divides **n** by 2, throwing away the remainder. The quotient is an integer (with no fractional part) and is stored back into **n**. Therefore, the value of **1/2** is 0, and the value of **7/2** is 3. Integer arithmetic is discussed more fully in Chapter 7.
- *Second inner box: incrementing the counter.* The operator **+=** is often used to increment loop counters, especially when counting by twos (or any increment not equal to 1). As seen in the next section, the operator **++** is more popular for adding 1 to a counter.

4.4   **Increment and Decrement Operators**

C contains four operators that are not present in most other languages because of the problems they cause, but they are very popular with C programmers because

Each time we halve a number, we eliminate one binary digit. If we halve it repeatedly until it reaches 0 and count the iterations, we know how many binary digits are in the number.

```c
#include <stdio.h>
void main( void )
{
    int k;              /* Loop counter. */
    int n;              /* Input - the number to analyze. */
    puts( "\n Halving and Counting\n " );
    printf( " Enter an integer: " );
    scanf( "%i", &n );
    printf( " Your number is %i,", n);

    k = 0;              /* Initialize the counter before the loop. */
    while (n > 0) { /* Eliminate one binary digit each time around loop. */
        n /= 2;         /* Divide n in half and discard the remainder. */
        k += 1;         /* Count the number of times you did this. */
    }
    printf( " it has %i bits when written in binary. \n\n", k );
}
```

Output:

```
Halving and Counting

Enter an integer:  37
Your number is 37, it has 6 bits when written in binary.
```

Figure 4.11.   Arithmetic combinations.

they are so convenient. These are the pre- and postincrement (++) and pre- and postdecrement (--) operators, which let us add or subtract 1 from a variable with only a few keystrokes. The increment operator most often is used in loops, to add 1 to the loop counter. Decrement sometimes is used to count backward. Both normally are used with integer operands, but they also work with variables of type `double`.

The same symbols, ++ and --, are used for both pre- and postincrement, but the former is written before the operand and the latter after the operand. The actions they stand for are the same, too, except that these actions are executed in a different order. Collectively, we call this group the *increment operators*; they are listed in Figure 4.12.

The increment and decrement operators cause side effects; that is, they change values in memory. The single operand of these operators must be a variable or storage location. The prefix operators both associate right to left; the postfix operators associate left to right.

Fixity	Symbol	Example	Meaning	Precedence
Postfix	++	j++	Use the operand's value in the expression, then add 1 to the variable	16
	--	j--	Use the operand's value in the expression, then subtract 1 from the variable	16
Prefix	++	++j	Add 1 to the variable then use the new value in the expression	15
	--	--j	Subtract 1 from the variable then use the new value in the expression	15

Figure 4.12.   Increment and decrement operators.

4.4.1   Parsing Increment and Decrement Operators

The increment operators have two properties that, when put together, make them unique from the operators considered earlier. First, they are unary operators, and second, they modify memory. The parse diagrams for these operators reflect these differences.

To diagram an increment or decrement operator, bracket it with its single operand (which must be a variable or a reference to a variable), drawing a stem under the operator and an assignment arrowhead to show that the variable will receive a new value. That value also is passed on, down the parse tree, and can be used later in the expression. See Figure 4.13 for examples.

When postincrement or postdecrement is used, it is also possible to have prefix unary operators applied to the same operand. In this case, the postfix operator is parsed first (it has higher precedence), then the prefix operators are done right to left. Thus, the expression (- **x** ++) parses to (- (**x** ++)). The

The parse trees are shown for each of these operators. The arrowheads indicate that a value is stored back into memory.

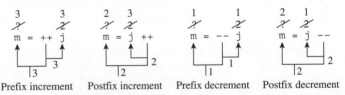

Prefix increment   Postfix increment   Prefix decrement   Postfix decrement

Figure 4.13.   Increment and decrement trees.

next program example (Figure 4.14) shows a typical use of preincrement in a counting loop.

Notes on Figure 4.14. Using increment in a loop.

- *First box.* We initialize these two variables in their declarations. This style is legal and saves two lines of code, but it is more error prone than the style we generally use. Since the `while` loop in the second box relies on these initializations, we normally would put the initializations immediately before the `while` statement.

We use the increment and `+=` operators to sum a series.

```c
#include <stdio.h>
void main( void )
{
    int N;
    int x = 0;                  /* Loop counter. */
    double sum = 0.0;           /* Sum of terms 1/x. */

    puts( "\n Summing 1.0/x for x between 1 and N.\n" );
    printf( " Please enter an integer N greater than 1: " );
    scanf( "%i", &N );

    if (N <= 1) {               /* Screen out faulty inputs. */
        printf( "\n Input value %i is too small.\n\n", N );
    }
    else {                      /* Compute terms and sum series. */
        while (x < N) {
            ++x;
            sum += 1.0 / x;
        }

    }
    printf( " The sum is %g \n\n", sum );
}
```

Output:

```
Summing 1.0/x for x between 1 and N.

Please enter an integer N greater than 1: 3
The sum is 1.83333
```

Figure 4.14.   Using increment in a loop.

- *Outer box.* We use the usual `if...else` to validate the data. We prefer to handle the easy case first so we can focus all attention on the more complex case. In this program, handling erroneous inputs is easy (we can do it in one line), so we do it first and leave the more complicated process of handling good inputs for the `else` clause, which contains an entire loop and the program's output statement.
- *Middle box.* This is a summation loop, which is a variation of the counted loop studied in Chapter 3. We will look at this kind of loop in more detail in Chapter 6.
- *Innermost box.*

    1. In this context, pre- and postincrement operators would do the same thing, because the `++` is the only operator in the expression.
    2. On entry to this loop, the value of `x` is 0. We increment it before the division, so `x` will equal 1 and the `sum` will equal 1 after the first addition. Thus, we will sum the fractions from `1/1` to `1/N`.
    3. Since the precedence of `/` is higher than `+=`, the division will be performed first then the result will be added to the current value of `sum` and the result will be stored back into `sum`; we say that `sum` *accumulates* the total.

4.4.2   Prefix versus Postfix Operators (Advanced Topic)

For simplicity, we will explain the differences between pre- and postfix operators in terms of the increment operators, but everything is equally true of decrement operators; simply change "add 1" to "subtract 1" in the explanations.

Both *prefix* and *postfix increment* operators add 1 to a variable and return the value of the variable for further use in an expression. For example, `k++` and `++k` both increase the value of `k` by 1. If a prefix increment or a postfix increment operator is the only operator in an expression, the results will be the same. However, if an increment operation is embedded in a larger expression, the result of the larger expression will be different for prefix increment and postfix increment operators. Both kinds of increment operator return the value of `k`, to be used in the larger expression. However, the prefix form increments the variable *before* it returns the value, so that the value in memory and the one used in the expression are the same. In contrast, postfix increment returns the original, unincremented value of the variable to the larger expression and increments the value in memory *afterward*. Thus, the value used in the surrounding expression is 1 smaller than the value left in memory and 1 smaller than the value used in the prefix increment expression.

A further complication with postfix increment is that the change in memory does not have to happen right away. The compiler is permitted to postpone the store operation for a while, and many do postpone it in order to generate more efficient code.[7] This makes postfix increment and decrement somewhat tricky to use properly. However, you can depend on two things: First, if you execute **x++** three times, the value of **x** will be 3 greater than when you started. Second, by the time evaluation reaches the semicolon at the end of the statement, all incrementing and decrementing actions will be complete.

Because of the complications with side effects, increment and decrement operators can be tricky to use when embedded in a complex expression. They are used most often in isolation to change the values of a loop counter, as in Figure 4.14. The following are some guidelines for their use that will help beginners avoid problems:

1. Use prefix increment and decrement operators because they are less confusing than postfix increment and decrement operators and cause less trouble for beginners.
2. Do not mix increment or decrement operators with other operators in an expression.

Mixing increment or decrement with other operators (advanced topic).

An increment operator is an easy, efficient way to add 1 to the value of a memory variable. Most frequently, increment and decrement operators are used in isolation. However, both also can be used in the middle of an expression because both return the value of the variable for use in further computation.

New programmers often write one line of code per idea. For example, in the summation loop from Figure 4.14, the first line of the loop body increments **x** and the second line uses the new value:

```
x = 0;          /* Sum 1/x for x = 1 to N */
while (x < N) {
    ++x;
    sum += 1.0 / x;
}
```

This two-line version is easy for a beginner to understand and use. Some even prefer to write the assignment statement the long way:

```
sum = sum + 1.0 / x;
```

An advanced programmer is more likely to write the following version, which increments **x** and uses it in the same line. The parse tree and evaluation of the assignment expression are shown in Figure 4.15.

```
x = 0;          /* Sum 1/x for x = 1 to N */
while (x < N) sum += 1.0 / ++x;
```

---

[7]The exact rules for this postponement are complex. To explain them, one must first define sequence points and how they are used during evaluation. This explanation is beyond the scope of the book.

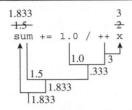

Figure 4.15.   Evaluating an increment expression.

As you can see, mixing an increment with other operators in an expression makes the code "denser"—more actions happen per line—and it often permits us to shorten the code. By using two side-effect operators, we have reduced the entire loop to one line. However, this happens at the expense of some clarity and, for beginners, at the risk of writing something unintended.

When using an increment or decrement in an expression, the difference between the prefix and postfix forms is crucial. If you use the postfix increment operator, the value used in the rest of the expression will be one smaller than if you use the prefix increment. For example, the loop shown previously sums the fractions $1/1 \ldots 1/N$. If a postfix increment were used instead of the prefix increment, it would try to sum the fractions $1/0 \ldots 1/(N-1)$ instead. Of course, dividing by 0 is a serious error that causes immediate program termination on some systems and meaningless results on others. Therefore, think carefully about whether to use a prefix or postfix operator to avoid using the wrong value in the expression or leaving the wrong value in memory. When these operators are used in isolation, such problems do not occur.

4.5   Relational Operators

The **relational operators** (`==`, `!=`, `<`, `>`, `<=`, and `>=`), with their meanings and precedence values, are listed in Figure 4.16. These operators perform comparisons on their operands and return an answer of **true** or **false**. To control program flow, we compare the values of certain variables to each other or to target values. We then use the result to select one of the clauses of an **if** statement or control a loop.

The semantics of comparison.   A relational operator can be used to compare two values of any simple type[8] or two values that can be converted to the

---

[8] Types **double** and **int** are simple. Nonsimple types are compounds with more than one part such as strings, arrays, and structures. These will be discussed in later chapters.

All operators listed here associate left to right.

Arity	Usage	Meaning	Precedence
Binary	x < y	Is x less than y?	10
	x <= y	Is x less than or equal to y?	10
	x > y	Is x greater than y?	10
	x >= y	Is x greater than or equal to y?	10
	x != y	Is x unequal to y?	9
	x == y	Is x equal to y?	9

Figure 4.16.   Relational operators.

same simple type. The result is always an `int`, no matter what types the operands are, and it is always either a 1 (`true`) or a 0 (`false`).

A common error among inexperienced C programmers is to use the assignment operator = instead of the comparison operator ==. The expression `x == y` is not the same as `x = y`. The second means "make x equal to the current value of y", while `x == y` means "compare the values of x and y". Therefore, if a comparison is done after the inadvertent assignment operation, of course, the values of the two variables *will be* equal. It may help you to pronounce these operators differently; we use "compares equal" for == and "gets" for =.

In other languages, such an error would be trapped by the compiler. In C, however, assignment is an "ordinary" operator that has precedence and associativity like other operators and actually returns a value (the same as the value it stores into memory). A C compiler has no way of knowing for sure whether a programmer meant to write a comparison or an assignment. Some compilers give a warning error comment when the = operator is used within an `if` or `while` statement; however, doing so is not necessarily an error, so the comment is only a warning, not fatal, and the compiler should produce executable code.

4.6   Logical Operators

Sometimes we want to test a more complicated condition than a simple equality or inequality. For example, we might need an input value between 0 and 10 or require two positive inputs that are not equal to each other. We can create compound conditions like these by using the logical operators `&&` (AND), `||` (OR), and `!`(NOT). The former condition can be written as `x >= 0 && x <= 10` and the latter as `x > 0 && y > 0 && x != y`. **Logical operators** let us test and combine the results of comparison expressions.

4.6.1 True and False

C has no special, different data type for truth values. Truth values are integers, and every integer has a **truth value**: The integer 0 represents *false* and anything else is interpreted as *true*. The integer 1 is the "standard true value"; that is, when C generates a true value as the result of an operator, that value is always 1.

A program in which the numeral **1** is used to represent both the number one and the truth value **true** can be difficult to read and interpret. For this reason, it is much better style to write **true** when you mean a truth value and reserve **1** for use as a number. To make this style convenient, the following two definitions can be included at the top of your program:[9]

```
#define false 0
#define true  1
```

You can then use these defined constants directly in comparisons, expressions and assignment statements where the logical values are desired.

All the comparison and logical operators produce truth values as their results. For example, if you ask **x == y**, the answer is either 0 (**false**) or 1 (**true**). The meanings of **&&**, **||**, and **!** are summarized by the **truth table** in Figure 4.17. The first two columns of the *truth table* show all possible combinations of the truth values of two operands. **T** is used in these columns to mean **true**, because an operand can have any value, not just 1 or 0. The last three columns show the results of the three logical operations. In these columns, true answers are represented by 1 because C always uses the standard **true** to answer questions.

Let us look at a few examples to learn how to use a truth table. Assume **x = 3** and **y = -1**. Then both **x** and **y** are **true**, so we would use the last line of the table. To find the answer for **x && y**, use the fourth column. To find

---

C uses the value 1 to represent **true** and 0 to represent **false**. The result of every comparison and logical operator is either 0 or 1. However, any value can be an input to a logical operator; all nonzero operands are interpreted as **true**. In the table, T represents any nonzero value.

Operands		Results		
x	y	!x	x && y	x || y
0	0	1	0	0
0	T	1	0	1
T	0	0	0	1
T	T	0	1	1

Figure 4.17.   Truth table for the logical operators.

---

[9]It is not necessary to do this in C++, since the Boolean values are defined by the C++ standard.

x || y, use the fifth column. As a second example, suppose x=0 and y=-1; then x is false and y is true, so we use the second row. Therefore, x || y is true (1) and x && y is false (0).

4.6.2 Parse Trees for Logical Operators

The precedence and usage of the three logical operators are summarized in Figure 4.18. Note that && has higher precedence than || and that both are quite low in the precedence table. If an expression combines arithmetic, comparisons, and logic, the arithmetic will be parsed first, the comparisons second, and the logic last. The practical effect of this precedence order is that we can omit many of the possible parentheses in expressions. Figure 4.19 gives an example of how to parse an expression with operators of all three kinds. Before beginning the parse, we note the precedence of each operator used. Beginning with the highest-precedence operator and proceeding downward, we then parenthesize or bracket each operator with its operands.

   A small circle, called a **sequence point**, is written on the parse tree under every && and || operator. The order of evaluation of the parts of a logical expression is different from other expressions, and the sequence points remind us of this difference. For these operators, the part of the tree to the left of the sequence point is always evaluated before the part on the right.[10] This fact is very important in practice because it permits us to use the left side of a logical expression to "guard" the right side, as explained in the next section.

4.6.3 Lazy Evaluation (Advanced Topic)

Logical operators have a special property that makes them different from all other operators: You often can know the result of an operation without even looking at the second operand. Look again at the truth table in Figure 4.17, and note that the answer for x && y is always 0 when x is false. Similarly, the answer for x || y is always 1 when x is true. This leads to a special method of computation, called **lazy evaluation**, that can be used only for logical operators. Basically,

Arity	Usage	Meaning	Precedence	Associativity
Unary	!x	logical-NOT x (logical opposite)	15	right to left
Binary	x && y	x logical-AND y	5	left to right
	x || y	x logical-OR y	4	"

Figure 4.18. Precedence of the logical operators.

---

[10] Two other operators, the question mark and the comma, have sequence points associated with them. For all other operators in C, either the right side of the tree or its left side may be evaluated first.

We parse the expression `y = a < 10 || a >= 2 * b && b != 1` using parentheses and a tree.

Parenthesizing in precedence order:

Precedence level is listed above each operator.

```
Level 13: y = a < 10 || a >= (2 * b) && b != 1
Level 10: y = (a < 10) || (a >= (2 * b)) && b != 1
Level 9:  y = (a < 10) || (a >= (2 * b)) && (b != 1)
Level 5:  y = (a < 10) || ((a >= (2 * b)) && (b != 1))
Level 4:  y = ((a < 10) || ((a >= (2 * b)) && (b != 1)))
Level 2:  (y = ((a < 10) || ((a >= (2 * b)) && (b != 1))))
```

```
        2    10   4    10  13 5    9
        y =  a <  10 || a >= 2 * b && b != 1
```

Figure 4.19.   Parsing logical operators.

the left operand of the logical operator is evaluated then tested. If that alone decides the value of the entire expression, the rest is skipped. We show this skipping on the parse tree by writing a diagonal *pruning mark* on the branch of the tree that is skipped. You can see these marks on the trees in Figures 4.21 and 4.23. To further emphasize the skipping, a loop is drawn around the skipped portion. Note that *no operator* within the loop is executed.

Logical-AND.   Figure 4.20 summarizes how lazy evaluation works for logical-AND, and Figure 4.21 illustrates the most important use of lazy evaluation: guarding an expression. The left side of a logical-AND expression can be used to "guard" the right side. We use the left side to check for "safe" data conditions; if found, the left side is **true** and we execute the right side. If the left side is **false**, we have identified a data value that would cause trouble and use lazy evaluation to avoid executing the right side. In this way, we avoid computations that would cause a machine error or program malfunction. For example, in Figure 4.21, we want to test a condition with **x** in the denominator. But dividing by 0 is an error,

x	y	x && y
0	?	0 and skip second operand
T	0	0
T	T	1

- To evaluate an **&&** operator, first evaluate its *left* operand. This operand might be a simple variable or literal, or it might be a complicated expression.
- Look at the truth value. If it is **false**, return 0 as the answer to the **&&** operation and skip the next step.
- Otherwise, we do not yet know the outcome of the expression, so evaluate the right operand. If it is **false**, return 0. Otherwise, return 1.

Figure 4.20.   Lazy truth table for logical–AND.

We evaluate a logical expression twice with different operand values.

(1) Evaluation with **x = 3.1** and **b = 4**. All parts of the expression are evaluated because the left operand is **true**.

```
   3.1         4    3.1
   x != 0  &&  b  /  x  <  1.0
    |__|       |_____|
    T|1         1.29|__|
                    F|0
         |_____|
           F|0
```

The **/** and **<** operators are evaluated and their results are written under the operators on the tree.

(2) Evaluation with the values **x = 0.0** and **b = anything**. Skipping happened because the left operand is **false**.

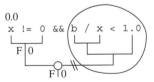

The "pruning mark" on the tree and the looped line show the part of the expression that was skipped.

Figure 4.21.   Lazy evaluation of logical–AND.

so we should check the value of **x** before testing this condition. If it is 0, we skip the rest of the test; if it is nonzero, we go ahead.

Logical-OR.   Figure 4.22 summarizes how lazy evaluation works for logical-OR, and Figure 4.23 illustrates how lazy evaluation can be used to improve program efficiency.   Logical-OR often is used for data validation.   If one validity condition is fast to compute and another is slow, we can save a little computation time by putting the fast test on the left side of the logical-OR and the slow test on the right.   Or we could put the most common problem on the left and an unusual problem on the right.

x	y	x || y
T	?	1 and skip second operand
0	0	0
0	T	1

- To evaluate an || operator, first evaluate its *left* operand. This operand might be a simple variable or literal or it might be a more complicated expression.
- Look at the truth value. If it is **true**, return 1 as the answer to the || operation and skip the next step.
- Otherwise, we do not yet know the outcome of the expression so evaluate the right operand. If it is **false**, return 0. Otherwise, return 1.

Figure 4.22.   Lazy truth table for logical–OR.

We evaluate a logical expression twice with different operand values. The first time, the entire expression is evaluated. The second time, a shortcut is taken.

(1) Evaluation with **vmax = 6**. All parts of the expression are evaluated because the left operand is **false**.

6   5   6   10
vmax < LOWER || vmax > UPPER

The < and > operators are both evaluated and their results are written under the operators on the tree.

(2) Evaluation with **vmax = 3**. The left side is **true**, which causes skipping.

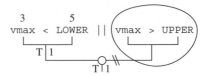

The pruning mark on the tree and the looped line show the part of the expression that was skipped.

Figure 4.23.   Lazy evaluation of logical-OR.

Figure 4.23 shows two evaluations of a logical-OR expression that is used in the next program. If the input data fails the first test, the second test determines the result of the expression. If the data passes the first test, we save time by skipping the second test and return the result of the left side.

4.7   An Example: A Voltage Ramp

Figure 4.24 gives the problem specification for a simple program that is part of the interface between a motor and an engineer running an experiment using the motor. Logical and relational operators are used to ensure that the input is valid; increment and decrement operators are used to control the loops. The program is given in Figure 4.25 and its flow diagram in Figure 4.26.

Problem scope: Generate a series of voltage levels that will be used to control an electric motor in an experiment. The level is to start at 0, increase by 1 volt repeatedly until it reaches a maximum, then decrease until it again reaches 0 volts. In this program, we simply display the voltage value at each step, with the exception of the final 0 value.

In a real application, the voltage would be sent to the device that controls the experiment and the program would contain a time delay between each increase or decrease to allow the motor to change speed.

Input: The maximum voltage, **vmax**.

Limitations: 5 volts <= **vmax** <= 10 volts.

Output required: A series of integer voltages that increase then decrease.

Figure 4.24.   Problem specification: Voltage ramp.

The problem specification is given in Figure 4.24.

```
/* ------------------------------------------------------------------
** Output a series of voltage values that ramp up from 0 to some maximum
** and then back down to 0 again in one volt increments.
*/
#include <stdio.h>
#define LOWER 5
#define UPPER 10
void main( void )
{
    int vmax;                      /* Voltage maximum of ramp */
    int volts;                     /* Current voltage value   */

    printf( "\n Enter the maximum voltage for the ramp: " );
    scanf( "%i", &vmax );
    while (vmax < LOWER || vmax > UPPER) {   /* Check for valid input. */
        printf( "\n Input=%i is not between %i and %i."
                "\n Try again.  Please enter a voltage: ",
                vmax, LOWER, UPPER );
        scanf( "%i", &vmax );
    }

    puts( "\n" );

    volts = 0;                     /* We will start and end at zero volts */
    while (volts < vmax) {         /* Ramp up */
        printf( " Voltage = %i\n", volts );
        volts++;
    }

    puts( "\n" );                  /* Voltage is now at maximum. */
    while (volts > 0) {            /* Ramp down */
        printf( " Voltage = %i\n", volts );
        --volts;
    }                              /* Voltage is back down to 0. */
}
```

Figure 4.25.   Ramp up and down.

Notes on Figures 4.25 and 4.26. Ramp up and Down.

- *Figure 4.25, first box, and Figure 4.26, first column: input validation.*

    1. The `while` test asks whether the input is outside the range of 5 to 10.
       The user will see this dialog if the input is not within the range:

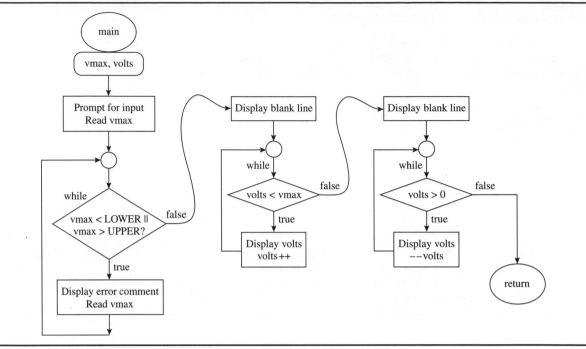

Figure 4.26.   Flowchart for the voltage ramp.

```
Enter the maximum voltage for the ramp: 3

Input=3 is not between 5 and 10.
Try again.   Please enter a voltage: 6
```

2. This loop checks the input data and keeps asking the user to retype it until a legal voltage is entered. Loops like this are a good idea.
3. Do not forget the `scanf()` inside the loop. Without it, you have an infinite loop that keeps asking for data but provides no chance to enter it.
4. A sample output corresponding to correct input is below.

```
Enter the maximum voltage for the ramp: 6

Voltage = 0
Voltage = 1
Voltage = 2
Voltage = 3
Voltage = 4
Voltage = 5
```

```
Voltage = 6
Voltage = 5
Voltage = 4
Voltage = 3
Voltage = 2
Voltage = 1
```

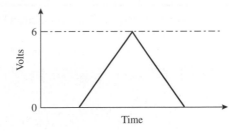

- *Figure 4.25, second box, and Figure 4.26, second column: ramp up.*

  1. We start with the voltage at 0 and quit when it equals the maximum.
  2. Each time around the loop, we print the voltage then increment it.
  3. We want minimum and maximum values of the voltage to appear only once on the ramp, so we do not print the maximum here.

- *Figure 4.25, third box, and Figure 4.26, third column: ramp down.*

  1. When we get to this box the voltage equals the maximum, so we print it.
  2. Each time around the loop, we print the voltage and decrement it.
  3. When it reaches 0 again, we quit without printing. (We printed the 0 value as part of the up ramp.)
  4. The second and third boxes could be enclosed in a larger loop to produce an up-and-down zigzag voltage pattern.

4.8   Case Study: Using a Parse Tree to Debug

When a program seems to work but gives the wrong answers, the problem sometimes lies in the expressions that calculate those answers. Drawing a parse tree can help **debug** the program; that is, help a programmer find the error. We illustrate this technique through a case study for which Figure 4.27 gives the full specification. In this problem, a circuit is wired with three resistances connected in parallel, as shown in the specification. We must calculate the electrical resistance equivalent, r_{eq}, for this part of the circuit.

Step 1. Making a test plan.   Making a **test plan** first is a good way to understand the problem. It forces us to analyze the formulas, look at the details, and think about what kind of data might cause problems. We look at the problem specification to decide what the test plan should be.

The first test case should be something that can be computed in one's head. We note that the arithmetic is very simple if all the resistances are 2 ohms, so we enter this case in the test chart, which follows. We want to test inputs with fractional values and note that we can easily compute the answer for three resistances of 0.1 ohm each. Then we notice that, if two inputs are 0, the denominator of the

---

Problem scope: Find the electrical resistance equivalent, r_{eq}, for three resistances wired in parallel.

Input: Three resistance values, r_1, r_2, and r_3.

Formula:

$$r\_eq = \frac{r_1 * r_2 * r_3}{r_1*r_2 + r_1*r_3 + r_2*r_3}$$

Constants: None.

Output required: The three inputs and their equivalent resistance.

Computational requirements: The equivalent resistance should be a real number, not an integer.

Figure 4.27.   Problem specification: Computing resistance.

fraction will be 0. Since division by 0 is undefined, this will cause trouble. Since no limitations on input values are specified, it is unclear what to do about this. Resistances that are 0 or negative make no realistic sense, so we decide to warn the user and trust him or her to enter valid data. Next, we enter an arbitrary set of values, just to see what the output will look like for the typical case. We use a pocket calculator and a pencil to do the computation by hand. We now have three tests in our test plan, which is enough for a very simple program.

r_1	r_2	r_3	r_{eq}
2	2	2	$8.0/12.0 = 0.666667$
0.1	0.1	0.1	$0.001/0.03 = 0.033333$
75	40	2.5	2.28137

Step 2. Starting the program.   Write the parts that remain the same from application to application. We write the `#include` statement and the first and last lines of `main()` with the opening and closing messages. The dots $(\ldots)$ represent the unfinished parts of the program.

```
#include <stdio.h>
...                     /* Space for #defines.*/
void main( void )
{   ...                 /* Space for declarations.*/
    puts( "\n Computing Equivalent Resistance \n" );
    ...                 /* Space for I/O and computations.*/
    puts( "\n Normal termination." );
}
```

Step 3. Reading the input.   We need to read three resistance values; we could do this with three calls on **scanf()** or with one. We choose to use one call because one input step is faster for the user and we do not think the user will be confused by giving three answers for one prompt in this situation. To store the three values, we need three variables, which we name **r1**, **r2**, and **r3**. We declare these as type **double** (not **int**) because the answer will have a fractional part. We write a declaration for three doubles:

```
double r1, r2, r3; /* input variables for resistances */
```

Now we are ready for the prompt and the input. In the format for **scanf()**, we write three percent signs because we will be reading three values. Since we are reading **double** values, we write **lg** (the letter l, not the numeral 1) after the percent signs. We remember to write the ampersand before the name of each variable that needs to receive an input value.

```
printf( "\n Enter resistances #1, #2, and #3 (ohms).\n"
        " All resistances must be greater than 0: " );
scanf( "%lg%lg%lg", &r1, &r2, &r3 );
```

Finally, we write a **printf()** statement to echo the three input values. In the output format, we again write three percent signs, for three values. However, the correct output code for type **double** is **g**, without the **l**. At the end of the format we remember to write a newline character. After the format we list the names of the variables to print, without ampersands. (Reading into a variable requires an ampersand; writing does not.)

```
printf( "\n    r1= %g    r2= %g    r3= %g\n", r1, r2, r3 );
```

Step 4. Computation and output.   Now we transcribe the mathematical formula into C notation, changing the fraction bar to a division sign and writing the subscripts as part of the variable names. In the process, we note that we need a variable for the result and declare another **double**. Then we write a **printf()** statement to print the result. We have

```
double r_eq;                 /* equivalent resistance */
...
r_eq = r1 * r2 * r3 / r1 * r2 + r1 * r3 + r2 * r3;
printf( " The equivalent resistance is %g\n", r_eq );
```

Step 5. Putting it together and testing it.   We now type in all the parts of the program. The code compiled successfully after correcting a few typographical errors; the result is shown in Figure 4.28. We then ran the program and entered the first data set. The output was

```
/* ------------------------------------------------------------
** Compute the equivalent resistance of three resistors in parallel
*/
#include <stdio.h>

void main( void )
{
    double r1, r2, r3;   /* input variables for three resistances */
    double r_eq;         /* equivalent resistance */
    puts( "\n Computing Equivalent Resistance\n" );
    printf( "\n Enter values of resistances #1, #2, and #3 (ohms).\n"
            " All resistances must be greater than 0: " );
    scanf( "%lg%lg%lg", &r1, &r2, &r3 );
    printf( "      r1= %g    r2= %g    r3= %g\n", r1, r2, r3 );

    r_eq = r1 * r2 * r3 / r1 * r2 + r1 * r3 + r2 * r3;
    printf( " The equivalent resistance is %g\n\n", r_eq );


    puts( "\n Normal termination." );
}
```

Figure 4.28.   Computing resistance.

```
Computing Equivalent Resistance

Enter values of resistances #1, #2, and #3 (ohms).
All resistances must be greater than 0: 2 2 2
     r1= 2    r2= 2    r3= 2
The equivalent resistance is 16

Normal termination.
```

Comparing the answer to the answer in our test plan, we see that it is wrong. The correct answer is 0.667. What could account for the error? There are three possibilities:

1. The input was read incorrectly. This could happen if the format were inappropriate for the data type of the variable or if we forgot to write an ampersand in front of the variable name.
2. The answer was printed incorrectly. This could happen if the format were inappropriate for the data type of the variable or if we wrote the wrong variable name or put an ampersand in front of it.
3. The answer was computed incorrectly.

We eliminate the first possibility immediately; we echoed the data and know it was read correctly. This is why every program should echo its inputs. Then we look carefully at the final `printf()` statement and see no errors. We think this is not the problem. The remaining possibility is that the computation is wrong, so we need to analyze the formula we wrote.

Step 6. Correcting the error. The best way to analyze a computation is with a parse tree, so we copy the expression on a piece of paper and begin drawing the tree (see Figure 4.29).

1. The `*` and `/` are the highest precedence operators in the expression so they are parsed first using left-to-right associativity, as shown in Figure 4.29.
2. At the `/` sign, we see that the right operand is `r1`, which does not correspond to the mathematical formula. The error becomes clear; the denominator for `/` should be the entire subexpression `r1 * r2 + r1 * r3 + r2 * r3`, not just `r1`.
3. The error is corrected by adding parentheses as shown in Figure 4.30, so that it now corresponds to the mathematical formula.

We correct the program, recompile it, and retest it. The results are

```
Computing Equivalent Resistance
Enter values of resistances #1, #2, and #3 (ohms).
All resistances must be greater than 0: 2 2 2
     r1= 2     r2= 2     r3= 2
The equivalent resistance is 0.667

Normal termination.
```

We see that the first answer is now correct. Before going on, we also consider the appearance of the output. Is it neat and readable? Does every number have a label? Should the vertical or horizontal spacing be adjusted? We decide to add a blank line before the final answer, so we insert a `\n` at the beginning of the format. The boxed section of the program now is

```
r_eq = r1 * r2 * r3 / (r1 * r2 + r1 * r3 + r2 * r3);
printf( "\n The equivalent resistance is %g\n", r_eq );
```

We recompile the program and go on with the test plan. The program produces correct results for the other two test cases:

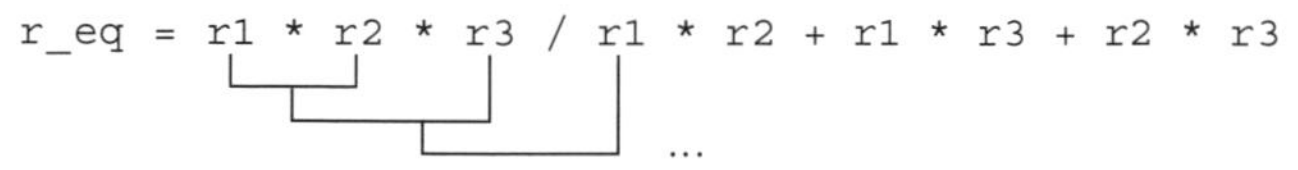

Figure 4.29. Finding an expression error.

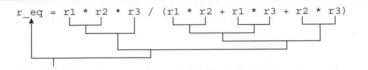

Figure 4.30.   Parsing the corrected expression.

```
Enter values of resistances #1, #2, and #3 (ohms).
All resistances must be greater than 0: .1 .1 .1
    r1= 0.1     r2= 0.1     r3= 0.1

The equivalent resistance is 0.033
--------------------------------------------------

Enter values of resistances #1, #2, and #3 (ohms)
All resistances must be greater than 0: 75 40 2.5
    r1= 75     r2= 40     r3= 2.5

The equivalent resistance is 2.281
```

The output is correct, neat, and readable, so we declare the program finished.

4.9   What You Should Remember

4.9.1 Major Concepts

This chapter is concerned with how to create and name objects, how to use types to describe their properties, and how to combine the objects with operators to form expressions. These concepts are summarized here.

- Types and objects:

  Variables and constants are objects; their names are used like nouns in English as the subjects and objects of actions.

  Every object has a type. Types are like adjectives in English: The type of an object describes its properties and how it may be used.

  A declaration is used to create and name an object.

  An object has a location and a value. The compiler assigns the location for the object. We can give it a value by initializing it in the declaration. An object that has not been given a value is said to be *uninitialized* or to contain *garbage*.

  A constant object must be initialized in the declaration and its value cannot be changed.

- Operators:

  Operators are like verbs: They represent actions and can be applied to objects of appropriate types. An expression is like a sentence: It combines operators with the names of objects to specify a computation.

  Precedence, associativity, and parentheses control the structure of an expression. The precedence of C operators follows normal mathematical conventions.

  A few operators have side effects; that is, they modify the value of some variable in memory. These include the assignment operator, assignment combinations, increment, and decrement.

- Diagrams:

  Diagrams are used to visualize the parts of a program and how they interact. They become increasingly important as the more complex features of C are introduced. We have now introduced three ways to visualize the aspects of a program:

  1. A flow diagram (introduced in Chapter 3) is used to depict the structure of an entire program and clarify the sequence of execution of its statements.
  2. A parse tree is used to show the structure of an expression and can be used to manually evaluate the expression.
  3. An object diagram is used to visualize a variable. Simple object diagrams were introduced in this chapter; more elaborate diagrams will be introduced as new data types are presented.

4.9.2 Programming Style

- Names: You must name every object and function you create. The compiler does not care what names you use as long as they are consistent. However, people do care. Obscure names, silly names, and unpronounceable names hinder comprehension. A program with bad names takes longer to debug.
- The length of a name: Extremely long and short names are poor choices. Except in unusual circumstances, a one- or two-letter name does not convey enough information to clarify its meaning. At the other extreme, very long, wordy names are distracting and often obscure the structure of an expression.
- Long expressions: Very long, complex expressions are difficult to write correctly and difficult to debug. When a formula is long and complex

Group	Operators	Complication
Assignment combinations	+=, etc.	These operators use the value of a memory variable, then change it. Although C permits more than one of these operators to be used in a single expression, you should limit your own expressions to one.
Prefix increment and decrement	++, --	If you use a side-effect operator, do not use the same variable again in the same expression.
Postfix increment and decrement	++, --	Remember that these operators return one value for further use in expression evaluation and leave a different value in memory.
Comparison	==	Remember not to use =.
Logical	&&, ||, !	Remember that all negative and positive integers are considered **true** values. The only **false** value is 0.
Logical	&&, ||	There are special sequencing and lazy evaluation rules for expressions that contain these operators.

Figure 4.31.   Difficult aspects of C **operators.**

or has repeated subexpressions, it is a good idea to break it into several separate assignment statements.

- Parentheses: Use parentheses to clarify the structure of your expressions by enclosing meaningful subexpressions. Use them when you are uncertain about the precedence of operators. However, use parentheses sparingly; too many can be worse than too few. When three and four parentheses pile up in one part of an expression, they can be hard to "pair up" visually. In this situation, moderation is the key to good style.

- Increment and decrement operators: These operators can give nonintuitive results because of C's complicated rules about the order in which parts of an expression are evaluated. Until you fully understand the evaluation rules, restrict your use to very short expressions and avoid combining these operators with logical && and ||.

4.9.3   Sticky Points and Common Errors

This has been a long chapter, filled with many facts about C semantics and C operators. The table in Figure 4.31 gives a brief review of the difficult aspects of C operators to assist you in program planning and debugging.

4.9.4   New and Revisited Vocabulary

The following C keywords and operators were introduced or discussed in this chapter:

`#define`	`+, -, *, /`	`++x` (preincrement)
`const`	`=, +=, -=, *=, /=`	`x++` (postincrement)
`sizeof`	`&&, ||, !`	`--x` (predecrement)
`(...)`	`<, <=, >, >=`	`x--` (postdecrement)
	`==, !=`	

These are the most important terms and concepts presented in this chapter:

modifier	undefined value	arithmetic operators
declaration	garbage	assignment operator
data type	precedence	combination operators
data value	associativity	postfix operator
identifier	arity	prefix operator
local name	precedence table	side effect
variable	binary operator	logical operators
constant	operand	truth value
literal constant	expression	truth table
symbolic constant	parse tree	lazy evaluation
initializer	debug	relational operators
object diagram	test plan	increment operators

4.10   Exercises

4.10.1   Self-Test Exercises

1. What is wrong with each of the following declarations?

   a. `int d; a = 5;`

   b. `doubel h;`

   c. `int h = 2.5;`

   d. `const double g;`

   e. `integer k = 0;`

   f. `double h = 2.0 * g;`

2. Look at the parse tree in Figure 4.8. Make a list that shows each operator (one per line) with the left and right operands of that operator.

3. Each of the following items gives two expressions that are alike except that one has parentheses and the other does not. You must determine whether the parentheses are optional. For each pair, draw the two parse trees and compare them. If the parse

trees are the same, the two expressions mean the same thing and the parentheses are optional.

```
a. d = a - c + b ;   d = a - (c + b) ;

b. e = g * f + h ;   e = g * (f + h) ;

c. d = a + b * c ;   d = a + (b * c) ;

d. e = f - g - h ;   e = (f - g) - h ;

e. d = a < b && b < c;   d = a < (b && b) < c;
```

4. Using the following data values, evaluate each expression and say what will be stored in **d** or **e**:

```
int d, a = 5, b = 4, c = 32;
double e, f = 2.0, g = 27.0, h = 2.5;
```

```
a. d = a + c - b ;

b. d = a + c * b ;

c. d = a * c - b ;

d. e = g * 3.0 * (- f * h) ;

e. d = a <= b ;

f. e = f - (g - h) ;

g. e = g / f ;

h. e = 1.0; e += h ;

i. d = (a < c) && (b == c) ;

j. d = ++a * b-- ;
```

5. Using the given data values, parse and evaluate each of the following expressions and say what will be stored in **k**. Start with the original values for **k** and **m** each time. Check your precedence table to get the ordering right.

```
double k = 10.0;
double m = 5.0;
```

```
a. k *= 3.5;

b. k /= m + 1;

c. k += 1 / m;

d. k -= ++m;
```

6. In the following program, circle each error and show how to correct it:

```
#include "stdio"
#define PI 3.14159;
void main (void)
{    double v;
```

```
        printf( "Self-test Exercise/n" );
        printf( "If I don't get going I'll be late!!";
        puts( "Enter a number:   " );
        scanf( %g, v );
        w = v * Pi;
        printf( "w = %g \n", w );
}
```

7. Write a C expression to compute each of the following formulas:

   a. Metric unit conversion: Liters = ounces / 33.81474

   b. Circle: Circumference = $2\pi r$

   c. Right triangle: Area = $\dfrac{bh}{2}$

8. Draw complete parse trees for the following expressions:

   a. `t = x >= y && y >= z ;`

   b. `x = (y + z) || v == 3 && !(z == y / v) ;`

4.10.2   Using Pencil and Paper

1. Draw parse trees for the following expressions. Use the trees to evaluate the expressions, given the initial values shown. Assume all variables are type **double**.

   a. `a = 5; b = 4; c = 32;     d = a + c / b ;`

   b. `w = 3; x = 30; y = 5;     z = y + x / (- w * y) ;`

   c. `f = 3; g = 30; h = 5;     d = f - g - h ;`

   d. `f = 3; g = 27; h = 2;     d = f - (g - h) ;`

2. Explain why you need to know the precedence of the C operators to find the answer to question 1a. Explain why you need to know more than precedence to find the answer to question 1c. What else do you need to know?

3. Look at the parse tree in Figure 4.29. Make a list that shows each operator (one per line) with the left and right operands of that operator.

4. Using the given data values, parse and evaluate each of the following expressions and say whether the result of the expression is **true** or **false**.

```
int h = 0;
int j = 7;
int k = 1;
int n = -3;
```

   a. `k && n`

   b. `!k && j`

   c. `k || j`

d. `k || !n`

e. `j > h && j < k`

f. `j > h || j < k`

g. `j > 0 && j < h || j > k`

h. `j < h || h < k && j < k`

5. Write a C expression to compute each of the following formulas:

   a. Circle: Diameter $= 2r$

   b. Flat donut: Area $= \pi \times ($outer_radius$^2 -$ inner_radius$^2)$

   c. Metric unit conversion: cm $= ($feet $\times 12 +$ inches$) \times 2.54$

6. Using the given data values, parse and evaluate each of the following expressions and say what will be stored in **k** and in **m**. Start with the original value for **k** each time.

   `int m, k = 10;`

   a. `m = ++k;`

   b. `m = k++;`

   c. `m = -- k / 2;`

   d. `m = 3 * k --;`

7. In the following program, circle each error and show how to correct it:

```
#include (stdio.h)
void main (void)
{
    integer k;
    double x, y, z

    printf( Enter an integer: );
    scanf( "%i", k );
    printf( "Enter a double: );
    scanf( "%g", &X );
    printf( "Enter two integers: );
    scanf( "%lg", &y, &z );
    printf( "k= %i X= %g \n", &k, &x );
    printf( "y= %i z= %g \n" y, z );
}
```

8. (Advanced) Draw parse trees for the following logical expressions and show the sequence points. Use the trees to evaluate the expressions, given the initial values shown. For each one, mark any part of the expression that is skipped because of lazy evaluation.

   a. `w = 1; x = 5; y = 1;`   `y && w != y && x`

   b. `w = 1; x = 5; y = 3;`   `w <= x && x <= y`

c. x = 3; y = 0; z = 0;   z != 0 || y && !x

d. r = 5; w = 0; x = 5; y = 0;   y || r || x && !w

4.10.3   Using the Computer

1. Your own size.
   Write a short program in which you use the **sizeof** operator to find the number of bytes used by your C compiler to store values of types **int** and **double**.

2. Miles per gallon.
   Write a program to compute the gas consumption (miles/gallon) for your car if you are given, as input, **miles**, the number of miles since the last fill-up, and **gals**, the number of gallons of gas you just bought. Start with a formal specification for the program, including a test plan. What is the appropriate type for **miles**? For **gals**? For the answer? Explain why.

3. Centimeters.
   Write a program to convert a measurement in centimeters to feet and inches. The numbers of centimeters should be read as input. There are 2.54 centimeters in each inch, and 12 inches in each foot. Start with a formal specification for the program, including a test plan. Turn in the source code and the output of your program when run using the data from your test plan.

4. Ascending order.
   Write a program to input four integers and print them out in ascending numeric order. Use logical operators when you test the relationships among the numbers.

5. A piece of cake.
   Write a complete specification for a program to calculate the total volume of batter needed to half fill two layer-cake pans. The diameter of the pans is N and they are 2 inches deep. Read N as an input. Write a test plan for this program, then write the program and test it. The formula for the volume of a pan is

$$\text{Volume} = \pi \times \frac{\text{diameter}^2}{4.0} \times \text{height}$$

6. Circles.
   Write a problem specification and a complete test plan for a program that calculates facts about circles. Prompt the user to enter the diameter of the circle. If the input is less than 0.0, print an error comment. Otherwise, calculate and print the radius, circumference, and area of the circle. Make your output attractive and easy to read, and check it using your test plan.

7. Slope.
   The slope of a line in a two-dimensional plane is a measure of how steeply the line goes up or down. This can be calculated from any two points on the line, say $p_1 = (x_1, y_1)$ and $p_2 = (x_2, y_2)$ such that $x_1 < x_2$, as follows:

$$\text{Slope} = \frac{y_2 - y_1}{x_2 - x_1}$$

Write a specification and test plan for this problem. Then write a program that will input two coordinates for each of two points, validate the second x coordinate, and print out the slope of the line.

8. What's the difference?

Each term of an arithmetic series is a constant amount greater than the term before it. Suppose the first term in a series is a and the difference between two adjacent terms is d. Then the kth term is $a + (k - 1) \times d$. The sum of the first k terms is

$$\text{Sum} = \frac{k}{2} \times (2a + d \times (k - 1))$$

Write a program that prompts the user for the first two terms of a series and the desired number of terms, k, to calculate. From these, calculate d and the sum of the first k terms. Display a, d, k, and the sum.

9. Summing squares.

The sum of the squares of the first k positive integers is

$$1 + 4 + 9 + \ldots + k^2 = \frac{k \times (k + 1) \times (2k + 1)}{6}$$

Write a program that prompts the user for k and prints out the sum of the first k squares. Make sure to validate the value of k that is entered.

CHAPTER
5

Using Functions and Libraries

In this chapter, we introduce the most important tool C provides for writing manageable, debuggable programs: the function. In modern programming practice, programs are written as a collection of functions connected through well-defined interfaces. We show how to use standard library functions, functions from a local library, and the programmer's own (user-defined) functions.

Functions are important because they provide a way to modularize code so that a large complex program can be written by combining many smaller parts. A **function** is a named block of code that performs a specified task when called. Many functions require one or more arguments. Each **argument** is an object or piece of information that the function can use while carrying out its specified task. Four functions were introduced in Chapter 3: `puts()`, `printf()`, `scanf()`, and `main()`. The first two perform an output task, the third performs input, while the fourth exists in every program and indicates where to begin execution.

Building a program is like building a computer. Today's computer is built by connecting boards. Each board is a group of connected chips, which consist of an integrated group of circuit components constructed by connecting logic elements.

A large program is constructed similarly. At the top level, the program includes several modules, where each module is developed separately (and stored in a separate file.) Each module is composed of object declarations and functions. These functions, in turn, call other functions.

In a well-designed program, the purpose, or task, of each function is clear and easy to describe. All its actions hang together and work at the same level of detail. No function is very long or very complex; each is short enough to comprehend in its entirety. Complexity is avoided by creating and calling other functions to do subtasks. In this way, a highly complex job can be broken into short units that interact with each other in controlled ways. This allows the whole program to be constructed and verified much more easily than a similar program written as one massive unit. Each function, then each module, is developed and debugged before it is inserted into the final, large program. This is how professional programmers have been able to develop the large, sophisticated systems we use today.

5.1   Libraries

We use functions from a variety of sources. Many come to us as part of a library, which is a collection of related functions that can be incorporated into your own code. The **standard libraries** are defined by the C language standard and are part of every C compiler. In addition, software manufacturers often create proprietary libraries that are distributed with the C translator and provide facilities not covered by the standard. Often, a group of computer users shares a collection of functions that become a **local library**. An individual programmer might use functions from all of these sources and normally also defines his or her own functions that are tailored to the tasks of a particular program.

Using library functions lets a programmer take advantage of the skill and knowledge of experts. In modern programming practice, code libraries are used extensively to increase the reliability and quality of programs and decrease the time it takes to write them. A good programmer does not reinvent the wheel.

5.1.1   Standard Libraries

C has about a dozen standard libraries; we use six of them in this text. The first one encountered by a beginning C programmer is the standard input/output library (**stdio**), which contains the functions **scanf()**, **printf()**, and **puts()** we have been using since Chapter 3. This library also contains functions for the input and output of specific data types, which will be explained as those types are introduced, as well as functions for file handling, which will be explained in Chapter 15.

The second most commonly used library is the mathematics library (**math**). This library contains implementations of the mathematical functions listed in Figure 5.1. The program examples in this chapter illustrate the use of several of these functions.

Another important library is the standard library (**stdlib**). It contains functions for generating random numbers; a definition for **abs()**, the absolute value

Name	Function	Argument type(s)	Return type
`fabs(x)`	Absolute value	`double`	`double`
`ceil(x)`	Round x up	`double`	`double`
`floor(x)`	Round x down	`double`	`double`
`rint(x)`	Round x to nearest integer	`double`	`double`
`cos(x)`	Cosine of x	`double`	`double`
`sin(x)`	Sine of x	`double`	`double`
`tan(x)`	Tangent of x	`double`	`double`
`acos(x)`	Arc cosine of x	`double`	`double`
`asin(x)`	Arc sine of x	`double`	`double`
`atan(x)`	Arc tangent of x	`double`	`double`
`cosh(x)`	Hyperbolic cosine of x	`double`	`double`
`sinh(x)`	Hyperbolic sine of x	`double`	`double`
`tanh(x)`	Hyperbolic tangent of x	`double`	`double`
`exp(x)`	e^x	`double`	`double`
`log(x)`	Natural log of x	`double`	`double`
`log10(x)`	Base 10 log of x	`double`	`double`
`sqrt(x)`	Square root	`double`	`double`
`pow(x, y)`	x^y	`double, double`[1]	`double`
`fmod(x,y)`	$x - N \times y$ for largest N such that $N \times y < x$	`double, double`[1]	`double`

[1]Use of two arguments with this function is discussed in Chapter 9.

Figure 5.1.   Functions in the math library.

function for integers; and a variety of general utility functions. Several of these will be introduced as the need arises in later chapters. Other libraries that we use are the time library (`time`), the string library (`string`), and the character-handling library (`ctype`).

5.1.2   Local Libraries

The standard C libraries contain many useful functions for input and output, string handling, mathematical computations, and systems programming tasks. Many C implementations have additional libraries; for example, a graphics library for building screen displays. These libraries provide expert solutions for common needs, but they cannot cover every possible need. The standard libraries contain only a fraction of the useful functions that might be written. The library functions are general-purpose utilities; many were designed for the convenience of programmers creating the UNIX operating system. They are not tailored to the needs of students or scientists and engineers who write C programs in the course of their work.

Programmers define their own functions to meet their needs. Some are special-purpose functions written for one application and not relevant to other

Functions

Name	Purpose	Argument types	Return type
`banner()`	Print an output heading	`void`	`void`
`hold()`	Pause until user hits Enter key	`void`	`void`
`bye()`	Print a termination message	`void`	`void`
`fatal()`	Print an error message and terminate	Same as `printf()`	`void`

Constants

Name	Value	Purpose
`PI`	3.1415927	Ratio of circle circumference to diameter
`ENATURAL`	2.7182818284590451	Base of natural logarithms
`GRAVITY`	9.80665	Gravitational force at sea level, latitude 45°
`NAME`	Student should enter his or her own name, in quotes.	
`CLASS`	Student should enter his or her course number and title in quotes.	

Figure 5.2.   Some items in the tools library. To use these functions and constants `#include` `"tools.h"` **and compile with** `tools.c`.

jobs. However, every programmer builds a collection of function definitions that are useful again and again. These usually are simple functions that save a little writing, simplify a repetitive task, or make a programmer's job easier. Often, such a collection is shared with coworkers and becomes a local library.

We have collected several functions of this nature into a local library named **tools**. In this library are functions to help you begin and end programs, display error messages, read the time and date from the system's clock, and do other common tasks. The use and purpose of each constant or function in the **tools** library will be explained when it is first used in a program example; the source code will be presented later when it can be understood. Figure 5.2 lists a few of the functions and constants in the **tools** library; Appendix F provides a more complete description and gives instructions for installing the tools on your own system.

5.2   Using Libraries

5.2.1   Prototypes

Every data object has a type. The type of a literal is evident from its form; the type of a variable is declared along with the variable name. Similarly, every function has a type, called a **prototype**, which must be known before the function can be used. The prototype defines the function's **interface**; that is, how it is supposed to interact with other functions. It declares the number and types of arguments that must be provided in every call and the kind of answer that the function computes and returns (if any). This information allows the compiler to check for syntax errors in the function calls.

Header files.   Each standard library has a corresponding header file whose name ends in `.h`. The **header file** for a library contains the prototype declarations for all of the functions in that library. It may also define related constants. The header files for the libraries we have mentioned so far are

Standard input/output library: `<stdio.h>`   Standard library: `<stdlib.h>`

Mathematics library: `<math.h>`   Time library: `<time.h>`

Character handling: `<ctype.h>`   String library: `<string.h>`

Local tools library: `"tools.h"`

To use one of the library functions in a program, you must include the corresponding header file in your program. This can be done explicitly, by writing an `#include` command for that library. However, the header file for the `tools` library includes the header files for all other standard libraries that will be used. If you write the command `#include "tools.h"`, there is no need to include the headers for the standard libraries separately.

In an `#include` command, angle brackets `<...>` around the name of the header file indicate that the header and its corresponding library are installed in the compiler's standard library area on the hard disk. We use quotation marks instead of angle brackets for local libraries like `tools` that are stored in the programmer's own disk directory rather than in the standard system directory.

5.2.2   Function Calls

A **function call** causes the function's code to be executed. The normal sequential **flow of control** is **interrupted**, and control is transferred to the beginning of the function. At the end of the function, control returns to the point of interruption. To call a function, write the name of the function followed by a pair of parentheses enclosing a list of zero or more arguments. In the following discussion, we refer to the function that contains the call as the **caller** and to the called function as the **subprogram** or, if there is no ambiguity, simply the **function**. Copies of the argument values are made by the caller and sent to the subprogram, which uses these arguments in its calculations. At the end of function execution, control returns to the caller; a **function result** also may be returned.

The function call must supply an argument value for each parameter defined by the function's prototype. The form of a simple prototype declaration is shown in Figure 5.3. It starts with the type of the answer returned by the function. This is followed by the function name and a pair of parentheses. Within the parentheses are zero or more **parameter declaration** units, consisting of a type

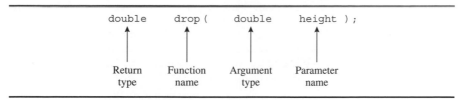

Figure 5.3. Form of a simple function prototype.

and an identifier. The type tells us what kind of argument is expected whenever the function is called. The identifier is optional in a prototype (but required in a function definition).

The C compiler checks every function call to ensure that the correct number of arguments has been provided and that every argument is an appropriate type for the function, according to the function's prototype. It also checks that the function's result is used in an appropriate context. Generally, if a mismatch is found between the function's prototype and the function call, the compiler generates an error comment and does not produce a translated version of the code. Some type mismatches are legal according to the type rules of C but they may not be meaningful in the context of the program. In such cases, the compiler generates a warning comment, continues the translation, and produces an executable program. However, the programmer should never ignore warnings; most warnings are clues about logic errors in the program.

Calling library functions. The program example in Figure 5.4 demonstrates how to include the library header files in your code and how to call the library functions. It uses standard I/O functions, the **sqrt()** function from the mathematics library, and two functions from the **tools** library to improve the human-computer interface. The **banner()** function prints a neat output header with the programmer's name and the current time and date. The **bye()** function prints a termination message and (in systems where this is needed) waits for the user to type the Enter key before returning to the operating system. This gives the user a chance to read the output before it disappears from view.

Notes on Figure 5.4. Calling library functions.

- *First box: the* **#include** *command.*

  1. The commands to **#include <stdio.h>** and **<math.h>** are written in **tools.h**. This saves us the trouble of writing these **#include** commands in every program.
  2. Since the local library, **tools**, is not standard, we use quotation marks to indicate the header file and library are found in the programmer's disk directory.

```
/* ------------------------------------------------------------------- */
/* Determine the time it takes for a grapefruit to hit the ground when it */
/* is dropped from a helicopter hovering at height h, with no initial    */
/* velocity.  Also determine the velocity of the fruit at impact.        */

#include "tools.h"

void main( void )
{
    double h;                    /* height of fall (m) */
    double t;                    /* time of fall (s) */
    double v;                    /* terminal velocity (m/s) */

    banner();

    puts( "\n Calculate the time it would take for a grapefruit\n"
          " to fall from a helicopter at a given height.  \n" );

    printf( " Enter height of helicopter (meters): " );
    scanf( "%lg", &h );          /* keyboard input for height */
    if (h < 0) {                 /* exit gracefully after error */
        fatal( " Error: height must be >= 0.  You entered %g", h );
    }

    t = sqrt( 2 * h / GRAVITY );/* calculate the time of fall */
    v = GRAVITY * t;             /* velocity of grapefruit at this time */
    printf( "    Time of fall = %g seconds\n", t );
    printf( "    Velocity of the object = %g m/s\n", v );
    bye();
}
```

Figure 5.4.   Calling library functions.

- *Second box: a tool for beginning a program.*

  1. The function **banner()** is defined in **tools.c**; its prototype is in **tools.h**. We use **banner()** to print a visually attractive header for the output. This function positions the cursor at the upper-left corner of the output screen and displays the programmer's name, course number, and the current date. In a later chapter, an exercise asks you to extend this definition by adding a title for the program.
  2. To print your own name as part of the banner, modify the **#define**s on the first three lines of the **tools.h** file. See Appendix F for instructions.

- *Third box: calling* `fatal()`.

  1. The function `fatal()` is defined in `tools.c`; its prototype is in `tools.h`. It prints an error comment, waits for the user to notice the error and respond, then exits from the program in the proper way. Although it most commonly is used to handle input errors, it could be called after any error that makes continuation meaningless.

  2. The `fatal()` function takes the same parameters as `printf()`; that is, a format and zero or more data items to be printed. It performs the print operation then ends program execution.[2]

  3. We use a simple `if` statement to test for errors and call `fatal()` if an error is found. No `else` statement is needed because `fatal()` takes control immediately and directly to the end of the program. In the flow diagram (Figure 5.7), it is diagrammed as a bolt of lightning because it "short-circuits" all the normal control structures.

  4. In response to an error, the following output is displayed and the system waits for a period and Enter key to be typed before continuing:

```
Calculate the time it would take for a grapefruit
to fall from a helicopter at a given height.

Enter height of helicopter (meters): -2
Error: height must be >= 0.  You entered -2

Error exit; press '.' and 'Enter' to continue.
```

- *Fourth box: calling* `sqrt()`.

  1. The `sqrt()` function computes the square root of its argument. To call this function, we write the argument in parentheses after the function name. In this call, the argument is the value of the expression `2*h/GRAVITY`. The multiplication and division will be done, and the result will be sent to the `sqrt()` function and become the value of the `sqrt()`'s parameter. Then the square root will be calculated and returned to the caller. When a function returns a result, the caller must do something with it. In this case, it is stored in the variable named `t`, then used in the next two lines of `main()`.

  2. A function prototype describes the function's interface; that is, the argument(s) that must be brought into the function and the type of result that is sent back. In this case, one argument is brought in and one result is returned. We can diagram the passage of information to and from the function like this:

---

[2]This function calls `exit()`, which flushes output buffers and closes any open streams. Streams, buffers, and `exit()` will be covered in later chapters.

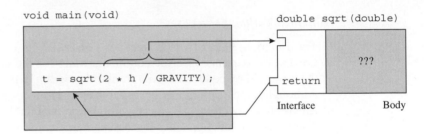

void main(void)   double sqrt(double)

t = sqrt(2 * h / GRAVITY);   return

???

Interface   Body

3. In general, spacing makes no difference to the compiler. We could have written

```
t=sqrt( 2*h/GRAVITY); or
t =sqrt (2 *h / GRAVITY); or
t= sqrt (2* h/GRAVITY);
```

However, spacing makes an important difference in the readability of a program. You should use spacing selectively to make formulas as readable as possible. Current style guidelines call for spaces after the opening parenthesis and before the closing parenthesis.

- *The output.* The following output is displayed when valid data are entered:

```
-----------------------------------------------------------
        Patience S. Goodenough
        CS 110
        Thu Feb 10 2000  22:41:46
-----------------------------------------------------------

Calculate the time it would take for a grapefruit
to fall from a helicopter at a given height.

Enter height of helicopter (meters): 30
   Time of fall = 2.47352 seconds
   Velocity of the object = 24.2569 m/s

Normal termination.
```

- *Fifth box: the closing message.*

1. In some systems, the user's output window disappears instantly when the program finishes, giving the user no chance to read or study the output. Even if the window can be brought back into view, the disappearance is annoying. In such systems, the **bye()** function provides a more satisfying way to end a program. It prints a closing comment and waits for the user to read the output. Typing a period and a newline returns control to the system.

2. This program demonstrates a pattern you should remember and follow; it starts by calling `banner()` and ends by calling `bye()`. Remember this idiom and use it to make convenient user interfaces.

5.3 Function Types

Functions can take no arguments or many, of any combination of types, and can return or not return values. The type of a function is a composite of the type of value it returns and the set of types of its arguments. We begin the study of functions by introducing two function types: double:double and void:void.

Double:double functions. Some functions calculate and return values when they are called. For example, in Figure 5.4, the function `sqrt()` calculates a mathematical function and returns the result to `main()`, which stores it in a variable and later prints it. The functions `sqrt()`, `log()`, `sin()`, and `cos()` all accept an argument of type `double` and return an answer of type `double`. We say, informally, that these are **double:double functions** because their prototypes are of the form `double funcname(double)`. A double:double function must be called in some context where a value of type `double` makes sense. Often, these functions are called from the right side of an assignment statement or from a `printf()` statement. Examples of calls on double:double functions follow:

```
t = sqrt( 2 * h / GRAVITY );
printf( "The natural log of %g is %g\n", x, log( x ) );
```

Void:void functions. Some functions return no value to the calling program. Their purpose is to cause a side effect; that is, perform an input or output operation or change the value of some memory variable. These functions are called *void functions* because their prototypes start with the keyword `void` instead of a return type. *Void* means "nothing"; it is not a type name, but we need it as a placeholder to fill the space a type name normally would occupy in a prototype. If the return-type field in a function header is left blank, the return type defaults to `int`.[3]

Some `void` functions require arguments; others, such as `banner()` and `bye()`, do not. These functions, called **void:void functions**, have prototypes of the form `void funcname(void)`. To call a void:void function, write the function name followed by empty parentheses and a semicolon. Normally, the function call will stand by itself on a line.

---

[3]This default makes no sense in ISO C; it is an unfortunate holdover from pre-ISO days, when C did not even have a type `void`. The default to type `int` was kept in ISO C to maintain compatibility with old versions of C.

| 5.4 | **User-Defined Functions** |

Functions serve three purposes in a program: They make it easy to use code written by someone else; they make it possible to reuse your own code in a new context; most important, though, they permit breaking a large program into small pieces in such a way that the interface between pieces is fixed and controllable. A programmer may (and generally does) modularize his or her program by dividing the entire job into smaller tasks and writing a **user-defined function** for each task.

A function has two parts: a prototype and a definition. The definition, in turn, has two parts: a **function header** (which must correspond to the prototype) and a **function body**, which is a block of code enclosed in curly brackets. The body consists of a series of (optional) declarations. These create local variables and constants for use by the function. The local declarations are followed by a series of program statements that use the local variables and the arguments (if any) to compute a value or perform a task. The body may contain one or more `return` statements, which return a value to the calling program.

The complete set of rules for creating and using functions in C is extensive and complex; it is presented in some detail in Chapter 9. In this section, we begin by writing the two types of functions discussed in the previous section. We illustrate how to define these function types, write prototypes for them, call them, and draw flowcharts (using barred boxes) to show the flow of control. We give a few examples and some brief guidelines so that the student may begin using functions in his or her own programs. The next figures illustrate, in context, how to write the parts of void:void and double:double functions.

5.4.1   Defining Void:Void Functions

We show how to write void:void functions first, using Figure 5.5 to illustrate the discussion. This program uses a void:void function to print user instructions and error comments. We ask the user to enter the number of passengers in a car. If the input number is greater than 5, we print an error message and beep four times.

Notes on Figure 5.5. Calling void:void functions.

- *First box: the prototypes.*

    1. Either a prototype declaration or the actual function definition should occur in a program before any calls on the function.[4]
    2. When we include prototypes at the top of a program, either explicitly or by including a header file, the corresponding functions can be called

---

[4]If a function is called before it is declared, the C compiler will construct a prototype for that function that may or may not work properly.

```
/* Include header files for tools and several standard libraries.  */
#include "tools.h"

/* Prototype declarations for the user-defined functions. ------- */
void instructions( void );          /* No arguments, no return value. */
void beep( void );
```

```
void main( void )
{
    int n_pass;                     /* Number of passengers in car. */

    banner();                       /* Display output headings. */
    instructions();                 /* Display instructions for the user. */

    scanf( "%i", &n_pass );

    if (n_pass > 5)  beep();  /* Error message: too many passengers */

    else printf( " OK! \n" );   /* Success message for good entry */
    bye();
}
/* --------------------------------------------------------------------- */
void instructions( void )                          /* function definition --- */
{
    printf( "\n Legal-passenger-load tester for 6-seat sedans.\n"
            " Number of passengers you will transport: " );
}

/* --------------------------------------------------------------------- */
void beep( void )                                  /* function definition --- */
{
    printf( " Bad data!  \n\a\a\a\a\n" );          /* error message and beeps */
}
```

Figure 5.5.   Calling void:void functions.

anywhere in the program. The prototypes for the tools library and the standard I/O library are brought into the program by the **#include** statement.

3. In addition, we must write prototypes for the two functions defined at the bottom of this program, **instructions()** and **beep()**.

4. The prototype for every void:void function follows the simple pattern shown here: the word **void** followed by the name of the function,

followed by the word **void** again, in parentheses. Every prototype ends in a semicolon.

- *Second, third, and fourth boxes: the function calls.*

   1. These lines each call a void:void function. The call consists of the function name followed by empty parentheses. Often, as with the calls on **instructions()**, **banner()**, and **bye()**, the function call will stand alone on a line.
   2. Often a void:void function is used to give general instructions or feedback to the user, as in the second and fourth boxes here. Sometimes, as in the third box, one is used to inform the user that an error has happened, as is the case with the **beep()** function. Such calls often form one clause of an **if** statement. Here is the output from two test runs (the second banner has been omitted):

```
------------------------------------------------
      Patience S. Goodenough
      CS 110
      Thu Feb 10 2000  22:46:38
------------------------------------------------

Legal-passenger-load tester for 6-seat sedans.
Number of passengers you will transport: 3
OK!

Normal termination.
------------------------------------------------
Legal-passenger-load tester for 6-seat sedans.
Number of passengers you will transport: 7
Bad data!

Normal termination.
```

- *Fifth and sixth boxes: the function definitions.*

   1. We define two void:void functions: **instructions()** and **beep()**. We use a comment line of dashes to mark the beginning of each function so that it is easy to locate on a video screen or printout.
   2. Each function definition starts with a header line that is the same as the prototype except that it does not end in a semicolon. Following each header line is a block of code enclosed in curly brackets that defines the actions of the function.
   3. Most void:void functions, like these two, perform input or output operations. The symbol \a, used in the **beep()** function, is the ASCII

code for a beeping noise. Many systems will emit an audible beep when this symbol is "printed" as part of the output. Other systems print a small box instead of emitting a sound.

5.4.2   Defining a Double:Double Function

We use Figures 5.6 through 5.8 to illustrate the construction and call of a double:double function, which is somewhat more complicated than a void:void function because information must be passed into the function and a result returned to the caller. For this purpose, we need a result type, a parameter type, and a parameter name.

Notes on Figure 5.6. The grapefruit returns.

- *First box: writing the prototype.* A prototype for a double:double function gives the function name and specifies that it requires one **double** parameter and returns a **double** result. The general form is

  ```
  double function_name( double parameter_name );
  ```

  where the parameter name is optional. This box contains a prototype declaration for the function named **drop()**. It states that **drop()** requires one argument of type **double** and returns a **double** result. This information permits the C compiler to check whether a call on **drop()** is written correctly.
- *Second box: the function call.* The prototype for **drop()** was given in the first box and the function is defined in Figure 5.8. The second box contains a call on **drop()**. The form of any function call must follow the form of the prototype. When we call a double:double function, we must supply one argument expression of type **double**. In this call, the argument expression is a simple variable name, **h**. When we call **drop()**, we send a copy of the value of **h** to the function to be used in its calculations.

  A function call interrupts sequential execution and sends control into the function. Figure 5.7 depicts this interruption as a dotted arrow going from the function call to the beginning of the function. From there, control flows through the function to the return statement, which sends control back to the point of interruption, as shown by the lower dotted arrow. When a double:double function returns, it brings back a **double** value, which should be either used or stored. In this example, we store the result in the **double** variable **t**.
- *Program output.* Here is one set of output from the grapefruit program (the banners and termination messages have been omitted):

A grapefruit is dropped from a helicopter hovering at height **h**. This continues development of the program in Figure 5.4. The **drop()** function is shown in Figure 5.8.

```
/* ----------------------------------------------------------------- */
/* Determine the time it takes for a grapefruit to hit the ground when it */
/* is dropped from a helicopter hovering at height h, with no initial    */
/* velocity.  Also determine the velocity of the fruit at impact.  Use a */
/* separate function to compute the time of travel of the grapefruit     */
#include "tools.h"

double drop( double height );    /* Prototype declaration of drop. */

void main( void )
{
    double h;                    /* height of fall (m) */
    double t;                    /* time of fall (s) */
    double v;                    /* terminal velocity (m/s) */

    banner();
    puts( "\n Calculate the time it would take for a grapefruit\n"
          " to fall from a helicopter at a given height.\n" );
    printf( " Enter height of helicopter (meters): " );
    scanf( "%lg", &h );          /* keyboard input for height */

    t = drop( h );               /* Call drop.  Send it the argument h. */

    v = GRAVITY * t;             /* velocity of grapefruit at this time */
    printf( "    Time of fall = %g seconds\n", t );
    printf( "    Velocity of the object = %g m/s\n", v );
    bye();
}
```

Figure 5.6.   The grapefruit returns.

```
Calculate the time it would take for a grapefruit
to fall from a helicopter at a given height.

Enter height of helicopter (meters): 906.5
    Time of fall = 13.5969 seconds
    Velocity of the object = 133.34 m/s
```

Notes on Figure 5.8. Definition of the **drop()** **function.**   We show how to write the definition of a double:double function.

- *First box: the comment block and the function header.* Every function should start with a block of comment lines, the **function comment block**, that separate the definition from other parts of the program and describe

This is a flow diagram of the program in Figures 5.6 and 5.8. Function calls are depicted using a box with an extra bar on the bottom to indicate a **transfer of control**. The dotted lines show how the control sequence is interrupted when the function call sends control to the beginning of the `drop()` function. Control flows through the function then returns via the lower dotted line to the box from which it was called. The call on `fatal()` (after an error) ends execution immediately and returns control to the operating system.

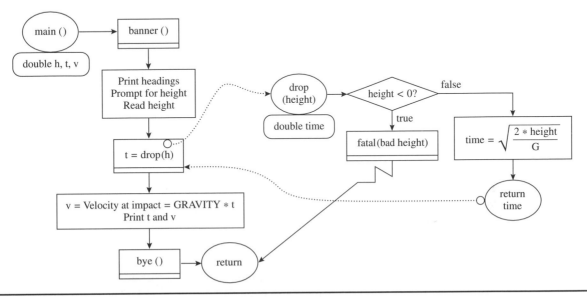

Figure 5.7.   Flow diagram for the grapefruit returns.

the purpose of the function. Comment marks (`/*...*/`) begin the first line and end the last line of the block comment. These comments provide a neat and visible heading for the function. The first line of a function definition is called the *function header*. It must be like the prototype except that the parameter name is required (not optional) in the header and the header does not end with a semicolon. A parameter can be given any convenient name, which need not be the same as the name of the argument that will appear in future function calls. A new variable is created for the parameter and can be used only by the function itself.

When a function is called, the expression in parentheses is evaluated and its value passed into the function and used to initialize the parameter variable. This value is called the *actual argument*. Within the function, the parameter name is used to refer to the argument value. In the function call, the argument was `main()`'s variable `h`, but the `drop()` function's parameter is named `height`. This is no error. *A double:double function can be called with any `double` argument value.* The argument can be the result of an expression, a variable with the same name, or a variable with

This function is called from Figure 5.6.

```
/* ------------------------------------------------------------------ */
/* Time taken for an object dropped from height meters to hit the ground. */
double drop ( double height )

{
    double time;

    if (height < 0) {                         /* exit gracefully after error. */
        fatal( " Error: height must be >= 0.  You entered %g", height );
    }
    time = sqrt( 2 * height / GRAVITY ); /* calculate the time of fall */

    return time;

}
```

Figure 5.8.   Definition of the `drop()` **function.**

a different name. Within the function, the parameter name (`height`) is used to refer to the argument value.

- *Second box: a local variable declaration.* The code block of a function can and usually does start with declarations for **local variables**. Memory for these variables will be allocated when the function is called and deallocated when the function returns. These variables are for use only by the code in the body of the function; no other function can use them. In the example program, we declare a local variable named `time`.
- *Third box: the function code.* Statements within the function body may use the parameter variable and any local variables that were declared. References also may be made to constants defined globally (at the top of the program). The use of global variables is legal but strongly discouraged in C. The statements in this function are like the corresponding lines of Figure 5.4 except that they use the parameter name and local variable name instead of the names of the variables in the main program.
- *Inner box: calling another function.* An error has been detected, so we call the `fatal()` function to handle it. The arguments to `fatal()` are just like the arguments to `printf()`. It will print the message you supply and terminate the program immediately.
- *Last box: the* `return` *statement.* On completion, a double:double function must return a result of type `double` to its caller. This is done using the `return` statement. A `return` statement does two things: it sends control

immediately back to the calling program and it tells what the return value (the result) of the function should be. It does not need parentheses. In Figure 5.8, the result from `sqrt()` is stored in the local variable `time`. To make that answer available to the caller, we return the value of `time`. On executing the `return` statement, the value of `time` is passed back to the caller and control is returned to the caller at the statement containing the function call, as depicted by the dotted line in Figure 5.7.

5.5 Math Library Application: Roots of a Quadratic Equation

Given a quadratic equation

$$a \times x^2 + b \times x + c = 0$$

where a is nonzero and $b^2 - 4 \times a \times c$ is nonnegative, we can find its roots by using the quadratic formula

$$x = \frac{-b \pm \sqrt{b^2 - 4 \times a \times c}}{2 \times a}$$

However, to write a general program that finds the roots of any quadratic equation, we must handle several special cases. Figure 5.9 defines the general problem of finding the roots of a quadratic equation. The program that implements this specification is in Figures 5.10 and 5.11. It is a good example of the use of library functions and also using a series of `if...else` statements.

Problem scope: Find the roots of a quadratic equation with any coefficients a, b, and c. Test for degenerate equations and account for single roots and complex roots.

Formulas:

A linear equation, $b \times x + c = 0$, has one root at $\frac{-c}{b}$.

The value $d = b^2 - 4 \times a \times c$ is called the *discriminant* of the equation.

If $d > 0$, the equation has two real roots at $x = \frac{-b \pm \sqrt{d}}{2 \times a}$

If $d = 0$, the equation has one real root at $x = \frac{-b}{2 \times a}$. We consider this situation to be a degenerate case of two equal real roots.

If $d < 0$, the equation has two complex roots at $x = \frac{-b \pm i \times \sqrt{|d|}}{2 \times a}$

Inputs: The user will enter the coefficients a, b, and c.
Output required: Echo the coefficients. If $a = 0$ and $b = 0$, there is no equation; this should be noted. Otherwise, print the root or roots. Print headings and a closing message.

Figure 5.9.   Problem specification: Roots of a quadratic equation.

Solve a quadratic equation with any coefficients a, b, and c. Test for degenerate equations and account for single roots and complex roots. Part of the program is in Figure 5.11.

```
#include "tools.h"
void main( void )
{
    double a, b, c;                      /* Coefficients of the equation. */
    double d, two_a, sroot;              /* Working storage. */
    double xreal, ximag, x1, x2;         /* Answers. */

    banner();
    puts( " Find the roots of ax*x + bx + c = 0" );
    printf( " Enter the values of a, b, and c: " );
    scanf( "%lg%lg%lg", &a, &b, &c );
    printf( "\n The equation is %g *x*x + %g *x + %g = 0\n", a, b, c );

    --- The code that belongs here is in Figure 5.11 ---

    bye();
}
```

Figure 5.10.   Quadratic roots.

Notes on Figures 5.10 and 5.11. Finding quadratic roots.

- *Outer box: a series of* **if...else** *statements.*

    1. This block of **if** statements is diagrammed in Figure 5.12.
    2. The first **if** statement tests for and eliminates nonequations of the form $c = 0$.
    3. Here is the output for one nonequation:

       ```
       Find the roots of ax*x + bx + c = 0
       Enter the values of a, b, and c: 0 0 0

       The equation is 0 *x*x + 0 *x + 0 = 0
       Degenerate equation -- no roots
       ```

    4. The second **if** statement is in the **else** clause of the first **if** statement. It tests for and solves linear equations of the form $b \times x + c = 0$. Here is the output for a linear equation:
       ```
       Find the roots of ax*x + bx + c = 0
       Enter the values of a, b, and c: 0 3 1

       The equation is 0 *x*x + 3 *x + 1 = 0
       Linear equation -- root at -c/b = -0.333333
       ```

This is the main portion of the program that begins in Figure 5.10.

```
if (a == 0 && b == 0) {
    printf( " Degenerate equation -- no roots\n" );
}
else if (a == 0) {
    printf( " Linear equation -- root at -c/b = %g\n", -c/b );
}
else {
    two_a = 2*a;
    d = b*b - 4*a*c;              /* discriminant of equation. */

    sroot = sqrt( fabs(d) );

    if (d < 0) {                  /* If d is negative, roots are complex. */
        xreal = -b / two_a;
        ximag = sroot / two_a;
        printf( " The roots are x = %g + %g i \n          and "
                "x = %g - %g i \n", xreal, ximag, xreal, ximag );
    }
    else if (d == 0) {            /* There is only one root. */
        printf( " Single real root at x = %g \n", -b / two_a );
    }
    else {                        /* If d is positive, roots are real. */
        x1 = -b / two_a + sroot / two_a;
        x2 = -b / two_a - sroot / two_a;
        printf( " The real roots are x = %g and %g \n", x1, x2 );
    }
}
```

Figure 5.11.   Quadratic roots, main portion.

5. The **else** clause of the second **if** statement contains the computations for true quadratic equations. First, it calculates some common subexpressions, then tests whether the two roots are real or complex and solves the equation.

- *First inner box: calling library functions.*

  1. The **fabs()** function computes the absolute value of a floating-point number.
  2. The **sqrt()** function computes the square root.
  3. Both functions are in the math library.

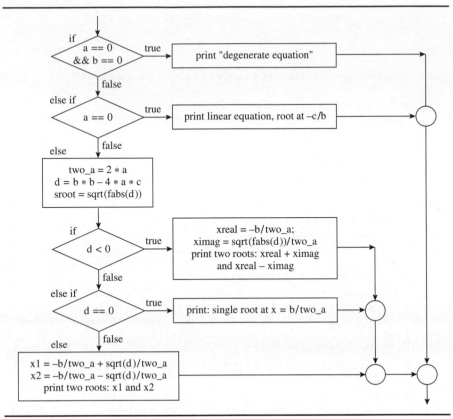

Figure 5.12.   Diagram for the `if...else` statements in Figure 5.11.

- *Second inner box: actual computation of the roots.*

  1. The value *d* is called the *discriminant* of the equation. If it is negative, the roots are complex. If it is 0 there is a double real root. Otherwise, there are two real roots.
  2. In the flow diagram, note that this series of `if...else` statements is contained entirely within the `else` clause of the earlier statement.
  3. Here are the results from three runs of this program:

```
Find the roots of ax*x + bx + c = 0
Enter the values of a, b, and c: 1 1 1

The equation is 1 *x*x + 1 *x + 1 = 0
The roots are x = -0.5 + 0.866025 i
          and x = -0.5 - 0.866025 i
----------------------------------------
Find the roots of ax*x + bx + c = 0
Enter the values of a, b, and c: 2 4 2
```

```
The equation is 2 *x*x + 4 *x + 2 = 0
Single real root at x = -1
----------------------------------------------
Find the roots of ax*x + bx + c = 0
Enter the values of a, b, and c: 1 0 -1

The equation is 1 *x*x + 0 *x + -1 = 0
The real roots are x = 1 and -1
```

5.6   A User-Defined Function: Numerical Integration by Summing Rectangles

We introduce the topic of integration with a simple integration program where the function to be integrated is coded as part of the main program. The definite integral of a function can be interpreted as the area under the graph of that function over the interval of integration on the x-axis. If a function is continuous, we can approximate its integral by covering the area under the curve with a series of boxes and adding up the areas of these boxes. Several methods for numerical integration are based on a version of this idea:

- Divide the interval of integration into a series of subintervals.
- For each subinterval, approximate the area under the curve in that interval by a shape such as a rectangle or trapezoid whose area is easy to calculate.
- Calculate and add up the areas of all these shapes.

The simplest way to approximate the integral of a function is to use rectangles to approximate the area under the curve in each subinterval; the diagram in Figure 5.13 and the program in Figure 5.14 illustrate this approach. For each subinterval, we place a rectangle between the curve and the x-axis such that the upper-left corner of the rectangle touches the curve and the bottom of the rectangle lies on the x-axis. In this example, we calculate the integral of the function $f(x)$:

$$f(x) = x^2 + x, \qquad \text{where } 0 \le x \le b$$

by summing 100 rectangular areas, each of width $h = b/100$, as shown by Figure 5.13. For example, the area of the rectangle between $2h$ and $3h$ is $h \times f(2h)$. Generalizing this formula, we get

$$\text{Area}_k = h \times f(k \times h)$$

Now, summing over 100 rectangles, we get

$$\text{Area} = \sum_{k=0}^{99} h \times f(k \times h)$$

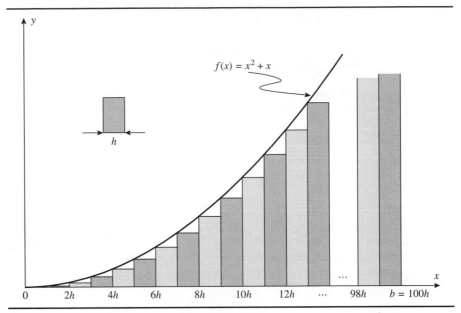

$f(x) = x^2 + x$

$$0 \quad 2h \quad 4h \quad 6h \quad 8h \quad 10h \quad 12h \quad \cdots \quad 98h \quad b = 100h$$

Figure 5.13.   The area under a curve.

Notes on Figures 5.13 and 5.14: Integration by Rectangles.

- *First box: the function definition.* This is the entire definition of the function we will integrate. Short functions can be written on one line.

- *Second box: declarations with initializations.*

  1. In this initial example, we integrate a single fixed function over a fixed interval using a fixed number of rectangles. Later, we present other integration programs that do the job in more general and more accurate ways.
  2. We integrate the function over the interval $0 \ldots 1$.
  3. We divide this interval into 100 parts of length **h** = **.01**.

- *Third box: initializations for the loop.*

  1. Although we could combine these initializations with the declarations, that is bad style. For trouble-free development of complex programs, all loop initializations should be placed immediately before the loop.
  2. To prepare for the loop, we initialize the **sum** that will accumulate the areas.
  3. The loop variable for this **while** loop is **k**. The first rectangle lies between a and $a + 1 \times h$, so we initialize **k** to 0. Since $a = 0.0$, the first rectangle we sum starts at $x = 0.0 + 0 \times h = 0.0$.

```
#include "tools.h"
#define N 100

double f( double x ){ return x*x + x; }

void main( void )
{
    double a = 0.0;        /* Lower limit of integration. */
    double b = 1.0;        /* Upper limit of integration. */
    double h = (b - a)/N;  /* Width of one of the N rectangles summed. */

    double x;              /* Current function argument; a <= x < b. */
    double sum;            /* Total area of rectangles. */
    int k;                 /* Loop counter. */

    banner();
    printf( " Integrate x*x + x from %g to %g. \n", a, b );

    sum = 0.0;
    k = 0;

    while(k < N) {              /* Add up N rectangles. */
        x = a + k * h;          /* Lower left corner of kth rectangle. */
        sum += h * f( x );      /* Area of rectangle at x. */
        ++k;
    }

    printf( " The area is %g\n", sum );

    bye();
}
```

Figure 5.14. Integration by summing rectangles.

- *Fourth box: the loop.*

    1. We execute the loop from `k` = `0` until (but not when) `k` = `100`. Therefore, we do it 100 times.
    2. The last rectangle summed starts at $x = a + 99h$ and goes to $x = a + 100h$.
    3. We use the `++` operator to increment `k` each time around the loop.
    4. Note how convenient the `+=` operator is for adding a new term to a sum.

- *Fifth box: the summary.*

    1. At the end of a calculation loop, you normally see either a **return** or a **printf()** statement that delivers the answer to the user.

2. The *exact* area under this curve for the interval $0 \ldots 1$ is .833333. Since we are calculating an approximate answer, it will be slightly different.

3. The output is

```
Integrate x*x + x from 0 to 1.
The area is 0.82335
```

5.7   What You Should Remember

5.7.1   Major Concepts

- Functions can be used to break up programs into modules of manageable complexity. In this way, a highly complex job can be broken into short units that interact with each other in controlled ways. These modules should have the following properties:

  The purpose of each function should be clear and simple.

  All its actions should hang together and work at the same level of detail.

  A function should be short enough to comprehend in its entirety.

  The length and complexity of a function can be minimized by calling other functions to do subtasks.

- Function definitions can come from the standard C libraries such as the **stdio** and **math** libraries or from local libraries such as the **tools** library that accompanies this text. Functions also can be defined by the programmer. This chapter presented two kinds of user-defined functions (void:void and double:double). Additional types of library functions and user-defined functions are introduced in subsequent chapters as additional data types are discussed.

- Some functions compute and return values; others do not. A function with no return value is called a **void** function. Such functions normally perform input or output of some sort.

- A call to a function that returns a value normally is found in an assignment statement, an expression, or an output statement.

- The basic components of a function are the prototype and the function definition, which consists of a header and a body.

- Arguments are the means by which a calling program communicates data to a function. Parameters are the means by which a function receives the communicated data. When a function is called, the actual arguments in the function call are passed into the function and become the values of the function's formal parameters.

- After passing the parameter values, control is passed into the function. Computation starts at the top and proceeds through the function until it is finished, at which time the result is returned and control is transferred back to the calling program. A more detailed look at functions will be given in Chapter 9.
- The name of the parameter in a function does *not* need to be the same as the name of a variable used in calling that function.
- Functions allow an application program to be constructed and verified much more easily than a similar program written as one massive unit. Each function, then each module, is developed and debugged before it is inserted into the final, large program. This is how professional programmers have been able to develop the large, sophisticated systems that we use today.

5.7.2   Programming Style

- Keep the main program and all function definitions short. An entire function should fit on one video screen, so that the programmer can see the declarations and the code at the same time. When a function begins to get long, this often is a sign that it should be broken into two or more functions.
- Every function definition should start with a distinctive and highly visible comment. We use a dashed line followed by a brief description of the purpose of the function. This comment block helps you to find each portion of your program quickly and easily, both on screen and on paper.
- Function names should be descriptive, distinctive, and not overly long.
- All the object names used in a function should be either parameter names or defined locally as variables. This provides maximum isolation of each function from all others, which substantially aids debugging.

5.7.3   Sticky Points and Common Errors

- The prototype must match the function header. If there is a mismatch, the program will not compile correctly.
- Prototypes end in semicolons. If the semicolon is missing, the compiler "thinks" that the prototype is the function header. This will cause many meaningless error comments.
- Definitions must *not* have a semicolon after the function header. If a semicolon is written there, the compiler "thinks" the header is a prototype and will give an error comment on the next line.
- If the prototype is missing or comes after the first function call, the compiler will construct a prototype using the types of the parameters given in the first function call. The return type always will be `int`, which may or

may not be correct. If the constructed prototype is wrong, it will cause the compiler to give error comments on lines that are correct.

5.7.4   New and Revisited Vocabulary

These are the most important terms and concepts that were introduced or discussed in this chapter:

function	transfer of control	user-defined function
standard library	function call	function definition
local library	caller	function comment block
header file	argument	function header
prototype (declaration)	void:void function	function body
interface	double:double function	local variable
interrupted flow	parameter	function return

The following C keywords, phrases, and library functions were discussed in this chapter:

`return` statement	`<stdlib.h>`	`log()` (from `math`)
`<stdio.h>`	`abs()` (from `stdlib`)	`"tools.h"`
`scanf()` (from `stdio`)	`<math.h>`	`banner()` (from `tools`)
`printf()` (from `stdio`)	`fabs()` (from `math`)	`fatal()` (from `tools`)
`puts()` (from `stdio`)	`sqrt()` (from `math`)	`bye()` (from `tools`)

5.8   Exercises

5.8.1   Self-Test Exercises

1. Declare a variable name for the phrase on the left in each item. Then write a C expression to compute the formula on the right and store the result in the variable you defined.

   a. Right triangle: Hypotenuse $= \sqrt{\text{base}^2 + \text{height}^2}$

   b. Rectangular to polar coordinates: $\theta = \text{arc tangent}(y/x)$ for $x \neq 0$

   c. Polar to rectangular coordinates: $y = r \times \cos(\theta)$

2. Write the prototype that corresponds to each function definition:

   a. `double cube( double x ) { return x*x*x; }`

   b. `void three_beeps() { beep(); beep(); beep(); }`

3. Write a double:double function that computes each of the formulas that follow and returns the result:

a. Tangent of angle $x = \dfrac{\sin(x)}{\cos(x)}$

b. Surface area of a sphere with radius $r = 4 \times \pi \times r^2$

4. Explain the difference between

a. An argument and a parameter

b. A prototype and a function header

c. A header file and a source code file

d. A local library and a standard library

e. A function declaration and a function call

f. A function declaration and a function definition

5. What happens on your compiler when a prototype for a user-defined function is omitted? To find out, start with the code from Figures 5.6 and 5.8 and delete the prototype above the main program.

5.8.2   Using Pencil and Paper

1. List everything you must write in your program when you want to *use* (not define) each of the following:

a. A user-defined void:void function named **help()**

b. The **fatal()** function

c. The **sqrt()** function

2. Declare a variable name for the phrase on the left in each item. Then write a C expression to compute the formula on the right and store the result in the variable you defined.

a. Sum of angles: $\sin(x + y) = \sin(x)\cos(y) + \cos(x)\sin(y)$

b. Sine: $\sin(x) = \sqrt{1 - \cos^2(x)}$

c. Tangent: $\tan(2x) = \dfrac{2\tan(x)}{1 - \tan^2(x)}$

3. Write a double:double function that computes each of the following formulas and returns the result:

a. Diagonal of a square with side $s = \sqrt{2 \times s^2}$

b. Volume of a sphere with radius $r = \dfrac{4\pi}{3} \times r^3$

4. What happens on your compiler when a required **#include** command is omitted? Will a program compile? Will it work correctly?

5. Write the prototype that corresponds to each function definition. Then define appropriate variables and write a legal call on the function.

   a. `double inches( double cm ) { return cm / 2.54; }`

   b.
   ```
   void beeps( int n )
   {    int k = 0;
        while (k < n) {
             beep();
             ++k;
        }
   }
   ```

5.8.3   Using the Computer

1. Geometric mean.
   Given terms $k - 1$ and $k + 1$ in a geometric progression, find term k and find the
   common ratio, R. Term k is called the *geometric mean* between the other two terms.
   Refer to Figure 2.2 for the definition of a geometric progression. The formulas for
   the kth term and common ratio are

   $$R = \sqrt{\frac{t_{k+1}}{t_{k-1}}} \quad \text{and} \quad t_k = R \times t_{k-1}$$

2. Numerical integration.
   The program in Figure 5.14 integrates the function $f(x) = x^2 + x$ for $0 \leq x \leq 1.0$.
   Modify this program to integrate the function $f(x) = x^2 + 2x + 2$ for $-1.0 \leq x
   \leq 1.0$. If you have studied symbolic integration, compare your result to the exact
   analytical answer.

3. Precision of numerical computations.
   Figure 5.14 gives a program that integrates a function by rectangles. Keep the function
   `f()` and modify the main program so that the integration process will be repeated
   using 10, 20, 40, 80, 160, and 320 rectangles. Print a neat table of the number of
   rectangles used and the results computed each time. Compare the answers. What can
   you say about their accuracy?

4. Sales tax.
   Write a double:double function whose parameter is a purchase price. Calculate and
   return T, the total price, including sales tax. Define the sales tax rate as a **const** R
   whose value is 6%. Write a main program that will read P, the before-tax amount of
   a purchase, call your function to calculate the after-tax price, and print out the answer.
   Both prices will be in units of dollars and cents. What are the appropriate types for
   P, R, and T? Why? Use the program in Figure 5.6 as a guide.

5. Take-home pay.
   Write a double:double function whose parameter is an employee's gross pay for one
   month. Compute and return the take-home pay, given the following constants:

   Medical plan deduction $= \$75.65$

   Social security tax rate $= 7.51\%$

Federal income tax rate $= 16.5\%$

State income tax rate $= 4.5\%$

United Fund deduction $= \$15.00$

The medical deduction must be subtracted from the gross pay before the tax amounts are computed. Then the taxes should be computed and subtracted from the gross. As each one is computed, print the amount. Finally, subtract the United Fund contribution and return the remaining amount.

6. Compound interest.

   a. Write a function to compute the amount of money, A, that you will have in n years if you invest P dollars now at annual interest rate i. The formula is

   $$A = P(1 + i)^n$$

   b. Write a main program that will permit the user to enter P, i, and n. Compute and print out A. Echo the inputs as part of the output.

7. Probability.
   A statistician needs to evaluate the probability, p, of the value x occurring in a sample set with a known normal distribution. The mean of the distribution is $\mu = 10.71$ and the standard deviation is $\sigma = 1.14$.

   a. Write a double:double function with parameter x that computes the value of the probability formula for a normal distribution, which follows. To compute e^x, use the **exp()** function from the math library; its prototype is **double exp(double x)**.

   $$p = \frac{1}{\sigma \times \sqrt{2\pi}} \times e^{-d}, \qquad \text{where } d = \frac{[(x - \mu)/\sigma]^2}{2}$$

   b. Write a main program to input the value for x, call your probability function, and print the results.

8. A spherical study.
   Write four functions to compute the following properties of a sphere, given a diameter, d, which is greater than or equal to 0.0:

   a. Radius $r = d/2$

   b. Surface area $= 4 \times \pi \times r^2$

   c. Circumference $= \pi d$

   d. Volume $= \dfrac{4\pi}{3} \times r^3$

   Write a main program that will input the diameter of a sphere, call all four functions, and print out the four results. Do not accept inputs less than 0.0.

9. Harmonic motion.
   A sphere of mass m (kg) is attached to the top of a flat steel spring. A sideways force puts the sphere in simple harmonic motion, back and forth. The period, in seconds,

of the the oscillation is independent of the force and given by

$$\text{Period} = 2 \times \pi \times \sqrt{m/k}$$

where k (N/m) is a constant associated with the particular spring used.

a. Design a program to calculate and print the period of oscillation of a sphere attached to a spring, given the mass of the sphere. In your design, specify the following requirements:

Scope of the problem.

Input or inputs required.

Output required.

Computational requirements and formulas.

Constants required, if any.

Meaningful limits on the range of legal inputs.

b. Design a test plan for this program; include enough inputs to verify the correctness of the program and calculate the output that corresponds to each.

c. Write a double:double function named **period()** to compute the period of oscillation, given the mass.

d. Using Figure 5.6 as a guide, write a program to input a mass **m**, call your **period()** function, and output the period. The spring constant **k** for this is 50 N/m. The program should test the input and process only inputs that are in the meaningful range, giving an error message for those that are not. Compile your program and carry out the test plan to demonstrate that it works correctly.

10. Orbits.

Consider a simple model of a hydrogen atom with a proton nucleus and an electron moving in a circular orbit. The proton and electron each carries a charge of magnitude 1.60×10^{-19} coul. The force of attraction between them is given by Coulomb's law to be

$$F = \frac{K \times q_p \times q_e}{r^2}$$

where q_p and q_e are the charges for the proton and electron, r is the radius of the orbit (m), and $K = 9.0 \times 10^9$ Nm^2/coul^2. This force also is equal to the centripetal force on the electron of mass $m = 9.11 \times 10^{-31}$ kg; that is,

$$F = \frac{mv^2}{r} \quad \text{and} \quad v = \sqrt{\frac{rF}{m}}$$

a. Make a complete specification and test plan for this problem.

b. Write a double:double function **velo()** that takes the radius of the orbit of an electron as an argument and calculates the velocity, **v**, of the electron. Use Figure 5.8 as a guide.

c. Write a main program that will prompt for and read a value for **r**; do not accept inputs of $r > 6 \times 10^{-11}m$. Call your **velo()** function and print the results. Use Figure 5.6 as a guide.

CHAPTER

6

More Repetition and Decisions

T his chapter continues the discussion of control statements, which are used to alter the normal top-to-bottom execution of the statements in a program. As each new kind of statement is covered, its corresponding flow diagram will be shown. We present the syntax, flowcharts, and examples of use for these statements.

There are three kinds of loop statements in C, each of which is used to repeat a block of code. The **while** loop was introduced in Chapter 3. This chapter presents two additional loop statements, **for** and **do...while**. We also discuss various ways that loops can be used.

Conditional control statements are used to determine whether to execute or skip certain blocks of code. The C language has three kinds of conditional control statements: the **if...else** statement and the simple **if** statement without an **else** clause, which are introduced in Chapter 3, and a multibranched conditional statement, the **switch** statement. In this chapter we examine the **switch** statement and a new way to use the simple **if** statement.

We briefly cover the **break** and **continue** statements, which interrupt the normal flow of control by transferring control from inside a block of code to its end or its beginning. C also supports the **goto** control statement. However, we neither explain it nor illustrate its use, because it is almost never needed in C and its unrestricted nature makes it error prone. Using a **goto** statement is considered very poor programming practice because it leads to programs that are hard to both debug and maintain.

New Loops

6.1.1 The `for` Loop

The `for` loop in C has a distinct syntax and a different flow diagram from that of the `while` loop, but it implements the same control pattern and the same semantics. Anything that can be done by a `while` loop can be done in the same way using a `for` loop and vice versa. Therefore, the `for` loop can be thought of as a shorthand notation for a `while` loop; it is not really a necessary part of the language. However, it probably is more widely used than either of the other loops because it is very convenient. In a `while` loop, the initialization(s), the loop test, and the update step are written as separate statements before and throughout the loop. In the `for` loop, these elements are combined into a control unit at the top of the loop, as shown in Figure 6.1. After gaining some experience, most programmers prefer using the `for` statement for many kinds of loops, especially for **counted loops** like that in Figure 6.1.

The `for` statement starts with the keyword `for`, followed by a control unit (in parentheses) and a body. The **control unit** has three parts, which are separated by semicolons: an initialization expression, a condition, and an update expression. All three expressions can be arbitrarily complicated. Usually, however, the first part is a single assignment, the second is a comparison, and the third is an increment expression.

In this simple `while` statement and its corresponding `for` statement, `k` is used as a counter to keep track of the number of loop repetitions. When `k` reaches `10`, the body will have been executed 10 times and the loop will exit. Following the loop, the values of `k` and `sum` will be printed. The output will be `10 45`.

```
Initializations:                                    sum = k = 0;
            ┌ Condition ....................        while (k < 10) {
while       │                                           sum += k;
statement:  ┤ Body ┤ Update ................            ++k;
            │                                        }
Next statement:                                     printf( "%i %i\n", k, sum );


for         ┌ Initializations; condition; update:   for (sum = k = 0; k < 10; ++k) {
statement:  ┤                                            sum += k;
            └ Body: ┤                               }
Next statement:                                     printf( "%i %i\n", k, sum );
```

Figure 6.1. The `for` **statement is a shorthand form of a** `while` **statement.**

A flow diagram for `for`.   Figure 6.2 is the flow diagram of a `for` loop. The separate initialization, condition, and update boxes in a `while` flow diagram now are combined into one multipart control box with a section for each part of the control unit. Control enters through the initialization section at the top, then goes through the upper diagonal line into the condition section on the right. If the condition is true, control leaves through the lower exit, going through the boxes in the body of the loop, coming back into the update section of the `for` box, and finally, going through the lower diagonal line into the test again. If the test is false, control leaves the loop through the upper exit. The flow diagrams in Figure 6.3 compare the equivalent `while` and `for` loops of Figure 6.1. Both the statement syntax and the diagram for the `for` loop are more concise—fewer parts are needed and those parts are more tightly organized—than in a corresponding `while` loop.

Initializing the loop variable.   An initialization statement must be written before a `while` loop so that the loop variable has some meaningful value before the loop test is performed the first time. In a `for` loop, this initialization is written as the first expression in the control unit. When the `for` loop is executed, this expression will be evaluated only once, before the loop begins.

The , (comma operator) can be used in a `for` loop to permit more than one item to be initialized or updated. For example, the loop in Figure 6.1 could be written with separate initializations for `sum` and `k`:

```
for (sum = 0, k = 0; k < 10; ++k) {
    sum += k;
}
```

The general form of a `for` flow diagram is shown here. Control passes through the loop in the order indicated by the arrows. Note that this order is not the same as the order in which the parts of the loop are written in the code.

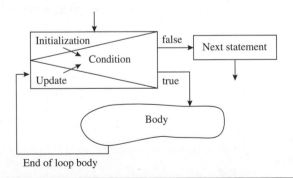

Figure 6.2.   A flow diagram for the `for` **statement.**

The flow diagram for the `while` loop in Figure 6.1 is shown on the left and the diagram for the `for` loop is on the right. Note that the parts of the two loops are executed in exactly the same order, as control flows into, through, and out of the boxes along the paths indicated by the arrows.

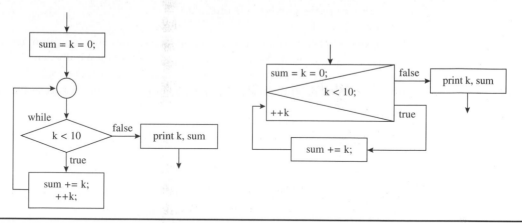

Figure 6.3.   Diagrams of corresponding `while` **and** `for` **loops.**

Technically, both assignment and comma are operators. They build expressions, not complete statements, so we are permitted to use either or both any time the language syntax calls for an expression.

The loop test and exit.   The condition in a `for` statement obeys the same rules and has the same semantics as that of a `while` condition. It is executed after the initializations, when the loop is first entered. On subsequent trips through the loop, it is executed after the update. If the condition does computations or causes side effects, such as input or output, those effects will happen each time around the loop. (This programming style is not recommended. It may be concise, but it sacrifices clarity and does not work well with some on-line debuggers.) Finally, note that the body of the loop will not be executed at all if the condition is false the first time it is tested.

Updating the loop variable.   The update expression is evaluated every time around the loop, after the loop body and before re-evaluating the loop condition. Note the mismatch between *where* the update is written on the page and *when* it happens. It is written after the condition and before the body, but it happens after the body and before the condition. Beginning programmers sometimes are confused by this inverted order. Let the flow diagram be your guide to the proper order of evaluation.

In a counted `for` loop with loop variable `k`, the update expression often is as simple as `k++` or `++k`. A lot of confusion surrounds the question of which of these is correct and why. The answer is straightforward: As long as the update section is just a simple increment or decrement expression, it does not matter whether you use the prefix or postfix form of the operation. Whichever way it is written, the loop variable will be increased (or decreased) by 1 after the loop body and before the condition is retested.

The loop body.   The loop body is executed after the condition and before the update expression. In Figure 6.1, compare the `for` loop body, which contains only one statement, with the two-statement body of the `while` loop. The update expression must be in the body of a `while` loop but becomes part of the control unit of a `for` loop, shortening the body of the loop by at least one statement. Often, this reduces the body of a `for` loop to a single statement, which permits us to write the entire loop on one line, without brackets, like this:

```
for (sum = 0, k = 0; k < 10; ++k) sum += k;
```

An extremely simple program containing a `for` loop is shown with its output in Figure 6.4. This illustrates how a loop should be laid out in the context of a program.

6.1.2   The `do...while` Loop

The `do...while` loop implements a different control pattern than the `while` and `for` loops. The body of a `do...while` loop is executed at least once; this is illustrated by the flow diagram in Figure 6.5. The condition, written after the keyword `while`, is tested after executing the loop body. Therefore, unlike the `while` and `for` loops, the body of a `do...while` loop can initialize the variables used in the test. This makes the `do...while` loop useful for repeating a process, as shown in Figure 6.12.

```
/* ----------------------------------
**    Counting with a for loop.                The output is
*/
#include <stdio.h>                              0
void main( void )
{                                               1
    int k;
    for (k = 0; k < 5; ++k) {                   2
        printf( " %i \n", k );
    }                                           3
    puts( "-----\n" );
}                                               4

                                                -----
```

Figure 6.4.   A simple program with a `for` statement.

The general form of a **do...while** flow diagram is shown on the left. Control passes through the loop body before reaching the test at the end of the loop. On the right is a diagram of a summing loop, equivalent to the loops in Figure 6.3 that use **while** and **for** statements.

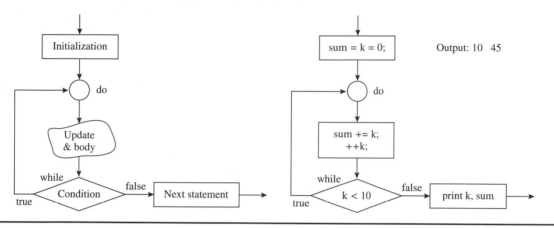

Figure 6.5.   A flow diagram for the do...while **statement.**

6.1.3 Loops That break

C supports three statements whose purpose is to transfer control to another part of the program. Two of these, **break** and **continue**, are used in conjunction with loops to create additional structured control patterns. The third, **goto**, has little or no place in modern programming and should not be used. Neither **break** nor **continue** is necessary in C; any program can be written to avoid them. However, when used skillfully, a **break** or **continue** statement can simplify program logic and shorten the code. This is highly desirable because decreasing complexity decreases errors.

The break statement.   The **break** statement is diagrammed as an arrow because it interrupts the normal flow of control, transferring control from inside a loop to its end. An **if** statement whose true clause is a **break** statement is commonly used inside a **while** loop or a **for** loop. We will call this combination an **if...break** statement. It is diagrammed as an arrow that leaves the normal control path at an **if** statement inside the loop and rejoins at a circular connector on the loop's exit arrow. The skeleton of a **for** loop with an **if...break** is shown below and diagrammed on the left in Figure 6.6.

```
for (initialization; condition; update) {
        statements
        if (condition) break;
        more statements
}
next statement /* Control comes here after the break. */
```

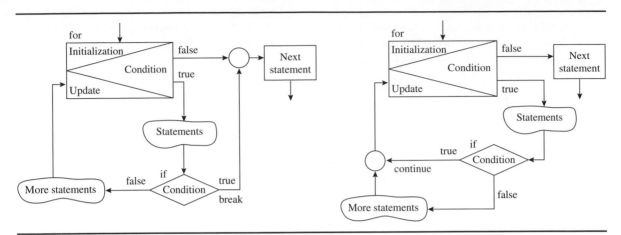

Figure 6.6.   Loops with `break` **and** `continue` **conditions.**

A loop that exits by means of an `if…break` statement has one big advantage over an ordinary loop: The resulting loop body can have some statements before the loop test and more statements after it. This flexibility makes it easier to write code in many situations: it provides an easy, clear, nonredundant way to do jobs that are awkward when done with other loops. It has two primary applications: to stop the looping action when a goal has been reached or when an error has occurred.

For example, consider a loop that reads and processes data items and stops when some maximum number of inputs has been processed. This control pattern can be conveniently implemented using a `for` loop. Now suppose, in addition, that you wish to end the loop prematurely if an error happens or some special value is entered. The `if…break` statement can be used to provide the **premature exit**. The program in Figure 6.7 illustrates the simplest version of this control pattern. It reads and echoes a series of numbers and quits (without the echo) when a 0 is entered.

To implement the combined control pattern with `while` or `for` statements, copies of the prompt and input statements would have to be written before the loop. To implement it with a `do…while` statement, an `if` statement with a copy of the loop exit test would be needed before the call on `printf()` so that the termination signal would not be processed. Using an `if…break` statement, the loop can be written without duplicating code and with its statements in the intuitively correct order.

"Infinite" `for` loops.   The `while` and `for` loops provide repetition patterns with the loop's exit test at the top, before the body; the `do…while` loop has a body

```
#include <stdio.h>
void main( void )
{
    int k, input;
    puts( "\n Enter up to 10 numbers."
          "\n Use 0 to quit early." );
    for (k = 0; k < 10; ++k) {
        printf( "> " );
        scanf( "%i", &input );
        if (input == 0) break;
        printf( "\t Input:  %i\n", input );
    }
    printf( " You entered %i numbers.\n", k );
}
```

The output is

```
Enter up to 10 numbers.

Use 0 to quit early.

> 3

    Input:   3

> 17

    Input:   17

> -2

    Input:   -2

> 0

You entered 3 numbers.
```

Figure 6.7.   Breaking out of a loop.

followed by an exit test. Some languages have a general loop that permits the exit test to be anywhere between the beginning and end. This control structure can be achieved in C by combining the **if...break** statement with a degenerate form of the **for** loop. A **for** statement usually has an expression for initialization, a test, and an update in its control unit. However, none of these parts is required; any one or all of them can be omitted, thus: **for (;;) { <loop body> }**. This degenerate statement sometimes is called an **infinite for loop** because it has no test that can end the execution of the loop.

A real infinite loop is not particularly useful because it never ends. However, an infinite **for** loop normally contains an **if...break** statement and, therefore, is not infinite because the **if...break** provides a way to leave the loop. Applications of the infinite **for** loop will be shown in Figure 6.15, where it is used for data validation, and in Figure 13.27, where an infinite loop is combined with a **switch** to implement a complex control structure.

6.1.4 Loops That `continue` (Optional Topic)

The **continue** statement interrupts the normal flow of control by transferring control from inside a loop to its beginning. If it is within a **for** loop, execution continues with the increment step. In a **while** or **do...while** loop, execution continues with the loop test.

The **continue** statement is diagrammed as an arrow. An **if...continue** statement is diagrammed as an arrow that leaves the normal control path at the

if statement and rejoins the loop at a circular connector just inside the loop at the top. If it is a **for** loop, this connector comes before the increment step, as shown on the right in Figure 6.6.

The **continue** statement is not commonly used but occasionally can be helpful in simplifying the logic when one control structure is nested within another, as when a loop contains a **switch** statement. This control pattern is used in menu processing and will be illustrated in Chapter 13 where **continue** is used within the switch to handle an invalid menu selection.

6.1.5 Defective Loops

If a loop does not update its loop variable, it will loop forever and be called an **infinite loop**. The most common cause of an infinite loop is that the programmer simply forgets to write a statement that updates the loop variable. Another source of error is missing or misplaced punctuation. The body of a loop starts at the right parenthesis that ends the condition. If the next character is a left curly bracket, the loop extends to the matching right curly bracket. Otherwise, the body consists of the single statement that follows the condition and the loop ends at the first semicolon. Figure 6.8 shows two loops that are infinite in nature because they do not update their loop variable. The loop on the left is like the **while** loop in Figure 6.1 except that the curly brackets are missing. Because of this, the loop ends after the statement **sum += k;** and does not include the **++k** statement. This kind of omission will not be caught by the compiler; it is perfectly legal to write a loop with no curly brackets and with only one statement in its body. The compiler does not check that the programmer has updated the loop variable.[1]

The loop on the right has an extraneous semicolon following the loop condition. This semicolon ends the loop, resulting in a null or empty loop body, which is legal in C. Since **k**, the loop variable, is not updated before this semicolon, it never changes. (The bracketed series of statements that follows the semicolon is outside the loop.) One way to avoid this kind of error is to write the left curly

---

Brackets missing: Extraneous semicolon:

```
int sum = 0, k = 0;  >.......... Prior code (initializations).......... <  int sum = 0, k = 0;
while (k < 10)       } .......... while statement ................ <  while (k < 10);
    sum += k;                                                          {   sum += k;
    ++k;             >.......... Next statement ................     ++k;
printf( "%i %i\n",k,sum );                                           }
                                                                    printf( "%i %i\n",k,sum );
```

Figure 6.8.   No update and no exit: Two defective loops.

---

[1] A mathematical technique, called a *loop invariant*, can be used to find loops that do not accomplish the design goals. This technique is beyond the scope of an introductory textbook.

bracket that begins the loop body *on the same line* as the keyword `while`. The left bracket is a visible reminder that the line should not end in a semicolon.

6.2

Applications of Loops

Knowing the correct syntax for writing a loop is important but only part of what a programmer needs to understand. This chapter and later ones present several common applications of loops and paradigms for their implementation in C. These applications include

- *Counted loops.* Introduced in Figure 3.13 and treated in greater depth in Section 6.2.1.
- *Query loops.* Presented in Section 6.2.2.
- *Input validation loops.* Introduced in Figure 3.14 and revisited in Section 6.2.3.
- *Sentinel loops.* Presented in Section 6.2.4.
- *Delay loops.* Presented in Section 6.2.7.
- *Search loops.* Introduced in Section 6.2.6 and illustrated in several later chapters.

Table processing loops are introduced in Chapter 14, and *end-of-file loops* are introduced in Chapter 15.

6.2.1   Counted Loops

Many loops are controlled by a counter. In such a **counted loop**, an initialization statement at the top of the loop usually sets some variable, say `k`, to 0 or 1. The update statement increments `k`, and the loop test asks whether `k` has reached or exceeded some goal value, `N`. To calculate the **trip count**, that is, the number of times the loop body will be executed,

- Let the initial value of the loop variable be I and the goal value be N.
- If the loop test has the form `k  <  N`, the trip count is $N - I$.
- If the loop test has the form `k  <=  N`, the trip count is $N - I + 1$.

The loops diagrammed in both Figures 6.3 and 6.9 are counted loops. In the first example, the loop variable is `k`, the initial value is 0, and the test is `k<10`; so this loop will be executed 10 times, with `k` taking on the values $0 \ldots 9$, successively. If an initial value of 1 and a loop test of `k  <=  N` were used, the loop body still would be executed 10 times, but the sum would be different, because `k` would have the values $1 \ldots 10$. Both patterns of loop control are common. A frequent source of program error is using the wrong initial value or the wrong comparison operator in the loop test.

A summation loop.   Our next example, in Figure 6.9, shows how a counted loop can be used to sum a series of numbers. This example demonstrates a typical

This program computes the sum of the first N terms of the series $1/n$.

```
#include "tools.h"
#define N   10

void main( void )
{
    int n;                      /* Loop counter */
    double sum;                 /* Accumulator  */

    banner();
    printf( "\n Summing 1/n where n goes from 1 to %i \n", N );

    sum = 0.0;                          /* Start accumulator at 0. */
    for (n = 1; n <= N; ++n) {   /* Sum series from 1 to N.    */
        sum = sum + 1.0 / n;
    }

    printf( " The sum is %g.   \n", sum );

    bye();
}
```

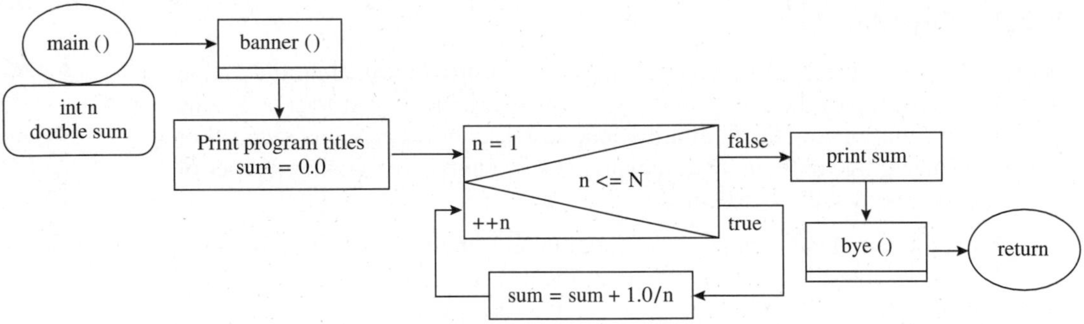

Figure 6.9.   Summing a series.

programming pattern in which two variables are used: a *counter* (to record the number of repetitions) and an *accumulator* (to hold the sum as it is accumulated). Both variables are initialized before the loop begins and both are changed on every trip through the loop. The flow diagram for this program (shown following the code) is very similar to that in Figure 6.3, since the same loop structure is being used.

Notes on Figure 6.9. SumUp.

- *First box: the declarations.*

  1. The type `int` is appropriate for counters such as `n`, which will be used to count the repetitions of the loop.
  2. An accumulator is a numeric variable used to accumulate the sum of a series of values. These might be computed values, as here, or input values, illustrated in Figure 6.16. We use a variable of type `double` for the accumulator because it will be used to compute the total of various fractions.

- *Second box: the loop.*

  1. Before entering any loop, the variables used in the loop must be initialized. We set `n = 1` because we want to sum the series from 1 to 10. We set `sum = 0.0`.
  2. The `for` statement is ideally suited for counted loops because the control unit organizes all the information about where the counter starts and stops and how it changes at each step. Each time around the loop, we add `1.0/n` to the sum. This loop starts with `n` equal to 1 and ends when `n` reaches 11. Therefore, the loop body will be executed $11 - 1 = 10$ times, summing the fractions `1.0/1 ... 1.0/10`.
  3. Note that `n` will have the value 1 (not 0 or 2) the first time we compute `1.0/n`. This is important. First, we do not want to start computing the series at the wrong point. Second, we need to be careful to avoid dividing by 0.
  4. We are permitted to divide the `double` value 1.0 by the integer value `n`. The result is a fractional value of type `double`. It is important that the constant 1.0 be used rather than 1 in this expression, because the latter will give an incorrect result. The reason for this is discussed in Chapter 7.

- *Third box: the output.*

  1. We use the format `%g` to print the `double` value. Up to six digits (C's default precision) will be printed with the result rounded to the sixth place. Trailing 0's, if any, are suppressed after the decimal point.
  2. The output from this program (with the banner omitted) is

```
Summing 1/n where n goes from 1 to 10
The sum is 2.92897.

Normal termination.
```

  From now on, we omit the termination message from the example output of most programs.

6.2.2 Query Loops

If the loop variable is either initialized or updated by `scanf()` or some other input function, we say that it is an **input-controlled loop**. Such loops are very important because they allow a program to respond to the real-world environment. There are several variations on this theme, including query loops, sentinel loops (Section 6.2.4), and input validation loops (Section 6.2.3).

A useful interactive technique, the **repeat query**, is introduced in Figure 6.10 and used in Figure 6.12. (It will be refined, later, in Chapter 11.) To develop and debug a program, the programmer must test it with several sets of input so that its performance with different kinds of data can be checked. We use a repeat query loop to automate this process of rerunning a program. Until now, you have needed to execute a program once for each line in your test plan. After each run, the output must be captured and printed. At best, the process is awkward. At worst, the programmer is tempted to shortcut the testing process. A typical program with a query loop follows the general form shown in Figure 6.10.

The testing process can be simplified by writing a function that processes one line of the test plan. The main program contains a `do...while` loop that calls the function once and asks whether the user wishes to do it again. This provides a simple, convenient way to let the user decide whether to continue running the program or quit, rather than restarting it every time. Furthermore, all the output for all of the tests ends up in one place at one time. The basic technique is illustrated in Figures 6.10 through 6.13.

Many programs perform a process repeatedly, until the user asks to stop. This is the general form of such a program. The process is performed by a function called from the main loop.

```
/* Comments that explain the purpose of the program.  */
#include and #define commands.

void main( void )
{
    Declaration of variable for query response;

    Output statement that identifies the program;
    do {
        Process one data set or call a function to do so;
        Ask the user whether to continue (1) or quit (0);
        Read the response;
    } while (response != 0);

    Print program results and termination comment;
}
```

Figure 6.10.   Form of a query loop.

This is a flow diagram of the program in Figures 6.12 and 6.13. The dotted lines show how the control sequence is interrupted when the function call sends control to the beginning of the function. Control flows through the function then returns via the lower dotted line to the box from which it was called.

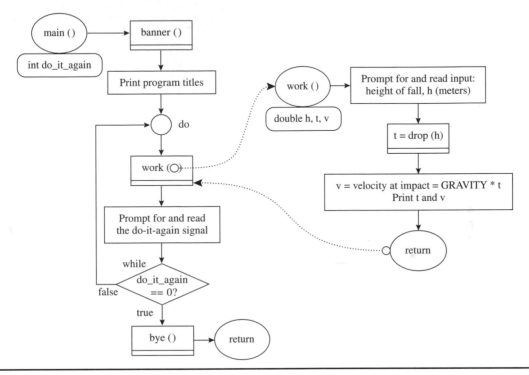

Figure 6.11.   Flow diagram for repeating a process.

Notes on Figure 6.10. Form of a query loop.

- Programs that use this technique will have a few statements at the beginning of **main()** that may open files, clear the screen, or print output headings.
- At the end are statements to print final results and any closing message.
- In between is a **do...while** loop. The loop body consists entirely of a call on a function that performs the work of the program, followed by a prompt to ask the user whether or not to repeat the process. The response is read and immediately tested. If the user enters the code 0,[2] control leaves the loop. If 1 (or an erroneous response) is entered, the process is repeated.

---

[2]We use a 1 or 0 response here because it is simple. In Chapter 11, we show how to process y or n responses.

This main program consists of statements to print the program titles and a loop that will repeatedly call the `work()` function, given in Figure 6.13, until the user asks to quit. This main program can be used to repeat any process by changing the titles and the `work()` function.

```
/* --------------------------------------------------------------------
** Determine the time it takes for a grapefruit to hit the ground when it
** is dropped, with no initial velocity, from a helicopter hovering
** at height h.  Also determine the velocity of the fruit at impact.
* --------------------------------------------------------------------- */
#include "tools.h"          /* include commands and user defined utilities */

void work( void );
double drop( double height );

void main( void )
{
    int do_it_again;         /* repeat-or-stop switch */

    banner();
    puts( "\n Calculate the time it would take for a grapefruit\n"
          " to fall from a helicopter at a given height.\n" );

    do { work();

        printf( " \n Enter '1' to continue or '0' to quit: " );
        scanf( "%i", &do_it_again );
    } while (do_it_again != 0);

    bye();
}
```

Figure 6.12.   Repeating a calculation.

Figure 6.11 shows a diagram of a query loop (on the left) used to repeat a calculation (the function diagrammed on the right). The dotted lines show how control goes from the function call to the entry point of the function and from the function return back to the call box.

Notes on Figure 6.12. Repeating a calculation.   We put almost all of the program's code into a function called `work()`. The main program contains only greeting and closing messages, a loop that calls the `work()` function to do all the work, and the input statements needed to control the loop. Figure 6.11 is a flow diagram of this program.

• *First box: prototypes for the two programmer-defined functions.* Two programmer-defined functions that follow the main program in the source

The `work()` function is called from the program in Figure 6.12. The `drop()` function is a more concise version of the one in Figure 5.8.

```
/* ----------------------------------------------------- */
/* Perform one gravity calculation and print the results. */
void
work( void )
{
    double h;              /* height of fall (m) */
    double t;              /* time of fall (s) */
    double v;              /* terminal velocity (m/s) */

    printf( " Enter height of helicopter (meters): " );
    scanf( "%lg", &h );

    t = drop( h );         /* Call drop with the argument h. */
    v = GRAVITY * t;       /* velocity of grapefruit at impact */
    printf( "    Time of fall = %g seconds\n", t );
    printf( "    Velocity of the object = %g m/s\n", v );
}
/* ----------------------------------------------------- */
/* Calculate time of fall from a given height. ---------- */
double
drop( double height )
{
    if (height < 0) return 0;
    else return sqrt( 2 * height / GRAVITY );
}
```

Figure 6.13.   The `work()` **and** `drop()` **functions.**

code file are shown in Figure 6.13. The `work()` function is called from `main()`. It, in turn, calls `drop()`.

- *Outer box: the main process loop.*

1. Compare this version of the program to the versions in Figures 3.8 and 5.6. The input, calculations, and output have been removed from `main()` and placed in a separate function, named `work()`. These lines have been replaced by a loop that will call the `work()` function repeatedly (inner box), processing several data sets. This keeps the logic of `main()` simple and easy to follow.

2. We use a loop because we expect to process a series of inputs. Since we do not know how many will be needed ahead of time, we ask the user to tell us what to do after each loop repetition.

3. We prompt for a 1 to do the process again or a 0 to quit; the response is read into the variable `do_it_again`.

4. As long as the values we read for **do_it_again** are nonzero, we call the **work()** function to read another input value and perform the computation and output processing. If the user's input is an error, that is, it is neither a 0 nor a 1, this program continues; it quits only if the user enters 0. (An improved version of this loop, which uses a y or n response, will be presented in Chapter 11.)

Notes on Figure 6.13: The work() and drop() functions.

- *Background.* Most of the code from the **main()** program in Figure 5.6 has been moved into the **work()** function. This reduces the complexity of **main()** and makes it easy to repeat the gravity calculations with several inputs. The **work()** function contains all the declarations and code that relate to the computation. The **main()** program contains only start-up code, termination code, and the loop that calls the **work()** function.
- *The flow of control.* The function call in **main()** sends control into the **work()** function, where we read one input and calculate the time of fall by calling the **drop()** function. After returning from **drop()**, we calculate the terminal velocity and print the time and velocity. Then we return to **main()**. In the flow diagram (Figure 6.11), these shifts of control are represented by dotted lines.
- *The output.* Lines printed by the **main()** program are intermixed with lines from the **work()** function. Here is a sample dialog (the banner and termination comment have been omitted):

```
Calculate the time it would take for a grapefruit
to fall from a helicopter at a given height.

Enter height of helicopter (meters): 20
    Time of fall = 2.01962 seconds
    Velocity of the object = 19.8057 m/s

Enter '1' to continue or '0' to quit: 1
Enter height of helicopter (meters): 906.5
    Time of fall = 13.597 seconds
    Velocity of the object = 133.34 m/s

Enter '1' to continue or '0' to quit: 2
Enter height of helicopter (meters): 2000.5
    Time of fall = 20.1987 seconds
    Velocity of the object = 198.082 m/s

Enter '1' to continue or '0' to quit: 0
```

As you begin to write programs, incorporate a processing loop into each one. It then will be convenient for you to test your code on a variety of inputs and demonstrate that it works correctly under all circumstances.

6.2.3 Input Validation Loops

Figure 6.14 contains a validation loop based on a `while` statement. It provides good user feedback but is long and requires duplicating lines of code. We can write a shorter, simpler validation loop that uses a `do...while` statement. However, this kind of validation loop has a severe defect: It gives the same prompt for the initial input and for re-entry after an error. This is a human-engineering issue. The error may go unnoticed if the program does not give distinctive feedback. A third kind of validation loop can be written with `for` and `if...break` statements that combines the advantages of the other two forms; it avoids duplication of code and provides informative feedback when the user makes an error (see Figure 6.15).

Notes on Figure 6.14: Input validation using a `while` statement.

1. The input prompt `scanf()` and calculation statements are written before the loop and again in the body of this loop. This duplication is undesirable because both sets of statements must be edited every time the prompt or input changes. The duplication is unavoidable, though, because the loop variable, `hours`, must be given a value before the `while` test at the top of the loop. It then must be given a new value within the loop.
2. The `while` test checks whether the value of `hours` is within the legal range. If not, we enter the body of the loop, print an error comment, and prompt for and read another input. Then control returns to the top of the loop to test the data again.

This input validation loop is a fragment of the miles-per-hour program in Figure 3.14. Some output from the loop and the following `printf()` statement follow.

```
printf( " Duration of trip in hours and minutes: " );
scanf( "%lg%lg", &hours, &minutes );
hours = hours + ( minutes / 60 );
while (hours < 0.0) {
    printf( " Please re-enter; time must be >= 0: " );
    scanf( "%lg%lg", &hours, &minutes );
    hours = hours + ( minutes / 60 );
}
```

Output:

```
Duration of trip in hours and minutes: -148 43
Please re-enter; time must be >= 0: 1 -70
Please re-enter; time must be >= 0: 148 -17
Average speed was 1.94291
```

Figure 6.14.   Input validation using a `while` statement.

3. Since only a legal input will get the user out of this loop, an informative prompt is very important. If the user is not sure what data values are legal, the program may become permanently stuck inside this loop and it may be necessary to reboot the computer to regain control.

Notes on Figure 6.15. Input validation using a `for` statement.
Compare the code in Figure 6.15 to the validation loop in Figure 6.14.

1. The original input prompt is written before the loop because it will not be repeated. (The error prompt is different.)
2. In contrast to the **`while`** validation loop, there is no need to write the **`scanf()`** and computation before the loop. Thus, we avoid duplication of code.
3. The input and calculation statements are done before the loop test, which is in an **`if...break`** statement. If the input is valid, control leaves the loop.
4. If not, we print an error prompt, return to the top of the loop, and read new data.
5. Since only a legal input will get the user out of this loop, an informative prompt is very important. If the user is not sure what data values are legal, the program may become permanently stuck inside this loop, and it may be necessary to reboot the computer to regain control.

6.2.4 Sentinel Loops

A **sentinel loop** keeps reading, inspecting, and processing data values until it comes across a predefined value that the programmer has designated to mean "end of data." Looping stops when the program recognizes this value, which is called a **sentinel value**, because it stands guard at the end of the data.

The value used as a sentinel depends on the application; to choose an appropriate sentinel value, the programmer must understand the nature of the data. Most functions that process strings use the null character as a sentinel value.

Compare this input validation loop to the version in Figure 6.14 that is built on the **`while`** statement. This form is simpler and avoids duplication. The output is identical to the output from Figure 6.14.

```
printf( " Duration of trip in hours and minutes: " );
for (;;) {
    scanf( "%lg%lg", &hours, &minutes );
    hours = hours + ( minutes / 60 );
    if (hours >= 0.0) break;                  /* Leave loop if input is valid. */
    printf( " Please re-enter; time must be >= 0: " );
}
```

Figure 6.15. Input validation loop using a `for` statement.

Loops that read and process input data often use the newline character as a sentinel. If the data values are integers and a program processes only nonzero data values, then 0 can be used as a sentinel. If all data values are nonnegative, then −1 can be used as the sentinel. If every integer is admissible, the value INT_MAX (the largest representable integer) often is used as a sentinel.

In all cases, a sentinel value must be of the same data type as the ordinary data values being processed, because it must be stored in the same type of variable or read using the same conversion specifier in a format string. Also, a sentinel must not be contained in the set of legal data values because it must be an unambiguous signal that there are no more data sets to process.

Sentinel loops are used

- For input, to read a series of data sets.
- To process string data.[3]
- To process data that are stored in an array[4] or a list in which the sentinel value is stored at the end of the data.

A sentinel loop is used when the number of data items to be processed varies from session to session, depending on the user's needs, and cannot be known ahead of time. A simple program with a sentinel loop follows this general form:

```
/* Comments that explain the purpose of the program. */
#include and #define commands.

void main( void )
{
    Declaration of input variable and others.
    Output statement that identifies the program.
    Use scanf() to initialize the input variable.
    while (input != sentinel value) {
        Process the input data.
        Prompt for and read another input.
    }
    Print program results and termination comment.
}
```

Most sentinel loops are implemented with **while** or **for** (;;) statements rather than a **do...while** statement because it is important not to try to process the sentinel value. The **do...while** statement processes every value before making the loop test, whereas the **while** loop makes the test before processing the value. Thus, a **while** loop can watch for the sentinel value and leave the loop when it appears without actually processing it.

---

[3] Strings will be introduced in Chapter 13.

[4] Arrays will be introduced in Chapter 10.

Compute the sum of a series of prices entered by the user.

```
#include "tools.h"
#define SENTINEL  0.0

void main( void )
{
    double price;                                   /* The input variable */
    double sum = 0.0;                               /* Accumulates the sum. */

    printf( "\n Please enter prices.  When finished,"
        "type 0 to quit.\n The total price will be"
        " printed.\n \t Price: " );

    scanf ( "%lg", &price );       /* Read first price. */
    while (price != SENTINEL) {    /* Sentinel value is 0.0 */
        sum += price;
        printf( "\t Price: " );
        scanf( "%lg", &price );
    }

    printf( "\n The total price is %g \n", sum );
    bye();
}
```

The output is

```
Please enter prices.  When finished, type 0 to quit.
The total price will be printed.
        Price: 3.10
        Price: 29.98
        Price: 2.34
        Price: 0

The total price is 35.42
```

Figure 6.16.   A cash register program.

Some sentinel loops are input loops; that is, the loop processes input values, and the sentinel is entered to end the input process. In such programs, the user prompts must give clear instructions about the "magic" value. Otherwise, the user will be unable to end the loop. For example, consider the cash register program in Figure 6.16. The initial prompt gives clear instructions about how to end the processing loop.

6.2.5   A Counted Sentinel Loop

Earlier in this section, we discussed a sentinel loop based on **while**. A more elegant version can be implemented using **for** and following this general form:

```
for (;;) {
    Prompt for and read an input.
    if (input == sentinel-value) break;
    Process the input data.
}
```

Often, we combine the sentinel test with a loop counter to make a counted sentinel loop, where **LIMIT** is the maximum number of times the loop should be repeated, and **k** is the loop counter. The general form of a counted sentinel loop is

```
for (k = 0; k < LIMIT; ++k) {
    Prompt for and read an input.
    if (input == sentinel-value) break;
    Process the input data.
}
```

The program in Figures 6.17 and 6.18 uses a counted sentinel loop. It is a simple interactive game in which the player is given a limited number of turns to guess (and enter) the hidden number. The game ends sooner if the player's input equals the program's hidden number, which is the sentinel value. The **for** and **if...break**

This is a flow diagram of the program in Figure 6.18.

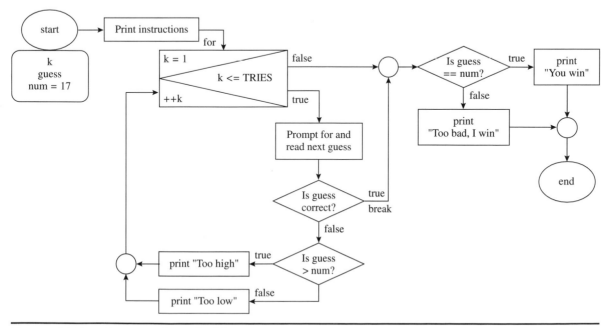

Figure 6.17.   A counted sentinel loop.

This program shows how to use **break** to leave a loop. Figure 6.17 is a flow diagram for this program, which is a simplified version of a number-guessing game that will be presented in its traditional form in Chapter 7.

```
#include "tools.h"
#define TRIES 5

void main( void )
{
    int k = 0;              /* Loop counter. */
    int guess;              /* User's input. */

    int num = 17;

    printf( " Can you guess my number?  It is between 1 and 30.\n"
            " Enter a guess at each prompt; You have %i tries.\n", TRIES );

    for (k = 1; k <= TRIES; ++k) {
        printf( "\n Try %i: ", k );
        scanf( "%i", &guess );

        if (guess == num) break;

        if (guess > num) printf( " No, that is too high.\n" );
        else printf( " No, that is too low.\n" );
    }

    if (guess == num) printf( " YES!!  That is just right.  You win!  \n" );
    else printf( " Too bad --- I win again!\n" );
    bye();
}
```

Figure 6.18.   A sentinel loop using for **and** if...break **statements.**

statements are used in typical ways to implement a counted loop with a possible early exit.

Notes on Figures 6.17 and 6.18: A sentinel loop using for and if...break statements.

- *The diagram: Figure 6.17.*

  1. A **break** statement is represented by an arrow and a connector, not by a box. Note the word **break** on the **true** arrow of the **if** condition diamond. The circular connector on the loop's exit arrow is for the **break**.
  2. The **if...break** statement is the first diamond in the **for** loop. If the guess is not correct, control stays in the loop and enters the **if...else**

statement at the end of the loop body. If the guess is correct, control flows out of the loop along the **break** arrow and enters the code that follows the loop.

- *First box, Figure 6.18: the concealed number.* This program is a simplification of an old game that asks the user to guess a concealed number. The computer responds to each guess by telling the user whether the guess was too large, too small, or right on target. In a complete program, the concealed number would be randomly chosen and the number of guesses allowed would be barely enough (or not quite enough) to win the game every time. We give a full version of this program in Chapter 7. In this simplification, we arbitrarily choose 17 as the concealed number. The five guesses allowed are enough to uncover this number if the user makes no mistakes.

- *Outer box: operation of the loop.*

  1. This **for** loop prompts for, reads, checks, and counts the guesses. It will allow the user up to five tries to enter the correct number. On each trial, the program gives feedback to guide the user in making the next guess. After the fifth unsuccessful try, the loop test will terminate the loop.
  2. We initialize the loop counter to 1 (rather than the usual 0) because we want to print the counter value as part of the prompt. The computer does not care about the counter values, but users prefer counters that start at 1, not 0.
  3. We use **<=** to compare the loop counter to the loop limit because the loop variable was initialized to 1, not 0, and we want to execute the loop when the counter equals the number of allotted trials.
  4. Each guess has three possibilities: It can be correct, too low, or too high. To check for three possibilities, we need two **if** statements. The first **if** statement is in the inner box. If the input matches the concealed number, the break is executed. Control will leave the loop and go to the box below it. The second **if** statement prints an appropriate comment depending on whether the guess is too high (the true clause) or too low (the false clause). Control then goes back to the top of the loop.

- *Inner box:* There are two ways to leave the loop: either the guess was correct or the guesser was unable to find the hidden number in the number of tries allowed. Here, we test the number of guesses that were used to distinguish between these two cases, then print a success or failure comment. This is a typical way to handle a loop with two exit routes.

6.2.6   Search Loops (Optional Topic)

A **search loop** examines a set of possibilities, looking for one that matches a given "key" value. The data items being searched can be stored in memory or calculated. The key value could be the entire item or part of it and it could be of any data type. The requirements for searching are almost identical in all cases:

- The program must know what key value to look for.
- There must be some orderly way to examine the possibilities, one at a time, until all have been checked.
- The loop must compare the key value to the current possibility. If they match, control must leave the loop.
- The search loop must know how many possibilities are to be searched or have some way to know when no possibilities remain. The loop must end when this occurs.

Therefore, the search loop will terminate for two possible reasons: The key item has been found or the possibilities have been used up. The most straightforward way to implement this control pattern is to use a counted sentinel loop. The **for** statement cycles through all the possibilities and an **if...break** statement within it terminates the loop when the key is found. The general pattern of a search loop is

```
Read or select the key value.
for (counter = 0; counter < LIMIT; ++counter) {
    Calculate or select the next item to be tested.
    if (current_data == key_value) break;
}
```

Search loops based on computed possibilities are illustrated in Figures 8.12 and 12.19. Search loops become increasingly important when there are large amounts of stored data. Loops that search arrays are illustrated in Chapter 16.

6.2.7   Delay Loops (Optional Topic)

A loop that executes many times but does nothing useful can be used to make the computer wait for a while before proceeding. Such a loop is called a **delay loop**. Delay loops often are used like timers to control the length of time between repeated events (see Figure 6.19). For example, a program that controls an automated factory process might use a delay loop to regulate sending analog signals to (or receiving them from) a device such as a motor generator.

Notes on Figures 6.19 and 6.20. Delaying progress, the delay() function.   The **tools** library contains a function used here for the first time: **delay()**. The **delay()** function implements a delay loop (see Figure 6.20). It calls the C library function **time()** to read the computer's real-time clock and return the current time, in units of seconds, represented as an integer so that we can do arithmetic with it. The type **time_t** is defined by the C system to be the kind of integer[5] that the local system uses to store the time.

---

[5]The various kinds of integers are discussed in Chapter 7.

```
#include "tools.h"
void main( void )
{
    int j, max, seconds;

    printf( "This is an exercise program.\n\n"
            "How many pushups are you going to do? " );
    scanf( "%i", &max );
    if (max < 0) fatal( "Can't do %i pushups", max );

    printf( "How many seconds between pushups? " );
    scanf( "%i", &seconds );
    if (seconds < 3) fatal( "Can't do a pushup in %i seconds", seconds );

    printf( "OK, we will do %i pushups, one every %i seconds.\n",
            "Do one pushup each time you hear the beep.\n", max, seconds );

    for (j = 1; j <= max; ++j) {
        printf( "%i \a\n", j );        /* Do one. */
        delay( seconds );              /* Wait specified # of seconds. */
    }

    puts( "Good job.  Come again." );
}
```

Figure 6.19.   Using a delay loop.

We add the desired number of seconds of delay to the current time to get
the goal time, then store it in the variable `time()`. The loop calls `time()` contin-
uously until the current time reaches the goal time. This loop is all test and no
body. Technically, it is called a **busy wait** loop because it keeps the processor
busy while waiting for time to pass. It is busy doing nothing, that is, wasting
time[6]. On a typical personal computer, the `time()` function might end up being
called 100,000 times or more during a delay of a few seconds. Busy waiting is an
appropriate technique to use when a computer is dedicated to monitoring a single

This function is in the `tools` library.
```
#include <time.h>
void delay( int seconds )
{
    time_t goal = time( NULL ) + seconds;    /* Add seconds to current time. */
    do {     /* Nothing */
    } while (time( NULL ) < goal);
}
```

Figure 6.20.   Delaying progress, the `delay()` function.

---

[6]This is legal in C; a loop is not required to have any code in its body.

experiment or process. It is not a good technique to use on a shared computer that is serving other purposes simultaneously.

A delay loop usually is used inside another loop, which must perform a process repeatedly at a particular rate that is compatible with human response or a process being monitored. For example, the boxed loop in Figure 6.19 is used to time repetitions of an exercise. It outputs a beep, then calls `delay()`, which waits the number of seconds specified by the user before returning. The output looks like this:

```
This is an exercise program.

How many pushups are you going to do? 5
How many seconds between pushups? 3
OK, we will do 5 pushups, one every 3 seconds.
Do one pushup each time you hear the beep.
1
2
3
4
5
Good job.  Come again.
```

6.3   The `switch` Statement

6.3.1   Syntax and Semantics

A `switch` statement is like a nested `if` statement.   A `switch` statement is much like a series of `if...else` statements. Both select one action from a series of possible actions. If there are only two alternatives, or if more complex comparisons must be made, we use the `if...else` statement. To use a `switch` statement, all the possible choices must have simple identifying codes. These must be single characters in quotes, integers, or enumeration constants.[7] Note that the `switch` statement is an inherently simpler way to implement a series of more than two choices and should be used whenever possible, but it cannot replace an `if...else` statement when a series of distinct tests must be made.

The syntax of a `switch` statement.   To illustrate the syntax and use of the `switch` statement, we use a program whose specification is given in Figure 6.21 and program code in Figure 6.24. A `switch` statement starts with the keyword `switch` followed by an expression in parentheses, followed by brackets enclosing a series of labeled `cases` ending in an optional `default` case. The

---

[7] These are covered in Chapter 11.

Problem scope: A contractor wants to automate the process of selecting an appropriate gauge wire for extension cords and temporary wiring at construction sites. Various long wires are used to supply electricity to power tools and other appliances at the site. All wires are standard annealed copper; calculations are to be made for a standard temperature of 20°C. There is a voltage drop in an extension cord due to the resistivity of its wire; heavier cords (lower-numbered gauges) have lower resistivity and incur less drop than lighter cords (higher-numbered gauges). The voltage drop is proportional to the length of the wire, so the drop can be significant in a long wire. This is an issue because appliances designed to operate at one voltage may overheat if operated at a voltage that is significantly lower. This program should evaluate a proposed wiring scheme and answer whether the wire will be adequate for its intended purpose.

Formula: An extension cord n meters long contains $2n$ meters of wire. The voltage drop is

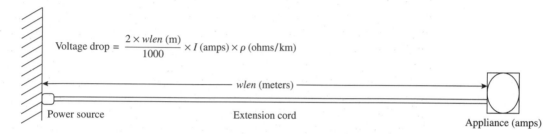

where $wlen$ is the length of the extension cord (in meters), ρ (rho) is the resistivity of the wire, and I is the current flowing in the wire, in amperes.

Constants: A voltage drop of up to 5 volts is acceptable. The resistivity, ρ, of copper wire at 20°C for the gauges used by this contractor are

Gauge	ρ
12	5.211
14	8.285
16	13.17
18	20.95

Inputs: The contractor will type in the length of the extension cord he needs, the wire gauge, and the current rating (amps) of the appliance he will be using. The program should reject any gauge that is not in the table above.

Output required: Program headings and a termination message should be printed. Input values should be echoed. The voltage drop and the answer (gauge is adequate or not adequate) should be given. Three digits of precision are adequate.

Figure 6.21.   Problem specification: Wire gauge adequacy evaluation.

expression must compute a value of some integral type[8] and the case labels must be constants or constant expressions of the same type. (A **constant expression** is composed of operators and constant operands.) If several cases require the same processing, several case labels may be placed before the same statement. The last label may be `default`.

When a `switch` is executed, the expression is evaluated and its value compared to the case labels. If any case label matches, control will go to the statement following that label. Control then proceeds to the following statement and through all the statements after that until it reaches the bottom of the `switch`. This is *not* normally what a programmer wishes to do. It is far more common to want the cases to be mutually exclusive. This is why each group of statements normally ends with a `break` statement that causes control to skip around all the following cases and go directly to the end of the `switch` statement. Programmers sometimes absentmindedly forget a `break` statement. In this case, the logic flows into the next case below it instead of to the end of the `switch` statement. Remember, this is not an error in the eyes of the compiler and it will not cause an error comment.

If no case label matches the value of the expression, control goes to the statement following the `default` label. If there is no `default` label, control just leaves the `switch` statement. This does not cause an error at either compile time or run time.

Diagramming a `switch` statement.   The diagram of a nested `if...else` statement has a series of diamond-shaped `if` boxes, each enclosing a test, as in Figure 6.22. The `true` arrow from each box leads to an action and the `false` arrow leads to the next `if` test. These tests will be made in sequence until some result is `true`.

In contrast, the diagram of a `switch` statement has a single diamond-shaped test box with a branching "out" arrow. This box encloses an expression whose value will be compared to the case labels. One branch is selected and the corresponding actions in the body of the `switch` statement are executed. Each set of actions must end in a `break` statement. Control normally enters a box from the case label and leaves by an arrow that goes directly to the connector at the end of the `switch` statement. Figure 6.23 shows the diagram for the `switch` statement in Figure 6.24. Compare this `switch` diagram to the `if...else` diagram in Figure 6.22. They implement the same logic; however, the version that uses `switch` is simpler.

---

[8] C has several integral types in addition to `int`; they will be introduced in the next few chapters. These include `char`, `short`, `long`, `unsigned short`, `unsigned int`, and `unsigned long`.

We diagram a series of **if...else** statements that implements the specification in Figure 6.21.

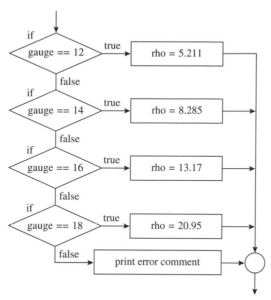

Figure 6.22. Diagram for a nested conditional.

6.3.2 An Application

Figure 6.24 shows a program that implements this **switch** statement to solve the problem specified in Figure 6.21. It illustrates "messy" integer case labels; that is, they are not consecutive numbers starting at 0 or 1.

Notes on Figure 6.24: Using a **switch**.

- *First box: input for the switch.* We display a list of available gauges and prompt the user for a choice. The user sees this set of choices:

```
Wire Gauge Adequacy Evaluation

Please choose gauge of wire:
    12 gauge
    14 gauge
    16 gauge
    18 gauge
Enter selected gauge:
```

A diagram for the same logic as in Figure 6.22, using a **switch** statement instead of an **if...else** statement.

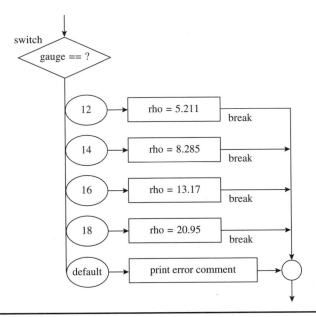

Figure 6.23.   Switching to a switch statement.

- *Second box: the* **switch** *statement.*

  1. A **switch** that processes an integer input must have integer constants for case labels. This **switch** has four cases to process the four gauges plus a **default** case for errors.
  2. Each "correct" case contains one assignment statement that stores the resistivity value for the selected gauge wire. Each assignment is followed by a **break** that ends the case. A **default** case does not need a **break** because it is always last.
  3. If more extensive processing is needed, a program might call a different function to process each case.
  4. Error handling is done smoothly in this program. The **default** case intercepts inputs that are not supported and calls **fatal()** to print an error comment and abort the program. By calling **fatal()**, we avoid printing meaningless answers. An example would be

```
Enter selected gauge: 11
Gauge 11 is not supported.

Error exit; press '.'  and 'Enter' to continue.
```

The specifications for this program are in Figure 6.21.

```
#include "tools.h"
#define   MAXDROP   5.0        /* volts */

void main( void )
{
    int gauge;        /* selected gauge of wire */
    double rho;       /* resistivity of selected gauge of wire */
    double amps;      /* current rating of appliance */
    double wlen;      /* length of wire needed */
    double drop;      /* voltage drop for selected parameters */

    banner();
    puts( "\n Wire Gauge Adequacy Evaluation" );

    printf( "\n Please choose gauge of wire:\n"
            "\t 12 gauge \n\t 14 gauge \n"
            "\t 16 gauge \n\t 18 gauge \n"
            " Enter selected gauge: " );
    scanf( "%i", &gauge );


    switch (gauge) {
      case 12:  rho = 5.211;    break;
      case 14:  rho = 8.285;    break;
      case 16:  rho = 13.17;    break;
      case 18:  rho = 20.95;    break;
      default:  fatal( " Gauge %i is not supported.", gauge );
    }


    printf( "\n Enter current rating for appliance, in amps: " );
    scanf ( "%lg", &amps );
    printf( "\n Enter the length of the wire, in meters: " );
    scanf ( "%lg", &wlen );
    drop = 2 * wlen / 1000 * rho * amps ;


    printf( "\n For %i gauge wire %g m long and %g amp appliance,\n"
            " voltage drop in wire = %g volts.  (Limit is %g.)  \n"
            gauge, wlen, amps, drop, MAXDROP );
    if (drop < MAXDROP)
        printf( "\n Selected gauge is adequate.\n" );
    else
        printf( "\n Selected gauge is not adequate.\n" );

    bye();
}
```

Figure 6.24.   Using a `switch`.

- *Third box: calculating the voltage drop.*

  1. Control goes to this box after every `break`. It does not go here after executing the `default` clause because that clause calls `fatal()`, which aborts execution.
  2. This box prompts for and reads the rest of the input data. This is done after the `switch` statement, not before, because the menu selection can be an invalid choice and there is no point reading the rest of the data until we know the gauge is one of those listed in the table.
  3. We calculate the voltage drop as soon as all the data have been read. The formula for voltage drop uses the resistivity value selected by the `switch` statement. We divide by 1,000 because ρ is given in ohms/kilometer and the wire length is given in meters. We multiply by 2 because each extension cord contains a pair of wires running its full length.

- *Fourth box: the answers.* We ran the program and tested two cases. Each time the program was run, the greeting comment, menu, and termination comment were printed; for brevity, these are not repeated here. Dashed lines are used to separate the runs.

```
Enter selected gauge: 12

Enter current rating for appliance, in amps: 10

Enter the length of the wire, in meters: 30

For 12 gauge wire 30 m long and 10 amp appliance,
voltage drop in wire = 3.1266 volts.   (Limit is 5.)

Selected gauge is adequate.
----------------------------------------------------

Enter selected gauge: 16

Enter current rating for appliance, in amps: 10

Enter the length of the wire, in meters: 30

For 16 gauge wire 30 m long and 10 amp appliance,
voltage drop in wire = 7.902 volts.   (Limit is 5.)

Selected gauge is not adequate.
```

6.4   Counted Loop Application: Integration by Simpson's Rule

Section 5.5.1 showed how to approximate the integral of a function by summing a series of rectangles. This method for approximating an integral is appealing because it is easy to understand. However, it is not very accurate unless the number of intervals is very large (and therefore h is very small).

The rectangle method is a special case of the general method of approximating the area under a function using a polynomial to connect points on the curve.[9] If we use a zeroth-order polynomial in this general method, we have integration by rectangles. If we use a first-order polynomial, we have the more accurate method of integration by trapezoids. To improve the accuracy further, we can take each segment, obtain the midpoint for each, and use a second-order polynomial (i.e., a parabola) to connect the three points. The result of this type of approximation applied to the entire interval of the function is called **Simpson's 1/3 rule**. The sketch in Figure 6.25 illustrates all three concepts.

This section develops a program that implements Simpson's 1/3 rule; the formula is shown in Figure 6.26. The method is much less intuitive than integration by rectangles but provides a substantially more precise answer.

Steps 1 and 2. Specification and test plan.   The program specification is given in Figure 6.26, but before beginning to write the program, we should plan how to test it.

For the first text case, we use the same function and the same limits of integration used in Section 5.5.1. As a second test case, we use a straight line because we can calculate its integral easily. Note that the definition of function $f()$ and two `printf()` statements must be changed, and we must recompile the program each time we change the function we are integrating.

We approximate a function $f(x)$ over an interval of width h by three shapes: a rectangle, a trapezoid, and a shape whose top edge is a parabola. The parabola gives the closest approximation.

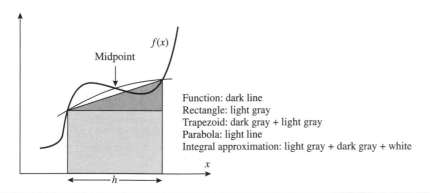

Figure 6.25.   Integration by polynomial approximation.

---

[9] S. Chapra, *Numerical Methods for Engineers*, 2d ed. (New York: McGraw-Hill, 1988), equation 15.18.

Problem scope: The interval over which we wish to integrate the function is divided into N subintervals with lower bounds $x_0, \ldots, x_{n-1}$. For each subinterval except the first and the last, a second-order polynomial is used to approximate the actual curve between a middle point x_k and its two neighboring points. The final answer is a weighted average of areas based on these polynomials.

Function: The function to be integrated, $f(x)$, must be defined within the program file.

Inputs: The lower and upper bounds of the interval of integration.

Constant: Divide the integration interval into 100 subintervals.

Formula: For Simpson's 1/3 rule for integrating the function $f(x)$ on the interval from a to b, we have the general equation

$$\text{Area} = (b-a) \times \frac{f(a) + f(b) + 4 \times \sum_{k=1,3,5,\ldots}^{n-1} f(a + k \times h) + 2 \times \sum_{k=2,4,6,\ldots}^{n-2} f(a + k \times h)}{3 \times n}$$

where n is the number of subintervals.

Output required: Echo the inputs and print the integral.

Computational requirements: The calculations should be done with the maximal possible precision. Six digits of precision should be printed.

Figure 6.26.   Problem specification: Integration by Simpson's rule.

Next, we add test cases (Figure 6.27) to verify that the integral of the sum of two functions is the same as the sum of two integrals; the fourth test item is the sum of the second and the third. Finally, we add a case to test error handling; the upper limit given is lower than the lower limit. This should be detected and handled in some reasonable way.

Step 3. Starting the program.   We start by writing the parts that remain the same from program to program; that is, the `#include` statement and the first and last lines of `main()` with the greeting and closing messages. We also add a `#define` command for the constant listed in the specification and a one-line definition of the function we will integrate. The dots in the code represent the unfinished parts of the program that will be filled in by later coding steps.

Function	Lower	Upper	Integral
$x^2 + x$	0.0	1.0	0.833333
x	0.0	2.0	2.0
x^2	0.0	2.0	2.666667
$x^2 + x$	0.0	2.0	4.666667
$x^2 + x$	2.0	0.0	Error

Figure 6.27.   Test plan: Simpson's rule.

```
#include "tools.h"
#define NUMBER  100

/* This is the function that we will integrate.  ------- */
double f( double x )  {   return x * x + x;   }


void main( void )
{   ...                 /* Space for declarations. */
    puts( "\n Integration by Simpson's rule.\n" );
    ...                 /* Space for I/O and computations. */
    bye();
}
```

Step 4. Reading valid data.   We need to read in the lower and upper bounds for integration. We declare two variables to store the data, using type **double** because that gives us maximal precision. We put these declarations at the top of **main()**.

```
double lower, upper;    /* Limits of integration. */
```

Then we write statements to prompt for and read the integration limits:

```
printf( " The function to integrate is: f(x)=x*x+x \n"
        " Enter lower and upper bounds for integration: " );
scanf( "%lg%lg", &lower, &upper );
```

If the inputs are given in the wrong order, the program will malfunction. So we test for this possibility and interchange the inputs, if necessary. We define another variable for the swapping process. Finally, we echo the inputs.

```
double swap;               /* For interchanging limits.*/

if (upper < lower) { swap=lower; lower=upper; upper=swap; }
printf( "\n Integrating f(x)=x*x+x from %g to %g\n",
          lower, upper );
```

Step 5. The computation.   The formula for computing an integral by Simpson's rule is long and complex enough to justify writing it as a separate function whose parameters are the lower and upper bounds of integration and whose result is the area. We name this function **simpson()**. We define a variable to hold the result, call **simpson()**, and print the answer:

```
double area;               /* Result of integration. */

area = simpson( lower, upper );
printf( " Area = %g \n", area );
```

```
#include "tools.h"

#define N   100
double f( double x )  {   return x*x+x;   } /* f(x) to integrate. */

void main( void )
{
    double lower, upper;       /* Limits of integration. */
    double swap;               /* For interchanging limits. */
    double area;               /* Result of integration. */
    banner();
    puts( "\n Integration by Simpson's rule.\n" );

    printf( " The function to integrate is: f(x)=x*x+x \n"
            " Enter lower and upper bounds for integration: " );
    scanf( "%lg%lg", &lower, &upper );


    if (upper < lower) { swap=lower; lower=upper; upper=swap; }
    printf( "\n Integrating f(x)=x*x+x from %g to %g\n",
            lower, upper );


    area = simpson( lower, upper );
    printf( " Area = %g \n", area );

    bye();
}
```

Figure 6.28.   Integration by Simpson's rule.

We complete the main program by combining all the parts in the appropriate order. The result, with comments added, is shown in Figure 6.28.

Step 6. The `simpson()` function.   We start by writing the skeleton of the function, including initial comments, the function header, and the closing bracket:

```
/* -------------------- Integration by Simpson's Method */
double
simpson( double low, double high )
{
    ...
}
```

The area formula uses the width of the subintervals, which is the width of the entire integration interval divided by the number of subintervals. We define a variable to store this value and compute it before we begin the main summation process:

```
double h;                /* Interval for integration. */
h = (high - low) / N;
```

The formula in the specification involves two large sums: one over the odd-numbered intervals, the other over the even-numbered intervals. To compute two sums, we must define two summation variables (**odds** and **evens**) and initialize them to 0.0. We also define variables for **area** (the result of the entire formula), a loop counter (**k**), and **x**, the point at which the function will be evaluated each time around the loop.

```
double odds, evens;    /* Sums for odd and even intervals. */
double area;           /* Weighted sums of all intervals. */
double x;              /* Evaluate function at this point. */
int k;                 /* Loop counter. */
```

A **for** loop is the easiest way to do the summation because the mathematical notation translates directly into the **for** control unit: The first index value, last index value, and index step size become its three fields. The body of the loop then computes the formula and adds it to the summation variable. The two summation loops are

```
odds = 0.0;              /* initial value of odd sum */
for (k = 1; k < N; k += 2) {
    x = low + k * h;
    odds += f( x );
}
evens = 0.0;             /* initial value of even sum */
for (k = 2; k < N; k += 2) {
    x = low + k * h;
    evens += f( x );
}
```

Once the even and odd sums have been computed, we can add all the terms in the formula and return the answer.

```
area = (high - low) / (3 * N) *
       (f( low ) + f( high ) + 4 * odds + 2 * evens);
return area;
```

We complete the function by combining all the parts in the appropriate order. The result is shown in Figure 6.29.

```
/* ------------------------------ Integration by Simpson's Method */
double
simpson( double low, double high )
{
    double h;                    /* Interval for integration. */
    double odds, evens;          /* Sums for odd and even intervals. */
    double x;                    /* Evaluate function at this point. */
    int k;                       /* Loop counter. */
    double area;                 /* Weighted sums of all intervals. */
    h = (high - low) / N;
    odds = 0.0;                  /* initial value of odd sum */
    for (k = 1; k < N; k += 2) {
        x = low + k * h;
        odds += f( x );
    }
    evens = 0.0;                 /* initial value of even sum */
    for (k = 2; k < N; k += 2) {
        x = low + k * h;
        evens += f( x );
    }
    area = (high - low) / (3 * N) *
            (f( low ) + f( high ) + 4 * odds + 2 * evens);
    return area;
}
```

Figure 6.29.   Summing areas by Simpson's rule.

Step 7. Testing the code.   We compile the program and run it using the
test plan. The first output agrees with the expected answer:

```
Integration by Simpson's rule.

The function to integrate is: f(x)=x*x+x
Enter lower and upper bounds for integration: 0 1

Integrating f(x)=x*x+x from 0 to 1
Area = 0.833333
```

Note that the answer is substantially more precise than the area calculated by
the rectangles method, Figure 5.14, which is accurate to only one decimal place.
Continuing with the test, we verify that the expected answers are produced for all
cases. In the last case, the error was detected and the limits were swapped. The
result was correct, that is, the same as the fourth case.

```
Integrating f(x)=x from 0 to 2
Area = 2
-------------------------------------------------------

Integrating f(x)=x*x from 0 to 2
Area = 2.66667
```

```
Integrating f(x)=x*x+x from 0 to 2
Area = 4.66667
```

6.5

Sentinel Loop Application: Interpolation (Optional Topic)

A common numerical problem often faced by scientists and engineers concerns finding a continuous function to approximate a set of discrete data values. Consider a set of data points $p = (x, f(x))$, where x is the controlled variable and $f(x)$ is the experimental reading for input x. The data can be used in several ways to calculate a function $f_{approx}(x)$, which approximates the true function, $f(x)$. Methods include linear and quadratic interpolation, least-squares curve fitting, and spline curve fitting.

As an introduction to this topic, consider the **linear interpolation** between two data points in which the true function, $f(x)$, is approximated by a straight line, $f_{approx}(x) = mx + b$, as shown in Figure 6.30. At x_1, we have $y_1 = f(x_1) = mx_1 + b$; and at x_2, $y_2 = f(x_2) = mx_2 + b$. Subtracting, $y_2 - y_1 = m(x_2 - x_1)$, so $m = (y_2 - y_1)/(x_2 - x_1) =$ slope. After solving for b at x_1, we get

$$y = f_{approx}(x) = y_1 + \left(\frac{y_2 - y_1}{x_2 - x_1} \right) (x - x_1)$$

Figure 6.33 gives a simple implementation of the linear interpolation specification in Figure 6.30. It has two phases: In the first phase, the user enters the two points used to determine the approximation function. In the second phase, a series of x values is entered and the program responds by printing the value of $f_{approx}(x)$ for each.

6.5.1   Program Design

Step 1. A test plan.   This program has two phases. In the first phase, the endpoints of a line segment are entered. In the second phase, several x values on that line segment are entered and the corresponding $f_{approx}(x)$ value is calculated. Therefore, each test case should specify a line for phase I, give the equation calculated from that line, and list a series of x values to test during phase II. The plan should cover all kinds of lines and test all the special cases we can think of. The ones that follow are shown in Figure 6.31.

The first test case should be something that can be computed in one's head. We note that the arithmetic is very simple if we start with two points on the line $f(x) = x$, which is a diagonal line. The equation is even simpler if the first x coordinate is 0. So we enter the points $(0, 0)$ and $(5, 5)$ in the chart to define the diagonal line, then add four test points for it: the two ends, a point in the middle, and a point that is out of range so that it causes termination.

Problem scope: Given two points in the form $(x, f(x))$, calculate the equation of a straight line through those points. In a second program phase, read the x coordinates of a series of points and use the linear equation to obtain an approximation for $f(x)$ for each input.

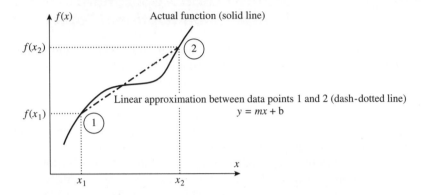

Input: In phase I, two points, $(x_1, f(x_1))$ and $(x_2, f(x_2))$. In phase II, a series of x values.

Formulas:

$$\text{Slope} = \frac{f(x_2) - f(x_1)}{x_2 - x_1}$$

$$f_{\text{approx}}(x) = f(x_1) + \text{slope} \times (x - x_1)$$

Output required: In phase I, echo the inputs and print the values $f(x_1)$, slope, and x_1 for the equation of the line through the two initial points. In phase II, echo the x-value inputs and print the value of $f_{\text{approx}}(x)$ for each. If the x-value is not in the defined range, print an error message and terminate the program.

Computational requirements: All the inputs will be real numbers with no more than six digits of precision. The outputs should be real numbers.

Limits on inputs: The point coordinates in phase I will be less than 1,000. It should be true that $x_2 > x_1$. The x values entered in phase II must be between the values x_1 and x_2 entered in phase I; that is, $x_1 \leq x \leq x_2$. If not, the program should terminate.

Figure 6.30.   Problem specification: Linear interpolation.

Next, we test a horizontal line. For the phase II inputs, we give a point in the middle of the line and a point barely out of range to test the termination condition. We also need to test the program with negative input, so we enter a

Phase I			Phase II	
Input Points		**Output Equation**	**Input**	**Output**
p_1	p_2	$f_{approx}(x)$	x	$f(x)$
$(0, 0)$	$(5, 5)$	$f(x) = x$	3	3
			0	0
			5	5
			−1	End
$(0, 0)$	$(5, 0)$	$f(x) = 0$	3	0
			−0.001	End
$(-1, -3)$	$(1, 2)$	$f(x) = -3 + 2.5(x + 1)$	0	−0.5
			1.00001	End
$(1, 0)$	$(1, 2)$	Error		
$(1, 2)$	$(-1, -3)$	Error		
$(2.0, 7.923)$	$(5.5, -2.6739)$	$f(x) = 7.923 - 3.028(x - 2)$	2.0	7.923
			5.5	−2.674
			1.99999999	7.923
			1.9999999	End

Figure 6.31.   Test plan: Linear interpolation.

line with one endpoint at $(-1, -3)$. In phase II, we test an input that is barely past the right endpoint of this line to terminate this test.

Next come a few special cases. The first is a vertical line, defined by **x₁ == x₂**. If not handled properly, this case would generate a division by 0 when computing the slope. The program should check for this case and display an error message if it occurs. Related to this is the case where $x_1 > x_2$. This violates the assumptions about the input and should be corrected before processing continues.

At this point, we believe that we have thought of all the special cases, so we now test an arbitrary line with a negative slope. To calculate the correct equation here, we use a pocket calculator. In phase II, we enter the endpoints of the line segment to be sure we get back the same values for $f(x)$ we started with. We plan to terminate this run by finding the maximum acceptable value for x that will end execution. We know that this will be 1.99..., adding some number of nines; we start with a long series of nines and decrease the number until the program terminates. This experiment will reveal the precision of the internal representation for type **double**.

Step 2. The program skeleton.   Some parts of the program remain the same from application to application: the **#include** command, the first line of `main()`, the curly brackets that open and close the program, and the closing message. We start by writing these parts (Figure 6.32); the dots represent the unfinished parts of the program.

The opening message must explain the purpose of the program and give instructions for its use. In this application, the opening message will be fairly long, so we write the instructions as a separate function (Figure 6.32), inserting a prototype at the top and a function call in `main()`.

Step 3. Input and echo for phase I.

We need to read two points of the form $(x, f(x))$, so we start by declaring four variables. We choose to use type `double` because it provides adequate precision for our purposes.

```
double x1, fx1;    /* Point with smaller x-coordinate. */
double x2, fx2;    /* Point with larger x-coordinate. */
```

Now we are ready to read the two points. However, we cannot just read them and be done. From our test plan, we know that we must look out for two error conditions: vertical lines and reversed x coordinates. To make our program more user-friendly, we decide that we would like to give the user a second chance to enter new coordinates if the first set were in error.

A typical approach to this is to develop a loop that will continue to prompt the user for new values until he or she gets it right. This is known as an *input validation loop*. In this case, getting it right is defined by $x_1 < x_2$, which actually takes care of both of the error cases, since the vertical line is defined by $x_1 == x_2$.

```
#include "tools.h"
void instructions( void );

void main( void )
{     …       /* Space for declarations.*/
      instructions();
      …       /* Space for input, output, and computations.*/
      bye();
}
/* -------------------------------------------------------------------- */
void instructions( void )
{
   banner();
   puts( "\n\n Linear Interpolation\n"
         "    Use a straight line to approximate an unknown function, \n"
         "    f(x).  The user enters x and f(x) for two points.  The \n"
         "    program calculates the formula for f_approx(x), the \n"
         "    straight line through these two points.  \n" );
}
```

Figure 6.32.   Skeleton for the linear interpolation program.

So the test that keeps us in the loop is x_1 >= x_2. Inside the loop we read each set of data. We decide to read one point at a time, so we write two prompts and two calls on `scanf()`. We instruct the user to enter the smaller x value first, hoping that correct data will be entered on the first attempt. After reading two proper sets of coordinates, we echo the data:

```
do {
    printf( " Enter smaller x and f(x) for that value: " );
    scanf( "%lg%lg", &x1, &fx1 );
    printf( " Enter larger x and f(x) for that value: " );
    scanf( "%lg%lg", &x2, &fx2 );
    if (x1 >= x2) puts( " First x must be < second.\n" );
} while ( x1 >= x2 );
printf( "\n\t For p1=(%g, %g) and p2=(%g, %g)\n",
        x1, fx1, x2, fx2 );
```

Step 4. Phase I computation and output.   We can now calculate the equation for a line by plugging the four input values into the given formula:

```
slope = (fx2 - fx1) / (x2 - x1);
printf( "\n\t f_approx(x) = %g + %g * (x - %g)\n",
        fx1, slope, x1 );
```

While coding this calculation, we note that we need a variable to store the slope of the line and add the following declaration, completing phase I of the program.

```
double slope;
```

Step 5. Input and computation for phase II.   Now we are ready to accept a series of x coordinates and calculate $f_{approx}(x)$ for each. We note that we need a variable for the input and one for the answer:

```
double x, fx;
```

To process several values, we need a loop, and every loop must have a termination condition. The specification says to reject phase II inputs that are not within the line segment defined by the phase I data, so we decide to use a sentinel loop where any value outside the allowable range will act as the sentinel. In our code, we compare each x value entered to both the left and the right ends of the line segment and leave the loop if the input is outside these limits. We write a prompt that gives instructions to the user, a `scanf()` statement, and the skeleton of a loop. Since this loop is supposed to process a new input value each time, we write another `scanf()` statement at the very end of the loop to prepare for the next data set.

```
printf( "\n Enter x-values between %g and %g\n", x1, x2 );
printf( "\t f_approx(x) will be printed for each x. \n"
        "\t To quit, enter value outside this range. \n" );
scanf( "%lg", &x );
while (x1 <= x && x <= x2) {
    ...
    scanf( "%lg", &x );
}
```

Now we must write the code for processing a legal input. We use the given formula to calculate $f_{approx}(x)$ and print the results:

```
fx = fx1 + slope * (x - x1);
printf( "\t x=%g   f_approx(x)=%g\n", x, fx );
```

6.5.2   Program Testing

The completed program is shown in Figure 6.33. We compile, execute, and test it with the first item in our test plan. The output is

```
Linear Interpolation
    Use a straight line to approximate an unknown function,
    f(x).  The user enters x and f(x) for two points.  The
    program calculates the formula for f_approx(x), the
    straight line through these two points.

Enter smaller x and f(x) for that value: 0 0
Enter larger x and f(x) for that value: 5 5

    For p1=(0, 0) and p2=(5, 5)

    f_approx(x) = 0 + 1 * (x - 0)

Enter x-values between 0 and 5
    f_approx(x) will be printed for each x.
    To quit, enter value outside this range.
3
    x=3   f_approx(x)=3
5
    x=5   f_approx(x)=5
0
    x=0   f_approx(x)=0
-1
```

We see that these answers are correct, as were the responses for the other test cases in our plan. The final data set produced the results that follow, which demonstrate

The user is asked to enter x and $f(x)$ for two points. The program uses a straight line to approximate an unknown function, $f(x)$, through these two points. The `instructions()` function is shown in Figure 6.32.

```
#include "tools.h"
void instructions( void )

void main( void )
{
    double x1, fx1;              /* Point with smaller x-coordinate. */
    double x2, fx2;              /* Point with larger x-coordinate. */
    double slope, x, fx;

    instructions();

    /* Phase I.----------------------------------------------------- */
    do {
        printf( " Enter smaller x and f(x) for that value: " );
        scanf( "%lg%lg", &x1, &fx1 );
        printf( " Enter larger x and f(x) for that value: " );
        scanf( "%lg%lg", &x2, &fx2 );
        if (x1 >= x2) puts( "First x must be < second.\n" );
    }   while (x1 >= x2);
    printf( "\n\t For p1=(%g, %g) and p2=(%g, %g)\n",
            x1, fx1, x2, fx2 );


    slope = (fx2 - fx1) / (x2 - x1);
    printf( "\n\t f_approx(x) = %g + %g * (x - %g)\n",
            fx1, slope, x1);


    /* Phase II.---------------------------------------------------- */
    printf( "\n Enter x-values between %g and %g\n", x1, x2 );
    printf( "\t f_approx(x) will be printed for each x.  \n"
            "\t To quit, enter value outside this range.\n" );

    scanf( "%lg", &x );
    while (x1 <= x && x <= x2) {
        fx = fx1 + slope * (x - x1);
        printf( "\t x=%g    f_approx(x)=%g\n", x, fx );

        scanf( "%lg", &x );
    }

    bye();
}
```

Figure 6.33. Linear interpolation.

the error handling. Note that the `%g` format specifier causes input values to be rounded to six significant digits when they are printed and suppresses trailing zeroes.

```
Linear Interpolation
    Use a straight line to approximate an unknown function,
    f(x).  The user enters x and f(x) for two points. The
    program calculates the formula for f_approx(x), the
    straight line through these two points.

Enter smaller x and f(x) for that value: 2.0 7.923
Enter larger x and f(x) for that value: 5.5 -2.6739

    For p1=(2, 7.923) and p2=(5.5, -2.6739)

    f_approx(x) = 7.923 + -3.02769 * (x - 2)

Enter x-values between 2 and 5.5
    f_approx(x) will be printed for each x.
    To quit, enter value outside this range.
2.0
    x=2    f_approx(x)=7.923
5.4999999
    x=5.5    f_approx(x)=-2.6739
1.9999999999999999999999
    x=2    f_approx(x)=7.923
5.5000001

Normal termination.
```

6.6   What You Should Remember

6.6.1   Major Concepts

- The `while` loop tests the loop exit condition before executing the loop body. The body, therefore, is executed zero or more times.
- The `while` loop is used for sentinel loops, delay loops, processing data sets of unknown size, and data validation loops when it is important to give the user an error comment different from an ordinary prompt.
- The `for` loop implements the same control pattern as the `while` loop but has a different and more compact syntax.
- The `for` loop is used for counted loops and processing any set of data whose exact size or maximum size is known ahead of time.

- The **do...while** loop executes the loop body before performing the loop exit test. Therefore, the body is always executed one or more times.
- The **do...while** statement is used to form query loops that call a **work()** function repeatedly. It also can be used for data validation.
- A **continue** statement within any kind of loop transfers control back to the top of the loop.
- An **if...break** statement can be used to leave any kind of loop but normally is used to leave a **for** loop before the iteration limit is reached.
- Any one or all the expressions in the control unit of a **for** statement can be omitted. If the loop test is omitted, an **if...break** is used to end the loop. This combination is used for data validation loops.
- The **switch** statement has several clauses, called *cases*, each labeled by a constant. At run time, a single value is compared to each constant and the clause corresponding to the matching constant is executed. A **default** case will be executed if none of the case constants match.
- Every case in a **switch** statement (except the last one) must end with a **break** statement.

6.6.2   Programming Style

Many programs can be improved by eliminating useless work and simplifying nested logic. The resulting code always is simpler and easier to debug and usually is substantially shorter. Some specific suggestions for improving program style follow:

- The golden rule of style is this: Indent your code consistently and properly.
- Line up the first letter of **for**, **while**, or **switch** with the curly bracket that closes the following block of statements. Indent all the statements within the block.
- Use the **switch** statement instead of a series of nested **if...else** statements when the condition being tested is simple enough.
- Do not compute the same expression twice—compute it once and save the answer in a variable. Any time you do an action twice and expect to get the same answer, you create an opportunity for disaster if the program is modified.
- If two statements are logically related, put them near each other in the program. Examples of this principle are

    Initialize a loop variable just before the beginning of the loop.

    Do the input just before the conditional that tests it.

- Use the **for** loop effectively, putting all initializations and increment steps in the control part of the loop.

- When one control unit is placed within the body of another, we call it *nested logic*. For example, a `switch` statement can be nested inside a loop, and a loop can be nested inside one clause of an `if` statement. Most real applications require the use of nested logic. Some generally accepted guidelines are these:

  Keep it simple. An `if` statement nested inside another `if` statement inside a loop has excessive complexity. Many times, the `if` statement can be moved outside the loop or the second `if` statement can be eliminated by using a logical operator.

  Establish a regular indenting style and stick to it without exception.

  Limit the number of levels of nesting to two or three.

  If your application seems to require deeper nesting, break up the nesting by defining a separate function that contains the innermost one or two levels of logic.

- To improve efficiency, move everything possible outside of a loop. For example, when you must compute the average of some numbers, use the loop to count the numbers and add them to a total. Do not do the division within the loop. Moving actions out of the loop frequently shortens the code; it always simplifies it and makes it more efficient. In poorly written programs, "fat loops" account for many of the extra lines. Take advantage of any special properties of the data, such as data that may be sorted, may have a sentinel value on the end, or may be validated by a prior program step and not need validation again when processed.

- During the primary debugging phase of an application, every loop should contain some screen output. This allows the programmer to monitor the program's progress and detect an infinite loop or a loop that is executed too many or too few times. Debugging output lines should print the loop variable, any input read within the loop, and any totals or counters changed in the loop.

6.6.3   Sticky Points and Common Errors

- *Semicolons in the wrong places.* The loop control clause of a `for` loop or the condition clause of a `while` loop or an `if` statement is, normally, *not* followed by a semicolon.
- *Off-by-one errors.* The programmer must take care with every loop to make sure it repeats the correct number of times. A small error can cause one too many or one too few iterations. Every loop should be tested carefully to ensure that it executes the proper number of times. In some counted loops, the loop counter is used as a subscript or as a part of a computation. In these loops, the results may be wrong even when the loop

is repeated the correct number of times. This kind of error happens when the value of the loop counter is **off by one** because it is not incremented at the correct time in relation to the expression or expressions that use the counter's value. Consider these two counted loops:

```
for (sumj = j = 0; j < 10; ++j)
    sumj += j;                      /* Sum from 0 to 9 */

sumk = k = 0;
while (k < 10) {                    /* Sum from 1 to 10 */
    ++k;
    sumk += k;
}
```

These loops are very similar, but **k** is incremented before adding it to **sumk** and **j** is incremented after adding it to the sum. A programmer must decide which timing pattern is correct and be careful to write the correct form.

- *Infinite loops.* The **for** loop with no loop test sometimes is called an *infinite loop*, although most such loops contain an **if..break** statement that stops execution under appropriate conditions. Such loops are useful tools. However, a real infinite loop is not useful and should be avoided. Such loops are the result of forgetting to include an update step in the loop body. (In a counted loop, the update step increments the loop variable. In an input-controlled loop, it reads a new value for the loop variable.) During the construction and debugging phases of a program, it is a good idea to put a **puts()** statement in every loop so that you can easily identify an infinite loop when it occurs.

- *Nested logic.* When using nested logic, the programmer must know how control will flow into, through, and out of the unit. Statements such as **break** and **continue** affect the flow of control in ways that are simple when single units are considered but become complex when control statements are nested. Be sure you understand how your control statements interact.

6.6.4 New and Revisited Vocabulary

These terms and concepts have been defined or expanded in the chapter:

control unit	infinite loop	search loop
counted loop	input-controlled loop	delay loop
trip count	repeat query	busy wait
off-by-one error	input validation loop	constant expression
premature exit	sentinel loop	Simpson's 1/3 rule
infinite **for** loop	sentinel value	linear interpolation

The following C keywords, phrases, and library functions were discussed in this chapter:

for loop	**break** statement	**switch** statement
, (comma operator)	**if...break** statement	**case** statement
do...while loop	**continue** statement	**default** clause

6.7   Exercises

6.7.1   Self-Test Exercises

1. Explain the fundamental differences between a series of **if...else** statements and a **switch** statement. Under what conditions would you use a **switch** statement? Give an example of a problem for which you could not use a **switch** statement.

2. Explain the fundamental differences between a **while** loop and a **do...while** loop. In what situation would you use each?

3. The following program contains a loop. What is its output? Rewrite the loop using **for** instead of **while**. Make sure the output does not change.

```
#include <stdio.h>
void main ( void )
{   int k, sum;

    sum = k = 0;
    while (k < 10) {
        sum += k;
        ++k;
    }
    printf( "A. %i %i \n", k, sum );
}
```

4. The following program contains a loop. What is its output? Rewrite the loop using **while** instead of **do...while**. Make sure the output does not change.

```
#include <stdio.h>
void main ( void )
{   int k, sum;

    printf( " Please enter an exponent >= 0: " );
    scanf( "%i", &k );
    sum = 1;
    do {
        if (k > 0) sum = 2*sum;
        --k;
    } while (k > 0);
    printf( "B. %i \n", sum );
}
```

5. Given the following fragment of a flow diagram, write the code that corresponds to it and define any necessary variables:

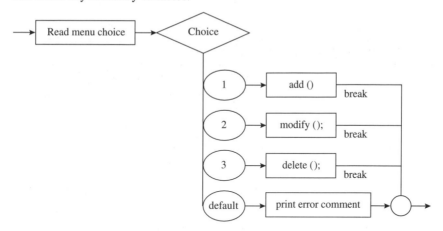

6. Draw a flow diagram for the linear interpolation program in Figure 6.33.

7. Rewrite the following **switch** statement as an **if...else** sequence. (Write code, not a flowchart.)

```
switch (k) {
    case 2:
    case 12:  puts( "You lose" ); break;
    case 7:
    case 11:  puts( "You win" ); break;
    default:  puts( "Try again" );
}
```

8. Analyze the following loop and draw a flow diagram for it. Then trace the execution of the loop using the initial values shown. Use a storage diagram to show the succession of values stored in each variable. Finally, show the output, clearly labeled and in one place.

```
for (k = 0,j = 1; j < 3; j++)  {
    k += j;
    printf( "\t %i\t %i\n", j, k );
}
printf( "\t %i\t %i\n", j,k );
```

9. What does each of the following loops print? They are supposed to print the numbers from 1 to 3. What is wrong with them?

a. `for(k = 0; k < 3; ++k) printf( "k = %i", k );`

b. ```
k = 1;
do {
    printf("k = %i", k);
    k++;
} while (k < 3);
```
```

6.7.2 Using Pencil and Paper

1. Explain the fundamental differences between a counted loop and a sentinel loop. What C statement would you use to implement each?

2. Explain the fundamental similarity between a **while** loop and a **for** loop. In what situation would you use each?

3. Rewrite the following **if...else** sequence as a **switch** statement. Write code, not a flowchart.

```
if (i == 0) puts( "bad" );
else if (i >= 1 && i < 3) puts( "better" );
else if (i == 4 || i == 5) puts( "good" );
else puts( "sorry" );
puts("------"):
```

4. Draw a flow diagram for the Simpson's method program in Figure 6.28.

5. Given the following fragment of a flow diagram, write the code that corresponds to it and define any necessary variables. What number will be printed by the last box?

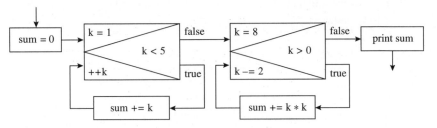

6. The following program contains a loop. What is its output? Rewrite the loop using **do...while** instead of **for**. Keep the output the same.

```
#include <stdio.h>
void main ( void )
{   int k, sum;
    for ( sum = k = 0; k < 5; ++k ) sum += k;
    printf( "C. %i %i \n", k, sum );
}
```

7. The following program contains a loop. What is its output? Rewrite the loop without using **break**. Keep the output the same.

```
#include <stdio.h>
void main ( void )
{   int k, sum;
    for (sum = k = 1 ; k < 10; k++) {
        sum *= k;
        if (sum > 10*k) break;
    }
    printf( "D. %i %i \n", k, sum );
}
```

8. What does the following loop print? It is supposed to print out the numbers from 1 to 3. What is wrong with it?

```
for(k=1; k<=3; ++k);
    printf( "k=%i", k );
```

9. Analyze each loop that follows and draw a flow diagram for it. Then trace execution of the loop using the initial values shown. Use a storage diagram to show the succession of values stored in each variable. Finally, show the output from each exercise, clearly labeled and in one place.

   a.
```
k=2;
do { printf("\t %i\n", k); --k; } while (k>=0);
```
   b.
```
j=k=0;
while (j<3){ k+=j; printf("\t %i\t %i\n", j, k); ++j; }
```

6.7.3 Using the Computer

1. Sum a series.
   Write a program that uses a **for** loop to sum the first 100 terms of the series $1/x^2$. Use Figure 6.9 as a guide. Develop a test plan and carry it out. Turn in the source code and output of your program when run on the test data.

2. Sum a function.
   Write a function with parameter x that will compute the value of $f(x) = (3 \times x + 1)^{\frac{1}{2}}$. Write a main program that sums $f(x)$ from $x = 0$ to $x = 1{,}000$ in increments of 2. Use a **for** loop. Print the result.

3. Find the best.
   Write a program that will allow an instructor to enter a series of exam scores. After the last score, the instructor should enter a negative number as a signal that there is no more input. Print the average of all the scores and the highest score entered.

4. Gas prices.
   The example at the end of Chapter 3 (Figure 3.17) is a program that converts a Canadian gas price to an equivalent U.S. gas price. This program does the calculation for only one price. Modify it so that it can convert a series of prices, as follows:

   a. Remove the price-per-liter input, computation, and output from the main program and put them in a separate function, named **convert()**.

   b. In place of this code in the main program, substitute a query loop that will allow you to enter a series of Canadian prices. For each, call **convert()** to do the work.

5. An increasing voltage pattern.
   Write a program that will calculate and print out a series of voltages.

a. Prompt the user for a value of $vmax$ and restrict it to the range **12 <=** $vmax$ **<= 24**. Let time **t** start at **0** and increase by 1 at each step until the voltage $v > 95\%$ of $vmax$; **v** is a function of time according to the following formula. Print the time and voltage at each step.

$$v = vmax \times \left(1 - e^{(-0.1 \times t)}\right)$$

b. Add a delay loop so that the voltage output is timed more slowly. See Figure 6.19.

6. Sine or cosine?

a. Write a double:double function, **f()**, with one **double** parameter, **x**, that will evaluate either $f_1(x) = x^2 \sin(x) + e^{-x}$ if $x \leq 1.0$ or $f_2(x) = x^3 \cos(x) - \log(x)$ if $x > 1.0$, and return the result. Write a prototype that can be included at the top of a program.

b. Start with the main program in Figure 6.12. Modify the program title and write a new **work()** function that will input a value for **x**, call **f()** using the value of **x**, and output the result.

c. Design a test plan for your program.

d. Incorporate all the pieces of your program in one file and compile it. Then carry out the test plan to verify the program's correctness.

7. A voltage signal.
An experiment will be carried out repeatedly using an ac voltage signal. The signal is to have one of three values, depending on the time since the beginning of the experiment:

For time $t < 1$, $\text{volts}(t) = 0.5 \times \sin(2t)$.

For time $1.0 \leq t \leq 10.0$, $\text{volts}(t) = \sin(t)$.

For time $t > 10.0$, $\text{volts}(t) = \sin(10.0)$.

a. Write a function named **volts()** with t as a parameter that will calculate and return the correct voltage. Use the function in Figure 5.8 and the **if...else** statements in Figure 5.11 as guides.

b. Using Figure 6.12 as a guide, write a main program that starts at time 0. Use a loop to call the **volts()** function and output the result. Increment the time by 0.5 after each repetition until the time reaches 12. Print the results in the form of a neat table.

8. Quadratic interpolation.
Following the program example and formulas in Section 6.5, write a program that will prompt the user to enter three points: $(x_1, f(x_1))$, $(x_2, f(x_2))$, and $(x_3, f(x_3))$. Output the formula for $f_{\text{approx}}(x)$ based on a quadratic interpolation, then accept inputs for values of x between x_1 and x_3 and output the values of $f_{\text{approx}}(x)$ for each value of x. Create an appropriate test plan and make sure to validate the input data.

The formula for quadratic interpolation among three points is

$$f_{\text{approx}}(x) = f(x_1) \cdot \frac{(x - x_2)}{(x_1 - x_2)} \cdot \frac{(x - x_3)}{(x_1 - x_3)} + f(x_2) \cdot \frac{(x - x_1)}{(x_2 - x_1)} \cdot \frac{(x - x_3)}{(x_2 - x_3)}$$
$$+ f(x_3) \cdot \frac{(x - x_1)}{(x_3 - x_1)} \cdot \frac{(x - x_2)}{(x_3 - x_2)}$$

9. Flow past a flat plate.
   A solar collector is installed 3 meters from the leading edge of a roof and flush with
   the roof surface, as follows. The collector is 1 m on each side. The solar collector
   has a constant surface temperature of 54°C and air flows over it at a speed of 1.5 m/s
   at a temperature of 0°C. We want to find the total amount of heat that the collector
   loses to the air above it.

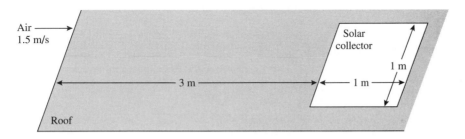

This problem is a special case of flow past a flat plate, where the starting length
(the roof part) is unheated. To solve this problem, use the appropriate equations for
heat transfer from a flat plate aligned with the flow[10] along with the properties of air
at atmospheric pressure to obtain the total rate of heat loss from a collector of this
size and temperature:

$$\text{Total rate of heat loss} = 129.06 \times \int_3^4 \frac{x^{-0.5}}{\left[1 - \left(\dfrac{3}{x}\right)^{0.75}\right]^{\frac{1}{3}}} \, dx \text{ (watts)}$$

where x is the distance in meters from the leading edge of the roof.

a. Define a function **loss()** with one **double** parameter, **x**, that computes the
   formula that must be integrated (between the integral sign and the dx).

b. Write a main program that will obtain a value for the rate of heat loss by using
   Simpson's rule to evaluate the **loss()** function between the limits of 3 and 4.
   Multiply the result by 129.06 and print the total rate of heat loss.

---

[10]F. Incropera and D. DeWitt, *Fundamentals of Heat and Mass Transfer*, 4th ed. (New York: Wiley,
1996).

10. Drag on a car.

An electric car of mass 2,000 kg can generate a constant maximum power output of P watts. As it moves forward at speed u, the main force retarding its motion is wind drag.

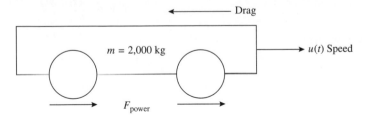

The wind drag is proportional to u^2 as

$$\text{Drag} = 0.25u^2$$

where u is measured in m/s and drag is in N. The force transmitted by all four wheels, which moves the car forward, is related to the maximum power as

$$F_{\text{power}} = P/u \quad (N)$$

Applying Newton's law to the car, we have

$$\sum F = ma$$

where acceleration, a, is

$$a = du/dt$$

It follows that

$$F_{\text{power}} - \text{Drag} = m \ du/dt$$

$$\frac{P}{u} - 0.25u^2 = 2,000 \ \frac{du}{dt}$$

$$2,000 \ \frac{du}{dt} = \frac{P - 0.25u^3}{u}$$

$$dt = \frac{2,000u}{P - 0.25u^3} \ du$$

The time t (s) required to reach a speed of 30 m/s, starting from rest, can be found by integrating the preceding formula. We have

$$t = 2,000 \int_0^{30} \frac{u}{P - 0.25u^3} \ du$$

Adapt the program for Simpson's rule, which was given in Figure 6.28, to obtain and print the numerical value for the preceding integral when $P = 10,000$ watts. Then extend your program by adding a loop around the main process. Let this loop generate values of motor power from 10,000 to 40,000 watts in increments of 10,000 watts. Print a table of the output, in seconds, for each power.

Basic Data Types

CHAPTER
7

![horizontal bar]

Using Numeric Types

Two kinds of number representations, integer and floating point, are supported by C. The various **integer types** in C provide exact representations of the mathematical concept of "integer" but can represent values in only a limited range. The **floating-point types** in C are used to represent the mathematical type "real." They can represent real numbers over a very large range of magnitudes, but each number generally is an approximation, using a limited number of decimal places of precision.

In this chapter, we define and explain the integer and floating-point data types built into C and show how to write their literal forms and I/O formats. We discuss the range of values that can be stored in each type, how to perform reliable arithmetic computations with these values, what happens when a number is converted (or cast) from one type to another, and how to choose the proper data type for a problem.

7.1   Integer Types

To accommodate the widest variety of applications and computer hardware, C integers come in two varieties and up to three sizes. We refer to all of these types, collectively, as the *integer types*. However, more than six different names are used for these types, and many of the names can be written in more than one form. In addition, some type names have different meanings on different systems. If this sounds confusing, it is.

Common Name	Full Name	Other Acceptable Names	
`int`	`signed int`	`signed`	
`long`	`signed long int`	`long int`	`signed long`
`short`	`signed short int`	`short int`	`signed short`
`unsigned`	`unsigned int`		
`unsigned long`	`unsigned long int`		
`unsigned short`	`unsigned short int`		

Figure 7.1. Names for integer types.

The full type name of an integer contains a sign specifier, a length specifier, and the keyword `int`. However, there are shorter versions of the names of all these types. Figure 7.1 lists the commonly used name, then the full name, and finally other variants.

A C programmer needs to know what the basic types are, how to write the names of the types needed, and how to input and output values of these types. He or she must also know which types are portable (this means that the type name always means more or less the same thing) and which types are not (because the meaning depends on the hardware).[1]

Short and long integers. Integers come in two[2] lengths: `short` and `long`. On most modern machines, short integers occupy 2 bytes of memory and long integers use 4 bytes. The resulting value **representation ranges** are shown in Figure 7.2. As you read this list, keep the following facts in mind:

- The ranges of values shown in the table are the minimum required by the ISO C standard.
- On many machines the smallest negative value actually is $-32,768$ for `short int` and $-2,147,483,648$ for `long int`.
- Unsigned numbers are explained more fully in Section 18.1.
- On PCs, `int` usually is the same as `short int`. On workstations and larger machines, it is the same as `long int`.
- The constants `INT_MIN`, `INT_MAX`, and the like are defined in every C implementation in the header file `limits.h`. This header file is required by the C standard, but its contents can be different from one installation to the next. It lists all of the hardware-dependent system parameters that relate to integer data types, including the largest and smallest values of each data type supported by the local system.

---

[1] A programmer also may need to be aware of the way a value is stored in memory as a sequence of bits. The interested reader can refer to Appendix E for more on this topic.

[2] Or three lengths, if you count type `char` (discussed in Chapter 11), which actually is a very short integer type.

Data Type	Names of Constant Limits	Range
int	INT_MIN...INT_MAX	Same as either **long** or **short**
short int	SHRT_MIN...SHRT_MAX	$-32,767\ldots32,767$
long int	LONG_MIN...LONG_MAX	$-2,147,483,647\ldots2,147,483,647$
unsigned int	0...UINT_MAX	Same as **unsigned long** or **short**
unsigned short	0...USHRT_MAX	$0\ldots65,535$
unsigned long	0...ULONG_MAX	$0\ldots4,294,967,295$

Figure 7.2.   ISO C **integer representations.**

The type **int** is tricky. It is defined by the C standard as "not longer than **long** and not shorter than **short**." The intention is that **int** should be the same as either **long** or **short**, whichever is handled more efficiently by the hardware. Therefore, many C systems on Intel 80x86 machines implement type **int** as **short**.[3] We refer to this as the **2-byte int model**. Larger machines implement **int** as **long**, which we refer to as the **4-byte int model**.

The potential changes in the limits of an **int**, shown in Figure 7.2, can make writing portable code a nightmare for the inexperienced person. Therefore, it might seem a good idea to avoid type **int** altogether and use only **short** and **long**. However, this is impractical, because the integer functions in the C libraries are written to use **int** arguments and return **int** results. The responsible programmer simply must be aware of the situation, make no assumptions if possible, and use **short** and **long** when it is important.

Signed and unsigned integers.   All sizes of integers come in two varieties: **signed** and **unsigned**. The difference is the interpretation of the leftmost bit in the number's representation. For signed numbers, this bit indicates the sign of the value. For unsigned numbers, it is an ordinary magnitude bit. In one common representation of a 2-byte signed integer, a 1 in this position indicates a negative number and 0 means a positive number. In an unsigned integer, the bit's place value is 32,768. Therefore, the largest **unsigned int** (see Figure 7.2) is 32,768 greater than the largest **signed int**. Every unsigned 2-byte number larger than 32,767 has the same bit pattern as some negative-signed 2-byte number. For example, in most PCs, the bit patterns of 32,768 (unsigned) and $-32,768$ (signed) are identical.

So why bother with two kinds of integers? FORTRAN, Pascal, and Java have only signed numbers. For most purposes, signed numbers are fine. Some applications, though, seem more natural using unsigned numbers. Examples

---

[3] However, the Gnu C compiler running under the Linux operating system on the same machine implements type **int** as **long**.

In this table, we assume that the type `int` is the same length as `short`, and that the maximum representable `int` is 32,767.

Literal	Type	Reason for Type
0	`int`	Number is less than 32,767
200	`int`	Number is less than 32,767
255U	`unsigned`	It uses the `U` code
255L	`long`	It uses the `L` code
255UL	`unsigned long`	It uses the `UL` code
32767	`int`	Largest possible 2-byte `int`
32768	`long`	Too large for a 2-byte `int`
32767L	`long`	It uses the `L` code
3000000000	`unsigned long`	3 billion, too large for `long`
6000000000	Compile-time error	6 billion, too large for any integer type

Figure 7.3.   Integer literals in base 10.

include applications where the actual pattern of bits is important, negative values are meaningless or will not occur, or one needs the extra positive range of the values.

Integer literals.   An **integer literal** constant does not contain a sign or a decimal point. If a number is preceded by a - sign or a + sign, the sign is interpreted as a unary operator, not as a part of the number. When you write a literal, you may add a type specifier, `L`, `U`, or `UL` on the end to indicate that you need a `long`, an `unsigned`, or an `unsigned long` value, respectively. (This letter is not the same as the conversion specifier of an I/O format.) If you do not include such a type code, the compiler will choose between `int`, `unsigned`, `long`, and `unsigned long`, whichever is the shortest representation that has a range large enough for your number. Figure 7.3 shows examples of various types of integer literals. Note that no commas are allowed in any of the literals.

7.2   Floating-Point Types in C

In traditional **scientific notation**, real numbers are written with two parts: a signed **mantissa** and a signed base-10 **exponent**, as in 1.4112×10^3. A floating-point number is represented similarly inside the computer by a sign bit, a mantissa, and a signed exponent.[4] At the end of each floating-point computation, the result is

---

[4]Floating-point representation is presented in more detail in Appendix E.

normalized: The mantissa is shifted right or left so that exactly one nonzero bit remains to the left of the decimal point. The exponent is adjusted appropriately; that is, incremented (or decremented) by 1 each time the mantissa is shifted left (or right) by one bit position. In this way, the significant information "floats" to the left end of the mantissa.

C has a great variety of integer types. Fortunately, the set of floating-point types is not so extensive. There are only three: `float`, `double`, and `long double`. We use the terms *float* or *floating point* to refer to a variable of any of these types. There are no unsigned floating-point types. The only real difference among the types is the number of bits used in the representation, which directly affects the range and number of possible digits of precision. Figure 7.4 shows the minimum properties of the `float` and `double` types defined by the IEEE standard,[5] which many C implementations support.

An IEEE `float` needs at least 8 bits for the exponent and 24 for the mantissa. Because of this limited number of bits, many values cannot be stored as type `float` with adequate precision for common numerical computations. An IEEE `double` uses 11 bits for the exponent and 53 for the mantissa, increasing both the range of exponents and the precision. This is a minimum standard; the actual range of real values supported by hardware may be greater than this standard requires, due to slight variations in the way the hardware and software treat floating-point numbers.[6] The actual precision and exponent range for a local implementation can be found in the local version of the file `float.h`. The third floating-point type, `long double`, is new in ISO C and identical to `double` on most systems. The standards do not define a minimum length for it, although 12 bytes are used on some systems. Since `double` is sufficient for most

These are the minimum value ranges for the IEEE floating-point types. The names given in this table are the ones defined by the C standard.

Type Name	Digits of Precision	Name of C Constant	Minimum Value Range Required by IEEE Standard
`float`	6	±FLT_MIN...±FLT_MAX	±1.175E−38 ... ±3.402E+38
`double`	15	±DBL_MIN...±DBL_MAX	±2.225E−308 ... ±1.797E+308

Figure 7.4.   IEEE **floating-point types.**

---

[5] The ISO C standard is less demanding than the IEEE standard.

[6] In our C system, both the range and the precision are slightly larger than the IEEE standard requires.

calculations and few machines have the specialized hardware to support `long double`, the longer type is rarely used. All the computations in this book will use the standard `float` and `double` types.

Floating-point literals.   In traditional mathematical notation, we write real numbers in one of two ways. The simplest notation is a series of digits containing a decimal point, like 672.01. The other notation, called base-10 scientific notation, uses a base-10 exponent in conjunction with a mantissa: we write 672.01 as 6.7201×10^2.

In C, real literals also can be written in either decimal or a variant of scientific notation: we write `6.7201E+02` instead of 6.7201×10^2. A numeric literal that contains either a decimal point or an exponent is interpreted as one of the floating-point types; the default type is `double`. (A literal number that has no decimal point and no exponent is an integer.) There are several rules for writing literal constants of floating-point types:

1. You may write the number in everyday decimal notation: Any number with a decimal point is a floating-point literal. The number may start or end with the decimal point; for example, `1.0`, `0.1`, `120.1`, `.1416`, or `1.`.

2. You may use scientific notation. When you do so, write a mantissa part followed by an exponent part; for example, `4.50E+6`. The mantissa part follows the rules for decimal notation, except that it is not necessary to write a decimal point. Examples of legal mantissas are `3.1416`, `341.0`, `.123`, and `89`.

   The exponent part has a letter followed by an optional sign and then a number.

   - The letter can be `E` or `e`.
   - The sign can be `+`, `-`, or it can be omitted (in which case, `+` is assumed).
   - The exponent number is an integer of one to three digits in the proper ranges, as given in Figure 7.4. If your system does not follow the standard, the ranges may be different.

3. Following the literal value a **floating-point type-specifier** may be used, just as for integers. (This letter is not the same as the conversion specifier of an I/O format.) The specifiers `f` and `F` designate a `float`, while `l` and `L` designate a `long double`. If a floating-point literal has no type specifier, it is a `double`.

Figure 7.5 shows some examples of floating-point literals and the actual number of bytes used to store them.

Literal	Type	Size in Common Implementations
3.14	double	8 bytes
1.05792e+05	double	8 bytes
65536E-4f	float	4 bytes
1.01F	float	4 bytes
.021	long double	8, 10, or 12 bytes
171.L	long double	8, 10, or 12 bytes

Figure 7.5.   Floating-point literal examples

7.3   Reading and Writing Numbers

Two factors must be considered when choosing a format for reading a number: the type of the variable in which the value will be stored and the way the value appears in the input. Similarly, when printing a number, its type and the desired output format must be considered. In previous examples, we used only a few of the many possible formats for numeric input and output, which we now discuss.

7.3.1   Integer Input

Each type of value requires a different **I/O conversion specifier** in the format string. An integer conversion specifier starts with a `%` sign, followed by an optional field-width specifier (output only), and a code for the type of value to be read or written. Figure 7.6 summarizes the options available for signed[7] integers; the use of `%hi` and `%li` is illustrated by the program in Figure 7.17. The `%i` code is

Context	Conversion	Meaning and Use
`scanf()`	`%d`	Read a base-10 (decimal) integer (traditional C and ISO C)
	`%i`	Read a decimal or hexadecimal integer (ISO C only)
`printf()`	`%d`	Print an integer in base 10
	`%i`	Same as `%d` for output
`scanf()`, `printf()`	`%hi` or `%hd`	Use a leading `h` for `short int`
`scanf()`, `printf()`	`%li` or `%ld`	Use a leading `l` for `long int`

Note: The code for short integers is **h** instead of **s**, because **s** is used for strings (see Chapter 13).

Figure 7.6.   Integer conversion specifications.

---

[7]Input and output for unsigned numbers will be discussed in Chapter 18, which deals with hexadecimal notation and bit-level computation on unsigned numbers.

new in ISO C,[8] supplementing the traditional `%d`. With `%i`, input numbers can be entered in either decimal or hexadecimal notation (see Chapter 18), whereas `%d` works only for decimal (base-10) numbers. A representational error[9] will occur if an input value has more digits than the input variable can store. The faulty input will be accepted, but only a portion of it will be stored in the variable. The result is a meaningless number that will look like garbage when it is printed. When a program's output clearly is wrong, it always is a good idea to echo the input on which it was based. Sometimes, this uncovers an inappropriate input format or a variable too short to store the required range of values.

7.3.2   Integer Output

For output, the `%d` and `%i` conversion codes can be used interchangeably. We use `%i` in this text because it is more mnemonic for "integer" and therefore less confusing for beginners.

When designing the output of a program, the most important things to consider are that the information be printed correctly and labeled clearly. Sometimes, however, spacing and alignment are important factors in making the output clear and readable. We can control these factors by writing a **field-width** specification (an integer) in the output format between the `%` and the conversion code (`i`, `li`, or `hi`). For example, `%10i` means that the output value is an `int` and the printed form should fill 10 columns, while `%4hi` means that the output value is a `short int` and the printed form should fill 4 columns. If the given width is wider than necessary, spaces will be inserted to the left of the printed value. To print the number at the left edge of the field, a minus sign is written between the `%` and the field width, as in `%-10i`. The remainder of the field is filled with blanks.[10] If the width is omitted from a conversion specifier or if the given width is too small, C will use as many columns as are required to contain the information and no spaces will be inserted on either end (therefore, the effective default field width is 1). Using a field-width specifier allows us to make neat columns of numbers, as will be illustrated by the program in Figure 7.29.

7.3.3   Floating-Point Input

In a floating-point literal constant (Figure 7.5), a letter (called the **type specifier**) is written on the end to tell the compiler whether to translate the constant as a `float`, a `double`, or a `long double` value. An input format must contain this same information, so that `scanf()` will know how many bytes to use when storing the input value. In a `scanf()` format, the input conversion specifier

---

[8] Older compilers may not support `%i`.

[9] Other sources of representational error will be discussed in Chapter 8.

[10] A format string may specify a nonblank character to use as a filler.

for type **float** is **%g**; for **double**, it is **%lg**; and for **long double**, it is **%Lg**. Figure 7.7 summarizes the basic conversion specifiers for real numbers. For input, all the basic specifiers **%g**, **%f**, and **%e** have the same meaning and can be used interchangeably, although the current convention is to use **%g**.

The actual input value may be of large or small magnitude, contain a decimal point or not, and be any number of decimal digits long. The number will be converted to a floating-point value using the number of bytes appropriate for the local C translator. (Commonly, this is 4 bytes for **%g**, 8 bytes for **%lg**, and 8 bytes or more for **%Lg**.) However, sometimes, the number stored in the variable is not exactly the same as the input given. This happens whenever the input, when converted to binary floating-point notation, has more digits of precision (possibly infinitely repeating) than the variable can store. In this case, only the most significant digits are retained, giving the closest possible approximation.

7.3.4   Floating-Point Output

Output formats for real numbers are more complex than those of integers because they have to control not only the field width but also the form of the output and the number of significant digits printed. There are three basic choices of conversions: **%f**, **%e**, and **%g**. The **%f** conversion prints the value in ordinary decimal form, the **%e** conversion prints it in scientific notation, and the **%g** conversion tries to choose the "best" way to present the number. This may be similar to **%f**, **%e**, or even **%i**, depending on the size of the number relative to the specified field width and precision. Whatever precision is specified and whatever conversion code is used, floating-point numbers will be rounded to the last position printed.[11]

All three kinds of conversion specifiers (**%f**, **%e**, and **%g**) can include two additional specifications: the total field width (as described for an integer) and a precision specifier. These two numbers are written between the **%** and the letter, separated by a period, as in **%10.3f**. In addition, either the total field width or the

Context	Conversion	Meaning and Usage
scanf()	**%g**, **%f**, or **%e**	Read a number and store in a **float** variable
	%lg, **%lf**, or **%le**	Read a number and store in a **double** variable
	%Lg, **%Lf**, or **%Le**	Read a number and store in a **long double** variable
printf()	**%f**	Print a **float** or a **double** in decimal format
	%e	Print a **float** or a **double** in exponential format
	%g	Print a **float** or a **double** in general format

Figure 7.7.   Basic floating-point conversion specifications.

---

[11] Note that this is different from the rule for converting a real number to an integer, which will be discussed later in this chapter. During type conversion, the number is truncated, not rounded.

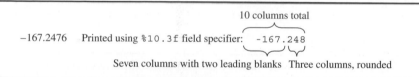

Figure 7.8.   The %f output conversion.

precision specifier can be used alone, as in **%10f** or **%.3f**. The default precision
is 6, and the default field width is 1 (as it is for integers). If the field is wider than
necessary, the unused portion will be filled with blank spaces.

The %f and %e conversions.   For the **%f** and **%e** conversions, the precision
specifier is the number of digits that will be printed after the decimal point. When
using the **%f** conversion, numbers are printed in ordinary decimal notation. For
example, **%10.3f** means a field 10 spaces wide, with a decimal point in the
seventh place, followed by three digits. An example is given in Figure 7.8.

In a **%e** specification, the mantissa is *normalized* so that it has exactly one
decimal digit before the decimal point, and the last four or five columns of the
output field are occupied by an exponent (an example is given in Figure 7.9). For
a specification such as **%.3e**, one digit is printed before the decimal point and
three are printed after it, so a total of four significant digits will be printed.

The %g conversion is unpredictable.   The result of a **%g** conversion can
look like an integer or the result of either a **%f** or **%e** conversion. The precision
specifier determines the maximum number of significant digits that will be printed.
The **printf()** function first converts the binary numeric value to decimal form,
then it uses the following rules to decide which output format to use. Here, assume
that, for a number N, with D digits before the decimal point, the precision specifier
is S.

- If $D == S$, the value will be rounded to the nearest integer and printed
  as an integer (an example is given in Figure 7.10).
- If $D > S$, the number will be printed in exponential format, with one digit
  before the decimal point and $S - 1$ digits after it (an example is given in
  Figure 7.11).

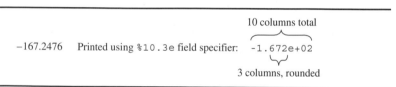

Figure 7.9.   The %e output conversion.

−167.2476   Printed using %10.3g field specifier: -167

10 columns total with three digits of precision.

Figure 7.10.   Sometimes %g output looks like an integer.

- If $D < S$ and the exponent is less than −4, the number will be printed in exponential format, with one digit before the decimal point and $S − 1$ digits after it.
- If $D < S$ and the exponent is −4 or greater, the number will be printed in decimal format with D digits before the decimal point and $S − D$ digits after it (an example is given in Figure 7.12).

In all four cases, the precision specifier determines the *total* number of significant digits printed, including any nonzero digits before the decimal point. Therefore, **%.3g** will print one less significant digit than **%.3e**, which always prints three digits after the decimal point. Also, **%.3g** may print several digits fewer than **%.3f**.

Finally, the **%g** conversion strips off any trailing zeros or decimal point that the other two formats will print. Therefore, the number of places printed after the decimal point is irregular. This leads to an important rule: The **%g** conversion is not appropriate for printing tables. Usually **%f** is used for tables, unless the values are of very large magnitude.

Figure 7.13 shows how the input values of 32.1786594, 2.3, and 12345678 might look if they were read into a **float** variable, and then printed in a variety of formats. Each input was read using **scanf()** with the **%g** specifier. The actual converted value stored in a **float** variable is shown beneath that. Output of these values was produced by **printf()**, using the conversion formats shown.

Notes on Figure 7.13. Output conversion specifiers.   When examining the various results, note the following details:

- *First line*. This line shows the values entered from the keyboard. In the first column, we input more than the six or seven significant digits that a **float** variable can store; the result is that the last digits of the internal value (on the next line) are only an approximation of the input.

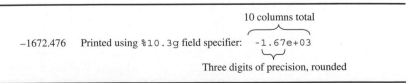

10 columns total

−1672.476   Printed using %10.3g field specifier: -1.67e+03

Three digits of precision, rounded

Figure 7.11.   Sometimes %g looks like %e.

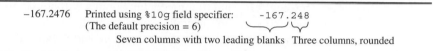

−167.2476   Printed using %10g field specifier: −167.248
              (The default precision = 6)
                        Seven columns with two leading blanks   Three columns, rounded

Figure 7.12.   Sometimes %g looks like %f.

- *Second line*. This line shows the actual values stored in three **float** variables. Due to the limited number of bits, the first two values cannot be represented exactly inside the computer. This may not seem surprising for the first value, since a **float** has only six digits of precision, but even the value of 2.3 is not represented exactly. This is because, just as there are repeating fractions in the decimal system (like 1/7), when certain decimal values are converted into their binary representation, the result is a repeating binary fraction. The stored internal value of 2.3 is the result of **truncating** this repeating bit sequence. By chance, even though it is more than six digits long, the third value, 12345678, could be represented exactly. Even though the stated level of precision is six decimal digits, longer numbers sometimes can be represented exactly, while some shorter ones can only be approximated.
- *Main portion of table.*
    1. All output values are rounded to the last place that is printed.
    2. An output too wide for the field is printed anyway, it just overflows its boundary, as in some of the values in the last column.
    3. The **default output precision is six decimal places**, so you get six digits after the decimal point with %f and %e unless you ask for more or fewer. With %g, you get a maximum of six significant digits.
    4. The %g conversion specifier works similar to %f for numbers that are not too large or too small. The primary differences are that

Input at keyboard	%g	32.1786594	2.3	12345678
Internal bit value		32.17865753173828125	2.2999999523162841796875	12345678
Output using	%f	32.178658	2.300000	12345678.000000
	%e	3.217866e+01	2.300000e+00	1.234568e+07
	%g	32.1787	2.3	1.23457e+07
	%.3f	32.179	2.300	12345678.000
	%.3e	3.218e+01	2.300e+00	1.235e+07
	%.3g	32.2	2.3	1.23e+07
	%10.3f	32.179	2.300	12345678.000
	%-10.3f	32.179	2.300	12345678.000

Figure 7.13.   Output conversion specifiers.

trailing zeros and trailing decimal points will not be printed and that the precision specifies significant digits, not actual digits after the decimal point. For very large and very small numbers, `%g` works almost like `%e` except that one fewer significant digit will be printed. Therefore, the number 12345678 printed in `%.3e` becomes 1.235e+07, but printed in `%.3g`, it is 1.23e+07.

The programs in Figures 7.21 and 7.28 illustrate some ways in which format specifiers can be used to achieve desired output results. To get a good sense of what the C language does with different floating-point types, experiment with various input values and changing the formats in these programs.

Alternate output conversion specifiers (advanced topic).   Some compilers will accept `%lg` (or `%lf` or `%le`) in a `printf()` format for type `double`. However, `%g` is correct according to the standard and it is poor style to get in the habit of using nonstandard features. The standard is clear on this issue. All `float` values are converted to type `double` when they are passed to the standard library functions, including `printf()`. By the time `printf()` receives the `float` value, it has become a `double`. So `%g` is used with `printf()` when printing both `double` and `float` values.

However, this is not true for `scanf()`. According to the ISO C standard, you *must* use `%g` for `float`, `%lg` for `double`, and `%Lg` for `long double` in input formats.

7.4   Integer Operations

Modern computers have two separate sets of machine instructions that perform arithmetic: one for integers, the other for floating-point numbers. We say that the operators, `*`, `/`, `+`, and `-`, are *generic*, because they have more than one possible translation. When a C compiler translates a generic operator, it uses the types of the operands to select either an integer or a floating-point operation. The compiler will choose integer operations when both operands are integers; the result will also be an integer. In all other cases, a floating-point operation will be chosen.

7.4.1   Integer Division and Modulus

Division.   Like the other arithmetic operators, the division operator `/` is generic; its meaning depends on the types of its operands. However, each of the operators `*`, `+`, and `-` symbolizes a single mathematical operation, even though it is performed in two different ways on the two kinds of number representations. In contrast, `/` represents two different mathematical operations: **real division** (where the answer has a fractional part) and **integer division** (where there are two parts of the answer, the quotient and the remainder). Here, the instruction used makes a significant difference. With floating-point operands, only real division is meaningful. However, with integer operands, both real and integer division are useful and a programmer might wish to use either one. In C, if both operands are integers, the integer quotient is calculated and the remainder is forgotten. A programmer who needs the remainder of the answer can use the modulus operator, %, which is described shortly. If the entire fractional answer is needed, one of the operands must first be converted to floating-point representation. (Data type conversion techniques are covered later in this chapter.)

Division by 0. Attempting to **divide by 0** will cause an error that the computer hardware can detect. In most cases, this error will cause the program to terminate.[12] It always is wise to check for this condition before doing the division operation in order to make the program as robust as possible; that is, it does something sensible even when given incorrect data.

Indeterminate answers (optional topic). A further complication of integer division is that the C standard allows two different correct answers for x/y in some cases. When x is not an even multiple of y and either is negative, the answer can be the integer either just larger than or just smaller than the true quotient (this choice is made by the compiler, not the programmer). This indeterminacy is provided by the standard to accommodate different kinds of hardware division instructions. The implication is that programs using division with signed integers may be nonportable because the answer produced depends on the hardware. This "feature" of the language is worse in theory than in practice; we tested C compilers running on a variety of hardware platforms and found that they all truncate the answer toward 0 (rather than negative infinity). However, the careful C programmer should be aware of the potential problem here.

Modulus. When integer division is performed, the answer has two parts: a quotient and a remainder. C has no provision for returning a two-part answer from one operation, so it provides two operators. The **integer modulus** operator, named *mod* and written %, performs the division and returns the remainder, while / returns the quotient. Figure 7.14 shows the results of using % for several positive values; Figure 7.15 is a visual presentation of how mod is computed. Note the following properties of this operator:

- Mod is defined for integers x and y in terms of integer division as: $x \% y = x - y \times (x/y)$.
- If x is a multiple of y, the answer is 0.
- If x is smaller than y, the answer is x.
- The operation $x \% y$ is a cyclic function whose answer (for positive operands) always is between 0 and $y - 1$.

---

[12]More advanced techniques, beyond the scope of this book, can be used to take special action after the termination.

x	y	x % y		x	y	x % y
10	3	1		3	10	3
9	3	0		3	9	3
8	3	2		7	2873	7
7	3	1		7	7	0
6	3	0		7	1	0
5	3	2		7	0	Undefined

Figure 7.14.   The modulus operation is cyclic.

- This operator has no meaning for floating-point operands.
- If y is 0, x % y is undefined. At run time a division by 0 error will occur.
- The results of / with negative values is not fully defined by the standard; implementations may vary. For example, $-5/3$ can equal either -1 (the usual answer) or -2. Since the definition of % depends on the definition of /, the result of x % y is indeterminate if either x or y is negative. Therefore, **-5** % **3** can equal either -2 or 1.

A program that uses integer / and % is given in the next section, and one that uses the % operator to help format the output into columns as in Figure 7.29.

7.4.2   Applying Integer Division and Modulus

We normally count and express numbers in base 10, probably because we have 10 fingers. However, any number greater than 1 can be used as the base for a positional notation.[13] Computers use base 2 (binary) internally and the C language lets us write numbers in bases 8 (octal) and 16 (hexadecimal) as well as

---

To calculate **a** % **b**, we distribute **a** markers in **b** columns. The answer is the number of markers in the last, partially filled row. (If the last row is filled, the answer is 0.)

```
operation:  12 % 5        15 % 5        4 % 5        5 % 4        10 % 4
            ---------------------------------------------------------------
            x x x x x     x x x x x     x x x x .    x x x x     x x x x
            x x x x x     x x x x x                  x . . .     x x x x
            x x . . .     x x x x x                              x x . .
            ---------------------------------------------------------------
answer:     1 2 3 4 0     1 2 3 4 0     1 2 3 4 0    1 2 3 0     1 2 3 0
                  ↑                 ↑            ↑    ↑                ↑
```

Figure 7.15.   Visualizing the modulus operator.

---

[13]Theoretically, negative bases can be used, too, but they are beyond the scope of this text.

base 10 (decimal). These number representations and the simple algorithms for converting numbers from one base to another are described in Appendix E. The next program shows how one can use a computer to convert a number from its internal representation (binary) to any desired base. The algorithm used is based on the meaning of a positional notation:

- Each digit in a number represents a multiple of its place value.
- The place value of the rightmost position is 1.
- The place value of each other position is the base times the place value of the digit to its right.

Therefore, given a number N (in the computer's internal representation) and a base B, `N % B` is the digit whose place value is $B^0 = 1$ when expressed in positional notation using base B. We can use these facts to convert a number N to the equivalent value N' in base B.

The algorithm is a simple loop that generates the digits of N' from right to left. On the first pass through the conversion loop, we compute `N % B`, which is the rightmost digit of N'. Having done so, we are no longer interested in the 1's place, so we compute $N = N/B$ to eliminate it and prepare for the next iteration. We continue this pattern of using `%` to generate digits and integer division to reduce the size of N until nothing is left to convert. An example is given in Figure 7.16, and a program that implements this algorithm is in Figure 7.17.

Notes on Figure 7.17. Number conversion.

- *First box: selecting the right data type.*

    1. We have restricted the acceptable number bases to the range 2...10, which restricts the possible digits to the range 0...9. We use type

---

Any number N can be expressed in positional notation as a series of digits:

$$N = \ldots D_3 D_2 D_1 D_0$$

If the number's base is B, then each digit is between 0 and $B - 1$ and the value of the number is

$$N = \ldots B^3 \times D_3 + B^2 \times D_2 + B^1 \times D_1 + D_0$$

Now, if $N = 1234$ and $B = 10$, we can generate all the digits of N by repeatedly taking `N % B` and reducing N by a factor of B each time:

$$
\begin{aligned}
D_0 &= 1234 \;\%\; 10 = 4 & N_1 &= 1234/10 = 123 \\
D_1 &= 123 \;\%\; 10 = 3 & N_2 &= 123/10 = 12 \\
D_2 &= 12 \;\%\; 10 = 2 & N_3 &= 12/10 = 1 \\
D_3 &= 1 \;\%\; 10 = 1 & N_4 &= 1/10 = 0
\end{aligned}
$$

Figure 7.16.   Positional notation and base conversion.

Convert an integer to a selected base and print it using place-value notation.

```
#include "tools.h"
void main( void )
{
    long n;            /* input: the number to convert */
    short base;        /* input: base to which we will convert n */
    short rhdigit;     /* right-hand digit of n-prime */
    int power;         /* loop counter */

    banner();

    printf( " Read an integer and express it in a given base.\n"
            " Please enter a base between 2 and 10: " );
    scanf( "%hi", &base );
    if (base < 2 || base > 10) fatal( " Base is not in required range." );

    printf( " Enter the number to convert: " );
    scanf( "%li", &n );
    if (n < 1) fatal( " Number must be greater than 0." );

    /* ------------ Generate digits of converted number, right to left. */
    for (power = 0; n != 0; ++power) {
        if (power == 0) {           /* Echo input before first term, */
            printf( "%12li = ", n );
        }
        else {                      /* and print a + before other terms. */
            printf( "             + " );
        }
        rhdigit = n % base;     /* Isolate right-hand digit of n.    */
        n /= base;              /* then eliminate right-hand digit. */

        printf( "%hi * %hi^%i \n", rhdigit, base, power );
    }

    bye();
}
```

Figure 7.17.   Number conversion.

short int for the variables **base** and **rhdigit** because they store only very small numbers.

2. We use **long int** for the number to be converted because it allows a greater range of possible inputs than type **short** and (on some machines) type **int**.

3. We use type `int` for the loop counter, because we do not need large values and type `int` is supposed to be the most time efficient of the integer types on the local machine.

- *Second box: selecting a valid base and the number to convert.*

  1. This algorithm could be used to convert a number to any base. We demonstrate it here only for bases of less than 10 because we wish to focus attention on the conversion algorithm, not on the representation of digits greater than 9.
  2. We use 2 as the minimum base value; 1 and 0 cannot be used as bases for a positional notation.
  3. The following output shows an example of error handling:

```
Read an integer and express it in a given base.
  Please enter a base between 2 and 10: 0
  Base is not in required range.

Error exit; press '.' and 'Enter' to continue.
```

- *Third box (outer): converting to the selected base.*

  1. We start by generating the coefficient of B^0, so we set **power** = 0. After each iteration, we increment **power** to prepare for converting the coefficients of B^1, B^2, and so forth.
  2. We reduce the size of N on each iteration by dividing it by the target base; we continue until N is reduced to 0.
  3. Note that a loop test need not always involve the loop counter; it is necessary only that the value being tested change somewhere within the loop.
  4. We first print the number itself (in base 10) and then an = sign before the first term of the answer. We indent and print a + before all other terms.

- *Inner box: decomposing the number, digit by digit.* As explained, we use `%` to generate each digit of N'. Then we use integer division to reduce N by removing the extracted digit and shifting the others one position to the right. This prepares N for the next iteration. Real division would not work here; the algorithm relies on the fact that the remainder is discarded.
- Two examples of the output are

```
Read an integer and express it in a given base.
Please enter a base between 2 and 10: 10
Enter the number to convert: 143
        143 = 3 * 10^0
            + 4 * 10^1
            + 1 * 10^2
```

```
Read an integer and express it in a given base.
Please enter a base between 2 and 10: 6
Enter the number to convert: 143
        143 = 5 * 6^0
            + 5 * 6^1
            + 3 * 6^2
```

7.5   Mixing Types in Computations (Advanced Topic)

Since we have introduced both the integer and floating-point data types that are typically used in calculations, it is time to discuss how to use them effectively and convert values from one data type to another.

7.5.1   Basic Type Conversions

Two basic types of data conversion can occur, a length conversion and a representation conversion. The **length conversion** occurs between two values of the same data category; that is, between two integers or between two reals. These are **safe conversions** if they lengthen the data representation and thereby do not introduce any representational error. For example, any number that can be represented as a `float` can be represented with exactly the same precision using the `double` type. **Unsafe conversions** may happen if the data representation is shortened.

A **representation conversion** involves switching between two categories, from integer to real or real to integer. Even in systems where a `float` value and an integer value have the same number of bits, their patterns are very different and incompatible. The computer hardware cannot add a `float` to a `long`—one of them must first be converted to the other representation. Depending on the direction of the conversion, it might be classified as safe or not. Therefore, let us examine the basic properties of type conversions more closely.

Safe conversions.   Converting from a "short" version of a data type to a "long" version is considered to be a safe operation. All the bits stored in the shorter version still can be stored in the longer form, with extra padding in the appropriate positions. Converting from a longer form to a shorter one may or may not be safe. For integers, if the magnitude of the value in the longer form is within the representation range of the shorter one, everything is fine. For real numbers, not only must the magnitude be within the proper range, but the number of significant digits in the mantissa must be small enough as well.

Converting from a `float` to a `double` is safe but the effects can be misleading. The value is lengthened, but it does not increase in precision. A `float` has six or seven decimal places of precision, and the precision of a lengthened value will be the same; the extra bits in the **double** representation will be meaningless zeros. For example, one-tenth is an infinitely repeating fraction in binary. We can store only a finite portion of this value in a **double** and even less in a **float**. Consider the code in Figure 7.18. We initialize both **f** and **d** to 0.1. In both cases, the number actually stored in the variable is only an approximation to 0.1. However, the approximation stored in **d** is more precise. It is accurate up to the 17th place after the decimal point, while **f** is accurate only up to the 8th place. When the value of **f** is converted to type **double** and stored in **x**, it still is accurate only to eight places. The precision does not increase because there is no opportunity to recompute the value and restore the lost bits.

Converting from an integer type to a floating-point type usually is safe, in the sense that most integers can be represented exactly as **floats** and all can be represented exactly as **doubles**. The opposite is not true; most floating-point values cannot be represented exactly as integers.

Unsafe conversions.   When a value of one type is converted to a shorter type, the number being converted can be too large to fit into the smaller type. We call this condition **representation error**. This is handled quite differently for integers and floating-point numbers.

When a large integer is converted to a smaller integer type, only the *least* significant bits are transferred, resulting in garbage. Converting a negative signed number to an unsigned type is logically invalid. Similarly, it is a logical error to convert an unsigned integer to a signed type not long enough to contain the value. The programmer must be careful to avoid any type conversions of this nature, because the C system gives little or no help with detecting the error. Some

```
#include <stdio.h>
void main( void )
{
    float  f = 0.1;   /* Precision limited to about 7 decimal places. */
    double d = 0.1;   /* Precision limited to about 15 decimal places. */
    double x = f;     /* Converted float; same precision as original value. */

    printf( "0.1 as a float  = %.17f\n", f );
    printf( "0.1 as a double = %.17f\n", d );
    printf( "0.1 converted from float to double = %.17f\n", x );
}
```

Output:

```
        0.1 as a float  = 0.10000000149011612
        0.1 as a double = 0.10000000000000001
        0.1 converted from float to double = 0.10000000149011612
```

Figure 7.18.   Converting a float **to a** double.

compilers will display a warning message when potentially unsafe conversions are discovered, others will not. At run time, if such an error happens, no C system will stop and give an error comment.

The shortening action that happens when a **double** value is converted to a **float** has two potential problems. First, it truncates the mantissa, discarding up to nine decimal digits of precision. Second, if the exponent of the value is too large for type **float**, the number cannot be converted at all. In this case, the C standard does not say what will happen; the result is "undefined" and you cannot expect the C system to warn you that this problem has occurred. If it happens in a program, you might observe that some of the output looks like garbage or that certain values are displayed as **Infinity** or **NaN**.[14]

When a floating-point number is converted to an integer type, the fractional part is lost. To be precise, it is *truncated*, not rounded; the fractional part is discarded, even if it is .999999. To maintain the maximum possible accuracy in calculations, C avoids converting floating-point values to integer types and does so only in four situations, which are listed and explained in the next section. Remember that, in these cases, rounding does not happen, so the floating-point value **1.999999999** will be converted to **1**, not to **2**.

A last source of unsafe conversions is the use of incorrect conversion specifiers in a **scanf()** statement. For example, using a **%g** (for **float**) in a **scanf()** format when you need **%lg** (for **double**) will not be detected by most compilers as an error. On these systems, the faulty program will compile with no warnings but will not run correctly. It will read the data from the keyboard and convert it into the representation indicated by the format. The corresponding bit pattern, whether the right length or not, will be stored into the waiting memory location without further modification. This will put the wrong information into the variable and inevitably produce garbage results.

7.5.2   Type Casts and Coercions

All the different conversions just mentioned can be invoked explicitly by the programmer by writing a type cast. They might also be produced by the compiler because of a type-mismatch in the program code; we call this **type coercion**.

Type casts.   A **type cast** is an explicit operation that performs a type conversion. A cast is written by enclosing a type name in parentheses and writing this unit before either a variable name or an expression. Any type name can be made into a cast and used as an operator in an expression. Technically, a type cast is a unary operator with precedence lower than all other unary operators but higher than all the binary operators. When applied to an operand, it tells the system to convert the operand to the named type, if possible. Sometimes this adjusts the

---

[14]More is said about these error conditions in Chapter 8.

length of the operand, sometimes it alters the representation, and sometimes it just changes the type labeling. Examples of casts are shown in Figure 7.19.

A cast from a floating-point type to an integer type truncates the value; it does not round to the nearest integer. If rounding is needed, it must be done explicitly, by adjusting the floating-point value before the conversion is done. The standard C library has no function for this purpose, so a `round()` function is included in the `tools` library. This function is shown in Figure 7.20 and calls on it are shown in Figure 7.21.

Figure 7.21 also contains a simple example of how information can be lost unintentionally during type conversions. We start with a `float` value, convert it into an `int`, and then convert it back again. The values of `y` and `x` are different because information was lost when the value of `y` was cast to `int`. That information cannot be recovered by converting it back again.

Notes on Figure 7.21. Rounding and casting.

- *First box: rounding.* This box contains two calls on `round()`; the output, which follows, demonstrates that it works correctly on both positive and negative numbers.

```
Rounding: y=  17.70  m=  18
Rounding: z= -17.70  n= -18
Casting:  y=  17.70  k=  17  x=  17.00
```

- *Second and third boxes: casting.* The `double` value of `y` is cast to type `int` and stored in `k`. This truncates the fractional part of the number, which is lost permanently. If we then take the value of `k` and cast it back

---

These examples of casts use the following declarations:

```
float x;     double t;        long k;        unsigned v;
```

The starred casts can cause run-time errors that will not be detected by the system and may cause the user's output to be meaningless.

	Cast	Nature of Change
*	`(float)t;`	Shortening (possible precision loss, magnitude too large)
	`(double)x;`	Lengthening (safe)
	`(double)t;`	No change (this is legal)
	`(float)k;`	Representation conversion (usually safe)
	`(int)x;`	Representation conversion (fractional part is lost)
*	`(short)k;`	Shortening (error if value of **k** is larger than 32,767)
*	`(signed)v;`	Type relabeling only (error if **v > INT_MAX**)
*	`(unsigned)k;`	Type relabeling only (error if **k** is negative)

Figure 7.19.   Kinds of casts.

This function rounds its argument to the nearest integer. It is included in the **tools** library.

```
/* --------------------------- Round a double to the nearest integer. */
int
round( double d )
{
    if (d >= 0.0) return (int)(d + 0.5);
    else          return (int)floor(d + 0.5);
}
```

Figure 7.20.   How to round.

to type **double**, the fractional part is not restored. Once it is gone, it is gone. The third line of the preceeding output demonstrates these results.

Automatic type coercion.   All of the arithmetic operators defined in Figure 4.5, except **%**, can be used with floating-point types. Within the representational limits of the computer, these operators implement the mathematical operations of addition, subtraction, multiplication, and division. If both operands are **float**s, the result is a **float**. If both are **double**s, the result is a **double**. The results of mixing different types of operands in an expression is discussed in the next section.

This program demonstrates how to use the **round()** function from the **tools** library, the syntax for type casts, and the effects of rounding and casting.

```
#include "tools.h"

void main( void )
{
    double x, y = 17.7, z = -17.7;
    int k, m;

    m = round( y )    /* Round y to nearest integer. */
    n = round( z );   /* Round z to nearest integer. */

    printf( "Rounding: y= %6.2f   m= %3i \n", y, m );
    printf( "Rounding: z= %6.2f   n= %3i \n", z, n );

    k = (int) y ;      /* Casting float to int truncates. */

    x = (double) k ; /* Casting back does not restore the fractional part. */

    printf( "Casting: y= %6.2f   k= %3i   x= %6.2f\n", y, k, x );
}
```

Figure 7.21.   Rounding and casting.

A type coercion is a type conversion applied by the compiler to make sense of the types in an expression. C will insert the conversion code before it compiles the operation that requires it. However, it is not wise to depend on coercion unless you are sure that the resulting conversion will be safe. Coercions happen in three basic cases:

1. When the type of the value in a **return** statement does not match the type declared in the function's prototype. If you are performing your calculations carefully, this case should not happen often. For instance, in Figure 7.20, if the explicit type cast (**int**) were removed, the **double** value would be coerced to type **int** during the function-return process.

2. When the type of an argument to a function does not match the type of the corresponding parameter in the function's prototype. Many of the functions in the math library have **double** parameters and frequently **int** or **float** arguments are passed to them. This is seen in Figure 7.22, line C, where the **float** value of **x** is coerced to type **double**. This kind of coercion may be safe or unsafe.

3. When an arithmetic or comparison operator is used with operands of mismatched types, such as

   (a) When the value of an expression is being saved into a variable using an assignment statement, as in Figure 7.22, line A. This conversion from the expression type (**float**) to the target type (**int**) is

---

This program demonstrates the effects of some type coercions. Unlike the program in Figure 7.21, automatic type conversions (not explicit casts) cause the values to change here.

```c
#include <stdio.h>
#include <math.h>

void main( void )
{
    float t, w; float x = 17.7;
    int k;

    k = x;          /* A. The = coerces the float value to type int. */
    t = k + 1.0;    /* B. The + coerces value of k to type double. */
                    /*    The = coerces the sum back to float. */
    w = sin( x );   /* C. Calling sin() coerces x to type double and */
                    /*    = coerces the double result of sin() to float. */
    printf( "x= %.2f   k= %3i   t= %.2f   w= %.2f\n", x, k, t, w );
}
```

The output is

```
x= 17.70   k=  17   t= 18.00   w= -0.91
```

Figure 7.22.   Type coercion.

automatic and performed whether safe or not. Examples of coercing a **double** value to type **float** are given in lines B and C. Note that neither of the explicit casts used in Figure 7.21 was necessary. The compiler would have coerced the values into the new formats automatically because a value of one type was being stored in a variable of a different type.

(b) When an operator has two real operands or two integer operands, but the operands have different lengths. The shorter value is converted to the type of the longer value, so that no information is lost. Therefore, **short** is converted to **int**, **int** to **long**, and **float** to **double**. The result of the operation will have the longer type.

(c) When an operator has operands of mixed representations, as in Figure 7.22, line B. The compiler must convert one value to the type of the other. The rule here is that the conversion always must be done safely, if possible. Therefore, the less inclusive type is converted into the more inclusive type (say, integer to **float** or **double**), so that usually no information is lost. Because of this, most expressions that have a real operand will produce a real result, and many of these are in the **double** format.

7.5.3   Diagramming Conversions

We use parse trees to help us understand the structure of expressions as well as to manually evaluate them. Since coercions and casts affect the results of evaluation, we need a way to show them in a parse tree. Both will be noted on a parse tree as small black squares. Figure 7.23 shows an example of each. Figure 7.24 diagrams casts and coercions within larger expressions.

The examples use these declarations:

```
int k;
double x = 3.14;
```

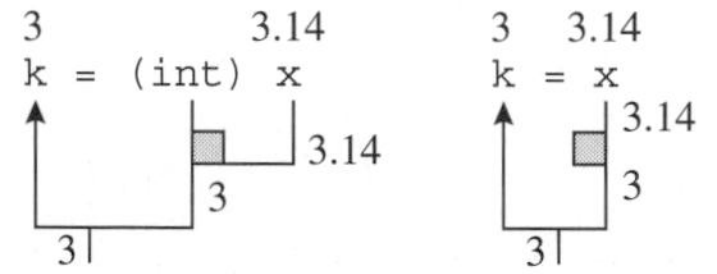

The diagram on the left is a cast; on the right is a coercion.

Figure 7.23.   Diagramming a cast and a coercion.

The examples use these declarations:

```
int k=3, r1=1, r2=2;  float w=1.57080;  double x, r_eq;
```

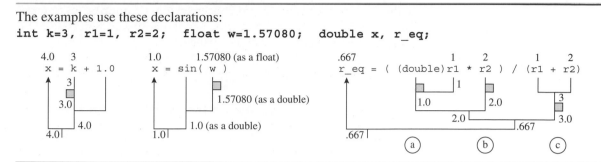

Figure 7.24.   Expressions with casts and coercions.

Notes on Figure 7.23. Diagramming a cast and a coercion.

- *Diagram on left: a cast.* A type cast is a unary prefix operator; we diagram it with the usual one-armed unary bracket. In addition, we write a black box on the bracket to denote a type conversion. In this example, the real value 3.14 is on the tree above the box; it is converted at the box and becomes the integer 3 below the box.
- *Diagram on right: a coercion.* When a real number is stored in an integer variable, it must be coerced first. We represent the coercion by a black box on a branch of the parse tree. Even though no cast is written here, the real value 3.14 above the box is converted at the box to become the integer 3 below the box. The result is the same as if it had been cast.

Notes on Figure 7.24. Expressions with casts and coercions.

- *Leftmost diagram: coercion of left operand of +.* The first operand of + is an **int**, the second is a **double** literal. The integer will be coerced to type **double** and real addition will be performed. The result is a **double** stored in **x** with no further conversion.
- *Middle diagram: coercion of an argument.* The trigonometric functions in the standard mathematics library are **double:double** functions whose arguments must be given in radians. Here we call **sin()** with a **float** argument, which is coerced to **double** before calling **sin()**. The result is a **double** that is stored in **x** with no further conversion.
- *Right diagram: a larger expression.* The formula from the third box in Figure 7.26 is diagrammed on the right. In this example, the operand **r1** is explicitly cast (a) from **int** to **double**. This forces the second operand **r2** to be coerced (b) so that real multiplication can happen, producing a **double** value for the numerator of the fraction. The result of the addition

in the denominator is an `int`; it is coerced to type `double` (c) to match the numerator. Real division is done and the `double` result is stored in `r_eq`, a `double` variable, with no change.

7.5.4   Using Type Casts to Avoid Integer Division Problems

As discussed earlier, division is an operation whose meaning is quite different for integers and reals; a programmer needs to be aware of these differences. At times, integer division (keeping only the quotient) is a desirable outcome; but at many other times, it is not. Often, even when dividing one integer by another, the fractional part of the answer is needed for the application. Therefore, be careful when writing expressions; divide one integer operand by another only when an integer answer is needed. Otherwise, one of the integers must be cast to a floating-point type before the division. Figure 7.26 illustrates an application in which the use of a cast operation on `int` values achieves the necessary precision in the answer.

A division application: Computing resistance.   Figure 7.25 is a simplification of the problem presented in Figure 4.27; it computes the equivalent resistance of two parallel resistors (rather than three). In Figure 7.26, we show how precision can be lost due to careless use of integer divison to calculate `r_eq`. Then we compare this answer to a second value calculated using floating-point variables.

Problem scope: Find the electrical resistance equivalent, r_{eq}, for two resistors wired in parallel.

Input: Two integer resistance values, r_1 and r_2.

Limitations: The resistances will be between 1 and 1,000 ohms.

Formula:

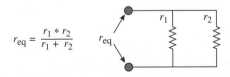

$$r_{eq} = \frac{r_1 * r_2}{r_1 + r_2}$$

Output required: The two inputs and their equivalent resistance.

Computational requirements: The equivalent resistance must be accurate to two decimal places.

Figure 7.25.   Problem specification: computing resistance.

We show how to use a type cast or coercion to solve the problem specified in Figure 7.25.

```
#include <stdio.h>
void main( void )
{
    int r1, r2;             /* integer input variables for two resistances */
    double r1d, r2d;        /* double variables for two resistances */
    double r_eq;            /* equivalent resistance of r1 and r2 in parallel */

    printf( "\n Enter integer resistances #1 and #2 (ohms): " );
    scanf( "%i%i", &r1, &r2 );
    printf( "    r1 = %i    r2 = %i \n", r1, r2 );


    r_eq = (r1 * r2) / (r1 + r2);              /* Oops!  Integer division. */
    printf( "    The truncated resistance value is %g\n", r_eq );


    r_eq = ((double)r1 * r2) / (r1 + r2);   /* Better:  we cast first. */
    printf( "    We cast to double first and get %g\n", r_eq );


    r1d = r1;                          /* Coerce to type double... */
    r2d = r2;                          /* by copying into double variables */
    r_eq = (r1d * r2d) / (r1d + r2d); /* and compute using doubles. */
    printf( "    The true value of equivalent resistance is %g\n", r_eq );
}
```

Figure 7.26.   Computing resistance.

Notes on Figure 7.26. Computing resistance.

- *First box: the input.*

  1. We use one prompt and one `scanf()` statement to read two input values; the format contains two `%` codes and we supply two addresses. As long as it is logical and causes no confusion, it is better human engineering to combine the inputs on one line, because this is faster and more convenient for the user.
  2. We use integer input here because we want to illustrate a potential problem with integer arithmetic. However, the inputs could have been read directly into **double** variables, avoiding the need for the casts or coercions demonstrated next.

- *Second box: the integer calculation.*

  1. Since **r1** and **r2** are integers, integer arithmetic will be used throughout the expression and the result will be an integer. The result will be

coerced to type `double` after the calculation and before being stored in `r_eq`. Two serious problems arise with this computation, as it is written, that can cause the answer to be less accurate than desired.

2. First, the programmer intended to have a real result. You might think that, since the answer is stored in a `double`, it would have a fractional part. But that is not how C works. It does not look at the context surrounding the division to find out what kind of division to perform; it looks only at the two operands, both of which are integer expressions in this case. For two integer operands, it performs integer division, so the fractional part of the result stored in `r_eq` will be 0.

3. Second, on a machine with 2-byte `int`s, the result of the multiplication could be a number too large to be represented as an `int`, even when the inputs are relatively small. If this occurs, the overall result will be wrong due to the overflow, a condition we discuss in Chapter 8.

- *Third box: using a cast.*

1. If any one of the original four operands or the resulting numerator or denominator is cast to a floating-point type, real division will be performed, as demonstrated by the fractional portion of the output.

2. Here we cast the first operand of the numerator to `double`, thereby causing real multiplication to be used. Integer addition still will be performed, however, because neither of the operands in the denominator was cast. The result of the addition will be coerced to type `double` before the division is done.

- *Fourth box: using `double` variables and coercion.*

1. The output from two runs of this program is shown below. The fractional parts of the correct answers are lost when integer division is used. However, correct answers are obtained when floating-point operations are performed.

2. When we assign a value to a variable of a different type, the compiler coerces the value to the type of the variable. The integer values entered into the program are transferred from `int` variables into `double` variables. This tells C to find the `double` representation of the numbers `r1` and `r2`. Since integers are a subset of the real numbers, this type conversion is usually safe.

- *Output.* Here is some sample output:

```
Enter integer resistances #1 and #2 (ohms): 20 24
   r1 = 20    r2 = 24

   The truncated resistance value is 10
   We cast to double first and get 10.9091
   The true value of equivalent resistance is 10.9091
```

```
Enter integer resistances #1 and #2 (ohms): 1 2
   r1 = 1     r2 = 2

The truncated resistance value is 0
We cast to double first and get 0.666667
The true value of equivalent resistance is 0.666667
```

7.5.5   Application of Mixed-Type Arithmetic: A Projectile

Figure 7.27 gives the specification for a program that calculates the horizontal
distance travelled by a ball shot out of a cannon. The resulting program is given
in Figure 7.28. Note that three different data types were chosen to represent the
various values. Since the input firing angle is given in whole degrees, an integer
was used. For those variables used to send arguments to or receive results from
the math library functions, the **double** type was appropriate. For the other input
and output values that did not require extended precision, **float** variables were
sufficient. We now discuss a few more of the program's details.

Notes on Figure 7.28. A projectile.

• *First box: the prompting.* The input prompts and responses for a sample
  run are

```
Enter the initial velocity (m/s): 25.36
Enter firing angle from the horizontal, in degrees: 20
```

• *Outer box: validating input.*

  1. The **if...else** sequence is used to verify that the input values
     are in the proper ranges before any calculations are performed.
  2. The first test checks whether the input angle is out of range. Since
     the value could be either too large or too small, two separate
     tests are combined using the logical OR operator. If the input
     is invalid, an error message is printed and no further processing
     occurs.
  3. A similar test ensures that the initial velocity is in the proper
     range.
  4. If both error tests fail, then all input is valid and the normal
     calculations are performed.
  5. A more robust program would use validation loops.

• *First inner box: mixed-type arithmetic.*

  1. The header file for the math library is included by **tools.h**, the
     header file for the **tools** library. The constants **PI** and **GRAVITY**
     also are defined there.

Problem scope: A solid ball is fired from a cannon at some angle, α, from the horizontal with a known initial velocity. Find the horizontal distance, x, that the ball will travel from the cannon, neglecting air friction (see following diagram).

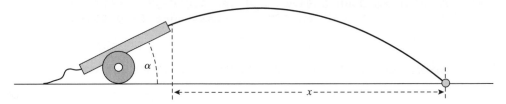

Inputs: α, the angle in whole degrees from the horizontal, and vel_0, the initial velocity in meters per second.

Constants required: π and G, the universal gravitational constant.

Formulas:

$$\alpha_{rad} = \alpha \times \frac{\pi}{180} \qquad\qquad \text{Firing angle, in radians}$$

$$vx = vel_0 \times \cos(\alpha_{rad}) \qquad \text{Initial horizontal velocity component}$$

$$vy = vel_0 \times \sin(\alpha_{rad}) \qquad \text{Initial vertical velocity component}$$

$$x = vx \times 2 \times \frac{vy}{G} \qquad\quad \text{Horizontal distance traveled}$$

Output required: Echo the inputs and print x, the horizontal distance traveled.

Computational requirements: The input angle will be a whole number, and the initial velocity will be a real number with no more than six digits of precision. The output should be printed to three decimal places.

Limits on inputs: The angle must be between 0° and 90°; the initial velocity will not exceed 100 meters per second.

Figure 7.27.   Problem specification: A projectile.

2. An **int** like **alpha** and a **double** constant like **PI** can be mixed in a formula. The **int** value automatically is coerced to type **double** before doing the multiplication. Similarly, the **float** value **vel_o** is converted to a **double** format before the computations.

3. The **sin()** and **cos()** functions are part of the standard ISO C math library. They compute the mathematical sine and cosine functions and return **double** answers. The input argument (an angle) is converted to type **double**, if necessary. Also the angle must be expressed in radians rather than degrees.

A solid ball is fired out of a cannon at some angle, **alpha**, from the horizontal. It has an initial velocity of **vel_o** meters per second. Find the distance, **x**, the ball will travel from the cannon.

```
#include "tools.h"

void main( void )
{
    int alpha;          /* firing angle of ball from horizontal, in degrees */
    float vel_o;        /* initial velocity in m/s */
    float x;            /* horizontal dimension of travel */
    double vx, vy;      /* x and y components of initial velocity */
    double a_rad;       /* angle alpha, in radians */
    double t;           /* time in seconds for ball to hit ground */

    banner();

    printf( "\n Enter the initial velocity (m/s): " );
    scanf( "%g", &vel_o );
    printf( " Enter firing angle from the horizontal, in degrees: " );
    scanf( "%i", &alpha );

    if (alpha < 0 || alpha > 90)        /* check for bad firing angle */
        printf( "Error: Firing angle must be in range 0..90 degrees." );
    else if (vel_o < 0 || vel_o > 100)  /* check for bad velocity */
        printf( "Error: Initial velocity must be in range 0..100 m/s." );
    else {                              /* inputs are valid */

        a_rad = alpha * PI / 180;       /* convert angle to radians. */
        vx = vel_o * cos( a_rad );      /* components of velocity. */
        vy = vel_o * sin( a_rad );

        t = 2 * vy / GRAVITY;           /* time of travel */
        x = vx * t;                     /* distance of travel */

        printf( "\n For initial velocity = %.3f m/s"
                "\n    and firing angle from the horizontal = %i degrees"
                "\n    The ball travels %.3f meters \n", vel_o, alpha, x );
        bye();
    }
}
```

Figure 7.28.   A projectile.

4. We do the intermediate computations with **double** values so
   that we maintain all possible precision. Every time a **double** is
   converted to a **float**, we risk losing precision.

5. Usually a calculation can be performed using **double** values and storing the final answer in a **float** variable. The answer automatically is shortened for you. This could be disastrous, though, if the number were too big (out of the range or too many significant digits) to fit into a **float**.

6. If **x** possibly could be larger than 10^{+38}, it would be better (safer) to declare **x** as a **double** variable. In this case, given the limitations in Figure 7.27, **x** cannot become that large. And since the final output is printed to only three decimal places, there is no worry about losing too much precision before printing the final answer.

- *Second inner box: the results.* Note that we print the answer with only three digits after the decimal point, which is appropriate for our input. When we use a **%.***n***f** specifier to print a **float** value, we should limit *n* to 7 because a **float** does not have more than six or seven places of precision. Given the preceeding input, the output from this box is

```
For initial velocity = 25.360 m/s
   and firing angle from the horizontal = 20 degrees
   The ball travels 42.155 meters
```

7.6   Pseudo-Random Numbers

7.6.1   Generating Random Numbers

Many computer applications (experiments, games, simulations) require the computer to make some sort of random choice. To serve this need, programs called *pseudo-random number generators* have been devised. These start with some arbitrary initial value (or values), called the **seed**, and apply an algorithm to generate another value that seems unrelated to the first. Then this first result will be used as the seed for the next value and so on, as long as the user wishes to keep generating values.

The numbers generated by these algorithms are called **pseudo-random numbers** because they are not really random but the output of an algorithm and an initial value. If the same algorithm is run again with the same starting point, the same series of "random" numbers will be produced. The goal, therefore, is to find an algorithm and a seed that will produce a long series of numbers with no detectable pattern and without duplicating the seed. Repeating a seed would cause the series to enter a cycle.

The C function **rand()** generates pseudo-random integers, which might be 2 or 4 bytes long, depending on the local definition of type **int**. (The actual range of values is 0 ... **RAND_MAX**, which is commonly the same as **INT_MAX**.) This function does not implement the best known algorithm but is good enough for many purposes. The function is found in the **standard** library; to use it you must

`#include <stdlib.h>`. Before calling `rand()` the first time, you must call another function, `srand()` to supply an initial seed value. This seed could be any integer value, such as a literal constant or a number entered by the user. However, in general, the user should not be bothered with selecting a seed, and a constant seed is undesirable because it always will result in the same pseudo-random series. (A constant seed can be useful during the debugging process so that error conditions can be repeated.) What therefore is needed for most applications is a handy source of numbers that are constantly changing and nonrepetitive. One such source is attached to most computers: the real-time clock. Therefore, it is quite common to read the clock to get an initial random seed. This technique is illustrated in Figure 7.29.

7.6.2   How Good Is the Standard Random Number Generator?

The next program generates a large quantity of random integers and counts the occurrences of 0. According to probability theory, if we generate numbers in the range $0 \ldots n - 1$, approximately $1/n$ of the values should be counted. No single program run can confirm whether the generator is fair. However, repeated trials or larger sample sizes will give some feeling for the quality of the random number generator being used. If the results are close to the expected value most of the time, the generator is performing well; otherwise, its behavior is questionable.

Notes on Figure 7.29. Generating random numbers.

- *First box: initializing the random number generator.*

    1. C provides a function in the `time` library that permits a program to read the system's real-time clock (if there is one). The return value of `time()` is an integer encoding of the time that has type `time_t` (an integer of some system-dependent length defined in `time.h`).
    2. The argument in the call to `time()` normally is the address of a variable where we want the time stored. The function `time()` stores the current time into the given address in the same way that `scanf()` stores an input value into a variable whose address is given to it.[15] However, this function also returns the same time value through the normal function return mechanism. Since we only need this information once, we use a special constant value, `NULL`, as the argument; this is legal and tells the function that we

---

[15] How this actually is done, using call by address, is discussed in Chapter 12.

We generate a series of pseudo-random numbers and print them in neat columns. When finished, we also print the number of zeros generated and the number expected, based on probability theory.

```
#include "tools.h"
#define HOW_MANY 500 /* Generate HOW_MANY random numbers */
#define NCOL 10        /* Number of columns in which to print the output. */
#define MAX 100        /* Upper limit on size of random numbers generated */
void main( void )
{
    long num;          /* a randomly generated integer */
    short select;      /* input:  upper limit on range of random numbers */
    short n;           /* # of random numbers generated */
    int count;         /* # of zeros generated */

    banner();

    srand( (unsigned) time( NULL ) );/* seed random number generator. */

    printf( " Generate %i random numbers in the range 0..n-1. \n"
            " Please choose n between 2 and %i: ", HOW_MANY, MAX );
    scanf( "%hi", &select );
    if (select < 2 || select > MAX) fatal( " Number is out of range." );

    /* Generate random numbers and test for zeros. -------------------- */

    count = 0;                        /* Count zeros generated. */
    for (n = 0; n < HOW_MANY; ) {     /* Generate HOW_MANY random numbers. */

        num = rand();                 /* Generate a random long integer. */
        num %= select;                /* Scale to range 0..select-1. */

        ++n;                          /* Count the trials and... */
        printf( "%5li", num );        /* ...print all numbers generated. */
        if (n % NCOL == 0) puts( "" ); /* End line every NCOL outputs. */

        if (num == 0) ++count;        /* ..count the zeros. */
    }

    if (count % NCOL != 0) printf( "\n" );   /* End last line of output. */
    printf( "\n %5i   zeros were generated.", count );
    printf( "\n %7.1f are expected on average.\n", HOW_MANY/(float)select );
    bye();
}
```

Figure 7.29.   Generating random numbers.

don't want a second copy of the information stored anywhere in memory.

3. Our purpose here is not to know the actual time. Rather, we use the clock as a convenient source of a seed for the random-number generator. A good seed is an unpredictable number that never is the same twice, and the time of day suits this purpose very well.

4. The type cast operator, **(unsigned)**, in front of the call on the **time()** function is used to convert the **time_t** value returned by the **time()** function into the **unsigned int** form expected by **srand()**. Using an explicit cast instead of the standard automatic coercion eliminates a compiler warning message on some systems.

- *Second box: data input and validation.* We eliminate divisors less than 2 because they are meaningless. We also set an arbitrary upper limit on the range of numbers that will be generated. Since the limit is relatively small, we can use a short integer to store it and there is space for printing many columns of numbers. Here is an example of the error handling:

```
Please choose n between 2 and 100: 1
Number is out of range.

Error exit; press '.' and 'Enter' to continue
```

A validation loop could be used here. We take the simpler approach of using **fatal()** because little effort has been invested so far in running this program and little is wasted by restarting it after an error.

- *Large outer box: generating and testing the numbers.* This loop calls **rand()** many times and collects some information about the results. With the constant definitions given, we will generate 500 integers in the range $0 \ldots n - 1$, where $n <= 100$. These numbers will be printed in 10 columns. Occurrences of 0 will be counted.

- *First inner box: generating the numbers.*

    1. The function **rand()** returns a number between 0 and **RAND_MAX**. According to the standard, this number may vary, but it is at least 32,767. We must scale this number to the desired range **0..n-1**.

    2. The modulus operator is exactly what we want for a scaling operation, since its result is between 0 and the modulus -1. We compute **num % select** and store the result back in **num**.

- *Second inner box: lines of output.*

    1. The counter **n** keeps track of the total number of random numbers produced so far.

    2. We want the output printed in columns, so we use a fixed field width in the conversion specifier: **%7li**. Ten columns, each

seven characters wide, will fit conveniently onto the usual 80-column line.

3. We want to print a '\n' after every group of NCOL numbers but not after every number. To do this, we count the output items as they are produced and print a newline character every time the counter is an even multiple of NCOL; that is, n % NCOL == 0.

● *Third inner box: counting the zeros.* To assess the "fairness" of the random-number generator, we can count the number of times a particular result shows up. If numbers in the range $0 \ldots n - 1$ are being generated, then each individual number should occur HOW_MANY / n times. In this program, we expect each number in the possible range $1 \ldots$ select-1 to occur approximately 500/select times. The following are the first and last lines of output from three runs. Note that the number of zeros generated on two of three trials differs substantially from the number expected. This is an indication that the rand() function does not produce a very even distribution of numbers on our computer.

```
Generate 500 random numbers in the range 0..n-1.
Please choose n between 2 and 100: 25
       7    19    24     8    18    20     8    10     4     5
       5    18    14    19     5    11    24    17    11     5
       ...
       2     0     5    21    22     3    21     7    23    18

      18    zeros were generated.
      20.0 are expected on average.
--------------------------------------------------------
Please choose n between 2 and 100: 33
       ...
      12    zeros were generated.
      15.2 are expected on average.
--------------------------------------------------------
Please choose n between 2 and 100: 33
       ...
      20    zeros were generated.
      15.2 are expected on average.
```

7.7   Application: A Guessing Game

In a classic game, one player thinks of a number and a second player is given a limited number of tries to guess it. The first player must say whether the guess is too small, correct, or too large. We illustrated a simple example of this game in Figure 6.18. Now, we implement the full game in the next program example, with the computer taking the part of the first player.

7.7.1   Strategy

Even if a person has never seen this game, it does not take long to figure out an optimal strategy for the second player:

- Keep track of the smallest and largest remaining possible value.
- On each trial, guess the number midway between them.

The computer's response to each guess will eliminate half the remaining values, allowing the human player to close relentlessly in on the hidden number.

Figure 7.30 illustrates a game in which the range is 1...1,000 and the hidden number is 458. The player makes an optimal sequence of guesses, halving the range of remaining values each time: 500, 250, 375, 437, 468, 453, 461, 457, 459, 458. In this example, 10 guesses are required to home in on the hidden number. In fact, with this strategy, this also is the maximum number of trials required to find any number in the given range. Half the time the player will be lucky and it will take fewer guesses. The code for the program that implements this game is given in Figures 7.31 (**main()**) and 7.32 (**one_game()**, which handles the sequence of guesses).

7.7.2   Playing the Game

Choosing and scaling the number.   We can call **rand()**, as was done in Figure 7.29, to get a number in the range **0..INT_MAX**. In this game, however, we require a random number between 1 and 1,000, so the number returned by **rand()** must be scaled and adjusted to fall within the desired range. To do this, we use the **%** (modulus) operator. For instance, **rand() % TOP** gives us a

---

In this example, the total range of possible values is 1...1,000. The hidden number, *num* = 458, is represented by a dashed line. The solid vertical lines represent the guesses of a player using an optimal strategy; only the first five guesses are shown.

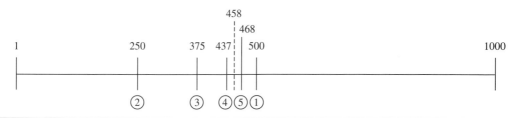

Figure 7.30.   Halving the range.

random number in the range (`0..TOP-1`). We then adjust it to the desired range simply by adding 1. This formula is used in the first box of Figure 7.32.[16]

Setting a limit on the number of guesses.   The strategy shown in Figure 7.30 is an example of an important algorithm called **binary search**,[17] because we search for a target value by dividing the remaining set of values in half. If N values were possible in the beginning, the second player always could discover the number in T trials or fewer, where $N \leq 2^T$. Another way to say this is that

$$T = \lceil \log_2 N \rceil$$

where $\lceil \ldots \rceil$ means that we round to the next higher integer. Paraphrased, the maximum number of trials required will be the base-2 logarithm of the number of possibilities, rounded up to the next larger integer. In our case, this is

$$\lceil \log_2 1000 \rceil = \lceil 9.96578 \rceil = 10$$

To introduce an element of luck into the game, set the maximum number of guesses to something smaller than T. This, in fact, is what we do in Figure 7.31; we round *down* instead of *up*, allowing too few guesses about half of the time. This "stacks" the game in favor of the computer.

Calculating a base-2 logarithm.   The C math library provides two logarithm functions: one calculates the base-10 log, the other the natural log (base e). Neither of these is what we want, but you can use the natural log function to compute the log of any other base, B, by the following formula:

$$\log_B(x) = \frac{\log_e(x)}{\log_e(B)}$$

In C, the natural log function is named `log()`, so to calculate the base-2 log of 1,000, we write

```
log( 1000 ) / log( 2 )
```

This formula is used in the second box of Figure 7.31.

Notes on Figure 7.31. Can you guess my number?

- *First box: guessing range.* In this game, the player will try to guess a number between 1 and `TOP`.

---

[16]For reasons too complex to explain here, this formula has a slight bias toward lower numbers in the range. However, if the range is small compared to **RAND_MAX**, the bias is insignificant.

[17]Other examples of binary search are given in Chapters 12 and 21.

This main program calls the function in Figure 7.32. It repeats the game as many times as the player wishes.

```
#include "tools.h"
void one_game( int tries );

#define TOP  1000                  /* Top of guessing range. */

void main( void )
{
    int do_it_again;                             /* repeat-or-stop switch */

    const int tries = log( TOP ) / log( 2 );    /* One too few. */

    banner();
    puts( "\n This is a guessing game.\n I will "
          "think of a number and you must guess it.\n" );

    srand( (unsigned)time( NULL ) );       /* seed number generator. */

    do {  one_game( tries );
          printf( "\n\n Enter 1 to continue, 0 to quit: " );
          scanf( "%i", &do_it_again );
    } while (do_it_again != 0);

    bye();
}
```

Figure 7.31.   Can you guess my number?

- *Second box: the number of trials.*

    1. We calculate `tries`, the maximum number of trials the user is allowed.
       It is defined as a **constant** because it depends only on `TOP` and does
       not change from one game to another. We use a **const** variable, rather
       than **#define**, because the definition is not just a simple number.[18]
    2. The result of the division operation is a **double** value that is coerced
       to type **int** when stored in `tries`.
    3. C permits us to use a formula to define the value of a constant. Such
       formulas can use literal constants (such as 2) and globally defined
       symbols (such as `TOP`). Inside a function definition, the parameter
       values also can be used in a constant expression.
    4. We calculate the base-2 logarithm of the number of possible hidden
       values and use this to set the maximum number of guesses. As de-
       scribed, we set this maximum so that the player will succeed about

---

[18]For reasons beyond the scope of this book, this is more efficient.

This function is called from Figure 7.31. It plays the number-guessing game once.

```
void
one_game( int tries )
{
    int k;                                        /* Loop counter. */
    int guess;                                    /* User's input. */

    const int num = 1 + rand() % TOP;             /* The hidden value. */

    printf( " My number is between 1 and %i;"
            " I will let you guess %i times.\n"
            " Please enter a guess at each prompt.\n", TOP, tries );

    for (k = 1; k <= tries; ++k) {
        printf( "\n Try %i: ", k );
        scanf( "%i", &guess );
        if (guess == num) break;
        if (guess > num) printf( " No, that is too high.\n" );
        else printf( " No, that is too low.\n" );
    }
    if (guess == num) printf( " YES!!  That is just right.  You win!  \n" );
    else printf( " Too bad --- I win again!\n" );
}
```

Figure 7.32.   Guessing a number.

half the time. The rest of the time, the player will be one guess short of success, even if he or she is using the optimal search strategy.

- *Third box: initializing the random number generator.* As in Figure 7.29, we initialize C's random number generator with the current time of day.

Notes on Figure 7.32. Guessing a number.   The one_game() function is called from main() in Figure 7.31 for each round of the game that the player wishes to play.

- *First box: the hidden number.* The first thing this function does is choose a hidden value. The value is defined as a constant because it does not change from the beginning of a round to the end of that round. In this case, the constant expression involves the value of a global constant. To calculate a random hidden number, we use the random number generator rand(), scaling and adjusting its value to the required range, as discussed earlier in this section.
- *Second outer box: playing the game.* The code in this box is almost identical to the earlier version in Figure 6.18. Correct guesses are handled

by an `if...break` in the inner box. When the loop exits, the program prints a failure message if the most recent guess was wrong.

- Here is some sample output (omitting output of `banner()`, the query loop, and `bye()`). The first two lines were printed by the main program, the rest of the dialog was printed by the `one_game()` function. In this sample game, the player was lucky and guessed the hidden number in only five tries. We expect this to happen only once in every 32 games.

```
This is a guessing game. I will think of a number and you must guess it.

My number is between 1 and 1000; I will let you guess 9 times.
Please enter a guess at each prompt.

Try 1: 500
No, that is too high.

Try 2: 250
No, that is too high.

Try 3: 125
No, that is too high.

Try 4: 62
No, that is too low.

Try 5: 93
YES!!  That is just right.  You win!
```

7.8   What You Should Remember

7.8.1   Major Concepts

Choosing the proper data type.

- *An integer type or a real type?* For most problems the details of the specification will make it rather obvious whether an integer or real data type should be used to represent a particular entity. Integers typically are used for such things as loop counters, simple quantities, menu choices, and answers to simple questions. Real variables more typically are used for measurements and mathematical calculations.
- *Type* `float` *vs.* `double`. Because a programmer can combine types `float` and `double` freely in expressions, most of the time, it does not matter which real type is used. Sometimes the degree of precision required for the data dictates the use of `double`. Since all the functions in the math library expect `double` arguments and return `double` results, some

programmers just find it easier to declare all real variables as **double**. However, two other important issues must be considered in choosing a data type: memory limitations and speed of execution. If you are processing large amounts of data and precision is not important, then **float** variables use only half as much space as **double**s and an **int** may use even less (depending on the compiler and computer system). If speed is of concern, integer arithmetic is performed more quickly than real computations on many machines. So if integers can be used, do so. Otherwise, in general, computations involving **float** values are faster than those using **double**s, due to the smaller amount of information (number of bits) being processed.

Representational properties.

- Integers come in many forms in C: **signed** and **unsigned**, **short** and **long**. An integer type permits us to represent a limited range of values exactly. The **short signed** integers can store numbers only up to 32,767. The largest **long signed** integer is 2,147,483,647. The largest **long unsigned** integer is 4,294,967,295. If numbers larger than this are needed, a floating-point type must be used.
- C supports floating-point numbers in two or three lengths. These types, named **float**, **double**, and **long double**, are used to represent real numbers. As with scientific notation, a floating-point number has an exponent that encodes the order of magnitude of the number and a mantissa that encodes the numeric value to a limited number of places of precision. The limits of floating-point representation were examined in Figure 7.4.
- The type **double** is the most important of the three floating-point types, because the C mathematics library is written to process **double** numbers (not **float** or **long double**) and does all its computations with **double**s. Type **float** exists to give the programmer a choice; **double** provides twice as much precision and a much larger range of exponents but takes twice as much storage space as **float** and may take twice as long to process in a computation. When memory space and processing time do not matter, many programmers use **double** because it provides more precision.
- Appendix E gives more detail about the floating-point number representations.

Computational issues.

- Integer division is not the same as division using real numbers; any remainder from an integer division is forgotten. The remainder, if needed, must be computed by using the modulus operator (**%**).
- There is some variation among compilers in the way floating-point types are handled. Sometimes the underlying computer hardware does not support floating-point arithmetic, in which case floating-point representation

and computation must be emulated by software. Emulation, of course, is much slower. Also, although all ISO C compilers must permit use of the type name **long double**, many simply make it a synonym for **double**.

Casts and mixed-type operations.

- C supports mixed-type arithmetic. Integer and floating-point types can be mixed freely in arithmetic expressions. When two values of differing types are used with an operator, the value with less precision automatically is coerced to the more precise representation.
- If an integer is combined with a **float** or a **double** in an expression, the integer operand always is converted to the type of the floating-point operand before the operation is performed; the result of the operation is a floating-point value.
- A type conversion may be "safe," in that it will cause no loss of information, or it may be "unsafe," because it can cause a loss of precision or simply result in total garbage. Knowing when a type conversion can be used safely is important. However, sometimes an unsafe conversion is exactly what the programmer needs.
- An explicit type cast must be used to perform real division with integer operands.

Random numbers.

- Applications such as games, experiments, and quiz programs require a program to make a series of randomized selections from a preset list of numbered options. To do this, we use an algorithm called a *pseudo-random number generator*, which generates a series of integers with no apparent pattern. The random number then is scaled to be in the proper range if it does not fall within the range of selection numbers.
- The **standard** library provides the functions **srand()** and **rand()**, which together implement a pseudo-random number generator.

7.8.2 Programming Style

- When using division or modulus, be sure that there is no possibility that the divisor is 0. Dividing by 0 causes an immediate program crash in many systems and produces incorrect results on others. If a 0 divisor is possible, test for it.
- It is appropriate to use integers for loop counters and customary to give them short names such as **j**, **k**, **m**, and **n**.
- Although the letters **i** and **l** have traditionally been used to name integer counters, they are poor choices, because they are easily mistaken for each other and for the numeral 1.

- Floating-point numbers traditionally have been given names starting with `f...h` and `r...z`.
- When implementing standard scientific or engineering formulas, it makes sense to use whatever variable names are used traditionally to express that formula, even when those names are single letters. Otherwise, use variable names long enough to convey the meaning or purpose of the variable.
- Use a `%f` conversion specifier if your output needs to be in neat columns. Use `%g` if you have no good idea whether the value to be printed is large or small. Use `%e` if the range of values is extreme.
- To print a table in neatly aligned columns, use a `%f` conversion specifier and include a field width. The `%g` conversion is not appropriate for tables.

7.8.3   Sticky Points and Common Errors

Operators.   The table in Figure 7.33 gives a brief summary of the difficulties that might be encountered when using C arithmetic operators and conversions.

Formats.   Using the wrong conversion specifier in a format can cause input or output to appear as garbage. Default length, `short`, and `long` integers have different conversion codes, as do `signed` and `unsigned` integers.

Group	Operators	Complications
Arithmetic	/	Division by 0 or 0.0 is undefined.
	/	Integer division is used if both operands are integers; the result is an integer. The fractional part is discarded.
	%	Not defined for floating-point values. For integers, the result is the remainder of an integer division.
	/, %	If both arguments are integers and one is negative, the result may be indeterminate.
Casts	(int)	Conversion from `double` or `float` will discard the fractional part.
	(short)	Conversion from a `long` will produce a garbage result if the value of the `long` is too great to fit into a `short`.
	(float)	Conversion from `int` is safe; from `double`, precision may be lost.
Coercions	=	Loss of precision does occur during assignment of a more-precise value to a less-precise variable.
	parameters	Argument values are coerced to match the declared types of the parameters.
	return values	The value returned by a function is coerced to match the declared function return type.

Figure 7.33.   Arithmetic operators and conversions in C.

Precision.   When using reals, there is no way to tell from the printed output whether a value came from a **double** or a **float** variable. If you specify a format such as **%.10f**, you might see 10 columns of nonzero digits printed, but that does not mean that all 10 are accurate. If the number came from a **float** variable, the eighth through tenth digits usually will be garbage. A similar problem happens when the precision specification of the output is made greater than the actual precision of the input. If an answer was calculated from input having two places of precision, all decimal positions in the output after the second will be meaningless. Remember that it is up to you to limit the columns of output to the precision of the number inside the machine or the known accuracy of the calculation, whichever is smaller.

Portability.   Some systems use 2 bytes to represent an **int**, others use 4 bytes. The two lengths of integers make portability of code a nightmare. Unless a programmer is aware of the different meanings of **int** and assiduously avoids relying on the size of his **int**s, it is very unlikely that his or her programs will run on each kind of machine without additional debugging. Furthermore, errors due to integer sizes are among the hardest to find because of the ever-present automatic size conversions all C translators perform.

It would be nice to avoid type **int** altogether and use only **short** and **long**. However, this is impractical because the integer functions in the C library are written to use **int** arguments and return **int** results. So what should the responsible programmer do?

1. Be aware.
2. Use **short** or **long** when the length is important in your application.
3. Do not rely on assumptions about the size of things.
4. Check all the possible data coercions and conversions and think about what can be done for those labeled *unsafe*.

7.8.4   New and Revisited Vocabulary

These are the most important terms and concepts discussed in this chapter:

representation range	scientific notation	type cast
integer literal	floating-point literal	type coercion
integer type specifier	floating-point type specifier	I/O conversion specifier
integer division	truncation	representational error
integer modulus	rounding	output field width
indeterminate results	safe conversions	default output precision
division by 0	unsafe conversions	constant expression
floating-point types	representation conversion	pseudo-random numbers
mantissa	length conversion	seed
exponent	2- and 4-byte models	binary search

The following types and conversion specifiers were discussed in this chapter:

`int`	`short int`	`float`
`i` and `d` conversions	`hi` and `hd` conversions	`long double`
`long int`	`signed int`	`e` and `le` conversions
`li` and `ld` conversions	`unsigned int`	`f` and `lf` conversions
`time_t`	`double`	`g` and `lg` conversions

The following operators, functions, prototypes, and library files were discussed in this chapter:

`const`	`limits.h`	`floor()`
`/` (operator)	`INT_MAX`	`log()`
`%` (operator)	`RAND_MAX`	`sin()`
`round()`	`float.h`	`cos()`
`stdlib.h`	`FLT_MIN`	int:int function
`srand()` and `rand()`	`FLT_MAX`	void:int function
`time.h`	`DBL_MIN`	int:double function
`time( NULL )`	`DBL_MAX`	int:void function

7.9   Exercises

7.9.1   Self-Test Exercises

1. The following functions and constants are all defined in the standard ISO C library or in the **tools** library. Name the specific header file that must be **#include**d to use each one. (Do not say **"tools.h"** if the function is in one of the standard libraries.)

   a. `time()`

   b. `fatal()`

   c. `INT_MAX`

   d. `srand()` and `rand()`

   e. `scanf()`

   f. `log()`

   g. `round()`

   h. `sin()` and `cos()`

2. What is the type of each of the following integer literals in a C compiler, where type **int** is the same length as type **short**? If the item is not a legal literal, say so.

   a. 33333

   b. 10U

   c. 32270

   d. −20

    e. 3000000000

    f. 100L

    g. 32,767

    h. 65432

3. We can represent all integer values using the **double** representation. List two situations in which we would still want to use the **int** data type.

4. Will the result of each of the following expressions be true or false? All variables are type **int**. Use the integer data values **k = 3, m = 9**, and **n = 5**.

    a. **m == k * 3**

    b. **k * (9 / k) == 9**

    c. **k * (n / k) == n**

    d. **k = n**

5. What will be stored in **k** or **f** by the following sets of assignments? Use these variables: **int h, k, m; float f; double g;**.

    a. **f=1.6;   k = f;**

    b. **f=1.4;   k = (int) f;**

    c. **g=5.1;   f = (float) g;**

    d. **g=9.6;   k = (float) g;**

    e. **g=9.7;   k = g + 1.8;**

    f. **h=13;   m=4;   f = (float) h / m;**

    g. **h=13;   m=4;   f = (float)(h / m);**

    h. **h=10;   m=3;   f = h / m + h % m;**

    i. **h=17;   m=5;   f = h / m;**

    j. **g=1.02;   f = 10.2   f == g * 10;**

6. Draw a parse tree for the following computation (include conversion boxes). Then use the tree to evaluate the expression. Use these variable declarations and initial values: **int k, j=70; double g=10.0; float f=32.08;**.

    k = g * (int) f + j;

7. Given the variable declaration **double x = 1234.5678;**, what is printed by the following statements?

    a. **printf("%e %f %g", x, x, x);**

    b. **printf("%10.3e %10.3f %10.3g %10.5g", x, x, x, x);**

8. Given the following variable declarations and input prompt, what is stored in **k, m, x,** or **d** by the following statements when the user enters the number shown on the left of each item? (If the result is garbage, say so.)

```
short int k;
long int m;
float x;
double d;
printf( " Please enter a number: " );
```

   a. 33   `scanf( "%hi", &k );`

   b. 33000   `scanf( "%hi", &k );`

   c. −44000   `scanf( "%li", &k );`

   d. 33   `scanf( "%li", &m );`

   e. 33   `scanf( "%g", &d );`

   f. 109e−02   `scanf( "%lg", &d );`

   g. 123.456789   `scanf( "%lg", &x );`

   h. −43.21098765   `scanf( "%f", &x );`

7.9.2   Using Pencil and Paper

1. Trace the execution of the following loop and show the actual output:

```
int num = 10;
while ( num > 5 ) {
    if ( num % 3 == 0 )   num -= num / 3;
    else if ( num % 3 == 1 )   num += 2;
    else if ( num % 3 == 2 )   num /= 3;
    else   num--;
    printf( "num = %i\n", num );
}
```

2. Draw a parse tree for the following computation (include conversion boxes). Then use the tree to evaluate the expression. Use these variable declarations and initial values:
`int k, j=10; double g=402.5; float f=32.08;.`

   `k = g - (int) f * j;`

3. Given the variable declarations, what is printed by the following statements?

```
int k = 1234;
float x = 1681.700612;
float y = 23.28765;
```

   a. `printf( "k =%i\n", k );`

b. `printf( "k =%10i\n", k );`

c. `printf( "k =%-10i\n", k );`

d. `printf( "x = %10.3f \n", x );`

e. `printf( "x = %10.4f \n", x );`

f. `printf( "x = %10.4e\n", x );`

g. `printf( "x = %.3g\n", x );`

h. `printf( "y = %.3g\n", y );`

4. Given the following variable declarations and input prompt, what is stored in **m**, **x**, or **d** by the statements when the user enters the number shown on the left of each item? (If the result is garbage, say so.)

```
long int m;
float x;
double d;
printf( " Please enter a number: " );
```

a. 33000   `scanf( "%li", &m );`

b. −44000   `scanf( "%hi", &m );`

c. 76.5   `scanf( "%g", &x );`

d. 5.12e20   `scanf( "%Lg", &d );`

e. −3000000033   `scanf( "%li", &m );`

f. 5,000,000,033   `scanf( "%li", &m );`

g. −3000000033   `scanf( "%li", &d );`

h. 333222111000.9   `scanf( "%lg", &d );`

5. Which operation (integer division or real division) will be used to evaluate each of the following divisions? Assume that **h**, **k**, and **m** are type **int** while **x** is type **double**.

a. `k = h / 3;`

b. `k = 3.14 / m;`

c. `x = h / m;`

d. `k = h / x;`

e. `h = x + k / m;`

f. `h = k + x / m;`

6. What will be stored in **k** by the following sets of assignments? All variables are integers.

a. `h=4;`   `m=5;`   `k = h % m;`

b. `h=14;`   `m=7;`   `k = h % m;`

   c. h=17;   m=5;   k = h / m;

   d. h=7;   m=-5;   k = h / m;

   e. h=10;   m=3;   k = h / m + h % m;

7. Show the output produced by the following program. Be careful about spacing.

```c
#include <stdio.h>
void main(void)
{
    int i = 0;
    float x = 1.2959;

    while (i < 4) {
        printf( "%6.2e %6.2f %6.2g \n", x, x, x );
        x *= 10;
        i++;
    }
}
```

7.9.3 Using the Computer

1. Turf.
   You are a building contractor. As part of a project, you must install artificial turf on some sports fields and the adjacent areas. The owner has supplied length and width measurements of the field in yards and inches. Your supplier sells turf in 1-meter-wide strips that are 4 meters long. Write a program that will prompt the user for a pair of measurements in yards and inches (use integers). Convert each to meters and print the answer with one decimal place of accuracy. (There are 39.37008 inches in a meter.) Calculate the number of strips of turf needed to cover the field. Round upward if a partial strip is needed.

2. Fence me in.
   A farmer has several rectangular fields to fence. The fences will be made of three strands of barbed wire, with fence posts no more than 6 feet apart and a stronger post on every corner. Write a complete specification, with diagram, for a program that will input the length and width of a field, in feet. Make sure that each input is within a meaningful range. If so, calculate the area of the field and the total length of barbed wire required to go around the field. Also calculate the number of fence posts needed (use the `ceil()` function from the **math** library). Now write a program that will perform the calculations and display the results.

3. Holy, holy, holy day.
   A professor will assign homework today and does not want it due on anybody's holy day. The professor enters today's day of the week (0 for Sunday, 1 for Monday, etc.) and the number of days, D, to allow the students to do the work, which may be several weeks. Using the % operator, calculate the day of the week on which the work would be due. If that day is someone's holy day—Friday (Moslems), Saturday (Jews), or

Sunday (Christians)—add enough days to D to reach the following Monday. Print the corrected value of D and the day of the week the work is due.

4. Rolling dice.
Over a large number of trials, a "fair" random number generator will return each of the possible values approximately an equal number of times. Therefore, in each set of 60 trials, if values are generated in the range $1 \ldots 6$, there should be about 10 ones and 10 sixes.

a. Using the loop in Figure 7.29 as a guide, write a function that will generate 60 random numbers in the range $1 \ldots 6$. Use **if** statements to count the number of times 1 and 6 each turns up. At the end, print out the number of ones and the number of sixes that occurred.

b. Following the example in Figure 6.12, write a main program that will call the function from part (a) 10 times. The main program should print table headings; the function will print each set of results under those headings. Look at your results; are the numbers of ones and sixes what you expected? Try it again. Are the results similar? Can you draw any conclusions about the quality of the algorithm for generating random numbers?

5. Summation.
A simple mathematical function can be defined by the equation

$$f(N) = \sum_{x=1}^{N} x \sin(x)$$

as x increases from 1 to N degrees in 1-degree increments. This equation will sum N terms, each of which multiplies x times a value of the **sin()** function. Write a function with a parameter N that will print a table of the N terms and return the value of $f(N)$. Write a main program that will input a value for N, then call the function $f(N)$, and print the result. Check to make sure that the value of N is positive. If not, give the user another chance to enter a valid value, until it is proper. Remember that the **sin()** function requires the angle to be in radians rather than degrees.

6. See your money grow.
Assume you are loaning money to a friend, who will pay it back as a lump sum at the end of the loan period, with interest compounded monthly. Write a program that will allow you to enter an amount of money (in dollars), a number of months, and an annual interest rate. From these data, first calculate a monthly interest rate (1/12 of the annual rate). Then print a table with one line per month, showing the month number, the amount of interest your money will earn that month, and the total amount of your investment so far after the interest is added. Print one line per month, from the time the loan is made until the time it is repaid. Print column headings and print all values in neat columns under them. Break your output into readable blocks by printing a blank line after every twelfth month. Be sure to test your program with a loan period greater than 12 months.

7. Greatest common divisor.
Some applications call for performing arithmetic on rational numbers (fractions). To do rational addition or subtraction, one must first convert the two operands to have

a common denominator. When doing multiplication or division with fractions, it is important to reduce the result to lowest terms. For both processes, we must compute the greatest common divisor (GCD) of two integers. A good algorithm for finding the GCD was developed by Euclid 2300 years ago. In Euclid's method, you start with the two numbers, X and Y, for which you want the GCD. It does not matter which number is greater. Set $x = X$ and $y = Y$, then perform the following iterative algorithm:

a. Let `r = x % y`.

b. Now set `x=y` and `y=r`.

c. Repeat steps (a) and (b) until `y == 0`.

d. At that time, `x` is the GCD of X and Y.

Write a function named *GCD* that will input two numbers from the user and calculate and print their greatest common divisor. Using Figure 6.12 as a guide, write a main program with a query loop that will call the GCD function as many times as the user wishes.

8. Loan payments.

Compute a table that shows a monthly payback schedule for a loan. The principle amount of the loan, the annual interest rate, and the monthly payment amount are to be read as inputs. Calculate the monthly interest rate as 1/12 of the annual rate. Each month, first calculate the current interest = the monthly rate × the loan balance. Then add the interest amount to the balance, subtract the payment, and print this new balance. Continue printing lines for each month until the normal payment would exceed the loan balance. On that month, the payment amount should be the remaining balance and the new balance becomes 0. Print a neat loan repayment table following this format:

```
Payment schedule for $1000 loan
at 0.125 annual interest rate
and monthly payment of $100.00
```

Month	Interest	Payment	Balance
1	10.42	100.00	910.42
2	9.48	100.00	819.90
...	...	...	...
10	1.66	100.00	60.99
11	0.64	61.63	0.00

9. Prime number testing.

A prime number is an integer that has no factors except itself and 1. The first several prime numbers are 2, 3, 5, 7, 11, 13, 17, and 19. Very large prime numbers have become important in the field of cryptography. The original public-key cryptographic algorithm is based on the fact that there is no fast way to find the prime factors of a 200-digit number that is the product of two 100-digit prime numbers. In this program, you will implement a simple but very slow way to test whether a number is prime.

One method of testing a number N for primality, is by calculating **N % x**, where x is equal to every prime number from 2 to $R = \sqrt{N}$. If any of these results equals 0, then N is not a prime. We can stop testing at $\sqrt{N}$, since if N has any factor greater than R, it also must have a factor less than or equal to R. Unfortunately, keeping track of a list of prime numbers requires techniques that have not yet been presented. However, a less efficient method is to calculate **N % x** for $x = 2$ and every odd number between 3 and $\sqrt{N}$. Some of these numbers will be primes, most will not. But if any one value divides N evenly, we know that N is not a prime.

Write a function that enters an integer N to test and prints the word **prime** if it is a prime number or **nonprime** otherwise. Write a main program with a query loop to test many numbers.

10. Scheduled time of arrival.

Airline travelers often want to know what time a flight will arrive at its destination in the local time of the destination. This can be calculated given the following data:

- The scheduled takeoff time, in hours and minutes on a 24-hour clock.
- The number of time zone boundaries the flight will cross. This number should be negative if traveling from East to West, positive if going West to East.
- Whether the international date line will be crossed. This number should be +1 if it is crossed traveling from East to West, −1 if crossed while going West to East, and 0 if it is not crossed.
- The scheduled duration of the flight, in hours and minutes.

Write a function, named **arrival()**, that will input these data values from the user and print the scheduled time at which the flight should arrive at its destination. This time is calculated as follows:

- Starting with the takeoff time, add or subtract an hour for each time-zone change.
- Then add the duration of the flight to this time.
- Finally, adjust the time by adding or subtracting a day if the flight crossed the international date line.
- Use integer division and the modulus operator to convert minutes to hours + minutes, and hours to days + hours.

Print the local time of arrival using a 24-hour clock. Also print **-1 day** if the flight will land the day before it took off or **+1 day** if it will land the day after it took off (both are possible). Write a main program with a query loop that will call this function as many times as desired.

CHAPTER
8

*The Trouble
with Numbers*

N ow that we better understand the limitations of the various data types and
how conversions between the types occur automatically or at our instruction, we need to consider how to use this knowledge to our advantage. In
this chapter, we discuss how to deal with some computational problems, such as
how to properly compare two numbers and what happens when a computed value
is outside of the representable range of the data type.

8.1   Floating-Point Comparisons

When two integers are compared, they are either equal or not; this is because
we use an exact representation for integers, and they are discrete values (each
one differs by exactly 1 from the next). In contrast, the real numbers are not
discrete; they are continuous. This makes the comparison of two real numbers
much harder.

8.1.1   Representational Error

An infinite number of real values lie between any two we care to write. We can
represent some of those numbers exactly but most can be represented only by an

approximation. The difference between the true value and its representation is called **representational error**. Types `float` and `double` are **approximate representations** for the real numbers, but with differing precision. As an example, consider this code fragment:

```
float w = 4.4;      double x = 4.4;

printf( " Is x == (double)w? %i \n", (x == (double)w) );
printf( " Is (float)x == w? %i \n", ((float)x == w) );
```

The output, shown below, is unexpected if you forget that the two numbers are represented with limited, and different, **precision** and that the `==` operator tests for exact bit-by-bit equality.

```
Is x == (double)w? 0
Is (float)x == w? 1
```

When the more-precise value is cast to the less-precise type, the extra bits are truncated and the numbers are exactly equal. When the shorter value is cast to the longer type, it is lengthened by adding zero bits at the end of the mantissa, not by recomputing the additional bit values. In general, these zeros are not equal to the meaningful bits in the `double` value.

Computation also can introduce representational error, as shown by the next code fragment. We start with **y**, divide it by a number, then multiply it by the same number. According to mathematics, the result should be the same real number we started with. According to our computer it is, but only sometimes, as with this first set of initial values:

```
float w;
double x,  y = 11.0,  z = 9.0;

x = z * (y / z) ;
w = y - x;
printf( "\n w=%g  x=%.10f \n", w, x );
```

The results from computing this on our system are

```
w=0   x=11.0000000000
```

But if we change the initial values to **y = 15.0** and **z = 11.0**, the results are different and the value of **w** is nonzero:

```
w=1.77635e-15   x=15.0000000000
```

Why does this happen? The answer to a floating-point division has a fractional part that is represented with as much precision as the hardware will allow. However, the precision is not infinite and there is a tiny amount of truncation error after most calculations. Therefore, the answer to **y / z** may have error in it, and that error is increased when we multiply by **z**. This is why the answer to **z * (y / z)** does not always equal the number **y** that we started with.

8.1.2 Making Meaningful Comparisons

The question then arises, when are two floating-point numbers really equal? The answer is that they should be called *equal* if both are approximations for the same real number, even if one approximation has more precision than the other. Therefore, an approximate test for equality is necessary to compare values that are approximations.

Practical problems often require comparing a calculated value to a specific constant or setpoint or comparing two calculated values that should be equal. Such a comparison is not as simple as it seems, because even simple computations with small floating-point values can have results that differ from the mathematically correct versions. If you read two identical floating-point values into variables of the same floating type and compare them, the values will be equal. However, as soon as you begin to compute, truncation and round-off error can happen. Any computed value could be affected by floating-point representational error. Further, two computed values could be affected by different amounts and in different directions.

Although truncation itself always results in a value smaller than it should be, using a truncated answer as a divisor gives a quotient that is too large. It takes considerable expertise to analyze how severely a number might be affected and in what way. In the example of representational error given previously, doing **y - (z * (y / z))** gave a nonzero answer for **y = 15.0** and **z = 11.0** because of round-off error due to the division, but the same computation on other values of **y** and **z** gave the answer 0.0. There was no obvious pattern to these zero and nonzero answers when the test was tried with other inputs.

Even though we know that the various results of **z * (y / z)** will be very close to the value of **y**, the **==** operator tests for exact, not approximate, equality. Since any floating-point value that results from a computation may be imprecise, we cannot use **==** and **!=** on **float**s and **double**s. We can get around this comparison problem by comparing the *difference* of the two numbers to a preset epsilon value, as in Figure 8.1. We call this an **approximate comparison** for equality with an **epsilon test**. For any given application, we can choose a value of epsilon that is slightly smaller than the smallest measurable difference in the data. We then ask if the absolute value of the difference between the values is less than epsilon—if so, we say the operands are equal. This can be done in one **if** statement by using the absolute value function, **fabs()**, as shown in Figure 8.2.

In addition to testing for equality, occasionally we also need to test for a greater-than or less-than condition. In a one-sided test, we still need an epsilon value to compensate for representational error, but the **fabs()** can be omitted. This kind of test is used in Figure 8.4.

With the epsilon shown (2 mph), we say that speed$_1$ = 49.0 equals 50.0 because it is within epsilon of 50.0, but speed$_2$ = 54.0 does not equal 50.0 with this value of epsilon.

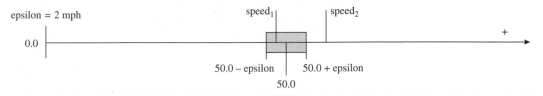

Figure 8.1.   An approximate comparison.

8.1.3   Application: Cruise Control

Sometimes different actions are required for values below, above, and equal to a target, so we need to use a series of **if** statements to test for these conditions. The program specified in Figure 8.3 and written in Figure 8.4 demonstrates this technique. The figures present an initial version of a cruise control program that would run on a computer embedded in the acceleration system of an automobile to regulate the setting of the automobile throttle. A real cruise control would need to be more complex to avoid drastically overshooting and undershooting the target speed.

Notes on Figure 8.4. Cruise control.

- *First box: the constants.*

   1. We define **eps** to be small so that the cruise control system can regulate the speed within a narrow range.
   2. The throttle setting ranges between 0.0° (horizontal) and 90.0° (vertical); we adjust it by 5° each time we need to raise or lower the car's speed.

Use an epsilon test with the absolute value function to compare floating-point values for equality. Note, the **fabs()** function is part of the **math** library and is used with real numbers, as opposed to **abs()**, which is used with integers.

```
double epsilon = 1.0e-3;
double number, target;

if (fabs( number - target ) < epsilon)    /* fabs is floating abs. */
    /* then we consider that number == target */
else
    /* we consider the values significantly different. */
```

Figure 8.2.   Comparing floats for equality.

Problem scope: A simple version of a cruise control program that would run on a computer embedded in the acceleration system of an automobile.

Inputs: These come from the functions `read_on_switch()`, `read_speed()`, `read_throttle()`, and `read_brake()`, which are attached to the car's sensors. Prototypes for these functions are in the file `throttle.h`. There is no direct interaction with a user.

Formulas: Increasing or decreasing the angle of the throttle affects the speed. An angle of 0° corresponds to a horizontal throttle and high speed, while the maximum angle of 90° corresponds to a vertical throttle and low speed. At 90°, we assume that some air still can enter the system because the throttle plate is designed to be smaller than the diameter of the tube. We need some air at all times for combustion of the gas-air mixture.

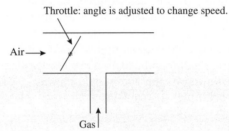

Constants required: `eps` = 2.5 mph, the "fuzz factor" for the speed comparison, and `delta` = 5°, the incremental correctional change in throttle setting.

Output required: No output report is displayed on a screen. Instead the output is in the form of appropriate calls on the `set_throttle()` function, which controls the position of the car's throttle.

Figure 8.3.   Problem specification: Cruise control.

- *Second box: waiting for the "set" signal.*

    1. When the cruise control first is turned on, it waits for the driver to press the "set speed" switch. This is performed by the one-line loop that repeats until the "set" signal is received. Note that no actual statement is being executed each time through the loop. The loop simply repeats the test until the test is false. This typically is called a *busy wait loop* and was discussed in Chapter 6.
    2. As soon as the "set" switch is recognized, we leave the loop and get the input values by calling functions to read the current speed and throttle settings.

The car's throttle setting is increased or decreased in response to the measured speed being too low or too high.

```c
#include <stdio.h>
#include "throttle.h"      /* Prototypes for switch and throttle functions. */

void main( void )
{
    const float eps = 2.5;         /* Fuzz factor for comparison.            */
    const float delta = 5.;        /* Change for throttle setting, in degrees.*/

    float throttle;                /* Current throttle setting.              */
    float target;                  /* Desired speed setpoint.                */
    float speed;                   /* Current speed.                         */
    float dif;                     /* Target speed - current speed.          */

    while (! read_on_switch()); /* Leave loop when driver sets speed.        */
    target = read_speed();         /* Initial speed and throttle settings.   */
    throttle = read_throttle();

    while (! read_brake()){              /* Leave loop when driver hits brake. */
        speed = read_speed();

        dif = target - speed;           /* Compare current speed to target    */
        if (dif > eps){
            puts( "Speed is too low; open throttle." );
            throttle -= delta;
            if (throttle > 90.0) throttle = 90.0;
        }
        else if (dif < -eps){
            puts( "Speed is too high; close throttle." );
            throttle += delta;
            if (throttle < 0.)  throttle = 0.;
        }
        else puts( "Speed is ok; do nothing." );

        set_throttle( throttle );
    }
}
```

Figure 8.4.   Cruise control.

- *Outer box: responding to conditions.*

    1. This loop will monitor the car's progress. The cruise control will remain active until the driver touches the brake.
    2. While active, it continually reads the current speed and compares it to the target speed.

3. After computing the new throttle setting in the inner box, we generate the output signal of the program by calling the `set_throttle()` function.

- *Inner box: adjusting the throttle.*

   1. Because the speed is a `float`, we use an epsilon test; that is, we declare the numbers to be equal if they differ by less than epsilon (2.5 mph).
   2. Here it is not just important to know whether the speeds are the same but, when they are different, which is greater. We use an `if...else` sequence to handle this.
   3. If the current speed is slower than the target speed minus epsilon, we subtract delta from the throttle setting. If the current speed is too fast, we add delta. (An actual cruise control algorithm would use more information than just the current speed to make this decision.) If both these tests fail, then the speeds would be "equal" according to our original approximate-equality test.

8.2   Calculation Errors (Advanced Topic)

The integer types provide a precise representation for numbers within a restricted range. The restriction is particularly severe for short integers, which are not large enough to store the results of many computations. While the overall range of numbers that can be represented by floating-point types is vastly greater, it still is finite and the representation used is an approximation of the real number with limited precision. We saw some of this precisional error in the last section. The various mathematical operations can produce inaccurate or completely incorrect results if the operands are either too large or too small or if the two operands differ greatly in size. These computational problems are demonstrated in more detail by the following short programs.

8.2.1   Overflow

Overflow is the error condition that occurs when the result of an operation becomes larger than the limits of the representation, as described in Figures 7.2 and 7.4. How this error condition is detected and handled differs for the integer and real data types. These overflow situations are a serious problem. They cannot be detected by the compiler. The compiler cannot predict that a result will overflow because it cannot know what data will be used later, at run time, to make calculations. Also, a C system will not detect the error at run time and will not give any warning that it has happened. It usually is possible to look at the results of calculations on the screen and notice when something has gone wrong, but this is far from a desirable solution.

Integer overflow and wrap.   Expressions that cause **integer overflow** are fairly common on small computers because the range of type `int` is so restricted. Integer calculations like addition, subtraction, and multiplication with large numbers are likely to exceed the maximum limit, perhaps by quite a lot.[1]

On a 16-bit machine, if a computation causes overflow and the result is stored in a variable, only the rightmost (least significant) 16 bits of the overlarge answer will be stored; the rest will be truncated. If the result then is printed, it will appear much smaller than the mathematically correct result (or even negative). Noticing the faulty value is the only way for a user to detect an overflow.

For example, suppose that the 2-byte integer variable `k` contains the number 32300 and you enter a loop that adds 100 to `k` seven times. The value stored in `k` would be, in turn, 32400, 32500, 32600, 32700, -32736, -32636, and finally -32536. The value has **wrapped** around and become negative, but that does not stop the computer! The program will continue running with a faulty number that is not even approximately correct. For these reasons, 2-byte integers (type `int` on smaller machines and type `short int` on most machines) are not very useful for serious numeric work. We generally use type `long` if we want to use integers in these calculations. But even though type `long`, with a range up to 2.1 billion, can handle many more calculations properly, it still is limited to 10 digits.

Floating-point overflow and infinity.   The phenomenon of wrap is unique to integers; floating-point overflow is handled differently. The IEEE **floating-point standard** defines a special bit pattern, called `Infinity`, that will result if overflow occurs during a computation. (The exponent field of this value is set to all 1 bits, the mantissa to 0 bits.) The constant `HUGE_VAL`, defined in `math.h`, is set to be the "infinity" value on each local system. Therefore, one way an overflow can be detected is by comparing a result to `HUGE_VAL` or `-HUGE_VAL`. The other way is that, on some systems, the output from `printf()` for such a value will be the message `+Infinity` or `-Infinity`. These techniques are a real help, but they are available only in systems that implement the full standard (many systems do not).

Factorial: A demonstration of overflow.   As an illustration of what all this means in practice, consider the mathematical factorial operation:

$$N! = 1 \times 2 \times \ldots \times (N-2) \times (N-1) \times N$$

Factorial, by its nature, is a function that grows large very rapidly. Figure 8.5 shows a version of the factorial program that computes $N!$ for values of N ranging from 1 to 40. The computation is made with variables of five different types so that we can compare the range and precision of these types.

---

[1] Unlike the `*`, `+`, and `-` operators, integer division cannot cause overflow. The smallest integer value you can divide by is `1`, which will not increase the magnitude of the value being divided.

We compute the factorial function using five different types so that we can compare their range and precision.

```
#include <stdio.h>
void main( void )
{
    int N;                          /* Loop counter. */
    short int        facts = 1;     /* We compute factorial using 5 types. */
    short unsigned   factu = 1;     /* 0! is defined to be 1. */
    long int         factl = 1;
    float            factf = 1.0;
    double           factd = 1.0;

    puts( "\n N    N factorial \n        short unsigned \n"
        "           int    short int  long int \t float \t\t\t double \n" );

    /* Compute N! using each type, quit after 40 factorial.   */
    for (N = 1; N <= 40; ++N) {
        facts *= N;   factu *= N;   factl *= N;
        factf *= N;   factd *= N;

        if (N <= 9)
            printf( "%3i %7hi %7u ", N, facts, factu );
        else
            printf( "%3i                    ", N );
        if (N <= 17)
            printf( "%12li", factl );
        else
            printf( "             " );
        printf( "  %18.12g  %23.22g\n", factf, factd );
    }
}
```

Figure 8.5.   Computing N!.

Wrap error.   The output on the first seven lines is fully correct. (Horizontal spacing has been reduced.)

| N | N factorial | | | | |
	short int	unsigned short int	long int	float	double
1	1	1	1	1	1
2	2	2	2	2	2
3	6	6	6	6	6
4	24	24	24	24	24
5	120	120	120	120	120
6	720	720	720	720	720
7	5040	5040	5040	5040	5040

However, 7! is the largest factorial value that can be stored in a short signed (16-bit) integer. From line 8 on, the numbers in the first column are meaningless; overflow has happened and the answer wraps around to become a negative number. This will not always occur, but when it does, it is a good indication of trouble.

	short int	unsigned short int	long int	float	double
8	-25216	40320	40320	40320	40320
9	-30336	35200	362880	362880	362880
10			3628800	3628800	3628800
11			39916800	39916800	39916800

One more value, 8!, can be stored in a short unsigned integer. But, beginning with 9!, the answer overflows into the 17th bit position and the number stored in the variable **factu** is garbage. When working with unsigned numbers, as in the second column, there is not even a negative sign to warn us about the wrap. Nonetheless, the numbers are wrong from line 9 on. This is what makes it so difficult to detect this error in practice. The program suppresses output in these two columns after line 9.

	long int	float	double
11	39916800	39916800	39916800
12	479001600	479001600	479001600
13	1932053504	6227020800	6227020800
14	1278945280	87178289152	87178291200
15	2004310016	1.30767427994e+12	1307674368000

Using long integers, as in the third column, we get correct answers all the way up to 12!, the largest N for which the calculation can be made using either signed or unsigned long integers. Starting at line 13, the answer for long integers is garbage; it should be the same as the value in the other columns. Here, we get no negative sign to warn us that wrap has occurred, because the value has wrapped past all of the negatives and into the positives again.

Representational error.   Between $N = 14$ and $N = 34$, using type **float**, we encounter the limits of the IEEE **float**'s precision, rather than its range. Although we can compute the factorial function for $N > 13$, the answers are only approximations of the true answer. (The **float** value computed for $N = 14$ is 87,178,289,152; this is close to, but smaller than, the true answer, 87,178,291,200, shown in the last column for the **double** calculation.) The **float** simply lacks enough bits to hold all the significant digits, even though the maximum **float** value has not been reached. We say that such an answer is **correct but not precise**. It may be a fully acceptable approximation to the true answer, but it differs in the last few digits. Whether the precision is adequate depends on the application.

	float	double
15	1.30767427994e+12	1307674368000
16	2.0922788479e+13	20922789888000
17	3.55687414628e+14	355687428096000
18	6.40237353042e+15	6402373705728000
19	1.21645096004e+17	121645100408832000
20	2.43290202316e+18	2432902008176640000
21	5.10909408372e+19	51090942171709440000
22	1.12400072481e+21	1124000727777607680000
23	2.58520174446e+22	2.585201673888497821286e+22

Using type **double** (as in the last column) instead of **float** extends the range of accuracy. The same factorial program goes up to 22! with total precision; this number has 18 nonzero digits. For $N = 23$, the last few digits show evidence of the error, they should be 664000 not 821286.

	float	double
33	8.68331850985e+36	8.683317618811885938716e+36
34	2.95232822997e+38	2.952327990396041195551e+38
35	+Infinity	1.033314796638614422221e+40
36	+Infinity	3.719933267899011774924e+41

At $N = 35$, floating-point overflow happens, for the **float** number format where **3.402e+38** is the maximum representable number. However, this does not stop the program, which continues to try to compute the numbers up to 40!. If we continued, we would find that values up to 170! can be approximated using the **double** format before an overflow.

8.2.2   Underflow

The opposite problem of overflow is **underflow**, which occurs when the magnitude of the number falls below the smallest number in the representable range. This cannot occur for integers, only for real numbers, since the minimum magnitude of an **int** is 0. For real numbers, underflow happens when a value is generated that has a 0 **exponent** and a nonzero **mantissa**. Such a number is referred to as **denormalized**, which means that all significant bits have been shifted to the right and the number is less than the lowest number specified by the standard. This effect is shown in the left column of the last few lines of output from the division program in Figure 8.6:

N= 43	frac= 9.9492191e-44	1+frac=	1
N= 44	frac= 9.8090893e-45	1+frac=	1
N= 45	frac= 1.4012985e-45	1+frac=	1
N= 46	frac= 0	1+frac=	1
N= 47	frac= 0	1+frac=	1

This program continually divides a number by 10 until the result is too small to store as a normalized `float`.

```c
#include <stdio.h>

void main( void )
{
    int N;
    float frac = 1.0;

    puts( "\n Dividing by 10; frac=1/(10 to the Nth power)\n" );
    for (N = 0; N < 25; ++N) {
        printf( " N=%3i    frac= %13.8g    1+frac= %13.8g\n",
                N, frac, 1+frac );
        frac = frac / 10;
    }
}
```

Figure 8.6.   Floating-point underflow.

The program continually divides a value by 10. The actual lower limit of the representation range is 1.175e−38, and some systems will generate the 0 value when this limit is reached. Others, like the one shown here, still use the denormalized values. But even these, at $N = 46$, have all the bits shifted so far to the right that the result becomes 0.

Underflow can result from several kinds of computations:

- Dividing a number by a very large number or repeated division, as just illustrated.
- Multiplying a small number by a near-zero number, which has the same effect as dividing by a very large number.
- Subtracting two values that are near the smallest representable `float` and ought to be equal but are not quite equal because of round-off error.

8.2.3   Orders of Magnitude and Other Problems

The limits of `float` precision can be a problem with addition as well as with multiplication. For example, if you attempt to add a small `float` number to a large one, and their exponents differ by more than 10^7 (or 7 **orders of magnitude**), the addition likely will have no effect. The answer will be the same large number that you started with. This is because the floating-point hardware starts the operation by lining up the decimal points of the two operands. In the process, the mantissa bits of the smaller value get denormalized (shifted to the right). But the hardware register in which this happens has a finite width, so the least significant (rightmost) bits of the smaller operand "fall off" the right end of the register and are lost. If the difference in exponents between the operands is great enough, all of the mantissa bits of the smaller value will be lost and only a value of 0 will be left when the addition happens. You can add a millimeter to a kilometer in single precision, but the answer is still 1 kilometer.

This effect is illustrated in the right column of the first few lines of output from the program in Figure 8.6:

```
Dividing by 10; frac=1/(10 to the Nth power)
```

```
N=  0    frac=                1    1+frac=                2
N=  1    frac=              0.1    1+frac=              1.1
N=  2    frac=   0.0099999998    1+frac=             1.01
N=  3    frac= 0.00099999993    1+frac=            1.001
N=  4    frac=   9.999999e-05    1+frac=           1.0001
N=  5    frac= 9.9999988e-06    1+frac=          1.00001
N=  6    frac= 9.9999988e-07    1+frac=         1.000001
N=  7    frac= 9.9999987e-08    1+frac=        1.0000001
N=  8    frac= 9.9999991e-09    1+frac=                1
N=  9    frac= 9.9999986e-10    1+frac=                1
```

It starts with the value 1.0, divides it repeatedly by 10, and adds each fractional result to 1. After only nine divisions, the original fraction is so small that the addition has no effect. We say that the fraction is insignificant in comparison to 1.0. Sometimes the order in which a set of calculations is performed can cause an error if these differences in magnitude are not taken into account, while the same operations done in a different order can be correct.

Last, a special value called `NaN`, which stands for "not a number," can be generated through operations such as `0 / 0`. This is another special bit pattern that does not correspond to a real value. The IEEE standard specifies that any further operation attempted using a `NaN` or `Infinity` as an operand will return the same value. This was seen for `+Infinity` in the factorial example. On our system, the hardware computes `Infinity` and `NaN` values correctly and C's `stdio` library prints them (as was shown) instead of printing meaningless digits.

8.3   Optional Application: Finding the Real Roots of an Equation

Three simple, common algorithms for finding the real root (or roots) of an equation are the bisection method, the secant method, and Newton's method. Each method has advantages and drawbacks; all three methods fail on certain kinds of input; and the type of information and inputs required for each are different. In this section, we present Newton's method and show how to use it. (Bisection is covered in Chapter 12 and secant in Chapter 23.) This program is an excellent example of why we must be aware of the limitations of numerical algorithms on real computers: The method can fail to converge on a root either because of an unlucky initial guess, because of the limited precision of floating-point arithmetic, or because the particular function is unsuitable for the method. Fortunately, the method works well for many common functions.

8.3.1   Newton's Method

Newton's method is an iterative process. The programmer supplies the function, $f(x)$; its derivative, $f'(x)$; and epsilon, an arbitrarily small tolerance interval. At run time, the user supplies an arbitrary initial value for x. The algorithm starts with that value and improves it, step by step. If all goes well, this iterative process gives us a series of values $x_0, x_1, \ldots, x_n$, such that x_0 is an arbitrary starting point and for $k = 1, 2, \ldots, n$; x_k is computed from x_{k-1} and is closer to a root of the function. We continue the process until we find a value, x_n, that is within a predefined small epsilon of the actual root.

Think of the function $f(x)$ as a series of "hills" on the xy plane. For any value, x, $f(x)$ is a point on the hill; and the derivative of the function, $f'(x)$, is the slope of the hill at that point. The **roots of the equation** are the points at which it crosses the x axis. In intuitive terms, Newton's method works by "sliding downhill" (or uphill) from the starting point to the nearest root.

To use Newton's method, we start by guessing some value x_0 that we hope is close to a root of $f(x)$. Then we calculate $y_0 = f(x_0)$ and $y'_0 = f'(x_0)$. We then take a line with slope $f'(x_0)$ that is tangent to the curve at $f(x_0)$ and calculate the value x_1 at which that tangent line will cross the x axis (see Figure 8.7). To compute x_1 we use the formula for the slope of a line:

$$\text{Slope} = \frac{\Delta y}{\Delta x} = \frac{y_1 - y_0}{x_1 - x_0}$$

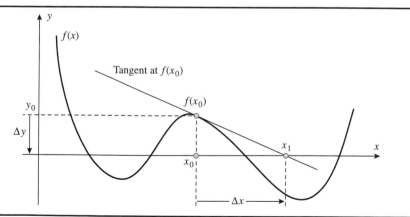

Figure 8.7.   Newton's method: Terminology.

But $y_0 = f(x_0)$ and $y_1 = 0$ because x_1 is the point at which the tangent line crosses the x axis, so

$$\text{Slope} = \frac{-f(x_0)}{x_1 - x_0}$$

The derivative of a function, $f'(x_0)$, also is the slope of the tangent line at the point (x_0, y_0). Combining these facts, we get

$$f'(x_0) = \frac{-f(x_0)}{x_1 - x_0}$$

Solving for x_1,

$$f'(x_0)(x_1 - x_0) = -f(x_0)$$
$$x_1 - x_0 = -\frac{f(x_0)}{f'(x_0)}$$
$$x_1 = x_0 - \frac{f(x_0)}{f'(x_0)}$$

Therefore, to compute x_1, we simply compute $\Delta x = -f(x_0)/f'(x_0)$ and add it to x_0. This process is depicted in Figure 8.8.

We repeat this process, using each x value to find the next, until $|x_n - x_{n-1}| < \epsilon$ and we have converged on a root or until we identify one of the error situations described next. A program that implements Newton's method is given in Figure 8.11.

Problems with Newton's method.   To use Newton's method, the program must contain a function that computes $f(x)$, whose roots are sought, and a second function that computes the derivative, $f'(x)$. Therefore, we cannot use this method unless we can write a program to compute both the function and the derivative.

We continue the search for a root using the value for x_1 found in Figure 8.7.

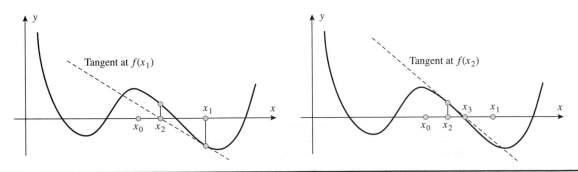

Figure 8.8.   Newton's method: Finding the next x value.

Second, some functions simply cannot be solved by Newton's method. To be suitable, a function must be continuous and differentiable; that is, its graph must have no breaks and no corners. Also, there is a class of symmetric functions that meet these criteria, such as the one in Figure 8.9, for which the method will not terminate. The function graphed here is $f(x) = -\sqrt{|x|}$ if $x < 0$ and $f(x) = \sqrt{|x|}$ if $x \geq 0$. Such functions have the property that, no matter what the user guesses for x_0, the next point, x_1, is the symmetrically opposite point and x_2 is the same as x_0. Newton's method will not converge on this function; it will bounce back and forth between the initial guess and its opposite point. Because of this possibility, our program contains a limit on the number of iterations that will be attempted.

Newton's method can fail to converge if $f(x)$ has a "hump" that does not intersect the x axis, as in Figure 8.10, and if our initial guess happens to be on this noncrossing hump. As we try to slide down this hill, we may seesaw back and forth until we find that x_n is near the peak of the hump. At this point, the tangent line is nearly horizontal and crosses the x axis far away, on a different part of the curve. It also is possible for overflow to happen when we compute Δx with such a slope. In either case, the process does not converge in the normal way.

Finally, when the iteration converges to a value x_n, it is difficult to tell for sure what that means. Because of the limited precision of floating-point arithmetic, x_n will approximate a root, but it rarely will be an exact root and may not even be within epsilon of the root. For this reason, our program prints the

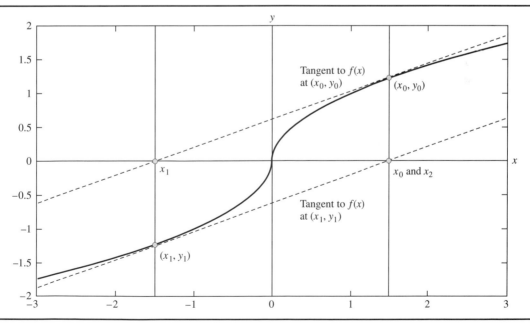

Figure 8.9.   Failure to converge.

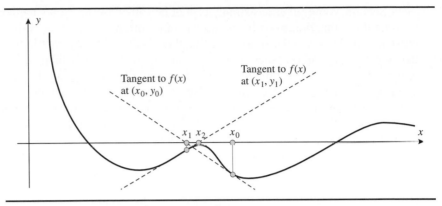

Figure 8.10.   Failure by converging on a near root.

actual values of x_n, $\Delta x = x_n - x_{n-1}$, $f(x_n)$, and $f'(x_n)$. If $f'(x_n)$ is large, the value x_n may be very close to x_{n-1} but further than epsilon from a root. If it is 0 or near 0, there may be a double root at x_n; this happens when $f(x)$ has a "hump" tangent to the axis at x_n or if the function comes very close to the x axis but does not cross it, as in Figure 8.10. It may be possible, although unlikely, to "find" a root that does not exist. This could happen if the numbers in the computations come close to the limits of precision of the computer. Figures 8.11 and 8.12 are a program using Newton's method to find $f(x)$.

```
#include "tools.h"

#define EPSILON     .000001        /* Convergence tolerance.         */
#define TRIES       100            /* Give up after 100 iterations.  */

void newton (void);

void main( void )
{
    int do_it_again;                   /* repeat-or-stop switch */

    banner();

    puts( "\n Solve f(x) = x*x + 3*x - 3 by Newton's method." );

    do { newton();
        printf( " \n\n Enter 1 to continue, 0 to quit: " );
        scanf( "%i", &do_it_again );
    } while (do_it_again != 0);
    bye();
}
```

Figure 8.11.   Using Newton's method to find a root.

This function is called from the main program in Figure 8.11.

```
/* ----------------------------------------------function to be solved */
double f (double x) {   return x*x + 3*x - 3;   }
/* ------------------------------------------------ derivative of f */
double fprime (double x) {   return 2*x + 3;   }
```

```
/* -------------------------------------------------------------------
** Find one root of function f using Newton's method.
*/
void newton( void )
{
    int k;                 /* Iteration counter. */
    double x;              /* Current guess. */
    double delta_x;        /* Difference between successive guesses. */
```

```
    printf( " Enter x0, the initial guess: " );
    scanf( "%lg", &x );
```

```
    for (k = 0; k < TRIES; ++k) {          /* Give up after TRIES times. */
        delta_x = -f(x) / fprime(x);
        if (!finite( delta_x )) break;              /* Overflow. */
        x += delta_x;
        if (fabs( delta_x ) < EPSILON) break;    /* Convergence. */
    }
```

```
    /* Analyze reason for leaving loop and print results.  -------------- */
    if (k == TRIES)
        printf( "\t No convergence in %i iterations.\n", TRIES );
    else if (!finite( delta_x ))
        printf( "\t Overflow on delta_x.\n" );
    else
        printf( "\t Process converged.\n" );
```

```
    printf( "\t x = %g,  delta_x = %g. \n", x, delta_x );
    printf( "\t f(x) = %g,  f'(x) = %g. \n", f(x), fprime(x) );
}
```

Figure 8.12.   Sliding downhill.

Notes on Figures 8.11 and 8.12. Newton's method.

- *First box, Figure 8.11: constants.*

    1. EPSILON is the convergence tolerance. We terminate the iterations
       when the new x value is within EPSILON of the old one.

2. We need a way to end the iteration process when it is not converging. The constant **TRIES** is the maximum number of trials that we will make with one initial guess. It is an arbitrary number. Newton's method usually converges very quickly, if it converges at all, so 100 iterations should be more than enough.

- *Second box, Figure 8.11, and first box, Figure 8.12: the function and its derivative*. The functions **f()** and **fprime()** must be supplied by the programmer. To find the roots of a different function, the output string in the second box of Figure 8.11 must be changed, the new functions must be supplied in Figure 8.12, and the program must be recompiled.
- *Second box, Figure 8.12: the initial guess*. The first guess is arbitrary. For most functions, any initial guess will work. However, after finding one root of the function or a failed attempt, the next initial value should be somewhat distant from the first.
- *Third box, Figure 8.12: ending*. There are three ways to end this iteration. We test for various conditions here and break out of the loop if we find one. We print the appropriate comment later, in the fourth box.

1. The **for** loop will terminate after a fixed number of iterations. This prevents an infinite loop in the case of a divergent or repetitive series of **x** values.
2. To compute a new **x** value, the function, its derivative, and their quotient all must be computable. If any one of these computations causes floating-point overflow, a system that conforms to the IEEE standard will return a value **+Infinity** or **-Infinity** as the answer to that calculation and any further calculations based on that number. If one of these conditions has happened, there is no point in continuing. We can test for this condition by comparing the result to the constant **HUGE_VAL**, which is the standard C name for **Infinity**.
3. In systems that support the IEEE floating point standard, it is more elegant to test for overflow using the function **finite()**:

```
if (!finite( delta_x )) break;
```

4. If Newton's method converges at all, it converges rapidly. In the beginning, **delta_x** (the change in **x** values) is large. As **x** approaches a root, it shrinks. Finally, when it is smaller than the convergence tolerance, **EPSILON**, we have found a candidate for a root and break out of the loop. Further analysis is required to be sure that it actually *is* a root.
5. The loop finds the next **x** by calculating **delta_x** and adding it to the old **x**.

- *Fourth and fifth boxes, Figure 8.12: case analysis and the answers*. Three paths leave the iteration loop. At this point, we need to identify which one actually happened and print the appropriate comment. In all cases, the fourth box prints all the relevant results.

1. We know that the iteration did not converge if the loop counter equals the maximum allowed number of trials. In this case, we have not found a root. For example, assume we replaced the function given in Figure 8.12 with one that does not cross the x axis and, therefore, has no real roots:

```
Solve f(x) = x*x + EPSILON/2.0 by Newton's method.
Enter x0, the initial guess: 1
    No convergence in 100 iterations.
    x = 1.06182e-05,   delta_x = 0.000707.
    f(x) = 5.00112e-07,   f'(x) = 2.12364e-05.
```

We get the same result with this function by starting with $x_0 = .00001$ and $x_0 = -1$. However, starting with $x_0 = 0$, the result was different, as shown in the next case.

2. We cannot continue and, therefore, leave the loop, if the calculation for **delta_x** causes an overflow. This can happen when the function approaches very close to the x axis without crossing it and the tangent line is horizontal or nearly so, as in the next case.

```
Solve f(x) = x*x + EPSILON/2.0 by Newton's method.
Enter x0, the initial guess: 0
    Overflow on delta_x.
    x = 0,   delta_x = -Infinity.
    f(x) = 5e-07,   f'(x) = 0.
```

We get the same results if we use the function $f(x) = x^2 - \epsilon/2$, which has two roots close to 0, when we start with an initial value of 0.0. If the function is tangent to the x axis (for instance, $f(x) = x^2$), the tangent at the root is horizontal and overflow will happen if **x** ever takes on the exact value of the root. In this case, the last line of the printout lets us know that a root has been found:

```
Solve f(x) = x*x by Newton's method.
Enter x0, the initial guess: 0
    Overflow on delta_x.
    x = 0,   delta_x = NaN.
    f(x) = 0,   f'(x) = 0.
```

3. If the process converges, we print the final values of **x**, **delta_x**, **f(x)**, and **f'(x)** so that the user can see how close we are to a root. Since this algorithm only approximates the root, we may get slightly different results with different starting values. For the function $f(x) = x^2 - \epsilon/2$, we get

```
Solve f(x) = x*x - EPSILON/2.0 by Newton's method.
Enter x0, the initial guess: 1
```

```
    Process converged.
    x = 0.000707,  delta_x = -1.31555e-08.
    f(x) = 1.73068e-16,  f'(x) = 0.001414.

Enter 1 to continue, 0 to quit: 1
Enter x0, the initial guess: 0.000707
    Process converged.
    x = 0.000707,  delta_x = 1.06789e-07.
    f(x) = 1.14039e-14,  f'(x) = 0.001414.
```

Finally, note that the user needs to keep searching for roots by trial and error until all the roots have been discovered. For the actual function in the program, we have a quadratic polynomial, so we search until both roots are found:

```
Solve f(x) = x*x + 3*x - 3 by Newton's method.
Enter x0, the initial guess: 3
    Process converged.
    x = 0.791288,  delta_x = -7.17961e-08.
    f(x) = 5.32907e-15,  f'(x) = 4.582576.

Enter 1 to continue, 0 to quit: 1
Enter x0, the initial guess: -4
    Process converged.
    x = -3.791288,  delta_x = 5.94117e-11.
    f(x) = 1.77635e-15,  f'(x) = -4.582576.
```

8.4   What You Should Remember

8.4.1 Major Concepts

- When making calculations with large integers, the programmer must be wary of integer overflow and wrap. If a variable contains the maximum integer value, adding 1 will cause the value to wrap. The answer will be the minimum representable negative value (farthest from 0).
- Floating-point computations also can cause overflow. This happens when you divide by a near-zero value or multiply two very large numbers. The number will have an exponent of all 1 bits. On some systems, this will be printed as +Infinity or -Infinity; on others, it will be a number with a very large exponent.
- An underflow error condition happens when a real number becomes very close to 0 but does not exactly equal 0. In this situation, some systems store the number in a denormalized form, others simply set the result to 0.

- Computations on real numbers commonly introduce small and somewhat unpredictable representational errors. For this reason, all comparisons between computed real numbers should be made using a tolerance.
- Newton's method is one way to find the roots of an equation. It generally is a good method as long as the derivative of the function can be calculated.

8.4.2   Sticky Points and Common Errors

Algorithms.   Know the weak points in your algorithm as well as any assumptions on which the calculations might be based. If the algorithm can "blow up" at any point, guard against that possibility.

Debugging.   Insert printouts into your program after every few calculations to spot potential calculation errors.

Magnitude errors.   Do not try to add or subtract values of widely differing magnitudes.

Handling error conditions.   The C standard does not specifically cover how a compiler must handle the special values `NaN`, `+Infinity`, and `-Infinity`; it leaves these results officially "undefined." This means that a particular compiler may do anything convenient about the problem. Many do nothing; a garbage result is returned and the user is not notified of an error. However, most computer hardware will set an error indicator when the various floating-point problems occur. This permits a program to test for a particular result and thereby discover the illegal operations. The user can get control by defining a signal handler[2] to trap these types of signals and process them. However, most programmers have no idea how to do this, and most user programs don't attempt to use the interrupt system. Avoidance is the best policy for the ordinary programmer. The careful programmer takes these precautions:

- An output with a huge, unreasonable exponent probably is the result of an overflow. Each programmer needs to be able to recognize the overflow and undefined values that will be printed by the local compiler and system. If these values appear in the output, the programmer should identify and correct the erroneous computation that caused them.
- If a divisor possibly could be 0, test for it.
- Define an epsilon value, related to the precision of the input, that is the smallest meaningful value in this context. Any number whose absolute value is smaller than epsilon should be considered 0 and any two numbers whose difference is less than epsilon can be considered equal.

---

[2]This subject is beyond the scope of this text.

8.4.3 New and Revisited Vocabulary

These terms and concepts are discussed in this chapter.

integer overflow	representational error	factorial
wrap	normalized and denormalized	overflow
IEEE floating-point standard	order of magnitude	underflow
exponent	approximate comparison	roots of an equation
mantissa	epsilon test	Newton's method
precision	correct but not precise	convergence

The following keywords, functions, and symbols were discussed in this chapter:

`fabs()`	`+Infinity`	`HUGE_VAL`
`abs()`	`-Infinity`	`NaN`
	`finite()`	

8.5   Exercises

8.5.1 Self-Test Exercises

1. Draw a parse tree for each of the following expressions. Include coercion boxes. Then use the given data values to evaluate each expression and record the final values stored in the variables **J**, **L**, and **F**. Indicate if overflow occurs during an evaluation.

   ```
   short int J, K=100;
   long int L, M=2000;
   float F;
   ```

   a. `J = L = K * K * K;`

   b. `L = M * M * M;`

   c. `F = M * M * M;`

   d. `F = (float) M * M * M;`

2. Answer the following questions about the computer you use. Write a short program to find the answers, if necessary.

   a. What is the largest **int** that you can enter on your machine and print correctly?

   b. What is the biggest **unsigned int** you can read and write?

   c. When is $x + 1 < x$?

3. Write one or a few lines of code that will cause integer overflow and wrap to happen.

4. Say whether each of the following computations will give a meaningful answer or is likely to cause overflow, underflow, or a serious precisional error.

   ```
   float f;
   float g = 0.1;
   float h = cos(0); /* This should be 1.0 */
   ```

a. `f = 0.000001 - pow(g, 5);`

b. `f = 233344455.5 * .1;`

c. `f = 233344455.5 + .1;`

d. `f = pow(3.14159, 100);`

5. When a floating-point number is printed in `%e` format, it is printed in normalized form, with exactly one digit to the left of the decimal point. Rewrite the following numbers in normalized scientific notation:

   a. `75.23`

   b. `.00012`

   c. `.9998`

   d. `32,767`

6. Each item that follows compares two numbers. For each, answer whether the result is `true`, `false`, or indeterminate and explain why. To get the correct answers, you must know about the type conversions used in mixed-type expressions.

```
float w = 3.3;
int j = w, k = 3;
double x = 3.0, y = 3.3, z = 4.2;
```

   a. `x == k`

   b. `y == k`

   c. `x != y`

   d. `w == j`

   e. `w == y`

   f. `x == w`

   g. `(float)x == w`

   h. `y == z * (y / z)`

   i. `x + 1.0 == k + 1`

   j. `x == .3 * 10`

8.5.2   Using Pencil and Paper

1. Define the following and give an example of code that might cause it:

   a. Integer overflow error

   b. Floating-point underflow error

   c. **NaN** error

   d. Precision error

2. Several problems are associated with doing calculations with real values. Which of these do you believe occurs most often? Which of these, even if it does not occur often, causes the most trouble and why?

3. For each computation that follows, say whether overflow will occur if integers are 2 bytes long? If they are 4 bytes long?

```
int J, K=100, M=2000;
```

a. `J = K * K * K;`

b. `J = (float)K * K * K;`

c. `J = 30 * M / K * M;`

d. `J = M * M * M;`

4. Show how the following normalized numbers would look when printed in `%.3f` format:

a. `3.245E+02`

b. `1.267E-03`

c. `3.14E+04`

d. `1.02E-03`

5. Say whether each computation that follows will give a meaningful answer or is likely to cause overflow, underflow, or serious precisional error.

```
float c = 80000;
float d = 1.0e-5;
float f;
```

a. `f = pow( c, 5 ) / d;`

b. `f = ceil( d ) * 2e-90;`

c. `f = d + sqrt( 100 * c );`

d. `f = sqrt( 10 * d );`

6. Something is wrong with the following tests for equality. For each item, explain why the answer will be different from the intended answer.

```
short int s=1, t=32767;
long int k=65536;
float w=3.3;
double x=3.3, y=33.0, z;
```

a. `x == w`

b. `x*10.0 == y`

c. `s == (short)k`

d. `32769 == (int)t + 2`

8.5.3   Using the Computer

1. Finding roots.
   Using Newton's method and the function $f(x) = x^3 - 2.5 \times x^2 - 0.5 \times x + 3.0$ find the three real roots. Compare your approximate results to the exact roots, which are -1, 1.5, and 2.0.

2. Precision and convergence.
   The program given for Newton's method uses **EPSILON** = **.000001**. Modify this program to allow the user to enter an epsilon value and print the number of iterations required to converge on a root. Run your program with several epsilon values, starting with 0.001, and make a neat chart that summarizes the results.

3. Bubbles.
   The internal pressure inside a soap bubble depends on the surface tension and the radius of the bubble. The surface tension is the force per unit length of the inner and outer surface. The equation for the pressure inside the bubble relative to the air pressure outside is

$$P = \frac{4\sigma}{r} \quad (\text{lb/ft}^2)$$

   where σ is the surface tension (lb/ft) and r is the bubble radius (ft).
   Define a function, **bubble()**, that will compute the pressure P given a value of r and assuming the constant σ to be 0.002473 lb/ft. Then write a main program that will input a value for r, call the **bubble()** function to compute the pressure, convert the units of pressure from lb/ft^2 to psi (pounds per square inch, lb/in^2), and print the answer. Make sure that the input radius is valid; that is, greater than 0. Allow the user to continue entering values until the radius is valid.

4. How functions grow.
   Write a program that will ask the user to enter an integer, $Nmax$, then print a table like the following one, with $Nmax$ lines. If $Nmax$ is less than 1 or more than 20, print an error comment and ask the user to reenter $Nmax$. Store the result of all calculations in variables of type **int**. Use the **pow()** function in the math library to calculate 2^N. The C system will coerce the **double** result of **pow()** to an integer for you. Are all the results correct when you use $N = 20$? If not, why not?

N	sum(1..N)	N squared	2 to the power N
1	1	1	2
2	3	4	4
3	6	9	8
...	...	...	...

5. Capacitance.
   A capacitor is a charge storage device consisting of two electrodes separated by a space occupied by a dielectric. We can connect three capacitors in series:

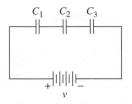

In this circuit, the equivalent capacitance is

$$C_{eq} = \frac{1}{\frac{1}{C_1} + \frac{1}{C_2} + \frac{1}{C_3}} \quad \text{(picofarads)}$$

where C_1, C_2, and C_3 are the three capacitors. Given an applied voltage, v, the electric charge, q, on each is

$$q = C_{eq} \times v \times 10^{-12} \quad \text{(coul)}$$

a. Start with the main program in Figure 6.12 and modify it for this problem. Then write a new **work()** function that will input a voltage and three capacitances from the keyboard, calculate both C_{eq} and q and print the results. Use type **int** for all variables. Beware of division by 0.

b. Write a second **work()** function that uses type **double** variables. Compare the accuracy of this function's results to those of the first version and explain why they are different.

6. Fibonacci numbers.

A Fibonacci sequence is a series of numbers such that each number is the sum of the two preceding numbers in the sequence. For example, the simplest Fibonacci sequence is: 1, 1, 2, 3, 5, 8, 13, 21, ... In this sequence, the first two terms are, by definition, 1. Write a program to print the terms of this sequence in five columns, as follows:

```
0.  1        1.  1        2.  2        3.  3        4.  5
5.  8        6.  13       7.  21 ...
```

Hint: Consider having three variables in your loop, called **current**, **old**, and **older**. After computing the new current value, shift the old values from one variable to the next to prepare for the next iteration. Run your program and determine experimentally how many terms of the Fibonacci series can be computed on your machine before an overflow if you use variables of type **short**, **long**, **float**, and **double** to hold the results.

7. A table.

Write a program that will ask the user to enter a real number, N, then print a table showing how certain functions grow as N doubles. For $N = 3.14$, the output should start thus:

N	1/N	N * log(N)
1	3.14	3.184713e-01	3.592860e+00
2	6.28	1.592357e-01	1.153868e+01
...	...	...	...

Let all your variables be type **float**. Continue computing and printing lines until an underflow occurs in the column for $1/N$ *and* an overflow occurs in the last column. Use the **log()** function, which computes the natural log of a number, and use the constant **HUGE_VAL** from the **math** library to test for an overflow. Remember that a value becomes 0.0 when an underflow occurs.

8. Summing a convergent series.
   The natural logarithm of x can be approximated by summing the first several terms of the infinite series

   $$\ln(x) = \sum_{n=1,2,3,...}^{\infty} \frac{1}{n} \times \left(\frac{x-1}{x}\right)^n \quad \text{for } x > \frac{1}{2}$$

   Write a program to compute the terms of the series and sum them until the current term is less than a value epsilon. Have the user enter the values for x and epsilon. Prepare a table of the results. At each step, print the number of the step, the current term, and the current sum. Then print out the value of $\ln(x)$ computed by calling the **log()** function in the **math** library. Run your program several times with different values for epsilon, starting with 0.01 and getting smaller. Summarize your results in a neat chart with columns for epsilon, the approximation for $\ln(x)$, and the number of iterations needed to converge with that value of epsilon.

9. Square root.
   Over 2000 years ago, Euclid invented a fast, iterative method for approximating the square root of a number. Let N be a positive number and *est* be the current estimate of its square root. (Initially, let *est* $= N/2$.) At each step of the iteration, let *quotient* $= N/est$. If *quotient* equals *est*, they are the square root of N and the iteration should end. Otherwise, let the new *est* be the average of *quotient* and the old *est* and repeat the calculation until *quotient* equals *est* within some epsilon value. Print a table showing the iteration number and the current values of *est* and *quotient*. Let the user enter the values of N and epsilon. Then print the value calculated using the standard **sqrt()** function. Run your program several times with epsilon equal to 0.01, 0.001, 0.0001, and so on. Summarize your results in a neat chart with columns for epsilon, the approximation for $\sqrt{x}$, and the number of iterations needed to converge with that value of epsilon.

10. Summing a Fourier series.
    Many mechanical and electrical devices involve quantities such as displacement or voltage that are periodic functions of time. These functions can be represented by an infinite series of sine and cosine terms called a *Fourier series*. To approximate the value of the function, we calculate and sum the terms at the beginning of the infinite series.

    In a typical Fourier series, the kth term is a quotient that is a function of k and another independent variable (usually t or x). The terms in the series get gradually smaller and smaller, but they do not decrease steadily because the terms are built from sine and cosine expressions, which are periodic. For example, the Fourier series for a square wave (which follows) is

    $$f(t) \approx \frac{4A_0}{\pi} \times \sum_{k=1}^{n} \frac{\sin[(2k-1) \times \omega \times t]}{2k-1}$$

where A_0 is the magnitude of the wave and ω is the frequency. To find the value of $f_n(t)$ at any specified time t, we substitute values for A_0 and t and sum n terms of the series. We want to approximate $f(t)$ for the wave below at $A_0 = 2.0$, time $t = 0.5$ second, and $\omega = 1.0$ rad/sec (so the square wave completes a cycle every 2π seconds):

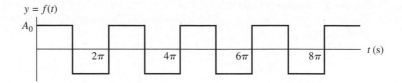

Write a program to sum the terms of this series for the values of A_0, t, and ω given above. Continue summing until six consecutive terms are within 0.001 of 0. After evaluating each term, print one line of a table like this:

Sum of the Fourier Series for a Square Wave:

n	nth term	sum, n terms	~f(t)
1	0.479426	0.479426	1.220847
2	0.332498	0.811924	2.067547
3	0.119694	0.931618	2.372346
4	-0.050112	0.881506	2.244738

Hint: Extend the technique of exercise 6, using several variables to remember past term values.

CHAPTER
9

Program Design

This chapter discusses modular organization and the ways that parts of a modular program must relate to each other. It formalizes many aspects of functions presented in preceding chapters, including prototypes, function definitions, function calls, and how these elements must correspond. The concepts of local, global, and external names are presented. Function call graphs are presented as a way to visualize the relationships among functions. The process of designing a modular program is described and illustrated with a programming example.

9.1   Modular Programs

When a program has only 20 or 50 lines, a programmer can keep the entire program structure in mind at once. Many programs, though, have thousands of lines of code. To deal with this complexity, it is necessary to divide the code into relatively independent modules and consider each module in isolation from the others, usually with a main program in one module and groups of closely related functions in others. Each module is composed of functions and declarations that relate to one identifiable phase of the overall project. This is the way professionals have been able to develop the large, sophisticated systems that we use today.

A **module** is a file containing programmer-defined types, data object declarations, and function definitions. The order of these parts within the module is quite flexible; the only constraint is that *everything must be declared before it is used*. The modules themselves and the functions within them serve several purposes: They make it easy to use code written by someone else or reuse your own code in a new context. Far more important, though, is that they permit us to break a large program into manageable pieces in such a way that the interface among pieces is fixed and controllable. Functions, their prototypes, and header files make this possible in C; class definitions make it easier in C++.

Each **function** is a block of code that can be invoked, or called, from another function and will perform a specific, defined task. All its actions should hang together and work at the same level of detail. For example, some functions "specialize" in input or output. Others calculate mathematical formulas or do error handling. No function should be very long or very complex. Complexity is avoided by calling other functions to do subtasks.

One guideline for good style is to keep each function short enough that its parameters, local variable declarations, and code will fit on the video screen at the same time. This limits functions to about 20 lines of code on many computers. Following this guideline, any moderate-sized program will have many functions that are organized into several code modules or classes, with each module or class in a separate source file. The question then arises of where various objects should be declared: in which module and where within the module. This level of design is touched on in Chapter 23; we consider only the organization of a single module here.

9.1.1 Organization of a Module

Generally, a program has a `main()` function that calls several other library and programmer-defined functions. To compile `main()`, the compiler needs to know the **prototype** of every function called. One way this information can be supplied is by putting `main()` at the bottom of the module, while the definitions of the other functions come before it. However, many programmers dislike having the main program at the end of the file and it is customary, in C, to put `main()` at the top. When this is done, prototypes for all the functions that `main()` calls must be written above[1] it. This pattern has been followed in every program example given so far. There is one major exception to this organizational guideline: When a function is so simple that its entire definition can fit on one line, the function itself often is written at the top of the file in place of a prototype.

When you call a function from one of the C libraries, you use code that is already compiled and ready to link to your own code (see Chapter 5). Header files such as `stdio.h` and `math.h` contain prototypes (not C source code) for the precompiled library functions. When your code module uses a **library** function you `#include` the library header file at the top. This causes the preprocessor to insert all the prototypes for the library functions into your module, making it possible for the compiler to properly check your calls on the library functions.

---

[1] The prototypes also may be written inside the calling function. However, we wish to discourage this practice.

The order of parts, from the top of the source file to the bottom follows. These principles lead to the following layout for the parts in a simple program:

- `#include` commands for header files.
- Constant definitions and type declarations.[2]
- Prototypes (function declarations) and one-line functions.
- `main()`, which contains function calls.
- Function definitions, possibly containing more calls.
- Figure 9.1 illustrates the principles with a complete program and two functions.

A function's prototype may be given first, then the call, and finally the full definition of the function, like function `f()` here. Alternatively, the function may be fully defined before it is called; for example, function `g()` is defined before `main()`, which calls it.

```
#include "tools.h"
#define MIN    10.5
#define MAX    87.0

float f( float y );               /* Prototype for function f, defined below. */
float g( float y ) { return( y * y + y ); }  /* Definition of function g. */

void main( void )
{
    float x, z;

    banner();
    printf( "\n Enter a value of x between %.2f and %.2f: ", MIN, MAX );
    scanf( "%g", &x );
    z = f( x ) ;
    printf( "\n The value of x * exp(x) is: %g \n", z );
    printf( "\n The value of x * x + x  is: %g \n", g( x ) );
    bye();
}

/* ---------------------------------------------------------------------- */
/* Definition of function to calculate f = y * e to the power y. ----- */
float
f( float y )
{
    return y * exp( y ) ;
}
```

Figure 9.1.   Functions, prototypes, and calls.

---

[2]Type declarations will be discussed in Chapters 11, 13 and 14.

Notes on Figure 9.1. Functions, prototypes, and calls.

- *First box: things that precede* **main()** *in a code module.*

  1. When the C compiler reaches the **#include** command, it puts a copy of the **tools.h** file into this program. This file contains prototypes for the functions in the **tools** library, including **banner()** and **bye()**, called in this program.

  2. Included files often contain other **#include** commands. For example, the **tools.h** file contains **#include** commands for the library header files, **stdio.h**, **math.h**, **string.h**, **time.h**, and **ctype.h**. If we include **tools.h** in a program, we need not write separate include commands for these other library header files.

  3. This program uses two constants, representing the minimum and maximum values acceptable for input. These constants are defined after the **#include** command and before the prototypes.

  4. We need a prototype for a function if a call on it comes before its definition in the file. Function **f()** is called (second box) from **main()** and defined after **main()** (fourth box). Therefore, **f()** needs a prototype, which is given on the fourth line of this box.

  5. The actual definition of function **g()** is given here, rather than a prototype. When a function definition comes before any use of that function, no prototype is needed. This often is done when a function is so simple that all its work is done in the **return** statement and so short that it can be written on one line.

- *Second and third boxes: Calls on the programmer-defined functions.*

  1. We create **f()** and **g()** as two functions separate from **main()**, so that it is easy to change them when we need to do some other calculation. A good modular design keeps the calculation portion of a program separate from the user-interaction portion.

  2. In the second box, we set **z** equal to the result of calling function **f()** with the value of the variable **x**. Function **f()** was only prototyped before **main()**, so when the compiler reaches this box, the full definition of **f()** will not be known to it. However, the prototype for **f()** already was supplied, so the compiler knows that a call on **f()** should have one **float** argument and return a **float** result. This information is necessary to translate the call properly.

  3. In the third box, the function **g()** is called, and its return value is then passed directly to **printf()**. Since **g()** already was fully defined, the compiler has full knowledge of **g()** when it reaches this line and, therefore, is able to compile this call correctly.

  4. A sample output from this program, excluding the banner and closing comment, is

```
Enter a value of x between 10.50 and 87.00: 13.2

The value of x * exp(x) is: 7.13281e+06

The value of x * x + x  is: 187.44
```

- *Fourth box: Definition of programmer's function **f ()**.*

  1. Here we define **f ()**. The return type and parameter list in the function definition must agree with the prototype given earlier.
  2. Function definitions should start with a blank line and a comment describing the action or purpose of the function. Discipline yourself to do this. The dashed line provides a visual separation and helps the programmer find the beginning of the function definition. This is extremely useful in a long program; make it a habit in your work.
  3. Compare this definition to the previous one-line definition of **g ()**. The definition of **f ()** begins with a descriptive header. The code itself is spread out vertically, with only one program element on each line, according to the accepted guidelines for good style. The definition of **g ()** is written compactly on one line; that style is used only for very simple functions.

- *Inner box: A call on a library function.*

  1. We call the function **exp ()**, which is in the **math** library. We can do this because the header file, **math.h**, was included by **tools.h**, which was included in this file.
  2. The variable **y** is a **float**. The prototype for **exp ()** says that its parameter is a **double**. The type mismatch here is not a problem. The compiler will note the mismatch and automatically compile code to convert the **float** value to a **double** format during the calling process.

9.2   Communication Between Functions

In Chapter 5, we introduced the concepts of functions and function calls and defined some basic terminology. In this chapter, we review that terminology, extend the rules for defining and using functions, and discuss how the necessary communication actually happens. We use the program in Figure 9.1 and the diagram in Figure 9.2 to illustrate these topics as we discuss them.

One function in every program must be named **main ()**; it is often called the *main program*. The **main program** can call other functions and those functions can call each other, but none can call **main ()**. We use the term **caller** to refer to the function that makes the call and **subprogram** to refer to the called function. For example, in Figures 9.1 and 9.2, **main ()** is the caller and **f ()** is the subprogram.

This illustrates the function calls in Figure 9.1.

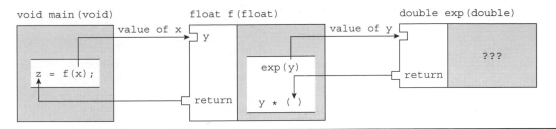

Figure 9.2.   A function is a black box.

9.2.1 The Function Interface

Each function has a defined **interface**, which includes a **parameter list** through which it receives information from the caller. Information then can be returned to the caller either through the parameter list or through the function's **return value**.[3]

A programmer must know about a function's interface to call it correctly. This information is supplied in a header file and by the documentation that normally accompanies a software library. **Header files** are used to keep the interface between the modules consistent and permit functions in one module to call functions in another.

A function's interface is defined by its prototype, which lists one or more parameters and a return type. Either the parameter list or the return type may be replaced by **void**. Each parameter listed in the prototype becomes a separate communication path by which the caller can send information into the function.[4] The function's result or return value (if not **void**) is another communication path from the subprogram back to the caller.

A **function call** consists of the name of the function followed by a list of arguments, in parentheses. Some functions have no parameters; in which case, the parentheses in the function call still must be written but with nothing between them. During the calling process, two kinds of information are sent from the caller into the subprogram:

- One argument value for each declared parameter. During a function call, the C run-time system allocates memory for the parameter variables and stores the argument values in these locations.

---

[3]Information also can be passed between a caller and a subprogram through global variables, which will be discussed in Section 9.4. However, this practice is discouraged and should be avoided wherever possible. Extensive use of global variables can make a program undebuggable.

[4]If a parameter is a pointer, it also can be a communication path by which the subprogram can send information back to the caller. This communication method will be explained in Chapter 12.

• The return address, which is the address of the first instruction in the *caller* after the function call. This address is passed by the caller to the subprogram on every call so that the function knows where to go when its execution is finished.

Control is then transferred to the **entry point** of the function, which is the first line of code in its body. Execution of the subprogram begins and continues until the last line of code is completed or control reaches a `return` statement. Control then returns to the caller at the **return address**, taking along any return value produced.

The **return type** declared in the prototype is the type of value that will be returned. If the **return statement** returns an answer of some other type, C will convert it to the declared type and return the converted value. If such a conversion is not possible, the compiler will issue an error comment. For example, in function `f()` in Figure 9.1, the value calculated by the expression in the `return` statement is of type `double` (the math-library functions always return `double`s). However, the prototype for `f()` says that it returns a `float`. What happens? The C compiler will notice the type mismatch and compile code to coerce the `double` value to a `float` format during the return process.

In Figure 9.2, the body of each function is shaded, indicating that it may appear as a "black box" to the programmer. The inner workings of a function frequently are hidden from the programmer, like those of `exp()` in this case. You need not know the details of what is inside a function to be able to use it.

In contrast, interfaces are white. This symbolizes that the programmer can (and must) know the details of the interface. The passage of information into the subprogram is represented by right-facing arrows. Function execution begins at the entry point and, when complete, control returns to the caller along a left-facing arrow, which ends at the return address in the caller. The caller continues processing from that point. The function also may return a result along the left-facing arrow.

9.2.2   Arguments and Parameters

Function parameters introduce variability into the behavior of a function. A void:void function without parameters always does the same thing in the same way.[5] In contrast, introducing even one parameter permits the actions of a function and its results to depend on the data being processed. By parameterizing a piece of code, we can make it useful under a much more general set of circumstances.

Formal parameters are part of a function definition and specify a set of unknowns; **arguments** are part of a function call and supply values for those

---

[5] An exception to this occurs if the function uses global variables or user input.

unknowns. In Figure 9.2, parameters are represented by notches along the left edge of each function's interface. Right-facing arrows connect each argument to the notch of the corresponding parameter; these arrows represent the direction in which information flows from the caller to the subprogram.

The function `f()` has one parameter, a `float` value named `y`. Even if other objects in the program have the same name, the parameter `y` in `f()` will be a distinct object, occupying a separate memory location. It is quite common to have two objects with the same name defined in different functions.

Looking at the list of library functions in Figure 5.1, we see that the `exp()` function has one parameter of type `double`. The name of this parameter is not known because `exp()` is a library function and its details have been concealed from us. During the calling process, the argument value is stored in the parameter variable, making a complete object.

A function can be `void` or have one or more parameters. Its prototype defines the correct **calling sequence**; that is, the number, order, and types of the arguments that must be written in a call. The call must supply one argument expression per parameter;[6] if the number of arguments does not match the number of parameters, the program will not compile. When a function call is executed, each argument expression in the call will be evaluated and its value will be passed from the caller to the subprogram, where it will be stored in the corresponding parameter. For example, the argument in the call on `f()` is the value of the variable named `x` in the main program. This value is a `float`, so it can be stored in the `float` parameter with no conversion.

Inside a function, the parameter names are used to refer to the argument values; the first parameter name in the function header refers to the first argument in the function call, and so on. In Figure 9.2, when `main()` makes the call `f(x)`, the value of `x` is copied into the parameter named `y`. Within the body of `f()`, the value stored in this parameter will be used wherever the code refers to the name `y`. During execution of `f()`, this value is further copied and stored in the parameter variable of `exp()`.

9.2.3 Returning Results from a Function

A function that returns a value is fundamentally different from a `void` function. A `void` function simply causes some side effect, such as output, like `banner()` in Figure 9.1. The call on such a function forms a separate statement in the code. In contrast, a function that returns a value interacts with the rest of the program by creating information for further processing. A `return` statement is used to send a result from a function back to the caller. It is represented in the diagram in

---

[6] Some functions accept a variable number of arguments; `scanf()` is an example. However, the details of how this is accomplished are beyond the scope of this text.

Figure 9.2 as a tab sticking out of the function's interface. A `return` statement can be placed anywhere in the function definition, and more than one `return` statement can be used in the same function.[7]

A function that returns a value can be called anywhere in a C statement that a variable name or literal of the same type would be permitted. Often, as in the call on `f()` in Figure 9.1, a function is called in an assignment statement. The return address for this call is in the middle of the statement, just before the assignment happens. When the value is returned from the call, `main()` will resume execution by assigning the returned value to the variable `z`.

If a function is called in the middle of an expression, the result of the function comes back to the calling program in that spot and is used to compute the value of the rest of the expression. The call on `exp()` in Figure 9.1 illustrates this. The function is called from the middle of a `return` statement: `return y * exp(y)`. The return address for this call is in the middle of the statement, just before the multiplication happens. After a value is returned by `exp()`, it will be multiplied by the value of `y` and the result returned to `main()`.

Finally, as in the call on `g()` in Figure 9.1, a function can be called from the argument list of another function. It is quite common to nest function calls in this way.

Other function returns (advanced topic).   The results of a subprogram must be passed back to the caller. Depending on the function's purpose, there may be no, one, or more results. We have given many examples of functions that return no result (such as `banner()`) or return a single result through a `return` statement. Unfortunately, only one result can be returned this way.[8] If more information must be returned to the caller, it can be returned through the parameter list using a call-by-address mechanism. However, most arguments in C are passed **by value**.[9] This means that a copy of the value of the argument is sent into the subprogram and becomes the value of the corresponding parameter. The function does not know the address of the argument, which could be a variable or the result of an expression. If the argument is a variable, the subprogram cannot change the value stored there. For example, in Figure 9.1, the subprogram `f()` receives the value of `main()`'s variable `x` but not the address of `x`. The code in the body of `f()` can change the value of its own parameter, `y`, but doing so will not change the value stored in `main()`'s `x`. Information cannot be passed back to the caller through an ordinary parameter.

In contrast, with **call by address**, the address of a variable is passed into the subprogram, which then can both use and change the information at the argument

---

[7] However, we strongly recommend using a single `return` statement at the end of the function.

[8] Only one object can be returned. However, this may be a compound object, such as a structure, containing many pieces of information. Structures are discussed in Chapter 14.

[9] The exceptions are arrays (Chapter 10) and functional arguments (Chapter 20), for which the address of the beginning of the object is passed.

address. An example of a function that sometimes must return more than one piece of information is `scanf()`. It uses the return value to return an error code, which we have ignored so far,[10] and it returns one or more data items through **address arguments**. When we call `scanf()`, we send it the address of each variable to be read. It reads the data, stores the input(s) in the given address(es), and returns a success or failure code. A programmer also can define such functions with address parameters; we explain how in Chapter 12.

9.3   Declaration-Call Correspondence

The syntax for writing a function call parallels the syntax for the prototype and the function header. However, no two of these three things follow exactly the same rules. Worse yet, ISO C and older C implementations differ extensively on the rules for function declarations and definitions. The purpose of this section is to clarify the relationships among definitions, declarations, and calls in ISO C and eliminate confusion about the details.

9.3.1   Prototypes and Parameter Type Checking

The general rule in C is that everything must be declared before it is used. There are two ways to "declare" a function: Either supply a prototype or give the complete function definition. To guarantee correctness, one or the other must occur in your program before any call on that function. The compiler uses a prototype for two purposes: checking whether the call is legal and compiling any type conversions necessary to make the argument types match the parameter types.

Missing prototypes.   The C compiler must know the prototype of a function to check whether a call is legal. Sometimes, however, a programmer forgets to either `#include` a necessary header file or write a prototype for a locally defined function. Sometimes the prototype is in the file but in the wrong place, coming after the first call on the function.

In any of these cases, the compiler does *not* just give an error comment about a missing prototype and quit. The first time it encounters a call on a nonprototyped function it simply *makes up* a prototype and continues compiling. The compiler will use the types of the actual arguments in the call to construct a prototype that matches, but all such created prototypes have the return type `int`. Sometimes this prototype is exactly what the programmer intended; other times it is wrong because the call depends on an automatic type conversion or contains an error. In any case, the constructed prototype becomes the official prototype for the function and is used throughout the rest of the program. If it has an incorrect parameter

---

[10]This will be explained in Chapter 15.

or return type, the compiler will compile too many or too few type coercions for each function call.

   If a misplaced prototype is found later in the file and it is the same as the prototype constructed by the compiler, there is no problem. However, if it is different, the compiler will give an error comment such as *type conflict in function declaration* or *illegal redefinition of function type*. This can be an astonishing error comment if the programmer does not realize that the problem is *where* the prototype was written, not *what* was in it. If the prototype really is missing, not just misplaced, a similar error comment may be produced when the compiler reaches the actual function definition. If you see such an error comment, check that all functions have correct prototypes and that they are at the top of the program.

Number of arguments.   If the number of arguments in a function call is appropriate, the compiler considers each parameter-argument pair, one by one, comparing the parameter type declared in the prototype to the type of the argument expression. If they match exactly, code is compiled to copy the argument values into the subprogram's parameters and transfer control to its entry point. If the number of arguments supplied by a function call does not match the number declared in the prototype, the compiler prints an error comment.

Type coercion of mismatched arguments and parameters.   If the number of arguments is the same as the number of parameters but their **types do not match** exactly, the compiler will attempt to convert each argument to the declared parameter type according to the standard type-conversion rules. We already discussed a large number of variations of the basic integer and floating-point types: `short`, `unsigned short`, `int`, `unsigned int`, `long`, `unsigned long`, `float`, `double`, and `long double`. In addition, there are three character types: `char`, `signed char`, and `unsigned char`. Taken as a set, these are called the **arithmetic types**. An argument of any arithmetic type can be coerced to any other arithmetic type, if needed, to make the argument's type match the type declared in the function's prototype. As an instance of such **type coercion**, in the last box of Figure 9.1, the argument in the call on `exp()` is a `float`, while the parameter is a `double`. The C compiler will include code to convert the `float` argument value to type `double` as part of the function call, and the function will receive the `double` value that it expects.

Type coercion of returned values.   The declared return type also is compared to the actual type of the value in the `return` statement. If they are different, the value will be coerced to the declared type before it is returned. The compiler generates the conversion code automatically. Conversion is possible if there is a meaningful relationship between the two types, such as both being numbers. If conversion is not possible, the compiler will issue a fatal error comment.[11] The

---

[11] If the function has an ANSI prototype, the coercions allowed for arguments and return values are the same as those allowed for assignment statements.

rule in C is that any numeric type can be converted to any other numeric type. Therefore, a `short int` can be converted to a `long int` or an `unsigned int` or a `float` and vice versa. Some kinds of argument coercions are very common and compilers simply include code for the conversion and do not notify the programmer that it was necessary. For example, normally no warning would be given when a `float` value is coerced to type `double`. At other times, compilers warn the programmer that a conversion is occuring. This happens when an unusual kind of argument conversion would be required or the conversion might result in a loss of information due to a shortening of the representation, as when a `double` value is converted to type `float`. The warning you get depends on the nature of the type mismatch, the severity of the possible consequences, and your particular compiler.

9.3.2 A Review of Familiar Prototypes

In previous chapters, we saw several examples of functions with various kinds of prototypes. These are summarized in Figures 9.3 and 9.4.

We continue by considering other kinds of prototypes and the rules for the required correspondence among a function's prototype, definition, and call. We look at a series of short functions with different configurations of parameters and results and show how the prototypes and calls relate to the function definition. In this discussion, we also cover the rules for parameter naming, parameter order, and type checking.

9.3.3 Formal Parameter Names

An ISO C prototype states the name of a function, the types of its parameters, and the return type. The parameters also may be named in the prototype, but such names are optional and often omitted. The function header (which is the first line of the function definition) states the same information, except that parameter names *are required* in the function header. They provide the only way for the programmer to refer to the argument values in the function's code.

Any legal name may be given to a formal parameter. It may be the same as or different from the name of a variable used in the function call, and both can

---

Here are examples of the kinds of `void` functions already covered, showing the prototype and corresponding call. Note that the word `void` must appear in the prototype but does not appear in the call.

Category	Prototype	Sample Call
Void:void	`void beep(void);`	`beep();`
Void:one parameter	`void srand(unsigned);`	`srand((unsigned)time(NULL));`

Figure 9.3.   **Review of prototypes for** `void` **functions.**

Here are two examples selected from the non-**void** functions we covered. Note the correspondence between the number of parameters declared in the prototype and the number of argument expressions in the call.

Category	Prototype	Sample Call
Int:void	`int rand(void);`	`num = rand();`
Double:one parameter	`double sqrt(double);`	`t = sqrt( 2 * h / GRAVITY );`

Figure 9.4.   Review of prototypes for functions that return a value.

be the same as or different from the optional name in the function's prototype.[12] The names chosen do not affect the meaning of the program because argument values are matched up with parameters by position, not by name. To illustrate this principle, we introduce a main program (Figure 9.5) that calls a function named **n_stars()** (Figure 9.6). Our discussion focuses on how a parameter enables the behavior of a function to vary.

Notes on Figure 9.5. Calling a one-parameter function.

- *First box: the function prototype.* An ISO prototype for **n_stars()** can be written two ways, with or without the optional parameter name:

This program demonstrates the syntax and use of a **void** function with one parameter.

```c
#include <stdio.h>
#include <math.h>
void n_stars( double n );       /* Function prototype. */
void main( void )
{
    double x, y;
    printf( "\nEnter the value of x: " );
    scanf( "%lg", &x );
    n_stars( x );                   /* Call the function to print x asterisks. */
    printf( "The value of x = %.2f,", x );
    y = sqrt( x );
    printf( " the square root of x = %.2f \n", y );
    n_stars( y );                   /* Call function to print sqrt(x) asterisks. */
}
```

Figure 9.5.   Calling a one-parameter function.

---

[12] However, it is good style to use the same name in the prototype and the function header.

```
void n_stars( double n )       /* Function definition: display n stars. */
{
    int k;                     /* Number of stars already printed. */
    putchar( '\n' );
    for (k = 0; k < n; ++k) putchar( '*' );       /* Print n stars. */
    printf( "\n\n" );                    /* Flush output to screen. */
}
```

Figure 9.6.   Parameters enable variations in behavior.

```
void n_stars ( double n );
void n_stars ( double );
```

This name even could be different from the actual parameter name given in Figure 9.6. This difference would not matter to the compiler because it ignores the name in the prototype. However, we prefer to include the parameter names given in the definition, so that the prototype will be an exact copy of the function header, differing only by the semicolon on the end of the prototype.

- *Second and third boxes: the function calls.* The main program calls the **n_stars()** function twice, using different argument values:

```
n_stars( x );
n_stars( y );
```

In both calls, the expression will be evaluated and its value passed into the function, where it will be stored in the parameter **n**. The argument name does not match the parameter name in either call; name matching is not required.

Notes on Figure 9.6. Parameters enable variations in behavior.

- *The function definition.* The parameter is a **double** named **n**; it is used in the loop body to control the loop that prints stars. (Printing stops after **n** stars have been printed.)
- *Output.* A sample output from this program is

```
Enter the value of x: 51

****************************************************

The value of x = 51.00, the square root of x = 7.14

********
```

9.3.4   Function Syntax: The General Case

We studied a variety of **void** and non-**void** functions having either no parameters or one parameter and discussed the essentials of prototypes, parameters, type matching rules, and the function interface. Most functions, though, have more than one parameter, so we need to study the few remaining facets of the syntax for defining and calling functions with a more complex interface. Figure 9.7 summarizes the syntax for functions with two parameters and a return value. The forms for three or more parameters follow the same pattern, with additional clauses added to the parameter list. We illustrate these rules for the general format of a C function using **cyl_vol()** in Figure 9.8. This function takes two parameters, performs a simple computation, and returns the answer.

Notes on Figure 9.8. Two parameters and a return value.

- *First box: the prototype.*

    1. As always, the prototype for the **cyl_vol()** function may be written with or without parameter names. The first box in Figure 9.8 shows one way to write the prototype for this function, with parameter names included, but the prototype also could be written this way:

       ```
       double cyl_vol( double, double );
       ```

    2. You also could write the prototype on two lines, like the function header in the third box, but there is no good reason to do so. Remember, in C, you can break a line anywhere except within a quoted string. Other line breaks are ignored by the compiler and should be used by the programmer to make the code easier to read.

This table summarizes the ISO rules and options for functions that return a value and take two parameters. Forms are given for prototypes with and without parameter names. In this figure, angle brackets are used to enclose syntactic categories: ⟨f-name⟩ means any function name; ⟨p-type⟩ means the type of a parameter, ⟨p-name⟩ means the name of a parameter, ⟨r-type⟩ means the type returned by the function, ⟨var⟩ means the name of a variable, and ⟨exp⟩ means any expression of the correct type.

Prototype syntax:	⟨r-type⟩	⟨f-name⟩	(⟨p1-type⟩ ⟨p1-name⟩,	⟨p2-type⟩ ⟨p2-name⟩);
Example:	double	cyl_vol	(double d,	double h);
Prototype syntax:	⟨r-type⟩	⟨f-name⟩	(⟨p1-type⟩,	⟨p2-type⟩);
Example:	double	cyl_vol	(double,	double);
Definition syntax:	⟨r-type⟩	⟨f-name⟩	(⟨p1-type⟩ ⟨p1-name⟩,	⟨p2-type⟩ ⟨p2-name⟩){...}
Example:	double	cyl_vol	(double d,	double h){...}
Call syntax:	⟨var⟩	=⟨f-name⟩	(⟨exp1⟩,	⟨exp2⟩);
Example:	volume	= cyl_vol	(diam,	height);

Figure 9.7.   Summary: Non-void functions with two parameters.

This program illustrates the usage of a two-parameter non-**void** function.

```
#include "tools.h"

double cyl_vol( double d, double h );                /* function prototype */

void main( void )
{
    double diam, height, volume;

    banner();
    printf( "\n Enter diameter and height of cylinder: " );
    scanf( "%lg%lg", &diam, &height );


    volume = cyl_vol( diam, height );
    printf( "\t The volume of this cylinder = %.2f \n", volume );

    bye();
}

/* -------------------------------------------------------------- */
double                          /* We return the volume of a cylinder */
cyl_vol( double d, double h ) /* with diameter=d and height=h;       */
{
    double r;                   /* r is the radius of the cylinder.   */

    r = d / 2;
    return PI * r * r * h;
}
```

Figure 9.8.   A function with two parameters and a return value.

- *Second box: the function call and output.*

    1. Since **cyl_vol()** returns a value, calls will be in the context of an assignment statement or in the argument list of another function call. This call is part of an assignment.
    2. First, we call the function and save the answer in **volume**. Then, on the next line, we send the value of **volume** to **printf()**. The calculation could be combined with the output and condensed into one statement by putting the call on **cyl_vol()** directly into the argument list for **printf()**, thus:

       ```
       printf( "\t The volume of this cylinder = %.2f \n",
               cyl_vol( diam, height ) );
       ```

    3. It is a matter of personal style which way you write this code. The one-line version is more concise and takes slightly less time and space. The two-line version, however, is easier to modify, works better with an

on-line debugger, and enhances seeing and understanding the technical calculation.

- *Third box: the function definition.*

  1. Following modern guidelines for style, we prefer to write the return type, alone, on the first line of the function definition. The second line starts with the function name on the left. Using this style makes it somewhat easier to find the function names when you scan a long program and allows writing a comment about the return value. Of course, these two lines also could be combined, thus:

     ```
     double cyl_vol( double d, double h )
     ```

  2. The code in the body of this function uses only three variable names: **d, h**, and **r**. The first two are parameters to the function, the third is defined at the top of the function's block of code. All three objects are local to the function; that is, these variables are defined by the function and only this function can access them. Every properly designed function follows this pattern and confines its code to use only locally defined names. All interaction between the function and outside variables happens through the parameter list or the function's return value.

  3. A sample output from this program, excluding the banner and closing comment is

     ```
     Enter diameter and height of cylinder:   2.0 10.0
     The volume of this cylinder = 31.42
     ```

9.3.5 Parameter Order

The order of the arguments in a function call is important. If a function's parameters are defined in one order and arguments are given in a different order in a call, the results generally will be nonsense. There is no "right" order for the parameters in a function definition; this is a design issue. However, once the definition has been written, the order of the arguments in the call must be the same. If the program has several functions that work with the same parameters, the designer should choose some order that makes sense and consistently stick to that order when defining the functions to avoid absentmindedly writing function calls with the arguments in the wrong order.

Sometimes a compiler, by performing its normal parameter type checking, can detect an error when a programmer scrambles the arguments in a function call. More often, this is not possible. For example, the function **cyl_vol()** in Figure 9.8 has two parameters, the diameter and height of a cylinder. Since the parameters are the same type, the compiler cannot tell when the programmer writes them in

the wrong order. The result will be a program that compiles, runs, and produces
the wrong answer. To further demonstrate the kind of nonsense that can result
from mixed-up arguments, we will add a second parameter to the **n_stars()**
function, adding a second dimension of variability to the function's capabilities.
The resulting function, named **n_marks()**, prints a variable character instead of
only asterisks. Figure 9.9 illustrates the **n_marks()** function and a main program
that calls it twice, correctly. The output is

This program illustrates how important it is to provide arguments in the proper order in a function call. The
boxes highlight the changes necessary to add a second parameter to the **n_stars** program in Figures 9.5
and 9.6.

```
#include <stdio.h>
#include <math.h>

void n_marks( double n, char ch );     /* function prototype */

void main( void )
{
    double x, y;                        /* How many characters to print */
    char ch1, ch2;                      /* The characters to print */

    printf( "\nEnter two characters to print: " );
    scanf( "%c %c", &ch1, &ch2 );

    printf( "\nEnter the value of x: " );
    scanf( "%lg", &x );

    n_marks( x, ch1 );                  /* Call the function to print x ch1's */

    printf( "The value of x = %.2f,", x );

    y = sqrt( x );
    printf( " the square root of x = %.2f \n", y );

    n_marks( y, ch2 );                  /* Call function to print sqrt(x) ch2's */
}
/* --------------------------------------------------------------- */
void n_marks( double n, char ch )       /* Print n copies of character ch. */
{
    int k;                              /* # of marks already printed */
    putchar( '\n' );
    for (k = 0; k < n; ++k) putchar( ch ); /* print n marks */
    printf( "\n\n" );                   /* flush output to screen */
}
```

Figure 9.9.   The importance of parameter order.

```
Enter two characters to print: 9$

Enter the value of x: 55.552

99999999999999999999999999999999999999999999999999999999

The value of x = 55.55, the square root of x = 7.45

$$$$$$$$
```

Each call prints a different mark and a different quantity of that mark. Compare this output to the output from the erroneous call in the next paragraph.

Parameter coercion errors.   When the compiler translates a function call, it either accepts the arguments as given, coerces them to the declared type of the parameter, or issues a fatal error comment. This automatic conversion can result in some weird and invalid output. For example, suppose a programmer called the `n_marks()` function but wrote the arguments in the wrong order:

```
n_marks( ch1, x );
```

The output would be

```
Enter two characters to print: 9$

Enter the value of x: 55.552

7777777777777777777777777777777777777777777777777777777777

The value of x = 55.55, the square root of x = 7.45

$$$$$$$$
```

This call certainly is not what a programmer would intend to write. However, according to the ISO C standard, this is a legal call. The standard dictates that the character `ch1` will be converted first to an `int` and then to a `double`, while the `double x` will be converted first to an `int` and then to a `char` to match the parameter types in the prototype `void n_marks( double, char )`. Using this input, the programmer would expect to see a line of 56 nines, but instead a line of 57 sevens is printed because of the conversions: The ASCII code for `9` is 57, which will be converted to 57.00, and the 55.552 will be converted to 55, which is the code for `7`. Some compilers at least may give a warning comment about these two "suspicious" type conversions, but all standard ISO C compilers will compile the conversion code and produce an executable program. When you try to run such a program, the results will be nonsense, as shown.

9.4   Data Modularity

A large program may contain hundreds or thousands of objects (functions, variables, constants, types, etc.). If a programmer had to remember the name, purpose, and status of this many objects, large programs would be very hard to write and harder to debug. Happily, C supports modular programming. Each module has its own independent set of objects and interaction between modules can be strictly controlled. The same name can be used twice, in different modules, to refer to different objects, so a programmer need not keep a mental catalog of the hundreds of names that might have been used. C's accessibility and visibility rules determine *where* a variable or constant may be used and *which* object a name denotes in each context. We use the program in Figures 9.10 and 9.11 to illustrate these concepts and the related concept of scope.

9.4.1   Scope and Visibility

The **scope** of a name is the portion of the program in which it exists. The three levels of scope are local, global, and external; respectively meaning that access to an object can be restricted to a single program block or function, shared by all functions in the same file or program module, or shared by parts of the program in different files or program modules. More specifically,

- Parameters and variables defined within a function are completely **local**; no other functions have access to them.
- We are permitted to declare variables outside of the function definitions, either at the top of a file or between functions. These are called **global** variables. They can be used by other modules and all the functions in the code module that occur after their definition in the file. It is possible (but not the default) to restrict the use of these symbols to the module in which they are defined.
- All global names and all the functions defined in a module default to **extern**; that is, they are **external** symbols unless declared otherwise. This means that their names are given to the system's linker and all the modules linked together in a complete program can use these variables.[13]

We say that a locally declared variable or parameter is **visible**, or **accessible**, from the point of its declaration until the block's closing }. This means that the statements within the block can use the declared name, but no other statements can (i.e., the scope and visibility of a local variable are the same). A global or external variable is visible everywhere in the program after its definition, *except* where another, locally declared variable bears the same name. If a function has a parameter or local variable named **x** and a statement **x = x+1**, the local **x** will be

---

[13]External linkage will be discussed in Chapters 21 and 23.

This program calculates the pressure of a tank of CO gas using two gas models. The functions in Figure 9.11 are part of this program and should be in the same source file.

```
#include "tools.h"
#define R    8314              /* universal gas constant */
float ideal( float v );       /* prototypes */
float vander( float v );

float temp;                    /* GLOBAL variable:  temperature of CO gas */
```

```
void main( void )
{
    /* Local Variables ----------------------------------- */
    float m;                      /* mass of CO gas, in kilograms */
    float vol;                    /* tank volume, in cubic meters */
    float vmol;                   /* molar specific volume */
    float pres;                   /* pressure (to be calculated) */

    banner();

    printf( "\n Input the temperature of CO gas (degrees K): " );
    scanf( "%g", &temp );
    printf( "\n The mass of the gas (kg) is: " );
    scanf( "%g", &m );
    printf( "\n The tank volume (cubic m) is: " );
    scanf( "%g", &vol );

    vmol = 28.011 * vol / m;        /* molar volume of CO gas */
    pres = ideal( vmol );               /* pressure; ideal gas model */
    printf( "\n The ideal gas at %.3g K has pressure "
            "%.3f kPa \n", temp, pres );
    pres = vander( vmol );          /* pressure; Van der Waal's model */
    printf( "\n Van der Waal's gas has pressure "
            "%.3f kPa \n\n", pres );

    bye();
}
```

Figure 9.10.   Gas models before global elimination.

used no matter how many other objects named **x** are in the program's "universe." Therefore, the visibility of a global variable is that portion of its scope in which it is not masked or hidden by a local variable. This is a very important feature; it is what frees us from concern about conflicts with the names of all the hundreds of other objects in the program.

These functions are part of the gas models program in Figure 9.10 and are found at the bottom of the same source code file.

```
/* ------------------------------------------------------------------
** Pressure of CO gas in a tank, using the ideal gas equation Pv = RT.
*/
float
ideal( float v )
{
    float p;                     /* LOCAL variable DECLARATION */

    p = R * temp / v;           /* pressure in Pascals */
    return p / 1000.0;          /* pressure in kilo Pascals (kPa) */
}
```

```
/* ------------------------------------------------------------------
** Pressure of CO gas in a tank, using Van der Waal's equation,
** P = RT/(v-b) - a/(v*v).
*/
float
vander( float v )
{
    float p;                          /* LOCAL declaration, not same p as above */
    const float a = 1.474E+05;                       /* constants for CO gas */
    const float b = .0395;

    p = R * temp / (v - b) - a / (v * v);       /* pressure in Pascals */
    return p/1000.0;                            /* kPa pressure */
}
```

Figure 9.11.   Functions for gas models before global elimination.

9.4.2 Global and Local Names

Insofar as possible, all variables should be declared locally in the function that uses them. Information used by two or more functions should be passed via parameters. The use of global variables usually is a bad idea; any variable that can be seen and used by all the functions in a program might be changed erroneously by any part of the program. When global variables are in use, no one part of the program can be fully understood or debugged without considering the entire thing.

    While global variables are not encouraged, constants and types usually are declared at the top of a file because they are necessary to coordinate the actions of different parts of a program. Since the values of **const** variables and **#define**d symbols cannot be changed, their global visibility does not foster the same kind of problems as a global variable. Further, declaring constants and types at the top of a file makes them easier to locate and revise, if necessary.

A function prototype can be declared globally or locally in every function that calls it. Each style of organization has its advantages. In this text, we declare most prototypes globally because it is simpler. We illustrate some of these issues using the program in Figure 9.10, which has two subprograms (Figure 9.11) and a variety of local and global declarations (Figure 9.12).

Notes on Figures 9.10, 9.11, and 9.12. Gas models before global elimination.

We use a main program, two functions, a global constant, and a global variable to examine the scope and visibility of names in C. Figure 9.12 illustrates the scope of the symbols defined in this program.

- *First box, Figure 9.10: global declarations and included files.*

  1. The `#include "tools.h"` means that everything in the file `tools.h` will be copied into this program at this point. All the objects declared in `tools.h`, therefore, will have a global scope in this program.
  2. The constant `R` and the variable `temp` are declared globally. In Figure 9.12, these names are written in the gray box, which represents the global scope. Here, they are visible and can be used by any function in this file; that is, by `main()`, `ideal()`, and `vander()`. The functions `ideal()` and `vander()` also can be called from any part of this file.

The diagram shows the scope of the functions, variables, and constants defined in the gas models program from Figures 9.10 and 9.11. Each box represents one scope; the gray box represents the global scope. Local scopes are white boxes; within each, parameters are listed above the dotted line and local variables and constants below it. Symbols defined in the gray area are visible everywhere in the program where they are not masked. Symbols in the white boxes are visible only within the scope that defines them.

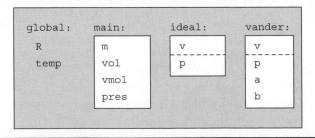

Figure 9.12.   Name scoping in gas models program, before global elimination.

3. It is considered very bad style to use a global variable such as `temp`. We do so only to demonstrate the meaning of global declarations and show how to eliminate them.

4. A global constant such as `R` creates fewer problems than a global variable. It is common for a program to use global constants and is not considered bad style.

- *Second box, Figure 9.10: declarations for* `main()`.

  1. The four variables `m`, `vol`, `vmol`, and `pres` are local to `main()` and therefore visible only within `main()`. In Figure 9.12, the leftmost white rectangle represents the scope created by `main()`. Inside it is a list of `main()`'s local variables, which are "visible" only within the function `main()`.

  2. The functions `ideal()` and `vander()` cannot access the values in `m`, `vol`, `vmol`, and `pres` because the values are local within `main()`.

- *Third box, Figure 9.10: code for* `main()`.

  1. This code can use the definitions included by the first box and the global variable and constant defined in the first box as well as the variables defined in the second box.

  2. This code cannot use the parameters, variables, or constants defined by the two functions in Figure 9.11. If we tried to use `v`, `p`, `a`, or `b` here, it would cause an undefined-symbol error at compile time.

  3. The two inner boxes contain the calls on the functions `ideal()` and `vander()`. These functions will need to be modified to eliminate the use of the global variable.

  4. Sample output from this program (banner and closing message have been omitted) is

```
Input the temperature of CO gas (degrees K): 28.5

The mass of the gas (kg) is: 1.2

The tank volume (cubic m) is: 3

The ideal gas at 28.5 K has pressure 3.385 kPa
Van der Waal's gas has pressure 3.357 kPa
```

- *First box, Figure 9.11: code for the function* `ideal()`.

  1. Because this function is compiled at the same time as the code in Figure 9.10, it can use any object, such as `R` or `temp`, that is defined (or included) in the first box in Figure 9.10.

  2. In Figure 9.12, the center rectangle represents the scope created by `ideal()`. Inside it are `ideal()`'s parameter `v` and the local variable

p, which are visible only within **ideal()** and cannot be used outside this function.

- *Second box, Figure 9.11: code for the function* **vander()**.

1. This function also can use objects such as **R** and **temp** that are defined (or included) in the first box in Figure 9.10.
2. In Figure 9.12, the rightmost rectangle represents the scope created by **vander()**. Inside it are **vander()**'s parameter **v** and the local variables **a**, **b**, and **p** (**a** and **b** actually are constants). These are visible only within **vander()** and cannot be used outside this function.
3. Each parameter or local variable declaration creates a new object. Therefore, the **p** defined here is a different variable than the **p** defined in **ideal()**, with its own memory location, even though they have the same name.
4. If the local variable **p** had been named **temp**, this function would compile but not work properly because the local variable would mask the global variable. Every reference to **temp** in **vander()** would access the local variable, and the information in the global **temp** would not be accessible within the function. The next section shows how to improve the lines of communication so that these difficulties do not occur.

9.4.3 Eliminating Global Variables

We introduced a programming style in which interaction with the user is done by one function and calculations by another. This separation of work makes a program maximally flexible and easier to modify at a later date. However, since one function reads the input data and another uses it for calculations, the data value must be communicated from the first to the second.

A beginning programmer often will be tempted to use a global variable because it provides one way to solve this communication problem. A global variable is visible to both the data input function and the calculation function, so nothing special has to be done to communicate the value from the first to the second.

In a small program, using global variables might seem easy and communicating through parameters might seem to be a nuisance. However, global variables almost always are a mistake,[14] because they allow unintended interactions between distant parts of the program. They make it hard to follow the flow of data through the process, and they make it harder to modify and extend the program. In a large program, global variables become a debugging nightmare. It is hard to know what parts of the program change them and under what conditions. There-

---

[14]The program in Figure 12.15 shows an instance where the use of global variables is acceptable.

fore, it is important, from the beginning, to avoid global variables and learn to use parameters effectively.

We will use the program in Figures 9.10 and 9.11 to demonstrate the technique for eliminating global variables. The result is shown in Figures 9.13 and 9.14. Parameters are the right way to solve the communication problem. They

---

This program is a revised and improved version of the gas models program in Figures 9.10 and 9.11; it solves the communication problem by using a parameter instead of a global variable. The functions in Figure 9.14 are part of the revised program and should be in the same source file.

```c
#include "tools.h"
#define R   8314              /* universal gas constant */

float ideal( float v, float temp );
float vander( float v, float temp );

void main( void )
{
    /* Local Variables ------------------------------------- */
    float temp;               /* Temperature of CO gas */
    float m;                  /* mass of CO gas, in kilograms */
    float vol;                /* tank volume, in cubic meters */
    float vmol;               /* molar specific volume */
    float pres;               /* pressure (to be calculated) */

    banner();
    printf( "\n Input the temperature of CO gas (degrees K): " );
    scanf( "%g", &temp );
    printf( "\n The mass of the gas (kg) is: " );
    scanf( "%g", &m );
    printf( "\n The tank volume (cubic m) is: " );
    scanf( "%g", &vol );

    vmol = 28.011 * vol / m;                /* molar volume of CO gas */
    pres = ideal( vmol, temp );    /* pressure; ideal gas model */
    printf( "\n The ideal gas at %.3g K has pressure "
            "%.3f kPa \n", temp, pres );
    pres = vander( vmol, temp );   /* pressure; Van der Waal's model */
    printf( " Van der Waal's gas has pressure "
            "%.3f kPa \n\n", pres );

    bye();
}
```

Figure 9.13. Eliminating the global variable.

These functions illustrate how to eliminate a global variable from Figure 9.11. The boxes highlight the changes necessary to replace the global variable by adding a parameter to each function.

```
/* ----------------------------------------------------------------------
** Pressure of CO gas in a tank, using the ideal gas equation Pv = RT.
*/
float
ideal( float v, float temp )
{
    float p;                    /* LOCAL variable DECLARATION */

    p = R * temp / v;           /* pressure in Pascals */
    return p / 1000.0;          /* pressure in kilo Pascals (kPa) */
}
/* ----------------------------------------------------------------------
** Pressure of CO gas in a tank, using Van der Waal's equation,
** P = RT/(v-b) - a/(v*v).
*/
float
vander( float v, float temp )
{
    float p;                         /* LOCAL declaration, not same p as above */
    const float a = 1.474E+05;
    const float b = .0395;                 /* constants for CO gas */

    p = R * temp / (v - b) - a / (v * v);  /* pressure in Pascals */
    return p / 1000.0;                     /* kPa pressure */
}
```

Figure 9.14.   Functions for gas models after global elimination.

make the sharing of data explicit and they prevent unintended sharing with un-related functions. In general, global variables should be replaced by parameters. The transformation works for globals used to send information into a function; a variant of this technique[15] is needed if the function also uses the global variables to send information back out.

Notes on Figures 9.13 and 9.14. Eliminating the global variable.

We start with the main program in Figure 9.10 and the two functions in Figure 9.11, which communicate through a global variable. To eliminate this variable and replace it by a parameter, we need to change five lines in Figure 9.10 and two lines in Figure 9.11.

---

[15] This variation uses pointer parameters, which will be covered in Chapter 12.

- *First box of Figure 9.13.* The prototypes for the functions `ideal()` and `vander()` found in the first box of Figure 9.10 need to be changed to include an additional parameter of the same type as the global variable.
- *Second box of Figure 9.13.* The declaration of `temp` must be moved out of the global area where it was defined in Figure 9.10 and into `main()`'s local area.
- *Third and fourth boxes of Figure 9.13.* The function calls in these boxes must be modified to include an additional argument, the value of the former global variable, which is now a local variable in `main()`.
- *First box of Figure 9.14.* A new parameter was added to the parameter list in the prototype for `ideal()`. We also must add the parameter to the function header.
- *Second box of Figure 9.14.* We must add the new parameter to the list for `vander()` as well. It is important to be consistent about parameter order when adding parameters, to avoid the problems mentioned earlier.

9.5   Function Call Graphs

We use flow diagrams to visualize the flow of control through the statements of a single function or the transition from one function to another during execution. Another kind of diagram, a **function call graph**, is useful for showing the relationships between functions established by function calls. In a function call graph (see Figure 9.15), a box at the top is used to represent the function `main()`. Below it, attached to the branches of a bracket, is one box for each of the functions called by the main program.[16] As far as possible, these are listed left to right in the

---

This is a function call graph for the gas pressure program in Figure 9.13.

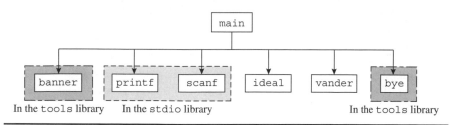

Figure 9.15.   A simple function call graph.

---

[16] Various elaborations of this basic scheme are in use. In one version, the function arguments are written on the arrows. We choose to introduce the concepts by using the simplest scheme.

This is a function call graph for the functions, prototypes, and calls of the program in Figure 9.1.

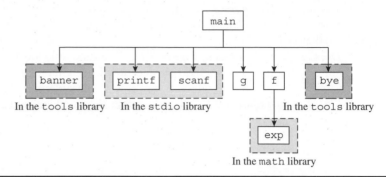

Figure 9.16.   Function call graph with two levels of calls.

order in which they appear in the program. Each function has only one box; if it is called several times, there is no sign of that in the diagram. A very simple program is charted in Figure 9.15. We have added shading around the boxes to indicate which functions are in the standard libraries and which are in the **tools** library.

The pattern of one box pointing at others is repeated when diagramming a more complex program; a box and a connection are drawn for each function called by a first-level function. In Figure 9.1, the main program calls a programmer-defined function, **f()**, which in turn, calls a function named **exp()** from the **math** library. The resulting function call graph, shown in Figure 9.16, has boxes at three levels. In a large program, a function call graph will have many boxes at several levels and may have complex dependencies among the functions (arrows may point from a lower level to an upper level). We use call graphs to visualize the relationships among functions in future program examples. The graph becomes more and more important as the number of functions increases and the interactions among functions become more complex.

In some programs it becomes beneficial to add information to the call graph concerning what is being passed between the functions. This would require an arrow for every parameter in every function call. If a program makes many function calls, this can get very complicated very quickly. Therefore, for the sake of clarity, we omit parameter and return information from the call graphs presented in this text.

9.6   Program Design and Construction

In the gas pressure example, we started with a program and its two functions and analyzed it section by section. This is a good way to understand how a given program works, but it gives little perspective on how a program with functions is developed. In this section, we reverse the process and show how to develop a program and its subprograms from the specification.

9.6.1 The Process

The first step in designing a program is to decide what you want the program to do and specify it as precisely as possible. If there is any doubt about the specifications or any missing information, this must be cleared up before proceeding.

Start with `main()` and the `work()` function.   To design and construct the program, we start by analyzing the requirements at the most general level, then we add detail, one area at a time, until the program is complete. Program elements that are simple and straightforward are written immediately. Those that seem complex or require more thought are deferred and written as a programmer-defined subprogram.

The `main()` program follows a basic form with a few variations that should be familiar by now. We develop a `main()` function by following these steps:

1. *The skin.* Write the necessary `#include` commands. Write the first and last lines of `main()`. Decide what greeting message and headings you need. Write output statements to do this job. At the bottom, write a call on `bye()` or some other appropriate termination code.

2. *Multiple data sets.* Will there be more than one data set? If so, write a processing loop with a call on a `work()` function (as in Figure 6.12) that will repeat the process until the user chooses to quit.

3. *The skeleton.* Next, prepare the **function skeleton**; that is, fill in the middle section of `main()` or write the `work()` function, if there is one. Start by listing the major phases in processing a single data set. Generally these phases are input, calculation, and output; but one of these phases might not be needed and the calculation phase may have multiple steps. Write the code to perform each phase if it is only one or two lines long.

4. *Major subsystems.* For longer or more complex processing tasks, invent a name for a function to do a task and write a call on that function with whatever arguments you think it will need. It is not necessary to get the argument list exactly right at this stage; you will return to complete this call later, after you have designed the function interface. If your function returns a value, store it in a variable and write a declaration for that variable.

5. *Declarations.* Go back to the top of `main()` and make sure there is a declaration for every object you have named. Write a comment explaining the purpose of each variable or constant. If you wrote declarations as you went along, move them all to the top of `main()`.

6. *The call graph.* Draw the first level of a function call graph showing how your functions relate to `main()`.

Designing the functions.   We describe the process of designing one function; it must be repeated, on each function in turn, until all the functions have been designed and coded. To begin, choose one of the functions you have named and focus your attention on it. It often is helpful to start with the first one called.

1. *The idea.* Write a comment block for the top of the function that describes its purpose. Include a brief description of the result returned (if any) or the side effects of the function (input, output, changes in memory variables that can be accessed by the caller).

2. *The interface.* What parameters are needed for this function? Choose a name and type for each and write a comment that describes its meaning and purpose. Write a prototype for the function. Make sure your return type agrees with the type expected by the caller. Write the first and last lines of the function below the comment block.

3. *Preconditions.* Does your code make any assumptions about the data? If so, add comments at the top of your function listing these assumptions. These are called the **preconditions** for your subprogram. Can every possible argument value allowed by the preconditions be processed, or is it necessary to restrict the argument values in some way? If a restriction is necessary, write a test for the illegal argument value and code to display an appropriate error message or return an error code.

4. *The skeleton.* List, in order, the specific tasks that this function must do and figure out a method to do each step. If some part of this description becomes long or complex, invent another function name to do the task. Add the new function to your function call graph.

5. *Declarations.* Are any constants needed to do these tasks? If so, define them. Also define any variable that you are certain you will need.

6. *Information.* Do your parameters provide enough information to carry out the required tasks? If not, go back to step 2 and add another parameter to the prototype.

7. *The muscles.* Write the code to fill in the skeleton for your algorithm. If you have decided to use a lower-level function to do part of the job, write a tentative call on it and postpone its design until later.

8. *More declarations.* Add declarations for any variables that were used in step 7 but not yet defined.

9. *Foreign relations.* Go back to all the functions that call this function and correct the argument lists in all the tentative function calls that you previously wrote. Update the prototype.

Testing and debugging.   Testing can and should happen at many stages of the program construction process. This, of course, requires a test plan giving several data sets with corresponding final answers. For a complex program, the test plan should also include some data sets with correct intermediate results that will be produced by some of the functions called during the calculation process.

Begin trying to compile and test the code as soon as the `main()` and `work()` functions are complete. Of course, at this stage, the program cannot produce meaningful results. However, it is important to know that the outer framework of the program is free from compile-time errors and at least can print greetings and instructions and begin the task of processing the data. Two techniques, testing by amputation and stub testing, are used to test partially complete programs.

After completing the main program and one function, testing should begin. Assume that your code also contains a call on a second function that has not been written. The program cannot be compiled as it stands because of this call. One solution is **testing by amputation**, in which you temporarily "amputate" the call. If the function is a **void** function, this can be done easily by enclosing the call in a comment. Amputating a non-**void** function requires an additional step: Wherever the return value would have been used, substitute an arbitrary (but recognizable) constant value. Then compile the program, fix any compilation errors, and run it. Check the output, looking for the correct general form and correcting any visible errors. The amputated call should be restored when you are ready to develop the code to process it. This process can be repeated until all necessary functions are written.

A second method used to manage large programs is called **stub testing**. In this method, the code for the `main()` function is written and "dummy" definitions are supplied for the other functions. A dummy function definition, called a **function stub**, consists of the function header and a statement that prints a comment such as *entering function foo, parameters are:* ... If the function is supposed to return a value, let it return a constant of the proper type. This technique lets you start compiling and debugging your program early, while the program is still small, thus making it easier to find and fix errors. Function stubs are replaced one by one as their corresponding functions are developed.

When all parts of the program are complete and compiled, we run the program using the data in the test plan and verify that the output is exactly what we expected. Any differences from the expected values should be explored. Sometimes slight differences occur because of round-off error; these can be ignored. However, the cause of any major discrepancy must be found and corrected.

Finally, the appearance of the output should be polished and the comments and other documentation, such as instructions for the user, should be checked over to make sure that they adequately explain the program.

9.6.2 Stepwise Development of a Program

We now apply the design steps from Section 9.6.1 to develop a program for a real problem: calculating the temperature of a cooling fin, diagrammed in Figure 9.17.

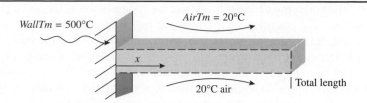

Problem scope: A cooling fin of rectangular cross section extends out from a wall, as shown. Print a table of temperatures every 0.005 m along the fin.

Formulas: The cooling properties of a fin depend on temperatures of the wall and the air and a fin constant, *FinC*, which is a function of the film coefficient of the air and the thermal conductivity and cross-sectional area of the fin. A fin is slender if its length is an order of magnitude greater than the height or width of its rectangular cross section. Given a long, slender fin with a rectangular cross section, the temperature of the fin at a distance x from the wall is given by the equation

$$\text{Temperature}(x) = AirTm + (WallTm - AirTm) \times \frac{\cosh[FinC \times (len - x)]}{\cosh(FinC \times len)}$$

Constants required: Temperature of the air, $AirTm = 20°C$; temperature of the wall at the base of the fin, $WallTm = 500°C$; fin constant $FinC = 26.5$.

Input: Length of the fin, len, in meters.

Output required: Print column headings `Distance from base (m)` and `Temperature (C)`. Beneath the headings print a table of temperatures starting with the temperature at the wall ($x = 0$). Print one line for each increment of 0.005 m up to the length of the fin.

Computational requirements: Print the distance from the wall to three decimal places and the temperature to one.

Figure 9.17.   Problem specification: fin temperature.

The specification.   This problem arose from a real application: designing the cooling apparatus for a piece of machinery. The problem specification comes directly from the set of engineering principles and formulas in use by the designer.[17] Figure 9.17 is a diagram of the required cooling fin and specifications for a program to analyze its temperature gradient. We now develop a `main()` program for the fin application.

---

[17] F. Incropera and D. DeWitt, *Fundamentals of Heat and Mass Transfer*, 4th ed. (New York: Wiley, 1996).

Steps in writing `main()`.

1. *The skin.* We start by writing the usual `#include` commands and the first and last few lines of `main()` (the greeting message and termination code):

```
#include "tools.h"
void main( void )
{
    banner();
    puts( " Temperature Along a Cooling Fin" );
    /* Program code will go here. */
    bye();
}
```

2. *Multiple data sets.* We will write this program for only one data set, so we do not need a processing loop or a `work()` function.

3 and 4. *The skeleton and major subsystems.* Next we fill in the middle section of `main()`. We need two basic steps:

   (a) Input a fin length.
   (b) Print a temperature table for that length.

   We write the code for step a directly because it is only two lines; however, step b is more complex so we invent the function `print_table()` to perform the task.

```
float len;              /* Length of the cooling fin. */
printf( " Please enter length of the fin (m): " );
scanf( "%g", &len );
print_table( len );
```

5 and 6. *Declarations and the call graph.* The first draft of the main program is now complete; it is shown in Figure 9.18 with the corresponding call graph.

This main program contains one call on a function that has not yet been written. We would like to use the C compiler to check the work so far but we cannot compile the program as it stands because the definition of `print_table()` is missing. So we create a stub for `print_table()`. This consists of an identifying comment, a function header that matches the call, and a single output statement to let the programmer track the program's progress. We put this stub at the end of the program and a matching prototype at the top (see Figure 9.19). The stub served its purpose when we compiled this file. There were a few errors, but the program is so short that they were easy to find and fix. It ran successfully, producing this output:

This code was written piece by piece in development steps 1 through 6. The corresponding call graph follows.

```
#include "tools.h"
void print_table( float N );
void main( void )
{
    float len;                            /* Length of the cooling fin (m). */
    banner();
    puts( " Temperature Along a Cooling Fin" );
    printf( " Please enter length of the fin (m): " );
    scanf( "%g", &len );
    print_table( len );
    bye();
}
```

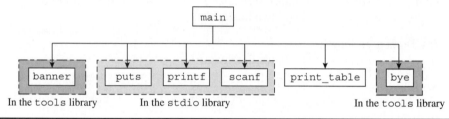

Figure 9.18.   First draft of `main()` **for the fin program.**

```
Temperature Along a Cooling Fin
Please enter length of the fin (m): .06
>>> Entering print_table with parameter 0.06
```

From this, we can see that the program is starting and ending properly and receiving its input correctly. We now can start work on the functions.

```
/* Stub:  ----------------------------------------------------------------
** Print a table of temperatures for a fin that is N meters long.
*/
void
print_table( float N )
{
    puts ( " >>> Entering print_table with parameter %g", N );
}
```

Figure 9.19.   A `print_table()` **stub for the fin program.**

Writing the function to print the table.

1. *The idea.* We wrote the comment block for `print_table()` when we generated its function stub.

2 and 3. *The interface and preconditions.* We already wrote a prototype and a function stub for `print_table()`. This function has no return value and only one parameter, the length of the fin, which must be a positive number. We named the parameter *N* and declared it a `float` when we created the function stub.

Since *N* must be positive, we add a line to the comment block at the beginning of the stub to document this precondition. We now have this skeleton:

```
/* ----------------------------------------------------
** Print a table of temperatures for a fin N m long.
**       N must be greater than 0.
*/
void print_table( float N ) { /* Code goes here */ }
```

If "bulletproof" code were needed, we would add a test for negative values of *N* and print an error message if they are detected.

4. *The skeleton and the call graph.* To print a table, we must (a) print table headings, (b) print several lines of detail, and (c) print table footings. To print the detailed lines, we need a loop that will produce one line on each iteration. For each line, we must compute and print the temperature at the current distance, *x*, from the wall. We invent a function named `compute_temp()` to compute the temperature. Our revised function call graph is shown in Figure 9.20.

5. *Declarations.* We need a constant in this function: the step size for the loop. The specification says that the temperature should be calculated every 0.005 meter, but it always is unwise to bury constants like that in the code. We define the step size as a local constant so that it will be easy to modify in the future. It is obvious that we also need at least

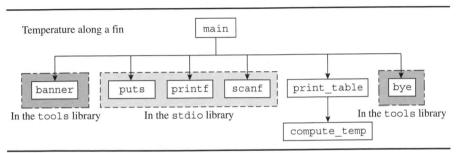

Figure 9.20.   Final call graph for fin program.

one variable, **x**, to hold the current distance from the wall and another, **temp**, to hold the result of the **compute_temp()** calculation:

```
const float step = .005;    /* Step size for loop. */
float x;                    /* Distance from wall. */
float temp;                 /* Temperature at x. */
```

6. *Information.* We have completed the first draft of **print_table()** and discovered no need for additional parameters, so we are finished for now.

7. *The muscles.* Next, we write the code for the tasks listed in step 4. We do this in a layered fashion: at each step we do what is obvious and defer the less obvious parts of the job. Tasks 4a and 4c are simple so we start by coding them:

```
printf(
   "\n Distance from base (m)      Temperature (C) \n"
   " ---------------------      --------------- \n" );
   /* loop will go here */
printf(
   " ---------------------      --------------- \n" );
```

Printing the detailed lines requires a loop that starts at distance 0.0 from the wall and increases to the length of the fin in increments of the defined step size. Since the loop variable, **x**, is not an integer, we need an epsilon value for the floating comparison that ends the loop. This epsilon must be smaller than the step size; we arbitrarily set it to half the step size:

```
float epsilon = step/2.0;        /* Tolerance */
```

We are ready to code the loop. We start with the loop skeleton and defer the computation and printout:

```
for (x = 0.0; x < N + epsilon; x += step) {/*Defer*/}
```

Now we approach the loop body. The loop prints the lines of the table one at a time. For each one, we must compute the current distance, x, from the wall and the temperature at distance x. The distance computation is handled by the loop control; the remaining tasks are to call **compute_temp()** and print the result:

```
temp = compute_temp( x );
printf( "%12.3f %24.1f \n", x, temp );
```

In the format, we use **%f** conversion specifiers because we want a neat table with the same number of decimal places printed for every line (3 for **x** and 1 for **temp**). We supply a field width so that the output will appear in neat columns. To find the correct field width, we either count the letters in the headings or guess; a guess that is too big or too small can be adjusted after we see the output. We now have completed the first draft of the code for **print_table()**; it is shown in Figure 9.21.

```
/* -----------------------------------------------------------
** Print a table of temperatures for a fin that is N meters long.
**       N must be greater than 0.
*/
void
print_table( float N )
{
    const float step = .005;        /* Step size for loop. */
    float epsilon = step / 2.0;     /* Tolerance. */
    float x;                        /* Distance from wall; 0.0..N. */
    float temp;                     /* Temperature at x. */

    printf( "\n Distance from base (m)     Temperature (C) \n"
            " ----------------------     --------------- \n" );
    for (x = 0.0; x < N + epsilon; x += step) {
        temp = compute_temp( x );
        printf( "%12.3f %24.1f \n", x, temp );
    }
    printf( " ----------------------     --------------- \n" );
}
```

Figure 9.21.   Fin program: First draft of `print_table()` **function.**

8. *Foreign relations.* We did not change the parameter list, so the call on
   `print_table()` inside `main()` still is correct. Therefore, we need not
   go back to `main()` at this time and modify the prototype and the call.
   (However, we might need to do this later.)

We have completed a main program and one function with a tentative call
on a second function that has not been written. It is time to compile again. We
cannot compile the program as it stands because of the call on `compute_temp()`.
Although we could write another function stub, in this case we choose to temporarily "amputate" the call on `compute_temp()` by enclosing it in a comment
and setting the variable `temp` to an arbitrary (but recognizable) constant value:

```
temp = 1.1;   /* compute_temp( x ); */
```

Now we compile the program, fix any compilation errors, and run it. Our
program ran successfully, producing the output that follows (only the first and
last few lines are shown). Looking at this table, we see that the number of rows
printed is correct and the numbers are adequately centered under the headings.
The numbers in the first column are correct and the numbers in the second column
are the constant value we used when we amputated the call on `compute_temp()`.

```
Temperature Along a Cooling Fin
Please enter length of the fin (m): .06
```

```
Distance from base (m)     Temperature (C)
----------------------     ---------------
        0.000                    1.1
        0.005                    1.1
        0.010                    1.1
         ...                     ...
        0.050                    1.1
        0.055                    1.1
        0.060                    1.1
```

Designing the `compute_temp()` function.   We write the temperature computation function following the usual steps:

1–3. *The idea, the interface, and preconditions.* The `compute_temp()` function must calculate the temperature of the fin at a distance x from the wall. Tentatively, we have given it one parameter, a `float` named x, which will range between 0 meters and the length of the fin. The function must return a `float` value to `print_table()`. We write a comment block and the shell of the function:

```
/* ----------------------------------------------------
** Compute temperature at distance x from wall.
**       x must be between 0 m and length of fin.
*/
float compute_temp( float x ){/* Code goes here. */}
```

4–7. *The skeleton, the muscles, and missing information.* We compute the temperature using the formula in the specifications (see Figure 9.17) and return the answer. This is a simple task that need not be broken down further. Here is the resulting statement:

```
return AirTm + (WallTm - AirTm)
       * cosh( FinC * (N-x) ) / cosh( FinC * N );
```

Looking at this formula, we see that it involves several variables (wall temperature, air temperature, fin constant, and length of the fin), not just the distance x from the wall. However, the first three values are given as constant numbers in the problem specification. We could write constants for these quantities in our formula, but the program would be much more useful if these values could be varied. Therefore, we choose to define all three constants in `main()` and add them to the parameter lists of both `print_table()` and `compute_temp()`. By placing all these constants in `main()`, we make them easy to find and modify. It also would be easy to change them into input variables if that were desired. Last, the fin length is a missing parameter; it is read in `main()` and we must pass it from `main()` through `print_table()` to this function. Similarly, we must pass the constants from `main()` to `compute_temp()`. To do so, we need to change the prototypes of both functions and correct two function calls.

8. *Foreign relations.* We have three constants and one input variable that must be passed from `main()` to `compute_temp()` as parameters. Although the order of the new parameters is not crucial, we want an order that makes some sense and can be remembered, so we put all the properties of the fin together. Our new prototypes are

```
void print_table( float, float, float, float );
float compute_temp( float,float,float,float,float );
```

Next, we add three constant definitions to `main()` and change the call on `print_table()` to use them:

```
const float FinC = 26.5;    /* Fin constant. */
const float WallTm = 500.0; /* Wall temperature, C */
const float AirTm = 20.0;   /* Air temperature, C */
print_table( len, FinC, WallTm, AirTm );
```

Last, the function call in `print_table()` must also be changed:

```
temp = compute_temp( x, N, FinC, WallTm, AirTm );
```

The completed `compute_temp()` function is shown in Figure 9.22; the rest of the adjusted program is in Figure 9.23. The first and last few lines of the output (with banner and termination line omitted) are

```
Temperature Along a Cooling Fin
Please enter length of the fin (m): .06

Distance from base (m)     Temperature (C)
----------------------     ---------------
       0.000                     500.0
       0.005                     445.5
       0.010                     398.5
       ....                      .....
       0.055                     209.6
       0.060                     208.0
----------------------     ---------------
```

The problem specifications are given in Figure 9.17 and the program in Figures 9.23 and 9.21.

```
/* -------------------------------------------------
** Compute the temperature at distance x from wall.
**       x must be between 0.0 m and length of fin.
*/
float
compute_temp( float x, float N, float FinC, float WallTm, float AirTm )
{
    return AirTm + (WallTm - AirTm) * cosh( FinC*(N-x) ) / cosh( FinC*N );
}
```

Figure 9.22. Fin program: The `compute_temp()` function.

The problem specifications are given in Figure 9.17 and the `compute_temp()` function in Figure 9.22.

```c
#include "tools.h"

void print_table( float, float, float, float );
float compute_temp( float, float, float, float, float );

void main( void )
{
    float len;                          /* Length of the cooling fin (m). */
    const float FinC = 26.5;            /* Fin constant. */
    const float WallTm = 500.0;         /* Wall temperature, C. */
    const float AirTm = 20.0;           /* Air temperature, C. */

    banner();
    puts( " Temperature Along a Cooling Fin" );
    printf( " Please enter length of fin (m): " );
    scanf( "%g", &len );
    print_table( len, FinC, WallTm, AirTm );
    bye();
}
/* ------------------------------------------------------------------
** Print a table of temperatures for a fin that is N meters long.
**      N must be greater than 0.
*/
void
print_table( float N, float FinC, float WallTm, float AirTm )
{
    float x;                            /* Distance from wall. */
    float temp;                         /* Temperature at x. */
    const float step = .005;            /* Step size for loop. */
    const float epsilon = step/2.0;     /* Tolerance. */

    printf( "\n Distance from base (m)    Temperature (C) \n"
            " ---------------------    --------------- \n" );
    for (x = 0.0; x < N + epsilon; x += step) {
        temp = compute_temp( x, N, FinC, WallTm, AirTm );
        printf( "%12.3f %24.1f \n", x, temp);
    }
    printf( " ---------------------    --------------- \n" );
}
```

Figure 9.23.　Temperature along a cooling fin.

We should compare these results to the ones in the test plan to know that we are fully finished.

What You Should Remember

9.7.1 Major Concepts

- *Modular design.* Large programs are organized into modules, which contain related sets of functions and constants. It is the compiler's job to properly compile and link together the files containing the modules. The organization of a module follows a stylistic pattern. Modular design is a skill worth learning if you intend to write programs of any substantial size.

- *Parameter and return value type conversion.* The type of a function argument in a call should match the type of the corresponding formal parameter in the prototype. If they are not identical, the argument will be coerced (automatically converted) to the parameter's type, if that is possible. Any numeric type (including `char`) can be converted to any other numeric type. Similarly, the value returned by a function will be converted to the declared return type. Normally, this type coercion causes no trouble. However, converting from a longer representation to a shorter one can cause overflow or loss of precision and converting from `char` to anything except `int` usually is wrong.

- *Parameter names.* The name of a parameter is arbitrary. It identifies the parameter value within the function and therefore should be meaningful, but it has no connection to anything outside the function, even if other objects have the same name. The order in which arguments are given in the call, not their names, determines which parameter receives each argument value.

- *Parameter order.* The order of parameters for a function is arbitrary. However, related parameters should be grouped together, and when several functions are defined with similar parameters, the order should be consistent. The number and order of arguments are not arbitrary. Parameters and arguments are paired according to the order in which they are written (not by name or type).

- *Call graphs.* A function call graph is a diagram that shows the caller-subprogram relationships of all the functions in a program. More sophisticated forms may include descriptions of the information being sent into and out of the subprogram.

- *Scope and visibility.* The scope of an object is the portion of a program in which it exists. The visibility of an object is the portion of its scope in which it can be accessed. An object can have external, global, or local scope, meaning that it is available to the entire program, restricted to a single module, or restricted to a single function, respectively.

- *Stub testing.* When a program is long and has many functions, stub testing often is the best way to construct and debug it. In this technique, the main program is written first, along with a stub for each function it calls. The stub is a function header, some comments, and only enough code to print the parameter values. If not a **void** function, it also must return some fixed and arbitrary answer. After the main function compiles and runs correctly by calling the stubs, the stubs are filled in, one at a time, with real code. This code, in turn, may require the construction of new stubs. After one or a few stubs have been fleshed out, the code is compiled and tested again. This is repeated until all stubs have been replaced by complete functions. This technique is important because it forces the programmer to work in a structured way; it ensures that all parts of the program are kept consistent with each other as they are developed. Also, compiler errors are easier to find and fix because there is never a large amount of new code being compiled for the first time.

9.7.2   Programming Style

- *Monolithic vs. modular.* If you cannot look at a function on your computer screen and understand what it is doing, it is too long, too complex, or both. Keep function definitions short enough to see the beginning and the end at the same time. Generally, it is good to keep code for user interaction and code for mathematical computation in separate functions. Modular development also aids the compiling and debugging process.
- *Placement of prototypes in the file.* The easiest way to be sure that the compiler uses the correct prototype to translate every function call is to write all the **#include** commands and all your prototypes at the top of each code module. Although other arrangements may be legal, according to C's rules, putting the prototypes at the top is the easiest way to avoid errors caused by misplaced prototypes, missing arguments, and incorrect argument order in function calls.
- *Global vs. local.* Define variables locally, not globally, wherever possible. This tactic makes logical errors easier to locate and fix because it limits unintentional interaction between parts of a program. In general, parameters should be used for interfunction communication. Global definitions should be used only for new type definitions and constants shared by several parts of a program.
- *Function documentation.* Every function should start with a highly visible comment line, such as a row of dashes. This line is very useful during debugging because it helps you find the functions quickly. You should be able to give a succinct description of the purpose of each function. This description should start on the second line of the comment at the top of the function definition. This comment also must make clear the purpose of each parameter and include a discussion of any preconditions.

- *Parameter and argument consistency.* If more than one function uses the same set of parameters, reduce confusion by being consistent in their order and naming.
- *Function layout.* The parts of a function definition can be arranged in many ways. The layout recommended here is the easiest to read and extends best to advanced programming in C++.

  1. Every function definition should start with a comment block, as described previously. The first line of code should be the return type and a comment, if needed, that describes the meaning of the return value (nothing else).
  2. The second line of code should start with the name of the function, followed by a left parenthesis. If all parameters will fit on one line, they should come next, ending with a right parenthesis. Otherwise, put each parameter on a separate line, with a comment. Put the closing right parenthesis on a line by itself, aligned directly under the matching left parenthesis.
  3. On the next line, write the left curly bracket in the first column.
  4. Next come the declarations with their comments; indent them two to four columns. Then leave a blank line and write the function body, indented similarly. Increase the indentation for each conditional or loop statement.
  5. Write the right curly bracket that ends the function in the leftmost column on a separate line.

9.7.3 Sticky Points and Common Errors

- *Parameter order.* The arguments in a function call must be written in the same order as the matching parameters in the definition. If the order is scrambled, the code often will compile and run but produce incorrect results. Using an incorrect number of arguments can lead to confusing errors at compile time.
- *The declaration must precede the call.* Either a function prototype or the complete function definition must precede all calls on the function. If this is not done, the compiler will construct a prototype automatically, which often will be wrong. This normally results in an error comment about an *illegal function redefinition* when the function definition is translated.
- *Call vs. prototype vs. definition.* Beginning programmers often confuse the syntax of a function call with the syntax of the corresponding prototype and header. These have parallel but different forms. The function call supplies a list of argument values; although each value has a type, the type names are not written in the call. In contrast, the function prototype and header do not know what values eventually will be supplied by future calls,

so they list the types of the parameters. In addition, the function header must give parameter names, so that the code can refer to the parameters and use them. Last, a semicolon is found at the end of a prototype but not at the end of a function header.

- *A global vs. local mix-up.* Having global variables leads to trouble for a variety of reasons. One scenario is the following: A local variable declaration is omitted, and it happens to have the same name as a global variable. The compiler cannot detect the omission and will use the global variable. Any assignments to this variable will change the global value, causing unexpected side effects in other parts of the program. Such errors are hard to track down because they are not in the part of the program that seems to be wrong and produces incorrect results.

9.7.4   New and Revisited Vocabulary

A large number of terms relating to functions and function calls have been introduced in this chapter. This list is provided as a review of the new concepts covered.

main program	function call	return type
subprogram	calling sequence	return value
function	caller	scope
module	call graph	visibility
library	argument	accessibility
header file	call by value	local
prototype	type coercion	global
function definition	arithmetic types	external
interface	call by address	preconditions
formal parameter	address argument	function skeleton
parameter list	entry point	foreign relations
parameter order	return address	function stub
type matching	`return` statement	stub testing
type conflict	missing prototype	testing by amputation

9.8   Exercises

9.8.1   Self-Test Exercises

1. Local and Global. Look at the program for Newton's method in Figures 8.11 and 8.12. Fill in the following chart listing the symbols *defined* (not used) in each program scope. List the global symbols on the first line and add one line below that for each function in the program; remember that every function definition creates a new scope. The line for `main()` has been started for you.

Scope	Parameters	Variables	Constants
global	—		
main()	—		

2. **Local names.** List all the local symbols defined in the main program in Figure 9.9. List the parameters and local variables in the function named **n_marks()**.

3. **Call chart.** The main program, which follows, calls two of the functions declared at the top. Which standard libraries would need to be included to compile this program? Draw a function call graph for this program.

```c
#define MAX 7
void pattern( int p );
void stars( int n );
void space( int m, int n );
int odd( int n ) { return n % 2; }

void main( void )
{
    int k;
    for (k = 0; k < MAX; ++k) {
        if (k < 2 || k >= MAX-2) stars( MAX );
        else pattern( k );
        printf( "\n" );
    }
}

void stars( int n )
{
    int k;
    for (k = 0; k < n; ++k) printf( "*" );
}

void space( int m, int n )
{
    int k;
    for (k = 0; k <= n; k += 2) printf( " %i", m );
}

void pattern( int p )
{
    stars( 1 );
    space( p, MAX-4 );
    if (odd(MAX)==1) printf( " " );
    stars( 1 );
}
```

4. Tracing calls. Trace the execution of the code in problem 3. Make a list of the function calls, one per line, listing the name, arguments, and return value for each. Show the program's output as well.

5. Visibility. List all the variable names used in the function named `cyl_vol()` in Figure 9.8. For each, say whether it is a parameter or a local variable.

6. Control flow. Draw a flow diagram for the fin temperature program in Figures 9.22 and 9.23.

7. Prototypes and calls. Given the prototypes and declarations that follow, say whether each of the lettered function calls is legal and meaningful. If the call would cause a type conversion of either a parameter or the return value, say so. If the call has an error, fix it.

```
void    squawk( int );
int     triple( int );
double power( double, int );

int j, k;
float f, g;
double x, y;
```

a. `squawk( 3 );`

b. `squawk( f );`

c. `triple( 3 );`

d. `f = triple( k );`

e. `j = squawk( k );`

f. `y = power( 3, x );`

g. `y = power( x, 3 );`

h. `x = power( double y, int k );`

i. `y = power( triple( k ), x );`

j. `printf( "%i %i", k, triple( k ) );`

9.8.2   Using Pencil and Paper

1. Control flow. Draw a flow diagram for the Newton's method program in Figures 8.11 and 8.12.

2. Call chart. Draw a call graph for the **n_marks** program in Figure 9.9.

3. Prototypes and calls. Given the prototypes and declarations that follow, say whether each of the lettered function calls is legal and meaningful. If the call would cause a type conversion of either a parameter or a return value, say so. If the call has an error, fix it.

```
double rand_dub( void );
int half( double );
int series( int, int, double );

int j, k;
float f, g;
double x, y;
```

a. `half( 5 );`

b. `rand_dub( y );`

c. `x = rand_dub();`

d. `j = half();`

e. `f = half( x );`

f. `j = series( x, 5 );`

g. `j = series( 5, (int)x, y );`

h. `y = series( j, k, rand_dub() );`

i. `printf( "%g %g", x, half( x ) );`

j. `printf( "%i %g", k, rand_dub( k ) );`

4. **Call chart.** The main program that follows calls the three functions defined at the top. Which standard libraries would need to be included to compile this program? Draw a function call graph for this program.

```
double f( double x ) { return x / 2.0; }
double g( double x ) { return 1.0 + x; }
double h( double x ) { return x * 3.0; }

void main( void )
{
    double x = 1;
    double sum = 0.0;

    while (sum < 100) {
        x = h( x );
        printf( " %6.2f \t", x );
        sum += x;
        if (fmod( x, 2.0 ) == 0) x = f( x );
        else x = g( x );
        printf( " %6.2f \n", x );
    }
    printf( " ------\n %6.2f \n", sum );
}
```

5. **Tracing calls.** Trace the execution of the program in exercise 4. Make a list of the function calls, one per line, listing the name, arguments, and return value for each. Show the program's output as well.

6. Local and Global. Look at the main program for fin temperatures in Figure 9.23 and its functions in Figures 9.22 and 9.23. Fill in the following table, listing the symbols that are *defined* (not used) in each program scope. List the global symbols on the first line and add one line below that for each function in the program (the line for **main()** has been started for you).

Scope	Parameters	Variables	Constants
global	—		
main()	—		

7. Visibility. The diagram that follows depicts a main program with three functions: **one()**, **two()**, and **other()**. Within the box for each function, parameters are shown above the dashed line, local variables below it. All functions return an **int** result. All variables and parameters are type **int**. The global constant, **RATE**, and global variable, **color**, also are type **int**.

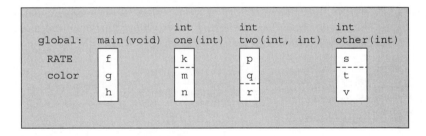

For each function call shown that follows, say whether it is legal or illegal. Fix any illegal statements.

a. In **main()**: **f = one(RATE);**.

b. In **main()**, after calling **one()**: **f = two(g, k);**.

c. In **one()**: **n = two(m);**.

d. In **one()**: **n = two(color, m);**.

e. In **one()**: **n = other(k);**.

f. In **two()**, after being called from **one()**: **r = other(k);**.

9.8.3   Using the Computer

1. A function.
   Write a function to compute the formula

$$f(x) = (3x + 1)^{\frac{1}{2}}$$

Write a main program that will sum $f(x)$ for the values $x = 0$ to $x = 1000$ in steps of 50. Print out the value of $f(x)$ and the current sum at every step in a nice neat table.

2. Tables.
   Write a program that contains two function definitions:

   $$f1(n, x) = e^{\sqrt{nx}} \times sin(nx)$$
   $$f2(n, x) = e^{\sqrt{nx}} \times cos(nx)$$

   where n is an integer and x is a **double**. In the main program, input a value for x and restrict it to the range $0.1 \leq x \leq 2.5$. Print a neat table showing the values of $f1(n, x)$ and $f2(n, x)$ as n goes from 0 to 30. Print column headings above the first line. Show all numbers to three decimal places.

3. Bubbles.
   Modify your program from computer exercise 3 in Chapter 8; change the **bubble()** function so that it takes both σ and r as parameters. Then change the **main()** function to ask the user to enter a value for σ as well. Define an error function that prints a message "Input out of range." Use it to screen out values of σ less than 0.001 or greater than 0.003 lb/ft and values of r less than 0.0002 or greater than 0.015 ft. Call this function from **main()**.

4. An arithmetic series.
   Each term of an arithmetic series is a constant amount greater than the term before it. Suppose the first term in a series is a and the difference between two adjacent terms is d. Then the kth term is $t_k = a + (k - 1)d$. Write a function **term()** with three parameters, a, d, and k, that will return the kth term of the series defined by a and d. Use type **long int** for all variables. Write a program that prompts the user for a and d, then prints the first 100 terms of the series, with 5 terms on each line of output, arranged neatly in columns. Quit early if integer overflow occurs.

5. A geometric series.
   A *geometric progression* is a series of numbers in which each term is a constant times the preceding term. The constant, R, is called the *common ratio*. If the first term in the series is a, then succeeding terms will be aR, aR^2, aR^3, ... The kth term of the series will be $t_k = aR^{k-1}$. Write a function **term()** with three parameters (a, R, and k) that will return the kth term of the series defined by a and R. Use type **double** for all variables, since the terms grow large rapidly when R is greater than 1. Write a main program that prompts the user for a and R, then prints the terms of the series they define until either 50 terms have been printed, 5 terms per line, or floating-point overflow or underflow occurs.

6. Torque.
   Given a solid body, the net torque T (Nm) about its axis of rotation is related to the moment of inertia I and the angular acceleration acc (rad/s^2) according to the formula for the conservation of angular momentum:

   $$T = I \cdot acc$$

The moment of inertia depends on the shape of the body; for a disk with radius r, it is

$$I = 0.5mr^2$$

a. Write a function named **moment()** to calculate and return the moment of inertia of a solid disk. It should take two parameters: the radius and mass of the disk.

b. Write a **work()** function that will prompt the user to enter the radius, mass, and angular acceleration of a disk. Limit the inputs to be within these ranges:

$$0.093 \le r \le 0.207$$
$$0.088 < m \le 11$$

Compute and print the torque of the disk, calling **moment()** to compute I first.

c. Write a main program that will allow the user to compute several torques.

7. A real drag!
The force on a solid body due to air flowing past it is called *aerodynamic drag*. This force depends on the geometrical shape of the solid, the density ρ (kg/m^3) of the air, and the speed U (m/s) of the air flow. The equation relating drag force D (N) to these parameters is

$$D = C \left(\frac{\rho A\, U^2}{2} \right)$$

where C is the drag coefficient of the shape and A is the frontal area (m^2) of the solid.

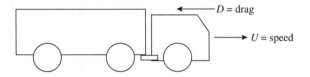

For tractor trailer trucks, the values of the drag coefficient are[18]

Standard	$C = 0.96$
With fairing	$C = 0.76$
With fairing and gap seal	$C = 0.70$

Write a program that will calculate and print a drag force table. Assume that air density at 15°C is 1.23 kg/m^3 and an estimate of the frontal area of the truck is 7 m^2. Make one column for the speed and separate columns for each kind of truck. Let the speed vary from $U = 10.0$ to 40.0 m/s by increments of 1.0. Write a single function with two parameters, C and U, that computes D. Call this function three times for each row of the table.

---

[18] B. Munson, D. Young, and T. Okiishi, *Fundamentals of Fluid Mechanics*, 2nd ed. (New York: Wiley, 1994).

8. **An AC circuit.**
   An AC circuit that you have designed is operating at a voltage V (rms volts) alternating at a frequency f (cyc/s). It is constructed of a capacitor C (farads), inductor L (henrys), and a resistor R (ohms) in series. Some important properties of this circuit are

Impedance:	$Z = \left[R^2 + \left(2\pi f L - \dfrac{1}{2\pi f C} \right)^2 \right]^{0.5}$	(ohms)
Current:	$I = \dfrac{V}{Z}$	(rms amps)
Power used:	$\text{Power} = \dfrac{V \times I \times R}{Z}$	(watts)

   Write a function to compute an answer for each formula. Assume that f is a constant 120 cyc/s and $C = 0.00000001$ farads. Then write a main program that will input values for V, L, and R and output the impedance, current, and power used. Validate the inputs and ensure that they are within the following ranges:

   $$60 \leq V \leq 200$$
   $$0.1 \leq L \leq 10$$
   $$100 \leq R \leq 1000$$

9. **An air duct.**
   The duct pictured here is used to heat air flowing inside it. The surface of the duct is maintained at a constant temperature of $T_s = 450°$K, which generates an average air temperature inside the duct of about 300°K. A table follows the diagram for the properties of air at 1 atmosphere pressure and 300°K.

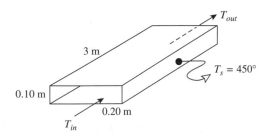

Air constants at 1 atmosphere, 300°K	
Specific heat	$C_p = 1007$ J/kg K
Thermal conductivity	$k = 0.0263$ W/m K
Prandtl number	$\text{Pr} = 0.707$
Density	$\rho = 1.1614$ kg/m^3
Viscosity	$vis = 15.89e\text{-}06\text{m}^2/\text{s}$

If the air enters the duct at temperature T_{in}, and at a mass flow rate of 0.25 kg/s, we can establish a set of calculation steps that will compute the outlet temperature of the air flowing in the duct and the total heat transferred. These steps are

Area of end of duct:	oe_area = duct_height × duct_width
Perimeter of end of duct:	oe_peri = 2 × duct_height + 2 × duct_width
Velocity:	v = mass_flow_rate/(ρ × oe_area)
Hydraulic diameter:	D_h = 4 × oe_area/oe_peri
Reynolds number:	$R = (v \times D_h)/vis$
Film coefficient:	$h = k \times \dfrac{0.023 \times R^{0.8} \times Pr^{0.4}}{D_h}$
Exponent:	$\text{expo} = \dfrac{\text{oe\_peri} \times \text{duct\_length} \times h}{\text{mass\_flow\_rate} \times C_p}$
Output temperature:	$T_{out} = T_s - (T_s - T_{in}) \times e^{-\text{expo}}$
Heat transfer:	$Q_{tot} = \text{mass\_flow\_rate} \times C_p \times (T_{out} - T_{in})$

Write a separate function for each of these formulas. Then write a main program that will input T_{in} in degrees Kelvin and output the computed values of T_{out} and Q_{tot}. Assume that these constants and approximations are accurate only if T_{in} is in the range 250–300°K, so ensure that the value entered by the user falls within this range.

10. Heat in a solid.
    The heat, Q, gained by a solid is related to its physical properties and the change in temperature experienced by the solid:

$$Q = m \times c \times (T_{final} - T_{initial}) \quad \text{(Joules)}$$

where m is the mass (kilograms), c is the specific heat (J/kgC), and the values of T (C) are the initial and final temperatures of the solid. The specific heat also is a function of T. For cobalt, we have the following values of c for the temperature ranges given:

Temperature Range	c (J/kgC)
$0 \leq T \leq 200$	452
$200 < T \leq 400$	498
$400 < T \leq 600$	548
$600 < T \leq 800$	594

a. Write a function named **spec_heat()** with two **double** parameters, the initial and final temperatures of a solid object. Return a value for c that is the average of the c values in the table for the ranges in which **T_initial** and **T_final** fall.

b. Write a **work()** function that inputs the mass and the two temperatures of a solid object (**T_initial** and **T_final**). Calculate and print the heat gained by calling your **spec_heat()** function to compute the value for c.

c. Write a main program that will allow the user to compute several Q values.

CHAPTER
10

An Introduction to Arrays

The data types we have studied so far have been simple, predefined types and variables of these types are used to represent single data items. The real power of a computer language, however, comes from its ability to define complex, multipart, structured data types that model the complex properties of real-world objects. For example, to model the periodic table of the elements, we would need a collection of 110 objects that represent elements; each object would have several parts (name, symbol, atomic number, atomic weight, etc.). We call such types *compound types* or **aggregate types**. An array is an aggregate whose parts are all the same type. In this chapter, we study how to define, access, and manipulate the elements of an array.

10.1   Arrays

In many applications, each data item is processed once, just after it is read, and never needs to be used again. In such programs, an array can be used to store the data, but it is not necessary. In contrast, some programs must read all the data, perform a calculation, then go back and process the data again. In these programs, we must store all the data between reading it and reprocessing it.

Consider the problem of assigning grades to a class based on the average score of an exam. If we were computing only the exam average, this could be done without storing the data in an array; all that is needed is a summation loop. However, to assign a grade, we must have both the exam score and the average. The scores must be processed once to compute the average, then we must go back and reprocess the scores to assign the grades. In between we need to store the values.

We could do this using individual variables. For instance, in the example of computing the average of three numbers in Figure 2.8, we used three separate variables to hold the numbers. While this works well for only three numbers, it does not work on larger data sets. Imagine how tedious it would be to write a `scanf()` statement and a formula with many variable names. We can solve this problem by using an array. For example, a program to compute the average temperature over a 24-hour period might store 24 temperature readings in an array named `temperature`. An array used to determine the average high temperature for one year would have 365 (or 366) entries, each containing a daily high temperature.

An **array** is a consecutive series of variables that share one variable name. We will call these variables the **array slots**; the data values stored there are called the **array elements**. The number of slots in a *one-dimensional array* is called the **array length**. Arrays with two or more dimensions also can be defined; these will be studied in Chapter 17. The variables, or slots, that form an array have a uniform type called the **base type**.

An array object, as a whole, is given a name. We can refer to the entire array by this name or to an individual slot by appending a number in square brackets to the name. This number is called the *subscript*. A **subscript** is an integer expression enclosed in square brackets that, when written after an array name, designates a particular slot in the array.

In C, all arrays start with slot 0 (rather than 1) because it is easier and more efficient for the system to implement. This means that the first element in an array named `ary` would be called `ary[0]`; the next one would be `ary[1]`. If this array had six elements, the last one would be `ary[5]`.

10.1.1 Array Declarations and Initializers

Declarations. An array variable is declared and initialized very much like a simple variable. The **array declaration** starts with the base type, which can be any type—simple or compound. Thus, we can have an array of `int`s, an array of `char`s (also known as a *string*), or even an array of arrays. Following the base type in the declaration is the array name and a pair of square brackets enclosing the length, which must be an integer constant or an integer **constant expression** (an expression with only constant operands). The length determines the number of slots in the array. Figure 10.1 shows the declaration for an array named `pressure` containing five `float`s. This creates a series of five `float` variables that we can

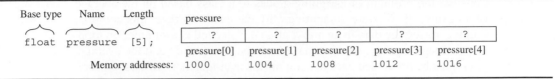

Figure 10.1.   Declaring an array of five floats.

refer to as **pressure[0]**, **pressure[1]**, **pressure[2]**, **pressure[3]**, and **pressure[4]**. These five **float**s will be stored in a contiguous set of memory locations with **pressure[0]** at the location with the lowest memory address, 1000, in this case. In later chapters, the address of each slot may also be of interest; if so, we write the address above or below the slot, as shown in Figure 10.1.

To diagram an array, we draw a row of connected boxes that are the right size for the base type. We write the name of the array above and the subscripts below this row. If there is an initializer, as in Figure 10.2, we copy the initial values into the boxes. Otherwise, as in Figure 10.1, we leave them blank or write a question mark.

Initial values.   An array can be declared with no initial values, like the array named **pressure** in Figure 10.1. The contents of an uninitialized array are as unpredictable as ordinary variables.[1]

Alternatively, it may have an **array initializer**, which is a list of values enclosed in curly brackets. The values will be stored in the array slots when the array is created, as illustrated in Figure 10.2. The values in the initializer list must be constants or constant expressions. The types of values in the initializer must be appropriate for the base type of the array.[2]

If an initializer *is* given, the array length may be omitted from the square brackets. The C translator will count the number of initial values given and use that number as the length; exactly enough space will be allocated to store the given values. Note the absence of the length value in the declaration for **temperature** in Figure 10.3.

What if both a length and an initializer are given and the sizes do not match? This is an error if the initializer contains too many values; the compiler will detect this error and comment on it. However, if an initializer list is too short, it is not an error. In this case, the values provided are used for the first few array slots and the value 0 is used to initialize all remaining slots. The declaration for **inventory** on the third line in Figure 10.3 illustrates an initializer that is shorter than the array. It also is possible to initialize an entire array to zeros by supplying an empty set of brackets, as in the initializer for **instock** in Figure 10.3.

---

[1] Global arrays and static local arrays are initialized to 0 values.

[2] The initializer type must match or be coercible to the array base type.

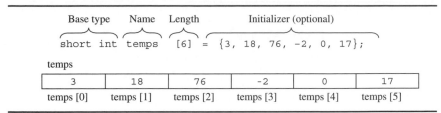

Figure 10.2.   An initialized array of short ints.

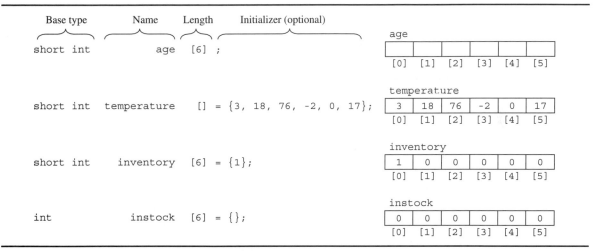

Figure 10.3.   Length and initializer options.

10.1.2 The Size of an Array (Advanced Topic)

Two different aspects of an array's size are important: its length and the total number of bytes of memory required to store it. When we use **sizeof** with an array variable, we get the number of bytes, which is the product of the array's length and the size of one element of its base type.

While knowing the number of slots is necessary to write an array declaration, a programmer will not always know the **size of the array**, because that depends on the size of the base type, which may vary from one machine to another. The program in Figure 10.4 shows the sizes of the arrays declared in Figures 10.1, 10.2, and 10.5. An output from this program is

```
pressure: sizeof(float)  is 4 * length 5 = sizeof array 20
temps:    sizeof(short)  is 2 * length 6 = sizeof array 12
vec2:     sizeof(double) is 8 * length 3 = sizeof array 24
```

Often, the first portion of an array will hold data, while the last portion is not in use. This happens when the array is intended to hold a variable amount

```
#include <stdio.h>

#define DIMP 5      /* Lengths of the arrays. */
#define DIMT 6
#define DIMV 3

void main( void )
{
    float pressure[DIMP] = { .174, 23.72, 1.111, 721.2, 36.3 };
    short int temps[DIMT] = { 3, 18, 76, -2 };
    double vec2[DIMV] = { 2.0, 0.0, 1.0 };

    printf( " pressure: sizeof(float)  is %i * length %i ="
            " sizeof array %i \n", sizeof(float), DIMP, sizeof(pressure) );
    printf( " temps:    sizeof(short)  is %i * length %i ="
            " sizeof array %i \n", sizeof(short), DIMT, sizeof(temps) );
    printf( " vec2:     sizeof(double) is %i * length %i ="
            " sizeof array %i \n", sizeof(double), DIMV, sizeof(vec2) );
}
```

Figure 10.4.   The size of an array.

of information and its length is set to the maximum length that might ever be needed. Even in this case, the size returned by **sizeof** is the total amount of memory allocated including both the portion in use and the unused portion. This is illustrated by the array **temps** in Figure 10.4.

When an array is passed as an argument to a function, (see Section 10.4) the size information does not travel along with it. No operation in C will give us the actual length of an array argument inside a function. If you apply **sizeof** to an array parameter, the result always will be the number of bytes needed to store the starting address of the array. Unfortunately, an array-processing function frequently needs the information to work properly. For this reason, the programmer, who knows the array's length when it is declared, must make the information available for use by every part of the program that operates on the array. One way to do this is to declare the array length using a **#define** at the top of the program, as in our first several examples.

10.1.3   Accessing Arrays

The elements of an array can be accessed in two ways: by using pointers or by using subscripts. Both ways are important in C and need to be mastered. Pointers often are used when the slots of an array will be used in sequential numeric order, because this technique can lead to greater efficiency. While subscripts can be used for this purpose, too, they are better at accessing the elements in a random order. Since pointer processing techniques are harder to master than those based

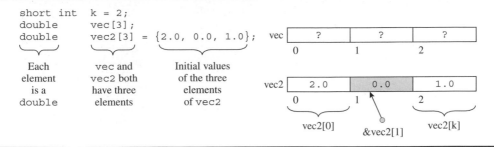

Figure 10.5.   Simple subscripts.

on subscripts, using pointers will be deferred until Chapter 20, while subscripting is explained in this chapter.

Subscripts.   Figure 10.5 shows how constant subscripts are interpreted. It shows two arrays named **vec** and **vec2**, which represent vectors in a three-dimensional space. The first slot of **vec2** is **vec2[0]** and represents the x-component of the vector, containing the value 2.0. The y-component has the value 0.0 and is stored in **vec2[1]**, the shaded area in the diagram. In an object diagram, we use an arrow to represent an address. The arrow in Figure 10.5 represents **&vec2[1]**, the address of the shaded area. When both an ampersand and a subscript are used, the subscripting operation is done first and the "address of" operation is applied to the single variable selected by the subscript.[3] These addresses are important when using arrays as function arguments, as demonstrated in Section 10.4.

We also can use an expression involving a variable to compute a subscript (Figure 10.6). A subscript expression can be as simple as a constant or as complex as a function call, as long as the final value is a nonnegative integer less than the length of the array. The most frequently used subscript expression is a simple variable name, which also is illustrated in Figure 10.5. The phrase **vec2[k]** means that the current value of **k** should be used as a subscript for the array. Since **k** contains a 2 here, **vec2[k]** means **vec2[2]**, which contains the value 1.0. The flexibility and versatility of these subscript rules enables a variety of powerful array-processing techniques.

Notes on Figure 10.6. Computed subscripts.   Figure 10.6 demonstrates how we can use computed subscripts. It depicts an array containing the

---

[3] Appendix B contains a precedence table that includes both subscript (**[]**) and address of (**&**) operators. Note that the precedence of subscript is higher, and therefore, the subscript will be applied to the array name before the address operator.

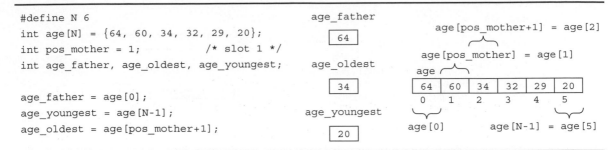

Figure 10.6.   Computed subscripts.

ages of *N* members of a family: father, mother, and children, in order of age. The array length is #defined. Often this is done so that it can be used for calculations throughout the code yet modified easily if the program's needs change.

The variable **pos_mother** is used here to store the position in the array of the mother. In the last line on the left, the expression **pos_mother+1** is used to find the age of the oldest child. Also, we often need to use the subscript of the last element in an array. To compute this, we subtract 1 from the array length. Therefore, **age[N-1]** is the age of the last (youngest) child in the family.

The example in Figure 10.7 declares an array variable named **vec** and shows simple input, computation, and output statements that operate on the array elements.

Notes on Figure 10.7. Subscript demo, the magnitude of a vector.

- *First box: input into an array.* When we call **scanf()** to read the value of a variable, we write **&** before the variable's name to refer to its address. Similarly, we can use **&** to refer to the address of a single slot of an array. To read just one value into the first component, we would write **scanf("%lg", &vec[0]);**.
- *Second box: computation on array elements.*

  1. We can use a subscripted array name like a simple variable name in any expression.
  2. Here, to compute the magnitude of a vector, we add the squares of the three components, take the square root of the sum, and store the result in **magnitude**. The easiest and most efficient way to square a number is to multiply it by itself.

- *Third box: output from an array.*

  1. To print an array element, give the array name and the subscript of the element.

This brief demonstration program shows how to do input, output, and computation with the elements of an array.

```
#include "tools.h"

void main( void )
{
    double vec[3];          /* A vector in 3-space. */
    double magnitude;

    puts( "\n Subscript Demo: The Magnitude of a Vector" );

    printf( " Please enter the 3 components of a vector: " );
    scanf( "%lg%lg%lg", &vec[0], &vec[1], &vec[2] );

    magnitude = sqrt( vec[0] * vec[0] + vec[1] * vec[1] + vec[2] * vec[2] );

    printf( "    The magnitude of vector ( %g, %g, %g ) is %g \n",
            vec[0], vec[1], vec[2], magnitude );

    bye();
}
```

Figure 10.7.   Subscript demo, the magnitude of a vector.

2. You cannot print the entire contents of an array with just one format field specifier. Here, we use three separate **%g** specifiers to print the three array elements. A loop would be used to print all the elements of a large array,

3. The output from two runs of this program is

```
Subscript Demo: The Magnitude of a Vector
Please enter the 3 components of a vector: 1 0 1
    The magnitude of vector ( 1, 0, 1 ) is 1.41421
-----------------------------------------------------

Subscript Demo: The Magnitude of a Vector
Please enter the 3 components of a vector: 1 2 0
    The magnitude of vector ( 1, 2, 0 ) is 2.23607
```

10.1.4   Subscript Out-of-Range Errors (Advanced Topic)

One important reminder and caution: It is *up to the programmer* to ensure that all subscripts used are legal. C does not help you confine your processing to the array slots that you defined. C uses the subscript value to compute a memory address called the **effective address** according to this formula:

$$\texttt{effective\_address} = \text{address of beginning of the array} +$$
$$\text{subscript} \times \texttt{sizeof} \text{ (base type of array)}$$

If you use a subscript that is negative or too large, C will compute the theoretical "address" of the nonexistent slot and use that address even though it will not be between the beginning and the end of the array. C does absolutely no subscript range checking. The compiler will give no error comment and there will be no error comment at run-time either. Your program will run and either access a memory location that belongs to some other variable or attempt to access a location that does not exist.

10.2   Using Arrays

A common array processing pattern involves a counting loop, where the loop variable starts at 0 and stops before **N**, the length of the array. The loop variable is used as a subscript to access each array element, in turn. This kind of loop is seen again and again in programs that use arrays to process large amounts of data. Often, one loop is used to read data into the array, another to process the data items, and a third loop to print them all.

10.2.1   Array Input

The best way to read data into an array is with a **for** loop, where the loop counter starts at 0, increments through the subscripts of the array, and ends at **N**, the declared length of the array. The loop does not try to process slot **N**, which is past the end of an **N**-element array. This simple idiom is illustrated in Figure 10.8.

Notes on Figure 10.8. Filling an array with data.

- *Outer box: the* **for** *loop.* Since the loop counter takes on the values from 0 to **N** and the loop ends when **k == N**, all **N** array slots (with subscripts 0...**N-1**) will be filled with data.
- *Inner box: reading data into one slot.* Within the loop, a **scanf()** statement reads one data value on each iteration and stores it in the next array slot. Note that both an ampersand and a subscript are used in the **scanf()** statement to get the address of the current slot.
- *Sample output.*

  ```
  Array Input Demo: the Volume of a Box
  Please enter dimensions of box in cm when prompted.
  ```

```
#include <stdio.h>
#define N 3

void main( void )
{
    int k;                  /* Loop counter. */
    float dimension[N];     /* Dimensions of a box. */
    float volume;           /* The volume of the box. */

    printf( "\n Array Input Demo: the Volume of a Box \n"
            " Please enter dimensions of box in cm when prompted.\n" );

    for (k = 0; k < N; ++k) {   /* End loop when k reaches length of array. */
        printf( " > " );
        scanf( "%g",  &dimension[k]  );
    }

    volume = dimension[0] * dimension[1] * dimension[2] / 1e6;
    printf( " Volume of the box ( %g * %g * %g ) is %g cubic m.\n\n",
            dimension[0], dimension[1], dimension[2], volume );
    bye();
}
```

Figure 10.8.   Filling an array with data.

```
        > 100
        > 100
        > 100
        Volume of the box ( 100 * 100 * 100 ) is 1 cubic m.
```

10.2.2 Walking on Memory

A loop that runs amok can cause diverse kinds of trouble. One common outcome is that variables that occupy nearby memory locations are overwritten with information that was supposed to go into one of the array's slots. Afterward, any computation or output that uses these variables will be erroneous.

If you write a loop to print the values in an array and it loops too many times, you will start printing the values stored adjacent to the array in memory. When reading data, you will start erasing other information when the loop exceeds the array bounds. This is demonstrated by the program in Figure 10.9 (a modification of the program in Figure 10.7), which reads input into an array named **v**. Figure 10.10 is a diagram of memory for this program. It shows the variables and the memory addresses that a typical compiler might assign. The array is colored gray.

This program is a modification of the vector magnitude program in Figure 10.7. It demonstrates how an incorrect loop can destroy the value of a variable and result in unpredictable behavior.

```
#include "tools.h"
void main( void )
{
    int k;                 /* Loop counter. */
    float v[3];            /* A vector in 3-space. */
    float sum;             /* The sum of the squares of the components. */
    float magnitude;

    puts( "\n Subscript Demo: Walking on Memory" );
    printf( " Please enter one float vector component at each prompt.\n" );

    for (sum = 0.0, k = 0; k <= 3; ++k) {       /* Loop goes too far. */

        printf( "\tv[%i]: ", k );
        scanf( "%g", &v[k] );
        sum += v[k] * v[k];
    }
    magnitude = sqrt( sum );
    printf( "    The magnitude of vector ( %g, %g, %g ) is %g \n",
            v[0], v[1], v[2], magnitude );
    bye();
}
```

Figure 10.9.   Walking on memory.

The array has three slots, but the loop was written to execute four times, with subscripts 0 through 3. The last time, the effective address calculated for v[k] actually is the address of k, and the input value, wrongly, is stored on top of the loop counter. Here is the output from one run:

```
Subscript Demo: Walking on Memory
Please enter one float vector component at each prompt.
        v[0]: 0.0
        v[1]: 1.0
        v[2]: 2.0
        v[3]: 0.0
        v[1]: 5.0
        v[2]: -1.0
        v[3]: 4.5
Segmentation fault
```

The upper diagram in Figure 10.10 shows the values of the variables just after the third trip around the loop. All the array slots have been filled, and k has

These diagrams illustrate the contents of memory while processing the input sequence described in the text.

After filling the array on the third trip around the loop:

1008	1012	1016	1020	1024	1028
	5.0	0.0	1.0	2.0	3
magnitude	sum	v[0]	v[1]	v[2]	k

After exceeding array bounds on the fourth trip around the loop:

1008	1012	1016	1020	1024	1028
	5.0	0.0	1.0	2.0	0.0
magnitude	sum	v[0]	v[1]	v[2]	k

Running amok, incrementing k before the fifth trip around the loop:

1008	1012	1016	1020	1024	1028
	5.0	0.0	1.0	2.0	1
magnitude	sum	v[0]	v[1]	v[2]	k

Figure 10.10.   Before and after walking on memory.

been incremented to 3 and is ready for the loop exit test. However, since the test was written incorrectly (with a `<=` operator instead of a `<` operator), the loop does not end.

The middle diagram shows what happens during the next loop iteration, as the subscript goes beyond the end of the array. The input value of 0.0 is stored in the variable that follows the array, which is the memory location used for the loop counter. This destroys the value of the loop counter and leaves the input value in its place. In this example, the input is 0, which then gets incremented to 1 by the `for` loop (bottom diagram). The loop still does not terminate, because now **k** is 1. It continues taking input until some input value is stored in **k** that satisfies the loop exit test or until an abnormal termination happens, as occurs here.

In this example, storing input on top of the loop counter causes unpredictable behavior that depends on the data entered by the user. Usually, as in the output shown, the program crashes; other times it continues and terminates normally but produces erroneous results. Be sure to check the limits of array processing loops to minimize these problems.

Random locations and memory faults (optional topic).   Sometimes, a faulty subscript causes the program to try to use a memory location that is not legal for that program to access; the result is an immediate hardware error (a memory fault, bus error, or segmentation fault) that terminates the program. Usually, the system displays a message to this effect, as was seen in the last program.

If a program continues to run after a subscript error, it generally produces erroneous output. The cause of the errors may be difficult to detect because the value of some variable can be changed by a part of the program that does not refer to that variable at all, and output based on the mistake may not occur until long after the destructive deed. Prevention is the best strategy for developing working code. It is up to the programmer to use subscripts carefully and ensure that every subscript is legal for its array. With this in mind, remember that

- Arrays start with subscript 0, so the largest legal subscript is one less than the number of elements in the array.
- An input value must be checked before it can be used as a subscript. Negative values and values equal to or larger than the array length must be eliminated.
- A counting loop that processes an array should terminate when the loop counter reaches the number of items in the array.

10.3   Parallel Arrays

The next program (specified in Figure 10.11 and given in Figure 10.12) uses a set of **parallel arrays**, all of the same length, to implement a table of data. Each array in the set represents one column of the table and each array subscript represents one row of data. In this example, the first column is a list of student ID numbers. Parallel to it are three other arrays containing data about the students. The data at subscript k in each of these arrays corresponds to the student with subscript k in the ID array. This is illustrated by the declarations and diagram in Figure 10.13.

Problem scope: Given the ID number and two exam scores (midterm and final) for each student in a class, compute the weighted average of the two scores. Also, compute the overall class average and the difference between that and each student's average.

Input: ID numbers will be long integers and exam scores will be integers.

Limitations: The class cannot have more than 16 students.

Formula: Weighted average $= 0.45 \times$ midterm score $+ 0.55 \times$ final score

Output and computational requirements: All inputs should be echoed. In addition, for each student, print the exam average and the difference between that average and the overall average for the class, both to one decimal place. The overall exam average of the class should be printed using two decimal places.

Figure 10.11.   Problem specifications: Exam averages.

```
#include "tools.h"
#define MAX 16
void main( void )
{   int k;                /* Loop counter. */
    int n;                /* Number of students in class. */
    long id[MAX];         /* Students' ID numbers. */
    short midterm[MAX], final[MAX];      /* Exam scores. */
    float average[MAX]; /* Average of exam scores. */
    float avg_average;    /* Average of averages. */
    float diff;           /* Student's average minus class average. */
    banner();
```

```
    printf( " Exam average = .45*midterm + .55*final.\n"
            " How many students are in the class? " );
    scanf( "%i", &n );
    if (n > MAX || n < 1) fatal( "Size must be between 1 and %i.", MAX );
```

```
    printf( " At each prompt, enter an ID# and two exam scores.\n" );
    for (k = 0; k < n; ++k) {
        printf( "\t > " );
        scanf( "%li%hi%hi", &id[k], &midterm[k], &final[k] );
        average[k] = .45 * midterm[k] + .55 * final[k];
    }
```

```
    for (avg_average = 0, k = 0; k < n; ++k) avg_average += average[k];
    avg_average /= n;
    printf( "\nAverage of the averages = %.2f\n", avg_average );
```

```
    puts( "\nID num    mid    fin    average   +/- " );
    puts( "------------------------------- " );

        for (k = 0; k < n; ++k) {
            diff = average[k] - avg_average;
            printf( "%li %5hi %5hi %8.1f %6.1f \n",
                    id[k], midterm[k], final[k], average[k], diff );
        }

    puts( "---------------------------------" );
```

```
    bye();
}
```

Figure 10.12.   Using parallel arrays.

This is a diagram of the memory for the program in Figure 10.12. A set of parallel arrays is used to represent the exam scores and exam average for a class. A common subscript, **k**, is used to subscript all four arrays. The maximum number of students this table can hold is 16, but this class has only 13 students, so the last three array slots are empty.

		id	midterm	final	average
`#define MAX 16`	MAX:16	0	825176	80	85	82.8
	k	1	825301	72	68	69.8
`int k;`	3	2	824769	97	90	93.2
`int n;`	n	3	826162	57	66	62.0
`long id[MAX];`	13					
`short midterm[MAX];`		4	824388	88	92	90.2
`short final[MAX];`		5	825564	42	61	52.5
`float average[MAX];`		6	825923	75	62	67.8
		7	823976	82	81	81.4
		8	824662	91	94	92.7
		9	824478	68	80	74.6
		10	826056	82	71	75.9
		11	826178	95	97	96.1
		12	825743	51	57	54.3
		13				
		14				
		15				

Figure 10.13.   Parallel arrays can represent a table.

When a table is implemented as a set of parallel arrays, the same variable is used to subscript all of them. We can apply this principle here. A loop is used to select the array slots. For each slot, first, input is read into three of the arrays at the selected position, then an average is calculated and stored in the fourth array. After the input loop, we scan this last array to compute several more values.

Notes on Figure 10.12. Using parallel arrays.

- *First box: limiting the subscripts.*

  1. Serious errors result from using a subscript beyond the end of the array. To avoid this, we check that the class size is within the limits we are prepared to handle. If it is too large, we abort. We also abort if the size is negative or 0, because these values are meaningless.
  2. If a class really had more than 16 students, this program would need to be edited to make **MAX** larger and then recompiled.

3. The function `fatal()`, defined in `tools.c`, is used to print an error comment and end execution gracefully. The parameters for `fatal()` are the same as for `printf()`: a format and a list of values to output.

- *Second box: the input phase.*

1. Our input loop counts from 0 up to the class size the user has entered. Since this count has been validated, we can be sure that all array subscripts are legal.
2. On each iteration we enter all the data for one student. Three numbers are read and stored in the corresponding slots of the first three arrays.
3. Sometimes the input loop does only input and other loops are used to process the data. In this example, the loop both reads the input and calculates the weighted average, which is part of a student's record and based directly on the input. This average is stored in the fourth array (the fourth column of the table). Merging these actions leads to a slightly more efficient program. However, if the additional calculations are lengthy, efficiency can be sacrificed for the added clarity of splitting the tasks into separate loops.
4. The prompts and input process look like this:

```
Exam average = .45*midterm + .55*final.
How many students are in the class? 13
At each prompt, enter an ID# and two exam scores.
        > 825176 80 85
        > 825301 72 68
        > 824769 97 90
        > 826162 57 66
        > 824388 88 92
        > 825564 42 61
        > 825923 75 62
        > 823976 82 81
        > 824662 91 94
        > 824478 68 80
        > 826056 82 71
        > 826178 95 97
        > 825743 51 57
```

5. We will echo the input data later, along with calculated values.

- *Third box: the average calculation.*

1. We sum the weighted averages as the first step of computing the overall class average. This task also could have been done as part of the input loop but was written as a separate loop because it has no direct connection to the input process or a single student's record.

2. We use a one-line `for` loop, because summing the values in an array is a simple job that corresponds to a single conceptual action.

3. Note how convenient the `+=` operator is for summing the elements of an array. The `/=` operator provides a concise way to say "now divide the sum by the number of students."

4. The output from this box is

`Average of the averages = 76.40`

• *Fourth and fifth boxes: the output phase.*

1. In the outer box, we print table headings before the output loop and print a line to terminate the table after the loop.

2. In the inner box, we print each student's record by including one value from each of the parallel arrays and a final value computed from the average array. Note that we use `%f` in the `printf()` format to make nicely aligned columns.

3. The final output of the program is

```
ID num   mid   fin   average   +/-
----------------------------------
825176    80    85     82.8     6.3
825301    72    68     69.8    -6.6
824769    97    90     93.2    16.8
826162    57    66     62.0   -14.5
824388    88    92     90.2    13.8
825564    42    61     52.5   -24.0
825923    75    62     67.8    -8.6
823976    82    81     81.4     5.0
824662    91    94     92.7    16.2
824478    68    80     74.6    -1.8
826056    82    71     75.9    -0.5
826178    95    97     96.1    19.7
825743    51    57     54.3   -22.1
----------------------------------
```

4. The input data is printed side by side with the final output to make it easier to check whether the computations are correct.

10.4   **Array Arguments and Parameters**

No data type is very useful in a programming language unless it can be used in a function call to pass information into and out of a function. Therefore, we need to know how to write a function with an array parameter and how to call such a function with an array argument. C does not permit a function to *return* an array value.[4]

Array arguments in C are handled differently from other types of arguments. When an `int` or `double` is passed to a function, its value is copied into the parameter variable that has been created for the function. However, when an array is passed to a function, only the *address* of the first slot of the array, not its entire list of values, is copied into the function's memory area. This permits a large amount of data to be made available to a function efficiently (since the actual data are not copied) and also allows the function to store information into the array. Therefore, a program can pass an empty array into a function, which then will fill it with information. When the function returns, that information still is in the original array's memory and can be used by the caller. This is similar to the way that `scanf()` works. The address of a variable is passed to `scanf()`, which fills it with information from the keyboard, and this information remains in the variable even after `scanf()` finishes.

To call a function with an **array argument**, the caller simply writes the name of the array and does *not* write a subscript or the square subscript brackets. Also, no `&` operator is used in front of the array name, because the array name automatically is translated into its starting address. To declare the corresponding **array parameter**, however, we use empty square brackets (with no length value). The length may be written between the brackets but it will be ignored by the compiler. This is done in C so the function can be used with arrays of many different lengths.

For example, if the actual argument were an array of `double`s, a formal parameter named `ara` would be declared as `double ara[]`. Within the function, the parameter name is used with subscripts to address the corresponding argument values.

The next program illustrates the basic array operations described so far: input, output, access, calculation, and the use of an array parameter. In it, the term `FName` means function name and `AName` means array name. We introduce and demonstrate the use of three new forms of function prototypes that manipulate arrays:

• `void FName( double AName[], int n );`
   A prototype of this form is used when the purpose of the function is to read data into the array or print the array data. The `get_data()` function in the next example has this form; its prototype is

   `void get_data( double x[], int n );`

   This function takes two parameters, an array of `double`s called `x` and an integer that gives the length of the array. Since the declaration of the

---

[4]However, it is possible to return a pointer to an array. This topic is deferred until a later chapter.

parameter **x** contains no length, we need a limiting value. This can be the globally defined constant that was used to declare the array object. Often, though, we do not use the entire array, and a parameter is used to communicate the amount of the array currently in use. The `get_data()` function fills the array with input values that remain in it after the function returns. This is one way of returning a large number of values from a function to the calling program. Since there is no other return value, the return type is declared as **void**.

- `double FName( double AName[], int n );`
  A prototype of this form is used when an array contains data and we wish to access those data to calculate some result, which then is returned. The function named **average()** in the next example has this form; its prototype is

  `double average( double x[], int n );`

  It again takes two parameters, the array of **double**s and the current length of the array. The function calculates the average (mean) of those values and returns it to the caller via the **return** statement. Therefore, the function return type is declared as **double**.

- `double FName( double AName[], int n, double Arg );`
  We use a prototype of this form when we need both an array of data and another data value to perform a calculation. The function named **variance()** in the next example has this form; its prototype is

  `double variance( double x[], int n, double mean );`

  It takes three parameters, the same array **x**, its length **n**, and the mean of those values, which was previously calculated. It uses the array values and the mean to calculate the variance of the values. The variance is returned, so the function return type is declared as **double**.

10.4.1   An Array Application: Statistical Measures

In many experiments, the measured values of the experimental variable are distributed about the mean value in a bell-shaped curve centered on the **mean value of the array**; that is, the arithmetic average of the data values. Such a distribution is called a *normal*, or *Gaussian*, *distribution*.

The **variance** and **standard deviation** of a set of data are measures of how significantly the measured values differ from the true mean of the distribution. To compute these measures accurately, we need at least 20 data values. For fewer than 20 data points, we use the slightly different formulas, shown in Figure 10.14, to estimate the variance and standard deviation. In these equations, $x_1, x_2, x_3, \ldots, x_N$ are the data values and $N - 1$ is called the *degree of freedom* of the data.

Problem scope: Calculate the arithmetic mean, variance, and standard deviation of N experimentally determined data values.

Input: The user will specify the number of data values, N, then N data values will be typed in. These will be real numbers.

Restrictions: No more that 50 data values will be processed.

Formulas:

$$Mean = \frac{\sum_{k=1}^{N} x_k}{N}$$

$$Variance = \frac{\sum_{k=1}^{N} (x_k - mean)^2}{N - 1} \quad \text{for } N < 20$$

$$Variance = \frac{\sum_{k=1}^{N} (x_k - mean)^2}{N} \quad \text{for } N \geq 20$$

$$Standard\ deviation = \sqrt{Variance}$$

Output required: The mean, variance, and standard deviation of the N points, accurate to at least two decimal places.

Figure 10.14.   Problem specifications: Statistics.

In the next program example, we introduce a method for computing these statistical measures for N data values: $x_1, x_2, x_3, \ldots, x_N$.[5] The program specification is given in Figure 10.14 and the main program is shown in Figure 10.15. To keep the flow of logic in all parts of the program simple and uniform, major phases of the computation have been written as separate functions that work with a data array. We call **get_data()** to read the data into an array, then pass that array to the **average()** and **variance()** functions, and finally, print the answers. A call graph is given in Figure 10.16 and the three array-processing functions are found in Figures 10.17 and 10.18.

Notes on Figure 10.15. Mean and standard deviation.

- *First and third boxes: the data array.* The length of the array is controlled by the definition of **N** at the top of the program (first box). We easily can increase or decrease the length by changing only the **#define** at the top of the program. In this case, since **N** is defined to be 50, the array slots are named **x[0]** through **x[49]**. This is one of the most important ideas in computing: By using loops and arrays, we can process a virtually

[5]J. P. Holman, *Experimental Methods for Engineers*, 3rd ed. (New York: McGraw-Hill, 1978).

The specification for this program is in Figure 10.14 and the call graph is in Figure 10.16. The three programmer-defined functions are in Figures 10.17 and 10.18.

```c
#include "tools.h"

#define N    50                     /* Maximum number of data values.   */

void   get_data( double x[], int n );
double average ( double x[], int n );
double variance( double x[], int n, double mean );

void main( void )
{
    double x[N];                    /* Array for data values. */

    int num;                    /* Actual number of data values. */
    double mean;                /* The mean of the values in array x. */
    double var;                 /* Variance of the data in array x. */
    double stdev;               /* Standard deviation of the data in array x. */

    banner();

    printf( "\n Enter number of values in data set (2..%i): ", N );
    for(;;) {
        scanf( "%i", &num );
        if (num > 1 && num <= N) break;
        printf( "Error: %i is out of legal range, try again: \n", num );
    }
    printf( " Computing statistics on %i data values.\n", num );

    get_data( x, num );
    mean = average( x, num );
    var = variance( x, num, mean );
    stdev = sqrt( var );

    printf( "\n The mean of the %i data values is = %.2f \n", num, mean );
    printf( " The variance is = %.2f \n", var );
    printf( " The standard deviation is = %.2f \n", stdev );

    bye();
}
```

Figure 10.15.   Mean and standard deviation.

This graph is for the program found in Figures 10.15, 10.17, and 10.18

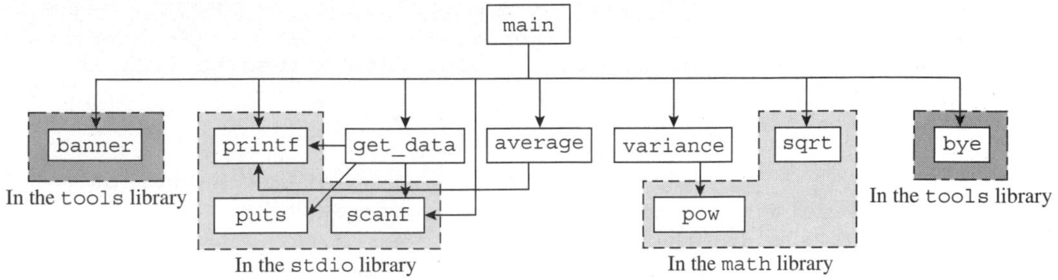

Figure 10.16. **Call graph for the mean and standard deviation program.**

unlimited number of data items. Files that store large amounts of data are the final element needed in this application. We will revisit this example in Chapter 15 to show how such data can be read from a file.

- *First box: the definition of N.* Every part of this program uses the value of *N* to define the number of data values that are to be read, processed, or output.
- *Fourth box: the actual amount of data.* It is rare that the maximum number of data values is used, since the value of *N* usually is set to a comfortably large value. Therefore, the user needs to specify the size of the current data set. This value, rather than *N*, will serve as the processing limit in each of the array functions.
- *Second and fifth boxes: the function prototypes and function calls.*

  1. Every programmer-defined function needs a prototype. The second box provides prototypes for the three functions in Figures 10.17 and 10.18.
  2. The function calls (fourth box) must correspond to the prototypes. Each call must have the same number of arguments (of the same type and in the same order) as the parameters declared by the prototype. All three of these functions have an array parameter and an integer parameter that gives the size of the data set. Note that the square brackets must be used for an array in the parameter declaration, but they are omitted in the function call.
  3. The formula for variance also depends on the mean, so we send the value of **mean** as a third argument to the **variance()** function.
  4. Last, we call **sqrt()**, a function from the mathematics library, to compute the standard deviation, given the variance.

- *Output.* The **main()** function prints headings, reads the number of data items, calls the four functions, and then prints the answers. The following

This function is called from the main program in Figure 10.15.

```
/* ------------------------------------------------------------------ */
/* Given an empty array of length n, input data values to fill it.  */
void
get_data( double x[], int n )
{
    int k;                              /* Loop counter and subscript. */
    puts( "Please enter data values when prompted." );
    for (k = 0; k < n; ++k) {
        printf( "x[%i] = ", k );    /* Prompt for kth value. */
        scanf( "%lg", &x[k] );      /* Read into array slot k. */
    }
}
```

Figure 10.17.   The `get_data()` **function.**

output is produced by **main()** when given the following 10 data values: 77.89, 76.55, 76.32, 79.43, 75.12, 64.78, 79.06, 78.58, 75.49, and 74.78.

```
Enter number of values in data set (2..10): 10
Computing statistics on 10 data values.
Please enter data values when prompted.
... output from get_data() and average() is here ...

The mean of the 10 data values is = 75.80
The variance is = 17.75
The standard deviation is = 4.21
```

Notes on Figure 10.17. The `get_data()` **function.**

This function and the two in Figure 10.18 follow a common pattern used for processing an array sequentially. Each function uses a **for** loop to perform an operation (input or calculation) on every array element, starting with the first and ending with the last. A programmer can use arrays for a wide variety of applications by following this pattern and varying the operation.

1. When control enters this function, the parameter array is empty. Before entering the loop, we ask the user to enter a series of data values.
2. We use a **for** loop to process the array. The variable **k** is used as the counter for the loop and also to subscript the array (the usual paradigm for processing arrays). We initialize **k** to 0 and leave the loop when **k** exceeds the last valid subscript, based on the current number of array slots that are in use.
3. On each repetition of the loop, we read one data value directly into **&x[k]**, the **k**th slot of the array **x**. At the end of each repetition, we

increment **k** to prepare for processing the next array element. Each time around the loop the variable **k** contains a different value between 0 and **n-1**; after **n** iterations, data fill the first **n** array slots and the remaining slots still contain garbage.

4. Within the loop, we prompt individually for each value.   This is a clear and convenient interactive user interface. In the future, when we read data from a file, this will not be necessary. During execution of **get_data()**, the user will see something like this:

```
Please enter data values when prompted.
x[0] = 77.89
x[1] = 76.55
x[2] = 76.32
x[3] = 79.43
x[4] = 75.12
x[5] = 64.78
x[6] = 79.06
x[7] = 78.58
x[8] = 75.49
x[9] = 74.78
```

5. After the last data value has been read, control returns to the caller and the caller can use the values stored in the array by the function.

Notes on Figure 10.18. Functions average() and variance().

- *First box: the average() function.*

  1. The **summing loop** was introduced in Figure 6.9. We use one here to sum the data values stored in array **x**. As always, the loop counter and accumulator must be initialized before entering the loop and the array-length parameter must be used to terminate the loop.

  2. As in the **get_data()** function, the variable **k** is used as both loop counter and subscript. On each repetition, we add a data value. We also echo it and its subscript as a double check that the value was entered properly. The output from our example is

```
x[0] = 77.89
x[1] = 76.55
x[2] = 76.32
  ...      ...
x[7] = 78.58
x[8] = 75.49
x[9] = 74.78
```

These functions are called from the main program in Figure 10.15. We use summing loops to calculate the mean and variance of **n** experimentally determined data values stored in the array **x**.

```
/* ---------------------------------------------------------------------
** Given an array of n values, print the values and calculate the mean.
*/
double
average( double x[], int n )
{
    double sum;
    int k;                                   /* Loop counter and subscript. */

    for (sum = k = 0; k < n; ++k) {       /* Echo and sum the k values. */
        printf( "\n    x[%i] = %.2f", k, x[k] );
        sum += x[k];
    }
    return sum / n;
}
```

```
/* ---------------------------------------------------------------
** Given an array of values and their mean, calculate the variance.
*/
double
variance( double x[], int n, double mean )
{
    double divisor, sum;
    int k;

    for (sum = k = 0; k < n; ++k) {     /* Compute and sum the k squares. */
        sum += pow( (x[k] - mean), 2 );
    }
    if (n < 20) divisor = n - 1;
    else divisor = n;
    return sum / divisor;
}
```

Figure 10.18.   Functions average() **and** variance().

3. Once all **n** values have been summed, we can calculate the average and return it to **main()**. The division that computes the mean is after the loop, rather than within it, because there is no need to perform a division on every repetition. We need not worry about division by 0 because **n** has been validated in **main()**.

- *Second box: the* **variance()** *function.*

    1. This function is very much like the **average()** function, but with two differences: We do not print any data in this loop and we are summing a different expression.
    2. The **pow()** function is in the **math** library. It raises a **double** value to a **double** power and returns a **double** result. In this call, the integer 2 will be coerced to type **double** before it is passed to the function. The result will be the square of the first argument.
    3. Once all **n** squares have been summed, we set the divisor to **n** or **n-1**, according to the specifications, then perform the division and return the result to **main()**. Again, we need not worry about division by 0, since **n** was validated in **main()**.

10.4.2   Linear Regression (Optional Topic)

Linear **regression** is a technique that is used to fit a line to a set of data points. This is done by finding the **least squares fit** of the data; that is, the line that minimizes the sum of the squares of the distance from each data point to the line. This is a generalization of the problem of linear interpolation between two points presented in Chapter 6. In this example, assume the data values are the result of an experiment in which distance was measured as a function of time. For example, Figure 10.19 includes a graph of seven data values (t_k, y_k). We want to find the equation of the straight line that best approximates these points; that is, we want to calculate the constants for the slope (m) and intercept (b) of the equation $(y(t) = \text{slope} \times t_k + \text{intercept})$ so that the line fits the data as closely as possible. For any particular data point, we can define the error between the actual point and the line as[6]

$$err_k = |y(t_k) - y_k| \qquad \text{where } y(t_k) = \text{slope} \times t_k + \text{intercept}$$

If we minimize the sum of the squares of the error values, err_k, for all the points, we have the least squares fit for the data. The result of such a minimization process (not explained here) is the set of equations presented in Figure 10.19 that specify the desired line's slope and intercept, as well as a "goodness of fit" measure, r. If $r = 1$, we have a perfect fit. When $0.9 < r < 1$, the fit is considered good. Anything less makes us suspect whether or not the data really represent a line. Figure 10.19 gives the full problem specification for the regression calculations, which are implemented and shown in Figures 10.20 through 10.23.

---

[6]Other possible error measures can be used; for example, the perpendicular distance from the point to the line.

Scope: Fit a straight line to a set of paired data values consisting of distance y vs. time t, such that the error in the y values is minimized.

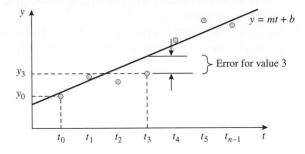

Input: A set of (no more than 100) experimental data points provided by the user, one at a time, using double values for t (in seconds) and y (in meters).

Formulas: Let k range over all n data values in the summations. Define

$$\texttt{t\_mean} = \frac{\sum t_k}{n}$$

$$\texttt{y\_mean} = \frac{\sum y_k}{n}$$

$$\texttt{sum\_ty} = \sum t_k \times y_k - n \times \sum t_k \times \sum y_k = \sum (t_k - t_{mean})(y_k - y_{mean})$$

$$\texttt{sum\_tt} = \sum t_k \times t_k - n \times \sum t_k^2 = \sum (t_k - t_{mean})^2$$

$$\texttt{sum\_yy} = \sum y_k \times y_k - n \times \sum y_k^2 = \sum (y_k - y_{mean})^2$$

As a result of error minimization, the slope and the y-intercept of the regression line are

$$Slope = \frac{\texttt{sum\_ty}}{\texttt{sum\_tt}}$$

$$Intercept = y_{mean} - slope \times t_{mean}$$

The "goodness" of the fit is measured by the **correlation coefficient**, r, as

$$r = \frac{\texttt{sum\_ty}}{\sqrt{(\texttt{sum\_tt} \times \texttt{sum\_yy})}}$$

Output: The data pairs will be echoed. An equation in the form ($y = slope \times t + intercept$) will be printed with the calculated values of slope and intercept inserted. The correlation coefficient for the data set also will be printed.

Figure 10.19.   Problem specifications: Linear regression.

This program calculates the least-squares line to fit a collection of data points. The main program calls the `get_data()` and `regression()` functions in Figures 10.21 and 10.22.

```
#include "tools.h"

#define NMAX    100              /* Maximum number of data values. */

/* Prototypes ------------------------------------------------- */
int get_data( double t[], double y[] );
void regression( double t[], double y[], int n );

void main( void )
{
    int n;                       /* Actual number of values. */

    double t[NMAX], y[NMAX];     /* Parallel arrays of data values. */

    banner();
    puts( "\n Least squares fit of straight line\n" );

    n = get_data( t, y );        /* Read data values. */

    regression( t, y, n );       /* Do regression analysis, print answers. */

    bye();
}
```

Figure 10.20.   Linear regression.

Notes on Figure 10.20. Linear regression.

- *First and second boxes: definitions.*

  1. As in the preceding program, we may wish to use this program to process data sets of various sizes, so we declare an array length large enough for the largest data set we expect to process. Chapter 19 discusses more sophisticated techniques for reducing the amount of storage wasted.
  2. We need to store a series of data values. Here, we define two parallel arrays so that corresponding positions contain the *t* and *y* values for a data point. In Chapters 14 and 17, other methods of storing the data points will be presented.

- *Third box: the input phase.*

  1. The function `get_data()` reads the point data into the pair of arrays in a manner similar to that in the previous statistical program.

This function is called from Figure 10.20.

```
/* Read in data value pairs from the keyboard until sentinel input. */
int get_data( double t[], double y[] )
{
    int k;                                  /* Number of points to be fit. */
    puts( " Enter data values when prompted, (-1, -1) to quit.\n" );

    for (k = 0; k < NMAX; k++) {
        printf( "\tEnter (t[%i] y[%i]): ", k, k );  /* Enter data pair. */
        scanf( "%lg%lg", &t[k], &y[k] );
        if (t[k] == -1 && y[k] == -1) break;        /* Quit for sentinel. */
    }

    return k;                               /* Return actual number of data items. */
}
```

Figure 10.21.   The `get_data()` **function: Read the input data.**

2. Array parameters, as defined in the prototypes, can be filled in by `get_data()` and returned to the main program through the array arguments.
3. In general, the number of data points entered will be smaller than the maximum number for which we have allocated space. In the previous program, we asked the user to type in the number of data items to process and used that number to control looping in `get_data()`. Here, the function counts and returns the actual number of points read, which is then stored in **n**.

- *Fourth box: computing the answers.*

  1. We call the **regression()** function in Figure 10.22 to compute a regression line. Here the data in the array parameters are being sent to the function rather than being filled in and returned. The function needs to know how many actual points exist, so the value of **n** is transmitted as well.
  2. The final results are displayed in **regression()**. In Chapters 12 and 14, we explore how all of the answers calculated in this function can be returned to **main()**, for further processing or display.

Notes on Figure 10.21. The `get_data()` function.

- *The box: an input loop.*

  1. As in the statistical program, data are read directly into the array locations. This **scanf()** call assumes that the *t* and *y* values have a

This function is called from Figure 10.20 and calls the **average()** function in Figure 10.18 and the **sq_sum()** function in Figure 10.23. It computes the slope and intercept of the regression line and the correlation coefficient for the values in the arrays **t** and **y** and displays them.

```
/* Prototypes ----------------------------------------------------------- */
double average( double x[], int n );
double sq_sum( double a[], double b[], int n, double a_mean, double b_mean );
```

```
void regression( double t[], double y[], int n )
```

```
{
    int k;                          /* subscript for loops. */
    double t_mean, y_mean;          /* means of coordinate data values. */
    double tt, ty, yy;              /* sums of t*t, t*y, y*y */
    double slope, intercept;        /* line slope, intercept, and */
    double correlation;             /* correlation coefficient */

    t_mean = average( t, n );           /* Means of coordinate values */
    y_mean = average( y, n );           /* and sums of squares. */
    tt = sq_sum( t, t, n, t_mean, t_mean );
    ty = sq_sum( t, y, n, t_mean, y_mean );
    yy = sq_sum( y, y, n, y_mean, y_mean );

    slope = ty / tt;                    /* Compute best-fit line parameters. */
    intercept = y_mean - slope * t_mean;
    correlation = ty / sqrt( tt * yy );

    puts( "\n For the following data values" );
    for (k = 0; k < n; k++)             /* Echo print the data */
            printf( "\tData[%2i]: t = %.2f, y = %.2f \n", k, t[k], y[k] );
    printf( "\n The least squares equation is: y = %.2f * t + %.2f \n",
            slope, intercept );
    printf( " The correlation coefficient is: r = %.3f \n", correlation );
}
```

Figure 10.22.   The regression() **function: Calculate the regression line.**

space between them. If a comma is present in the keyboard input, the program will not work correctly. Methods of dealing with this kind of input error will be presented in Chapter 15.

2. A **for** loop with an **if...break** structure is used to implement a sentinel loop because we do not know in advance how many values will be entered. The arrays have **NMAX** slots, so we use a loop limit of **NMAX** to ensure that we do not read beyond the end of it. Here we choose to

enter the point $(-1, -1)$ as a sentinel because it could never be actual data (time cannot have a negative value). Ending with a sentinel value often is more convenient than asking the user to count the data sets.

Notes on Figure 10.22. The `regression()` function.

- *First box: the prototypes.* This function uses two subfunctions to keep its total length reasonable. These two functions are found in Figures 10.18 and 10.23.
- *Second box: the function header.* This function computes the slope and intercept of a line and a correlation coefficient. To do this, the number of valid entries in the arrays is needed. Both data arrays also are needed, and they are passed as defined in this chapter. The order of the arguments is kept consistent with the `get_data()` function.
- *Third box: the summations.*

    1. It is good design practice to reuse appropriate functions where possible. In this program, it is possible to reuse the function **average()** from the statistical program, calling it twice to compute the two means. However, we do not want each array's data printed separately, so we deleted the **printf()** statement from the earlier version when we included it in this program. It is not reprinted here.
    2. We call the **average()** function twice to get the average of the **t** and **y** values. These must be computed before the sums are calculated in the third line.
    3. We write a new function, **sq_sum()**, to compute the summations. Its parameters are two arrays, the data set size, and two means. As we will see, this lets us compute either squares of the values in one array or the product of two different arrays.

Compute the sum of the products of the differences from the means.

```
double
sq_sum( double a[], double b[], int n, double a_mean, double b_mean )
{
    double sum;    /* Accumulator for final answer.  */
    int k;         /* Loop counter.  */

    for (sum = k = 0; k < n; k++) sum += (a[k] - a_mean) * (b[k] - b_mean);

    return sum;
}
```

Figure 10.23.   The `sq_sum()` function.

4. We call this function three times to compute the three formulas. The second call sends two different array arguments and two different mean values into the function. However, the first and third calls send the same array twice. This is legal. The result is that both parameter names in the function will refer to the same array argument, and we will sum the squares of the differences between the elements in that array and the corresponding mean.

- *Fourth box: the regression line and output.*

1. Once all the sums are computed, we can use the formulas given in the problem description to calculate the answers. None of these is overly complex, so we need not create more subfunctions.

2. The input data are echoed to the screen for the user to review. Then the equation for the line fit to the data is printed along with the accompanying correlation coefficient to determine the goodness of the fit. The output for a sample set of seven data points follows:

```
Least squares fit of straight line

Enter data values when prompted, (-1, -1) to quit.

        Enter (t[0] y[0]): 0 0.85
        Enter (t[1] y[1]): 1 4.72
        Enter (t[2] y[2]): 2 7.05
        Enter (t[3] y[3]): 3 9.43
        Enter (t[4] y[4]): 4 12.69
        Enter (t[5] y[5]): 5 17.2
        Enter (t[6] y[6]): 6 20.41
        Enter (t[7] y[7]): -1 -1

For the following data values
        Data[ 0]: t = 0.00, y = 0.85
        Data[ 1]: t = 1.00, y = 4.72
        Data[ 2]: t = 2.00, y = 7.05
        Data[ 3]: t = 3.00, y = 9.43
        Data[ 4]: t = 4.00, y = 12.69
        Data[ 5]: t = 5.00, y = 17.20
        Data[ 6]: t = 6.00, y = 20.41

The least squares equation is: y = 3.19 * t + 0.77
The correlation coefficient is: r = 0.995
```

Notes on Figure 10.23.   The sq_sum() function.   Summing the squares:

1. The summation formula uses two delta values, the difference between the first coordinate value and the mean of all first coordinates and the same difference for the second coordinate.

2. We sum the product of these two deltas for all coordinates in the array and return the sum.

10.5   What You Should Remember

10.5.1   Major Concepts

- *Arrays and their use.* An array in C is a collection of variables stored in order, in consecutive locations in the computer's memory. The array element with the smallest subscript (0) is stored in the location with the lowest address. We use arrays to store large collections of data of the same type. This is essential in three situations:

    1. When the individual data items must be used in a random order, as with the items in a list or data in a table.
    2. When each data value represents one part of a compound data object, such as a vector, that will be used repeatedly in calculations.
    3. When the data must be processed in separate phases, as with the calculation of mean and variance in this chapter. In this program, all the data were first read and then summed to calculate the mean. Then all the original data were processed a second time, using the mean, to calculate the variance.

- *Parallel arrays.* A multicolumn table can be represented as a set of parallel arrays, one array per column, all having the same length and accessed using the same subscript variable. Multidimensional arrays also exist and are discussed in Chapter 17.

- *Array arguments and parameters.* An array name followed by a subscript in square brackets denotes one array element whose type is the base type of the array. This element can be used as an argument to a function that has a parameter of the base type. To pass an entire array as an argument, write just the array name with no subscript brackets. The corresponding formal parameter is declared with empty square brackets. When the function call is executed, the address of the beginning of the array will be passed to the function. This gives the function full access to the array; it can use the data in it or store new data there.

- *Array initializers.* C allows great flexibility in writing array initializers; we summarize the rules here:

    1. An array initializer is a series of constant expressions enclosed in curly brackets. These expressions can involve operators, but they must not depend on input or run-time values of variables. The compiler must be able to evaluate the expressions at compile time.
    2. If there are too many initial values for the declared length, C will give a compile-time error comment.

3. If there are too few initial values, the uninitialized areas will be filled with 0 values of the proper type: an integer 0, floating value 0.0, or pointer **NULL**.

4. The length of an array may be omitted from the declaration if an initializer is given. In this case, the items in the initializer will be counted and the count will be used as the length of the array.

10.5.2   Programming Style

- Use a defined constant to declare the length of an array. This way the use and the array declarations will be consistent and easily changed if the need arises.

- A **for** loop typically is used to process the elements of an array. The values of the loop counter go from 0 to the length of the array (which is given by a defined constant or a function parameter); for example, **for (k=0; k<N; ++k) printf("%g ", volume[k]);**. Note that this loop paradigm stops before attempting to process the nonexistent element **volume[N]**.

- Variable names such as **j** and **k** typically are used as array subscripts since they are commonly found in mathematical formulas.

10.5.3   Sticky Points and Common Errors

- *Array length vs. highest subscript.* The number given in an array declaration is the actual number of slots in the array. Since array subscripts start at 0, the highest valid subscript is one less than the declared length. Often, though, there are more slots than valid data. This happens during an input operation and whenever the total amount of data entered falls short of the maximum allowed. In such situations, another variable is used to store the number of actual data elements in the array.

- *Caution: do not fall off the end of an array.* Remember that C does not help you confine your processing to the array slots that you defined. When you use arrays, avoid any possibility of using an invalid subscript. Input values must be checked before using them as subscripts. Loops that process arrays must terminate when the loop counter reaches the number of items in the array.

- *Array parameters.* To pass an entire array as an argument, write just the name of the array, with no ampersands or subscript brackets. The ampersand operator is not necessary for an array argument because the array name automatically is translated into an address. The corresponding array parameter is declared with the same base type and empty square brackets. A number can be placed between the brackets, but it will be ignored.

- *Array elements as parameters.* A single array element also can be passed as a parameter. To do this, write the array name with square brackets and a subscript. If the function is expected to store information in the array slot, as **scanf()** might, you must also use an ampersand in front of the name.

10.5.4   New and Revisited Vocabulary

These are the most important terms and concepts presented in this chapter:

aggregate type	array declaration	sequential array processing
array	array initializer	mean value of an array
base type	constant expression	variance
array slot	effective address	standard deviation
array element	walking on memory	regression
array length	memory error	least-squares fit
size of an array	array argument	correlation coefficient
subscript	array parameter	**pow()**
parallel arrays	summing loop	**get_data()**
		sqrt()

10.6   Exercises

10.6.1   Self-Test Exercises

1. Which occupies more memory space, an array of 15 **short int**s or an array of 3 **double**s? Explain your answer.

2. An array will be used to store temperature readings at four-hour intervals for one day. It is declared thus: **float temps[6];**

    a. Draw an object diagram of this array.

    b. What is its base type? Its length? Its size?

    c. Write a loop that will read data from the keyboard into this array.

    d. Write an **if** statement that will print **freezing** if the temperature in the last slot is less than or equal to 32°F and **above freezing** otherwise.

3. Array and function declarations.

    a. Write a declaration with an initializer for the array of **float**s pictured here.

    ff
1.9	2.5	-3.1	17.2	0
[0]	[1]	[2]	[3]	[4]

    b. Write a complete function that takes this array as a parameter, looks at each array element, and returns the number of elements greater than 0.

c. Write a prototype for this function.

d. Write a `scanf()` statement to enter a value into the last slot of the array.

4. In the indicated spots below, write a prototype, function header, and call for a function named **CHKBAL** that computes and returns the balance in a checking account. Its parameters are an initial account balance and an array of check amounts. You need not actually write a whole function to compute the new account balance; just fill in the indicated information.

```
#define  X   5
/* insert prototype here */

void main( void )
{
    float check_amounts[X];    /* $ amounts of checks */
    float start_balance;       /* balance before checks */
    float end_balance;         /* balance after checks */
    /* put call here */
}
/* put function header here */
```

5. The following are two declarations and a **while** loop.

```
int ara[13] = {1, 2, 4, 8, 16, 32, 64,
                128, 256, 512, 1024, 2048, 4096};
int k = 12;
while (k > 0) {
    printf( "%2i: %i \n", k, ara[k] );
    k -= 2;
}
```

a. What is the output?

b. Rewrite the code using a **for** loop instead of the **while** loop.

6. Given the following declarations, the prototypes on the left, and the calls on the right, answer *good* if a function call is legal and meaningful. If there is an error in the call, show how you might change it to match the prototype.

```
int j, a[5];
float f, flo[10];
double x, dub[4];
```

a. `double fun( double d[] );`   `x = fun( dub[] );`

b. `void fill( double d );`   `x = fill( dub );`

c. `int fix( float f ) ;`   `fix( flo[5] );`

d. `int hack( int a[] );`   `j = hack( a );`

e. `double q( double d[], int n );`   `x = q( dub[0], a[0] );`

7. Use the following definitions in this problem:

```
#define   LIMIT 5
int j;
double load[LIMIT];
```

a. Draw an object diagram for the array named **load**; identify the slot numbers in your drawing. Also show the values stored in it by executing the following loop:

```
for ( j=0; j<LIMIT; j++ ) {
    if ( j % 2 == 0 ) load[j] = 10.2 * (j + 1);
    else load[j] = (j + 1) * 2.5;
}
```

b. Trace the following loop and show the output exactly as it would appear on your screen. Show your work.

```
for (j = 0; j < LIMIT; ++j) {
    if (j <= LIMIT / 2)  printf( "\t%6.3g", load[j] );
    else printf( "\t%5.2f", load[j] -.05 );
}
```

10.6.2   Using Pencil and Paper

1. Draw a flow diagram for the main program in Figure 10.15 and for the **average()** function in Figure 10.18 (you may omit the details of the other two functions). In your diagram, show how control flows from one function to the other and back again.

2. An array will be used to store the serial numbers of all the printers in the lab. It is declared thus: **long printer_ID[10];**.

   a. Draw an object diagram of this array.

   b. What is its base type? Its length? Its size?

   c. Write a loop that will read data from the keyboard into this array; the loop should end when the user enters a negative number. Store the actual number of data items in the variable named **count**.

   d. Write a loop that will print out all **count** data items from the array.

3. Array and function declarations.

   a. Write a declaration with an initializer for the array of small integers pictured here:

   scores

96	68	79	93
[0]	[1]	[2]	[3]

b. Write a complete function that takes this array and an integer **n** as parameters, tests each array element, and prints all array elements greater than **n**.

c. Write a prototype for this function.

4. Use the following definitions in this problem:

```
#define  LIMIT 7
int j;
short puzzle[LIMIT], crazy[LIMIT];
```

a. Draw an object diagram for the array named **puzzle**; identify the slot numbers in your drawing. Also show the values stored in it by executing the following loop:

```
for (j = LIMIT; j > 0; --j) {
    if (j+4 > j*2) {
        puzzle[j] = j*2;
        crazy[LIMIT-j] = j + 2;
    }
    else {
        puzzle[j] = j/2;
        crazy[LIMIT-j] = j - 2;
    }
}
```

b. Trace the following loop and show the output exactly as it would appear on your screen. Show your work.

```
for (j = 0; j < LIMIT; ++j) {
    if (j % 2 == 1)
        printf( "\t%5i %3i", puzzle[j], crazy[j] );
    else  printf( "\t%3i %5i", crazy[j], puzzle[j] );
}
```

5. The following are two declarations and a **for** loop.

```
int a[12] = {2, 4, 8, 3, 9, 27, 4, 16, 64, 5, 25, 125};
int k;
for (k = 1; k < 10; k += 2) printf("%i: %i \n", k, a[k]);
```

a. What is the output?

b. Rewrite the code using a **while** loop instead of the **for** loop.

6. Given the following declarations, the prototypes on the left, and the calls on the right, answer *good* if a function call is legal and meaningful. If there is an error in the call, show how you might change it to match the prototype.

```
int j, ary[5];
float f, flo[10];
double x, dub[4];
```

```
a. double list( double d[] );        x = list( ary );
b. void handle( int k );             handle( ary[5] );
c. void bank( float f, int n );      bank( flo[5], j );
d. int days( int a[] );              j = days( &flo );
e. int area( double d );             x = area( dub[0] );
```

7. In the spots indicated below, write a prototype, function header, and call for a function named **MISSING**. Its parameters are an array of student assignment scores and the number of assignments that have been graded and recorded. The function will look at the data and return the number of nonzero scores in the array. You need not actually write the whole function, just fill in the indicated information.

```
#define  MAX  10
/* insert prototype here */

void main( void )
{
    int assignments[MAX];    /* grades */
    int actual;              /* # of assignments so far. */
    int done;                /* # of nonzero grades. */
    /* put call here */
}

/* put function header here */
```

10.6.3   Using the Computer

1. Seeing bits.
   The program in Figure 7.17 shows how to convert an integer to any selected base. Obviously, this program works for base 2, binary notation. Modify this program so that it inputs a number and prints the equivalent value in binary notation. Do not print it in the expanded form of the previous program, but as a series of ones and zeros. You will need to store the binary digits in an array and print them later in the opposite order, so that the first digit generated is the last printed. For example, if the input were 22, the output should be 10110.

2. Global warming.
   As part of a global warming analysis, a research facility tracks outdoor temperatures at the North Pole once a day, at noon, for a year. At the end of each month, these temperatures are entered into the computer and processed. The operator will enter 28, 29, 30, or 31 data items, depending on the month. You may use −500 as a sentinel value after the last temperature, since that is lower than absolute 0. Your main program should call the **read_temps()**, **hot_days()**, and **print_temps()** functions described here:

a. Write a complete specification for this program.

b. Write a function, **read_temps()**, that has one parameter, an array called **temps**, in which to store the temperatures. Read the real data values for one month and store them into the slots of an array. Return the actual number of temperatures read as the result of the function.

c. Write a function, **hot_days()**, that has two parameters: the number of temperatures for the current month and an array in which the temperatures are stored. Search through the temperature array and count all the days on which the noon temperature exceeds 32°F. Return this count.

d. Write a function, **print_temps()**, with the same two parameters plus the count of hot days. Print a neat table of temperatures. At the same time, calculate the average temperature for the month and print it at the end of the table, followed by the number of hot days.

3. Exam grades.
   Start with the program in Figures 10.15 through 10.18; modify it as follows:

a. In the main program, declare an array to store exam scores for a class of 15 students. Print out appropriate headings and instructions for the user. Call the appropriate functions to read in the exam scores and calculate their mean and standard deviation. Print the mean and standard deviation. Then call the **grades()** function described here to assign grades to the students' scores and print them.

b. Modify the **average()** function so that it does not print the individual exam scores during its processing.

c. Write a new function, named **grades()**, with three parameters: the array of student scores, the mean, and the standard deviation. This function will go through the array of exam scores again and assign a letter grade to each student according to the following criteria. Using one line of output per student, print the array subscript, the score, and the grade in columns. The grading criteria are

   - A, if the score is greater than or equal to the mean plus the standard deviation.
   - B, if the score is between the mean and the mean plus the standard deviation.
   - C, if the score is between the mean and the mean minus the standard deviation.
   - D, if the score is between the mean minus the standard deviation and the mean minus twice the standard deviation.
   - F, if the score is less than the mean minus twice the standard deviation.

   If a score is exactly equal to one of these boundary limits, give the student the higher grade.

4. The tab.
   An office with six workers maintains a snack bar managed on the honor system. A worker who takes a snack records his or her ID number and the price on a list. Once a month, the snack bar manager enters the data into a computer program that calculates the monthly bill for each worker. No item at the snack bar costs more than $2, and monthly totals are usually less than $100.

a. Write a complete specification for this program.

b. Using a top-down development technique, write a main program that will call functions to generate a monthly report. These functions are described here. Declare an array of **float**s named **tabs** to store total purchase amounts for each member and the guests.

c. The **purchases()** function should have one parameter, the **tabs** array. This function should allow the manager to enter two data items for each purchase: the price and the ID number of the worker who made the purchase. The ID numbers must be integers between 1 and 6. In addition, the code 0 is used for guests, whose bills are paid by the company. As each purchase is read, the amount (in dollars and cents) should be added to the array slot for the appropriate worker. When the manager enters an ID code that is not between 0 and 6, it should be considered a sentinel value and a signal to end the loop and return from the function. At that time, the array should contain the total purchases for each worker and for the guests.

d. The **bills()** function should have one parameter, the **tabs** array. Print a bill for each worker, giving the ID number and the amount due.

5. Payroll.
The Acme Company has some unusual payroll practices and keeps the information in its personnel database in a strange way. The firm never has more than 200 employees and pays all its employees twice a month, according to the following rules:

- If the person is salaried, the pay rate will be greater than $1,000. There are 24 pay periods per year, so for one period, **earnings = payrate / 24**.
- If the person is paid hourly, the pay rate will be between $5 and $100 per hour and the earnings are calculated by this formula:
  earnings = payrate * hours.
- A pay rate less than $5 per hour or between $100 and $1,000 per hour is invalid and should be rejected.

a. Write a complete specification for this program.

b. Using a top-down development process and following the example of Figure 10.12, write a main program that prints the bimonthly payroll report. Since the number of employees changes frequently, **main()** should prompt for this information. Then call functions to perform the calculations and produce a report. Use the functions suggested here, and add more if that seems appropriate. You will need a set of parallel arrays to hold the ID number, pay rate, hours worked, and earnings for each employee.

c. Following the example of Figure 10.21, write a function, **get_earnings()**. Read the data for all the employees from the keyboard into the parallel arrays.

d. Write a function, named **earn()**, that uses the pay rate and hours worked arrays to calculate the earnings and fill in the earnings array.

e. Write a function, named **pay()**, to calculate and return the earnings for one employee. If the pay rate is invalid, print an error comment and return 0.0.

   f. Write a function, named **payroll()**, that prints a neat table of earnings, showing all the data for each person. Also calculate the total earnings and print that value at the end of the list of employees.

6. Sorting boxes.
A set of boxes are on the floor. We want to put them in two piles, those larger than the average box and those smaller than or equal to the average box. Write a program to label the boxes in the following manner:

   a. Rewrite the **get_data()** function in Figure 10.17 so that you can enter data into three arrays rather than one. These arrays should hold the length, width, and height of the boxes, respectively.

   b. Write a function, named **volume()**, to compute and store the volume of each box in a fourth parallel array. The volume of a box is the product of its length, width, and height.

   c. Compute the average volume of the boxes using the **average()** function in Figure 10.18. Then write a function, **print_boxes()**, that will print the data for each box in a nice table, including a column containing the appropriate label, **big** or **small**, depending on whether the volume of the box is larger or smaller than the average volume.

7. Guess my weight.
At the county fair a man stands around trying to guess people's weight. You've decided to see how accurate he is, so you collect some data. These data are a set of number pairs, where the first number in the pair is the actual weight of a person and the second number is the weight guessed by the man at the fair. You decide to use two different error measures in your analysis: absolute error and relative error. Absolute error is defined as $E_{abs} = W_{guess} - W_{real}$, where W_{guess} and W_{real} are the guessed and real weights, respectively. The units of this error are pounds. The relative error is defined by $E_{rel} = 100 \times E_{abs}/W_{real}$, where the result of this equation is a percentage. Write a program that will input the set of weight pairs you accumulated, using a function with a sentinel loop to read the data. The number of weight pairs should be between 1 and 100. Write another function that will calculate both the absolute and relative errors of the guesses and display them in a table. Finally, compute and print the average of the absolute values of the absolute errors and the average of the absolute values of the relative errors.

8. Having fen.
Ms. Honeywell, an American businessperson, is preparing for a trip to Beijing, China, and is worried about keeping track of her money. She will take a portable computer with her, and wants a program that will sum the values of the Chinese fen (coins and bills) she has and convert the total to American dollars. Fen come in denominations of 1, 5, 10, 20, 50, 100, 200, 500, 1,000, and 2,000. The exchange rate changes daily and is published (in English) in the newspaper and on television. Write a program for Ms. Honeywell that will prompt her for the exchange rate and then for the number of fen she has of each denomination. Total the values of her fen and print the total as well as the equivalent in American dollars. Implement the table of fen values as a global constant array of integers.

9. Moving average.

Some quantities, such as the value of a stock, the size of a population, or the outdoor temperature, have frequent small fluctuations but tend to follow longer-term trends. It is helpful to evaluate such quantities in terms of a moving average; that is, the average of the most recent N measurements. (N normally is in the range $3 \ldots 10$.) This technique "smoothes out" the most recent fluctuations, exposing the overall trend. Write a program that will compute a moving average of order N for the price of a given stock on M consecutive days, where $M > N + 4$. To do this, first read the values of N and M from the user. Next read the first N prices and store them in an array. Then repeat the process below for the remaining $M - N$ prices:

   a. Compute and print the average of the N prices in the array.

   b. If all M values have been processed, quit and print a termination message.

   c. Otherwise, eliminate the value in array slot 0 and shift the other $N - 1$ values one slot leftward.

   d. Read a new value into the empty slot at the end of the array.

10. Find the lines.

The linear regression program in this chapter produces the equation of a line given a set of points. Consider the following set of points:

X	0	1	2	3	4	5	6	7
Y	2.8	4.7	7.2	8.9	11.6	13.1	14.7	17.5

We want to analyze how the equation of the line that fits these points will change as different combinations of points are used. Write a program to do the following:

   a. Compute and display the line fitted to these eight points, along with the corresponding correlation coefficient, which indicates the goodness of the fit.

   b. Then randomly pick one point, remove it from the set and recompute the line equation. Randomly remove another point and recompute. Continue this until you generate a line equation for only two remaining points.

   c. Display all these line equations in a table, with the number of points used to generate each and the corresponding correlation coefficients. Looking at the numbers in this table, what observations can you make concerning how well the linear regression process works?

CHAPTER

11

Character Data and Enumerations

This chapter is concerned with the character data type. We show how characters are represented in a program and in the computer; how they can be read, written, and used in a program; and how they are related to integers.

Enumerated types are also introduced. Enumerations are used to create symbolic codes for collections of conditions or objects. They can be useful in a variety of situations, such as handling error conditions, where they list and name the possible types of outcomes. Characters are the only built-in enumerated type.

11.1   Representation of Characters

A character is represented using a single byte (8 bits). We have shown how numeric values (integers and reals) are represented using the binary number system. Characters also are represented by bits. However, when we think of a text character, a binary number is not the first thing that comes to mind. There is no obvious way in which numbers or bit patterns correspond to the letters, digits, and special characters on a keyboard. So people have invented arbitrary codes to represent these characters. The most common of these is the ASCII (American Standard Code for Information Interchange) **code**, which is listed in a table in Appendix A.

Data type	Define Constant Limits	Range
signed char	SCHAR_MIN..SCHAR_MAX	$-128\ldots127$
unsigned char	0..UCHAR_MAX	$0\ldots255$
char	CHAR_MIN..CHAR_MAX	Same as **signed** or **unsigned char**

Figure 11.1. Character types.

Each ASCII character is represented by 7 bits,[1] which are stored on the rightmost side of a byte. You can think of the value of this byte either as a character or an integer.

The ASCII characters are listed in the appendix in numeric order, according to the value of their bit representations. We can find a character in the table and see its code or use a numeric code as an index into the table to determine the associated character. For historical reasons, the indexing number often is listed in two forms, decimal and hexadecimal.[2] The codes from 33 to 126 represent printable characters; most of these are letters of the alphabet in upper or lower case.

11.1.1 Character Types in C

In reality, characters are just very short integers in C; the single byte of a character holds a number. Anything you can do with an integer, you can do with a character. Anything you can do with a character, you can do with 1 byte of an integer. *There is no difference between a character and an integer* except the number of bytes used and the format specifiers used to read and print the two types.

11.1.2 The Different Interpretations

Figure 11.1 lists the character types defined by the C standard. The type **signed char** is not used often, and when used, it is generally thought of as a very short **int**. The more common type, **unsigned char**, is useful primarily when a program must store large quantities of small positive integers in memory and conserve storage to avoid running out of it. In this case, the **unsigned char** actually is being used as a very short **unsigned int**. A program that does image processing is an example of such an application (see Chapter 17). The type **char** is used for most character-handling applications.

---

[1] International ASCII uses 8 bits to represent each character.

[2] The hexadecimal number system is discussed in Chapter 18 and in Appendix E.

A character code such as ASCII uses a fixed number of bits to represent the letters of the alphabet, numerals, punctuation marks, special symbols, and control codes. ASCII uses 7 bits and therefore can represent 128 codes. The C standard permits type `char` to be defined either as signed or unsigned values; the compiler manufacturer makes that decision. Normally, it is of no concern to the programmer, since the index values for the ASCII table (0–127) are present in both forms, so there is not such a **portability** problem as there is with `int`. However, an international version of the ASCII code uses all 256 index values. The extra codes are used to represent additional letters and special symbols used in various European languages. In systems that use International ASCII, `char` is implemented as an unsigned type.

11.1.3 Character Literals

Most often **character literals** are written in C using single quotes, like this: `'A'`. However, nothing in C is simple. The character literal inside the quotes can be written two ways, as shown in Figure 11.2:

- If it is an ordinary printable character, we write it directly in quoted form. Thus, the first letter of the alphabet is written as `'a'` (lower case) or `'A'` (upper case).
- Some characters are written with an **escape code** or escape sequence. This consists of the \ (escape) character followed by a code for the character itself. The predefined symbolic escape codes are listed in Figure 11.3, a few of which we already used in output formats.

Escape code characters are included in C for two different reasons: to resolve ambiguity and to provide visible symbols for invisible characters. Three of the escape codes, `\'`, `\\`, and `\"`, are used to resolve lexical and syntactic ambiguity.

Character constants can be written symbolically or numerically. The symbolic form is preferable because it is portable; that is, it does not depend on the particular character code of the local computer.

Meaning	Symbol (Portable)	Decimal Index (ASCII Only)
The letter A	`'A'`	65
Blank space	`' '`	32
Newline	`'\n'`	10
Formfeed	`'\f'`	12
Null character	`'\0'`	0

Figure 11.2.   Writing character constants.

Code	Meaning	Code	Meaning	Code	Meaning
\0	Null	\a	Attention	\"	Double quote
\n	Newline	\b	Backspace	\'	Single quote
\r	Return	\f	Formfeed	\\	Backslash (escape)
\t	Horizontal tab	\v	Vertical tab		

Figure 11.3.   Useful predefined escape sequences.

The backslash (also called *escape*), single quote, and double quote characters have special meaning in C, but we also need to be able to write and process them as ordinary characters. The escape character tells C that the following keystroke is to be treated as an ordinary character, not as an element of C syntax.

The other escape characters are invisible; their purpose is to cause a side effect. For example, the *attention* code, \a, is used to alert the user that something exceptional has happened that needs attention. (Note that '\a' and 'a' are very different; the first means "attention" and should cause most computers to beep; the second is an ordinary letter.) A very important escape code is the *null character*, \0, which is used to mark the end of every character string and will be discussed further in Chapter 13.

One set of escape code characters that we use frequently are called **white-space** *characters*; they affect the appearance of the text but leave no visible mark themselves. The list includes newline, \n; return, \r; horizontal tab, \t; vertical tab, \v; formfeed, \f; and the ordinary space character. The two tab characters insert horizontal spaces or vertical blank lines into the output (the precise number of horizontal or vertical spaces depends on the system). Whitespace characters often are treated as a group in C and handled specially in a variety of ways.[3]

11.2   Input and Output with Characters

Character input and output can be performed using the standard `scanf()` and `printf()` functions. In addition, other special functions exist just for characters. Some of these functions have subtle difficulties associated with them, which we discuss.

11.2.1   Character Input

The standard library functions for reading characters are

---

[3] These ways will be explained as they become relevant to the text.

1. `getchar()`. This function has no parameters. It reads a single character of input and returns it.[4] Normally, the value returned by `getchar()` is used in an assignment statement.

   Example: `ch = getchar();`

2. `scanf()` *with a* `"%c"` *conversion specifier*. In this format, there is *no space* between the opening quotation mark and the `%c` specifier. This will read the next input character, whether or not it is whitespace, and store it in the address provided. This version is equivalent to using the `getchar()` function.

   Example: `scanf( "%c", &ch );`

3. `scanf()` *with a* `" %c"` *conversion specifier*. In this format, there is a space in the format string before the `%c` specifier. The space causes `scanf()` to skip leading whitespace (if any exists) before reading a single nonwhitespace character and storing it in the address provided. This is similar to the manner in which other data types are scanned.

   Example: `scanf( " %c", &ch );`

Keyboard input is buffered.   Whether you are entering numeric or character data into a program, your input is not sent immediately to the program. Until you hit the Enter key, it is displayed on the screen but remains in a holding tank called the **keyboard buffer** so that you can inspect and change it, if necessary. It is not the case that as soon as you type a character the program will read it and begin processing. Some languages provide this feature, but C is not one of them.[5] After you hit Enter, your input moves to another area called the **input buffer** and becomes available to the program. The program will read as much or as little as called for by the `scanf()` or `getchar()` statement. Unread data remain in the input buffer and will be read by future calls on `scanf()` or `getchar()`.

Whitespace characters complicate input.   When reading integers or floating-point numbers, `scanf()` skips over leading whitespace characters and starts reading with the first data character. However, with the `"%c"` specifier, leading whitespace is not ignored. If the first unread character is whitespace, that is what the system reads and returns. The function `getchar()` does the same thing. It reads a single character, which might be whitespace. Reading data in this manner leads to surprising behavior if the input contains unexpected whitespace characters such as `\n` and `\t`. Since these are not visible, it is easy to forget that they may be present.

---

[4]Technically, the value returned by `getchar()` is an `int`. The character is stored in the rightmost part of that `int`, and bytes to the left of the character are filled with **padding** bits. When the padded value is stored in a character variable, the padding is discarded. This process of adding and stripping off padding is automatic, and transparent, and can be ignored by beginning programmers.

[5]Some PC compiler systems do provide this feature, but it is not supported by the C standard and so it is not portable.

As mentioned previously, the behavior of `scanf()` can be changed by adding a single blank to the format: `" %c"`. The space inside the quotes and before the `%c` tells `scanf()` to skip over leading whitespace, if any exists. However, there is no way to force `getchar()` to skip over these invisible characters. For this reason, we usually use `scanf()` rather than `getchar()` to input single characters interactively.

11.2.2 Character Output

Character output is relatively straightforward. The `stdio` library provides two ways to display or print a single character:

1. `putchar()`. When only one character of output is needed, `putchar()` is the easiest way to do the job; we simply pass it the character we want to display. For example, to move the screen cursor to the beginning of the next line, we might say `putchar( '\n' );`. Note that the `putchar()` function does not automatically move the cursor to the next line as `puts()` does.
2. `printf()` *with a* `%c` *conversion specifier*. When printing a character mixed in with other kinds of data, we use `printf()` with the `%c` format specifier. Example:
    `printf( "Child is %c, %i years old.", gender, age );`
    Of course, a specific (nonvariable) character can be included in the format string itself. As with the other data types, it is possible to specify a field width between the `%` and the `c`, and the printed character will be right or left justified in the field area, depending on the sign of the width specifier.

Since characters *are* integers, it is legal to read or print them as integers. When you read an integer that is the ASCII code of a letter and print that number using a `"%c"` format or `putchar()`, you see the letter. Conversely, when you read a letter and print it using a `"%i"` format, you see a number.[6] This technique is demonstrated in Figure 11.4.

Notes on Figure 11.4. Printing the ASCII codes.

*   *First box: declaration*. We declare a `char` variable. In the remaining code, we use it to perform both character and integer output.
*   *Second box: character input*. We read a character (one keystroke); its ASCII code is stored as a binary integer in the `char` variable. The character is not read until the Enter key is pressed.

---

[6]It also is possible to print the hexadecimal form of the character's index by using a `%x` conversion specifier. See Chapter 18.

```
#include <stdio.h>
void main( void )
{
    char ch;

    puts( "\n Demo: Printing the ASCII codes." );
    printf( "\n Please type a character then hit ENTER: " );
    ch = getchar();

    printf( " The ASCII code of %c is %i \n\n", ch, ch );
}
```

Figure 11.4.   Printing the ASCII **codes.**

- *Third box: output.* We print the input character twice: first as a character, using `%c`; then as an integer, using `%i`. Sample program output looks like this:

```
Demo: Printing the ASCII codes.

Please type a character then hit ENTER: A
The ASCII code of A is 65
```

11.2.3   Using the I/O Functions

The program in Figure 11.5 illustrates the use of the four character input and output functions and demonstrates how a simple program can produce very confusing output if the problem of whitespace in the input is not addressed.

Notes on Figure 11.5. Character input and output.

- *First box: character output.*

    1. The function `putchar()` prints a single character. Its argument can be a character variable, a literal character, or an integer. If the argument is an `int`, the rightmost byte of its value is interpreted as an index for the ASCII code table, and the character in that position is printed. The command `putchar( 42 )` prints an asterisk because 42 is the ASCII code for `*`.
    2. We also can print a single character using `printf()` with `%c`; in this case, we print a dollar sign. If we try to print an integer with a `%c` conversion specifier, we see the character that corresponds to that integer's index in the code table. For example, the output from `printf( "%c", 42 )` would be an `*`.

We demonstrate various ways to read and write single characters and how a whitespace character in the input can cause unexpected results.

```
#include <stdio.h>
void main( void )
{
    char input;
    char money = '$';
    char star  = '*';

    putchar( '\n' );  putchar( star );  putchar( 42 );   putchar( '\n' );
    printf( " Do you need %c (y/n)? ", money );

    scanf( "%c", &input );

    while (input == 'y') {
        printf( " Here is %c5.00\n", money );
        printf( "\n Do you need more (y/n)? " );
        input = getchar();
    }

    printf( " OK --- Bye now.  %c \n", '\a' );
}
```

Figure 11.5.   Character input and output.

- *Second box: reading the first response.*

  1. The line `scanf( "%c", ...  )` reads a single character of input.
  2. When a program begins executing, the input buffer is empty. Normally, the user will not enter any input until prompted, so the user's response to the first prompt will be the only thing in the input buffer. The first character of that response will be read, while the newline character generated by the Enter key will remain in the buffer. We presume that the user will type **y**, causing control to enter the loop.

- *Third box: the loop.*

  1. In this loop, we "give" $5.00 to the user and prompt for another response:

     ```
     Here is $5.00

     Do you need more (y/n)?
     ```

  2. This time we use `getchar()` to read the next input character. If it is **y**, we will stay in the loop; for any other input (including whitespace), we leave the loop.

3. This logic seems simple enough, but *it does not work.* As shown in the following output, the user sees the second prompt but the program quits and says goodbye without giving that user a chance to enter anything. The reason for this problem is explained in the following section.

4. The complete output for this run is

```
**
Do you need $ (y/n)? y
Here is $5.00

Do you need more (y/n)?   OK --- Bye now.
```

- *Fourth box: the closing message.* The `%c` "prints" the escape character `\a`. On some systems, if the computer has a sound generator and the volume is turned up, you should hear a ding when you print the attention character, but you see nothing. On other systems, the output may be visible (for instance, a small box) but not audible.

Problems with `getchar()`.   A common programming error was illustrated in Figure 11.5. After `scanf()`, the program initially performs as expected; if the input is `y`, it enters the loop and "gives" the user $5.00. Then the loop prompts the user to enter another (`y/n`) response. However, when the second prompt is displayed, the system does not even wait for the user to respond; it simply quits. Why?

When entering the answer to the first question (above the loop), the user types `y` and hits the Enter key. This puts the character `y` and a newline character into the input buffer. The newline character is necessary because, in most operating systems, the system does not send the keyboard input to the program until the user types a newline. The `scanf()` above the loop reads the `y` but leaves the `\n` in the buffer. At the end of the first time around the loop, that `\n` still is sitting in the input buffer, unread. The loop prompts the user for a choice, but the program does not wait for a key to be hit because input already is waiting. The `getchar()` then reads the `\n`, emptying the buffer. Since `\n` is not equal to `y`, the loop ends and the program says goodbye.

Now, if the user had typed `yyy` followed by a newline instead of a single `y` at the first prompt, the characters waiting in the input buffer would have been `yy\n`. The input to the second prompt then would have been `y`, and the program would have given the user another $5.00 bill. Altogether, the user would get three bills before the program could read the newline and leave the loop, all with no further typing by the user. The resulting output would be

```
**
Do you need $ (y/n)? yyy
Here is $5.00

Do you need more (y/n)?   Here is $5.00
```

```
Do you need more (y/n)?   Here is $5.00

Do you need more (y/n)?   OK --- Bye now.
```

Using `scanf( "%c", &input )` in place of `input = getchar()` does not solve the problem, because `scanf()` with `"%c"` works the same way as `getchar()`. However, we can solve this whitespace problem by using a single space in the format for `scanf()`. Replace the call on `getchar()` in Figure 11.5 by this call on `scanf()`:

scanf(" %c", &input);

Note space in format

With this change, everything will work as intended: The program will query the user, wait for a response every time, and do the appropriate thing. A typical output would look like this:

```
**
Do you need $ (y/n)? y
Here is $5.00

Do you need more (y/n)? y
Here is $5.00

Do you need more (y/n)? n
OK --- Bye now.
```

If the user initially were to type **yyy**, the output would begin as shown earlier, but after three times through the loop, the user would have a chance to enter responses again.

11.3   Operations on Characters (Advanced Topic)

11.3.1   Characters Are Very Short Integers

The basic operations defined for characters are the same operations that are defined for integers because, technically, characters *are* integers in the range $0 \ldots 255$ or $-128 \ldots 127$. Some kinds of data (such as digital images) are composed of a very large number of very small integers. In such cases, it is useful to minimize the amount of storage occupied by the data, so the data are stored as type **char** or **unsigned char** rather than **short int** or **int**. In such applications, it is important that all the integer operations can be applied to variables of type **char**.

The common use of type `char`, however, is to represent characters. Even then, many integer operators are useful; These are summarized in Figure 11.6. A little caution is warranted here; some integer operations are legal but not useful with characters. For example, it makes no sense to multiply or divide one character by another. Unfortunately, useless or not, the compiler will not identify such expressions as errors. In addition to the basic integer operators, there is also a set of functions in the `ctype` library that can manipulate character values. We now examine some of the library functions and take a closer look at the operators in Figure 11.6.

11.3.2 Assignment

We have seen that the values of both character and integer variables can be assigned to a `char` variable. As long as the integer value is not too big, everything will be fine (large values lead to overflow). Automatic coercion will shorten the integer and a single byte will be assigned. Literal characters also can be assigned to `char` variables. The columns of Figure 11.2 show two different values that will assign the same character code to a variable.

Commonly used character operations are listed here. The phrase *alphabetical order* used here means "the order defined by the ASCII code or whatever code is in use on the local hardware." This normally is an extension of ordinary alphabetical order to include all of the characters in the local character set.

Operation	Meaning and Use
`char c1, c2;`	Declare two character variables
`c1 = c2;`	Copy the value of `c2` into `c1`
`c1 == c2`	Do `c1` and `c2` contain the same letter?
`c1 != c2`	Do `c1` and `c2` contain different letters?
`c1 < c2`	Does `c1` come before `c2` in alphabetical order? The `<=`, `>`, and `>=` operators also are defined for characters
`c1 + 1`	The letter that follows the value of `c1` in the alphabet
`c1 - 1`	The letter that precedes the value of `c1` in the alphabet
`++c2;`	Change `c2` from its current value to the next letter in the alphabet. All four increment and decrement operators are defined for characters
`c2 - c1`	Assuming that `c2 > c1`, this is the number of letters in the alphabet between `c1` and `c2`

Figure 11.6.   Character operations.

11.3.3   Comparing Characters

The operators == and != are used to test whether two characters are equal. These operators are straightforward and portable; that is, they work identically on all systems. The other four comparison operators, <, >, <=, and >=, also are useful for characters, but their results can vary because they depend on the local computer system.

ASCII and International ASCII are the two codes used most commonly in personal computers today, but some systems use different underlying character codes. The particular code in use on the local system determines the "alphabetical order" on that system. (The technical terms for alphabetical order are **collating sequence** and **lexical order**.) Numerals and letters of the English alphabet are arranged in the usual order in most codes, but the special symbols may be arranged in arbitrary and incompatible ways. Therefore, two dissimilar machines might produce different results for some character comparisons.

11.3.4   Character Arithmetic

The operators +, -, ++, and -- are used in **character arithmetic** to compute the next (or prior) letters of the alphabet. The operator - can be used to determine how far apart two letters are in the alphabet. All these operations are useful for text processing programs and all depend on the collating sequence of the machine.

11.3.5   Other Character Functions

One of the standard C libraries is the character processing library, whose header file is `ctype.h`. This library contains a group of functions essential to a system programmer, including ones to test whether a character is in a particular set, such as the alphabet, as well as certain transformation routines. Several of these functions are frequently useful, even in simple programs:

1. `isalpha()`. This function takes one argument, a character. If the character is an alphabetic character (A ... Z or a ... z), the value **true** (1) is returned; otherwise, **false** (0) is returned.
2. `islower()`. This function takes one argument, a character. If the character is a lower-case alphabetic character (a ... z), the value **true** (1) is returned; otherwise, **false** (0) is returned.
3. `isupper()`. This function takes one argument, a character. If the character is an upper-case alphabetic character (A ... Z), the value **true** (1) is returned; otherwise, **false** (0) is returned.
4. `isdigit()`. This function takes one argument, a character. If it is a digit (0 ... 9), **true** (1) is returned; otherwise, **false** (0) is returned.

5. `isspace()`. This function takes one argument, a character. If the character is a whitespace character (space, newline, return, formfeed, horizontal tab, or vertical tab), **true** is returned; otherwise, **false** is returned.
6. `tolower()`. This function takes one argument, a character. If the character is an upper-case alphabetic character (between A and Z), the return value is the corresponding lower-case character (between a and z). If the argument is anything else, it is returned unchanged.
7. `toupper()`. This function is the opposite of `tolower()`. If the argument is a lower-case character, the return value is the corresponding upper-case character. If the argument is anything else, it is returned unchanged.

When an input buffer might contain an unpredictable sequence of input items, a program can use the functions `isalpha()`, `islower()`, `isupper()`, `isdigit()`, and `isspace()` to analyze each input character and handle it appropriately.

The functions `toupper()` and `tolower()` often are used in conjunction with testing character input, so that it does not matter whether the user types an upper-case or lower-case character. The programmer chooses one case to use for processing (often, it does not matter which) and converts all input characters to that case. By doing so, the logic of the program can be simplified. An example of this use of `tolower()` follows; `toupper()` is illustrated by the program in Figure 11.7.

Suppose that a program needs to read a character into a variable named **ch** and use it to select one action from a set of actions. We could write the code like this:

```
scanf( " %c", &ch );

if (ch == 'x' || ch == 'X') {         /* X actions here */ }
else if (ch == 'y' || ch == 'Y') { /* Y actions here */ }
else if (ch == 'z' || ch == 'Z') { /* Z actions here */ }
else {                                /* default actions */ }
```

By using a case-shift function, we can eliminate one comparison in each test:

```
scanf( " %c", &ch );
ch = tolower( ch );

if (ch == 'x') {          /* X actions go here */  }
else if (ch == 'y') {  /* Y actions go here */  }
else if (ch == 'z') {  /* Z actions go here */  }
else {                    /* default actions go here */  }
```

We improve the user interface of the main program from Figure 6.12 by permitting a `y/n` or `Y/N` response to the question, "Do you want to continue?" The `work()` function can be found in Figure 6.13.

```
#include "tools.h"
void work( void );              /* function prototypes */
void title( void );

void main( void )
{
    char more;                  /* repeat-or-stop switch */
    banner();
    title();                    /* print program title and instructions */
    do { work();
         puts( "\n Do you want to continue (Y/N)? " );
         scanf( " %c", &more );
         more = toupper( more ) ;
    } while (more != 'N');

    bye();
}

void title( void )  /* Print program title. ------------------ */
{
    puts( " Calculate the time it would take a grapefruit\n"
          " to fall from a helicopter at a given height.\n" );
}
```

Figure 11.7.   Improving the workmaster.

11.4   Character Application: An Improved Processing Loop

In Chapter 6, Figure 6.12, we demonstrate how a process can be repeated using a query loop until the user chooses to quit. Using the codes 1 to continue and 0 to quit is adequate, but it is not good human engineering and not customary. Now that we have shown how to read a single input character and how to force that character into a particular case, it is possible to improve the human interface by giving the more usual prompt: `Do you want to continue (y/n)?` and accepting either an upper-case or lower-case answer. The next program implements this improved interface using `toupper()` and `scanf( " %c", ... )`. Since it is a revision of the main program from Figure 6.12, we comment on only the aspects that have changed.

Notes on Figure 11.7. Improving the workmaster.

- *First box: the* `char` *variable.* We now use a character variable rather than an integer to store the user's response.
- *Outer box: the repetition loop.* We change the `do...while()` termination condition to test for the letter `'N'` instead of the number 0. This is more natural for the user. However, to make this test work reliably, we need to change two things in the inner box.
- *Inner box: reading input.* To read the input, we use a `scanf()` format that will skip whitespace in the input buffer. This is important in a loop that controls a `work()` function, because the input operations performed by that function usually leave whitespace (at least one newline character) in the input buffer.
- *Innermost box: case conversion.* Even when instructions call for a `Y` or `N` response, many users will type `y` or `n` instead. Good human engineering dictates that the program should accept upper-case and lower-case letters interchangeably. We achieve this by using `toupper()` to force the response into upper case. This permits us to make a simple check for an upper-case response instead of the more complex test for either a lower-case or upper-case letter. To achieve the same result without `toupper()`, we would have to write the loop test as

  ```
  while (more != 'n' && more != 'N').
  ```

- *Fifth box: the* `title()` *function.* The statement that prints the program title has been removed from `main()` and placed in a function. By doing this, we create a main program that, literally, can be used from program to program without any changes. All the task-specific code is found in `work()` or `title()`.
- *Output.* A sample of the output follows. Note that whitespace and case differences are ignored.

  ```
  Calculate the time it would take a grapefruit
  to fall from a helicopter at a given height.

  Enter height of helicopter (meters): 19.9
      Time of fall = 2.015 seconds
      Velocity of the object = 19.756 m/s

  Do you want to continue (Y/N)? Y
  ```

```
Enter height of helicopter (meters): 175
   Time of fall = 5.974 seconds
   Velocity of the object = 58.586 m/s

Do you want to continue (Y/N)?     n
```

11.5   Enumerated Types[7]

The use of **#define** to give a symbolic name to a constant is familiar by now. It is a simple way to define a symbolic name for an isolated constant such as π or the force of gravity. Sometimes, though, we need to define a set of related symbols, such as codes for the various kinds of errors that a program can encounter. We wish to give the codes individual names and values and declare that they form a set of related items. The **#define** command lets us name values individually but gives us no way to associate them into a group of codes whose meaning is distinct from all other defined symbols. For example, suppose we wanted to have symbolic names for the possible ways that a data item could be illegal. We could define the following four symbolic constants:

```
#define DATA_OK   0
#define TOO_SMALL   1
#define TOO_BIG   2
#define NO_INPUT -1
```

11.5.1   Type Definitions

Variable names are like nouns in English; they are used to refer to objects. Type names are like adjectives; they arc used to describe objects but are not objects themselves. A type is a pattern or rule for constructing future variables. Types such as **int**, **float**, and **double** have names defined by the C standard. These are all simple types, meaning that objects of these types have only one part. We have also studied arrays, which are aggregate objects.

Other important types that we use all the time, such as string, do not have standard names in C; they must be defined by type specifications. A **type specification** describes how a new type is constructed out of previously defined elements. The most convenient way to define a new type is within a **typedef** declaration, which enables us to attach a name to the newly constructed type. Naming a type makes code easier to read and understand because type names permit the programmer to work on a conceptual plane instead of working at the level of implementation detail.

---

[7]This section can be deferred until structures are introduced in Chapter 14.

11.5.2   Enumerations

The character data type really is an enumeration. The ASCII code maps the literal forms of the characters to corresponding integer values. This particular enumeration is built into the C language, so you do not see its construction. But it is possible to create new types using the **enumeration specification**, the keyword **enum** followed by a bracketed list of symbols called **enumeration constants**. Enumerations normally are defined within a **typedef** declaration, as shown in Figure 11.8.

Although the **enum** and **#define** mechanisms produce similar results, using an **enum** declaration is superior to using a set of **#define** commands because we can declare that the enumeration codes listed form the complete set of relevant codes and thus use the enumerated type to define the set of valid values a variable may have or a function may return. Using **enum** rather than **#define** improves readability with no cost in efficiency.

The enumeration symbols will become names for the constants, much as the symbol in a **#define** becomes a name for a constant. By default, the first symbol in the enumeration is given the underlying value 0; succeeding symbols are given integer values in ascending numeric order, unless the sequence is reset by an explicit assignment. Such an assignment is illustrated by the third declaration in Figure 11.9. Such an explicit initializer resets the sequence, which continues from the new number, so it is possible to leave gaps in the numbering or have two constants represented by the same code, which normally is undesirable. Therefore, the programmer must be careful when assigning specific representations to enumeration constants.

Inside a C program,[8] enumeration values are treated as integers in all ways, as is true for characters. The compiler makes no distinction between a value of an enumeration type and a value of type **int**. Since enumeration constants are translated into integers, all the integer operators can be used with enumeration values. Although most integer operators make no sense with enumeration constants, increment and decrement operators sometimes are used, as they are with

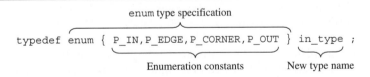

The underlying values of **P_IN...P_OUT** are 0, 1, 2, 3 respectively.

Figure 11.8.   The form of an enum declaration.

---

[8]This is not true in C++, where enumerated types are distinct from integers.

```
typedef enum { P_IN, P_SIDE, P_CORNER, P_OUT } in_type;
typedef enum { NO_ROOT, ROOT_OK } status_t;
typedef enum { DATA_OK, TOO_SMALL, TOO_BIG, NO_INPUT=-1 } error_t;
typedef enum { false, true } bool;
```

Figure 11.9.   Four enumerations.

type **char**. However, unlike **char**, C provides no way to automatically read or print enumeration values; they must be input and output as integers. This complication leads to extra work to devise special input and output routines for values of an enumeration type. This extra hassle sometimes discourages the programmer from using an **enum** type. However, the added clarity in a program normally is worth the effort, and in truth, the values of many such types never actually are input or output, but merely used within the program to send information back and forth between functions.

Why use enumerations?   We use enumerations (rather than integer constants) to distinguish each kind of code from ordinary integers and other codes. This enables us to write programs that are less cryptic. Someone reading the program sees a symbol that conveys its meaning better than an integer that encodes the meaning. The reader understands the program more easily because the use of **enum** clarifies which symbols are related to each other. By using an **enum** constant rather than its associated integer, we make it evident that the object is a code, not a number.

Notes on Figure 11.9. Four enumerations.   This figure declares four enumerated types that give names to conditions that are somewhat complex to characterize but easy to understand once they are named. These types will be used in various programs in the remainder of the text.

- *Type* **in_type***: answer codes.* The first **typedef** declares a set of codes that will be used in an application in Chapter 14. This program processes a point and a rectangle in the xy plane, determining where the point is located with respect to the rectangle. One function does the analysis and returns an answer of type **in_type** to the main program, which then interacts with the user. The code **P_IN** is used if the point is inside the rectangle; the codes **P_SIDE**, **P_CORNER**, and **P_OUT**, respectively, mean that the point is on a side, on a corner, or outside of the rectangle.
- *Type* **status_t***: status codes.* The second declaration in Figure 11.9 is an enumeration of codes used in a program that finds the roots of an equation. In this program (Figure 12.16) the main program prompts the user for equation parameters, then calls a function to do the actual work. The function returns the root (if found) and a success-or-failure code, **ROOT_OK** or **NO_ROOT**. The descriptive nature of these symbols makes the program logic clearer.

We declare an enumeration variable and use it to store an error code after testing an input value.

```
double x;
error_t status;

scanf( "%lg", &x );
if (x < 0) status = TOO_SMALL;
else status = DATA_OK;
```

Figure 11.10.   Using an enumeration to name errors.

- *Type* `error_t`: *error codes.* The third declaration in Figure 11.9 is an enumeration of **error codes**, which can be used to simplify the management of input errors. The symbols `DATA_OK`, `TOO_SMALL`, and `TOO_BIG` carry the underlying integer values 0, 1, and 2, respectively. The last symbol, `NO_INPUT`, is followed by an assignment, so the symbol `NO_INPUT` will be represented by the code -1 rather than 3. Figure 11.10 illustrates a code fragment that applies this enumerated type. These statements test for an input error and set the value of a variable to indicate whether it was detected. Further input error processing is described in Chapter 15.

- *Type* `bool`: *Boolean variables and functions.* The last declaration in Figure 11.9 is taken from the `tools` library. It defines **type** `bool`, short for "Boolean," and its two truth values, `false` and `true`. Many languages (such as C++) have this type built into the language. It is used to represent the answers to yes-no questions such as, "Is the data value legal?" and "Are two objects the same?" ISO C has no separate data type called `bool`; instead, the integer 1 is used to represent `true` and 0 is used to represent `false`.[9] This sometimes leads to confusion about whether an object's value represents a number or a truth value. The clarity of such code can be improved by using the type `bool` instead of `int` to declare variables and functions that involve decisions and by using the symbols `false` and `true` for truth values instead of the numbers 0 and 1.

The next application is a prime number generator that illustrates how to use the type `bool` as the result of a function. The task specifications are given in Figure 11.11, the main program in Figure 11.12, and the Boolean function in Figure 11.13.

Notes on Figure 11.12. Calculating prime numbers.

- *First box: prototype.* The `divisible()` function tests whether a number is a prime and returns a result of type `bool`. This type is defined in `tools.h` as `enum {false, true}`, with `false=0` and `true=1`.

---

[9]This is not true in C++, where the type `bool` is standard. We introduce `bool` here in a way that is fully compatible with C++. Some newer C compilers may also predefine the type.

Problem scope: Print a list of all prime numbers, starting with 2, and continuing until **MANY** primes have been printed. A prime number is an integer that has no proper divisors except itself and 1.

Constant: MANY, the number of primes to be found and printed.

Restrictions: MANY must be small enough that an array of **MANY** integers can fit into memory and the last prime calculated is less than the maximum integer that can be represented.

Input: None.

Output required: A neat list of primes, one per line.

Figure 11.11.   Problem specifications: A table of prime numbers.

```
/* Calculate and print a table of the first MANY prime numbers. */

#include "tools.h"
#define MANY 3000

void print_table( int primes[], int num_primes );

bool divisible( int candidate, int primes[], int n ); /* Is it nonprime? */

void main( void )
{
    int k;                       /* Integer being tested. */

    int primes[MANY] = {2}; /* Start with the only even prime in table. */
    int n = 1;                   /* Number of primes in table. */

    banner();

    /* Fill table with the first MANY prime numbers ----------------------*/
    for (k = 3; n <= MANY; k += 2) {     /* Test the next odd integer. */
                                         /* Quit when table is full. */
        if (!divisible(k, primes, n)) { /* If it is a prime... */
            primes[n]=k;                 /* ... put it in the table... */
            ++n;                         /* ... and count it. */
        }
    }

    print_table( primes, MANY );         /* Print table of primes. */

    bye();
}
```

Figure 11.12.   Calculating prime numbers.

Type `bool` was defined in Figure 11.9. We use it here as the return type and to declare a local variable in a function that tests whether an integer is a prime number.

```
/* ----------------------------------------------------------------
// Test candidate number for divisibility by primes in the table.
// Return true if proper divisor is found, false otherwise.
*/
bool divisible( int candidate, int primes[], int n )
{
    int m;                      /* Loop counter */
    int last = (int) sqrt( candidate );
    bool found = false;         /* Set=true later if divisor is found. */

    /* Divide by every prime < square root of candidate. */
    for (m = 0; m < n && primes[m] <= last; ++m) {
        if (candidate % primes[m] == 0) {
            found = true;
            break;
        }
    }

    return found;
}
/* ----------------------------------------------------------------
// Print the list of prime numbers, one per line.
*/
void print_table( int primes[], int num_primes )
{
    int m;                   /* Loop index for primes table */
    printf( "\n The First %i Primes"
            "\n --------------------\n", num_primes );
    for (m = 0; m < num_primes; m++) printf( "%10i\n", primes[m] );
    printf( " --------------------\n" );
}
```

Figure 11.13.   Functions for the prime number program.

• *Second box: the table of primes.*

1. The table will be filled in with prime numbers. The list will be generated in order by testing every possible odd number, starting with 3. As primes are discovered, we store them in the table. To test each integer, we use the previously computed portion of the table.
2. We choose an arbitrary constant for the length of this table. Computing more primes requires more time and storage space. This method

is limited by the space available and the largest integer that can be represented in the ordinary way. The latter limit usually occurs first.

3. The first prime, and the only even prime, is 2. We initialize the first slot in the table to 2 so that the computation loop can be limited to testing odd numbers. The rest of the prime table will be initialized to 0.

4. We already have stored one prime in the table, so we initialize **n** to 1. It will be incremented each time a new prime is found.

- *Third box: filling the table.*

  1. We use a **for** loop that starts at 3 and counts by twos to test all the odd numbers.

  2. This is a very unusual loop. While we initialize **k** and increment it each time around the loop, we use **n**, the number of primes, to end the loop. We want to continue searching for primes until the table is filled; that is, **n==MANY**. Since we do not know how big **k** will be at that time, we do not use **k** to terminate the loop.

- *Inner box: calling the function to test for primality.*

  1. By definition, N is prime if it has no divisors except itself and 1. If N did have a divisor, it would have to have two, and one of them would have to be less than or equal to $\sqrt{N}$. Also, if N did have a divisor, D, either D would be a prime number or D itself would have at least two other divisors smaller than itself. Thus, we can show that N is a prime by showing that it is not divisible by any prime less than or equal to $\sqrt{N}$.

  2. If **divisible()** returns **true**, **k** is not a prime. If it returns **false**, we put **k** into the table and increment **n**.

- *Last box: printing the table.* The output is printed by calling **print_table()**. The first and last portions of it are

```
The First 3000 Primes
---------------------
          2
          3
          5
          7
         11
         13
         17
         19
        .....
      27427
      27431
      27437
      27449
---------------------
```

Notes on Figure 11.13. Functions for the prime number program.
The `divisible()` function can identify primes up to the square of the largest
prime currently stored in the table. Its parameters are `candidate` (a number to
test), `primes` (a table of primes), and `n` (the current length of the table).

- *First box: the Boolean variable.*

  1. We define a variable of type `bool`, whose value will be returned later
     as the result of the function. We initialize the variable to `false` and
     later set it to `true` if we find what we are searching for; that is, a
     number that evenly divides the candidate.
  2. This is a common control pattern and especially useful when several
     tests must be made and any one of them could terminate processing.

- *Second box: the search loop.*

  1. We use the modulus operator to test whether one number is divisible
     by another; *a* is divisible by *b* if the remainder of `a/b` is 0; that is, if
     `a%b == 0`.
  2. To test a candidate number, we divide it by all the numbers in the table
     up to the square root of the candidate and leave the search loop with a
     `break` statement the first time we find a proper divisor.
  3. If no divisor is found, one of two conditions will terminate the loop:
     Either we have tested every prime in the table or the next prime in the
     table is greater than the square root of the candidate.

- *Last box: the return statement.* We return the value of the `bool` variable,
  which will be either `true` or `false`.
- *The* `print_table()` *function.* This function follows the usual pattern;
  it prints a table heading, uses a `for` loop to print the data in the array, and
  finishes with a table footer.

11.6   **What You Should Remember**

11.6.1   Major Concepts

- ASCII is a character code. It uses 7 bits to represent the set of 128 characters that are part of the code. International ASCII is an 8-bit code that
  represents 256 characters. These codes are used with the `char` data type.
- Character literals are written between single quotemarks.
- Escape codes are used to write literals for invisible characters.
- There are several whitespace characters, including space, horizontal and
  vertical tabs, and newline.

- An enumerated type specification allows you to define a set of related symbolic constants.
- Use **typedef** declarations to name enumerations.
- Type **char** is the most commonly used enumerated type and type **bool** is the most common programmer-defined enumerated type.

11.6.2 Programming Style

- *Escape codes.* Most ASCII characters are printable characters; that is, they leave a visible mark when displayed on a video screen or a printer. These characters correspond to keys on a typical computer keyboard. Some keys, such as the space bar, the Tab key, and the Enter key, do not represent printable characters but are used for their effect on the printed text. These, called *whitespace* characters, are represented in a C program by symbolic escape codes. There also are nonprintable ASCII characters that have no symbolic escape codes; they are used infrequently but may be referenced, if necessary, by using the underlying value. To be sure that your program is portable, use only the literal form of a character or a symbolic code.
- *Enumerations.* Use enumerations wisely. Use an enumeration any time you have a modest sized set of codes to define. It might be a set of error codes, conditions, or codes relating to the data. Use **#define** for isolated constants. Often, it is wise to include one item in the enumeration to designate an appropriate value to use when an unexpected error occurs. Names of the enumeration constants should reflect their meaning, as with any constant or variable. For example, an enumeration for "gender" might be **enum { male, female, unknown }**.
- *Truth values.* Many functions and operators return truth values (**false** or **true**). Learn to test truth values directly rather than making an unnecessary comparison; for example, write **if (error_flag)** rather than **if (error_flag == true)**.
- *Avoiding errors.* Use character processing for a better human interface, like that in the revised **work()** function. Use functions like **toupper()** and **tolower()** to handle both upper-case and lower-case responses.

11.6.3 Sticky Points and Common Errors

- **char** *vs.* **int**. Technically, characters are very short integers in C. Conceptually, though, they are a separate type with separate operations and different methods for input and output. Be sure not to do meaningless operations like multiplying two characters and avoid potentially nonportable operations like <. Every C implementation uses the character code built into the underlying hardware. For most modern machines, that code is either International ASCII or ASCII, which is given in Appendix A.

- *Character input.* Whitespace can be a confusing factor when doing character input. The `scanf()` input conversion process for numeric types automatically skips leading whitespace and starts storing data only when a nonwhitespace character is read. However, `getchar()` returns the first character, no matter what it is; and `scanf()` with a `"%c"` does the same thing. To skip leading whitespace, you must use `scanf()` with a `" %c"` specifier (a space inside the format and before the percent sign). If this space is omitted, the program is likely to read whitespace and try to interpret it as data, which usually leads to trouble. Therefore, a programmer must have a clear idea of what he or she wishes to do (read whitespace or skip it) and choose the appropriate input mechanism for the task.

- *Enumeration constants are not strings.* The words that you write in an `enum` definition are literal symbols, not strings. Use them directly; do not enclose them in quotes. Because of this, you cannot input or output the symbols directly; you must use the underlying integer values for these purposes.

11.6.4   New and Revisited Vocabulary

These are the most important terms and concepts presented in this chapter:

character literal	input buffer	character arithmetic
escape code	whitespace	enumerated type
portability	improved `work()` function	enumeration constant
ASCII code	padding	type `bool`
collating sequence	type specification	`true` and `false`
lexical order		error codes

The following C keywords, functions, and symbols are discussed in this chapter:

`\n` (newline)	`getchar()`	`ctype.h`
`\r` (return)	`putchar()`	`isalpha()`
`\b` (backspace)	`printf()`	`isupper()`
`\t` (horizontal tab)	`scanf()`	`islower()`
`\v` (vertical tab)	`"%c"` conversion	`isspace()`
`\f` (formfeed)	`" %c"` conversion	`isdigit()`
`\a` (attention)	`typedef`	`tolower()`
`\0` (null character)	`enum`	`toupper()`

11.7   Exercises

11.7.1 Self-Test Exercises

1. Explain the difference between `'6'` and `6`. Explain the difference between `"true"` and `true`.

2. What is a whitespace character? List three of them. What is an escape code character? List three of them.

3. Show the output produced by the following program. Be careful about spacing.

```
#include <stdio.h>
void main( void )
{
    int k;
    for (k = 1; k <= 5; k += 2) {
        printf( "    %i:", k );
        putchar( '0'+k );
    }
    putchar( '\n' );
}
```

4. What will be stored in **k**, **c**, or **b** by the following sets of assignments? Use these variables:

   `int k;      char c, d;      bool b;`

   a. `d = 'b';    c = d+1;`

   b. `d = 'b';    c = d--;`

   c. `d = 'E';    c = toupper( d );`

   d. `d = '7';    k = d - '0';`

   e. `b = isalpha( '@' );`

   f. `b = 'A' == 'a';`

5. What will be stored in each of the variables by the input statements on the right, given the line of input on the left. If the combination is an error, say so. Use these variables:

   `int k;   char d;`

   a. `a     scanf( "%c", &d);`

   b. `66    scanf( "%c", &d);`

   c. `70 C  scanf( "%i%c", &k, &d);`

   d. `F     scanf( "%i", &k);`

e. go!   d = getchar();

f. \n   scanf("%c", &d);

6. Write a **void** function named **er_out()**, which has one parameter, a constant from the enumerated type **error_t** defined in Figure 11.9.   Use a **switch** to print a message that is appropriate for the argument value.

7. What is the output from the following program if the user enters **Z** after the input prompt?

```
#include <stdio.h>
void main( void )
{
    char ch;
    printf( "\n Type a character and hit ENTER: " );
    ch = getchar();
    printf( "%3i %c \n ", ch, ch );
    putchar( ch ); putchar( '\n' );
}
```

11.7.2   Using Pencil and Paper

1. What will be stored in **k**, **c**, or **b** by the following sets of assignments?   Use these variables:

```
int k;     char c, d;     bool b;
```

a. d ='A';   k = d;

b. d ='c';   c = toupper(d);

c. d ='@';   c = tolower(d);

d. k = 66;   c = k-1;

e. b = isupper('A');

f. b = 'A' < 'a';

2. What will be stored in each of the variables by the input statements on the right, given the line of input on the left. If the combination is an error, say so. Use these variables:

```
int k, m;   char c, d;
```

a. a   scanf("%c", &k);

b. 126   scanf("%c", &d);

c. 70 D   scanf("%i %c", &k, &d);

d. 70 71   scanf("%i%i", &k, &m);

e. U2   scanf("%c%i", &d, &k);

f. I O   c = getchar();   d = getchar();

3. Without running the following program, show what the output will be. Use your ASCII table.

```c
#include <stdio.h>

void main( void )
{
    int upper = 65;
    int lower = upper + 32;
    int limit = 26;
    int step = 0;

    puts( " Do you read me?" );
    while ( step < limit ) {
        printf( "%2i.    %c  %c\n", step, upper, lower );
        ++upper;
        ++lower;
        ++step;
    }
    printf( "=========\n" );
}
```

4. Two declarations and a **while** loop follow:

```c
char ara[14] = {'y','c','u','h','k','e',
                'y','e','u','r','k','s','!'};
int k = 1;
while (k < 12) {
    printf( "%i %c \n", k, ara[k] );
    k += 2;
}
```

   a. Make a diagram of the array showing the array slots, subscripts, and values stored in those slots.

   b. What is the overall output from the **printf()** statement in the **while** loop?

5. What is the output from the following program if the user enters 80 after the input prompt?

```c
#include <stdio.h>
void main( void )
{
    int k;
    printf( "\n Enter a number 65 ... 126: " );
    scanf ( "%i", &k );
    printf( " %3i %c \n", k, k );
    putchar( k ); putchar( '\n' );
}
```

6. Write a code fragment to compare two character variables and print **true** if both are alphabetic and they are the same letter, except for possible case differences. Print **false** otherwise.

7. Write a type definition that defines an enumerated type for the days of the week. Call the type **day_type**.

11.7.3   Using the Computer

1. Character manipulation practice.
   Write a program to prompt the user once for a series of characters. Read the characters one at a time using **scanf(" %c", ...)** in a loop. Generate the following output, based on the input, one response per line:

   • Echo the input character.
   • Call **isalpha()** to find out whether it is alphabetic.
   • If so, call **toupper()** to convert it to an upper-case letter and print the result. If not, print an error comment.
   • If the character is a period, print a statement to that effect and quit.

2. Palindromes.
   This program will test whether a sentence is a palindrome; that is, whether it has the same letters when read forward and backward. First, prompt the user to enter a sentence. Read the characters one at a time using **getchar()** until a period appears. As they are read,

   • Echo the input character.
   • Call **tolower()** to convert each character to lower case.
   • Count the number of characters read (excluding the period).
   • Store the converted character in the next available slot in an array.

   When a period appears, start from both ends of the array and compare the letters. Compare the first to the last, the second to the second-last, and so forth. If any pair fails to match, leave the loop and announce that the sentence is not a palindrome. If you get to the middle, stop, and announce that the input is a palindrome. Assume that the input will be no more than 80 characters long.

3. Boolean algebra.
   Using the **bool** data type defined in **tools.h**, write a program to generate and print the truth tables for the AND, OR, and NOT operations defined in Chapter 4. Use the actual operators to generate the values for the table. Pass the truth values to a function named **bool_out()**, which will print **T** or **F**, depending on its argument.

4. Tooth fairy time.
   This program will "pronounce" an ordinary sentence with a lisp. Prompt the user to enter a sentence. Read the characters, one at a time, until a period appears. As they are read, convert everything to lower case and test for occurrences of the character **'s'** and the pair **"ss"**. Replace each **'s'** or **"ss"** by the letters **'t'** and **'h'**. Print the converted message using **putchar()**. For example, given the sentence **I see his house**, the output would be **I thee hith houthe**.

5. Detecting character?
   The character classification functions can be used to separate characters into one of several categories: capital letters, lower-case letters, digits, whitespace, and other symbols. Define an appropriate enumerated type for these categories. Write a function that takes a **char** argument, tests it, and returns a constant from this enumerated

type. In your main program, read in a sequence of characters until a period is encountered. Echo each input and print the label appropriate for it. Also count the number
of instances of each category. Process and count the period, then print the totals and
quit. Suggestion: use an array of integer counters that parallels your enumeration
and use the enumeration constants as subscripts for that array when you increment
the counters.

6. Fancy guessing.
   Redo the guessing game program in Figures 7.31 and 7.32. Define an enumerated
   type to represent the result of a guess (too small, just right, too large, impossible,
   illegal). Make the following improvements:

   - Use characters in the user interface instead of numbers.
   - Help the user make valid guesses by calling the **good_guess()** function de-
     scribed here and using the result to print an appropriate message.
   - Write a function named **good_guess()** that will take as arguments the user's
     guess, the target number, and the maximum and minimum of the current remaining
     possibilities. Analyze the guess. Test whether the guess is outside the original
     range of numbers or impossible at this time because the range of possibilities has
     been narrowed already. If the guess makes sense, test whether it is less than, equal
     to, or greater than the target value. Return an appropriate value from the result-type
     enumeration.

7. A tall story.
   Develop a program for a baker who makes wedding cakes. These cakes have multiple
   layers, and the layers have different shapes. The top layer always is circular, with a
   diameter of 6 inches. The next layer down is square, each side 7.5 inches long. The
   third layer would be circular again, with a diameter of 8 inches; and the fourth layer
   is a 9.5-inch square. The shapes continue to alternate in this pattern and get bigger
   until the bottom layer is reached. In addition, each layer is 2 inches thick, so the area
   of its side is 2" × the perimeter of the layer. The baker wants to know how much
   frosting to make for the cake to frost the entire top and side of every layer. Write a
   program that will read in the number of layers desired for a cake, and then print the
   total square inches of cake to be covered with frosting. Break up your program as
   follows:

   a. Write a function called **surface_area()**. This function has two parameters.
      One is a character with the value **C** for circle or **S** for square. The other is an
      integer that represents either the diameter for a circle or the length of a side of a
      square. This function will compute the sum of the top area and the side area of
      either a circular or a square layer, depending on the character value.

   b. Write a main program that first will read in the number of layers of the cake. Then
      it will call the **surface_area()** function for each layer of the cake and total
      the areas. Finally, print the total.

8. Areas.
   Write a program to calculate areas. Start by writing three double:double functions
   for three geometric shapes:

   - **circle()**. The argument is the radius of a circle. Calculate and return its area.

- **square()**. The argument is the length of one side of a square. Calculate and return its area.
- **right_triangle()**. The argument is the length of the base of a right triangle whose height is equal to its base. Calculate and return its area.

Write a program that will permit the user to compute the area of several shapes. Use a **do...while** loop to prompt the user to enter a letter choice (**c**, **s**, **t**, or **q** in either upper or lower case), to select a shape, or to quit. Read the letter in such a way that whitespace does not matter. Test the input in such a way that upper-case and lower-case differences do not matter. If the letter is **q**, terminate the program. Otherwise, read and validate a real number that represents the size of the figure. If this length is 0 or negative, print an error comment. If it is positive, call the appropriate area function and print the answer it returns. If the letter entered is not **c**, **s**, **t**, or **q**, print an appropriate error message.

9. Temperatures.

    Write a program and three functions that will convert temperatures from Fahrenheit to Celsius or vice versa. The main program should implement a work loop and use the improved interface of Figure 11.7. The **work()** function should prompt the user to enter a temperature, which consists of a number followed by optional whitespace and a letter (**F** or **f** for Fahrenheit, **C** or **c** for Celsius). Appropriate inputs might be **125.2F** and **-72 c**. Read the number and the letter, test the letter, and call the appropriate conversion function, described here. Test the converted answer that is returned and print an error comment if the return value is −500. Otherwise, echo the input temperature and print the answer with the correct unit, **F** or **C**. (Note that there is no difficulty reading an input in the form **125F**; **scanf()** stops reading the digits of the number when it gets to the letter and the letter then can be read by a **%c** specifier.)

    Write two functions: **Fahr_2_Cels()** converts a Fahrenheit argument to Celsius and returns the converted temperature; **Cels_2_Fahr()** converts a Celsius argument to Fahrenheit and returns it. Both functions must test the input to detect temperatures below absolute 0 (−273.15°C and −459.67°F). If an input is out of range, each function should return the special value −500.

10. Try it, I dare you!

    Write a program that will display the ASCII code in a table that looks like the one in Appendix A. Be sure not to try to print the unprintable characters directly. Omit the column that lists the hexadecimal codes.

CHAPTER
12

An Introduction to Pointers

In this chapter, we introduce the final remaining primitive data type, the pointer, which is the address of a data object. We show how to use pointer literals and variables, explain how they are represented in the computer, and present the three pointer operators: &, *, and =. We explain how, using pointer parameters, more than one result can be returned from a function. Pointers are covered here only at an introductory level and will be considered in greater depth in later chapters.

12.1   A First Look at Pointers

A **pointer** is like a pronoun in English; it can refer to one object now and a different object later. Pointers are used in C programs for a variety of purposes:

- To return more than one value from a function (using call by address).
- To create and process strings.
- To manipulate the contents of arrays and structures.
- To construct data structures whose size can grow or shrink dynamically.

In this chapter we study only the first of these uses of pointers; the others will be explored in Chapters 13, 14, 19, and 20.

12.1.1 Pointers Are Addresses

A pointer is the address (i.e., a specific memory location) of an object. A pointer in C acts much like a pronoun in English. It gives us flexibility in writing, because it can refer to different objects at different times. If **p** is a pointer variable and the address of **k** is stored in **p**, then we say **p** *points at* **k** or **p** *is a reference to* **k** or **p** *refers indirectly to* **k**. In the other direction, we say that **k** *is pointed at by* **p** or **k** *is the* **referent** *of* **p**. In object diagrams, we represent pointers as arrows and pointer variables as boxes from which arrows originate. The tail of each pointer arrow is a small circle that can be "stored" in a pointer variable; the head of the arrow points at its referent. The leftmost diagram in Figure 12.1 shows a pointer variable that points at the integer variable **k**, which itself has a value of 31.

Pointer variables. To declare a **pointer variable**, we start with the **base type of the pointer**; that is, the type of object it can reference. After the type comes a list of pointer variable names, each preceded by an asterisk, as shown in Figure 12.2. A common mistake is to omit the asterisk in front of **p2**. This makes it a simple integer rather than a pointer. The asterisk must be written before each name, not just appended to the base type. A pointer can refer only to objects of its base type. Although a given pointer can refer to different objects at different times, we cannot use it to refer to an **int** at one moment and a **double** later. Therefore, both **p1** and **p2** in the diagram can be used to refer to an integer variable **k**, but neither could refer to a **char** or a **double**. When we use pointers in expressions, the base type of the pointer lets C know the actual type of the values that can be referenced, so that it can compile appropriate operations and conversions.

Pointer initialization. When a pointer is declared without an initializer (as an **unitialized pointer**), memory is allocated for it but no address is stored there, so any value previously stored in that memory location remains. Therefore, a pointer always points at *something*, even when that thing is not meaningful to the current program. It could be an actual object in the program, a random memory address in the middle of the code, or an illegal address that does not

---

We diagram a pointer variable as a box containing an arrow (a pointer). Here, we diagram three pointer variables. The first points at an integer, the second is uninitialized, and the third contains the **NULL** pointer.

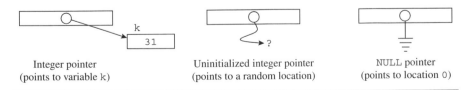

| Integer pointer (points to variable k) | Uninitialized integer pointer (points to a random location) | NULL pointer (points to location 0) |

Figure 12.1. Pointers.

Two uninitialized pointer variables are declared.

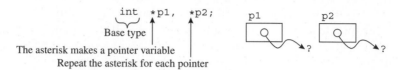

Figure 12.2.   Declaring a pointer variable.

even correspond to a memory location the program is allowed to access. Most C compilers will not detect or give error comments about uninitialized pointers. If a program unintentionally uses one, the consequences will not be discovered until run time and can be quite unpredictable, depending on the random contents of memory when the program begins execution. Anything can happen, from apparently correct operation to strange output results to an immediate program crash. To emphasize the unknown consequences of using such pointers, we diagram an uninitialized pointer as a wavy arrow that ends at a question mark, as in the middle diagram in Figure 12.1.

The NULL pointer.   Many data types include a literal value that means "nothing": for type **double** this value is 0.0, for **int** it is 0, and for **char** it is \0. There also is a "zero" value for pointer types, the **NULL pointer**, and it is defined in **stdio.h**. We store the value **NULL** in a pointer variable as a sign that it points to nothing. **NULL** is represented in the computer as a series of 0 bits and, technically, is a pointer to memory location 0 (which contains part of the operating system). In diagrams, we represent **NULL** using the electric "ground" symbol, as shown in the rightmost part of Figure 12.1, or an arrow that loops around, crosses itself, and ends in midair. One of the basic uses of **NULL** is to initialize a pointer, to avoid pointing at random memory locations. We often initialize pointers to **NULL** (see Figure 12.3). This indicates that the pointer refers to nothing, as opposed to something undefined.

Which nothing is correct?   A pertinent question is, What is the difference between 0.0, 0, \0, and **NULL**? First, even though all are composed entirely of 0 bits, they are of different lengths. A **double** 0.0 often is 8 bytes long, but the character \0 is only 1 byte long. The **NULL** pointer is the length of pointers on

---

An integer pointer variable is declared and initialized to **NULL**.

```
int  *p = NULL;
```
Base type | Initializer
The asterisk makes a pointer variable

Figure 12.3.   Initializing a pointer variable.

the local system, which, in turn, is determined by the number of bytes required to store a memory address on that system. Second, these zero values have different types and a C compiler treats them like other values of their type when it produces compile-time error comments. For example, if the value 3.1 would be legal in some context, then the value 0.0 also would be legal. The value 0 would be acceptable and require conversion, while the value **NULL** would be inappropriate and cause a compile-time error.

The implementation of pointers.   A pointer variable is a storage location in which a pointer can be stored. The pointer itself is the address of another variable. Thus, a *pointer variable* has an address and also contains an address; a *pointer* is the address of its referent. The dual nature of pointers can be confusing, even to experienced programmers. Sometimes it helps to understand how pointers actually are implemented in the computer at run time. The basics are illustrated in Figure 12.4. There, we declare two integer variables and two integer pointers, then diagram the variables created by the declarations. (We assume that an **int** fills 2 bytes and a pointer 4.) Hypothetical memory addresses are shown above the boxes to help explain the actions of certain pointer operations in the next section.

12.1.2   Pointer Operations

C has three basic operators[1] that deal with pointers: **&**, *****, and **=**. While each operation is straightforward, sometimes the use of pointers can be confusing.

```
int *pt = NULL;    /* An int pointer variable, initialized to NULL.  */
int *p;            /* A pointer variable that can point at any int.  */
int k = 17;        /* An integer variable initialized to 17.         */
int m;             /* An uninitialized integer variable.             */
```

Storage for these variables might be laid out in the computer's memory as follows:

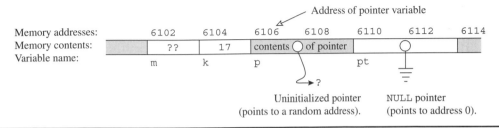

Figure 12.4.   Pointers in memory.

---

[1] Pointers to aggregate types follow different syntactic rules than pointers to simple variables and use an additional operator. The differences are explained in Chapters 14 and 20.

References and indirection.   The expression &k (the **&** **of a variable**) gives us the address of the variable k, also called a *reference to* k. The **dereference operator**, *, also called **indirection**, is the inverse of &; that is, *p means the referent of p (the object at which p points). Since, by definition, & and * are inverse operations, *&k == k and &*p == p.[2]

The expression *p stands for the referent the same way a pronoun stands for a noun. If k is the referent of the pointer p, then m = *p means the same thing as m = k. We say that we *dereference* p *to get* k. Similarly, *p = n means the same thing as k = n. Longer expressions also can be written; anywhere that you might write a variable name, you can write an asterisk and the name of a pointer that refers to the variable. For example, m = *p + 2 adds 2 to the value of k (the referent of p) and stores the result in m. Since the dereference operator and the multiply operator use the same symbol, *, the C compiler distinguishes between them by context. If the operator has operands on both the left and right, it means "multiply." If it has only one operand, on the right, it means "dereference."

Pointer assignment.   As just seen, a pointer can be involved in an assignment operation in three ways:

1. We can make an assignment directly *to* a pointer, as in p = &k.
2. We can access a value *through* a pointer and assign it to a variable, as in m = *p.
3. We can use a pointer to make an *indirect assignment* to its referent, as in *p = m+2.

Direct assignments are useful for string manipulation (Section 13.1). Indirect assignment and access through a pointer are used with call-by-address parameters (Section 12.2). Figure 12.5 illustrates the three kinds of pointer assignment using the variables declared in Figure 12.4.

Notes on Figure 12.5. Pointer operations.   To show the actual relationship between a pointer variable, its contents, and its referent, the addresses and contents of each pointer and variable in this program have been printed and diagrammed.

- *First box: pointer declarations.* Figure 12.4 contains a diagram of the initial contents of the two pointers and the variables declared here.
- *Second box: direct pointer assignments.* There are two ways to assign a value to a pointer: assign either the address of a variable of the correct base type or the contents of another pointer of a matching type.
  1. The base type of p is the same as the type of k, so we are permitted to make p refer to k with the assignment p = &k. In the diagram below the output, note that the address of k is written in the variable p and

---

[2]The combinations *&k and &*p, therefore, are silly and not written in a program.

This short program connects the program fragments from this section and adds output statements that show the contents and addresses of the variables.

```
#include <stdio.h>

void main( void )
{
    int * pt = NULL;     /* An int pointer variable, initialized to NULL. */
    int * p;             /* A pointer variable that can point at any int. */
    int   k = 17;        /* An integer variable initialized to 17. */
    int   m;             /* An uninitialized integer variable. */

    p = &k;              /* Use & to set a pointer to k's memory location. */
    pt = p;              /* Copy a pointer. */

    m = *p + 2;          /* Add 2 to value of p's referent; store result in m. */
    *p = m;              /* Copy the value of m into p's referent. */

    printf( "address of  p:  %i contents of  p:  %i\n", (int)&p, (int)p );
    printf( "address of pt:  %i contents of pt:  %i\n", (int)&pt, (int)pt );
    printf( "address of  k:  %i contents of  k:  %i\n", (int)&k, k );
    printf( "address of  m:  %i contents of  m:  %i\n", (int)&m, m );
}
```

When compiled and run on a system with 2-byte integers, the following output was produced:

```
address of  p: 67106106   contents of  p: 67106104
address of pt: 67106110   contents of pt: 67106104
address of  k: 67106104   contents of  k: 19
address of  m: 67106102   contents of  m: 19
```

This corresponds to the memory layout that follows. Here, only the last four digits of the memory addresses are shown.

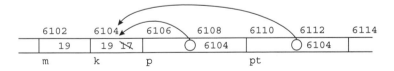

Figure 12.5.   Pointer operations.

that the arrow coming from **p** ends at **k**. We say that **p** *refers to* (or *points at*) **k**.

2. Pointers **p** and **pt** are the same type, so we can copy the contents of **p** into **pt** with the assignment **pt** = **p**. This causes the contents of **p**

(which is the address of **k**) to be copied into **pt**. In the diagram, you can see that both **p** and **pt** contain arrows with heads pointing at **k**.

- *Third box: indirect pointer assignments.*

  1. The first line dereferences **p** to get **k**, then fetches the value of **k** and adds 2 to it. The result (19) is stored in **m**; the value stored in **k** is not changed at this time. It is not necessary to use parentheses in this expression because ∗ has higher precedence than +.
  2. The second line copies the value of **m** into the referent of **p**, which still is **k**. This changes the value of **k** from 17 to 19, as diagrammed.

- *Output.* The output shows how memory might be laid out in a system with 2-byte integers. The memory addresses and contents were printed after completing all the assignments. Compare the output to the memory diagrams, shown in Figures 12.4 and 12.5.

12.2   Call by Address

Most parameter values are passed from the caller to a function using **call by value**; that is, by copying the argument value from the caller's memory area into the parameter variable within the function's memory area. However, there are three situations in C in which call by value is not used, cannot be used, or is inefficient:

1. When an array of any size is being passed (discussed in Chapter 10).
2. When a function needs to return more than one result (discussed in this section).
3. When a large structure is being passed (discussed in Chapter 14).

All these situations are handled in C by using **call by address**. In this form of call, the address of a variable or a pointer to a variable is sent from the caller to the function and stored in a pointer parameter in the function's memory area. This gives the function full access to the variable that belongs to the caller. Since call by address does not isolate the caller from the subprogram, we use call by value wherever possible. Even so, call by address is quite important in C and frequently must be used.[3]

12.2.1   Address Arguments

Address arguments let the function read from and write to variables that *belong to the caller*. By reading the caller's variables, the function obtains the values placed

---

[3] This is a defect of C. It is corrected in C++, which supports a third form of parameter passing, termed *call by reference*.

there by the calling program. By writing (storing) into the caller's variables, the function can pass values back to the calling program, since when the function ends, the values that it wrote still are in those variables. We use the term **output parameter** to mean an address argument that is used by a function only to store information in the caller's variable. Similarly, the term **in-out parameter** refers to an address argument that is used to both read from and write into the caller's variable. The term **input parameter** designates a call-by-value parameter (such as those used up to this point) that carries information only into the function and not in the other direction.

Array arguments always are passed by address, not by value. When we pass an array as an argument, only the **memory address** of the first array slot, not the array's list of values, is passed into the function. This makes a large amount of data available to the function efficiently and allows the function to store information into the array. As demonstrated in Section 10.4, a program can pass an empty array into a function, which then fills it with information. When the function returns, that information is in the array and can be used by the caller.

Arguments of simple types also can be passed by address. The calling program must supply the address of the variable it wants the function to use, and the function must have a corresponding parameter of a pointer type. To pass the address of a simple variable, the caller writes an **&** followed by the name of the variable. For example, if **x** is an integer variable, then **&x** is the address of **x**. You already are familiar with one function that requires an address argument: **scanf()**. When calling **scanf()**, we use an **&** with arguments of simple types such as **long** and **double**. Another way to pass the address of a simple variable is to write the name (with no ampersand) of a pointer variable that refers to the variable. In this case, the value of the pointer, which is the address of its referent, is passed.

12.2.2   Pointer Parameters

A function declares that it is expecting an address argument from the caller by declaring the corresponding parameter with a pointer type. When the argument is an array, as in the statistics program of Figures 10.15 through 10.18, the corresponding parameter can be declared either as a pointer or as an array with an unspecified dimension. For example, if the actual argument were an array of integers, a formal parameter named **ara** could be declared as either **int* ara** or **int ara[]**. The two declarations are identical in most respects, but it is cleaner style to use the latter for arrays. In either case, the parameter name can be used with subscripts within the function to reference the array elements.

For nonarrays, a **pointer parameter** is declared with an asterisk. When the function is called, the address argument is copied into the corresponding pointer parameter. The base type of the pointer parameter must match the type of the address argument. For example, if a function expects to receive the address of an integer variable, it should declare the corresponding parameter to be of type **int*** (as in Figure 12.6).

This short program illustrates call-by-address syntax and gives examples of in-out and output parameters.

```c
#include <stdio.h>
void f1( int * xp );
void f2( int * xp );

void main( void )
{
    int k = 1;        /* An int variable, initialized to 1. */
    printf( "Original value of k: %i\n", k );
    f1( &k );          /* This function changes the value of k. */
    printf( "Changed value of k: %i\n", k );
    f2( &k );          /* This function changes the value of k. */
    printf( "Input is stored in k: %i\n", k );
}
/* --------------------------------------------------------------- */
void f1( int * xp ) /* xp is an in-out parameter. */
{
    *xp = *xp + 2;   /* add 2 to the old value of xp's referent. */
}
/* --------------------------------------------------------------- */
void f2( int * xp ) /* xp is an output parameter. */
{
    printf( "Enter an integer: " );
    scanf( "%i", xp );
}
```

Sample output:

```
Original value of k: 1
Changed value of k: 3
Enter an integer: 25
Input is stored in k: 25
```

Figure 12.6.   Call by address.

Notes on Figure 12.6. Call by address.   Here we have two simple functions that illustrate two techniques for altering the value of a variable in the caller's memory area.

- *First box: prototypes.* Both functions have the same prototype, having one parameter that is an integer pointer.

- *Second box: function calls by address.*

  1. The value of **k** is displayed before and after each call to show the effects.
  2. Each function is called by passing **&k**, the address of **k**, as the argument to the pointer parameter. This value will be stored in the memory locations for each **xp** parameter as each call occurs, so **xp** will refer to **k**.

- *Third box: indirect reference through an in-out parameter.*

  1. In the functions, ***xp** means the value of **k**. Here, we fetch that value, add 2 to it, and store the result back into **k**.
  2. We call **xp** an *input* parameter because we use the information that the caller stored in it. We call it an *output* parameter because we change that information. Thus, it is an in-out parameter.

- *Fourth box: indirect assignment through an output parameter.*

  1. We want to pass the address of **k** to **scanf()** so that input can be stored in **k**. We could do this by writing **&*xp** as the argument, but this simplifies to just **xp**, which contains the original address of **k** as it was passed into the function. The **scanf()** call stores a value directly into **main()**'s variable **k**.
  2. We use **xp**, an output parameter here, to return a value from **scanf()** back to the caller. The new value is printed in **main()** after the function call.

12.2.3 A More Complex Example

In some situations, call by value does not provide enough information to enable a function to do its task. The simplest example consists of a function that wants to swap the values of its two parameters. In Figures 12.7 through 12.9, we examine two possible versions of this simple **swap function**. The first fails to swap the values; the second works properly.

Notes on Figures 12.7, 12.8, and 12.9. Seeing the difference in the swap functions.

- *First and second boxes, Figure 12.7: the first version of the swap.* The first box declares two parameters as type **double**, not **double***, so the arguments will be passed by value. When **main()** calls **badswap(x,y)** (second box), the current values of **x** and **y** are copied into **badswap()**'s parameters **f1** and **f2**. The function receives these values, not the addresses of the variables. This is shown in the diagram for **badswap()** on the left side of Figure 12.9.
- *Third box, Figure 12.7: the bad swap.* When **badswap()** swaps the values, it swaps the copies stored in the parameters, not the originals. In

This version of swap does not work because call by value is used to pass the parameters.

```c
#include "tools.h"
void badswap( double f1, double f2 );
void main( void )
{
    double x = 10.2, y = 7;
    printf( "Before badswap: x=%5.1g  y=%5.1g\n", x, y );
    badswap( x, y );
    printf( "After badswap:  x=%5.1g  y=%5.1g\n", x, y );
}

void badswap( double f1, double f2 )
{
    double swapper = f1;
    f1 = f2;
    f2 = swapper;
}
```

Figure 12.7.   A swap function with an error.

This version of swap works because call by address is used to pass the parameters.

```c
#include "tools.h"
void swap( double * fp1, double * fp2 );
void main( void )
{
    double x = 10.2, y = 7;
    printf( "Before swap: x=%5.1g  y=%5.1g\n", x, y );
    swap( &x, &y );
    printf( "After swap:  x=%5.1g  y=%5.1g\n", x, y );
}
/* ------------------------------------------------------- */
void swap( double * fp1, double * fp2 )
{
    double swapper = *fp1;
    *fp1 = *fp2;
    *fp2 = swapper;
}
```

Figure 12.8.   A swap function that works.

The memory use for Figure 12.7 is diagrammed on the left. Each function has its own memory area, and values of the arguments are copied from variables of **main()** into the parameters of **badswap()**. Assignments change only the values in the parameters.

The memory use for Figure 12.8 is diagrammed on the right. The arguments here are pointers to variables of **main()**. Indirect assignments made through these pointers change the underlying variables.

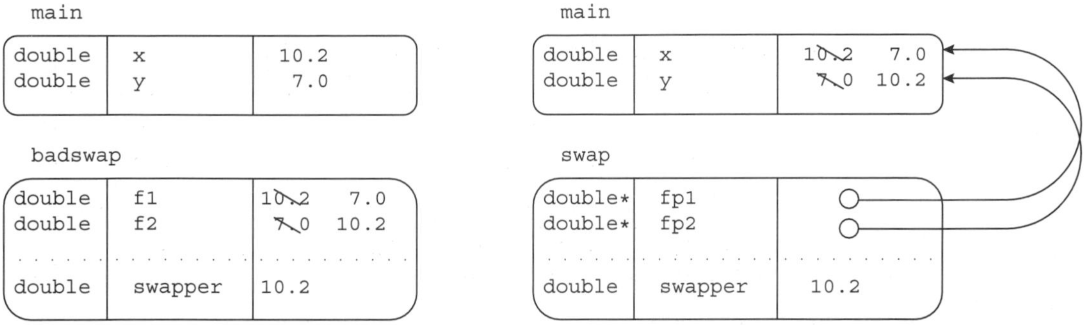

Figure 12.9.   Seeing the difference.

the diagram, note that the assignments in **badswap()** cause no changes to the variables of **main()**. The program output is

```
Before badswap: x= 10.2   y=   7.0
After badswap:  x= 10.2   y=   7.0
```

- *First and second boxes, Figure 12.8: the good version of swap.* In contrast, this version uses call by address (first box). The arguments are two addresses (second box), which are stored in the **swap()** parameters **fp1** and **fp2**. In the diagram, you can see that the parameters of **swap()** are pointers to the variables of **main()**.
- *Third box, Figure 12.8: the good swap.* The function receives pointers to the variables, not copies of their values. When **swap()** says **swapper = *fp1**, it copies the value of the referent of **fp1** into **swapper**. When it executes ***fp1 = *fp2;**, it copies the value of the referent of **fp2** into the referent of **fp1**. This changes the value of the corresponding variable in **main()**, not the pointer in the **swap()** parameter. We say that ***fp1 = *fp2;** fetches the value *indirectly through* **fp2** and stores it *indirectly through* **fp1**. The final output from this program is

```
Before swap: x= 10.2   y=   7.0
After swap:  x=  7.0   y= 10.2
```

12.2.4   Returning Multiple Function Results

The program in Figures 12.10 and 12.11 illustrates a typical use of call by address to return multiple results from a function. It reexamines the quadratic root program presented in Chapter 5 and shows how the logic can be simplified by using a function and an enumerated type to solve the equation.

Notes on Figures 12.10 and 12.12. Returning three results.

- *First box, Figure 12.10:* **status code enumeration** *of cases.* We define an enumerated type to represent the five possible ways in which a quadratic equation can have or not have roots:

  NONE means the equation is inconsistent; it has a nonzero constant term but no variable terms.

  LINEAR means the equation is linear because the coefficient of x^2 is 0.

  SINGLE means the two real roots of this equation are the same; if graphed, the function would be tangent to the x axis at the root value.

  REAL means there are two real roots; if graphed, the function would cross the x axis twice.

  COMPLEX means there are two complex roots; if graphed, the function would not touch or cross the x axis.

- *Second box, Figure 12.10: calling the* **solve()** *function.* This function call takes three arguments (the three coefficients of the equation) into the function, passing them by value. It also supplies two addresses in which to store the roots of the equation, should they exist. The value returned directly by the function will be one of the status codes from the enumeration in the first box. In Figure 12.12, note that the values of the first three arguments have been copied into the memory area of the function, but addresses (pointers) are stored in the last two parameters.

- *Third box, Figure 12.10: interpreting the results.* The status code returned by the function is stored in **n_roots**. We use a **switch** statement to test the code and select the appropriate format for displaying the answers. It is quite common to use a **switch** statement to process an enumerated-type result because it is a simple and straightforward way to handle a complex set of possibilities. It is not necessary to use a default case, since all of the enumerated type's constants have been covered. This programming technique also has the advantage that it separates the user interaction from the algorithm that computes the answers, making both easier to read and write.

- *Output.* The output is like that for the previous version of this program. We show only one data set here:

This is a revision of the quadratic root program from Chapter 5. In this version, the main program does only user interaction; the equation is solved by a function, which must then return one, two, or three results, depending on the coefficients of the equation.

```c
#include "tools.h"

typedef enum { NONE, LINEAR, SINGLE, REAL, COMPLEX } root_type;
root_type solve( double a, double b, double c, double* rp1, double* rp2 );

void main( void )
{
    double a, b, c;                    /* Coefficients of the equation. */
    double r1, r2;                     /* Roots of the equation. */
    root_type n_roots;                 /* How many roots the equation has. */

    banner();
    puts( " Find the roots of a*x^2 + b*x + c = 0" );
    printf( " Enter the values of a, b, and c: " );
    scanf( "%lg%lg%lg", &a, &b, &c );
    printf( "\n The equation is %.3g *x^2 + %.3g *x + %.3g = 0\n", a, b, c );

    n_roots = solve( a, b, c, &r1, &r2 );

    switch (n_roots) {
      case NONE:
            printf( "\n Degenerate equation -- no roots\n" );
            break;
      case LINEAR:
            printf( "\n Linear equation -- root at -c/b = %.3g\n", r1 );
            break;
      case SINGLE:
            printf( "\n Single real root at x = %.3g \n", r1 );
            break;
      case REAL:
            printf( "\n The real roots are x = %.3g and %.3g \n", r1, r2 );
            break;
      case COMPLEX:
            printf( "\n The roots are x = %.3g + %.3g i and "
                    "x = %.3g - %.3g i \n", r1, r2, r1, r2 );
    }

    bye();
}
```

Figure 12.10.   Returning three results.

This function is called from the quadratic root program in Figure 12.10. One result is returned by a `return` statement; the other two (if they exist) are returned through pointer parameters.

```
#define EPS   1e-6
bool iszero( double x ) { return fabs( x ) < EPS; }
```

```
root_type      /* Returns enum constant for number and type of roots. */
solve( double a, double b, double c, double * rp1, double * rp2 )
{
    double d, two_a, sroot;       /* Working storage. */
    if (iszero( a ) && iszero( b )) return NONE;   /* Degenerate cases. */
    if (iszero( a )) {
        *rp1 = -c / b;
        return LINEAR;
    }

    two_a = 2 * a;
    d = b * b - 4 * a * c;       /* discriminant of equation. */
    if (iszero( d )) {           /* There is only one root. */
        *rp1 = -b / two_a;
        return SINGLE;
    }

    sroot = sqrt( fabs( d ) );/* fabs is floating point absolute value. */
    if (d > EPS) {               /* There are 2 real roots. */
        *rp1 = -b / two_a + sroot / two_a;
        *rp2 = -b / two_a - sroot / two_a;
        return REAL;
    }
    else {                       /* There are 2 complex roots. */
        *rp1 = -b / two_a;
        *rp2 = sroot / two_a;
        return COMPLEX;
    }
}
```

Figure 12.11.   The quadratic root function.

```
Find the roots of a*x^2 + b*x + c = 0
Enter the values of a, b, and c: 1 0 -1

The equation is  1 *x^x + 0 *x + -1 = 0

The real roots are x = 1 and -1
```

We diagram the storage allocated for the quadratic root program in Figures 12.10 and 12.11. The diagram on the left shows the contents of memory just after calling the **solve()** function and before its code is executed. The diagram on the right shows the situation during the function return process, just before the function's storage disappears.

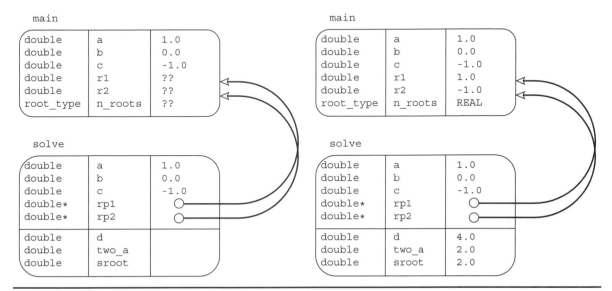

Figure 12.12.   Memory for the quadratic root program.

Notes on Figures 12.11 and 12.12. The quadratic root function.

- *First box: A zero test.*

    1. We use **double** values for the coefficients of the equation. To make the program more robust and useful in various circumstances, we use an epsilon test for all comparisons. We arbitrarily choose an epsilon value of 10^{-6}, which is compatible with the default precision of **printf()**.
    2. The **iszero()** function uses the **EPS** value to compare its argument to 0. We write the code as a separate function to remove repetitive clutter from the **solve()** function, making it shorter and clearer.
    3. This function returns a **bool** result, which can be used directly in an **if** statement or a logical expression.

- *Second box: degenerate cases.*

    1. We test for coefficients that do not represent quadratic equations and return the appropriate code from the enumerated type. A tolerance of **EPS** is used, here and later, when we test for zero values.
    2. By using the **if…return** control structure, we eliminate the need for **else** clauses and nested conditionals. Contrast the simplicity of this

approach with the nested logic in the original version of the program, Figures 5.10 and 5.11.

- *Third box: A double root.*

  1. We compute and store the values of **two_a** and **d** because these subexpressions are used several times in this box and the next. Factoring out these computations increases run-time efficiency and shortens the code.
  2. If the equation is quadratic, it can have two separate roots, real or complex, or one repeated real root. We look at the discriminant of the equation, **d**, to identify how many roots are present. If **d** equals 0, the equation has only one distinct root, which we then compute and return through the first pointer parameter.
  3. The function return value tells the main program that only one of the pointer parameters has been given a value (the other is unused).

- *Fourth box: Two different roots.*

  1. We compute **sroot** once and use the stored value to compute the roots in each of the two remaining cases.
  2. In both cases, two **double** values are returned to **main()** by storing them indirectly through the pointer parameters. The function return value tells **main()** how to interpret these two numbers.
  3. The **REAL** case is illustrated in Figure 12.12 and the corresponding output is shown in the notes for the main program. Note that the values of **r1** and **r2** in **main()** have been changed by storing numbers indirectly through the two pointer parameters.

12.2.5 Summary: Returning Results from a Function

We have now demonstrated three ways to return a result from a function:

1. By using the **return** statement.
2. By using a pointer parameter.
3. By storing the results in an array parameter.

The first method is simple and it supports a total separation between the "territory" of the calling program and the actions of the function. The function need not receive an address from the caller to use **return**. This kind of separation is a highly important debugging tool and should be maintained wherever possible. Unfortunately, the **return** statement is limited to one result.[4]

The second method can be used for multiple results, as in the previous program, but it involves the use of the address-of operator (**&**) in the function call,

---

[4] This one result however can be a complex object, such as a structure that contains multiple components. Structures will be discussed in Chapter 14.

the dereference operator ($*$) in the function body, and a pointer declaration in the function's prototype and header. Using these operators is somewhat awkward and can become confusing. Sometimes the required stars and ampersands are omitted accidentally. More significant, though, is that each pointer parameter supplies the function with an address in the memory area that belongs to its caller. Each such address can be a source of unintended damaging interaction between the two code units. Therefore, we prefer to pass parameters by value wherever possible.

Finally, returning large numbers of results of the same type is possible by using an array. It generally is convenient, efficient, and not confusing. However, the array parameter still is an address of storage that belongs to the caller. Therefore, an array parameter (like a pointer parameter) reduces the isolation of one part of the program from the other, potentially making debugging harder.[5]

12.3   Application: The Bisection Method (Advanced Topic)

The **bisection method** is an iterative method for finding a root of a function. The user supplies a function, $f(x)$, and the endpoints, x_1 and x_2, of an interval on the x axis that, hopefully, contains a root of the function. Figure 12.13 contains specifications for this problem. The success or failure of this method depends on the user's skill or luck in guessing an interval that contains an odd number of roots. If the original interval specified by the user contains an even number of roots (possibly 0), then $f(x_1)$ and $f(x_2)$ have the same sign. In this case, *the bisection method fails immediately.* If either $f(x_1)$ or $f(x_2)$ actually is a root, the method succeeds immediately. Otherwise, the root finder carries out an iterative search for the root, narrowing the range of possible values on each iteration, until the root is trapped between two points that are nearly equal.

One other limitation of this algorithm is that it is designed to find the roots of one-parameter functions. It is the user's responsibility to supply a function of one variable that serves the purpose. This is a common restriction when interfacing to a software package you cannot alter. Unfortunately, this is not always easy, as our next example will show.

Figure 12.14 gives a specification for a function that will solve a heat transfer problem. This is actually a situation in which the solution depends on two variables, the material's conductivity and the pipe radius. Only one of these can be chosen as the search variable; the other must be given a value prior to the search.

The two-variable function can be handled in different ways. First, the second variable could be defined as a constant. This is the most restrictive, because changing it would require recompiling the program. A second way would be to

---

[5] Clearly, none of these three mechanisms is an ideal solution to the problem. For this reason, the reference parameter, a fourth method of returning results, was implemented in C++.

Problem scope: Given a function, $f(x)$, determine if a specified interval contains a root (the function value is 0).

Function: The function to be solved, $f(x)$, must be defined within the program file.

Input: The lower and upper bounds of the search interval (real values); and the function to be analyzed, $f(x)$ (defined using C code within the program file).

Constants:

LIMIT $= 10^{-10}$, the value of $f(x)$ that is close enough to 0.

EPS $= 10^{-5}$, the difference between the search interval endpoints that is close enough to 0.

Formulas: Given three increasing values of x: low, mid, and high, the following is true:

(1) If $f(x) = 0$, then x is a root.

(2) If $f(low) \cdot f(high) > 0$, an even number of roots are between low and high.

(3) If $f(low) \cdot f(mid) < 0$, an odd number of roots are between low and mid.

(4) If $f(mid) \cdot f(high) < 0$, an odd number of roots are between mid and high.

Output required: The value, x, that causes the function, $f(x)$, to be 0 within the specified interval. If there is no such value, a message indicating this should be displayed.

Limitations: Only roots of functions of one variable can be found. The found root will be either within EPS of the actual root or the function value at the root will be less than LIMIT, but the program cannot guarantee both.

Figure 12.13.   Problem specifications: Root finding by the bisection method.

define the variable as global. In this manner its value could be established during execution before the search. Even though global variables have been discouraged in this text, the interface of this code to that of predetermined software actually is an instance in which the use of global variables is acceptable.[6]

In this implementation of the function, the pipe radius, PIPE_R, is defined as a constant and the variable conductivity is defined globally, leaving thickness as the search variable. We implemented the final formula as the function f(), given in Figure 12.15. We ask the user to enter the conductivity at the keyboard in main(), then use the root finder to solve for the thickness. Before describing the details of the bisection algorithm, we develop the main program (Figure 12.16) that will interact with the user and call the bisection function to find a root of f().

---

[6]There are other ways in which the bisection program could be made more general to handle functions of more than one variable, but the complexity of these methods is beyond the scope of this text.

A pipe with a radius of 0.333 foot is to be insulated with a material having heat conductivity k. We wish to find r, the radius of the insulation that solves the heat transfer equation to within a 1% error. Note that r must be greater than 0.333 foot. Also compute t, the thickness of the insulation needed to achieve that radius.

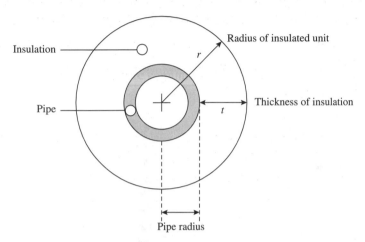

A heat transfer analysis of this situation gives the following equation for the radius of the outer insulation layer for a specified heat loss per unit length:

$$\frac{1}{k} \times \ln\left(\frac{r}{\text{pipe radius}}\right) + \frac{1}{r} = \frac{2}{\text{pipe radius}}$$

The terms $1/r$ and 2/(pipe radius) were derived based on assumptions about the geometry of the problem, the temperatures of parts of the setup, and the desired level of heat loss. Stating this equation as a function of r, we get

$$f(r) = \frac{1}{k} \times \ln\left(\frac{r}{\text{pipe radius}}\right) + \frac{1}{r} - \frac{2}{\text{pipe radius}}$$

Figure 12.14.   A heat transfer problem.

Notes on Figures 12.16 and 12.17. Calling the bisection root finder.

- *First box: properties of the heat function and the search process.*

  1. **LIMIT** is a fuzz factor. We want to find a root of the function `f()`; that is, some value of **x** for which `f(x)` is 0. Since the computation will be done using floating-point numbers, the function values always will be approximate and never may exactly equal 0. This constant defines the amount of imprecision acceptable: If |`f(x)`| is less than this limit, we declare that it *is* 0.

This function implements the heat transfer equation specified in Figure 12.14.

```
/* ------------------------------------------------------------
** Heat transfer in an insulated pipe.
*/
double conductivity;       /* depends on insulation used. */

double
f( double r ) {
    return (1.0 / conductivity) * log( r / PIPE_R ) + 1.0 / r - 2 / PIPE_R;
}
```

Figure 12.15.   A heat transfer function.

2. `EPS` is the error tolerance; the difference between the answer returned and the actual root of the function should be less than `EPS`. The main program, not the bisection function, defines `EPS` because the precision needed varies from one application to another.

3. `PIPE_R` is relevant only to the particular function being analyzed. Other functions might need other constants in their calculations. For this reason, it might seem logical to define `PIPE_R` within the function `f()`. However, this value also is used by the user interface in setting the search limits, so it must be made accessible to both routines; therefore, it is defined at the top of the file.

• *Second box: codes for interfunction communication.*

1. The symbols `NO_ROOT` and `ROOT_OK` are defined so that `bisect()` and `main()` have a clear and identical understanding about the meaning of the code returned by `bisect()`.

2. The bisection method starts with an interval on the x axis having endpoints r_1 and r_2. If this interval does not contain an odd number of roots, `bisect()` will return immediately with the failure code `NO_ROOT`. Otherwise, a root will be found and `bisect()` will return the success code, `ROOT_OK`.

• *Third box: prototypes.*

1. The `main()` function reads search limits from the keyboard and passes them as arguments to `bisect()`, as illustrated in Figure 12.17. The function `bisect()` is a general root finder, designed to solve a broad class of functions. It is explained in Figure 12.18.

2. The prototype `double f( double )` indicates that we can solve only functions that take one `double` argument and return a `double` result. Any function `f()` that has this prototype could be used in place of the particular `f()` defined in Figure 12.15 for the heat transfer problem.

We call the function `bisect()` (Figure 12.18) to use the bisection method to find a root of the heat transfer equation in Figure 12.15.

```
#include "tools.h"
```

```
#define LIMIT 1.0e-10 /* how close to 0 a number must be to say it is 0. */
#define EPS .00001     /* solution must be this close to actual root. */
#define PIPE_R 0.333   /* radius of pipe */
```

```
typedef enum { NO_ROOT, ROOT_OK } er_type;
```

```
                          /* prototype for bisection root finder */
er_type bisect( double r1, double r2, double* root );
double f( double r ); /* prototype for the function we are solving. */
void swap( double* fp1, double* fp2 );    /* Prototype for number swapping */
```

```
void main ( void )
{
    double r1, r2;          /* end points of interval */
    double root;            /* value of root, to be computed. */
    er_type success_code;   /* result error code from bisect() */


    banner();
```
```
    printf( "\n Thermal conductivity of insulation (BTU/h ft F): " );
    scanf( "%lg", &conductivity );

    do {      /* enter search limits in correct order and valid range */
        printf( " Enter interval limits (>= %.3f ft): ", PIPE_R );
        scanf( "%lg%lg", &r1, &r2 );
        if (r2 < r1) swap( &r1, &r2 );    /* check order and range */
        if (r1 < PIPE_R) puts( "\n Error: must be outside pipe radius." );
    } while (r1 < PIPE_R);
```
```
    success_code = bisect( r1, r2, &root );
    if (code == ROOT_OK) {                    /* A root was found. */
        printf( "\n The root is %g ft \n", root );
        printf( " The thickness of the insulation is %.3g inches\n",
                (root-PIPE_R) * 12 );
    }
    else printf( "\n No root found; try a different interval.\n" );
```
```
    bye();
}
```

Figure 12.16.   Calling the bisection root finder.

In this program, **main()** (Figure 12.16) calls **bisect()** (Figure 12.18) and **bisect()** returns two answers to **main()**. The diagram shows the ways in which information is communicated between **main()** and **bisect()**.

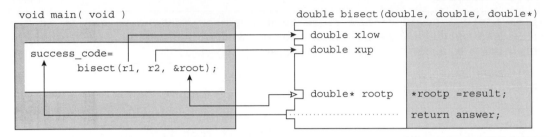

Figure 12.17.   Communication between functions bisect() **and** main().

3. To solve a different function, the user simply changes the function definition, recompiles the program, and runs it with the new function. User prompts may have to be changed to ask for values of additional or different parameters for the new function.

4. We use the corrected **swap()** routine defined in Figure 12.8.

- *Fourth box: inputs.*

   1. The conductivity variable is declared globally because it must be both set by **main()** and used by **f()**. Normally, such a value would be a second parameter sent from **main()** to **bisect()** and from **bisect()** to **f()**, but we cannot do this here because **bisect()** is designed to solve only one-parameter functions.

   2. The bisection algorithm needs to know an interval on the x axis in which it should search for the root. Whether the method succeeds or fails depends very much on this interval; it will succeed only if there are an odd number of roots in the interval. We ask the user to guess the general vicinity of a root and supply the endpoints of an interval $r_1 \ldots r_2$ that we hope brackets the root.

   3. The **bisect()** function depends on the fact that r_1 *is less than* r_2. It will malfunction if the endpoints are supplied in the wrong order. Therefore, if the user accidentally enters values in the wrong order, we interchange them by calling the **swap()** function from Figure 12.8.

   4. It also is important that the interval be in the physically meaningful range of values for the problem; namely, **r1 > PIPE_R**. Therefore, we use the **do...while** loop to accomplish the data validation.

- *Fifth box and Figure 12.17: interacting with* **bisect()**.

   1. The function's parameters and variables are completely separate from the variables of **main()** and even are called by different names. When

This part of the program receives the user's inputs and checks for special cases and the failure condition. In these situations, it quickly returns either a ROOT_OK or NO_ROOT result. Otherwise, it calls go_find() in Figure 12.19 to actually find the root, then returns both the root and a ROOT_OK success code.

```
er_type      /* ROOT_OK (success) or NO_ROOT (failure) */
bisect( double xlow, double xup, double* rootp )
{
    double go_find( double xlow, double fxlow, double xup );

    double fxlow, fxup;                  /* f(x) at xlow and xup */
    double result;                       /* root of function */
    er_type answer;                      /* success or failure code */

    answer = ROOT_OK;
    fxlow = f( xlow );
    fxup = f( xup );

    if (fabs( fxlow ) < LIMIT) {         /* xlow is the actual root */
        result = xlow;
    }
    else if (fabs( fxup ) < LIMIT) {  /* xup is the actual root */
        result = xup;
    }

    else if (fxup * fxlow < 0) { /* true if they have opposite signs. */
        /* We know there is a root in the interval -- so find it. */
        result = go_find( xlow, fxlow, xup );
    }

    else answer = NO_ROOT;

    *rootp = result;     /* Store root value in main's variable. */
    return answer;       /* Return error code. */

}
```

Figure 12.18.   The bisect() function.

a variable name or an expression is used as a call-by-value argument, it only carries information into the subprogram; it allows no other kind of interaction among the modules.

2. When we call bisect(), the values of r1 and r2 and the address of the variable root are copied into the parameter variables that belong to the bisect() function. Copying a value is represented in the diagram by an arrow with one black arrowhead. Sending an address is

represented by an arrow with two heads, because it permits two-way communication between the program units. The right-facing arrow-head is white in this program, indicating that the initial value of this variable is not used by the function. The left-facing arrowhead is black because this connection is used to carry information from `bisect()` back into `main()`.

3. If `bisect()` successfully finds a root, the variable `root` will contain an *x* value corresponding to one root of the function, calculated to within a tolerance of `EPS` of the true root or such that `f( root )` is within `LIMIT` of 0.

4. Then `bisect()` uses the `return` statement to send a success or failure code back to `main()`, where it will be stored in `success_code`.

5. If a root is found, the thickness of the insulation is computed and displayed. To find additional roots, the user would need to run the program again and enter a different initial interval. Improving this program by embedding the main process in a query loop is left as an exercise for the reader.

• *Output.* We ran this program three times using a conductivity of cork = 0.025. The essential output from these runs follows:

```
Thermal conductivity of insulation (BTU/h ft F): .025
Enter interval limits (>= 0.333 ft): .3 .5

Error: must be outside pipe radius.
Enter interval limits (>= 0.333 ft): .333 .5

The root is 0.361107 ft
The thickness of the insulation is 0.337 inches
---------------------------------------------------------
Thermal conductivity of insulation (BTU/h ft F): .025
Enter interval limits (>= 0.333 ft): .35 .333

No root found; try a different interval.
---------------------------------------------------------
Thermal conductivity of insulation (BTU/h ft F): .025
Enter interval limits (>= 0.333 ft): .333 .35

No root found; try a different interval.
```

This output shows that the validation tests for reversed entries and values in a proper range are functioning. Also, output for trials ending in both failure and success are given.

Notes on Figure 12.18. The `bisect()` function.
We assume that all code in this series of figures is written in the same file with the `#include` and

#define commands grouped at the top of that file. The symbols NO_ROOT and ROOT_OK, defined by the enumeration in Figure 12.16, are visible everywhere.

- *First box: calling* bisect().

    1. The bisect() function receives the lower and upper ends of the interval in which to search for the root. It calls these *x* values xlow and xup. The last parameter is rootp, containing the address of a location in which bisect() will store the answer and main() will look for it when bisect() is done.
    2. Only one piece of information can be returned via the return statement. Since bisect() always returns an error code but only sometimes finds a root, we return the error code through the return statement and the root through a pointer parameter. This is a common practice in C.

- *Second box:* go_find() *prototype.* Generally, we have placed all of the function prototypes at the top of the code file. This is because, until now, most of the functions we have written have been called from main(). Here, we have extra levels in our call graph. Because go_find() is called only by bisect(), its declaration can be more local, inside bisect(). However, we cannot do this for the function f(), because it is called by both bisect() and go_find().

- *Third box: dealing with special cases.*

    1. One of the user's two initial guesses, by chance, might be the root of the function. The third box evaluates the function first at xlow, which is the root if f(xlow) is zero. In this case, bisect() stores xlow in the temporary result variable and leaves the success code set to its initial value of ROOT_OK. Otherwise, f(xup) is similarly evaluated and tested, setting the result to xup if f(xup) == 0.
    2. Since we are working with floating-point numbers, we cannot meaningfully ask whether f(x) == 0. Instead, we use a "fuzzy comparison" and ask whether the absolute value of f(x) < LIMIT, which is a constant that defines the required precision.

- *Fourth box: solving the general case.*

    1. If the function has an odd number of roots in the interval between xlow and xup, f(xlow) and f(xup) will have opposite signs and their product will be negative. We test the sign of the product to find out whether a root exists between the two ends of the initial interval. If so, we begin the bisection process, which repeatedly narrows the interval and "traps" the root between the shifting low and high ends.

2. The `go_find()` function defined in Figure 12.19 carries out this algorithm as illustrated in Figure 12.20. We pass along to `go_find()` some, but not all, of the parameters passed from `main()` to `bisect()`. The `go_find()` function will return a root of the function to `bisect()`, which will store it in `result`.

- *Fifth box: failure.* If the product of `f( xlow )` and `f( xup )` is positive, either no roots or an even number of roots are in the given interval. In either case, the bisection method cannot be applied, so we set the answer to the failure code, `NO_ROOT`, before it is returned.
- *Sixth box: returning the answers.*

  1. We return the actual root value (if any was set) by storing it into `main()`'s variable indirectly, *through* the address argument. If no root was found, this value will be garbage.
  2. We return the appropriate success or failure code to `main()` through the normal function return mechanism. The code `NO_ROOT` tells `main()` not to use the meaningless value stored in `root`.

This code is called by `bisect()` in Figure 12.18 after screening out trivial and impossible cases. The operation of this function is illustrated in Figure 12.20.

```
double                          /* perform bisection iteration */
go_find( double xlow, double fxlow, double xup )
{
    double xmid;                /* midpoint of interval */
    double fxmid;              /* value of function at midpoint of interval */

    do {            /* continue until interval too small */
        xmid = .5 * (xup + xlow);
        fxmid = f( xmid );
        if (fabs(fxmid) < LIMIT) break; /* quit; we are close enough! */

        else if (fxmid * fxlow < 0) {   /* root is between xlow and xmid */
                xup = xmid;             /* use xmid as new upper bound */
        }

        else {                          /* root is between xmid and xup */
            xlow = xmid;                /* use xmid as new lower bound */
            fxlow = fxmid;
        }
    } while ( (xup - xlow) > EPS );

    return xmid;
}
```

Figure 12.19.   Iteration for the bisection method.

This function has five roots (it crosses the *x* axis five times) and three of these roots are in the initial interval. We will find one of these three roots using the bisection method. In this case, we divide the interval in half repeatedly until we pin down the exact location of the root. The gray area in each diagram marks the new search interval at each iteration. The function in Figure 12.19 implements this algorithm.

Step 0. The initial interval must contain at least one root.

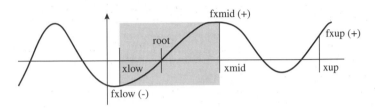

Step 1. Since `fxlow * fxmid < 0`, at least one root is in the left half of the original interval. Let the value of `xmid` become the new value for `xup`.

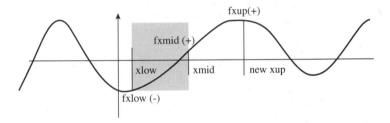

Step 2. Again, the root is in the left half of the interval; let `xmid` be the new `xup`.

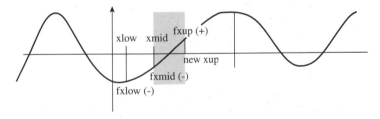

Step 3. This time `fxlow * fxmid > 0`, meaning the root is in the right half of the interval and the value of `xmid` will become the new value for `xlow`.

Step ... We continue this process, changing either `xup` or `xlow` each time, until `fxmid` is within a tolerance of 0.0 or the difference between `xlow` and `xup` becomes suitably small.

Figure 12.20.   Finding a root by bisection.

Notes on Figures 12.19 and 12.20. Iteration for the bisection method.

- *Outer box: the iteration.*

  1. This is a typical two-exit search loop. The **do...while** loop normally ends when no interval is left to search. The **if...break** statement ends the loop early if a root is found at the midpoint of the interval, before the interval becomes too small to continue.
  2. On each repetition, the algorithm divides the current interval in half, evaluates the function at both endpoints and the middle, and identifies which half still contains an odd number of roots by the sign test. This algorithm converges rapidly because the interval's size is halved on each repetition.
  3. We continue cutting the distance between **xlow** and **xup** in half until they are within a distance, **EPS**, of each other. Since the root must be trapped between these two limits, it is then known to acceptable accuracy.
  4. The series of diagrams in Figure 12.20 illustrates how the algorithm progressively narrows the interval in which the root must lie until we know the root with acceptable accuracy.

- *First inner box: calculating a potential root.*

  1. Each time around the iteration loop we calculate **xmid**, the point halfway between **xlow** and **xup**, then calculate the value of the function at that point.
  2. If **fxmid** is near 0 within the required limit of accuracy, then **xmid** is the root and we break out of the loop. This method of exiting the loop does not occur often; it depends on the relative magnitudes of the tolerances **LIMIT** and **EPS**.
  3. A **do...while** loop (rather than a **while** loop) is used so that **xmid**, the value returned, is guaranteed to have an assigned value.

- *Second inner box: the root is in the left half of the interval.*

  1. If the signs of **fxlow** and **fxmid** are different, their product will be less than 0. This again indicates that there is one root or an odd number of roots in the left half of the interval.
  2. In this case, the current midpoint is used as the new right endpoint for the next iteration. In the example shown in Figure 12.20, this happens the first two times through the loop, as seen in the upper two graphs.

- *Third inner box: the root is in the right half of the interval.*

  1. If the signs of **fxlow** and **fxmid** are the same, their product will be greater than 0. This indicates that either no roots or an even number

of roots are in the left half of the interval. Therefore, there must be a root we can find in the right half of the interval.

2. In this case, the current midpoint is used as the new left end of the interval on the next iteration. This happens, in the example, during the third iteration and is shown in the last graph in Figure 12.20.

3. Here, when we reset the left end position, we also reset the left end function value. This saves us the effort of computing the value every iteration.

12.4   What You Should Remember

12.4.1 Major Concepts

- A pointer is the address of a variable. If **p** is a pointer, then the base type of **p** determines how the compiler will interpret the data stored in the referent of **p**. For example, if a **float** pointer is dereferenced, the result is treated like a **float**.

- There are two major pointer operators, **&** and *****, which are the inverses of one another. The address operator, **&**, is used to refer to the memory location of its operand. The dereferencing operator, *****, uses the address in the pointer operand to either retrieve or store a value at that location.

- Pointer variables, like all others, can have garbage in them if they are not initialized. Sometimes this garbage could be an accessible memory location and other times not. The value **NULL** often is used to initialize pointers. Any attempt to reference this location on a properly protected system will cause an immediate and consistent run-time error that can be tracked down more easily than the intermittent errors caused by using a random address.

- When a parameter is a pointer variable, the corresponding argument must be an array, a pointer, or an address. The called function then can store data at that address and, by doing so, change the value in a variable that belongs to the caller. We call this method of parameter passing *call by address*.

- Using pointer parameters, one can return multiple results from a single function. An array parameter is translated as a pointer and lets us pass a large amount of data to or from a function efficiently.

- Binary search is a common technique used in many circumstances, including the bisection algorithm. It is more efficient than an ordinary search but requires that the things being looked through be ordered in some manner. Binary search will be discussed in more detail in Chapter 21.

12.4.2 Programming Style

- In this text, pointer variable declarations place the * next to the base type (as in `float* f`) or let it float (as in `float * f`) between the type and the name. However, it is quite common, for various historical reasons, for programmers to use the style `float *f`, in which the asterisk is attached to the variable name. We prefer the style `float* f` because it clarifies that the data type of the variable is a pointer type.
- To avoid confusion about which variables are pointers and which are not, it is best to declare only one pointer per line. This lets you maintain our preceding style convention and provides space for a comment. If you declare more than one pointer on the same line, be sure to use an * for each one.
- Use the correct zero literal. For pointers, use `NULL`. Reserve `0` for use as an integer.
- It is good practice to initialize pointers to `NULL`, which makes pointer usage errors easier to find.
- Do not use the operator combinations `&*` and `*&`. Since the operators cancel each other out, there is no need for either.
- In a function definition, put the parameters that bring information into the function first and the call-by-address parameters that carry information out of the function last. Any in-out parameters can be placed in between.
- Minimizing the use of call by address increases the separation between caller and subprogram, which is helpful when debugging. However, call by address is an important mechanism. Learn to use it wisely.
- Do not use a global variable to pass information into or out of a function unless you must use a piece of pre-existing code that you cannot change. In all other cases, pass the information as a parameter.
- When using both the return value and pointer parameters to return results from a function, use the return value for a result that *always* is meaningful, such as a status code. Use parameters for results that may or may not be meaningful, depending on circumstances.
- If a function, `f()`, is not called by `main()` and is called by only a single other function, then the prototype for `f()` may be written inside the function that calls it. This properly limits its accessibility to the scope the programmer intended.

12.4.3 Sticky Points and Common Errors

- The most common pointer error is an attempt to use a pointer that has not been set to refer to anything. Sometimes such pointers have a `NULL` value; sometimes they contain garbage. In both cases, the attempt to use such a pointer is an error. On some systems, this causes an immediate crash. On others, execution may continue indefinitely before anything unexpected happens. Pointers are like pronouns; until they are initialized to point at specific variables, they must not be used. Be careful with your pointers and check them first when a program that uses pointers malfunctions.

- There can be confusion between the multiply and dereference operators. It should be clear from the context which is being used. If, by accident, an operand is omitted in an expression, the compiler might interpret the * as multiplication (when dereference was intended) without generating an error message. Using redundant parentheses can help the compiler interpret your code as you intended, but excess parentheses can clutter the expression, potentially causing other kinds of errors. Some compromise in style is needed.

- Do not reverse the use of & and *. Using the wrong operator always leads to trouble.

- When using call by address, a common oversight is to omit some of the required asterisks in the function or the ampersand in the call. This can produce a variety of compile-time error comments that may warn you about a type mismatch between argument and parameter but not tell you exactly what is wrong. For example, if the omission is in the parameter declaration, the error comment actually will be on the first line in the function where that parameter is used. Sometimes a beginner "corrects" the thing that was not wrong, which leads to different errors, and so on, until the code is a mess. When you have a type mismatch error, think carefully about why the error happened and fix the line that actually is wrong. Sometimes drawing a memory diagram can help clear up the confusion.

- Even if you have no type mismatches between arguments and parameters, you may not have the kind of communication you want. If you want call by address, you must declare things properly; otherwise, you get functions like `badswap()` in Figure 12.7. Still other times you might omit the * where it is needed inside the function, and the address in a pointer parameter will be changed rather than the contents of the other memory location. The compiler may not complain about this, but it certainly will affect the logic of your program. Also, forgetting the & in front of an argument for a pointer parameter may not generate a compiler error, but the value of the parameter during execution will be nonsense and usually cause the program to crash. Some compilers give warnings about errors like this.

12.4.4   New and Revisited Vocabulary

These are the most important terms, concepts, and keywords presented in this chapter.

pointer	memory address	call by value
pointer variable	& of a variable	call by address
base type of pointer	* operator	address argument
NULL pointer	indirection	pointer parameter
uninitialized pointer	output parameter	swap function
referent	input parameter	status code enumeration
dereference	in-out parameter	bisection method

12.5   Exercises

12.5.1   Self-Test Exercises

1. Complete each of the following C statements by adding an asterisk, ampersand, or
   subscript wherever needed to make the statement do the job described by the comment.
   Use these declarations:

```
float x, y;
float s[4] = {62.3, 65.5, 41.2, 73.0};
float * fp;
```

   a. fp = y;   /* Make fp refer to y. */

   b. fp = s;   /* Point fp at slot containing 65.5. */

   c. x = fp;   /* Copy fp's referent into x. */

   d. fp = y;   /* Copy y's data into fp's referent. */

   e. fp = s[];   /* Copy 73.0 into fp's referent. */

   f. scanf("%g", x);   /* Read data into x. */

   g. scanf("%g", fp); /* Read data into fp's referent. */

   h. printf("%g", s); /* Print value of second slot. */

2. a. Given the following diagram of four variables, write code that declares and initial-
      izes them, as pictured. On this system, an **int** occupies two bytes.

Memory addresses:	1000	1002	1004	1006	1008	1010
Memory contents:		◯		3	0		◯
Variable name:	ptr1		m	n	ptr2	

   b. Now write two or three direct or indirect pointer assignment statements to change
      the memory values to the configuration shown here:

Memory addresses:	1000	1002	1004	1006	1008	1010
Memory contents:		◯		3	9		◯
Variable name:	ptr1		m	n	ptr2	

3. Consider the function prototype that follows. Write a short function definition that
   matches the prototype and the description above it. Then write a main program that
   declares any necessary variables, makes a meaningful call on the function, and prints
   the answer.

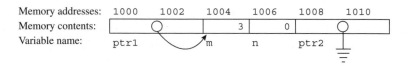

```
/* Return true via out1 if in1 == in2, false otherwise. */
void same( int in1, int in2, bool* out1 );
```

4. All the questions that follow refer to the given partially finished program.

```
#include "tools.h"
void freeze( int temperatures[], int n );
void show( int temperatures[], int n );

void main( void )
{
    int max = 6;
    int degrees[6] = { 34, 29, 31, 36, 37, 33 };
    freeze( degrees, max );
    printf( "\n After freeze: max = %i\n", max );
    .........................

}
/* ------------------------------------------------ */
void freeze( int temperatures[], int n )
{   int k;
    for(k = n-1; k >= 0; --k)
        if (temperatures[k] >= 32) --n;
}
```

a. The second parameter of the **freeze()** function is supposed to be a call-by-address parameter. However, the programmer forgot to write the necessary ampersands and asterisks in the prototype, call, function header, and function code. Add these characters where needed so that changes made to the parameter **n** actually change the underlying variable **max** in the main program.

b. Write a function named **show()**, according to the prototype given, that will display all the numbers in the array on the computer screen. Write a call on this function on the dotted line in **main()**.

c. Draw a storage diagram similar to the one in Figure 12.9 and use it to trace execution of the call on **freeze()** and the following **printf()** statement. On your diagram, show every value that is changed.

d. What is the output from this program after the additions?

5. Look at the main program and the function **solve()** for the quadratic root program in Figures 12.10 and 12.11. Fill in the following table, listing the symbols that are *defined* (not used) in each program scope listed.

Scope	Input Parameters	Output Parameters	Variables	Constants
global	—	—		
main()	—	—		
solve()				
iszero()				

6. Trace the execution of the quadratic root program in Figures 12.10 and 12.11 twice. First, let the input data be 0 3 1. The second time use 0 0 1. List the function calls, giving the function's name, input arguments, return value, and values returned through output parameters. Show the program's output separately.

7. (Advanced question) Trace the execution of the program that follows. Make a memory diagram following the example of Figure 12.9 and showing each program scope in a separate box. On your diagram, show the value given to each parameter when a function is called, how the values of its variables change as execution proceeds, and the value(s) returned by the function. Show the output produced on a separate part of your page.

```c
#include <stdio.h>
int y = 2, z = 3;              /* Global variables! */

int func1( int* x, int* y );
void func2( int* x ){  *x = y;  y = z;  z = *x;  }

void main( void )
{
    int x = func1( &y, &x );
    printf( "X = %i  Y = %i  Z = %i\n", x, y, z );
}

int func1( int* x, int* y )
{
    *y = z+1;
    *x = *y;
    func2( y );
    z = *x+2;
    return *y;
}
```

12.5.2   Using Pencil and Paper

1. Complete each of the following C statements by adding an asterisk, ampersand, or subscript wherever needed to make the statement do the job described by the comment. Use these declarations:

```c
short s, t;
short age[] = { 30, 65, 41, 23 };
short * agep, * maxp;
```

a. agep = age; /* Make agep refer to first age in array */

b. s = agep; /* Copy value of agep's referent into s. */

c. agep = age[]; /* Copy 65 into agep's referent. */

d. maxp = agep; /* Make maxp refer to agep's referent. */

```
e. agep = (age[]+age[])/2;   /* Store mean of 2nd and last
                                ages in agep's referent. */

f. scanf( "%hi", age[] );   /* Read into third array slot. */

g. scanf( "%hi", agep );    /* Read into agep's referent. */

h. printf( "%hi", agep );   /* Print agep's referent. */
```

2. a. Given the diagram of three variables and an array, write code that declares the variables and initializes the array and the pointers, as pictured.

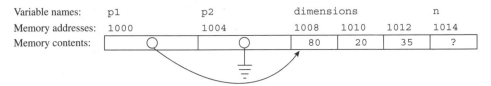

Variable names:	p1	p2	dimensions			n
Memory addresses:	1000	1004	1008	1010	1012	1014
Memory contents:			80	20	35	?

   b. Write a function that takes the **dimensions** array as its parameter. Use a nested **if...else** statement to identify the smallest dimension and return the subscript of its slot.

   c. Now call the function and store the result in **n**, then use **n** to set **p2** to point at the smallest dimension.

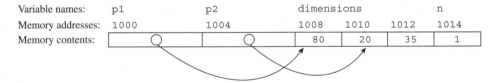

Variable names:	p1	p2	dimensions			n
Memory addresses:	1000	1004	1008	1010	1012	1014
Memory contents:			80	20	35	1

3. All the questions that follow refer to the given partially finished program.

```
#include "tools.h"
#define MAX 10
void count( int ages[], int adults, int teens );

void main( void )
{
    int family[MAX] = {44, 43, 21, 18, 15, 13, 11, 9, 7};
    int Nadults=0, Nteens=0, Nkids=0;

    puts( "\nFamily Structure" );
    count( family, Nadults, Nteens );
    Nkids = MAX - (Nadults + Nteens);
    printf( "Family has %i adults, %i teens, %i kids\n",
              Nadults, Nteens, Nkids );
    puts( "------------------------------------------\n" );
}
```

```
void count( int ages[], int adults, int teens )
{
    int k;
    for (k = 0; k < MAX; ++k) {
        if ( ages[k] >= 18 ) ++adults;
        else if ( ages[k] >= 13 ) ++teens;
    }
}
```

a. The second and third parameters of the **count()** function need to be pointer parameters. However, the programmer forgot to write the necessary ampersands and asterisks in the prototype, call, function header, and function code. Add these characters where needed so that changes made to the parameters **adults** and **teens** actually change the underlying variables in the main program.

b. Draw a storage diagram similar to the one in Figure 12.9 and use it to trace execution of the corrected program. On the diagram, show every value changed and show the output on a separate part of the page.

4. Draw a call graph for the bisection program. Include all the functions in Figures 12.8, 12.15, 12.16, 12.18, and 12.19.

5. Look at the main program and functions for the bisection program in Figures 12.8, 12.15, 12.16, 12.18, and 12.19. Fill in the following table, listing the symbols *defined* (not used) in each program scope. List global symbols on the first line. Allow one line below that for each function in the program (**main()** has been started for you).

Scope	Input Parameters	Output Parameters	Variables	Constants
global	—	—		
main()	—	—		
...				

6. Trace the execution of the quadratic root program in Figures 12.10 and 12.11 when the input data are 1 2 3. Make a list of the function calls, one per line. For each call, list the function's name, input arguments, return value, and values returned through output parameters. Show the program's output separately.

7. Consider the function prototype that follows. Write a short function definition that matches the given prototype and description. Write a main program that declares necessary variables, makes a meaningful call on the function, and prints the answer.

```
/* Set the referent of dp to its own absolute value. */
/* Return +1 if it was positive, 0 if it was zero, */
/* and -1 otherwise. */
int signum( double* dp );
```

12.5.3   Using the Computer

1. Pointer and referent.
   Write a program that creates the integer array `int ara[]` = `{11, 13, 17,`
   `19, 23, 29, 31}`. Also create an integer pointer `pt` and make it point at the
   beginning of the array. Write `printf()` statements that will print the address and
   contents of both `ara[0]` and `pt`. Use this format:

   ```
   printf( "address of pt: \t %li   contents:\t %li\n",
           (long)&pt, (long)pt );
   ```

   Then write 10 similar `printf()` statements following the same format to print the
   address and contents of the slots designated by the following expressions: `(*pt+3)`,
   `*pt`, `(pt[3])`, `*&pt`, `*pt[3]`, `&*pt`, `*(pt+3)`, `(*pt++)`, `*(pt++)`,
   `(*pt)++`. Some of these will cause compile-time errors when printing the address field, the contents field, or both; in such cases, delete the illegal expression and
   print dashes instead of its value. When the program finally compiles and runs, use the
   output to complete the following table, grouping together items that have the same
   memory address:

	Address	Contents
pt		
ara		
...		

   Finally, make four lists: (a) illegal pointer expressions, (b) expressions that have
   identical meanings, (c) expressions that change pointer values, and (d) expressions
   that change integer values. It will require careful reasoning to get the last two lists
   correct.

2. Finding roots.
   First use the quadratic root program to find the roots of this equation:

   $$t^2 - 4t + 3 = 0$$

   Then write a function, `f(t)`, to represent this equation and use the bisection program to find the roots of the equation. Try search intervals of 0...4, 0.6...1.75, and
   2.933...3.421. Explain the answers.

3. Positive and negative.
   Write a function, named `sums()`, that has two input parameters; an array, `a`, of
   `float`s; and an integer, `n`, which is the number of values stored in the array. Compute
   the sum of the positive values in the array and the sum of the negative values. Also
   count the number of values in each category. Return these four answers through
   output parameters. Write a main program that reads no more than 10 real numbers and
   stores them in an array. Stop reading numbers when a 0 is entered. Call the `sums()`

function and print the answers it returns. Also compute and print the average values of the positive and negative sets.

4. More stats.

   Start with the statistics program in Figures 10.15 through 10.18. Add a parallel array for the student ID numbers, which should be read as input. Add functions to do these three tasks:

   a. Find the maximum score and return the score and its array index through pointer parameters.

   b. Find the minimum score and return the score and its array index through pointer parameters.

   c. Find the score that is closest to the average and return the score and its array index through pointer parameters.

   In **main()**, call your three functions and print the student ID number and score for the best, closest to average, and weakest student.

5. Sorting.

   Write a **void** function, named **order()**, that has three integer parameters: a, b, and c. Compare the parameter values and arrange them in numerical order so that $a < b < c$. Use call by address so the calling program receives the values back in order. In addition, the function **order()** should start by printing the addresses and contents of its parameters, as well as the contents of the locations to which they point. Write a main program that enters three integers, prints their values and addresses, orders them by calling the function **order()**, and prints their values again after the call. Add a query loop to allow testing several sets of integers.

6. Compound interest.

   a. Write a function to compute and return the amount of money, A, that you will have in n years if you invest P dollars now at annual interest rate i. Take n, i, and P as parameters. The formula is

   $$A = P(1 + i)^n$$

   b. Write a function to compute and return the amount of money, P, that you would need to invest now at annual interest rate i in order to have A dollars in n years. Take n, i, and A as parameters. The formula is:

   $$P = \frac{A}{(1 + i)^n}$$

   c. Write a function that will read and validate the inputs for this program. Using call by address, return an enumerated constant for the choice of formulas, a number of years, an interest rate, and an amount of money, in dollars. All three numbers must be greater than 0.0.

   d. Write a **main** program that will call the input routine to gather the data. Then, depending on the user's choice, it should call the appropriate calculation function and print the results of the calculation.

7. Cool it.

Refrigerators and heat pumps are modeled thermodynamically as reversible (i.e., no frictional effect) cycles that convert work energy to heating or cooling energy. For such cycles, we have a measure of efficiency, the coefficient of performance (*cop*), that is the ratio of cooling or heating divided by the work input required. The values of *cop* are as follows:

$$\text{Refrigeration cycle:} \quad cop = \frac{T_c}{T_h - T_c}$$

$$\text{Heat pump:} \qquad\qquad cop = \frac{T_h}{T_h - T_c}$$

where T_c and T_h are the absolute temperatures (K) of cold and hot reservoirs.

a. Write a function to enter and return the temperatures of the cold and hot reservoirs in degrees Celsius; return them through pointer parameters. Make sure that both are greater than absolute 0 (allow the user to correct any errors) and that they have the proper relationship to one another; that is, $T_h > T_c$ (if not, swap them).

b. Write a function to convert a Celsius temperature to an absolute temperature in degrees Kelvin. Absolute 0 is $-273.15°C$.

c. Write a function, named **cop()**, that will compute both values of **cop**, given the T_h and T_c, and return the results using call by address.

d. Write a main program that will calculate and print the value of *cop* for either a refrigerator or a heat pump. Use a query loop to repeat the process, asking the user to select one or the other computation or "quit." Do the input and calculations using functions described above. Although the **cop()** function returns two results, print only the result that the user requested.

8. Viscous flow.

We have two equations for the friction factor f for viscous fluid flow in a smooth pipe. The laminar flow equation applies to flows with a Reynolds number, Re, less than 2000; the turbulent flow equation applies when the Reynolds number is between 4000 and 100,000. The equations are[7]

$$\text{For laminar flow:} \quad f = \frac{64}{\text{Re}}$$

$$\text{For turbulent flow:} \quad f = \frac{0.316}{\text{Re}^{0.25}}$$

Write a single function that will compute both friction factors for a given value of Re. Write a main program containing a loop that will generate a random series of Re values between 1 and 100,000. Print this information in a flow table with four columns, the Re value; the resulting laminar, f; and the corresponding turbulent, f. The value of Re tells you which f value is supposed to be correct, if any. The fourth

---

[7]F. White, *Fluid Mechanics*, 2nd ed. (New York: McGraw-Hill, 1986). For $2000 < \text{Re} < 4000$, we have transitional flow and neither equation is valid.

column of the output should be a relative error value that compares the correct f value to the other one. *Relative error* is defined as the difference of the two values divided by the correct one. Print dashes in the last column if Re is between 2000 and 4000.

9. Inductance of an electrical circuit.
   Consider this electrical circuit, which consists of a resistance R (ohms), a capacitor C (farads), and an inductor L (henrys).

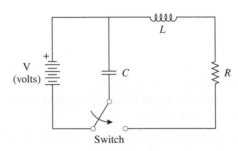

Reasonable Limits on Circuit Parameters

Property	Unit	Minimum	Maximum
V	volts	5	15
R	ohms	50	500
L	henrys	1×10^{-3}	1×10^{-1}
C	farads	1×10^{-5}	1×10^{-4}

The charge q on the capacitor is obtained by solving a second-order differential equation resulting from applying Kirchhoff's law at each node. This law states that the sum of all the currents entering and leaving the node is 0. The result of this analysis gives the charge q as:

$$q = VCe^{-\frac{R}{2L}t} \times \cos\left\{\left[\frac{1}{LC} - \left(\frac{R}{2L}\right)^2\right]^{0.5} t\right\}$$

This function depicts an oscillating signal that decays in magnitude over time in a manner similar to that sketched here:

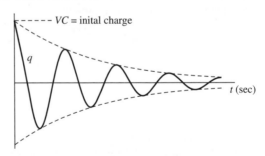

a. Write a main program that will use a query loop to do a series of circuit simulations. For each, call the functions described next to get parameters for the simulation and the circuit and to carry out the simulation.

b. Write a function, named **q()**, to evaluate q and return the answer.

c. Write a function, named **sim()**, that simulates the decay of the signal by calculating and printing q for a series of time steps. Call **q()** to do each calculation.

d. Write a function, named `timer()`, that asks the user to enter the length of time to simulate the circuit and the size of the time step to use. Use call by address to return these values to the caller.

e. Write a function, named `circuit()`, to read in and validate the circuit properties V, R, L, and C. Use call by address to return these values to the caller. Reasonable ranges are given in the table.

10. Bisection improvement.
Start with the completed, working root-finding program in Figures 12.8 and 12.15 through 12.19. Note that it allows you to enter only a single guess for the interval that contains a root. Thus, it will find either no roots or one root, depending on your skill or luck at guessing. Improve this program as follows:

a. Remove the function `f()` and replace it by a function representing this equation:

$$e^t - 3.6945t = 0$$

b. Modify `main()`. Remove all code that deals with conductivity or pipes. Write a loop that repeats the process of entering an interval and calling `bisect()` until the user supplies an interval that contains a root.

c. Make a table of the answers you get for different search intervals.

11. Search and display.
Many functions have more than one real root; a good root-finding program should allow the user to enter different intervals until all the roots have been found. Improve the bisection program in Figures 12.8 and 12.15 through 12.19 so that it can help you find multiple roots.

a. Start with the completed, working bisection program and modify `main()`. Remove all code that deals with conductivity and pipes. Replace it with code that will read values for the components R and C of the circuit diagrammed in problem 9. Reasonable ranges are given in the table. In order to find the inductance required to reduce the initial charge to 5% of its original value after 10 seconds, we need to find the root of the following function for the given values of R and C:

$$\text{Induct}(L) = e^{-10\left(\frac{R}{2L}\right)} \times \cos\left\{10\left[\frac{1}{LC} - \left(\frac{R}{2L}\right)^2\right]^{\frac{1}{2}}\right\} - 0.05$$

b. Add a query loop to `main()` that calls `bisect()` repeatedly until the user is satisfied, permitting the user to guess a different interval each time. Display the result of each trial.

c. Remove the function `f()` and replace it with a function representing the inductance equation. Use your program to find at least three roots of this function.

Structured Data Types

CHAPTER
13

Strings

I n this chapter, we begin to combine the previously studied data types into more complex units: strings and arrays of strings. A pointer type expression is used with **typedef** to define and name the type **string**, which is a fundamental type in C, but is not given a name by the standard. Strings combine the features of arrays, characters, and pointers discussed in the three preceding chapters. String input and output are presented, along with the most important functions from the standard **string** library, as well as the portions of the **tools** library that apply to strings.

Strings and arrays are combined to form a data structure called a *ragged array*, which is useful in many contexts. Examples given here include a menu-driven user interface and a technique for printing enumeration constants symbolically.

13.1   String Representation

We have used literal strings as formats and output messages in virtually every program presented so far but have never formally defined the type *string*. It is a necessary type and fundamental. C reference manuals talk about strings and the standard C libraries provide good support for working with strings. The functions in the **stdio** library make it possible to read and write strings in simple ways, and the functions in the **string** library let you manipulate strings easily. Within C, though, the implementation of a **string** is not simple; it is defined as a pointer to a null-terminated array of characters. The goal in this section is to learn certain fundamental ways to use and manipulate strings and to learn enough about their representation to avoid making common errors.

For instance, suppose we want a string that contains different messages at different times. There are two ways to do this. First, the pointer portion of the string can be switched from one literal array of letters to another. Second, it is possible to simply have an array of characters, each of which can be changed individually to form a new message. These two representations have very different properties and different applications, leading directly to programming choices, so we examine them more closely.

13.1.1 String Literals

A **string literal** is a series of characters enclosed in double quotes. String literals are used for output with `puts()`, as formats for `printf()` and `scanf()`, and as initializers. Ordinary letters and escape code characters such as `\n` may be written between the quotes, as shown in the first line of Figure 13.1. In addition to the characters between the quotes, the C translator adds a null character, `\0`, to the end of every string literal when it is compiled into a program. Therefore, the literal `"cat"` actually occupies 4 bytes of memory and the literal `"$"` occupies 2.

Two-part literals.   Often, prompts and formats are too long to fit on one line of code. In old versions of C, this constrained the way programs could be written. The ANSI C standard introduced the idea of *string merging* to fix this problem. With **string merging**, a long character string can be broken into two or more parts, each enclosed in quotes. These parts can be on the same line of code or on different lines, so long as there is nothing but whitespace or a comment between the closing quote of one part and the opening quote of the next. The compiler will join the parts into a single string with one null character at the end. An example of a two-line string literal is shown in the second part of Figure 13.1.

Quotation marks.   You can even put a quote mark inside a string. To put a single quotation mark in a string, you can write it like any other character. To insert double quotes, you must write `\"`. Examples of quotes within a quoted string are shown in the last line of Figure 13.1.

A simple string literal: `"George Washington\n"`
A two-part string literal: `"was known for his unswerving honesty "`
                              `"and became our first president."`
One with escape codes: `"He said \"I cannot tell a lie\"."`

Figure 13.1.   String literals.

Strings and comments.   The relationship between comments and quoted strings can be puzzling. You can put a quoted phrase inside a comment and you can put something that looks like a comment inside a string. How can you tell which situation is which? The translator reads the lines of your source code from top to bottom and left to right. The symbol that occurs first determines whether the following code is interpreted as a comment or a string. If a begin-comment mark is found after an open quote, the comment text, enclosed between /* and */, becomes part of the string. On the other hand, if the /* occurs first, followed by an open quote, the following string becomes part of the comment. In either case, if you attempt to put the closing marks out of order, you will generate a compiler error. Examples of these cases are shown in Figure 13.2.

The null string and the null character.   The **null string** is a string with no characters in it except the null character. It is denoted in a program by two adjacent double quote marks, `""`. It is a legal string and often useful as a placeholder or initializer. The **null character** (eight 0 bits), or **null terminator**, plays a central role in all string processing. When you read a string with `scanf()`, the null character automatically is appended to it for you. When you print a string with `printf()` or `puts()`, the null character marks where to stop printing. The functions in the `string` library all use the null character to terminate their loops.

13.1.2   A String Is a Pointer to an Array

We have said that a string is a series of characters enclosed in double quotes and that a string is a pointer to an array of characters that ends with the null character. Actually, both these seemingly contradictory statements are correct: When we write a string in a program using double quotes, it is translated by the compiler into a pointer to an array of characters.

A `typedef` for strings.   Some important types that we use all the time, such as "string" and "stream," have no standard names; they must be defined by **type expressions**. For example, although the C standard refers many times to strings, it does not define `string` as a type name; the actual type of a string in C is `char*`, or "pointer to character." If we want to use *string* as a type name in our program, we can write a `typedef` statement that defines `string` as a synonym for the character pointer expression:

A comment in a string:	`"This /* is not a comment */ it is a string."`
A string in a comment:	`/* Here's how to put "a quote" in a comment. */`
Overlap error:	`"Here /* are some illegal" misnested delimiters. */`
Overlap error:	`/* We can't "misnest things */ this way, either."`

Figure 13.2.   Quotes and comments.

```
typedef  char*  string;
```

This type definition is in the **tools** library. When you include this definition or include **tools.h** in your program, you can use **string** as if it were an ordinary type name. We use it often in the programs presented in this text. Even so, you must also be comfortable with using **char*** instead, since you will see this in many programs.

String pointers.   One way to create a string is to declare a variable of type **string** or **char*** and initialize it to point at a string literal.[1]   Figure 13.3 illustrates a **string variable** named **word**, which contains the address of the first character in the sequence of letters that makes up the literal **"Holiday"**. The pointer variable and the letter sequence are stored in different parts of memory. The pointer is in the user's memory area and can be changed, as needed, to point to a different message. In contrast, the memory area for literals cannot be altered. C forbids us to change the letters of **"Holiday"** to make it into **"Ponyday"** or **"Holyman"**.

Using a pointer to get a string variable.   We can use the pointer form of a string variable and **string assignment** to select one of a set of predefined messages and remember it for later processing and output. The string variable acts like a finger that can be switched back and forth among a set of possible literals.

For example, suppose you are writing a simple drill-and-practice program and the correct answer to a question, an integer, is stored in **target_answer** (an integer variable). Assume that the user's input has been read into **input_answer**. The output is supposed to be either the message "**Good job!**" when a correct answer is entered or "**Sorry!**" for a wrong answer. Let **response** be a string variable, as shown in Figure 13.4. We can select and remember the correct message by using an **if** statement and two pointer assignment statements, as shown.

```
typedef char* string;
string word = "Holiday";
```

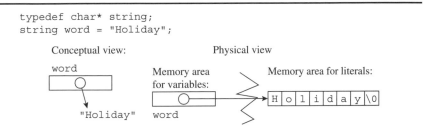

Figure 13.3.   Implementation of a string variable.

---

[1] Dynamically allocated memory also can be used as an initializer. This advanced topic is left for Chapter 19.

```
if (input_answer == target_answer) response = "Good job!";
else response = "Sorry!";
```

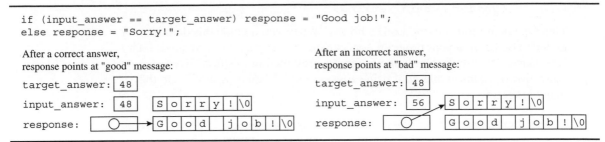

Figure 13.4.   Selecting the appropriate answer.

13.1.3   Declare an Array to Get a String

To create a string whose individual letters can be changed, as when a word is entered from the keyboard, we must create a character array big enough to store the longest possible word. Figure 13.5 shows one way to do this with an array declaration.[2] Here, the variable **president** is a character array that can hold up to 17 letters and a null terminator, although only part of this space is used in this example.

Initializers.   A character array can be declared with or without an initializer. This initializer can be either a quoted string or a series of character literals, separated by commas, enclosed in curly brackets. The array **president** in Figure 13.5 is initialized with a quoted string. The initializer also could be

```
= {'A','b','r','a','h','a','m',' ',
   'L','i','n','c','o','l','n','\0'}
```

This kind of initializer is tedious and error prone to write, and you must remember to include the null character at the end of it. Because they are much more convenient to read and write, quoted strings (rather than lists of literal letters) usually are used to initialize **char** arrays. The programmer must remember, though, that every string ends in a null character, and there must be extra space in the array for the **\0**.

An array of 18 **char**s containing the letters of a 15-character string and a null terminator. Two array slots remain empty.

Figure 13.5.   An array of characters.

---

[2]The use of **malloc()** for this task will be covered in Chapter 19.

Using character arrays. If you define a variable to be an array of characters, you may process those characters using subscripts like any other array. Unlike the memory for a literal, this memory can be updated.

It also is true that an array name, when used in C with no subscripts, is translated as a pointer to the first slot of the array. Although an array is not the same as a string, this representation allows the name of a character array to be *used* as a string (a `char*`). Because of this peculiarity in the semantics of C, operations defined for strings also work with character arrays. Therefore, in Figure 13.5, we could write `puts( president )` and see `Abraham Lincoln` displayed.

However, an array that does not contain a null terminator must not be used in place of a string. The functions in the `string` library would accept it as a valid argument; the system would not identify a type or syntax error. But it would be a semantic error; the result is meaningless because C will know where the string starts but not where it ends. Everything in the memory locations following the string will be taken as part of it until a byte is encountered that happens to contain a 0.

13.1.4 Array vs. String

Typical uses of strings are summarized in Figure 13.6. Much (but not all) of the time, you can use strings without worrying about pointers, addresses, arrays, and null characters. But often confusion develops about the difference between a string and an array of characters. A common error is to declare a string variable as a `char*` and expect it to be able to store an array of characters. However, a string variable is only a pointer, which usually is just 4 bytes long. It cannot possibly hold an entire word like `"Hello"`. If we want a string to store alphabetic data, we need to allocate memory for an array of characters. These issues can all be addressed by understanding how strings are implemented in C.

Figure 13.7 shows declarations and diagrams for a character array and a string variable, both initialized by quoted strings. As you can see, the way storage is allocated for the two is quite different. When you use an array as a container for

---

Use type `char*` for these purposes:

- To point at one of a set of literal strings.
- As the type of a function parameter where the argument is either a `char*` or a `char` array.

Use a `char` array for these purposes:

- To hold keyboard input.
- Any time you wish to change some of the letters individually in the string.

Figure 13.6. Array vs. string.

These declarations create the objects diagrammed here:

```
char    ara[7] = "Monday"; /* 7 bytes total. */
string str     = "Sunday"; /* 11 bytes total, 4 for pointer, 7 for chars. */
```

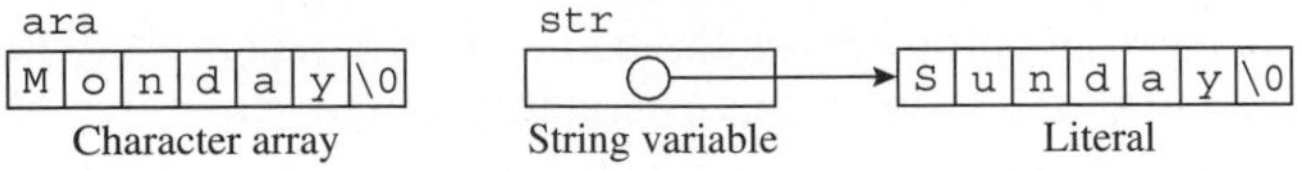

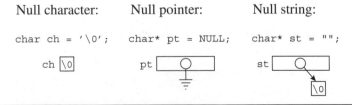

Figure 13.7.   A character array and a string.

a string, space for the array is allocated with your other variables, and the letters of an initializing string (including the null) are copied into the array starting at slot 0. Any unused slots at the end of the array are left untouched and therefore contain garbage. In contrast, two separate storage areas are used when you use a string literal to initialize a pointer variable such as **str**. A string pointer typically occupies 4 bytes while the information itself occupies 1 byte for each character, plus another for the null character. The compiler stores the characters and the null terminator in an unchangeable storage area separate from the declared variables, and then it stores the address of the first character in the pointer variable.

Null objects.   The null character, the null pointer, and the null string (pictured in Figure 13.8) often are confused with each other, even though they are distinct objects and used in different situations. The null string and the null character have different types (pointer vs. **char**), have different sizes (4 bytes vs. 1 byte), and certainly are not interchangeable in any way. Both the null pointer and the null string are pointers, but the first is all 0 bits, the address of machine location 0, and the second is the nonzero address of a byte containing all 0 bits.

- The null character is 1 byte (type **char**) filled with 0 bits.
- The null pointer is a pointer filled with 0 bits (it points to address 0).
- The null string is a pointer to a null character. The address in the pointer is the nonzero address of some byte filled with 0 bits.

Null character: Null pointer: Null string:

```
char ch = '\0';     char* pt = NULL;     char* st = "";
```

ch \0   pt [O]   st [O]
                        =   \0

Figure 13.8.   Three kinds of nothing.

13.2 String I/O

Even though the string data type is not built into the C language, functions in the standard libraries perform input, output, and other useful operations with strings.

13.2.1 String Output

We have seen two ways to output a string literal: `puts()` and `printf()`. The `puts()` function is called with one string argument, which can be either a literal string, the name of a string variable, or the name of a character array. It prints the characters of its argument up to, but not including, the null terminator, then *adds* a newline (`\n`) character at the end. If the string already ends in `\n`, this effectively prints a blank line following the text. We can call `printf()` in the same way, with one string argument, and the result will be the same except that a newline will not be added at the end. The first box in Figure 13.9 demonstrates calls on both these functions with single arguments.

String output with a format. We can also use `printf()` with a `%s` conversion specifier in its format to write a string. The string still must have a null terminator. Again, the corresponding string argument may be a literal, string variable, or `char` array. Examples include

```
string fname = "Henry";
printf( "First name: %s\n", fname );
printf( "Last name:  %s\n", "James" );
```

The output from these statements is

```
First name: Henry
Last name:  James
```

Further formatting is possible. A `%ns` field specifier can be used to write the string in a fixed-width column. If the string is shorter than **n** characters, spaces will be added to fill the field. When **n** is positive, the spaces are added on the left; that is, the string is **right justified** in a field of n columns. If **n** is negative, the string is left justified. If the string is longer than **n** characters, the entire string is printed and extends beyond the specified field width. In the following example, assume that `fname` is `"Andrew"`:

```
printf( ">>%10s<<\n", fname );
printf( ">>%-10s<<\n", fname );
```

Then the output would be

```
>>    Andrew<<
>>Andrew    <<
```

```
#include "tools.h"
void main( void )
{
    string s1 = "String demo program.";
    string s2 = "Print this string and ring the bell.\n";
```

```
    puts( s1 );
    printf( "\t This prints single ' and double \" quotes.\n" );
    printf( "\t %s\n%c", s2, '\a' );
```

```
    puts( "These two quoted sections " "form a single string.\n" );
    printf( "You can break a format string into pieces if you\n"
            "end each line and begin the next with quotes.\n"
            "You may indent the lines any way you wish.\n\n" );
```

```
    puts( "This\tstring\thas\ttab\tcharacters\tbetween\twords.\t" );
    puts( "Each word on the line above starts at a tab stop. \n" );
    puts( "This puts()\n\t will make 3 lines of output,\n\t indented.\n" );
```

```
    printf( " >>%-35s<< \n >>%35s<< \n",
            "left justify, -field width", "right justify, +field width" );
    printf( " >>%10s<< \n\n", "not enough room?  Field gets expanded" );
}
```

Figure 13.9.   String literals and string output.

Notes on Figure 13.9. String literals and string output. In this program, we demonstrate a collection of string-printing possibilities.

- *First box: ways to print strings.*

    1. On the first line, we use **puts**() to print the contents of a string variable.
    2. The second line calls **printf**() to print a literal string. When printing just one string with **printf**(), that string becomes the format, which always is printed. This line also shows how escape characters are used to print quotation marks in the output.
    3. The third line prints both a string and a character. The **%s** in the format prints the string **"Print this string and ring the bell."** and then goes to a new line; the **%c** prints the character code **\a**, which results in a beep with no visible output on our system.

4. The output from this box is
```
String demo program.
            This prints single ' and double " quotes.
            Print this string and ring the bell.
```

- *Second box: adjacent strings are united.*
  1. The **puts()** shows that two strings, separated only by whitespace, become one string in the eyes of the compiler. This is a very useful technique for making programs more readable. Whitespace refers to any nonprinting character that is legal in a C source code file. This includes ordinary space, newline, vertical and horizontal tabs, formfeed, and comments. If we were to write a comma between the two strings, only the first one would be used as the format, the second one would cause a compiler error.
  2. The output from this box is
  ```
  These two quoted sections form a single string.

  You can break a format string into pieces if you
  end each line and begin the next with quotes.
  You may indent the lines any way you wish.
  ```
  3. When we have a long format in a **printf()** statement, we just break it into two parts, being sure to start and end each part with a double quote mark. Where we break the format string and how we indent it have no effect on the output.

- *Third box: escape characters in strings.*

  1. The output from this box is shown below a tab line so you can see the reason for the unusual spacing:

  ```
  This     string has    tab      characters    between words.
  ```

  ```
  Each word on the line above starts at a tab stop.
  ```

  ```
  This puts()
          will make 3 lines of output,
          indented.
  ```

  2. Note that the tab character does not insert a constant number of spaces, it moves the cursor to the next tab position. Where the tab stops occur is defined by the software (an eight-character stop was used here). In practice, it is a little tricky to get things lined up using tabs.
  3. The presence or absence of newline characters controls the vertical spacing. The number of lines of output does not correspond, in general, to the number of lines of code.

- *Fourth box: using field-width specifiers with strings.*

  1. The output is

     ```
     >>left justify, -field width            <<
     >>           right justify, +field width<<
     >>not enough room?  Field gets expanded<<
     ```

  2. Spaces are used to pad the string if it is shorter than the specified field width. Using a negative number as a field width causes the output to be left justified. A positive field width produces right justification.
  3. If the string is longer than the field width, the width specification is ignored and the entire string is printed.

13.2.2   String Input

String input is more complicated than string output. The string input functions in the standard I/O library offer a bewildering variety of options; only a few of the most useful are illustrated here. One thing common to all string input functions is that they take one string argument, which should be the name of a character array or a pointer to a character array. *Do not use a variable of type* **char*** *for this purpose unless you have previously initialized it to point at a character array.*

For example, the diagram in Figure 13.10 shows two before-and-after scenarios that cause trouble. The code fragment on the left is wrong because the pointer is uninitialized, so it points at some random memory location; attempting to store data there is likely to cause the program to crash. The code on the right is wrong because C does not permit a program to change a literal string value. The diagrams in Figure 13.11 show two ways to do the job right. That on the left uses the name of an array in the **scanf()** statement; that on the right uses a pointer initialized to point at an array.

Also, an array that receives string input must be long enough to contain all the information that will be read from the keyboard plus a null terminator. The

Both these **scanf()** statements are errors:

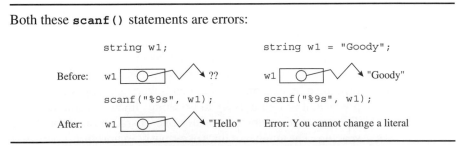

Figure 13.10.   You cannot store an input string in a pointer.

Here are two correct and meaningful ways to read a string into memory:

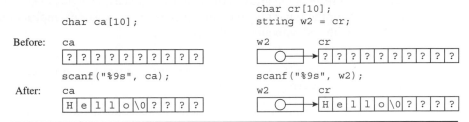

Figure 13.11.   You need an array to store an input string.

input, once started by the user hitting the Enter key, continues until one of two conditions occurs:

1. The input function reads its own termination character. This varies, as described next, according to the input function.
2. The maximum number of characters is read, as specified by some field-width limit.

After the read operation is over, a null character will be appended to the end of the data.

Reading an entire line.   The get-string function has the prototype `string gets ( char s[] )`. It reads characters (including leading whitespace) from the buffer into the array part of **s** until the first **\n** is read. The newline character terminates reading but is *not* stored in **s**. A null terminator then is stored in the array at the end of the input characters. The variable **s** must refer to an array of **char**s long enough to hold the entire string and the null character. Otherwise, the function will store the extra characters beyond the array bounds and wipe out the contents of adjacent memory variables. For example:

```
char course_name[20];
gets( course_name );     /* Error if input > 19 chars. */
```

Here, we ignore the return value of `gets()`. Normally this is just a pointer to the **char** array, but it is set to **NULL** when an input error occurs. For the time being, we continue to ignore such error-return codes; full error checking will be taken up in Chapter 15.

Reading a string with `scanf()`.   For string input, we also may use `scanf()` with either a **%s** or **%ns conversion specifier**. In both cases, leading whitespace characters are skipped, then input characters are read and stored at the address given in the input list until more whitespace is encountered. The integer **n** in the **%ns** field specifier is the field-width limit. When **%ns** is used, the read operation will stop after reading **n** input characters, if whitespace was not found first. For example, **%9s** will stop the read operation after nine characters are read; the corresponding array variable must be at least 10 bytes long to allow enough space for the input plus the null terminator. Here are examples of calls on **scanf()** with and without a field-width limit:

```
char name[10];
scanf( "%s", name );     /* dangerous; overflow possible */
scanf( "%9s", name );    /* safe */
```

Note that there is no ampersand before the variable name; the **&** must be omitted because **name** is an array.

The brackets conversion.   If the programmer wants some character other than whitespace to end the read operation with **scanf()**, a format of the form **%[^?]** or **%n[^?]** may be used instead of **%s** or **%ns** (**n** is still an integer denoting the field length). The desired termination character replaces the question mark and is written inside the brackets following the carat character, **^**.[3] Some examples:

```
scanf( "%29[^\n]", street );
scanf( "% 29[^,], %2[^\n]", city, state );
```

A complete input would be

```
122 E. 42nd St.
New York, NY
```

The first example stops the read operation after 29 characters have been read, sooner if a newline character is read (but it does not stop for other kinds of whitespace). The second example reads characters into the array **city** until a comma is read. It then discards the comma and reads the remaining characters into the array **state** until a newline is entered.

Combining input formats.   A format for **scanf()** can have more than one string conversion specifier. Blanks can be included in the format to tell **scanf()** to ignore whitespace characters in the input. Anything else in an input format that is not part of a conversion specifier *must* be present in the input for correct operation. When that part of the format is interpreted, characters are read from the input buffer, compared to the characters in the format, and discarded if they match. If they do not match, it is an input error and they are left in the buffer. This is another error condition that will be discussed in Chapter 15.

In the second example above, the program reads two strings (city and state) that are on one input line, separated by a comma and one or more spaces. The comma is detected first by the brackets specifier but not removed from the buffer. The comma and spaces then are read and removed from the buffer because of the

---

[3]A variety of effects can be implemented using square brackets. We present only the most useful here. The interested programmer should consult a standard reference manual for a complete description.

" , " in the format. Finally, the second string is read and stored. These comma and whitespace characters are discarded, not stored in a variable. Whenever a nonwhitespace character is used to stop an input operation, that character must be removed from the buffer by including it directly in the format or through some other method. Figure 13.12, in the next section, shows these calls on `scanf()` in the context of a complete program.

Using `gets()` **vs. using** `scanf()`. The basic differences between `gets()` and `scanf()` are the following:

* The `gets()` function reads an entire line up to the first newline character, whereas `scanf()` with `%ns` stops at the first whitespace character or after n characters have been read. We can make `scanf()` act more like `gets()` by using the `%[^\n]` conversion specifier. However, there is no way to make `gets()` limit its input to just n characters.
* The `scanf()` function skips leading whitespace characters, whereas `gets()` reads and stores any character, including whitespace, up to the first newline character. This is much like the difference between `getchar()` and `scanf()` with the `" %c"` specifier.

The `gets()` function typically is used to read entire lines of text of a known length. For more specialized processing, `scanf()` can be used to read single words, phrases delimited by a specified character, or fragments of text that are up to n characters long. If either input method is used and the array is too short to hold the entire data string, the input will overflow the storage area provided and overwrite adjacent memory variables.

13.2.3 Other String Functions

The C standard supports a library of functions that process strings. In addition, programmers can define their own string functions. In this section, we first examine how strings are passed as arguments and used as parameters in functions. Then we explore the many built-in string functions and how they can be used in text processing.

13.2.4 Strings as Parameters

The program example in Figure 13.12 demonstrates the proper syntax for a function prototype, definition, and call with a string parameter.

Notes on Figure 13.12. A string parameter.

* *First box: string input.*

    1. The safe methods of string input described in the previous section are used here in a complete program. In every case, a call on `scanf()` limits the number of characters read to one less than

This program demonstrates a programmer-defined function with a string parameter. It also uses several of the string input and output functions in a program context.

```c
#include "tools.h"
void print_upper( string s );

void main( void )
{
    char first[15];
    string name = first;
    char street[30], city[30], state[3];

    printf( " Enter first name: " );
    scanf( "%14s", name );                      /* read one word only */
    printf( " Enter street address: " );
    scanf( " %29[^\n]", street );               /* read to end of line */
    printf(" Enter city, state: " );            /* split line at comma */
    scanf( " %29[^,], %2[^\n]", city, state );

    putchar( '\n' );
    print_upper( name );
    printf( "\n %s %s, ", street, city );
    print_upper( state );
    puts( "\n" );
}

/* -------------------------- Print letters of string in upper case. */
void print_upper( string s )
{
    int k;        /* loop counter */
    for (k = 0; s[k] != '\0'; ++k) putchar( toupper( s[k] ) );
}
```

Figure 13.12.   A string parameter.

the length of the array that receives them, leaving one space for the null terminator.

2. In the first call, the argument to **scanf()** is a string variable initialized to point to a character array. It is the correct type for input using either the **%s** or **%[^?]** conversion specifiers.

3. In the other two calls, the argument is a character array. This also is a correct type for input using these specifiers.

- *Second box: character and string output.*

  1. Both **putchar()** and **puts()** are used to print a newline character. The arguments are different because these functions have different types of parameters. The argument for **putchar()** is the single character, **\n**, while the string **"\n"** is sent to **puts()**, which prints the newline character and adds another newline.

  2. Inner boxes: calls on **print_upper()**. The programmer-defined function **print_upper()** is called twice to print upper-case versions of two of the input strings. In the first call, the argument is a string variable. In the second, it is a character array. Both are appropriate arguments when the parameter has type **string**. We also could call this function with a literal string.

  3. Sample output from this program might be

  ```
  Enter first name:  Maggie
  Enter street address:  180 River Rd.
  Enter city, state:  Haddon, Ct

  MAGGIE
  180 River Rd.  Haddon, CT
  ```

- *Last box: the **print_upper()** function.*

  1. The parameter here is type **string**. The corresponding argument can be the name of a character array, a literal string, or a string variable. It could also be the address of a character somewhere in the middle of a null-terminated sequence of characters.

  2. Since a string is a pointer to an array of characters, those characters can be accessed by writing subscripts after the name of the string parameter, as done here. The **for** loop starts at the first character of the string, converts each character to upper case, and prints it. The original string remains unchanged.

  3. Like most loops that process the characters of a string, this loop ends at the null terminator.

13.3 The String Library

The standard C **string library** contains many functions that manipulate strings. Some of them are beyond the scope of this book, but others are so basic that they deserve mention here:

- **strlen()** finds the length of a string.
- **strcmp()** compares two strings.

- **strncmp()** compares up to *n* characters of two strings.
- **strcpy()** copies a whole string.
- **strncpy()** copies up to *n* characters of a string. If no null terminator is among these *n* characters, do not add one.
- **strcat()** copies a string onto the end of another string.
- **strncat()** copies up to *n* characters of a string onto the end of another string. If no null terminator is among these *n* characters, add one at the end.
- **strchr()** finds the leftmost occurrence of a given character in a string.
- **strrchr()** finds the rightmost occurrence of a given character in a string.
- **strstr()** finds the leftmost occurrence of a given substring in a string.

We discuss how these functions can be used correctly in a variety of situations.

The length of a string.   Because a string is defined as a **two-part object** (recall the diagrams in Figure 13.7), we need different methods to find the sizes of each part. Figure 13.13 illustrates the use of both operations. The operator **sizeof** returns the size of the pointer part of a string, while the function **strlen()** returns the number of characters in the array part, not including the null terminator. (Therefore, the string length of the null (empty) string is 0.) Figure 13.24 shows further uses of **strlen()** in a program.

```
#include "tools.h"    /* contains definition of type string */
#define N 5
void main( void )
{
    string w1 = "Annette";
    string w2 = "Ann";
    char w3[20] = "Zeke";
    printf( " sizeof w1 is %2i   string is \"%s\"\t strlen is %i\n",
            sizeof w1, w1, strlen( w1 ) );
    printf( " sizeof w2 is %2i   string is \"%s\"\t\t strlen is %i\n",
            sizeof w2, w2, strlen( w2 ) );
    printf( " sizeof w3 is %2i   string is \"%s\"\t strlen is %i\n\n",
            sizeof w3, w3, strlen( w3 ) );
}
```

The output of this program is

```
sizeof w1 is  4    string is "Annette"    strlen is 7
sizeof w2 is  4    string is "Ann"        strlen is 3
sizeof w3 is 20    string is "Zeke"       strlen is 4
```

Figure 13.13.   The size of a string.

Notes on Figure 13.13. The size of a string.

1. The variables `w1` and `w2` are strings. When the program applies `sizeof` to a string, the result is the size of a pointer on the local system. So `sizeof w1 == sizeof w2` even though `w1` points at a longer name than `w2`.

2. In contrast, `w3` is not a string; it is a `char` array used as a container for a string. When the programmer prints `sizeof w3`, we see that `w3` occupies 20 bytes, which agrees with its declaration. This is true even though only 5 of those bytes contain letters from the string. (Remember that the null terminator takes up 1 byte, even though you do not write it or see it when you print the string.)

3. To find the number of letters in a string, we use `strlen()`, string length, not `sizeof`. The argument to `strlen()` can be a `string` variable, a string literal, or the name of a character array. The value returned is the number of characters in the array part of the string, up to but not including the null terminator.

Comparing two strings.   Figure 13.14 shows what happens when we try to compare two strings or `char` arrays using `==`. Unfortunately, only the addresses get compared. So if two pointers point at the same array, as with `w5` and `w6`, they are equal; if they point at different arrays, as with `w4` and `w5`, they are not equal, even if the arrays contain the same characters.

To overcome this difficulty, the C `string` library contains the function `strcmp()`, which compares the actual characters, not the pointers. It takes two arguments that are strings (pointers) and does a letter-by-letter, alphabetic-order comparison. The return value is a negative number if the first string comes before the other alphabetically, a 0 if the strings are identical up through the null characters, and a positive number if the second string comes first. We can use `strcmp()` in the test portion of an `if` or `while` statement if we are careful. Because the intuitively opposite value of 0 is returned when the strings are the same, we must

---

```
char w4[6] = "Hello";      w4 | H | e | l | l | o |\0|     w5 | O | ───▶ "Hello"
string w5 = "Hello";
string w6 = w5;                                            w6 | O |
```

Compare address of `w4` to address stored in `w5`. Output: `No, not ==`

```
if (w4 == w5)
    puts( "Yes, ==" );
else puts( "No, not ==" );
```

Compare address stored in `w5` to address stored in `w6`. Output: `Yes, ==`

```
if (w5 == w6)
    puts( "Yes, ==" );
else puts( "No, not ==" );
```

Figure 13.14.   Do not use `==` with strings.

remember to compare the result of `strcmp()` to 0 in a test for equality. Figure 13.15 shows a proper test for equality. Two other string comparison functions also deserve mention:

1. The function `strncmp()` is like `strcmp()` except that it compares up to the first *n* characters of the strings. A call takes three arguments and has the form `strncmp( s1, s2, n )`. If *n* is greater than the length of the strings, it works identically to `strcmp()`.
2. The `tools` library contains a definition that makes `strcmp()` more convenient and intuitive to use. It defines `strequal()`,[4] which has two string arguments. It returns `true` when the strings are equal and `false` when they are unequal. Figure 13.15 shows a sample call on `strequal()` that is equivalent to the prior call on `strcmp()`. Figure 13.24 shows its use in a program.

Character search.   The function `strchr( string s1, char ch )` searches `s1` for the first (leftmost) occurrence of `ch` and returns a pointer to that occurrence. If the character does not appear at all, `NULL` is returned. The function `strrchr( string s1, char ch )` is similar, but it searches `s1` for the last (rightmost) occurrence of `ch` and returns a pointer to that occurrence. If the character does not appear at all, `NULL` is returned. Figure 13.16 shows how to call both these functions and interpret their results.

Substring search.   The function `strstr( string s1, string s2 )` searches `s1` for the first (leftmost) occurrence of substring `s2` and returns a pointer to the beginning of that substring. If the substring does not appear at all, `NULL` is returned. Unlike searching for a character, there is no library function

---

```
char w4[6] = "Hello";          w4  H e l l o \0

string w5 = "Hello";           w5  [ O ]──→ "Hello"
```

Use function from **string** library to compare **"Hello"** with **"Hello"**. Output: `Yes, str=`

```
if (strcmp( w4, w5 ) == 0)
    puts( "Yes, str=" );
else puts( "No, not str=" );
```

Use function from **tools** library to compare **"Hello"** with **"Hello"**. Output: `Yes, str=`

```
if (strequal( w4, w5 ))
    puts( "Yes, str=" );
else puts( "No, not str=" );
```

Figure 13.15.   Two functions for comparing strings.

---

[4]`strequal()` is actually not a function but a macro. This is an alternative way of defining certain operations using the compiler's preprocessor. However, we will not explore this aspect of macros in this text.

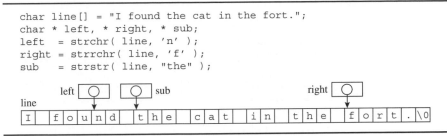

```
char line[] = "I found the cat in the fort.";
char * left, * right, * sub;
left  = strchr( line, 'n' );
right = strrchr( line, 'f' );
sub   = strstr( line, "the" );
```

Figure 13.16.   Searching for a character or a substring.

that searches for the last occurrence of a substring. Figure 13.16 gives an example of using **strstr()**.

Copying a string.   What does it mean to copy a string? Do we copy the pointer or the contents of the array? Both. We really need two copy operations because sometimes we want one effect, sometimes the other. Therefore, C has two kinds of operations: To copy the pointer, we use the assignment operator; to copy the contents of the array, we use **strcpy()** or **strncpy()**.

Figure 13.14 diagrams the result of using a pointer assignment; the expression **w6 = w5** copies the address from **w5** into **w6**. After the assignment, **w6** points at the same thing as **w5**. This technique is useful for output labeling. For example, in Figure 13.4 the value of **response** is set by assigning the address of the correct literal to it.

Copying the array portion of a string also is useful, especially when we need to extract data from an input buffer and move it into a more permanent storage area. The **strcpy()** function takes two string arguments, copies the contents of the second into the array referenced by the first, and puts a null terminator on the end of the copied string. It is necessary, first, to ensure that the receiving area is long enough to contain all the characters in the source string. This technique is illustrated in the second call of Figure 13.17. Here, the destination address is actually the middle of a character array.

The **strncpy()** function is similar to **strcpy()** but takes a third argument, an integer **n**, which indicates that copying should stop after **n** characters. Setting **n** equal to one less than the length of the receiving array guarantees that the copy operation will not overflow its bounds. Unfortunately, **strncpy()** does not automatically put a null terminator on the end of the copied string; that must be done as a separate operation unless the null character is copied by the operation. Or we can let a succeeding operation handle the termination, as happens in the example of Figure 13.17.

String concatenation. The function **strcat(string s1, string s2)** appends **s2** onto the end of **s1**. Calling **strcat()** is equivalent to finding the end of a string, then doing a **strcpy()** operation starting at that address. If the position of the end of the string already is known, it actually is more efficient to use

```
char line[20];
strncpy( line, "Hotdog", 3 );
strcpy( &line[3], " diggety" );
strcat( line, " dog!" );
```

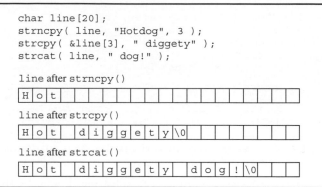

Figure 13.17.   **Copy and concatenate.**

strcpy() rather than **strcat()** to append **s2**. In both cases, the array in which **s1** is stored must have enough space for the combined string. The **strcat()** function is used in the last call in the example of Figure 13.17 to complete the new string.

The function **strncat()** is like **strcat()**, except that the appending operation stops after at most **n** characters. A null terminator *is* added to the end of the string. (Therefore, up to $n + 1$ characters may be written.) The careful programmer uses **strncpy()** or **strncat()**, rather than **strcpy()** or **strcat()**, and sets **n** to the number of storage slots remaining between the end of **s1** and the end of the array.

13.3.1   Three String Tools (Optional Topic)

The standard **time** library supplies functions that read the computer's internal clock to determine the current date and time. The function **time()** returns a relative time in the form of a long integer that must be decoded before it can be understood. Fortunately, this can be done using another function in the **time** library called **ctime()**. It converts the encoded date and time into a string of the form **"Sat Jun 10 09:56:55 2000\n"**. These functions are somewhat awkward and confusing to use. Also, sometimes we want the time without the date or the date without the time. No functions in the **time** library do this. However, the **tools** library contains three additional time-date functions that use the standard library functions and format the time and date separately. The first function, **today()**, returns the date as a string in the form **"Mon Aug 21 2000"**. This function actually is called by **banner()** to get the date. The second, **oclock()**, returns only the time in the form **"11:58:47"**, while **when()** returns both the date and time as separate strings. Use of these three **string tools** is illustrated in Figure 13.18 and their code is given in Appendix F.

```
#include "tools.h"
void main( void )
{
      char date[16];      /* Array for date with 16 chars. */
      char time[9];       /* Array for time with 9 chars. */

      printf( "\n Date: %s \n", today( date ) );
      printf( " Time: %s \n", oclock( time ) );

      when( date, time );
      printf( "\n Today is %s at %s \n", date, time );
}
```

Figure 13.18.   Printing the date and time.

Notes on Figure 13.18. Printing the date and time.

- *First box: the variables.* The program allocates a 16-character array for the date to hold a string in the format **"Wed Jan 13 2004"** which consists of 15 characters and the terminating null character. Similarly, it allocates a nine-character array for the time, which will be returned in the form **"19:01:51"**, meaning 19:01 and 51 seconds on a 24-hour clock.
- *Second box: calling* **today()** *and* **oclock()**. When the **today()** function is called with an empty array as its argument, the function reads the date, formats it, and copies it into the array for later use. It also returns a pointer to the date.[5] This lets the program print the date value directly, as shown on the first line. The **oclock()** function is similar. The prototypes of these two functions are

```
string today( char[] );
string oclock( char[] );
```

The program also could call them as if they were **void** functions, then print the date and time later, as is done with the **when()** function.
- *Third box: calling* **when()**. The **when()** function must be used differently because it is a **void** function; its prototype is

```
void when( char[], char[] );
```

When this function returns, the first argument will contain the date and the second, the time. The date and time can be printed separately. Typical output from this program is

---

[5] Certain other functions in the standard C libraries (not mentioned here) also have this return behavior.

```
Date: Thu Mar 13 2003
Time: 11:58:07

Today is Thu Mar 13 2003 at 11:58:07
```

13.4   Arrays of Strings

An important aspect of C, and all modern languages, is that aggregate types such as strings and arrays can be compounded. Thus, we can build arrays of arrays and arrays of strings. An **array of strings**, sometimes called a **ragged array** because the ends of the strings generally do not line up in a neat column, is useful for storing a list of names or messages. This saves space over a list of uniform-sized arrays that are partially empty.

We can create a ragged array by declaring an array of strings and initializing it to a list of string literals.[6] For example, the following declaration creates the data structure shown in Figure 13.19:

```
string word[3] = { "one", "two", "three" };
```

This particular form of a ragged array does not permit the contents of the entries to be changed. Making a ragged array of arrays that can be updated is explained in a later chapter. The programs in Figures 13.21 and 13.25 demonstrate the use of ragged arrays in two different contexts.

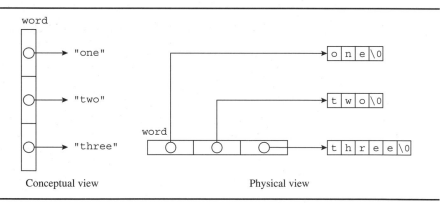

Conceptual view   Physical view

Figure 13.19.   A ragged array.

---

[6]In a later chapter, we show how to create a ragged array dynamically.

13.4.1   Printing Enumeration Codes

Enumerated types were introduced in Chapter 11 as a way to define a set of related codes or symbols. Enumerations were used as status codes and function return values both there and in Chapter 12, but no real attempt was made to output them. Since enumeration constants are represented by integers in C, we could print them as integers. However, the purpose of using an enumeration is to give meaningful symbolic names to status codes, so we certainly do not want to see a cryptic integer code in the output. Rather, we want to see an English word.

Symbolic output is achieved easily using a ragged array. An array of strings is declared that is parallel to the enumeration. Each word in the array is the English version of the corresponding symbol in the enumeration. We use the symbol (an integer) to subscript the ragged array and select the corresponding string, which then is used in the output. The array of strings is defined in the same program scope as the enumeration, so that any function that uses the enumeration has access to the output strings. Since enumerations usually are defined globally, the string array also is global. An important precaution with any global array is to begin the declaration with the keyword **const** so that no part of the program code can change it accidentally. As an example, consider an enumeration defined in Chapter 11:

```
typedef enum { P_IN, P_SIDE, P_CORNER, P_OUT } in_type;
```

We can define output strings thus:

```
const string in_labels[] = { "inside", "on a side of",
        "on a corner of", "outside" };
```

To show how to use this array of strings, assume we have a variable, **position**, that contains a value of type **in_type**. We write the following lines to insert the English equivalent of the value of **position** into the middle of a sentence and display the result on the screen:

```
in_type position;
...
printf( " Point is %s square.\n", in_labels[position] );
```

The output might look like this

```
Point is on a corner of square.
```

13.4.2   The Menu Data Structure

In computer programs, a menu is a list of choices presented interactively to a computer user. Each choice corresponds to some action or process that the program can carry out and the user might wish to select. In a modern windowing system, the user may make selections using a mouse. The other standard approach is to display an alphabetic or numeric code for each option and ask the user to enter the selected code from the keyboard. When execution of an option is complete, the menu is presented again for a new choice. Because they are easy to code and create an attractive interface, menus now are a component of programs in virtually every application area. Here, we present an easy way to set up your own menu-driven applications.

To use a menu, several things must occur:

- A title or some general instructions should be presented.
- Following that should be a list of possible choices and the input selection code for each. It is a good idea to include one option that means "take no action" or "quit."
- Then the user must be prompted to enter a choice, and the choice must be read and validated.
- Finally, the program must carry out the user's chosen intent.

Often, carrying out the chosen action means using supporting information specific to the choice. This information may be stored in a table implemented as a set of parallel arrays. In the menu display, each menu item can be shown next to its array subscript. The user is asked to choose a numbered item, and that number is used as a subscript for all of the arrays that form the table.

13.4.3   An Example: Selling Ice Cream

The program in Figure 13.21 illustrates the use of a menu of ice cream flavors and a parallel array of prices, as depicted in Figure 13.20. A loop prints the menu.

```
#define CHOICES 6

string flavor[CHOICES] = {"Empty","Vanilla",
                          "Pistachio","Rocky Road",
                          "Fudge Chip","Lemon" };
float price[CHOICES] = {0.00,1.00,1.50,1.35,1.25,1.20};
```

flavor[0]	○ →	"Empty"	price[0]	0.00
flavor[1]	○ →	"Vanilla"	price[1]	1.00
flavor[2]	○ →	"Pistachio"	price[2]	1.50
flavor[3]	○ →	"Rocky Road"	price[3]	1.35
flavor[4]	○ →	"Fudge Chip"	price[4]	1.25
flavor[5]	○ →	"Lemon"	price[5]	1.20

Figure 13.20.   A menu array.

This program calls the **menu()** function in Figure 13.22.

```
#include "tools.h"
#define CHOICES 6
int menu ( string title, int max, string menu_list[] );

void main( void )
{
    int choice;                                 /* The menu selection. */
    string greeting = " I'm happy to serve you.  Our specials today are: ";
    string flavor[CHOICES] = { "Empty", "Vanilla", "Pistachio",
                               "Rocky Road", "Fudge Chip", "Lemon" };
    float price[CHOICES] = { 0.00, 1.00, 1.50, 1.35, 1.25, 1.20 };

    choice = menu( greeting, CHOICES, flavor );

    printf( "\n Here is your %s cone.\n That will be $%.2f.  ",
            flavor[choice], price[choice] );

    puts( "Thank you, come again." );
}
```

Figure 13.21.   Selecting ice cream from a menu.

The loop variable is used as the subscript to print each menu item and is displayed as the selector for that item. When the user enters a choice, the number is used to subscript two **parallel arrays:** the **flavor** array and the **price** array. The program then prints a message using this information (and we imagine that ice cream and money change hands).

Notes on Figure 13.21. Selecting ice cream from a menu.

- *First box: creating a menu.*

  1. The first string declared here is the greeting that will appear at the top of the menu.
  2. Second, we declare an array of strings named **flavor** and initialize it with the menu selections we want to offer.
  3. Another array, **price**, parallel to **flavor**, lists the price for a cone of each flavor. The position of each price in this array must be the same as the corresponding item in **flavor**.
  4. Making the menu longer or shorter is fairly easy: Just change the value of **CHOICES** at the top of the program, add or delete a string to or from the **flavor** array, and add or delete a corresponding cost to or from the **price** array.

5. Since this is a relatively small program, the declarations have been placed in `main()`. Alternative placements are discussed as they occur in other examples in this chapter.

- *Second box: calling the* `menu()` *function.*

  1. Since the `menu()` function, defined in Figure 13.22, will be used for all sorts of menus in various programs, the program must supply, as an argument, an appropriate application title to be displayed above the menu items.
  2. The second argument is the number of items in the menu. In C, the number of items in an array must be an argument to any function that processes the array; the function cannot determine this quantity from just the array itself.
  3. The third argument is the name of the array that contains the menu descriptions. These descriptions will be displayed for the user next to the selection codes.
  4. The return value from this function is the index of the menu item that the user selected. The `menu()` function returns only valid selections, so we can safely store the return value and use it as a subscript with no further checking.

- *Third box: the output.*

  1. The variable `choice` is used to subscript both arrays. The program prints the chosen flavor and the price for that flavor using the vali-

---

This function is called from the main program in Figure 13.21.

```
int menu( string title, int max, string menu_list[] )
{
    int choice;
    int n = 0;                    /* Loop counter for menu display. */
    printf( "\n %s\n ", title );
    for (n = 0; n < max; ++n)  printf( "\t %i. %s \n", n, menu_list[n] );

    printf( " Please enter your selection: ");
    for(;;) {                     /* Prompt for and validate a menu selection. */
        scanf( "%i", &choice );
        if (choice >= 0 && choice < max) break;   /* Accept valid choice. */
        printf( " Please enter number between 0 and %i: ", max - 1 );
    }

    return choice;
}
```

Figure 13.22.   A menu-handling function.

dated menu selection as a subscript for the `flavor` and `price` arrays, respectively.

2. Below the menu presented on the screen (shown later), the user will see his or her selection, as well as the results, displayed like this:

```
Please enter your selection: 3

Here is your Rocky Road cone.
That will be $1.35.  Thank you, come again.
```

Notes on Figures 13.22. A menu-handling function.

- *First box: the function header.*

  1. The first parameter is a string that contains a title for the menu. This should be declared with the menu array, as in Figure 13.21.
  2. The second parameter is the number of choices in the menu. This number is used to control the loop that displays the menu and determine which index inputs are legal and which are out of bounds.
  3. The final parameter is an array of strings that contains the list of menu items.
  4. The return value will be a legal subscript for the arrays that contain the menu and price information.

- *Second box: displaying the menu.*

  1. First, the program prints the title for the menu with appropriate vertical spacing.
  2. Then it uses a loop to display the menu. On each repetition, the loop displays the loop counter and one string. This creates a numbered list of items, where each number displayed is the array subscript of the corresponding item.
  3. The actual menu display follows. Note that choice 0 permits an escape from this menu without buying anything. It is a good idea to include such a "no operation" alternative. A "quit" option is not necessary in this menu since it is displayed only once by the program.

```
I'm happy to serve you.  Our specials today are:
        0.  Empty
        1.  Vanilla
        2.  Pistachio
        3.  Rocky Road
        4.  Fudge Chip
        5.  Lemon
```

- *Third box: the prompt, input, and **menu selection validation.***

  1. The original prompt is written outside the loop, since it will be displayed only once. If the first selection is invalid, the user will see an error prompt.

2. This `for` loop is a typical data validation loop. It is very important to validate an input value before using it as a subscript. If that value is outside the range of legal subscripts, using it could cause the program to crash. The smallest legal subscript always is 0. The second argument to this function is the number of items in the menu array, which is one greater than the maximum legal subscript. The program compares the user's input to these bounds: If the selection is too big or too small, it displays an error prompt and asks for a new selection.

3. A good user interface informs the user of the valid limits for a choice after he or she makes a mistake. Otherwise, the user might not understand what is wrong and have to figure it out by trial and error.

4. When control leaves the loop, `choice` contains a number between `0` and `max-1`, which is a legal subscript for a menu with `max` slots. The function returns this choice. The calling program prints the chosen flavor and the price for that flavor using this number as a subscript for the `flavor` and `price` arrays.

5. The following output demonstrates the validation process. The `menu()` function does not return to `main()` until the user makes a valid selection. After returning, `main()` uses the selection to print the chosen flavor and its price:

```
I'm happy to serve you.   Our specials today are:
          0. Empty
          1. Vanilla
          2. Pistachio
          3. Rocky Road
          4. Fudge Chip
          5. Lemon
Please enter your selection: -3
Please enter number between 0 and 5: 6
Please enter number between 0 and 5: 5

Here is your Lemon cone.
That will be $1.20.   Thank you, come again.
```

13.4.4   Subscript Validation

The `menu()` function in Figure 13.22 must validate the input because C does not guard against use of meaningless subscripts. To demonstrate the effects of using an invalid subscript, we removed the data validation loop from the third box, leaving only these two lines:

```
printf( " Please enter your selection: " );
scanf( "%i", &choice );
```

Compiling and running the resulting program on a variety of invalid inputs produced the following output lines at the end of the program:

```
Here is your POXO-@ .6D cone.

Here is your MACHTYPE=m68k cone.

Here is your (null pointer) cone.

Here is your #9DO
$,R`nx[u cone.

Here is your
I'm happy to serve you.  Our specials today are:  cone.

Segmentation fault

Bus error
```

As you can see, C calculates a machine address based on any subscript given it and uses that address, even though it is not within the array bounds. The results normally are garbage and should be different for each illegal input. On some computer systems, the last two messages indicate errors that will cause the program to crash and may force the user to reboot the computer. A well-engineered program does not let an input error cause a system crash or garbage output. It validates the user's response to ensure that it is a legal choice, as in Figure 13.22.

13.4.5 The `menu_i()` and `menu_c()` Functions

The process of displaying the menu and eliciting a selection is much the same for any menu-based program. The content of the menu changes from application to application but the processing method remains the same. This commonality enables us to write a general-purpose menu-handling function such as **menu()**. The **tools** library contains two functions similar to **menu()**: **menu_c()** handles menus where the selection code is a character and **menu_i()** handles numeric selections. The code for **menu_c()** is given in Figure 13.23, while the code for **menu_i()** is shown in Appendix F. The **menu_i()** function is much like **menu()** except that it incorporates a complete input error handling process (several more topics must be presented before this code can be understood).

In Figure 13.23, we show the source code of the **menu_c()** function from the **tools** library. Like **menu()**, it receives a menu title, the number of menu items, and the menu as arguments, where each menu string now consists of a

This function in the **tools** library displays a menu, then reads and returns a nonwhitespace character.

```
char menu_c( string title, int n, const string menu[] )
{
    int k;                          /* Loop counter */
    char ch;                        /* User's selection */

    printf( "\n%s\n\n", title );

    for (k = 0; k < n; ++k)  printf( "\t %s \n", menu[k] );

    printf( "\n Enter letter of desired item: " );
    scanf( " %c", &ch );            /* Skip leading whitespace. */
    return ch;
}
```

Figure 13.23.   The menu_c() **function.**

selection code character and a phrase describing the menu item. The function displays the strings from the menu array, one per line, then reads and returns the menu choice in the form of a single nonwhitespace character.[7] This function will be used in the program of Figure 13.27 in the next section.

Notes on Figure 13.23. The menu_c() **function.**

- *First box: the title.* This function displays a title in the same manner as **menu()**.
- *Second box: the counting loop.* The menu array is the third parameter of **menu_c()**. This is an array of strings, where each string has a code character for the menu choice and a phrase describing the choice. No subscript is displayed before the menu line, as was done for **menu()**, because the character choice is embedded in the string. These codes probably will be processed by a **switch** statement, as in the program of Figure 13.27.
- *Third box: the selection and return.*

  1. The **printf()** prompts the user to make a selection. It lets the user know that a character (not a number) is expected this time.
  2. We use **scanf()** with **" %c"** to read the user's response. The space before the **%c** is important because the input stream probably contains

---

[7] In contrast, **menu_i()** reads and returns an integer response that can be used directly as a table subscript.

a newline character from some prior input step.[8] The program must skip over that character to reach the user's current input.

3. The program returns whatever nonwhitespace character the user enters. This function has no way to validate the selection because it does not know what selection codes are legal. Although these codes are present in the menu's item labels, they are part of larger menu strings and not extracted easily by this function for use in validation.

13.5   String Processing Applications (Optional Topic)

In this section, we examine two applications that use many of the string processing functions presented in the chapter.

13.5.1   Password Validation and Message Construction

The following program uses some of the string functions in a practical context; namely, requiring the user to enter a password to access a sensitive database on the computer. In this case, the database is somewhat fanciful: a list of guys and their girlfriends and an automated system for composing love letters.

The love letter is a form letter consisting of a series of sentence fragments with three kinds of blanks to be filled in to make it complete. The data to use are defined as a set of parallel arrays giving information about each guy (and his girlfriend) who wants to use the love letter facility.

Figure 13.24 implements the password validation phase of this program. Figure 13.25 contains the text for a form "love letter"; a larger database could be created using additional header files with different messages and different lists of couples. Finally, Figure 13.26 composes the letter using this text, the user's selections, and functions from the standard **string** library.

Notes on Figure 13.24. Comparing and copying strings.

- *First box: the output message.*

    1. When the user types the wrong password, the incorrect input will be echoed, followed by the string **no_go**.
    2. We calculate the length of **no_go** so that we know how much extra space to leave in the input buffer to provide empty array slots for appending the "No entry" message onto the end of the incorrect password.

---

[8] Review the discussion of these issues concerning problems with **getchar**() following Figure 11.5.

This program calls the `compare()` function in Figure 13.26.

```
#include "tools.h"

#define PASSW "LoveForEver"
void compose( void );

void main( void )
{
    string no_go = " is not the password; No Entry!  \n";
    const int k = strlen( no_go );

    char word[80 + k];       /* Buffer for the password and comment. */
    printf( "\n Please enter the password: " );
    scanf( "%79[^\n]", word );

    if (strequal( word, PASSW )) {
        puts( " Password is correct; go ahead\n" );
        compose();
    }
    else {
        strcat( word, no_go );   /* Join no_go to end of input word */
        printf( " %s\n", word );
    }
}
```

Figure 13.24.   Password validation: Comparing and copying strings.

3. We define **k** to be a constant, since it is used later in the declaration of **word**, and only constant expressions can be used to define array lengths.

- *Second box: string input.*

    1. The variable **word** is defined to be big enough to hold an entire line of character input plus the error message in **no_go**.
    2. The **scanf()** function reads all the characters typed, up to but not including the end-of-line character, and stores them in **word**. A maximum of 79 characters will be read, to avoid overflowing the buffer. If more characters are typed, the extra ones will remain, unread, in the input stream.

- *Third (outer) box: the comparison.*

    1. **strequal()** takes two string arguments of any variety.

2. The password entered by the user is compared to the constant `PASSW`, which is the current password. If they are equal, `strequal()` returns the value 1 (true). The same test could be expressed using the standard `string` library function `strcmp()` as

```
strcmp( word, PASSW ) == 0
```

People often forget to compare the result of `strcmp()` to 0, making the test the exact opposite of what is intended. The use of `strequal()` reduces this confusion.

3. If the password is correct, the fourth box is executed; if not, the fifth box is.

- *Fourth box: doing the work.* The user now has gained entry into the protected part of the program, which calls the `compose()` function, that actually does the desired work. When the correct password is entered, the beginning of the output of this program is

```
Please enter the password: LoveForEver
Password is correct; go ahead
```

- *Fifth box: processing an incorrect password.*

1. Before printing a response, the error message is appended (using `strcat()`) onto the end of the buffer that contains the erroneous password.
2. This will work without difficulty because the input buffer was declared as a character array with enough slots to hold an entire line of input plus the error message.
3. Here is a sample of beginning output that resulted from entering an incorrect password:

```
Please enter the password: passme
passme is not the password; No Entry!
```

Notes on Figure 13.25. The guys and their message.

- *First and second boxes: guys and their girls.*

1. The first box defines `N`, the number of guys who will be using this program, and `MAXINSERT`, the maximum length of any name in the second box.
2. The second box contains an array of names, one for each guy who wants to use the automated letter writer. If someone is added or deleted, the constant `N`, in the first box, must be adjusted. Also, if a name is longer than `MAXINSERT` letters, that constant must be increased.
3. Parallel to the array of guys are two arrays for their girlfriends' names and nicknames. These must be adjusted simultaneously if any changes are made to the array of guys.

This header file is named `love.h`. It is included by the program in Figure 13.26. It defines a message form, a list of guys who want to send it, and names for the girls who should receive the message.

```
#define N 4                        /* Number of couples */
#define MAXINSERT 15               /* Maximum length of name or pet name */
```

```
/* -----------------------------------------------------------
** Warning:  every name must be no larger than MAXINSERT characters.
*/
const string guys[N] = {"Harold", "Jim", "Jerry", "Charles"};
const string girls[N] = {"Annie", "June", "Leila", "Desiree"};
const string petnames[N] = {"baby", "bug", "lover", "doll"};
```

```
#define L 8                        /* Number of lines in message array */
#define MAXMESSAGE 80              /* Maximum length of line in message array */
```

```
/* -----------------------------------------------------------
** Warning:  every line must be no larger than MAXMESSAGE characters
** and any insertion must be at the end of a line.
*/
const string message[L] = {  /* Insertions must be at end of line. */
    "\n\n ***",
    ",\n\n I need you!  ",
    "\n Every moment without my xxx",
    " is empty!\n Let me back into your life, ***",
    "!  Talk to me!\n You will always be my ***",
    "-xxx",
    "!\n\n ",
    "-- @@@"
};
```

```
#define KISSES "\n XOXOXOX\n "
```

Figure 13.25.   The guys and their message.

    4. Since these arrays will be global after this file is included in a program, we use the `const` qualifier to ensure their integrity.

- *Third and fourth boxes: the message.*

    1. There may be as many sentence fragments as needed, but the actual number must be defined as `L` in this header file.

2. Also given is the constant **MAXMESSAGE**; no line of text in the message array should be longer than this.

3. Each sentence fragment may have at most one field to fill in, and it must be at the end. Newline characters may be anywhere and are used to format the letter so that it reads nicely. Therefore, there is not a one-to-one correspondence between array lines and lines in the final letter.

4. The substring **@@@** will be replaced by a guy's name, while ******* stands for the name of his girlfriend and **xxx** for her pet name.

- *Fifth box:* **KISSES**. This is the traditional symbol for hugs and kisses. This string is appended by default to any line that does not contain an insertion slot.

Notes on Figure 13.26. Composing the love letter.

- *First box: the header file.* We must include the header file that contains the message and the names of the guys and their girls. The **#include** statement is written above this function because none of the rest of the program uses these data arrays. Technically, it could have been written within the function, but that is not considered good style. A separate file was used for these declarations because of the large number and the changeable nature of the database they represent. By using a separate file, we avoid the danger of accidentally changing the source code when intending to change only the database. The **tools.h** file was included at the top of the program. The code in Figure 13.26 will be placed at the end of the program.

- *Second box: the line buffer.* The program constructs and prints the form letter one line at a time. A fully constructed line will contain one string from the message array plus either a name or a string of hugs and kisses. We declare the line buffer as a character array long enough to contain both.

- *Third box: who wants a letter written?* We call the **menu_i()** function to let the user choose one of the **N** guys in the list. Since this function validates the menu choice, we are guaranteed that the return value is OK and can be used safely as a subscript for the parallel name arrays. The output from this part of the program is

```
Form Love Letter

Who needs a letter?
        0. Harold
        1. Jim
        2. Jerry
        3. Charles

Enter number of desired item: 3
```

This function is called from `main()` in Figure 13.24, which asks for and validates a password before it allows entry to this part of the program. The include file is given in Figure 13.25.

```
#include "love.h"

void compose( void )
{
    int k;                      /* line counter */
    int who;                    /* number of guy selected from menu */
    string guy, girl, petname;  /* pointers for fill-in locations */
    char line[MAXMESSAGE + MAXINSERT];   /* Construct output here. */
    puts( "\n Form Love Letter" );
    who = menu_i( " Who needs a letter?", N, guys );

    for (k = 0; k < L; ++k) {
        strcpy( line, message[k] );

        guy = strstr( line, "@@@" );
        girl = strstr( line, "***" );
        petname = strstr( line, "xxx" );

        if (guy != NULL) strcpy( guy, guys[who] );
        else if (girl != NULL) strcpy( girl, girls[who] );
        else if (petname != NULL) strcpy( petname, petnames[who] );
        else strcat( line, KISSES );

        printf( "%s", line );
    }
    puts( "\n" );
}
```

Figure 13.26.   Composing the love letter.

- *Fourth box and inner boxes: filling in the form.*

  1. In the outer box, every message has **L** lines that are constructed and printed one at a time using a loop.
  2. To construct a line, the program first copies the original form, with its substitution markers, into the line buffer, which is long enough to contain this original line plus an insertion. This permits us to modify a copy of the string. We cannot modify the original because it is a literal.

3. The first inner box finds an insertion spot. The function **strstr()** searches a string for a given substring and returns two kinds of information: *whether* the substring occurred in the string and, if so, *where* it starts. The program calls **strstr()** three times to find out whether to substitute a guy's name, a girl's name, or a petname. At most, one of the results will be non-**NULL**. Since only one of these three things can occur, for efficiency's sake, we could write the program to avoid the second and third searches if the first one is successful. However, implementing this strategy complicates the program's logic considerably, so we use the simple but slightly less efficient algorithm.

4. The second inner box substitutes the name. We test the **guy** pointer first to learn whether the current line ends with the substring **"@@@"**. If so, we want to replace the **@** signs by a name from the **guys** array. The **guy** pointer will point at the first **@** sign, so we want to start copying the name in that position and continue to the end of the name. Since the **@** signs always are at the end of the message line and the line buffer is amply long, the name of any guy in the array can be accommodated. For example, for the last line of the letter, the **guy** pointer will be non-**NULL**. We then call **strcpy(guy, guys[who])** to copy the name of the selected guy (Charles, in this case) and its **\0** terminator into the buffer, starting at position **guy**, thus:

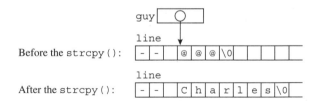

If the **guy** pointer is **NULL**, we test the **girl** pointer (and maybe the **petname** pointer) to identify the insertion slot.

5. If a line contains no insertion spot, the **else** clause appends a line of kisses to it. The following diagram shows how the line buffer would look before and after concatenating the kisses onto the end of the seventh line of the message array:

6. The resulting love letter looks like this:

```
Desiree,

I need you!
XOXOXOX

Every moment without my doll is empty!
Let me back into your life, Desiree!   Talk to me!
You will always be my Desiree-doll!


XOXOXOX
-- Charles
```

13.5.2   Menu Processing and String Parsing

The `switch` statement was introduced back in Section 6.3 as a method of decision making. Putting a `switch` inside a loop is an important control pattern used in menu processing, especially when the menu choices are characters rather than numbers. The loop is used to display the menu repeatedly, until the user wishes to quit, while the `switch` is used to process each selection. One option on the menu should be to quit, that is, to leave the loop.

An example of this control structure is given in Figures 13.27 and 13.28. The program in Figure 13.27 presents a menu and processes selections until the user types the code `q` or `Q`. It illustrates the use of a `for` loop with a `switch` statement inside it to process the selections, a `continue` statement to handle errors, and a `break` statement to quit. This program also shows a use of `strchr()` and `strrchr()` in context.

Notes on Figures 13.27 and 13.28. Magic memo maker and its flow diagram.

- *First box: the menu.*

  1. As usual, a menu consists of an integer, **N**, and a list of **N** strings to be displayed for the user. This menu is designed to be used with `menu_c()`, so each string incorporates both a single-letter code and a brief description of the option.

  2. To add another menu option, we must increase **N**, add a string to the array, and add another case in the switch statement (second box). To make such modifications easier, the declarations have been placed at the top of the program. The `const` qualifier is used to protect them from accidental destruction, since they are global.

- *Second box: the menu loop.* This menu-processing loop is typical and can be adapted to a wide variety of applications. Its basic actions are

This program calls the `compose()` function from Figure 13.29. Its control flow is diagrammed in Figure 13.28.

```
#include "tools.h"      /* contains definition of type string */

void compose( string name, string re, string event );  /* Modifies name. */

#define N 4     /* Number of memo menu choices */
const string menu[N] = {"P  Promote", "T  Trip", "F  Fire", "Q  Done"};

void main( void )
{
    char memo;            /* Menu choice.  */
    string re, event;     /* Subject and main text of memo. */
    char name[52];        /* Employee's complete name. */

    puts( "\n Magic Memo Maker" );

    for(;;) {
        memo = toupper( menu_c( " Next memo:", N, menu ) );
        if (memo == 'Q') break;        /* Leave for loop and end program. */

        switch (memo) {
          case 'P': re = "Promotion";
                    event = "You are being promoted to assistant manager.";
                    break;
          case 'T': re = "Trip";
                    event = "You are tops this year "
                            "and have won a trip to Hawaii.";
                    break;
          case 'F': re = "Downsizing";
                    event = "You're fired.\n "
                            "Pick up your final paycheck from personnel.";
                    break;
          default:  puts( "Illegal menu choice" );
                    continue;
        }

        printf( " Enter name: " );
        scanf( " %51[^\n]", name );
        compose( name, re, event );
    }

    bye();
}
```

Figure 13.27.   Magic memo maker.

This is a flow diagram of the program in Figure 13.27.

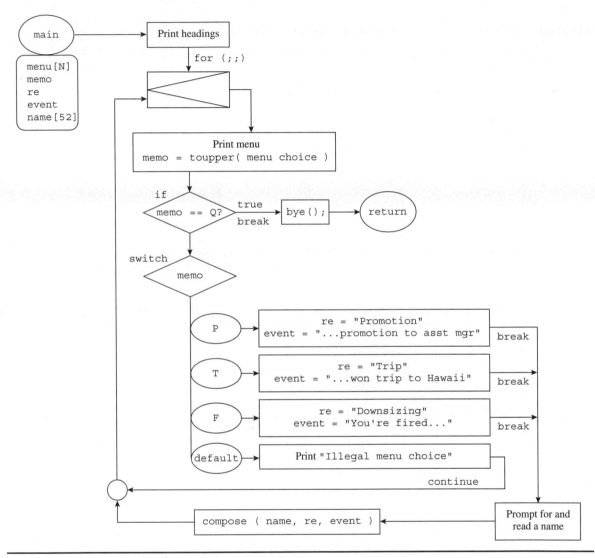

Figure 13.28.   Flow diagram with a menu loop.

1. The first inner box reads the user's choice. We use **menu_c()** to display a menu, return a selection, and break out of the **for** loop to call **bye()** if the user chooses the "Quit" option.
2. The second inner box validates the choice and sets the variables. We use a **switch** to process other possible selections. For each legal

choice, a case should be available that will call a function to process that case or set up the variables needed to process the case later. Here, we set the value of the string **re** for the memo generator:

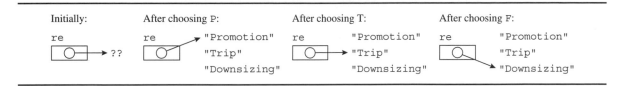

The **break** at the end of each valid case takes control to the processing statements at the bottom of the loop.

3. The default case should print an error comment and **continue**. By going directly back to the loop start, the program avoids the processing actions that come at the end of the loop body. In the flow diagram (Figure 13.28), note how the arrow for **continue** returns to the top of the loop for the menu display rather than going through the process boxes.

4. In the third inner box the request is processed. The common actions for generating the memo are performed after the end of the **switch**. When control reaches this point, invalid menu choices have been eliminated and valid ones fully set up. In this program, we call the **compose()** function to process the request.

- The output from the main program begins like this:

```
Magic Memo Maker
Next memo:

        P    Promote
        T    Trip
        F    Fire
        Q    Done

Enter letter of desired item: T
Enter name: Harvey P. Rabbit, Jr.
```

In Figure 13.29, the memo is composed and processed.

Notes on Figure 13.29. Composing and printing the memo.

- *First box: memo header.*

  1. The program prints a memo header that contains the employee's entire name, the boss's name, and the subject of the memo.
  2. The boss's name is supplied by a **#define** command. The other information is passed as arguments from **main()**.

This function is called from Figure 13.27. As a side effect, the first argument, `name`, is modified.

```
#define BOSS  "Leland Power"
void compose( string name, string re, string event )
{
    string extra, last;            /* Pointers used for parsing name. */
    printf( "\n\n To: %s\n", name );
    printf( " From: The Big Boss\n" );
    printf( " Re: %s\n\n", re );

    extra = strchr( name, ',' );        /* Find end of last name. */
    if (extra != NULL) *extra = '\0';   /* Mark end of last name. */

    last = strrchr( name, ' ' );        /* Find beginning of last name. */
    if (last == NULL) last = name;
    else ++last;

    printf( " Dear M. %s:\n %s\n\n -- %s\n\n", last, event, BOSS );
}
```

Figure 13.29.   Composing and printing the memo.

- *Second box: finding the end of the last name.*

  1. A name can have up to four parts: first name, middle initial (optional), last name, and a comma followed by a title (optional).
  2. For the salutation, we wish to print only the employee's last name, omitting the first name, middle initial, and any titles such as Jr. or V.P. Since the initial and titles are optional, it is a nontrivial task to *locate* the last name and separate it from the rest of the name.
  3. The last name is followed by either a comma or the null terminator that ends the string. We search the name for a comma thus:

```
extra = strchr( name, ',' );
if (extra != NULL) *extra = '\0';
```

  If the result of `strchr()` is `NULL`, we know that the last name is the last thing in the string. Otherwise, the result of `strchr()` is a pointer to the comma. The following diagram shows how the `extra` pointer would be positioned for two sample inputs, with and without "extra" material at the end:

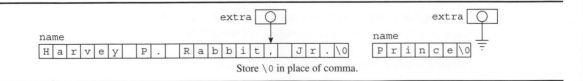

Store \0 in place of comma.

We replace the comma, if it exists, with a null character, using ***extra = '\0'**. We now know for certain that the last name is followed by a null character. This has the side effect of changing the value of the first argument of **compose()** by shortening the string. The part cut off is colored gray in the next diagram. This is an efficient but generally risky technique. Documentation must be provided to warn programmers not to call the function with constants, literal strings, or strings that will be used again. For a safe alternative, see Figure 13.26, where the string is first copied into a local buffer. The local copy then is modified; the original remains unchanged.

- *Third box: the beginning of the last name.*

  1. To find the beginning of the last name, use **strrchr(name, ' ')** to search the (newly shortened) string for the rightmost space. The result is indicated by a dashed arrow in the diagram that follows.

```
last = strrchr( name, ' ' );
if (last == NULL) last = name;
else ++ last;
```

  2. If a space is found, as in the diagram on the left, the last name will be between that space and the (newly written) null terminator. The program then increments the pointer one slot so that it points at the first letter of the name.
  3. If the name has only one part, like Midori or Prince, the result of **strrchr()**, which is stored in **last**, will be **NULL**. In that case, the last name is the first and only thing in the string, so we set **last = name**.

- *Fourth box: printing the memo.* The program now has located the last name and is ready to print the rest of the memo. The event (an input parameter) and the boss's name (given by a **#define** command) are used. Here is a sample output memo:

```
To: Harvey P. Rabbit, Jr.
From: The Big Boss
Re: Trip

Dear M. Rabbit:
You are tops this year and have won a trip to Hawaii.

-- Leland Power
```

Application: A Gas Pressure Table

In this section we develop a program that uses the ideal gas equation to find the pressure of a gas whose volume, mass, and temperature are given. The user will be asked to choose a gas from a menu; this choice will be used to select the proper molecular weight and chemical formula from arrays that parallel the menu array. The problem specifications are given in Figure 13.30.

13.6.1   Step 1. The Test Plan

We list the gases in the menu in alphabetic order, as shown in Figure 13.31. This permits us to write actual menu choice numbers as part of the test plan. Given the constants needed to compute gas pressures using the formulas in the specification, no combination of data values will be easy to calculate in one's head. We can minimize the complexity of one computation for the first test by choosing 1 as the

---

Problem scope: Use the ideal gas equation to find the pressure of 1 cubic meter of a selected gas whose mass and temperature are inputs. The gases to be used are carbon dioxide, carbon monoxide, nitrogen, oxygen, and steam.

Inputs: On each repetition, a gas will be selected from a menu. Its mass and temperature will be entered from the keyboard. Input values will have no more than six digits of precision.

Limitations: Inappropriate menu selections are disallowed. The temperature and mass should be nonnegative.

Constants: $R = 8314$ (Nm/kmol K), the universal gas constant; $V = 1$ cubic meter of gas; also the chemical formula and molecular weight of each gas on the menu.

Formulas:

$$\text{Moles} = \frac{m}{mwt}$$

where m is mass (kg) and mwt is the molecular weight of the gas.

$$\text{Pressure} = \frac{\text{moles} \times R \times t}{V \times 1000}$$

where t is the temperature (degrees Kelvin) and V the volume of the gas (cubic meters). The pressure will be in units of kilopascals (kPa).

Output: The volume, mass, and temperature of the gas should be echoed to two decimal places; the calculated pressure, in kPa, should be printed to three significant digits.

Figure 13.30.   Problem specifications: Gas pressure.

Name of Gas	Menu Choice	Formula	Temperature in Degrees Kelvin	Mass in Kilograms	Calculated Results	
					Moles	Pressure (kPa)
Carbon dioxide	0	C_O2	100	1.00	0.02272	18.88941
Carbon monoxide	1	C_O	1	0.01	0.000357	0.002968
(Error)	5					
(Error)	−1					
(Error)	2		−1	1		
(Error)	1		1	−1		
Nitrogen	2	N2	250	2.00	0.07140	148.39539
Oxygen	3	O2	500	0.50	0.01563	64.95515
Steam	4	H2_O	200	1.00	0.05551	92.30086

Figure 13.31.   Test plan for the gas pressure program.

mass and 100 as the temperature. One division and one multiplication on a pocket calculator give us an answer for the first line of the test plan. On the second line of the plan, we enter a different gas and very small inputs. Then we test illegal menu choices, with one selection too large and one too small. Finally, we test the three remaining menu selections with varying input values (some invalid) to fill in the final lines of this plan.

13.6.2   Step 2. The Main Program

The specification calls for a series of inputs, so we decide to use a `work()` function to separate the repetition from the process itself. We write the entire `main()` function by only slightly modifying the improved workmaster in Figure 11.7 to include a new table of constant definitions. The result is shown in Figure 13.32.

13.6.3   Step 3. The Gas Table

We need one column (one array) in the gas table for each gas property used in the equations and one line in the menu (therefore, one element in each array) for each gas handled. We start by defining `N` to be 5, the number of gases, and declaring an array named `menu` to contain the names of the `N` gases (quoted strings). We also declare an array of molecular weights named `mwt` that is parallel to the `menu` array.

Representing chemical formulas is not as straightforward as representing names or numbers, because the formulas contain subscripts that cannot be printed in ordinary computer fonts. We decided to separate elemental components with an underscore and follow a component with a numeral where a subscript normally would be. The final declarations follow:

The specification is in Figure 13.30; the `work()` function is in Figure 13.33.

```
#include "tools.h"

#define R  8314              /* universal gas constant (Nm/kmol · K) */
#define V  1.00              /* Use volume of 1 cubic meter */

void work( void );

void main( void )
{
    char do_more;

    banner();
    puts( "\n Gas Pressure Calculation" );
    do {
        work();
        printf( "\n Do you want more calculations (y/n)? " );
        scanf( " %c", &do_more );
    } while (tolower( do_more ) != 'n');
    bye();
}
```

Figure 13.32.   Gas pressures.

```
/* ------ Table of gases for the pressure program.  ---- */
#define N 5       /* number of gases in the menu */
string menu[N] ={ "carbon dioxide", "carbon monoxide",
                  "nitrogen", "oxygen", "steam"};
string formula[N] = { "C_O2", "C_O", "N2", "O2", "H2_O" };
float mwt[N] =  { 44.011, 28.011, 28.013, 31.999, 18.015 };
```

We group the `#define` with these three arrays to form the gas table and write a comment as a heading. This table will become part of the `work()` function, since no other function needs access to it.

13.6.4 Step 4. The `work()` Function

The `work()` function is in Figure 13.33. The work to be done is choose a gas, input its temperature and mass, calculate the pressure, and print the answer. We will approach these steps in order, defining constants and variables as needed.

Using the menu.   Because it is much easier than writing out the code to present a menu, we decide to use the `menu_i()` function. We must declare a variable named **choice** to store the value returned by `menu_i()`. The call on `menu_i()` requires three arguments:

1. A title for the menu; we write this as a string literal in the function call.

2. The length, **N**, of the menu.
3. The name of an array that contains the menu items, in this case, **menu**.

The resulting code is

```
int choice;              /* for the menu selection */
choice = menu_i( " Please choose a gas:", N, menu );
```

Input. The specification calls for two input values. We declare variables and write the appropriate prompts and **scanf()** statements. A simple test is made for illegal inputs; if found, an error response is given and control is returned to the query loop in main.

```
float temp;              /* temperature of gas, Kelvin */
float mass;              /* mass in kilograms */
printf( "\n Input the temperature in Kelvin: " );
scanf( "%g", &temp );
printf( "\n Input the mass in kilograms: " );
scanf( "%g", &mass );
if (temp <= 0 || mass <= 0) {
    printf( " Inputs can't be negative, try again.\n" );
    return;
}
```

Computation. To implement the formulas, we need two more variables:

```
float moles;             /* number of kmol of gas */
float pres;              /* pressure, in kilopascals */
```

We already added a definition of the constant **R** at the top of the file. The formula for pressure uses the volume of the gas, which was specified as 1 cubic meter. We could have substituted 1.0 for *V* in the formula. However, we chose to **#define** **v** as 1.0 instead, in case we want to extend this program or change the volume later. This definition also is placed at the top of the file. The formula for moles uses the molecular weight of the selected gas. We get this weight by using the menu choice as a subscript for the **mwt** array. The rest of the computations are routine and we arrive at this code:

```
moles = mass / mwt[choice];                /* kmol */
pres = (moles * R * temp) / (V * 1000);    /* kPa */
```

Output. Following good output design principles, we incorporate the input values as part of the output. We also display the formula for the chosen gas, which we get by using the menu choice as a subscript into the array of formulas. We make sure to format the numbers with the specified precision.

```
printf( "\n For %.2f kg of %s\n", mass, formula[choice] );
printf( "    in %.2f cubic meters at %.2f K,\n", V, temp );
printf( "    pressure is %.3g kPa.\n", pres );
```

This function is called from Figure 13.32 and carries out the specification in Figure 13.30. Each box encloses the results of one development step.

```c
void work( void )
{
    int choice;              /* for the menu selection */
    float temp;              /* temperature of gas, Kelvin */
    float mass;              /* mass in kilograms */
    float moles;             /* number of kmol of gas */
    float pres;              /* pressure, in kilopascals */

    /* ------ Table of gases for the pressure program.  ------ */
    #define N 5              /* number of gases in the menu */
    string menu[N] =     { "carbon dioxide", "carbon monoxide",
                           "nitrogen", "oxygen", "steam"};
    string formula[N] = { "C_O2", "C_O", "N2", "O2", "H2_O" };
    float mwt[N] =       { 44.011, 28.011, 28.013, 31.999, 18.015 };

    choice = menu_i( " Please choose a gas:", N, menu );

    printf( "\n Input the temperature in Kelvin: " );
    scanf( "%g", &temp );
    printf( "\n Input the mass in kilograms: " );
    scanf( "%g", &mass );
    if (temp <= 0 || mass <= 0) {
        printf( " Inputs can't be negative, try again.\n" );
        return;
    }

    moles = mass / mwt[choice];                /* kmol */
    pres = (moles * R * temp) / (V * 1000);    /* kPa */

    printf( "\n For %.2f kg of %s\n", mass, formula[choice] );
    printf( "    in %.2f cubic meters at %.2f K,\n", V, temp );
    printf( "    pressure is %.3g kPa.\n", pres );
}
```

Figure 13.33.   Calculating gas pressure.

13.6.5   Step 5. Testing the Program

The **main()** function from Figure 13.32 is entered into a file, followed by the completed **work()** function, shown in Figure 13.33. We compile them, correcting typographical and syntax errors in the process, and begin execution with the first line of the test plan. The output of the first test case is shown here without the banner:

```
Gas Pressure Calculation

Please choose a gas:
        0. carbon dioxide
        1. carbon monoxide
        2. nitrogen
        3. oxygen
        4. steam

Enter number of desired item: 0

Input the temperature in Kelvin: 100
Input the mass in kilograms: 1.00

For 1.00 kg of C_O2
   in 1.00 cubic meters at 100.00 K,
   pressure is 18.9 kPa.

Do you want more calculations (y/n)?
```

We compared the hand-calculated answer (18.88941) to the program's answer (18.9). They are equal up to the third significant digit, which was rounded off to fit the `%.3g` field specifier. To continue with the plan, we keyed in a **y** (the results of the remaining tests are not shown here). The erroneous menu choices were trapped properly by the **menu_i()** function, which redisplayed the menu, until a correct choice was made. The negative inputs were trapped properly by the data validation test. The rest of the testing was uneventful. Answers displayed by the program agreed with the calculated answers when they were rounded to three digits of precision. The output was acceptably neat and readable, so we pronounced the program finished. Had we made mistakes, we would have detected and corrected the problem when the result of a particular line in the test plan produced an unexplained result. If better output formatting were needed, we would have improved it as a last step.

13.7   What You Should Remember

13.7.1 Major Concepts

- The type **string** is not a built-in data type, but C has functions to support many of the basic operations that exist for built-in types.
- The standard **string** library, whose header file is **string.h**, contains many useful functions for operating on strings. In this chapter, we note the following:

To find the number of characters in a string, use **strlen()**. (Note that **sizeof** gives the size of the pointer part.)

To search a string for a given character or substring, use **strchr()**, **strrchr()**, and **strstr()**.

To compare two strings for alphabetic order, use **strcmp()** and **strncmp()**. (Note that **==** tells only whether two string pointers point at the same slot in an array.)

To copy a string or a part of a string, use **strcpy()**, **strncpy()**, **strcat()**, and **strncat()**. (Note that **=** copies only the pointer part of the string and cannot be used to copy an array.)

- A character array may be initialized with a string literal. The length of the array must be at least one longer than the number of letters in the string to allow for the null terminator.
- Literal strings, string variables, and character arrays all are called *strings*. However, these objects have very different properties and are not fully interchangeable.
- In memory, a string is represented as a pointer to a null-terminated array of characters.
- A string variable is a pointer and must be set to point at some referent before it can be used. The referent can be either a quoted string or a character array.
- The operators that work on the pointer part of a string are different from the functions that do analogous jobs on the array part.
- An array of strings, or ragged array, is a compound data structure that often saves memory space over an array of fixed-length strings. Common uses include printing enumerated types and representing menus.
- An essential part of interactive programs is the display of a menu to provide choices to the user. A **switch** statement embedded in a loop is a common control structure for processing menus. The menu display and choice selection continue until the user picks a termination option.

13.7.2 Programming Style

- A loop that processes all of the characters in a string typically is a sentinel loop that stops at the null terminator. Many string functions operate in this manner.
- Use the "zero" literal of the correct type. Use **NULL** for pointers, \0 for characters, and **" "** for strings. Reserve **0** for use as an integer.
- Use the **typedef** name **string** instead of **char*** for variables. This definition is in **tools.h**; when you include this file in your program, you can use **string** as an ordinary type name without writing your own **typedef** statement.

- You can use a string literal to initialize a character array or a string variable. For the array, this is preferable to a sequence of individually quoted characters.
- It is not possible to change the contents of a string literal.
- Adjacent string literals will be merged. This is helpful in breaking up long output formats in a `printf()` statement.
- Use `char[]` as a parameter type when the argument is a character array that may be modified. Use `char*` when the argument is a literal or a string that should not be modified.
- Declare a `char` array to hold text input or for character manipulation and take precautions that the operations will not go past the last array slot. Do not attempt to store input in a `char*` variable.
- Using the brackets specifier makes `scanf()` quite versatile, allowing you to control the number of characters read as well as the character or characters that will terminate the input operation.
- A menu-driven program provides a convenient, clear user interface. To use a menu, a list of options must be displayed where each option is associated with a code. The user is instructed to select and key in a code, which then is used to control the program's actions. Having one option on the menu to either quit or do nothing is common practice. User selections should be validated.
- One or more data arrays parallel to a menu array can be used to make calculations based on a table of data. Each array in the set represents one column in the table that relates to one data property. If integer selections are used, the items in the arrays can be indexed directly using the choice value.
- The process of using a menu is much the same for all menu applications. The `tools` library contains two menu functions that automate the process, `menu_i()` for numeric codes and `menu_c()` for alphabetic codes. The ragged arrays used for menus should be declared as `const` if they are defined globally.

13.7.3   Sticky Points and Common Errors

These errors are based on a misunderstanding of the nature of strings.

- *Ampersand errors.* When using `scanf()` with `%s` to read a string, the argument must be an array of characters. Do *not* use an ampersand with the array name, because all arrays are passed by address. A character pointer (a string) can be used as an argument to `scanf()`, but it first must be initialized to point at a character array. Do *not* use an ampersand with this pointer because a pointer already is an address, and `scanf()` does not want the address of an address.

- *String input overflow.* When reading a string as input, limit the length of the input to one less than the number of bytes available in the array that will store the data. (One byte is needed for the null character that terminates the string.) C provides some input operations, such as `gets()`, that should not be used in cases of unknown input length because there is no way to limit the amount of data read. If an input operation overflows the storage, it will destroy other data or crash the program.
- *No room for the null character.* When you allocate an array to store string data, be sure to leave space for the null terminator. Remember that most of the library functions that read and copy strings store a null character at the end of the data.
- *A pointer cannot store character data.* Be careful to distinguish between a character array and a variable of type `char*`. The first can store a whole sequence of characters; the second cannot. A `char*` variable can only be used to point at a literal or a character array that has already been created.
- *Subscript validation.* If the choice for a menu is not validated and if it is used to index an array, then an erroneous choice will result in accessing a location outside of the array bounds. This may cause almost any kind of error, from garbage in the output to an immediate crash.
- *The correct string operator.* Strings can be considered in memory as two-part objects. The operations used on each part are different:

  To find the size of the pointer part, use `sizeof`; for the array part use `strlen()`.

  Remember to use the `==` operator when comparing the pointer parts, but use `strequal()` or `strcmp()` to compare the array parts. When using `strcmp()` remember to compare the result to 0 when testing for equality.

  To copy the pointer part of a string, use `=`; to copy the array part, use `strcpy()` or `strncpy()`. Make sure the destination array is long enough to hold the result.

The following table summarizes the syntax for initializing, assigning, or copying a string:

Operation	With a `char` Array	With a `char*`
Initialization	`char word[10] = "Hello";`	`char* message = "circle";`
Assignment	Does not copy the letters	`message = "square";`
	Cannot do `word = "Hello"`	
		`char* message = word;`
String copy	`strcpy( word, "Bye" );`	`strcpy( message, "Thanks" );`
String comparison	`strcmp( word, "Bye" )`	`message = word`

• *Quoting.* A string containing one character is not the same as a single character. The string also contains a null terminator. Be sure to write single quotes when you want a character and double quotes when you want a string. The double quotes tell C to append a null terminator. You can embed quotation marks within a string, but you must use an escape character. Also, be careful to end all strings properly, or you may find an unwanted comment in the output.

13.7.4 New and Revisited Vocabulary

These are the most important terms and concepts presented or discussed in this chapter:

string	null string	C `string` library
string literal	**NULL** pointer	string `tools`
string merging	conversion specifier	array of strings
two-part object	right and left justification	ragged array
type expression	string variable	enumerated type
null terminator	string assignment	parallel arrays
null character	string comparison	menu selection validation

The following keywords, C library functions, and functions from the `tools` library are discussed in this chapter.

`puts()`	`strcmp()`	`==` (on strings)
`\"` and `\0`	`strncmp()`	`=` (on strings)
`char *`	`strcpy()`	`strequal()`
`typedef`	`strncpy()`	`time()`
`gets()`	`strcat()`	`ctime()`
`char []`	`strncat()`	`today()`
`printf()` `%s` conversion	`strchr()`	`oclock()`
`scanf()` `%s` conversion	`strrchr()`	`when()`
`scanf %[^?]` conversion	`strstr()`	`menu_c()`
`strlen()`	`sizeof` a string	`menu_i()`

13.8   Exercises

13.8.1 Self-Test Exercises

1. a. Given the following declarations and `printf()` statements, what is printed?

```
string s[4] = {"hello", "help", "save me", "groan"};
char t[] = "help";
string p = s[3];
```

```
printf( "%4s?\n", s[0] );
printf( "%s!  ", p );
printf( "%10s ", s[2] );
printf( "%i", t == s[1] );
printf( "%c!\n", s[0][0] );
```

b. The following statement will compile with no errors, but it will not work properly. What is wrong?

```
char t[5] = "wait";
strcpy( t, "finished" );
```

2. You wish to read either a single word or a name consisting of two or three words separated by spaces. Given the declarations shown, find and fix the errors in the following **scanf()** statements.

```
char word[10], name[20];
string w = word; /* Make w point at first char in word */
string t;
```

a. scanf("%s", t);   /* Read a single word. */
b. scanf("%9s", &word);   /* Read a single word. */
c. scanf("%19s", name);   /* Read first, middle, last. */
d. scanf("%9s", &w);   /* Read a single word. */
e. scanf("%[^\n]", name); /* Read entire name. */

3. Using these variables,

```
string message;
int v;
```

write an **if** statement that will select the string **"good"** if the value of **v** is between 1 and 10, and the string **"bad"** otherwise. Then write a single **printf()** statement that will print the selected message.

4. Given the declarations shown, find and fix the errors in the following statements.

```
char name[12] = "";
char word[10] = "harmony";
string w = word; /* Make w point at first char in word */
string t;
```

a. if (strequal(t, w)) puts("Same words here.");

b. t = '\0';

c. name = word;

d. strncpy(word, name, 10);

e. if (strcmp(name, word)) puts("Same words here.");

f. strcpy(w, &name);

5. Given the declarations shown for exercise 4, determine whether each of the following statements is true or false. If false, supply the correct answer.

a. `sizeof` **w** is 4.

b. `sizeof` **name** is 12.

c. `sizeof` **word** is 8.

d. `strlen( w )` is 10.

e. `strlen( name )` is 0.

f. `strlen( word )` is 10.

6. Trace the program that follows and show the output produced. Also, make a diagram (or several) of the message string. Use it to show the referent of each pointer after a string operation and the change in the letters of the message after each assignment.

```
#include "tools.h"

void main( void )
{
    char mess[] =
        "Yes, I would truly love to see you on Friday.";
    string p1, p2, p3, p4, p5;

    p1 = strstr( mess, "to" );   *p1 = 'd';
    p2 = strchr( p1, 'y' );
    p3 = strchr( p2, ' ' );       *p3 = p1[2] = '\0';

    p3 = strrchr( mess, 'l' );   *(p1-1) = *(p3-1) = '\0';
    p4 = strchr( mess, ' ' );    *p4 = '\0';   p4++;
    p5 = strchr( p4, 't' );

    printf( "%c %s %s\n", *p4, p3, p2 );
    printf( "%s %c %s\n", mess, *p4, p1 );

    strcpy( mess, "Drew" );
    printf( "%c %s %s %s %s!\n", *p4, p3, p2, p5, mess );
}
```

7. You are writing an interactive program to be used by the Baloo Balloon telephone order service. Right now, you are implementing only the user interface. The operator will answer the phone and take care of customers' needs. The program eventually will have functions for taking orders, canceling orders, checking on standing orders, and making complaints. At the end of the day, the operator must shut down the program before going home.

a. Define an array of strings to implement a menu for the operator's use.

b. Write a loop containing a call on a menu function to display the menu and a `switch` statement to process the menu selection. Assume that you will have functions to do the four tasks listed above. Be sure that invalid responses are handled properly, either here or by the menu function.

c. Draw a flowchart of your loop.

8. The following partially completed program analyzes whether a box is big enough in each dimension to hold some piece of equipment whose dimensions are given by the array **mindims**. A box can be impossible, too short, too skinny, too flat, or big enough. Fill in some of the missing parts as follows:

a. Define an array of output messages parallel to the **dim_type** enumeration given in the code.

b. Define an array of strings for the names of the dimensions that can be used to print a comment when a dimension is too small. Your comment should be like this: **" Your length is 2.6; minimum is 12 "**.

c. Write a function, **analyze()**, according to the prototype given. It should use a loop to compare each actual dimension with the corresponding minimum. Print an error comment for each inadequate dimension, using your string array and the format **"Your %s is %g; minimum is %g\n"**. Return an appropriate enumeration constant (if more than one is appropriate, return any one).

d. Complete the **printf()** statement on the last line to print out the results of the dimensional analysis. Print one of the labels from your message array.

```c
#include <stdio.h>
typedef enum {ERROR, SHORT, SKINNY, FLAT, GOOD} dim_type;

dim_type analyze( double box[], double min[] );

void main( void )
{
    double mindims[] = {12, 10, 6};   /* l*w*h */
    double box[3];    /* Dimensions of the box. */
    dim_type result; /* Are dimensions big enough? */

    printf( " Enter the box dimensions: " );
    scanf( "%lg%lg%lg", &box[0], &box[1], &box[2] );
    result = analyze( box, mindims );
    printf( ... );
}
```

13.8.2   Using Pencil and Paper

1. You are writing an interactive program to search a database. At any time, the user will have several options: quit, ask for help, or perform a search based on title, author, or subject.

a. Define an array of strings to implement a menu for this program.

b. Write a call on a menu function to display the menu and receive a response.

c. Write a **switch** statement to process the menu selection. Pretend that there are functions you can call to process each case. Be sure that invalid responses are handled properly, either here or by the menu function.

2. The following are a set of declarations, a list of tasks (on the left), and input lines (on the right). Write a single **scanf()** statement that can perform each task correctly if given the corresponding input.

```
char sentence[80], w1[10], w2[10], c1, c2;
```

(a) Read entire line into **sentence**.   The house, I know, is red.
(b) Read the first word into **w1**, safely.   Paderewski's dog is black.
(c) Using different conversion specifiers,   Ho! Where did you come from?
     read the first two words into **w1** and **w2**.
(d) Read all but the last word into **sentence**.   Happy day, I can get zzzzz.
(e) Read the initials into **c1** and **c2** and the   T. P. Hammond
     name into **w1**.

3. Trace the program that follows. After each of the three groups of statements, diagram the array and the positions of the pointers **p1**, **p2**, and **p3** relative to the message array.

```
#include "tools.h"
void main( void )
{
    char mess[] = "Murphy Brown had a baby "
                  "and the President had a cow.";
    string p1, p2, p3;

    p1 = strstr( mess, "ow" );
    p2 = strstr( p1, "ow" );
    p3 = strstr( p1+1, "ow"  );

    p1 = strchr( mess, ' ' );
    p2 = strchr( p1, 'r' );
    p3 = strrchr(p1, 'r' );

    p1 = strstr( mess, " and" ) ;
    *p1 = '\0';
    p2 = strrchr( mess, ' ' );
    strcpy( p2, " zoo" );
}
```

4. What is the **sizeof** each of the following:

a. `char a[] = { 'Z', 'e', 'r', 'o' };`

b. `char a[] = "One";`

c. `char a[6] = "Two";`

d. `string c = "Three";`

e. `string d[3];`

5. Show the output produced by the following program:

```
#include "tools.h"
void main( void )
{
    int k;
    string p;
    char line[80] = "";
    string word[] =
        {" attention","like","sleep","eat","dogs "};
    for (k = 4; k >= 0; --k) {
        strcat( line, word[k] );
        if (k < 4 && k > 1) strcat( line, " and " );
    }
    printf( "%s.\n", line );

    strcpy( line, "I want to eat horses." );
    strncpy( &line[10], "seek", 3 );
    p = strrchr( line, 'r' );
    *p = 'u';
    puts( line );
}
```

6. What is the output from the following program?

```
#include "tools.h"
void stutter( char w[], int n );

void main( void )
{
    string s = "Hello";
    char word[10] = "Goodbye";
    puts( "\n--------------" );
    stutter( s, 3 );
    stutter( word, strlen( s ) );
    puts( "\n--------------" );
}
/* ------------------------------------- */
void stutter( char w[], int n )
{
    int k;
    for(k = 0; k < n; ++k) printf( "%s", w );
}
```

7. Given the variables **action** and **task** declared in the following, determine whether each of the listed operations is legal and meaningful.

```
char t[10] = "wait";
string action = t;
char* task = "mail"
```

a. `action = "go";`

b. `*action = 'b';`

c. `scanf( "%9s", action );`

d. `printf( "%s\n", action );`

e. `task = "go";`

f. `*task = 'b';`

g. `scanf( "%9s", task );`

h. `printf( "%s\n", task );`

13.8.3   Using the Computer

1. A better banner.

   a. Get a copy of **banner()** from **tools.c**. Write a new version to print the following output header that is customized to include your lab assignment number and title, as well as your name, course number, and the date. The revised banner will look like this:

   ```
   - - - - - - - - - - - - - - - - - - - - - - - - - - - - - - - - - - -
                   Mary Jane Talmadge
                   CS 110
                   Lab 8: My New Banner
                   Mon Jul 29 2004  11:40:18
   - - - - - - - - - - - - - - - - - - - - - - - - - - - - - - - - - - -
   ```

   The new function should take the lab number and title as parameters (the other information still is in the **#define** statements in **tools.h**). The new prototype should be

   `void banner( int lab_no, string title );`

   b. Put your **banner()** function into **tools.c** in place of the simple version already there. Call it at the beginning of each program you write from now on.

   c. Put the new prototype for **banner()** into **tools.h** in place of the old one.

   d. Test your function by calling it from some program you have already debugged. Revise the call on **banner()** in that program by adding appropriate arguments (the number and name of that program).

2. A string search.
   Write a function, **rightmost()**, that has two input parameters (a character and a string) and one output parameter (an integer). Search the argument string for copies of the specified character and count the number of occurrences. If the number is nonzero, return the subscript of the rightmost occurrence through the output parameter. Return the number of occurrences as the value of the function. Write a main program with a query loop to permit you to test the **rightmost()** function.

3. Which is longer?

   a. Write a function, `lencmp()`, that has two string parameters. It should return a positive number if the first string is longer than the second, 0 if they are the same length, and a negative value if the second is longer.

   b. Write a function, `longer()`, that has two **string** parameters and returns a value of type **string**. It should call `lencmp()` to compare the lengths of the two strings and return a pointer to the longer one.

   c. Write a main program with a query loop to permit you to test these two functions.

4. Substitution.
   Write a function, `substitute()`, that has three parameters: two characters and a string. It should search the string for copies of the first character, and change them all to the second character. Return the number of times a substitution was made. This function might be part of a larger hangman or cryptogram program.

   Write a main program with a query loop to permit you to replace several letters in the same sentence. For each data set, prompt the user to enter two characters, the letter to find, and its replacement.

5. Cost estimate.

   a. Define a pair of parallel arrays that will be used for estimating the cost of a repair job. The first array should contain the names of various parts; the second array, the price of each part. For example, these arrays might contain data like this:

   ```
   { "muffler", "oil filter", "spark plugs", ... }
   { 39.95, 4.95, 6.00, ... }
   ```

   b. Write a program that will present a menu of parts for the user, then permit him or her to select any number of parts from the menu. After selecting a part, the program should prompt for the quantity of that part (one or more) that will be used for the repair, calculate the price for those parts, and add it to a total price. When the user selects "Done" from the menu, print the total price of all parts needed, with a sales tax of 6%.

6. Waves.
   A tight string (e.g., a guitar string) exhibits transverse wave motion when plucked. Write a program to compute the wave speed for a plucked string according to the following instructions.

   • The **main()** function should use a menu to input the string type from the following list, then prompt for the diameter and tension of the string, testing for valid entries (all greater than 0). Use a parallel array to store the densities of the metals given in the table.

Metal	Density in kg/m^3
Copper	8933
Aluminum	2702
Platinum	21450
Steel	7854
Lead	11340

Retrieve the appropriate density using a subscript and use it to call the **mass()** function to compute m_{len}. Then call the **speed()** function to compute the wave speed for these inputs. Finally, print the wave speed and the metal type.

- Define a function, **mass()**, that has two parameters, ρ and d, which will compute m_{len}, the mass per unit of length, according to this formula:

$$m_{len} = \frac{\pi \times \rho \times d^2}{4}$$

where ρ is the density (kg/m^3) of the string and d is its diameter (m).

- Define a function **speed()** to take two parameters: F and m_{len}. Compute the speed of movement of a string according to the formula:

$$\text{Speed} = \left(\frac{F}{m_{len}}\right)^{\frac{1}{2}} \quad \text{(m/s)}$$

where F is the tension (N) in the string and m_{len} (kg/m) is the mass per unit length of the metal string.

7. Metric to English.

The following table lists the factors for converting a variety of metric measurement units to the English equivalents. To perform the opposite conversion, you simply divide (rather than multiply) by the given factor. Implement this table as three global arrays of constant strings with a parallel array of constant **double**s.

To Convert	From	To	Multiply By
Acceleration	m/s^2	ft/s^2	3.281
Area	m^2	ft^2	10.76
Density	kg/m^3	lbm/ft^3	0.06243
Energy	J	Btu	9.478E$-$4
Force	N	lbf	0.2248
Length	m	ft	3.281
Length	m	mile	6.214E$-$4
Mass	kg	lbm	2.205
Power	W	hp	1.341E$-$3
Pressure	N/m^2	lb/in^2	1.450E$-$4
Velocity	m/s	ft/s	3.281
Velocity	m/s	mph	2.237

Write a program that will present a menu of possible conversions to the user and permit selection of one. Then ask whether he or she wishes to convert from metric to English units or from English to metric. Finally, prompt the user to enter a measurement and convert it. Continue presenting the menu until the user selects the "Quit" option.

8. Compression.

A spark ignition internal combustion engine can be modelled thermodynamically as an Otto cycle. An analysis of this cycle can be made by assuming that the ideal gas equation of state is valid, no frictional effects occur, and no gases are lost through intake or exhaust valves. The efficiency of the cycle, eta, is defined to be the net work produced divided by the heat added. We can calculate it thus:

$$\text{Eta} = 1 - \frac{1}{r^{k-1}}$$

where r is the compression ratio (volume in cylinder at bottom dead center divided by volume at top dead center) and k is the specific heat ratio of the gas.

a. Define a function, **eta()**, with two parameters, r and k, that will compute the efficiency of the cycle.

b. Write a main program as follows:

- Implement a menu to let the user choose one of the following gases. Also, define a parallel array for the specific heat values.

Gas	k Value
Air	1.401
Hydrogen	1.416
Oxygen	1.398
Carbon dioxide	1.314

- Implement the calculations using Figure 13.33 as a guide. Let the user select a gas and use the choice number as a subscript to get its k value.
- Obtain output for values of $r = 1, 2, 3, 5, 10, 100,$ and $1,000$. Note that eta approaches 1 (i.e., 100%) as r increases. Print the efficiency values returned by **eta()** in a neat table.

9. Deflection of a Cantilever Beam for Different Cross Sections and Materials. Write a program that will calculate the deflection of the end of a cantilevered steel beam projecting horizontally from a vertical wall as follows. The beam is a solid having a cross section in the shape of a rectangle, a circle, or an equilateral triangle. An analysis of the beam based on Hooke's law of stress and strain gives an equation for δ (delta), the deflection of the end of the beam due to a vertical downward force, F:

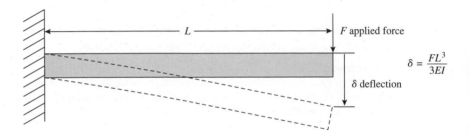

where F is the applied force (N), L is the beam length (m), E is Young's modulus (a property of the material, N/m^2), and I is the moment of inertia (a property of the geometry of the cross-sectional area, m^4).

a. Write three functions, one for each of the cross-sectional areas, as shown. Each function should prompt for the values of **b**, **h**, or **a**, as appropriate, and validate that the inputs are positive. Return the moment of inertia to the main program. Use the formulas for moments of inertia shown adjacent to each shape.

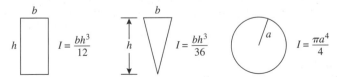

b. Use an array to store Young's modulus, E, for the following materials:

Material	$(E \times 10^9$ N/m$^2)$
Steel (cold rolled)	204
Brass (70–30)	109
Aluminum alloy	68.9
Molybdenum	345

c. The main program should ask the user to choose from one menu for materials, then from a second menu for the cross-section shape (**r=rectangle**, **t=triangle**, or **c=circle**). Use a numeric menu for the first choice, a character menu for the second. Last, prompt the user for the length and applied force (both must be greater than 0.0). Use validation loops for all inputs. Use a **switch** statement to call the appropriate cross-section function based on the second menu choice and compute the deflection amount based on a value of E from the first choice, I computed for the second choice, and the input values of F and L. Finally, print the resulting value of δ.

10. Resistance.
The electrical resistance of a pure metal increases with temperature. In the temperature range most commonly considered in engineering and science, it is observed that this relationship is a linear function: $R_T = R_0(1 + aT)$, where R_T is the resistance, in ohms, at any temperature; T (°C); R_0 is the resistance at 0°C; and a is the temperature resistance coefficient (1/°C). The value of the constant a for some common substances is given in this table:

Metal	a	ρ
Aluminum	0.00403	2.828E−02
Brass	0.00150	6.210E−02
Copper	0.00393	1.724E−02
Mercury	0.00089	96.8E−02
Steel	0.00160	15.9E−02

Using simple algebra, we can use this equation to find a formula for R_T/R_0. In addition, at a fixed temperature, T, resistance also is a function of the length of the wire, L (m); its cross-sectional area, A (m^2); and the resistivity, ρ (ohm -m), given in the table. The full equation is

$$R_p = (\rho \times L/A) \times 10^{-6} \quad \text{(ohms)}$$

Using Figures 13.32 and 13.33 as a guide, and following these steps, write a program that will calculate the resistance of a wire:

a. Define a set of global constant parallel arrays to implement the columns of the table. These constant arrays should go at the top of your program, above **main()**.

b. Following the form of Figure 13.32, write a main program that will repeat a resistance calculation (the work) as many times as desired.

c. In your **work()** function, incorporate a menu that will display the list of metal names and read the number of a chosen metal. Then display a second menu that will permit the user to choose to calculate *either* the ratio R_T/R_0 or R_p. Based on the choice, call one of the functions described next. Echo the inputs and constants used from the table and print the chosen result.

d. Write a function with one parameter, the menu choice, that calculates the ratio R_T/R_0. Read a temperature, $-20°C \leq T \leq 500°C$, then calculate the value of R_T/R_0 using the argument value to get a from the table.

e. Write another function with one parameter, the menu choice, that calculates R_p. Read the length of the wire, $1 \text{ m} \leq L \leq 1000 \text{ m}$, and its cross-sectional area, $0.0 < A \leq 0.1 \text{ m}^2$. Then use the preceding formula to calculate R_p for the given inputs and ρ from the table.

CHAPTER

14

Structured Types

We have discussed two kinds of aggregate data objects so far: arrays and strings. This chapter introduces a third important **aggregate type**: structures. Unlike an array, in which all parts have the same type, the components of a **structure** generally are of **aggregate** (mixed) **types**. Also, while the elements of an array are numbered and referred to by a subscript, the parts of a structure are given individual names. We examine how structures are represented, which operations apply to them, and how to combine arrays with structures in a compound object.

14.1 Declarations

Structures provide a coherent way to represent the different properties of a single object. A `struct` variable is composed of a series of slots, called **members**, each representing one property of the object. Members also may be called *fields* or *components*.

A structure type specification starts with the keyword `struct`, followed by an optional identifier called the **tag name**, followed by the member declarations enclosed in curly brackets. All this normally is written as part of a `typedef` declaration, which gives another name, the **typedef name**, to the type. The members can be almost any combination of data types, as in Figure 14.1. Members even can be arrays or other types of structures. However, a structure cannot contain

```
                        Tag name
                         ⌒
    typedef struct BOX {
                        int length, width, height;  ⎫
                        float weight;               ⎬ Members
                        ...                         ⎪
                        char contents[32];          ⎭
    } box_type;
      ‿‿‿‿‿‿
      typedef name
```

Figure 14.1. Modern syntax for a `struct` declaration.

a member of the type it is defining (the type of a part cannot be the same as the type of the whole). A new type name, defined using **typedef** and **struct**, may be used like a built-in type name to

1. Declare and initialize a structured variable.
2. Create and, optionally, initialize an array of structures.

Before the **typedef** was introduced into C, the tag name was the only way to refer to a structured type. Using tag names is syntactically awkward because the keyword **struct** must be used every time the tag name is used. For example, a type definition and variable declaration might look like this:

struct NAME { char first[16]; char last[16]; } boy;

or they could be given separately, like this:

struct NAME { char first[16]; char last[16]; };
struct NAME boy;

Today, tag names are not used as much because **typedef** is less error prone and serves most of the purposes of tag names. Tag names have two remaining important uses. If one is given, some on-line debuggers provide more informative feedback. They also are useful for defining recursive types such as trees and linked lists.[1] When present, the tag name should be related to the **typedef** name. Naming style has varied; the most recent seems to be to write tag names in upper case and **typedef** names in lower case. We supply tag names with no further comment for the types defined in this chapter.

Structure members.   Member declarations are like variable declarations: Each consists of a type, followed by a list of member names ending with a semicolon. Any previously defined type can be used. For example, a structure listing the properties of a piece of lumber is defined in Figure 14.2. We represent

---

[1] In such types, one member is a pointer to an object of the **struct** type currently being defined. These topics are beyond the scope of this text.

A `struct` type specification creates a type that can be used to declare variables. The `typedef` declaration names this new type.

```
typedef struct LUMBER {      /* Type for a piece of lumber. */
    char type[11];           /* Type of wood.               */
    short int height, width; /* In inches.                  */
    short int length;        /* In feet.                    */
    float price;             /* Per board, in dollars.      */
    int quantity;            /* Number of items in stock.   */
} lumber_t;
```

The members of `lumber_t` will be laid out in memory in this order:

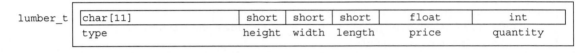

Figure 14.2.   A `struct` type declaration.

the dimensions of the board as small integers (a $2 \times 4 \times 8$ board is cut at the sawmill with a cross section of approximately 2×4 inches and a length of 8 feet). We use the types `float` to represent the price of the lumber and `int` to represent the quantity of this lumber in stock. Figure 14.2 also shows a memory diagram of the structure created by this declaration. The result of a `typedef struct` declaration is a "pattern" for creating future variables; it is not an object and does not contain any data. Therefore, you do not include any initializers in the member declarations.

The **member names** permit us to refer to individual parts of the structure. Each name should be unique and convey the purpose of its member but do so without being overly wordy. (This is good advice for any variable name.) A member name is used as one part of a longer compound name; it needs to make sense in context but need not be complete enough to make sense if it stood alone.

A component **selection expression** consists of an object name followed by one or more member names, all separated by the dot operator. Because such expressions can get lengthy, it is a good idea to give each member a brief name.

Declaring and initializing a structure.   We can declare a structured variable and, optionally, initialize it in the declaration. The two declarations in Figure 14.3 use the structured type declared in Figure 14.2 to declare variables named `sale` and `plank`. The variable `sale` is uninitialized, so the fields will contain unknown data. The variable `plank` is initialized. The **structured variable initializer** is much like that for an array. It consists of curly brackets enclosing one data value, of the appropriate type, for each member of the structure. These are separated by commas and must be placed in the same order as the member

We use the type declared in Figure 14.2.

```
lumber_t sale;
lumber_t plank = { "white oak", 1, 6, 8, 5.80, 158 };
```

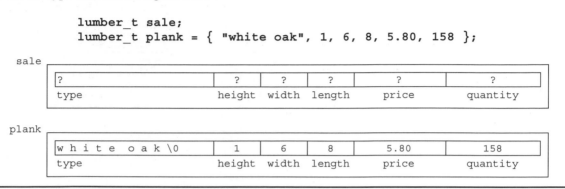

Figure 14.3.   Declaring and initializing a structure.

declarations. The arrangement of the values in **plank** is diagrammed in the figure. Like an array, if there are too few initializers, any remaining member will be filled with 0 bytes.

14.2   Operations on Structures

ISO C supports a variety of **operations on structures**; older, pre-ANSI C compilers support some but not all of these operations. Therefore, what you are permitted to do with a structure depends on the age of your compiler. ISO C compilers permit the following operations:

1. Set a pointer's value to the address of a structure.
2. Access one member of a structure.
3. Use assignment to copy the contents of a structure.
4. Return a structure as the result of a function.
5. Pass a structure as an argument to a function, by value or address.
6. Include structures in larger compound objects, such as an array of structures.
7. Access one element in an array of structures.
8. Access one member of one structure in an array of structures.

One important and basic operation is not supported in C: comparison of two structures. When comparison is necessary, it must be implemented as a programmer-defined function. The remainder of this section isolates and explains each of these operations. Figures 14.7, 14.8, 14.9, and 14.11 contain function definitions that are part of the complete program in Figures 14.12 and 14.13.

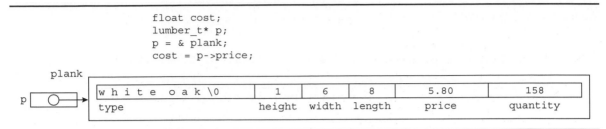

```
              float cost;
              lumber_t* p;
              p = & plank;
              cost = p->price;
```

Figure 14.4.   Set and use a pointer to a structure.

14.2.1 Structure Operations

Set a pointer to a structure.   We can declare a pointer and set its value to the address of a **struct**. In Figure 14.4, the address of the structure named **plank**, defined in Figure 14.3, is stored in the pointer variable **p**. The address used is the address of the first member of the structure, but the pointer gives access to the entire structure, as illustrated.

Access one member of a structure.   The members of a structure may be accessed either directly or through a pointer. The **dot** (period) **operator** is used for direct access. We write the variable name followed by a dot, followed by the name of the desired member. For example, to access the **length** member of the variable **plank**, we write **plank.length**. Once referenced, the member may be used anywhere a simple variable of that type is allowed.

The **arrow operator** is used to access the members of a structure through a pointer. We write the pointer name followed by -> (arrow) and a member name. For example, since the pointer **p** is pointing at **plank**, we can use **p** to access one member of **plank** by writing **p->price**. This is illustrated by the last line in Figure 14.4. We use both access operators in Figure 14.5 to print two members of **plank**. The output from these two print statements is

```
Plank price is $5.80
Planks in stock: 158
```

Structure assignment.   ISO compilers let us copy the entire contents of a structure in one assignment statement. A structure assignment copies all of the values of the members of the structure on the right into the corresponding

```
  printf( " Plank price is $%.2f\n", plank.price );   /* direct access */
  printf( " Planks in stock: %i\n", p->quantity );    /* indirect access */
```

Figure 14.5.   Access one member of a structure.

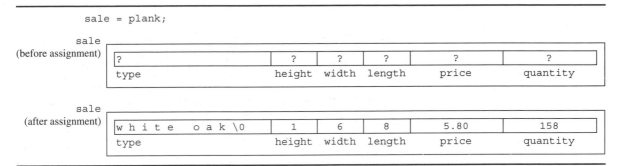

Figure 14.6.   Structure assignment.

members of the structure variable on the left (which must be the same type).[2]
Figure 14.6 gives an example.

14.2.2 Using Structures with Functions

Three functions are given in this section to illustrate how structures can be passed
into and out of functions. Calls on these functions are incorporated into the
program in Figures 14.12 and 14.13.

Returning a structure from a function.   The same mechanism that allows us to do structure assignment lets us return a structure as the result of a

```
lumber_t read_lumber( void )
{
    lumber_t board;
    puts( " Reading a new stock item." );
    printf( " Enter the three dimensions of a board: " );
    scanf( "%hi%hi%hi", &board.height, &board.width, &board.length );
    printf( " Enter the type of wood: " );
    scanf( "%10[^\n]", board.type );
    printf( " Enter the price: $" );
    scanf( "%g", &board.price );
    printf( " Enter the quantity in stock: " );
    scanf( "%i", &board.quantity );
    return board;
}
```

Figure 14.7.   Returning a structure from a function.

---

[2]This actually is a "shallow" copy. If one of the members is a pointer to an object, assignment makes
a copy of the address but not the object it references. Deep copies, which duplicate both pointer and
referent, are beyond the scope of this text.

```
void print_lumber( lumber_t b )
{
    printf( " %-11s  %hi\" x %hi\" x %2hi feet   $%.2f  stock: %i\n",
            b.type, b.height, b.width, b.length, b.price, b.quantity );
}
```

Figure 14.8.   Call by value with a structure.

function. For example, in Figure 14.7, we declare a function, **read_lumber()**, that reads the data for a piece of lumber into the members of a local structured variable. In these **scanf()** statements, we do not need parentheses around the entire member name. The dot operator has higher precedence than the address operator, so we get the address of the desired member. When all input has been read, we return a copy of the contents of the local structure as the function's value. This is yet another way to return multiple values from a function.

Call by value with a structure.   We can pass a structure as an argument to a function. When we use call by value to do this, all the members of the caller's argument are copied into the members of the function's parameter variable, just as if each were a separate variable. In Figure 14.8, we declare a function, **print_lumber()** with a structure parameter. It formats and prints the data in the structure. Because the parameter is a structure (not a pointer), we use the dot operator to access the members.

Calls on **read_lumber()** and **print_lumber()** might look like this:

```
sale = read_lumber();
print_lumber( sale );
```

The input would be read into a local variable in the **read_lumber()** function, then copied into **sale** when the function returns. It would be copied a second time into parameter **b** in **print_lumber()**. The output produced by this interaction might be

```
void sell_lumber( int sold, lumber_t* board )
{
    int n = board->quantity;
    if (n >= sold) {
        board->quantity -= sold;
        printf( " OK, sold %i\n", sold );
        print_lumber( *board );
    }
    else printf( " Error: cannot sell %i boards (only have %i).\n",
                 sold, n );
}
```

Figure 14.9.   Call by address with a structure.

```
Reading a new stock item.
Enter the three dimensions of a board: 2 3 6
Enter the type of wood: fir
Enter the price: $4.23
Enter the quantity in stock: 16
fir         2" x 3" x 6 feet   $4.23   stock: 16
```

Call by address with a structure.   We can pass a pointer to a structure, or the address of a structure, as an argument to a function. This, **call by address**, gives us more functionality than call by value. In Figure 14.9, we declare a function named **sell_lumber()** that takes an integer (the item number) and a structure pointer as its parameters and checks the inventory of that item. If the supply is adequate, the quantity on hand is reduced by the number sold; otherwise an error comment is printed. The following sample calls illustrate two ways to call this function:

```
sell_lumber( 200, p );                /* p points to plank. */
sell_lumber( 2, &sale );
```

The output would look like this:

```
Error: cannot sell 200 boards (only have 158).
OK, sold 2
fir         2" x 3" x 6 feet   $4.23   in stock: 14
```

On the first line of **sell_lumber()**, we use the parameter (a pointer) with the arrow operator to access a member of the structure. Within the code is a call on **print_lumber()** to show the reduced quantity on hand after a sale. Note that the pointer parameter of **sell_lumber()** is the wrong type for **print_lumber()**, because the argument for **print_lumber()** must be an item, not a pointer. We overcome this incompatibility by using a dereference operator in the call to **print_lumber()**. The result of the dereference is a structured value.

Value vs. address parameters.   The three functions just discussed, as well as the **boards_equal()** function in Figure 14.11 have been implemented using call by value wherever possible; it was necessary to use a pointer parameter (call by address) for **sell_lumber()**, because the function updates its parameter to return information to the caller. The prototypes are

```
lumber_t read_lumber( void );
void print_lumber( lumber_t );
void sell_lumber( int, lumber_t* );
bool boards_equal( lumber_t, lumber_t );
```

Pointer parameters also could have been used in **print_lumber()**, **read_lumber()**, and **boards_equal()**. This would have both advantages and disadvantages. Call by address does not isolate the caller from the subprogram, so the subprogram can change the value stored in the caller's variable. This is a disadvantage for functions like **print_lumber()** and **boards_equal()** that use, but do not modify, their parameters. A lack of isolation between caller and subprogram makes accidental mistakes harder to track and correct.

On the other hand, using call by address can save time and memory space, because only a pointer, not an entire structure, must be copied into the function's parameter. The time for copying can be significant for large structures. The same is true of the time consumed by returning a structured result from a function like **read_lumber**(). If the structure has many members or contains an array of substantial size as one member, it usually is better to use call by address to send the information to a function and to return information. The revised prototypes for a large structure in this program would be

```
void read_lumber( lumber_t* );
void print_lumber( lumber_t* );
void sell_lumber( int, lumber_t* );
bool boards_equal( lumber_t*, lumber_t* );
```

14.2.3 Arrays of Structures

It is possible to include one aggregate type within another. In the definition of the **struct** for **lumber_t**, we include a character array. A **struct** type also may be the base type of an array. Thus, we can declare and, optionally, initialize an **array of structures**. An initializer for an array of structures is enclosed in curly brackets and contains one bracketed set of values for each item in the array,

```
lumber_t stock[4] = { { "spruce", 2, 4, 12, 8.20, 27 },
                      { "pine", 2, 3, 10, 5.45, 11 },
                      { "pine", 2, 3, 8, 4.20, 35 },
                      { "" /* Remaining members will be set to 0. */ }
                    };
```

stock

[0]	s p r u c e \0	2	4	12	8.20	27
	type	height	width	length	price	quantity

[1]	p i n e \0	2	3	10	5.45	11
	type	height	width	length	price	quantity

[2]	p i n e \0	2	3	8	4.20	35
	type	height	width	length	price	quantity

[3]	\0	0	0	0	0.00	0
	type	height	width	length	price	quantity

Figure 14.10.   An array of structures.

separated by commas.[3] An example and its diagram are shown in Figure 14.10, where we declare and initialize an array of `lumber_t` structures.

Accessing one structure in an array of structures.   The name of the array and a subscript are needed to access one element in an array of structures, shown in the following code. The first line assigns a structured value to the last item of an array, the second calls `print_lumber()` to display the result. To send one structure from the array, by address, to a function that has a structure pointer parameter, the argument needs both a subscript and an ampersand, as shown by the call on `sell_lumber()` on the third line.

```
stock[3] = read_lumber();      /* Read into one element. */
print_lumber( stock[3] );      /* Print one element. */
sell_lumber( 3, &stock[3] );   /* Call by address. */
```

A sample of the interaction and output is:

```
Reading a new stock item.
Enter the three dimensions of a board: 1 4 10
Enter the type of wood: walnut
Enter the price: $29.50
Enter the quantity in stock: 10
walnut     1" x 4" x 10 feet  $29.50   stock: 10
OK, sold 3
walnut     1" x 4" x 10 feet  $29.50   stock: 7
```

Accessing a member of one structure in an array.   We also can access a single member of a structure element. Both a subscript and a member name must be used to access an individual part of one structure in an array of structures. Again, no parentheses are needed because of the precedence of the subscript and dot operators. Write the subscript first, because the overall object is an array. The result of applying the subscript is a structure to which the dot operator is applied. The final result is one member of the structure. For example, to print the `price` of the second piece of lumber in the `stock` array, we would write this:

```
printf( "Second stock item: $%.2f\n", stock[1].price );
```

This statement's output is

```
Second stock item: $5.45
```

Arrays of structures vs. parallel arrays.   In Section 10.3, we used a set of **parallel arrays** to implement a table. In this representation, each array represented one column of the table, and each array position represented one row. An array of structures can represent the same data: Each structure is a row of the table and the group of structure members with the same name represents one column.

---

[3] In addition to the commas between members, it is legal to have a comma after the last one. This sometimes makes it easier to create large data tables with a word processor, without having to remember to remove the comma from the last one.

A modern approach to representation would favor grouping all the columns into a structure and using an array of structures. This combines related data into a coherent whole that can be passed to functions as a single argument. The method is convenient and probably helps avoid errors. The argument in favor of using parallel arrays is that the code is simpler. The column's array name and a subscript are enough to access any property. In contrast, with an array of structures, the array name, a subscript, and a member name are needed.[4] The other factor is whether the functions in the program process mainly rows or columns of data. Row processing functions favor the structure, while column processing functions are most practical with the parallel arrays. A mixed strategy also may be used: We might define an array of menu items for use with `menu_i()` or `menu_c()`, but group all other data about each menu choice into a structure and have an array of these structures parallel to the menu array.

14.2.4   Comparing Two Structures

Unfortunately, there is one useful operation that no C compiler supports: **comparing** two **structures** in one operation. If we wish to know whether **sale** and **plank** have the same values in corresponding members, we cannot write this:

```
if (sale == plank) …/* Not legal in C. */
```

Instead, to find out whether two structured variables are equal, each member must be checked individually. A function that does such a comparison is shown in Figure 14.11.

Type **bool** was defined in Figure 11.9. We use it here as the return type of a function that compares two structured variables for equality.

```
bool boards_equal( lumber_t board1, lumber_t board2 )
{
    bool same = true;

    if (!strequal( board1.type, board2.type )) same = false;
    else if (board1.height != board2.height) same = false;
    else if (board1.width != board2.width) same = false;
    else if (board1.length != board2.length) same = false;
    else if (board1.price != board2.price) same = false;
    else if (board1.quantity != board2.quantity) same = false;

    return same;
}
```

Figure 14.11.   Comparing two structures.

---

[4] Interestingly, a C++ class provides the best of both worlds; an array of class objects is a coherent object itself, but class functions can refer to individual members of the object simply, without using a dot or arrow. Further examination of this topic is beyond the scope of this book.

In the `boards_equal()` function, we compare two structured variables of type `lumber_t` and return the value `true` or `false`, depending on whether the structures are equal or unequal, respectively. We use a series of `if` statements to make this comparison. To begin, we assume that the two structured arguments are equal and initialize the local `bool` variable `same` to `true`. Then we compare each pair of members. Comparing members may be as simple as using `!=`; more complicated, as in calling `strequal()`; or complex, as calling another function to compare two structured components. As long as each successive pair matches, we continue testing. If any pair is unequal, we store `false` in the `bool` variable and skip the rest of the comparisons. The last line of the function returns the final value of this variable.

Calling the comparison function.   We combine several structure operations in the next example, a loop that processes an entire array of structures, comparing each item to a sale item while printing everything.

```
for (k = 0; k < 4; ++k) {              /* Process every slot. */
    if (boards_equal( sale, stock[k] )) printf( "Sale: " );
    else printf( "       " );
    print_lumber( stock[k] );
}
```

The output from this code fragment is

```
       spruce     2" x 4" x 12 feet   $8.20    stock: 27
       pine       2" x 3" x 10 feet   $5.45    stock: 11
Sale:  pine       2" x 3" x  8 feet   $4.20    stock: 35
       walnut     1" x 4" x 10 feet   $29.50   stock: 10
```

These declarations are in the file `"lumber.h"`. They are used by the program in Figure 14.13. The type declaration was discussed in Figure 14.2.

```
#include "tools.h"

typedef struct LUMBER {        /* Type for a piece of lumber. */
    char type[11];             /* Type of wood.               */
    short int height, width;   /* In inches.                  */
    short int length;          /* In feet.                    */
    float price;               /* Per board, in dollars.      */
    int quantity;              /* Number of items in stock.   */
} lumber_t;

lumber_t read_lumber( void );
void print_lumber( lumber_t b );
void sell_lumber( int sold, lumber_t* board );
bool boards_equal( lumber_t board1, lumber_t board2 );
```

Figure 14.12.   Declarations for the lumber program.

This program incorporates the declarations and code fragments used to demonstrate structure declarations and operations in Sections 14.1 and 14.2. The included file **"lumber.h"** is given in Figure 14.12. Function definitions are in Figures 14.7, 14.8, 14.9, and 14.11.

```
#include "lumber.h"
void main( void )
{   int k;    /* Loop counter. */
    /* Structured object declarations:  Figures 14.3, 14.4, 14.10.*/
```

```
    lumber_t sale;
    lumber_t plank = { "white oak", 1, 6, 8, 5.80, 158 };
    lumber_t* p;
    lumber_t stock[4] = { { "spruce", 2, 4, 12, 8.20, 27 },
                          { "pine", 2, 3, 10, 5.45, 11 },
                          { "pine", 2, 3, 8, 4.20, 35 },
                          { "" /* Remaining members will be set to 0. */ }
                        };
```

```
    puts( "Demo program for structure operations.\n" );
    /* Access parts of a structure:  Figures 14.4, 14.5.        */
```

```
    p = &plank;                     /* Make p point at plank.        */
    printf( " Plank price is $%.2f\n", plank.price );   /* direct access */
    printf( " Planks in stock: %i\n", p->quantity );  /* indirect access */
    sell_lumber( 200, p );
```

```
    /* Function calls using structs:  Section 14.2.2.        */
```

```
    sale = read_lumber();       /* Return a structured result.   */
    print_lumber( sale );       /* Call by value.                */
    sell_lumber( 2, &sale );    /* Call by address.              */
```

```
    /* Accessing an array of structures:  Section 14.2.3.    */
```

```
    sale = stock[2];                /* Copy a structure.         */
    stock[3] = read_lumber();       /* Input into an array slot. */
    print_lumber( stock[3] );       /* Print one array element.  */
    sell_lumber( 3, &stock[3] );  /* Call by address.            */
    printf( "\n Second stock item: $%.2f\n\n", stock[1].price );
```

```
    /* Test if two structures are equal:  Section 14.2.4.        */
```

```
    for (k = 0; k < 4; ++k) {       /* Process every slot of array.  */
        if(boards_equal( sale, stock[k] )) printf( " Sale:  " );
        else printf( "         " );
        print_lumber( stock[k] );
    }
}
```

Figure 14.13.   Structure operations.

14.2.5 Putting Some Pieces Together

Throughout the previous sections, many declarations, statements, and functions have been discussed. Most of these have been gathered together into a single program. A header file, `lumber.h`, is shown in Figure 14.12; it contains the `lumber_t` structure definition and the function prototypes. The remaining declarations, initializations, and statements are found in Figure 14.13. The function definitions are in Figures 14.7, 14.8, 14.9, and 14.11. Each block of code in the program has a comment noting the section in which it was discussed; we do not duplicate any of that discussion here. A full run of the program generates the following output sequence:

```
Demo program for structure operations.

Plank price is $5.80
Planks in stock: 158
Error: cannot sell 200 boards (only have 158).

Enter the three dimensions of a board: 2 3 6
Enter the type of wood: fir
Enter the price: $4.23
Enter the quantity in stock: 16
fir        2" x 3" x  6 feet   $4.23   stock: 16
OK, sold 2
fir        2" x 3" x  6 feet   $4.23   stock: 14

Reading a new stock item.
Enter the three dimensions of a board: 1 4 10
Enter the type of wood: walnut
Enter the price: $29.50
Enter the quantity in stock: 10
walnut     1" x 4" x 10 feet   $29.50   stock: 10
OK, sold 3
walnut     1" x 4" x 10 feet   $29.50   stock: 7

Second stock item: $4.20

        spruce     2" x 4" x 12 feet   $8.20   stock: 27
        pine       2" x 3" x 10 feet   $5.45   stock: 11
Sale:   pine       2" x 3" x  8 feet   $4.20   stock: 35
        walnut     1" x 4" x 10 feet   $29.50   stock: 7
```

14.3 Application: Points in a Rectangle

The next program example uses a structure to represent a point on the xy plane. It illustrates a variety of operations on structures, including assignment, arithmetic, and function calls.

An elementary part of any CAD (computer-aided design) program or graphics windowing package is a function that determines whether a given point in the

xy plane falls within a specified rectangular region. In a mouse-driven interface, the mouse is used to select the active window, "grab" scrolling buttons, and "click on" action buttons and menu items. All these rectangular window elements on the screen are represented inside the computer by rectangles, and the mouse cursor is represented by a point. So, quite constantly, a mouse-based system must answer the question, "Is the point P inside the rectangle R?"

We present a program that answers this simple but fundamental question. The problem specifications are given in Figures 14.14 and 14.15. Figure 14.16 outlines a test plan. The various portions of the program are contained in Figures 14.17 and 14.19 through 14.22 and Figure 14.18 diagrams the structured data types used in this application. Structures are used to define both points and rectangles in this program. A point is represented by a pair of **doubles** (its x and y coordinates) and a rectangle is represented by a pair of points (its diagonally opposite corners). We use the first structured type (**point**) to help define the next. This is typical of the way in which complex **hierarchical data structures** can be constructed by combining simpler parts.

Just as some programs take simple objects as input and operate only on those simple objects (**floats** or **ints**), conceptually, this program takes structured objects as data and operates on these structured objects. Because operations on compound objects are more complex than those on simple objects, functions are introduced to perform these operations. This keeps the main flow of logic simple and lets us focus separately on the major operations and the details of the structured objects. New function prototypes are introduced in which the **struct** and **enum** data types are used to declare both parameters and return types. Specifically, we use the enumerated type **in_type** declared in Figure 11.9, which has one code for each way that a point's position can relate to a rectangle.

A test plan for points in a rectangle.   The specifications in Figure 14.15 ask us to analyze the position of a point relative to a rectangle. They require us

Use this diagram to understand the next program.

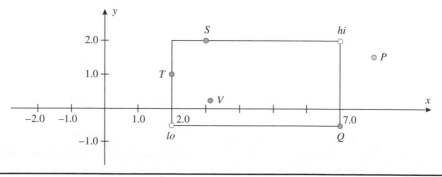

Figure 14.14.   A rectangle on the xy-plane.

Refer to the diagram in Figure 14.14.

Problem scope: Given the coordinates of a rectangle in the xy plane and the coordinates of a series of points, determine how the position of each point relates to the rectangle. As an example, in the diagram in Figure 14.14, R has diagonally opposite corners at $lo = (2, -0.5)$ and $hi = (7, 2)$. Point $P = (7.9, 1.35)$ is outside the rectangle, $Q = (7, -0.5)$ is at a corner, $S = (3, 2)$, and $T = (2, 1)$ are on two of the sides, and $V = (3.15, 0.4)$ is inside the rectangle.

Limitations: The sides of the rectangle will be parallel to the x and y axes. Thus, two diagonally opposite corners are enough to completely specify the position of the rectangle.

Input: In Phase 1, the user enters the x and y coordinates (real values) of points lo and hi, the lower left and upper right corners of the rectangle. In Phase 2, the user enters the x and y coordinates of a series of points. An input point at the same position as lo will terminate execution.

Output: In Phase 1, echo the actual coordinates of the corners of the rectangle that will be used. In Phase 2, for each point entered, state whether the point is outside, at a corner of, on a side of, or inside the rectangle.

Formulas: A point is outside the rectangle if either of its coordinates is less than the corresponding coordinate of lo or greater than the corresponding coordinate of hi. It is inside the rectangle if its x coordinate lies between the x coordinates of lo and hi and the point's y coordinate lies between the y coordinates of lo and hi. The point is on a corner if both of its coordinates match the x and y coordinates of one of the four corners. It is on a side if only one of its coordinates equals the corresponding x or y coordinate of a corner and the point is not outside nor on a corner.

Computational requirements: If the user accidentally enters the wrong corners of the rectangle or enters the corners in the wrong order, the program should attempt to correct the error. The program also must function sensibly if the rectangle is degenerate; that is, if the x coordinates of lo and hi are the same, the y coordinates of lo and hi are the same, or lo and hi are both the same. The first two cases define a line; the last defines a point. If rectangle R is a single point, then point P must be either "on a corner" or "outside" R. If the rectangle is a straight line, P can be "on a corner," "on a side," or "outside" R. When comparing the coordinates, consider two coordinates to be the same if they differ by less than an epsilon value of .000001.

Figure 14.15.   Problem specifications: Points in a rectangle.

to handle any point in the xy plane and any rectangle with sides parallel to the x and y axes. Degenerate rectangles (vertical lines, horizontal lines, and points) must be handled appropriately. A suitable test plan, then, will include at least one example of each case.

Type of Rectangle	Lower Left (x, y)	Upper Right (x, y)	Point (x, y)	Position (answer)
Normal	$(2, -0.5)$	$(7, 2)$	$P = (7.9, 1.35)$	Outside
			$Q = (7, -0.5)$	Corner
			$S = (3, 2)$	Horizontal side
			$(5, -0.5)$	Horizontal side
			$T = (2, 1)$	Vertical side
			$(7, -0.1)$	Vertical side
			$V = (3.15, 0.4)$	Inside
			$lo = (2, -0.5)$	Corner, end of test
x coordinates, reversed	$(2, 0)$	$(-1, 5)$	$(1, 1)$	Inside
x coordinates, corrected	$(-1, 0)$	$(2, 5)$	$(-1, 0)$	Corner, end of test
y coordinates, reversed	$(-1, 5)$	$(2, 0)$	$(-1, 5.00001)$	Outside
y coordinates, corrected	$(-1, 0)$	$(2, 5)$	$(-1, 0)$	Corner, end of test
Vertical line	$(1, 0)$	$(1, 3)$	$(1, 3)$	Corner
			$(1, 2)$	Side
			$(1, 0)$	Corner, end of test
Horizontal line	$(0, 1)$	$(3, 1)$	$(3, 1)$	Corner
			$(2, 1)$	Side
			$(2, 0.0001)$	Outside
			$(0, 1)$	Corner, end of test
Point	$(1, 3)$	$(1, 3)$	$(2, 0.0001)$	Outside
			$(1, 3)$	Corner, end of test

Figure 14.16.   The test plan for points in a rectangle.

We construct such a plan, shown in Figure 14.16 by starting with the sample rectangle and points given in Figure 14.14. We then add points that lie on the other two vertical and horizontal sides. The last input for this rectangle is a point equal to the lower-left corner, which should end the processing of this rectangle. This part of the test plan is shown in the top portion of Figure 14.16. Next, we add two rectangles whose corners have been entered incorrectly, to ensure that the program will swap the coordinates properly and create a legitimate rectangle. Finally, we need to test three degenerate rectangles: a vertical line, a horizontal line, and a point.

Notes on Figure 14.17. Main program for points in a rectangle.
Figure 14.17 contains the type declarations and function prototypes for the program. Corresponding function definitions are found in Figures 14.19 through

The program specification is in Figure 14.15. This part of the program declares the necessary types, constants, and functions and calls the functions in Figures 14.19, 14.20, 14.21, and 14.22, all of which would be stored in the same source-code file, following `main()`.

```
#include "tools.h"
```

```
typedef struct POINT { double x, y; } point_type;
typedef struct RECTANGLE { point_type lo, hi; } rect_type;
typedef enum { P_IN, P_SIDE, P_CORNER, P_OUT } in_type;
const string answer[4]={"inside","on a side of","at a corner of","outside"};
```

```
void test_points( void );
rect_type get_rect( void );
bool equal( point_type p1, point_type p2 );
in_type in_or_out( point_type P, rect_type R );
void swap( double* fp1, double* fp2 );
```

```
void main( void )
{
    char again;            /* For user response in test_points loop. */

    banner();
    puts( " Given a rectangle with a side parallel to the x axis \n"
          " and a series of points on the xy plane,\n"
          " say where each point lies in relation to the rectangle." );
    do {   test_points();
           printf( " Do you want to test another rectangle (y/n)? " );
           scanf( " %c", &again );
    } while (tolower( again ) != 'n');
    bye();
}
```

Figure 14.17.   Main program for points in a rectangle.

14.22. The code in `main()` prints program titles and executes the usual work loop.

- *First box: type declarations.*

  1. Most type declarations are written at the top of the program, above `main()`. This placement permits all the functions defined in the same program file to use the newly defined types.

  2. The type `point_type` represents the coordinates of a point in the xy plane. We define it as a `struct` containing a pair of `double`s, `x` and `y`. We also could define this type as an array of two `double`s. If we did so, the coordinates of a point `P` would be called `P[0]` and `P[1]`.

However, for clarity, we would rather refer to the coordinates as `P.x` and `P.y`. We declare this type as a *structure* of two **double**s so that we can name the parts, not number them. In other circumstances, we might make the opposite choice. This type is diagrammed on the left in Figure 14.18.

3. According to the problem specifications, a rectangle is defined by the two points at its opposite corners. The type **rect_type**, therefore, is defined as a structure of two **point_type** variables, called **lo** (the lower-left corner) and **hi** (the upper-right corner). The compound type is diagrammed on the right in Figure 14.18. We could have used an array of four **double**s or a structure of four **double**s, but neither captures the fundamental nature of the problem as well as a pair of points (lower and upper corners), where each point has two coordinates (**x** and **y**).

4. To reference the members of this structure, we choose brief but suggestive names so that the code will not be too wordy. For example, to access the *x* coordinate of the lower-left corner of rectangle **R**, we write **R.lo.x**.

5. The third **typedef** declares **in_type**, an enumeration of the positions a point can have relative to a rectangle. Each time a point is entered, the function **in_or_out()** is called to test its position, and one of these codes is returned as the result of the function. These codes permit us to return the position information from a function with greater ease and clarity. The order in which the codes are listed here does not matter. To allow convenient output of the results, we declare a parallel array of strings, as discussed in the previous chapter.

- *Second box: the prototypes.*

1. The first prototype is for the **test_points()** function in Figure 14.19. It reads a rectangle description and a series of points and locates those points relative to the rectangle.

2. The second prototype is for the function **get_rect()** in Figure 14.20, which reads, validates, and returns the coordinates of a rectangle in a structure.

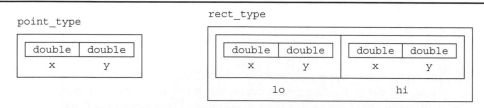

Figure 14.18.   Two structured types.

3. The third prototype is for the function **equal()**, which is defined in Figure 14.21. It has two **point_type** parameters. This comparison function tests whether the coordinates of the two points are equal (within a small margin of error) and returns a **true** or **false** answer.

4. The fourth prototype is for **in_or_out()**, which is defined in Figure 14.22. The parameters are a point and a rectangle. The result of the function is an **in_type** value; this means that the function will return one of the constants from the **in_type** enumeration.

5. Last, we use the **swap()** function defined in Figure 12.8.

- *The main program.*

  1. The main program contains a loop that processes a series of rectangles. Each time **test_points()** is called, it reads one rectangle and a series of points, whose locations are determined relative to that rectangle. This is continued as long as the user wishes.

  2. Note that the main program is not involved with any of the details of the representation or processing of rectangles and points. All that **work is delegated** to other functions, and each of them accomplishes just one part of the overall job. This kind of modular program construction is the foundation of modern programming practice.

Notes on Figure 14.19. Testing points.   We illustrate some basic techniques for using enumerations and structures: variable declarations, output, and function calls that use and return structured data.

- *First box: the rectangle.* The program must read the definition of one rectangle and compare it to a series of points. A rectangle is a compound structure with several parts, so we define a separate function to read and validate the part values and return a valid rectangle. The **get_rect()** function returns a **rect_type** answer, which we store in **R**. We use this function to "hide" all the details of reading and validation. This simplifies the logic of the **test_points()** function and lets us focus on processing points.

- *Second box: processing points.*

  1. We use a **do…while** sentinel loop to process a series of points. On entering the loop, the program prompts for and reads a point, explaining clearly how to end the loop (by entering the point **lo** as a sentinel). When reading data into a structured variable (or printing from it), it is necessary to list each member of the structure separately. The program cannot scan data directly into **pt** as a whole but must scan into **pt.x** and **pt.y**. Similarly, it cannot print the lower-left corner of **R** by printing **R.lo**; it must print the individual members, **R.lo.x** and **R.lo.y**.

This function analyzes the position of point **pt** with respect to rectangle **R** in the xy plane. It is called from Figure 14.17. In turn, it calls functions in Figures 14.20 through 14.22.

```
void test_points( void )
{
    rect_type R;            /* The rectangle. */
    point_type pt;          /* The points we will test. */
    in_type where;          /* Position of point relative to rectangle. */

    R = get_rect();

    puts( "Please enter a series of points when prompted." );

    do {
        printf( "\n Enter x and y (%g %g to quit): ", R.lo.x, R.lo.y );
        scanf ( "%lg%lg", &pt.x, &pt.y );

        where = in_or_out( pt, R );

        printf( " The point (%g, %g) is %s the rectangle.\n",
                pt.x, pt.y, answer[where] );

    } while (! equal( pt, R.lo ) );

}
```

Figure 14.19.   Testing points.

2. In the first inner box, the program calls the function **in_or_out()** to determine the position of point **pt** relative to rectangle **R**. The two arguments are structured values. A structured argument is passed to a function in the same manner as an argument of a simple type; that is, by copying all of the structure's members. This function returns an **in_type** value, which is stored in **where**, an **in_type** variable.

3. Since enumerated types are represented by small integers, the program could print the **in_type** value directly, in an integer format. However, this would not be very informative to the user. Instead, we use the integer as a subscript to select the proper phrase from the parallel array of answers defined in Figure 14.17. The **printf()** statement prints the resulting string using a **%s** format.

4. In the second inner box, the program calls the **equal()** function to determine whether the point **pt** is the **sentinel value**; that is, the same point as the lower-left corner of the rectangle. If so, we end the loop. This function returns a **true** or **false** answer, which can be tested directly in a **while** or **if** statement. Since we cannot use **==** to com-

This function is called from Figure 14.19; the type `rect_type` is defined in Figure 14.17.

```
rect_type get_rect( void )
{
    rect_type R;              /* To store coordinates as they are read. */

    printf( "\n Enter x and y for lower left corner: " );
    scanf ( "%lg%lg", &R.lo.x, &R.lo.y );
    printf( " Enter x and y for upper right corner: " );
    scanf ( "%lg%lg", &R.hi.x, &R.hi.y );

    /* If corners were not entered correctly, swap coordinates. */
    if (R.lo.x > R.hi.x) swap( &R.lo.x, &R.hi.x );
    if (R.lo.y > R.hi.y) swap( &R.lo.y, &R.hi.y );

    printf( "\n Using lower left = (%g, %g), "
            "upper right = (%g, %g).\n", R.lo.x, R.lo.y, R.hi.x, R.hi.y );

    return R;
}
```

Figure 14.20.   Reading a rectangle.

pare two points, we simplify and clarify the logic of `test_points()` considerably by putting the testing details into the `equal()` function.

Notes on Figure 14.20. Reading a rectangle.   The function in Figure 14.20 illustrates input, validation, and output of a structure.

- *First box: reading the coordinates.*

  1. The program prompts the user to enter both the *x* and *y* coordinates of a single corner at the same time, because these two numbers are closely related logically. The two numbers should be separated by whitespace. If a user enters a comma between the numbers, the program will not work. This error condition will be addressed in Chapter 15.
  2. The program prompts for the rectangle's two corners one at a time. It would be possible to read both corners (all four coordinates) in one statement, but entering four inputs at one prompt is likely to cause confusion or omissions.

- *Second box: testing for valid input.*

  1. The correct operation of the algorithm depends on having the coordinates of the lower-left corner be less than or equal to the coordinates

of the upper-right corner. The user is instructed to enter the points in this order. However, trusting a user to obey instructions of this sort is never a good idea. A program that depends on some relationship between data items should test for that relationship and ensure that the data are correct.

2. If the user enters the wrong corners (upper left and lower right) or enters the correct corners in the wrong order, the program still has the information needed to continue the process. That information, though, is stored in the wrong members of the rectangle structure. So we test for this kind of an error and swap the coordinates if necessary.

3. The tests in the `if` statements show why we choose short names for the parts of the structures, instead of longer names like `upper_right` and `x_coordinate`. Since we may have to write a long list of qualifying member names to specify an individual component, even short names can result in long phrases. These become too hard to read and make it difficult to write entire statements on one line. It is much easier to read a brief expression like the first version that follows than a long-winded version like the second:

```
R.lo.x > R.hi.x
Rectangle.lower_left.x_coordinate >
        Rectangle.upper_right.x_coordinate
```

- *Third box: printing the rectangle's coordinates.*

1. The program prints the coordinates of the rectangle's opposite corners after testing for errors because they might have been swapped. A program always should echo its input so that the user knows what actually is being processed. This is essential information during debugging, when the programmer is trying to track down the cause of an observed error. Being certain about the data used reduces the number of factors that must be considered. Echoing the input also gives the user confidence that the program is progressing correctly.

2. As an example, if two points were entered incorrectly, the user might see the following dialog. Note that the *y* coordinates get corrected:

```
Enter x and y for lower left corner: -1 5
Enter x and y for upper right corner: 2 0

Using lower left = (-1, 0), upper right = (2, 5).
```

- *Fourth box: returning the rectangle.* A `rect_type` variable is declared at the top of this function and used to contain the coordinates as they are entered. When control reaches the `return` statement, that variable contains four `double`s, representing the two points at the lower-left and upper-right corners of a rectangle. The `return` statement sends back a

This function is called from the `test_points()` function in Figure 14.19.

```
#define epsilon 0.000001
bool equal( point_type p1, point_type p2 )
{
    bool answer = true;
    if (fabs( p1.x - p2.x ) > epsilon || fabs( p1.y - p2.y ) > epsilon)
        answer = false;
    return answer;
}
```

Figure 14.21.   Comparing structured data.

structured value containing these four coordinates in proper order. This structured value then must be stored in a `rect_type` variable by the calling program, as in `test_points()`.

Notes on Figure 14.21. Comparing structured data.   The parameters to the function in Figure 14.21 are the two structures we wish to compare; the return value is type `bool`. We need this separate function because we cannot compare two structures using `==`. We use the usual method for comparing structured variables:

- Initially, set a `bool` variable to `true`.
- Then compare each corresponding pair of members and set the `bool` variable to `false` if a mismatch is found.
- Finally, return the `bool` value, whatever it is.

In this application, we compare floating-point numbers, so we use a fuzzy comparison with an epsilon value. An **epsilon test** is necessary in this situation because the program prompts the user to re-enter the lower-left point to end the processing loop. Sometimes, the number displayed in the prompt is only an approximation to the number stored in the memory because the last decimal digit was rounded during the output process. We use an approximate comparison so that, if the user enters the number shown in the prompt, it will be "equal to" the number stored in memory. The epsilon value used here is 0.000001, because we are using an output format that prints up to six decimal places. We write the epsilon constant's definition near the `equal()` function since it is the only function that uses epsilon.

Notes on Figure 14.22. Point location.   The brief but logically complex function in Figure 14.22 is called from the `test_points()` function in Figure 14.19.

- *The function header.*
    1. The two parameters are `struct` types, the return value is an enumerated type.

This function is called from the `test_points()` function in Figure 14.19.

```
in_type                                /* Where is P with respect to R? */
in_or_out( point_type P, rect_type R )
{
    in_type place;                     /* Set to out, in, corner, or side. */
    if (P.x < R.lo.x || P.x > R.hi.x || P.y < R.lo.y || P.y > R.hi.y)
        place = P_OUT;                 /* Point is outside rectangle. */
    else if (P.x > R.lo.x && P.x < R.hi.x && P.y > R.lo.y && P.y < R.hi.y)
        place = P_IN;                  /* Point is inside rectangle. */
    else if ((P.x==R.lo.x || P.x==R.hi.x) && (P.y==R.lo.y || P.y==R.hi.y))
        place = P_CORNER;              /* Point is on a corner. */
    else place = P_SIDE;               /* Point is on one side of rectangle. */
    return place;
}
```

Figure 14.22.   Point location.

2. We use short names for the parameters because the task of this function requires using logical expressions with several clauses. Short names let us write the entire expression on one line in most cases.

- *Testing for containment.*

    1. The logic of this function could be organized in many different ways. We choose to ask a series of questions, where each question completely characterizes one of the locations.
    2. If a case tests **true**, the program stores the corresponding position code in an **in_type** variable. Otherwise, it continues the testing.
    3. Each test is a logical expression with four clauses that compares the two coordinates of **P** to the four coordinates of **R**.
    4. The first two tests use one logical operator repeatedly. They will be parsed and executed in a strictly left-to-right order. The third test uses both || and && operators and requires parentheses to achieve the correct parse tree:

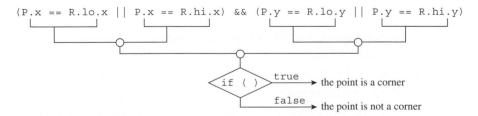

5. The most complicated case to identify occurs when a point lies on one of the sides of the rectangle. A logical expression to identify this case would be even longer than the three other expressions. However, by leaving this case to last, we can identify it by the process of elimination. The final **else** clause handles this case.

Program testing.   The test plan presented in Figure 14.16 tests all possible kinds of rectangles (ordinary and degenerate) with points in all possible relationships to each rectangle. We show some, but not all, the test results here.

    With an ordinary rectangle, the output will appear as follows. The first three lines are from **main()**, the next three from **get_rect()**, the point processing is from **test_points()**, and the final question is again from **main()**.

```
Given a rectangle with a side parallel to the x axis
and a series of points on the xy plane,
say where each point lies in relation to the rectangle.

Enter x and y for lower left corner: 2 -.5
Enter x and y for upper right corner: 7 2

Using lower left = (2, -0.5), upper right = (7, 2).
Please enter a series of points when prompted.

Enter x and y (2 -0.5 to quit): 7.9 1.35
The point (7.9, 1.35) is outside the rectangle.

Enter x and y (2 -0.5 to quit): 7 -.5
The point (7, -0.5) is at a corner of the rectangle.

Enter x and y (2 -0.5 to quit): 3 2
The point (3, 2) is on a side of the rectangle.

Enter x and y (2 -0.5 to quit): 2 1
The point (2, 1) is on a side of the rectangle.

Enter x and y (2 -0.5 to quit): 3.15 .4
The point (3.15, 0.4) is inside the rectangle.

Enter x and y (2 -0.5 to quit): 2 -.5
The point (2, -0.5) is at a corner of the rectangle.
Do you want to test another rectangle (y/n)? y
```

A specified requirement is that the program perform sensibly with a "rectangle" that is a straight line. We tested such a degenerate rectangle; an excerpt from the output is

```
Enter x and y for lower left corner: 1 0
Enter x and y for upper right corner: 1 3

Using lower left = (1, 0), upper right = (1, 3).
Please enter a series of points when prompted.

Enter x and y (1 0 to quit): 1 3
The point (1, 3) is at a corner of the rectangle.

Enter x and y (1 0 to quit): 1 2
The point (1, 2) is on a side of the rectangle.

Enter x and y (1 0 to quit): 1 0
The point (1, 0) is at a corner of the rectangle.
Do you want to test another rectangle (y/n)? n
```

14.4   Application: The Monte Carlo Method (Optional Topic)

In this section, we do the top-down development of a program that uses structured data in a numerical setting.

14.4.1   Problem Description, Specifications, and Testing

The **Monte Carlo method** can be used to determine the approximate area of any shape on the xy plane, as long as there is some method (such as the function in the previous program) for determining whether a randomly selected point is inside or outside the figure. In this method, a bounding box B of known area is drawn around the figure F, whose size is to be estimated. Then random points are generated that lie within B. We ask whether each one also is within F. By keeping track of the total number of points generated that are in B and counting those that also are inside F, we can estimate the proportion of B covered by F.

A figure F and bounding box B follow, for both a circle and an irregular shape. Here, points a and c are outside the figures, while points b and d are inside.

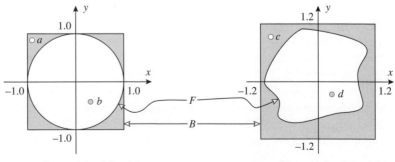

Area of box = $2.0 \times 2.0 = 4.0$ Area of box = $2.4 \times 2.4 = 5.28$

After hundreds of trials, the ratio of points found to be inside the figure F to the total number of trials will approach the ratio of the area of F to the area of the bounding box B:

$$\frac{\text{Area of } F}{\text{Area of } B} \approx \frac{\text{Number of points inside } F}{\text{Total number of trials}}$$

By solving for the unknown, the area of F, we get the formula shown in the program specifications in Figure 14.23. To demonstrate and test this method, we choose a very simple figure, a unit circle, whose exact area is known and can be compared to the experimental results.

Testing. The quality of this approximation depends greatly on the number of points used and whether the random number generator selects points evenly distributed over the area of the bounding box. For ease of experimentation, we have allowed the user to enter the number of random trials to conduct. The nature and limitations of this method can be illustrated by using it to approximate the area of a figure that also can be calculated exactly. We use the example mentioned in the specification, a unit circle; that is, one with radius $= 1.0$, and, therefore, area $= \pi$. This circle can be bounded by a box tangent to it, as illustrated previously. The length of a side of this bounding box is 2.0.

Problem scope: We can use a technique, Monte Carlo simulation, to estimate the area of a figure F on the xy plane with reasonable accuracy no matter how complex or irregular F is.

Input: The user will enter the number of random trials to conduct.

Output required: The approximate area of the figure will be printed to four digits of precision.

Formula: As discussed in the text, the unknown area is approximately

$$\text{Area of } F \approx \text{Area of } B \times \left(\frac{\text{Number of points inside } F}{\text{Total number of trials}} \right)$$

Items specific to the figure F: The user needs to provide a function, `inside()`, that takes a point $P = (x, y)$ on the plane as its parameter and returns `true` if P is inside F and `false` otherwise. The user must also use `#define BOX_SIDE` to supply a constant that is the length of one side of a square box that bounds F. A point $P = (x, y)$ is inside a circle if the distance between P and the center of the circle is less than the radius of the circle. If the circle's center is at $(0, 0)$, the distance from the center to P is

$$Distance = \sqrt{(P.x)^2 + (P.y)^2}$$

Figure 14.23.   Specifications: Monte Carlo approximation of an area.

14.4.2 Developing the Main Program

As usual, we start by writing the `#include` commands and the beginning and ending lines of `main()` (the greeting and termination code). We also write an incomplete definition of `BOX_SIDE`. (This is required by the specifications and will need to be completed later). Since we make only one estimate of the area per run, we do not need a query loop.

```
#include "tools.h"
#define BOX_SIDE ???
void main( void )
{   ...
    banner();
    puts( " Monte Carlo Estimate of Area of Unit Circle" );
    ...         /* Program code will go here. */
    bye();
}
```

The next step is to add problem-specific elements. We use the same type specification for a point that we used for the rectangle program. We also add a prototype for the `inside()` function (at the top of the program) and a call on `srand()` to initialize the random number generator (inside `main()`, after the headings).

```
typedef struct POINT { double x, y; } point_type;
bool inside( point_type p );
...
    srand( (unsigned)time( NULL ) );
```

We continue by filling in the middle section of `main()`. We need three steps:

1. Read the number of trials to use.
2. Run the simulation with that number of trials.
3. Print the answers.

We write the code for the first and third steps directly because they are only one or two lines each. In the process, we see that two variable declarations are needed and add them. The second step is more complex so we defer it for a moment.

```
double area;       /* Approximate area of unit circle. */
int trials;        /* Loop limit. */
...
printf( " Number of random trials to use = " );
scanf( "%i", &trials );                      /* step 1 */

...
printf( " With %i trials, estimated circle area = %.4g\n",
        trials, area );                      /* step 3 */
```

For step 2, a `simulate()` function must know the length of one side of the bounding box and how many trials to carry out. The return value will be the estimate of the area of the figure. With this in mind, we can write a prototype and a call for `simulate()`.

```
double simulate( int max, double box_side );
...
area = simulate( trials, BOX_SIDE );              /* step 2 */
```

The main program, shown in Figure 14.24, now is complete.

14.4.3   Developing the Functions

Now we need to write two functions, `inside()` and `simulate()`. The `inside()` function for this example is simple and specific to a unit circle. The `simulate()` function is more general. We start with the simple one.

The `inside()` function.   This function must answer the question, "Is the current, randomly chosen point inside the figure?" A different version of `inside()`

This program implements the specifications in Figure 14.23, assuming the figure is a unit circle and the side of the bounding box is length 2. It calls the functions in Figure 14.26.

```
#include "tools.h"
typedef struct POINT { double x, y; } point_type;
#define BOX_SIDE 2                   /* Length of side of bounding box. */
bool inside( point_type p );
double simulate( int max, double box_side );

void main( void )
{
    double area;                     /* Approximate area of unit circle. */
    int trials;                      /* Loop limit. */

    banner();
    puts( " Monte Carlo Estimate of Area of Unit Circle" );
    srand( (unsigned)time( NULL ) );   /* seed random number generator */

    printf( " Number of random trials to use = " );
    scanf( "%i", &trials );

    area = simulate( trials, BOX_SIDE );
    printf( " With %i trials, estimated circle area = %.4g\n",
            trials, area );
    bye();
}
```

Figure 14.24.   A Monte Carlo approximation.

is needed for each figure whose area is to be calculated. If we were calculating the area of an irregular figure, the `inside()` function could be very long and complicated. In extreme cases, we might even display the figure and the point graphically and ask a user to answer whether each point is inside or outside.

The `inside()` calculation for a unit circle is particularly simple: a point $P = (x, y)$ is inside the circle if its distance from the center of the circle is less than the radius of the circle. We use the distance formula in the specification. The `return` statement computes the distance from the center of the circle (the origin) to point `P` and compares that distance to the radius of a unit circle (distance < 1.0). The answer, either `true` or `false`, is returned as the result of the function.

```
bool inside( point_type p )
{
    return sqrt( p.x * p.x + p.y * p.y ) < 1.0;
}
```

We also must provide a constant to define the length of one side of a square, centered on the origin, that bounds the figure. We place the figure so that its center is at or near the origin. Then we implicitly "draw" a square bounding box around the figure, using horizontal and vertical lines, such that the center of the square is at the origin and the sides of the square are outside or tangent to the figure.

This is very easy with a circle; the side of the square that encloses the circle is the circle's radius times 2. Every point $P = (x, y)$ with $-1.0 \leq x \leq 1.0$ and $-1.0 \leq y \leq 1.0$ lies inside a square with side length $= 2$ and most, but not all, of these points also lie inside the circle. We can now finish the definition at the top of the program:

```
#define BOX_SIDE   2.0    /* Bounding box side length. */
```

The `simulate()` function.   We start by writing the skeleton of the function to correspond with the given prototype:

```
double simulate( int max, double box_side ) {
   ...
}
```

The task of this function is to test whether a large number (specified by the first parameter, `max`) of random points are inside the figure whose area we are estimating. The flowchart in Figure 14.25 expresses this logic. To implement the process, we need a point variable, a counted loop, and a counter for successful, trials:

```
point_type random;      /* The point we select. */
int k;                  /* Loop counter. */
int count = 0;          /* Number of successful trials. */
for (k = 0; k < max; ++k) { ... }
```

This is a diagram of the function in Figure 14.26.

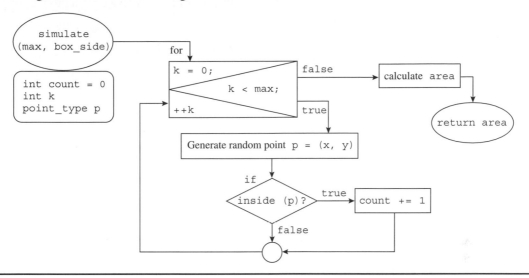

Figure 14.25.   Flow diagram for the Monte Carlo loop.

To generate a point, we need two randomly selected coordinates. Each should be a **double** value between **-BOX_SIDE/2** and **+BOX_SIDE/2**, which are the edges of the bounding box. C's random number function, **rand()**, gives us integers in the range **0...RAND_MAX**. Before using the results, we have to convert to type **double**, divide by **RAND_MAX** to scale the number to the range **0.0...1.0**, shift the number range so it is centered on the origin, and rescale the value to the box's dimension. We use a function named **randy()** from the **tools** library to call **rand()** and do the initial scaling and conversion:

```
/* ----------------------------------------------- */
/* Generate a random value between 0 and 1. */
double randy() {   return rand() / (double)RAND_MAX;   }
```

The result from **randy()** is in the range **0.0...1.0**, but we want a range centered on 0.0, so we shift the range by subtracting 0.5. Finally, the scale operation is accomplished by multiplying the result by **BOX_SIDE**. Using this formula, we generate a random point:

```
/* Get random x and y coordinates for point. */
random.x = (randy() - .5) * box_side;
random.y = (randy() - .5) * box_side;
```

Once generated, we must test whether the point is inside the figure and, if so, add 1 to the variable that counts the successes:

```
if (inside( random )) count += 1;
```

After generating and testing all the points, we calculate the percentage inside the figure and return an estimate of the area of the figure according to the formula in the specification:

```
return (box_side * box_side) * ((double)count / max);
```

The complete code for `simulate()` is shown in Figure 14.26.

14.4.4   Testing, Output, and Evaluation

We expect to achieve better and better estimates of the area as we perform more and more random trials. The accuracy of the estimate also depends on the quality of the random number generator being used. We ran this program several times with various numbers of random trials. Part of the output follows:

```
Monte Carlo Estimate of Area of Unit Circle
Number of random trials to use = 100
With 100 trials, estimated circle area = 3.12
------------------------------------------------------------
Number of random trials to use = 100
With 100 trials, estimated circle area = 3.28  ± .33
```

The loop in `simulate()` is diagrammed in Figure 14.25. The `randy()` function is in the `tools` library.

```
/* Is point p inside a unit circle? ------------------------------- */
bool inside( point_type p )
{
    return sqrt( p.x * p.x + p.y * p.y ) < 1.0;
}
/* Carry out the random trials. ----------------------------------- */
double simulate( int max, double box_side )
{
    point_type random;                /* The point we select. */
    int k;                            /* Loop counter. */
    int count = 0;                    /* Number of successful trials. */

    for (k = 0; k < max; ++k) {
        /* Get random x and y coordinates for point.  */
        random.x = (randy() - .5) * box_side;
        random.y = (randy() - .5) * box_side;
        if (inside( random )) count += 1;   /* +1 if inside circle. */
    }
    return box_side * box_side * ((double)count / max);
}
```

Figure 14.26.   Functions for the Monte Carlo simulation.

```
---------------------------------------------------------
Number of random trials to use = 1000
With 1000 trials, estimated circle area = 3.076
---------------------------------------------------------
Number of random trials to use = 5000
With 5000 trials, estimated circle area = 3.153        ± .044
---------------------------------------------------------
Number of random trials to use = 10000
With 10000 trials, estimated circle area = 3.122       ± .031
```

Note that the results are quite inconsistent and we are achieving only between two and three digits of precision, whether we use 1,000 or 10,000 random trials. This indicates that the random number generator supplied by the C system *← not true !* does not produce a very even distribution of random values.

14.5   What You Should Remember

14.5.1   Major Concepts

- A structured type can be used to represent an object with several properties. Each member of the structure represents one property and is given a name that reflects its meaning.
- A **struct** type specification does not create an object; it creates a pattern from which future variables may be created. Such patterns cannot contain initializations.
- The basic operations on structures include member access, assignment, use as function parameters and return values, and hierarchical object construction.
- Structured types can be combined with each other and with arrays to represent arbitrarily complex hierarchical objects. A table of data can be represented as an array of structures.
- An entire structured object can be used in the same ways as a simple object, with three exceptions. Input, output, and comparison of structured objects must be accomplished by operating on the individual components.

14.5.2   Programming Style

- *Structure declarations.* Declare all structures within **typedef** declarations. This simplifies their use and makes a program less error prone. Using a tag name in a **struct** specification is an advantage with some on-line debuggers.
- *Long-winded names.* The names of the members of a structure should be as brief as possible while still being clear. They must make sense in the context of a multipart name, but they need not make sense in isolation.

- *Using* **typedef** *wisely.* Type declarations can be overused or underused; try to avoid both pitfalls. Use of **typedef** should generally follow these guidelines:

  1. Use a structured type and **typedef** for a collection of related data items that will be used together and passed to functions as a group.
  2. Any type named using **typedef** should correspond to some concept with an independent meaning in the real world; for example, a point or a rectangle.
  3. Each **typedef** should make your code easier to understand, not more convoluted. Names of types should be concise, clear, and not too similar to names of objects.

- *Call by value vs. call by address.* Some structured objects are quite large. In such cases, using call by value for a function parameter consumes a substantial amount of run time during the function call because the entire structure must be copied into the parameter. This becomes significant because functions generally are used for input, output, and comparison of structures and so are called frequently. To increase program efficiency, use call by address for functions that process large structures. Remember, however, that this increases the likelihood of inadvertently modifying portions of the structure.

- *Array vs. structure.* Use a structure to represent an aggregate type with heterogeneous parts. For example, the **lumber_t** in Figure 14.2 is defined as a structure because its five members serve different purposes and have different types. If all parts of an aggregate are of the same type, we can choose between using an array and using a structure to represent it. In this case, the programmer should ask, "Do I think of the parts as being all alike or do the various parts have different purposes and must be processed uniquely?"

  For example, assume you want to measure the temperature once each hour and keep a list of temperatures for the day. This is best modeled by an array, because the temperatures have a uniform meaning and will be processed more-or-less in the same manner, likely as a group.

  Sometimes either technique can be used. For example, the rectangle defined in Figure 14.17 could have been defined as an array of four **double**s. However, each **double** has a different meaning, and the numbers in the first pair must be less than the numbers in the second pair. Giving unique symbolic names to the lower and upper corners, as well as to the *x* and *y* coordinates of each corner, makes the program easier to write and understand.

- *Parallel arrays vs. an array of structures.* These two ways to organize a list of data objects are syntactically quite different but similar in purpose. Most applications based on one could use the other instead. Parallel arrays require somewhat less writing and are well suited for menu processing.

However, an array of structures provides a better model for the data in a table and is considered more modern.

14.5.3   Sticky Points and Common Errors

- *Call by value.* If a parameter is not a pointer (and not an array), changes made to that parameter are not passed back to the caller. Be sure to use call by address if any part of a structured parameter is modified by the function.
- *The dot and arrow operators.* Two C operators are used to access members of structures: the dot and the arrow. If `obj` is the name of a structured variable, then we access its parts using the dot. If `p` is a pointer to a structured variable, we use the arrow.

    Even so, programmers sometimes become confused because the same object is accessed sometimes with one operator and sometimes with the other. For example, suppose a program passes a structured object to a function using call by address. Within the main program, it is a structure and its members are accessed using dot notation. But the function parameter is a pointer to a structure, so its members are accessed within the function using an arrow. Another function might use a call-by-value parameter and would access the object using a dot.

    For these reasons, it is necessary to think carefully about each function parameter and decide whether to use call by value or address. This determines the operator to use (dot or arrow) in the function's body. If you use the wrong one, the compiler will issue an error comment about a type mismatch between the object name and the operator.
- *Comparison and copying with pointers.* When working with pointers to structures remember that the result is a two-part object like a string. If one pointer is assigned or compared to another, only the pointer part is affected, not the underlying structure. To do a structure assignment through a pointer, you must dereference the pointer. To do a structure comparison, you must write a comparison function and call it.

14.5.4   New and Revisited Vocabulary

These are the most important terms and concepts presented in this chapter:

structure	selection expression	operations on structures
aggregate type	dot operator (member access)	comparing structures
member	arrow operator (member access)	hierarchical structures
member name	call by value or address	array of structures
tag name	pointer to a structure	parallel arrays
`typedef` name	sentinel value	delegating work
member declaration	epsilon test	Monte Carlo method
structured initializer		

The following keywords, C library functions, and functions from the **tools** library were discussed or used in this chapter:

struct	**&** (address of)	**srand()**
typedef	***** (dereference)	**rand()**
fabs()	**->** (dereference and member access)	**randy()**
tolower()	**.** (member access)	**strequal()**

14.6   Exercises

14.6.1 Self-Test Exercises

1. a. Give an example of a situation in which you could use either an array or a structure but the array would be better.

   b. Give an example of a situation in which you could use either an array or a structure but the structure would be better.

   c. Give an example of a situation in which you could use a set of parallel arrays but an array of structures would be better.

   d. Give an example of a situation in which you could use an array of structures but parallel arrays would be better.

2. Write a **typedef** declaration for the pictured structured type, which will be used to fill in a doctor's appointment calendar with the patient's name and appointment time.

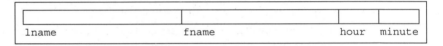

```
lname                          fname                    hour   minute
```

3. a. Write a **typedef** declaration that defines an enumerated type for the days of the week. Call the type **day_type**.

   b. Write a **typedef** declaration for a structure named **today_type** with members for the name of the day of the week, the year, month, and day. The year, month, and day should be integers.

   c. Declare a **today_type** variable with an initializer containing today's date.

4. Given these **typedef** declarations, find and fix any errors in the statements that follow. (Hint: One statement is valid.)

```
typedef enum STATE { CT, ME, MA, NH, RI, VT } state_t;
string name[] = { "Connecticut","Maine","Massachusetts",
        "New Hampshire","Rhode Island","Vermont" };
typedef struct TRIP {  state_t start, end;
                       short days;  } trip_t;


a. trip_t CT, vacation;    /* Variables for two trips. */

b. scanf( "%11s", vacation.start );
```

c. `vacation.end = "VT";`

d. `vacation->days = 3;`

e. `printf( "Begin at: %s\n", name[vacation.start] );`

5. a. Define a type named **point** that represents a point on a computer screen as a horizontal coordinate between 0 and 1599 and a vertical coordinate between 0 and 1199.

   b. Define a type named **line** that represents a line on a computer screen as two points and an integer between 0 and 15 that represents the thickness of the line.

   c. Declare an object named **corners** of type **line** and initialize it to the coordinate limits and the maximum thickness just given.

   d. Write a function named **get_line()** that will read all the data for a line and return it through an output parameter that is a pointer to a **line**. It should take **corners** as an input parameter and use it to validate all parts of the data.

6. Using the types and the string array defined in problem 4, diagram the array named **trip** created by the following code. In this diagram, show some possible values that might be stored in the object by the loop.

```
#define DAYS 3
trip_t trip[DAYS];
int k;
trip[0].start = menu_i( " Trip begins at: ", 6, name );
trip[DAYS-1].end = trip[0].start;
for (k = 0; k < DAYS-1; ++k) {
    printf( "Day %i begins at: %s",
            k, name[trip[k].start] );
    trip[k].end = menu_i( " Day ends at: ", 6, name );
    trip[k].days = 1;
    trip[k+1].start = trip[k].end;
}
```

14.6.2   Using Pencil and Paper

1. Assume you have a grading program that reads a student's ID number and three exam grades so that it can compute the exam average.

   a. Write a **typedef** declaration for an entire student record containing an ID number, an array of three grades, and an average.

   b. Write a variable declaration for an array of 20 student records named **class**. Initialize this array to hold all 0 values.

2. a. Write a **typedef** declaration for an enumerated type that lists the kinds of wood kept in stock at a lumber company. These include maple, pine, oak, mahogany, teak, walnut, and fir.

   b. Modify the specification of **lumber_t** in Figure 14.2 to use the enumerated type instead of a string.

c. Declare an array of boards named **stock**; initialize it to these values:

```
stock
```

wood	height	width	length	price	quantity
maple	1	6	4	8.00	27
maple	1	8	6	16.00	70
pine	2	6	8	15.65	198

3. a. Define a type named **xyz_point** that represents a point in three-dimensional space as a structure of three numbers.

   b. Define a type that represents a tetrahedron in three-dimensional space as a structure of four **xyz_point**s. Call the type **tetra**.

   c. Given these **typedef** statements, declare a tetrahedron variable, **T**, and initialize it in the declaration so that one corner lies at the origin and each of its other three corners are 1 unit from the origin in the positive direction along each of the three axes.

4. a. Redo the last declaration in the previous problem to declare a tetrahedron object as an array of four **xyz_point**s. Initialize this object, as described previously.

   b. Redo the object declaration with no type definitions. Declare three parallel arrays, for the x, y, and z coordinates, and initialize them to the same values.

   c. Which of the three styles of object representation do you prefer? Why?

5. Given these **typedef** declarations and function prototype, find and fix the errors in the statements that follow.

```
typedef enum STATE {AWFUL, BAD, OK, GOOD, FINE} state_t;
typedef struct JUNK {
    char name[16];
    short size; float price; state_t status;
} junk_t;
string label[] = {"Awful", "Bad", "Ok", "Good", "Fine"};

void analyze( junk_t j );
```

   a. `JUNK heap;    /* Variable for info about my junk. */`

   b. `scanf("%15s%hi%g", heap);   /* Read junk's name,
                                        size, price. */`

   c. `heap.state_t = BAD;`

   d. `analyze( junk_t heap );`

   e. `printf("%s: condition = %s\n", heap.name, heap.status);`

6. You are writing a program as part of an inventory system for a very small store. Given the declarations shown, write statements that do each task. Assume that all flowers are sold in packages that contain between 1 and 100 plants.

```
typedef enum {WHITE, YELLOW, PURPLE, PINK, RED} color_t;
typedef struct GARDEN {
      char what[12]; color_t hue; float cost; short count;
} flower_t;
```

a. Declare an array named **stock** that can hold the data for all of the flowers in stock; assume the store never has more than 200 kinds of flowers.

b. Write a loop that will read the data for up to 200 flowers. Within this loop, write one **scanf()** statement that will read a flower's name, price, and the number per package and store them in the next slot of the array. Present the user with a menu from which to select a color, and store that color in the structure.

c. Write a function, **buy()**, that will take a **flower_t** structure as its parameter. In this function, prompt the user for the quantity of the flower he or she wishes to buy. Figure out how many packages are needed to fill the order, and return the total price of that many packages.

7. Using the types defined in exercise 5, diagram the object created by the following code. In this diagram, show possible values that might be stored in the object by the loop.

```
junk_t j[3] = {{"rug",0,0},{"chair",0,0},{"table",0,0}};
int k;
for (k = 0; k < 3; ++k) {
    printf( "\n Next item: %s ", j[k].name );
    j[k].status = menu_i( " Condition: ", 5, label );
    printf( "Price of item: " );
    scanf( "%g", &j[k].price );
}
```

14.6.3   Using the Computer

1. Gas pressures revisited.
   Rewrite the gas pressures program that begins in Figure 13.32 to use an array of structures, instead of parallel arrays, for the table of data.

2. Wages earned.
   You are writing a program that is part of a payroll system for a very small store. Given these declarations, write a program that does the tasks listed. Assume that all workers are paid by the hour.

```
typedef enum { MANAGER, STOCKER, CLERK, BAGGER } job_t;
typedef struct WORKER {
      char name[20]; job_t title;
      float payrate; float hours;
} worker_t;
```

a. In **main()**,

   • Declare an array object to hold the data for 10 workers.

- Print titles and report headings, then call the input function described next to fill in the data array.
- Write a loop that processes pay for all the workers in the array. Within this loop, use **hours** and the worker's pay rate to calculate the employee's weekly pay. Print the worker's name and pay, and keep sums of the total wages earned by the employees in each of the four categories.
- At the end of the loop, print the total pay for each category of workers and the grand total for all workers.

  b. In the input function, write a loop that reads the data for all 10 workers. An array to hold these data should be a parameter to the function. Within this loop, write one **scanf()** statement that reads a worker's name, pay rate, and hours worked, and store them in the current slot of the array. Then present a menu of job types and store the response in the record.

3. A point in a circle.

Develop a program to determine whether a point is inside a circle defined in the xy plane. The circle is represented by a single point C, its center, and a length, its radius. A point P is defined to be inside a circle if the distance from it to the center, C, is less than the radius of the circle. It is on the circle if the distance equals the radius and outside otherwise. The distance D between two points, C and P, is given by the following formula, derived from the Pythagorean theorem:

$$D = \sqrt{(P.x - C.x)^2 + (P.y - C.y)^2}$$

Model your solution after the rectangle program that begins in Figure 14.17.

  a. Write program specifications that include a discussion of limitations and degenerate cases. Provide a diagram that defines the variable names.

  b. Write a test plan that is complete and adequate to test the program fully, including degenerate cases.

  c. Write a program that determines the locations of a series of points relative to a circle, for possibly many circles. Use functions to perform tasks similar to those in the rectangle program.

  d. Compile the program and test it using your test plan.

4. Triangle shapes.

Develop a program to determine whether a triangle is equilateral (all sides are the same length), isosceles (two sides are equal), or scalene (no sides are equal).

  a. Write program specifications that include a discussion of limitations and degenerate cases. Provide a diagram that defines the variable names.

  b. Write a test plan that is complete and adequate to test the program fully, including degenerate cases.

  c. Define a type to represent a triangle as three points, where each point has an x and y coordinate. Also define an enumerated type, **shape_t**, and a parallel array of output labels to represent the three possible triangle shapes: **equilateral**, **isosceles**, and **scalene**.

d. Write a function, **get_triangle()**, to input the three corners of a triangle and return a triangle structure.

e. Write a function, **classify()**, that will analyze the shape of a triangle. The argument should be one triangle; the result should be a value of type **shape_t**.

f. Write a program that will permit the user to enter a series of triangles. For each, echo the input, call the **classify()** function, and print the triangle's shape.

5. Area of a quadrilateral.
A convex quadrilateral is a four-sided planar polygon with the property that any two points within it can be connected by a line that does not cross the border of the polygon.

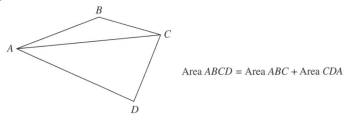

Area $ABCD$ = Area ABC + Area CDA

To compute the area of any convex quadrilateral, you can divide it into two triangles by drawing either diagonal and sum their areas. For example, the area of the quadrilateral $ABCD$ is the sum of the areas of the two triangles ABC and CDA. The area of a triangle can be calculated easily if its three coordinates are known. Suppose triangle $A_1 = ABC$ has coordinates $A = (x_a, y_a)$, $B = (x_b, y_b)$, and $C = (x_c, y_c)$. Its area is

$$A_1 = \frac{|x_a \times y_b - x_b \times y_a + x_b \times y_c - x_c \times y_b + x_c \times y_a - x_a \times y_c|}{2}$$

a. Write a program with a **work()** function that processes a series of quadrilaterals. From the **work()** function, call the three functions listed next to calculate and print the area of the quadrilateral.

b. Write a **get_quad()** function to input the four corners of a quadrilateral from the keyboard. Tell the user to enter the points in a clockwise direction. Verify that the quadrilateral's four points are all different (write a subfunction to do this).

c. Write a **print_quad()** function to output the quadrilateral's points.

d. Write an **area()** function that calculates and returns the area of a triangle; the parameters should be three points.

6. Cylinders.
We have a set of small cylinders filled with various substances and wish to calculate some statistics about these cylinders. We are given the diameter, height, mass, and contents of each cylinder (a string of up to 15 characters). We wish to calculate their volume and density.

a. Write a **typedef** for **cyl_type** that defines a **struct** with members for these six properties. The common symbol for density is the Greek letter ρ (rho).

b. Declare **barrels** to be an array of **cyl_type** with 20 slots.

c. Write a void function, **read_barrel()**, with an address parameter. It will read the diameter (cm), height (cm), mass (g), and contents for one cylinder into the members of its parameter. After reading the data, calculate the volume, V, and density, ρ, of the barrel and store the answers in the appropriate members. Use these formulas, where d is the diameter, h is the height, and m is the mass of the cylinder (the contents plus the barrel itself):

$$V = \pi \times \left(\frac{d}{2}\right)^2 \times h \quad (\text{cm}^3)$$

$$\rho = \frac{m}{V} \quad (\text{g/cm}^3)$$

d. Write a **bool** function, **floats()**, that returns **true** if a barrel floats on water, **false** otherwise. An item floats on water if its density is less than the density of water. Use 1.0 g/cm^3 as the density of water.

e. Write a main program. It must contain a sentineled loop that will read the data for up to 20 barrels and store the number of barrels actually read. It then should print a neat table showing all six member values for each cylinder. The seventh column of the table should say *Floats* or *Sinks*, based on the results of the **floats()** function. Calculate the total mass and the total volume of the barrels and print these at the bottom of the table.

7. Torque.

Given a solid body, the net torque, $T(\text{Nm})$, about its centroidal axis of rotation is related to the moment of inertia, I, and the angular acceleration acc (rad/s^2), according to the formula for the conservation of angular momentum:

$$T = I \times acc$$

The moment of inertia depends on the shape of the body:

Solid	Moment of Inertia	
Cone	$0.3 \times \text{mass} \times r^2$	r is the radius of the cone's base
Sphere	$0.4 \times \text{mass} \times r^2$	r is the radius of the sphere
Disk	$0.5 \times \text{mass} \times r^2$	r is the radius of the disk

a. Define an enumerated type and a parallel array of labels for the three shapes.

b. Define a structure type to represent the five constants associated with each shape: one constant from the formula in the preceding table, plus the four limits from the following table:

Solid	Correct r Values (m)	Correct Mass Values (kg)
Cone	$0.024 \leq r \leq 0.070$	$0.23 < \text{mass} \leq 9.7$
Sphere	$0.015 \leq r \leq 0.045$	$0.11 < \text{mass} \leq 10$
Disk	$0.093 \leq r \leq 0.207$	$0.088 < \text{mass} \leq 11$

Declare and initialize an array of structures to store the constants from these tables.

c. Write a program with a **work()** loop so that you can conveniently test several data sets. In this loop, present a menu of shapes. Then call the **get_data()** function (described next), with the appropriate row of limits from the table, using the menu choice as a subscript. Use the data it returns to compute the moment of inertia and the torque. Echo the data and print both answers.

d. Write a function named **get_data()** to read one data set. Prompt for and read values for the angular acceleration, *r*, and *m*. Take one line from the table of constants as an input parameter and screen out values of *r* and *m* outside the ranges listed. Return the three results through pointer parameters.

8. Rational numbers.

A *rational number*, in everyday terminology, is a fraction. It has two parts, a numerator and a denominator. Most calculations can be done quite satisfactorily with either integers or floating-point numbers. However, occasionally, rational arithmetic is desirable because both numerator and denominator are represented as integers and no precision is lost by truncating the number after the division. Of course, rational arithmetic is much slower than arithmetic with data types that are built into the hardware. Define a type **rational** as a structure with a numerator, **n**, and a denominator, **d**. Then build a set of functions for handling rational numbers; include all functions whose prototypes are listed here. Finally, write a main program to call and test each function in the package. The test plan should include at least two test cases per operation and a final expression that combines several operations.

a. **long gcd(long n, long d)**. Compute and return the greatest common divisor of **n** and **d**, as follows:

```
begin loop:
  Let r be n % d.
  If r == 0, leave loop and return d as the answer.
  Otherwise, set n = d, d = r, and go to top of loop.
end loop.
```

b. **rational reduce(rational r)**. Reduce **r** to its lowest terms and return the result. To do this, compute the greatest common divisor (gcd) of **r**'s numerator and denominator. The numerator of the result is the original numerator divided by the gcd. The denominator of the result is the original denominator divided by the gcd.

c. **rational getr(void)**. Read a numerator *n* and a denominator *d*. Use a validation loop to eliminate zero values for *d*. If *d* is negative, set it to its absolute value and set *n* to $-n$. Store *n* and *d* in a local variable of type **rational** and call **reduce()** to reduce it to lowest terms. Return the result.

d. **void putr(rational r)**. Print a **rational** number as (n / d).

e. **rational negate(rational r)**. Negate the numerator and return the result.

f. **rational product(rational r, rational s)**. Create a new **rational** number with numerator equal to the product of the two numerators and denominator equal to the product of the denominators. Call **reduce()** and return the result.

g. `rational invert( rational r )`. Create a new **rational** number whose numerator is the denominator of **r** and vice versa. Return the result.

h. `rational sum( rational r, rational s )`. Adding two **rational** numbers is done in two steps. First, compute the two parts of the answer:

```
numerator = r.n * s.d + s.n * r.d;
denominator = r.d * s.d;
```

Call **reduce()** to eliminate common factors from the numerator and denominator. Return the result.

9. Complex numbers.

Complex numbers are used in many scientific calculations. They are an important built-in data type in FORTRAN but not in C. Imagine that your professor needs to do complex mathematics and has asked you to create a complex-number package. Define a type **complex** as a structure with a real part named **rp** and an imaginary part named **ip**. Then build a set of functions for handling **complex** numbers; include all functions whose prototypes follow. Finally, write a main program to call and test each function in the package. The test plan should include at least two test cases per operation and a final expression that combines several operations.

a. `complex getx( void )`. Read two **double** values, the real part, **rp**, followed by the imaginary part, **ip**. Store them in a local variable of type **complex** and return the result.

b. `void putx( complex z )`. Print a **complex** number as (**rp + i*ip**).

c. `complex sum( complex c, complex d )`.   Return the following **complex** number:

```
real part = sum of real parts of c and d.
imaginary part = sum of imaginary parts of c and d.
```

d. `complex product( complex c, complex d )`. Return the following **complex** number:

```
real part = c.rp * d.rp - c.ip * d.ip
imaginary part = c.rp * d.ip + c.ip * d.rp
```

e. `complex square( complex z )`. Return the result of the call `product( z, z )`.

f. `complex inverse( complex z )`. Return the following **complex** number:

```
real part = z.rp / (square(z.rp) + square(z.ip))
imaginary part = -z.ip / (square(z.rp) + square(z.ip))
```

g. `complex negate( complex z )`. Return the **complex** number whose parts are the negation of the two parts of **z**.

    h. `complex conjugate( complex c )`. Return the `complex` number with the same real part and the negation of the imaginary part.

    i. `double cabs( complex z )`. Return the square root of `z`'s real part squared plus `z`'s imaginary part squared.
Note: `cabs( z ) = product( z, conjugate(z) )`.

10. Do you have the time of day?
Working with time is well understood but has many tricky aspects. In this program, you will implement a simple representation for a time and a few basic operations on times.

    a. Define an enumerated type named **APD** to represent the options AM, PM, and duration.

    b. Define a structured type to represent a time in the 24-hour system as four short integers (hours, minutes, seconds, days).

    c. You can represent a duration using the same type. For example, 3 hours, 2 minutes, and 30 seconds could be represented as 3:2:30. The days member will not be used for duration.

    d. Write a function to input a duration in the format 3:2:30 *d* or a time in the 12-hour system in the format 1:25:00 *a* or 10:9:00 *p*. Validate all three fields, convert the time to the 24-hour system, and set the days field to 0. Store the appropriate **APD** constant in the record. Return the result as a structured value.

    e. Write a function to print a 24-hour time in a 12-hour format. If the days field is nonzero, print that information last. Your output might look like this:
Time: 12:20:00 PM + 2 days.

    f. Write a function named **add()** whose parameters are a time and a duration. Add the duration to the time and return a time. For example, if you add 1:25:00 *a* and 3:2:30 *d*, you get 4:27:30 *a*. After adding each part, adjust the answer so that a number of seconds greater than 59 carries into the minutes member. Similarly, more than 60 minutes should carry into the hours member. If the hour number is greater than 23, let it wrap back to 0 and set the days field appropriately.

    g. Write a test plan that includes difficult cases as well as ordinary ones.

    h. Write a main program that will call the functions. Test it thoroughly.

CHAPTER
15

Streams and Files

We have been using the input function `scanf()` and the output functions `puts()` and `printf()` since Chapter 3. In this chapter, we introduce the concept of streams, the three predefined streams, and programmer-defined streams. We also present several additional input and output functions, go more deeply into the complexities of the I/O system, consider I/O errors, and present an example of a crash-resistant, programmer-defined input function.

Even with no compile-time errors and all the calculations correct, a program's output can be wrong because of run-time errors during the input or output stages. Such errors can be caused by format errors, incorrect data entry, or human carelessness. Hardware devices also occasionally fail. Three ways to detect certain input errors have been used since the beginning of this text:

1. Echo the input data to see what the program actually is processing for its computations. The values displayed may not be the values the user intended to enter.
2. Use `if` or `while` statements to test whether the input values are within acceptable ranges.
3. Write a test plan that lists important categories of input with the corresponding expected output. Use these examples of input to test the program and inspect the output to ensure correctness.

We describe one more important method of detecting input errors and show a variety of ways to recover from these mistakes.

Streams and Buffers

To understand the complexities of I/O, it is necessary to know about streams and buffers. In this section we describe these basic components of the I/O system.

15.1.1 Stream I/O

The input or output of a program is a sequence of data bytes that comes from or goes to a file, the keyboard, the video screen, a network socket,[1] or, possibly, other devices. A C stream is the conduit that connects a program to a device and carries the data into or out of the program.

You can think of a stream as being like a garden hose. To use a hose, we must find an available one or purchase a new one. Before water can flow, the hose must be attached to a source of water on one end and the other end must be aimed at a destination for the water. Then, when the valve is opened, water flows from source to destination (see Figure 15.1). When we open a stream for reading, it carries information from the source to our program. A stream opened in write or append mode carries data from the program to a destination. Calling an input function to read the data or an output function to write them, is like turning on the valve and letting the water flow.

Standard streams.   Three streams are predefined in C: **stdin**, **stdout**, and **stderr**. These streams are defined by **stdio.h** and connected, by default, to the keyboard and monitor screen as shown in Figure 15.2. These default connections provide excellent support for interactive input and output. Additional **streams** can be created by a program and attached to sources or destinations outside the program by using the **fopen()** function, which is covered in the next

---

An output stream connects a program to a file or an output device. Calling an output function is like opening the valve: It lets the data flow through the stream to their destination.

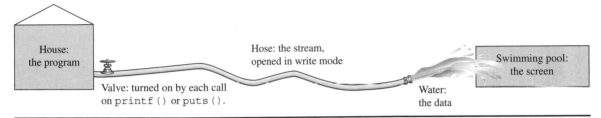

Figure 15.1.   A stream carries data.

---

[1] A network socket is used to connect an input or output stream to a network.

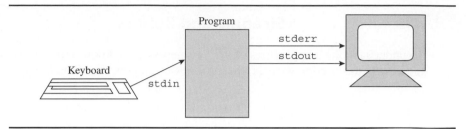

Figure 15.2.   The three default streams.

section. Also, the default connections can be changed by a technique called **file redirection**, so that the streams become attached to files rather than the interactive devices.

- The **stdin** stream is the standard input stream. It is used whenever we call **scanf()**, **getchar()**, or **gets()**. Normally, **stdin** is connected to the user's keyboard, although most systems permit it to be redirected so that data come from a file instead.

- The **stdout** stream is the standard output stream. It is used by **printf()**, **putchar()**, and **puts()**. Normally, **stdout** is connected to the user's video screen, although most systems permit it to be redirected so that data go to a file instead.

- The **stderr** stream is the standard error stream. It is used by the operating system to display error comments, although any program can write output, instructions, and error messages into **stderr**. The error stream normally is connected to the user's video screen; although it can be redirected, it seldom is. There is no standard function that uses only **stderr**. However, two functions in the **tools** library write to **stderr**: **fatal()** (which we already discussed) and **say()**. The function **say()** displays information to **stderr** in exactly the same manner as **fatal()**, but it does not call **exit()** to abort the program. Both functions use **fprintf()** (defined in an upcoming section). The details of these functions are described in Appendix F.

Stream redirection (optional topic).   The streams **stdin** and **stdout** allow the user to run programs interactively. During the debugging process, this interaction is important so that the programmer can monitor the progress of the job. However, it can also be quite useful to run a program noninteractively; that is, taking its input from a file or sending its output to a file.

For example, a complete set of test data for a complex program may require many lines of input. Most programs must be tested again and again before they are fully debugged. The easiest, surest way to perform a series of identical tests is to enter the input data into a file and cause the program to read from that file as if it were the keyboard. Similarly, it can be very helpful to have the output recorded in a file for later review.

Most operating systems permit the user to run a program both interactively and noninteractively without changing the program. This is done from the system shell using a facility called *file redirection*. For example, assume you are using a UNIX system and want to run the program `myroot`. Figure 15.3 shows possible commands to run the program with `stdin` or `stdout` redirected to files.

Notes on Figure 15.3: File redirection in UNIX.

- *First run*. The first run of the program is fully interactive; the user types just the name of the executable file to start the program, then sees user prompts and enters the data from the keyboard.
- *Second run*. The second run is fully noninteractive; both input and output are redirected. The less-than sign before the file name `my.in` is the `stdin` redirection symbol; the greater-than sign before the file name `my.out` is the `stdout` redirection symbol. Redirection is in force throughout the duration of the program; the user sees nothing until the system prompt reappears, unless the program uses `stderr`.
- *Third run*. The third run takes its input from the file `my.in` and puts its output on the screen. This style of operation is useful during program testing, especially if a lot of data are needed for a test.
- *Fourth run*. The last run takes interactive input but sends the output to the file `my.out`. Redirecting output but not input is not particularly useful for a program designed to be interactive because the user sees none of the normal input prompts and must guess or remember what to enter and when. However, some programs are designed specifically to work with redirection. User information may be sent to `stderr` while the primary output goes to `stdout` (see Figure 15.4).

At the system prompt, (`~>`), one can give any of these four UNIX commands to run the program `myroot`, with different outcomes. Similar commands work in recent versions of DOS.

```
~> myroot
~> myroot < my.in > my.out
~> myroot < my.in
~> myroot > my.out
```

Figure 15.3.   Stream redirection in UNIX.

By redirecting **stdout**, we separate it from **stderr**. User instructions then are written to **stderr** and the primary output to **stdout**.

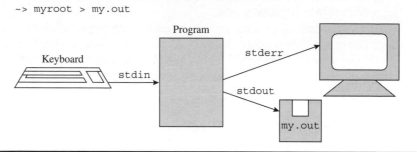

Figure 15.4.   Redirecting stdout.

15.1.2   Buffering

Water moves through a garden hose in a continuous stream. In contrast, a C stream generally is buffered, causing the data to flow through it in blocks. A **buffer** is a sequence of memory locations that is part of every stream. It lies between the producer and the consumer of the data, temporarily storing data after they are produced and before they are consumed, so that the characteristics of the I/O devices can be matched to the operation of the program.

The system reads or writes the data in blocks, through the stream, even if the user scans or prints data one item at a time. This buffering normally is transparent to the programmer. However, there are some curious and, perhaps, tricky aspects of C input and output that cannot be understood without knowing about buffers.

Input buffering.   An input stream is illustrated in Figure 15.5. The data in a stream flow through the buffer in blocks; at any time, part of the data in the buffer already will have been read by the program and part remains waiting to be read in the future.

An input stream delivers an ordered sequence of bytes from its source to the program on demand. When the buffer for an input stream is empty and the user calls for more input, an entire unit of data will be transferred from the source into the buffer. The size of this unit will vary according to the data source. For example, if the stream is connected to a disk file, at least one disk cluster (often 1,024 or 2,048 characters) will be moved at a time. When that data block is used up, another will be retrieved.

Keyboard input actually goes through two buffers. The keyboard, itself, has a buffer. When you enter data for an interactive program, the keystrokes remain in the keyboard buffer until you press Enter. If you make an error, you can use the Backspace key to correct it. Using the Enter key causes the line to go from the

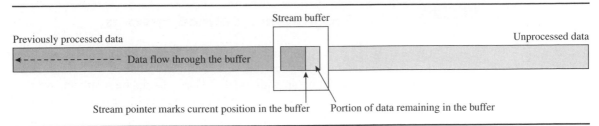

Figure 15.5.   A buffer is a window on the data.

keyboard buffer into the stream buffer. Then your program takes the data from the stream buffer one item at a time.

Output buffering and flushing.   An output stream delivers an ordered sequence of bytes from the program to a device. Items will go into a buffer whenever `printf()`, `puts()`, or another output function is called. The data then are transferred to the device as a block, whenever the output stream is flushed, which may occur for several reasons. Information written to `stdout` normally stays in the buffer until a newline character is written or the program switches from producing output to requesting input. At that time, the contents of the buffer are flushed to the screen and become visible to the user. For other output streams, the system will send the output to its destination when the buffer is full. All output buffers are flushed automatically when the program exits. A program also can give an explicit command to flush the buffer, using the `fflush()` function, which takes a stream as its only parameter and sends the data in that stream's buffer to its destination immediately.

Unbuffered I/O (advanced topic).   Some systems support a function that will read unbuffered keyboard input. For example, Turbo and Borland C supply a function, `getche()`, that returns a single character without waiting for the Enter key to be hit. In Microsoft C, the function `kbhit()` returns a signal when some key on the keyboard is hit. Unfortunately, using functions like these makes a program nonstandard and entirely nonportable and so their use is generally not recommended.

In contrast to `stdout`, `stderr` is an **unbuffered** output **stream**. Messages sent to it are passed on to their destination immediately. When both standard streams are directed to the same video screen, it is possible for the output to appear in a different order than that which was written. This could happen when a line sent to `stdout` does not end in a newline character and is held in the buffer indefinitely, until a newline is written or the program ends. Other material sent to `stderr` during this holding period will appear on the screen first.

| 15.2 | **Programmer-Defined Streams** |

The streams `stdin`, `stdout`, and `stderr` are defined by default. A programmer who wishes to read or write data from or to a file can either redirect one of these standard streams or define an additional stream. To define a stream, we must give it a name and open it (this causes it to be connected to a specified source or destination file for data).

Streams can be opened in text mode or binary mode. (**Binary files** are used for executable code, bit images, and the compressed, archived versions of text files.) In this chapter, we concentrate on using text files; binary data files are explored in Chapter 17. **Text files** (in character codes such as ASCII or International ASCII) are used for most purposes, including program source files and many data files.

15.2.1 Defining and Using Streams

A variety of constants and functions are used to set up and control stream I/O. We discuss many of them in this chapter, as they are needed. We already have seen `fflush()`; the two basic stream management functions, `fopen()` and `fclose()`, are discussed next.

p663

Although the concept of a stream exists in C, the word `stream` is not a predefined type name. However, the type name `FILE` is defined by `stdio.h`, and the stream input and output functions expect arguments of type `FILE*`. Since it always is awkward and error prone to use type names that include an asterisk (such as `char*` and `FILE*`), we use a `typedef` statement to define the name `stream` and use `stream` in our programs.

- `stream fopen( string filename, string mode )`. This is used to open a file with the given name, attach it to a stream name, and declare the mode of the file. The most common **stream modes** are to read text (`"r"`), read binary (`"rb"`), write text (`"w"`), write binary (`"wb"`), and write and append text (`"a"`).
- `int fclose( stream s )`. Here, we flush the data buffer for this stream and close the file. Since this is done automatically when a program terminates normally, the primary use for this function is to close streams that are used only early in a program. Closing a stream releases the buffer's memory space and allows the file to be used by others.

Figure 15.6 illustrates how streams can be declared and opened, resulting in the configuration shown in Figure 15.7.

Notes on Figure 15.6. Streams and `fopen()`.

- *First box: declaring the type stream.* The `typedef` in the first box allows us to use `stream` as a type name and makes `stream` a synonym for `FILE*`. This type declaration is given in `tools.h`, as was the definition of `string`.

We define four streams and open them for input or output.

```
typedef FILE* stream;

stream f_in, f_out, s_in, s_out, b_in, b_out;

f_in = fopen( "prog4.in", "r" );
s_in = fopen( "a:\\cs110\\my.in", "r" );
b_in = fopen( "image1.in", "rb" );

f_out = fopen( "prog4.out", "a" );
s_out = fopen( "a:\\my.out", "w" );
b_out = fopen( "image1.out", "wb" );
```

Figure 15.6.　Streams and `fopen()`.

This shows the three default stream assignments, plus the streams **s_in** and **s_out**, which were declared and opened in Figure 15.6.

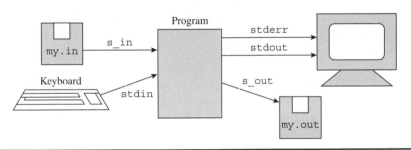

Figure 15.7.　Programmer-defined streams.

- *Second box: stream variables.* We declare six stream variables here: **f_in**, **f_out**, **s_in**, **s_out**, **b_in**, and **b_out**. When opened properly, these stream names will allow us access to six different files. Figure 15.7 shows the configuration that would be created if only **s_in** and **s_out** were opened.

- *Third box: opening input streams.* The function **fopen()** is used to open all kinds of streams. It creates a data structure of type **FILE**, which is managed by the system, not by the programmer. It creates memory for the stream's buffer, a pointer to the current position in the buffer, flags for error and end-of-file conditions (discussed later), and anything else it needs to maintain and process the stream. The programmer never accesses the **FILE** object directly, so it is not necessary to know exactly how it is implemented. Rather, a pointer to this structure is returned from **fopen()**, and it should be stored in a **stream** variable that then is used with C's input or output functions. Usually a limit (determined by the local system) is placed on the number of files that can be open simultaneously; however, this limit is generous and rarely becomes an issue. In the third box of Figure 15.6, we open two input streams for text data. The **"r"** designates them as input streams (**"r"** means "read"). One stream is attached to the file **prog4.in**, which must be in the current directory, normally, the directory containing the executable code for the program. The assignment operator stores the stream pointer in the variable **f_in**. If the file is not in the current default directory, its entire pathname must be written between the quotes. The second call on **fopen()** opens an input stream for the file **my.in**, located in subdirectory **cs110** on a diskette in the A drive. Because backslash is the C escape character, it is necessary to write two backslash characters in the code to get one in the pathname. The third stream, **b_in**, is opened for input in binary mode and attached to a binary image file. This stream's data could be read using **fread()**, as we demonstrate in Chapter 17.

- *Fourth box: opening output streams.* We open a stream, **s_out**, and attach it to the file **my.out**. The **"w"** mode means "write" and makes this an output stream. If the file does not already exist in the named directory, it will be created. If it does exist, the old version will be destroyed. For this reason, some caution is advised; when selecting a name for an output file, it should not duplicate the name of another file in the same directory. The append mode **"a"** is like the write mode except that the new material will be written at the end of the existing file's contents. We open the output stream **f_out** in the append mode and attach it to the file **prog4.out**. If the file does not yet exist, it is created and the stream shifts to write mode. The third stream in this box, **b_out**, is opened for output in the binary mode and attached to a file that will receive a binary image. This stream's data could be written using **fwrite()**, as we also demonstrate in Chapter 17.

15.2.2   File Management Errors

The **fopen()** function has a return type of **FILE***. Under normal conditions, the return value is the address of the **FILE** record for the stream. But what if something goes wrong and the file cannot be opened? If this happens, an error indicator is returned.

Stream-opening errors.   Several things must be done to open a stream; if any one of them goes wrong, the "opening" action will fail. These include

- An appropriate-sized buffer must be allocated for the stream. If space for this buffer is not available in the computer's memory, **fopen()** will fail. If allocation is successful, the address of the buffer is stored as a member of the **FILE** object.

- For input, the operating system must locate the file. If the file is protected or no file of that name exists in the designated directory, **fopen()** will fail. Otherwise, the location of the beginning of the file is stored in the **FILE** object.
- For output, the operating system must check whether a file of that name already exists. If so, it is deleted. Then space must be found on the disk for a new file. This process can fail if the disk is full, the file is protected, or the user lacks permission to write in the specified directory.

If a stream cannot be opened properly, **fopen()** returns a value of **NULL**. It is a very good idea to check for this condition before trying to use the newly opened stream. Otherwise, you are likely to "hang" or crash your program and may be forced to reboot your computer. Such a check is simple enough: Simply compare the stream pointer to **NULL** and take appropriate action if a failure is detected. This technique is shown in the remaining programs in this chapter.

Stream-closing errors.   Closing a file causes the system to flush the buffer and do a little bookkeeping. It is rare that something will go wrong with this process; a full disk is the main cause for problems. Both **fflush()** and **fclose()** return integer error indicators. However, since trouble occurs infrequently, programs rarely check for them. We will not do so in this text.

15.3   Stream Output

Once a stream has been properly opened in write or append mode, data can be sent from the program to the stream destination. When we wrote to the **stdout** stream, we used the functions **printf()**, **puts()**, and **putchar()**, which implicitly use **stdout**. Another set of functions, analogous to these, let us specify the stream. Most of these new functions have names like the name of the old function preceded by **f** (for "file"). Their first argument often is the name of the stream to use. Each function is described below in a form similar to a prototype, with the return type first followed by the function name and an indication of the number, type, and order of the parameters. An **output list** is a list of expressions whose values are to be output.

15.3.1   Output Functions

Here we describe the functions used to handle text output to a specified stream. All three of these functions return the value **EOF**[2] if an error occurs. As write

---

[2]Traditionally, **EOF** is represented by -1. However, the ISO C standard requires only that it is some negative integer. This constant is used by some **stdio** functions to announce that some problem, such as a write error, has occurred.

errors are infrequent and usually do not lead to more serious hidden consequences, the values returned by the output functions generally are ignored and we do so in this text.

- **int fprintf(stream st, string format, output-list);**
  This function is like `printf()`, except that the output goes to the stream `st`, instead of to `stdout`. Each expression in the output list is evaluated, and the result is converted to ASCII, according to the specifiers given in the format, and written to stream `st`. After correct operation, it returns the number of characters actually written. For example,

  ```
  fprintf( myfile, "name:   %s   time=%g \n", fname, t );
  ```

- **int fputs(string s, stream st);**
  This function writes the characters of **s** (not including the `\0`) to the specified output stream. Unlike `printf()`, it cannot output numbers. Also, unlike `puts()`, it adds no newline at the end of the output. After correct operation, a nonnegative value is returned. For example,

  ```
  fputs( address, my_out );
  fputs( "Error:   file cannot be opened", stderr );
  ```

- **int fputc(int outchar, stream st);**
  This function behaves like `putchar()`, except that the character is written to the specified stream instead of `stdout`. After correct operation, the value of the first parameter is returned. For example,

  ```
  fputc( 'Z', my_out );
  ```

15.3.2   Writing Data to a File

Output files are used for a variety of reasons. Some of the most common are these:

- Many experiments are monitored by a computer and produce data that are written into a file for later analysis, often by another program. The data might need special formatting.
- Sometimes we need two kinds of output from the same program. For example, the program might interact with the user through the screen and write a finished table or report in a file.

Each of these situations occurs in the problem specified in Figure 15.8. The program in Figure 15.9 computes a table of voltage values for a resistor-capacitor circuit and writes these values to a file in one of two formats, selected by the user.

Writing a literal string in an I/O function call is not the only way to write a format; a string variable can be used instead. Here, we need two different

Problem scope: Calculate the measured voltage across the capacitor in the following circuit as time increases from $t = 0$ to $t = 1$ second, in increments of
1/15th second, assuming the switch is closed at time 0. Write the resulting data
into a predetermined file in one of two formats.

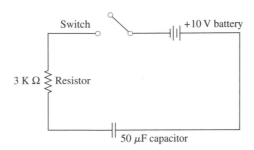

Input: The user selects the format of the output with a **y/n** response.
Output required: The results are stored in the file **voltage.dat**. If the user
selects a table format, headings should be printed, with two columns of data
representing the time and the voltage value, v. Otherwise, the data should be
written as a series of point coordinates of the form (t, v), for later use by a
graphing program. Two decimal places of precision are appropriate.
Constants: In this circuit, $V = 10$ volts, $R = 3,000$ ohms, and $C = 50 \times 10^{-6}$
farads. The circuit has a time constant τ (tau), which depends on the resistance,
R, and the capacitance, C, as $\tau = R \times C = 0.15$ second.
Formula: If the switch is closed at time 0, the voltage across the capacitor is
given by the following exponentially increasing equation:

$$v(t) = V \times \left(1 - e^{-\frac{t}{\tau}}\right)$$

Figure 15.8.   Specifications: Writing a date file from an experiment.

formats. The string output format is set to the user's choice of format; since both
formats expect the same arguments, the string variable can be used in the call on
fprintf() to specify the format. This technique is easily extended if more than
two formats are needed.

Notes on Figure 15.9: Writing a file of voltages.

- *First box: the #define commands.* These symbols **step** and **epsilon**
  are defined by expressions rather than by simple constants. An expression
  is permitted so long as it involves only known values, not variables. However, because of the way the preprocessor translates **#define**, an expression

Compute voltage as a function of time for the circuit in Figure 15.8.

```
#include "tools.h"
#define V 10                       /* battery voltage */
#define TAU 0.15                   /* time constant for this circuit (s) */
#define step (1.0 / 15.0)     /* time step for lines of table */
#define epsilon (step / 2.0) /* for floating comparison to end loop */

double f( double t ) {  return V * (1 - exp( - t / TAU )) ;  }
void main( void )
{
    double t;                      /* time since switch closed */
    double v;                      /* voltage at time t */
    char table;                    /* 'y' for table, else coordinate format */
    string format = "(%.2f, %.2f)\n";    /* format for coordinate output */

    stream myfile = fopen( "voltage.dat", "w" );
    if (myfile == NULL)  fatal( "Cannot open voltage.dat" );

    printf( "\n Write output in table form (y/n)? " );
    scanf( " %c", &table );
    if (tolower( table ) == 'y') {
        fprintf( myfile, "    time          voltage \n\n" ); /* headings */
        format = "%8.2f %14.2f\n";
    }

    printf( "\n Writing table to file voltage.dat\n" );
    for (t = 0.0; t <= (1.0 + epsilon); t += step) {
        v = f( t );
        fprintf( myfile, format, t, v );
    }

    fclose( myfile );
    bye();
}
```

Figure 15.9.   Writing a file of voltages.

sometimes can lead to unintended precedence problems. To avoid this, enclose the definition in parentheses, as shown here, or use a **const** variable.

- *Third box: declaring and opening the output stream.*

  1. We need to declare a stream for the output; here, we create one named **myfile**. The type **stream** is defined in **tools.h**. The name of the

stream pointer is arbitrary and need not resemble the actual name of the data file we write.

2. As part of the declaration, we initialize the stream **myfile** by opening it for writing with mode **"w"**. It will be attached to the file **voltage.dat** in the current default directory. This file will be created if it does not already exist. If it does exist, the former contents will be lost.

3. The value **NULL** is returned by **fopen()** if any of the steps in creating a stream goes wrong. We check the return value to be sure the open command was successful and abort if it was not. The function **fatal()**[3] provides a succinct and convenient way to print an error message, close all streams, and terminate execution. It should be used whenever an error has been identified and the programmer does not know how to continue meaningful execution.

- *Second and fourth boxes: the variable format.*

  1. In the second box, we define a **string** variable that will be used as a format and initialize it to one of the two formats that are supported. The default format produces output in coordinate format, like this:
```
(0.00,  0.00)
(0.07,  3.59)
 ...    ...
```

  2. If the file opening was successful, we come to the fourth box. Here, we ask the user what format to use. If table format is chosen, we print table headings and change the format variable. The format selected here will be used for all the output.

- *Fifth box: writing the table to the output file.*

  1. We use **printf()** to display a greeting to let the user know that all is well. This is the last output that will be displayed until the closing message.

  2. Each pass through the loop writes one line of output into the file. Because the step size is a noninteger amount, the loop termination test incorporates a fuzz factor to make sure the final value of **t=1** is processed.

  3. Inside the loop, the program prints lines using the format variable set earlier. This substantially simplifies the logic of the loop, which otherwise would need to contain an **if...else** statement with two **fprintf()** statements.

  4. The first and last few lines of output from this program follow, with table format on the left and coordinate format on the right.

---

[3]The function **fatal()** expects the same kind of arguments as **printf()**: a format string and a list of things to print. It passes these arguments on to **fprintf()** to print on the **stderr** stream, then finishes by calling **exit(1)**.

time	voltage	
0.00	0.00	(0.00, 0.00)
0.07	3.59	(0.07, 3.59)
0.13	5.89	(0.13, 5.89)
0.20	7.36	(0.20, 7.36)
...	...	... ...
0.87	9.97	(0.87, 9.97)
0.93	9.98	(0.93, 9.98)
1.00	9.99	(1.00, 9.99)

- *Sixth box: cleaning up.* As a matter of good style, the program closes the stream, and therefore the file, as soon as it is done with it. If the programmer fails to close a file, the system will close it automatically when the program exits.

15.4   Stream Input

In the previous section, we studied a set of file output functions, each of which is the analog of one of the familiar **stdout** functions. In this section, we examine the file input functions that are counterparts of the **stdin** functions and use them in an example of input file processing.

15.4.1   Input Functions

In this section, we introduce the functions provided by **stdio** for reading text files. An **input list** is a list of addresses in which to store the data. The functions are

- **int feof(stream st);**

  This function is used to test whether an end-of-file condition has occurred for an input stream. It reads the stream's status flag and returns **true** (1) if the flag is *on* and **false** (0) otherwise. This status flag is not turned on when the program finishes reading the last data item, only when an attempt is made to read *beyond* the final piece of data. During this "bad" read, the value of the input variable is not changed. For this reason, **feof()** always should be used after a read operation and prior to processing the data. See the program in Figure 15.10 for an example of correct usage.

- **int fscanf(stream st, string format, input-list);**

  This function is similar to **scanf()** except that the data come from the specified input stream **st** rather than **stdin**. The argument **st** must be declared as type **stream** and be open for reading.

  A **status code** is returned by **fscanf()** (and also by **scanf()**); it is the number of items that were successfully read, converted, and stored into the variables of the input list. The `fscanf()` function also may return the constant value **EOF** indicating that end of file occurred before any input happened. If the number returned is smaller than expected, an error or end of file occurred in the middle of the input operation. The error status code may be ignored, as in the first example below, and often this is done. However, if the program needs to be crash-proof, the status code should be saved and later tested, then appropriate action should be taken. Since most input statements read only one data item, any return code less than 1 signals some sort of error. Use of the status code is taken up in Section 15.5.5.

As with `scanf()`, a percent-sign field in a format indicates a conversion. Further, a space in the format instructs `fscanf()` to skip zero or more spaces in the input stream and start the input operation with the next nonwhitespace character. Also, if a format contains any character other than whitespace or a conversion specifier, that character must appear in the input stream. If it does, the character is removed from the stream and discarded. If not, an error code is returned. The use of space and extra characters in the format string occurs frequently in file processing, where the data fields often are delimited by special characters in a prearranged manner; for example,

```
fscanf( my_in, "%g", &x );
fscanf( my_in, "%c. %23s", initial, name );
status_code = fscanf( datain, "%15s%i", state, &zip );
```

In the first line above, the program reads one real number. In the second, the format has a period and would be appropriate for an input like **"A. Fischer"**. In the third example, two items are read, and the status code is stored so that we can check for errors.

- `string fgets( char ar[], int n, stream st );`

  This function reads up to **n-1** characters from input stream **st** and stores them in array **ar**. It does not skip leading whitespace. As with `gets()`, if a newline occurs before **n-1** characters have been read, the program terminates reading. Unlike `gets()`, the newline character *is stored in the array* before the \0 terminator. As with `gets()`, a pointer to **ar** is returned after a normal read and **NULL** if an error or end of file occurred. The return value can be ignored if `feof()` is used to check for end of file.

  Because `fgets()` lets us specify n, the maximum length string to read, it often is used in preference to `gets()`, which lacks the ability to impose a limit. Using `fgets()` helps us avoid storing characters past the end of the input array; for example,

```
fgets( ar, 79, my_file ); /* Read my_file into ar. */
fgets( ar, 79, stdin );   /* Read stdin into ar. */
```

The second line indicates a safer way of reading strings from the keyboard than using `gets()`; the length limit should be one less than the length of the array, leaving space for the null terminator.

- `int fgetc( stream st );`
  This function reads a single character from the given stream, returning the character as an `int` value. Leading whitespace characters are not stripped away.[4] An example is

  ```
  ch = fgetc( my_in );
  ```

15.4.2 Detecting End of File

The program examples so far have relied on the user to enter data at the keyboard. This works well when the amount of data is minimal or each input depends on the results of previous inputs. It does not work well for programs that must process large masses of data or data that have been previously collected and written into a file for later analysis. For these purposes, we need file input. File input raises a new set of problems that require new solution techniques. These problems include recognizing the end of the data and handling input errors.

When you are using keyboard input, running out of data is usually not an issue. Programs typically provide an explicit way for the user to indicate when to quit. Until the quit signal is given, the system will continue to prompt for input and simply wait, forever if necessary, until the user types something. However, when your data come from a file, the file does have a definite end, and the end of data must be recognized as the signal to quit.

The best way to check for the end-of-file condition is to use the system function `feof()`, which is completely portable and simple. There are other methods of detecting end of file, such as testing the status code returned from an input function, but they get tangled in special cases and multipurpose error codes. The next section gives an example of a properly used end-of-file test.

15.4.3 Reading Data from a File

The next example (Figure 15.10) incorporates two important techniques: opening a file whose name is entered from the keyboard and handling an end-of-file condition. It often is necessary to retrieve analytical or experimental data stored in a file. These values usually are analyzed or processed in some manner. However, in this example, we just send them to the screen.

The program prompts the user to enter the name of a data file. This offers more flexibility than simply writing the file name as a literal constant in the

---

[4] Another name for this function is `getc()`, which is analogous to `getchar()`.

Read and process a file that has two numbers on each line in point coordinate format (x, y).

```c
#include "tools.h"
void main( void )
{
    double t, v;
    char file_name[80];      /* Full pathname of file to be read. */
    stream flop;

    banner();
    printf( " What file do you want to read? " );
    scanf( " %79[^\n]", file_name );                /* Read entire line. ----- */
    flop = fopen( file_name, "r" );
    if (flop == NULL) fatal( "Cannot open %s for reading.\n", file_name );

    for (;;) {
        fscanf( flop, " (%lg,%lg)", &t, &v ); /* Read next input. ------ */
        if (feof( flop )) break;                /* Test stream status  --- */
        printf( "%8.2f %14.2f \n", t, v );    /* Echo input. ----------- */
        /* Process the input here, if processing is needed. ----------- */
    }

    fclose( flop );
    bye();
}
```

Figure 15.10.   Reading a data file.

program since it permits the program to be used with a variety of input sources. However, it introduces a new opportunity for error: the user could give an incorrect name. For the sake of this program, we assume that the file consists of pairs of numbers in the output format generated by the program in Figure 15.9.

Notes on Figure 15.10. Reading a data file.

- *First box: declarations.*

  1. Since the name of the file will be entered from the keyboard, we need to declare a character array long enough to hold whatever file name the user enters. We make it 80 characters long to be on the safe side.
  2. We also declare a **stream**, **flop**, for the input.

• *Second box: open the stream and check for errors.*

1. The program prompts the user and reads the name of a file. If the file exists in the current default directory, the user needs only to type its name. However, if it is somewhere else in the file system, the user must supply either a complete pathname or a pathname relative to the current directory. To make sure the array does not overflow, we stipulate a maximum of 79 characters.

2. The / is used in UNIX pathnames to separate directory names; in DOS, a \ would be used. Since backslash is the escape character in C, you must write \\ *in the code* to mean backslash. However, a single backslash is enough if the pathname is part of a string that is read as input.

3. The program opens the stream **flop** for reading (**"r"**). It will be attached to whatever file the user named. A run-time error will occur if this file does not exist, if it exists in a directory other than the one specified, or if the user lacks permission to read it. All these conditions will be indicated by a **NULL** value in **flop**. The user will see this dialog:

```
What file do you want to read? none.in
Cannot open none.in for reading.
```

This code could be enhanced by embedding it in a validation loop that would repeat until a valid file name is entered.

• *Third box: reading and echoing the data.*

1. Each pass through the loop reads and echoes one line in the file. Further processing could be inserted in the indicated position.

2. If we put any character other than the **%** fields in the format, the system will try to match that character to the input. (A space character in the format matches zero or more whitespace characters in the input.) If the spacing or content of the input line does not match, there will be a read error. For this reason, it is better to use the simplest possible input formats as shown here.

3. The two numbers on each input line are enclosed in parentheses and separated by a comma. The input format includes these characters to indicate that they should be read from the input stream and discarded.

4. There is a newline character that must be handled on the end of each line. To do so, we put a space at the beginning of the format. This causes **fscanf()** to skip the newline character at the end of the prior line before looking for the parenthesis that begins the current line.

5. We need not put a space between the **%lg** specifiers, even though spaces are in that position in the file. This is because **fscanf()** always skips leading whitespace when the conversion specifier is **%lg** (or any other numeric code).

- *Third box: End-of-file processing.*

    1. The function `feof()` tests a flag set by the system when the program attempts to read data that are not there; to detect an end-of-file condition, we must try to read beyond the end of the data then call `feof()` *after* the read operation. If `feof()` returns `true`, the end-of-file flag is on and there is no more data to process. To be valid, the `feof()` test should be made only after a read command has been executed and it should be made after every read command.

    2. This loop shows the proper order in which to call `fscanf()`, `feof()`, and `printf()`. The `for` loop starts by calling `fscanf()` and, immediately after that, calls `feof()` to check for end of file. All processing activities of the loop follow the `feof()` test.

    3. Here is some sample output, run on the file `voltage.dat` written by Figure 15.9 (dashes indicate lines that have been omitted):

```
What file do you want to read? voltage.dat
    0.00              0.00
    0.07              3.59
    0.13              5.89
----------------------------
    0.93              9.98
    1.00              9.99


Normal termination.
```

15.5   Errors and Exceptions

In programming lingo, an **exception condition** is some event that happens rarely and requires unusual handling. Files that are supposed to exist but seem not to, disk errors during reading, input conversion errors, and end-of-file conditions are exceptions that might occur. A **robust program** anticipates exceptions, checks for them, applies an appropriate recovery strategy, and continues processing if possible. Any exception that cannot be handled routinely should be **flagged**; that is, the operator should be notified of the nature of the problem and the specific data that caused it. In this section and the next two, we look closely at **error detection** and how we may protect programs against some errors.

15.5.1   Format Errors

The formats in C are quite unforgiving and must be precisely correct to work properly. We can make few generalizations about the results of incorrect formats, except to say that things will go wrong in unpredictable ways. Some kinds of

format errors can even cause a program to crash or go into an infinite loop. A format bug in a program also can be very hard to find, because the debugging printouts may make no sense if their formats, or the variables they print, are affected.

The format strings used by `printf()`, `scanf()`, and their file I/O counterparts are *not* checked by many compilers.[5] Each call on `scanf()` contains a format and a list of addresses, called the *input list*. Each call on `printf()` has a format and a list of expressions to be printed, called an *output list*. Many compilers just pass the format string to the run-time system without checking whether the conversion specifiers are appropriate in either number or type for the items on the I/O list. We now look at a few problems this can generate.

When is a big number small? (advanced topic)   A big number is small when a large integer value is printed in a `short` format instead of a `long` format. One way to cause this error is changing the declaration of a variable without changing every format. Another (probably the most frequent) way is to omit the length specifier when printing a `long int` or a `short int`. Why is this a problem? When `printf()` is called, it receives the format and a list of values to print. The number of items in a list varies, and the actual values can be of assorted sizes and types. All these are stored end to end in a memory area reserved for the arguments of `printf()`, which takes them out of this area and prints them one at a time. For this process, `printf()` must know the type of each one and where it ends. The format is used as a "key" to separate and decode the list of output values; it is the sole source of this information for `printf()`. Therefore, if the format says the next value is a `short int`, `printf()` will remove 2 bytes and print them. For a `long int`, it removes 4 bytes. If we lie to `printf()` about what is there, it will do as the program tells it and probably print garbage for that field and every field following it. Clearly, the moral of this tale is this: *If your output seems to make no sense at all, check the formats carefully*.

Figure 15.11 and its output illustrate some of this behavior. All the format specifiers in the first `printf()` statement are correct and the output is what we would expect. In the second, the specifiers do not match the corresponding arguments. The program compiles and runs but the results are wrong.

Notes on Figure 15.11. Correct and mismatched formats.

- *First box: correct format.*

  1. The output from this box is

     ```
     Here are the variables printed with correct formats
             k=55       j=117440518       f=4.4
     ```

---

[5]The gcc compiler from the Free Software Foundation checks these formats if an option to print all warning messages is turned on.

```
#include "tools.h"

void main( void )
{
    long int j = 117440518L;   /* Has 1 bits near both ends, 0's between. */
    short int k = 55;
    float f = 4.4;
```

```
    printf( "\nHere are the variables printed with correct formats\n\t"
            "k=%hi     j=%li     f=%g \n\n", k, j, f );
```

```
    printf( "Here are the results of some format errors\n\t"
            "k=%li     j=%hi     f=%c     f=%g \n", k, j, f, f );
```

```
}
```

Figure 15.11.   Correct and mismatched formats.

2. We use `%hi` for short integers and `%li` for long integers. A short integer uses 2 bytes on almost all systems; a long integer uses 4 bytes.

- *Second box: an inappropriate format.*

1. Here are results from one system with 2-byte integers,[6] where type `int` is the same size as `short int`:

   ```
   Here are the results of some format errors
           k=370700     j=6     f=     f=-26738688
   ```

2. In the declarations, `j` is a `long int` with a very large value and `k` is a `short int` with a small value. In the format, the situation is reversed. Altogether, they contain 6 bytes of information.
3. The value printed for `k` is much too large. The 4 bytes printed included two from the value of `k` and the high-order 2 bytes of `j`.
4. The value printed for `j` is much too small. What we see is the value of the low-order 2 bytes of the representation of `j`. The other 2 bytes were omitted because `%hi` expects a `short int` and so used the next 2 bytes from the argument list.
5. It is obvious that the third value printed is nonsense; you cannot print a `float` (meaningfully) as a `char`. The `%c` used fewer than 4 bytes from the first copy of `f`, leaving the remaining bytes to be processed by the next conversion specifier.
6. It seems that the last value should be correct, since we gave an appropriate format field for a `float` value. However, the faulty `%c` caused a

---

[6] This output was produced on a machine that stores the leftmost (high-order) byte of a number in the lowest memory address. This is known as *big-endian architecture*.

misalignment. A combination of bytes from the first and second copies of `f` are merged and interpreted as a value. The remaining bytes from the end of the second `f` are never used.

7. Here are two sets of results from the same program compiled and run on two systems[7] where type `int` is the same size as type `long int`:

```
Here are the results of some format errors
      k=55        j=6       f=        f=-1.49166e-154
-------------------------------------------
Here are the results of some format errors
      k=55        j=117440518      f=        f=-0
```

The results are wrong here, too, but in different ways and for different reasons. This clearly demonstrates that the results of an error depend on the hardware and software architecture of the system. The common factor is that the items printed often bear little resemblance to the actual values.

Input format errors.   At run time, `scanf()` and `fscanf()` receive a format and a list of addresses from the caller. They scan the format and the input stream, looking in the stream for characters that can be combined to form the data items described by the format. Unfortunately, `scanf()` has no way to check whether the format field specifications are appropriate for the corresponding memory addresses and their associated variables. After scanning and conversion, each data value is stored in the address of the next variable on the input list, whether or not the types match. A mismatch might be detected later, when a garbage value is retrieved from a variable. Sometimes the mismatch is not detected until the output from the program is checked.

15.5.2   File Processing Errors

The paradigm for reading input from a file, presented in Figure 15.10, is simple and works reliably as long as the data file contains appropriate data. However, three kinds of errors in the data file will cause this program to malfunction.

A missing newline.   If the newline character at the end of the last line of data is missing, the end-of-file flag will be turned on when the last item is read successfully. This is one read operation sooner than expected. The loop will test the flag before processing the last data set and the program will end immediately without processing the data. The result is shown here—the last line is missing:

---

[7] The first output was produced on a big-endian machine. The second is from a Pentium-class machine, which stores the rightmost (low-order) byte of a number in the lowest memory address. This is known as *little-endian architecture*.

```
What file do you want to read?  volts2.dat
    0.00            0.00
    0.07            3.59
    0.13            5.89
---------------------------
    0.87            9.97
    0.93            9.98
```

```
Normal termination.
```

But this is not a programming error; it is a data file error. It *is* normal to end
each line of a file with a newline character. The program is "correct" because it
handles a correct data file properly.

It is possible to write the input loop so that it does the "right" thing, whether
or not the final newline is present. However, this complicates the code considerably. This kind of error handling is discussed in the next section.

An illegal input character.   Even worse behavior will happen if the format
calls for a numeric input and the file contains a nonnumeric character. The
character causes a conversion error, and **scanf()** will return without doing the
rest of the read operation. Values read before the conversion error will be stored
correctly in their variables, but the variable being processed when the conversion
error happened will not be changed and still will contain the data from the prior
line of input. The results of a run using a file **voltsbad.dat** follow:

```
What file do you want to read?  voltsbad.dat
    0.00            0.00
    0.07            3.59
    0.07            3.59
    0.07            3.59
    ....            ....
```

This file was created by taking a correct input file and replacing the 0 at the
beginning of 0.13 by the character **o**. Because of this, the third data set cannot be
read. Even worse, C will do *nothing* to correct the error; the offending character
is not removed from the input stream. Repeated attempts to read another line will
continue to fail due to a format mismatch. The program, therefore, will be in an
infinite loop, processing the last pair of correct data values again and again.

Fortunately, the C programmer is not helpless in dealing with these problems. As shown in section 15.5.6, after each read operation, the program can
check a series of error codes and respond to any error detected. This should be
done if the application is important and possible failure must be avoided.

Data omission.   Similar errors can occur if some portion of a multipart data
set is missing. In some cases, this will be detected when the next input character

does not match the next specific character in the format. For instance, if part of a line in the file **voltage.dat** was missing, the next parenthesis would not be in the expected place. In simpler file formats, such as lists of numbers separated by whitespace, the program would not detect an error, but a misalignment in data groupings would cause the output of the program to be meaningless.

15.5.3   Error Recovery

In general, a programmer should decide what level of error handling is appropriate for each application. If a program will be used many times or used in a context where failure is damaging, it becomes important to try to recover from input errors. If it will be used casually or restarting is very little trouble, the program still should check for input errors but can simply announce an error and abort, rather than implement an automatic **error recovery** strategy. The following sections present a couple of these error-recovery schemes.

15.5.4   A Tool for Error Recovery: `cleanline()`

The function shown in Figure 15.12 is part of the **tools** library. It can be used to help recover from an input error that arises when the contents of the current input line do not match the format. This function takes one argument, an input stream. It reads and skips over all of the characters remaining in that stream, up to and including the next newline character. (Informally, it *cleans out* or *flushes* the rest of the current input line.)

Every stream has a pointer to the next unread character in its input buffer; let us call this the *current-position pointer*. When a read error occurs, the stream's current-position pointer is left pointing at the offending character. Because of this, we cannot simply handle the error by repeating the operation; the bad character still is there and the same error will happen again. Before proper reading can resume, the program must take corrective action to clear the erroneous character(s) from the input stream. This is the purpose of the **cleanline()** function. A similar function, **clean_and_log()**, also will clear the input buffer and, in addition, echo the bad portion of the input line to an error stream. This function is presented in Appendix F.

p1020

Notes on Figure 15.12. The `cleanline()` function.

• The purpose of the boxed loop is to read and discard the remainder of the current line of input from the stream designated by the parameter. The characters read are simply discarded. (In **clean_and_log()**, the characters are echoed to a stream designated by a second parameter, to assist the user in error correction.)

This function from the **tools** library is intended for use in error recovery; it flushes the specified input stream up to the end of the current line. A sample call can be found in Figure 15.13.

```
void cleanline( stream sin )
{
    char ch;                            /* Character under input scanner */

    do { ch = fgetc( sin );                 /* Read next character */
    } while (!feof( sin ) && ch != '\n');   /* Quit at first newline */
}
```

Figure 15.12.   The cleanline() **function.**

- Each time around the loop, the function reads a single character from the specified input stream. The **do...while** statement tests the character at the bottom of the loop and quits if it is a newline.
- A special case occurs if the line in question is the last line of the file and it does not end properly with a newline character. The additional test for end of file is an exit condition that handles this situation.

15.5.5   Using the Return Value of scanf()

During a **scanf()** operation, an error occurs if the contents of the stream are not appropriate for the conversion format or an end-of-file condition occurs prematurely. In either case, **scanf()** returns immediately and does not change the contents of the remaining memory variables. Previously, we used **scanf()** as if it were a **void** function. However, **scanf()** does return a value, and that value must be checked to implement proper error handling. *The value returned by* **scanf()** *is the number of data items successfully read, converted, and stored.* If no errors occur, this number will be equal to the number of **%** signs in the format string, as well as the number of addresses in the input list. If there is a hardware error, a conversion error, or an end-of-file condition, this number will be lower than expected.

Certain errors can be detected by comparing the value that **scanf()** returns to the number of items it was supposed to read. For example, suppose you are processing the **scanf()** command in Figure 15.13. If you entered the line of data " 39 !67.5 63.2 ", **scanf()** will read the value 39 correctly but detect an error when it tries to read the second number and encounters the nonnumeric character ! instead. This is illustrated in Figure 15.14. The value returned by **scanf()** will be 1 and only the first variable's contents will be changed. Figure 15.15 shows how an error at the end of a numeric value might not be detected until the next value is read. In this case, the 71 will be read correctly for the first

```
ok = scanf( "%hi%g%g", &age, &weight, &height );
if (ok == 3) {
    /* No error occurred; all variables contain new data. */
    printf( "\t\tOK: %hi values read: %hi %g %g\n",
            ok, age, weight, height );
}
else {
    /* Error occurred; values of some variables are not valid. */
    cleanline( stdin );                     /* Flush rest of line. */
    printf( "\t\tError: %hi values read: %hi %g %g\n",
            ok, age, weight, height );
}
```

Figure 15.13.   Testing the code returned by `scanf()`.

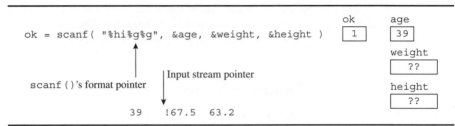

Figure 15.14.   Error reading second value.

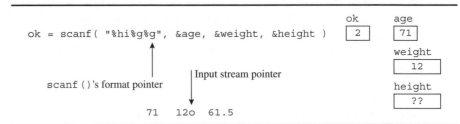

Figure 15.15.   Error reading third value.

number. The second number will be 12, because the letter **o** is not numeric and stops the read operation just like whitespace. However, no error occurs until we attempt to read the third number and get the **o** instead. Here, `scanf()`'s return value will be 2. In either situation, the remaining code in Figure 15.13 will handle the recovery process, using `cleanline()` to flush the remainder of the offending line so processing can continue.

15.5.6   A Combined Technique for Error Recovery

Data files often are organized so that each line of the **file** represents one **data set;** that is, a group of values that, taken together, form one set of inputs to be processed. (Occasionally, a data set is too long to fit on a single line and is recorded on a group of lines.) A file-based program usually reads an entire data set with one call on **scanf()**. Unlike interactive input, there is no need to prompt for and validate each data item one at a time.

Input errors are far less likely during file processing than interactive work because so many files are generated mechanically or can be verified before they are processed. However, if an application is critically important, the program must include thorough error detection and implement a recovery scheme that will allow correct results to be produced in a timely manner.

The **stdio** library provides three ways to detect errors and exceptions:

1. All input functions return success or failure codes.
2. The function **feof()** returns **true** if an attempt has been made to read past the end of the file; that is, read data that do not exist.
3. Another function, **ferror()**, returns **true** when the stream's underlying I/O device has failed during a previous attempt to read data. For example, this could happen if a disk drive became disconnected or a speck of dust on the disk caused a part of it to become unreadable.

Garbage in, information out.   A robust program performs according to reasonable expectations no matter what kind of input it is given. It does not follow the old rule of garbage in, garbage out. Rather, it detects erroneous inputs and does something constructive about them. Most important, if answers are produced, those answers are based on meaningful data.

Figure 15.16 shows how all the file processing and error recovery techniques discussed so far can be combined to form a robust file-processing loop. This program detects and recovers from each of the errors described previously. If data can be read according to the given format, it is processed; otherwise, it is cleaned out of the stream and sent to a **log file**. The program terminates properly, having processed the last valid data item, whether or not the last line contains valid data and a newline. No detectable errors are ignored, and the program "gives up" and aborts only when there is a hardware failure from which no recovery is possible. This is the kind of algorithm that is needed to make a robust file-processing program.

Notes on Figure 15.16. Handling end-of-file and file input errors.

*   *First box: declarations and opening the files.*

    1. We declare one variable to hold the input data and one to save the error code returned by **fscanf()**.

This example shows how to test for an error or end-of-file condition after using the common input routines. It represents a complete error-recovery strategy.

```
#include "tools.h"
#define in_name   "feet2.in"
#define log_name  "feet2.log"

void main( void )
{
    int data, flag;
    stream f_in = fopen( in_name, "r" );
    stream f_log = fopen( log_name, "w" );

    if (f_in == NULL) fatal( "Cannot open file %s for input.", in_name );
    if (f_log == NULL) fatal( "Cannot open file %s for output.", log_name );

    for (;;) {                              /* Main data processing loop. */
        flag = fscanf( f_in, "%i", &data ); /* Read next item. */
        if (flag == 1) {                    /* Test for successful read. */
            printf( " Data: %i\n", data );
            /* Process the data here. */
        }

        else if (feof( f_in )) break;       /* End of file -- leave loop. */

        else if (ferror( f_in )) fatal( " Hardware error on input file." );
        else {                              /* Flag error and do recovery. */
            fprintf( f_log, "\a Bad data: " );
            clean_and_log( f_in, f_log );   /* Flush & echo rest of line. */
        }
    }
    bye();
}
```

Figure 15.16.   Handling end-of-file and file input errors.

2. We also declare a stream, **f_in**, for input and initialize it in the declaration by opening the stream for input and attaching the file **feet2.in**. This file has been constructed by starting with a list of integers, one per line, and introducing a wide variety of errors.

3. Similarly, we declare and open a stream named **f_log** for the error log.

4. In this program, the file names are supplied by **#define** statements at the top of the program, where they are easy to find if a file name needs

to be modified. This technique is better than writing the name directly in the **fopen()** call but less flexible than reading the file name from the input stream.

- *Second box: detecting file-opening failures.*

  1. If the open command fails, a **NULL** value will be returned instead of a file pointer, so we check for incorrect operation by comparing **f_in** and **f_log** to **NULL**. Failure to open correctly is a common error, so it is important for programs to check this condition.
  2. If there is an error, we call **fatal()** to print an error comment and exit. We might use a data validation loop if the file name was to be entered interactively.

- *Third box: Reading and processing the input.*

  1. The **for** loop keeps repeating until the data in the file are used up. Normally, it stops after trying to read past the end of the data, which causes the **feof()** function to return the value **true**. This loop will be executed at least once for each line in the file, and more than once if multiple correct items are on the same line.
  2. The first thing we do in the loop is try to read the next data item. This **fscanf()** statement reads a single integer, but the techniques shown here apply to a format that calls for any kind or amount of data.
  3. The **fscanf()** function will read the next string of decimal digits in the input stream. Anything else (such as a letter or a period) stops the input. The function then returns a success or failure code, which is stored in the variable **flag**. The number returned is the number of data items correctly read and stored in memory. This number should be equal to the number of **%** signs in the format (one, in this case).

- *First inner box: valid data.* We compare the error flag to 1 to test whether or not one valid data item has been received. If we were reading two data items per line, the test would be **if (flag == 2)**. If the program has data, it processes them. In this demonstration, the processing is simply to echo the data to the screen.

- *Second inner box: end of file.* We test for end-of-file only after testing for invalid data and processing the valid inputs. This permits the program to process the last data line correctly, even if the final newline is missing. After processing the last data item, the program breaks out of the processing loop and ends.

- *Third inner box: other errors.* If we did not read valid data and have not reached the end of the file, then an error of some sort has occurred. There are two possibilities. The first is a hardware failure, which is extremely unlikely; if it happens, the program cannot recover from it. We test for this type of error by calling **ferror()** and abort if **true** is returned.

The left column shows the input file processed by the program in Figure 15.16. The middle and right columns show the output lines produced by processing each input line.

Input File (`feet2.in`)	Corresponding Screen Output	Log File (`feet2.log`)
23.5	Data: 23	Bad data: .5
1	Data: 1	
3.28084 abc 2	Data: 3	Bad data: .28084 abc 2
39 10	Data: 39	
	Data: 10	
a		Bad data: a
.00001		Bad data: .00001
421.8 20	Data: 421	Bad data: .8 20
37012x	Data: 37012	Bad data: x

Figure 15.17.   Error report for recovery.

Otherwise, we know from the `fscanf()` return code that the program did not successfully read an entire data set. And, after using `feof()` and `ferror()`, we know that end-of-file and hardware errors were not the cause of failure. The remaining possibility is a conflict between the format specification and the actual contents of the file. This could be due to an error in another program that created the file or a format error in the current program. In either case, we call `clean_and_log()` to write the information in the log file and flush the rest of the faulty line from the input stream. In a different application, where each data set contained more than one item, it would be important to write the entire faulty data in the log file, including any part that was read correctly before the error was detected.

• *The output.* This program was tested on the file `feet2.in`, which contains a mixture of correct data (integers) and incorrect data (decimal points, letters). The contents of this file, with the output and log file entries corresponding to each line, are shown in Figure 15.17. The program reads and accepts the part of each line that precedes the decimal point or letter, and "cleans" the rest out of the way. If two integers occur on the same line, both are read normally and processed. Blank lines are ignored.

15.6   File Application: Random Selection Without Replacement

The need to randomize the order of a list of items arises in certain game programs; for example, those that shuffle an imaginary deck of cards and deal them. The same problem also arises in serious applications, such as the selection of data

Problem scope: Write a drill-and-practice program to help students memorize the symbols for the chemical elements.

Input file: The list of element names, symbols, and atomic numbers to be memorized. One element should be defined on each line of the file, with the number first, followed by the name and symbol, all delimited by blanks.

Keyboard input: When prompted, the user will type in an element's atomic number and symbol.

Output: The program will display the names of the elements in random order and wait for the user to type the corresponding number and symbol. After the last question, the number of correct responses will be printed.

Limitations: Restrict the program to 20 elements.

Figure 15.18.   Problem specifications: A quiz.

for an experiment where a randomly selected subset of data items must be drawn from a pool of possible items.

The automated quiz program presented here is a good example of the use of files, random selection, and an array of structures. Each question in the drill-and-practice quiz is represented as one structure in an array. The program presents the questions to the user, checks the answers, and keeps score. It uses C's pseudo-random number generator[8] and a "shuffling" technique to randomize the order of the questions. Program specifications are given in Figure 15.18, the main program in Figure 15.19, and a call chart for the final solution in Figure 15.20. The purpose of this particular quiz game is to help the user learn about the periodic table of elements. However, the data structures and user interface easily can be modified to cover any subject matter.

The complete program discussed here was developed using top-down design; the main program in Figure 15.19 begins and ends the quiz, calling two major subprograms to do the work. The result is a highly modular design, as shown in the call chart of Figure 15.20. (Calls to functions in the **tools** library are surrounded by light gray boxes, calls to the **math** library are in dark gray boxes, and calls to **stdio** functions are omitted.)

Notes on Figure 15.19. An elemental quiz.

- According to the specification, 20 questions are enough for a drill-and-practice program, so we set the maximum array length at 20.
- We define the type **question_t** to hold the name, symbol, and atomic number of one element. Using this base type, we build a table that stores a list of elements for the quiz. These data will be read from a file that has one element's information written on each line.

---

[8] This was presented in Chapter 7, Figure 7.29.

This main program implements the specification in Figure 15.18. It calls functions in Figures 15.21 and 15.22.

```c
#include "tools.h"

/* Type information -----------------------------------------------------*/
#define MAXQ 20                      /* Maximum number of questions in the quiz */
typedef struct { short number; char name[16]; char symbol[4]; } question_t;

/* Prototypes -----------------------------------------------------------*/
int get_quiz( int n, question_t qu[] );
int do_quiz( int nq, question_t quiz[] );

void main( void )
{
    question_t quiz[MAXQ];       /* Array of questions and answers. */
    int nq;                      /* Number of questions in the quiz. */
    int right;                   /* Number of correct answers. */

    banner();
    printf( "\n Chemical Element Quiz\n" );

    nq = get_quiz( MAXQ, quiz );   /* Read nq quiz questions from a file. */
    printf( "\n This quiz has %i questions.\n", nq );
    printf( " For each element name, enter its symbol and number.\n" );

    right = do_quiz( nq, quiz );
    printf( "\n You gave %i correct answers on %i questions.\n", right, nq );

    bye();
}
```

Figure 15.19.   An elemental quiz.

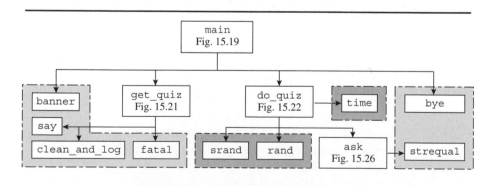

Figure 15.20.   A call chart for the quiz program.

- The type definition must come before the two function prototypes that use the new type.
- The body of **main()** is simple. It calls the two subprograms **get_quiz()** and **do_quiz()** in Figures 15.21 and 15.22 and reports the results.

Notes on Figure 15.21. The get_quiz() function. This function reads a set of quiz-question data from a designated input file and stores them in an array of structures. The array and the number of valid entries in it are returned to **main()**. The three items that form each data set are read directly into the three parts of the **struct** for the current slot of the data array.

- *First box: opening the file.* Prior to the loop, we abort the program if the data file cannot be opened. An error output would look like this:

This function is called from Figure 15.19.

```
int get_quiz( int n, question_t qu[] )
{
    char filename[256];        /* Name of input file holding questions. */
    stream fin;                /* Input stream for questions. */
    int items;                 /* For the code returned by fscanf. */
    int k;                     /* Number of questions in the quiz. */
    printf( "\n What quiz file do you want to use? " );
    scanf( "%255s", filename );
    fin = fopen( filename, "r" );
    if (fin == NULL) fatal( " Error: cannot open file %s", filename );

    for (k = 0; k < n; ) {
        items = fscanf( fin, "%hi%15s%3s",
                        &qu[k].number, qu[k].name, qu[k].symbol );

        if (items == 3) ++k;        /* all is well -- count the item. */
        else if (feof( fin )) break;
        else {
            say( " Bad data while reading slot %i: ", k );
            clean_and_log( fin, stderr );
        }
    }
    return k;
}
```

Figure 15.21.   The get_quiz() function: Read the quiz data from a file.

This function is called from the main program in Figure 15.19. It calls the `ask()` function in Figure 15.26.

```c
int do_quiz( int nq, question_t quiz[] )
{
    bool ask( question_t qu );   /* Prototype for subfunction. */

    int many = nq;              /* Number of questions not yet asked. */
    int score = 0;              /* Number of correct answers so far. */
    int k;                      /* Subscript of selected question. */
    srand( time( NULL ) );      /* initialize random number generator. */
    while (many > 0) {
        k = rand() % many;      /* Choose subscript of next question. */
        if (ask( quiz[k] )) {   /* Ask question, check answer. */
            score++;
            printf( "\t YES ! Score one.\n" );
        }
        else {
            printf( "\t Sorry, the answer is %s %hi \n",
                    quiz[k].symbol, quiz[k].number );
        }

        /* Now remove the question from further consideration. */
        --many;                     /* Decrement question counter. */
        quiz[k] = quiz[many];       /* Move last question into vacant slot. */
    }
    return score;                   /* Number of correct answers. */
}
```

Figure 15.22. The `do_quiz()` function: Ask quiz questions in random order.

```
Chemical Element Quiz

What quiz file do you want to use? q1
Error: cannot open file q1
```

- *Second box: reading one line from the file.*

  1. To read a number into the address of one member of a structure in an array of structures, we use an ampersand and the full name of the field, including the object name (`qu`), a subscript(`[k]`), and a member name (`.number`). We do not use an ampersand to read the element's name or symbol, because these members are character arrays.
  2. We assume that the data fields in the input stream are delimited by whitespace, so we use the `%s` specifier (with a length limit) rather than the `[ ]` specifier in the format.

- *Third box: input error checking and handling.*

  1. In the loop, we increment the array index only when **fscanf()** reads three members successfully.
  2. Otherwise, we identify the nature of the exception. Reading the end of file ends the loop. For a data error, we call **clean_and_log()** to eliminate both the input character that caused the error and any part of the data set that remains on that line of the input stream. Eliminating this bad data set shortens the quiz but permits the program to work properly. In this program, the erroneous characters are echoed to **stderr**, but they could be sent to a file instead. The **say()** function works like **puts()** except that the message is displayed on **stderr** instead of **stdout**.

- *Fourth box: ending the loop.*

  1. Each time around the **for** loop, the program reads one data set from the file. It stops if the array becomes full (**k == n**), whether or not the entire file has been read. If an end-of-file condition occurs before this, the program breaks out of the loop.
  2. The value of **k** after the loop ends is the actual number of valid data sets stored in the array. This count is returned to the main program so that it will ask only valid questions and not try to use the uninitialized portion of the array.
  3. The following array contents would be the result of reading data from the file **q0.in**, containing eight data sets, into an array with 20 slots. We use these data for the remainder of the discussion. Figures 15.23 through 15.25 show how the array contents change during the quiz.

quiz	.number	.name	.symbol
[0]	12	magnesium	Mg
[1]	13	aluminum	Al
[2]	14	silicon	Si
[3]	15	phosphorus	P
[4]	16	sulphur	S
[5]	17	chlorine	Cl
[6]	18	potassium	K
[7]	20	calcium	Ca
[8]	?	??	??
	...	...	...
[19]	?	??	??

Notes on Figure 15.22. The do_quiz() function.   This function administers the quiz and keeps score. Each pass through the main loop calls the **ask()** function in Figure 15.26 to ask a randomly selected question, then overwrites its data with that of an unused question from the end of the array.

- *First box: a prototype.*

    1. In most prior examples, function prototypes have been placed at the top of the program. When the prototype is inside a function definition, the subfunction is known only to the function that contains the prototype.
    2. We define `ask()` as a separate function to keep the detail of how to ask a question separate from the logic of asking all the questions and keeping score. We define it as a subfunction of `do_quiz()`, because asking a question is part of administering the quiz and has no relevance outside of this context.

- *Second box: select and present a question.*

    1. The following is the presentation of the first question from one run of the program: the first two lines are produced by `main()`, the next three from `ask()`, and the last one from `do_quiz()`:

    ```
    This quiz has 8 questions.
    For each element name, enter its symbol and number.

    Element: sulphur
             symbol ? S
             atomic number ? 16
             YES !  Score one.
    ```

    2. At any given time, the beginning portion of the data array contains the unused questions, while the last part contains garbage (duplicate copies of questions and uninitialized slots). The value of `many` is the number of questions not yet asked and also the subscript of the first slot in the last portion of the array.
    3. We generate a random number in the range `0..many-1` by taking the result of `rand()` modulo the current value of `many`. We use this random number as a subscript to select the next question to ask. This works because the unasked questions are always kept at the beginning of the array.

- *Third box: remove the question from further consideration.*

    1. Figures 15.23 through 15.25 show the state of the question array after asking each of the first six questions of our sample quiz. The first three were answered correctly, but only one of the next three was right.
    2. After each question is asked, we decrement `many`, shortening the part of the array containing the unasked questions. Just after the decrement operation, `many` is the subscript of the last unused question. We copy this question's data into slot `k`, overwriting the data of the question that was just asked.
    3. In the diagrams, we represent the shortening by coloring the discarded slots gray. Note in Figure 15.24 that, after three questions are asked,

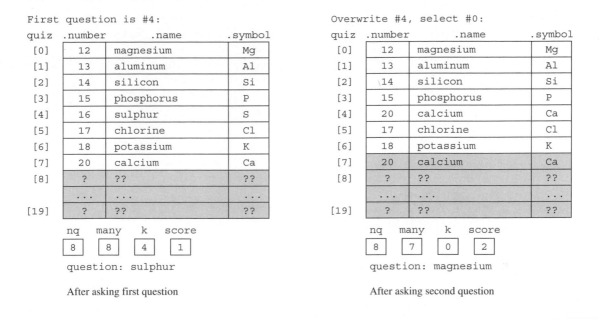

Figure 15.23. The array after two questions.

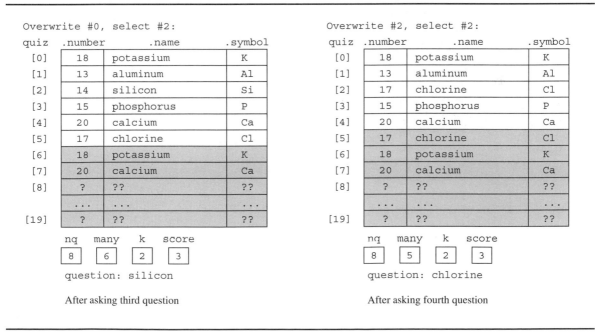

Figure 15.24. The array after four questions.

Overwrite #2, select #3:

quiz	.number	.name	.symbol
[0]	18	potassium	K
[1]	13	aluminum	Al
[2]	20	calcium	Ca
[3]	15	phosphorus	P
[4]	20	calcium	Ca
[5]	17	chlorine	Cl
[6]	18	potassium	K
[7]	20	calcium	Ca
[8]	?	??	??
...	...	...	...
[19]	?	??	??

nq	many	k	score
8	4	3	3

question: phosphorus

After asking fifth question

Overwrite #3, select #0:

quiz	.number	.name	.symbol
[0]	18	potassium	K
[1]	13	aluminum	Al
[2]	20	calcium	Ca
[3]	15	phosphorus	P
[4]	20	calcium	Ca
[5]	17	chlorine	Cl
[6]	18	potassium	K
[7]	20	calcium	Ca
[8]	?	??	??
...	...	...	...
[19]	?	??	??

nq	many	k	score
8	3	0	4

question: potassium

After asking sixth question

Figure 15.25.   The array after six questions.

three elements no longer appear in the white part of the array and all the unused questions have been shifted up so they do appear in the white area. The contents of the gray part of the array no longer matter; they will not be used in the future because the program always selects the next question from the white part (slots 0..many-1).

4. Here is the sample dialog for questions 4 and 5, which were answered incorrectly:

```
Element: chlorine
        symbol ? Cl
        atomic number ? 16
        Sorry, the answer is Cl 17

Element: phosphorus
        symbol ? Ph
        atomic number ? 15
        Sorry, the answer is P 15
```

5. Note that, after the fifth question is asked in Figure 15.25, the question replacement operation effectively does nothing, since this is the last question in the list. We could have saved the effort of doing the copy

operation, but a test to detect this special case would end up being more complex and more work in the long run than the unnecessary copying operation.

6. The quiz continues until all questions have been presented. The last two questions have not been illustrated.

- *Fourth box: The return.* When all the questions have been asked, `do_quiz()` returns the score to `main()`, which prints the results:

```
You gave 5 correct answers on 8 questions.
```

Notes on Figure 15.26. The `ask()` function.

- *The function header.*

  1. The argument is one element selected from the remaining unused questions; it is not the entire array, because only one element is needed here. It is good programming style to pass exactly what is needed and no more.
  2. The return value will be `true` if the answer is correct, `false` otherwise. If it is `true`, the final score will be incremented in `do_quiz()`.

- *First box: prompting for an answer.*

  1. First, the name of the selected element is displayed. Since `qu` is a structure, its name field is selected by writing `qu.name`.
  2. We prompt separately for the two parts of the answer, because individual prompts are less likely to confuse the user.

This function is called from the function in Figure 15.22. It presents a single quiz item to the user, reads the response, checks the answer, and returns the score.

```c
bool ask( question_t qu )
{
    char symb[4];              /* User response for atomic symbol. */
    short number;              /* User response for atomic number. */

    printf( "\n Element: %s\n", qu.name );
    printf( "\t symbol ? " );
    scanf( "%3s", symb );
    printf( "\t atomic number ? " );
    scanf( "%hi", &number );

    return strequal( symb, qu.symbol ) && number == qu.number;
}
```

Figure 15.26.   The `ask()` function: A question and an answer.

- *Second box: checking for correctness.*

  1. The correctness test compares the symbol and name entered by the user to the corresponding members of the parameter **qu**. If they both match, a **true** answer is returned, **false** otherwise.
  2. Remember that **strequal()** or **strcmp()** must be used to compare strings for equality. If we tried to use **==**, the pointer parts of the strings would be compared, not the characters that were typed, and the answer would be **false**.
  3. The result of the test is returned directly, because this is the simplest way to handle the answer.

15.7   Application: Measuring Torque (Optional Topic)

We do a top-down development of a program to conduct and monitor a torque experiment. In the process, we use all three standard streams (**stdin**, **stdout**, and **stderr**), as well as a programmer-defined stream.

This experiment examines a simple rod subject to a torque to model the response of a shaft (such as a motor shaft) that could produce a power output. One end of the experimental rod is attached to a stationary base plate, the other to a handle through which a force can be applied. The force causes the rod to twist through some angle, θ (theta), as diagrammed in Figure 15.27. Under ideal conditions, the theoretical twist angle is $\theta = FbL/JG$. (Ideal conditions mean that the shaft is perfectly circular, the cross sections of the shaft are planar and remain planar while the shaft twists, the rod is made of a uniform material, and the induced stress is proportional to the strain.) The task of the program is to generate force inputs for the experiment and monitor and record the twist angles that the equipment produces. The program specifications are given in Figure 15.27 and the main program in Figure 15.28.

Development step 1, Figure 15.28. The main() program.   We write the usual **#include** command, pertinent constant definitions, and the opening and closing lines for **main()**. We also write statements to display the opening and closing remarks. These must be displayed on **stderr**, because **stdout** will be used to communicate with the experimental equipment. Therefore, we use **say()** and **bye()**, not **puts()**.

- *First box: creating and opening an output stream.* The program specifications call for an output file, so we declare a name (at the top) for the output stream and write the code to open it, checking for an opening failure. We use **say()** to keep the user informed about what is happening.

Problem scope: The program should conduct and monitor an experiment in which a force is applied to a bar attached to the end of a circular steel shaft, as diagrammed here. This causes twisting. We can measure the angle of rotation caused by the force, F; compare it to a theoretical value; and categorize those values that are theoretically correct and those that are not.

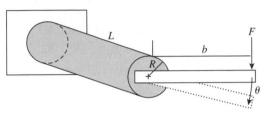

Modulus of rigidity, $G = 12 \times 10^6$ (lbf/in.^{2}) for steel

Radius of shaft, $R = 0.125$ in.

Length of shaft, $L = 12$ in.

Length of handle, $b = 3.0$ in.

Polar moment of inertia, $J = \dfrac{\pi R^4}{2}$ for a solid shaft

Formula: In theory, and under ideal conditions, the angle of twist of the shaft is given by the formula $\theta = FbL/JG$ (radians), where the specific terms are defined above. The torque is the quantity Fb.

Limitations: In this experiment, we want to verify the accuracy of this equation for a shaft subject to forces between 10 and 30 lbf. For this range of forces, we expect a twist angle between 4° and 14° for a steel shaft.

Input: A number of experimental trials will be conducted. For each trial, the program should randomly select a force (in lbf) in the target range and output that force on **stdout**. This force will be applied and the resulting θ measured by the apparatus and input to the program on **stdin**.

Constants:

TRIALS=1000, the number of trials to conduct.

MINF=10 lbf, the minimum force to be applied.

MAXF=30 lbf, the maximum force to be applied.

EPS=.1 rad, allowable deviation of actual twist angle from theoretical value.

Output required: Any input of a θ value outside the expected range should be recorded by an appropriate error comment on **stderr**. Other valid inputs and their corresponding forces should be written to a file called **theta.out** for later analysis.

Figure 15.27.   Problem specifications: Twisting of a circular shaft.

- *Second box: preparing to generate random numbers.* The specification calls for random numbers. This means that the random number generator must be initialized, or seeded. Since this action needs to happen only once, we do it at the beginning of **main()**.
- *Third box: repeating the experiment.* The specification calls for the process to be repeated, so we declare a counter to control the repetition loop (at the top of the program) and write the framework of this loop. In the process, we realize that we need a constant for the loop termination test and a function for the loop body. We invent names for these and write a framework that includes all of the required parts of a loop: the

```
#include "tools.h"
#define TRIALS 1000
void try_once( stream s );

void main( void )
{
    stream fout;           /* For the experimental data. */
    int k;                 /* Loop counter for the process repetition. */

    say( "Measuring Torque" );
    say( "\n Opening file theta.out for output." );
    fout = fopen( "theta.out", "w" );
    if (fout == NULL) fatal( "Cannot open theta.out." );

    srand( time( NULL ) );              /* seed random number generator */

    say( "\n Ready to begin torque experiment." );
    for (k = 0; k < TRIALS; ++k) try_once( fout );

    bye();
}
```

Figure 15.28.   Torque program: The first step.

initialization, the exit test, a function call for the loop body, and the update step. We define the number of trials to be conducted at the top of the program.

- *Inner box: doing one experimental trial.* We have not yet defined `try_once()` (see Figure 15.29), the function that will conduct the experimental trials. However, we know that it is supposed to write output to the file we created, so we know the stream must be an argument in the call. Given this information, we write a tentative prototype for `try_once()` at the top of the program and insert a call as the loop body.

Development step 2, Figure 15.29. The `try_once()` function.

- *The function interface.* We start by writing the first and last lines of `try_once()` so that it is consistent with the call and prototype written in the `main()` program in Figure 15.28:

```
void try_once( stream s )
{   /* Function body will go here. */
}
```

- *First and second boxes: constants that define the experiment.* We write `#define` commands and constant declarations for the various constants and formulas given in the problem specifications:

```
#define MINF  10.0          /* minimum force */
#define MAXF  30.0          /* maximum force */
#define EPS   .1            /* permitted variation */
#define G  12E06            /* psi for steel */
#define R  0.125            /* radius of shaft */
#define L  12.0             /* length of shaft */
#define b  3.0              /* length of handle */
const double J = PI * pow( R, 4 ) / 2;
```

These `#define`d constants could be placed at the top of `main()`. However, all of the remaining details of the experiment are part of the
`try_once()` function, so we place the constant definitions at the top
of `try_once()` to keep them close to the formulas that depend on them.
The constant variable must be placed inside a function definition, because
it calls a function from the `math` library. The C compiler does not permit
a global constant initializer to call library functions.

- *Second box: variables for the experiment.* Now we focus our attention on
  conducting one experimental trial. The specifications call for generating
  a random force in a specified range, sending this value to the experimental apparatus, and receiving back an angle of twist. Although the
  acceptable range of values for the force is stated using integers, normally
  floating-point representations are used for physical quantities of this nature. Therefore, we declare two `double` variables, `F` for the force applied
  and `theta` for the resulting twist angle. We also need a variable to hold
  the theoretical twist amount (calculated from the applied force), which
  we call `theta_t`:

```
double F;       /* Force: input for experiment. */
double theta;   /* Twist angle; output. */
double theta_t; /* Twist angle; theoretical value. */
```

- *Third box: generating a random number.* Next, we must generate a
  random force, `F`, in the desired range. The `randy()` function (defined
  in the `tools` library and explained in Section 14.4) returns a random
  `double` in the range `0.0...1.0`. We multiply this result by $(30.0 - 10.0)$
  to expand the range to match the span of our target values. Then, by
  adding 10.0 to this, we shift the values to match the required range of
  `10.0...30.0`. Of course, all these limits are expressed using `#define`d
  constants so that they easily may be changed if we modify the parameters
  of the experiment. So we get this formula for F:

```
F = randy() * (MAXF - MINF) + MINF;
```

This is the finished function that is developed step by step in this section. Each box encloses a code fragment written during one of the development stages.

```
#define MINF   10.0          /* minimum force */
#define MAXF   30.0          /* maximum force */
#define EPS   .1             /* permitted variation */
#define G  12E06             /* psi for steel */
#define R  0.125             /* radius of shaft */
#define L  12.0              /* length of shaft */
#define b  3.0               /* length of handle */
```

```
void try_once( stream s )
{
    const double J = PI * pow( R, 4 ) / 2;    /* polar moment of inertia */
    double F;          /* Force: randomly selected input for experiment. */
    double theta;    /* Twist angle; experimental output. */
    double theta_t; /* Twist angle; theoretical value. */

    F = randy() * (MAXF - MINF) + MINF;    /* Get and scale random force. */

    printf( "%g\n", F );                    /* Send force to apparatus. */
    scanf( "%lg", &theta );                 /* Receive measured result. */

    theta_t = (F * b * L) / (J * G);
    if (theta > theta_t - EPS && theta < theta_t + EPS)
        fprintf( s, "%g %g\n", F, theta );
    else
        say( " Angle %g outside possible range for force %g.", theta, F );
}
```

Figure 15.29.   Torque program, step 2: The `try_once()` **function.**

- *Fourth box: interacting with the experimental apparatus.* We calculated a random force; now we send it to the apparatus. In reality, the program would send this force to the apparatus by using a digital-analog interface board, which would convert the digital value of F to an actual output voltage. This voltage then could operate some device that would produce the required force. Finally, an optical encoder could be used to send back the number of "counts" or a potentiometer could send back a voltage that corresponds to the resulting twist angle, θ.

    Since we have no such equipment readily available, we emulate the hardware by writing each force value to **stdout** and receiving the measurement of the resulting twist angle from **stdin**.

```
printf( "%g\n", F );    /* Send force to apparatus. */
scanf( "%lg", &theta ); /* Receive measured result. */
```

- *Fifth box: monitoring the experiment.* Finally, the measured value of
  theta must be checked for reasonableness. If the value is OK, the data
  are written to the output file. If not, an error comment is displayed on
  stderr. *Reasonableness* is defined as a tolerance of plus or minus **EPS**
  about the theoretical value, which is calculated first:

```
theta_t = (F * b * L) / (J * G);
if (theta > theta_t - EPS && theta < theta_t + EPS)
    fprintf( s, "%g %g\n", F, theta );
else
    say( " Angle %g outside possible range for"
         " force %g.", theta, F );
```

The finished function is shown in Figure 15.29. Due to the fact that
interaction with the device is only emulated, no sample output will be
given.

15.8   What You Should Remember

15.8.1 Major Concepts

Streams and files.

- A file is a physical collection of information stored on a device such as
  a disk or tape. It has a name and its own properties. A stream is a data
  structure created and used during program execution to connect to and
  access a file or any other input source or output destination.
- There are three standard predefined streams—**stdin, stdout**, and
  stderr—which are connected by default to the keyboard, monitor, and
  monitor, respectively. These can be reconnected using the process of redirection. A programmer can define additional streams. A call on **fopen()**
  opens a stream, specifying its direction (in or out) and attaching it to some
  device that will supply or receive the data. A call on **fclose()** terminates
  the connection.
- Once open, a stream can be used to transfer either ASCII text or data in
  binary format. All of the I/O functions presented in this chapter operate
  in text mode. Binary I/O is introduced in Chapter 17.
- Except for **stderr**, streams are buffered. On input, bytes do not come
  directly from a device into the program. Rather, a block of data is transferred from the device into a buffer and waits there until the program is
  ready for it. Typically, it is read by the program in many smaller pieces.
  On output, bytes that are written go first into a buffer and stay there until

the buffer is full or flushed for some other reason, such as an explicit call on `fflush()`. If a program crashes, everything waiting in the output buffers is lost. The corresponding files are not closed and, therefore, not readable.

- Three file-oriented input functions were introduced: `fscanf()`, `fgets()`, and `fgetc()` (which also can be called `getc()`). The input functions that use `stdin` are specializations of these routines.
- Three file-oriented output functions were introduced: `fprintf()`, `fputs()`, and `fputc()` (which also can be called `putc()`). The output functions that use `stdout` are specializations of these routines.
- When reading data from a file, certain types of errors and exceptions are likely to occur:

1. The `fopen()` function may fail to open the file properly.
2. The end of the file can be reached.
3. An incorrect character may have been inserted into the file, polluting the data on that line.
4. Data from a multipart data set may have been omitted, causing alignment errors.

Methods and functions exist to detect and recover from these types of errors. A robust input routine was presented that incorporates detection and recovery methods.

New tools.   A few more items from the `tools` library have been introduced or explained in this chapter. These include

- The type `stream` is defined by a `typedef` statement as a synonym for `FILE*` (Figure 15.6).
- The function `say()` writes a message to the `stderr` stream (Section 15.1).
- The function `cleanline()` reads and discards characters from the designated stream until a newline character is encountered (Figure 15.12).
- The function `clean_and_log()` reads characters from the first designated stream until a newline character is encountered and writes them to the specified output stream. (This function is shown in Appendix F and used in Figure 15.16.)

15.8.2   Programming Style

- *Function follows form.* When choosing a data structure for a program, its form must follow that of the real-world object the program is modeling. Within the program, processing of those data should follow the form established by the data structure. When dealing with an entire structured item, operations should be performed by calling a function. This keeps the details of the representation separate from the main flow of program logic. Modules should be designed to permit the programmer to think and talk about the problem on a conceptual level, not at a detailed level. For example, the quiz program in Figure 15.19 operates on an array of structures. It uses functions to call up a quiz (operating on the whole array), administer a quiz (operating on the whole array), and ask a single question (operating on a single item).

- *Opening files.* Failure to be able to open a file is a common experience. This leads to the following maxim: Always check that the result of **fopen()** is a valid stream. Further, if a program uses files, all of them should all be opened "up front," even if they will not be used immediately. This avoids the situation in which human effort and computer time have been spent entering and processing data, only to find that it is impossible to open an output file to receive the results. The general principle is this: Acquire all necessary resources before committing human labor to a project.

- *Interaction and redirection.* Some programs, particularly those that analyze large amounts of data, are designed to take their data from files. These generally contain minimal user feedback. Other programs are designed to be used interactively. Typically, these supply generous prompts to guide the user through the process of entering input. Without these prompts, using a program interactively is quite confusing. Any program can be run using the default stream assignments or redirection. However, unless the program was designed with redirection in mind, this may lead to problems such as the user being expected to "type blind"; that is, enter data without seeing the prompts. This problem can be avoided by writing user prompts to **stderr** if the programmer expects to use redirection on **stdout**.

- *Closing streams.* All streams are closed automatically when the program exits. However, the **stdio** library provides the **fclose()** function to permit a stream to be closed before the end of the program. Closing an input file promptly releases it for use by another program. Closing an output file promptly protects it from loss of data due to possible program crashes later in execution. Closing a stream releases the memory space used by the buffers. The **fflush()** function is defined only for output streams. It is used automatically when a stream is closed. Normally, a programmer has no need to call it explicitly.

- *End of file.* The function **feof()** should be used to detect the end of an input file. This condition occurs when you attempt to read data that are not there, so test for end of file only *after* an input operation, not before it. It is simpler and more reliable to use **feof()** than to test for a return code of **EOF** from the input routines.

- *Exceptions and errors.* File-based programs typically handle large amounts of prerecorded data. It is important for these programs to detect file input errors and inform the user of them. The input functions in the **stdio** library return error codes of one form or another. These should be checked and appropriate action taken if it is important for a program to be robust. Also, an error log file can be kept. It should record as much information as possible about each input error, so that the user has some way to find the faulty data and correct them. The input routine developed in Figure 15.16 robustly handles many types of input errors. The order in which the error tests are made is important; use this example as a template in your programs.

15.8.3   Sticky Points and Common Errors

- Keep in mind the difference between a stream name and a file name. The file name identifies the data to the operating system. A stream name is used within a program. The **fopen()** function connects a stream to a file and the argument to **fopen()** is the only place the file name ever appears in a program.

- A common cause of disaster is to create an output file with the same name as an already existing file, which will "blow away" the earlier file. The most common "victims" of this error are the program's own source code or input file, whose name absentmindedly is typed in by the user. For this reason, we recommend using **.in** as part of every input file name and **.out** as part of every output file name.

- Another common mistake is to write the wrong conversion specifiers in a format string. For output, this may produce incorrect results from valid calculations. Input errors simply invalidate all of the processing. Check for such errors early when strange answers are being produced.

- An input file must be constructed correctly for the program that reads it. Most programs expect the last line of a file to end with a newline character.

- The first unprocessed character in an input stream's buffer often is the whitespace character that terminated the previous data item. Input formats must take this into account, especially when working with character or string input.

- Input errors, incorrectly formatted data, and end-of-file problems are frequently encountered exception conditions. Any program that is to be used by many people or for many months needs to test for and deal with these conditions robustly. Failure to do so can lead to diverse disasters, including machine crashes and erroneous program results.

- A nonnumeric character in a numeric field can throw a program into an infinite loop unless detected and dealt with. Minimally, a character-oriented function such as **fgetc()** must be called to remove the character that caused the error from the input stream. The function **cleanline()** removes the faulty character along with the rest of the current line.

- When using **gets()**, **fgets()**, **scanf()**, or **fscanf()** to read a string, the input variable must be declared as a character array long enough to hold all of the characters that will be read. If the array is too short, the extra characters will overlay something else in memory. The functions `fgets()`, `scanf()`, and `fscanf()` provide ways to limit the number of input characters read so that it does not exceed the number that can be stored. These should be used regularly.

15.8.4   New and Revisited Vocabulary

These are the most important terms and concepts discussed in this chapter:

stream I/O	mode of stream	flag
buffer	input list	error detection
unbuffered stream	output list	format errors
file	end of file	error recovery
file redirection	status code	data set
text file	exception condition	log file
binary file		robust program

The following keywords, C library functions, and functions from the **tools** library are discussed in this chapter:

`stream`	`feof()`	`fprintf()`
`FILE*`	`ferror()`	`printf()`
`stderr`	`fflush()`	`fputs()`
`stdin`	`fscanf()`	`puts()`
`stdout`	`scanf()`	`fputc()` or `putc()`
`NULL`	`fgets()`	`putchar()`
`EOF`	`gets()`	`say()`
`fopen()`	`fgetc()` or `getc()`	`clean_and_log()`
`fclose()`	`getchar()`	`cleanline()`

15.9 | Exercises

15.9.1   Self-Test Exercises

1. What is the difference between

   a. `scanf()` and `fscanf()`

   b. `say()` and `printf()`

   c. `say()` and `fatal()`

   d. `fgetc()` and `getc()`

2. Happy Hacker tried to write his own version of `cleanline()`. He produced the following code, which seems to work. When he turned in the code, his teacher gave it a poor grade and said it had a potentially serious error. What is it?

```
void mycleanline( stream sin )
{
    char ch;  /* Character under input scanner */
    while (!feof( sin ) && ch != '\n') ch = fgetc( sin );
}
```

3. Each item that follows gives an input statement on the left and the data on the input stream on the right. Say what will be stored in **ok** and each of the variables on the input list. Declarations are at the top. Assume that the stream **nin** is open for input.

```
int ok, j, k;      float x, y, z;
```

a. ok = scanf("%i %i", &j, &k);   37.21   46

b. ok = scanf("%g %g %g", &x, &y, &z);   24.5   17   -.22

c. ok = fscanf(nin, "%i %i", &k);   37   71   26

d. ok = fscanf(nin, "%i %i", &j, &k);   66 (end of the file)

e. ok = fgetc(nin);   Hello

4. What (if anything) is wrong with these **fopen()** statements? Consider potential usage and style errors as well as syntax.

a. **fin = fopen("text.in", "w");**

b. **myimage = fopen("image1.in", "bw");**

c. **my_input_file = fopen(data.in, "r");**

d. **fout = fopen("c:jones.cs110.labs", "w");**

e. **fout = fopen("myprog.c", "wb");**

5. Write an input statement to read each line of data on the left from a stream named **fin** into the variables listed on the right.

```
char code, name[24], title[24], company[32], label[32];
int age;
float t, x, y, z;
```

a. **Al E. Neumann, #1 Idiot, MAD Inc.**   name, title, company

b. **38 47.1 26**   x, y, z

c. **98.6F normal body temperature**   t, code, label

d. **And so it goes!**   title

e. **Gail Bailey, F 23**   name, code, age

6. Many programs test the return value from **scanf()** to identify an end-of-file condition. However, experts advise using **feof()** for that purpose, rather than testing for a return value of **EOF**. Explain what **feof()** can do that using **EOF** cannot and explain the way in which an **EOF** return value can mean something other than end of file.

7. What is the difference between buffered and unbuffered streams? What are the advantages of buffering? Why is `stderr` unbuffered?

15.9.2   Using Pencil and Paper

1. What is the difference between

   a. `fgetc()` and `getchar()`

   b. `fgets()` and `fscanf()` for strings

   c. `say()` and `puts()`

   d. `fatal()` and `printf()`

   e. `"w"` mode and `"a"` mode

2. Variable declarations follow. Assume that the stream `nin` is open for input. Each item gives an input statement on the left and the data on the input stream on the right. Say what will be stored in `ok` or `p` and in each of the variables on the input list.

   ```
   int ok, k;        float x, y, z;
   char ar[80];      char* p;
   ```

   a. `ok = scanf( "%g %g %g", &x, &y, &z );`   46 2o5 4.2

   b. `ok = scanf( "%g %g %g", &x, &y, &z );`   46.2 215 4.2x

   c. `ok = fgetc( nin );`   (end of file)

   d. `ok = fscanf( nin, "%i", &k );`   a newline (end of file)

   e. `p = fgets( ar, 79, nin );`   (end of file)

3. Write a line of data that is formatted properly to be read from the stream `fin` by each input statement that follows.

   ```
   char code, name[24], title[24], word1[24], word2[24];
   int age;
   double t;
   ```

   a. `fscanf( fin, "%23[^:]:  %i %23s", name, &age, title );`

   b. `fgets( name, 23, fin );`

   c. `code = fgetc( fin );`

   d. `fscanf( fin, "%lg %i %c", &t, &age, &code );`

   e. `fscanf( fin, "%23s %23s", word1, word2 );`

4. What is the output from the following code fragment?

   ```
   string squeeze = "%i %i %i \n";
   string spread = "%8i %8i %8i \n";
   int p = 1000 / 3, q = -15, r = 32767L;
   ```

```
printf( squeeze, p, q, r );
printf( spread, p, q, r );
```

5. Betty Beginner tried to write a program to copy a file and produced the following code, which almost works but does not seem to terminate properly. What is the problem? How can she fix it?

```
#include "tools.h"
void main( void )
{
    char ch[80];
    stream sin, sout;

    sin = fopen( "my.in", "r" );
    sout = fopen( "my.out", "w" );
    while (!feof( sin )) {
        fgets( ch, 79, sin );
        fputs( ch, sout );
    }
    fclose( sout );
}
```

6. Write an **fopen()** statement for each purpose that follows.

   a. Open a stream named **nin** to read a text file named **n.in** in the same directory as the program.

   b. Open a stream named **im_out** to write a binary image in a file named **image1.b**.

   c. As part of a program that uses itself as data, open a stream, **cannibal**, to read the source code for the program itself from the file **prog.c**.

   d. Open a stream, **adopt**, to read a text file **babe** in a directory **daughter** that is a subdirectory of the current directory.

   e. As part of a program that copies executable files, open a stream, **clone**, to read an executable code file, **a.out**.

7. Your program's input is the file **member.dat** in which each line represents one member of a club. On each line, the person's name is listed first, followed by a comma. After that, separated by spaces, are an age and a single-character code (**M** or **F**) for the gender. Your club needs a program that will be run on January 1 of each year. The program will add 1 to the age field on every record and write the updated record to a new file, **memnew.dat**. Write statements that will declare and open the necessary streams, a statement that will read one data set, and a statement that will write the updated data set to the output file.

15.9.3 Using the Computer

1. Using files.
   The program in Figure 15.30 takes input from **stdin** and writes output on **stdout**. It evaluates $f(x) = x^3 - x^2 - 3x + 12$ from a defined initial value to a defined

final value of **x** in increments of 0.1. Following the boxed instructions, modify this program to read the initial and final values of **x** from an input file, **my.in**, and write the table of values of **f(x)** into an output file, **my.out**. Comments in the boxes suggest the additions and changes you need to make. Then create a file **my.in** containing two real values for the table limits. Test your program, including all of the error comments. Hint: You can cause an opening error for the output file by trying to open a file in a directory that does not exist.

2. Speedy streams?
   In this problem, you perform some timing experiments on the speed of your computer's memory and four kinds of streams, as listed. To perform these experiments, you need to call the function **time()** from the standard **time** library, which reads the computer's internal clock and returns the time in the form of a long integer. Store the result in a variable of type **time_t**, which is a **typedef** name for the correct kind

```
#include "tools.h"
#define x_init 0.0
#define x_final 1.0

double f( double x ) { return pow( x, 3 ) - pow( x, 2 ) - 3 * x + 12; }
void main( void )
{
    double x, y;

    /* Delete the #defines for x_init and x_final. */
    /* Declare x_init and x_final as double variables. */
    /* Declare an int variable for the error code returned by fscanf(). */
    /* Declare streams for your input and output files. */

    banner();

    /* Open your input and output files; exit if either statement fails. */
    /* Read values from your input file for x_init and x_final. */
    /* Exit with an appropriate message if there is a read error. */

    /* Change the next line to use your output stream instead of stdout. */
    printf( "\n      x                y \n\n" );

    for (x = x_init; x <= x_final; x += 0.1) {
        y = f( x );

        /* Change the next line to use your out stream instead of stdout. */
        printf( "%8.2f %15.2f \n", x, y );
    }
    /* Close your streams. */
    bye();
}
```

Figure 15.30.   Program for Exercise 1.

of integer on your local system. To time a portion of code, call `time()` immediately before and after the lines of interest, then difference the times. The result will be an integer giving the elapsed time in seconds. Your program might contain code like this:

```
time_t start, finish;    /* Integer time encodings. */
int elapsed;             /* Elapsed time in seconds. */

start = time( NULL );    /* Read system date and time. */
...                      /* Do the experiment. */
finish = time( NULL );   /* Get the time again. */
elapsed = finish - start;
```

Each experiment will consist of processing an `int` value, **V**, repeatedly. This same number will be read or written **N** times, where **N** is some very large number selected by the user to be compatible with his or her computer's speed. On our computer, 500,000 is appropriate. We suggest that you debug the program using 100 and work your way up to a number that is large enough to measure the differences among streams. In the program, declare an input stream, **nin**, and an output stream, **nout**. Define **V** to be an integer variable and initialize it to a multidigit constant such as 32,000. Prompt the user to enter **N**. Then code and time these five experiments and print the results in a neat table:

a. Store **V** in some other memory location **N** times.

b. Write **V** to **stdout** **N** times (this is buffered screen output).

c. Write **V** to **stderr** **N** times (this is unbuffered screen output).

d. Open the file **test.out** using **nout** before recording the start time, then write **V** to **nout** **N** times (this is buffered file output).

e. Close the file **test.out** and reopen it for input using **nin**; using **nin**, read each of the **N** numbers from **test.out** into **V** (this is buffered file input).

3. Units conversion.
    In the usual terminology, a *filter* is a program that reads a file, makes some small conversion to the data's format, and writes the data to another file in the converted form. Filters often are used to make the output of one program compatible with the input requirements of another. For example, suppose we want to run a program that analyzes the lengths of items in a set and have a data file containing the proper input information. However, the measurements are recorded in feet and the program requires them to be in meters. Write a short program that will read the existing data from a file named **feet.in**, convert each length to meters (divide by 3.281), and write the new data to a file named **meters.out**.

4. Text file conversion.
    Text file formats on UNIX and DOS systems are incompatible in a minor way. Each line of a UNIX text file ends with a newline character (`\n`), while each line of a DOS text file ends with both newline and return characters (`\n\r`). Programmers who use more than one machine frequently need to move programs and data from one kind of system to the other, which requires that the files be converted from one format to the other. As a first step at creating a general utility program, write a program, **u2d**, that

will convert a file from UNIX format to DOS format. Prompt the user for the names of the input and output files. Read the input file and echo every character to the output file. Also, after writing each newline character, write an additional carriage return character.

5. Computation and error handling.

   a. Write a function, `cubic()`, that will calculate and return the value of the function

   $$f(x) = x^3 \cdot e^{x \cdot \sin(x)}$$

   b. Write a main program that will read and validate a series of values for x from a file, `expermnt.in`. If a value read from the file is not numeric, less than 10, or greater than 20, write the nature of the error as well as the bad data to an error log file. For valid inputs, call `cubic()` and write both the number and the function value to the file `expermnt.out`. Use Figures 15.16 and 15.29 as guides.

6. A deck of cards.
   The output of this program should be a file in which you will store 52 lines, each line representing one card in a deck of 52 cards. There is no input. Define enumerated types for the 13 face values and four suits of cards, as well as a structure type to represent a card. Define an array of 52 cards and fill it in systematically with four suits of 13 cards each. Output a shuffled version of the deck to the file, using the random selection and replacement technique presented in the quiz program (Section 15.6). This file will be used by other game-playing programs, so the format of a card in the output file should be a pair of integer constants from your enumerated type. In addition, display the cards on the screen in an English format such as "king of hearts."

7. Partitioning a data set.
   The input of this program will be a file in which each line represents one person. The person's name is first, followed by a comma. After that, separated by spaces, are an age and a single-character code (**M** or **F**) for the gender. This file contains records of people of all ages and both genders. You work for a school system that needs to produce one file containing the names of males of school age (**5...18**) and another for females of school age. The program must be able to read the data from the input file and select the specified items. Write data for school-age males to the file `male.out` and data for school-age females to `female.out`. Log bad data sets on the file `error.log`. Ignore any input data for children younger than 5 and adults older than 18.

8. Barrels of barrels.
   A primary use of computers is to process large amounts of data. To make this realistic, the data should be in a file, not entered interactively. In Chapter 14, exercise 6, specifications were given for a program about cylinders. Redesign this program to read its data from a file called `cyl.in` until the end of the file is reached or the array is full. Write the output on a file, `cyl.out`, in one of two forms, either a table of the results as before or simply seven columns of data per line, each separated by whitespace. Allow the user to select the form of the output, following the example of Figure 15.9.

9. A multiline data set.
   Design a program to print mailing labels. Each label will have two blank lines, three or four address lines, and two or three more blank lines. Each address line may contain up to 30 characters. The addresses will be printed in a single column on strips

of gummed label stock, so the spacing is critically important. Be sure that each label has a total of eight lines. The addresses to be printed are stored in a file, **mail.adr**. Each data set is composed of three or four lines, where each line has a code in column 1 and column 2 is blank. The actual data start in column 3. The codes in column 1 are used to determine which lines belong in the data set and to ensure that all required lines are present. The first three lines are required and have codes **A**, **B**, and **C**. The fourth line is optional and has code **D**. The program should

a. Declare a type, **address**, to hold an entire data set.

b. Read complete lines of data from the file **mail.adr**, making sure that the input array is long enough for long lines. If any data line has more than 30 characters, log the exception and echo the extra characters to a log file, **mail.log**. Print only the first 30 characters. (Hint: You can store a null terminator in the 31st slot.)

c. Reject and log any address that has its lines out of order or has a required line missing.

d. For each complete data set, print a label to the file **mail.lbl**. Print only the actual address, not the codes in the first column. Make sure to print eight lines per label.

e. After the end of the input file is encountered, display (on the screen) the number of valid labels that were printed and the number of errors found.

10. Gas pressures.
    The state of an ideal gas is given by the equation $PV = nRT$, where n is the number of moles, R is the universal gas constant, V is the volume, P is the absolute pressure, and T is the absolute temperature. Consider heating a rigid sealed tank initially containing an ideal gas at pressure P_1 and temperature T_1. Since n, V, and R remain constant, pressure will be proportional to temperature. We get the simplified relation:

$$\frac{P_2}{P_1} = \frac{T_2}{T_1}$$

a. Write a pair of double:double functions to convert temperatures to absolute units. The argument to **abs_temp_metric()** is a temperature in degrees Celsius; the argument to **abs_temp_english()** is in degrees Fahrenheit. Recall that the two equations for absolute temperature are Kelvin = Celsius + 273 and Rankine = Fahrenheit + 460.

b. Write a program that will input data sets from a file, **pressure.in**. Each data set will consist of an input pressure **P1** (kPa or psi) followed by a code (**C** for Celsius or **F** for Fahrenheit), then an initial temperature (in Celsius or Fahrenheit) and a final temperature. Validate all inputs as they are read and display an error message on **stderr** for invalid inputs. (A pressure is not allowed to be negative and a temperature is not allowed to be below absolute 0.) Call the appropriate conversion function to change the temperatures to absolute units and calculate the final pressure using the preceding equation. Create an output file, **press.out**, where each line will contain a pressure (input), the converted temperatures, and the calculated gas pressure, all separated by spaces.

CHAPTER

16

Simple Array Algorithms

Chapter 10 introduces arrays, shows how to write array declarations and initializers, and uses arrays with subscripts for input, output, and simple array processing. This chapter continues the development of arrays by presenting several fundamental array algorithms. Chapter 17 introduces two-dimensional arrays and their applications.

16.1 Searching an Array Data Structure

A common application of arrays is to store a table of data that will be searched, and possibly updated repeatedly, in response to user inputs. In the noncomputer world, a table has at least two columns: a column of index values and one or more columns of data. For example, in a periodic table of the elements, the atomic numbers (1...109) might be used as the **index column**, then the atomic weights and chemical symbols would be the **data columns**. For other purposes involving these elements, a different column, such as the element's name, might be chosen as the index column.

A table can either be sorted or unsorted. The data in a **sorted table** are arranged in ascending or descending order, according to some comparison function defined on the values in the index column. For example, a periodic table is sorted in ascending order by the atomic number. A dictionary is sorted in ascending alphabetic order. The typical university course catalog is sorted in ascending order by department code, and within a department, by course number.

To implement a table in the computer, we can use either a set of parallel arrays or an array of structures. When we implement a table as a set of **parallel arrays**, we use one array to represent the index column and one more for each data column in the table. If the table is modeled as an **array of structures**, the structure has one member for each column in the table. The array of structures usually is considered a better style because it is more coherent; that is, it groups together all the values for a table entry. The relative merits of these two approaches are discussed in Chapter 14.

If the index values are consecutive small integers, or numbers that easily can be converted into small integers, we need no separate index column. We can use the array subscripts for this purpose. This actually is the kind of table we have been using for menu applications. In menus, the index values and the subscripts are equal. This lets us access the table entries directly, without searching, by using the index value as a subscript. In contrast, if the index values are not small integers or are irregular, we must search the index column to find the position (subscript) of the data item we want.

16.1.1 Searching a Table

As discussed in Chapter 6, a typical **search loop** examines a set of possibilities, looking for one that matches a given key value. A sequential search of a table examines the index column for an entry that matches the key, one item after another. In every table-searching application, we find the following elements:

- A table, consisting of an index column and one or more data columns.
- A **search key**, the input value that must be compared to the entries in the index column of the table.
- The **position variable**, the output from the search process, set to the subscript that identifies the value in the index column matching the key value.
- A **success or failure code**, sometimes a separate output value, other times failure may be indicated by setting the position variable to a value either too large or too small to be a legal subscript.

Chapter 6 introduces the idea of a search loop. Figure 16.1 shows a complete **sequential search** function that uses such a search loop.

Notes on Figure 16.1. Sequential search.

- *First box: the header.* The parameters include elements required for a search algorithm: a table and a search key. The table is a simple integer array containing **n** values. The return value will be a failure code or the subscript of the key value in the array if it exists.

A simple sequential search function for an unsorted table.

```
int sequential_search( int data[], int n, int key )
{
    int scan;        /* Loop counter and array index. */
    for (scan = 0; scan < n; ++scan) {
        if ( data[scan] == key ) return scan;
    }

    return -1;
}
```

Figure 16.1.   Sequential search.

- *Second box: the loop.* A counted loop is used to examine the data items. If a match is found for the key, the loop terminates; otherwise, all **n** values are checked.
- *First inner box: the comparison.* Each item is compared to the key. With integers, the **==** operator is appropriate, but other comparison functions would be necessary for types such as strings and structures.
- *Second inner box: success.* If a match is found, we need to leave the loop. Sometimes this is done with a **break** statement. In this case, we use **return** because the function needs to do nothing more. The answer is the current item's subscript.
- *Last box: failure.* If the loop goes past the last data item without finding a match, the search has failed. Failure is indicated by returning a subscript of **-1**, which is invalid for any array.

This function assumes that the data are unsorted and that all items must be checked before we can conclude that the search has failed. When searching a table sorted in ascending (descending) order, the search can be terminated before reaching the end of the data if the key value is found to be greater than (less than) the current index value.

The Chauvenet's statistics example in the next section describes and illustrates a simple sequential search algorithm for a sorted array or for an array of structures sorted with respect to an index column.[1]

---

[1]Discussion of the binary search algorithm, which is more complex but much faster for sorted arrays, is deferred until recursion is introduced in Chapter 21.

16.1.2   Masking

At times, when we search through a table of data, we are not looking for a specific item but a set of items that have particular characteristics. Further processing will be applied only to this subset of the data. These "relevant" items sometimes are copied into a separate array or separate file. An alternative is to leave the items where they are and label each one, so that later processing steps can easily and efficiently identify the relevant data. More generally, several categories of data may be labeled differently and used later for different purposes.

A technique called **masking** implements this strategy. In this technique, we have an array of data and, parallel to it, an array that contains a label value, which indicates whether to use each item in the data array or ignore it. Alternatively, the data and the mask could be members of a structure in an array of structures.[2]

Masking allows us to eliminate data items from further consideration without physically removing them from the table and closing the gap. In the beginning, the mask flag for every item is initialized to `true`. When an item no longer is needed, its mask flag is set to `false`. Every function that works with the data should examine the mask before including a data item in a computation.

The programs in this chapter work with two different masking techniques. In the next small program, we use a menu with a parallel mask array. Each menu item is marked `false`, and therefore eliminated, after it has been selected. The result is that fewer and fewer possibilities are displayed on the menu as the process proceeds. In the application in Section 16.2, each data item is represented by a structure with two members: the data and the mask. If the mask value is `false`, the item is considered "bad" and therefore ignored.

Enhanced menu processing.   In prior chapters, we used menu functions that display a list of choices repeatedly, asking the user to select one option each time. The program found in Figures 16.2 and 16.3 elaborates on this simple process by adding a mask array parallel to the menu array. The mask is used to suppress display of items previously chosen and ensure that the user chooses one of the items currently displayed.

The application itself is a simple carnival guessing game. A player pays a small amount for the chance to win prizes of greater value. The computer selects a random number and sets that as the player's value limit but does not let the player know what that limit is. The player then selects a series of "prizes" from the menu. A player who stops before exceeding the limit gets to keep all the prizes. A player who goes over the limit loses everything. To make the game more challenging, the player is not told the value of the prizes, although clearly some are worth more than others.

---

[2] Actually, several data members could be controlled by the same mask. Masking will be revisited in Chapter 18 where the data objects and the masks are arrays of bits, rather than arrays of numbers.

We use a mask to eliminate items, one at a time, from a menu. This main program calls the function in Figure 16.3.

```c
#include "tools.h"
#define PRIZES 10
typedef struct ITEMS { char name[20]; int price; } item;
int choose( item inventory[], bool mask[] );

void main( void )
{
    int count = 0, total = 0; /* Number and value of prizes picked so far. */
    int pick;                 /* Player's selection. */
    char yesno;               /* Continue or quit flag. */
    int max;                  /* Player's random limit. */

    item inventory[PRIZES] = { {"ball",5}, {"bear",15},
        {"doll",10}, {"gorilla",15}, {"hat",1}, {"kazoo",3},
        {"lollipop",3}, {"spider",1}, {"squirt gun",10}, {"stickers",1}
    };
    bool mask[PRIZES] = {true,true,true,true,true,true,true,true,true,true};

    banner();
    puts( " Prize Giveaway Game" );

    max = (time( NULL ) % 10) + 6;      /* Choose the random limit. */

    for (yesno = 'y'; tolower( yesno ) == 'y'; scanf( " %c", &yesno )) {
        pick = choose( inventory, mask );

        total += inventory[pick].price;
        if (total > max) break;

        ++count;
        printf( " Do you want to keep going? " );
    }

    if (total > max) printf( " You ran out of luck!  You lose.\n" );
    else printf( " You are a lucky stiff!  \n"
                 " You have %i prizes worth %i tickets!\n", count, total );

    bye();
}
```

Figure 16.2.   A carnival game.

Notes on Figure 16.2. A carnival game.

- *First box: the menu and mask array.*

    1. The **inventory** stores the available "prizes" and the cost of each (in terms of tickets, not dollars). For development purposes, a short array initialized in the program is enough to define the list of prizes. In a more realistic program, the data for the table would be read from a file.
    2. The mask array parallels the prize array; all of its elements are initialized to **true**. This indicates that all of the prizes will be available when the game begins. As play progresses, elements of this array are set to **false** when the corresponding prize is selected.

- *Second box: The hidden limit.* The formula for selecting the hidden maximum is based on two factors: The player pays 5 tickets to enter the game, and the values of the prizes range from 1 to 15 tickets, with most being less than 10. This formula first generates a random number in the range $0 \ldots 9$, then adds a constant to shift that range to $6 \ldots 15$. So, technically, it is possible to win any of the prizes, but unlikely that anyone will ever get the gorilla or the bear. The carnival does not lose money on this deal because many players will keep going until they lose everything. Far fewer will walk away with prizes worth more than they paid.

- *Third box: The game loop.*

    1. On each pass through the loop, the user is allowed to choose another prize and its cost is added to his current total in hopes that it will not exceed the limit. This loop has two exit paths. First, it ends if the current total exceeds the limit. Second, the player may quit while ahead.
    2. This loop is a query loop, not a counted loop, and therefore is somewhat different than the usual **for** loop. The loop variable, which must be updated after each pass through the loop, is **yesno**. This variable is updated using **scanf()** (not increment), so we place the **scanf()** in the loop's update position. We initialize **yesno** to **y**, so that we will enter the loop the first time. After that, we continue as long as the user's response is **y**.
    3. In the first inner box, the **choose()** function presents a menu, elicits a choice, validates it, and updates the mask array so that the prize will not be offered again. The choice is returned and stored in **pick**.
    4. The second inner box adds the price of the current selection to the total and compares it to the hidden limit. If the total is higher, control leaves the loop and the game ends in a loss.

This function is called from the main program in Figure 16.2.

```
int
choose( item inventory[], bool mask[] )
{
    int k;
```
```
    puts( " Here are the remaining prizes:" );
    for (k = 0; k < PRIZES; ++k)
        if (mask[k]) printf( "%2i: %s\n", k, inventory[k].name );
```
```
    printf( " Your choice? " );
    scanf( "%i", &k );
    while (k < 0 || k >= PRIZES || mask[k] == false) {
        puts( " Hey, can't you read?  \n Choose a number on the list!" );
        scanf( "%i", &k );
    }
```
```
    mask[k] = false;
    return k;
```
```
}
```

Figure 16.3.   Masked menu function for the carnival game.

- *Last box: winning or losing.* After leaving the loop, the program prints a losing message or congratulations, depending on the reason for leaving the loop. Here, we tested **total**; it would work equally well to test the contents of **yesno**.
- *Sample output.* Here is sample output from two runs, showing how the menu gets shorter after each turn, and demonstrating a variety of responses from the program. Read the left column before the right one.

```
Prize Giveaway Game                     Here are the remaining prizes:
                                        1: bear
Here are the remaining prizes:          2: doll
0: ball                                 3: gorilla
1: bear                                 4: hat
2: doll                                 5: kazoo
3: gorilla                              6: lollipop
4: hat                                  7: spider
5: kazoo                                8: squirt gun
6: lollipop                             9: stickers
7: spider                               Your choice? 5
8: squirt gun                           Do you want to keep going? n
9: stickers                             You are a lucky stiff!
Your choice? 0                          You have 2 prizes worth 8 tickets!
Do you want to keep going? y
```

```
Prize Giveaway Game

Here are the remaining prizes:
0: ball
1: bear
2: doll
3: gorilla
4: hat
5: kazoo
6: lollipop
7: spider
8: squirt gun
9: stickers
Your choice? 10
Hey, can't you read?
Choose a number on the list!
3
You ran out of luck!  You lose.
```

Notes on Figure 16.3. Masked menu function.

- *First box: displaying the menu.* Both the menu and mask arrays are passed to the function. We omit the array length from the parameter list because it is defined as a global constant. The `for` loop is like the menu loop studied earlier, except that it checks the mask value for each selection and displays the menu item only if the mask value is `true`.

- *Second box: selecting a prize.* The program prompts the user for a choice, reads the response, then enters a validation loop. As usual, a response is invalid if it is not a legal subscript for the array. In addition, it must correspond to one of the remaining menu choices. The mask array was used to display the remaining selections and is used again to test whether the choice is valid. If not, an error prompt is given and the loop repeats.

- *Third box, returning the results.* Since the mask defines what *valid choice* means, it must be updated each time a valid choice is made. We use the number selected to store `false` in the mask, then return the choice to the caller. Since the mask is an array parameter, it carries the updated information back to the caller.

16.2   Application: Screening out Faulty Data (Optional Topic)

In Section 10.4.1, we wrote a program to calculate some statistics about a set of data values. The standard deviation and variance of a set depend on all of the values in the set. However, experimental error, equipment malfunction, and recording errors sometimes result in one or two "bad" data values in a set. The question for a set of n experimental measurements, then, becomes how to distinguish between a faulty reading due to equipment failure and an exceptional situation that results in a validly deviant data value.

16.2.1   Chauvenet's Algorithm

We use a method called **Chauvenet's criteria** to screen out statistically invalid values.[3] This technique is based on the assumption that the collected data have a **Gaussian error distribution**. It calculates, for each value, whether the value differs from the mean by an acceptable amount that might result from experimental error or whether the deviation from the mean is much more than the majority of the values. To use Chauvenet's criteria, we first compute the deviance ratio for each value:

- Let the data values be $x_1 \ldots x_n$.
- Let sd be the standard deviation of the set.
- Let dr_k be the deviance ratio for value x_k.
- Then $dr_k = |(x_k - \text{mean})/sd|$

The ratio dr_k is some indication of the "badness" of the value x_k. We can reject a value, x_k, if dr_k is greater than the allowable ratio listed in the Chauvenet table (Figure 16.4). The larger the set of values we are using, the smaller is the effect of a single "bad" value on the statistics and the better we can tolerate such values. Therefore, as the number of data values grows, the maximum acceptable value of dr_k also grows.

Number of Values	Allowable Maximum Value of dr_k
3	1.38
5	1.65
10	1.96
15	2.13
25	2.33
50	2.57
100	2.81
300	3.14
500	3.29

Figure 16.4.   Chauvenet's table.

---

[3] J. Holman, *Experimental Methods for Engineers*, 3rd ed. (New York: McGraw-Hill, 1978).

To apply this statistical test, we first need to know the mean and standard deviation for the set of values. Then each value can be examined for acceptability. This is no problem, since we can store all of the data values in an array.

Setting up the Chauvenet table.   In this program, we implement Chauvenet's table as an array of structures: One column, **n_vals**, contains the index values; the second column, **ratio**, contains the data we want to retrieve. The type definition and an object declaration with initializers are shown in Figure 16.5. We can load data into such a table either by reading data from a stream or by writing initializers for the array that forms the table. If a table is short and its contents are constants that cannot change, the easiest way to load data into it is with initializers, as we do here. If this example were extended to handle larger data sets, it might become worthwhile to read the table data from a file.

This is the function that, given the number of values in a data set, identifies the appropriate deviance ratio for use in evaluating the quality of those values. It is called from the main program in Figure 16.8.

```
/* ----------------------------------------------------------------
** Precondition:   n must be greater than 2.
*/
double
chauv_ratio( int n )
{
   int k;                                  /* position variable for search loop. */
```

```
   typedef struct { int n_vals; double ratio; } table_type;
   #define L 9                              /* Length of Chauvenet's table */
   static const table_type chauv[L] = {{  3, 1.38}, {  5, 1.65}, { 10, 1.96},
                                        { 15, 2.13}, { 25, 2.33}, { 50, 2.57},
                                        {100, 2.81}, {300, 3.14}, {500, 3.29}
                                        };
```

```
   /* Compare actual number of data items to numbers in table. */
   /* Stop search when proper place in table is located.   */
   for (k = 0; k < L; ++k) {
       if (n < chauv[k].n_vals) break;
   }
```

```
   return chauv[k-1].ratio;    /* We've gone too far; back up one slot. */
```

```
}
```

Figure 16.5.   Searching the Chauvenet table.

Notes on Figure 16.5. Searching the Chauvenet table.

- *First box: the Chauvenet table.*

    1. In most previous examples, types have been defined at the top of the program and tables have been declared as global constants. That is not desirable here because the type and the table are relevant only to the `chauv_ratio()` function. Therefore, we will define the type, the table length, and the table itself inside the function, making them the private property of `chauv_ratio()`.
    2. The `typedef` defines a two-part structure with members named `n_vals` and `ratio`. If we make an array of this type, we get a two-column table that looks like the table in Figure 16.4.
    3. The object `chauv` is an array of structures. Its initializer has one unit for each slot in the array, and each unit (enclosed in curly brackets) has an initial value for `n_vals`, followed by one for `ratio`.
    4. To access one cell of the table, we need the object name, a subscript, and a component name: `chauv[3].n_vals` or `chauv[k].ratio`.
    5. The array is declared as `static const`; we use `static` because it is more efficient. A **static variable** is initialized only once, at the beginning of execution, and stays available. It is not reinitialized every time the function is called. This is ideal for a table of constant values defined inside a function. Static storage is discussed more in Chapter 21.

- *Second box: searching the table.* In addition to defining the Chauvenet table, we need to search it. The elements of the search application are

    The table is named `chauv`, the index field is `.n_vals`, and the data field is `.ratio`.

    The key value is `n`, the number of values in the data set being analyzed.

    The position variable is `k`; when the search is complete, `chauv[k-1]` will contain the appropriate Chauvenet ratio for the given data set.

    No success or failure code is needed because the last entry in the table will be used whenever `n` is greater than 500.

    We want to locate the row of the Chauvenet table with the largest index value less than or equal to the number of data values in the input array. We do this by locating the first row whose index value is too big and, if it exists, then backing up one row.

    1. Normally, we use a `for` statement with an `if...break` to search a table, as we do here. The control unit of the `for` loop steps through the entries in the array one by one and stops when there are no more entries.
    2. There are two ways to leave this loop: search through all of the table entries or break out in the middle of the search.

3. The `for` test ends the loop if **k** has stepped *past* the end of the table. This happens when the number of data values in the sample is greater than or equal to the largest index value in the table (500, in this case). When this happens, we use the last entry in the table. We can access this row after we finish the search loop by decrementing **k**.
4. The `if` statement in the loop body tests whether the value of `chauv[k].n_vals` is greater than the number of values in the data array. If so, we `break`; if not, we continue. When we break, the search index has gone one step too far, so we also need to decrement **k** to position it at the preceding array slot.

- *Third box: the* `return` *statement.*

1. Control comes here after leaving the loop for either reason. Also, whichever reason caused the loop exit, **k** is one too large. So we return the value from the table at slot **k-1**.
2. If the parameter **n** is smaller than 3, there are not enough data values to consider eliminating any. We rely on the calling program to detect this potential problem and take appropriate action instead of calling `chauv_ratio()`. The comment block at the top of the function documents this precondition of the function.

The `chauv_test()` function in Figure 16.6 is called from a loop in Figure 16.11. Given a value from Chauvenet's table, this function computes the actual deviance ratio of a data item and makes a comparison. That is, it tests whether a single data value, **x**, "fits" the distribution of a set of values.

Notes on Figure 16.6: Using Chauvenet's ratio.

- The function header.

1. The value of the first parameter, **x**, is to be compared to the distribution of values whose mean and standard deviation are contained in the

---

This function is called from the function `chauv_ar()` in Figure 16.11. It tests whether a data value, **x**, fits the given distribution of values.

```
bool                    /* Return true for good values, false for bad values. */
chauv_test( double x, stat_t st, double ratio )
{
    double dr = fabs( (x - st.mean) / st.stdev ); /* deviation ratio */
    /* Compare ratio to ratio from Chauvenet's table.   */
    /* Return true if dr is small enough, false otherwise.  */
    return ratio > dr;
}
```

Figure 16.6.   Using Chauvenet's ratio.

stat_t structure (defined in Figure 16.8) given as the second parameter. The mean and standard deviation values will be extracted from the structure, as needed.

2. A bad value has a deviance ratio greater than the value of the last parameter, **ratio**. When this function is called, the parameter will be the value selected from Chauvenet's table (using **chauv_ratio()**) as appropriate for the size of the data set.

- *The computation.*

1. The deviance of a data value is the difference between it and the mean of the distribution.
2. The deviance ratio, **dr**, of a value is its deviance divided by the standard deviation of the distribution.
3. We compare the absolute value of the deviance ratio to the criterion from Chauvenet's table and return **true** if **dr** is small enough, indicating that we do not consider **x** to be an "outlying" value.

16.2.2   The Chauvenet Program

In the program of Figure 10.15, we compute statistics for a small set of data values. We now extend the original statistics program to process a large amount of data stored in a file and eliminate deviant data values. Once this is done, the statistics originally computed to do the testing no longer are accurate for the remaining values; if accurate statistics are needed, we have to recompute them. This suggests that we should use a separate function to compute the statistics so that we need not write the same code twice. We also use a structure to package the three statistical values into a coherent unit. Finally, we use the masking techniques discussed in Section 16.1.2.

This is the call chart for the statistics program in Figures 16.5 through 16.13. Calls on functions in **stdio** have been omitted.

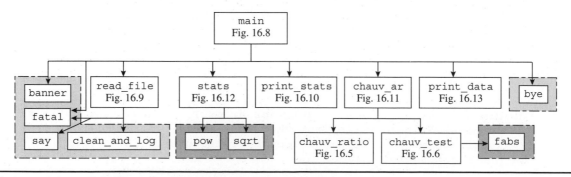

Figure 16.7.   Call chart for computing better statistics.

A data set is analyzed, and statistics for it are produced after deviant data values have been eliminated. The program calls functions in Figures 16.5 through 16.13, directly or indirectly. The call chart of Figure 16.7 diagrams the relationships among the functions in the application.

```
#include "tools.h"
```
```
#define N   500                 /* maximum number of data values */
typedef struct VALUE { double data; bool mask; } value_t;
typedef struct STATS { double mean, var, stdev; } stat_t;
```
```
int     read_file  ( value_t x[], int nmax );
void    print_data ( value_t x[], int n );
stat_t  stats      ( int n, int n_good, value_t x[] );
void    print_stats ( string when, int n, stat_t st );
int     chauv_ar   ( int n, value_t x[], stat_t st );
bool    chauv_test ( double x, stat_t st, double ratio );
double  chauv_ratio ( int n );

void main( void )
{
```
```
    value_t x[N];       /* array for the data values */
    int num;            /* initial number of data values */
    int n_good;         /* number of values after eliminating "bad" ones */
    stat_t answer;      /* Statistical results for array x. */
```
```
    banner();
```
```
    num = read_file( x, N );                    /* read data from file */
    if (num < 3) fatal( " Too few data items for meaningful analysis." );
```
```
    answer = stats( num, num, x );              /* compute initial stats */
    print_stats( "before", num, answer );       /* and print them */
```
```
    n_good = chauv_ar( num, x, answer );        /* test values */
```
```
    answer = stats( num, n_good, x );           /* recompute stats */
    print_stats( "after", n_good, answer );     /* print new stats */
    print_data( x, num );                       /* print results */
```
```
    bye();
}
```

Figure 16.8.   Computing better statistics.

Figures 16.5 to 16.13 constitute the revised application, as shown in Figure 16.7. We examine the new main program first (Figure 16.8), then discuss the functions developed to support it. Since this program elaborates on an earlier program, we comment primarily on the new parts.

Notes on Figure 16.8. Computing Better Statistics.

- *First box: definitions.*

    1. We increase the possible number of data values we can handle to 500, since the Chauvenet table goes that far and data will be read from a file instead of the keyboard.
    2. We use an array of `value_t` structures, rather than a simple array of numbers. This provides a second column in the table to use as a mask. A value will be marked "bad" if it differs too radically from the rest of the data and, therefore, is likely to be an error. Otherwise, it will be marked "good."
    3. We use type `bool` when we want to store a truth value or return one from a function. In C, this type is completely compatible with type `int`, and if necessary, a `bool` value can be treated like an integer.
    4. The structure `stat_t` is introduced here to package together the three statistical measures: mean, variance, and standard deviation. By doing this, the program can pass one argument, instead of two or three, to the many functions that use these statistics. This also eliminates the need for call-by-address parameters, since the function that computes the statistics can pass them back as a single structured return value. Overall, the code becomes simpler, and simpler code is less prone to error.

- *Second box: declarations.*

    1. The variable `x` now is an array of up to `N` structures, in which each row of the array contains a number and a mask. The actual number of data items in the array will be stored in `num`, which could be smaller than `N`.
    2. Initially, we mark all the data values as good. After testing the data, some will be marked as bad and discarded. The variable `n_good` will be used to hold the count of the good values.

- *Third box: initializing the data array.*

    1. The tasks of opening a stream, reading data from the file into an array, and handling input errors are routine and much the same for any array application. By shifting the file-handling code to a function, we remove all these details from the main flow of program logic. The function `read_file()` is shown in Figure 16.9.
    2. We call `read_file()` to read up to `N` data values into the array `x`. The number of data items successfully read and stored in the array is returned from this function and saved in `num`. This number is passed to all functions that process the data and used to control processing loops throughout the rest of the program.
    3. If the number of data items is less than 3, the data set is too small for analysis with Chauvenet's criteria, so we abort.

- *Fourth box: initial statistics.* We call a new function to compute the initial statistics and another to print them. The body of the **stats()** function contains the code from the old **average()** and **variance()** functions, modified to use an array of structures (values with masks) instead of a simple array. For the data set echoed below, the initial statistics are

```
Stats before eliminating bad values:
        For 17 data values
        mean = 76.32
        variance = 24.20
        standard deviation = 4.92
```

- *Fifth box: elimination of deviant data.* We use the initial mean and standard deviation to apply Chauvenet's criteria. The operation of the **chauv_ar()** function is discussed shortly. When it returns, each data value in the array **x** will have been evaluated and marked as good or bad using the mask field. The number of good data values is returned. We then are ready to compute the final statistics.

- *Sixth box: the final answers.*

  1. The **stats()** function is called again to compute the statistics on the corrected set of values. It checks the mask of each value and excludes those marked as bad.

  2. The second call to **stats()** is almost the same as the call in the fourth box; only the second argument differs. This time it is the number of good items, which was computed by **chauv_ar()** and stored in **n_good**. This number is used to compute the mean.

  3. Last, we call the **print_stats()** and **print_data()** functions to output the revised statistics and the labeled data table. The final output is

```
Stats after eliminating bad values:
        For 15 data values
        mean = 76.34
        variance = 9.09
        standard deviation = 3.01

Evaluation of data:
        x[ 0] = 77.89 is good
        x[ 1] = 76.55 is good
        x[ 2] = 76.32 is good
        x[ 3] = 79.43 is good
        x[ 4] = 75.12 is good
        x[ 5] = 64.78 is bad
        x[ 6] = 79.06 is good
        x[ 7] = 78.58 is good
        x[ 8] = 75.49 is good
        x[ 9] = 74.78 is good
```

```
x[10] = 78.43 is good
x[11] = 75.42 is good
x[12] = 67.78 is good
x[13] = 79.96 is good
x[14] = 87.58 is bad
x[15] = 76.49 is good
x[16] = 73.78 is good
```

16.2.3   I/O Utility Functions

The functions that read from the data file and print the statistics to the screen are adaptations of familiar code from previous examples. The major change is

---

This function is called by the main program in Figure 16.8.

```
int
read_file( value_t x[], int nmax )
{
    int k;                  /* subscript variable for loop */
    char filename[80];      /* name of input file */
    stream fin;             /* stream for input file */
    int flag;               /* for fscanf() return value */

    printf( " Name of data file: " );
    scanf( "%s", filename );
    fin = fopen( file_name, "r" );
    if (fin == NULL) fatal( " Fatal error: cannot open %s.", filename );
    printf( " Reading data from %s.\n", infile );

    for (k = 0; k < nmax; ) {           /* Don't read beyond end of array. */
        flag = fscanf( fin, "%lg", &x[k].data );
        if (flag == 1) {
            x[k].mask = true;       /* Point is "good" until proven bad. */
            ++k;                    /* all is well -- count the item. */
        }
        else if (feof( fin )) break;/* no more data is available. */
        else {                          /* bad data - note, skip, continue. */
            say( " - - Bad data while reading slot %i: ", k );
            clean_and_log( fin, stderr );
        }
    }

    fclose( fin );
    return k;
}
```

Figure 16.9.   From file to masked array.

that these functions work with structures rather than simple numeric parameters. They are presented here with minimal comment.

The program's data are a set of real values stored in a file, one item per line. All the details of file-handling and input error checking are encapsulated in the function shown in Figure 16.9, which is a minor modification of the file-handling code in Figure 15.21.

Notes on Figure 16.9. From file to masked array.

- *The function header and local declarations.* The address of an empty array of structures and its length are parameters to this function. The function reads real values from the file and stores them in the `.data` fields of the array.
- *First box: the file.* We define stream-handling variables and open the stream locally, because the stream will be used and closed entirely within this function. Variables include an array for the file name, the name of the input stream, `fin`, and `flag`, which will hold the value returned by `fscanf()`. The name of the data file is read interactively, then the input stream is opened. We test for a valid open stream and supply feedback, positive or negative.
- *Second box: the input loop.*

    1. The `for` statement uses the variable `k` to subscript the data array. It processes array slots `0...nmax-1`, if that much data exist. If the end of the file occurs before the array is full, the `feof()` test takes control out of the loop. In both cases, the value of `k` after exiting the loop is the actual number of data items correctly read and stored in the array. This number is returned to the calling program explicitly, using the `return` statement. The data values and masks are returned through the array parameter.
    2. The order in which a data item is read and error indicators are checked is very important. The tests must be made in the order shown here to guarantee correct operation under all circumstances.
    3. *Inner box: good data.* If an error occurs while reading a data value, that value is not stored. Therefore, we do not want the program to increment the array subscript, `k`. Because of this, the program increments `k` only when a correct value has been read, rather than doing it in the usual update position of the control line of the loop. The other structure member, `x[k].mask`, is initialized to `true` so that the value will be used to calculate the initial statistics. Each data item is considered good until proven otherwise.

Notes on Figure 16.10: The `print_stats()` function.   The body of the function in Figure 16.10 is a single `printf()` statement formerly found in `main()`. All the relevant statistics are extracted from the structure parameter in which they are packaged. Normally, we do not write a separate function for one

This function is called from the fourth and sixth boxes of the main program in Figure 16.8.

```
void
print_stats( string when, int n, stat_t st )
{
    printf( "\n Stats %s eliminating bad values:\n"
            "\t For %i data values \n\t mean = %.2f \n"
            "\t variance = %.2f \n\t standard deviation = %.2f \n\n",
            when, n, st.mean, st.var, st.stdev );
}
```

Figure 16.10.   The `print_stats()` function.

statement. This one is written as a separate function, however, because this single statement is long and tedious to write, and we want to print the statistics twice. It is easier and better style to write it once and call it twice, instead of writing identical copies of the statement in two places in the program.

16.2.4   Identifying Bad Data

From `main()`, we call the `chauv_ar()` function (Figure 16.11) to test each data value and record whether it is good or bad in its mask component. This uses the `chauv_test()` function (Figure 16.6), which evaluates only a single data value. Here, we evaluate and mark the entire array as well as count the number of good values. A few key parts of the routine are examined.

Notes on Figure 16.11: The `chauv_ar()` function.

- *First box: the header.* The array **x** brings a table of **n** data records into this function, with the **n** data values in the first column of the table.
- *Second box: The ratio.* It is more efficient to test all the values at the same time, because we need to search the Chauvenet table only once. A ratio is selected from the table that is appropriate for the number of data values and stored in the variable **ratio**. It then is used to label all of the values without further searching.
- *Third box: The labeling.* We embed the Chauvenet computations in a loop, which we execute **n** times. The loop evaluates the `.data` member of each element of **x** and stores **true** or **false** in the corresponding `.mask` field. At the same time, it counts the number of "good" values and (after exiting the loop) returns that number to `main()`. The mask values are returned to `main()` through the array parameter.

16.2.5   Eliminating Bad Data

When statistical computations were introduced in Chapter 10, the main program did part of the calculations and short functions were used to compute the mean and

This code is called from **main()**.   It calls the **chauv_ratio()** function in Figure 16.5 and the **chauv_test()** function in Figure 16.6.   It tests all of the values in an array of structures, storing **true** (for good values) and **false** (for bad values) in the mask member of each structure.

```
int                                   /* Return number of good values. */
chauv_ar( int n, value_t x[ ], stat_t st )
{
    double  ratio;                    /* Chauvenet ratio for n values */
    int     k;                        /* subscript for data table */
    int     n_good = 0;               /* number of good values */

    ratio = chauv_ratio( n );         /* get proper ratio for n values */

    for (k = 0; k < n; ++k) {         /* Analyze values one at a time */
        x[k].mask = chauv_test( x[k].data, st, ratio );
        if (x[k].mask) ++n_good;      /* count number of "keepers" */
    }

    return n_good;
}
```

Figure 16.11.   The `chauv_ar()` **function: Creating the mask array.**

variance. Now, however, we need to compute these things twice, before and after identifying faulty data. Moreover, the calculations are more complex, because they involve a mask. The **stats()** function in Figure 16.12 gathers together all these parts into a function that computes all three statistical measures for the good data values and returns them in a single structure.

Notes on Figure 16.12: The `stats()` function.

- *First box: the function interface.*

    1. This function has three parameters. The first is the actual number of data values in the array. The second is the number of data values currently considered to be good. This number could be recomputed by the function, but it is slightly more efficient to pass it as a parameter.
    2. When **stats()** is called the first time, the array argument, **x**, contains **n** data values and **n** mask values set to good. The second time, fewer values are likely to be good. The data will be used by **stats()** but not changed.

- *Second box: the structured result.* The **stats()** function must compute and return three values: the mean, variance, and standard deviation of the set of values. Since only one result can be sent back through the normal function return mechanism, all three are packed into a structured variable

This function is called from the fourth and sixth boxes of the main program in Figure 16.8. It computes the mean, variance, and standard deviation for the set of good values in the array **x**.

```
stat_t
stats( int n, int n_good, value_t x[] )
{
    int k;                       /* subscript for data array */
    double sum1;                 /* sum of values */
    double sum2;                 /* sum of squares */
    double divisor;
    stat_t local;                /* local storage for answers */

    for (sum1 = k = 0; k < n; ++k)          /* Sum "good" data values. */
        if (x[k].mask) sum1 += x[k].data;

    local.mean = sum1 / n_good;             /* Mean of "good" values. */
    for (sum2 = k = 0; k < n; ++k)          /* Sum difference^2 of "goods". */
        if (x[k].mask) sum2 += pow( (x[k].data - local.mean), 2 );

    if (n_good < 20) divisor = n_good - 1;
    else             divisor = n_good;
    local.var = sum2 / divisor;
    local.stdev = sqrt( local.var );
    return local;                           /* Return struct containing the stats. */
}
```

Figure 16.12.   The stats() **function.**

and returned as one object. To do this, we need a local variable of the structured type, which we call **local**.

- *Third box: calculating with the good values.*

  1. In previous versions of this program, we used all the values in computing each sum. Here, we first test whether a value is good (meaning **x[k].mask** has the value **true**) before we include it in a computation. Bad values are ignored in both summation loops.

  2. As each part of the structured answer is computed, the program **packs the results into a structure**, named **local**. This is like packing a suitcase. When it is full, the whole structure is returned to **main()**, where it is either unpacked or sent on to other functions.

- *Fourth box: computing and returning the answers.*

  1. The program uses **n_good** in these calculations (not **N** or **n**) because it is processing only the good values. For small data sets, **n_good-1** is used as the divisor, according to accepted statistical principles.

This function performs the final output for the statistics program in Figure 16.8.

```
void
print_data( value_t x[], int n )
{
    int k;
    string answer;              /* set to "good" or "bad" for output */
    printf( " Evaluation of data:\n" );
    for (k = 0; k < n; ++k) {
        if (x[k].mask) answer = "good";
        else answer = "bad";
        printf( "\t x[%2i] = %.2f is %s\n", k, x[k].data, answer );
    }
}
```

Figure 16.13.   The `print_data()` **function.**

2. We compute the variance and standard deviation and store them, respectively, in the second and third fields of **local**. This fills our result "suitcase," which is returned to **main()**.

In the earlier statistics program (Chapter 10), the **average()** function printed the data values as they were summed. In this program, we want them printed after identifying the deviant values, and we need to know which values were used to compute the final statistics. For clarity, this has been placed in a separate function, **print_data()**, in Figure 16.13.

Notes on Figure 16.13. The `print_data()` **function.**   We use the typical counted loop to step through the array from beginning to end. However, like every other function that processes masked data, this loop checks the mask to know how to print each item. Here, the mask is translated into an English word to make the output more readable. If the mask value is **true**, the string variable is set to point at **good**. A **false** mask is translated into the word **bad**. Then a line is printed containing the array subscript, the data value, and the verdict on its quality.

16.3   Sorting by Selection

A common operation performed on arrays is sorting the data they contain. Many sorting methods have been invented: Some are simple, some complex, some efficient, some miserably inefficient. In general, the more complex sorting algorithms are the most efficient, especially if the array is very long. However, a simple algorithm, **insertion sort**, has been shown to be the fastest sort of all when

p 852

used on short arrays (fewer than 10 items) and therefore has a place in any sort library. We present this algorithm in Chapter 20. The **quicksort** (discussed in Chapter 21) is a much better way to sort moderate length and long arrays.

In this section, we look at **selection sort**, which can be used on a small number of items. It is one of the simplest sorting methods, but also one of the slowest. Nonetheless, selection sort has the advantage that, if you stop in the middle of the process, the initial part of the array is fully sorted, so it is a reasonable way to find the either the largest or smallest few items in a long array.[4]

16.3.1   The Selection Sort Algorithm

Problem specifications for selection sort are given in Figure 16.14. To sort an array of n values in ascending order, we begin with the entire array and make repeated trips through smaller and smaller portions of it. On each trip, we locate the smallest remaining value in the unsorted part of the array, then move it to the end of the sorted area by swapping it with whatever value happens to be there. After k trips, the k smallest items have been selected and placed at the beginning of the array. After $n - 1$ trips, the array is sorted.

A program to implement this algorithm is developed easily by a top-down analysis. We design such a program to read numbers from a user-specified file (the numbers will be type **float**), sort the numbers, and output the sorted list to another user-specified file. As we go through the top-down analysis, keep in mind that, at any time, the array consists of a sorted portion on the left (which is initially empty) and an unsorted portion on the right (which initially contains all of the items).

16.3.2   The Main Program

A well-designed main program is like an outline of the process; it calls on a series of functions to do each phase of the actual job. This kind of design is easy to plan, easy to read, and easy to debug. The sorting task has three major phases: input (read the numbers), processing (sort them), and output (print the sorted list). For each phase, the program should call a function to do the job and display a comment that reports the progress. Programs that contain arrays and loops often take a while to debug; during that time, generous feedback helps the programmer identify the location and nature of the errors.

We start by writing the obvious parts of **main()**. Since we are using an array to hold the numbers, we **#define** the array length and declare an array named **data_list**. This algorithm works for any kind of numeric data; we

---

[4]Two other simple sorts, bubble sort and exchange sort, have truly bad performance for all applications. They are not presented here and should not be used.

Problem scope: Given a file of numbers, read and sort the numbers, then write the sorted list to another file.

Input: The name and contents of an input file and the name of an output file.

Limitations: The numbers will be real numbers with two decimal places of accuracy and values in the range 0…1000.

Output: When the numbers are sorted, write them to the named output file. Also, print messages after each major stage of processing so that the user can monitor the progress of the program. For instance, if the input or output file cannot be opened, print a message and abort.

Algorithm: Use a selection sort, as follows:

1. Let **n** be the number of items to be sorted (a parameter). Let **start** and **where** be subscripts.
2. Set **start** to 0. This is the subscript of the first item in the array and also the beginning of the unsorted portion of the array. All processing will be restricted to the part of the array between subscripts **start** and **n-1**.
3. Repeat the following actions $n - 1$ times:
   - Let **where** be the subscript of the minimum-valued element in the array between subscripts **start** and **n-1**.
   - Swap the element at position **where** with the element at position **start**. The currently smallest value will now be in its proper sorted position. Increment **start** so that it again points to the first unsorted item.

Figure 16.14.   Problem specifications: Sorting numbers in ascending order.

choose to write the program to sort type **float**, but it can be modified easily to sort other types.

```
#include "tools.h"
#define LENGTH 20
void main( void )
{
    float data_list[LENGTH];    /* Data to be sorted. */
    banner();
    ...
    bye();
}
```

Input.   The basics of reading an input file were covered in Figure 15.10. A function, **read_file()**, to read a file and store the data in an array of structures is developed from the basic pattern given in Figure 16.9. We develop the new function by copying `read_file()` into a new source code file and changing everything that depends on the base type of the array. This includes

- The type `value_t` changes to `float` in the prototype and the function header. The revised prototype becomes

  ```
  int read_file( float x[], int nmax );
  ```

- The conversion specifier in the `fscanf()` statement changes from `%lg` to `%g`, because the program is reading `float`s, not `double`s. In the input list, the reference to a member of a structure must be replaced by a simple reference. The resulting statement is

  ```
  flag = fscanf( fin, "%g", &x[k] );
  ```

- The masking code in the `if` statement must be removed. This leaves a simple one-line `if` statement:

  ```
  if (flag == 1) ++k;    /* all is well--count item. */
  ```

Looking at the description of `read_file()`, we see that it will prompt for the name of a file, open it, use it, and close it again. We also must supply the name and length of the data array in the call on `read_file()`. From the documentation, we see that the function will read data into this array until end of file occurs or `nmax` items have been read. Data will remain unread if the file is longer than the array. The actual number of data items read (a number between `0` and `nmax`) will be returned. So we declare a variable to store the actual number of data items and write the call on `read_file()`:

```
int n;              /* # of data items; will be <=LENGTH. */
...
n = read_file( data_list, LENGTH );
```

Processing.   We invent the name `sort_data()` for the selection sort function. The routine needs to know what array to sort and the length of that array. It rearranges the data within the array and returns the sorted values in the same array, with no need for any additional return value. We write a prototype (at the top) and a call for this function inside `main()`:

```
void sort_data( float data[], int n );
...
printf( " %i items were read; beginning to sort.\n", n );
sort_data( data_list, n );
```

Output.   When sorting is finished, we need to write the sorted data to a file. We name the output function `write_file()` and decide to put all the file and stream-handling code within it. It will need only two parameters, the data array and the number of items in it. We defer the actual construction of `write_file()` and write the prototype, user feedback statement, and call in `main()`:

```
void write_file( float data[], int n );
...
puts( " Data sorted, ready for output" );
write_file( data_list, n );
```

The completed **main()** function is shown in Figure 16.15. The three boxes correspond to the three phases of processing. A call chart for the overall program is given in Figure 16.16.

16.3.3   Developing the `write_file()` Function

Writing the data to a file is simpler than sorting it, so we attack that job first. We have a prototype already, so we can write the skeleton of the function:

```
void write_file( float data[], int n )
{
}
```

This program calls the sort function in Figure 16.18, the output function in Figure 16.17, and a modification of the input function in Figure 16.9.

```
#include "tools.h"
#define LENGTH 20

int read_file( float x[], int nmax );
void sort_data( float data[], int n );
void write_file( float data[], int n );

void main( void )
{
    int n;                         /* # of data items; will be <=LENGTH. */
    float data_list[LENGTH];   /* Data to be sorted. */

    banner();
    n = read_file( data_list, LENGTH );

    printf( " %i items were read; beginning to sort.\n", n );
    sort_data( data_list, n );

    puts( " Data sorted, ready for output" );
    write_file( data_list, n );

    bye();
}
```

Figure 16.15.   Main program for sorting.

This diagram shows the relationships among the functions in Figures 16.15 through 16.21.

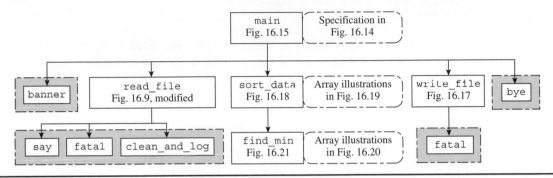

Figure 16.16.   Call chart for selection sort.

At the top of the function, we must prompt the user to enter a file name, then open an output stream connected to that file and check for successful opening. At the end of the function, we close the stream:

```
stream fout;
char filename[80];

printf( " Name of output file: " );
scanf( " %79[^\n]", filename );
fout = fopen( filename, "w" );
if (fout == NULL)
    fatal( " Fatal error: cannot open %s.", filename );
...
fclose( fout );
```

Finally, we need a loop to copy all the data from the array into the file. Since we know exactly how much data exist, we can write a simple counted **for** loop. We remember to write a declaration for the loop counter. The **fprintf()** statement uses a **%7.2f** format so that the output in the file will be neatly aligned and easy to read. Four places before the decimal point and two after are enough to match the specified range of input accuracy.

```
int k;                          /* Subscript variable for loop. */
...
for (k = 0; k < n; ++k) {/* Don't print past data end. */
    fprintf( fout, "%7.2f\n", data[k] );
}
```

The complete code for the **write_file()** function is shown in Figure 16.17.

16.3.4 Developing the `sort_data()` Function

We must start with a thorough understanding of the algorithm. This is defined carefully in Figure 16.14 and illustrated in Figures 16.19 and 16.20. Once the

This function is called from the main program in Figure 16.15.

```
void write_file( float data[], int n )
{
    int k;                          /* Subscript variable for loop.  */
    stream fout;
    char filename[80];

    printf( " Name of output file: " );
    scanf( " %79[^\n]", filename );
    fout = fopen( filename, "w" );
    if (fout == NULL)
        fatal( " Fatal error: cannot open %s.", filename );

    for (k = 0; k < n; ++k) {  /* Don't print past data end. */
        fprintf( fout, "%7.2f\n", data[k] );
    }

    fclose( fout );
}
```

Figure 16.17.   Writing the data to a file.

method is understood, we are ready to implement the **sort_data()** function.
We begin with the function skeleton and declare the variables mentioned in step
one of the algorithm in the problem specifications.

```
void sort_data( float data[], int n )
{
    int start, where;
    float smallest;
    ...
}
```

The loop skeleton.   Steps 2 and 3 of the specification call for a process to
be repeated $n - 1$ times, starting with array subscript 0. We write a **for** loop that
implements this control pattern:

```
for (start = 0; start < n - 1; ++start) {
    ...
}
```

Now we need to write the body of the loop. Finding the minimum value in an array
is an easy but nontrivial task, so we invent a function, **find_min()**, to do the job.
This function needs to know what array to search and where to start and end. So we
pass it three parameters: the array name, the subscript at which the search should
begin, and the number of items in the array. The function locates the minimum

value and returns its subscript. We write the prototype for `find_min()` *inside* the `sort_data()` function, because it is a private subprogram of `sort_data()`:

```
int find_min( float data[], int begin, int n );
```

Next, we write a call on `find_min()` inside the sorting loop and swap the small value at position `where` with the value at position `start`:

```
where = find_min( data, start, n );
smallest = data[where];
data[where] = data[start];
data[start] = smallest;
```

This completes the `sort_data()` function; the finished code is shown in Figure 16.18. An illustration of the operation of `sort_data()` is given in Figure 16.19 for a sample data set of 10 items. The state of the array and the local variables are shown during the middle of each pass. The gray portion of the array is the slowly growing sorted portion. Figure 16.20 illustrates operation of the `find_min()` function.

Finding the minimum.   The remaining task is to write the `find_min()` function, which searches the portion of the data array between `start` and `n-1` and identifies the subscript of the minimum data element. We use the following strategy (illustrated in Figure 16.20):

1. We put a finger on the first slot in the area being searched. This slot contains the smallest value found so far.
2. Now we search the rest of the array looking for something smaller. Using a cursor, we step through the array slots, one by one, until the end of the search area.

This function is called from the main program in Figure 16.15.

```
    void
    sort_data( float data[], int n )
    {
        int find_min( float data[], int begin, int n );
        int start, where;
        float smallest;

        for (start = 0; start < n - 1; ++start) {
            where = find_min( data, start, n );
            smallest = data[where];
            data[where] = data[start];
            data[start] = smallest;
        }
    }
```

Figure 16.18.   Sorting by selecting the minimum.

We illustrate the state of the data array and position variables during the middle of each pass of the loop in Figure 16.18, after **smallest** has been set. The part of the array in gray is the sorted section.

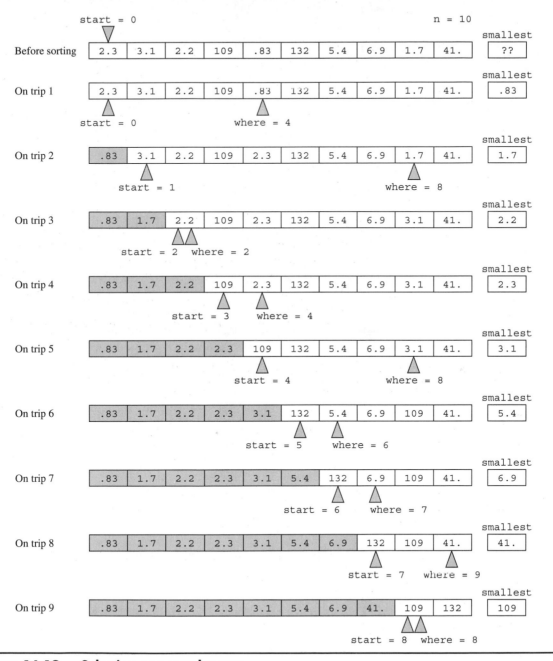

Figure 16.19.   Selection sort step by step.

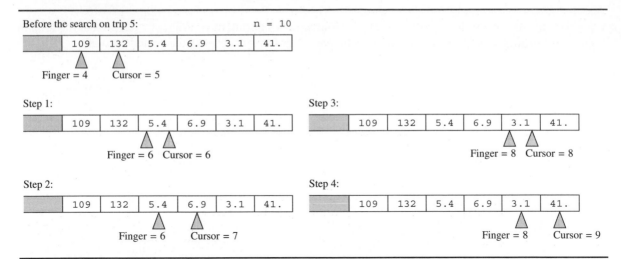

Figure 16.20.   Finding the minimum step by step: `find_min()`.

3. At each step, we ask whether the value under the cursor is smaller than the value under our finger. If so, we move the finger to the cursor's slot.
4. When the entire area has been searched, the finger will be pointing at the minimum value. We return the subscript of this value.

In Figure 16.20, the array shown is the white area from the selection sort trip 5 of Figure 16.19. We can implement the strategy with a short **for** loop that moves the cursor from the starting point to the end of the array. The function skeleton, local variable declarations, and loop control look like this:

```
int find_min( float data[], int begin, int n )
{
    int finger = begin;
    int cursor;
    for (cursor = begin + 1 ; cursor < n; ++cursor) {
        ...
    }
    return finger;
}
```

All that remains is to check whether the current value is less than the previous minimum. We compare the two values; if the new value is smaller, we put our finger on it:

```
if (data[cursor] < data[finger]) finger = cursor;
```

The finished code is listed in Figure 16.21.

We combined all of the pieces of the sort program, compiled it, and ran it on the file **sele.in**, which contains the data listed in Figure 16.19. The contents

This function is called from the function in Figure 16.18. It returns the subscript of the smallest value in the array between positions `begin` and `n`.

```
int
find_min( float data[], int begin, int n )
{
    int finger = begin;
    int cursor;
    for (cursor = begin + 1 ; cursor < n; ++cursor) {
        if (data[cursor] < data[finger]) finger = cursor;
    }
    return finger;
}
```

Figure 16.21.   Finding a minimum element.

of the files `sele.in` (on the left) and `sele.out` (on the right) are shown here, followed by the screen output:

Input file	Output file
2.3	0.83
3.1	1.70
2.2	2.20
109	2.30
.83	3.10
132	5.40
5.4	6.90
6.9	41.00
1.7	109.00
41.	132.00

```
Name of input file: sele.in
Reading data from sele.in.
10 items were read; beginning to sort.
Data sorted, ready for output
Name of output file: sele.out
```

16.4   What You Should Remember

16.4.1   Major Concepts

Searching.   Many methods can be used to search an array for a particular item or one with certain characteristics. A sequential search starts at the beginning of a table and compares a key value, in turn, to every element in the index column. The search ends when the key item is found or after each item has been examined.

The typical control structure for implementing a sequential search is a `for` loop that moves a subscript from the beginning of the array to the end. In the body of this loop is an `if...break` statement that compares the key value to the current table element.

The search can either succeed (find the key value) and break out of the loop or fail (because the key value does not match any item in the table). A sequential search for a specific item is slow and appropriate for only short tables. It is slightly more efficient when the table is in sorted order, because failure can be detected prior to reaching the end of the table. However, binary search (see Chapter 21) is an even faster algorithm for use with sorted data.

If the data are sorted according to the search criterion, shortcuts may be possible. However, a sequential search is necessary when the order of the data in the array is unrelated to the criterion because all the data items must be examined. For example, finding the longest word in a dictionary would require looking at every word (a sequential search) because a dictionary is sorted alphabetically, not by word length.

Masking.   Once data values are stored in a table, moving them around can be slow and inefficient. However, sometimes we must delete items from a table or exclude them temporarily. A mask can be used to mark items as deleted selectively without actually moving other data items to close up the gap. A mask column in a table contains `true` for data items that are currently "good" and `false` for items that have been deleted. In a masked data structure, all functions that process the data must be designed to check the mask component first and ignore any deleted items. The mask values may be kept in a separate array, or as a member of a structure containing the data. Applications such as the selective menu presentation and Chauvenet data labeling can make good use of masking techniques.

Sorting.   Locating a particular item in a table can be done much more efficiently if the information is sorted. Many sort algorithms have been devised and studied; among the simplest (and slowest) is the selection sort. It sorts n items by selecting the minimum remaining element $n - 1$ times and moving it to a part of the array that will not be searched again. Other more efficient techniques such as the insertion sort (Chapter 20) and the quicksort (Chapter 21) are examined later.

16.4.2   Programming Style

- *Names*. When writing a program that sorts, it is very helpful to use meaningful names for the subscript variables. You are much more likely to write the code correctly in the first place, and then get it debugged, if you use names like `cursor` and `finger` rather than single-letter variable names such as `i` and `j`.
- *Local vs. global*. Constants should be declared globally if they are used by more than one function or if they are purely arbitrary and likely to

be changed. If a constant is used by only one function, it may be better to declare it locally. However, a large set or table of such constants will incur large setup times each time the function is called. These constants should be declared as **static const** values, which are only initialized once.

- *Don't talk to strangers.* Each object name used in a function should represent an object that fits into one of the following categories:

    1. A global constant, **#define**d at the top of the program, or like **NULL** and **true**, in a header file.
    2. A parameter, declared and named in the function header.
    3. A local variable or constant, declared and named within the function (an object should be local if it is used only within a function and does not carry information from one function to another).
    4. A global function whose prototype is at the top of the program or in a header file.
    5. A local function, declared within the function and defined after it (a function should be declared locally if it is used only within that function. This does not cause any run-time inefficiency).

- *Modularity.* We wrote a **sort_data()** function as a loop that calls the **find_min()** function. Within that function is another loop. When written like this, the logic of the program is completely transparent and easily understood. In many texts, this algorithm is written as a loop within a loop. This second form takes fewer lines of code and executes more efficiently, because no time is spent calling functions. However, it is not so easy to understand. Which form is better? The modular form. Why? Because it can be debugged more easily and is less likely to have persistent bugs. Doesn't efficiency matter? It often does, but if so, a better algorithm (such as quicksort) should be used instead. It is a false economy to use bad programming style to optimize a slow algorithm.

- *Sorted vs. unsorted.* If the data we wish to search already are sorted, by all means we should take advantage of this. If not, we need to decide whether to sort the data before searching. This issue will be addressed to some extent in later chapters. However, it is a complex issue involving the data set size, how fast the data set changes, which data structures and algorithms are used, and how many times a search will be performed. The general topic of data organization and retrieval is the subject of dozens of books on data structures and databases.

- *Software reuse.* Do not waste time trying to reinvent the wheel. If a library routine meets your need, use it. If you have previously written a function that does almost what you need, modify it as necessary. If someone else has developed a solution for a certain task, such as sorting, go ahead and use it, after you have verified that any assumptions it makes are satisfied by your data and structures.

16.4.3 Sticky Points and Common Errors

- *Subscript errors.* Programmers accustomed to other languages often are surprised to learn that C does absolutely no subscript range checking. If a subscript outside the defined range is used, there will be no error comment from the compiler or at run-time. The program will run and simply access a memory location that belongs to some other variable. For example, if we write a loop to print the values in an array and it loops too many times, the program starts printing the values adjacent to the array in memory. At best, this results in minor errors in the results; at worst, the program can crash.

- *Ampersand errors.* Arrays and nonarrays are treated differently in C. An array argument always is passed to a function by address. We do not need to use an ampersand with an unsubscripted array name.

- *Sorting.* Writing a sorting algorithm can be a little tricky. It is quite common to write loops that execute one too many or one too few times. When debugging a sort, be sure to examine the output closely. Check that the items at the beginning and end of the original data file are in the sorted file and that the output has the correct number of items. Examine the items carefully and make sure all are there and in order. It is common to make an error involving the first or last item. Test all programs on small data sets that can be thoroughly checked by hand.

- *Parallel arrays.* A table can be implemented as a set of parallel arrays. When sorting such a table, it is important to keep the arrays all synchronized. If the items in one column are swapped, be sure to swap the corresponding items in all other columns. Using an array of structures may solve this problem, but this solution may have its own drawbacks, which we have discussed previously.

- *Masking.* When using a masked data structure, make sure that *all* functions use the mask. If we fail to do so, the results are likely to be inconsistent. Make sure that the mask array is properly initialized to indicate that all the data are valid in the beginning.

16.4.4 New and Revisited Vocabulary

These are the most important terms and concepts presented or discussed in this chapter:

index column	search loop	Chauvenet's criteria
data column	sequential search	`static` variable
sorted table	search key	pack results into a structure
parallel arrays	position variable	selection sort
array of structures	masking	finding the minimum

16.5   Exercises

16.5.1   Self-Test Exercises

1. Consider an array containing six data items that you must sort using the selection sort algorithm. How many data comparisons does the algorithm perform in the `find_min()` function? How many times is `find_min()` called, and how many comparisons are made (total) during all these calls? How many (total) data swaps does `sort_data()` perform?

2. Suppose you are searching for an item in a sorted array of N items. Using a sequential search algorithm, how many items are you likely to check before you find the right one? Is this number the same whether or not the item is present in the array? Express the answer as a function of N.

3. The selection sort in the text generated a list of values in ascending order. How would you change the algorithm to generate numbers in descending order?

4. Consider the following list of numbers: 77, 32, 86, 12, 14, 64, 99, 3, 43, 21. Following the example in Figure 16.19, show how the numbers in this list would be sorted after each pass of the selection sort algorithm.

5. Rewrite the `find_min()` function in Figure 16.21 to have an array of strings as its data parameter. Have it find the minimum string; that is, the one that comes first in alphabetical order. Use `strcmp()`. Return the subscript of that string.

6. The following diagram shows an array of odd integers. Declare and initialize a parallel array of type `bool` that contains `true` in the slot corresponding to every prime number, and `false` for the nonprime numbers.

3	5	7	9	11	13	15	17	19	21	23	25

7. (Advanced topic). Write a function with two parameters, the data and mask arrays in the preceding prime problem. This function should be able to print the prime numbers in the set the first time it is called and the nonprime numbers the second time. The caller must not modify the mask array between calls.

16.5.2   Using Pencil and Paper

1. Define a structured type named `person_t` that will store a name (a character array) and an age (integer). Write a function, `old_enough()`, that has four parameters: an age `A` (integer), the number of people (integer), an array of `person_t` records, and an empty parallel array of type `bool`. This function should test the ages in the people array and fill in slots of the Boolean array with `true` if the corresponding age is greater than or equal to `A`, and `false` otherwise.

2. Write a function that generates a three-way mask array for the data in the `person_t` array of the previous problem. For the mask, use an enumerated type with three values: child (under 18), adult (between 18 and 55), and senior (greater than 55). The function should set the values of the mask array according to these criteria.

3. An unsuccessful search for an item in sorted and unsorted data arrays will require different numbers of comparisons. Compare a sequential search on these two types of data and explain why they are different (in terms of the number of comparisons performed).

4. Modify the code in the sequential search function in Figure 16.1 so that it assumes the data in the array are sorted in descending order. Do not search any more positions than necessary. Still return a value of **-1** if the key value cannot be found.

5. Consider an array containing N data items that you must sort using the selection sort algorithm. How many data comparisons does the algorithm perform? How many data swaps does it perform? Express the answer as a function of N.

6. Consider the following list of numbers: 77, 32, 86, 12, 14, 64, 99, 3, 43, 21. Following the example in Figure 16.19, show how the numbers in this list would be sorted after each pass of a selection sort algorithm that sorts numbers in *descending* order. Use the algorithm developed in self-test exercise 3.

7. Suppose you want to sort personnel records by pay rate. Each record has the employee's name, social security number (both strings), and an hourly pay rate (a real number).

    a. Define a structured type for these data.

    b. Rewrite the **find_min()** function in Figure 16.21 to have an array of this type as its data parameter. Have it find the subscript of the employee with the lowest pay rate. Return this subscript.

16.5.3   Using the Computer

1. Class average and more.
   An instructor has a set of exam scores stored in a data file. Not only does he want a report containing the average and standard deviation for the exam, he wants lots of other statistics. These include the high score, the low score, the median score, and the coefficient of variation, cv. The *median score* is defined to be the middle one in the array of scores, if that array is sorted. This *coefficient of variation* relates the "error" measured by the standard deviation to the "actual" value measured by the arithmetic mean as $cv = $ stdev/mean. Write a program that will read, at most, 100 exam scores from a user-specified file and print out the indicated statistics. Use portions of the statistics programs in this chapter and Chapter 10, as appropriate.

2. The mode of a set.
   Another instructor who teaches huge classes does grading in a different way. She assigns the grade B for the score that is the *mode* of the class; that is, the score that occurs most often. Write a program that will compute the mode of a data set containing, at most, 500 exam scores that have been stored in a user-specified data file. Since exam scores occur in the range 0 to 100, an easy way to find the mode is to use an array of counters with subscripts 0 to 100; that is, a histogram. Each counter is used to keep a separate total of the number of times that a particular score has occurred. After you finish tallying the exam scores, the mode is the subscript of the maximum value in the array of totals. Write a program that computes a histogram of the scores and determines the mode. Display the counts of scores in the histogram that are not 0. Label the score that is the mode.

3. Average students.
   Yet another instructor wants to know just how many students in his class are average, where average is defined as having an exam score in the range of the mean ± one-half the standard deviation. Write a program that will read the exam scores of, at most, 100 students from a user-specified file. Then write out the scores of those students labeled as average into one user-specified file and the scores of the remaining students into another file. Also display on the screen the mean of the scores of the average students and see how it differs from the mean of all of the students.

4. Ordering the points.
   Assume that a file contains a set of (x, y) point coordinates, one point per line, in this point-coordinate format. Write a program that reads this point data into an array of structures, where each structure holds one point's coordinates. Then sort the points in descending order with respect to their x coordinates and print the sorted point set. Modify the selection sort code in this chapter to implement this program.

5. Sorting and resorting.
   Assume that a file contains a set of (x, y) point coordinates, one point per line, in this point-coordinate format. Write a program that first reads this point data into a pair of parallel arrays, one for the x coordinates and one for the y coordinates. Sort the points in ascending order with respect to their x coordinates and print the sorted point set. Then sort the points again in descending order with respect to their y coordinates and print them again. Consider modifying the code in this chapter to handle two arrays, where the first contains the index values, and the other gets swapped in parallel with every swap done in the index array.

6. A function defined by a table.
   In the Chauvenet program, looking up a value in the Chauvenet table was done using a function. Write a similar function that computes a tax rate based on earned salary according to the following table. In this function, if the salary value is not given exactly, rather than choose the value from the next lowest index, approximate the value using linear interpolation. That is, find the two index positions the salary is between and compute an approximate tax rate using linear interpolation (see Figure 6.33) between these two values.

Salary ($)	Tax Rate (%)
0	0
10,000	5
20,000	12
30,000	20
40,000	33
50,000	38
60,000	45
70,000	50

   Write a small program that will input a salary from the user, call your function to compute the tax rate, and then print the tax rate and the amount of tax to be paid. Validate the input salary so that it does not fall outside of the salary range in the table.

7. Sorting the keepers.

Currently the Chauvenet program displays its final results on the screen. Somebody has written another program that we want to operate on the good values of our data set. This program requires that the values be stored in a file in ascending order for it to work properly. Modify the Chauvenet program, by combining it with the selection sort algorithm, to read in a data set from a user-specified file, make a pass to remove the bad values, sort the remaining good values in ascending order, and finally write the sorted data into a user-specified file.

8. A bidirectional sort.

Another sorting algorithm is similar to the selection sort, the "cocktail shaker" sort. This algorithm differs from the selection sort in the way it selects the next item from the array. Selection sort picks either the maximum or minimum value from the remaining values each time (depending on the sort order) and swaps it into the end of the sorted portion. For the cocktail shaker sort, the first pass finds the maximum data value and moves it to one end of the array. The second pass finds the minimum remaining value and moves it to the other end of the array. Subsequent passes alternate choosing the maximum and minimum values from the remaining data and moving that value to the appropriate end of the array. Eventually the two ends meet in the middle and the data are sorted. Write a program that implements the cocktail shaker sort just described and uses it to sort data sets containing up to 100 values read from a user-specified file. Write the sorted set to another file.

9. Deadbeats.

Consider a club that charges membership dues but currently has a large group of members delinquent in paying their dues. The club wants to send out weekly reminders to these people until they have paid, at which time they will not be bothered until the next set of dues should be paid. The club wants a computer program to handle the process of generating the appropriate form letters for those who have yet to pay. Write a program that provides the user a menu to perform the following tasks:

a. Initialize the list of people that need to pay. This information will be read from a file called **dead.in**. Each line in this file will contain two pieces of information. The first is a string for the person's name (no longer than 30 characters), followed by a comma as the delimiter. After that is a real number specifying the amount of money owed. These data should be read from the file and stored in an array of structures. Initially, a mask array should be initialized to indicate that everyone owes money.

b. Remove a person from the list. Someone who has paid can be taken off the deadbeat list. The program should ask the user for the person's name, find this in the list, and change the corresponding entry in the mask array to exclude this person from future mailings.

c. Generate a mailing list. A list of the remaining people who have not paid, along with the amount that they owe, should be displayed on the screen. At the bottom, display the current number of "deadbeats" and the amount they owe, as well as the number of people who have paid so far and the total amount of dues collected so far.

d. Quit and write the file. Write an output file containing the remaining people who have not paid, along with the amount that each one owes. Make sure the format is the same as that of the input file so that this file can be used as input the next time.

10. Dewpoint.
   The *bubble point* of a liquid mixture is the temperature at which it begins to vaporize, or boil. The *dew point* of a gas mixture is the temperature at which it begins to condense. In this problem, you will use a simple binary search algorithm to calculate the dew point of a mixture of N gasses. Let $X(i)$ = the mole fraction of component i in a mixture in the liquid state, and let $Y(i)$ = the mole fraction of component i in the gaseous state. The mole fractions in each phase should sum to 1.00; that is,

$$\sum_{i=1}^{n} X(i) = \sum_{i=1}^{n} Y(i) = 1.00$$

A set of constants A, B, and C describes the properties of a gas and can be read from Figure 16.22, a table of gas constants.[5] Given these, we can calculate $P_{vap}(i)$, the

Gas	Formula	C Temperature Range	A	B	C
Acetaldehyde	C_2H_4O	45 to 70	6.81089	992.0	230
Acetone	C_3H_6O	—	7.02447	1161.0	224
Benzene	C_6H_6	—	6.90565	1211.033	220.790
Chlorobenzene	C_6H_5Cl	0 to 42	7.10690	1500.0	224.0
Chlorobenzene		42 to 230	6.94504	1413.12	216.0
Ethyl acetate	C_4H_8O	20 to 150	7.09808	1238.71	217.0
Ethyl alcohol	C_2H_6O	—	8.04494	1554.3	222.65
Ethylbenzene	C_8H_{10}	—	6.95719	1424.255	213.206
Isopentane	C_5H_{12}	—	6.78967	1020.012	233.097
Methyl alcohol	CH_4O	20 to 140	7.87863	1473.11	230.0
Methyl ethyl ketone	C_4H_8O	—	6.97421	1209.6	216
n-Heptane	C_7H_{16}	—	6.90240	1268.115	216.900
n-Hexane	C_6H_{14}	—	6.87776	1171.530	224.366
n-Pentane	C_5H_{12}	—	6.85221	1064.63	232.000
Styrene	C_8H_8	—	6.92409	1420.0	206
Toluene	C_7H_8	—	6.95334	1343.943	219.377
Water	H_2O	0 to 60	8.10765	1750.286	235.0
Water		60 to 150	7.96681	1668.21	228.0

Figure 16.22.   Antoine equation constants.

---

[5] Reprinted from R. Felder and R. Rousseau, *Elementary Principles of Chemical Processes*, 2nd ed. (New York: Wiley, 1986). A dash in the third column means that the constants are valid for any temperature.

vapor pressure of gas component i, by Antoine's equation:

$$P_{vap}(i) = \frac{A_i - B_i}{T + C_i}$$

where T is the temperature of the gas. Assuming ideal behavior of the liquid and gas phases of a mixture and given the mole fraction of component i in the gaseous phase, we can calculate its mole fraction in the liquid phase as follows, where P_{tot} is the sum of the individual gas pressures:

$$X(i) = \frac{Y(i) \times P_{tot}}{P_{vap}(i)}$$

Given this, we can discuss how to compute the dew point of a gas. Assume N components are in the mixture and an array of N structures holds the identity and mole fraction of each gas component. We can use a simple interactive algorithm to calculate T_{dew}. To begin, let the user arbitrarily select two temperatures, T_{high} and T_{low}. Then iterate the following steps:

- Calculate $T = (T_{high} + T_{low})/2.0$.
- For each gas component, i, calculate $P_{vap}(i)$. Then compute P_{tot} and $X(i)$ for each component and calculate S, the sum of the values of $X(i)$.
- If $S > 1$, T is too low. Replace T_{low} with T to prepare for the next iteration.
- If $S < 1$, T is too high. Replace T_{high} with T to prepare for the next iteration.
- Stop the process if the size of the remaining interval is less than a desired relative error tolerance; that is,

$$\frac{T_{high} - T_{low}}{T_{low}} \leq tolerance$$

Write a program to solve the problem, as follows:

a. Define an enumerated type and a parallel array of constant strings for the gas names in Figure 16.22. Define a **struct** type for the three **double** constants associated with each gas, A, B, and C. Finally, define a structured type, **fracs_t**, with two members: a gas code and the fraction of that gas in a mixture, called Y in the formulas.

b. Declare and initialize the gas table as a global constant. In the main program, first declare an array of type **fracs_t** to hold the list of gasses and the fraction of each that makes up the mixture we are processing. Then call the functions **mixture()** and **dewpoint()** (defined later) and print the final composition of the mixture in its liquid phase and its dew point.

c. Write a function, **mixture()**, to initialize the contents of its parameter, which is an empty array of **fracs_t** structures. This function will read N, the number of gasses in the mixture (no more than 10). It then presents a menu of gasses N times, letting the user select N gasses. Do not allow the user to select the same gas twice. For each gas except the last, prompt the user to enter the mole fraction of that gas in the mixture, making sure that the sum of these fractions never exceeds 1.0. For the last gas, set the fraction to 1.0 minus the sum of the preceding fractions. This information is returned through the array parameter. The number N is returned via a **return** statement.

d. Write a function, **v_pressure()**, to calculate the vapor pressure of each gas component and then the sum P_{tot}. The parameters should be the temperature T and the gas table that contains the constants A, B, and C.

e. Write a function, **mole_fraction()**, to calculate the liquid phase mole fractions of the components in the mixture, given the vapor pressures and gaseous mole fractions.

f. Write a function, **dewpoint()**, that takes the array of gas components initialized by **mixture()** and calculates the dew point of the mixture according to the algorithm. Use the functions **v_pressure()** and **mole_fraction()**. The acceptable relative error tolerance is 0.01.

g. Test the program with one of the following realistic mixtures:

   • Isopentane, n-heptane, n-hexane, and n-pentane.
   • Benzene, toluene, styrene, chlorobenzene, and ethylbenzene.
   • Acetaldehyde, acetone, ethylacetate, ethylalcohol, methyl alcohol, and methylethyl ketone.

CHAPTER
17

Two-Dimensional Arrays

Two-dimensional arrays commonly are used in applied physics, engineering, and mathematics to hold numerical data and represent two-dimensional (2D) physical objects. In this chapter, we explore two different data structures, the matrix and the array of arrays, both of which are implemented as two-dimensional arrays. A third kind of two-dimensional array, the array of pointers to arrays, requires dynamic allocation and is left for Chapter 19. Here we also use arrays of strings, which are introduced in Chapter 13. We explore applications of these compound arrays, the type definitions used to facilitate their construction, and two-dimensional array processing.

17.1   Nested Loops: Printing a Table

As noted before, function follows form. A primary use of counted loops is to process arrays. When arrays are nested within larger arrays to form a 2D data structure, the code that processes them is built from loops **nested** within **loops**. For processing two-dimensional arrays, a `for` loop within a `for` loop is the dominant control pattern. This control structure is illustrated in a simple but general form by the program in Figure 17.1, which prints a 10-by-12 multiplication table. Its flow diagram is given in Figure 17.2.

This program prints a multiplication table with 10 rows and 12 columns. The line number and a vertical line are printed along the left margin.

```
#include "tools.h"
#define R 10
#define C 12

void main( void )
{
    int row, col;

    banner();
    printf( "\n\n Multiplication Table \n\n" );

    for (row = 1; row <= R; ++row) {          /* Print R rows. */
        printf( "%2i.  |", row );             /* Print left edge of row. */

        for (col = 1; col <= C; ++col) {      /* Print C columns in each row. */
            printf( "%4i", row * col );
        }

        printf( "\n       |\n" );             /* Print blank row. */
    }

    printf( "\n\n" );
    bye();
}
```

Figure 17.1.   Printing a table with nested for loops.

Notes on Figure 17.1. Printing a table with nested for loops.   This program prints an *R*-by-*C* multiplication table, where R and C are #defined as 10 and 12.

- *Outer box: The* **row** *loop.* The outer loop is executed 10 times, once for each row of the table. Its body consists of the code to process one row; it prints a row label, processes all columns (the inner loop), and finishes the row by printing a newline and a vertical bar on the next line. This is a very typical processing pattern for a nested loop that does output. The output from one repetition, one row of numbers followed by a blank row looks like this:

```
1.  |   1   2   3   4   5   6   7   8   9  10  11  12
    |
```

- *Inner box: the column loop.* The output from each repetition of the inner loop is one column of one row of the table, consisting of two or three spaces and a number. The **printf()** in the inner loop will be executed 12 times per trip through the outer loop. After the 12th number has been

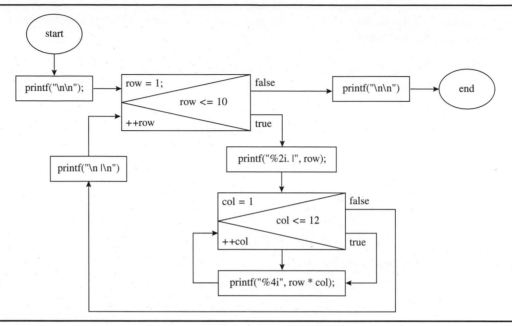

Figure 17.2.   Flow diagram for the multiplication table program.

printed, the inner loop exits and control goes to the `printf()` at the end of the outer box.

- *After 120 trips.* In this program, control goes through the outer loop 10 times. For each trip through the outer loop, control goes through the inner loop 12 times. Therefore, control passes through the body of the inner loop (a `printf()` statement) a total of 120 times, processing every column in every row of the table. After finishing the 10th row, control goes to the final `printf()` and the `bye()` statement. The complete output is

```
Multiplication Table

1.  |   1   2   3   4   5   6   7   8   9  10  11  12

2.  |   2   4   6   8  10  12  14  16  18  20  22  24

3.  |   3   6   9  12  15  18  21  24  27  30  33  36

4.  |   4   8  12  16  20  24  28  32  36  40  44  48

5.  |   5  10  15  20  25  30  35  40  45  50  55  60
```

```
  6.   |     6   12   18   24   30   36   42   48   54   60   66   72
       |
  7.   |     7   14   21   28   35   42   49   56   63   70   77   84
       |
  8.   |     8   16   24   32   40   48   56   64   72   80   88   96
       |
  9.   |     9   18   27   36   45   54   63   72   81   90   99  108
       |
 10.   |    10   20   30   40   50   60   70   80   90  100  110  120
       |
```

17.2   Introduction to Two-Dimensional Arrays

17.2.1   Declarations and Memory Layout

Figure 17.3 shows a two-dimensional array, sometimes called a **matrix**, used to implement a 4-by-4 multiplication table. We declare such an array by writing an identifier followed by two integers in square brackets. The first (leftmost) number is the row dimension; the second is the column dimension. Visually, **rows** are horizontal cross sections of the matrix and **columns** are vertical cross sections.

We initialize a two-dimensional array with a set of values enclosed in nested curly brackets; each pair of inner brackets encloses the values for one *row*. The result can be viewed, conceptually, as a rectangular matrix, but physically, it is laid out in memory as a flat data structure, sequentially by row. Figure 17.4 shows two views of a 3-by-4 array of characters: The two-dimensional conceptual view and the linear physical view. Technically, we say it is stored in **row-major order**. All the slots in a given row will be adjacent in memory; the slots in a given column will be separated. This can have practical importance when dealing with large matrices: Row operations always will be efficient; column operations may not be as efficient because adjacent elements of the same column might be stored in different memory segments.

We refer to a single slot of a matrix using **double subscripts**: the row subscript first, followed by the column subscript. Each subscript must have its own

```
short mult_table[4][4]={{1,  2,  3,  4},      mult_table  [0]   [1]   [2]   [3]
                        {2,  4,  6,  8},       [0]    1     2     3     4
                        {3,  6,  9,12},        [1]    2     4     6     8
                        {4,  8,12,16}          [2]    3     6     9    12
                       };                      [3]    4     8    12    16
```

Figure 17.3.   A two-dimensional array.

The conceptual view of a 3-by-4 array of characters is shown on the left; the subscripts of each cell are written in the corner of the cell. Note that subscripts are used to refer to individual cells but are not actually stored in the cell. The actual storage layout of this array is shown on the right with the subscripts under each cell.

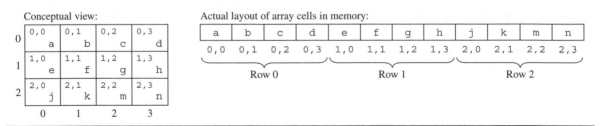

Figure 17.4.   Layout of an array in memory.

set of square brackets. For example, to refer to the first and last slots of the matrix in Figure 17.3, we would write `mult_table[0][0]` and `mult_table[3][3]`.[1]

17.2.2   Using `typedef` for Two-Dimensional Arrays

A programmer may create and use arrays, strings, and multidimensional arrays without defining any new type names. We never actually *need* to use a `typedef`, because it just creates an abbreviation or synonym for a type description. However, `typedef` often should be used with array types in place of the basic syntax, because `typedef` helps simplify the code and clarify thinking. More important, it often enables a programmer to work at a higher conceptual level and have less involvement with the actual implementation of a data structure. There are two conceptually different kinds of two-dimensional arrays, and the appropriate type definitions are quite different for the two varieties, although they are initialized and stored identically.

17.2.3   A Matrix

In one kind of 2D array, the data are a homogeneous, two-dimensional collection. Columns and rows have equal importance, and each data element has as close a relationship to its column neighbors as to its row neighbors. Programs that process this data structure typically have no functions to process a single row or column. Instead, they might process single elements, groups of contiguous elements, or

---

[1] Experienced programmers who are new to C must take care. They might be tempted to write `mult_table[j,k]`, which is correct in FORTRAN and Pascal. This means something in C, and it will compile without errors. However, it does not mean the same thing as `mult_table[j][k]`. (The comma will be interpreted as a comma operator, which is beyond the scope of this text.)

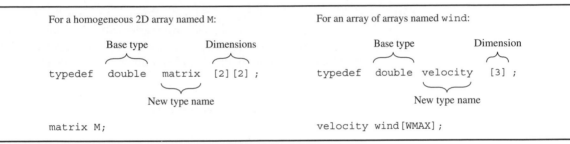

Figure 17.5.   Using `typedef` for 2D arrays.

the entire matrix. For example, consider an image-processing program in which each element of a matrix represents one pixel in a digital image. A **pixel**, which is short for "picture element," is one dot in a rectangular grid of dots that, taken together, form a picture. That pixel has an equally strong relationship to its vertical and horizontal neighbors. Functions operate on entire images or on a rectangular subset of the elements, called a **processing window**. Rows and columns are equally important.

The general form of the **typedef** declaration for this kind of data structure is given on the left in Figure 17.5; note that the dimensions, not the type name, are written last. An example of its use for image processing is given in Section 17.4.

Using a matrix.   The next program example illustrates the use of a 2D array for a practical purpose. Many road atlases have a table of travel times from each major city to other major cities, such as that in Figure 17.6. To use such a table, you find the row that represents the starting city and the column that represents

This is the matrix of city-to-city travel times that stores the input for the program in Figure 17.7.

		0	1	2	3	4
Albany	0	0	194	330	145	193
Boston	1	194	0	524	115	265
Buffalo	2	330	524	0	475	506
Hartford	3	145	115	475	0	150
New York	4	193	265	506	150	0
		Alb	Bos	Buf	Hfd	NY

Figure 17.6.   Travel time matrix.

the destination. The number in that row and that column is the time that it should take to drive from the first city to the second. We implement a miniature version of this matrix and use it to calculate the total driving time for a two-day trip, where you start in city 1, stay overnight in city 2, and end up in city 3. The program is in Figure 17.7.

Notes on Figure 17.7. Travel time for a two-day trip.

- *First box: the matrix and its index variables.*

  1. The names of the cities covered by the table are defined as an array of strings that will be used as a menu. The menu will be displayed three times to permit the user to select the source city (`city1`), layover city (`city2`), and destination city (`city3`). These cities will be used as subscripts for the travel-time matrix.
  2. The table of travel times will be a square matrix with one row and one column for each city. The value in each slot will be the number of minutes needed to drive from the row-index city to the column-index city.
  3. The integers `row` and `col` will be used in nested `for` loops to read the travel times from a file.

- *Second box: reading the input file.*

  1. The nested `for` loops used here are a typical control structure for processing a matrix.
  2. We keep this example simple by omitting normal error checking. We assume that the data in the file are not damaged and that the file contains the correct number of data values. In a realistic application, some error detection would be necessary.

- *Third box: choosing three cities.* These three statements permit the user to select three cities from the `towns` list. The city numbers will be used to access both the list of cities and the matrix of travel times.

- *Fourth box: calculating and printing the travel time.* We access one time from the table by giving two subscripts; the number of the source city is the row subscript and the number of the destination city is the column subscript. The total time is the sum of the times on each of the two days. Sample output follows (repetitions of the menu have been replaced by dashed lines):

```
Travel Time

Where will your trip start?
-------------------------------
Enter number of desired item: 0
Where will you stay overnight?
```

This program uses the input data illustrated in Figure 17.6.

```
#include "tools.h"
#define NTOWNS 5
#define INFILE "minutes.in"

void main( void )
{
    stream minutes; /* Data for travel-time matrix */
    string towns[NTOWNS]={"Albany","Boston","Buffalo","Hartford","New York"};
    int timetable[NTOWNS][NTOWNS];
    int row, col;
    int city1, city2, city3; /* Cities along route of trip. */

    int time;

    banner();
    printf( "\n Travel Time \n" );
    minutes = fopen( INFILE, "r" );
    if (minutes == NULL) fatal( " Cannot open %s for reading.", INFILE );

    for (row = 0; row < NTOWNS; ++row) /* Read travel-time matrix. */
        for (col = 0; col < NTOWNS; ++col) {
            fscanf( minutes, "%i", &timetable[row][col] );
        }

    city1 = menu_i( " Where will your trip start?", NTOWNS, towns );
    city2 = menu_i( " Where will you stay overnight?", NTOWNS, towns );
    city3 = menu_i( " What is your destination?", NTOWNS, towns );

    time = timetable[city1][city2] + timetable[city2][city3];
    printf( "\n Travel time from %s to %s to %s\n\t will be %i minutes.\n",
            towns[city1], towns[city2], towns[city3], time );

    bye();
}
```

Figure 17.7.   Travel time for a two-day trip.

```
-------------------------------
Enter number of desired item: 1
What is your destination?
-------------------------------
Enter number of desired item: 4
Travel time from Albany to Boston to New York
        will be 459 minutes.
```

17.2.4   An Array of Arrays

In the other kind of 2D array, an **array of arrays**, the data are a collection of rows, where each row has an independent meaning. The data elements in each row relate to each other but not to the corresponding elements of nearby rows. Programs that process this data structure typically have functions that process a single row. The general form of the **typedef** declaration for this data structure is given on the right in Figure 17.5.

For example, consider a program that makes weather predictions. One of its data structures might be an array of winds measured by weather stations in a series of locations. Each wind is represented by an array of three **double** values, which give the magnitude and direction in Cartesian coordinates (x, y, z). In Figure 17.8, we use **typedef** to give the name **velocity** to this kind of array. The variable **wind** is an array of velocities, representing the winds in several locations. The first coordinate of each wind is related to the second and third; taken together, they specify one physical object. However, the first coordinate of one wind has little relationship to the first coordinate of the next wind. You would expect various functions in this program to have parameters of type **velocity**, as does the function **speed()** in Figure 17.9.

Using an array of arrays.   The program in Figure 17.9 implements a sample wind array representing five locations. Altogether, it contains 15 **double** values, five locations with three coordinates each. In this example, **wind[1]** is the entire velocity array for Bradley Field and **wind[2][0]** is the x coordinate of the velocity at Sikorsky Airport.

Weather stations at five locations phone in their instrument readings daily to a central station running this program. When a weather station reports its data, the data are recorded in the wind table for that day. The program accepts a series of readings, then prints a table that summarizes the data and the wind speeds at the locations that have reported in so far.

Notes on Figure 17.9. Calculating wind speed.

- *First box: the type declaration.* We declare a type to represent the velocity of one wind. We use this type to build a two-dimensional array (several winds with three components each) and to pass individual winds to the **speed()** function.

```
typedef double velocity[3]; /* Type velocity is an array of 3 doubles. */
double speed( velocity v ); /* Given velocity, calculate wind speed. */

velocity calm = {0, 0, 0};  /* No wind.  */
velocity wind[5];            /* The winds for 5 towns.  */
```

Figure 17.8.   Declaring an array of arrays.

This program creates a table of wind velocities at several weather stations, calculates the wind speeds, and prints a report. It calls the function in Figure 17.10.

```
#include "tools.h"
#define N 5

typedef double velocity[3];

double sqr( double x ) { return x * x; }
double speed( velocity v ){ return sqrt(sqr(v[0]) + sqr(v[1]) + sqr(v[2])); }

void print_table( string names[], bool mask[], velocity w[] );

void main( void )
{
    int city;
    double windspeed;

    velocity wind[N];
    bool mask[N] = { false };   /* Initialize all masks to false. */
    string names[N+1] = { "Tweed", "Bradley", "Sikorsky",
                          "Hamden MS", "Bridgeport", "--finish--" };

    banner();
    printf( "\n Wind Speed \n" );

    for (;;) {
        city = menu_i( " Station reporting data:", N + 1, names );
        if (city == N) break;                        /* User selected "quit" */

        printf( " Wind components for %s: ", names[city] );
        scanf( "%lg%lg%lg", &wind[city][0], &wind[city][1], &wind[city][2] );
        mask[city] = true;

        windspeed = speed( wind[city] );

        printf( "\t Wind speed is %g.\n", windspeed );
    }
    print_table( names, mask, wind );

    bye();
}
```

Figure 17.9.   Calculating wind speed.

- *Second box: the data structure.*

    1. Three objects are declared here as parallel arrays. Together, they form a masked table of wind velocities for several weather locations, whose names are listed in a form that can be passed to `menu_i()`.

2. The array of names has one extra item on the end to make it simple to end menu processing and finish the program.
3. The mask array is initialized to **false** values (0) to indicate that, initially, no stations have called in their data. Recall that if an initializer is given that is too short for the array, all remaining array locations will be initialized to 0.

- *Third box: entering the data.*

1. The **name** and **mask** arrays are parallel to the **wind** array. Once a city is chosen, that city number is used to subscript all three. When the wind information for that city is entered, the corresponding mask is set to **true**. If the same city reported a second set of data, it simply would replace the first.
2. Even though **wind** is declared as an array of arrays, not a matrix, a single velocity component is accessed using two subscripts.
3. For simplicity, error checking is omitted here. In a realistic application, the numbers entered would be tested for being reasonable and an error recovery strategy would be implemented to recover from accidental input of nonnumeric data.

- *Fourth box: calculating one wind speed.* The argument to the **speed()** function is a single wind velocity vector, not the whole array of winds, because that calculation involves only one velocity. By passing only the relevant row of the wind array, we simplify the code for **speed()**. Inside the function, we focus attention on that single wind and can access the individual velocity components using only one subscript.
- *Fifth box and Figure 17.10: printing the wind speed table.* The parameters to the **print_table()** function are the three parallel arrays that make up the wind table. We use the **names** array to print the locations

This function is called from Figure 17.9.

```
void
print_table( string names[], bool mask[], velocity w[] )
{
    int k;
    puts( "\n Wind Speeds at Reporting Weather Stations" );

    for (k = 0; k < N; ++k) {
        if (mask[k])
            printf( " %-15s (%7.1f %7.1f %7.1f ) speed: %6.1f\n",
                    names[k], w[k][0], w[k][1], w[k][2], speed( w[k] ) );
    }
}
```

Figure 17.10.   Printing the wind speed table.

and the **mask** array to avoid printing "garbage" values for weather stations that have not reported in. Sample output follows, with dashed lines replacing repetitions of the menu:

```
Wind Speed

Station reporting data:
        0. Tweed
        1. Bradley
        2. Sikorsky
        3. Hamden MS
        4. Bridgeport
        5. --finish--

Enter number of desired item: 0
Wind components for Tweed: 1.50 2.00 0.00
        Wind speed is 2.5.


-------------------------------
Enter number of desired item: 2
Wind components for Sikorsky: 1.30 2.10 -1.10
        Wind speed is 2.7037.


-------------------------------
Enter number of desired item: 5

Wind Speeds at Reporting Weather Stations
Tweed            (    1.5    2.0    0.0 ) speed:    2.50
Sikorsky         (    1.3    2.1   -1.1 ) speed:    2.70
```

17.2.5   Reading and Writing Binary Matrix Data

The program in Figure 17.7 read the data for a matrix from a file in text mode. An alternative, especially for very large arrays, is to read matrix data in binary mode. One reason this is done is because data in binary files can be read and written faster, since the ASCII to binary conversion is not necessary. Furthermore, the number of bytes needed to store values in binary format often is less than the number needed for an ASCII encoding. A number in ASCII format requires 1 byte for every digit in the number. A number in binary format occupies the same amount of space on disk as in memory. For example, the number $-1,234,567,890$ occupies 11 bytes when stored in ASCII but only 4 bytes when stored as a long integer. The space saved by using binary formats can be very helpful, especially for large data sets such as digital images. Compact size is even more important when such data are transmitted over a network.

Two functions from the **stdio** library are used to perform binary I/O:

```
int fread( void* ar, size_t sz, size_t count, stream s );
int fwrite( void* ar, size_t sz, size_t count, stream s );
```

In addition, to open a file for binary I/O, we use a **"b"** as part of the mode specifier:[2]

```
bin = fopen( "myimage.in", "rb" );
bout = fopen( "myimage.out", "wb" );
```

Examples of using the **fread()** and **fwrite()** functions to read and write data from a digital image file will be given in Section 17.4.

Reading binary data.   The **fread()** function is used to transmit data in binary format through an input stream specified by the last parameter. The first parameter of **fread()** is a pointer to the array in which the data will be stored. The data type **void*** is used because the function must be able to read data into a memory array of any base type. The type name **void*** is used to describe such an array, whose type is unknown. The **fread()** function need not know the base type of the array, because it simply copies the bytes of data directly from the stream into the memory; no conversion is done.

The second and third parameters are of type **size_t**, which is defined by every C system to be some kind of integer, often a long unsigned integer. The second parameter specifies the size of the base type of the data being read; for example, 8 bytes for a **double**. The third parameter indicates how many data items will be read in one input operation. The product of these two values determines the total number of bytes that should be read. As with **fscanf()**, a status code is returned; namely, the number of bytes that actually were read. If this value is different from the intended amount, some type of error has occurred.

Writing binary data.   The counterpart of **fread()** is **fwrite()**, which is used to transmit data in binary format through an output stream. The set of parameters used is virtually identical. The first specifies the memory address from which the data will be taken, the next two indicate the size of each data element (in bytes) and the total number of data items to transmit, while the last tells which output stream to use. The returned status code indicates exactly how many bytes were transmitted successfully, almost always the same amount as intended. An example of using the **fwrite()** function to write a digital image file will be given in Figure 17.19.

17.2.6   Multidimensional Arrays

Scientists and engineers use multidimensional arrays to model physical processes with multiple parameters. As in the two-dimensional case, a distinction should be made between multidimensional objects and arrays of matrices or matrices of

---

[2] In UNIX systems, no distinction needs to be made between opening a file in binary or text mode, because both kinds of files are handled in the same manner. The use of **fscanf()** or **fread()** determines the *mode* of operation. However, it always is permissible to use binary mode explicitly in UNIX. Most other operating systems require the explicit specification of binary mode.

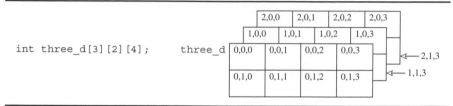

Figure 17.11.   A three-dimensional array.

arrays. C supports all these multidimensional data structures. Usage should be the guiding factor in deciding which to implement.

When using arrays of matrices or matrices of arrays, the rules for type compatibility of array parameters can become confusing. It is especially helpful to use **typedef** to define names for the subtypes, such as rows, and use those names to declare function parameters. The manipulation of uniform multidimensional structures can be more straightforward.

Three-dimensional arrays.   The **dimensions** of a three-dimensional (3D) array usually are called *planes, rows,* and *columns.* The layout in memory is such that everything in plane 0 is stored first, followed by plane 1, and so forth. Within a plane, the slots are stored in the same order as for a two-dimensional matrix. Figure 17.11 shows a diagram of a 3D array with its subscripts.

When declaring a 3D array or a type name for a 3D type, each dimension must have its own square brackets, as shown in Figure 17.11. A 3D object may be referenced with zero, one, two, or three subscripts, depending on whether we need the entire object, one plane, one row of one plane, or a single element. For example, the middle plane in Figure 17.11 is **three_d[1]**. This plane is a valid two-dimensional array and could be an argument to a function that processes 2-by-4 matrices. Three-dimensional arrays are referenced analogously to matrices. For example, the last row of the last plane is **three_d[2][1]** and the last slot in that row is **three_d[2][1][3]**. A 3D function parameter is declared using a **typedef** name or with three sets of square brackets. Of these, the leftmost may be empty, but the other two must give fixed dimensions.

A **typedef** for a 3D array would extend the form for two dimensions, with the additional dimension, in square brackets, at the end. Multidimensional arrays may be initialized through nested loops or by properly structured initializers; a **3D initializer** would use sets of brackets nested three levels deep.

17.3   Application: Transformation of 2D Point Coordinates

An interesting application of two-dimensional arrays is the production of graphic images on the screen, often animated images. To move "objects" around on the screen, it may be necessary to rotate or translate them from their current position.

Problem: Write a program that reads in a set of points representing an object and produces another set of points based on a 2D transformation (rotation and translation) of the original.

Input: (1) The name of a data file containing point coordinates, one point per line, each line containing two numbers, the x and y coordinates of the point, separated by a space. (2) The transformation will be entered in the form of a counterclockwise (ccw) rotation angle, θ, and two numbers that are the translational changes in the x and y directions. The diagram shows a rotation angle of 15 degrees and translation of $(10, 6)$.

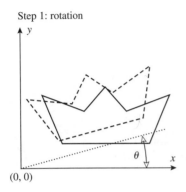
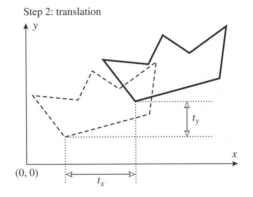

Constant: π.

Formula: The transformation usually is represented in symbolic matrix form as

$$p_{new} = R \; p_{old} + T$$

where p_{new} and p_{old} are given by (x, y) coordinate pairs, R is a 2-by-2 rotation matrix for an object rotating counterclockwise (left) or clockwise (right) through angle θ:

$$R_{ccw} = \begin{bmatrix} \cos\theta & -\sin\theta \\ \sin\theta & \cos\theta \end{bmatrix} \quad \text{or} \quad R_{cw} = \begin{bmatrix} \cos\theta & \sin\theta \\ -\sin\theta & \cos\theta \end{bmatrix}$$

and T is a translation given by another (x, y) pair. Expanded, the matrix formula for counterclockwise rotation becomes two equations:

$$p_{new_x} = p_{old_x} \cdot \cos\theta - p_{old_y} \cdot \sin\theta + T_x$$
$$p_{new_y} = p_{old_x} \cdot \sin\theta + p_{old_y} \cdot \cos\theta + T_y$$

The **sin()** and **cos()** functions are in the standard **math** library, which is included by **tools.h**.

Output: The original point coordinates are echoed to the screen in a table, and next to them are the new point coordinates that have resulted from the transformation. Display two decimal places.

Limitations: It is assumed either that the data file contains ten or fewer total points, or if not, that only the first ten points will be processed.

Figure 17.12.   Problem specifications: 2D point transformation.

This requires transforming the coordinates of the points constituting the object. In this section, we show a program that reads a set of point coordinates representing an object from a file and produces a new, transformed set of points.

A two-dimensional transformation is composed of two parts: a rotation and a translation. First, the object is **rotated** counterclockwise about the origin by an angle θ. Then it is **translated.** This is a straight-line motion described by offsets in position along each of two orthogonal axes (usually the x and y axes). Given these three values, an appropriate equation can be written for calculating the transformed coordinates of a point based on its original location. This situation is depicted in Figure 17.12 along with the specifications for the 2D transformation. The main program is listed in Figure 17.13, and the supporting functions are shown in Figures 17.14 and 17.15.

Notes on Figure 17.13. 2D point transformation—main program.

- *First box: defining an object.*

    1. An object is defined hierarchically, being composed of a set of points. Each point is a set of double-precision coordinates.
    2. In Chapter 14, a point was defined using **struct**. Here a point is defined as an array of coordinates. This is done so that the processing code can take advantage of array properties. The program is written with the possibility of expanding it to more than two-dimensional objects. In such cases, the loops that perform the calculations can remain the same, only the value of **DIM** needs to change. If a structure were used, more code would need to be changed.
    3. This is an example of a 2D array defined as an array of arrays. It is done in this manner because each point is considered logically to be an independent entity within the overall grid of coordinates.

- *Second box: array types.*

    1. Both one- and two-dimensional arrays are used; for convenience, the common names of **vector** and **matrix** are associated with them.
    2. In the **typedef** statements, note that the length of the arrays are specified after the type name, not before the name as with other kinds of type definitions.
    3. Note also that the definitions of types **vector** and **point** are the same: both are one-dimensional (1D) arrays. Although a single type definition could have been used, points and vectors have different semantic meanings in the program, and therefore the code is more comprehensible with two type names.

- *Third box: gathering input data.*

    1. The interactive input sessions are performed by separate functions so that the flow of the main program can remain relatively straightforward.

This program is specified in Figure 17.12. It calls functions can be found in Figures 17.14 and 17.15.

```
#include "tools.h"

#define MAXPOINTS 10                 /* maximum number of points */
#define DIM 2                        /* points are 2D */

typedef double point [DIM];          /* type point is an array */
typedef point object [MAXPOINTS];    /* an object is many points */


typedef double vector [DIM];         /* vector is for translation */
typedef double matrix [DIM][DIM];    /* matrix is for rotation */

int read_points( object obj );
void display_points( object obj1, object obj2, int numpts );
void get_transform( matrix R, vector t );
void transform_point( point p, matrix R, vector t, point newp );

void main( void )
{
    object old_obj, new_obj;         /* point sets before and after */
    vector translation;              /* transformation movement */
    matrix rotation;                 /* transformation rotation matrix */
    int num_points;                  /* actual number of points */
    int k;                           /* loop counter */

    banner();
    puts( "Welcome to the 2D point transformation program" );

    num_points = read_points( old_obj ); /* input points and transform */
    get_transform( rotation, translation );


    for (k = 0; k < num_points; ++k)
        transform_point( old_obj[k], rotation, translation, new_obj[k] );

    display_points( old_obj, new_obj, num_points ); /* print result table */
    bye();
}
```

Figure 17.13.   2D point transformation—main program.

2. The function **read_points**() returns the number of points extracted from the input file, which will be no larger than the length of the array. If fewer points are read, a portion of the array will go unused. Eliminating wasted space will be a topic of a later chapter.

3. The transformation information is gathered in `get_transform()`, which also computes the elements of the rotation matrix before returning.

- *Fourth box: transforming the object.*

  1. Every point on the object must undergo the same transformation. A `for` loop is appropriate for this task.
  2. Each point is a vector in and of itself. Since the transformation equation requires vectors and matrices, each point is passed as a single argument, rather than passing individual point coordinates that have been extracted from its array.
  3. A second array is used for the new object's coordinates. This makes the equations easier to compute, and lets us display both old and new points in the final output.

Notes on Figure 17.14. Reading and displaying the data.

- *First box: opening the data file.*

  1. Since the data file contains the point coordinates of the object, it first must be opened using `fopen()` with mode `"r"` to generate the input stream.
  2. In the event that the file name is incorrect or permission is not granted to use the file, a **NULL** value is returned. If an error occurs, one approach to fixing it would be to repeatedly read file names until a correct one is given. For simplicity this program simply terminates with an informative message using `fatal()`.

- *Second outer box: file processing.*

  1. Reading the data can end in one of three ways: The maximum number of points has been read in, all data in the file have been read, or the data in the file were found to be corrupted.
  2. The `for` loop terminates reading if all of the slots in the data array have been filled, even if the end of the file has not been encountered.
  3. The function `fscanf()` returns the number of valid data items it read, using the specified format string. Since we cannot directly read in an entire array with one format code, each point coordinate is read and stored individually.

- *Inner box: error handling.*

  1. If the number of items read does not agree with the quantity requested, an error has occurred. These errors are handled in different manners.
  2. The end of a file is detectable only after a data read error has occurred. Not all data read errors indicate an end of file, however. The **break** statement is used to exit the `for` loop immediately when no more data exist in the file.

These functions are called from Figure 17.13. The function `read_points()` enters the (**x, y**) coordinates of a point set from an indicated file. It reads as many points as there are or until the data array is full. At the end, `display_points()` prints a table of original and transformed point coordinates.

```
int
read_points( object obj )
{
    char filename[80];                     /* name of data file */
    stream f_in;                           /* input stream to read data */
    int count;                             /* number of data values read */
    int k;                                 /* loop counter */

    printf( "\nPlease enter name of file containing object points: " );
    scanf( "%79s", filename);

    f_in = fopen( filename, "r" );         /* open file in read mode */
    if (f_in == NULL) fatal( "Can't open %s for input.", filename );

    /* read data points until array is full, end of file or error occurs */

    for (k = 0; k < MAXPOINTS; ++k) {
        count = fscanf( f_in, "%lg %lg", &obj[k][0], &obj[k][1] );

        if (count != 2)                     /* if bad read */
            if (feof( f_in )) break;        /* End of file, leave loop */
            else fatal( "Error reading file %s", filename );
    }

    fclose( f_in );

    return k;
}
/* ------------------------------------------------------------------- */
void display_points( object obj1, object obj2, int numpts )
{
    int k;                                                 /* loop counter */
    puts( "\n\t Transformation of coordinates \n");
    puts( "Pt\t Old X\t Old Y\t\t New X\t New Y" );
    for (k = 0; k < numpts; ++k)              /* put both points on one line */

        printf( "%2i \t%7.2f %7.2f \t%7.2f %7.2f\n",
                k+1, obj1[k][0], obj1[k][1], obj2[k][0], obj2[k][1] );

}
```

Figure 17.14.   Reading and displaying the data.

These functions are called from Figure 17.13. The function **get_transform()** inputs a rotation angle and a translation vector from which the 2D transformation is constructed, assuming a ccw rotation of the object. The function **transform_point()** applies this transformation to a single passed point and returns new coordinates.

```
void get_transform( matrix R, vector t )
{
    double theta;                     /* rotation angle in degrees */
    for (;;) {                        /* read rotation angle */
        printf( "Number of degrees to rotate object counterclockwise: " );
        scanf( "%lg", &theta );

        if (theta >= 0 && theta <= 360) break;

        puts( "Error:  Angle must be in the range 0 - 360 degrees" );
    }

    theta = PI * theta / 180.0;    /* convert angle to radians for math */


    R[0][0] = cos( theta );         /* compute rotation matrix elements */
    R[0][1] = -sin( theta );
    R[1][0] = sin( theta );
    R[1][1] = cos( theta );

    printf ( "Please enter the translation amount ( X, Y ): " );
    scanf( "%lg %lg", &t[0], &t[1] );
}
/* ------------------------------------------------------------------ */
void transform_point( point p, matrix R, vector t, point newp )
{
    int r, c;                         /* loop counters */
    for (r = 0; r < DIM; ++r) {   /* multiply row by point for new pt */
        for (newp[r] = 0, c = 0; c < DIM; ++c)      /* do dot product */
            newp[r] += R[r][c] * p[c];
    }
    for (r = 0; r < DIM; ++r)         /* add translation vector to point */
        newp[r] += t[r];

}
```

Figure 17.15.   The transformation.

3. If the line containing a point's coordinates is corrupted, the count returned by **fscanf()** will be wrong but the end-of-file flag will not be set. In designing this program, a decision was made to simply

terminate the program if this occurs. A different application might decide to ignore the corrupted data on the line and proceed to the next data item.

- *Third box: closing a file.* Even though the run-time system closes all files when a program terminates, it always is a good idea to close the data stream when the program finishes using the file. Closing the file releases it for other programs to use and releases the buffer space.
- *Final box: output formatting.*

  1. As with array input, it is not possible to display an entire array's contents using one format code, so each point coordinate is printed as a separate field.
  2. We want to print the data in neat columns. Tab characters are used to set starting columns for each field, while the `%7.2f` code provides the common fixed-point format.

Notes on Figure 17.15. The transformation.

- *First box: input validation.* The rotation angle is restricted to be in the traditional range of $0° - 360°$. Actually, this is not necessary, since the trigonometric functions can handle values outside this range. However, it is understood more easily by the user. Validation is done using an infinite **for** loop containing an **if...break** statement.
- *Second box: math library function arguments.* All the trigonometric functions in the standard **math** library accept an argument measured in radians. Therefore, the input angle is converted from degrees to radians.
- *Third box: generating the rotation matrix.*

  1. The elements of the rotation matrix are computed based on the equations presented in Figure 17.12.
  2. Even though the values of the matrix elements are simple in nature, it is more efficient to compute them once and use them in the transformation calculations, rather than recompute the formulas for every point processed.

- *Fourth box: applying the rotation transformation.*

  1. The rotational part of the transformation is applied first, followed by translation.
  2. Each coordinate of the new point requires a separate calculation, but because the terms in the equation have been stored in arrays, it is a simple matter to use nested loops to do the work. The outer loop processes each coordinate of the point.
  3. The inner loop calculates the *dot product* of two vectors. Corresponding elements of the matrix row and point array are multiplied and the terms are summed. Compare this to the formulas in Figure 17.12.

- *Fifth box: applying the translation transformation.* The translation of the point is done using vector addition; the rotated point coordinates are added to the translation vector.

Results of transforming a point set.   The program was run on a data set defining the crownlike object originally shown in Figure 17.12. The object was rotated ccw by 15° and moved 6 units in the x direction and 10 units in the y direction. This would move the crown a little to the right and somewhat more upward. The output from the program follows. It is left to the reader to connect the dots.

```
Welcome to the 2D point transformation program

Please enter name of file containing object points: crown
Number of degrees to rotate object counterclockwise: 15
Please enter the translation amount ( X, Y ): 6 10

          Transformation of coordinates

Pt         Old X     Old Y        New X      New Y
1           2.00      8.00         5.86      18.25
2           6.00      7.00         9.98      18.31
3          10.00      9.00        13.33      21.28
4          14.00      7.00        17.71      20.38
5          18.00      8.00        21.32      22.39
6          16.00      2.00        20.94      16.07
7           4.00      2.00         9.35      12.97
```

17.4   Application: Image Processing

One task for which we use computers is the analysis of digital images. An example of image processing is the restoration of corrupted pictures. For example, consider the "snow" you see on the screen of a TV set with a poor antenna. Removing the snow, thereby producing a clearer picture, makes other image processing tasks easier. This image restoration can be accomplished using many different techniques, both simple and complex, with varying levels of success. The program we develop here performs a simple technique known as *image smoothing*.

Inside the computer, a picture must be stored in a discrete form. The format of a **digital image** typically is a grid of numbers, called pixels, where each number corresponds to the amount of light captured at that location by a camera. These numbers are typically scaled to a range of $0 \ldots 255$, where 0 corresponds to black, 255 is white, and the levels in between are shades of gray. This scaling is done so that each pixel can be stored in memory using only a single byte, a great memory savings when a typical image grid could be a square of size 512-by-512 numbers.

Problem scope: Write a program that will read in a digital image stored in a computer file, and produce a new image by smoothing the pixel values of the original image.

Input: (1) The name of a data file that contains a digital image of size 128-by-128 pixels. (2) The name of a data file into which the new digital image will be stored. (3) The size of a processing window centered about each pixel, defining the neighborhood of values to be used in the averaging calculation. The format of the image representation and the processing window follow:

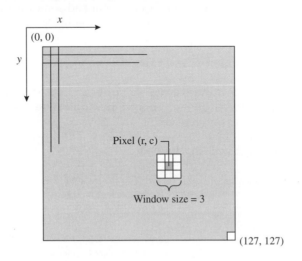

Constants: Image dimension: 128 pixels square.

Formula: The average value of a processing window is the sum of the pixel values in the window divided by the number of pixels in the region. This formula does not hold for pixels around the border of the image, for which the window does not fit completely in the image. In such cases, the dimensions of the window must be cropped to confine the window within the bounds of the image.

Output: A new image is to be generated, where each new pixel value is the average value of the pixels in the window of the old image that is centered at the corresponding location.

Limitations: Input image size is limited to 128-by-128. The input file must have the proper amount of data in it, stored linearly in a rowwise manner. The processing window size should be an odd number in the range 3...11.

Figure 17.16.   Problem specifications: Image smoothing, main program.

The idea behind **smoothing** is that, in general, most pixel values are similar to those of their neighbors and the image intensity changes gradually across the picture. If one of the pixels in the image is corrupted, then its value probably has become quite a bit different than the values of the pixels surrounding it. Therefore, perhaps, a better value for the pixel would be based on its neighbor's values. The simplest kind of smoothing calculation is to replace every pixel value

This program is specified in Figure 17.16. It calls functions that can be found in Figures 17.18, 17.19, and 17.20.

```
#include "tools.h"

#define SIZE 128
typedef unsigned char pixel;              /* image element is a pixel */
typedef pixel picture[SIZE][SIZE];        /* image is a square, 128 X 128 */


typedef struct pt { int x, y; } point;
typedef struct rect { point ul, lr; } window;        /* processing mask */

void setup( stream* infile, stream* outfile, int* masksize );
void read_image( stream infile, picture image );
void write_image( stream outfile, picture image );
void smooth_image( picture im_in, picture im_out, int ms );
pixel average( picture image, window w );

void main( void )
{
    picture image, new_image;    /* original and processed images */
    stream infp, outfp;          /* streams for input and output images */
    int mask_size;               /* dimension of processing mask */

    banner();
    puts( "This program will smooth a greyscale image" );

    setup( &infp, &outfp, &mask_size );

    read_image( infp, image );
    smooth_image( image, new_image, mask_size );
    write_image( outfp, new_image );
    bye();
}
```

Figure 17.17.   Image smoothing—main program.

by the average pixel value in a small square window centered about the pixel's location. If a pixel is corrupted, this average should be much closer to the true value than the original value. If it is not corrupted, the true value will be changed slightly. The resulting image typically does not include the extremely erroneous pixel values, but some blurring of the picture does occur, especially for larger calculation windows.

Specifications for an image smoothing program are given in Figure 17.16, along with a more specific description of an image's representation. The various functions that compose the program's implementation are shown in

Figures 17.17–17.20. The `fread()` and `fwrite()` functions are used in these functions to read and write binary data files.

Notes on Figure 17.17. Image smoothing—main program.

- *First box: picture definition.*

    1. Each pixel has a value in the range 0 . . . 255. This range corresponds directly to that represented by the **unsigned char** data type, which only uses 1 byte.
    2. Since the image array data type is used quite frequently as a function parameter, a **typedef** is used to make the code more presentable. This application works with true two-dimensional data, so we use the typical 2D array **typedef**.

- *Second box: processing window definition.*

    1. We compute each new pixel by averaging the pixels within a processing window centered on the old pixel. Each processing window requires four values to describe its bounds. Rather than use four separate variables, we use a structured rectangle type similar to that used in Chapter 14. This makes it easier to pass window values as arguments.
    2. Because of the coordinate system used for the image (see Figure 17.16), it is easy to define the rectangle using the upper-left and lower-right corners.

- *Third box: getting program input.*

    1. The overall form of the main program is the typical three-step process: input, calculations, and output. The input stage has two phases: getting those values needed to start and reading the complete image to process.
    2. Note that each of the arguments is passed by address; all three will be used to return values to the main program.

Notes on Figure 17.18. Reading program input data.

- *First box: opening a binary file for reading.*

    1. The input data file contains the image to process. The **fopen()** function is used to generate the input stream for the pixel values.
    2. When a function parameter is passed by address, the dereference operator (asterisk) must precede the parameter name every time it is used. The address parameter here is named **infile**; by assigning the stream value to ***infile**, we send the stream back to **main()** so that **main()** can use it.
    3. Note that the stream is opened in **"rb"** mode. Here the **"r"** still denotes that the stream is used for reading, while the **"b"** indicates that a binary-mode transfer will occur.

This function is called from Figure 17.17. It reads in the name of the input image file to process, the output file to send the results to, and the desired processing mask size. It checks the data files and the mask size for validity. Errors are fatal.

```
void
setup( stream* infile, stream* outfile, int* masksize )
{
    char filename[80];                /* name of image file */
    printf( "Please enter name of image file to open: " );
    scanf( "%79s", filename );
    *infile = fopen( filename, "rb" );   /* open binary file in read mode */
    if (*infile == NULL)
        fatal( "Error: couldn't open input file %s\n", filename );

    printf( "Please enter name of file for result image: " );
    scanf( "%79s", filename );
    *outfile = fopen( filename, "wb" ); /* open binary file in write mode */
    if (*outfile == NULL)
        fatal( "Error: couldn't open output file %s\n", filename );

    printf( "Enter size of square smoothing mask: " );
    scanf( "%i", masksize );     /* should be 3, 5, 7, 9, or 11 */

    if ( *masksize % 2 == 0 )
        fatal( "Error: mask size must be an odd number.\n" );
    if (*masksize < 3 || *masksize > 11)
        fatal( "Error: mask size must be in range 3 - 11.\n" );
}
```

Figure 17.18.   Reading program input data.

4. As usual, the program terminates if the file cannot be opened.

- *Second box: opening a binary file for writing.* Opening an output stream is similar to creating an input stream except that the `"w"` flag is used to indicate write mode. The `"b"` still denotes binary data, which is appropriate for a new image file.
- *Third box: reading the mask size with* `scanf()`. The dereference operator is not used with the parameter name in the `scanf()` statement, neither is the ampersand, normally used with `scanf()` for integer input variables. The ampersand and asterisk are inverse operations and, if written together, would cancel each other, so we write neither.

These functions are called from Figure 17.17. Image data are either read from a data file into a 2D array or written from the array to a data file. Errors in the I/O process are fatal.

```
void
read_image( stream infile, picture image )
{
    int num_bytes;            /* actual number of bytes read from file */

    num_bytes = fread( image, sizeof(pixel), SIZE * SIZE, infile );

    if (num_bytes != SIZE * SIZE)
        fatal( "Error:  input file not of size %3i X %3i\n", SIZE, SIZE );
    fclose( infile );
}
/* ------------------------------------------------------------------ */
void
write_image( stream outfile, picture image )
{
    int num_bytes;            /* actual number of bytes written to file */

    num_bytes = fwrite( image, sizeof(pixel), SIZE * SIZE, outfile );

    if (num_bytes != SIZE * SIZE)
        fatal( "Error:  unable to write entire output file." );
    fclose( outfile );
}
```

Figure 17.19.   Reading and writing image files.

- *Fourth box: odds and evens.*

  1. The input window size should be an odd number so that the window can be centered about a pixel. Therefore, a validation test is needed. For efficiency reasons, we limit the size of the processing window to no more than 11.
  2. Odds and evens are tested most easily using the `%` operator. The result of an odd number `%2` is 1, an even number `%2` is 0. Again, the dereference operator must be used with the variable `masksize`.

Notes on Figure 17.19. Reading and writing image files.

- *First box: using* `fread()`.

  1. Each pixel value is stored in a single byte. The image data, when stored in a 2D array in memory, really is just a sequence of bytes, stored row after row. If the pixels are stored in the data file in the same

The function **smooth_image()** is called from Figure 17.17 and in turn calls **average()**. Pixel values in the original image are recomputed based on calculating the average pixel value in a window of dimensions $ms \times ms$ centered about each image pixel.

```
void
smooth_image( picture im_in, picture im_out, int ms )
{
  int row, col;        /* image indices */
  window mask;         /* boundary limits of processing mask */

  for (row = 0; row < SIZE; ++row)
    for (col = 0; col < SIZE; ++col) {
      /* Window is normally centered about the current pixel.  If */
      /* pixel is near the image boundary, the complete mask may */
      /* not fall entirely within the image and must be resized. */

      mask.ul.x = col - ms/2; if (mask.ul.x < 0) mask.ul.x = 0;
      mask.ul.y = row - ms/2; if (mask.ul.y < 0) mask.ul.y = 0;
      mask.lr.y = row + ms/2; if (mask.lr.y >= SIZE) mask.lr.y = SIZE-1;
      mask.lr.x = col + ms/2; if (mask.lr.x >= SIZE) mask.lr.x = SIZE-1;

      im_out[row][col] = average( im_in, mask );   /* compute value */
    }

}
/* ------------------------------------------------------------------- */
pixel
average( picture image, window w )
{
  const int rmin = w.ul.y, rmax = w.lr.y,   /* unpack row limits */
            cmin = w.ul.x, cmax = w.lr.x;   /* unpack column limits */

  int r,c;                                   /* image indices */
  int sum = 0, count = 0;                    /* sum and pixel count */

  for (r = rmin; r <= rmax; ++r)
    for (c = cmin; c <= cmax; ++c) {
      sum += image[r][c];
      count++;
    }

  return sum / count;
}
```

Figure 17.20.   The smoothing calculation.

order, one single read statement can be used to get the entire image at once. Therefore, the second and third parameters of `fread()` are used to specify the total quantity of bytes to read.

2. Using `fread()` is the most efficient way of reading the image data using the `stdio` library. These same data could be scanned using `fscanf()`, byte by byte, but this would take much longer.

3. The number of bytes actually read is returned and can be used as an error check to see if the image file was the correct size and read without error.

- *Second box: using* `fwrite()`.

  1. The resulting image is stored into a file using `fwrite()`. Since we are just reversing the direction of data flow, the parameters here are the same as used in `fread()`, with the output stream used in place of the input stream.

  2. Again, an error check is possible using the return value, which indicates the number of bytes actually written to the disk. This could be less than the expected number if the disk became full during the operation.

Notes on Figure 17.20. The smoothing calculation.

- *First outer box: nested processing loops.*

  1. The nested loop structure in this function follows the typical form for processing a 2D array.

  2. Each pixel must be processed independent of the others. It is necessary to save the results of processing each pixel into a new image; otherwise, the processing of successive pixels would incorporate both old and new pixel values, which would give a distorted result. The original image and the bounds of the processing window are passed to the `average()` function to do this calculation.

- *Second (inner) box: determining window bounds.*

  1. The processing window is centered about the pixel in question. The bounds of the window extend out half the specified size in each direction. Integer division by 2 makes sure that integer limits are generated.

  2. Around the borders of the image, portions of the window may extend past the image boundary. Since there are no pixels in these areas to use, the window bounds must be restricted to stop at the edges. The set of `if` statements tests each computed limit and resets it if necessary.

- *Third box: using structure parameters.*

  1. It would be possible to use the members of the structure that represent the window bounds directly in the `for` statements as the starting and ending values of the loop counters. However, this is avoided for two

reasons: One is clarity, the loops are clearer with the shorter names; the other is efficiency, the loop-ending expression is computed every time the loop test is performed. It takes longer to extract a value from a nested structure than to read from a simple variable. When repeated as many times as it is here, the time difference can be noticeable. Therefore, we extract the values from the structure once and store them in local variables.

2. Since the bounds are constant within the function, we use the `const` qualifier. Doing so may enable the compiler to produce more efficient code.

3. We pass the four window bounds using a structure for clarity. They could be passed separately, but this becomes awkward, especially in functions where additional parameters are needed.

- *Fourth box: computing the average.* The nested summation loops used to compute the total of all pixel values and the number of pixels in the window are a direct extension of the simple summation loops used in previous chapters for one-dimensional arrays.

Results of smoothing an image.   The program was run on a sample image. The results are shown in Figure 17.21. The original image on the left was corrupted by a small amount of "snow." A window size of 3 was chosen for processing, which produced the image on the right. As can be seen, the extreme white values have been removed, but the image has been blurred. Other image restoration techniques, which are more complex, can remove the corrupted values without the blurring.

Original image with "snow"   Smoothed image

Figure 17.21.   Results of image smoothing program.

17.5 What You Should Remember

17.5.1 Major Concepts

- The nature of control structures follows the form of the data being processed. Using 1D arrays requires a single loop control structure. Using 2D arrays requires nesting one loop within another to process all data elements. This effect continues as the data complexity increases.
- A **typedef** name stands for the entire type description, including all the asterisks and array dimensions. In the basic syntax, this information is scattered throughout a variable declaration, with variable names written in the middle. This makes C declarations hard to read and easy to misunderstand. When you use a **typedef** name, all the type information goes at the beginning of the line and all the variable names come at the end.
- A table of data can be represented conceptually in two different manners. An array of arrays implies a unity of the elements in each of the rows in the table, whereas a matrix implies that each element in the table is independent of the others.
- Whether declared as an array of arrays or a matrix, the data elements are still stored sequentially in memory in row-major order. This layout can be exploited when filling or removing data from the structure, as in reading and writing data from files using **fread()** and **fwrite()**.
- The C language allows for arrays of many dimensions, although in practice using more than three or four dimensions is unusual.
- Example applications of 2D arrays include matrix arithmetic and image processing. Matrix arithmetic uses both 1D vectors and 2D matrices in various calculations. Image processing programs use 2D arrays of various sizes and typically store the data in binary files.

17.5.2 Programming Style

- Avoid deeply nested control structures. If the nesting level is greater than three, the logic can be very difficult to follow. It is better to break up the code by defining a new function that performs the actions of the inner loops on the particular data items selected by the outer loops.
- The processing of data in a 2D array typically is done using two **for** loops. Other loop combinations can be used, but the double **for** loop has become almost standard.
- The programmer must take care when using nested loops to make sure that the outer and inner loops each process the appropriate dimension of a 2D array. It helps a great deal to use meaningful identifiers for the subscripts, such as **row** and **col**, rather than the simpler **j** and **k**.

- In a set of nested loops, the number of times the innermost loop body is executed is the product of the number of times each loop is repeated. It is important to make the innermost statements efficient, since they will occur many times.
- Use `#define` appropriately. As with 1D arrays, defining the array dimensions as constants at the top of the program makes later modification simple.
- Using `typedef` to name the parts of nested array types makes the code correspond to your concepts. This makes it easier to write, compile, and debug a program, because it allows you to declare parameters with the correct types and enables the compiler to help you write the appropriate number of subscripts on array references and arguments.
- Any legal C identifier may be used as the type name in a `typedef`. Some caution should be used, however, to avoid names that sound like variables or C keywords. Types are classes of objects, so the type name should be appropriate for the general properties of the class.
- Usually a choice must be made as to whether to use an array of arrays or a matrix. If each of the data elements is independent of the others, then the matrix is the appropriate structure. If the data in a single row have a meaning as a group, then it is correct to use the array of arrays. When data in a column also have a meaning, either structure can be used.
- Continuing the preceding reasoning, always pass the proper parameter. When using a function to process a multidimensional array, pass only the part of the array that is needed, if possible. When a function works on all elements of the array, the parameter should be the entire array. The same is true if the function processes one entire column. However, if a function processes only one row, simply pass the single row, not the whole matrix. And if a function processes a single array element, pass just that element.

17.5.3 Sticky Points and Common Errors

- When using nested loops, it is fairly common to write a statement at the wrong nesting level. The action then will happen either too often or not often enough. Use curly brackets where necessary to make sure statements are in the correct loop.
- As always, all subscripts, even in a multidimensional array, start at 0, not 1.
- The programmer must be careful always to use subscripts within the bounds of the array. When using a 2D array, it is possible for a column subscript to be too large and still have the referenced element be within the memory area of the array. This is a serious error and usually harder to find than simply referencing outside the array's memory.

- Always beware of using subscripts in the wrong order. This may cause you to access outside the array's memory, or it might not. Using meaningful subscript names reduces the frequency of these errors.
- It also is important to use the proper number of subscripts. Because legally you can reference a single row in a matrix, most such references are not deemed incorrect by the compiler and may generate only a warning. However, rather than get the data item you desire, you will be using a memory address in your calculations.
- Use correct C syntax: `a[row][col]` rather than the syntax common in other languages: `a[row,col]`.

17.5.4   New and Revisited Vocabulary

These are the most important terms, concepts, keywords, and C library functions discussed in this chapter:

matrix	double subscripts	binary data
array of arrays	row	`"rb"` and `"wb"` modes
2D and 3D initializers	column	`fread()`
array `typedef`	nested loop	`fwrite()`
vector	row-major order	digital image
dimension	2D transformation	smoothing
plane	rotate	pixel
multidimensional array	translate	processing window

17.6   Exercises

17.6.1   Self-Test Exercises

1. Assume your program contains this code:

```
short int box[5][4];
int j, k;

for (k = 1; k <= 3; k++)
    for (j = 1; j <= 3; j++)
        box[j][k] = 2*j-k;
```

a. Draw a flowchart of this code.

b. Make a diagram of the array **box** showing the array slots and subscripts. In the diagram, write the values that would be stored by the **for** loops. If no value is stored in a slot, write a question mark there.

c. What are the subscripts of the slot in **box** in which the value **5** is stored?

d. What is **sizeof box**?

e. Which array slot will have the lower memory address, **box[1][2]** or **box[2][1]**? Why?

f. What happens if you execute this line: **box[5][4] = 10;**?

2. Diagram the array created by the following declarations. In the drawing, identify the slot numbers and show the values stored in those slots by the loops that follow. Also, write a new declaration statement that has an initializer to set the contents of the array to that produced by these loops.

```
#define Y 4
#define Z 3
int a, b;
float lumber[Z][Y];

for (a = 0; a < Z; ++a)
    for (b = 0; b < Y; b++) {
        if (b > a)            lumber[a][b] = 0;
        else if (b == a)      lumber[a][b] = 2.5;
        else                  lumber[a][b] = (a + b) / 2.0;
}
```

3. Trace the execution of the following code using a table like this one:

m	
k	
Output	

Show the initial values of the loop variables. For each trip through a loop, show how these values change and what is displayed on the screen. In the table, draw a vertical line between items that correspond to each trip through the inner loop.

```
int k, m;
int data[4][3] = { {1,2,3}, {2,4,6}, {3,6,9}, {4,8,12} };

for (k = 0; k < 4; ++k) {
    for (m = k; m < 3; ++m)
        if (k != 1) printf( " %i ", data[m][k] );
        else printf( " %i ", data[k][m] );
    putchar( '\n' );
}
```

4. Trace the execution of the following loop, showing the output produced. Use the array **data** and initial values declared in the previous exercise. Be careful to show the output formatting accurately.

```
for (k = 0; k < 3; ++k) {
   for (m = 0; m < 3; ++m) {
      if ((k+m) % 2 == 0) printf( " %2i", data[m][k] );
      else                printf( "    " );
   }
   putchar( '\n' );
}
```

5. Write a function, **find_min()**, that has one parameter, **data**, that is a 10-by-10 matrix of **float**s. The function should scan the elements of the matrix to determine the element with the minimum value, keeping track of its position in the matrix. Return the value itself through the normal return mechanism and its row and column subscripts through pointer parameters.

6. Happy Hacker wrote and printed the following code fragment in the middle of the night, when some of the keys on his keyboard did not work. The next day, he looked at it and saw that it was not quite right: All of the curly brackets were missing, there was no indentation, there were too many semicolons, and the loops were a little messed up. The code is supposed to print a neat matrix with three columns and seven lines. In addition, the column and row numbers are supposed to be printed along the top and left sides of the matrix. Please fix the code for Happy.

```
#define Z 3
#define W 7
int k, m;

printf( "     " );
for (k = 0; k < Z; ++k);
printf( " %2i", k );
puts( "\n --------------" );
for (m = 0; m < Y; ++m);
printf( " %4i:", m );
for (k = 0; k < W; ++k);
printf( " %2i", mat[m][k] );
putchar( '\n' );
```

17.6.2   Using Pencil and Paper

1. The pair of loops that follow initialize the contents of a 2D array, **data**. Draw a picture of this array, labeling the subscripts and showing the contents of the slots after the loops are done.

```
int j, k;
int data[4][3];

for (k = 0; k < 4; k++)
   for (j = 0; j < 3; j++ )
      data[k][j] = j * k + 1;
```

2. Write a function, **count_zero_rows()**, with one matrix parameter. It should count and return the number of rows in the matrix that have all zero values. Assume the matrix is a square array of size N-by-N integers, where $N \geq 1$ and is defined as a global constant.

3. Given the following code,

```
#include <stdio.h>
void main( void )
{ int j,k;

    for (j = 1; j < 3; j++) {
        for (k = 0; k < 5; k += 2) {
            if (k != 4) printf( " %i, %i ", k, j );
            else k--;
        }
        putchar( '\n' );
        if (j % 2 == 1) printf( ">>> %i , %i <<<\n", j, k );
    }
}
```

a. Draw a flowchart that corresponds to the program.

b. Using a table like the one that follows, trace the execution of the program. Show the initial values of **j** and **k**. For each trip through a loop, show how the values of **j** and **k** change and what is displayed on the screen. Draw a vertical line between the columns that correspond to each trip through the inner loop.

j	
k	
Output	

4. Trace the following loop and show the output exactly as it would appear on your screen:

```
#define Z 3
int a, b;
char square[Z][Z+1] = { "cat", "ode", "dog" };

for (a = 0; a < Z; ++a) {
    printf ( "%i:  ", a );
    for (b = 0; b < Z; b++) {
        if (a == 0) printf( "%2c", square[a][b] );
        else printf( "%2c", square[b][a-1] );
    }
    putchar( '\n' );
}
```

5. Given the declarations and code that follow, show the output of the loops:

```
int k, m;
int data[4][3] = { {1,2,3}, {2,4,6}, {3,6,9}, {4,8,12} };

for (k = 0; k < 4; ++k) {
    for (m = 0; m < 3; ++m) {
        if ((k*m)%2==0) printf( " %2i", data[k][m] );
        else            printf( "   " );
    }
    putchar( '\n' );
}
```

6. Given the declarations and code that follow, trace the code and show the output of the loops:

```
#define Z 3
char square[Z][Z+1] = { "---", "---", "---" };
int r, c;

for (r = 2; r >= 0; --r) square[r][r] = '0';
for (r = 0; r < 3; ++r) square[r][(r + 1)%Z] = '1';
for (r = 0; r < 3; ++r) {
    for (c = 0; c < 3; ++c)
        printf( "%c ", square[r][c] );
    puts( "\n" );
}
```

17.6.3   Using the Computer

1. Sales Bonuses.
   A company with three stores, A, B, and C, has collected the total dollar amount of sales for each store for each month of the year. These numbers are stored in a file, **sales.in**, that has the information for January, then February, and so on. Within each month, the sales amount for store A is first, then store B, then store C. The company pays each store a $1,000 bonus if its sales exceed $30,000 in any particular month. Write a function, **bonus()**, that has one parameter, a matrix of **float** values. It returns an integer to the caller. In this function, search through the **sales** matrix, starting at the first month for the first store. Test each value in the matrix to see if the sales amount qualifies for a bonus. If it does, print the store name and month corresponding to the row and column, as well as the sales amount. Count and return the number of bonuses given. If no amount qualifies for a bonus, return 0. Next, write a function, **read_file()**, that will read in the data from the sales file and store the amounts in a matrix where each row represents a store and each column

represents a month. Finally, write a main program that first reads in all the data, then prints the sales amounts and total sales for each store in a neat table, with all of store A's sales first, followed by those of store B, and finally those of store C. Last, call the **bonus()** function to determine the bonuses for the year. Print the total sales amount, the number of bonuses awarded, and the total amount of bonus money that the company will give out.

2. Array averages.

An instructor teaches classes of up to 40 students, and needs to compute grade averages. He typically assigns between 5 and 10 projects each term.

a. Write a main program that will compute and print the grade averages. Represent a class as a set of parallel arrays (**name**, **grades**, **average**) where each element of the **grades** array is an array of scores, and each score is an integer between 0 and 200. Have the program interactively read in the number of students in a class (maximum 40) and the number of grades per student (maximum 10). Then call the **get_class()**, **get_grades()**, and **compute_average()** functions described here. Finally, print each student's name, grades, and grade average in a neat table.

b. The function **get_class()** should read all of the student names. The parameters are N, the number of students, and **class**, an array of character arrays. Read the names of N class members and store them in **class**. Each name can be limited to 20 characters. There is no return value.

c. The function **get_grades()** should input the grades for one student. The parameters are the name of one student (a string for printing), the number of grades to read for that student, and a one-dimensional array in which to store those grades. There is no return value.

d. The function **compute_average()** should compute the grade average for one student. The parameters are the number of grades to average and a one-dimensional array containing one student's grades. The return value is the average.

3. Matrix transpose.

a. Write a type definition for **matrix** as a two-dimensional square array of **double**s with **SIZE** rows and **SIZE** columns. Define **SIZE** as a constant.

b. Write a function, **transpose()**, to perform a matrix transpose operation, as follows:

- There will be one parameter, a matrix, M. The results will be returned through M.
- To transpose a matrix, swap all pairs of diagonally opposite elements; that is, swap the value in $M[I][J]$ with the value in $M[J][I]$ for all pairs of I and J.
- Try to accomplish the operation with a minimal number of swaps. Warning: This cannot be done by the usual double loop that executes the body I times J times.

When the operation is over, the original matrix should have been overwritten by its transpose. Elements with the same row and column subscripts will not change.

As an example, the 3-by-3 matrix on the left is transposed into the matrix on the right:

$$\begin{bmatrix} 1 & 2 & 3 \\ 4 & 5 & 6 \\ 7 & 8 & 9 \end{bmatrix} \quad \rightarrow \quad \begin{bmatrix} 1 & 4 & 7 \\ 2 & 5 & 8 \\ 3 & 6 & 9 \end{bmatrix}$$

c. Write a function, **read_matrix()**, to read in a **SIZE**-by-**SIZE** matrix of numbers from a user-specified file.

d. Write a function, **print_matrix()**, to print out a matrix of numbers in neat rows and columns. Assume that **SIZE** is small enough that an entire row will fit on one printed line.

e. Write a main program to test your functions. Using function calls, read in a matrix of numbers, print it, transpose it, and print it again to demonstrate the effects of the operation.

4. Matrix multiplication.

a. Write three type definitions for **matrix** that correspond to two-dimensional arrays of **double** values of size M-by-P, P-by-N, and M-by-N. Define M, P, and N as constants.

b. Write a function, **multiply()**, to perform a matrix multiplication operation, as follows:

- There will be three matrix parameters, **A**, **B**, and **C** of the sizes just mentioned. **A** and **B** are used as input and **C** is the resulting matrix.
- The result elements of **C** are defined as:

$$C_{ij} = \sum_{k=0}^{P-1} A_{ik} B_{kj}$$

where i is in the range $0 \ldots M - 1$ and j is in the range $0 \ldots N - 1$. This essentially is the dot product operation shown earlier in the chapter. An example calculation would be

$$\begin{bmatrix} 1 & 2 & 3 \\ 4 & 5 & 6 \end{bmatrix} \quad \times \quad \begin{bmatrix} 4 & 7 \\ 5 & 8 \\ 6 & 9 \end{bmatrix} \quad \rightarrow \quad \begin{bmatrix} 32 & 50 \\ 77 & 122 \end{bmatrix}$$

c. Write two separate functions to read in the matrices of size M-by-P and P-by-N from user-specified data files.

d. Write a function, **print_matrix()**, to write a matrix of size M-by-N to a data file of the user's choice. Also, write separate functions to print matrices of the various sizes to the screen.

e. Write a main program that will read in the two matrices of known size from user-specified files, perform matrix multiplication on them, write the results to a file, and then echo the input matrices and print the result matrix on the screen.

5. Bingo.

In the game Bingo, a playing card has five columns of numbers with the headings B, I, N, G, and O. There are five numbers in each column, arranged randomly, except that all numbers in the B column are between 1 and 15, all numbers in the I column are between 16 and 30, N has 31–45, G has 46–60, and O has 61–75. The word *FREE* is in the middle slot in the N column instead of a number. Your job is to create and print a Bingo card containing random entries in the proper ranges. Define a type, **card**, to be a 5-by-5 array of integers. Generate 25 random numbers and use them to initialize a card, **C**, as follows:

- Declare an array of length 15 named **ar**. Repeat the next step five times, with $x = 0, \ldots, 4$.
- Store the number $(1 + 15 \times x)$ in **ar[0]**, then fill the remaining 14 slots with the next 14 integers. Repeat the next step five times, once for each of the five rows on the Bingo card.
- Randomly select a number, **r**, between 1 and 15. If the number in **ar[r]** is not 0, copy it into column x of the current row of the Bingo card and store 0 in **ar[r]** to indicate that the number already has been used. If **ar[r]** already is 0, generate another **r** and keep trying until you find a nonzero item. This trial-and-error method works adequately because the number of nonzero numbers left in the array always is much larger than the number of zero items. You would have to be very unlucky to hit several used items one after another.
- When all 25 random numbers have been filled in, store a code that means FREE in the slot in the middle of the card. Print the resulting Bingo card as follows, with spaces between the numbers on each row and dashed lines between rows:

```
 B     I     N     G     O
------------------------------
 3    17    32    49    68
------------------------------
12    23    38    47    61
------------------------------
11    18   FREE   60    70
------------------------------
 2    29    36    50    72
------------------------------
 9    22    41    57    64
------------------------------
```

6. Surrounded items.

Define R and C as global constants of reasonable size. Define a type, **matrix**, with R rows and C columns of type **unsigned char** elements.

a. Write a function, **find_surrounded_elements()**, with two **matrix** parameters: one for input and the other for output. The function will do the following. The values in the input matrix will be either 1 or 0, representing **true** and **false**. The function will set each value of the output matrix to 1 or 0 according to whether the corresponding element in the input matrix is "surrounded." *Surrounded* is defined as follows. First, an element's value must be **true** for it to be surrounded. Second, there are potentially four meaningful neighbors of the test element as follows (up, down, left, right):

If three or more of the current element's four neighbors have a value of **true**, then the current element is surrounded. If the current element is on a border, but not in a corner, then only two neighbors have to be **true** to be surrounded. Corner elements need only one of their two neighbors to be **true** to be surrounded. If the given element is surrounded, then the corresponding element in the resulting matrix is set to **true**; otherwise, it is set to **false**. As an example, for the input matrix on the left, the resulting matrix is on the right:

T	T	F	F	F
T	T	T	T	F
T	F	T	T	T
F	T	F	T	T
F	T	F	T	F

$\longrightarrow$

T	T	F	F	F
T	T	T	F	F
F	F	F	T	T
F	F	F	T	T
F	F	F	F	F

b. Write a main program. Use functions similar to **read_image()** and **write_image()** in Figure 17.19 to handle the input of a matrix of values from a binary file and the return of the resulting matrix to a binary file of the user's choice. Assume the input file contains data for a matrix of the proper size. Process the elements of the input matrix using the function **find_surrounded_elements()** to produce the resulting matrix. In addition to saving the result in a file, display output similar to that above using T and F on the screen.

7. Bar graph.
A professor likes to get a visual summary of class averages before assigning grades. Her class averages are stored in a file, **avg.in**. You are to read the data in this file and from it make a bar graph, as follows:

- Your graph should have 21 lines of information, which are printed with double spacing.
- Down the left margin will be a list of 5-point score ranges: $0 \ldots 4$, $5 \ldots 9$, up to $100 \ldots 104$. Following this, on each line, should be a single digit (defined later) for each student whose average falls within that range. There may be scores over 100 because this professor sometimes curves the grades.

- Any negative scores should be treated as if they were 0. Any scores over 104 should be handled as if they were 104.

Represent this graph as a matrix of characters with 21 rows and 35 columns initialized to 0 (null characters). You may assume that the number of scores put into any single row will not exceed 35. Also, have an array of integer counters corresponding to the rows. As each average is read, determine which row, r, it belongs in by using integer division. Also, isolate the last digit, d, of each score; that is, for 98, $d = 8$ and for 103, $d = 3$. To record the score, convert digit d to the ASCII code for the digit by adding it to `'0'`. Store the resulting character in the next available column of row r and update the counter for row r. When the end of the file is reached, print the matrix on the screen using a two-column field width for each score, and a blank line between each row.

8. Local maxima in a 2D array.
   Assume that you have a data file, **max.in**, containing 1-byte integers in binary format. The file has 50 numbers, representing a matrix of values that has five rows containing 10 numbers each. The numbers are stored in a rowwise manner. Write a program that will do the following:

   a. Read the data values into a 2D array on which further processing can be performed.

   b. Call the **localmax()** function described next and print the values of both the input and output matrices.

   c. Write a function, **localmax()**, that takes two 2D arrays of integers as parameters. The first parameter is the input matrix; the second is an output matrix. Set the value at a particular location in the output matrix to 1 if the corresponding input value is a "local maximum"; that is, the value is larger than the four neighboring values to its left, right, above, and below. Set the output value to 0 if the corresponding position cannot be labeled as a local maximum. Matrix positions on a corner or an edge will have only two or three neighboring points, which must have lesser values for the given location to be a maximum. As an example, the input matrix on the left would generate the matrix on the right:

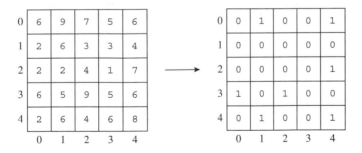

9. Local maxima and minima.
   In solving this problem, refer to the smoothing program in Figure 17.17 and generate a new program to do the following:

a. First, open up a user-specified ASCII file that contains a 10-by-10 matrix of integer values in the range 0–9 and store them in a 2D array.

b. Then generate a corresponding 10-by-10 array of character values, each of which is determined by the following:

- Generate a ′+′ if the value in the original array is a local maximum, where *local maximum* is defined as the highest value in a 3-by-3 area centered on that position in the matrix. For values on the border, examine only the portion of this area containing actual values.
- Generate a ′-′ if the value in the original array is a local minimum, where *local minimum* is defined as the lowest value in the same 3-by-3 area.
- Generate a ′*′ if the value in the original array is a saddle point, where *saddle point* is defined as a value higher than the neighboring values in the same column but lower than the neighboring values in the same row. Saddle points cannot occur on a border.
- Finally, if the value is not classified as any of the preceding three, simply convert the integer value of 0–9 into a character ′0′–′9′ by adding the number to the character value ′0′.
- As an example, using a 5-by-5 array,

$$
\begin{bmatrix} 0 & 2 & 3 & 2 & 4 \\ 6 & 5 & 6 & 0 & 3 \\ 7 & 4 & 1 & 2 & 3 \\ 5 & 8 & 7 & 4 & 8 \\ 1 & 2 & 9 & 3 & 2 \end{bmatrix} \rightarrow \begin{bmatrix} - & 2 & 3 & 2 & + \\ 6 & * & + & - & 3 \\ 7 & 4 & 1 & 2 & 3 \\ 5 & 8 & 7 & * & + \\ - & 2 & + & 3 & - \end{bmatrix}
$$

c. Display both the numeric matrix and the character matrix on the screen.

10. Computing the wind chill.

The wind-chill index is a measure of the increase in heat loss by convection from a body at a specific temperature. Consider the wind-chill table in Figure 17.22. Write a program that will read the wind-chill table from a text file, **chill.in**, and store it in a two-dimensional array (the column and row headings are not in the data file).

		Actual Air Temperature (F)									
		−10	**−5**	**0**	**5**	**10**	**15**	**20**	**25**	**30**	**35**
	5	5	5	5	5	4	4	4	3	3	2
	10	24	22	22	20	19	18	17	16	14	13
Wind	**15**	35	35	33	30	28	26	26	24	19	19
Speed	**20**	42	41	40	37	34	32	29	29	27	23
(mph)	**25**	48	47	45	42	39	37	35	32	30	28
	30	53	51	49	46	43	41	38	36	32	30
	35	57	55	52	48	45	42	40	38	34	32

Figure 17.22.   Effective temperature decrease due to wind chill.

Then enter a query loop that will call a function, **chill()**, to perform the main process as many times as the user wishes. The **chill()** function should have the prototype **void chill(matrix)**, where type **matrix** is a 7-by-10 array of integers. Within the **chill()** function do the following:

a. Prompt the user to enter real values for the actual temperature, t, and the wind speed, s. Use data validation loops to ensure that s is in the range $2.5 \le s < 37.5$ mph and the temperature is in the range $-12.5° \le t < 37.5°$ Fahrenheit. Use these values to look up the effective temperature decrease in the wind chill table as follows.

b. Calculate the row subscript. For any input wind speed, s, we want to use the closest speed that is in the table. If s is a multiple of 5 mph, the table entry is exactly right. If not, we must calculate the closest speed that is in the table. For example, if the speed is between 7.5 and 12.5 mph, we want to use the row for 10 mph, which is row 1. To calculate the correct row number, subtract 2.5 from s, giving a result less than 35.0. Divide this by 5.0 and store the result in an integer variable. Since fractional parts are discarded when you store a **float** in an integer, the integer will be between 0 and 6 and usable as a valid row number.

c. Calculate the column subscript. As for the wind speed, use the temperature in the table closest to the input temperature, t. For example, if the temperature is between $-2.5°$ and $+2.5°$, use the values for $0°$, which are in column 2. To calculate the correct column number, add 12.5 to t, giving a positive number less than 50.0. Divide this by 5.0 and store the result in an integer variable. This will give an integer between 0 and 9 that can be used as a valid column number.

d. Use the computed row and column subscripts to access the wind chill table and read the decrease in temperature. To compute the effective temperature, subtract this decreased amount from the actual air temperature. Echo the inputs and print the effective temperature.

CHAPTER
18

Calculating with Bits

Until now, we have used the basic numeric types and built complex data structures out of them. In this chapter, we look at numbers at a lower, more primitive level. We examine how bits are used to represent numbers and how we can operate on individual bits within a number.

Most C programs use the familiar base-10 notation for both input and output. The programmers and users who work with these programs can forget that, inside the computer, all numbers are represented in **binary** (base 2), not **decimal** (base 10). Usually, we have no need to concern ourselves with the computer's internal representation.

Occasionally, though, a program must deal directly with hardware components or the actual pattern of bits stored in the memory. Applications such as cryptography, random number generators, and programs that control hardware switches and circuits may relate directly to the pattern of bits in a number, rather than to its numerical value. For these applications, base-10 notation is very inconvenient because it does not correspond in an easy way to the internal representation of numbers. It takes a little work, starting with a large base-10 number, to arrive at its binary representation. Throughout this chapter and its exercises, whenever a numerical value is used and it is ambiguous as to which number base is being used, that value will be subscripted. For example, 109_{10} means 109 in base 10, while 109_{16} means 109 in base 16.

Ordinary arithmetic operators are inadequate to work at the bit level, because they deal with the values of numbers, not the patterns of bits. An entire additional set of operators is needed that operate on the bits themselves. In this chapter, we study the hexadecimal notation, **unsigned integers**, and the bitwise operators that C provides for low-level bit manipulation. Further details of the bit-level representation of signed and unsigned integers and algorithms for number-base conversion among bases 10, 2, and 16 are described in Appendix E.

18.1   Unsigned Numbers and Hexadecimal Notation

We use **hexadecimal** notation to write machine addresses and to interface with certain hardware devices. Using hexadecimal notation is the easiest way to do some jobs because it translates directly to binary notation. A programmer who wants to create a certain pattern of bits in the computer and cares about the pattern itself, not just the number it represents, should first write out the pattern in binary, then convert it to hexadecimal, and write a literal in the program. To properly use the hexadecimal notation, we need to store values in `unsigned int` or `unsigned long` variables. The following paragraphs describe the syntax for writing hexadecimal (hex) literals and performing input and output with hexadecimal values.

Hexadecimal literals.   Any integer can be written as either a decimal literal (base 10) or a hex **integer literal** (base 16).[1] As illustrated in Figure 18.1, a hex literal starts with the characters `0x` or `0X` (digit zero, letter ex). Hex digits from 10 to 15 are written with the letters `A`...`F` or `a`...`f`. Upper- and lower-case letters are acceptable for both uses and mean the same thing. A **hex character literal** is written as an escape character followed by the letter `x` and

An integer literal can be written in either decimal or hexadecimal notation:

Decimal	Hex	Decimal	Hex	Decimal	Hex
0	0x0	16	0x10	65	0x41
7	0x7	17	0x11	91	0x5b
8	0x8	18	0x12	127	0x7f
10	0xA	30	0x1E	128	0x80
11	0xB	33	0x21	255	0xFF
15	0xF	64	0x40	32767	0x7FFF

Figure 18.1.   **Hexadecimal numeric literals.**

---

[1] Octal literals can be used, too, but their use is not as prevalent and so they are omitted from this text.

the character's hexadecimal code from the ASCII table; a few samples are given in Figure 18.2. These numeric codes should be used only if no symbolic form exists because they may not be **portable**, that is, they depend on the particular character code of the local computer and may not work on another kind of system. In contrast, quoted characters are portable.

18.1.1   Unsigned and Hexadecimal I/O

Input and output in binary notation are not supported in C because binary numbers are difficult for human beings to read and use accurately. We do not work well with rows of bits; they make our eyes swim. Instead, all input and output is done in decimal, octal, or hexadecimal notation. When we read a number with `scanf()`, the `%i` or `%g` tells the system to read decimal digits and convert them to (respectively) binary integer or binary floating-point representation. All numbers are stored in binary. The opposite conversion (binary to decimal) is done by `printf()` when we output a number using `%i` or `%g`. These conversions are done automatically, and we often forget they happen. But on some occasions base-10 representation is not convenient for input or is confusing for output. For example, if a programmer needs to write a mask value or see the value of a pointer to debug a program, the value should be written as an unsigned integer and often is easiest to work with when written in hexadecimal form.

For these reasons, C supplies input and output methods for unsigned and hexadecimal numbers. In general, a `%u` or `%x` **conversion specifier** is used instead of `%i` for unsigned input and output. The appropriate conversion specifiers for `scanf()` and `printf()` are shown in Figure 18.3. If an input number contains the `0x` prefix, it can be read using `scanf()` with a `%i` conversion specifier (but

---

Character literals can be written symbolically as an escape character followed by the letter **x** and the character's hexadecimal code from the ASCII table:

Meaning	Symbol (portable)	Hex Escape Code (ASCII only)
The letter A	`'A'`	`'\x41'`
The letter a	`'a'`	`'\x61'`
Newline	`'\n'`	`'\xA'`
Formfeed	`'\f'`	`'\xC'`
Blank space	`' '`	`'\x20'`
Escape character	`'\\'`	`'\x1B'`
Null character	`'\0'`	`'\x00'`

Figure 18.2.   Hexadecimal character literals.

	int	long	short	char
Decimal input	`%u`	`%lu`	`%hu`	
Decimal output	`%u`	`%lu`	`%hu`	`%u`
Hex input	`%i` or `%x`	`%li` or `%lx`	`%hi` or `%hx`	
Hex output	`%04x` or `%08x`	`%08lx`	`%04hx`	`%02x`

Figure 18.3.   Conversion specifiers for unsigned values.

not `%d`) and it will be converted using hexadecimal-to-binary conversion. If hexadecimal digits are given without the prefix, a `%x` specifier must be used. For example, the value `0xA12` could be input using either `%i` or `%x`, but `A12` would require the `%x` format specification.

Hexadecimal output from `printf()` is achieved with `%x`; the length specifier `l` or `h` is added for long or short integers. Ordinarily, leading 0 digits are suppressed and spaces are printed instead. However, when using hexadecimal to print masks or bit patterns, it often is helpful to have one character printed for every 4 bits in the mask. To print leading zeros, write a 0 and a field-width specifier after the `%`. For example, if the short integer value `0x0F0F` were printed using `%x` format, the output would be `F0F`; using `%04x` format, the output would be `0F0F`.

Positive or negative?   If an unsigned integer has a bit in the high-order position and we try to print it in a `%i` format instead of a `%u` format, the result will have a negative sign and the magnitude may even be small. Unfortunately, most programmers eventually make this careless mistake. This section explains *why* it happens so that *when* it happens, you will understand what occurred.

We would like to think of numbers as integer values, not as patterns of bits in memory. This is possible most of the time when working with C because the language lets us name the numbers and compute with them symbolically. Details such as the length (in bytes) of the number and the arrangement of bits in those bytes can be ignored most of the time. However, inside the computer, the numbers *are* just bit patterns. This becomes evident when conditions such as integer overflow occur and a "correct" formula produces a wrong and meaningless answer. It also is evident when there is a mismatch between a conversion specifier in a format and the data to be written out.

Reading and writing unsigned integers.   The program in Figure 18.4 does input and output using both decimal and hex notations. It demonstrates how to write formats that read and write unsigned integers of various sizes. By showing numbers in both base 10 and base 16, we hope to build some understanding of the numbers and their representations.

This program demonstrates how unsigned integers of various sizes may be read and written.

```
#include <stdio.h>
void main( void )
{
    unsigned ui, xi;
    unsigned short sui;
    unsigned long lui;

    printf( "\n Please enter an unsigned int: " );
    scanf( "%u", &ui );
    printf( "    = %u in decimal and = %x in hex.\n", ui, ui );
    printf( "\n Please enter an unsigned int in hex: " );
    scanf( "%x", &xi );
    printf( "    = %u in decimal and = %x in hex.\n", xi, xi );

    printf( " short and long unsigned ints: " );
    scanf( "%hu%lu", &sui, &lui );
    printf( "     short in hu = %hu in hx = %hx\n",
               sui, sui );
    printf( "     long in lu = %lu in lx = %lx\n\n",
               lui, lui );

    printf( "    Error:  short unsigned in hi format = %hi\n", sui );
    printf( "    Error:  long unsigned in li format = %li\n", lui );

}
```

Figure 18.4.   Formatting unsigned integers.

Notes on Figure 18.4: Formatting unsigned integers.

- *First box:* unsigned int.

    1. The conversion codes for default length unsigned integers are %u for input or output in base 10 and %x for base 16. A sample output from this box is

    ```
    Please enter an unsigned int: 123
        = 123 in decimal and = 7b in hex.

    Please enter an unsigned int in hex: 0xa1
        = 161 in decimal and = a1 in hex.
    ```

    2. Note that a number always *looks* smaller printed in hex than printed in decimal.
    3. We run the program again and enter a signed number instead of an unsigned one. The faulty input is accepted and stored in the variable.

The output in base 10 looks like garbage but from the hexadecimal output, we see that the value has a 1 in the high-order position and, if interpreted as a negative signed integer, it would be a relatively small number:

```
Please enter an unsigned int: -132
    = 4294967164 in decimal and = ffffff7c in hex.

Please enter an unsigned int in hex: -0x10
    = 4294967280 in decimal and = fffffff0 in hex.
```

- *Second box:* `short int` and `long int`.

1. We use `%hu` for unsigned short integers and `%lu` for unsigned long integers.
2. A sample output from this box is

```
short and long unsigned ints: 4096 65548
    short in hu = 4096 in hx = 1000
    long in lu = 65548 in lx = 1000c
```

3. We run the program again and enter large values. We see from the leading `f`s in the hexadecimal output that these numbers are close to the largest value that fits into an unsigned short integer and an unsigned long integer. The output is

```
short and long unsigned ints: 65530 4294967200
    short in hu = 65530 in hx = fffa
    long in lu = 4294967200 in lx = ffffffa0
```

4. We run the program again and enter faulty data. The first input is too large to fit in a short integer; the second is negative. Again, the faulty input is accepted and stored in the variables but the output is garbage:

```
short and long unsigned ints: 65548 -65548
    short in hu = 12 in hx = c
    long in lu = 4294901748 in lx = fffefff4
```

5. The output shown for the unsigned short integer is too small by 2^{16} because the high-order bit of the value does not fit into the variable and, therefore, is dropped: $12 + 65536 = 65548$.
6. The negative number -65548 is entered for the long unsigned variable and converted with a `%lu` format. Even though the input format code was inappropriate for the input value, the hex output shows that the number was converted and stored correctly for a signed number. The garbage answer happened because of a mismatch between the stored value and the output format code. If we printed the same value with a `%i` format, the result would be the number we entered.

- *Third box: Unsigned data, signed specifier.* Here are two lines that print unsigned values in signed integer formats. If we use `%hi` instead of `%hu` or `%li` instead of `%lu`, the compiler will not give us an error comment and the program will work correctly until we try to print a number that is too large to fit in a signed variable of the same length. When we enter the values 65530 4294967200, the output in `%hi` and `%li` format is negative:

```
Error:  short unsigned in hi format = -6
Error:  long unsigned in li format = -96
```

This happens because the high-order bit in the unsigned number is interpreted as a negative sign during the signed integer conversion. The result is that the complement of the value is printed: $(65530 - 65536 = -6)$.

18.2   Bitwise Operators

C includes six operators whose purpose is to manipulate the bits inside a byte. For most applications, we do not need these operators. However, systems programmers use them extensively when implementing type conversions and hardware interfaces. Any program that must deal directly with a hardware device may need to pack bits into the instruction format for that device or unpack status words returned by the device. Another application is an archive program that compresses the data in a file so that it takes up less space in an archive file. A program that works with the DES encryption algorithm makes extensive use of bitwise operators to encode or decode information.

Bitwise operators fall into two categories: shift operators move the bits toward the left or the right within a byte, and **bitwise-logic** operators can turn individual bits or groups of bits on or off or **toggle** them. These operators are listed in Figure 18.5. The operands of all these operators must be one of the integer types (type **int** or **unsigned**; length **long**, **short**, or **char**). When using bitwise operators, we refer to operands of these types as **bit vectors**. We call them *vectors* because the bits in these data types are stored sequentially one after another; we do not call them *arrays* because we cannot use the subscript

Arity	Symbol	Meaning	Precedence	Use and Result
Unary	~	Bitwise complement	15	Reverse all bits
Binary	<<	Left shift	11	Move bits left
	>>	Right shift	11	Move bits right
	&	Bitwise AND	8	Turn bits off
	^	Bitwise exclusive OR (XOR)	7	Toggle bits
	|	Bitwise OR	6	Turn bits on

Figure 18.5.   Bitwise operators.

operator to reference the bits individually. We must use some combination of the bitwise operators to extract the value of a given bit in the vector.

18.2.1 Masks and Masking

When a program manipulates codes or uses hardware bit switches, it often must isolate one or more bits from the other bits that are stored in the same byte. The process used to do this job is called *masking*. In a masking operation, we use a bit operator and a constant called a **mask** that contains a bit pattern with a 1 bit corresponding to each position of a bit that must be isolated and a 0 bit in every other position.

For example, suppose we want to encode a file so that our competitors cannot understand it (a process called *encryption*). As part of this process, we want to split a short integer into four portions, A (3 bits), B (5 bits), C (4 bits), and D (4 bits), and put them back together in the scrambled order: C, A, D, B. We start by writing out the bit patterns, in binary and hex, for isolating the four portions. The hex version then goes into a `#define` statement. The table in Figure 18.6 shows these patterns. Then we use the `&` operator with each mask to decompose the data, shift instructions to move the pieces around, and `|` operations to put them back together in the new order. This simple technique for **encoding and decoding** is illustrated in the next section in Figures 18.16 and 18.17.

Bitwise AND (`&`) turns bits off.   The bitwise AND operator, `&`, is defined by the fourth column of the truth table shown in Figure 18.7, which is the same as the truth table for logical AND. The difference is that logical operators are applied to the truth values of their operands, and bitwise operators are applied to each pair of corresponding bits in the operands. Figure 18.8 shows three examples of the use of bitwise AND. To get the answer (on the bottom line) look at each pair of corresponding bits from the two operands above it, and apply the bitwise AND truth table to them.

The bitwise AND operator can be used with a mask to isolate a bit field by "turning off" all the other bits in the result. (None of the bitwise operators affect the value of the operand in memory.) The first column in Figure 18.8 shows that using a mask with 0 bits will turn off the bits corresponding to those zeros. The second column shows how a mask with a field of four 1 bits can be used to

Part	Bit Pattern	#define, with Hex Constant
A	11100000 00000000	`#define A   0xE000`
B	00011111 00000000	`#define B   0x1F00`
C	00000000 11110000	`#define C   0x00F0`
D	00000000 00001111	`#define D   0x000F`

Figure 18.6.   Bit masks for encrypting a number.

Operands		Results			
x	y	~x	x&y	x|y	x^y
0	0	1	0	0	0
0	1	1	0	1	1
1	0	0	0	1	1
1	1	0	1	1	0

Figure 18.7.   Truth tables for bitwise operators.

isolate the corresponding field of **x**. The third column of this figure illustrates the semantics of **&** by pairing up all combinations of 1 and 0 bits. Note that a bit in the result is 1 only if both of the corresponding bits in the operands are 1.

Bitwise OR (|) turns bits on.   Just as the bitwise AND operator can be used to turn bits off or decompose a bit vector, the bitwise OR operator, defined in the fifth column of Figure 18.7, can be used to turn on bits or reassemble the parts of a bit vector. Figure 18.9 shows three examples of the use of this operator. The first column shows how a mask can be used with | to turn on a single bit. The second column shows how two fields in different bit vectors can be combined into one vector with bitwise OR. The third column of this figure illustrates the semantics of | by pairing up all combinations of 1 and 0 bits. Note that a bit in the result is 1 if either of the corresponding bits is 1.

Complement (~) and bitwise XOR (^) toggle bits.   Sometimes we want to turn a bit on, sometimes off, and sometimes we want to simply change it, whatever its current state is. For example, if we are implementing a keyboard handler, we need to change from upper-case to lower-case or vice versa if the user presses the Caps Lock key. When we change a switch setting like this, we say we *toggle* the switch. The complement operator, ~, defined by the third column in Figure 18.7, toggles all the bits in a word, turning 1's to 0's and 0's to 1's.

The bit vectors used here are 1 byte long. A result bit is 1 if both operand bits are 1.

	Binary	Hex		Binary	Hex		Binary	Hex
x	1111 1111	0xFF	x	0111 1010	0x7A	x	0111 1010	0x7A
mask	0010 0000	0x20	mask	1111 0000	0xF0	y	1010 0011	0xA3
x & mask	0010 0000	0x20	x & mask	0111 0000	0x70	x & y	0010 0010	0x22

Figure 18.8.   Bitwise AND (&).

The bit vectors used here are 1 byte long. A result bit is 1 if either operand bit is 1.

	Binary	Hex		Binary	Hex		Binary	Hex
x	0000 0000	0x00	x	0000 1100	0x0C	x	0011 1110	0x3E
mask	0010 0000	0x20	mask	1111 0000	0xF0	y	1010 0111	0xA7
x | mask	0010 0000	0x20	x | mask	1111 1100	0xFC	x | y	1011 1111	0xBF

Figure 18.9.   Bitwise OR (|).

The bitwise XOR operator (^) can be used with a mask to toggle some of the bits in a vector and leave the rest unchanged. This is essential when several switches are packed into the same control word. The first two columns of Figure 18.10 show how to use XOR with a mask to toggle some of the bits in a vector but leave others unaffected. Of course, to actually change the switch setting, you must use = to store the result back into the switch variable. The last column of this figure illustrates the semantics of ^ by pairing up all combinations of 1 and 0 bits. Note that a bit in the result is 1 if the corresponding bits in the operands are *different*.

The three negations (advanced topic).   C has three unary operators that are alike but different. Figure 18.11 shows the operation of these operators: logical NOT, complement, and arithmetic negation. All of them compute some kind of opposite, but on most machines, these three "opposites" are different values. Normally, this is no problem, since you use the three operators for different types of operands and in different situations. This discussion is included for those who are curious about why we need three ways to say no.

The logical NOT operator (!) is the simplest (see the second row in Figure 18.11). It turns true values to **false** and false values to **true**. True is represented by the *integer 1*, which has many 0 bits and only a single 1 bit.

The complement operator, which toggles all the bits, is shown on the third row in Figure 18.11. Looking at the first column of Figure 18.11, note how the result of !x is very different from the result of ~x.

The bit vectors used here are 1 byte long. A result bit is 1 if the operand bits are different.

	Binary	Hex		Binary	Hex		Binary	Hex
x	1111 1111	0xFF	x	1100 1100	0xCC	x	0111 1010	0x7A
mask	0011 0000	0x30	mask	1111 0000	0xF0	y	1010 0011	0xA3
x ^ mask	1100 1111	0xCF	x ^ mask	0011 1100	0x3C	x ^ y	1101 1001	0xD9

Figure 18.10.   Bitwise XOR (^).

We illustrate the results of the three ways to say no: logical NOT, complement, and negate. The bit vectors used here are 1 byte long, the representation for negative numbers is two's complement.

	Decimal	Hex	Binary		Decimal	Hex	Binary		Decimal	Hex	Binary
x	0	0x00	0000 0000	x	1	0x01	0000 0001	x	−10	0xF6	1111 0110
!x	1	0x01	0000 0001	!x	0	0x00	0000 0000	!x	0	0x00	0000 0000
~x	−1	0xFF	1111 1111	~x	−2	0xFE	1111 1110	~x	9	0x09	0000 1001
-x	0	0x00	0000 0000	-x	−1	0xFF	1111 1111	-x	10	0x0A	0000 1010

Figure 18.11.   Just say no.

Most modern computers use two's complement notation to represent negative integers. The **two's complement** of a value is always 1 greater than the bitwise complement (also known as one's complement) of that number.[2] We can see this relationship by comparing the third and fourth lines in Figure 18.11.

18.2.2 Shift Operators

Once we have used & to decompose a bit vector or isolate a switch setting, we generally need to move the bits from the middle of the result to the end before further processing. Conversely, to set a switch or recompose a word, bits usually need to be shifted from the right end of a word to the appropriate position before using | to recombine them. This is the purpose of the right-shift (>>) and left-shift (<<) operators.

The left operand of a shift operator can be either a signed or unsigned integer. This is the bit vector that is shifted. The right operand must be a nonnegative integer;[3] it is the number of times that the vector will be shifted by one bit position. Figure 18.12 shows examples of both shift operations.

Left shifts.   Left shifts move the bits of the vector to the left; bits that move off the left end are forgotten, and 0 bits are pulled in to fill the right end. This is a straightforward operation and very fast for hardware. Shifting left by one position has the same effect on a number as multiplying by 2 but it is a lot faster for the machine. In the table, you can see that the result of n << 2 is four times the value of n, as long as no significant bits fall off the left end.

One thing to remember is that a shift operation does not change the number of bits in a vector. If you start with a 16-bit vector and shift it 10 places to the left, the result is a 16-bit vector that has lost its 10 high-order bits and has had 10 0 bits inserted on the right end.

---

[2]This is the definition of *two's complement*. Appendix E explains this topic in more detail.

[3]The C standard specifies that negative shift amounts are undefined.

The table uses 1-byte variables declared thus:

```
signed   char s;      /* A one-byte signed integer. */
unsigned char u;      /* A one-byte unsigned integer. */
```

Signed	Decimal	Hex	Binary	Unsigned	Decimal	Hex	Binary
s	15	0x0F	0000 1111	u	10	0x0A	0000 1010
s << 2	60	0x3C	0011 1100	u << 2	40	0x28	0010 1000
s >> 2	3	0x03	0000 0011	u >> 2	2	0x02	0000 0010
s	−10	0xF6	1111 0110	u	255	0xFF	1111 1111
s << 2	−40	0xD8	1101 1000	u << 2	252	0xFC	1111 1100
s >> 2	−3	0xFD	1111 1101	u >> 2	63	0x3F	0011 1111

Figure 18.12.   Left and right shifts.

Right shifts. Unfortunately, right shifts are not as simple as left shifts. This is because computer hardware typically supports two kinds of right shifts, signed right shifts and unsigned right shifts. In C, an **unsigned shift** always is used if the operand is declared to be unsigned. A **signed shift** is used for signed operands.[4]

A signed right shift fills the left end with copies of the sign bit (the leftmost bit) as the number is shifted, and an unsigned shift fills with 0 bits. The reason for having signed shifts at all is so that the operation can be used in arithmetic processing; with a signed shift, the sign of a number will not be changed from negative to positive when it is shifted. There is no difference between the effects of signed and unsigned shifts for positive numbers, since all have a 0 bit in the leftmost position anyway.

Analogous to left shift, a right shift by one position divides a number by 2 (and discards the remainder). A right shift by n positions divides a number by 2^n. In the table, you can see that `15 >> 2` gives the same result as `15 / 4`.

18.2.3 Example: Shifting and Masking an Internet Address

IP (Internet protocol) addresses normally are written as four small integers separated by dots, as in `32.55.1.102`. The machine representation of these addresses is an unsigned long integer. Figure 18.13 lists the specifications for decoding an IP address. The program in Figure 18.14 takes the hex representation of an

---

[4] According to the standard, an implementor could choose to use an unsigned shift in both cases. However, signed shifts normally are used for signed values.

Problem scope: Read a 32-bit Internet IP address in the form used to store addresses internally and print it in the four-part dotted form that we customarily see.

Input: A 32-bit integer in hex. For example: `fa1254b9`

Output required: The corresponding dotted form of the address. For the example given, this is: 250.18.84.185

Figure 18.13.   Problem specifications: Decoding an Internet address.

address, decodes it, and prints it in the four-part dotted form we are accustomed to reading.

Notes on Figure 18.14: Decoding an Internet address.

- *First box: the mask.* We define a mask to isolate the last 8 bits of a long integer. We can write the constant with or without leading zeros, as `0xffL` or `0x000000ffL`, but we need the `L` to make it a long integer.

The problem specifications are in Figure 18.13.

```
#include "tools.h"

#define  BYTEMASK  0xffL /* The L is to make a long integer. */

void main( void )
{
    unsigned long ip_address;
    unsigned f1, f2, f3, f4;

    banner();
    printf( "Please enter an IP address as 8 hex digits: " );

    scanf( "%lx", &ip_address );
    printf( "You have entered %08lx\n", ip_address );

    f1 = ip_address >> 24 & BYTEMASK;
    f2 = ip_address >> 16 & BYTEMASK;
    f3 = ip_address >>  8 & BYTEMASK;
    f4 = ip_address       & BYTEMASK;

    printf( "The IP address in standard form is: %i.%i.%i.%i \n\n",
            f1, f2, f3, f4 );
}
```

Figure 18.14.   Decoding an Internet address.

- *Second box: the variables.*

  1. We declare the input variable as **unsigned** so that unsigned shift operations will be used and **long** because the input has 32 bits.
  2. We use each of the other four variables to hold one field of the IP address as we decompose it. These can be short integers since the values are in the range 0...255.

- *Third box: hex input.*

  1. We read the input in long hex format, using **%lx**. Internally, the value will be stored in binary.
  2. The **0** in the **%081x** output conversion specifier tells C to print leading zeros.

- *Fourth box: byte decomposition.*

  1. The coded address contains four fields; each is 8 bits. The byte mask lets us isolate the rightmost 8 bits in an address.
  2. At the end of this section, we have stored each successive 8-bit field of the input into one of the **f** variables.
  3. To get **f1**, the first field of the IP address, we shift the address 24 places to the right so that all but the first 8 bits are discarded.
  4. If all machines used 32-bit long integers, we would not need the masking operation to compute **f1**. We include it to be sure that this code can be used on machines with longer integers.
  5. To get **f2** and **f3**, we shift the input by smaller amounts and mask out everything except the 8 bits on the right.
  6. Since **f4** is supposed to be the rightmost 8 bits of the IP address, we can mask the input directly, without shifting.

- The output from two sample runs is

```
Please enter an IP address as 8 hex digits: fa1254b9
You have entered fa1254b9
The IP address in standard form is: 250.18.84.185
-------------------------------------------------------
Please enter an IP address as 8 hex digits: ff001701
You have entered ff001701
The IP address in standard form is: 255.0.23.1
```

18.3   Application: Simple Encryption and Decryption

We have enough tools to write a simple application program that uses the bitwise operators. Let us return to the encryption example. Using the masks in Figure 18.6, we encrypt a short integer by breaking it into four portions, A (3 bits),

B (5 bits), C (4 bits), and D (4 bits), and putting them back together in a scrambled order: C, A, D, B. That is, we start with the bits in this order: `aaabbbbbcccccdddd` and end with the scrambled order: `ccccaaaddddbbbbb`. Figure 18.15 specifies the problem, Figure 18.16 is the encryption program, and Figure 18.17 is the program for subsequent decryption.

Notes on Figures 18.16 and 18.17. Encrypting and decrypting a number.

- *First boxes: the masks.*

  1. We refer to the bit positions with numbers 0...15, where bit 0 is the leftmost and bit 15 is the last bit on the right.
  2. We define one bit mask for each part of the number we want to isolate. The hex constants for encryption are developed in Figure 18.6.
  3. The bit masks for the decryption process allow us to isolate the same four fields in different positions within the word so that we can reverse the encryption process.

- *Second boxes: the interfaces for functions* `encrypt()` *and* `decrypt()`. We use type `unsigned` for all bit manipulation, so that the leftmost bit is treated just like any other bit. (With signed types, the leftmost bit is

---

Problem scope: Write a function to encrypt a short integer and a main program to test it. Write a matching decryption program.

Input: Any short integer.

Formula: Divide the 16 bits into four unequal-length fields (3, 5, 4, and 4 bits) and rearrange those fields within the space as shown:

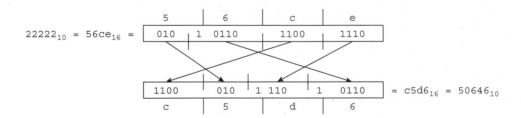

Output required: The input will be echoed in both decimal and hex; the encrypted number also will be given in both bases.

Figure 18.15.   Problem specifications: Encrypting and decrypting a number.

This program carries out the first half of the specifications in Figure 18.15.

```
#include "tools.h"
```

```
#define AE   0xE000      /* bits 0:2 end up as 4:6 */
#define BE   0x1F00      /* bits 3:7 end up as 11:15 */
#define CE   0x00F0      /* bits 8:11 end up as 0:3 */
#define DE   0x000F      /* bits 12:15 end up as 7:10 */
```

```
unsigned short encrypt( unsigned short n );
```

```
void main( void )
{
    short in;
    unsigned short crypt;
    printf( "\n Enter a short integer to encrypt: " );
    scanf( "%hi", &in );
    /* Cast the int to unsigned before calling encrypt. */
    crypt = encrypt( (unsigned short) in );
    printf( "\n The input number in base 10 is:      %hi \n"
            " The input number in hexadecimal is: %hx \n\n"

            " The encrypted number in base 10 is: %hu \n"
            " The encrypted number in base 16 is: %hx \n\n",
            in, in, crypt, crypt );
}
/* ---------------------------------------------------------------- */
unsigned short
encrypt( unsigned short n )
{
    unsigned short a, b, c, d;               /* for the four parts of n */
    a = (n & AE) >> 4;/* Isolate bits 0:2, shift to positions 4:6. */
    b = (n & BE) >> 8;/* Isolate bits 3:7, shift to positions 11:15. */
    c = (n & CE) << 8;/* Isolate bits 8:11, shift to positions 0:3.  */
    d = (n & DE) << 5;/* Isolate bits 12:15, shift to positions 7:10. */

    return c | a | d | b ;       /* Pack the four parts back together. */

}
```

Figure 18.16.   Encrypting a number.

treated differently because it is the sign.) We are working with 16-bit
numbers, so we use type **short**. Therefore, the argument type and the
return type are both **unsigned short**.

Decryption is the inverse of encryption. This program looks very much the same as the encryption program in Figure 18.16 except that every operation is reversed.

```
#include "tools.h"
```

```
#define AD   0x0E00         /* bits 4:6 goto 0:2 */
#define BD   0x001F         /* bits 11:15 goto 3:7 */
#define CD   0xF000         /* bits 0:3 goto 8:11 */
#define DD   0x01E0         /* bits 7:10 goto 12:15 */
```

```
unsigned short decrypt( unsigned short n );
```

```
void main( void )
{
    unsigned short in;
    short dcrypt;

    printf( "\n Enter an encrypted short int: " );
    scanf( "%hu", &in );
    dcrypt = (signed) decrypt( in );

    printf( "\n"
            "The encrypted input number in base 10 is: %hu \n"
            "Encrypted input number in hexadecimal is: %hx \n\n"

            "The decrypted number in base 10 is:       %hi \n"
            "The decrypted number in base 16 is:       %hx \n\n",
            in, in, dcrypt, dcrypt );
}
/* ------------------------------------------------------------------- */
unsigned short                         /* use unsigned for bit manipulation */
decrypt( unsigned short n)
{
    unsigned short a, b, c, d;              /* for the four parts of n */

    a = (n & AD) << 4;/* Isolate bits 4:6, shift to positions 0:2. */
    b = (n & BD) << 8;/* Isolate bits 11:15, shift to positions 3:7. */
    c = (n & CD) >> 8;/* Isolate bits 0:3, shift to positions 8:11.  */
    d = (n & DD) >> 5;/* Isolate bits 7:10, shift to positions 12:15. */

    return a | b | c | d ;       /* Pack the four parts back together. */

}
```

Figure 18.17.   Decrypting a number.

- *Third boxes: unpacking.*

  1. The & operation turns off all the bits of n except those that correspond to the 1 bits in the mask. This lets us isolate one bitfield so we can store it in a separate variable. We call this process **unpacking** the fields.

2. After masking, we shift the isolated bits to their new positions. To compute the shift amount, we subtract the original position of the first bit in the field from its new position. We use `>>` for positive shift amounts, `<<` for negative amounts.

3. We use four mask-and-shift expressions, one for each segment of the data.

- *Fourth boxes: packing.*

  1. We use the `|` operator to put the four parts back together. We call this process *packing*.
  2. It does not matter in what order the operands are listed in the `|` expression, we get the same result whether we write `a | b | c | d` or `c | a | d | b`.

- *Encryption.* The output from two encryptions follows:

```
Enter a short integer to encrypt: 22222

The input number in base 10 is:      22222
The input number in hexadecimal is: 56ce

The encrypted number in base 10 is: 50646
The encrypted number in base 16 is: c5d6
------------------------------------------

Enter a short integer to encrypt: -22222

The input number in base 10 is:     -22222
The input number in hexadecimal is: a932

The encrypted number in base 10 is: 14921
The encrypted number in base 16 is: 3a49
```

- *Decryption.* The output from decryption of the second example is

```
Enter an encrypted short int: 14921

The encrypted input number in base 10 is: 14921
Encrypted input number in hexadecimal is: 3a49

The decrypted number in base 10 is:      -22222
The decrypted number in base 16 is:      a932
```

18.4   Bitfield Types

A bitfield declaration defines a structured type in which the fields are mapped onto groups of bits rather than groups of bytes. **Bitfield structure** types are useful in programs that interface with and manipulate hardware devices, turning on and turning off individual bits in specific positions at fixed memory addresses. The bitfield declaration lets us represent and manipulate such devices symbolically, an important aid to processing them correctly.

A bitfield declaration has the same elements as any **struct** declaration, with the restriction that the base type of each field is **unsigned int** and there is a colon and an integer (field width, in bits) after each field name. The field name is optional. Fields can be any width, and the total size of a bitfield structure may exceed one byte. The precise rules and restrictions for bitfield declarations are implementation dependent, as is the order in which the fields will be laid out in memory. This is unavoidable: computer architecture is not at all standardized and dealing with memory below the byte level obviously involves the nonstandard aspects of the hardware.

The program in Figure 18.18 can be used to determine how your own hardware and compiler treat bitfields. It declares a bitfield object, initializes it, prints various information about it, and returns a hexadecimal dump of the contents so that the placement of information within the object can be determined. The packing diagram at the bottom of the figure shows the way this structure is implemented by the Gnu C compiler. Its treatment of bitfields is simple and logical and may well be the most common way to compile bitfield types. However, always be careful to check the conventions of the compiler doing the work when writing or porting bitfield programs.

Notes on Figure 18.18. Bitfield-structure demonstration.

- *First and third boxes: a bitfield type.*

    1. We declare a bitfield type, **demo_type**, that occupies a minimum of 37 bits. The compiler will add padding, as necessary, to meet the requirements of the local hardware.
    2. In the diagram, byte boundaries are indicated by divisions in the white strip at the bottom. Short-word boundaries are dark lines that cross the gray area, and field boundaries are indicated by the white boxes in the gray area. This implementation packs the bits tightly together starting at the left. Fields three and five cross byte boundaries, field four crosses a short-word boundary, and field six crosses a long-word boundary.
    3. Two bits of padding are added between fields four and five because of the unnamed 2-bit field declared there. This is the only instance in the language where a memory location can be declared without associating a name with it.
    4. Additional padding bits were placed after field six to fill the structure up to a short-word boundary, as required by the local compiler. Other compilers might add padding to reach a long-word boundary.

This program can be used to determine how a compiler and its underlying hardware treat bitfields. The packing used by the Gnu C compiler is diagrammed below.

```c
#include <stdio.h>
typedef struct DEMO {
        unsigned int one    : 1;
        unsigned int two    : 3;
        unsigned int three :10;
        unsigned int four   : 5;
        unsigned int        : 2;
        unsigned int five   : 8;
        unsigned int six    : 8;
} demo_type;

void main( void )
{
    int k;
    unsigned char* bptr;
    demo_type bit = { 1, 5, 513, 17, 129, 0x81 };

    printf( "\n sizeof demo_type = %lu\n", sizeof(demo_type) );

    printf( "initial values: bit = %u, %u, %u, %u, %u, %u\n",
            bit.one, bit.two, bit.three, bit.four, bit.five, bit.six );
    bptr = (unsigned char*)&bit;
    printf( "hex dump of bit: %02x %02x %02x %02x %02x %02x\n",
            bptr[0], bptr[1], bptr[2], bptr[3], bptr[4], bptr[5] );

    bit.three = 1023;
    printf( "\n assign 1023 to bit.three: %u, %u, %u, %u, %u, %u\n",
            bit.one, bit.two, bit.three, bit.four, bit.five, bit.six );
    k = bit.two;
    printf( "assign bit.two to k: k = %i\n", k );

}
```

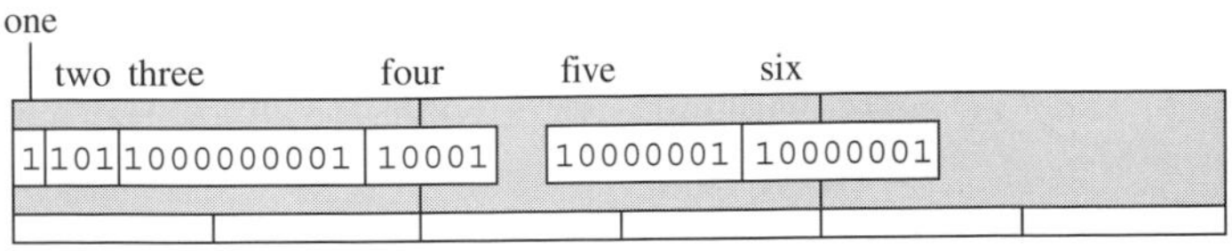

Figure 18.18.   Bitfield-structure demonstration.

5. The standard permits the fields to be assigned memory locations in left-to-right or right-to-left order and padding to be added wherever necessary to meet alignment requirements on the local system. Before using a bitfield structure, you must check how it works on your local system.

6. The third box prints out the size of the structure on the local system. In this implementation, it is 6 bytes (48 bits). Therefore, the last 11 bits are padding and this system uses *short-word alignment*; that is, all objects occupy an even number of bytes and begin on an even-numbered memory address.

- *Second box: a bitfield object.*

1. We declare a **demo_type** object, **bit**, and initialize its fields to distinctive values. Each initializer value has the correct number of bits needed to fill its field, and its value starts and ends with a 1 bit and has 0 bits in between. When we look at this in hexadecimal, we can see where each field starts and ends. From this information, we can determine the packing and padding rules used by the local compiler.

2. A 2-bit padding field lies between fields four and five. An initializer should not supply a value for a padding field; the compiler may store anything there that is convenient. Our compiler initializes these fields to 0 bits.

- *Fourth box: making the packing order visible.*

1. First we print out the contents of each field, simply to verify that the initializer works as expected. This is not always the case. Initializer values too large to fit into the corresponding fields are simply truncated (the leftmost bits are dropped). This is the output from the program in Figure 18.18 when compiled under the Gnu C compiler (gcc):

```
sizeof demo_type = 6
initial values: bit = 1, 5, 513, 17, 129, 129
hex dump of bit: d8 06 24 0c 08 00
```

2. We next use the object, **bptr**, to print out the bytes of **bit** in hexadecimal. We do this to verify the position of each field in the whole. At the top of **main()**, we declare **bptr** to be **unsigned** because we want to print the values in hexadecimal. We further declare it to be of type **char*** so that we can print individual bytes of the bit vector. The **2** in the conversion specifier (**%02x**) causes the values printed to be two columns wide, while the **0** before it means that leading zeros will be printed. This is the form in which the hexadecimal codes are easiest to convert to binary.

3. We set **bptr** to point at the beginning of **bit**. To avoid compiler warnings, we cast the address of **bit** to the type of **bptr**.

4. From the first line of output, we know that `bit` occupies 6 bytes. So
    we use `bptr` to print 6 bytes starting at the address of the beginning
    of `bit`. Any value of any type can be printed in hex in this way, by
    using an `unsigned char*`.

5. Below we rewrite the hex value from each output field in binary, with
    spaces separating the bits into groups of four that correspond to the
    hexadecimal output. We omit the last byte of zeros. The conversion
    values simply are filled in using the table values in Appendix E, Figure
    E.4. A `v` is written above the first bit of each of the 6 bytes. Long-word
    boundaries are marked by `L`, and short-word boundaries by `s`:

```
d8            06            24            0c            08
L                           s                           L
v             v             v             v             v
1101 1000 0000 0110 0010 0100 0000 1100 0000 1000
```

We now rewrite the bits using spaces to separate the bitfields. The
decimal value of each bitfield is written below it. Padding bits are
marked by `-`.

```
L                         s                 L
v           v             v         v       v
1 101 1000000001 10001 00 10000001 10000001 000
1 5   513        17    -- 129      129      ---
```

We produce the diagram in Figure 18.18 from this output.

- *Fifth box: using an individual field.*

  1. The assignment to `bit.three` demonstrates that an integer value may
      be assigned to a bitfield in the ordinary way. The C code positions the
      bits correctly and assigns them to the structure without disturbing the
      contents of other fields.

  2. The assignment `k = bit.two` shows that a bitfield may be assigned
      to an integer in the ordinary way. The C run-time system will lengthen
      the bitfield to the size of an integer.

      ```
      assign 1023 to bit.three: 1, 5, 1023, 17, 129, 129
      assign bit.two to k: k = 5
      ```

18.4.1   Bitfield Application: A Device Controller (Advanced Topic)

An artist has a studio with a high sloping ceiling containing skylights. Outside,
each skylight is covered with louvers that can be opened fully under normal
operation to let the light in or closed to protect the glass or keep heat inside the
room at night.

The louvers are opened and closed by a small computer-controlled motor, with two limit switches that sense when the skylight is fully open or fully closed. To open the skylight, one runs the motor in the forward direction until the fully open limit switch is activated. To close the skylight, one runs the motor similarly in the reverse direction. To know the current location of the skylight, one simply examines the state of the limit switches.

The motor is controlled by a box with relays and other circuitry for selecting its direction, turning it on and off, and sensing the state of the limit switches. The controller box has an interface to the computer through a multifunction chip using a technique known as *memory-mapped I/O*. This means that when certain main memory addresses are referenced, bits are written to or read from the multifunction chip, rather than real, physical memory.

In this program, we assume that the multifunction chip interfaces with the computer through two memory addresses: `0xffff7100` refers to an 8-bit data register (DR) and `0xffff7101` refers to an 8-bit data direction register (DDR). Each bit of the data register can be used to send data either from the chip to the program or vice versa. Data flows from chip to program through a bit if the corresponding bit of the DDR is 0 and from program to chip if the corresponding

---

Problem scope: Write a program to control a motor that opens and closes a skylight.

Output required: To the screen, a menu that will allow a user to select whether to open the skylight, close it, or report on its current position. To the motor controller, signals to start or stop the motor.

Input: The program receives menu selections from the user. It also receives signals directly from the motor controller via the memory-mapped address that is its interface to the controller.

Constants: The memory-mapped addresses used by the multifunction chip in this program are `0xffff7100` for the DR and `0xffff7101` for the DDR. Bit positions in the DR, which follow, are numbered starting from the right end of the byte.

Bit #	In or Out?	Purpose	Settings	
0	Output	Motor direction	0 = forward	1 = reverse
1	Output	Motor power	0 = off	1 = on
2	Input	Fully closed louver sensor	0 = not fully closed	1 = fully closed
3	Input	Fully open louver sensor	0 = not fully open	1 = fully open

Data register (DR): Motor is on and the louver is partly closed

Fully closed louver sensor ——— ——— Motor power
Fully open louver sensor ——— ——— Motor direction

				0	0	1	1

Data direction register (DDR)

Input: Output:
Chip to program Program to chip

				0	0	1	1

Figure 18.19. Problem specifications: Skylight controller.

bit is 1. Certain bits of the DR then are wired directly to the skylight controller box as shown in the specifications in Figure 18.19. The program for the skylight controller consists of three parts:

- A set of declarations (Figure 18.20) that define constants and types
- A `main()` function (Figure 18.21) that initializes the system, displays a menu in an infinite loop, and waits for a user to request some service
- A set of functions (Figure 18.22) that perform those services: opening the skylight, closing it, and asking about its current state

Notes on Figure 18.20. Declarations for the skylight controller: `skylight.h.`

- *First box: the bitfield type.*

  1. We use four bits to communicate with the multifunction chip; two are used by the program to receive status information from the chip and two are used to send control instructions to the chip. As shown in the register diagram, the leftmost four bits in the chip registers will not be used in this application. Therefore, the bitfield type declaration used to model a register begins with an unnamed field for the four padding bits, followed by named fields for two status bits and two control bits.
  2. We use pointer variables in the program to hold the addresses of the chip registers, so we declare a pointer type that references a register byte.
  3. The keyword **volatile** means that something outside the program (in this case, the controller box) may change the value of a register byte at unpredictable times. We supply this information to the C compiler so that its code optimizer does not eliminate any assignments or reads from the location that, otherwise, would appear redundant.

- *Second box: status and switch codes.*

  1. Throughout the code, we could deal with 1 and 0 settings, as specified in Figure 18.19. However, doing so makes the code error prone and very hard to understand. Instead, we define three enumerated types to give symbolic names to the various switch settings and status codes. An array of strings is defined, parallel to the third enumeration, to allow easy output of the device's status.
  2. Two of the enumerations are not within a **typedef**. They are used simply to give names to codes. A series of **#define** commands could be used for this purpose, but **enum** is better because it is shorter and it lets us group the codes into sets of related values. We do not intend to use them as variable or parameter types, so we really do not need a **typedef** name. It is not necessary to set the symbols equal to 0 and 1 here but it does make the bit-value correspondence more obvious.

These declarations are stored in the file **skylight.h**, which is used in Figures 18.21 and 18.22.

```
#include "tools.h"
```
```
/* -----------------------------------------------------------------
** Definitions of the registers on the multifunction chip
*/
typedef struct REG_BYTE {
    unsigned int                 : 4;
    unsigned int fully_open      : 1;
    unsigned int fully_closed    : 1;
    unsigned int motor_power     : 1;
    unsigned int motor_direction : 1;
} reg_byte;

typedef volatile reg_byte* device_pointer;
```

```
/* -----------------------------------------------------------------
** Definitions of the codes for the multifunction chip
*/
enum power_values      { motor_off = 0,      motor_on = 1 };
enum direction_values  { motor_forward = 0, motor_reverse = 1 };

string
position_labels[] = { "fully closed", "partially open", "fully open" };
typedef enum { fully_closed, part_open, fully_open } position;
```

```
/* -----------------------------------------------------------------
** Attach to hardware addresses and create initialization constants.
*/
device_pointer const DR = (device_pointer)0xffff7100;
device_pointer const DDR = (device_pointer)0xffff7101;
const reg_byte DDR_mask = {0,0,1,1};  /* select output bits */
const reg_byte DR_init = {0,0,0,0};   /* initialize motor off */
```

```
/* Prototypes for the control operations. */
position skylight_status( void );
void open_skylight( void );
void close_skylight( void );
```

Figure 18.20.   Declarations for the skylight controller: skylight.h.

- *Third box: setting up the registers.*

    1. We want a pointer variable **DR** to point at the address of the data register byte on the multifunction chip. We write its memory-mapped address

This program implements the specification of Figure 18.19. It uses the declarations in Figure 18.20 and calls functions in Figure 18.22.

```
#include "skylight.h"

void main( void )
{
    char choice;
    string menu[] = { "O: Open skylight", "C: Close skylight",
                      "R: Report on position", "Q: Quit" };

    /* Initialize chip registers used by application.----- */
    *DDR = DDR_mask;    /* Designate input and output bits. */
    *DR = DR_init;      /* Make sure motor is turned off. */

    for (;;) {
        choice = toupper( menu_c( " Select operation:", 4, menu ) );
        if (choice == 'Q') break;
        switch (choice) {
            case 'O': open_skylight();                    break;
            case 'C': close_skylight();                   break;
            case 'R': /* Report on position */
                      printf( " Louver is %s\n",
                              position_labels[skylight_status()] );
                                                          break;

            default:  puts( " Incorrect choice, try again." );
        }
    }
    puts( " Skylight controller terminated.\n" );
}
```

Figure 18.21.   A skylight controller.

as a hex literal, cast it to the appropriate pointer type, and store it in
DR. The keyword **const** after the type name means that **DR** always
points at this location and can never be changed.

2. Similarly, we set a pointer variable **DDR** to the address of the data
   direction register byte.

3. A bitmask is used when the program is started to initialize the data
   direction register. The rightmost two bits are used to send control
   information to the chip from the program, while the other two will be
   read by the program to check the chip's status.

4. Similarly a bitmask is used to deliver a command to initialize the motor
   to an off state.

- *Fourth box: prototypes.* This package is composed of a main program and three functions used to carry out the user's menu commands.

Notes on Figure 18.21. A skylight controller.

- *First box: chip initialization.* When the system is first turned on, the value {0,0,1,1} must be stored in the rightmost bits of the chip's data direction register to indicate the direction of data flow through the bits of the data register. Then the data register can be used to initialize the motor to an off state with a 0 bit vector.
- *Second outer box: an infinite loop.*

  1. The remainder of the program is an infinite loop that presents an operation menu to the user and waits for commands. The user can quit at any time (and thereby turn the system off) by choosing option Q.
  2. We use the `menu_c()` function from the `tools` library to display the menu and read a selection. Then we use `toupper()` so that the program recognizes both lower-case and upper-case choices in the `switch` statement.

- *First inner box: controller functions.*
  The system supports three operations: open the skylight, close it, and report on its position. There is a menu option and a function to call for each. The open and close commands change the state of the skylight. The report function checks on that state and returns a position code that `main()` uses to index the array `position_labels` and display the position for the user.
- *Second inner box: other user interactions.*
  The `switch` has a `default` case to handle input errors. This case is not necessary; without it an error would just be ignored. However, a good human interface gives feedback after every interaction, and an explicit error comment is helpful.

Notes on Figure 18.22. Operations for the skylight controller.

- *First box:* `skylight_status()`.

  1. There are three possible states: fully open, fully closed, and somewhere in between (represented by both status bits being off). This information is vital to the program because it must turn off the motor when the skylight reaches either limit.
  2. The status is tested by checking the appropriate bitfields in DR to see which of the mutually exclusive conditions exists and then returning the corresponding position code to `main()`.

These functions are called from Figure 18.21 and are in the same source code file.

```
/* ---Return skylight position------------------------------------------ */
position
skylight_status( void )
{
    if (DR->fully_closed) return fully_closed;
    else if (DR->fully_open) return fully_open;
        else return part_open;
}
```

```
/* ---Open skylight------------------------------------------------------ */
void
open_skylight( void )
{
    reg_byte dr = { 0, 0, motor_on, motor_forward };

    if (DR->fully_open) return;   /* don't start motor if already open */

    *DR = dr;

    while (!(DR->fully_open));     /* delay until open */

    dr.motor_power = motor_off;
    *DR = dr;

}
```

```
/* ---Close skylight----------------------------------------------------- */
void
close_skylight( void )
{
    reg_byte dr = { 0, 0, motor_on, motor_reverse };
    if (DR->fully_closed) return; /* don't start motor if already closed */
    *DR = dr;

    while (!(DR->fully_closed));  /* delay until closed */

    dr.motor_power = motor_off;
    *DR = dr;
}
```

Figure 18.22.   Operations for the skylight controller.

- *Second outer box:* `open_skylight()`.

    1. The basic steps of opening the skylight are turn on the motor, wait
       until the louvers are completely open, then turn off the motor.

2. Sometimes it is not necessary to turn on the motor. If a command is given to open the skylight when it is already open, control simply returns to the menu.
3. In between turning on the motor and turning it off, the program sits in a tight **while** loop, waiting for the open status bit in **DR** to change state due to the controller's actions. This is referred to as a *busy wait loop*.

- *First inner box: turning on the motor.* If the louver needs to be opened, the program turns on the motor in the forward direction, so both the direction and power bits of the control byte must be changed. To do this, we initialize these bits in a local **reg_byte**. The contents of this byte are copied to **DR** to initiate the motor's action.
- *Second inner box: turning off the motor.* A similar pattern is repeated to turn off the motor. The motor power bit in the local **reg_byte** is set to off and the byte is transferred to **DR**. The direction bit needs no adjusting since it is irrelevant when the motor is off.
- *Last box:* **close_skylight()**. The **close_skylight()** function is analogous to **open_skylight()**. It returns promptly if no work is needed. Otherwise, it turns the motor on in the reverse direction, waits for the **fully_closed** bit to be turned on by the controller, then turns the motor off.

To run this program in reality, we would need an automated skylight, a motor, a board containing the electronics necessary to drive the motor, and a multifunction chip attached to a computer. However, code always should be tested, if possible, before using it to control a physical device. This program was tested using a skylight simulator: a separate program that emulates the role of the real device, supplies feedback to the program written in this section, and prints periodic reports for the programmer. (This simulation program is too complex to present here in detail.)

Output from a simulation follows. The initial state of the simulated skylight is half open (the result of a power failure). When a line in the output starts with **SKYLIGHT**, we imagine we hear a motor running and see the louvers changing position. To reduce the total amount of output, repetitions of the menu have been replaced by dashed lines.

```
SKYLIGHT: louver is 47% open

Select operation:

O: Open skylight
C: Close skylight
R: Report on position
Q: Quit

Enter letter of desired item: r
```

```
Louver is partially open
-------------------------------
Enter letter of desired item: o
SKYLIGHT: louver is 60% open
SKYLIGHT: louver is 80% open
SKYLIGHT: louver is 100% open
SKYLIGHT: louver is 101% open
-------------------------------
Enter letter of desired item: o
-------------------------------
Enter letter of desired item: c
SKYLIGHT: louver is 100% open
SKYLIGHT: louver is 80% open
SKYLIGHT: louver is 60% open
SKYLIGHT: louver is 40% open
SKYLIGHT: louver is 20% open
SKYLIGHT: louver is 0% open
SKYLIGHT: louver is -1% open
-------------------------------
Enter letter of desired item: r
Louver is fully closed
-------------------------------
Enter letter of desired item: q
Skylight controller terminated.
```

Note that the motor always "overshoots" by a small amount. This happens because it takes a brief time to turn off the motor after the sensor says that the louver is fully open or fully closed. A real device would have to be calibrated with this in mind.

18.5   What You Should Remember

18.5.1   Major Concepts

- *Unsigned numbers.* At times, applications naturally use numbers whose range always is positive, such as memory addresses and the pixel values of digital images. In these cases, using an **unsigned** type allows for larger ranges and helps prevent errors during calculations.
- *Hexadecimal.* C supports input, output, and literals for hexadecimal integers. Hex notation is important because it translates directly to binary notation and, therefore, lets us work easily with bit patterns.
- *I/O conversions.* All built-in data types have format conversion specifiers. Unsigned data values are displayed using **%u** in decimal form and **%x** in hexadecimal form. For any data type, it is possible to specify a leading fill

character other than blank. This is useful for printing leading zeroes in hex values, as in `%08x`.

- *Bit vectors.* The bits in an integer data value can be viewed as a vector and manipulated using bitmasks and bitwise operators.

- *Bitmasks.* A mask is used to specify which bit or bits within an integer are to be selected for an operation. To create a mask, first write the appropriate bit pattern in binary, then translate it to hexadecimal and `#define` the result as a constant.

- *Summary of bitwise operators.* Bitwise operations are used with bitmasks expressed in hexadecimal notation to operate on both single bits and groups of bits within an integer. Figure 18.23 is a summary of these operators.

- *Bitfields.* Bitfield structures provide a symbolic alternative to the manual manipulation of bits using the bitwise operators. A structure can be declared with components that are smaller than a byte, and those components can be initialized like the fields of an ordinary structure and used like ordinary integers with small ranges. The compiler does all the shifting and masking needed to access the separate bits.

- *Encoding and decoding.* Information is encoded to save storage space and transmission time, or encrypted to preserve privacy. These applications make extensive use of bitwise operations.

- *Volatile.* When used in a variable declaration, this type qualifier indicates that an outside agent such as a hardware device may change the variable's value at any time. Using the qualifier instructs the compiler not to attempt to optimize the use of the variable.

18.5.2   Programming Style

- *Constants.* As with other constants, use `#define` for bitmasks to generate more understandable code.

Operator	Meaning and Use
~	Used to toggle bit values in vector.
|	Used to combine sections of a vector or turn on bits.
&	Used to isolate sections of a vector or turn off bits.
^	Used to compare two bit vectors or toggle bits on and off.
<<	Used to shift bits left; fills right end with 0 bits. Shifting an integer left by one bit has the same effect as multiplying it by 2.
>>	Used to shift bits right. Unsigned right shift fills left end with 0 bits; signed right shift fills left end with copies of the sign bit. Shifting an integer right by one bit has the same effect as dividing it by 2.

Figure 18.23.   Summary of bitwise operators.

- *Hexadecimal vs. decimal.* It is important to *understand* numbers written in hexadecimal, binary, and decimal notations. Since we cannot use binary constants in the code, we need to know when to *use* hexadecimal and when to use decimal notation. Use hexadecimal for literals when working with bitwise operators or interacting with hardware devices because the pattern of bits in the number is important and the translation from hex to binary is direct. Use decimal notation for most other purposes.
- *Proper data type.* In addition to using the appropriate literal form, the proper integer data type should be chosen. The range of needed values should help you to decide between signed and unsigned, as well as the shortest length necessary.
- *Bit vector vs. bitfield.* One must choose whether to use bit vectors or bitfield structures as a representation. Bitfield structures are appropriate for describing the bit layout of a hardware device interface that is unlikely to change. They enable us to use field names instead of bit positions to interact with the device more easily. When dealing with a series of bytes from a stream, it is more convenient to use bit vectors and the bitwise operations, as with the encoding and decoding of information.

18.5.3 Sticky Points and Common Errors

- Some pocket calculators provide a way to enter a number in base 10 and read it out in base 16 or vice versa. If yours does not, use the decimal to binary to hexadecimal method presented in Appendix E to do number conversions. The algorithm that converts directly from base 10 to base 16 relies on modular arithmetic, which is not supported by many calculators.
- When generating bitmasks beware of inverting the bit pattern. Make sure the ones and zeroes are appropriate for the bitwise operation being performed.
- Do not confuse the logical operators `&&`, `||`, and `!` with the bitwise operators `&`, `|`, and `~`. Logical operators do whole-word operations and return only the values `true` or `false`. Bitwise operators use bit vectors of varying length as both input and output.
- Do not confuse the use of `&` and `|` in an expression. Keep straight whether you are using the mask to select bits from a value or to introduce bits into it.
- Beware of shifting a bit vector in the wrong direction, either by using the incorrect operator or mistakenly using a negative shift amount.
- Remember that the data type determines whether a signed bit extension or unsigned zero-fill is performed during right shifts.
- Beware of the relative precedence of the bitwise operators. There are many different precedences, and not all seem natural to someone unfamiliar with manipulating bits.

- Beware of being off by one bit position. It is quite common when shifting or manipulating a particular bit to miss and be off by one position. Knowing the powers of 2 can help reduce the number of times this happens.
- When using bitfields that have nonstandard length, watch out for using values that do not fall in the representable range. The more significant bits will be truncated, leading to confusing results.

18.5.4   New and Revisited Vocabulary

These are the most important terms, concepts, keywords, and operators discussed in this chapter.

binary	~ (complement)	bit vector
decimal	<< (left shift)	mask
hexadecimal	>> (right shift)	toggle
unsigned integer	signed shift	unpack and recombine
hex integer literal	unsigned shift	encode and decode
hex character literal	& (bitwise AND)	encryption
%x (hex I/O conversion)	^ (bitwise exclusive OR)	bitfield structure
%u (unsigned conversion)	| (bitwise OR)	volatile
two's complement	portable notation	memory-mapped I/O

18.6   Exercises

18.6.1   Self-Test Exercises

1. a. What decimal numbers do you need to convert to get the following hexadecimal outputs: AAA, FAD, F1F1, and B00 ?

   b. Write the decimal numbers from 15 to 35 in hexadecimal notation.

   c. Write the decimal value 105 in hexadecimal notation.

   d. What hexadecimal number equals 101010 in binary?

   e. Write any string of 16 bits. Show how you convert this to a hexadecimal number. Then write this number as a legal C hexadecimal literal.

2. Compile and run the program in Figure 18.4. Experiment with different input and answer the following questions:

   a. What happens if you try to print a negative signed integer with a %hu format?

   b. What is the biggest **unsigned int** you can read and write? Note what it looks like in hexadecimal notation; you easily can see why this is the biggest representable integer. Explain it in your own words.

   c. You can read numbers in hexadecimal format using a %x format. Try this. Enter a series of numbers and experimentally find one that prints the value 117_{10}.

3. As part of a cryptographic project, 4-byte words are scrambled by moving around groups of 4 bits each. A scrambling pattern follows: it has three sets of bits labeled with the letters **x**, **v**, and **e**. The bits in the **x** positions do not move. All the **e** bits move 8 bits to the left, and the **v** bits go into bits 3...0.

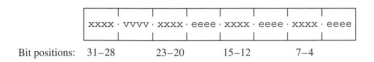

Bit positions: 31–28   23–20   15–12   7–4

   a. Define three AND masks to isolate the sets of fields **x**, **v**, and **e**.

   b. Write three AND instructions to decompose the word by isolating the three sets of bits and storing them in variables named **X**, **V**, and **E**.

   c. Write the two shift instructions required to reposition the bits of **E** and **V**.

   d. Write an OR instruction that puts the three parts back together.

4. A college professor is writing a program that emulates the computer he first used in 1960 (an IBM 704). He wants to use this program to teach others about the way in which hardware design has progressed in 40 years. The instructions on this machine were 36 bits long and had four parts:

        Operation code   bits 35–33

        Decrement field   bits 32–18

        Index register field   bits 17–15

        Address field   bits 14–0

op	decrement	index	address
35–33	32–18	17–15	14–0

Bit positions

In this machine, the decrement field is used as part of the operation code in some instructions and as a second address field in others. Write a **typedef** and bitfield structure declaration to embed this instruction layout in 6 bytes. Put the necessary padding bits anywhere convenient but make sure that the two 3-bit fields do not cross byte boundaries and the two longer fields cross only one boundary each.

5. Repeat problem 4 using bit masks. Assume that the op and index fields are stored together in one byte and the other fields occupy two bytes each.

6. What is stored in **w** by each line of the following statements? Write out the 8-bit vectors for each variable and show the steps of the operations. Use these values for the variables:

```
unsigned char v, w, x = 1, y = 2, z = 4;
const unsigned char mask = 0xC3;
```

a. `w = ~ x & x;`

b. `w = ~ x ^ x;`

c. `w = x | y & x | z;`

d. `v = y | z; w = (v<<3) + (v<<1);`

e. `w = x | y & x | z<<y ^ mask>>x;`

f. `w = ~ x | x;`

g. `w = 1;    w<<= 1;`

h. `w = x ^ ~ y;`

i. `w = x | y | z>>2;`

j. `w = x & y & ~ z;`

18.6.2 Using Pencil and Paper

1. Write your full name, including blanks, in the ASCII character code in hexadecimal literal form (refer to Appendix A).

2. As part of a cryptographic project, every 4 bytes of information in a data stream will be scrambled. One of the scrambling patterns follows: it has five fields labeled with four letters. The bits in the positions labeled **x** are not moved. The bit field labeled **n** swaps places with the field labeled **v**; the rightmost bit of **n** moves to position 5 and the leftmost bit of **v** shifts to position 27. The field labeled **e** moves 2 bits to the left to make space for this swap.

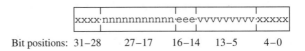

Bit positions: 31–28   27–17   16–14   13–5   4–0

   a. Define four AND masks to isolate the fields **x**, **n**, **e**, and **v**.

   b. Write four AND instructions to decompose the word, isolating the four sets of bits and storing them in variables named **X**, **N**, **E**, and **V**.

   c. Write the three shift instructions required to reposition the bits of **N**, **E**, and **V**.

   d. Write the OR instruction to put the four parts back together.

3. Repeat parts (a) and (b) of exercise 2 using a bitfield structure. Explain why parts (c) and (d) are easier to do using masks than using bitfields.

4. a. Write the numbers from 30_{10} to 35_{10} in binary notation.

   b. Write 762_{10} in hexadecimal notation.

   c. Write 762_{10} in binary notation.

   d. What hexadecimal number equals 11000011_2?

   e. What base-10 number equals 11000011_2?

   f. What decimal numbers equal the following hex "words": **C3b0**, **dab**, **add**, and **feed**?

5. (Advanced topic.) The following three riddles have answers related to the limitations of a computer and the quirks of the C language in representing and using the various integer types.

   a. When is $x + 1 < x$?

   b. When does a positive number have a negative sign?

   c. When is a big number small?

6. You are writing a program to analyze health statistics. A data set containing records for a small village has been collected, coded, and stored in a binary file. The data cover about 1,000 residents. Each person's data are packed into a single long unsigned integer, with fields (shown in the diagram) defined as follows:

ID code	bits 31–22	
Gender	bit 19	0 = male, 1 = female
Alive	bit 18	0 = dead, 1 = living
Marital status	bits 17–16	0 = single, 1 = married, 2 = divorced, 3 = widowed
Age	bits 14–8	
Disease code	bits 7–0	

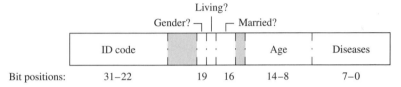

The remaining bit positions (gray in the diagram) are irrelevant to the current research and may be ignored. Write a **typedef** and bitfield structure declaration to describe these data.

7. Solve for **N** in the following equations. Show your work, using an 8-bit unsigned binary representation for the constants and the variables **N** and **T**. Give the answer to each item in binary and hexadecimal format.

   a. $N = 21_{16} \mid 39_{16}$ e. $N = 2A_{16} \;\&\; 0F_{16}$

   b. $3A_{16} \;\hat{}\; N = 00_{16}$ f. $N = 4C_{16} << 3_{16}$

   c. $N = \;\tilde{}\; AE_{16} \mid 39_{16}$ g. $N = A1_{16} \;\&\; 39_{16} \mid 1E_{16}$

   d. $N = 4C_{16} >> 1$ h. $T = 2A_{16};\; \tilde{}T >> 2 \;\hat{}\; N = 01_{16}$

18.6.3 Using the Computer

1. The case bit.
   In an alphabetic ASCII character, the third bit from the left is the *case-shift bit*. This bit is 0 for upper-case letters and 1 for lower-case letters. Except for this bit, the code of an upper-case letter is the same as its lower-case counterpart. Write a program that contains a bitmask for the case-shift bit. Read three lines of characters using **scanf(" %c", …)**. Do the operations described here and print the results. Assume that each line, including the last, will end with a newline character.

a. On the first line of input, use a mask and one bitwise operator to toggle the case of the input; that is, change **B** to **b** or **b** to **B**.

b. On the second line of input, use your mask and one bitwise operator to change the input to all uppercase.

c. On the third line of input, use your mask and one bitwise operator to change the input to all lowercase.

In these, make sure to change only alphabetic letters; do not alter the values of numerals, special symbols, and the like. Use the library function **isalpha()** for this.

2. Decomposing an integer.
One of the fastest methods of sorting is a *radix sort*. To use this algorithm, each item being sorted is decomposed into fields and the data set is sorted on each field in succession. The speed of the sort depends on the number of fields used; the space used by the sorting array depends on the number of bits in each field. A good compromise for sorting 32-bit numbers is to use four fields of 8 bits each, as in the following diagram. During the sorting process, the data are sorted first based on the least significant field (A, in the diagram) and last using the most significant field (D).

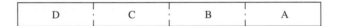

This problem focuses on only the decomposition, not the sorting. Assume you want to sort long integers and need to decompose each into four 8-bit portions, as shown in the diagram. Write a function, **get_key()**, that has two parameters: the number to be decomposed and the pass number, 0...3. Isolate and return the field of the number that is the right key for the specified pass. For pass 0, return field A; for pass 1, field B; and so forth. Write a main program that will let you test your **get_key()** function. For each data value, echo the input in both decimal and hexadecimal form, then call the **get_key()** function four times, printing the four fields in both decimal and hexadecimal format.

3. A computational mystery.

a. Enter the following code for the **mystery()** function into a file and write a main program that will call it repeatedly. The main program should enter a pair of numbers, one real and one positive integer; call the **mystery()** function; and print the result.

```
double mystery( double x, int n )  /* Assume n >= 0 */
{
    double y = 1.0;
    while (n > 0) {
        if (n & 1) y *= x;          /* Test if n is odd. */
        n >>= 1;
        x *= x;                      /* Square x. */
    }
    return y;
}
```

b. Manually trace the execution of the code for **mystery()**. Use the argument values **n = 5** and **x = 3.0**, then try again with **x = 2.0** and **n = 6**. On a trace chart, make columns for **x, y, n, n** in binary, and **n & 1**. Show how the values of each expression change every time around the loop.

c. Run the program, testing it with several pairs of small numbers. Chart the results. The **mystery()** function uses an unusual method to compute a useful and common mathematical function. Which mathematical function is it?

d. Turn in the program, some output, the chart of output results, the hand emulation, and a description of the mathematical function.

4. Binary to decimal conversion.
   Appendix E, Figure E.4 describes and illustrates one method for converting binary numbers to base 10. Write a program to implement this process, as follows:

   a. Write a function, **strip()**, that returns the value of the rightmost bit of its **long** integer argument. This will be either 0 (**false**) or 1 (**true**). Implement this using bit operations.

   b. Write a **void** function, **convert()**, that has one **long signed** integer argument. It should start by printing a left parenthesis and finish by printing a matching right parenthesis. Between generating these, repeatedly strip a bit off the right end of the argument (or what remains of it). If the bit is a 1, print the corresponding power of 2 and a **+** sign. Then shift the argument 1 bit to the right. Continue to test, print, and strip until the remaining argument is 0.

   c. Write a main program to test the conversion function, making it easy to test several data values. For each, prompt the user for an integer. If it is negative, print a negative sign and take its absolute value. Then call the **convert()** function to print the binary value of the number in its expanded form. For example, if the input was -25, the output should be $-(1 + 8 + 16)$.

5. Input hexadecimal, output binary.
   Appendix E, Figure E.5 describes and illustrates a method for converting hexadecimal numbers to binary. Write a program to implement this process, as follows:

   a. Define a constant array of strings to implement the bit patterns in the third column of the table in Figure E.5.

   b. Write a function, **strip()**, that has a call-by-address parameter, **np**, the number being converted. Use a masking operation to isolate the rightmost 4 bits of **np** and save this value. Then shift **np** 4 bits to the right and return this modified value through the parameter. Return the isolated hexadecimal digit as the value of the function.

   c. Write a **void** function, **convert()**, that has one **long signed** integer argument, **n**, and an empty integer array in which to store an answer. Remember that integers are represented in binary in the computer and 4 binary bits represent the same integer as 1 hexadecimal digit. Repeatedly strip a field of 4 bits off the right end of the argument (or what remains of it) and store the resulting hexadecimal digit in successive slots of the answer array. Do this eight times for a 32-bit integer.

d. Write a main program to test your conversion function, making it easy to test several data values. For each, prompt the user to enter a hexadecimal integer in the form **10A2**, and read it using a **%x** format specifier. Then call the **convert()** function, sending in the value of the number and an array to hold the hexadecimal expansion of that number. After conversion, print the number in expanded binary form. Start by printing a left parenthesis, then print the eight hexadecimal digits of the number in their binary form, using the array from part (a). Finish by printing a matching right parenthesis. For example, if the hexadecimal numbers −1 and 17 were entered, the output should be

```
( 1111 1111 1111 1111 1111 1111 1111 1111 )
( 0000 0000 0000 0000 0000 0000 0001 0111 )
```

6. Compressing an image—run length encoding.

Digital images often are large and consume vast amounts of disk space. Therefore, it can be desirable to compress them and save space. One simple compression method is *run length encoding*. This technique is based on the fact that most images have large areas of constant intensity. A series of three or more consecutive pixels of the same value is called a *run*. When compressing a file, any value in the input sequence that is not part of a run simply is transferred from the original sequence into the encoded version. When three or more consecutive values are the same, an encoding triplet is created. The first element of this triplet is an escape code, actually a character value not expected to be present in the data. The second value is the number of characters present in the run, stored as a 1-byte unsigned integer. The last value is the input value that is repeated the indicated number of times.

The compression process is illustrated below. A stream of characters is shown first in its original form, and below that in compressed form. The escape code characters are shown as gray boxes.

Original length : 27

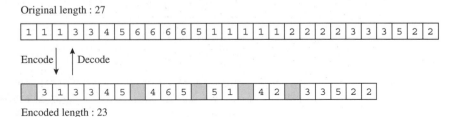

Encoded length : 23

When a compressed image is used, the encoding process must be reversed. All encoding triplets are expanded into a corresponding sequence of identical byte values. Write a program that will perform run length encoding and decoding. First, open a user-specified file for input (appropriately handle any errors in the file name) and another file for output. Then ask the user whether encoding or decoding should be performed. If encoding, read successive bytes from the input stream, noting any consecutive repetitions. Those occurring once or twice should be echoed to the output file, while runs of length three or more should be converted into an encoding triplet, which then is written to the output file. Use a value of **0xFF** (255) as the escape code for this problem. If a data value of 255 occurs, change it to 254. Any runs in the data longer than 255 should be broken into an appropriate number of triplets of that length, followed by one of lesser length to finish the description. If decoding, read successive bytes from the input stream, scanning for encoding triplets. All characters between these triplets should be copied directly into the output file. Encoding triplets should be expanded to the appropriate length and sent to the output file.

7. Encoding a file—uuencode.

One command in the UNIX operating system is *uuencode*, and its purpose is to encode binary data files in ASCII format for easy transmission between machines. The program will read the contents of one data file and generate another, taking successive groups of three input bytes and transforming them into corresponding groups of four ASCII bytes as follows:

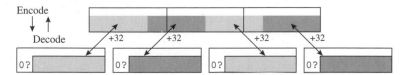

The original 3 bytes (24 bits) are divided into four 6-bit segments. The value of each segment is used to generate a single byte of data. The value of this byte is calculated by adding the value 32 to the 6-bit value and storing the result in a character variable. This creates a printable ASCII value that can be transmitted easily. In the event that the original file length is not divisible by 3, fill in the missing bytes at the end by bytes containing the value 0. The final byte triplet then is converted in the same manner.[5] Write a program that will perform the uuencode operation. First, open a file with a user-specified name for input (appropriately handle any errors in the file name). Open another file for output. Then read successive byte triplets from the input stream and write corresponding 4-byte chunks to the output stream, adding 0 bytes at the end, if necessary, to make 3 bytes in the final triplet.

8. Decoding a file—uudecode.

The matching command to the uuencode command discussed in the previous exercise is uudecode. It takes as input an ASCII file created using uuencode and produces the corresponding binary file. It simply reverses the encoding process just described, taking 4-byte groups as input and generating 3-byte groups as output. Write a program that will perform the uudecode operation. First, open a file with a user-supplied name for input (appropriately handle any errors in the file name). Open an output file as well. Perform the conversion process by transforming successive 4-byte input groupings into 3-byte output groups and writing them to the output file.

9. Set operations.

A set is a data structure for representing a group of items. The total collection of items that can exist in a set is referred to as the *set's domain*. A set with no items

---

[5]The real uuencode command also generates header and trailer information that is useful in decoding the file. For simplicity, we ignore this information in the exercise. Newer versions add 96 (not 32) to the null character.

in it is called an *empty set*, while one that contains all the items is called a *universal set*. Items can be added to a set, but if that item already exists in the set, nothing changes. Items also can be removed from the set. In addition, some operations create new sets: (1) *intersection* produces the set of items common to two sets, (2) *union* produces the set containing all items found in either of two sets, (3) *difference* produces the set containing those items in a first set that do not exist in a second set, and (4) *complement* produces the set containing those items in the domain that are not present in a set.

There are many ways to represent a set in C. In this exercise, define a set as a bit vector. Represent the domain of the set as an enumeration. Each bit position in the vector corresponds to an item in the domain. A bit value is 1 if that item is present in the set. Each of the various set operations can be performed by doing an appropriate bitwise operation on sets represented in this manner. Write a program that allows a user to define and manipulate sets in the following manner:

- Let the domain be the colors red, orange, yellow, green, blue, purple, white, and black. To map from a color to a bit in the set representation, start with a bit vector containing the integer value 1 and use the enumeration value as a left shift amount.
- Write a group of functions that will (a) add an element to a set, (b) remove an element from a set, (c) test if an element is in the set, and (d) print the contents of a set. These will be support functions for the rest of the program.
- Write a group of functions that perform set intersection, set union, set difference, and set complement.
- Write a main program that presents an initial menu to the user, the options being the four set operations just mentioned. When one of these options is chosen, the program should ask the user to supply the contents of the necessary sets, perform the operation, and print the contents of the resulting set. To supply the contents of a set, the user should be able to add and remove items from the set repeatedly until the desired group has been produced. When adding or removing an item, the user should be able to type the name of the item (a color) or select it from a menu and the program then should adjust the representation of the set accordingly.

10. Machine code disassembler.

The last phase of the compilation process is turning assembly language into machine language. Sometimes it is desirable to reverse this process by generating assembly language from machine code, or *disassembling*. This is similar to what happens in the instruction decoding step of the CPU. We describe a fictitious machine that has 16 assembly language instructions encoded in a 4-byte machine instruction. This 4-byte area can be decomposed into five pieces. The leftmost half (2 bytes) is split into 4-bit fields. The remaining half may be used in conjunction with the last 4-bit field from the left half to form another large field, as follows:

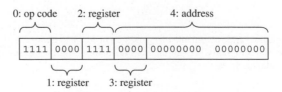

Instruction	Op Code	1st Register	2nd Register	3rd Register	Address	Description
Load	0000	R	—	—	M	Load **R** with contents of **M**
Store	0001	R	—	—	M	Store contents of **R** into **M**
Add	0010	Ri	Rj	Rk	—	`Rk = Ri + Rj`
Subtract	0011	Ri	Rj	Rk	—	`Rk = Ri - Rj`
Multiply	0100	Ri	Rj	Rk	—	`Rk = Ri * Rj`
Divide	0101	Ri	Rj	Rk	—	`Rk = Ri / Rj`
Negate	0110	Ri	Rj	—	—	`Rj = -Ri`
AND	0111	Ri	Rj	Rk	—	`Rk = Ri & Rj`
OR	1000	Ri	Rj	Rk	—	`Rk = Ri | Rj`
XOR	1001	Ri	Rj	Rk	—	`Rk = Ri ^ Rj`
NOT	1010	Ri	Rj	—	—	`Rj = ~Ri`
<	1011	Ri	Rj	Rk	—	`Rk = Ri < Rj`
>	1100	Ri	Rj	Rk	—	`Rk = Ri > Rj`
=	1101	Ri	Rj	Rk	—	`Rk = Ri == Rj`
Branch U	1110	—	—	—	M	Branch to address **M**
Branch C	1111	R	—	—	M	Branch to **M** if **R** true

Figure 18.24.   Problem 10.

The contents of these fields depend on the particular instruction, described in Figure 18.24. The operation code determines whether there is a third register number or those bits are to be used as part of a memory address. Write a program that prints the assembly language program described by a machine code file. First, open a user-specified binary file for input (appropriately handle any errors in the file name). Read successive groups of 4 bytes and treat each group as an instruction. Decode the instruction based on looking at the op code field and interpreting the remaining fields properly. Print an assembly language line describing this. Print register numbers as **R1** or **R15**. Print the 20-bit memory addresses in hexadecimal form. For instance, the two machine instructions on the left might be translated into the assembly instructions on the right:

```
00000101 00001111 11001101 01100100 → LOAD R5, 0xFCD64
00101101 00101011 00000000 00000000 → ADD R13, R2, R11
```

Advanced Techniques

CHAPTER
19

Dynamic Arrays

In Chapter 17, we explored the capabilities of two kinds of two-dimensional array data structures: the matrix and the array of arrays. Here we explore a third: the array of pointers to arrays. We also introduce another important part of the C language: dynamically allocated memory. We show how an array of unpredictable length can be allocated at run time and how dynamic allocation can be used to remove some of the limitations from algorithms that work with arrays.

19.1	Dynamic Memory Allocation

When an array is declared with a constant length, like the `data_list` array in Figure 16.15, the C translator calculates the size of the array at compile time. At run time, the predetermined amount of storage is allocated and the program must work within fixed array boundaries. In many applications, though, the amount of data to be processed and, therefore, the length of an array to store the data are not known ahead of time. A sort program is a good example of an application that may operate on a small or large amount of data; the operation of the program is not tied to any particular amount of data. However, defining a maximum array length at compile time limits the usefulness of a sort program to data sets smaller than that maximum.

We can eliminate this artificial restriction by using pointers and **dynamic memory allocation**. We can write a program that can sort any amount of data that will fit into the memory of the computer, so long as the amount of data is known before the data are read,[1] so we can allocate a block of storage. This makes the program much more flexible than one with a #defined array length. Image processing and graphics applications also profit from dynamically allocated memory, because images and graphical objects come in many sizes, from small to large, but the processing methods remain the same.

The C language contains a set of functions for creating and handling dynamically allocated memory. When given the required size of a memory area, these functions interact with the operating system and ask it to reserve an additional block of memory for the program's use. The beginning address of this block is returned to the program as a pointer value that can be saved and later used to access the memory. The dynamic-memory functions are listed in Figure 19.1 and described in more detail in the subsections that follow.

These functions are defined in the C standard library whose header is **stdlib.h**. They are included by **tools.h**.

Prototype	Action
`void* malloc( size_t sz );`	Mass memory allocation. Return a pointer to an uninitialized block of memory of the specified size, **sz** bytes.
`void* calloc( size_t n, size_t sz );`	Allocate and clear memory. Return a pointer to an array of memory locations that have been cleared to 0 bits. The array has **n** slots, each of size **sz** bytes.
`void  free( void* pt );`	Recycle a memory block. Return to the operating system the block of memory that starts at the address stored in **pt**. A block should be freed after it no longer is needed by the program.
`void* realloc( void* pt, size_t sz );`	Mass memory reallocation. Given a pointer, **pt**, to a memory block that was previously allocated by **malloc()** or **calloc()**, and given a new number of bytes, **sz**, that is different from the current size of that block, resize the block to the new length. If the new block cannot start at the same location as the old one, this will involve copying the entire contents of the old block to the new one.

Figure 19.1.   Dynamic memory allocation functions.

---

[1] It actually is possible to resize the memory allocation as a data file is being read, but this can be time consuming.

19.1.1   Mass Memory Allocation

When a programmer cannot predict the amount of memory that will be needed by a program, the **malloc()** function can be used at run time to allocate an array of bytes of the required size. Its prototype is

```
void* malloc( size_t sz );
```

where **size_t** is an unsigned integer type used by the local system to store the sizes of objects. Frequently, **size_t** is defined by **typedef** to be the same as **unsigned int** or **unsigned long**. The value returned by **malloc()** is a pointer to an array of bytes. The simplest way to call **malloc()** is with a literal constant, thus:

```
malloc( 20 )
```

This call allocates a memory area like the one diagrammed here:

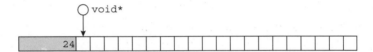

This memory is not initialized and still contains whatever data happened to be left over from a previous program. The gray area in the diagram represents additional bytes that the C system sets aside to store the total size of the allocated block (the size of a **size_t** value plus the size of the white area). The importance of these bytes becomes clear when we discuss **free()** and **realloc()**.

The type **void*** has not been discussed yet; it is a generic pointer type, which basically means "a pointer to something, but we don't know what." It is used because **malloc()** must be able to allocate memory for any type of object, and the function's prototype must specify a return type compatible with all kinds of pointers. Before the **void** pointer that is returned can be used, it must be either **explicitly cast**[2] to a specific pointer type, as shown next, or implicitly cast by storing it in a pointer variable, as shown in Figure 19.2.

```
(char*) malloc( 20 )
```

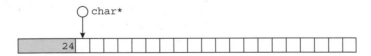

---

[2]The cast is not necessary, even to avoid warning messages, in ISO C. However, it was necessary in older versions of C and is a style that many experienced programmers prefer to follow.

Normally, **malloc()** is used to allocate space for a single object or an array of objects of some known type. Since the number of bytes occupied by a type can vary from one implementation to another, we usually do not call **malloc()** with a literal number as an argument. Instead, we use the **sizeof** operation to supply the correct size of the desired type on the local system:

```
malloc( sizeof(long) )
```

Note that the return type is still **void***, even though we use the type name **long** in the expression. The **sizeof** expression *inside* the argument list does not affect the type of the pointer that is returned.

To allocate an array of objects, simply multiply the size of the base type by the number of array slots. The next diagram illustrates this common usage, along with a cast that converts the **void*** value to a pointer with the correct base type:

```
(long*) malloc( 5 * sizeof(long) )
```

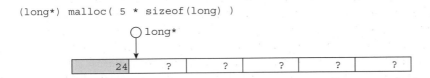

Although it is uncommon on modern systems, **malloc()** will fail if there is not enough available memory to satisfy the request. In this case, its return value is **NULL**. It is good programming practice to include a test for this condition and abort the program if it occurs, because no further meaningful processing can be done. An example of this is shown in Figure 19.2.

19.1.2 Cleared Memory Allocation

The **calloc()** function allocates an array of memory and clears all of it to 0 bits. It has two parameters, the length of the array and the size of one array element. A typical call and its results are

```
long* lptr;
lptr = calloc( 5, sizeof(long) );
```

No cast operator is needed here because the return value is stored immediately in a pointer variable of the correct type.

Even though `malloc()` and `calloc()` have different numbers of parameters, they essentially do the same thing (except for initialization) and return the same type of result. Like `malloc()`, `calloc()` returns a `void*` to the first memory address in the allocated area or returns **NULL** if not enough memory is available to allocate a block of the specified size.

19.1.3   Freeing Dynamic Memory

In many applications, memory requirements grow and shrink repeatedly during execution. A program may request several chunks of memory to accommodate the data during one phase then, after using the memory, have no future need for it. Memory use and, sometimes, execution speed are made more efficient by recycling memory; that is, returning it to the system to be reused for some other purpose. Dynamically allocated memory can be recycled by calling `free()`, which uses the number of bytes in the gray area at the beginning of each allocated block. This function returns the block of memory to the system's memory manager, which adds it to the supply of available storage and eventually reassigns it when the program again calls `malloc()` or `calloc()`. The use of `malloc()` and `free()` are illustrated by the simulation program beginning in Figure 19.8.

While each program is responsible for recycling its own obsolete memory blocks, a few warnings are in order. A block should be freed only once; a second attempt to free the same block is an error. Similarly, we use `free()` only to recycle memory areas created by `malloc()` or `calloc()`. Its use with a pointer to any other memory area is an error. Another common mistake, described next, is to attempt to use a block after it has been freed. These are serious errors that cannot be detected by the compiler and may cause a variety of unpredictable results at run time.

A **dangling pointer** is one whose referent has been reclaimed by the system. Any attempt to use a dangling pointer is wrong. Typically, this happens because multiple pointers often point at the same memory block. When a block is first allocated, only one pointer points to it. However, that pointer might be copied several times as it is passed into and out of functions and stored in data structures. If one copy of the pointer is used to free the memory block, all other copies of that pointer become dangling references. A dangling reference may seem to work at first, until the block is reallocated for another purpose. After that, two parts of the program will simultaneously try to use the same storage and the contents of that location become unpredictable.

If you do not explicitly free the dynamically allocated memory, it will be returned to the memory manager when the program completes. So, forgetting to perform a `free()` operation is not as damaging as freeing the same block twice. However, it still is good programming style to free memory that no longer is needed, especially when the memory is used for a short time by only one function. Because functions often are reused in a new context, they always should clean up after themselves.

19.1.4 Resizing an Array

By using the **malloc()** function, we can defer the decision about the length of an array until run time. However, array space still must be allocated before the data are read and, perhaps, before we know how many data items actually exist. Using **malloc()** to create an array makes a program more flexible, but it still cannot accommodate an amount of data greater than expected. Fortunately, the C library provides an additional function to solve the problem of too little space for the data. The function that **resizes the data array** is called **realloc()**. When given a pointer to a memory block that was created by **malloc()** or **calloc()**, it will reallocate the array, making it either larger or smaller, according to the newly requested size.

Making an array smaller causes no physical or logical difficulties. The excess space is taken off the end of the original area and returned to the system for recycling. The length count that is kept in the gray area at the head of the block is adjusted appropriately. For example, assume we have the following memory block before reallocation:

Then we give the reallocation command

```
lptr = realloc( lptr, 3 * sizeof(long) );
```

After reallocation, the picture becomes

Making an array longer causes a problem because the space at the end of the array already may be in use for some other purpose. The C system keeps track of the length of every area created by **malloc()** or **calloc()** and also knows what storage is free. If there is enough empty space after the end of an array, that storage area easily and efficiently can be added onto the end. This is what **realloc()** does, if possible. When the space after the array is unavailable, **realloc()** allocates a new area that *is* large enough, then copies the data from the old area into the new one, and finally frees the old area. For example, before reallocation, we have

After the reallocation command

```
lptr = realloc( lptr, 7 * sizeof(long) );
```

we have

Therefore, **realloc()** always succeeds unless the memory is full, but the reallocated array might start at a new memory address. The function returns the starting address of the current memory block, whether or not it has been changed. The program must store this address so it can access the storage.

Copying an entire array of information from one memory block to another is a costly operation and should be avoided if possible. It would not be a good idea to reallocate an array many times in a row, adding only a small number of slots each time. For this reason, successive calls on **realloc()** normally double the length of the array or at least add a substantial number of slots. An application of **realloc()** is given in the simulation program in Section 19.2.

Finally, **realloc()** is inappropriate for applications that have many pointers pointing into the dynamic array. Since the memory location of an array might change when it is reallocated, any pointers previously set to point at parts of the array are left dangling. If there are only a few such pointers, new memory addresses sometimes can be computed and the pointers reconnected properly. If not, **realloc()** should not be used.

19.1.5 Using Dynamic Arrays

A pointer to a dynamic array can be used with a subscript, just like the array itself, as shown in this code fragment that allocates space for **n** long integers, then reads that many numbers from **stdin**:

```
lptr = malloc( n * sizeof(long) );
if (lptr == NULL) fatal( "Memory allocation failure." );
for (k = 0; k < n; ++k) scanf( "%li", &lptr[k] );
```

The close relationship between an array pointer and an unsubscripted array name makes it very easy to take an application written for ordinary arrays and convert it to use dynamic arrays. As an example, consider the selection sort program from Figure 16.15. This program consists of `main()` and four other functions and uses an array whose length is defined at compile time. To allow this program to use dynamic allocation, only six lines in the main program need be changed; namely, the lines that determine the length of the array and allocate it. None of the function definitions or prototypes need to be modified. Figure 19.2 shows the revised main program.

Notes on Figure 19.2. Sorting using a dynamic array.   We comment on the differences between the selection sort program given earlier, which used an array whose length was fixed at compile time, and the version given here, where the array length is determined at run time. The three functions called by the main program will work correctly with no modification.

This main program was first presented in Figure 16.15. The boxed lines were changed to convert this program from using an ordinary array to a dynamically allocated array.

```c
#include "tools.h"

int read_file( float x[], int nmax );
void sort_data( float data[], int n );
void write_file( float data[], int n );

void main( void )
{
    int n;                          /* # of data items to be sorted. */
    float* data_list;

    banner();

    printf( " How many items need to be sorted? " );
    scanf( "%i", &n );
    data_list = malloc( n * sizeof(float) );
    if (data_list == NULL) fatal( "Not enough memory for %i items.", n );

    n = read_file( data_list, n );

    printf( " %i items were read; beginning to sort.\n", n );
    sort_data( data_list, n );

    puts( " Data sorted, ready for output." );
    write_file( data_list, n );

    free( data_list );

    bye();
}
```

Figure 19.2.   Sorting using a dynamic array.

- *Global definitions.* We eliminate the `#define` statement because the array length will be determined at run time. The prototypes do not need to be changed. When a parameter is declared as type `float[]`, the function expects the argument to be the address of an array (all array arguments are passed by address). The value of a pointer to a dynamic memory block is the address of the array, so it is the correct type.
- *First box: the array pointer.* In the earlier version of this program, `data_list` was declared as an array of fixed length. In this version, it is of type `float*` and used to point at an array whose length will be determined at run time.
- *Second box: allocating an array of the right size.* We prompt for and read `n`, the expected number of data items. If the actual number of data items is larger than this, we sort only the first `n` items. If the actual number is smaller, the program works correctly and all the data are sorted. We allocate enough memory for an array of `n` `float`s and test for allocation failure. The pointer returned by `malloc()` is stored in the variable `data_list`, which will be an argument to the input, sort, and output functions.
- *Third box: a pointer argument.* Since the array length now is variable, we remove the constant `LENGTH` from the call on `read_file()` and replace it with `n`, the array length entered as input and used to allocate space. The function still returns the number of items it actually reads, which might be less than the expected number. The main program stores the return value back into `n` because it might be different from the value of `n` that was the argument to `read_file()`. The `read_file()` function actually could be enhanced using `realloc()` to allow for a greater number of items than expected.
- *Fourth box: program termination.* We use `free()` to recycle memory allocated by `malloc()`. When a program terminates, all the memory allocated for it, whether static or dynamic, is supposed to be returned to the system automatically. However, using an explicit `free()` is a good habit.

19.1.6   Arrays of Dynamic Strings

A **ragged array** is a commonly used data structure. As introduced in Chapter 13, the strings used to initialize the ragged arrays were all literals. Now, however, we have seen how to allocate space dynamically and can extend the concept of a ragged array to include strings created from input data. The methods for building such a data structure are straightforward but not obvious, so we illustrate them with the short program in Figures 19.3 and 19.4. The resulting data structure is shown in Figure 19.5. This program is a preliminary version of a membership-management tool that will be used to maintain a club's database file. Here, we focus on issues related to dynamic allocation.

This is a preliminary version of a program that eventually will add a new family to a club database stored in a file. In this version, we focus on building a ragged array from interactively entered data. All potential file input and output have been "amputated" by enclosing the function calls in comments.

```c
#include "tools.h"
typedef struct FAMILY { int n; string* name; } family_t;
void get_names( string new[], int mem );
void print_family( family_t f );

void main( void )
{
    int mem;                            /* # of people in new family. */
    string* new;                        /* Names for newest family. */

    int fam = 0;                        /* # of families in the club. */
    family_t club[20];                  /* Membership roster. */

    puts( "\n Pleasant Lakes Club Membership List " );
    /* fam = read_file( club ); /* Read current members from file. */
    /* print_all( club, fam );  /* Print roster of current members. */

    printf( " Ready for new family data.  How many people? " );
    scanf( "%i", &mem );

    new = malloc( mem * sizeof(string) );
    if (new == NULL) fatal( "Not enough memory for new family." );

    club[fam].n = mem;
    club[fam].name = new;
    get_names( new, mem );

    print_family( club[fam] );

    fam++;

    /* write_file( club, fam );   /* Write file and free dynamic storage. */
    bye();
}
```

Figure 19.3.   A variable number of varying-sized objects.

A group of neighboring families got together, bought two cottages on a lake, and incorporated as the Pleasant Lakes Club. Their bylaws say that there must be no more than 20 families in the club, so that each family can use a cottage one week per summer. The club secretary has a database of member families. He has found that the sizes of families and the length of their names vary dramatically, so he decided that his database program will use dynamic allocation for this information. When a new family joins, an array is allocated with the one slot for each person. As each family member's name is entered, the size of the name is measured and the right number of bytes is allocated.

Notes on Figure 19.3. A variable number of varying-sized objects.

- *First box: the data.* Each family will be represented by a structure. In this example program, the structure contains only the number of family members and a list of their names. In a more realistic program, the structure would include an address and so forth.

- *Second box: the club database.* The club membership is represented as an array of families and a count of the current number of families actually in the club. In a final version of this program, `fam` will store the number of member families as read from an input file. Here, the call on `read_file()` is commented out, so we initialize `fam` in the declaration. When we begin, no families are in the database, so we use 0 as the initializer.

- *Third box: allocating an array for the family.*

  1. Before we can allocate an array, we need to know how long it should be. In this situation, we ask the user to supply the number of names that will be entered. We store this in `mem` and use it in the call on `malloc()`.

  2. We are building an array of strings; each slot in the array will contain a pointer to an array of characters. Therefore, the argument to `malloc()` must be `mem` times `sizeof(string)`.

  3. As always, we test for allocation failure and abort if there is trouble.

- *Fourth and fifth boxes: the member count.*

  1. The variable `fam` tells us the current number of families stored in the club array. Therefore, `club[fam]` is the first vacant slot. In that slot, we store the data for the new family: the number of family members and the pointer to the array just allocated. For convenience in coding, we also store this pointer in a local variable with a short name.

  2. The actual names of the family are input and stored by the `get_names()` function, which is discussed shortly.

  3. At this point, we have finished creating and installing another member family, so we increment the member count. The permanent database is not updated yet; that will be done by the `write_file()` function in the final version of the program.

- Sample output from a test run follows:

```
Pleasant Lakes Club Membership List
Ready for new family data.  How many people? 5
```

These functions are called by the main program in Figure 19.3.

```
void get_names( string new[], int mem )
{
    int k;              /* Loop index. */
    char buf[80];       /* For input of member names. */
    int len;            /* Name length. */
    puts( "\n Enter names at prompt, parents first.\n"
          " Surnames may be omitted if same as first." );

    for (k = 0; k < mem; ++k) {        /* Read & install new names. */
        printf( " > " );
        scanf( " %79[^\n]", buf );

        len = strlen( buf );           /* Measure name. */
        new[k] = malloc( len + 1 );    /* Allocate space. */
        strcpy( new[k], buf );         /* Copy name into space. */

    }
}
/* -------------------------------------------------------------------- */
void print_family( family_t f )
{
    int k;              /* subscript variable for loop */

    printf( "\n This family has %i members:\n", f.n );
    for (k = 0; k < f.n; ++k)   printf( "\t%s\n", f.name[k] );
}
```

Figure 19.4.   Building a ragged array.

```
        Enter names at prompt, parents first.
        Surnames may be omitted if same as the first.
        > Joseph M. Cotton
        > Alexandria S. Wisnewski-Cotton
        > Tara A. Wisnewski
        > Andrew K.
        > Mary M.

        This family has 5 members:
                Joseph M. Cotton
                Alexandria S. Wisnewski-Cotton
                Tara A. Wisnewski
                Andrew K.
                Mary M.
```

This data structure is built by the function in Figure 19.4 for the sample data shown in the text.

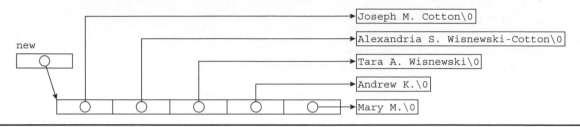

Figure 19.5.   A dynamic ragged array.

Notes on Figure 19.4. Building a ragged array.

- *First box: the header.* The parameters are **new**, an array of string pointers, and **mem**, the number of slots in that array. The task of the function is to read **mem** names, allocate space for them, copy the names into that space, and store the allocation pointers in the slots of the array **new**.
- *Second box: building the ragged array.*

  1. The program executes this loop once for each family member, installing **mem** new names in the data structure.
  2. Within the loop body, the program prompts for and reads a name into a local buffer. The brackets specifier and length are used in the format to ensure that all parts of the name are read safely.
  3. The three lines of the inner box create the rags. This is a paradigm that should be mastered. We want to allocate enough space to hold the name, so we use **strlen()** to measure its length. The result does not include space for the null terminator, so we add one to it and allocate this number of bytes of memory. The result of the allocation is a pointer, which we store in the current slot of our string array. Finally, we copy the input data from the buffer into the newly allocated space. There is no need to worry about overrunning the destination array because we have allocated exactly the right amount of storage. The resulting data structure generated for the sample run is diagrammed in Figure 19.5.

- *The* **print_family()** *function.* The information in the family array is extracted for printing by specifying the member name of the structure followed by the index of a specific person in the family.

19.2   Using Dynamic Arrays: A Simulation

A pointer to an array can be used with a subscript, just like the array itself. The difference between a pointer to an array and the name of an array is that the latter refers to a particular area of storage, while the former acts like a pronoun that can refer to any array. The technique we use in the next example, a simulation, involves two pointers, `old` and `new`, that switch back and forth between pointing at two arrays, first referring to one, then to the other. This lets us represent an indefinite series of arrays, where the array values in `new` at each time step are derived from the ones in `old`. There is no need to allocate a long series of separate arrays or constantly move the data values from one array to another; we just **swap array pointers** (or the addresses in them).

19.2.1   Transient Heat Conduction in a Semi-Infinite Slab

Problems that involve changes over time in a property of a solid or fluid often can be solved by analytical techniques when the geometry, boundary conditions, and material properties are simple. This is the preferred method, because a valid result can be determined at any continuous point inside the material at any time. However, when an analytical solution is not possible, numerical techniques can give an approximate solution at discrete points inside the material at specific times.

Transient heat conduction in a solid slab forms a class of problems suitable for **numerical approximation.** A slab, as shown in Figure 19.6, is divided by imaginary boundaries into equal-sized regions called *cells*. For each cell, the temperature is determined at a discrete point called its *node*. An energy equation

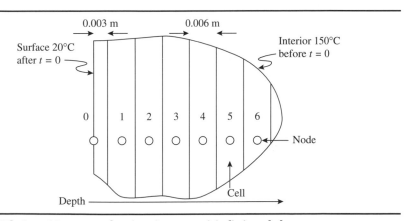

Figure 19.6.   Heat conduction in a semi-infinite slab.

is used to derive a formula for the temperature at the cell's node, for each cell at each time step, in terms of the temperature at each of the surrounding nodes on the previous time step. This **finite-difference equation** (a form of the heat conduction equation) for each cell can be modeled by a computer program.

For the specific example in Figure 19.6, the slab's initial uniform temperature is 150°C. It has a thermal diffusivity of $6 \cdot 10^{-7}$ m²/s. Suddenly, at time $t = 0$, it is exposed to a cooling liquid so that the surface is instantly cooled to 20°C, where it remains throughout the process.

We want to determine the temperature at various depths below the surface of the slab as time passes. As mentioned, this process can be represented by a partial differential equation. The numerical approach to solving it assumes that the slab can be split into cells and that each cell has the same uniform temperature throughout as at its node, which is at the midpoint of the cell. The nodes are labeled 0, 1, 2, 3, ... beginning at the surface and are spaced 0.006 meter apart. The set of finite-difference equations used to compute the temperature T at nodes 1, 2, 3 ... is

$$T_m^{t+1} = \frac{1}{2} \left(T_{m-1}^t + T_{m+1}^t \right) \qquad \text{for } m = 1, 2, 3, \ldots \quad \text{and} \quad t = 0, 1, 2, 3, \ldots$$

where m denotes the node and t is the number of elapsed time steps, each corresponding to a 30-second interval. That is, $t = 0$ at time 0, $t = 1$ after 30 seconds, $t = 2$ after 60 seconds, and so on.

At time 0 in the example, the cooling source at 20°C is applied at the edge of the slab, which initially is at a uniform temperature of 150°C. Therefore, the temperatures of the first four nodes at time 0 become $T_0^0 = 20$, $T_1^0 = 150$, $T_2^0 = 150$, $T_3^0 = 150$. At the next time step (30 seconds later), $t = 1$ and we can compute the nodal temperatures as

$$T_0^1 = 20$$

$$T_1^1 = \frac{1}{2} \left(T_0^0 + T_2^0 \right) = \frac{1}{2} (20 + 150) = 85 \qquad \text{at a depth of 0.006 m}$$

$$T_2^1 = \frac{1}{2} \left(T_1^0 + T_3^0 \right) = \frac{1}{2} (150 + 150) = 150 \qquad \text{at a depth of 0.012 m}$$

$$T_3^1 = \frac{1}{2} \left(T_2^0 + T_4^0 \right) = \frac{1}{2} (150 + 150) = 150 \qquad \text{at a depth of 0.018 m}$$

As time passes, the cooling effect penetrates deeper into the slab. The next time step corresponds to 60 seconds; at that time, the nodal temperatures are

$$T_0^2 = 20$$

$$T_1^2 = \frac{1}{2} \left(T_0^1 + T_2^1 \right) = \frac{1}{2} (20 + 150) = 85$$

$$T_2^2 = \frac{1}{2}\left(T_1^1 + T_3^1\right) = \frac{1}{2}\left(85 + 150\right) = 117.5$$

$$T_3^2 = \frac{1}{2}\left(T_2^1 + T_4^1\right) = \frac{1}{2}\left(150 + 150\right) = 150$$

After 90 seconds, node 3 will begin to cool. Eventually, if the cooling source remains constant, the cooling effect will reach the end of the slab, and the entire slab will begin to approach a steady-state temperature of 20°C.

19.2.2 Simulating the Cooling Process

A call chart for this application is shown in Figure 19.7. The main program is given in Figure 19.8 and the remaining functions are defined in Figures 19.9, 19.10, and 19.11.

Notes on Figures 19.8 and 19.9. A heat flow simulation.

- *First box of Figure 19.8: the variables.*

    1. The first four variables are used to hold the simulation parameters entered by the user.
    2. All parts of the simulation depend on the depth at which the temperature is to be monitored. We use this depth to calculate **slot**, the number of the node at the desired depth, which then controls memory allocation and looping.
    3. The **sim_cool()** function will simulate the heat flow process at successive time steps as the slab cools. It will stop when the selected node reaches a specified temperature. We also declare variables for the two items that **sim_cool()** returns to **main()**: a pointer to the array of nodal temperatures at the end of the simulation and the number of simulation steps required for the selected node to reach the goal

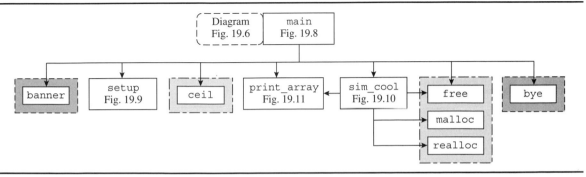

Figure 19.7.   A call chart for the heat flow simulation.

This code calls the functions from Figures 19.9, 19.10, and 19.11.

```c
#include "tools.h"
#define MAX_STEPS 1000
#define DEPTH_LIMIT .25

void setup( double* p_deep, double* p_init, double* p_last, double* p_surf );
double* sim_cool( int slot, double initial,
                  double goal, double surf, int* actual );
void print_array( double nodes[], int last );

void main( void )
{
    double init_temp, last_temp; /* Beginning and ending temperatures. */
    double surf;                 /* Temperature at surface of slab. */
    double depth;                /* Depth at which to monitor temperature. */
    int slot;                    /* Array slot at given depth. */

    int steps, seconds;          /* Simulation steps, time to reach goal. */
    double* nodes;               /* Array that holds final temperatures. */

    banner();
    puts( "\nSimulation of Heat Conduction in a Slab\n" );

    setup( &depth, &init_temp, &last_temp, &surf );
    slot = ceil( (depth - .003) / .006 );

    printf( "\nGoal temperature = %g at node %i\n\n", last_temp, slot );

    nodes = sim_cool( slot, init_temp, last_temp, surf, &steps );

    seconds = 30 * steps;
    printf( "\nTemperature of %g reached at node %i \n"
            "\tin %i seconds (= %.1f minutes or %.2f hours).\n",
            nodes[slot], slot, seconds, seconds/60.0, seconds/3600.0 );
    printf( "\nFinal nodal temperatures after %i steps: \n", steps );
    print_array( nodes, steps );

    free( nodes );
    bye();
}
```

Figure 19.8.   A heat flow simulation.

temperature. The actual time required to reach that goal is computed from the number of simulation steps.

- *Second box of Figure 19.8 and Figure 19.9: reading the parameters.*

  1. We call the **setup()** function in Figure 19.9 to prompt the user for the parameters of the simulation. Sometimes a main program handles all user interaction. In this program, however, several parameters are

This function is called from Figure 19.8 to read the simulation parameters from the user.

```
void
setup( double* p_deep, double* p_init, double* p_last, double* p_surf )
{
    double deep;                    /* Local variable for depth (input) */

    do {
        printf( "Enter depth to monitor (up to %g meters): ", DEPTH_LIMIT );
        scanf( "%lg", &deep );
    } while (deep < 0 || deep > DEPTH_LIMIT);
    *p_deep = deep;

    printf( "Enter initial temperature of the slab: " );
    scanf( "%lg", p_init );

    printf( "Enter target temperature for depth %g: ", *p_deep );
    scanf( "%lg", p_last );

    printf( "Enter temperature of cold outer surface: " );
    scanf( "%lg", p_surf );
}
```

Figure 19.9.   Parameters for the simulation.

    needed to initialize the simulation and one of them requires validation, so it makes sense to move all the input details out of the main program into a function. One address argument is needed for each parameter.

2. In the first box of **setup()**, Figure 19.9, the program prompts for, reads, and validates the depth at which to monitor the temperature. When **setup()** returns the depth, **main()** uses it to compute the node number (**slot**) to monitor. This will determine the amount of storage allocated, when to terminate the simulation, and how much output to print after each time step. If the depth value is large, the arrays used by the simulation will take up a lot of space, and each iteration will take more computation. The number of iterations needed to reach the goal temperature also will be very high and may exceed the predefined iteration limit, **MAX_STEPS**. If this happens, the simulation will be halted prior to reaching the goal. Therefore, as a practical matter, we limit the observation depth to 0.25 m and **#define** this constant (**DEPTH_LIMIT**) at the top of the program. Obviously, negative values are rejected. A local variable is used during this process because it is clearer and more efficient than making several references through the address parameter. When the user succeeds in entering a valid depth value, it is stored in **main()**'s variable.

3. In the second box of **setup()**, Figure 19.9, we prompt for and read the other parameters without validity checking. If the parameters are ridiculous or impossible, the simulation will be meaningless but

proceed and terminate normally. Remember that the address-of (`&`) and dereference (`*`) operators cancel each other in the `scanf()` calls.

4. An example of output produced by the setup portion of the program is

```
Simulation of Heat Conduction in a Slab

Enter depth to monitor (up to 0.25 meters): .055
Enter initial temperature of the slab: 100
Enter target temperature for depth 0.055: 85
Enter temperature of cold outer surface: 0

Goal temperature = 85 at node 9
```

5. On returning to the main program, the monitoring depth entered is used to calculate `slot`, the index of the node at the desired depth. The `ceil()` function (from the `math` library) returns the integer that is just larger than or equal to the floating-point argument. The value of `slot` is used throughout the remaining program to control allocation and looping.

*   *Third, fourth, and fifth boxes of Figure 19.8: doing the work.* We call functions to do the simulation, `sim_cool()`, and print the results, `print_array()`. The operation of these functions is discussed in the notes following each routine. When the simulation is done, the dynamically allocated memory no longer is needed and we call `free()` to recycle it.

Notes on Figure 19.10. Doing the heat flow simulation.   This simulation is an iterative process that will continue either for a specified number of steps (`MAX_STEPS`) or until the selected node (`slot`) reaches the goal temperature (`goal`). On each iteration, the new temperature at each node is computed, based on the temperatures of its neighboring nodes during the preceding time step. The array containing the final set of temperatures is sent back through the `return` statement via a pointer. The other function result, the number of iterations required to complete the simulation, is returned through a pointer parameter.

*   *First box: allocation and initialization.*

1. We use a finite array to model the temperatures in a semi-infinite slab. In each time step, the cooling process progresses one more slot toward the end of the array. Therefore, eventually, the number of slots in the array must be as great as the number of iteration steps needed to reach the final temperature goal. This is very difficult to predict without doing the simulation first, so we make an initial guess (three times the monitoring depth) about the number of slots needed and use `realloc()` later to extend the array if we guess too few. By this method, we can imitate a semi-infinite object until either the available time or memory runs out.

This function is called by the main program in Figure 19.8 to perform the steps of the simulation.

```
double*                    /* Pointer to array of nodes holding answers. */
sim_cool( int slot,        /* Number of node being monitored. */
          double initial,  /* Initial temperature of infinite slab. */
          double goal,     /* Stop when chosen slot <= goal temp. */
          double surf,     /* Temperature of the cold outer surface. */
          int* actual )    /* Actual number of iterations carried out. */
{
    int n = 3 * slot;      /* Current allocation length. */
    int p;                 /* Counter for time steps. */
    int k;                 /* Index for node array. */
    double* swap;          /* To swap old and new arrays. */

    double* old = (double*) malloc( n * sizeof(double) );
    double* new = (double*) malloc( n * sizeof(double) );

    new[0] = old[0] = surf;
    for (k = 1; k < n; ++k) new[k] = old[k] = initial;

    for (p = 1; p <= MAX_STEPS; ++p) {

        if (p == n - 1) {    /* If no neighbor exists on right, make one. */
            n *= 2;
            new = realloc( new, n * sizeof(double) );
            old = realloc( old, n * sizeof(double) );
            for (k = p + 1; k < n; ++k) new[k] = old[k] = initial;
        }

        for (k = 1; k <= p; ++k)    new[k] = (old[k-1] + old[k+1]) / 2.0;

        printf( "%3i. ", p );
        print_array( new, slot );

        if (new[slot] <= goal) break;

        swap = old; old = new; new = swap;

    }

    *actual = p;           /* Return the number of iterations executed. */
    free( old );
    return new;            /* This array holds results when goal is reached. */
}
```

Figure 19.10.   Iteration for the heat flow simulation, sim_cool().

2. We use two arrays in this simulation, representing the temperatures of the nodes on two successive time steps. We create these arrays using `malloc()` so that the array length can grow, if necessary, and so we can use a swapping technique with the array pointers (described later).

3. The array `new`, containing the final node temperatures, is passed back to `main()`. To begin the simulation the program initializes both arrays to the starting temperature of the slab (`initial`). Slot 0 in each array, which represents the surface, is set to `surf`, the temperature of the cooling source.

- *Second, third, and fourth boxes: the iteration loop.* The technique we use here involves two pointers, `old` and `new`, which point at dynamically allocated arrays. At any given time, `old` points at the array of node temperatures from the prior time step while `new` points at the array that is being calculated for the current time step.

  1. *Second box: Growing.* We can't compute the temperature of the last node in the array by averaging its two neighbors, because it has no right neighbor. We solve this problem using reallocation. On each time step, the cooling wave progresses one slot closer to the end. When the time step equals the subscript of the last slot in the array, the cooling wave has reached the end. We then must increase the size of both arrays and initialize the new portions to the starting slab temperature. The amount by which we should increase the array size is a difficult question to answer. If we reallocate too frequently, the potential cost of repeatedly copying the contents of the entire array becomes too great. But, if we increase by too much at one time, we allocate and initialize memory that may not be needed. If we were not concerned with time or space overhead, we could allocate a huge array at the start. By doubling the length of the array on each reallocation, we make a reasonable and simple compromise between copying data too often and wasting too much memory.

  2. *Third box: Calculating values for the next time step.* For all nodes except the first, the temperature at the current time step is the average of its two neighbors at the prior time step. Each time around the loop, two temperatures from the `old` array are used to compute one temperature in the `new` array for the current time step. The growing process, in the preceding box, ensures that this formula is valid, even for the last node. The temperature at node 0 remains constant due to the cooling source.

  3. *Fourth box: Swapping.* Two arrays are required at each time step. At the beginning of each time step, `old` points at data that will be used to compute the node values in the current step and `new` points at an array in which to store them (its current contents are not used and do not matter). At the end of each time step, `new` points at the newly

computed values and **old** points at data that are no longer needed. For the next time step, the current values must become the old values and room must be made for newer values. This problem is solved, in the fourth box, simply by swapping the referents of the two pointers, making them ready for the next iteration. So, **old** and **new** switch back and forth between the two arrays, first referring to one of the arrays, then to the other. No additional memory is needed.

- *Sample output.* The values in the **new** array from node 0 to the node being monitored are displayed after each time step, so that the user can observe the progress of the algorithm. The results of the first two time steps, given the input parameters shown earlier, look like this:

```
1.  [ 0] =    0.00  [ 1] =   50.00  [ 2] =  100.00  [ 3] =  100.00  [ 4] =  100.00
    [ 5] =  100.00  [ 6] =  100.00  [ 7] =  100.00  [ 8] =  100.00  [ 9] =  100.00


2.  [ 0] =    0.00  [ 1] =   50.00  [ 2] =   75.00  [ 3] =  100.00  [ 4] =  100.00
    [ 5] =  100.00  [ 6] =  100.00  [ 7] =  100.00  [ 8] =  100.00  [ 9] =  100.00
```

The iterations continue until the goal temperature is reached or the maximum number of steps is exceeded. If the goal is attained, the program breaks out of the loop and returns the number of iterations used and the array that contains the final temperature values. The printed results of the last two steps look like this:

```
38. [ 0] =    0.00  [ 1] =   12.86  [ 2] =   25.07  [ 3] =   37.29  [ 4] =   47.76
    [ 5] =   58.23  [ 6] =   66.32  [ 7] =   74.41  [ 8] =   80.04  [ 9] =   85.67


39. [ 0] =    0.00  [ 1] =   12.54  [ 2] =   25.07  [ 3] =   36.42  [ 4] =   47.76
    [ 5] =   57.04  [ 6] =   66.32  [ 7] =   73.18  [ 8] =   80.04  [ 9] =   84.61
```

- *Fifth box: returning the answers and cleaning up.*

  1. The number of iterations is returned through **actual**, an address parameter, which refers to the variable **steps** in **main()**. Therefore, writing ***actual = p** copies the value of **p** into **steps**.
  2. The programing is done using the **old** array so it is freed. The program should not free the **new** array yet, because it will be used to carry the results back to **main()**.
  3. The **return** statement sends the starting address of the **new** array back to **main()**, which stores it in the variable **nodes**. Afterwards, **nodes** can be used with a subscript to access the final temperatures of each node.

This function is called from **main()** in Figure 19.8 and from **sim_cool()** in Figure 19.10.

```
void
print_array( double nodes[], int last )
{
    int k;
    for (k = 0; k <= last; ++k) {
        printf( "[%2i] = %6.2f  ", k, nodes[k] );
        if (k % 5 == 4) printf( "\n     " );  /* Newline after five items. */
    }
    printf( "\n\n" );
}
```

Figure 19.11.   Print function for the heat flow simulation.

Notes on Figures 19.8 and 19.11. Print function for the heat flow simulation.

- Since we print values from two different arrays at different times and we print the entire array sometimes but only part of it at others, the array itself and the subscript of the last node to print must be the parameters to this function.
- If we printed the temperatures one per line, it would consume too many lines. On the other hand, all the parameters won't fit on one line, so we use modular arithmetic to print five values per line in formatted fields. If the array subscript mod 5 equals 4, we know that we have printed five values on this line, so we print a newline character and enough spaces to indent the beginning of the next line. For proper spacing between steps of the simulation we also need some newlines at the end of the entire table.
- *Fourth box of Figure 19.8: the final output.* When the simulation ends, we print out the number of steps used to cool the slab to the desired temperature, as well as the time this took. Then we call **print_array()** to show the final values in all of the slots used in the temperature array. These, too, are printed five per line. The nodes with temperatures shown here as 100.00 actually are slightly cooler; 100.00 is simply the rounded value of temperatures above 99.995. The final output is

```
Temperature of 84.614 reached at node 9
        in 1170 seconds (= 19.5 minutes or 0.33 hours).

Final nodal temperatures after 39 steps:
    [ 0] =    0.00  [ 1] =   12.54  [ 2] =   25.07  [ 3] =   36.42  [ 4] =   47.76
    [ 5] =   57.04  [ 6] =   66.32  [ 7] =   73.18  [ 8] =   80.04  [ 9] =   84.61
    [10] =   89.19  [11] =   91.93  [12] =   94.67  [13] =   96.15  [14] =   97.63
    [15] =   98.34  [16] =   99.05  [17] =   99.36  [18] =   99.66  [19] =   99.78
    [20] =   99.89  [21] =   99.93  [22] =   99.97  [23] =   99.98  [24] =   99.99
    [25] = 100.00  [26] = 100.00  [27] = 100.00  [28] = 100.00  [29] = 100.00
    [30] = 100.00  [31] = 100.00  [32] = 100.00  [33] = 100.00  [34] = 100.00
    [35] = 100.00  [36] = 100.00  [37] = 100.00  [38] = 100.00  [39] = 100.00
```

19.3   Dynamic Matrix: An Array of Pointers (Advanced Topic)

Dynamic allocation of memory is not limited to one-dimensional arrays. Since 2D arrays are stored in contiguous memory, they also can be allocated as a single large area, a **dynamic 2D array**. However, accessing a particular element using the normal, two-subscript notation is not possible. (A function to perform this operation is considered in an exercise on image processing.) Alternatively, a 2D object can be represented as an array of pointers to arrays, using `malloc()` repeatedly to allocate each part of the structure. The result is a **dynamic matrix** data structure in which the rows can be efficiently manipulated and swapped, as illustrated next. Elements of this matrix can be accessed using the matrix name and two subscripts, as if the entire matrix were allocated contiguously. This data structure is ideal for certain mathematical applications, as demonstrated in the next example.

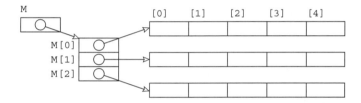

19.3.1   Application: Gaussian Elimination

Gaussian elimination is an algorithm for solving a system of m linear equations in m unknowns, as shown next. The goal is to find values for the variables $a, b, \ldots, m$ that simultaneously satisfy all the equations

$$c_{1,1}a + c_{1,2}b + \cdots + c_{1,m}m = X_1$$
$$c_{2,1}a + c_{2,2}b + \cdots + c_{2,m}m = X_2$$
$$\vdots$$
$$c_{m,1}a + c_{m,2}b + \cdots + c_{m,m}m = X_m$$

We can use an M by $M+1$ matrix to contain the coefficients of the variables in the M equations, one row for each equation, one column for each unknown, and a final column for the constant term. To find the set of variable values that satisfy the system, we apply to the coefficient matrix a series of arithmetic operations that are valid for systems of equations. These operations include

- *Scaling.* Both sides of an equation may be divided or multiplied by the same number. That is, if we divide or multiply all of the coefficients and the constant term of an equation by a single number, the meaning of the equation remains unchanged.

- *Subtraction.* We can subtract one equation E_1 in the system from another, E_2, and replace E_2 by the result, without changing the constraints on the variable values that satisfy the system.
- *Swapping.* Since the order of the equations in the matrix is arbitrary, we can exchange the positions of any two equations without changing the system. (But we cannot swap two columns because each column position is associated with a particular variable.)

An algorithm that uses these operations, Gaussian elimination, can be used to compute the variable values that solve the **system of equations**.

We implement this algorithm by writing a function to perform each of the preceding operations, and a function, `solve()`, that uses them appropriately. The algorithm solves the system of equations in stages. At stage k, we select one equation, place it on line k of the matrix, then scale it by dividing all of the row's entries by its own kth coefficient. This process leaves a value of 1 in the kth column of the kth row of the matrix. The new kth equation then is used by the scaling and subtraction functions to reset the kth coefficient of every other equation to 0 while simultaneously adjusting the other coefficients. After M such elimination steps, the matrix (except for the last column) has a single element with the value 1 in each row and in each column. This corresponds to a set of equations of the following form, in which the last column of the matrix contains the solution to the system of equations:

$$1 \cdot a = X'_1$$
$$1 \cdot b = X'_2$$
$$\cdots$$
$$1 \cdot m = X'_m$$

19.3.2   An Implementation of Gauss's Algorithm

The call chart in Figure 19.12 shows the structure of the Gaussian elimination program; the main program is in Figure 19.13 and functions are in Figures 19.14 through 19.20. To solve a particular system of equations using this code, the user must first create a data file, **gauss.in**, that contains the data. The number of equations must be on the first line. Following that must be the coefficients of the equations, one equation per line. The constant term of each equation is the last entry on a line. The file we use in the example looks like this:

```
4
1     2     2     1     10
3    -1     0     5     -4
2     2     3     0     15
0    .5    -1     7     -9
```

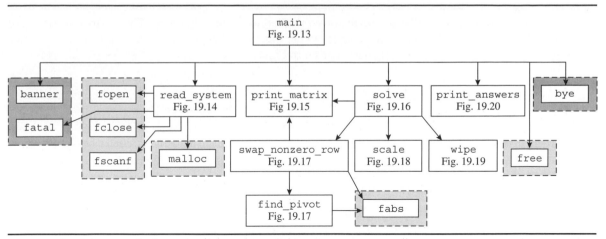

Figure 19.12.   A call chart for Gaussian elimination.

Notes on Figure 19.13. Solving a system of linear equations.

- *First box: the constant.* We need a comparison tolerance in certain portions of the algorithm to test whether coefficients equal (or nearly equal) zero. The **find_pivot()** function uses this constant to identify which equations have a nonzero coefficient in the current column. The tolerance is needed to avoid floating-point overflow caused by division by 0 or a nearly 0 value. The constant **EPS** is defined here, rather than in the function that uses it, to make it easy to find and change if the user requires more or less precision.

- *Second box: the type definitions.*

  1. The algorithm is based on matrix row operations; that is, operations on entire equations. Although we *could* use a two-dimensional array to hold the coefficients, this data structure does not reflect the nature of the problem well: The program really is working with an array of equations, not a two-dimensional array of numbers.
  2. We also wish to use dynamic allocation so we can solve a system of equations with any reasonable number of unknowns.
  3. For these two reasons, we define the type **equation** as an array of **double** coefficients and type **linear_system** as an array of equations. For the data file given earlier, the data structure eventually will look like this:

We show how to use Gaussian elimination to solve m equations in m unknowns. This figure contains type definitions, prototypes, declarations, and `main()`. Other functions that are part of the application are shown in Figures 19.14 through 19.20. A call chart is given in Figure 19.12.

```
#include "tools.h"

#define EPS   .0001                    /* Comparison tolerance for zero test. */


/* --------------------------------------------------------------- Types */

typedef double* equation;
typedef equation* linear_system;


/* ---------------------------------------------------- Prototypes */
linear_system read_system( int* unknowns );
void print_matrix( linear_system mat, int unknowns );
bool solve( linear_system mat, int unknowns );
bool swap_nonzero_row( linear_system mat, int unknowns, int k );
int  find_pivot( linear_system mat, int unknowns, int k );
void scale( equation eqn, int unknowns, int k );
void wipe( linear_system mat, int unknowns, int piv_row, int row );
void print_answers( linear_system mat, int unknowns );
/* ------------------------------------------------------------------ */
void main( void )
{
    int m;                          /* Number of equations. */
    linear_system matrix;           /* Array of equation pointers. */
    bool solvable;

    banner();
    puts( " Linear Equations to Solve:" );
    matrix = read_system( &m );

    print_matrix( matrix, m );
    solvable = solve( matrix, m );

    puts( " Equations after Elimination:" );
    print_matrix( matrix, m );
    if (!solvable) puts( " Equations inconsistent or not independent." );
    else print_answers( matrix, m );
    free( matrix );
    bye();
}
```

Figure 19.13.   Solving a system of linear equations.

```
matrix
 ┌─────┐              [0]    [1]    [2]    [3]    [4]
 │  O  │            ┌──────┬──────┬──────┬──────┬──────┐
 └─────┘            │ 1.0  │ 2.0  │ 2.0  │ 1.0  │ 10.0 │
                    └──────┴──────┴──────┴──────┴──────┘
matrix[0]  ┌───O─┐  ┌──────┬──────┬──────┬──────┬──────┐
matrix[1]  │   O─┤  │ 3.0  │ -1.0 │ 0.0  │ 5.0  │ -4.0 │
matrix[2]  │   O─┤  └──────┴──────┴──────┴──────┴──────┘
matrix[3]  │   O─┘  ┌──────┬──────┬──────┬──────┬──────┐
                    │ 2.0  │ 2.0  │ 3.0  │ 0.0  │ 15.0 │
                    └──────┴──────┴──────┴──────┴──────┘
                    ┌──────┬──────┬──────┬──────┬──────┐
                    │ 0.0  │ 0.5  │ -1.0 │ 7.0  │ -9.0 │
                    └──────┴──────┴──────┴──────┴──────┘
```

The **matrix** array and the four equation arrays are created by five separate calls to **malloc()** during the input process in the function **read_system()**.

- *The prototypes and* **main()**.
  This main program reads like an outline of the entire process. It first prints a heading, then calls functions to do each phase of the job: input the coefficients, manipulate the matrix using the Gaussian elimination algorithm, and print out the final solution. This is the right way to build a program: keep **main()** simple. The other functions, listed in the prototype section, do all the work. Each has been given a descriptive name to improve the readability of **main()**.

Notes on Figure 19.14. Reading the equations.

- *First box: the input stream.* The program opens and closes the data stream within this function because this is the only function that deals with input. It reads the equation coefficients from the file **gauss.in** in the current directory. Throughout this application, we are careful to do responsible error detection and print appropriate error comments. The first thing that must be read from the file is the number of equations in this linear system.
- *Second box: setting up the data structure.* We allocate storage for a **linear_system** object, **mat**, with one slot for each equation in the system. At this stage, this object is only an array of uninitialized equation pointers.
- *Third box: the main read loop.*

  1. The number of equations was read from the first line of the data file. This loop reads the data for the equations, one per line.
  2. *First inner box: allocate equation.* Each time around this loop, the program allocates space for one equation and stores the pointer returned by **malloc()** in the current slot of **mat**.
  3. *Second inner box:* **read_data()**. Using **current**, the program reads the data for one equation into the equation array (one coefficient for each unknown and one constant term). Again, we take care to detect and comment on any read errors.

This function allocates one array to represent the equation matrix and separate arrays for the coefficients of each equation. The coefficients of the equations are read from the input file into these arrays. This function is called from **main()** in Figure 19.13.

```
linear_system
read_system( int* unknowns )
{
    stream eq_in;
    linear_system mat;    /* Matrix is allocated and initialized here. */
    equation current;     /* Row currently receiving input. */
    int ok;               /* Return code from fscanf(). */
    int col, k;           /* Loop counters. */
    int m;                /* Number of unknowns. */

    /* Open input file and read number of equations. ------------------- */
    eq_in = fopen( "gauss.in", "r" );
    if (eq_in == NULL) fatal( " Cannot open gauss.in" );
    fscanf( eq_in, "%i", &m );

    /* Allocate equation array. ---------------------------------------- */
    mat = (linear_system) malloc( m * sizeof(equation) );
    if (mat == NULL) fatal( " Cannot allocate enough memory." );

    /* Read in all the equations. -------------------------------------- */
    for (k = 0; k < m; ++k) {

        /* Allocate space for equation. ------------------------------ */
        current = (equation) malloc( (m+1) * sizeof(double) );
        if (current == NULL) fatal( " Cannot allocate enough memory." );
        mat[k] = current;                     /* Attach array to matrix. */

        for (col = 0; col <= m; ++col) {      /* Read one equation. */
            ok = fscanf( eq_in, "%lg", &current[col] );
            if (ok < 1) fatal( " Read error or unexpected eof." );
        }

    }

    fclose( eq_in );      /* Done with input; close stream. */
    *unknowns = m;        /* Return number of equations. */
    return mat;           /* Return matrix. */
}
```

Figure 19.14.   Reading the equations.

4. Since the name of an array is translated as a pointer to the beginning of the array, using a pointer is no different from using the array name. Therefore, the program can use `current` with a subscript, just as if it were an array. This technique is used throughout the application.

5. Alternatively, the pointer could be stepped down the array as the loop progresses and used with the dereference operator instead of a subscript to access the loop elements. This technique is explained in Chapter 20.

- *The return values.* The program returns two things to `main()`: the matrix that has been constructed and the number of equations in the matrix, which was read from the file. An address parameter is used to return the integer, while the `return` statement handles the matrix.

Notes on Figure 19.15. Print the equations.   This function was very useful during the process of debugging the application. Extra calls that are not in the final code were inserted to print the matrix contents after each stage of the calculation. This made it possible to monitor the progress of the computation and spot the many errors originally in the code. The extra calls on `print_matrix()` were commented out after the code was debugged. In the finished program, it is called only twice from `main()`, before and after solving the equations.

- *First box: the outer loop.* The outer loop prints all the equations; the inner loop prints the coefficients of one equation. Each equation is placed on a separate line; we assume here that an equation will fit on one line. More thought would be necessary to decide how to display longer equations. Starting with our example data set, the output from the first call in `main()` looks like this:

```
Linear Equations to Solve:
-------------------------------------------------------------
   1.000 * a +     2.000 * b +     2.000 * c +     1.000 * d =    10.000
   3.000 * a +    -1.000 * b +     0.000 * c +     5.000 * d =    -4.000
   2.000 * a +     2.000 * b +     3.000 * c +     0.000 * d =    15.000
   0.000 * a +     0.500 * b +    -1.000 * c +     7.000 * d =    -9.000
-------------------------------------------------------------
```

- *Second box: the inner loop.*

1. Two "tricks" are used in the inner loop to format the output in a readable manner. To generate the names of the unknowns ($a, b, c, \ldots$) we "add" the column subscript to the letter `'a'` (of course, we really add the subscript to the integer ASCII code for `'a'`). When we print the result with a `%c` format specifier, we see the letters of the alphabet, in order.

2. We also want a `+` printed between every pair of terms except the last. For that one, we want an `=`. To achieve this, we use a character variable, `op`, which we initialize to `+` each time through the outer loop and change to `=` before printing the last term.

This function formats and prints the matrix as a system of equations. This code is part of the application that begins in Figure 19.13.

```
void
print_matrix( linear_system mat, int unknowns )
{
    int col, row;
    char op;               /* Char to print between terms in output equation. */
    equation current;      /* Pointer to new allocation. */

    printf( "-------------------------------------------------------------\n" );

    for (row = 0; row < unknowns; ++row) {   /* Print all equations. */
        current = mat[row];                      /* Next equation pointer. */
        op = '+';

        for (col = 0; col < unknowns; ++col) {
            if (col == unknowns - 1) op = '=';
            printf( "%8.3f * %c %c ", current[col], 'a' + col, op );
        }

        printf( "%8.3f\n", current[unknowns] );
    }

    printf( "-------------------------------------------------------------\n" );
}
```

Figure 19.15.   Print the equations.

3. Currently, when a term is negative, the program prints both a + and a
   - sign in front of it. For even fancier output, we could test the sign of
   each coefficient and print either a + sign or a - sign, but not both.

Notes on Figure 19.16. Gaussian elimination.   The main loop of
this function is executed once for each equation in the system. Its purpose is
to manipulate the matrix so that, eventually, it has ones on the main diagonal
(elements with the same row and column subscripts) and zeros elsewhere. To do
this it calls three functions (in the three boxes). We give a brief overview of the
calls here, then discuss each function individually.

- *First box and Figure 19.17: the pivot equation.*

  1. The first task is to select an equation, called the *pivot equation*, for the
     next phase of the process. On pass k, we look at all of the equations in
     rows k and greater. We select the equation with the largest coefficient
     in the kth column because this maximizes computational accuracy.
  2. The `swap_nonzero_row()` function calls `find_pivot()` to do this
     job, then swaps the chosen pivot equation with the one in the kth row
     of the matrix.

This function is called from **main()** in Figure 19.13. It performs the Gaussian elimination algorithm. It uses row operations to reduce the first *m* columns of the *m* by *m* + 1 matrix to an identity matrix, if possible. At that point, the last column contains the solution to the system of equations.

```
bool
solve( linear_system mat, int unknowns )
{
    int row, k;
    bool solvable;
    for (k = 0; k < unknowns; ++k) {

        solvable = swap_nonzero_row( mat, unknowns, k );
        if (!solvable) break;        /* Do all rows have 0 in column k? */

        scale( mat[k], unknowns, k );      /* Make a 1 in mat[k][k]. */
        /* print_matrix( mat, unknowns ); For debugging.   */

        /* Use the 1 in mat[k][k] to zero out the rest of column k. */
        for (row = 0; row < unknowns; ++row)
            if (k != row) wipe( mat, unknowns, k, row );

    }
    return solvable;
}
```

Figure 19.16.   Gaussian elimination.

3. **swap_nonzero_row()** returns **false** if all of the coefficients in column *k* of the remaining equations are zero or within the **EPS** tolerance of zero. This occurs when the system of equations has no solution, either because it contains inconsistent formulas, or because one of the equations is a linear combination of some of the others. If this occurs, we abort the process and return an error code to **main()**.

   If one of the equations is a linear combination of some of the others, there are not enough constraints to determine a unique solution. If the equations are inconsistent, there are too many constraints and they cannot be simultaneously satisfied. A system of inconsistent equations will be shown at the end of this section.

• *Second box and Figure 19.18: prepare the pivot row.* Once the pivot equation is in row *k*, the next step is to manipulate the equation into a form with a 1 in column *k*. To do this, we call **scale()** to divide the coefficients by the value in column *k*. During debugging, a call to **print_matrix()** was used to monitor the progress of the algorithm during each pass through the outer loop.

The `swap_nonzero_row()` function is called from `solve()` in Figure 19.16, which is called from `main()` in Figure 19.13. In turn, it calls `find_pivot()`.

```
bool
swap_nonzero_row( linear_system mat, int unknowns, int k )
{
    equation swap;          /* Used to interchange rows. */

    int row = find_pivot( mat, unknowns, k );

    /* Coefficient k of pivot equation must be nonzero. ---------------- */

    if (fabs( mat[row][k] ) < EPS) return false;

    if (row != k) { swap = mat[row]; mat[row] = mat[k]; mat[k] = swap; }

    /* print_matrix( mat, unknowns ); For debugging.  */
    return true;
}
/* ------------------------------------------------------------------- */

int                     /* Find equation with largest coefficient in column k. */
find_pivot( linear_system mat, int unknowns, int k )
{
    double coefficient = mat[k][k];        /* Largest value found so far. */
    int big = k;                           /* Index of current coefficient. */
    int row;                               /* Index for search loop. */

    for (row = k + 1; row < unknowns; ++row)
        if (fabs( mat[row][k] ) > coefficient) {
            coefficient = fabs( mat[row][k] ); /* A bigger coefficient. */
            big = row;                         /* Remember where it was found. */
        }
    return big;        /* Line number of equation with biggest coefficient. */
}
```

Figure 19.17.   Pivoting.

- *Third box and Figure 19.19: clear the pivot column.* Finally, we call the function `wipe()`, which will use the chosen pivot equation to clear (set to 0) the kth column of all the other equations in the matrix and adjust the other coefficients at the same time.

Notes on Figure 19.17. Pivoting.

- *The call on* `swap_nonzero_row()`. The `swap_nonzero_row()` function is called from the first box in Figure 19.16. On pass k of the elimi-

This function is called from `solve()` in Figure 19.16, which is called from `main()` in Figure 19.13.

```
void
scale( equation eqn, int unknowns, int k )
{
    int col;                              /* loop index */
    double factor = eqn[k];               /* scale factor */
    for (col = k; col <= unknowns; ++col)
        eqn[col] /= factor;
}
```

Figure 19.18.   Scaling the *k*th equation.

nation process, it searches for an acceptable pivot equation. If one exists, `swap_nonzero_row()` swaps it into row *k* of the matrix and returns `true`. If no pivot can be found, `false` is returned.

- *First box: Calling `find_pivot()`.*

  1. The first thing to do after selecting the pivot equation is to divide its nonzero coefficients by the coefficient in column *k* to produce a 1 in element `mat[k][k]`. Since dividing a number by 0 or a nearly 0 value results in a hardware error (floating-point overflow), we must try to select a pivot equation that has a nonzero value in column *k*. We actually select the equation with the largest available divisor on each step. This maximizes the overall precision of the computation.
  2. So, on pass *k* of the elimination loop, we search the equations that have not yet been selected as pivots for the one with the largest coefficient in column *k*.

- *Second box: failure to find a pivot.* If the largest coefficient left in this column is 0 or nearly 0, it means that an appropriate pivot equation does not exist and we cannot solve this system of equations. In this case, we return an error code, indicating that the equations are inconsistent. Otherwise, if we reach the last line of the function, we will have found a good pivot equation and placed it on the *k*th row of the matrix, so we can return `true`.

- *Third box: a good pivot.* If a good pivot is found, we ask if the pivot equation already is in row *k* of the matrix. If not, we put it there. Since the matrix is an array of pointers to equations, the program can exchange the positions of two entire equations by simply swapping values of the two equation pointers.

- *The result.* In the original example given, the second equation has the largest coefficient in column 0, so it is swapped with the first one, giving this intermediate result (the matrix is not printed at this stage by the final program):

```
----------------------------------------------------------------
    3.000 * a +    -1.000 * b +    0.000 * c +    5.000 * d =    -4.000
    1.000 * a +     2.000 * b +    2.000 * c +    1.000 * d =    10.000
    2.000 * a +     2.000 * b +    3.000 * c +    0.000 * d =    15.000
    0.000 * a +     0.500 * b +   -1.000 * c +    7.000 * d =    -9.000
----------------------------------------------------------------
```

- *Fourth box: The* `find_pivot()` *function.*

  1. We use the normal technique for finding a maximum: One variable is used as an index during the search loop. Two other variables, `coefficient` and `big`, are used to contain the largest value found so far and its index.
  2. We start the search at row k because all rows prior to that have already been processed and should not be moved.
  3. To search for a pivot, we initialize `coefficient` and `big` to the value and position of the coefficient in row k and then start the loop with row $k + 1$.
  4. At any stage of the search, if the current coefficient is bigger than `coefficient`, we discard the old value of `coefficient` and remember the new value and its row index.
  5. We eventually return the row number in which the largest coefficient was found.

Notes on Figure 19.18. Scale the *k*th equation.   Once a pivot equation has been selected and placed on the kth row of the matrix, we scale it so that the coefficient in column k is 1. To scale the equation, we divide all coefficients in columns $\geq k$ by the coefficient in column k. The coefficients to the left of this column already are 0 because of prior elimination steps. In our example, the matrix has these values after scaling the first equation:

```
----------------------------------------------------------------
    1.000 * a +    -0.333 * b +    0.000 * c +    1.667 * d =    -1.333
    1.000 * a +     2.000 * b +    2.000 * c +    1.000 * d =    10.000
    2.000 * a +     2.000 * b +    3.000 * c +    0.000 * d =    15.000
    0.000 * a +     0.500 * b +   -1.000 * c +    7.000 * d =    -9.000
----------------------------------------------------------------
```

Notes on Figure 19.19.   Using the pivot equation to clear coefficients.   This loop subtracts multiples of the current equation (row k) from the other equations. Before beginning the loop, we have scaled the kth equation so that `mat[k][k] == 1`. We use this equation now to set the kth coefficient of every other equation to 0, as follows:

This code is part of the application that begins in Figure 19.13. It is called from `solve()` in Figure 19.16.

```
void
wipe ( linear_system mat, int unknowns, int piv_row, int row )
{
    int col;
    double coefficient = mat[row][piv_row];
    for (col = piv_row; col <= unknowns; ++col)
        mat[row][col] -= coefficient * mat[piv_row][col];
}
```

Figure 19.19.   Using the pivot equation to clear coefficients.

For all equations where `row != k`,
and for all columns in that row where `col >= k`,
subtract `mat[row][k]` * `mat[k][col]` from `mat[row][col]`.

This sets `mat[row][k]` to 0 for `row != k`. The elimination loop processes only columns k and greater because coefficients in the columns to the left of k already are 0. The values in the columns to the right of k will be adjusted. In this example, after three calls on `wipe()` to process rows 1...3, column 0 is wiped out and the matrix has the values that follow (again, the final version of the program does not print the matrix at this stage):

```
1.000 * a +   -0.333 * b +    0.000 * c +    1.667 * d =   -1.333
0.000 * a +    2.333 * b +    2.000 * c +   -0.667 * d =   11.333
0.000 * a +    2.667 * b +    3.000 * c +   -3.333 * d =   17.667
0.000 * a +    0.500 * b +   -1.000 * c +    7.000 * d =   -9.000
```

The remaining stages of the elimination.   At this point, we have finished one trip through the main loop in `solve()`. The first column is cleared and we are ready to start work on the second column. The next three printouts show the contents of the matrix during and after clearing the second column. We select the third row as a pivot because it has the largest coefficient in the second column. We swap it into the second row, yielding this matrix:

```
1.000 * a +   -0.333 * b +    0.000 * c +    1.667 * d =   -1.333
0.000 * a +    2.667 * b +    3.000 * c +   -3.333 * d =   17.667
0.000 * a +    2.333 * b +    2.000 * c +   -0.667 * d =   11.333
0.000 * a +    0.500 * b +   -1.000 * c +    7.000 * d =   -9.000
```

We print the answers from the last column of the matrix, with labels. This code is called from **main()** in Figure 19.13.

```
void
print_answers( linear_system mat, int unknowns )
{
    int row;
    for (row = 0; row < unknowns; ++row)
        printf( "      %c = %8.3f\n", 'a' + row, mat[row][unknowns] );
}
```

Figure 19.20.   Printing the answers.

Next, we scale the second row to achieve a value of 1 in **mat[1][1]**:

```
------------------------------------------------------------
    1.000 * a +    -0.333 * b +    0.000 * c +    1.667 * d =    -1.333
    0.000 * a +     1.000 * b +    1.125 * c +   -1.250 * d =     6.625
    0.000 * a +     2.333 * b +    2.000 * c +   -0.667 * d =    11.333
    0.000 * a +     0.500 * b +   -1.000 * c +    7.000 * d =    -9.000
------------------------------------------------------------
```

Finally, we wipe the second column clear:

```
------------------------------------------------------------
    1.000 * a +     0.000 * b +    0.375 * c +    1.250 * d =     0.875
    0.000 * a +     1.000 * b +    1.125 * c +   -1.250 * d =     6.625
    0.000 * a +     0.000 * b +   -0.625 * c +    2.250 * d =    -4.125
    0.000 * a +     0.000 * b +   -1.562 * c +    7.625 * d =   -12.312
------------------------------------------------------------
```

After performing the pivoting, scaling, and wiping steps two more times, the solution matrix is in its final form and **solve()** returns to **main()** with a success code. In **main()**, a title is printed and the **print_matrix()** function is called. The screen output is

```
Equations after Elimination:
------------------------------------------------------------
    1.000 * a +     0.000 * b +    0.000 * c +    0.000 * d =     1.000
    0.000 * a +     1.000 * b +    0.000 * c +    0.000 * d =     2.000
    0.000 * a +     0.000 * b +    1.000 * c +    0.000 * d =     3.000
    0.000 * a +     0.000 * b +    0.000 * c +    1.000 * d =    -1.000
------------------------------------------------------------
```

Notes on Figure 19.20. Printing the answers.   If the elimination process is successful, the solution to the system of equations is contained in the

```
Linear Equations to Solve:
-------------------------------------------------------------
    1.000 * a +     2.000 * b +     2.000 * c +    1.000 * d =    10.000
    3.000 * a +    -1.000 * b +     0.000 * c +    5.000 * d =    -4.000
    2.000 * a +     2.000 * b +     3.000 * c +    0.000 * d =    15.000
    2.000 * a +     2.000 * b +     3.000 * c +    0.000 * d =    14.000
-------------------------------------------------------------
Equations after Elimination:
-------------------------------------------------------------
    1.000 * a +     0.000 * b +     0.000 * c +    2.600 * d =    -1.600
    0.000 * a +     1.000 * b +     0.000 * c +    2.800 * d =    -0.800
    0.000 * a +     0.000 * b +     1.000 * c +   -3.600 * d =     6.600
    0.000 * a +     0.000 * b +     0.000 * c +    0.000 * d =    -1.000
-------------------------------------------------------------
Equations inconsistent or not independent.
```

Figure 19.21.   A system of equations with no solution.

last column and `main()` calls `print_answers()` to display this solution. The program prints the names of the unknowns and their values in a column, using the same trick as in `print_matrix()` to display the character labels. The output, using these data, is

```
a =     1.000
b =     2.000
c =     3.000
d =    -1.000
```

At this time, the dynamically allocated memory no longer is needed, so the program calls `free()` then ends by calling `bye()`.

A system of equations with no solution.   As an example of a set of inconsistent equations, Figure 19.21 gives a linear system with conflicting constraints and, therefore, no solution. This system is inconsistent because the last two equations have the same coefficients for all the unknowns but different constant terms.

19.4   What You Should Remember

19.4.1 Major Concepts

- *Array allocation time.* If an array is declared with square brackets and a `#defined` length, its size is fixed at compile time and can be changed only by editing and recompiling the source code. At very little additional cost in terms of time and space, many programs can be made more flexible by using dynamic memory. The maximum expected amount of data is determined at run time, and storage is then allocated for an array of the appropriate size. Such an array is declared in the program as an uninitialized pointer variable, **p**. Then at run time, either **malloc()** or **calloc()** is called to allocate a block of memory, and the resulting starting address is stored in **p**. (Of course, this must be done before attempting to use **p**.)

• *The functions* **malloc()** *and* **calloc()**. The **malloc()** function allocates a block of memory of the requested size and returns a **void*** pointer to that block. If not enough memory is available to fill the request, the **NULL** pointer is returned. The **calloc()** function performs the same task and, in addition, clears the block to 0 bits.

• *Type* **void***. This is a pointer type with an unspecified base type. It is used to declare parameters and return values for generic functions such as **malloc()** and **calloc()**, that work on data of any type. A **void*** pointer must be cast, explicitly or implicitly, to a specific pointer type such as **char*** or **float*** before it can be used. Storing the **void*** value in a pointer variable causes an implicit cast.

• *Resizeable arrays.* By using **realloc()**, it is possible to resize a dynamic array, making it either longer or shorter. If the array is lengthened, it may be reallocated starting at a new memory address. In this case, the system must copy all the data from the old block to the new block. Resizing an array is an appropriate technique for applications in which the amount of data to be processed cannot be predicted until after processing has begun.

• *Recycling storage.* A program that uses dynamic memory is responsible for recycling that memory when no longer needed. Blocks used during only one phase of processing should be recycled by calling **free()** as soon as that phase is complete. Some memory blocks remain in use until the end of the program. If all is working properly, such blocks will be freed by the system automatically when the program ends, and so the program should not need to free them explicitly. However, relying on some other program to clean up after yours is risky. It is better if every program frees the dynamic storage it allocates. Recycling memory is especially important if a program requests either several very large memory blocks or many smaller ones. In some systems with less memory, failure to free salvageable blocks can cause program performance to deteriorate. In others, the available memory can become exhausted, causing a fatal run-time error.

• *A setup function.* In the heat slab simulation, we created a function, **setup()**, to initialize variables and allocate memory. This was done to remove the initial user dialog from **main()**, so that the higher-level steps of the algorithm would be more evident. This becomes more necessary as the complexity of a program increases. We continue to use this strategy throughout the remainder of the text.

- *Two kinds of matrix.* C supports two distinctly different dynamic implementations of a matrix. In one implementation, all of the memory is contiguous and allocated by a single call on `malloc()` or `calloc()`. In the other, the matrix is represented as an array of pointers each pointing at an array of data elements. Here, `malloc()` is called several times, once for the array of pointers and once for each of the arrays of elements.

- *The dynamic 2D array.* A dynamic 2D array is useful for applications such as image processing, in which data sets of varying sizes will be processed. The size is generally known at the beginning of run time and a properly sized block of storage can be allocated then. Unfortunately, the programmer has to write a function to do the address calculations for accessing a particular element. This calculation is examined in the exercises.

- *The dynamic matrix data structure.* A dynamic matrix is an array of pointers to arrays. Like static two-dimensional arrays, elements are accessed by using two subscripts. The first subscript selects a row from the array of pointers, the second selects a column from that row. This data structure is appropriate if rows of the matrix must be interchanged.

- *The ragged array.* An earlier chapter introduced the ragged array of strings, which was initialized by string literals in that chapter. It is even more versatile when implemented with dynamically allocated strings because each entry can contain new data and entries easily can be added or deleted. The amount of memory used is only slightly larger than the number of characters in the strings. This is much more economical than a nondynamic strategy, in which several arrays are declared, each long enough to hold the longest anticipated string.

- Gaussian elimination is a well-known method for solving systems of simultaneous linear equations in several unknowns. The algorithm is easily implemented using a dynamic matrix data structure and a set of functions that perform row operations on the equations.

19.4.2 Programming Style

- *Use the proper arguments.* If you are writing a function to process a row of a matrix, pass as the argument a row of the matrix. Do not send the entire matrix as the parameter along with a row index to be used by the function in accessing the data. Write your functions to pass the appropriate amount of data, no more.

- *Use type cast.* The `void*` pointer returned by `malloc()` and `calloc()` normally is stored in a pointer variable. While explicitly performing a type cast is not necessary, doing so can be a helpful form of documentation. Prior to the ANSI C standard, the explicit cast was necessary, and many programmers continue to use it out of habit.

- *Use* `free()` *properly.* It is a good practice to recycle memory at the first possible time. Sometimes it is possible to reuse a memory block for different purposes before giving it back. This can improve program performance because the memory manager need not be involved as often.
- *Check for allocation failure.* It is proper to check the pointer value returned by the allocation functions to make sure it is not **NULL**. If no memory is available, program termination is a logical course of action.
- *Use* `realloc()` *properly.* Do not use `realloc()` too often, because it can reduce the performance of a program if data are copied frequently. Therefore, choose a size that is appropriately large but not too large. A common rule of thumb is to double the current allocation size. A final call to `realloc()` can be made to return excess capacity to the system when the dynamic data structure is complete and all data have been entered.
- *Use the proper data structure.* It is important to choose which form of 2D structure you will use. Should it be defined at compile time or dynamically? Should it be a 2D matrix, an array of arrays, or an array of pointers to arrays? If the size is not known at compile time, dynamic memory is chosen. If the processing of rows is significant, one of the array structures is better suited. It is best to use a 2D matrix when the size can be defined at compile time and all the elements are treated equally.
- *Use a setup function* to organize data initialization and memory allocation statements. This improves code legibility and localizes much of the user interaction in one function.
- *Use one buffer for string input.* It is a common practice to have one large buffer for string input, since the lengths of such input vary greatly. Each data item is read, then measured (using `strlen()`). An appropriate amount of memory is allocated dynamically for the input, then the input is copied into the new memory block and attached to some data structure. This frees the single long buffer for reuse.

19.4.3 Sticky Points and Common Errors

- *Misuse of* `free()`. The two most common mistakes involving the use of `free()` are attempting to recycle a storage area that was not dynamically allocated and attempting to free a memory block that already has been recycled. Each of these is likely to result in a program that terminates unexpectedly.
- *Using a dangling pointer.* After a memory block has been freed, it never should be accessed again. When space is deallocated, it is logically "dead" but physically still there. If more than one variable is set to point at the area, a common error is to continue using the memory block. Once reassigned to a different portion of the program, the competing use eventually will corrupt the data.

- *Using* `realloc()`. The dangling pointer problem also arises with regard to `realloc()`. If a new memory block is assigned, pointers into the old memory block become obsolete. Care must be taken to save the new memory address and use it to reset other pointers to elements within the data block.
- *Uninitialized pointers.* It is easy to forget that every pointer needs a referent before it can be used. A pointer with no referent is like a pocket with a hole in the bottom; it looks normal from the outside but is not functional. A common error is to declare a pointer but forget to store in it the address of either a variable or a dynamically allocated memory block. This frequently results in a program crashing.
- *Remembering array sizes.* Whenever an array is used, the actual number of data items in it must be remembered. Functions that process arrays must have two parameters, the array and the count. The count commonly is forgotten. Logically, these two items always should be grouped. In the next chapter, we use a structure that contains these two members so that we can pass the structure to functions as a single entity.
- *Null character.* When allocating a memory block for an input string, remember to include space for the null character at the end.

19.4.4 New and Revisited Vocabulary

These are the most important terms and concepts presented in this chapter:

dynamic memory allocation	dynamic 2D array	`sizeof`
generic pointer	dynamic matrix (array of arrays)	`strlen()`
pointer cast	numerical approximation	`strcpy()`
recycling memory	simulation of a process	`malloc()`
dangling pointer	finite-difference equation	`calloc()`
resize the data array	Gaussian elimination	`realloc()`
ragged array	system of equations	`free()`
swapping array pointers		`void*`

19.5   Exercises

19.5.1 Self-Test Exercises

1. Given these declarations, explain what is wrong with the following allocation and deallocation commands:

```
float * fp;
double darray[] = { 1.7, -2.0, 5.12 };
int max = 20;
int* ip;
```

a. `fp = maaloc( 20 );`

b. `free( darray );`

c. `(int) calloc( 5, sizeof(int) );`

d. `fp = malloc( 5, sizeof(int) );`

e. `realloc( fp, max * sizeof(float) );`

f. `ip = (int*) calloc( 10 * sizeof(int) );`

g. `fp = (float) (max * sizeof(float) );`

h. `fp = realloc( max, sizeof(float) );`

2. Trace the following code and diagram the object that it creates, assuming that the user types this input: **Come with us to the party.**

```
int k;
string say[5];
printf ( "Enter a sentence: " );
for (k = 0; k < 5; ++k) {
    say[k] = malloc( 6 );
    scanf( "%5s", say[k] );
}
```

3. a. Would the functions **malloc()** and **free()**, taken together, be enough to do all dynamic memory operations if **calloc()** and **realloc()** were eliminated from the language? If not, why not? If so, how?

   b. What harm would it do, if any, to eliminate **free()** from the language?

4. Rewrite the following statement, possibly using more than one statement, to do exactly the same thing by using **malloc()** instead of **calloc()**:

   `p = calloc( 10, sizeof(int) );`

5. A basic step in many sorting programs is swapping two items in the same array. Write a function that has three parameters, an array of strings and two integer indexes. Within the function, compare the strings at the two specified positions and, if the first comes after the second in alphabetical order, swap the string pointers.

6. When a program uses dynamic storage, it is responsible for recycling it. Write a **void** function that has two parameters: an array of dynamically allocated strings and an integer that tells how many strings are in the array. Within the function, write a loop to properly recycle the dynamic memory, including the array and all the strings.

7. Compare the advantages and disadvantages of these three methods for creating a two-dimensional matrix: (a) declare it with two constant dimensions at the top of a program block, (b) allocate it dynamically by a single allocation call, (c) use a series of allocation calls to build an array of dynamically allocated arrays.

19.5.2 Using Pencil and Paper

1. Draw a diagram of the variable created by the following declarations:

```
typedef double* series;
series data[4] = { NULL };
data[1] = malloc( 5 * sizeof(double) );
data[1][1] = 3.2;
```

2. Write a function to read input into its parameter an array of 100 strings, named **paragraph**. Within the function, write a loop that will read a series of lines of text. Allocate an array of characters with exactly enough space for each line and store the string pointer in the next available slot of **paragraph**. Then copy the input text into the newly allocated array. Return from the function when the null string is read (do not store it in the array) and return the number of nonnull strings read and stored.

3. In the heat flow program (Figure 19.10), we begin the simulation by calculating the node n to be monitored, and then allocating two arrays that were $3 \times n$ nodes long. Then we doubled the length of the array each time the cooling wave reached the end of the array. Assume that we were monitoring node 9 and the simulation ran for 100 steps; how many times did we double the array? Altogether, how many **double** values were copied during the growing process? Assume, instead, that we began by allocating arrays that were just n nodes long and tripled the length of the array each time it grew. How many times would we triple it, and how many **double** values would be copied during the growing process?

4. a. Would the functions **malloc()**, **realloc()**, and **free()**, taken together, be enough to do all dynamic memory operations if **calloc()** were eliminated from the language? If not, why not? If so, how?

   b. Would the functions **realloc()** and **free()**, taken together, be enough to do all dynamic memory operations if **malloc()** and **calloc()** were eliminated from the language? If not, why not? If so, how?

5. Given these declarations, explain what is wrong with the following allocation and deallocation commands:

```
double* p, *q;
int arr[5];
```

   a. `free( arr );`

   b. `p = malloc( 20 );`

   c. `p = realloc( q, 200 );`

   d. `realloc( p, 200 );`

   e. `p = malloc( 5, sizeof(double) );`

   f. `recycle( p );`

```
g. p = calloc( 10,* sizeof(int) );

h. p = (double*) malloc( 10 * sizeof(int) );
```

6. Write the code needed to allocate the right amount of storage for a data structure with 20 rows of **double**s, in which the row with subscript n has $n + 1$ columns.

7. Write a function, **resize()**, that is similar to the **realloc()** function except that it always allocates a new memory block in a new location and copies the data. (It does not reuse all or part of the old memory block.)

19.5.3   Using the Computer

1. More matrices.
   Extend the program described in Chapter 17, exercise 4, to do matrix multiplication using arbitrary-sized matrices. Allow the user to specify the matrix size for each input file. Print an error message if the quantity of data in the file doesn't match.

2. Changing a figure.
   Extend the crown program (point transformation) described in Chapter 17 to permit the user to add a point to the figure between any two existing points or delete any point in the figure after it is originally constructed. Provide a menu so that the user can do several point transformations. When "quit" is selected, write out the new data set.

3. Simulation of heat conduction.
   Given the semi-infinite slab in Figure 19.6, determine the temperatures at nodes 1 through 30 inside the slab after time periods of 5, 10, 15, 20, 25, and 30 minutes have passed. Start with the functions in Figures 19.8 through 19.11 and modify them to print the results every 5 minutes and terminate after half an hour. Note that 30 minutes corresponds to $p = 60$. Print a hard copy of the final results.

4. A dictionary.
   Make a dictionary data structure by reading in the contents of a user-specified text file one word at a time. Allocate space dynamically for each word and store the string pointers in a resizeable array. Modify the **sort_data()** and **find_min()** functions from Figures 16.18 and 16.21 to compare and sort strings. When sorting, swap string pointers, not the contents of the character arrays. Print out the entries in your dictionary in alphabetical order, watching for duplicates. Do not display a word more than once. Instead, display a count of how many times each word appeared in the file.

5. Like the UNIX **sort**.
   Use a resizeable array of strings, starting with space to store four string pointers. Read a text file, one line at a time, and install the lines in this array. Use Figure 19.4 as a guide. Stop reading when end-of-file is reached. (Do not limit the array to a fixed number of lines.) During the input phase, double the length of the array each time it becomes full. Then sort the strings by using **strcmp()** and adapting the selection sort functions from Chapter 16 as described in exercise 4. Print the sorted list of lines.

6. String math.
   Write a program to read any two integers as character strings (with no limitation on the number of decimal digits). Hint: Read a number one character at a time, using `realloc()`, when necessary, to extend the input array length. Add the two numbers digit by digit, using a third character array to store the digits of the result. Print the input numbers and their sum. Hint: To convert an ASCII digit to a form that can be meaningfully added, subtract `'0'`. To convert a number 0 ... 9 to an ASCII digit, add `'0'`.

7. Easier said than done.
   Read in the contents of a file of real numbers for which the file length is not known ahead of time and could be large. Write the numbers to a new file in reverse order. Abort the program if the file is so long that the data cannot be held in the computer's memory. You may need to use `realloc()` creatively.

8. Variable-sized image processing.
   Convert the image processing program described in Chapter 17 to work on a variable-sized image, as follows:

   a. Write a type definition to implement a dynamic 2D matrix as a structure called a *matrix pack*. The matrix pack should have three fields: R, the number of rows in the matrix; C, the number of columns; and D, a pointer to a long array of **unsigned char**s for storing the pixels.

   b. Write a function, **sub()**, that has a matrix-pack parameter, MP, and two **short int** parameters, a row number and a column number. (Valid row numbers go from 0 to $R - 1$; columns go from 0 to $C - 1$.) This function should compute and return an integer, the subscript of the slot in D that corresponds to **MP[row][column]**. To compute this slot number, use the formula

   $$\text{Slot} = \text{row} \times C + \text{column}$$

   If the specified row or column number is not valid for the given matrix pack, return a **NULL** pointer.

   c. Rewrite the image processing program to prompt the user for the number of rows and columns in an image, then create and use a matrix pack instead of a fixed-size matrix throughout the program, making use of **sub()** to access the data.

9. Sparse matrix.
   Many applications involve using a matrix of numbers in which most entries are 0. We say that such a matrix is *sparse*. Assume that we are writing a program that uses a sparse 100 by 100 matrix of **double**s that is only 1% full. Thus, instead of 10,000 entries, there are only approximately 100 nonzero entries. However, the actual fullness varies, and there might be more than 100 nonzero entries. One representation of a sparse matrix is to store each nonzero entry as a structure of three members: the row subscript, the column subscript, and the value itself; that is, the value **20.15** in **matrix[15][71]** would be represented as the triple **{ 15, 71, 20.15 }**. When space is allocated for the matrix, we naturally allow for 100 of these structures and allocate an array with 100 slots. During processing, if this turns out to be too few, we reallocate the array and double its size. Implement a program as follows:

a. Write a type definition, **triple**, to implement the structure for one element of the sparse matrix.

b. Write a function, **get_mat()**, that has two parameters: an array with base type **triple*** and a pointer to the integer variable that stores the array's current maximum length. Write a sentinel loop that will read data sets (a pair of subscripts and a matrix value) from the keyboard until a negative subscript is entered. For each data set, allocate memory for a new triple, store the pointer in the next available array slot, and store the data in the triple. If the array is full, double its size by reallocation before storing the new data set and update the maximum length field through the pointer parameter. Return the actual number of data sets read and stored in the array.

c. Write a function, **show_mat()**, that prints the matrix as a table containing three neat columns (two subscripts and a value). The parameters should be the pointer to the array of **triple** pointers and the number of data sets actually stored in the array.

d. Write a main program that tests these functions. Testing programs on huge amounts of data is impractical. During development, define the initial number of element pointers to be 3, rather than 100. Declare **mat** to be of type **triple**
    and initialize it to a dynamically allocated array of length 3 of **triple** pointers. Define a variable, **max**, that is the current length of the array and initialize it to 3. Then call **get_mat()** and **show_mat()** to read and print the values of the matrix. To test this program, read at least seven data sets.

10. Partially sorting the matrix.
     Start with the matrix program in the previous problem. Add to it a function, **sort_mat()**, that sorts the array elements in increasing order by the first subscript. If two elements have the same first subscript, sort them in increasing order by their second subscripts. If both subscripts are equal, display an error comment. To perform the sort, adapt the sorting program in Chapter 16, printing the matrix before and after sorting.

CHAPTER
20

Working with Pointers

In many ways, a pointer in C is like a pronoun in English. Both can be attached, or bound, to an object and changed later to refer to a different object. This chapter covers two important advanced programming techniques: using pointers with arrays and using pointers to functions. The use of pointers in array processing is illustrated by a program for insertion sort.

The ability to create pointers to functions, store those pointers in arrays, and pass functions as parameters to other functions leads to more versatile programs. Some applications provide a menu of functions, using one or another, depending on the conditions. Such menus can be built using arrays of pointers to functions, as we will see in a calculator application.

20.1   Pointers—Old and New Ideas

This section collects, reviews, and elaborates on the material concerning pointers introduced in Chapters 12, 13, 14, and 19 and extends it to show new ways pointers may be used with arrays, strings, structures, and arrays of structures.

20.1.1   Pointer Declarations and Initialization

An asterisk can be used with a type name in a declaration to create a pointer variable. The declaration `int k`, with no `*`, creates an `int` variable, but `int* p` creates a pointer variable that can refer to an `int`. The type named is called the

We declare simple and structured variables and show how to set pointers to refer to them.

```
typedef struct {double x; double y;} point_t;

double w = 17.2;
double* wp = &w;
point_t corner = {1.5, -2.0};
point_t* cp = &corner;
double* yp;
yp = &corner.y;
```

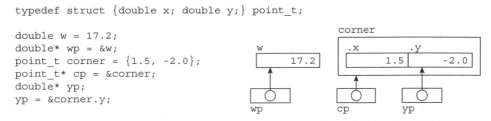

Figure 20.1. Pointing at a variable or a structure.

base type of the pointer, and the pointer can point meaningfully only at variables of that type.

The **referent** of a pointer (the address of an object of a matching type) can be set either by initialization or by assignment. Figures 20.1 through 20.4 give examples of declarations of several types of pointers. In the following paragraphs, we briefly summarize the syntax and meaning of these pointer assignments.

Simple objects and structures. Intuitively, a structure is like an array because both contain a list of data items (members or slots). Syntactically, though, a structure is more like a simple variable in C. To set a pointer to a simple object, an entire structure, or a part of a structure, an ampersand is needed. For example, in Figure 20.1, we can write `wp = &w`, `cp = &corner`, and `yp = &corner.y`. Remember that the **.** operator has higher precedence than the **&**, so we get the address of the **y** portion of the structure.

Pointing at an array. In C, an array is a sequence of variables that have the same type and are stored consecutively and contiguously in memory. When we point at an array, we actually point only at one of the elements (slots) in that array, not at the entire object. However, pointing at one slot gives us access to all the other slots that precede and follow it. Figure 20.2 illustrates pointing to an array.

To point at a single slot in an array, we use the array name with both an ampersand and a subscript, as in `wp = &z[2]`. To set a pointer to the beginning of an array, we could write `zp = &z[0]` or, more simply, omit both the ampersand and subscript and write `zp = z`. We normally use the second form. This simpler syntax works because, in C, the name of an array is translated as a pointer to the first slot of that array.[1] Similarly, there are two ways to set a pointer to the

---

[1] This nonuniform syntax causes confusion for many people. It permits an efficient implementation with an economy of notation at the expense of clarity. When C was a new language, efficiency was a major concern, and the C language developers expected only experts to use it.

We declare an array and show how to set a pointer to its first slot or to an interior slot.

```
double z[3] = {0.0, 1.0, 0.0};
double* wp, * zp = z;
wp = &z[2];
```

Figure 20.2.   Pointing at an array.

third array element: `zp = &z[2]`, as just discussed, and `zp = z+2`, which is discussed in a later section.

Pointing at a function (advanced topic).   Pointers also can refer to functions. Later in this chapter and again in Chapter 22, we show applications of this technique. For now, we focus only on the syntax. The top part of Figure 20.3 shows one way to declare a pointer to a function. The base type of a **function pointer** must match the prototype of the function it refers to. For example, since `pow()` has the prototype `double pow( double, double )`, `fp` must be declared as `double (*fp)( double, double );`. The function name in the prototype is replaced by parentheses enclosing an asterisk and the pointer name. Having declared `fp` this way, it could then refer to a function like `pow()` or any other double:(double, double) function. However, it could not refer to a function with different types of parameters, like `calloc()`, or to one with a different number of parameters, such as `sin()` or `cos()`.

We declare a pointer `fp` that could refer to any function with two **double** parameters and a **double** result:

```
double (*fp)( double, double );
```

As an alternative, we could declare a function pointer type using **typedef**, and use the new type to declare the function pointer:

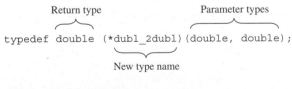

```
dubl_2dubl fp;
```

Figure 20.3.   Declaring a function pointer.

To initialize or assign a referent to a function pointer, use a **pointer as-signment** with the name of the function and nothing else[2] (no ampersand and no parentheses). A function name with no parentheses following it is translated as a pointer to that function. For example, since `fp` is a pointer variable with the same base type as `pow()`, we can write `fp = pow;`.

Type definitions for function pointers (advanced topic).   A decla-ration of a function pointer can be quite long and complex because it includes an entire function prototype. If a program will be using function pointers, it makes good sense to use `typedef` to define a concise name for the pointer type. The bottom of Figure 20.3 shows an example of using `typedef` for a function pointer type that could point at the `pow()` function. The form of this `typedef` is like the form of the declaration for a function-pointer variable. Both include the prototype of the function that will be the referent of the pointer. In place of a function name, though, is a unit consisting of parentheses, an asterisk, and the new type name. Finding an appropriate name for a function-pointer type is somewhat difficult. Generic type names such as `func_pointer` might be ap-propriate if only one type is used in a program. A more detailed name, such as `double_double_double` is more descriptive and easy to remember but very long. The name used in the example, `dubl_2dubl` is a compromise: it gives information about the function prototype but in a condensed way.

Using a function pointer (advanced topic).   To call a function using a pointer, the name of the pointer can be used in exactly the same way as the name of the function that is its referent; if `fp` points at `pow()`, then `fp( 3, 2 )` means the same thing as `pow( 3, 2 )`.[3] Figure 20.4 illustrates some declarations and calls for two types of function pointers. The resulting memory layout is diagrammed on the right; the output is given below the code.

20.1.2 Using Pointers

To use pointers skillfully, the meanings of several pointer operations must be understood. These include subscript, direct and indirect reference, direct and indirect assignment, input and output through pointers, and pointer arithmetic. The following paragraphs review or present these operations.

---

[2]Normally, in C, a name with an ampersand and a name without an ampersand mean different things. However, this is not true for functions; if you write an ampersand in front of a function name, it still is translated as a pointer to the function. Therefore the assignment `fp = sin` means the same thing as `fp = &sin`.

[3] We do not use `*fp( 3, 2 )` because the precedence of the function call is higher than the precedence of `*`. If we add parentheses, `(*fp)( 3, 2 )`, the resulting expression is correct but awkward and more complex than necessary. The asterisk, if present, is ignored; so we prefer the simpler syntax, `fp( 3, 2 )`.

We declare names for two function-pointer types and use them to declare and initialize two pointer variables. The pointer variables then are used to call the underlying functions and print the results.

```
typedef double (*dubl_2dubl)( double, double );
typedef double (*funcptr)( double );

dubl_2dubl fp = pow;
funcptr gp = exp;

printf( " 3^5 = %g\n", fp( 3.0, 5 ) );
printf( " e^5 = %g\n", gp( 5 ) );
```

fp   pow()

gp   exp()

The output is

```
      3^5 = 243
      e^5 = 148.413
```

Figure 20.4.   Using function pointers.

Pointers with subscripts.   Syntactically, there is no difference between using an array name and a pointer to an array. If the referent of pointer **p** is one of the slots within an array, then **p** can be used with a subscript to refer to the other slots of that array. For example, in Figure 20.2, the pointer **zp** refers to array element **z[0]**, so using a subscript with **zp** means the same thing as using a subscript with **z**, and **&zp[1]** means the same thing as **&z[1]**. The subscript used with a pointer is interpreted relative to the pointer's referent. In Figure 20.2, pointer **wp** refers to **z[2]**, so **wp[0]** means the same thing as **z[2]**, and **wp[1]** would be the slot after the end of the diagrammed array. The ability to use a **pointer with a subscript** is important because array arguments are passed by address. Within a function, the parameter is a pointer to the beginning of the array argument. The notational equivalence of arrays and pointers lets us use subscripts with array parameters.

Indirect reference.   Two operators in C dereference pointers: the asterisk (*****) and the arrow (**->**). The expression ***p** stands for the referent of **p**, the same way a pronoun stands for a noun. We say that we can use **p** to reference **k** *indirectly*. If **p** points at **k**, then **m = *p** means the same thing as **m = k**. Longer expressions also can be written; anywhere that you might write a variable name, you can write an asterisk and the name of a pointer that refers to the variable. For example, the expression **m = *p + 2** adds 2 to the value of **k** (the referent of **p**) and stores the result in **m**. Figure 20.5 shows two more examples of this indirect referencing.

The arrow operator, **->**, is used only for pointers that refer to structures. It gives a convenient way to dereference the pointer and select a member of the structure in one operation. Therefore, in Figure 20.5, the expression **cp->x**

An indirect reference accesses the value of the pointer's referent. These declarations create two **double** variables and two structured variables. The assignments change the values marked by a large X.

```
double x, w = 17.2;
double* wp = &w;
point_t corner = {1.5, -2.0};
point_t* cp = &corner;
point_t c2;

x = *wp;    /* Ind. ref. to double. */
c2 = *cp;   /* Ind. ref. to struct. */
w = cp->x;  /* Ind. ref. to member. */
```

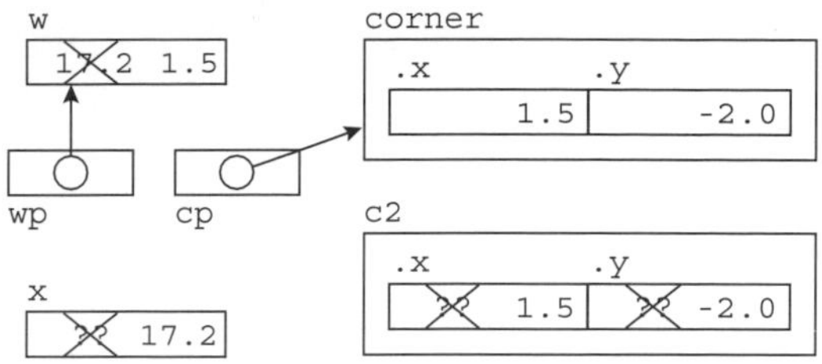

Figure 20.5.   Indirect reference.

would mean the same thing as (***cp**) **.x**; namely, "dereference the pointer **cp** and select the member named **x** from the structure that is the referent of **cp**." (When the expression is written with the asterisk instead of the arrow, parentheses are necessary because of the higher precedence of the **.** operator.) Pointers often are used to process arrays of structures; in such programs, the arrow operator is particularly convenient.

Direct reference.   Like any other variable, we can simply refer to the value of a pointer, getting an address. This address can be passed as an argument to a function, stored in another variable, and so forth. A statement like **p1 = p2;** is a simple example.

Direct and indirect assignment.   C permits assignment between any two simple variables, structures, or pointers that have the same type. The meaning is the same for any type: The value of the expression on the right is copied into the storage area for the object on the left. With pointers, an assignment can be either direct, as in **p2 = ??**, or indirect, as in ***p2 = ??**. A direct assignment changes the value stored in the pointer variable. In contrast, an **indirect assignment**, which is written with an asterisk in front of the pointer name, changes the value of the underlying variable. For example, if **p** points at **k**, then ***p = n** means the same thing as **k = n**. Figure 20.6 gives an example of each of these assignments.

Input and output.   Finally, let us look at the use of pointers with **scanf()** and **printf()**. When using **scanf()** to read an integer or a **double** value directly, we write an ampersand before the name of the variable that will receive the input; this passes the address of the variable to **scanf()**. But a pointer value *is* the address of its referent. Therefore, we can use a pointer to the variable (instead of an ampersand and the variable name) in a call on **scanf()**. This is illustrated in Figure 20.7, where the pointer **ap** refers to **a[0]**. To read input directly into **a[0]**, write **scanf("%lg", &a[0])**. We can do the same thing indirectly by writing **scanf("%lg", ap)**.

Indirect assignment changes the value stored in the pointer's referent; direct assignment changes the pointer itself.

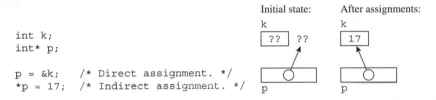

```
int k;
int* p;

p = &k;     /* Direct assignment. */
*p = 17;    /* Indirect assignment. */
```

Figure 20.6.   Direct and indirect assignment.

To print a value using a pointer, we must dereference the pointer in the call on **printf()**. Given the pointer **ap** and the array **a**, as shown, the statement **printf("%.2f", *ap)** has the same effect as **printf("%.2f", a[0])**. An exception to this would involve the output of strings, in which the pointer's value is used directly, not indirectly. The memory address contained in a pointer also can be printed, by casting it to an integer type, then using either a **%i** or **%x** format: **printf("Referent of p is %x \n", (unsigned)p)**. This technique can be useful when debugging a pointer program.

20.1.3   Pointer Arithmetic and Logic

Some, but not all, of the operations defined for numbers also are defined for pointers. Addition, subtraction, comparison, increment, and decrement are defined because these have reasonable and useful interpretations with pointers. Division, multiplication, modulo, and the logical operators are not defined for pointers because they have no meaning.

Two declarations are given on the left, resulting in the memory layout shown. On the right are calls on **scanf()** and **printf()** and their results.

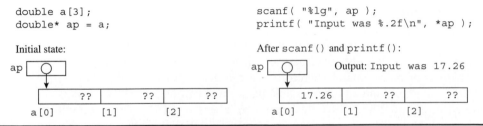

Figure 20.7.   Input and output through pointers.

Pointers can be set to refer to an element in an array using the array name and the element's index value. In the diagram, subscripts are given below the array and memory addresses above it.

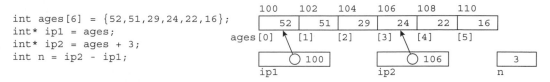

```
int ages[6] = {52,51,29,24,22,16};
int* ip1 = ages;
int* ip2 = ages + 3;
int n = ip2 - ip1;
```

Figure 20.8.   Pointer addition and subtraction.

Addition and subtraction with pointers.   All **pointer arithmetic** relates in one way or another to the use of pointers to process arrays. If a pointer points at some element of an array, then adding 1 to it makes it refer to the next array slot, while subtracting 1 moves a pointer to the prior slot. This is true of all arrays, not just arrays of 1-byte characters. A pointer and the array it points into must have the same base type, and the size of that base type is factored in when pointer arithmetic is performed. In Figure 20.8, **ip1** points at the beginning of the array, which has memory address 100. (The actual content of the pointer variable is the address 100.) Similarly, **ip2** points at the fourth slot of the array, which has memory address 106.

Adding **n** to a pointer creates another pointer **n** slots further along the array. In Figure 20.8, we set **ip1** to point at the beginning of the array **ages**. So **ip1 + 1** refers to the second array slot, at memory address 102. Now we can address any slot in the array by adding an integer to **ip1** or **ages**. As long as the integer is not negative and is smaller than the length of the array, the result always will be a pointer to a valid array slot.[4] For example, **ages[5]** is the last slot in the array. So, **ip1+5** refers to the same location as **ages[5]**.[5]

If two pointers point at slots in the same array, subtracting one from the other gives the number of array slots between them. In Figure 20.8, **ip2 - ip1** is 3. If a pointer **ip1** points at the beginning of an array and another pointer **ip2** points at the last slot that contains data, then **ip2-ip1+1** is the number of data items in the array. The result of the subtraction **ip2 - ip1** is 3, not 6, because all pointer arithmetic is done in terms of array slots, not the underlying memory addresses.

Increment and decrement with pointers.   Sometimes, pointers, rather than integer counters, are used to control loops. The increment and decrement operators make pointer loops easy and convenient. Increment moves a pointer

---

[4] Any address resulting from pointer arithmetic refers to the beginning (not the middle) of an array slot because C adds or subtracts a multiple of the size of the base type of the array.

[5] Both also are synonyms for **ages+5**, because the name of an array is translated as a pointer to slot 0 of the array.

A pointer can traverse the elements of an array using pointer arithmetic. In the diagram, subscripts are given below each array and memory addresses above it.

```
int ages[6] = {52, 51, 29, 24, 22, 16};
int* ip1 = ages;
ip1++;
```

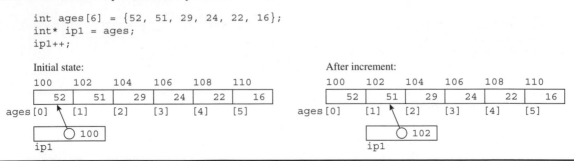

Figure 20.9.   Incrementing a pointer.

Comparing pointers or addresses is just like comparing integers.

```
int ages[6] = {52,51,29,24,22,16};
int* ip1 = ages;
int* ip2 = ages + 3;
if (ip1 == ip2) ...    /* false */
if (ip1 > ip2) ...     /* false */
if (ip2 < ip1 + 5) .../* true */
```

Figure 20.10.   Pointer comparisons.

to the next slot of an array; decrement moves it to the prior slot. For example, in Figure 20.9, the pointer **ip1** is initialized to the beginning of the array **ages**, then it is incremented. After the increment, it points to **ages[1]**.

Pointer comparisons.   All six comparison operators are defined for use with two pointers that refer to the same data type. Two pointers are equal (**==**) if they point to the same slot, unequal otherwise. In Figure 20.10, (**ip1 == ages**) is true but (**ip1 == ip2**) is false. In general, a pointer **ip1** is less than a pointer **ip2** if the referent of **ip1** is a slot with a lower subscript than that of the referent of **ip2**. Pointer arithmetic can be used in these **pointer comparisons**. In the diagram, (**ip1 < ip2**) is true, as is (**ip2 < ip1+5**).

20.2   Application: A Menu of Pointers to Functions (Advanced Topic)

Section 20.1.1 showed how to declare a function pointer and make it refer to a specific function. In this section, we demonstrate how to use function pointers in a menu-driven application, a simple calculator (see Figure 20.11). We define an

This program allows the user to choose which mathematical function to run, as one might on a calculator. The choice indexes an array of function pointers to run the selected operation.

```
#include "tools.h"

typedef double (*funcptr)( double );

double                          /* Base 2 logarithm */
log_2( double x ) { return log( x ) / log( 2 ); }

void main( void )
{
    int choice;                    /* user's function selection index */
    double x, fx;                  /* data input, calculated function value */
    funcptr fp;                    /* function chosen by user */

    #define CHOICES  7
    string greeting = " Select a function:";
    string names[CHOICES] = { "quit", "sine", "cosine", "tangent",
                              "natural log", "base 2 log", "e to the x" };
    funcptr function[CHOICES] = { NULL, sin, cos, tan, log, log_2, exp };

    banner();
    puts( " A Menu of Functions" );
    for (;;) {

        choice = menu_i( greeting, CHOICES, names );
        if (choice == 0) break;

        printf( " Enter x: " );
        scanf( "%lg", &x );
        fp = function[choice];
        fx = fp( x );

        printf( "\n %s(%g) = %g \n", names[choice], x, fx );
    }
    bye();
}
```

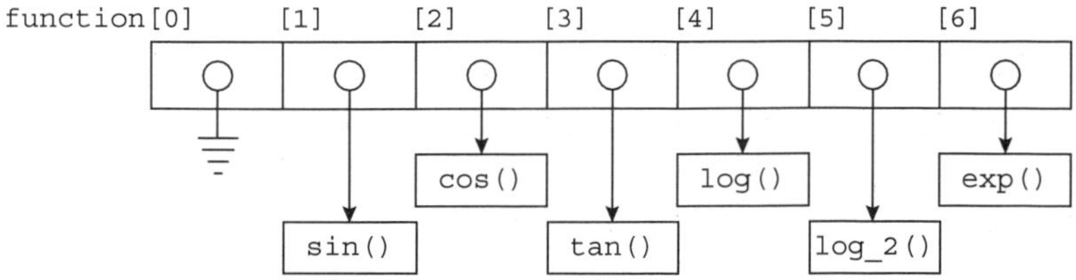

Figure 20.11.   Selecting a function from a menu.

array of function pointers that is parallel to an array of menu selections, then use each menu choice to select and execute the corresponding function.

Notes on Figure 20.11. Selecting a function from a menu.   This is a very simple program that illustrates how to both set a pointer to a function and call that function using the pointer.

- *First box: a* **typedef** *for a function pointer.* We define the type name **funcptr** for pointers to double:double functions.
- *Second box: a function for the menu array.* We offer a choice of six functions in the menu format. Five of them are defined in the standard **math** library, but the base-2 logarithm is not, so we must define it here in terms of the natural logarithm.
- *Third box: the menu.*

  1. The menu consists of a title, a **#define** command for the menu length, and a pair of parallel arrays. One array contains the strings displayed for the menu, and the other has the corresponding functions that are executed when selected.
  2. We use the new **typedef** name, **funcptr**, to declare the array of function pointers. To initialize this array, we list the names of the functions that correspond to the menu strings. (Remember, a function name with no parentheses following it is translated into a pointer to that function.) When the compiler translates this initializer, it will create the data structure illustrated below the code.
  3. We have placed the "quit" option in slot 0 of the menu array. We did this because it makes it easier to add or remove menu items in the future, and it also has the nice property that choosing option 0 means doing nothing. We write **NULL** in the first slot of the initializer because we must list something, and no function corresponds to a "quit" command. The **NULL** value can be used to represent a **NULL** (empty) **pointer** of any type, even a pointer to a function.
  4. Alternatively, it would be possible to write a function with the prototype double:double that performs the "quit" operation when called. But the "quit" action would not need a parameter and quitting from within a function is a little more complex than quitting from **main()**. Therefore, this solution lacks appeal.

- *Fourth box: using the menu.*

  1. The **menu_i()** function always returns a value in the range **0…(CHOICES-1)**. Except for the value of 0, this is an appropriate subscript for either the menu array or the function array.
  2. The **if** statement tests for a "quit" command and breaks out of the menu loop when it is selected. It is important to do this before trying

to use the function pointer, since the **NULL** value does not point to an executable function, and therefore we cannot dereference it.

- *Fifth box: calling the selected function.*

    1. The program prompts for and reads **x**, the argument of the chosen function.
    2. If we have an array of pointers to functions, then we can subscript that array to get a single function pointer. For example, **function[1]** is a pointer to the **sin()** function.
    3. The **menu_i()** function returned an integer that is used here to subscript the **function** array, thereby selecting one function pointer from it, which is stored in a function-pointer variable, **fp**.
    4. Since **fp** is a pointer, ***fp** refers to the function at which **fp** points and therefore **(*fp)(x)** would call that function with the argument **x**. Even though it is legal and meaningful to write **(*fp)(x)**, C syntax allows us to use just the function pointer, without writing the parentheses and the asterisk, and we prefer the simpler and cleaner syntax.
    5. On the last line in this box, we use the pointer variable to call the selected function and store the result in a **double** variable.
    6. When using a function pointer array, the phrase **function[1]** or **function[n]** denotes a single function pointer, so it too can be written in place of the function name in a call. Thus, the last two lines in this box could be combined into one line that both subscripts the array and calls the function:

    ```
    fx = function[choice]( x );
    ```

    Again, this is correct and legal but more complex than necessary; we prefer to set the pointer and use it in two separate steps.

- *The output.* The final **printf()** statement prints the name of the function, the value of **x**, and the computed result. Here is some sample output, with repetitions of the menu replaced by dashed lines:

    ```
    A Menu of Functions

    Select a function:
            0. quit
            1. sine
            2. cosine
            3. tangent
            4. natural log
            5. base 2 log
            6. e to the x
    ```

```
Enter number of desired item: 1
Enter x: 1.55

sine(1.55) = 0.999784


------------------------------
Enter number of desired item: 5
Enter x: 33

base 2 log(33) = 5.04439
------------------------------
Enter number of desired item: 0


Normal termination.
```

20.3   Using Pointers with Arrays

There is a very close relationship between pointers and arrays. As shown in Chapter 19, a pointer can be used with a subscript just like an array. In this section, we show how pointers can be used to process an entire array.

20.3.1   Scanners and Sentinels

A major use of pointers in C is sequential processing of arrays, especially dynamically allocated arrays. Three kinds of pointers are commonly used for this purpose: head pointers, scanning pointers, and tail pointers. A **head pointer** stores the address of the beginning of the array that is returned by `malloc()` when an array is allocated dynamically. The name of an array that is declared with dimensions can be treated like a head pointer in most contexts. A **tail pointer** is initialized to the end of an array. Both head and tail pointers, after they are set, remain constant during their useful lifetime, and the head pointer is used to free the storage. In contrast, a **scanning pointer**, or **cursor**, usually starts at the head of an array, points at each array slot in turn, and finishes at the end of the array.

We can use pointer arithmetic to cycle through the elements of an array with great efficiency and simplicity. The scanning pointer initially is set to the head of the array, as shown in Figure 20.12. The tail pointer, often called a *sentinel*, is used in the test that terminates the loop. It points either at the last slot in the array (**on-board sentinel**) or at the first location past the end of the array (**off-board sentinel**). During scanning, all unprocessed array elements lie between the cursor and the sentinel. To process the entire array, we use a **scanning loop** to increment the `cursor` value so that it scans across the array, dereferencing it (`*cursor`) to access each array element in turn. We leave the loop when the cursor reaches the

Suppose we start with the declarations on the left. Array **ages** contains six integers. A cursor is initialized to the head of **ages** and an off-board sentinel is set to point at its end.

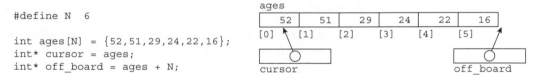

```
#define N   6

int ages[N] = {52,51,29,24,22,16};
int* cursor = ages;
int* off_board = ages + N;
```

Figure 20.12.   An array with a cursor and a sentinel.

end of the array; that is, when it surpasses an on-board sentinel or bumps into an off-board sentinel. Figure 20.13 shows such a loop that will print the contents of an array. The upper diagram shows the positions of the pointers after the first pass through the loop. The lower diagram shows the positions of the pointers after exiting from the loop.

On-board and off-board sentinels.   Figure 20.13 illustrates the use of an off-board sentinel. Using an on-board sentinel is similar but differs in two details:

Starting with the declarations in Figure 20.12, we write a loop to process the **ages** array:

```
for (cursor = ages; cursor < off_board; ++cursor) {
    printf( "%i ", *cursor );
}
```

After the first pass through the loop, the output is: **52**

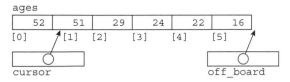

After exiting from the loop, the output is: **52 51 29 24 22 16**

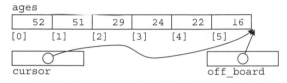

Figure 20.13.   An increment loop.

We subtract 1 in the initializing expression for the sentinel and we use a `<=` in the loop test. Figure 20.14 illustrates this option using a sentinel, `on_board`, set to the last slot of the array `ages`. All in all, using an off-board sentinel leads to slightly simpler code.

Measuring progress with pointer subtraction.   We can use pointer arithmetic to calculate how much of an array has been processed and how much remains. Remember that, if `pp1` and `pp2` are pointers and both are pointing at the same array, then `pp2 - pp1` tells us how many array slots lie between `pp1` and `pp2` (including one end of the range). Remember also that an unsubscripted array name is translated as a pointer to the beginning of the array. Therefore, if we are processing an array sequentially, we can calculate how many array slots already have been processed by subtracting the array name from a cursor pointing to the first unprocessed slot. For example, consider the loop in Figure 20.13. At the beginning of the loop, `cursor-ages == 0`; after the first pass through the loop, the cursor has been incremented so `cursor-ages == 1` and one data value has been printed. Similarly, subtracting the cursor from a sentinel tells us how many array slots are left to process between the cursor and the end of the array. For example, after the increment operation in Figure 20.13, `off_board-cursor` is `5`. Of course, similar calculations can be done using a subscripting index and the size of the array, if pointers are not being used.

Subscripts vs. pointers.   Programmers converting to C from other languages often prefer to use subscripts. However, experienced C programmers use pointers far more often, because once mastered, they are simple and convenient to use. Many or most applications of arrays use the array elements sequentially, visiting the slots in either ascending or descending order. For these situations, pointers provide a more concise and more efficient way to code the application. Every time a subscript is used, the corresponding memory address must be computed. To do so, the compiler generates code to multiply the subscript by the size of the base type, then adds the result to the base address of the array. In contrast, when you increment a pointer, the compiler generates code to add the size of the base type to the contents of the pointer. No multiplication is needed,

---

The following piece of code uses an on-board sentinel to scan the `ages` array and print the value in each array slot. Compare this to the loop using an off-board sentinel in Figure 20.13.

```
int* on_board = ages + N - 1;
for (cursor = ages; cursor <= on_board; ++cursor) {
    printf( "%i ", *cursor );
}
```

Figure 20.14.   An on-board sentinel.

just one addition. Also, once a pointer has been set to refer to a desired location, its value can be used many times without further computations. So, overall, sequential processing is more efficient with pointers than with subscripts. Therefore, experienced C programmers often prefer using pointers when an array is to be processed sequentially but use subscripts for nonsequential access to array elements.

20.3.2   Input and Output Functions Using Pointers

Every function that works with an array must know the effective length of the array. For an input function, it is the number of array slots that were allocated. For a processing or output function, it is the number of slots actually filled with data. Since an array and its lengths (maximum and actual) always are used together, it is a good idea to define a structure that will consolidate these three objects into one.[6] We call this new data type **data_pack**, because it packages together a data array and its bounds information. The general form of the type declaration is

```
typedef struct {
    BASETYPE* data;     /* Type of data stored in array. */
    int n;              /* Current number of items. */
    int max;            /* Allocation length of array. */
} data_pack;
```

In this definition, the word **BASETYPE** is a placeholder. When using this structure in a program, **BASETYPE** should be replaced by the type of data being processed. (This can be done using **typedef** or **#define**.)

To give some examples of using this structure, the functions **get_data()** in Figure 20.15 and **print_data()** in Figure 20.16 illustrate the use of a cursor and a sentinel to process a **data_pack**.

Notes on Figure 20.15. Input into an array.

- *First box: the function header.*

   1. The parameters of the function **get_data()** are an input stream and a data package. The **data_pack** consists of an already-allocated array to be filled with input, the maximum length of this array (a function input), and the number of data items stored in it (a function output). Since the data pack will be modified, it must be declared as a pointer parameter.
   2. This input function processes **float**s; we assume that the **BASETYPE** of the data pack is declared as type **float**.

---

[6]In an object-oriented language, this structure would be defined as a class.

Fill an array with data read from an input stream until encountering either the end of the stream or the end of the allocated array.

```
void
get_data( data_pack* sortp, stream instream )
{
    int stream_status;

    float* cursor = sortp->data;
    float* end = cursor + sortp->max;   /* off-board sentinel */

    for ( ; cursor < end; ++cursor) {
        stream_status = fscanf( instream, "%g", cursor );
        if (stream_status != 1) break;
    }

    sortp->n = cursor - sortp->data;   /* Actual # of items read, stored. */

}
```

Figure 20.15.   Input into an array.

- *Second box: the array pointers.* The variable **cursor** is initialized to the beginning of the array. The variable **end** is initialized as an off-board sentinel. The input process will terminate if **cursor** reaches **end**.
- *Third box: the input loop.*
  1. Since the initialization of **cursor** occurs in the declaration, we can omit the corresponding portion of the **for** loop.
  2. Processing will stop either when **cursor** == **end** or if the **break** statement in the body of the loop is executed because a legal **float** value was not read from the input stream. This will happen when the end of file is reached but could also happen because of a hardware read error or the presence of nonnumeric data in the **instream**.
  3. Until then, on each pass, the program reads a value into the slot under the cursor, then increments the cursor to point at the next slot.
  4. Note that we write **cursor**, not **&cursor**, when calling **fscanf()**. Since **cursor** is a pointer that points at the current slot in the array, its value *is* an address, so we don't need to (and must not) write **&** (address of) in front of it. (It would be correct but needlessly awkward to write **&*cursor**.)
- *Fourth box: the return value.* Before returning, we update the data pack to reflect the actual number of data items read and stored. We calculate

Print the array values, one per line, to the selected stream.

```
void
print_data( data_pack sort, stream outstream )
{

    float* cursor = sort.data;
    float* end = cursor + sort.n;      /* an off-board sentinel */

    for( ; cursor < end; ++cursor ){
        fprintf( outstream, "%.7g\n", *cursor );
    }

}
```

Figure 20.16.   Output from an array.

this number by subtracting the address of the beginning of the array from **cursor** (a pointer to the first unfilled slot). If the loop ends because **cursor** reaches the **end** pointer, n will be equal to **max**. If the loop stops because of an end of file or error condition, n will be smaller than **max**.

Notes on Figure 20.16. Output from an array.   Producing output from an array is simpler than filling it with input, because we know ahead of time exactly how many values must be processed, fewer local variables are needed, and the data package does not need to be updated.

- *First box: the function header.* The **print_data()** function lets us specify which data pack to print and where to write the output. Since the data will not be modified, the data pack can be declared as a value parameter. This means that all accesses to the structure members will use the **.** (dot) operator rather than the **->** (arrow).
- *Second box: the sentinel pointer.*

  1. As in the **get_data()** function, we define two local pointers: one for a sentinel at the tail of the array and one to scan from the head to the tail.
  2. As before, the **end** pointer is an *off-board sentinel*. It points to the first location after the end of the actual data in the array. This may be an empty array slot or just past the end of the array's allocation area; it doesn't matter which it is. All that matters is that we point just beyond the n array slots that contain data.

- *Third box: the printing loop.*

    1. In an output function, the printing ends when the data end, no sooner. Therefore, there is only one reason to end the loop: the `cursor` has bumped into the sentinel.
    2. In the `fprintf()` statement, we write `*cursor`, not `cursor`. Since `cursor` is a pointer, we must dereference it to reach the data in the array slot we want to print.

20.4	**Insertion Sort**

In this section, we look at the insertion sort algorithm and its implementation using pointers to process the data. In the **insertion sort** algorithm, the data array is divided into two segments: the sorted portion first, followed by the unsorted portion. (This much is similar to the strategy of the selection sort studied earlier.) For *n* data values, the sorted portion initially contains one item and the unsorted portion contains the remaining *n* − 1 items.

p678

An insertion strategy differs from a selection strategy in an important way. When doing selection, we repeatedly examine the remaining unsorted items and must look at all of them each time an item is selected. When performing insertion, we always pick the next unsorted item and then scan from the end of the list of sorted items to its beginning, looking for the correct position for the new item. As soon as we locate an item smaller than the one being inserted (assuming we sort in ascending order), we stop looking. On the average, this search for the correct insertion slot takes fewer comparisons than looking through the remaining unsorted items to find the next smallest item during a selection sort.

Unfortunately, we can't just create new space for a value between two others in an array; we have to move some of them to make space for an insertion. We do this by shifting each sorted data item one slot toward the end of the array as we pass it during our search, in essence moving a hole along the array, so that it is always adjacent to the item we are testing. When the proper insertion slot is found, we simply store the current value in our hole. This sequence of movements requires more work than the single data swap in a selection sort. However, because the number of comparisons needed is smaller, insertion sort usually is faster. The insertion algorithm is implemented by the function `sort_data()` listed in Figure 20.19.

We begin this implementation with a `main()` program (Figure 20.17) designed to work through file redirection, rather than by opening explicitly named files. Therefore, we will read from `stdin` and assume that data are supplied from a file by the operating system and the output sent to `stdout` should be saved in another file by the operating system. More specifically, we use the input and output functions just given in Figures 20.15 and 20.16. The `main()` program is also supported by the functions in Figures 20.18 and 20.19.

This program calls the I/O utility functions in Figures 20.15 and 20.16, the setup function in Figure 20.18, and the insertion sort function in Figure 20.19. A call chart follows.

```
#include "tools.h"

typedef struct { float* data;     /* Dynamic data array. */
                 int    n;        /* Data length. */
                 int    max;      /* Allocation length. */
} data_pack;

void setup( data_pack* sortp );                      /* Data-pack constructor. */
void get_data( data_pack* sortp, stream instream );   /* Fill data array. */
void print_data( data_pack sort, stream outstream ); /* Output array data. */
void sort_data ( data_pack sort );                    /* Insertion sort. */


void main( void )
{
    data_pack sort;             /* Data array package */
    banner();

    setup( &sort );

    say( "Reading data from stdin." );
    get_data( &sort, stdin );

    say( "%i data items read.", sort.n );
    print_data( sort, stderr );

    say( "Beginning to sort." );
    sort_data( sort );

    say( "Data sorted; writing to output stream." );
    print_data( sort, stdout );

    bye();
}
```

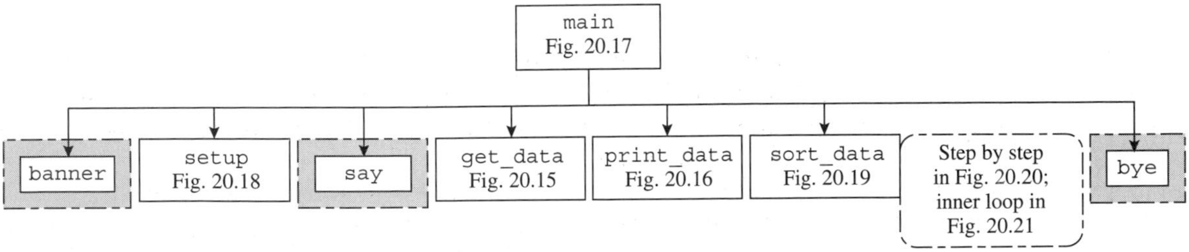

Figure 20.17.　The `main()` program for insertion sort.

Notes on Figure 20.17. The `main()` program for insertion sort.

- The function `say()` is called before each processing step to inform the user of the program's progress. Its output goes to the `stderr` stream, which should not be redirected, so that the user can get the messages.

- *First box: the setup.* In general, a **setup function** will open files, validate parameters, and allocate memory. It is analogous to a C++ constructor function. In this application, since we are using file redirection, `setup()` needs only to allocate memory for the array and initialize the members of the `data_pack` variable, `sort`.

- *Second box: the input.* The program reads data from `stdin` and expects the user to redirect `stdin` to a file that contains the data to be sorted. In this example, we used a file named `insr.in`. The `get_data()` function reads from the specified stream and stores data in `sort`. It returns the number of data items actually read by storing it in the `data_pack` member `n`. This value is used in all the other functions to set the sentinel pointers that control all processing loops.

- *Third and fifth boxes: the output.* First, the program echoes the unsorted data to `stderr` to provide user feedback. After sorting, it writes the values to `stdout`, which we expect to be redirected to a file. In this example, we used an output file named `insert.out`.

- *Fourth box: the sorting.* The only argument to `sort_data()` is the `data_pack` just constructed and initialized. The program passes this argument using call by value because nothing stored in `data_pack` itself will be changed by the function. The positions of the values in the data array will change, but the pack member named `data` is a pointer that provides read-write access to that array.

This function is called from the program in Figure 20.17. It sets up the `data_pack` structure for the rest of the program. Dynamic memory for the data array is allocated if sufficient memory exists.

```
#define LENGTH 20

void                         /* Allocate memory for data.  Errors are fatal.  */
setup( data_pack* sortp )
{
    sortp->max = LENGTH;  /* Read up to LENGTH items. */
    sortp->n = 0;         /* Array is currently empty.  */
    sortp->data = malloc( LENGTH * sizeof(float) );
    if (sortp->data == NULL)
       fatal( " Error:  not enough memory for %i floats\n", LENGTH );
}
```

Figure 20.18.   Setup for insertion sort.

Notes on Figure 20.18. Setup for insertion sort.

- This function's purpose is to create a valid data pack. Each member of the structure is initialized, including allocating a memory block of suitable size. In C++, this would be the constructor function for the class `data_pack`.
- *First box: the array size.* The constant **LENGTH** has been given a value of 20, which may be small for certain applications. Of course, it can be made quite large, but this will allocate a lot of memory that might not be used. If this is done, the `get_data()` function should be modified to include a call on `realloc()` to reduce the array size to **n** after the data have been read.

Sorting by insertion.   The strategy used here is to pick up the first data value in the unsorted section of the data array and insert it, in its proper position, into the sorted portion. This is repeated **n-1** times. After each of the **n-1** passes, the sorted part is one item longer and the unsorted part is one item shorter. An example is illustrated by the diagrams in Figure 20.20, which show the intermediate states of an array of 10 items after each pass.

　　To insert an item from the unsorted portion into the sorted part of the array, we pick up the value (call it **newcomer**), leaving a hole in the array where it had been. Then starting with the array slot just prior to **hole**, we search toward the head of the array for the proper insertion spot. The first value we examine will be the biggest we have found so far, since we are sorting in ascending order. As we move backward through the array, the values decrease. Eventually, we come to either the beginning of the array or to a value smaller than the current item. The **newcomer** must be inserted to the right of this value. This process is illustrated in Figure 20.21 for one of the middle passes through the data in Figure 20.20.

Notes on Figures 20.19, 20.20, and 20.21. Insertion sort for ascending order.

- *First box: the variables.* The **hole pointer**, `hole`, will be used as a cursor, traveling backward through the sorted data, while **pass** is a forward-moving scanner, pointing to the beginning of the unsorted data. The pointer named **end** is an off-board sentinel.

- *Second outer box: the pass loop.*

  1. The sorted part of the array initially consists of only the first item. Therefore, the first pass starts at the second value in the array.
  2. This algorithm makes **n-1** passes. On each pass, we perform the inner loop, which picks up the next unsorted item and inserts it into the

This function implements the insertion sort algorithm for putting items in ascending order. An example of this is diagrammed in Figures 20.20 and 20.21. The flowchart follows the actual code.

```
void
sort_data( data_pack sort )
{
    float* end = sort.data + sort.n;           /* Off-board sentinel. */
    float* pass;                     /* Starting point for pass through array. */
    float* hole;                     /* Array slot containing no data. */
    float newcomer;                  /* Data value being inserted on this pass. */

    for (pass = sort.data + 1; pass < end; ++pass) {
        newcomer = *pass;                        /* Pick up next item. */

        /* ...and insert into the sorted portion of the array. */
        for (hole = pass; hole > sort.data; --hole) {

            if (*(hole-1) <= newcomer) break;

            *hole = *(hole-1);
        }
        *hole = newcomer;
    }

}
```

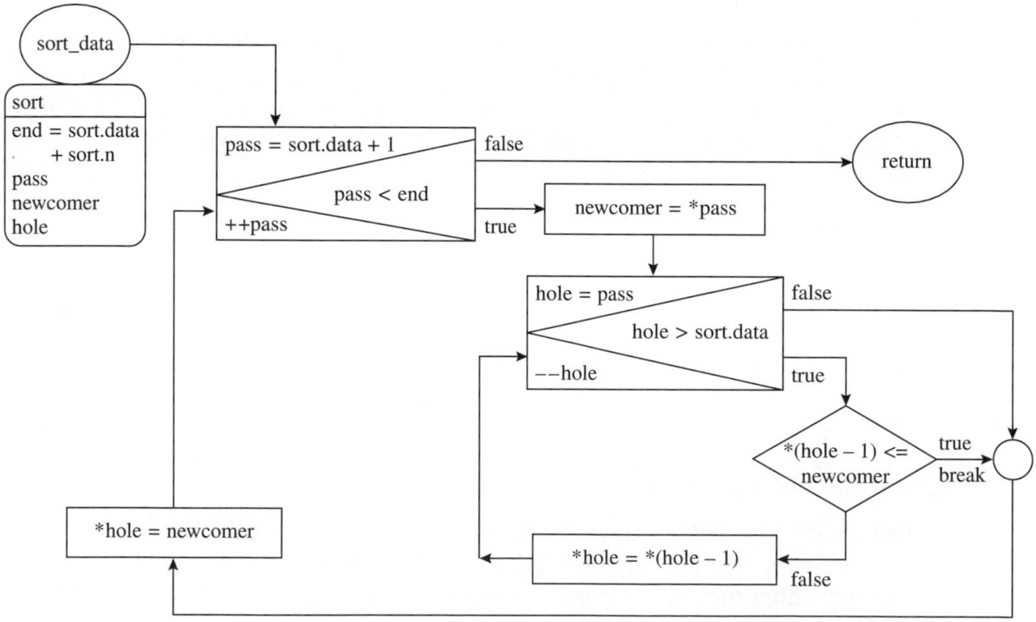

Figure 20.19.   Insertion sort for ascending order.

These diagrams show the data near the end of each pass through the outer loop of **sort_data()**, just before the value of **newcomer** is stored in the array. Details of the inner loop during one pass (the fifth) are shown in Figure 20.21.

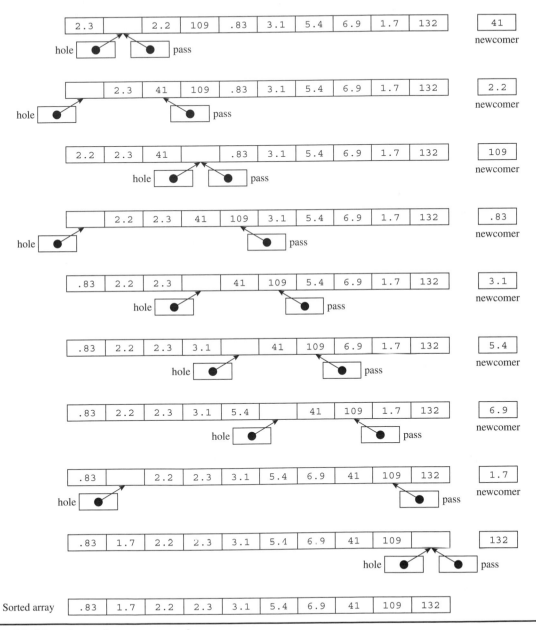

Figure 20.20.   Insertion sort step by step.

This illustrates the workings of the inner loop in Figure 20.19 for the fifth pass shown in Figure 20.20. We show how the data are tested and moved at each step of the search for the proper insertion slot for the `newcomer` value.

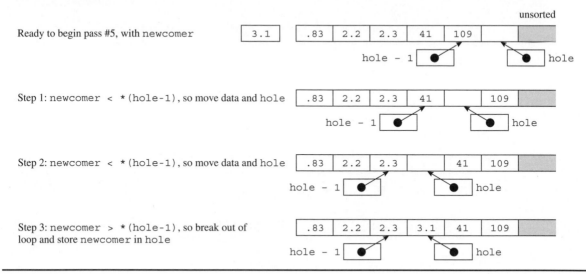

Figure 20.21.   Search and move.

growing list of sorted items. After `n-1` passes, we will have inserted every element into the sorted part of the array.

3. Instead of using an integer counter to mark the passes, we use a pointer named **pass** to mark the position of the first item in the unsorted portion of the array. The loop ends when **pass** equals **end**.

4. We copy the value under the **pass** pointer into **newcomer**, creating a hole in the array.

- *Middle inner box and Figure 20.21: the insertion loop.*

1. We initialize **hole** to the empty slot formerly occupied by **newcomer**.

2. We then step backward through the array, looking for the correct insertion slot. The first value we examine will be the biggest in the ascending-order set. On each step backward, the value just tested must be moved one slot to the right and the hole pointer must be decremented. Eventually, we come to either the end of the array or a slot containing a value smaller than **newcomer**. At this point, the current **hole** position is where **newcomer** must be inserted, so we terminate the inner loop.

3. We might shift as few as no items or as many as currently are in the sorted portion of the array. On the average, we move about half of the sorted items.

4. *Innermost box: finding the right slot.* During the search, `hole` always points to a blank slot and `(hole-1)` refers to the slot before `hole`. We compare the contents of the slot `(hole-1)` to `newcomer`; if the `(hole-1)` item is equal or smaller, we break out of the inner loop. Otherwise, the `hole` slot is *not* the proper insertion spot. So we move the data from `(hole-1)` into the `hole`, then move the `hole` pointer backward one step, and continue searching.

5. When the loop ends, the proper insertion spot has been found and we copy the value of `newcomer` into the `hole` slot.

- *The output.* The input file is echoed to `stderr` as part of the screen output, which follows. The output file is correctly sorted and printed to `stdout` in the order shown at the bottom of Figure 20.20.

```
Reading data from stdin.
10 data items read:
2.3
41
2.2
109
0.83
3.1
5.4
6.9
1.7
132
Beginning to sort.
Data sorted; writing to output stream.
```

20.5   What You Should Remember

20.5.1 Major Concepts

Pointer operations.   To use pointers skillfully, several pointer operations must be understood:

- *Direct assignment.* To set a pointer, `p`, to point at a selected referent, `r`, write `p = r` for arrays or functions but write `p = &r` for structures or simple variables.
- *Indirect assignment.* To assign a new value, `v`, to the referent of pointer `p`, use `*p = v` (`v` cannot be an array or function).
- *Direct reference.* To copy pointer `p` into another pointer `q` write `q = p`.
- *Indirect reference.* To use the referent of pointer `p` in an expression, write `*p` for simple variables and array elements, `p->member_name` if `p` points at a structure, and simply use `p (...)` if it points at a function.

- *Input.* To use `scanf()` to read information into the referent of a pointer, write `&p->member_name` to read into one member of a structure and simply `p` (with no ampersand) if the referent is a simple variable or one slot of an array (you cannot read data into a function).
- *Output.* To use `printf()` to write information from the referent of a pointer, use `p->member_name` to access one member of a structure and `*p` if the referent is a simple variable or one slot of an array.
- *Pointer increment.* To make pointer `p` point to the next (or previous) slot of an array, write `++p` (or `--p`).
- *Pointer arithmetic.* To calculate the number of array slots between two pointers, `p` and `q` (where `q` points to a later slot), write `q - p`. Accessing an array element has two equivalent forms; `*(p+5)` and `p[5]` reference the same value. The latter is preferred.
- *Pointer comparison.* To test whether two pointers, `p` and `q`, refer to the same object, simply use `p == q`. To compare the values of the referents, compare `*p` to `*q` using an appropriate comparison operator or function (`==`, `strcmp()`, or your own function for comparing two structures).

Pointers to functions.   C supports function pointers, which can be used, like pronouns, to refer to different functions at different times. The type of the function pointer must match the prototype of the function to which it points.

A function can be called through a pointer that refers to it, and function pointers can connect functions to data structures. The demonstration program given here used an array of function pointers to implement a menu-driven application. Another use, as functional parameters, will be discussed in Chapter 22.

Array representation.   Functions that process arrays typically need at least two pieces of information: the starting address of the array and the number of elements currently in the array. A data pack, a structure in which these and any other array properties are kept, is very useful. The array information is encapsulated and only one parameter needs to be sent to a function (sometimes using call by address, sometimes call by value).

Array and pointer semantics.   In a very strong sense, C doesn't really have array *types*. An array is simply a homogeneous, sequential collection of variables of the underlying type. We can do nothing with an array as a whole except initialize it and apply `sizeof` to it. When a pointer refers to an array, whether subscripted or not, it refers to only one slot at a time.

Sorting.   Insertion sort is a simple sorting algorithm, implemented here using a double loop that moves data within the array. The sorting strategy is to pick up items from the unsorted part of the data set and insert them, in order, into the sorted portion. Insertion sort should not be used for large data sets, because it is very slow compared to other sorts such as quicksort, which is covered in the next chapter. However, it is considered the best sorting algorithm for data sets of 10 items or less.

20.5.2 Programming Style

Data encapsulation.   Object-oriented languages such as C++ permit the programmer to define objects and data structures in a way that encapsulates everything about them. The use of a structure like **data_pack** is a step in this direction. When possible, gather together the information about an object into a structure and pass it as a single parameter to functions.

Coding idioms.   Errors with pointers are hard to track down because the symptoms may be so varied. Any computation or output that happens after the original error could be invalid because the program may be storing information in the wrong addresses and, thereby, destroying the data used by the rest of the program. This kind of error generally requires that the whole job be rerun and is doubly frustrating because the cause of the error can be hard to localize and, therefore, hard to fix. We address this problem by using coding idioms, presented throughout this chapter, that ensure all references to an array (either through subscripts or through pointers) refer to slots that are actually part of the array. A few of these are

- Initialize pointers to **NULL**. Using a **NULL** pointer should cause the program to terminate quickly and make the problem easier to find.
- Avoid useless operator combinations, such as **&***, when using **scanf()**.
- When referencing an element, **i**, of an array using a pointer, use the syntax **p[i]** rather than ***(p+i)**.
- Use a **typedef** declaration with a descriptive name to create function pointer types. This removes clutter from the function prototypes and variable declarations.
- When possible, use a sentinel to mark the end of an array for a pointer scanning loop. An off-board sentinel is slightly preferable to an on-board ending.

Pointers vs. subscripts.   A pointer can be used (instead of a subscript) to process an array. The scanning technique of using cursor and sentinel pointers is easy and very efficient when the array elements must be processed sequentially. When random access to elements is made, using a subscript is more practical with either an array name or a pointer to an array.

Sorting preferences.   Always use the appropriate sorting algorithm for a particular situation. Speed usually is the deciding factor. For small data sets, the insertion sort performs well. For larger data sets, a fundamentally different sort is needed, like the quicksort algorithms discussed in Chapters 21 and 22.

Menu choices.   When menus are developed, it can be prudent to establish choice 0 as the "quit" choice. It has fitting semantics and allows further options to be added onto the end of the list without affecting the prior ordering, as would be needed if "quit" were the last choice.

File redirection.   If you are redirecting data from a file into `stdin` and from `stdout` to a file, all other status or error messages should be sent to `stderr`. This unbuffered stream will display the messages as they are written, and they will not be interspersed with the data written to `stdout`.

20.5.3 Sticky Points and Common Errors

- *Pointers out of bounds.* One danger of pointers in C is pointing at something unintended. Common errors are to use a subscript that is negative or too large or to increment a pointer beyond either end of an array and then attempt to use the pointer's referent. You cannot use a declaration to restrict a pointer to point at a legitimate array element. Also, C does not "enforce" the boundaries of an array at run time. In general, it does not trap pointer errors. An attempt to use a pointer that is out of bounds (or `NULL`) may cause the program to crash but, on some systems, may not be detected at all; the program will simply walk on adjacent memory values.

- *Uninitialized sentinel.* Another common error is to use a pointer to process an array but forget to initialize the end pointer. The loop almost certainly will not terminate at the end of the array. After processing the actual array elements, the cursor will fall off the end of the array and keep going until, eventually, the program malfunctions or crashes. When you use a sentinel value, be careful to set your loop test correctly, depending on whether you are using an on-board or off-board pointer.

- *Pointers and arrays.* Since an array name, without subscripts, is translated as a pointer to the first slot in the array, some books say that "an array is a pointer." However, this clearly is not true. Since we can use an unsubscripted array name in almost any context where a pointer is expected,[7] we, accurately, could say that an unsubscripted array name becomes a pointer to the beginning of the array. But an array is not a pointer. A pointer requires only a small amount of storage, often 4

---

[7] For instance, we cannot do an assignment such as `arrayname = pointer`.

bytes.[8] In contrast, an array is a series of storage objects of some given type and can occupy hundreds of bytes. Conversely, a pointer certainly is not an array, it is not limited to use with arrays and cannot be used where an array is needed unless it refers to an array.

A common error of this sort is to attempt to use a string variable for input, but forget that an array must be declared to hold the characters that are read in. When the pointer is dereferenced, the program will usually crash.

- *Wrong reference level.* The most common reason for pointer programs to fail is that the wrong number of ampersands or asterisks is used in an expression. Although most compilers give warning comments about mismatched types, they still finish the translation and generate executable code. Do not ignore warnings about pointer type errors.

- *Incorrect referencing.* It also is common to write syntactically correct code with pointers that do not do what you intend. For example, you may wish to change the value of a pointer's referent and, instead, change the value of the pointer itself. Also, you may forget to insert parentheses in the proper places, such as using `*p+5` rather than `*(p+5)` to access an array element. Finally, you may attempt to use a pointer of one data type to access the memory area in which data of another type are stored. Dereferencing such a pointer will result in a garbage value.

- *Precedence.* When dereferencing a pointer using `*`, don't be afraid to use parentheses around the dereferenced value when other operators are involved, thereby making sure that the proper precedence is both understood by you and used by the computer. Watch out for the precedence of `*` in an expression involving pointers, such as `*p++`. Depending on the situation, this expression might have been intended to increment the contents of the address in `p`, but at other times it might have been necessary to increment the contents of `p` and then use the new address. Use parentheses where needed for clarity.

- *Pointer diagrams.* Errors sometimes stem from having an unclear idea about what the ampersand and asterisk operators really mean. The best way to avoid such trouble is to learn to draw diagrams of your pointers, objects, and intended operations, following the models at the beginning of this chapter. Having a clear set of diagrams can help reduce confusion when you begin to write code.

---

[8]This is true of many modern computers. However, some computers may have pointers of different lengths. Microprocessors in the Intel 80x86 family have two kinds of pointers, local (near pointers) and general (far pointers). The near pointer occupies only 2 bytes of storage. In the near future, computers may have such large memories that they will need more than 4 bytes for a pointer.

- *Pointer arithmetic and logic.* It is not meaningful to use address arithmetic on a pointer unless the pointer refers to an array. Similarly, it is not meaningful to compare or subtract two pointers unless they point at parts of the same array.

20.5.4   New and Revisited Vocabulary

These are the most important terms and concepts discussed in this chapter.

base type	pointer arithmetic	head pointer
referent	pointer comparisons	scanning loop
& (address of)	function pointer	**data_pack**
* (indirect reference)	**typedef** for function pointer	setup function
-> (dereference or select)	**NULL** pointer	insertion sort
pointer with subscript	scanning pointer (cursor)	hole pointer
pointer assignment	on- and off-board sentinels	reference level error
indirect assignment	tail pointer (sentinel)	file redirection

20.6   Exercises

20.6.1   Self-Test Exercises

1. Given the array of values that follows, show the positions of the values after each pass of a selection sort that arranges the data in descending order:

21	4	13	17	24	8	15

2. Repeat the previous problem on the data above using the insertion sort algorithm for ascending order.

3. Add the correct number of asterisks to the following declarations. Also add the correct number of ampersands in the initializers so that the declaration actually creates the object described by the phrase on the right. In the last item, replace the **???** by the correct argument.

   a. `char a[12] = "Ohio";`   An array of chars

   b. `char b[10];`   An array of char pointers

   c. `char p = b[0];`   A pointer to the first slot in
                                   an array of char pointers

   d. `char q = malloc( 12 );`   A pointer to a dynamically
                                   allocated array of 12 chars

   e. `char s = malloc( ??? );`   A pointer to a dynamically allocated
                                   array of 4 char pointers

4. Assume that **mat** is an *N* by *N* matrix of **float**s. Declare two pointers, **begin** and **end**, and initialize them to the first and last slots of **mat**. Declare a third pointer, **off**, and initialize it as an off-board pointer.

5. You are given the declarations and diagram that follow:

```
typedef struct { double x, y; } point_t;
double x;
point_t tri[3];

double* xp;
double* yp;
point_t* pp;
```

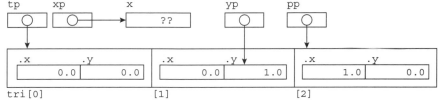

a. Change the declaration of **tri** to include an initializer for the values shown in the diagram.

b. Declare another pointer named **tp** and initialize it to point at the beginning of the array that represents the triangle, as shown.

c. Declare and initialize **tri_end**, an off-board sentinel for the triangle.

6. Use the diagram in the preceding exercise to write the following statements:

a. Write three assignment statements that make the pointers **xp**, **yp**, and **pp** refer to the objects indicated.

b. Using only these four pointers (and not the variable names **tri** and **x**), write an assignment statement that copies the **x** coordinate of the last point of the triangle **tri** into the variable **x**.

c. Using the array name **tri** and a subscript, store the value 3.3 in the referent of **yp**.

d. Using the pointer **tp** and no subscripts, print the **x** coordinate of the last point in the array.

7. Given the declarations and code below, show the output of the loops.

```
#define Z 3
char square[Z][Z];
char* p;
char* start = &square[0][0];
char* end = &square[Z-1][Z-1];

for (p = end; p >= start; p -= 2) *p = '1';
```

```
for (p = start; p < end; ++p) {
    ++p;
    *p = '0';
}

for (p = start; p <= end; ++p) printf( "%3c", *p );
puts( "\n" );
```

8. Using the representation for triangles diagrammed and described in problem 5, write a function, **tri_in()**, with no parameters that will read the coordinates of a triangle from the **stdin** stream. Dynamically allocate storage for the triangle within this function and return the completed triangle by returning a pointer to the first point in the array. Use pointers, not subscripts, throughout this function.

20.6.2 Using Pencil and Paper

1. Show the changes that must be made to adjust the insertion sort program to sort numbers in descending order. Then use the data array first presented in Figure 20.8 to trace the steps of execution of the new insertion sort algorithm, as was done in Figure 20.20.

2. Given the data structure in the following diagram, look at each of the statements. If the operation is valid, say what value is stored in **x** or in **p2** by each of these operations. If the operation is not valid, explain why. Assume that all numbers are of type **double** and all pointers are of type **double***.

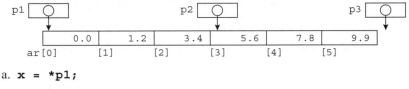

a. **x = *p1;**

b. **x = p1 + 1;**

c. **x = *(p2 + 1);**

d. **x = *p2 + 1;**

e. **p2 = p1[4];**

f. **p2++;**

g. **p2 = p1 + 1;**

h. **p2 = p3 - p1;**

3. Given the data structure diagrammed in the next problem, write a type declaration and the set of variable declarations to construct (but not initialize) the payroll structure, the pointer **scan**, and pointers (not illustrated) **end** and **p10**, which will be used to process the structure.

4. Given the data structure in the following diagram, write a statement for each item according to the instructions given. Assume that all numbers are type **float**. Declare the pointers appropriately.

a. Set **scan** to point to the first structure in the array, as illustrated.

b. Set **end** to be an off-board pointer for the array.

c. Move **scan** to the next array slot.

d. Set pointer **p10** to point at the slot with pay rate $10.00.

e. Give the last person a $.50 pay raise.

f. Calculate and store the pay for the person who is the referent of **p10**.

5. Rewrite the **get_data()** function from Figure 20.15 as follows:

a. The arguments remain the same. Assume the **data_pack** is initialized to the empty state by the caller, as before.

b. Read data from the stream argument into the **data_pack** argument until the end of the file is reached. Use **realloc()** to enlarge the array, if necessary.

c. When all of the data have been read, use **realloc()** to shrink the data array in the **data_pack** to exactly the right size, which could be either larger or smaller than its original size.

6. For each item that follows, write two C statements that perform the task described. Write the first using subscripts, the second using pointers and dereference. Explain which is clearer and easier to use and why. Use these declarations:

```
const int rows = 5, cols = 3;
int k, m;
float A[cols];
float M[rows][cols];
float* N = malloc( rows * cols * sizeof(float) );
float* p, * end;
```

a. Make **p** refer to the first slot of **A**.

b. Write a **for** loop to set all elements of **A** to one.

c. Double the number in **M[4][2]** and store it back in **M[4][2]**.

d. Set **end** as an off-board pointer for **M**.

e. Make **p** refer to the first **float** in **N**.

7. a. Define a type named **f_2strs** for a pointer that can refer to a function with two **string** parameters and a **string** result.

b. Declare **ps** as a pointer variable whose base type is a function of type **f_2strs**.

c. Set **ps** to refer to an appropriate function from the **string** library. (See Appendix G for a complete list.)

d. Call the selected library function using **ps** (not the function's name) and print the answer.

20.6.3 Using the Computer

1. String pointers.
A string pointer can point anywhere within a character array. Also, C permits us to do arithmetic with a string pointer, just like any other pointer. For example, this diagram shows the string variable **p2** after setting it equal to **p1+2**:

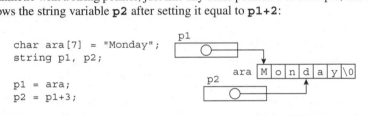

```
char ara[7] = "Monday";
string p1, p2;

p1 = ara;
p2 = p1+3;
```

Write a **void** function, **upper_word()**, that has one parameter, a string. Using the library function **toupper()**, convert all of the letters in the string to upper case. For example, the result of **upper_word(p2)** would be **"MonDAY"**. Write a program that reads text from **stdin** one line at a time, selects a random subscript between 0 and the end of each string, and converts the last portion of the string, starting at the selected position, by calling **upper_word()**. Display the changed line before reading the next line. Continue until a null string is entered. Reminder: A null string is a string of length 0.

2. Pointer selection.
Rewrite the selection sort program presented in Chapter 16 to use pointers for array searching and data accessing as in the insertion sort program in this chapter.

3. The right way to do it.
Modify the insertion sort program that begins in Figure 20.17 to sort an array of up to 100 strings in alphabetical order. Using appropriate functions, read the strings from a user-specified file, one per line, and allocate exactly enough space for each one. No string will be longer than 80 characters. Store the string pointers into the array by inserting each one into the sorted array as it is read. Quit when the null string is read and return the number of nonnull strings read and stored in the array. Write the sorted list to a user-specified output file. At the end of the program, free all dynamically allocated storage.

4. Trimming blanks.

   The **fgets()** function reads entire lines of input, including trailing whitespace and a newline character. When these strings are to become part of a data structure, though, the trailing whitespace is undesirable. Write a function, **trim()**, with one parameter, **s**, which is a pointer to an input buffer containing the result of a call on **fgets()**. The **trim()** function must find the last nonwhitespace character in **s** and trim the whitespace from the end of the string by storing a null terminator in the next array slot. When finished, return a pointer to the null terminator. Be careful to handle properly strings that contain no whitespace or all whitespace. Write a main program that calls this function repeatedly. After reading and trimming each string, display the final string length and the string itself. Test it using a variety of data.

5. Stripping blanks.

   Write a function, **no_space()**, with one string parameter, **s**, which is a pointer to a dynamically allocated array of characters. This function must remove all whitespace characters from **s**, shifting nonwhitespace characters to the left to close up the space. Be careful to handle properly strings that contain no whitespace or all whitespace. Hint: There is an efficient algorithm for this task that moves each character at most once, using two pointers. Write a program that reads text from a user-specified file, one line at a time, strips the whitespace, and writes the remaining characters back to another user-specified file. No line will be longer than 80 characters. When writing the output file, write a newline character at the end of each line.

6. The right substring.

   The C string library contains a function, **strstr()**, that searches for substrings. The parameters are two strings: the source string and the substring. It searches the source for the first occurrence of the substring and returns a pointer to the array slot at which it begins. If the substring does not occur, **NULL** is returned. Write a variation of this function, **strrstr()**, using the same parameters and the same return value, that finds the **rightmost** matching substring (instead of the leftmost). Implement the code using pointers, pointer arithmetic, and **strncmp()**. Write a program to prompt the user for a word to find and store it in an array, **find**. Then read lines of text from **stdin** and use your function to search each line for the last copy of **find**. No line will be longer than 80 characters. Echo the line of text back to the screen, except for the located substring. Echo that substring in upper-case letters. Stop processing when the null string is entered.

7. Substitution.

   Write a function with three string parameters, a sentence, **S**, a search string, **A**, and a substitution string, **B**. This function will form a new sentence by searching **S** for the first occurrence of **A** and replacing it by **B**. Use functions from the **string** library, and copy the nonreplaceable parts of **S**, as they are searched, into a dynamically allocated result array. When substring **A** is found, copy **B** into the result instead. Finally, copy the tail end of the sentence into the result array and return the pointer to the result string. Write a main program with a query loop to permit you to make several substitutions on one sentence.

8. Complex arithmetic.

   Define a structured type with real and imaginary parts to represent a complex number. Implement a menu-driven program that will first allow us to enter two complex numbers by entering their components, separated by whitespace, in the order $real_1$ $imag_1$ $real_2$ $imag_2$. Then present a menu with options to add, subtract, multiply, or divide. Display the input and the result after each operation. Write four functions to perform the complex operations defined next, and install them in an array of functions that can be called using the menu selection. These functions should accept two structured arguments, do the computations, store the answer in a local complex variable, and return the value of that variable. In these formulas, C_1 and C_2 are two complex numbers: $C_1 = a + bi$ and $C_2 = c + di$.

$$C_1 + C_2 = (a + c) + (b + d)i$$
$$C_1 - C_2 = (a - c) + (b - d)i$$
$$C_1 \times C_2 = (ac - bd) + (ad + bc)i$$
$$C_1 / C_2 = [(ac + bd) + (bc - ad)i] / (c^2 + d^2)$$

9. Matrix averages.
   Write a program that will input a matrix of numbers and output the row and column averages. More specifically,

   a. Read a file containing two integers on the first line: a number of rows and a number of columns. Then allocate memory for a matrix of **float**s with those dimensions. Read the rest of the data from the file, row by row, into the matrix.

   b. Allocate an array of **float**s whose length equals the number of rows and store the average of each row in the corresponding array slot.

   c. Allocate another array with one slot per column and store the average of each column in the corresponding array slot.

   d. Print the matrix in spreadsheet form, with row numbers on the left, row averages on the right, column numbers on top, and column averages at the bottom.

   Do all these operations using pointers and pointer increment, not subscripts.

10. Sorting a poker hand.
    This program asks you to begin implementing a program that runs a poker game. To start, you will need to define two types:

    a. Represent the suits of a deck of cards as an enumeration (clubs, diamonds, hearts, spades). Define two arrays parallel to this enumeration, one for input and one for output. The input array should contain one-letter codes: {'c', 'd', 'h', 's'}. The output array should contain the suit names as strings.

    b. Represent the card values as integers. The numbers on the cards, called *spot values*, are entered and printed using the following one-letter codes: {'2', '3', '4', '5', '6', '7', '8', '9', 'T', 'J', 'Q', 'K', 'A'}. These should be translated to integers in the range 2 ... 14. Any other card value is an error.

    c. Represent a card as a structure containing a suit and a spot value. A poker hand will be an array of five cards.

    d. Write a set of functions to process poker hands and a main program to test these functions. Implement the following functions:

- **void get_hand(card*)**. Read and validate five cards from the keyboard, one card per line. Each card should consist of a two-letter code such as **3H** or **TS**. Permit the user to enter either lower-case or upper-case letters. Return the data through the array of cards.
- **void sort_hand(card*)**. Sort the five cards in increasing order by spot value (ignore the suits when sorting). For example, if the hand was originally **TH, 3S, 4D, 3C, KS**, then the sorted hand would be **3S, 3C, 4D, TH, KS**. Use insertion sort and pointers.
- **void print_hand(card*)**. Display the five cards in a hand, one card per line. Each card should be printed in its full English form; that is, **9 of Hearts** or **King of Spades**, not **9h** or **KS**.

11. Beginner's poker.

   The object of poker is to get a hand with a better (less likely) combination of cards than your opponents. The scoring combinations are listed in Figure 20.22, in increasing order of value. Define an enumerated type to represent these values and a parallel array for output. Start with a program that can read, sort, and print a poker hand, as described in the previous problem. Add these functions to begin implementing the game itself:

   a. Write nine functions, one for each scoring combination. These functions will take a hand as a parameter and return **true** if the hand has the particular scoring combination that this function is looking for. (Return **false** otherwise.) Some of these functions will call others; for example, the full house function should call the triple and pair functions (carefully).

   b. **int value_hand(card*)**. Given a sorted hand, evaluate it using the scoring functions in Figure 20.22. Return the highest value that applies. For example, the hand **TS, JS, QS, KS, AS** is a royal flush, a straight flush, a flush, and a straight. Of these possibilities, royal flush has the highest value and should be returned.

Value	Description
Bust	Five cards that include none of the following combinations
One pair	The hand has two cards with the same spot value
Two pairs	The hand has two pairs of cards
Three of a kind	The hand has three cards with the same spot value
Straight	The spot values of all five cards are consecutive
Flush	All five cards have the same suit
Full house	The hand has one pair and three of a kind
Four of a kind	The hand has four cards with the same spot value
Straight flush	The suits all match and the spot values are consecutive
Royal flush	The suits all match and the spot values are **T, J, Q, K, A**

Figure 20.22. Poker hands.

c. Write a main program that reads two hands, calls the evaluation function twice, prints each hand and its value, then says which hand wins, that is, has a higher value. If two hands have the same value, then no one wins. (This is a slight simplification of the rules.)

12. Around and around and around she goes...

The gambling game roulette uses a wheel with 38 sections. Two green sections are numbered 0 and 00 (use 37 to represent 00). The other 36 sections are numbered 1 to 36. Half of these are black (2, 4, 6, 8, 10, 11, 13, 15, 17, 20, 22, 24, 26, 28, 29, 31, 33, 35); the other half are red. On this wheel is a small ball that runs around its edge. The wheel is spun and goes around and around for a while, during which time the bettors watch and wish, until the ball drops into a slot—and where she stops, nobody knows. You are to emulate a roulette game at a gambling casino, using the somewhat simplified betting scheme described in Figure 20.23. Bets are made based on where the ball will be when the wheel stops. The table describes most of the bets that a player can make and the payoff if a bet wins.

a. Define a type **color_t**, an enumeration of red, black, and green.

b. Define a type **section_t** to represent a section of the wheel using a number and a color. Define a global constant array, **wheel**, that has 38 sections and initialize it to the numbers **0...37** with the appropriate color for each number.

c. Write a function, **display()**, that has one parameter, a pointer to one section of the wheel. In a pleasing format at the top of the screen, display the number and color of that section.

d. Write a function, **pick()**, to get the next random section number. No parameters are needed. It should return a randomly selected integer between 0 and 37.

e. Write a function, **spin()**, to emulate a roulette wheel. The parameter should be the wheel array and return a pointer to the winning section of the **wheel**. Randomly select an integer N between **10** and **MAX** to represent the time during which the wheel is spinning. (Some experimentation will help you find the best value for **MAX**). Go around a loop N times, calling **pick()** each time (to choose a section of the wheel) and **display()** to show it. The user will see a rapidly changing display that stops spinning after a random amount of time. If the display spins too fast to see, call **delay()** to slow it down. When the wheel stops, also

A $1 Winning Bet	Pays
Red or black	$1
Odd or even	$1
High (19–36) or low (1–18)	$1
The dozen: 1–12, 13–24, or 25–36	$2
Two numbers (either one matches)	$17
One individual number	$35

Figure 20.23.   Roulette bets.

display whether the chosen section is high or low, odd or even (use the **%** operator), and in the first, second, or third dozen (use the integer / operator).

f. Write a main program that will display a menu to let the user choose a type of bet. Prompt the user for the number of dollars bet (a **float**). Then spin the wheel. When it stops, compare the results to the bet and tell the user whether he or she won or lost, and how much money was won or lost. The payoffs are listed in Figure 20.23.

13. Average students.

At Unknown University, the Admissions department has discovered that the best applicants usually go to big-name schools instead and the worst often do poorly in courses, so the school wants to concentrate recruitment efforts and financial aid resources on the middle half of the applicants. You must write a program that takes a file containing a list of applicants, in which each applicant has a name and a total SAT score, and prints an alphabetical list of the middle half of these applicants. (Eliminate the best quarter and the worst quarter, then alphabetize the rest.) This can be done using a simple iterative technique. First, read the data from a file named **apply.dat** into an array of structures (let N be the total number of applicants). Then begin a loop that eliminates applicants one at a time, until only half are left. Within this loop, let **first** be a pointer to the first array element that is still included, **last** be a pointer to the last one, and **r** (the number remaining) be initialized to N. Each time around the loop, either **first** is incremented or **last** is decremented and **r** decreases by 1. At each step,

a. If **r** is even, find the remaining applicant with the lowest SAT score and swap it with the applicant at position **first**. Then increment **first**, decrement **r**, and repeat.

b. If **r** is odd, find the remaining applicant with the highest SAT score and swap it with the applicant at **last**. Then decrement **last** and **r** and repeat.

c. Quit when $r \le N/2$. Return the values of **first** and **r**.

When only half the applicants are left, use any sort technique to sort them alphabetically. Write the sorted list to a user-specified output file.

CHAPTER
21

Recursion

This chapter presents **recursion**, a fundamental technique in which a function solves a problem by dividing it into two or more sections, calling itself to solve each portion of the original problem, continuing the self-calls until a subproblem's solution is trivial, and then building a total solution out of the partial solutions. We examine how to apply recursion to two familiar problems: searching and sorting.

Prior to this, as an aid to understanding how recursion works, we briefly survey C storage classes, giving a detailed description of how the `auto` storage class is used to implement recursive parameter passing.

21.1   Storage Classes

Every variable has a storage-class attribute in addition to its data type and perhaps a type qualifier like `const` or `volatile` as well. The **storage class** determines when and where a variable is allocated in memory, when it is initialized, how long it persists, and which functions may use it. There are four storage classes in C: `auto`, `register`, `extern`, and `static`. Of these, `register` relates to hardware registers and its use for object code optimization is beyond the scope of this text. The storage classes `auto`, `static` and `extern` are described here.

21.1.1 Automatic Storage

The automatic, or `auto`, storage class is used in C for function parameters. Local variables within functions also are labeled `auto` by default, unless declared to be `static`, as discussed in the next section. Whenever you call a function, memory for every `auto`-class variable is allocated in an area called the **run-time stack**, with other function call information. This memory is deallocated when the function returns. The stack memory is managed automatically and efficiently by the C system.

Automatic is the default storage class for local variables because it makes the most efficient use of computer memory. Good programmers use `auto` variables (rather than `static` local variables or global variables) wherever possible, because their lifetime is brief and their scope is restricted to one function. They provide an effective way to isolate the actions of each program unit from the others. Unintentional interference between functions is minimized, making it much easier to debug a large program. On the other hand, the constant allocation and deallocation of storage adds some overhead to the execution time. But, since allocation is done quite efficiently, the time wasted is minimal and the advantages of the added modularity are great. The characteristics of `auto` memory are discussed in greater detail in an upcoming section on the run-time stack, but briefly `auto` memory is

- **Allocated** on the run-time stack.
- **Initialized** during the function call.
- **Visible** only to the statements in the body of the declaring function.
- **Deallocated** during the function-return process. Local variables are freed by the called function and parameter storage is freed by the caller, both under the control of the C system.

21.1.2 Static Storage

The name *static* is derived from the word *stay;* it is used because `static` variables stay around from the beginning to the end of execution. In older computer languages, all variables were `static`. In C, local variables are `auto` by default but can be declared `static`. There are two purposes for `static` local variables: to remember the state of the subprogram and to increase time and space efficiency when a function uses a table of constants. The characteristics of `static` local memory are

- It is allocated in a portion of computer memory separate from the run-time stack, which we call the **static allocation area**. In many implementations, this immediately follows the memory block used for the program's code.

- It is initialized when the program is loaded into memory. Initializers must be constants or constant expressions; they cannot refer to non-**static** variables, even ones with a **const** qualifier.
- It is deallocated when the program exits and returns to the system.
- It is visible to the statements in the body of the function in which the **static** variable is declared.

Global variables default to **extern** but also may be declared **static**.[1] A **static** global variable is like a **static** local variable in almost every way. It is declared at the top of the source-code file and visible to all functions in that same file, as well as those in other source-code files that might be **#include**d by it.[2]

The state of a function.   In some complex situations, a function must remember a piece of data from one call to the next. For example, a function that assigns consecutive identification numbers to a series of manufactured objects would need to know the last number assigned before it could assign the next. We say that this last number is part of the **state** of the system. Since **auto** variables come and go as function calls are begun and completed, they cannot be used to store state information. Global variables can be used, but doing so is foolish because these variables can be seen and changed by other parts of the program. A **static** local variable is an ideal way to save state information because it is both private and persistent.

Tables of constants.   Normally, the time consumed by the allocating and initializing of automatic variables is minimal. It is not considered a waste because this allocation method guarantees that every function starts its computations with a clean slate. However, reinitializing a **table of constants** every time you enter a function that uses them can consume appreciable execution time. It also requires extra space, because the program code must contain a copy of the entire initializer for the table, which it then uses to reinitialize the local **auto** table every time the function is called. If the table truly is constant, certainly there is no need to keep recopying it.

We could solve this problem by declaring the table as a global constant. However, this is not really a good solution if the table is used by only one function. A general principle is that things used together should be written together in a program. If possible, a table should be defined by the function that uses it, not at the top of the program file, which may be several pages away. A better way to eliminate the wasted time and space is to declare the table inside the function with a **static** storage class. It will be visible only within the defining function and

---

[1] This makes a difference only in a multimodule application where the modules are compiled separately and linked before execution.

[2] The **static** variable is visible to functions from the included file only if the **#include** command follows the static declaration.

will not be re-created every time the function is called. Space will be allocated once (before program execution begins) and initialized at that time. Figure 16.5 first illustrated the use of **static** to define a table of constants.

21.1.3   External Storage (Advanced Topic)

A variable or function of the **extern** storage class is made known to the linker explicitly. This becomes useful when an application is so large that it is broken up into modules, often written by different people. Each module is a set of types, functions, and data objects in a separate source-code file. These files are compiled separately and joined into a single working unit by the linker. In such a program, many objects and functions are defined and used only within one subsystem. Others are defined in one module and used by others. They must be made known to the linker, so that it can make the necessary connections. This is known as **external linkage**.

   Functions, as well as global constants and variables, are labeled **extern** by default. These symbols are made known to the linker unless they are explicitly declared to be **static**. A **static** function or object is visible only within the code module that defines it.

Rules for extern declarations.   Developing large, multimodule programs is beyond the scope of this text. The following details are provided for general knowledge and as a basis for the small multimodule system developed in Chapter 23.

   An **extern** symbol must be declared in both the code file that supplies it and the ones that use it. One declaration defines the object and one or more declarations in other modules may import it. These two kinds of declarations are subtly different in several ways:

- *Creation.* A data object declaration with an initializer is the defining occurrence, whether or not the keyword **extern** is present. A function prototype is a defining occurrence but only if the function definition appears in the same code module.
- *Allocation and initialization.* The defining occurrence is allocated and initialized when its code module is loaded into memory. Initializers must be constants or constant expressions.
- *Deallocation.* External symbols are global in nature, therefore they are freed when the program exits and returns to the system.
- *Visibility.* The defining occurrence is visible in its own code module and any other code module that contains a matching declaration with the keyword **extern**. The importing occurrence must not include an initializer (if it is a data object) or a function definition (if it is a prototype).

| 21.2 | **The Run-Time Stack (Advanced Topic)** |

During a function call, the caller passes arguments that are stored in the called function's parameter variables, and these are used by the function in its computations. Static storage cannot be used for **parameters** in a language that allows functions to be recursive, because a recursive function may call itself an indefinite number of times. When a function calls itself, two or more sets of its argument values must coexist. At compile time, the translator cannot know how many times a recursive function will call itself, so it cannot know how much storage will be needed for all instances of its parameters. For this reason, C allocates space for parameters and local variables in a storage area that can grow dynamically as needed.

In C, as in most modern languages, a data structure called the *execution stack*, *run-time stack*, or simply, *stack* is used to store one *stack frame* for each function that has been called but has not yet returned since execution began. In this section, we look closely at the mechanism by which a function actually receives and stores its parameters.

21.2.1   Stack Frames

A function's **stack frame**, or **activation record**, holds its parameters, return address, and local variables. In it, there is one variable for each parameter listed in the function header. Before control is transferred from the caller to the function, the argument values specified by the function call are computed and copied into the parameter variables in the new stack frame, as follows:

1. Memory is allocated in the stack frame for the parameters.
2. Any argument expressions in the call are evaluated and the resulting values are written in order on the stack. If the type of an argument does not match the type of the corresponding parameter in the function's prototype, the argument value is converted to the required type.
3. Then control is transferred to the subprogram with a jump-to-subroutine machine instruction. One of the actions of this instruction is to store the return address in the stack.
4. On entry into the subprogram, an association is made between the defined parameter names and the arguments in the stack frame. More stack storage then is allocated and initialized for the local `auto` variables (storage for `static` variables was allocated at load time).
5. Control finally is transferred to the first line of code in the subprogram. Execution of the subprogram continues until a `return` statement is reached. If there is no `return` statement, execution continues until the last line of code is finished.

When execution of the function ends, the result is returned and storage is freed as follows:

1. The result of the **return** expression is converted (if necessary) to the return type declared by the function prototype. The return value then is stored where the caller expects to find it.
2. The local **auto** variable storage area is freed. (Local **static** variables are not freed until the program terminates.)
3. Control returns to the caller at the **return address** that was stored in the stack frame during the function call.
4. The caller picks up the return value from its prearranged location and frees the stack storage area occupied by argument values.
5. Execution continues in the calling program at the instruction after the jump-to-subroutine instruction.

21.2.2   Stack Diagrams and Program Traces

A **stack diagram** is a picture of the stack frames that exist at some given time during execution. We use stack diagrams to help understand what does and does not happen with function calls when we manually trace the execution of a program. They are particularly helpful in understanding recursion. Figure 21.1 shows a generic stack diagram. Figure 21.2 shows a more specific instance of a stack, which can be referred to during the following discussion.

To **trace** the operation of **a program**, start by drawing an area for global and **static** variables. Record the names and initial values of these variables. Set aside a second area for the program's output to simulate the screen. Begin the stack diagram at the bottom of the page with a frame for **main()** (new frames will be added above this one). Record the names and initial values of the variables of

---

The diagram on the left shows the arrangement of frames on the stack; the frame for **main()** is allocated first; a frame for each other function is added when the function is called and removed when it returns. The diagram on the right shows a more detailed view of the components of one stack frame.

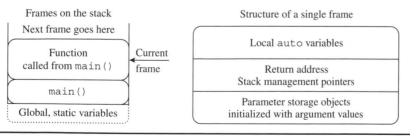

Figure 21.1.   The run-time stack.

These diagrams are pictures of the stack for the gas pressure program developed in Figure 9.10. The values shown for **temp**, **m**, and **vol** were entered by the user. On the left, the stack is shown during a call on the **ideal()** function, just before the function's **return** statement occurs. On the right, the stack is shown just before the return from **vander()**. The gray areas in each stack frame contain the function's return address and information used by the system for stack management.

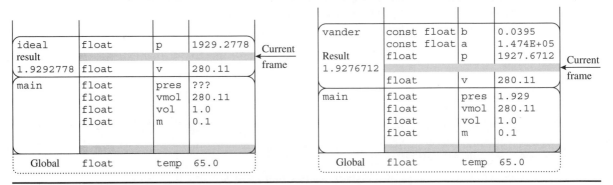

Figure 21.2.   The run-time stack for the gas pressure program.

main() in this frame. Make three columns for each variable, giving its type, its name, and the initial value (or a **?** if it is not initialized). Leave room to write in new values that might be assigned later.

Finally, start with the first line of code in **main()** and progress from line to line through the program code. Emulate whatever action each line calls for. If the line is an output command, write the output in your screen area. If the line is an assignment or input statement, change the value of the corresponding variable in the rightmost column of your stack diagram.

If the line is a function call, mark the position of the line in the calling program so that you can return to that spot. Add a frame to your stack diagram. Label the new frame with the function's name and record the argument values in it. Label these with the parameter names and add the local variables and their values. Then trace the code of the function until you come to the last line or a **return** statement. Write the function's return value under its name on the left side of the stack frame and draw a diagonal line through the function's stack frame to indicate that it has been freed.

For example, Figure 21.2 shows the stack at two times during the execution of the gas pressure program from Figure 9.10. The diagram on the left shows the stack during the process of returning from the **ideal()** function. In the next program step, the result will be stored in the variable **pres** of **main()** and the stack frame for **ideal()** will be freed. Later, **vander()** is called. The diagram on the right shows the stack when **vander()** is ready to return. The stack frame for **ideal()** is gone (it would be crossed out in your diagram), and a new stack frame for **vander()** is in its place.

21.3   **Iteration and Recursion**

In Chapter 12, we introduced the bisection method for finding a root of an equation that lies within a given interval. The implementation given used a loop to search for the root, dividing the remaining interval in half each time, discarding one half, until the root was trapped between the left and right ends of a very short interval. This process was a form of **binary search**, which we formalize in a later section. We were able to halve the unexplored territory each time because we knew on each step which subinterval, left or right, contained the root.

The bisection algorithm is an example of a general problem-solving approach called **divide and conquer**. If the problem is too difficult to solve when it is first presented, simplify it and try again. If this can be repeated, eventually the problem will become manageable. A loop, or **iteration**, is one way to repeat a process; recursion is another. We review the essentials of algorithms that iterate, then show how the problem simplification strategy is reflected in recursive processes.

21.3.1   The Nature of Iteration

Every loop consists of a control section and a body. The control section performs initialization and contains an expression, called the *loop condition*, that is tested either before or after every iteration. The loop ends when this condition has the value `false`. If we use a loop, something must change on each iteration (and that change must affect the loop condition) or the process will never end. We have seen infinite loops that fail to increment the loop variable or read a new input value; they simply repeat the same statements again and again until the user kills the process. Every programmer occasionally writes such a loop by mistake. In loops that are not controlled by the user's input, each iteration must make the remaining job smaller; that is, each trip around the loop must perform one step of a finite process, leaving one fewer step to do. Often progress is measured by the value of a variable that is incremented or decremented on each iteration, until a predetermined goal is reached.

21.3.2   The Nature of Recursion

A *recursive function* does its task by calling upon itself. Like a loop, a recursive function must reduce the size of the remaining task on every call, or the process will become mired in an infinite repetition of the same process step; this is called **infinite recursion**. Eventually, an infinite recursion will be detected by the system and the process aborted with a comment such as **stack overflow**, due to the allocation of too many stack frames or too much memory.

When one function calls another, argument values are passed into the subprogram, local storage is allocated on the stack for them, and an answer eventually is passed back to the caller. The same is true when a recursive function calls itself. The stack provides storage for parameters and local variables for each call on a function. We say that a **call is active** until the called function returns and its frame is discarded. Normally, there are several active functions at once, because one function can call a second one, and the second can call a third, and so forth. Therefore, at any given time, many frames can be on the stack. The computer always is executing the most recently called function, so it uses the most recent frame. When the task of a function is complete, its stack frame is eliminated and it returns control to its caller. The caller, which had been waiting for the subprogram to finish, resumes its own task, using its own stack frame, which is now on top of the stack. A recursive function calls itself, so the caller and the subprogram are two activations of the same function.

If a recursive function calls itself five times, six stack frames will exist simultaneously for it, each holding the parameters for one of the active calls. Each time one of the calls returns, its stack frame is discarded and control goes back to the prior invocation. That is, when the fifth active call returns, control goes back to the fourth active call. The fourth incarnation then resumes its work at the spot just after the recursive call. This process proceeds smoothly, just as with ordinary function calls, so long as each call *specifies a smaller task* than the previous call. In theory, if the job does not get smaller, the recursions will continue endlessly. Practically speaking, though, a recursion is unlikely to last forever because each stack frame requires memory, thereby making the stack longer. Eventually, all of the available memory is used up and the stack becomes too large to fit into memory. At this time, the system will report that the stack has overflowed and abort the user's process.

As with loops, every recursion must contain a condition used to determine whether to continue with more recursive calls or return to its caller. This condition often is referred to as the **base case**, because the action to take (usually to return) is basic and straightforward. Frequently, the entire body of a recursive function is just a single `if...else` statement, where the `if` contains the termination condition, the `true` clause contains the `return` statement, and the `else` clause contains the recursive call. The simplest and most common recursive strategy is

- Base cases: The function checks the first base case and returns if it is satisfied. If needed, it checks the second, third, and further base cases and returns if any one of them is satisfied.
- Recursive step: If no base case is satisfied, the function calls itself recursively with arguments that exclude part of the original problem. When the recursive call returns, the function processes the answer, if necessary, and returns to the caller.

The program in Figure 21.3 applies this recursive strategy to the task of finding the minimum value in a list of data items. On each recursive step, the function processes the first item on the list and calls itself recursively to process the rest of the list. Thus, each step reduces the size of the task by one item. This pattern is typical of recursion applied to a list or array of data items, and is called a **simple list recursion**.

21.3.3 Tail Recursion

If the recursive call is the last action taken before the function returns, we say it is a **tail recursion**. Once the returns start in a tail recursion, all the calls return, one after another, and all the stack frames are discarded one by one until control reaches the original caller. The value computed during the last call is sent back through each successive stack frame and eventually returned to the original caller. The binary search function in Figure 21.8 is tail recursive; the results of the recursive calls are returned immediately without further processing. Any tail recursive algorithm can be implemented easily, and more efficiently, as a loop. The bisection program in Chapter 12 that finds the roots of an equation is a form of binary search implemented using a `do...while` loop.

However, not all recursive algorithms are tail recursive. For example, the `array_min()` function in Figure 21.3 is not tail recursive because the result of the recursive call is compared to another value before returning. Although we can easily write an iterative algorithm to find the minimum value in a list, many recursive algorithms cannot be rewritten easily as iterative programs; they are essentially recursive and have no simple, natural, iterative form. The last program in this chapter, quicksort, falls into this category. It is one of the most important and easily understood of these inherently recursive algorithms.

21.4   **A Simple Example of Recursion**

The program in Figure 21.3 uses recursion to find the minumum value in an array of values. Compare it to the iterative minimum finding program in Figure 16.21. The iterative solution is better; it is just as simple and much more efficient. However, the recursive solution is useful for illustrating how recursion works and developing some intuition for it. Later examples will demonstrate that recursive solutions can be easier to develop than iterative versions in some cases.

Notes on Figure 21.3: A recursive program to find a minimum.

- *Second box: the* **recursive descent.** We want to find the minimum value in a set of values. But that requires some work, so we use a strategy of shrinking the size of the problem. At each step, we defer the action of examining the first value in the set (`a[0]`) and turn our attention to finding the minimum of the rest (`a[1]` to `a[n-1]`). If we do this recursively, we put aside the values one at a time, until only one value remains. Once

```
#include "tools.h"
#define N 15
int array_min( int a[], int n );

void main( void )
{
    int data[N] = { 19, 17, 2, 43, 47, 5, 37, 23, 3, 41, 29, 31, 7, 11, 13 };
    int answer;

    printf( "\n Find minimum in an array of %i positive integers.\n", N );
    answer = array_min( data, N );
    printf( "\n Minimum = %i\n\n", answer );
}
/* ------------------------------------------------------------------ */
int
array_min( int a[], int n )
{
    int tailmin, answer;

    printf( " Entering: n=%2i  head=%2i \n", n, a[0] );

    /* Base case. ------------------------------------------------- */
    if (n == 1) {
        printf( " ---- Base case ----\n" );
        answer = a[0];
    }

    /* Recursive step. ------------------------------------------- */
    else {
        tailmin = array_min( &a[1], n - 1 );
        if (a[0] < tailmin) answer = a[0];
        else answer = tailmin;
    }

    printf( " Leaving:  n=%2i  head=%2i  returning=%2i\n", n, a[0], answer );
    return answer;
}
```

Figure 21.3.   A recursive program to find a minimum.

we reach a set of one, we know (trivially) that this value is the minimum, so we can simply return it to the caller. This occurs halfway through the entire process. At this point, we have progressed, recursively, to the end of the array, and reached the base case of the recursion. Given the sample `data` array, the program output up until this point is

```
Find minimum in an array of 15 positive integers.
Entering: n=15  head=19
```

```
Entering:  n=14   head=17
Entering:  n=13   head= 2
Entering:  n=12   head=43
Entering:  n=11   head=47
Entering:  n=10   head= 5
Entering:  n= 9   head=37
Entering:  n= 8   head=23
Entering:  n= 7   head= 3
Entering:  n= 6   head=41
Entering:  n= 5   head=29
Entering:  n= 4   head=31
Entering:  n= 3   head= 7
Entering:  n= 2   head=11
```

Although we always print `a[0]`, it is not the same as `data[0]`, except on the very first call; it actually is the initial value of the portion of the array that is the argument for the current recursive call. During the processing, we repeatedly peel off one element and recurse. From the output, we can see that, after executing the first `printf()` statement 14 times, we have not yet reached the second `printf()` statement because of the recursions. Finally, `n` is reduced to 1 and we reach the base case.

- *First box: the base case.* When writing a recursive function that operates on an array, the base case usually happens when one item is left in the array. In this example, given a set of one element, that element is the minimum value in the set. Therefore, we simply return it. The `true` clause of the `if` statement contains a diagnostic `printf()` statement; it is executed midway through the overall process, after the recursive descent ends and before the returns begin. If we eliminate this `printf()` statement, the base case becomes very simple:

```
if (n == 1)    return a[0];
```

The diagnostic output from the base-case call shows us that we have reached the end of the array:

```
Entering:  n= 1   head=13
---- Base case ----
Leaving:   n= 1   head=13   returning=13
```

Now we begin returning. The stack frame of the returning function is deallocated and the stack frame of the caller, which had been suspended, again becomes current. When execution resumes, we are back in the context from which the call was made. When we return from the base case, we go back to the context in which there were two values in the set.

- *Second box revisited: ascent from the recursion.* At each step, we compare the value returned by the recursive call to `a[0]`. (Remember that `a[0]` is a different slot of the array on each recursion.) We return the smaller of these two values to the next level. Thus, at each level, we return with the minimum value of the tail end of the array and that tail grows by one element in length each time we return. When we get all the way back to the original call, we will have the minimum value of the entire array, which is printed by `main()`:

```
Leaving:    n= 2    head=11    returning=11
Leaving:    n= 3    head= 7    returning= 7
Leaving:    n= 4    head=31    returning= 7
Leaving:    n= 5    head=29    returning= 7
Leaving:    n= 6    head=41    returning= 7
Leaving:    n= 7    head= 3    returning= 3
Leaving:    n= 8    head=23    returning= 3
Leaving:    n= 9    head=37    returning= 3
Leaving:    n=10    head= 5    returning= 3
Leaving:    n=11    head=47    returning= 3
Leaving:    n=12    head=43    returning= 3
Leaving:    n=13    head= 2    returning= 2
Leaving:    n=14    head=17    returning= 2
Leaving:    n=15    head=19    returning= 2

Minimum = 2
```

• *Output without the diagnostic print statements.* If we remove all of the diagnostic `printf()` statements, the output reduces to

```
Find minimum in an array of 15 positive integers.

Minimum = 2
```

21.5   A More Complex Example: Binary Search

Searching an arbitrary array for the position of a key element is a problem that has only one kind of general solution, the sequential search. If the data in the array are in some unknown order, we must compare the key to every item in the array before we know that the key value is not one of the array elements. Sequential search works well for applications like the Chauvenet table, presented in Chapter 16, where only a few values are looked through. For an extensive data set such as a telephone book or an electronic parts catalog, sequential search is painfully slow and completely inadequate. Therefore, large databases are organized or indexed so that rapid retrieval is possible. One such way to organize data is simply to sort it according to a key value and store the sorted data in an array. We have seen algorithms for the selection and insertion sort so far. The quicksort algorithm will be discussed in the next section.

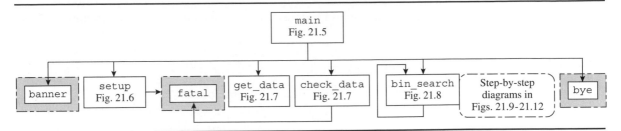

Figure 21.4.   Call chart for binary search.

Binary search is an algorithm that allows us to take advantage of the fact that the data in an array are sorted. (We simplify the following discussion by assuming that it is in ascending order. One of the exercises examines descending order.) The search can be implemented easily using either iteration or recursion. Both formulations are straightforward. The iterative version is a little more efficient, while the recursive version is a little shorter and easier to write. We will use the program in this section to illustrate both recursion and the binary search algorithm. The call chart in Figure 21.4 summarizes the overall structure of this program and where each piece can be found. Figures 21.5 through 21.8 contain a program that reads a sorted data file into an array, then searches for values requested by the user. We start with a **main()** program and its utility functions, then look at the recursive function last.

Notes on Figure 21.5. The binary search program.   The preliminary steps are setup, input, and input validation. After completing these, we can call the **bin_search()** function in Figure 21.8 to search the data for key values entered by the user. In the call chart, note the circular arrow that denotes the recursive call on **bin_search()**.

- *First box: setting up and reading the file.*
    1. It is not practical to use this program with file redirection, since it requires both interactive input and a data file. Moreover, a binary search program cannot function properly unless the data in the array are sorted in the correct order. This program assumes ascending[3] order. Therefore, reading the input really is a three-step process: (1) identify and open the file, (2) read the information, and (3) verify that it is properly sorted.
    2. The program calls the function **setup()** in Figure 21.6 to allocate memory for the data array and prepare it for input. It also opens a stream and connects it to the user-specified file of input data.

---

[3]Technically, we require nondescending order.

This **main()** program calls the search function in Figure 21.8 and the data functions in Figures 21.6 and 21.7.

```c
#include "tools.h"
#define NOT_FOUND  -1
typedef struct { int* data; int n; int max; } data_pack;

void setup      ( data_pack* spec, stream* infile );
int  get_data   ( data_pack* searchp, stream instream );
void check_data( data_pack search);
int  bin_search( int data[], int left, int right, int key );

void main( void )
{
    stream fin;                 /* Stream for the input file. */
    data_pack search;           /* Array data */
    int key;                    /* Number to search for. */
    int slot;                   /* Position at which key is found. */
    int stream_status;          /* For scanf()'s return value. */

    banner();
    puts( "\n Find a key value in an array of integers." );

    setup( &search, &fin );
    get_data( &search, fin );
    check_data( search );
    printf( " %i data items read; ready to search.\n", search.n );

    puts( "\n Enter numbers to search for; period to quit." );

    for(;;) {
        printf( " What number do you wish to find? " );

        stream_status = scanf( "%i", &key );
        if (stream_status < 1) break;

        slot = bin_search( search.data, 0, search.n - 1, key );
        if (slot == NOT_FOUND)
            printf( " Key value %i is not in table.\n\n", key );
        else printf( " Key value %i was found in slot %i.\n\n", key, slot );

    }
    bye();
}
```

Figure 21.5.   The binary search program.

3. The program uses `get_data()` from Figure 21.7 to read the data from the file into the data array. It reads until the data file is finished or the data array is full, whichever comes first.

4. Rather than take it on faith that the data in the file are in ascending order, the program calls the `check_data()` function from Figure 21.7 to make sure. Adjacent pairs of elements throughout the array are compared to see if they are in the proper relative order. If not, processing is terminated.

- *Second and third boxes: asking for search values.*

1. The loop will search for one data value each pass. Since no restriction is placed on the data items in the array, it is not really possible to use a sentinel loop that looks for a particular stopping value. Therefore, the loop looks for an invalid response; namely, a period. This is detected by noticing that `scanf()` does not return a `1`, which would indicate a valid data read occurred.

2. Even though the prompt says a period should be entered, any character that is not a valid digit will do.

- *Fourth box: calling the search function.*

1. The program calls the recursive function `bin_search()` just like any other function. The parameters tell it to search all the values in the data array, from slot 0 to slot $n - 1$, and return the position of the key value if it is present in the array.

2. When the original activation of `bin_search()` receives an answer from its recursive calls, it returns to `main()` and its answer is stored in the variable `slot`.

3. The binary search function returns either a valid subscript or an integer error code. We use a symbolic name for the error code, `NOT_FOUND`, rather than use the code itself, to make the program more readable.

4. An appropriate output response, indicating success or failure, is made based on the returned value.

- *Output.* The following is sample output from the program when used on the input file shown in Figure 21.9:

```
Find a key value in an array of integers.
Enter name of data file to be searched: binsearch
17 data items read; ready to search.

Enter numbers to search for; period to quit.
What number do you wish to find? 24
Key value 24 was found in slot 0.
```

This function is called from the `main()` program in Figure 21.5. It allocates memory for **MAX** data items, then reads in the name of the input file to be searched and opens the file. Errors are fatal.

```
#define MAX   1000
void setup( data_pack* spec, stream* infile )
{
    char filename[80];              /* For name of input file. */
    
    spec->max = MAX;                /* Space for MAX items.  */
    spec->n = 0;                    /* Currently empty.  */
    spec->data = malloc( MAX * sizeof(int) );
    if (spec->data == NULL)
        fatal( " Error: not enough memory for %i ints\n", MAX );
    

    printf( " Enter name of data file to be searched: " );
    scanf( "%79s", filename );
    *infile = fopen( filename, "r" );
    if (*infile == NULL)
        fatal( " Error: couldn't open input file %s\n", filename );

}
```

Figure 21.6.   Setting up the data structures.

```
                    What number do you wish to find? 276
                    Key value 276 was found in slot 4.

                    What number do you wish to find? 1899
                    Key value 1899 is not in table.

                    What number do you wish to find? .
```

Notes on Figure 21.6. Setting up the data structures.

- *First box: allocation.* A `data_pack` with elements of type `int` is allocated here, in the same manner as in the insertion sort program in Chapter 20, Figure 20.18.
- *Second box: the input stream.* If the data allocation is successful, a data stream is opened for the program. The function prompts the user for a file name and connects an input stream to that file. Failure to open the file is a fatal error. If the file is opened successfully, the stream is returned to `main()` by an indirect assignment through a pointer parameter, which stores it in `main()`'s stream, `fin`.

```
/* ---------------------------------------------------------------- */
void  /* Read up to max integers from input stream and store in array. */
get_data( data_pack* searchp, stream instream )
{
    int stream_status;                    /* For scanf()'s return value. */
    int* cursor = searchp->data;          /* Scanning pointer */
    int* end = cursor + searchp->max;     /* An off-board sentinel. */

    for ( ; cursor < end; ++cursor) {
        stream_status = fscanf( instream, "%i", cursor );
        if (stream_status != 1) break;
    }

    searchp->n = cursor - searchp->data;     /* Compute # of items read. */

}
/* ---------------------------------------------------------------- */
void          /* Make sure that the data are in ascending sorted order. */
check_data( data_pack search )
{
    int k;                                /* Loop counter. */
    int* head = search.data               /* Beginning of array pointer */

    for (k = 1; k < search.n; ++k) {
        if (head[k] < head[k-1])
            fatal( " Cannot continue, data in file are not sorted." );
    }

}
```

Figure 21.7.   Getting and checking the data.

- *Output.* A sample session with an error comment might be

  ```
  Find a key value in an array of integers.
  Enter name of data file to be searched: fake.in
  Error: couldn't open input file fake.in
  ```

Notes on Figure 21.7. Getting and checking the data.

- *First box: the parameters.* The parameters of **get_data()** arc a pointer to an empty **data_pack** and an input stream. The number of items read is returned through the member **n** of the **data_pack**, and this value is used throughout the rest of the program to limit the processing. The parameter of **check_data()** is passed by value since its members are not altered by the function.

- *Second box: reading.* Data items are read from the specified stream until either the array is full or **fscanf()** reports an exception condition. If the file contains too many items, only the first **MAX** are read. Fewer than that number are read if an end-of-file condition occurs prematurely, or there is a hardware failure or corrupted data in the file. We do not distinguish here among these cases; any of these events will end the input phase. This kind of shortcut would be inappropriate if we were writing a production-level program where failure to distinguish a file error could have bad repercussions.

- *Third box: the number of items.* To calculate how many items actually were read, the program subtracts the array's head pointer from the final value of the cursor. Since the cursor always points to the first unoccupied slot, the difference between the two pointers is the number of slots that have been filled. This is stored in the member **n** of **searchp**.

- *Fourth box: the loop check.*

    1. A pointer, **head**, is set to the start of the array and used as a cursor. Since the array is a member of a structure, it is more efficient to access it directly through the pointer rather than by using the structure's name with a dot operator.

    2. In the **check_data()** function, the program uses subscripts for accessing data in the array. Since it is accessing consecutive elements, we could write the test as **head[k] < head[k-1]** and increment **k** each time around the loop, or write ***head < *(head-1)**, and increment **head**. The first form is somewhat clearer.

    3. If each element in the input data is equal to or greater than its predecessor, the data are in the proper order. If not, the program calls **fatal()**.

    4. A sample error session ending with an error comment might be

       ```
       Find a key value in an array of integers.
       Enter name of data file to be searched: mixedup.dat
       Cannot continue, data in file are not sorted.
       ```

    5. This data check could have been written as part of the **get_data()** function. However, we wrote it as a separate processing step because **get_data()** is a general function that has been used before (see Figure 20.15) and will be used again. We prefer to use previously debugged code, wherever possible, rather than rewriting everything for every program. Also, if a modification is desired so that we can process descending order data, the change will be localized in **check_data()**.

Notes on Figure 21.8. The binary search function.

- *The function header.*

    1. The parameters to **bin_search()** are an array that must contain integers sorted in ascending order, the subscripts of the left and right ends

We search for the key value among the **n** values in the data array, which are assumed to be sorted in ascending order. This recursive function is called from the **main()** program in Figure 21.5.

```
int
bin_search( int data[], int left, int right, int key )
{
    int mid = (left + right) / 2;      /* Compute middle of search interval */

    /* Base cases:   (1) we found it or (2) it's not there */
    if (data[mid] == key)   return mid;
    if (left >= right)      return NOT_FOUND;

    /* Recursion:  search a smaller array */
    if (key < data[mid])    return bin_search( data, left, mid - 1, key );
    else                    return bin_search( data, mid + 1, right, key );
}
```

Figure 21.8.   The binary search function, bin_search().

of the portion of the array remaining to be searched, and a key value for which to search.

2. The array and key parameter values remain the same on all calls. The recursion eventually terminates if and only if, on each recursive call, the parameters **left** and **right** bracket a smaller portion of the array than on the prior call.

3. If the key value is in the array, the function returns its subscript. Otherwise, the failure code **NOT_FOUND** is returned.

- *First box: dividing the array.*

1. Each time through this recursion, the array is split in half by computing **mid**, the subscript of the item in the middle of the remaining interval of the array.

2. If an odd number of elements is in the interval, the **split point** is exactly in the middle, with an equal number of items on either side. If the number is even, the left portion has one fewer item than the right. The algorithm works equally well, whether the extra item is in the left or the right portion.

3. Figure 21.9 shows a sorted array of integers with the **left**, **right**, and **mid** subscripts initialized for the beginning of a binary search. Figures 21.10 through 21.12 trace the progress of this search.

4. Debugging a recursive function can be a challenge unless the programmer has enough information to track the progress of the recursion. To find and eliminate an error, the programmer needs to know the actual

We are prepared to begin a binary search of the array **data**, shown below, looking for the key value 270. The **left**, **right**, and **mid** subscripts are shown as they would be after making the first call at the beginning of this search.

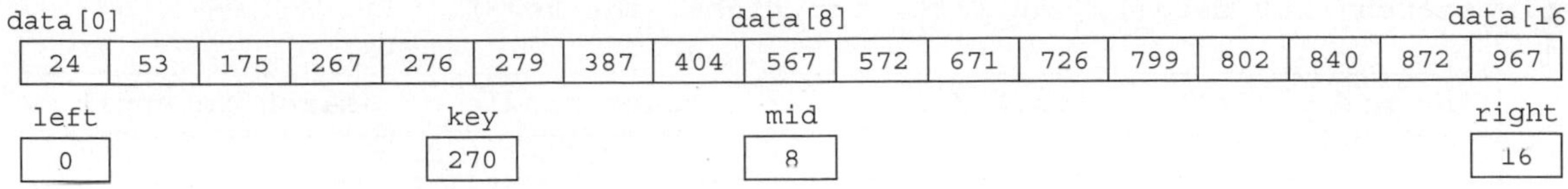
data[0]
data[8]
data[16]
24 53 175 267 276 279 387 404 567 572 671 726 799 802 840 872 967
left
0
key
270
mid
8
right
16

Figure 21.9. Beginning a binary search.

arguments in each recursive call. For this purpose, while debugging this program, the programmer inserted an output statement in this function just after the initialization of **mid**.

```
int mid = (left + right) / 2;
fprintf( stderr, "left=%i, mid=%i, right=%i\n",
         left, mid, right );
```

- *Second box: ending the recursion.*

  1. Any search might terminate in two ways: the key value could be found in the array or the key value might be missing from the array. Separate **return** statements are used in this function to handle each case, so that it can return either a valid subscript or a failure code.
  2. Each time through the recursion, the program checks for both possibilities and returns if either occurs. First, it checks whether it has found what it is looking for. If the item in slot **mid** equals the search key, it returns the subscript of that slot.
  3. We can guarantee that the recursion will eventually end by testing and eliminating the item at the split point on every call. This guarantees that each successive recursive call will be searching a shorter list of possibilities.

After comparing the key value 270 to the value of **data[mid]** (567), the program knows that the key should be in the left half. It calls **bin_search()** recursively to search an interval with the same left end but with **mid-1 = 7** as the right end. The situation now looks like this:

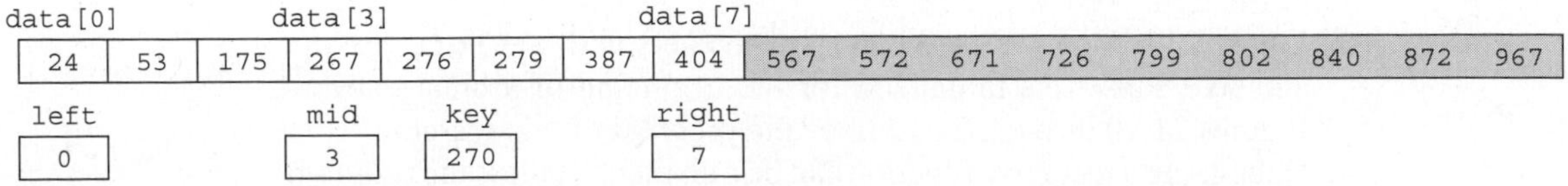
data[0]
data[3]
data[7]
24 53 175 267 276 279 387 404 567 572 671 726 799 802 840 872 967
left
0
mid
3
key
270
right
7

Figure 21.10. Second active call.

On this call, the left end of the remaining interval has been eliminated. The new left end is `mid+1` = `4`.

```
                 data[4]         data[7]
 24   53   175  267 | 276  279 | 387 | 404 | 567  572  671  726  799  802  840  872  967
                 left  mid       right   key
                  4     5          7     270
```

Figure 21.11.   Third active call.

4. The program knows that the key value is not in the array if it has searched the vicinity where the key should be and has not found it. Every stage of the recursion moves the `mid` index closer to the proper position of the key; and at every step, the program checks the value of the `mid` item. Eventually, the interval is reduced to one item and then `left`, `mid`, and `right` have the same value. If this item does not match the key, the key is not in the array.

5. This situation is illustrated by the third recursion (fourth active call) on `bin_search()` shown in Figure 21.12. On this call, both the parameters `left` and `right` are 4, so `mid` also is 4. Since `data[4]` does not equal `key`, the key is not in the array and so the program returns the failure code.

6. When the fourth active call returns, control goes back to the third activation, which receives the answer and returns this value immediately. Control (and the answer) then go back to the second instance, which returns the answer directly to the first, which then returns the answer to `main()`, where the answer finally is displayed for the user.

- *Third box: the recursive calls.*

  1. When the program reaches this box, there are two possibilities: the key value should be found to the left of the `mid` value if it is smaller than `data[mid]` or it belongs to the right of `mid` if greater. Figure 21.10 illustrates the result of a step in which the key belongs in the left half.

After determining that the key 270 must be in the left half, the program sets the right end to `mid-1` = `4`. Now only one array element remains to be searched and the key does not match the value in that slot. The program returns the failure code.

```
            return value: NOT_FOUND
 24   53   175  267 | 276 | 279  387  404  567  572  671  726  799  802  840  872  967
            left  mid  right            key
             4    4    4                270
```

Figure 21.12.   Fourth and last active call.

In this case, the program made a recursive call to search everything to the left of the middle by setting `right` to `mid - 1`. In the diagram, the middle element and those to its right are gray to indicate that they do not need to be considered further.

2. The program reaches the `else` clause when the key value is greater than `data[mid]`. This means the key value belongs in the right half. Figure 21.11 illustrates this case. During the second active call, the program eliminates the left half of the remaining interval by calling `bin_search()` with `mid + 1` as the left end argument.

3. During the third active call, only a few items are left to search, and the `mid` index is adjacent to the left end. When the program finds that the key is smaller than `data[mid]`, it again eliminates the middle element and everything to its right and makes another recursive call. The final situation, where both `left` and `right` are the same index, is shown in Figure 21.12. In the case illustrated, the key does not match the value at this position so the failure code is returned.

21.6   **Quicksort**

Even though computers become faster and more powerful each year, efficiency still matters when dealing with large quantities of data. This is especially true when large data sets must be sorted. Some sorting algorithms (selection sort, insertion sort) take an amount of time proportional to the square of the number of items being sorted and so are only useful on very short arrays (say, 10 items or fewer).[4] Even the fastest computer will take a long time to sort 10,000 items by one of these methods. The fastest known sorting algorithm, **radix sort**, takes an amount of time that is directly proportional to the number of items, but it requires considerable effort to set up the necessary data structures before sorting starts. Therefore, it is useful only when sorting very long arrays of data. In contrast, the **quicksort** algorithm is the fastest known way to sort an array containing a moderate number of data items (10 to 1000).

Quicksort is an example of the strategy of divide and conquer: Divide the problem repeatedly into smaller, simpler tasks until each portion is easy and quick to solve (conquer). If this can be done in such a way that the collection of small problems actually is equivalent to the original one, then after solving all of the small problems, the solution to the large one can be found. In particular, the quicksort algorithm works by splitting an array of items into two portions so that everything in the leftmost portion is smaller than everything in the rightmost portion, then it recursively works on each section. At each recursive step, the remaining part of the array is split again. This splitting continues until each

---

[4]The theory behind this is beyond the scope of this book.

segment of the array is very small (often one or two elements) and can be sorted directly. After all of the small segments have been sorted, the entire array turns out to be sorted as well, because every step put smaller things to the left of larger things.

There have been many implementations of quicksort, some very fast and others not so fast. In general, if an array of items is in random order, any of the quicksort implementations will sort it faster than a simple sort (selection, insertion, etc.). The version of quicksort presented here is especially efficient and one of the best, because its innermost loops are very short and simple. Further optimizations that can improve the efficiency of this algorithm have been omitted from the code in this section for the sake of clarity. However, two possible improvements are mentioned at the end of the section and explored in the exercises.

As an aid to following this example, a call graph is given in Figure 21.13. It includes references to the figures in which each function is defined or its actions are illustrated. We begin the discussion with the **main()** program in Figure 21.14, which calls the **quicksort()** function in Figure 21.15.

Notes on Figure 21.14. Calling the `quicksort()` function.

- *First box: an array of* **floats**. We use the **data_pack** structure again for this sort, so that we can pass data easily into and out of functions written previously for other sorts. The structure includes the number of items to be sorted and a pointer to a dynamically allocated array of **float**s containing that many items.

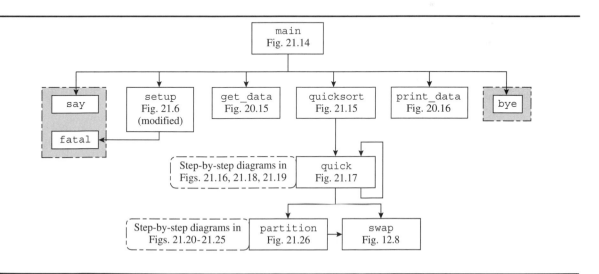

Figure 21.13.   Call graph for the quicksort program.

This **main()** program calls the **quicksort()** function in Figure 21.15.

```
#include "tools.h"
#define MAX   1000
typedef struct { float* data; int n; int max; } data_pack;

void setup( data_pack* spec, stream* infile, stream* outfile );
int  get_data( data_pack* sortp, stream instream );
void quicksort( data_pack sort );
void print_data( data_pack sort, stream outstream );

void main( void )
{
    stream in_str, out_str;        /* Streams for input and output. */
    data_pack sort;                /* Specifications for sort.   */

    say( "\n Quicksort program." );
    setup( &sort, &in_str, &out_str );

    get_data( &sort, in_str );
    say( " %i data items read; ready to sort.\n", sort.n );

    quicksort( sort );
    say( " Data sorted; writing to output stream." );

    print_data( sort, out_str );

    bye();
}
```

Figure 21.14.   Calling the quicksort() **function.**

- *Second box: specifications for the run.*

  1. The program uses **say()** to provide feedback for the user via the **stderr** stream, thereby separating the output of the sorted file from user feedback, making it possible for the program to be run with file redirection.

  2. A **setup()** function is used to open the input and output streams, as well as allocate memory for the data, so that these steps (and the necessary error checking) do not distract attention from the main flow of program logic. This function differs from the **setup()** function in Figure 21.6 in two ways. First, it opens an output stream in addition to the input stream. Second, the total number of array elements allocated

This function is called from the **main()** program in Figure 21.14. The array to be sorted must have one extra slot allocated at the right end; this function installs a sentinel in that slot and calls **quick()** in Figure 21.17 to sort *n* values starting at location **first**. Figure 21.16 shows the data configuration just after the call to **quick()** has been made.

```
#include <float.h>                        /* For the sentinel value, FLT_MAX */

/* Functions called directly or indirectly by quicksort() -------------- */
void    quick( float* first, float* last );
float* partition( float* first, float* last );
void    swap( float* fp1, float* fp2 );

void
quicksort( data_pack sort )
{
    float* sentinel = sort.data + sort.n; /* Create off-board sentinel  */

    *sentinel = FLT_MAX;                   /* with big value to stop loops. */

    quick( sort.data, sentinel - 1 );      /* Call quick() with pointers to */
}                                          /* beginning and end of data. */
```

Figure 21.15.   Getting ready to sort: quicksort().

is one more than before, although **MAX** remains the same. This extra slot is used to hold a special sentinel in **quicksort()** as described shortly. The function is not reprinted here.

- *Third and fifth boxes: input and output.* The functions **get_data()** and **print_data()** were well annotated in the previous chapter (Figures 20.15 and 20.16). They are used here with no modification and so require no further comment.
- *Fourth box: the call on* **quicksort()**. The argument to **quicksort()** is the **data_pack** structure filled with data. This function first sets up a special sentinel value in the extra allocated location at the end of the data array. It then calls the recursive function **quick()** in Figure 21.17 to do the real work.

Notes on Figure 21.15. Getting ready to sort: quicksort().

- *First and third boxes: the sentinel value.*

  1. The constant **FLT_MAX** is defined in the header file **float.h**. It is the largest value (short of infinity) that can be represented in a **float** variable.

The outer function, `quicksort()`, calculates the position of `last`, stores the sentinel value `FLT_MAX` in the next slot, and calls the recursive function `quick()` in Figure 21.17 with pointers to the beginning and end of the data. Here, we illustrate the status of the data array and pointers just after entering `quick()`.

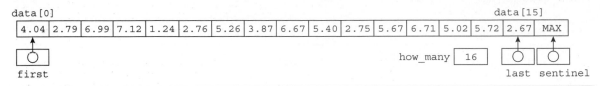

Figure 21.16.   Ready to sort.

2. This large value, which is larger than any other value in the data array, is appended after the last element, to help terminate data comparison loops correctly. This eliminates extra bookkeeping in the inner recursions and loops, resulting in improved performance for the algorithm. To allow room for the sentinel value, the array containing the data must have one extra slot at the right end. This was handled in `setup()`.

- *Second box: pointers.*

  1. To prepare for the recursion, `quicksort()` sets up a pointer to the end of the array. This will be passed to `quick()` at the end of the function.
  2. Figure 21.16 shows an example data array, the values of the `first` and `last` pointers, and the sentinel value as set up by `quicksort()` just after delivery to `quick()`. Processing of this example is continued in Figures 21.18 through 21.25 as the remaining details of the algorithm are discussed.

Notes on Figure 21.17: The `quick()` function performs the recursion.   This function is recursive; it calls itself again and again to sort shorter and shorter segments of the array. (The number of items to be sorted always decreases on each recursive call.) In this implementation, the program ends the recursive subdivision when two or fewer items remain, because we can sort these items directly. For three or more items, the program partitions the array and makes two more recursive calls with the two portions.

- *First box: the trivial base cases.*   Control comes to this box if there are zero, one, or two items in the part of the array being sorted. For one item or none, there is nothing more to do; it is sorted by definition. For two items, the program can compare them and swap, if necessary. The `swap()` function was given and discussed in Figure 12.8.
- *Second box: partitioning.*

  1. The heart of a quicksort is the **partition step**, which splits the array into two parts, separated by one item at the split point. The split is

p 452

This function is called from `quicksort()` in Figure 21.15. It calls the `partition()` function in Figure 21.26 and the `swap()` function in Figure 12.8.

```
void
quick( float* first, float* last )
{
    int how_many = last - first + 1;    /* The number of items left to sort */
    float* split;                       /* The dividing position */

    /* Base cases: ----------------------------------------------------- */
    if (how_many < 2)                   /* Nothing to do for 0 or 1 items left. */
    else if (how_many == 2) {           /* Stop recursive descent and -------- */
        if (*last < *first) swap( last, first );    /* swap if not in order. */
    }

    /* Recursive calls:  how_many > 2 -------------------------------- */
    else {

        split = partition( first, last ); /* Split into two areas. */


        quick( first, split - 1 );    /* Sort left portion (small items)  */
        quick( split + 1, last );     /* Sort right portion (large items) */

    }
}
```

Figure 21.17.   The `quick()` function performs the recursion.

done in such a way that everything in the left section is smaller than or equal to the value at the split point, and the split value is smaller than everything in the right section.

2. In this implementation, the task is performed by the function named `partition()` in Figure 21.26. The value returned by `partition()` is a pointer to the split position. This state is shown in the example in

The pivot value (located at the split point) now lies between small items on the left and large items on the right. It is in its final resting place and does not need to be considered in any further recursive calls. Thus, the sorting task has been reduced by at least one item.

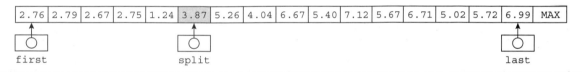

Figure 21.18.   Positions at the end of the first pass.

The function `quick()` makes two recursive calls on itself: to sort the smaller items and to sort the larger items.

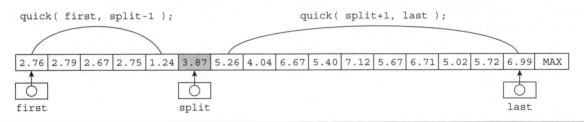

Figure 21.19.   The recursive calls.

Figure 21.18. This slot is gray to indicate that the value stored there is in its final, sorted position.

3. It is possible for the split point to be anywhere in the array interval, even at the ends. The most desirable division, of course, is an even split. Even so, wherever the split value ends up, it can be excluded from any future calls on `quick()`.

- *Third box: the recursive calls.* After partitioning the array, `quick()` makes two recursive calls, as shown in Figure 21.19, to sort the items before the split point (from `first` to `split - 1`) and the items after it (from `split + 1` to `last`). Each partition step places at least one item (the pivot value) at the split point in its proper slot, even if the split point is at one end or the other of an array interval. Using this fact, it is easy to prove that the number of items to be sorted eventually must decrease to two or fewer, causing the recursion to stop.

21.6.1   The Partition Step: Divide to Conquer

Partitioning a data set.   We start with data items in an array. We would like to end with these items in the same array but rearranged so that certain smaller values (in any order) are on the left, the median value (which we will call the **pivot**) is in the middle, and the remaining larger values are on the right (also in any order). If we always could find the median value and place it in the middle, the number of smaller values would roughly equal the number of larger values, maximizing the efficiency of the recursive sort.

However, without looking at all the data first, we cannot know even the general scale and range of the data values and, therefore, cannot guess what the median value might be. We could compute the median value, but that would take more time now than it would save later during the sorting process. Instead, we arbitrarily select a pivot value out of the middle of the array. If the array happens

This is the status of the data array and pointers just after `quick()` has called `partition()` for the first time. It shows the local pointers `lester`, which will scan from left-to-right along the array, and `rose`, which will scan from right to left. The pivot value is found at the location given by `mid`.

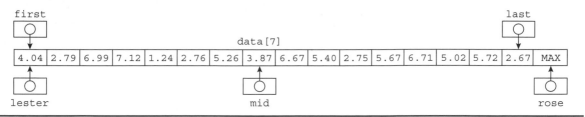

Figure 21.20.   Starting the sort.

to be sorted already, this value will be the median. If the values are in random order, the selected pivot could be anything, even the largest or smallest value in the array. With good luck, it will be a middle-sized value much of the time. Once the pivot is selected, the terms *smaller* and *larger* are defined in relation to it, and the remaining partition process is quite efficient.

To begin our description of the partition process, imagine two ushers, `lester` and `rose`, who work in a theater. Their job is to seat all the small people in the front and all the large people in the back. Unfortunately, everyone has already chosen a seat and they are out of order. Not knowing what collection of people are in the theater ahead of time, they arbitrarily select a teenager out of the middle of the crowd and use his height to define what *smaller* and *larger* mean. This height is the `pivot` value, and comes from location `mid`, as shown in Figure 21.20. Temporarily, they put this teenager in the first seat, and move the former occupant to the teenager's empty seat. This action is illustrated in Figure 21.21.

The function `partition()` puts the pivot value at the beginning of the array to act as a sentinel value for the scanner `rose` that moves from right to left.

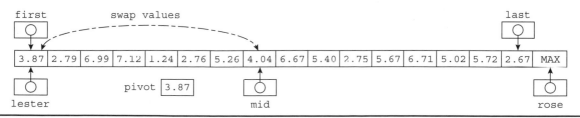

Figure 21.21.   Putting the pivot at the beginning.

Both the left and right scanners have stopped at elements that occupy slots in the wrong end of the array. The next action is to swap these values.

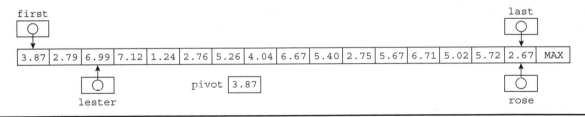

Figure 21.22.   Starting the scan.

One usher, **lester**, prefers short people. He starts at the front of the theater looking for people taller than the pivot height who don't belong in front. After searching a bit, he stops and points at the first taller person he finds. The other usher, **rose**, likes tall people; she starts from the back looking for short people (and other people whose height equals the pivot height) who don't belong in the back. She eventually stops and points at the first shorter person she finds. This scanning process is illustrated in Figure 21.22. They politely ask the two people that have been identified to swap places.

The scanning continues again from where it left off; **lester** scans toward the right, stopping at the next tall person, while **rose** scans leftward, stopping at the next short person. When they both have stopped, another two people are ready to swap places. This is illustrated in Figure 21.23.

Eventually, after having located and swapped several pairs, **lester** and **rose** meet somewhere in the middle of the theater, stopping just after they

The first swap is completed (dot-dashed line). The left and right scanners resume their movement and stop again. We are ready for the second swap.

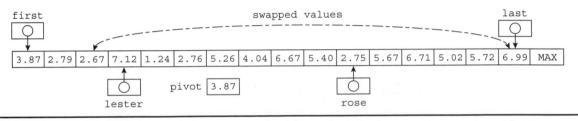

Figure 21.23.   Continuing the scan.

The second swap is completed (dot-dashed line). The left and right scanners resume their scan and stop again. But this time the scanners pass each other.

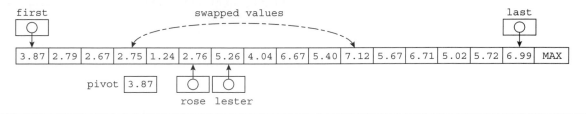

Figure 21.24.   The scanners meet.

pass each other (see Figure 21.24). We call **rose**'s position the *split point*. This is where the teenager whose height was used as the pivot value belongs. He swaps seats with the short person at the split point, who then moves up to the first seat. The ushers have now achieved what they set out to do: everyone ahead of the split point is shorter than the pivot height; everyone behind is taller. (If someone's height is equal to the pivot, that person goes in front with the shorter people.) This final state is shown in Figure 21.25.

Implementation of `partition()`.   The code for partitioning an array parallels this fanciful explanation very closely. The first task of the `partition()` function (see Figure 21.26) is to select a pivot element and move it to the beginning of the array. As mentioned, a variety of strategies can be used to select the pivot; the simplest is to use the first value in the array. While this works well enough on items in random order, it can lead to very bad performance on files that are nearly sorted. The version presented here selects a pivot from the middle of the array, which greatly improves the algorithm's performance on sorted or nearly sorted data. More sophisticated strategies attempt to choose the median value

The item under the right-to-left scanner, **rose**, is swapped with the pivot value (which was at the left end of the array). We return the pivot's new position to `quick()`.

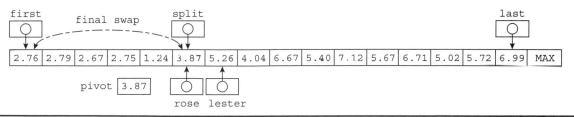

Figure 21.25.   Finishing the pass.

Choose a data value as the pivot then scan from both ends through the array putting smaller items on the left and larger ones on the right. This function is called from `quick()` in Figure 21.17. It calls `swap()` in Figure 12.8. The results, using the sample data set, were diagrammed in Figures 21.20 through 21.25.

```
float*
partition( float* first, float* last )
{
    float* lester = first;                      /* Data scanners */
    float* rose   = last + 1;
    float* mid = first + (last - first) / 2; /* Use mid element as pivot. */

    float pivot;                              /* pivot selection height */
    float* split;                             /* location of split point */

    /* Move pivot element to front end of array---copy remains in pivot. */
    pivot = *mid; *mid = *first; *first = pivot;


    for (;;) {
        while (*(++lester) <= pivot);      /* scan from left-to-right */
        while (*(--rose) > pivot);         /* scan from right-to-left */

        if (lester >= rose) break;         /* break if scanners meet */
        swap( rose, lester );              /* otherwise swap items */
    }

    split = rose;
    *first = *split; *split = pivot;       /* swap.  (pivot == *first) */
    return split;

}
```

Figure 21.26.   The `partition()` function.

or at least some value other than the maximum or minimum. This is discussed further shortly.

Notes on Figure 21.26. The `partition()` function.

- *First box: declarations.*

  1. We declare the pointer `lester` and initialize it to the beginning of the array (the slot that will soon be occupied by the pivot value).
  2. We declare the pointer `rose` and initialize it to the slot occupied by the sentinel at the end of the array.

3. We set a pointer **mid**, to the middle slot, by averaging the pointers to the beginning and end. The value in this slot is used as the pivot.
4. Figure 21.20 illustrates the sample data array at this point.

- *Second box: the pivot.*

1. The program swaps the items in the first slot and the middle slot and, in the process, makes a copy of the pivot value. Figure 21.21 illustrates the data array at this point.
2. The pivot value moves to the beginning of the array, where it will act as a sentinel for the right-to-left scanning loop. The right-to-left scanning loop stops each time **rose** finds a value equal to or smaller than the pivot. Therefore, a copy of the pivot at the beginning of the array guarantees the loop will stop before going off the end. This avoids the need to compare the pointer **rose** to the array boundary in the innermost scanning loop, which speeds up processing.
3. Similarly, **quicksort()** stores the sentinel value **FLT_MAX** at the right end of the array. This will stop the left-to-right scan, if necessary.

- *Third box (inner): the scans.*

1. Each scan is a one-line **while** loop statement, with all of the work being done in the test part and none in the body. Each test executes a shift of the pointer and a data comparison, all in one expression. When the loops exit, **lester** is pointing at a big value and **rose** at a small one. Figure 21.22 illustrates this first scanning step. Figure 21.23 shows the effects of the first data swap and the second scan.
2. This method of sorting is fast because these scanning loops (which do most of the work) are extremely efficient: Each loop pass consists only of a pointer increment or decrement and a comparison.

- *Third box (outer): rearranging the data.*

1. The **for** loop repeats the scan-and-swap sequence until **lester** and **rose** meet (or cross) in the middle. This situation is shown in Figure 21.24.
2. The **swap()** function works through the pointers and exchanges the array values to which they refer; it does not change the positions of the pointers.

- *Last box: placing the pivot value.*

1. The scanning pointers could meet anywhere in the array. When this happens, **rose** always is pointing at the rightmost small value, and this slot should become the split point.
2. The pivot value is swapped with the value at the split point and never is tested or moved again. This final state is shown in Figure 21.25.

21.6.2   Possible Improvements

The specific implementation just presented has been compared extensively to other variants of quicksort. It performs better in timed tests than almost all the others. With two improvements, this version becomes the fastest sort we have yet found for an array of length 10 to 1,000.

The first improvement would be to terminate the recursions in `quick()` when eight or fewer items are to be sorted, not just two. We can sort this small set of items using an insertion sort, which is the most efficient method for small sets of items. This improves the performance of the algorithm by replacing the overhead of recursion with iteration in dealing with the small groups of items. However, it increases the complexity of the code by adding the insertion sort function.

The second improvement would be to ensure that the pivot value is never the smallest or largest data value, guaranteeing some splitting of the data on every recursion. This can be done by inspecting three items (from the beginning, middle, and end of the array) and choosing the median of these three. Unfortunately, using stronger conditions, such as choosing the median value of five items or even finding the true median value, takes so long to execute that the potential benefits are minimal or nonexistent.

21.7	What You Should Remember

21.7.1   Major Concepts

Storage class.   C supports four storage classes: `auto`, `static`, `extern`, and `register`. Each class is associated with a different way of allocating and initializing storage, as well as different rules for scope and visibility.

- `auto` *storage*. Parameters and most local variables have storage class `auto` and are stored on the run-time stack. These objects are allocated and initialized each time the enclosing function is called and deallocated when the function completes.
- `static` *storage*. Global variables and `static` local variables are allocated and initialized when the program is loaded into computer memory and remain until the program terminates. The `static` variables can be used to store the state of the system. They also provide an efficient way to store a constant table that is local to a function.
- `extern` *variables*. Large applications composed of multiple code modules sometimes have external variables. These are defined and initialized in one module and used in others. They remain active until the program terminates. Functions are labeled `extern` by default, but may be declared to be `static` if their scope should be restricted to one code module.

Run-time stack. The state of a program is kept on the run-time stack. Every active function has a stack frame that contains its parameters, local variables, and a return address. All aspects of a function call are handled through communication via the stack. Drawing stack diagrams to use while performing a program trace is one method of debugging your software.

Recursion. A recursive function calls itself. Using the recursive divide-and-conquer technique, we can solve a problem by dividing it into two or more simpler problems and applying the same technique again to these simpler tasks. Eventually, the subproblems become simple enough to be solved directly and the recursive descent ends. The solution to the original problem then is composed from the solutions to the simpler parts. A storage area that can grow dynamically, such as the run-time stack, is necessary to implement recursion, because multiple activation records for the same function must exist simultaneously.

Binary search. Binary search is one of the fastest known algorithms for searching a sorted list. It can be implemented using either tail recursion or iteration. The strategy is to split the list of possibilities in half, based on the relative position of the key to the middle item in the remaining search range of the sorted data. This is done repeatedly, until we either find the desired item or discover that it is not in the list.

Quicksort. This is the best known algorithm for sorting a moderate number (10 to 1,000) of items. The algorithm uses a recursive divide-and-conquer strategy, sorting the data by repeatedly partitioning it into a set of small items on one end of the array and a set of large items on the other end, then recursively sorting both sets. Each partition step leaves one more item in its final sorted position between the sets of smaller and larger items.

21.7.2 Programming Style

- Streamline `main()` by delegating the details of opening and closing files, allocating and initializing data structures, and reading and printing data to separate functions. This improves the overall readability of the program.
- Write general functions and reuse them whenever possible. Try to separate and remove from routines those specific details that might make a function less reusable. Try and collect them into one function, which will not be reused.
- In general, using parameters rather than global variables to transmit information between functions is the preferred method. This aids the development and debugging of modularized code. Only rarely is it highly inconvenient to pass parameters.

- Use `static` local variables (not globals) to implement constant tables and remember state information from one call on a function to the next. Keep the constants that belong to a function with it if possible, rather than defining everything at the top of the file, especially if they are not likely to be changed.
- Global variables may be appropriate for saving state information shared between functions. For instance, the seed for the random number generator in C must be accessed by both `srand()` and `rand()`. However, this variable is `static`, not `extern`, and therefore can be accessed only by the functions in its defining code module.
- Failing to check for errors at every possible stage is irresponsible. This may mean checking for invalid input parameters, checking the return values of functions, and looking for invalid operations like dividing by 0. Try to think of all the special cases your program may deal with and devise some sort of response.
- Eventually, it is important to write efficient code. However, it is more important to write code that works properly. Many people spend too much time worrying about a program's efficiency and too little time worrying about getting a correct answer or appropriate error comment under all conditions.
- In general, if a problem can be solved using either iteration or tail recursion, a loop will be more efficient because it does not incur the overhead present in multiple function calls. In many situations, the recursive solution may be the most natural to devise. It then can be converted to an iterative form if speed is paramount. Unfortunately, for some problems, there may be no easy way to derive an equivalent iterative solution.
- Certain functions make assumptions about the nature of the input parameters. For instance, the binary search function assumes that the data are sorted in ascending order. It is a good idea to validate such assumptions and take corrective action if things are not right.
- Program efficiency can be improved most by looking at the amount of work done in the innermost loops. The less unnecessary work done in a loop that is executed many times, the faster the program will run. For instance, removing an array bounds check from the scanning loops of `partition()` makes the quicksort provided here very efficient.
- Don't use an inefficient tool if there is no need. For example, if the data array already is sorted, use a binary search rather than a linear sequential search. And, for moderate-sized data sets, use quicksort rather than insertion sort or selection sort. For small data sets, insertion sort usually is best.

21.7.3 Sticky Points and Common Errors

- *Recursion.* Recursion is a technique that can be difficult to understand at first. However, once new programmers understand it, they wonder what the fuss was about. To make it easier to trace a recursive program, pretend that, each time the recursive function calls itself, the new invocation has the same name but with a number appended. By having names with numbers you may be able to keep track more easily of what is going on.

- *Infinite recursions.* To avoid an infinite recursive descent, a recursive algorithm must reduce the "size" of the remaining problem on every recursive step. Degenerate and basic cases must be identified and handled properly to ensure that the stopping condition eventually will become true. Just as it can be tricky to get the limits of a loop correct, a common error with recursion is to stop either one step too early or one too late.

- *Storage types.* Probably the trickiest storage class to use is `static`. Mixing up `static` and `extern` can cause linker errors. Confusing `static` with `auto` may cause state information to be lost or extra copies of constants to be stored in memory.

21.7.4   New and Revisited Vocabulary

These are the most important terms and concepts discussed in this chapter:

storage class	run-time stack	recursive descent
`auto`	stack frame	infinite recursion
`extern`	activation record	stack overflow
`static`	parameters	list recursion
`register`	local variables	tail recursion
static allocation area	return address	divide and conquer
static visibility	stack diagram	binary search
initialization time	active call	split point
state	iteration	quicksort
table of constants	recursion	pivot
external linkage	base case(s)	partition step
program trace	recursive step	`data_pack`

21.8   Exercises

21.8.1   Self-Test Exercises

1. Describe the differences between `extern` and `static` storage classes. Discuss the differences between `static` and `auto`. Try to compare `extern` and `auto` as well.

2. Sort the data set in Figure 21.16 by hand into ascending order. Then show how the values of `left`, `right`, and `mid` change when using the binary search algorithm to look for the value 5.72. Repeat this for the value 2.1. Use a stack diagram to show the changing parameter values for each call.

3. The binary search function in Figure 21.8 has three `if` statements. These three statements could be arranged in six different orders. Explain whether or not the recursion will work and terminate properly for each of the five other possibilities.

4. The following program computes the sum of the first N numbers in the array **primes**. Trace the execution of this program, showing the stack frame created for each recursive call, the values stored in the stack frame, and the value returned.

```c
#include <stdio.h>
#define N 5
int sum( int a[], int n );

void main( void )
{
    int result;
    int primes[] = {2,3,5,7,11,13,17,19,23,29,31,37,41};

    printf( "\nCalculating sum of first %i primes\n", N );
    result = sum( primes, N );
    printf( "Sum = %i\n", result );
}

/* ------------------------------------------------------- */
int sum( int a[], int n )
{
    int partial;

    if (n == 1) partial = 0;
    else partial = sum( &a[1], n - 1 );
    return a[0] + partial;
}
```

5. Take the sorted data set in Figure 21.9 and scramble it up by hand. Then show the sequence of calls on **quick()** when using the quicksort algorithm to sort the data back into ascending order. Use a stack diagram to show the changing parameter values for each call.

6. The quicksort algorithm in this chapter reorders the left half of the array, then the right half. If the order of these two recursive calls is changed, will the algorithm still work? If so, prove it. If not, explain why not.

7. The following function iteratively computes the product of the first **n** elements of the array **a**. Write a recursive version of this function. Model your solution after the **sum()** function shown in exercise 4.

```c
long int product( int a[], int n )
{
    int k;
    long int prod = 1;

    for (k = 0; k < n; k++) prod *= a[k];

    return prod;
}
```

21.8.2 Using Pencil and Paper

1. Consider changing the binary search algorithm in this chapter to work on a data set in descending order. Indicate what lines need to be changed and how.

2. Sort the data set in Figure 21.16 by hand into descending order. Then show how the value of **mid** changes when using the new binary search algorithm developed in the previous exercise. Look first for the value 5.72, then for the value 2.1. Use a stack diagram to show the changing parameter values for each call.

3. The following program does some string manipulation. Trace its execution, showing the stack frame created for each recursive call, the values stored in the stack frame, and the value returned.

```c
#include "tools.h"
#define Z 3
string behead( string s, int n );

void main( void )
{
    string answer;
    char word[] = "distrust";

    printf( "\nBeheading the victim: %s?\n", word );
    answer = behead( word, Z );
    printf( "Now: %s!\n\n", answer );
}

string behead( string s, int n )
{
    if (n == 0) return s;
    else return behead( s + 1, n - 1 );
}
```

4. Consider changing the quicksort algorithm in this chapter so that the data set produced is in descending order. Indicate what lines need to be changed and how.

5. Scramble the sorted data set in Figure 21.9 by hand. Then show the sequence of calls on **quick()** when using the new quicksort algorithm developed in the previous exercise to sort the data into descending order. Use a stack diagram to show the changing parameter values for each call.

6. Write a recursive function that computes the value of **n!**. The definition of factorial was given in Chapter 8, Section 8.2.1.

7. Write an iterative version of the **bin_search()** function in Figure 21.8. In many ways, the result will be similar to the **go_find()** function in Figure 12.19, which searches for the root of a function using the bisection method.

21.8.3   Using the Computer

1. Running sum and difference.
   Write a recursive function, **sigma()**, that will return the result of an alternating sum and difference of the values in an array of **double**s. The first, third, fifth, and so forth calls on the function should add the next array element to the total. The second, fourth, sixth, and so on calls should subtract the next array element from the total. Write a **main()** function to read in values from a user-specified data file, compute the alternating sum and difference, and print the result. Assume no more than 1,000 inputs will be processed. Hint: During debugging, print the parameter values of the recursive function and print its result just before the **return** statement.

2. Fibonacci sequence.
   Write a short program that computes numbers in the Fibonacci sequence. This sequence is defined such that **fib(1)** = **0** and **fib(2)** = **1** and, for any other number in the sequence, **fib(n)** = **fib(n-1)** + **fib(n-2)**. Write a recursive function to compute the *n*th number in the sequence. Call this function from your main program. Use functions from the **time** library to determine how many seconds it takes to compute the 10th, 20th, and the 30th numbers in the sequence and output these times. Why does it take so long to compute the later numbers in the sequence? (See Chapter 15, computer exercise 2, for instructions on using the **time** library.)

3. Reversal.
   Write a short program that inputs a word or phrase of unknown length from the user, echoes it, and then prints it backward, exactly under the original. If the phrase is a *palindrome*, it will read the same forward as backward. Use a recursive function to peel off the letters and store them in a second array in reverse order. After reversing the string, compare it to the original and display the message **Palindrome** if the string is the same forward as backward. Otherwise, display **No palindrome**. For example, *pan a nap* is a palindrome; *banana* is not. Hint: The **behead()** function (given in an earlier exercise) may help you.

4. Two piles.
   Write a short program that separates negative and positive numbers, printing negative numbers on the first line and positive ones on the second line. Write a brief main program to prompt the user for a number *N* between 5 and 50. Then read *N* numbers into an array and call your recursive function (described next) to separate them. Write a recursive function named **neg_first()** to process the array. If an element is negative, the function should print it before making the next recursive call. If it is positive, the function should call itself recursively to print the other numbers and then print this number afterward.

5. Using recursion.
   Rewrite the iterative root-finding program from Section 12.3 to use tail recursion instead of a loop. Use the **bin_search()** function in Figure 21.8 as a model.

6. Proportional search.
   Modify the **bin_search()** function in Figure 21.8 as follows. Rather than always picking the value in the middle of the remaining array, assume that the data in the

array are distributed uniformly between the smallest and largest values, and let the next index position be determined proportionally, using this formula:

$$\text{index} = \frac{\text{key} - \text{data}_{\text{first}}}{\text{data}_{\text{last}} - \text{data}_{\text{first}}} \times (\text{last} - \text{first}) + \text{first}$$

After choosing an index and testing the corresponding value, continue the search as before. Compare the performance of this algorithm with the old binary search algorithm by searching for values in the example data set used in this chapter and noting how many calls each version makes. Which is better? Why?

7. A better quicksort.
   In Section 21.6.2, two possible improvements to the quicksort algorithm were given:

   * Terminate the recursions in **quick()** when eight or fewer items remain to be sorted, not two, and sort the items using an insertion sort.
   * Ensure that the pivot value is never the smallest or largest data value by inspecting three items (from the beginning, middle, and end of the array) and choosing the median of these three.

   Rewrite the quicksort algorithm given in this chapter to include these two improvements. To test which algorithm is more efficient, write a simple program to create a file of 10,000 random numbers. Time the execution of both versions of quicksort on the whole file and on just the first 100 items in it. Are the results what you expected? Explain.

8. The median value.
   The brute force method of finding the median value in a set is to sort the set first, then select the value in the middle. But sorting is a slow process. A more efficient algorithm, related to both quicksort and binary search, works as follows.

   * Let **N** be the number of values in the set, and let those values be stored in an array, **A**. If we sort the values in **A**, then by definition, the median value will be in slot **m** = **N/2**.
   * Perform the quicksort partitioning process on **A** once using the function in Figure 21.26. Store the return value (a pointer to the split point) in **p**.
   * Use pointer subtraction to compute **s**, the subscript corresponding to **p**. If **s==m**, we are done; we have found the median and it is in slot **m**. Everything to its left is smaller (or equal), everything to its right is larger, and **m** is in the middle of the array. If **s** is less than **m**, we know the median *is not* in the leftmost partition. Actually, it now is **m-s** positions from the left end of the right partition. So repeat the partition process with the right portion of the array starting at position **s+1** and reset **m** = **m-s**. If **s** is greater than **m**, we know the median *is* in the leftmost partition and still is **m** slots from the left end of the partition. So repeat the partition process beginning with the left end of the array and ending at position **s-1**.
   * Return the value in slot **m** after it has been found.

   Write a program that uses this algorithm to find the median value in a user-specified file containing an unknown quantity of real numbers.

9. Sorting Rectangles.
   Write a new program according to the following instructions:

- The **tools** library contains the function **randy()** that will return a random **double** value between 0 and 1. Write a short program that will open an output file, **rect.dat**, and call **srand()** to initialize the random number generator. Then write a loop that will call **randy()** 40 times, multiplying each result by 100. This will give you 40 random numbers in the range 0–100. Write these numbers into an output file, four per line. Use validation or swapping to ensure that the first number on each line is less than the third and the second is less than the fourth. This should produce a file that can represent 10 rectangles, one per line.
- Modify the **main()** program in Figure 21.14 to sort rectangles instead of **float**s. Sort the rectangles such that the *x* coordinates of the lower-left corners are in ascending order. The input, output, and comparison functions need modification. Write a new **get_data()** function that reads these data into an array of rectangles. Use either quicksort or insertion sort as the main sorting routine. Use the type definition for rectangles given in Figure 14.17 as

```
typedef struct POINT { double x, y; } point_t;
typedef struct RECTANGLE { point_t lo, hi; } rect_t;
```

- Use the revised program to sort the rectangles in **rect.dat**. Display both the input data and the sorted output data on the screen to verify that the program works properly. (The *x* coordinates of the lower-left corners must be in ascending order, and all numbers present in the input must be present in the output also.)
- Use the sorted list of rectangles to compute and display the bounding *x* coordinates of a single rectangle that would enclose all of the rectangles in the set. Do not worry about the *y* coordinates of the bounding box.
- Write a function, **overlap()**, whose parameters are pointers to two rectangles such that the first *x* coordinate of the first rectangle is less than the first *x* coordinate of the second. Return **true** if the rectangles overlap, **false** otherwise. If the rectangles have only a corner or a side in common, return **false**. Document the program with an explanation of the algorithm for testing the "overlap" property.
- Use the **overlap()** function to test all pairs of rectangles in the sorted set and print a list of pairs that overlap.

10. A path through a maze.
   Assume you have the following type definition:

```
typedef bool matrix[N][N];
```

   where **N** is a global constant. Also assume a variable of this type is initialized with a connected trail of elements containing the value **true**, going from a source element somewhere in the middle to a border element.

   a. Write a function, **print_trail()**, that will print out the row and column positions of the elements in this trail, from border to source, recursively. This function should have five parameters. The first is **grid**, a variable of type **matrix**. The next two are **row** and **col**; these are the subscripts of the current element of the trail. The last two are **old_row** and **old_col**, the subscripts of the preceding element. The initial call to **print_trail()** should have **row** and **col** set to the point at the beginning of the trail in the middle of **grid**, while **old_row** and **old_col** are both −1. To follow the trail, we can go up, down, right, or left.

Check the four directions, looking for an element with a value **true** and making sure not to pick the one with the location **[old_row][old_col]**. Then recursively call the **print_trail()** function to follow the rest of the trail from that position on. When a border element is reached, the recursion ends. This is the base case. As the function finishes and begins returning, it should print the location of the current element. This will print the trail elements in order from the border position to the middle position.

b. Write a program that will read an N-by-N maze matrix of ones and zeros from a user-specified file to initialize **grid**. From the next (and last) line of the file, read the row and column indexes at which the trail starts. Finally, call **print_trail()** with the starting position of the trail and have it print the trail.

CHAPTER
22

Making Programs General

T his chapter introduces an assortment of techniques for communicating with the operating system and using some advanced library functions. We show how a program can receive control information from the operating system through command-line arguments and how those arguments can be used to control the operation of a program. We also explore two standard library functions, `qsort()` and `bsearch()`, that are versatile and generalized because of their ability to process any type of array and accept functions as parameters.

22.1   Command-Line Arguments

In the examples presented so far, all communication between the user and the program has been either by interactive query and response or through data stored in a file. Both are useful and powerful ways to control a program and the only ways supported by some limited systems. However, most C systems provide a way to compile a program, link in the libraries, and store an executable form for later use. Such executable files can be started from the operating system's command shell without entering the compiler's development environment. When this option is available, the operating system's command line offers one way for the user to convey control information to a program.

The **command line** is an interface between the user and the operating system. Simple information such as the number of data items to process, the name of a file, or the setting of a control switch often is passed to a program through this mechanism. A command starts with the name of the application to execute, followed by an appropriate number of additional pieces of information, each separated by spaces. Some kinds of information on the command line may be intercepted and altered or used by the system itself; for example, wild-card patterns are expanded and file redirection commands are used. The rest of the information on the line is parsed into strings and delivered to the program in the form of **command-line arguments**.

22.1.1 The Argument Vector

To use command-line arguments, the programmer must declare parameters for `main()` to receive the following two arguments:

1. The **argument count**, an integer, customarily is named `argc`. This is the number of items, including the name of the program, that are on the command line after the operating system processes wild cards and redirection. Whitespace generally separates each item from the next. Certain grouping characters, such as quotation marks, often can be used to group separate words into one item.

2. The **argument vector**, an array of strings, customarily is named `argv`. Each element in the array is a pointer to a string containing one of the items the user wrote on the command line. (Note that this is the same data structure used for menus.) Element 0 points to the program name; the remaining elements are stored in the vector in the order they were typed.

Figure 22.1 shows an example of a command line and the argument data structure that `main()` receives because of it.

This is the argument data structure delivered to `main()` by the command-line processor.[1]

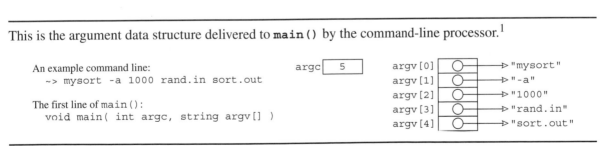

Figure 22.1.   The argument vector.

---

[1] This command line is for a UNIX system. The ~> is the UNIX system prompt.

22.1.2   Decoding Arguments

The first argument (`argv[0]`) is the first thing typed on the command line: the name of the executable program. This is used for making legible error comments. The other arguments can be arbitrary strings and have whatever sort of meaning the programmer devises. They have no preset meaning or order, other than that set up by the programmer; no hidden mechanism uses the command-line arguments to control a program. A program must decode and interpret the arguments itself and is well advised to check for all sorts of errors in the process. Potential errors include misspelled file names, missing or out-of-order arguments, and meaningless control switch settings. In this section, we show how a variety of command-line arguments can be decoded and used to affect the operation of a program. The program in Figure 22.2 allows the user to enter an assortment of information on the command line, including a number, two file names, and (optionally) a control switch. Figure 22.3 contains the `setup()` function that decodes the command line, and Figure 22.4 is a modified sort function.

Notes on Figure 22.2.   Using command-line arguments. Command-line techniques are illustrated by revising and extending the insertion sort program from Figure 20.17. The command line is used to specify the names of the input and output files, the number of items to sort, and the sorting order, either ascending or descending.

- *The* `main()` *function.* The `main()` function in Figure 22.2 is like that in Figure 21.14, which was extended from that in Figure 20.17 with minor changes in the output comments, the name of the sorting function, and an enumerated type. The major changes are found in the `setup()` function (Figure 22.3) and the `sort_data()` function (Figure 22.4). The functions given in Figures 20.15 and 20.16 for input to and output from a `data_pack` are reused with no change. In turn, this `main()` program will be reused in the next example, with only one change (the fourth box), the line that calls the sort function.
- *First box: an enumerated type.* This version of the program has the ability to sort data in either ascending or descending order, a choice made through use of a command-line control switch. The program uses an enumerated type as a choice value and has an accompanying label array for printing. It also adds a member, `order`, to the `data_pack` structure, since this information is needed by the sorting function.
- *Second box: the setup.* In keeping with the policy to remove setup details from `main()`, all the initial work is done by `setup()`. The additional command-line arguments must be passed as arguments so that `setup()` can decode them.
- *Third and fifth boxes: output.* Additional feedback is provided for the user by echoing his sort-order choice and the name of the output data file.

This program calls `get_data()` from Figure 20.15, `print_data()` from Figure 20.16, `setup()` from Figure 22.3 and `sort_data()` from Figure 22.4.

```
#include "tools.h"
typedef enum { ascend, descend } order_t;
string labels[] = { "ascending", "descending" };
typedef struct { float* data; int n; int max; order_t order; } data_pack;

void setup( int argc, string argv[],
            stream* inp, stream* outp, data_pack* sortp );
void get_data( data_pack* sortp, stream instream );
void print_data( data_pack sort, stream outstream );
void sort_data( data_pack sort );

void main( int argc, string argv[] )
{
    stream in_str, out_str;      /* Streams for input and output. */
    data_pack sort;              /* Pointer to array of numbers. */
    say( "\n Sort program." );
    setup( argc, argv, &in_str, &out_str, &sort );

    get_data( &sort, in_str );
    say( " %i data items read; sorting in %s order.",
         sort.n, labels[sort.order] );

    sort_data( sort );
    say( " Data sorted; writing to file %s.", argv[argc-1] );
    print_data( sort, out_str );
    bye();
}
```

Figure 22.2.   Using command-line arguments.

As explained in the notes for Figure 22.3, the output file name is the last argument, and therefore found in `argv[argc - 1]`.

- *Fourth box: sorting.* The program calls the modified insertion sort algorithm to order the data properly.

As with any `setup()` function, the goal is to set up the data structure that will be used for the rest of the application. In this case, the information needed to do so comes from the command line rather than from an interactive question-and-answer session. The files that will be used and the information to be put in each member of the `data_pack` is taken from the command line, tested, and processed. By the end of the function in Figure 22.3, we will have constructed a valid `data_pack`.

```
void
setup( int argc, string argv[], stream* inp, stream* outp, data_pack* sortp )
{
    char* last;                     /* To test for proper number conversion. */
    long int n;                     /* Number of data items. */
    int start = argc - 3;           /* First required argument. */

    if (argc < 4 || argc > 5)
        fatal( "\n Usage: %s [-ad] num infile outfile \n", argv[0] );

    /* ----------------------------------------------------- Open streams. */

    *inp = fopen( argv[start + 1], "r" );
    if (*inp == NULL)
        fatal( "\n Cannot open %s for reading.", argv[start + 1] );
    *outp = fopen( argv[start + 2], "w" );
    if (*outp == NULL)
        fatal( "\n Cannot open %s for writing.", argv[start + 2] );

    /* ---- Convert size from string to numeric format and allocate memory. */

    n = strtol( argv[start], &last, 10 );
    if (*last != '\0')
        fatal( "\n Error: %s is not an integer.", argv[start] );
    if (n < 2)
        fatal( "\n Error: %li is too few items to sort.", n );
    sortp->max = n;

    sortp->data = malloc( n * sizeof(float) );
    if (sortp->data == NULL)
        fatal( "\n Too little memory for %li floats.", n );

    /* --------------------------------- Pick up and check sort order. */

    if (argc == 5) {
        if (strequal( argv[1], "-d" )) sortp->order = descend;
        else if (strequal( argv[1], "-a" )) sortp->order = ascend;
        else fatal( "\n Sort order %s undefined.", argv[1] );
    }
    else sortp->order = ascend;              /* Default if switch is omitted. */
}
```

Figure 22.3.   Decoding command-line arguments.

Notes on Figure 22.3: Decoding command-line arguments.

- *First box: required arguments and usage comments.*

  1. The first step in command-line processing is to make sure that the required number of arguments has been provided. To do this, the program compares **argc**, the number of arguments supplied (including

the program's name), to the number of arguments that should be provided. If some **arguments** are **optional**, the number must be compared to both the minimum and maximum possible requirements.

2. In this program, the user is required to supply the last three arguments (an integer and two file names), and an optional sort-order flag, so the minimum value for `argc` is four and the maximum is five.

3. If `argc` is valid, the program begins getting and checking the individual arguments. If not, since the program cannot operate correctly, it is customary to display a **usage error** comment, which gives the program's name and summarizes the number, order, and nature of the arguments that should be present, with optional arguments listed in square brackets. An example of an erroneous command line and the resulting usage comment might be

```
~> mysort 10 rand.in

 Usage: mysort [-ad] num infile outfile
```

- *Second box: file name arguments.*

1. Input and output files often are named on the command line, as in this program. This eliminates the need to redirect I/O or query the user about file names.

2. Processing these arguments is straightforward: The program attempts to open each file named and displays an error comment if the file cannot be opened. When a command-line argument is the name of a file, it can be used directly in an `fopen()` statement. Since the required arguments are at the end of the command, we know what the subscript of each should be relative to the end of the list. In this program, the file names are the last two arguments.

3. Afterward, it is important to check that the `fopen()` command was completed successfully. The statements in this box demonstrate the proper way to handle file-name arguments.

4. As an example, two erroneous command lines follow, with the comments that were displayed. On the first run, the input file could not be opened because it did not exist; the name was `rand.in`. On the second run, the output file could not be opened because the path was invalid.

```
~> mysort -d 10 rand a:/sort.out

 Cannot open rand for reading.
--------------------------------------------------
~> mysort 10 rand.in a:/sort.out

 Cannot open a:/sort.out for writing.
```

- *Third box: numbers on the command line.*

1. If an argument is a number, it must be converted from a string of digits to a binary number before use. This is not done automatically by the system, as `scanf()` would do for keyboard input, but the `stdlib` library provides a function for this purpose.

2. The function `strtol()` (which stands for string-to-long) converts a `string` to a `long int`. Its first argument is the string to be converted and the third is the conversion base (10 for decimal, 16 for hexadecimal, etc.). The second argument is the address of a `char` pointer, which is set by `strtol()` to the first character in the conversion string that is not a legal digit.

3. In this context, the entire string should be a single number and the `last` pointer should be left pointing at the null terminator at the end of the argument. After attempting to convert the number, which is always the third-to-last argument, we check to be sure the string was convertible and, if it was, that the result is reasonable (at least two items). If so, the value is stored in the `max` member of the `data_pack`.

4. Here are the results of two faulty attempts at specifying the number of items:

```
~> mysort 3a rand.in sort.out

 Error: 3a is not an integer.
 --------------------------------------------------
~> mysort -a -10 rand.in sort.out

 Error: -10 is too few items to sort.
```

5. When the data set size is a legal and reasonable number, the program attempts to allocate the necessary memory. If the number ends up being too small for the amount of data provided in the file, the items at the end of the data file will not be read and sorted. If the command line specifies a number that is too large, no harm is done unless the number indicates an amount that exceeds the available memory of the computer. The last two statements of the third box in Figure 22.3 perform the memory allocation and check for success or failure of the allocation call.

6. On a personal computer, relatively small allocation requests actually may result in failure because the operating system itself occupies such a large portion of the memory. On a larger computer such as a workstation, virtual memory[2] generally is supported. Very large data struc-

---

[2] Virtual memory allows the computer to pretend that it has more main memory than it actually has. Only the portion of each program actively in use resides in the main memory; the rest is "paged out" to secondary memory (usually a hard disk).

tures can be created and used.[3] On such a system, even outrageous requests, such as memory for 70,000 numbers, can be satisfied.[4] The code examples in this text were tested on a UNIX workstation with paged virtual memory.[5]

7. As an example, here is the result of requesting space for 200 million `floats`:

```
~> mysort -d 200000000 rand.in sort.out

 Too little memory for 200000000 floats.
```

- *Fourth box: optional arguments and switches.*

  1. In a usage comment, square brackets [...] customarily are used to denote optional arguments. Often, optional arguments are used to set *switches*, which are single-letter codes used to convey control information. A dash usually precedes the letter and the code may be followed by additional information such as a file name.[6]

  2. Switches are used for a large variety of purposes: Their uses are limited only by the program designer's imagination. The documentation that accompanies a program must explain what switches are recognized, what each means, and whether they must have accompanying information. A usage error comment generally has a single pair of square brackets for the switches; within the brackets is a single - followed by all the acceptable single-letter switch options, in alphabetical order.

  3. In this example, we use an optional switch `-d` to request that the data be sorted into descending order. If no switch is present, the default is ascending order. However, to avoid confusion, the code `-a` also is accepted for ascending order. Therefore, the usage comment lists both options, `-a` and `-d`, in a single pair of brackets, like this:

     `Usage: mysort [-ad] num infile outfile`

  4. Because this argument is optional, the program must determine whether the user supplied it before decoding it. In this example, the switch will be the second thing on the command line, if it exists at all. If `argc` is five, we know that something optional was written. To determine whether it is a valid switch setting, the program compares the second argument, `argv[1]`, to the strings `"-a"` and `"-d"`. If it matches one

---

[3]The cost of such a scheme is the time required to move blocks of data back and forth between the main memory and the secondary memory.

[4]Unused portions of the data simply are never paged into memory and incur very little overhead.

[5]Code was compiled by gcc on a Linux operating system with 132 MB of virtual memory.

[6]This format is assumed by certain standard command-line processing functions that are beyond the scope of this text. The format is, therefore, familiar to UNIX users. It is customary to follow it in any program that uses the command line.

of these recognized options, the **order** member of the **data_pack** is set to the appropriate symbol (**ascend** or **descend**) from the enumerated type **order_t**. If the argument is anything else, the program calls **fatal()**.

5. If an application accepts optional arguments and none is provided on the command line, a default setting generally is provided by the system. In this program, the default sort order is ascending.

6. Here is the output from three calls on the sort program, one with and one without a valid optional argument and the last with an invalid argument:

```
~> mysort -d 10 rand.in sort.out

 Sort program.
 10 data items read; sorting in descending order.
 Data sorted; writing to file sort.out.
 -------------------------------------------------
~> mysort 10 rand.in sort.out

 Sort program.
 10 data items read; sorting in ascending order.
 Data sorted; writing to file sort.out.
 -------------------------------------------------
~> mysort -t 10 rand.in sort.out

 Sort program.
 Sort order -t undefined.
 -------------------------------------------------
```

The **main()** program in Figure 22.2 calls the **sort_data()** function in Figure 22.4, which is like the **insertion sort** in Figure 20.19, except that it can sort the array into either ascending or descending order. To accomplish this, we had to add an additional member to the data pack: **order**, the sort order, to pass this information along.

Notes on Figure 22.4. A revised sort function.

- The box focuses on finding the insertion position. In the heart of the original sort is the **if...break** statement that takes control out of the loop when the proper slot for an item has been found. In this revision, the simple one-line **if** from Figure 20.19 is expanded. It uses different comparison operators for ascending order (**<=**) and descending order (**>=**). The order flag is tested as part of the condition and controls which comparison operation actually is used.

This function is called by the program in Figure 22.2. It uses an insertion sort algorithm to sort *n* values into either ascending or descending order. The box encloses the lines that are different from the original algorithm in Figure 20.19.

```
void
sort_data( data_pack sort )
{
    float* end = sort.data + sort.n;            /* Off-board sentinel. */
    float* pass;                /* First unsorted item; begin pass here. */
    float* hole;                /* Array slot containing no data. */
    float newcomer;             /* Data value being inserted. */

    for (pass = sort.data + 1; pass < end; ++pass) {
        /* Pick up next item and insert into sorted portion of array. */
        newcomer = *pass;
        for (hole = pass; hole > sort.data; --hole) {
            if (sort.order == ascend && (*(hole - 1) <= newcomer))
                break;                       /* Insertion slot found... */
            else if (sort.order == descend && (*(hole - 1) >= newcomer))
                break;                       /* .... so leave loop. */
            else *hole = *(hole - 1);/* else move item back one slot. */
        }
        *hole = newcomer;                       /* Insert into sorted position. */
    }
}
```

Figure 22.4.   A revised sort function.

22.2   Functions as Parameters

Chapter 20 shows that it is possible to have a pointer set to point at a function. In this section, we present an additional application for function pointers. A very powerful aspect of C is that we can pass functions as arguments to other functions. A pointer parameter can point to a function as easily as to any other type. This property is useful in an application where the processing method does not depend on the particular function being used.

For example, the standard C library contains a general quicksort function, **qsort()**, that is capable of sorting any type of data, from simple integers to complex data types like structures. To do this, it must be told how to compare two objects of the type it is sorting. This information is delivered to **qsort()** in the form of a function, written by the application programmer, that does the comparison. A pointer to the comparison function is one of the arguments in the call to **qsort()**.

22.2.1   Using the System's `qsort()` Function

The function `qsort()` is written in a highly general way to sort objects of any type. Because of this generality, a call on `qsort()` is more complex than a call on a single-purpose sort function, like those we have presented, that is designed to sort a particular data type. **Generic functions** such as this require passing an argument of an arbitrary type, which is not supported by the normal ANSI C type-checking rules. Therefore, some type-casting "tricks" must be used to make it possible to call `qsort()`. The prototype for `qsort()` is:

```
void qsort( void* data, size_t n, size_t sz,
            int (*comp)( const void* p1, const void* p2 ));
```

In the definition of `qsort()`, the **generic type** name `void*` is used (instead of a specific type) to mean "a pointer to an object whose type is unknown."

Comparison functions.   Sorting is based on comparison. Each different type of data value needs an appropriate **comparison function** to define *greater than*, *less than*, and *equal to*. For instance, we use `strcmp()` with strings but need the operators `<`, `==`, and `>` to compare integers. Since `qsort()` cannot guess which function or operator is appropriate for the data it will receive, the appropriate comparison function must be supplied as one of its arguments. This function has a very special form:

1. It must have two parameters of type `const void*`. The function itself must cast these generic pointers to their actual type, before the arguments can be used. For example, when sorting an array of `float`s, the arguments must be cast to type `float*`.
2. After casting, the pointers must be dereferenced to get the actual values to be compared. Therefore, two local variables, `f1` and `f2`, are initialized to these values.
3. The comparison function must return an `int` that encodes a three-way outcome; that is, it must return distinct results for each of the cases in which the first argument is less than, equal to, or greater than the second argument. The `qsort()` function calls the comparison function, passing it a pair of pointers to data values. In return, for sorting in ascending order, it expects a positive integer if the first value is larger, a negative integer if the second is larger, and a zero value if they are the same. For descending order, the positive and negative outcomes are reversed.

The next program example shows how to use `qsort()` on an array of `float`s. To support this effort, Figure 22.5 shows a pair of comparison functions that will compare `float`s for ascending and descending order. The revised sorting program that calls `qsort()` is presented in Figure 22.6.

These functions are designed to be called by `qsort()` to compare two `floats`. The first is used for sorting in ascending order; the second is in descending order.

```
/* ------------------------------------------------------------------ */
/* Compare two floats for the qsort() function, for ascending order. --- */
int
sort_up( const void* fp1, const void* fp2 )
{
    float f1 = *(float*)fp1;
    float f2 = *(float*)fp2;

    if (f1 < f2) return -1;
    else if (f1 == f2) return 0;
    else return 1;
}
/* ------------------------------------------------------------------ */
/* Compare two floats for the qsort() function, for descending order. -- */
int
sort_down( const void* fp1, const void* fp2 )
{
    float f1 = *(float*)fp1;
    float f2 = *(float*)fp2;

    if (f1 > f2) return -1;
    else if (f1 == f2) return 0;
    else return 1;
}
```

Figure 22.5.   Two comparison functions for `qsort()`.

Notes on Figure 22.5. Two comparison functions for `qsort()`.

- The arguments passed from `qsort()` to the comparison function are pointers rather than values, because all pointers are the same size in C and so can be passed in a uniform fashion. These pointers have type `void*`, because `qsort()` does not know what type of data it is sorting.
- *The* `sort_up()` *function.*

  1. The arguments to `sort_up()`, `fp1` and `fp2`, point at the two numbers to be compared.
  2. First, the function must cast the `void*` arguments to pointers with the appropriate base type (`float*`) and extract the data using pointer indirection. These values are stored in local variables to make comparison easy.
  3. The return value is a positive number if `*fp1` is greater, a negative number if `*fp2` is greater, and 0 if they are equal.

This program calls I/O functions from Figures 20.15 and 20.16, `setup()` from Figure 22.3, and the `qsort()` function from the standard C library. It also uses the comparison functions from Figure 22.5. The `main()` program given here is identical to `main()` in Figure 22.2 except for the boxed lines. The `typedef` statements and prototypes at the top of Figure 22.2 are not repeated here.

```
int sort_up( const void* fp1, const void* fp2 );
int sort_down( const void* fp1, const void* fp2 );
```

```
void main( int argc, string argv[] )
{
    stream in_str, out_str;      /* Streams for input and output. */
    data_pack sort;              /* Pointer to array of numbers. */
    int (*compare)( const void*, const void* );    /* A function pointer. */

    say( "\n Qsort program." );
    setup( argc, argv, &in_str, &out_str, &sort );

    get_data( &sort, in_str );
    say( " %i data items read; sorting in %s order.",
        sort.n, labels[sort.order] );

    if (sort.order == ascend) compare = sort_up;
    else compare = sort_down;

    qsort( (void*)sort.data, sort.n, sizeof(float), compare );

    say( " Data sorted; writing to file %s.", argv[argc-1] );
    print_data( sort, out_str );
    bye();
}
```

Figure 22.6.   Using `qsort()` and a functional parameter.

4. Normally, a responsible program compares floating-point numbers using a tolerance, rather than the simple `==` operator. However, in this case, we really want 0 returned only when the two values are identical.

- *The `sort_down()` function.*

1. The function `sort_down()` gives the opposite answer, so a `>` operator is used instead of a `<` comparison.
2. There is an easier way to compute a positive, 0, or negative result when comparing integers, characters, or an enumerated type: subtraction. This technique is illustrated in Figure 22.8.

Notes on Figure 22.6. Using `qsort()` and a functional parameter.
Only a few changes are necessary to adapt the `main()` program from Figure 22.2 to use `qsort()` instead of `sort_data()`.

- *First box: prototypes.* First, the prototype for `sort_data()` (the last of the original prototypes) should be removed. We need not explicitly replace it by a prototype for `qsort()` because that prototype already is in `stdlib.h`, which is included by `tools.h`. However, we must add prototypes for the two comparison functions used by `qsort()` and defined in Figure 22.5.
- *Second and third boxes: pointing at a function.* Since there are two different comparison functions, we select one to send to `qsort()` based on the **command-line switch**. The selected function (in the third box) is assigned to the function pointer declared in the second box. No `typedef` was made for the function pointer type because its use is limited to `main()`.
- *Fourth box: calling* `qsort()`. It is necessary to pass four arguments to `qsort()`.

  1. The first parameter is an array of data. This must be unpacked from the `data_pack` and cast to type `void*` before passing it to `qsort()`. Type `void*` is used because the actual data could be of any type, and a meaningless parameter type is preferred to an incorrect type. The function `qsort()` does the appropriate indexing to access elements of the array, based on information about the array type passed to `qsort()` through the third argument.
  2. The second parameter is the number of data items to be sorted.
  3. The third parameter is the size of the base type of the array. This information is needed to correctly locate the items; that is, to know how far apart the items are in memory.
  4. Fourth is the **functional parameter**, a pointer to a function able to compare two elements of the base type according to the desired sorting order.

Thus, `qsort()` implements a **quicksort** algorithm that uses the specified comparison function to order pairs of array elements. Because `qsort()` is written in a highly general way and uses extensive type casting, it can be hard to understand how and why the code works. Because it calls a comparison function, which must work through pointers, its overall efficiency is decreased. For example, we cannot expect it to perform as well as the quicksort program in Figure 21.15. However, from direct observation, it clearly is a very fast function and can be used to sort anything. A programmer who understands how to write comparison functions may never need to write another sorting function again.

22.2.2   Using the System's `bsearch()` Function

The function `qsort()` is a generic sorting function. C also has a generic binary search function, `bsearch()`, which works in the same way, using `void*` parameters and a comparison function. Chapter 21 discusses the binary search algorithm; in Figure 22.7, we show how to perform a binary search by calling `bsearch()`.

Notes on Figure 22.7. Calling on `bsearch()`.   This program was adapted from the binary search program in Figure 21.5. Boxes enclose the few lines that were changed. It calls the comparison function in Figure 22.8.

- *First, third, and sixth boxes: the value returned by* `bsearch()`. The `bin_search()` function in Figure 21.5 returned an integer subscript. The system's function returns a pointer. This forces us to make three changes. First, the constant **NOT_FOUND**, defined at the top, needs to become **NULL** instead of **-1**, because that is what `bsearch()` returns to indicate a failed search. Second, since `slot` stores the value returned from `bsearch()`, it must be an `int*` rather than an `int`. Third, the output statement in the sixth box must subtract the address of the head of the data array from `slot` to compute the subscript at which the key value was found.

- *Second box: prototype.* We eliminate the prototype for `bin_search()` because we will call `bsearch()` instead. (Its prototype is in `stdlib.h`.) We also eliminate the prototype for `check_data()` because we will use `qsort()` instead. We add a prototype for a comparison function that is appropriate for comparing integers. This function is found in Figure 22.8.

- *Fourth box: calling* `qsort()`. A binary search cannot function properly unless the data values are in correct sorted order. In the earlier program, a function, `check_data()`, was called to verify that this was true and aborted if it was not. Here, a superior technique is used; the program simply sorts the data. We are guaranteed that the data will be in the correct order if `qsort()` is used to sort the data, then the same comparison function is used as an argument to `bsearch()`.

- *Fifth box: calling* `bsearch()`. The `bsearch()` function assumes that the data in the array to be searched are sorted in ascending order. A call has the same parameters as a call on `qsort()`, with one addition and a minor change. The first argument is the address of the search key, cast to type `const void*`. The second argument, the data array, is cast to `const void*`, not `void*`, because the values in the array will not be changed or moved around. The complete prototype for `bsearch()` is

```
void*
bsearch(
        const void* key, const void* data,
        size_t elements, size_t size,
        int (*compare)( const void*, const void* ) );
```

This program calls the standard search function **bsearch()** and the setup and input functions in Figures 21.6 and 21.7.

```
#include "tools.h"
#define NOT_FOUND   NULL

typedef struct { int* data; int n; int max; } data_pack;

void setup( data_pack* spec, stream* infile );
int  get_data( data_pack* searchp, stream instream );
int  sort_int_up( const void* ip1, const void* ip2 );

void main( void )
{
    stream fin;                  /* Stream for the input file. */
    data_pack search;           /* Array of data. */
    int key;                     /* Number to search for. */
    int* slot;                   /* Position at which key is found. */
    int stream_status;           /* For scanf()'s return value. */
    banner();
    puts( "\n Find a key value in an array of integers." );
    setup( &search, &fin );
    get_data( &search, fin );

    qsort( (void*)search.data, search.n, sizeof(int), sort_int_up );

    printf( " %i data items read; ready to search.\n", search.n );
    puts( "\n Enter numbers to search for; period to quit." );
    for (;;) {
        printf( " What number do you wish to find? " );
        stream_status = scanf( "%i", &key );
        if (stream_status < 1) break;

        slot = bsearch( (const void*)&key, (const void*)search.data,
                        search.n, sizeof(int), sort_int_up );

        if (slot == NOT_FOUND)
            printf( " Key value %i is not in table.\n\n", key );
        else

            printf( " Key value %i was found in slot %i.\n\n",
                    key, slot - search.data );

    }
    bye();
}
```

Figure 22.7.   Calling on bsearch().

This function is designed to be called by `qsort()` and `bsearch()` to compare two integers for ascending order. For `bsearch()`, the first argument is the sort key; the second is a value in the array being searched.

```
int
sort_int_up( const void* ip1, const void* ip2 )
{
    int i1 = *(int *)ip1;
    int i2 = *(int *)ip2;
    return i1 - i2;
}
```

Figure 22.8.   A comparison function for integers.

- *Sample output for a large file (not shown here).*

```
Find a key value in an array of integers.
Enter name of data file to be searched: rand.in

1000 data items read; ready to search.

Enter numbers to search for; period to quit.
What number do you wish to find? 35
Key value 35 is not in table.

What number do you wish to find? 2447
Key value 2447 was found in slot 233.

What number do you wish to find? .
```

Notes on Figure 22.8. A comparison function for integers.   A comparison function for integers can be simpler than one for `float`s. To compare two integers for ascending order, simply subtract the second argument from the first. For descending order, subtract the first argument from the second. This works because the result of a subtraction on these types is an appropriate positive or negative integer. We cannot use this technique to compare floating-point values because the comparison function returns an `int` and the result of a floating-point subtraction would be cast to type `int` before returning it. This would truncate the floating-point value and could turn a nonzero result into 0.

22.3   What You Should Remember

22.3.1 Major Concepts

The command line.   A program can receive information from the user either interactively, by reading a file, or (on systems that support it) through the command line. Command-line information is conveyed to the program in a data structure called the *argument vector*, which is an array of strings. The number of strings in the array (`argc`) and the array itself (`argv`) can be accessed in the program by declaring two parameters for `main()`: `main(int argc, string argv[])`. Decoding the contents of the command line may be straightforward if the relative positions of the information are known. Otherwise a decoding loop containing a `switch` statement is the typical processing strategy.

ASCII to number conversion.   When `scanf()` reads a number, it must read a series of ASCII characters and convert them to a numeric value before storing them in the caller's variable. When numbers are received through the command line, the program itself must do the conversion. For this purpose, the C libraries supply the functions `strtol()` and `strtod()`, which convert ASCII strings to numeric values of types `long int` and `double`, respectively.

Sorting and searching.   The C libraries provide two generic utility functions that can be used with arrays of any type of data: `qsort()`, which performs a quicksort, and `bsearch()`, which performs a binary search on an array sorted in ascending order. To use these functions, the programmer must supply a function that performs a three-way comparison on two values of the type being processed. Because these functions must be able to process any kind of data, their array arguments must be type cast to `void*` and the arguments received by the comparison function must be cast back to the proper data type. The size of the data elements in the array is an argument to the generic utilities and used to calculate appropriate index values for the array.

Functional arguments.   A function (technically, a pointer to a function) can be a parameter to another function. This enables us to write sort programs that can sort data into ascending or descending order and search programs that can search an array of any base type, using an appropriate comparison function.

Generic code.   A sophisticated programming technique can be used in C to implement certain general-purpose algorithms so that they can use data of any type. These techniques include

- One or more parameters of the generic algorithm are declared as type `void*`.
- In every call, the corresponding arguments must be cast to type `void*`.
- Other parameters of the generic function must contain all the information necessary to properly index arrays or members of structures, if those types are to be processed.
- One or more functional parameters may be needed so that appropriate operations can be applied to the generic type data. These operations are defined by the calling program to perform the generic operation (such as comparison or addition) on the actual type of data being processed.

22.3.2   Programming Style

- *Argument ordering.* It is possible to structure the order of command-line arguments in many ways. A typical convention is to place all the required arguments at the end of the list and the optional arguments between the actual command and the required arguments. The required arguments can be restricted into a particular order to ease decoding. The optional arguments, which typically are switches, must be able to appear in any order since any number may be present. Therefore, the processing strategy for these must be more robust.

- *Command line vs. interactive.* Information can be passed to the program either through command-line arguments or user interaction. If the list of information is short (and therefore easily remembered) and likely to change often, the command line is preferred. Such items as the names of files or settings of switches used to control execution are typical. Even so, the program should provide a usage error comment in case the user forgets. Also, if file redirection is expected to occur, user interaction is discouraged. For data-gathering sessions user interaction is preferred, since it is too easy to forget what to provide next. For large amounts of data, file input is best. Sometimes, having an interactive program makes a particular type of user feel better.

- *Avoiding casting confusion.* When using a function like **qsort()** or **bsearch()**, you must provide a comparison function appropriate for the type being processed. The comparison functions in this chapter provide sound patterns for writing your own. First, they cast the pointer parameters to the appropriate type and give appropriate names to the results. These names (rather than the generic parameter names) are used to write the actual comparisons. This helps avoid confusion about whether the comparisons are working on values or pointers and permits the type-checking system of C to assist the programmer in finding inappropriate operations.

- *Personalized vs. generic functions.* There is some question whether it is better to use the generic system sorting and searching functions or ones you write. First, the efficiency of these routines is reduced from what an experienced programmer could accomplish, due to the overhead processing involved with indirectly accessing data and repeated calls to a comparison function. In specialized situations, other sorting and searching algorithms might perform better. However, this is outweighed by the convenience of not having to write and debug functions, not to mention modify them each time a new data type is to be used. It is much easier to write a single comparison function than a whole sort program. So most people, unless execution speed is of overriding importance, will use generic functions if available.

22.3.3 Sticky Points and Common Errors

- *Casting correctly.* A pointer cast is not the same as a value cast: A value cast actually converts an object to a different representation. However, a pointer cast simply relabels the type of the object; it does not change the representation of either the pointer or its referent. For this reason, all the casting used to support generic code is done *on pointers.* Cast the pointer before trying to dereference it.

- *Comparison functions.* Two methods were given for writing a comparison function: (1) the long way, using **if...else if...else**, and (2) a short way, using subtraction. The short way is appropriate only for comparing integers and enumerated types. For floating-point data, the long way must be used. Also, make sure you have the correct tests. If you are trying to generate data in ascending order, getting the tests wrong will generate data in descending order.

- *Error checking.* Most functions return two types of values: valid responses as a result of the requested operation and an error code. If an error code can be returned, it is a mistake not to put code in your program to test for this possibility and take corresponding action. Similarly, a program must try to handle all the special cases that might occur. Even if the response is to terminate the program with an error message, this is better than an unexpected crash.

22.3.4 New and Revisited Vocabulary

These are the most important terms and concepts discussed in this chapter:

command line	**data_pack**	generic code
command-line arguments	**setup()**	type casting
argument count (**argc**)	insertion sort	**void***
argument vector (**argv**)	quicksort	**strtol()**
optional arguments	comparison function	**strtod()**
usage error comment	functional parameter	**qsort()**
command-line switch	generic type	**bsearch()**

22.4   Exercises

22.4.1 Self-Test Exercises

1. Consider the small sorting program designed at the beginning of this chapter. The following commands are intended to run this program but have errors in them. What is wrong with each one?

a. `mysor -a 10 in out`

b. `mysort -a in out`

c. `mysort -ad 10 in out`

d. `mysort -a -10 in out`

e. `mysort in out`

2. Consider the comparison function **sort_int_up()** defined in Figure 22.8. Think of another function, **sort_int_down()**, that swaps the two values in the **return** statement. What will happen to a combined sorting and searching program if

a. The function **sort_int_down()** is used first by **qsort()** and then by **bsearch()**

b. The function **sort_int_down()** is used by **qsort()** to prepare the data for searching, then **sort_int_up()** is used by **bsearch()** in the program

c. The function **sort_int_up()** is used by **qsort()** to prepare the data for searching, then **sort_int_down()** is used by **bsearch()** in the program

3. Think about the conversion function **strtol()**. Write a simple algorithm that describes how this function would work. Hint: Subtracting the ASCII code for **0** from each character digit will give you a numerical digit.

4. Happy Hacker was trying to adapt the **qsort()** program to sort a file of strings into ascending alphabetical order. Following the example of Figure 22.8, he wrote two versions of the **sort_up()** function (see the following) but neither worked. Assume you are the teaching assistant in his programming course and explain to him what he did wrong in each case.

a. This version gives four compiler warnings (assignment from incompatible pointer type, passing **arg** of **strcmp()** from incompatible pointer type), also, it does not change the order of the strings:

```
int sort_up( const string* st1, const string* st2 )
{    return strcmp( st1, st2 );  }
```

b. This version gives one compiler warning (assignment from incompatible pointer type) and does not change the order of the strings:

```
int sort_up( const void* st1, const void* st2 )
{    return strcmp( (char*)st1, (char*)st2 );  }
```

5. We have shown three ways to communicate data from a user to a program: by entering the data interactively, by reading data from a file, and through command-line arguments. Compare the strengths and limitations of these three communication methods and describe the kind of data for which each is most appropriate.

6. Design a command line for a program that searches for a single word in a text file. The program should have several options, such as find the first occurrence of the word, find all occurrences of the word, do case sensitive or insensitive matching, and have or not have verbose output.

22.4.2 Using Pencil and Paper

1. Consider the small sorting program designed at the beginning of this chapter. The following commands are intended to run this program but have errors. What is wrong with each one?

   a. `mysort -d 10 in in`

   b. `mysort -a -d 10 out`

   c. `mysort in 10 out`

   d. `mysort -t 10 out in`

   e. `mysort 10 in out -a`

2. Write a comparison function that can be used with `qsort()` to sort strings in descending order.

3. Think about the conversion function `strtod()` that converts a string of ASCII digits to a **double** number. Write an algorithm that describes how this function would work. Hint: Think about how `strtol()` works and extend the conversion process. Another hint: Consult the answers to the self-test exercises.

4. Design a command line for a program that acts like a simple calculator. It should perform the four basic math operations, as well as exponentiation and square root. One option should be the number of digits of precision to display for the answer.

5. Ima Intermediate was trying to adapt the `qsort()` program to sort a file of strings into ascending alphabetical order. Following the example of Figure 22.8, she wrote two versions of the `sort_up()` function (see the following), but neither worked. Assume that you are the teaching assistant in her programming course and explain to her what she did wrong in each case.

   a. This version gives two compiler warnings (assignment from incompatible pointer type) but it compiles and runs; it does not change the order of the strings:

   ```
   int sort_up( const string* sp1, const string* sp2 )
   {    return *sp1 - *sp2;  }
   ```

   b. This version gives a compiler warning (**dereferencing void* pointer**) and a fatal compile error (**void value not ignored as it ought to be**).

   ```
   int sort_up( const void* ip1, const void* ip2 )
   {    return (string)*ip1 - (string)*ip2;  }
   ```

6. Your company handles estate auctions and builds a database for each estate with about 5,000 inventory items. The data are in use from the time the auctioneer first estimates the value of the items until the auction transactions are closed, a period of about a month. The database is kept in a file. This file could be sorted or unsorted. Our best quicksort program sorts 5,000 items in about 13 time units. Our best insertion sort (Chapter 20) uses about 572 time units to sort the same data. For data retrieval, the sequential search (Chapter 16) can locate 1,000 items in 198 time units, and the recursive binary search can locate 1,000 items in 29 time units.

   a. If you sort the data, which sort should you use?

   b. If you expect to perform only 1,000 searches, should you use sequential search or sort the data and use binary search? Develop a formula to use in answering this question.

   c. What is the minimum number of searches that makes it worth the effort to sort the data?

7. a. Write a **typedef** and a prototype for a function, **f_fun()**, whose parameters are an integer N, two arrays of N **double**s, and a function that takes two **double** parameters and returns a **double** result. The **f_fun()** function should return a result of type **double***.

   b. Write an equivalent prototype for **f_fun()** without using the **typedef** name.

   c. Declare a variable that can store the result of **f_fun()**. Then write a call on it with the arguments 2.5, 3.14, and **pow()** and store the result in your variable.

   d. Declare a variable of the correct type to refer to **f_fun()**.

   e. Write another call on **f_fun()** using the function pointer from part d and the variable from part c.

22.4.3   Using the Computer

1. Search commands.
   In self-test exercise 6, we designed the command line for a program that searches a text file for a word. Implement this program, handling all the options described. The user specifies the text file and the search word on the command line. Read the file one line at a time and search that line for the given word. If you find an occurrence of the search word, print the line number on which you found it. To do case-insensitive matching, consider converting both the search word and the text file to the same case prior to comparing them. Verbose output would be an extensive report about whether the search word was found on each line of the file. Maximum line length is 80 characters.

2. Desk calculator.
   Write the program that acts like a simple calculator for which you designed a command line interface in pencil-and-paper exercise 4. Assume that the inputs are real numbers.

3. ASCII to integer conversion.
   Write a version of the **strtol()** function that implements the algorithm designed in self-test exercise 3. Include this in a program that reads two numbers from the command line as strings and produces their sum as output. Have the program compare the output of your function to the standard C **strtol()** function.

4. ASCII to floating point conversion.
   Write a version of the **strtod()** function that implements the algorithm designed in pencil-and-paper exercise 3. Include this in a program that reads two numbers from the command line as strings and produces their sum as output. Have the program compare the output of your function to the standard C **strtod()** function.

5. Command-line operation.
   Write a version of the binary search program, shown in this chapter, that uses a command-line interface. The user should be able to specify the name of the data file, the key value, and whether the file is sorted in ascending or descending order. The program should print the index position of the data item it found or an error message, if none was found.

6. Timed trials.
   Four different sorting programs have been given: selection sort, insertion sort, quicksort, and the standard **qsort()**. The goal of this exercise is to compare their performance on random data.

   a. The **tools** library contains the function **randy()**, which returns a random floating-point number between 0 and 1. Write a short program that will open an output file, **rand.flo**, then call **srand()** to initialize the random number generator. Write a loop that will call **randy()** 10,000 times and print the resulting values into your output file.

   b. Modify the **main()** program in Figure 22.6 as follows:

      • Use **rand.flo** for the input file and **sort.flo** for the output file.
      • Add a call on **time()** (from the C **time** library) before and immediately after the call on **qsort()**; store the two times in **long int** variables named **before** and **after**.
      • After sorting is complete, call **d = difftime(after, before);** to get the elapsed time in seconds and store the result in a variable. Display the elapsed time with appropriate labeling.

   c. By using the command line, run the program to sort 100, 1,000, 5,000, and finally 10,000 numbers from **rand.flo**. Make a table of the timing results.

   d. Now modify your program to use a different sorting algorithm and repeat the process. Perform timing tests on all four sorting methods mentioned, recording their performance. Present the results in the form of a neat table or graph. Which sorting algorithm was fastest on your system? The slowest? Are the results what you expected?

7. Summation.
   The method of taking a running sum or product of the elements of a vector is independent of the actual operation being performed. That is, the loop to compute a sum has the same structure as a loop to compute a product; only the operator is different.

   a. Write two short functions, **plus()** and **times()**. Each should have two **double** parameters and return their sum or product, respectively.

   b. Write a function, **running()**, that will accept an array of numbers, an integer that gives the length of that array, an initial value, and a pointer to one of the functions just described. When computing a sum, the initial value should be 0. For a product, it should be 1. The function should execute a loop to compute the running sum or product of the array values.

    c. Write a **main()** program that reads an array of real numbers from a file and calls the **running()** function twice, once to compute the running sum of the array and a second time to compute the product. Echo the input data and print the results.

8. Logical summation.
Modify the program specifications given in the previous exercise so that the base type of the array is **bool** and the operations implemented are running-AND and running-OR, using the logical operators. Determine what initial values are appropriate for these operations. Assume the input data are a series of ones and zeros representing **true** and **false**.

9. Generic code.
Generalize the **running()** function from the prior two exercises to work on an array of elements of any base type, when given an initial value of the same base type and a functional parameter appropriate for the type of data in the array. Write a **main()** program that tests this function by using the arrays of data and the operators from the previous two problems.

10. Interactive sorting.
Write a program that will sort an array of structures, as follows:

- Each structure should have three members: a name (type **string**), an ID number (**long int**), and a pay rate (**float**).
- Read data from a file named on the command line into an array of these structures. An upper limit on the amount of data to process also should be given on the command line. The input file should have one data item per line, with name, ID number, and pay rate in the order given, separated by commas.
- Prompt the user for the name of an output file. Open that file.
- Present a menu that lets the user select which field to sort on and whether the result should be in ascending or descending order.
- Sort the data in the manner selected and write the output to the specified file. Use whichever sorting algorithm you wish.
- Repeat the process. Prompt the user for another file name and another sort order. Resort and write another file. Continue until the user decides to quit.

Modular Organization

This chapter introduces a final assortment of techniques for organizing large applications and linking them with various useful libraries.

A well-designed large program is built in several modules, with a `main()` program at the top level that calls functions from other modules. When the application is designed, the purpose of each module is specified, as are the ways each module can interact with the others. Each then is developed separately (and stored in a separate file). The modules, in turn, are composed of programmer-defined types, data objects, and function definitions. Header files are used to keep the interface between the modules consistent and permit functions in one module to call functions in another. Source files contain the actual code. We further explore how the techniques presented so far extend into creating larger and more protected applications.

23.1   Constructing a Modular Program

Writing, compiling, and running a simple one-module program is very much the same in any system environment. The programmer creates a source file, then either types a compile command or selects a "compile" option from a menu. If compilation is successful, an execute or run command is given either from the command line or by selecting a menu option.

Writing and running a large program is much more complex and the process differs greatly from system to system. The design of a large program often includes several programmer-defined modules that perform different phases of the overall task, and these may be written by different people. Each module, in turn, is a set of related definitions and functions, written in separate source code and header files, and compiled into separate object files. The object files are linked together, along with the system libraries, to create an integrated executable program. In this section, we discuss some general principles and guidelines for **modular** program **design** and explain how to build a **multimodule program** in a UNIX environment.

23.1.1   File Management Issues with Modular Construction

Organizing and managing the files of a modular application and creating an executable program from them raises a group of problems related to efficiency, completeness, and consistency:

- We must be able to compile a module without linking it to anything, so that a debugged module can be stored much like a library. It is undesirable to recompile an entire large application every time a change is made in one small part of it.
- We must be able to link programs to object-code modules that were previously compiled, whether the module was produced locally or is part of a library package for which we do not have the source code.
- We must have access to the header files needed by each code module, whether these are our own or part of a library package.
- We must keep track of which object files and libraries are needed and make them all available to the linker at the appropriate time.
- We must avoid including the same header file twice in one module or the same source-code file twice in the linked program.
- We must have a way to determine whether a module is properly compiled and up to date and ensure we use the most recent version of each module. A systematic way to do this is vital if the modules are being developed independently.
- All modules must agree on the prototypes for shared functions, the values of common constants, the details of shared type definitions, and the names of included header files.
- We should have a way to test individual modules independently.

Once these problems are solved, modular design makes it truly easier and faster to create a large program. During debugging, modules can be changed one at a time, as errors are found. Only the corrected module then is recompiled and the linking step repeated. We avoid recompiling the other modules, which saves time for the programmer.

A variety of techniques have been developed to address the problems of **code management.** These include the use of subdirectories, system search paths, revision control systems, makefiles, project files, header files, compiler options, and preprocessor commands, just to mention a few. Different operating system environments provide alternate ways to organize files and perform the compilation tasks; the programmer must learn how the local environment works. We now discuss a few of these techniques.

Files and folders.   Four kinds of modules might be used as part of a project:

1. *System libraries* include both the standard C libraries and compiler-specific packages for graphics, sound, and the like.
2. User-defined library modules include both personal libraries and modules like **tools** that are shared among members of a group or employees of a company.
3. The programmer's main module containing the function **main()**.
4. Other modules that are defined to support this particular application.

To keep all of these parts organized and avoid conflict with the parts of other programs, a subdirectory, or folder, should be established for each multimodule project. This folder will contain all of the user's code modules, header files, relevant input data and output files, and ideally, a document file that explains how to use the program. Very large projects may have a subdirectory for each module, especially if modules are being developed by different people. Depending on your system, the relevant programmer-defined library modules and header files also may go in this subdirectory. Alternatively, it may be more convenient to put local library files in a more central directory that is accessible to other projects. In this case, these files are accessed by setting up appropriate search paths. These will be in addition to the standard search paths that the compiler uses to locate system libraries and system header files.

Header files and source code files.   The best way to work with a large application is to break it up into subsystems, then implement each subsystem as a separate code module. Each one is likely to have functions and objects for internal use only, and others that are **exported** and used by other modules. The **module interface** consists of the set of definitions and function prototypes that are exported. We organize such a program module by splitting it into two sections: the internal code and the interface. The interface portion becomes a **header file** (usually with a **.h** extension). The code portion becomes a **source code file** (with a **.c** extension), which must **#include** its own header file as well as headers of other modules. Any module that uses things defined by another module's interface must also **#include** its header file.

Header files normally do not contain function code or variable declarations (external global variable declarations are the common exception). They do contain the definitions and prototypes that define the interface between their corresponding source code module and the programs that might **import** it. You can see how code files and header files work by examining **tools.c** and **tools.h** in Appendix F. All the function definitions for the `tools` library are in `tools.c`. Type definitions, constant definitions, and function prototypes (but no source code) are in `tools.h`. Both `tools.c` and user programs include `tools.h`.

When you `#include` a file in a program, the contents of the file are copied into that program during compilation. If a source code file is `#included`, all its code is inserted into the program and compiled as part of the program. This is not considered a good practice because it increases the possibility that functions in one code module might inadvertently interact with global objects in the other in unanticipated and damaging ways. When we `#include` a header file in a program, only the interface declarations (and no foreign source code) are copied into the program. This allows the compiler to verify and set up calls on the imported functions.

This, of course, is how the standard libraries work. When we include `stdio.h`, we do not include the source code for the whole library (which is massively large). Rather, we include the prototypes for the library and a variety of type definitions and constants. This is the information needed to compile our calls on the library functions. Only our own code is compiled, not the library's, which saves much compilation time during a long program's development.

In a properly constructed modular program, the code portion of each module is compiled to produce an object code module (usually having a `.o` extension), which later is linked with the object modules of the libraries and other user modules to form a **load module,** or executable program. During the linking stage, all calls on imported functions are linked to the appropriate function in the exporting module, making a seamless and connected whole, as if the library source code actually was part of that module. The linking operation will fail if the linker cannot find a module, among the set provided, that defines each imported function. It also fails if two definitions of that function are provided. For this reason, it is very important to avoid including two modules that define the same thing.

Avoiding header file duplication.   A header file may be included in several modules, and it may be included in other header files. This can become a problem because a module will not compile if it includes the same header file twice. In small- to moderate-sized programs, we can deal with this double-inclusion problem by being extremely careful. However, in a large program, the inclusion relationships can become quite complex and sometimes even circular. To eliminate this difficulty, we use the `#ifndef` command provided by the C preprocessor. The first two commands and the last line in `tools.h` are

```
#ifndef TOOLS
#define TOOLS
...
#endif
```

Between the `#define` and the `#endif` commands are the lines that form the interface for `tools.c`. A `#ifndef` command is the beginning of a **conditional**

compilation block that ends with the matching `#endif`. When the preprocessor phase of the compiler encounters the command `#ifndef TOOLS`, it looks for `TOOLS` in its table of defined symbols. If present, everything following the command is skipped up to the matching `#endif`, thereby ensuring that the tools are not included a second time. If `TOOLS` was not previously defined, this is the first inclusion of the file. The compiler enters the block and immediately defines `TOOLS`, preventing future double inclusion. Then it processes the other definitions and declarations in the file normally. All header files should be guarded by these three preprocessor commands. The symbol named in the `#ifndef` command is arbitrary, but it should be unique and, ideally, related to the name of the module.

23.1.2   Building a Multimodule Program

Once the issues of file organization have been resolved, the compilation process must be investigated. Here we discuss how the process is automated in a typical UNIX environment, where the steps involved are demonstrated most easily because they are explicit.

Compiling and linking.   In many systems, such as DOS and UNIX, the C compiler can be called directly from a command line. For instance, suppose we have a source code file, `lab1.c`, that we wish to **compile and link** with the standard C library functions. The traditional UNIX command to accomplish this is

```
~> cc -o lab1 lab1.c
```

The command starts with the name of the compiler (typically cc or gcc). Following that is a `-o` switch and an accompanying name (`lab1`) that will be given to the executable program. The last argument is the name of the source code file. When this command is executed, the compiler is called to translate `lab1.c`. If there are no fatal errors, an intermediate object file, `lab1.o`, is produced. Then the linker is called to join this object file with the object files for the standard library functions. If linking also is successful, the executable file, `lab1`, is produced. To run the program, the name of the file simply is typed at the command-line prompt:

```
~> lab1
```

Compilers offer many options, in addition to `-o`, which can be very useful. For example, the gcc compiler[1] produces helpful warning comments when the `-W` switch is used to turn on all error checking, as follows (we use this option for the remainder of this chapter):

```
~> gcc -o lab1 -Wall lab1.c
```

---

[1]Gnu C compiler from the Free Software Foundation; ~> is the UNIX system prompt.

The complete list of **compiler options** is too numerous to give here, but we describe a few commonly used options, as needed.

Separating compilation and linking.   A single-module program generally is compiled and linked in one step. However, in a large multimodule program, each module is compiled separately, as it is developed, and linking is done as a final step. To **compile only** (without linking), the -c switch is used instead of -o. For example, suppose a game program has two user-defined modules, **game** and **board**, and further it calls functions from the **tools** library. The three separate compilation commands would be

```
~> gcc -c -Wall game.c
~> gcc -c -Wall board.c
~> gcc -c -Wall tools.c
```

The upper part of the diagram in Figure 23.1 illustrates the relationships among the code files, header files, and these three compilation commands. The direct input to each step is the .c file that is listed in the gcc command. The .h files are indirectly included by each .c file and so are not listed explicitly in the command.

This diagram represents a game application with three modules (**game**, **board**, and **tools**). Rectangles represent the programmer's files, shaded ovals are executions of programs (the compiler, the linker, and the user's finished application).

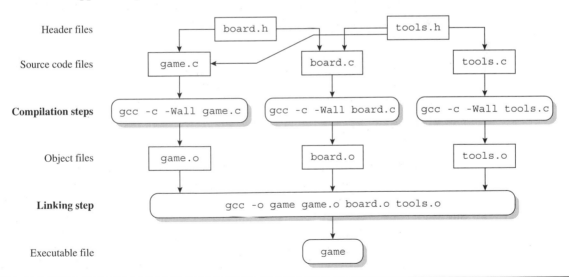

Figure 23.1.   Steps in building a program.

If there are no errors in the three source code modules, the result of the compilation commands will be three object files: `game.o`, `board.o`, and `tools.o`. These three files then can be linked with functions from the standard library by using the command

```
~> gcc -o game  game.o board.o tools.o
```

This step is illustrated by the bottom part of the diagram; the result is an executable program, `game`, that can be run from the command line by typing its name:

```
~> game
```

Dependencies.   The arrows in Figure 23.1 show how the object and executable files for an application **depend** on various combinations of source code and header files. For example, `game.o` depends directly on `game.c` and through it, indirectly, on `board.h` and `tools.h`. Similarly, `tools.o` depends on `tools.c` and `tools.h`. The executable program, which directly depends on all three `.o` files, indirectly depends on all five source code and header files. If one of these five files is changed, every file that depends on it becomes an **obsolete file** and needs to be rebuilt. Therefore, if we change `game.c`, `game.o` and `game` need to be regenerated. And if we change `tools.h`, all three object files and the executable program need to be rebuilt. The `.c` files need not be changed because they always include the version of the `.h` files current at compilation time. Keeping all the dependent files updated is important but can be tricky, especially if an application is large and has dozens of modules. This is the kind of detailed bookkeeping that human beings find difficult but is easy for a computer. Clearly, an automated system is needed.

A makefile automates the process.   Some integrated development environments provide automated support for making an "application" or "project." The programmer names the project and lists the source code files and any special libraries that compose it. Once the project has been defined, the programmer typically selects a menu option labeled **MAKE** or **BUILD** to compile and link the project. UNIX systems provide a "make" facility that is less user-friendly but more flexible. The programmer creates a file of compilation and linking commands, called a **makefile.** In any system, the project file or makefile represents the application as a whole and encodes the dependency information and compilation commands shown in Figure 23.1.

A **make facility** should provide several important services:

- It should allow the programmer to list the modules and libraries that compose the application and specify how to produce and use each one.
- For each module, it should allow the programmer to list the files on which it depends. In some systems, this list is automatically derived from the source code.

- When given the command **make**, the facility should generate the executable program. Initially, this means it must compile every module and link them together.
- When a source code module is changed, the corresponding object module becomes obsolete. The next time a **make** command is given, it should be recompiled.
- When a header file is changed, the object files for all modules that depend on it become obsolete. The next time a **make** command is given, they should be recompiled.
- When a module is recompiled, the corresponding executable program becomes obsolete, so the application should be relinked.

To explain the meaning and syntax for some basic commands in a makefile that accomplishes these services, we examine a makefile, shown in Figure 23.2,[2] for the hypothetical **game** program.

Notes on Figure 23.2. A UNIX **makefile for** game.   Appendix F provides a short discussion of the parts of a simple makefile that could be used with

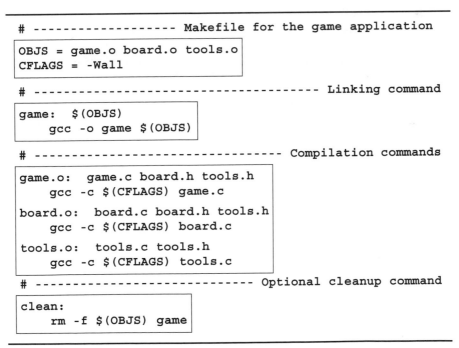

```
# ------------------ Makefile for the game application

OBJS = game.o board.o tools.o
CFLAGS = -Wall

# --------------------------------- Linking command

game:   $(OBJS)
    gcc -o game $(OBJS)

# ---------------------------- Compilation commands

game.o:   game.c board.h tools.h
    gcc -c $(CFLAGS) game.c

board.o:   board.c board.h tools.h
    gcc -c $(CFLAGS) board.c

tools.o:   tools.c tools.h
    gcc -c $(CFLAGS) tools.c

# -------------------------- Optional cleanup command

clean:
    rm -f $(OBJS) game
```

Figure 23.2.   A UNIX **makefile for** game.

---

[2] All UNIX systems provide similar make facilities; the particular one discussed here is the Gnu make program, from the Free Software Foundation.

the single-module programs developed up to this point. We review some of those points here and add a few more capabilities.[3]

A makefile contains a set of commands to compile and link an application, plus other information used to automate the process, maintain consistency, and avoid unnecessary work.

- The first line in this makefile is a comment; note that a comment starts with a **#** character, not C comment marks, and is limited to one line.
- *First box: symbol definitions.*

   1. A major goal of the make facility is to maintain consistency across all modules in the application. Another is to avoid omitting some essential file name or switch from one of the commands. To achieve this goal, a make facility lets us define symbolic names for phrases that must be used more than once in the set of compilation and linking commands. In this box, we define two symbols, **OBJS** and **CFLAGS**.

   2. These symbols are treated by the make facility in much the same way that a **const** variable is treated in C. They are defined by giving a symbol name followed by an equal sign and a defining phrase.

   3. We define **OBJS** to stand for the list of object files that form the application. We want a symbol to stand for this list because we use the list three times in the makefile and want to be sure the three copies are identical.

   4. When compiling a series of modules, we should be consistent about the compiler options used. To ensure consistency, we define a symbol, **CFLAGS**, as the list of compiler options we want to use for the application. In this example, we use only the error warning option, **-Wall**.

- *Second and third boxes: dependencies and rules.* These two boxes contain pairs of lines, which we will call **rules.** Each rule consists of a dependency declaration followed by a command used to compile or link. The dependency declaration encodes the arrows in Figure 23.1. It is used by the make facility to determine whether a dependent file is current or obsolete. (A file becomes obsolete whenever a file above it in the dependency tree is changed.)

- *Second box: the linking rule.*

   1. The linking rule should be the first rule in the makefile.

   2. The first line of this rule starts with the name that will be given to the finished application. Following that is a colon and a list of all the object files on which the application directly depends. In this example, we name the three object files by referring to the symbol **OBJS**, defined in the first box.

----

[3]A full discussion of makefile capabilities is beyond the scope of this text. These include archiving commands and ways to reduce the number of compilation commands that must be written.

3. The `$(...)` notation indicates that the symbol in the parentheses has been defined at the top of the makefile and the symbol's definition should be substituted for the `$(...)` unit. This process is almost identical to the way `#define` commands are used in C. After substitution, these lines would say:

```
game:  game.o board.o tools.o
    gcc -o game game.o board.o tools.o
```

4. The second line is the linking command. This command says that the object files listed in the first box must be linked with the standard C libraries to form the `game` application.

5. Note: The first keystroke on the line of any compilation or linking command in a makefile must be the tab character. The make facility will not work if spaces are used to indent the `gcc` command or if it is not indented.

- *Third box: the compilation commands.*

1. Since the application depends on three object files, there are three rules here that describe how to build them. The first line in each rule lists, as the set of dependencies, one source code file and all the programmer-defined header files that it includes.

2. The second line in each rule is the compilation command. All three of these use the list of options in `CFLAGS` defined in the first box. After substituting the flags for the `$(...)` unit in the first command, it would say

```
game.o:  game.c board.h tools.h
    gcc -c -Wall game.c
```

- *Fourth box: the cleanup command.*

1. This optional command automates the job of deleting all the object files and the executable file. The phrase `rm -f` is the UNIX command to remove (delete) a list of files. The `-f` flag says that the system should do it without prompting the user for verification on each file in the list. If a file is not there, the system also should not complain. We write `$(OBJS)` as an argument to delete all the object files listed in the first box. Then we add the name given to the executable file in the second box.

2. The first line of the rule gives a name by which this operation can be identified. There are no prerequisites to doing the deletion command, so the dependency list is left empty. It is helpful to have a cleanup command when the programmer wishes to archive the source modules or when the file creation times indicate that the executable file is newer than any of the files on which it depends, but the programmer wishes to recompile from scratch anyway. (This can happen for a variety of reasons, such as changing the list of compiler options in `CFLAGS`.)

3. To use the cleanup command, type

```
~> make clean
```

Using the makefile.   Only one makefile should be in a directory, and the files named in its dependency lists should be in the same directory. If this is true, we build the application by typing

```
~> make
```

The **make** program will look in the current default directory for a file named **makefile** and open it. Unless a specific rule name (such as **make clean**) has been given, it starts at the top of the makefile, interprets the definitions, and carries out the commands. It focuses on the first rule, which should be the linking rule. The name at the left side of its dependency line will be the name of the finished executable file. If that file does not exist or if it is older than one of the files on the dependency list, the linking should be redone. First, however, **make** must check whether the object files are all up-to-date.

   If an object file does not exist or is obsolete, the compilation command on the second line of its rule will be used to compile the file. Compilation is skipped when the object code file is newer than the source code and header files on its dependency list. When all the required object files are up to date, the linking command in the first rule finally is executed.

23.2   Modular Application: Finding the Roots of an Equation

Chapter 8 introduced the concept of finding roots by Newton's method and Chapter 12 introduced the **bisection method.** In this section, we look at a third method for finding the roots of an equation: the **secant method.** We write a function to perform this algorithm and combine it with the bisection function covered earlier to make a multimodule, general root-finding program.

23.2.1   The Structure of a Multimodule Application

Since all the root-finding methods fail under certain circumstances, a user might wish to try one method, then try a different method if the first fails. To make this convenient, we incorporate two methods into one root-finding application. The problem specification in Figure 23.3 describes the application we will build.

   At some point during the design process, after the problem has been divided into modules, a decision must be made about **module communication.** This decision is somewhat arbitrary and often based on the experience of the application designer or on the presence of pre-existing modules that can be reused. In this

Problem. Write a program that can be linked to a separately compiled function, `f()`. The program should permit the user to enter parameters for the function `f()`, then help the user find its roots.

Algorithms. Implement both the secant (Section 23.2.6) and bisection methods (Section 12.3).

Inputs.

1. The user will choose from a menu whose options include setting up parameters for the function `f()` and solving it by one of the two methods.
2. Once a root-solving method is chosen, the user will enter the appropriate initial values for that method.
3. If the setup option is chosen, the user will be prompted for new parameters for `f()`.

Constants and limitations.

- `LIMIT` $= 1 \times 10^{-10}$. Numbers with absolute value smaller than this will be treated as 0.
- `EPS` $= 1 \times 10^{-4}$. This is the precision within which the root should be calculated.
- `MAX_ITER` $= 50$. This is the loop limit for the secant method. The program should quit if a root has not been found within this many iterations.

Output. A menu is presented showing the choices: bisection search, secant search, setup `f()`, verbose mode, and quit. When a root is found, it will be displayed. Otherwise, an error comment will be displayed explaining the nature of the failure. If the user chooses **verbose output** from the menu, the results at each stage of the iterative search will also be displayed.

Figure 23.3.   Problem specifications: A general root finder.

case, we want a general program to find roots of double:double functions, and we already have a working program for finding roots by the bisection method. We wish to reuse this code with as few modifications as possible. Therefore, we decide not to change the prototype of either the `bisect()` function or the function `f()` that it is solving. These remain

```
er_type bisect( double x1, double x2, double* rootp );
double f( double r );
```

To build the desired application, we also need to write functions for the secant method that conform to the interface of the bisection method, and then redesign the `main()` program to use a menu. In addition, we want to make the new application fully modular and as general as possible. This means that everything dealing with a specific function, `f()`, must be removed from the main module. Last, we must create a makefile that will tie together the four modules and build the application.

To begin the actual construction process, we create a subdirectory, called the **application directory**, for the files that belong to the new package; we will call it `roots`. Everything needed for this application should be placed in the directory, except for the libraries shared by all applications. As each part of the application is found or constructed, we put it into the **roots** directory. These parts will include

1. Documentation, including a program specification.
2. The file **ffam.h** from Figure 23.4, which is the header file for **heat.c**.
3. The file **heat.c**, containing the function whose roots are to be found, shown in Figure 23.5.
4. The file **main.c**, containing the **main()** function, shown in Figures 23.6 and 23.7.
5. The file **root.h** from Figure 23.8, which is the header file for both methods.
6. The file **bisect.c**, containing the bisection method root finder from Figures 23.9 and 23.10.
7. The file **secant.c**, containing the secant method root finder from Figures 23.12 and 23.13.
8. The **makefile** in Figure 23.14.
9. The files **tools.h** and **tools.c**, documented in Appendix F.

We develop and discuss these program modules in the order just given.

23.2.2   Function to Solve: Heat Transfer Equation

To maximize the code we can reuse, we use the heat transfer equation presented in Chapter 12 to test the bisection method. However, this function now will be in its own, separately compiled module rather than bundled into the main module. This will make it possible to use the root-finding program, with no changes, to solve any other double:double function. Unfortunately, placing this equation in a separate module creates a problem of communication among the modules.

   Typically, a real-life function has one or more parameters in addition to the variable for which we are solving. Of course, these parameters could be defined as constant values, but a program that permits the user to change the parameters dynamically is much more useful. In Chapter 12, the **main()** program set the pipe radius to a constant value but prompted the user for the conductivity of the insulation, storing it in a global variable that could be accessed by the heat transfer function, **f()**. Once this heat function is in a different module, there is no reasonable way for the **main()** program to do this. It would be possible to make the global variable accessible to both **main()** and **f()**, but **main()** needs to be adaptable to a wide range of problems and only the author of the function module will know what parameters are needed for **f()**.

   One way to solve the communication problem is by adding a second function, **setup()**, to every function module that will be used with the root finder. The module contains all the code relevant to the function **f()** and is quite independent of the other parts of the program. This **setup()** function is called by **main()**;

```
#ifndef FFAM
#define FFAM
/* Interface for general function family ---------------------------- */

void setup( void );    /* Set up parameters for function f(). --------- */
double f( double r ); /* Mathematical function to solve. ------------ */
#endif
```

Figure 23.4.   Header file `ffam.h.`

it will prompt the user for as many or as few parameters as needed by `f()`. The prototypes for these two functions will be found in the header file `ffam.h` shown in Figure 23.4, while the specific code for the heat transfer problem is in the file `heat.c`, which is shown in Figure 23.5. This heat transfer function is the same as in Chapter 12, except that it has been generalized to have a second parameter: the radius of the pipe being insulated.

Notes on Figures 23.4 and 23.5. The heat transfer module and its header file.

- *Figure 23.4 and the first box of Figure 23.5: the header file.* The purpose of a header file is to define constants and types shared by more than one module and the interface that will enable one module to use functions or variables in another. The heat transfer module must provide a header file with prototypes for two functions that can be called **externally**. In this case, the header file is given a general name, `ffam.h`, because it is the interface to a general family of double:double functions that have supporting `setup()` functions.[4] We `#include` the header in the heat transfer module and in every module that will call either of its functions. The actual file is shown in Figure 23.4. Notice that the declarations are enclosed in a conditional compilation block as protection against double inclusion.

- *Second box: the* `static` *variables.* Values for the extra function parameters are stored in `static` **global variables** in the heat module. These variables are private within the module; that is, they can be used only by functions in that module and not by any others. This is ideal for our purposes. These variables cannot be local to a single function because the module has two functions that must access them: One establishes their values (third box), the other uses them (fourth box). Therefore, they must be global to the module. By making them `static`, we guarantee that no other module can change them and that they will retain the values of the parameters from one call to the next.

---

[4] This kind of modular independence is achieved more easily by using classes in an object-oriented language.

A pipe of user-specified radius is to be insulated with a material having a user-specified conductivity. Given the radius, `r`, of the outer insulation layer, the function `f()` calculates the difference between the heat loss per unit length and a specified heat loss.

```c
#include "tools.h"
```
```c
#include "ffam.h"
```

```c
static double conductivity;        /* thermal conductivity */
static double pipe;                /* radius of pipe (feet) */
```

```c
/* --------set up parameters for the heat transfer equation----------- */
void
setup( void )
{
    printf( "\n Thermal conductivity of insulation (BTU/h ft F): " );
    scanf( "%lg", &conductivity );

    printf( "\n Enter radius of pipe (feet): " );
    scanf( "%lg", &pipe );
}
```

```c
/* --------function to compute heat transfer discrepancy-------------- */
double
f( double r )
{
```
```c
    if (r < pipe)
        fatal( " Error--radius received is inside pipe dimensions." );
```
```c
    return log( r/pipe ) / conductivity + 1.0/r - 2.0/pipe;
}
```

Figure 23.5.   The heat transfer module `heat.c`.

- *Third box: the* `setup()` *function.* This function will be called from `main()` once before entering the menu loop and then again each time the user asks to set up a new set of parameters. The heat equation now uses two variables, `conductivity` and `pipe`, rather than a variable `conductivity` and a constant `radius`.
- *Fourth box: the function* `f()`. This function will be called many times from both the bisection and secant modules in the process of solving the function. The only change to the equation is to use the variable `pipe` rather than the defined constant `PIPE_R` used in the previous version in Chapter 12.
- *Inner box: error handling.* The return value is not computed for an invalid pipe radius. Instead, the program quits because something is drastically wrong. Formerly, this radius test was part of the input validation

in `main()`. Since this test is specific to the application and `f()`, it is moved out of `main()` and into this module. It cannot be done by the `setup()` function because many different `r` values are computed during the iteration. Calling `fatal()` actually is a bit harsh.[5] Ideally, we would like to return to `main()` to make another choice, but this is not possible.[6] A sample of error handling output follows, with the menu replaced by a dashed line.

```
Thermal conductivity of insulation (BTU/h ft F): .025

Enter radius of pipe (feet): .333
---------------------------------
Enter letter of desired item: s
Enter two initial estimates for the root: .2 .5
Error--radius received is inside pipe dimensions.

Press '.' and 'Enter' to continue.
```

23.2.3 Main Function for the Roots Package

The design of the `main()` program, shown in Figure 23.6, is straightforward: It must call the `setup()` function, then display a menu and process the selections appropriately. The specifications in Figure 23.3 list the options that must be offered: setup, verbose mode, bisection search, secant search, and quit.

Notes on Figure 23.6. The main module for the root finder.

- *First box: module interfaces.*

  1. This `main()` program calls functions from the heat transfer, bisection, secant, and `tools` modules. It must include the header files for each of these. (One header, `root.h`, is used to coordinate the `main()` program with two modules, bisection and secant.)
  2. The variable `verbose` is defined, used, and exported by `main()` and imported and used by bisection and secant. The declaration of an intermodule variable in an *exporting* module is different from the declaration in an *importing* module. The former should have an initializer and should not have the `extern` modifier. The latter must have the `extern` modifier and must not have an initializer. Because they are different and header files are included by both importing and exporting modules, we do not put the `extern` variable definition in a header file.

---

[5] The best way to handle this problem would be to use an exception handler. This exists in C++ but not in C.

[6] It is possible on some systems that support long-distance transfers of control facilities. These are beyond the scope of this text.

Processing begins here and continues with calls on functions in Figures 23.5, 23.9 and 23.12.

```
#include "tools.h"
#include "ffam.h"
#include "root.h"

/* Global external variable to control verbose output ----- */
bool verbose = true;
```

```
/* Menu of program options.  -------------------------------- */
static string menu[] = {
    "b find root using Bisection method",
    "s find root using Secant method",
    "n choose New parameters for function",
    "v",   /* completed later according to state of verbose flag */
    "q Quit"
};
#define VMENU 3   /* position of "v" item in menu */
```

```
/* -------------------------------------------------------------- */
void main( void )
{
    char c;                    /* menu choice */
    double root;               /* value of root */
    double x1, x2;             /* starting interval or end points */
    er_type return_code;       /* result error code */

    banner();
    puts( "Root finder program" );
    setup();                   /* get parameters for f(). */

    /* The menu-processing loop shown in Figure 23.7 goes here. */
    bye();
}
```

Figure 23.6.   The main module for the root finder.

   3. The need for two different declarations, either of which might be for-
       gotten, is another reason for avoiding shared, global variables.

 • *Second box: the menu choice.*

   1. We define an array of strings for the main menu and declare it as
       static so that it is private within this code module. Since **main()**
       is the only function in this module, the menu array will be its pri-

vate property. Therefore, it is unnecessary to declare it locally within `main()` to protect it from accidental tampering by other functions. In this situation, we prefer defining it at the top so that it will not clutter the function's basic algorithm.

2. This menu has one unusual aspect: the **v** option will be used as a toggle switch to turn **verbose** output on and off. When **verbose** is **true**, the algorithms print values computed on each iteration and the menu displays the string `"v turn off Verbose feedback"`. When the switch is **false**, only the final results are printed and the menu displays the string `"v turn on Verbose feedback"`. Each time this option is selected, the setting of the switch will be reversed.

3. **VMENU** is the subscript of the menu array slot that holds the string for the verbose option. This is used to provide direct access to the `"v"` pointer to update the message whenever the switch is toggled.

- *Third box: initial parameters.* The `main()` program calls `setup()`, in the heat transfer module, to read in initial parameters of the function `f()`. This must be done before `bisect()` or `secant()` can be called. To be sure this step is not overlooked, the program does it before entering the menu loop. The menu also provides an option by which the parameters later can be changed.

- *Fourth box: the menu loop.* The program enters a loop that displays the menu and processes selections until the quit option, **q**, is picked. The code for this loop is given in Figure 23.7.

Notes on Figure 23.7. The menu loop from `main()`.

- *First box: toggling the menu message.* Whether the **v** option displays the word **on** or **off** depends on the current setting of the global switch **verbose** and changes each time this option is selected. Before we can display the menu, we must install the right words in the array. Initially, **off** should be displayed since **verbose** is initialized to **true**.

- *Second box: the switch.* As usual, we call `menu_c()` and use a **switch** statement to process the result.

1. In the first inner box, the user looks for a root. The user who decides to search for a root by choosing **b** or **s** will be prompted for a pair of **x** values. The wording of the prompt depends on the algorithm chosen and is discussed in association with each method. Both functions store the root (if found) in the variable **root** and return a code that signals either a success or the nature of the failure. After completing one of these cases, control **break**s out of the **switch** and goes to the last box where the results are printed.

The code shown here belongs in the comment-filled box near the bottom of Figure 23.6.

```
do {
      /* update menu -------------------------------------------- */
      if (verbose)   menu[VMENU] = "v turn off Verbose feedback";
      else           menu[VMENU] = "v turn on Verbose feedback";


      /* display menu and get user selection ---------------------- */
      c = menu_c( " Select next option:", 5, menu );
      switch (c) {
            case 'b': printf( " Enter endpoints of search interval: " );
                      scanf( "%lg%lg", &x1, &x2 );
                      return_code = bisect( x1, x2, &root );
                      break;

            case 's': printf( " Enter two initial estimates for the root: " );
                      scanf( "%lg%lg", &x1, &x2 );
                      return_code = secant( x1, x2, &root );
                      break;


            case 'n': setup();   /* Read new parameters for function f(). */
                      continue;
            case 'v': verbose = !verbose;
                      continue;


            case 'q': continue;

            default:  cleanline( stdin );
                      continue;
      }


      if (return_code == ROOT_OK)
          printf( "\n The root is %g \n\n", root );
      else
          printf( "\n Failed to find root--%s\n\n", errmsg[return_code] );
} while (c != 'q');
```

Figure 23.7.   The menu loop from `main()`.

2. In the second inner box, the user changes the parameters. At any time, the user can ask to enter a new set of parameters for the function being searched or turn verbose feedback on or off. After processing either of these options, the program uses **continue** to go immediately to the loop test. It does not use **break** because neither option calculates a

result, so we do not want to execute the code in the last box that prints the answers.

3. Selecting q takes control directly to the loop test, which then evaluates to `false` and ends the loop and eventually ends the program. Selecting an invalid option, which is not in the menu, causes control to reach the `default` case, which flushes the rest of the input line to allow a fresh start with a new choice. Execution then resumes with the loop test, which still is `true`, and a redisplay of the menu.

• *Last box: The output.* If a root was found, the program prints it. Otherwise, it prints an error message from the list of messages in the array `errmsg` found in `root.h`. The following are some examples of typical output, with repetitions of the menu replaced by dashed lines:

```
Root finder program
Thermal conductivity of insulation (BTU/h ft F): .05

Enter radius of pipe (feet): .4

Select next option:

        b find root using Bisection method
        s find root using Secant method
        n choose New parameters for function
        v turn on Verbose feedback
        q Quit

Enter letter of desired item: b
Enter endpoints of search interval: 1 2

Failed to find root--no root in interval
---------------------------------------
Enter letter of desired item: v

Select next option:

        b find root using Bisection method
        s find root using Secant method
        n choose New parameters for function
        v turn off Verbose feedback
        q Quit

Enter letter of desired item: s
Enter two initial estimates for the root: .4 .6
During iteration 0:
    x1 =              0.4, y1 =              -2.5
    x2 =              0.6, y2 =         4.775969
    x3 =         0.468719, y3 =         0.304266
```

```
During iteration 1:
    x1 =              0.6, y1 =         4.775969
    x2 =         0.468719, y2 =         0.304266
    x3 =         0.459787, y3 =        -0.039116
During iteration 2:
    x1 =         0.468719, y1 =         0.304266
    x2 =         0.459787, y2 =        -0.039116
    x3 =         0.460804, y3 =         0.000294
During iteration 3:
    x1 =         0.459787, y1 =        -0.039116
    x2 =         0.460804, y2 =         0.000294
    x3 =         0.460797, y3 =      2.83502e-07

The root is 0.460797
```

23.2.4   The Roots Header File

In the file **root.h** (Figure 23.8), we have placed the information that needs to be common knowledge between the **main()** program and either of the root-finding functions. This header file will be included in three source files: **main.c**, **bisect.c**, and **secant.c**.

Notes on Figure 23.8. The **root.h** header file.

- *First box: tolerances.* The constants named in the program specification are defined here. The values given generally are appropriate for numerical calculation, but it is possible that some future application would require different values. The value of **EPS** really is a function of how the answer will be used. The value of **LIMIT** is specific to the scale of the function's equation; namely, the coefficients of the terms. The value of **MAX_ITER** may need to be increased for high-degree functions that vary wildly, as opposed to low-order polynomials, which tend to be well behaved. These definitions are placed in the header file to make them easy to locate and change, if necessary.
- *Second box: error return codes.* These codes are returned by the root-finding functions to indicate that a solution was found (**ROOT_OK**) or was not found. The enumeration is in the header file to ensure that the **main()** program and the root-finding function both have an identical understanding about the meaning of the codes. The symbols **ROOT_OK** and **NO_ROOT** are returned by the bisection method, which either fails immediately or finds a root, depending on the values of the function at the initial points. The values **ROOT_OK**, **BAD_INITIAL_POINTS**, **HORIZONTAL**, and **TOO_MANY_ITERATIONS** are used by the secant method, which can fail in three different ways, as will be demonstrated in Section 23.2.6.
- *Third box: error messages.* This array provides one message for each **error code** in the **er_type** enumeration. It is declared as **static** since

This is the header file for the bisection and secant modules.

```
#ifndef ROOTS
#define ROOTS
```

```
/* Constants for root finders ------------------------------------ */
/* Done when approximation is within EPS of root. */
#define EPS 1.0e-4

/* Numbers of smaller magnitude than this will be treated as zero. */
#define LIMIT 1.0e-10

/* Loop cutoff for secant method */
#define MAX_ITER 50
```

```
/* error codes returned by the roots modules and used by main() */
typedef enum {
    ROOT_OK, NO_ROOT, BAD_INITIAL_POINTS, HORIZONTAL, TOO_MANY_ITERATIONS
} er_type;
```

```
/* Table of error messages.  -------------------------- */
static string const errmsg[] = {
    "root found",
    "no root in interval",
    "initial points too close",
    "secant almost horizontal",
    "iteration limit exceeded"
};
```

```
/* root-finding methods called by main -------------- */
er_type secant( double x1, double x2, double *rootp );
er_type bisect( double xlow, double xup, double *rootp );
```

```
#endif
```

Figure 23.8.   The `root.h` **header file.**

otherwise it would default to **extern**, and the two modules that include this header would both contain defining instances of the same **extern** variable. Both modules would compile properly. However, linking would fail because of the double definition. The array is declared **const** because the string pointers do not change. The error code returned from one of the root-finding algorithms is used to subscript this array, which translates the error code into English so that the printed comment is informative.

- *Fourth box: prototypes.*

    1. This header file will be included by **main.c** so that the compiler will know the correct calling sequence for the two root-finding functions.

2. Both root finders take two `double` parameters. The parameters to the secant method are two initial estimates of the root. The parameters to `bisect()` are the endpoints of an interval on the *x* axis.

3. Both root finders return the root (if found) through the third parameter and both use the `return` statement to return an error code.

23.2.5   Adapting the Bisection Method

To create a module for the bisection method, we reuse the code developed in Chapter 12 with only a few changes. All these changes relate to the process of moving the bisection functions to a separate module and providing the optional verbose feedback. The entire module is reprinted, in Figures 23.9 and 23.10, but commentary is restricted to the changes.

Notes on Figures 23.9 and 23.10. The bisection module.

- *First box, Figure 23.9: imports and exports.* Whenever two modules interact, we include the same header file in both modules to be sure that all modules are consistent. The headers `tools.h` and `ffam.h` are included because those files supply the prototypes of functions that are called here. The header `root.h` contains information that this module "owns" and uses but also exports to the main module.

- *Third box: a `static` function.* In Chapter 12, this prototype was declared inside the `bisect()` function. By doing so, we declared that it was the private property of that function and no other function could call `go_find()`. We accomplish the same thing here by placing the prototype at the top of the file and declaring it to be `static`. This means it can be called from other functions within this module (of which there are none) but not by functions in other modules. In contrast, the `bisect()` function has no storage class declared, so it defaults to `extern` and can be called by any other module that includes its prototype.

- *Fourth box: error checking.* Previously, error checking was done in the `main()` function during the input stage. When we redesigned the program to be modular, the error check was removed from `main()` and placed here because the bisection method cannot work if the interval limits are backward. Each code module should make whatever tests are necessary to ensure that the code in that module functions reasonably and properly.

- *Second and fifth boxes, Figure 23.9, and first box, Figure 23.10: verbose output.* The `main()` program displays a menu that permits the user to turn verbose feedback on or off. In the verbose mode, some functions throughout the program print out intermediate results. This kind of feedback is useful during debugging and when the user is having trouble finding roots. The level of feedback desired is selected in `main()`, which stores this information in a variable that must be visible to all parts of the

This code and the `go_find()` function in Figure 23.10 form the file `bisect.c`.

```
#include "tools.h"
#include "root.h"          /* Interface between root-finders and main. */
#include "ffam.h"          /* Interface for function being solved. */
```

```
extern bool verbose;       /* Imported from main. */
```

```
static double go_find( double xlow, double fxlow, double xup );
```

```
er_type
bisect( double xlow, double xup, double *rootp )
{
    double fxlow, fxup;        /* function values at xlow and xup. */
    er_type answer = ROOT_OK;  /* Default result is successful search. */
    double swap;               /* To interchange interval end points. */

    if (xlow > xup) { swap = xlow; xlow = xup; xup = swap; }

    fxlow = f( xlow );   fxup = f( xup );

    if (verbose) {
        printf( "    x1 = %g, f(x1) = %g\n", xlow, fxlow );
        printf( "    x2 = %g, f(x2) = %g\n", xup, fxup );
    }

    if (fabs( fxlow ) < LIMIT) {         /* xlow is the actual root */
        *rootp = xlow;
    }
    else if (fabs( fxup ) < LIMIT) {   /* xup is the actual root */
        *rootp = xup;
    }
    else if (fxup * fxlow < 0) { /* true if they have opposite sign. */
        /* We know there is a root in the interval -- so find it. */
        *rootp = go_find( xlow, fxlow, xup );
    }
    else answer = NO_ROOT;
    return answer;
}
```

Figure 23.9.   The `bisect()` **function.**

program; it is a truly global switch setting that **main()** exports to other modules. This module imports the switch, named **verbose**, and uses it to control printing in **bisect()** and in **go_find()**. To import a variable from another module, the variable must be declared locally as storage class **extern** and have no initializer. When the application is linked, this

This code follows the function `bisect()` in the file `bisect.c`.

```c
double
go_find( double xlow, double fxlow, double xup )
{
    double xmid;        /* midpoint of interval */
    double fxmid;       /* value of function at midpoint of interval */

    do {                    /* Iterate until interval is too small.  */
        xmid = .5 * (xup + xlow);
        fxmid = f( xmid );
        if (verbose) printf( "   xmid = %g, f(xmid) = %g\n", xmid, fxmid );

        if (fabs( fxmid ) < LIMIT) break; /* quit; we are close enough! */
        else if (fxmid * fxlow < 0) {     /* root is between xlow and xmid */
            xup = xmid;                   /* use xmid as new upper bound */
        }
        else {                            /* root is between xmid and xup */
            xlow = xmid;                  /* use xmid as new lower bound */
            fxlow = fxmid;
        }
    } while ((xup - xlow) > EPS);

    return xmid;
}
```

Figure 23.10.   The `go_find()` **function.**

variable will be linked to the defining instance of **verbose**, which is in **main()**. The two declarations then refer to one variable, not two. When designing verbose output for an iterative application, it is helpful to print the parameters before iteration begins and print the results of each iteration. A sample of the output from the bisection module follows; dashed lines indicate that output is omitted.

```
Root finder program
Thermal conductivity of insulation (BTU/h ft F): .025

Enter radius of pipe (feet): .333

----------------------------------------------------
Enter letter of desired item: b
Enter endpoints of search interval: .4 .5
  x1 = 0.4, f(x1) = 3.82188
  x2 = 0.5, f(x2) = 12.2476

Failed to find root--no root in interval
```

```
-----------------------------------------------------
Enter letter of desired item: b
Enter endpoints of search interval: .333 .5
    x1 = 0.333, f(x1) = -3.008
    x2 = 0.5, f(x2) = 12.2476
    xmid = 0.4165, f(xmid) = 5.3397
    xmid = 0.37475, f(xmid) = 1.38211
    xmid = 0.353875, f(xmid) = -0.753093
    xmid = 0.364313, f(xmid) = 0.328677
    xmid = 0.359094, f(xmid) = -0.208572
    xmid = 0.361703, f(xmid) = 0.06095
    xmid = 0.360398, f(xmid) = -0.073585
    xmid = 0.361051, f(xmid) = -0.006261
    xmid = 0.361377, f(xmid) = 0.027358
    xmid = 0.361214, f(xmid) = 0.010552
    xmid = 0.361132, f(xmid) = 0.002146

The root is 0.361132
```

23.2.6   Using the Secant Method

The secant method is an iterative algorithm that starts with two estimates of the root of an equation and uses the value of the function at those two points to compute a new estimate. This process is repeated, always using the two most recent estimates, until a root is found. The specification for this algorithm is found in Figure 23.11.

Using the secant to compute the next estimate.   We call the original two estimates x_1 and x_2; the values of the function at these points are y_1 and y_2. The secant to the function at these points is the straight line between (x_1, y_1) and (x_2, y_2). Unless this line is horizontal, it crosses the x axis somewhere; we call this point x_3. For example, consider the function graphed in Figure 23.11; the points (x_1, y_1) and (x_2, y_2) have been used to find x_3. Note that x_3 is between x_1 and x_2 in this example, but this is not necessarily true.

From x_3 we calculate y_3. For the next iteration, we take the secant between (x_2, y_2) and (x_3, y_3) and use that line to find x_4. This process continues until the program quits or a root is found; that is, $f(x_n) <$ **LIMIT**, our limit for required computational accuracy. We present a program for this algorithm (Figure 23.12) and discuss the weaknesses of the method.

Notes on Figures 23.12 and 23.13.   The secant algorithm and verbose output.   In this example, we use the secant method to solve the heat transfer problem described in Figure 12.14.

- *The module interface.*

  1. We include **root.h**, the header file for secant; **ffam.h**, the header file for the function being solved; and **tools.h**.

Problem scope. Given a function, $f(x)$, find a root of the equation given two initial estimates of that root.

Function. The function to be solved, $f(x)$, must be defined within a separate module.

Input. Two initial estimates of the root of the function $f(x)$.

Constants:

- **LIMIT** $= 1 \times 10^{-10}$, the value of $f(x)$ that is close enough to 0.
- **EPS** $= 1 \times 10^{-4}$, the difference between search interval endpoints that is close enough to 0.
- **MAX_ITER** $= 50$, the maximum number of iterations to make before quitting.

Formulas. Given two estimates, x_1 and x_2, with corresponding function values $y_1 = f(x_1)$ and $y_2 = f(x_2)$, compute a new estimate as shown in the diagram.

$$x_3 = x_2 - y_2 \times \frac{x_2 - x_1}{y_2 - y_1}$$

Replace x_1 with x_2 and x_2 with x_3 and iterate the computation until

- $f(x_3) <$ **LIMIT**, in which case x_3 is taken as the root.
- $|x_3 - x_2| <$ **EPS**, in which case x_3 is taken as the root.
- $|y_2 - y_1| <$ **LIMIT**, in which case the method has failed.
- Success has not been achieved within the maximum number of iterations.

Output. The value x, which causes the function, $f(x)$, to be 0 within the specified tolerance. If no such value is found, a message should be displayed indicating the nature of the failure: initial points too close, secant has a horizontal slope, or too many iterations.

Limitations. Only roots of functions of one variable can be found. Either the found root will be within **EPS** of the actual root or the function value at the root will be less than **LIMIT**, but the program cannot guarantee both.

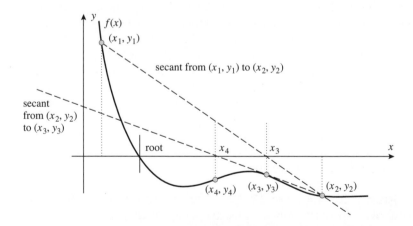

Figure 23.11.   Problem specifications: Root finding by the secant method.

This code and the **verbose_print()** function in Figure 23.13 form the file **secant.c**.

```
#include "tools.h"
#include "root.h"        /* Interface between roots module and main. */
#include "ffam.h"        /* Prototype for function to solve. */
extern bool verbose;     /* Imported from main. */

static void
verbose_print( int, double, double, double, double, double, double );

er_type
secant( double x1, double x2, double *rootp )
{
    int k;                          /* to count the number of iterations. */
    double x3;                      /* next estimate */
    double y1, y2, y3;              /* f(x) at points x1, x2, x3, resp. */
    double slope, delta;            /* line coefficients */

    if (fabs( x2 - x1 ) < EPS)    /* initial points too close together */
        return BAD_INITIAL_POINTS;
    y1 = f( x1 );    y2 = f( x2 );

    for (k = 0; k < MAX_ITER; k++) {
        slope = (y2 - y1) / (x2 - x1);
        if (fabs( slope ) < LIMIT)  return HORIZONTAL;

        delta = -y2 / slope;
        x3 = x2 + delta;                /* compute new estimate */
        y3 = f( x3 );
        if (verbose) verbose_print( k, x1, y1, x2, y2, x3, y3 );

        if (fabs( delta ) < EPS || fabs( y3 ) < LIMIT) {
            *rootp = x3;                /* Store root in caller's variable. */
            return ROOT_OK;            /* and return the success code. */
        }
        /* Get ready for the next iteration ---------------------- */
        x1 = x2;   y1 = y2;   /* Move old root estimate to older slot */
        x2 = x3;   y2 = y3;   /* Move new root estimate to old slot */
    }
    return TOO_MANY_ITERATIONS;
}
```

Figure 23.12.   The secant algorithm.

2. As in the bisection module, the **verbose** flag from the main module is imported by declaring it here as an **extern** variable.

3. The prototype for **verbose_print()** (Figure 23.13) is declared to be **static** because the function is purely local and should not be exported.

This code follows the code for the `secant()` function (Figure 23.12) in the file `secant.c`.

```
/* ------------------------------------------------------------- */
/* Function prints intermediate output if user selects verbose mode. */
void
verbose_print( int k, double x1, double y1, double x2, double y2,
               double x3, double y3 );
{
    printf( " During iteration %i:\n", k );
    printf( "    x1 = %15g, y1 = %15g\n", x1, y1 );
    printf( "    x2 = %15g, y2 = %15g\n", x2, y2 );
    printf( "    x3 = %15g, y3 = %15g\n", x3, y3 );
}
```

Figure 23.13.   The secant method: verbose output.

- *First box: preparation.*

    1. The secant method starts with two estimates of the root. It is very sensitive to the particular values provided. Some values cause immediate failure; others converge quickly.

    2. The secant algorithm cannot work if the two estimates, **x1** and **x2**, are the same point or almost the same point. Trying to compute the slope of a line between two almost-equal points gives a result that can be highly inaccurate and therefore not useful. The program uses an epsilon test here to compare the given points for equality. If they are too close together, the program returns the error code **BAD_INITIAL_POINTS**.

    3. Otherwise, it prepares to enter the loop by evaluating the function at both initial points.

- *Second box: the iteration.*

    1. The success code, **ROOT_OK**, is returned if the process converges and a root is found. The secant function can fail to find a root for two reasons other than having the starting points too close together. A different error code is returned to document each reason.

    2. The **for** loop repeats the estimation process until either its counter exceeds the given iteration limit or a root is found and the **return** statement (second inner box) is executed. If the iteration maximum is exceeded, the program leaves the loop and returns the error code **TOO_MANY_ITERTIONS**.

    3. On each iteration, the slope of the secant line is computed through the two most recent points. The program tests for slopes that are 0 or close to 0 because dividing by such a number will cause floating-point overflow or, at the very least, produce a new estimate too far away to be meaningful. If a near-zero slope is found, the program returns the error code **HORIZONTAL**.

4. Otherwise, the slope is valid and used to find the next estimate, **x3**, and repeat the process. For a well-behaved function and initial guesses somewhere in the vicinity of the root, this process can converge quite rapidly.

- *First inner box: computing the next estimate.*

  1. The program uses the slope to compute the point **x3** at which the secant crosses the *x* axis. Since this point is the new estimate, the program evaluates the function at **x3**.
  2. If the **verbose** flag is set to **true** by the caller, all three *x* values and their corresponding function values will be printed. This feedback is invaluable when the user is having trouble finding initial estimates with which the algorithm can succeed.
  3. It would certainly have been easier to just include the **printf()** statements in the **secant()** function directly, rather than making a new function, **verbose_print()**, with seven parameters. However, we still follow the principle that statements that essentially do not contribute to the flow of the algorithm should be extracted into functions.

- *Second inner box: a root?*

  1. If the new estimate equals the old estimate, within tolerances, the root has been found. If the new function value equals zero, within tolerances, the root has also been found.
  2. To return the answer, the program stores the most recent estimate in the address (***rootp**) that the caller provided.
  3. It also returns the success code so that the caller will know that the value in ***rootp** is the correct answer.

- *Third inner box: go around again.*

  1. We now have three estimates of the root: The two we had before beginning this iteration and the one new estimate just calculated. Before repeating the process, we must discard the oldest estimate.
  2. In this code, **x1** always refers to the oldest of the three current estimates and **x2** to the second oldest (except for the first pass, when they are of equal age). To be ready for the next time through the loop the program copies the values from **x2** and **y2** into the variables **x1** and **y1**, then **x3** and **y3** into **x2** and **y2**. This leaves **x3** and **y3** available for newly computed values on the next iteration.
  3. This technique of moving a pair of values "down the line" to prepare for the next pass is used commonly in iterative processes.

- *Successful output.*

  1. Following is the output from a run having the verbose feedback turned on. (The dashed line indicates omitted menu output.) Note that the algorithm achieved four decimal places of accuracy after only four it-

erations. The user prompts and inputs came from the `main()` program in Figure 23.6.

```
Root finder program
Thermal conductivity of insulation (BTU/h ft F): .2

Enter radius of pipe (feet): .333
-------------------------------------------------
Enter letter of desired item: s
Enter two initial estimates for the root: .4 .8
During iteration 0:
    x1 =                 0.4, y1 =          -2.59439
    x2 =                 0.8, y2 =         -0.378654
    x3 =            0.868357, y3 =         -0.067097
During iteration 1:
    x1 =                 0.8, y1 =         -0.378654
    x2 =            0.868357, y2 =         -0.067097
    x3 =            0.883079, y3 =         -0.002239
During iteration 2:
    x1 =            0.868357, y1 =         -0.067097
    x2 =            0.883079, y2 =         -0.002239
    x3 =            0.883587, y3 =      -1.36614e-05
During iteration 3:
    x1 =            0.883079, y1 =         -0.002239
    x2 =            0.883587, y2 =      -1.36614e-05
    x3 =             0.88359, y3 =      -2.79689e-09

The root is 0.88359
```

2. Below is the output for the same function parameters but with different initial guesses and the verbose feedback turned off. It converged after five iterations.

```
Enter letter of desired item: s
Enter two initial estimates for the root: 1 2

The root is 0.88359
```

Problems with the secant method.   Just like Newton's method, explained in Chapter 8, the secant iteration process can fail to converge on a root, even when that root exists, for several different reasons:

- The two current estimates can be too nearly equal, resulting in the **BAD_INITIAL_POINTS** error; for example:

```
Enter letter of desired item: s
Enter two initial estimates for the root: .4 .40003

Failed to find root--initial points too close
```

- The function values at the two current estimates are nearly equal. The computed secant therefore is nearly horizontal, making it impossible to compute another estimate. In this case, the **HORIZONTAL** error code is returned. This occurs when the function values at the current estimates are positioned on two sides of a "hill" or a "valley" in the function's graph and happen to be the same distance from the x axis. It is easy to generate such a situation purposely but unlikely for it to happen by chance, during the course of the iteration.

- Failure also can happen when the function has an inflection point near the x axis. In this case, a secant may be nearly horizontal (but not within our tolerance), meaning that the next value for x may be a long distance away. Succeeding values for x then are likely to oscillate wildly back and forth without closing in on the correct answer. In Figure 23.11, this begins to happen with the secant between (**x3, y3**) and (**x4, y4**); the value for **x5** will be off the graph to the right. After that, estimates may or may not settle down again in the vicinity of a root. For this reason, we limit the number of new estimates computed to **MAX_ITER**. The output from one such search follows. The function being searched was

```
double f( double r )
{
    double x = pow( fabs( r ), 0.333 );
    if (r < 0) return -x;
    else return x;
}
```

The output was:

```
Enter letter of desired item: s
Enter two initial estimates for the root: -1 2
During iteration 0:
   x1 =                 -1, y1 =                  -1
   x2 =                  2, y2 =            1.25963
   x3 =           0.327651, y3 =           0.689655
During iteration 1:
   x1 =                  2, y1 =            1.25963
   x2 =           0.327651, y2 =           0.689655
   x3 =           -1.69585, y3 =            -1.1923
During iteration 2:
   x1 =           0.327651, y1 =           0.689655
   x2 =           -1.69585, y2 =            -1.1923
   x3 =          -0.413874, y3 =          -0.745448
During iteration 3:
   x1 =           -1.69585, y1 =            -1.1923
   x2 =          -0.413874, y2 =          -0.745448
   x3 =            1.72474, y3 =            1.19903
-------------------------------------------------
```

```
During iteration 48:
    x1 =          -0.423763, y1 =         -0.751332
    x2 =           1.79709, y2 =          1.21555
    x3 =           0.424585, y3 =         0.751817
During iteration 49:
    x1 =           1.79709, y1 =          1.21555
    x2 =           0.424585, y2 =         0.751817
    x3 =          -1.80058, y3 =         -1.21633
```

```
Failed to find root--iteration limit exceeded
```

- A last mode of failure is that the search method generates a value of *x* for which the function cannot be properly evaluated. In this example, it would mean values that correspond to an insulation radius smaller than the pipe radius. There is a discontinuity in the function at that point. When this occurs, the program terminates, as illustrated in the notes on Figure 23.5.

23.2.7 Defining the Root Solver Application

A makefile or project file defines an application by listing its parts, how each part depends on the others, and how the entire program should be assembled. The makefile for this program (Figure 23.14) is very much like the one presented and

```
OBJS = main.o secant.o bisect.o heat.o tools.o
CFLAGS = -Wall
```

```
roots:   $(OBJS)
    gcc -o roots $(OBJS)
```

```
main.o:  main.c tools.h root.h ffam.h
    gcc -c $(CFLAGS) main.c

heat.o:  heat.c tools.h ffam.h
    gcc -c $(CFLAGS) heat.c

bisect.o:  bisect.c tools.h root.h ffam.h
    gcc -c $(CFLAGS) bisect.c

secant.o:  secant.c tools.h root.h ffam.h
    gcc -c $(CFLAGS) secant.c

tools.o:  tools.c tools.h
    gcc -c $(CFLAGS) tools.c
```

```
clean:
    rm -f $(OBJS) roots
```

Figure 23.14.   A makefile for roots.

explained in Figure 23.2: only the number of modules, their names, and their dependencies have been changed.

Notes on Figure 23.14: A makefile for `roots`.

- *First box: definitions.* As the components of this program, we list the four user modules (main, heat, bisect, and secant) as well as the **tools** library.
- *Second box: linking.* The modules just defined are linked and the name **roots** given to the executable program.
- *Third box: compiling.* Five compilation rules are given, one for each module. The dependency line of each rule lists one source code module and all the header files it includes. These lists easily are generated by examining the tops of the source files. Each compilation command uses the compiler flags defined in the first box.
- *Fourth box: cleanup.* A rule for deleting the `.o` and executable files from the working directory again is provided.

23.3   What You Should Remember

23.3.1 Major Concepts

- *Modular organization.* Large applications generally are broken up into several interacting modules, where the main module controls the overall sequence of program actions and calls functions from the subsidiary modules to do the work. Each subsidiary module implements an identifiable and coherent collection of services and is relatively independent of other modules. Dividing a problem solution into an appropriate set of modules, and designing their interfaces are tasks for the most skilled programmer in a group.
- *Importing and exporting things.* A subsidiary module consists of a source code file and a matching header file, which defines its interface with the rest of the application; that is, the set of types, constants, and functions it exports. It also is possible (but rarely appropriate) to export a variable. To import that variable into a different module, the importing module must have an **extern** declaration for it. To import functions and constants, a module must include the header file of another module that exports those capabilities. The information in the header file is used at compile time to validate function calls and set up automatic type conversions. The functions and variables declared at the top of a module are exported to the linker unless explicitly declared to be **static**. The linker matches the supply of available exports with the list of requested imports and makes the required intermodule connections.
- *Compiling and linking a multimodule application.* Project files and makefiles are used to identify the required parts of a multimodule application,

list the dependencies, and automate the process of compiling the modules and linking them. In addition, a project facility or make facility typically assists the programmer by recompiling and relinking a project if any of its component files have been changed.

* *The secant method for finding roots.* The secant method, a major algorithm for searching for the roots of an equation, was presented here. It is an iterative method much like Newton's method but does not require a second function that can compute the derivative of the function being searched. The Newton, bisection, and secant root-finding methods have problems with certain kinds of functions and some initial values. If one of them does not work in a particular situation, it often is helpful to switch to another. Developing alternative strategies to solve a problem is useful.

23.3.2   Programming Style

* Make it modular. Split a large project into modules, each of which can be fairly independent of the others, and supply a narrow set of functions in its interface. This will minimize the number of changes that one programmer in a group must make to accomodate the needs of the others.
* Define functions and objects in a module as `static`, where possible, which makes them private within the module.
* Organize a project by making a subdirectory for it and put in that subdirectory all of the files needed to make that project. Use a makefile or a project file to organize and automate the production of a big application.
* Occasionally, but rarely, there is a good use for a global variable. In the example given here, a `verbose` switch was used to control the global environment in which all functions operated. The switch was interpreted (or ignored) by each function in its own way. Such information could be passed as an additional parameter to every function, but doing so tends to obscure the structure of the program. It is properly handled as a global object that can be viewed, unobtrusively, by all interested functions.
* Debugging printouts are a good idea.

23.3.3   Sticky Points and Common Errors

* *Keep the interface stable.* When an application is built from many modules, the module interfaces are specified early in the design process. Members of the programming team then begin designing and constructing the modules. From that point on, it is important to keep the interfaces stable rather than "improving" them repeatedly. Getting the communication between modules to work correctly can be difficult. Doing it again and again is a bad use of a programmer's time.
* *Avoid double inclusion.* A module will not compile if the same header file is included twice; use `#ifndef…#endif` to avoid this. Even after

all modules have been compiled successfully, linking can fail if functions or external variables in two modules have the same name. Avoid this by limiting the use of external functions and variables to situations in which they are necessary.

- *Use external variables carefully.* Remember that the definition of an external variable in the exporting module should have an initializer, and the definition in an importing module must not have an initializer and must be declared **extern**.

- *List all module dependencies.* A makefile can operate correctly only if it contains complete and correct information. A common error is to omit one header file in the dependency list of a rule. Check the code at the top of each file carefully and be sure that every **#include** statement is reflected in the dependency list for that module. Also check every nonsystem file that is included.

- Tab characters (not spaces) are used to indent compile commands in a makefile.

- The linking rule should be the first rule in the makefile.

23.3.4   New and Revisited Vocabulary

These are the most important terms and concepts discussed in this chapter.

modular design	compile and link	module interface
multimodule program	compile only	exported definition
application directory	compiler options	imported variable
code management	**gcc -o, -c, -Wall**	module communication
source-code file	load module	**extern** variable
#include	make facility	**static** global variable
header file	makefile	**static** function
duplicate inclusion	project file	secant method
conditional compilation	dependencies	bisection method
#ifndef	rules	error codes
#define	obsolete file	**setup()**
#endif	**make** and **make clean**	verbose output

23.4   Exercises

23.4.1   Self-Test Exercises

1. Draw a relationship graph for the **roots** package developed in this chapter. Follow the example given in Figure 23.1 for the imaginary game program.

2. Draw a call graph for the **roots** package developed in this chapter. Include all functions, even those from the standard libraries. Comment on the relationship between this graph and the module relationship graph developed in exercise 1.

3. A particular three-module application contains a main module and two other modules, each of which has a corresponding header file. Assume that the main module calls functions from both other modules. Also, the first module calls functions from the second, but the second calls only local functions. In addition, functions in both modules use types declared in the main module's header file. The three code modules are named **main.c**, **mod1.c**, and **mod2.c**; list the header files that should be included by each.

4. The following is a sample makefile for the three module application described in the previous exercise. The executable application is supposed to be named **apple**. Unfortunately, the commands in this file have errors. Find them and fix them, based on the description of the problem and the **#include** commands that you wrote. The lines are lettered, for your convenience in writing the answers; the letters are not part of the makefile.

a. `OBJ = dummy.o mod1.o mod2.o`

b. `CFLAGS = -all`

c. `main.o:  main.c mod1.h mod2.h`

d. `    gcc -o $(CFLAGS) main.c`

e. `mod1.o:  mod1.c mod1.h`

f. `    gcc -c $(CFLAGS) mod2.c`

g. `mod2.o:  mod2.h main.h`

h. `    gcc -c (CFLAGS) mod2.h`

i. `apple:  $(OBJ)`

j. `    gcc -o main $(OBJ)`

k. `clean:`

l. `    rm -f $(OBJS) main`

23.4.2   Using Pencil and Paper

1. Consider the modular design of the **roots** package presented in this chapter. Develop a different method of subdividing the functions into modules, headers, and the like. Compare your solution to the one presented here.

2. The verbose option for the **roots** application was handled as an external variable exported from the main module to the others. This could have been handled by passing the variable as a parameter between functions. Decide where this variable should be defined and how it should be initialized. Show all the function calls that would need to be modified to pass this variable through the parameter lists. Which method is preferable? Why?

3. We want to include Newton's method as another root-finding method in the **roots** package. This method was given in Chapter 8. Start planning the Newton module, with an outline of the contents of the source and header file. Since Newton's method

requires a derivative function for the function being searched, adjust the heat module as well to add a function to do this. Add any other considerations you think are needed to integrate this module. Do not write any actual code for this problem. Extend and modify the makefile developed for the **roots** application shown in Figure 23.14 to include the Newton module.

4. Several games have been presented as exercises in preceding chapters. Now, we want to integrate them into a modular game package that lets the user choose a game from a menu and play it. The following is a proposed makefile for this application. It has a very short main module, a menu module, and one module each for bingo, poker, and roulette. Assume that the main module includes the header file of the menu module, the menu module includes the header files for the three game modules, and each of the game modules is entirely independent and has nothing to do with any other module. The commands in the makefile contain errors. Find them and fix them, based on the description here.

```
OBJ = menu.o bingo.o poker.o roulette.o
CFLAGS = -Wall

games: $(OBJ)
    gcc -o $(OBJS)

main.o: main.c  poker.h  bingo.h  roulette.h
    gcc -o $(CFLAGS) main.c

menu.o: menu.c  menu.h
    gcc -c $(CFLAGS) menu.c

poker.o: poker.c  poker.h
    gcc -c (CFLAGS)  poker.h

roulette.o: roulette.h  roulette.h
gcc -c (CFLAGS)  roulette.c

clean:
    rm -f $(OBJS) main
```

23.4.3   Using the Computer

1. Changing the function.
   In turbulent pipe flow, it is necessary to determine the friction factor, f, to calculate the energy loss. This f is a function of the pipe's inner surface roughness (alpha), the pipe diameter (d), and the Reynolds number (Re) of the flow (Re is the fluid velocity times the pipe diameter divided by the viscosity of the fluid). The Colebrook equation is used to determine f:

$$\text{Colebrook(f)} = \frac{1}{\sqrt{f}} + 2.0 \log_{10}\left(\frac{\text{alpha}/d}{3.7} + \frac{2.51}{\text{Re}\ \sqrt{f}}\right) = 0$$

a. Following the example in Figure 23.5, write a **setup()** function that will prompt for an input value of Re between 10,000 and 100,000 and the ratio alpha/*d* between .0001 and .01. Then write a function, **Colebrook()**, with one argument, the friction factor, f, that calculates the value of the Colebrook equation. Be sure to include an error check on the argument, f, which must be positive; otherwise, the square root operation will fail or we will divide by zero. Call **fatal()** if an invalid value of f is used.

b. Make a subdirectory containing the following files: the header file from Figure 23.4, your **Colebrook()** function and its **setup()** function in a file called **cole.c**, and the other components of the root-finding program from Figures 23.6 through 23.13.

c. If you are using a UNIX system, also create a makefile as shown in Figure 23.14. If you are using some other system, construct a multimodule project and install the source code files (but not the header files) as parts of that project.

d. Compile and link this program and use it to find the root of different Colebrook equations using both the bisection and secant methods. Compare your results.

2. Extending roots.
   Extend the **roots** application by adding a module for Newton's method according to the design developed in pencil-and-paper exercise 3. Use the functions defined in Chapter 8 as a basis. You also need to add a derivative function to the heat module. The derivative of the heat loss function defined in Figure 23.5 is given by $f'(r) = 1/kr - 1/r^2$, where k is the conductivity of the insulation. Compare the answers you get using Newton's method to those from the other two modules.

3. A modular search package.
   Develop an application similar to **roots** that searches for items in a data file. The three algorithms to use are the linear sequential search from Chapter 16, the binary search from Chapter 21, and the proportional search described in Chapter 21, computer exercise 6. Again, provide a menu that allows the user to choose the search method, provide verbose output, and change the data file from which to read the data. Assume that the data files contain a sorted list of integers. Normal output should be the location in the data array where the search element is found or an error message if it is not present. Verbose output should print out each location being searched until a search is over.

4. I can sort any way.
   Develop an application similar to **roots** that sorts integer data. The four algorithms to use are the selection sort, insertion sort, quicksort, and the generic **qsort()**. Provide a menu that allows the user to choose a sort method, turn verbose output on or off, change the input and output data files, or quit. Normal output should be sorted data written to an indicated file. Verbose output should consist of the amount of time that it took a particular sorting algorithm to process the data in the file. Instructions on how to calculate the execution time can be found in computer exercise 2 of Chapter 15.

Appendixes

APPENDIX A

The ASCII *Code*

Dec	Hex	Char		Dec	Hex	Char		Dec	Hex	Char		Dec	Hex	Char
0	0x00	null \0		32	0x20	space		64	0x40	@		96	0x60	`
1	0x01			33	0x21	!		65	0x41	A		97	0x61	a
2	0x02			34	0x22	", \"		66	0x42	B		98	0x62	b
3	0x03			35	0x23	#		67	0x43	C		99	0x63	c
4	0x04			36	0x24	$		68	0x44	D		100	0x64	d
5	0x05			37	0x25	%		69	0x45	E		101	0x65	e
6	0x06			38	0x26	&		70	0x46	F		102	0x66	f
7	0x07	bell \a		39	0x27	', \'		71	0x47	G		103	0x67	g
8	0x08	backspace \b		40	0x28	(		72	0x48	H		104	0x68	h
9	0x09	tab \t		41	0x29	)		73	0x49	I		105	0x69	i
10	0x0A	linefeed \n		42	0x2A	*		74	0x4A	J		106	0x6A	j
11	0x0B	vertical tab \v		43	0x2B	+		75	0x4B	K		107	0x6B	k
12	0x0C	formfeed \f		44	0x2C	,		76	0x4C	L		108	0x6C	l
13	0x0D	carriage return \r		45	0x2D	-		77	0x4D	M		109	0x6D	m
14	0x0E			46	0x2E	.		78	0x4E	N		110	0x6E	n
15	0x0F			47	0x2F	/		79	0x4F	O		111	0x6F	o
16	0x10			48	0x30	0		80	0x50	P		112	0x70	p
17	0x11			49	0x31	1		81	0x51	Q		113	0x71	q
18	0x12			50	0x32	2		82	0x52	R		114	0x72	r
19	0x13			51	0x33	3		83	0x53	S		115	0x73	s
20	0x14			52	0x34	4		84	0x54	T		116	0x74	t
21	0x15			53	0x35	5		85	0x55	U		117	0x75	u
22	0x16			54	0x36	6		86	0x56	V		118	0x76	v
23	0x17			55	0x37	7		87	0x57	W		119	0x77	w
24	0x18			56	0x38	8		88	0x58	X		120	0x78	x
25	0x19			57	0x39	9		89	0x59	Y		121	0x79	y
26	0x1A			58	0x3A	:		90	0x5A	Z		122	0x7A	z
27	0x1B	escape \\		59	0x3B	;		91	0x5B	[		123	0x7B	{
28	0x1C			60	0x3C	<		92	0x5C	\		124	0x7C	|
29	0x1D			61	0x3D	=		93	0x5D	]		125	0x7D	}
30	0x1E			62	0x3E	>		94	0x5E	^		126	0x7E	~
31	0x1F			63	0x3F	?		95	0x5F	_		127	0x7F	delete

Figure A.1.   The ASCII code.

The characters of the 7-bit ASCII code are listed, in order. The first two columns of each group give the code in base 10 and as a hexadecimal literal. The third column gives the printed form (if any) or a description of the character. Last is the escape code for the character, if one exists.

The Precedence of Operators in C

Arity	Operator	Meaning	Precedence	Associativity
	a[k]	Subscript	17	left to right
	fname(arg list)	Function call	17	"
	.	Struct part selection	17	"
	->	Selection using pointer	17	"
Unary	postfix ++, --	Postincrement k++, decrement k--	16	left to right
"	prefix ++, --	Preincrement ++k, decrement --k	15	right to left
"	sizeof	# of bytes in object	15	"
"	~	Bitwise complement	15	"
"	!	Logical NOT	15	"
"	+	Unary plus	15	"
"	-	Negate	15	"
"	&	Address of	15	"
"	*	Pointer dereference	15	"
"	(typename)	Type cast	14	"
Binary	*	Multiply	13	left to right
"	/	Divide	13	"
"	%	Mod	13	"
"	+	Add	12	"
"	-	Subtract	12	"
"	<<	Left shift	11	"
"	>>	Right shift	11	"
"	<	Less than	10	"
"	>	Greater than	10	"
"	<=	Less than or equal to	10	"
"	>=	Greater than or equal to	10	"
"	==	Is equal to	9	"
"	!=	Is not equal to	9	"
"	&	Bitwise AND	8	"
"	^	Bitwise exclusive OR	7	"
"	|	Bitwise OR	6	"
"	&&	Logical AND	5	"
"	||	Logical OR	4	"
Ternary	...?...:...	Conditional expression	3	right to left
Binary	=	Assignment	2	"
"	+= -=	Add or subtract and store back	2	"
"	*= /= %=	Times, divide, or mod and store	2	"
"	&= ^= |=	Bitwise operator and assignment	2	"
"	<<= >>=	Shift and store back	2	"
"	,	Left-side-first sequence	1	left to right

Figure B.1. The precedence of operators in C.

Keywords

C.1   Preprocessor Commands

The commands in the first group are presented in this text. The other commands are beyond its scope.

- Basic: `#include, #define, #ifndef, #endif`.
- Advanced: `#if, #ifdef, #elif, #else, defined(), #undef, #error, #line, #pragma`.
- Advanced macro operators: `#` (stringize), `##` (tokenize).

C.2   Control Words

These words control the order of execution of program blocks.

- Functions: `main, return`.
- Conditionals: `if, else, switch, case, default`.
- Loops: `while, do, for`.
- Transfer of control: `break, continue, goto`.

C.3   Types and Declarations

- Integer types: `long, int, short, char, signed, unsigned`.
- Real types: `double, float, long double`.
- An unknown or generic type: `void`.
- Type qualifiers: `const, volatile`.
- Storage class: `auto, static, extern, register`.

- Type operator: `sizeof`.
- To create new type names: `typedef`.
- To define new type descriptions: `struct`, `enum`, `union`.

C.4   Additional C++ Reserved Words

The following are reserved words in C++ but not in C. C programmers should either avoid using them or be careful to use them in ways that are consistent with their meaning in C++.

- Classes: `class`, `friend`, `this`, `private`, `protected`, `public`, `template`.
- Functions and operators: `inline`, `virtual`, `operator`.
- Kinds of casts: `reinterpret_cast`, `static_cast`, `const_cast`, `dynamic_cast`.
- Boolean type: `bool`, `true`, `false`.
- Exceptions: `try`, `throw`, `catch`.
- Memory allocation: `new`, `delete`.
- Other: `typeid`, `namespace`, `mutable`, `asm`, `using`.

C.5   An Alphabetical List of C and C++ Reserved Words

#	catch	goto	static
##	char	if	static_cast
#define	class	inline	struct
#elif	const	int	switch
#else	const_cast	long	template
#endif	continue	mutable	this
#error	default	namespace	throw
#if	defined()	new	true
#ifdef	delete	operator	try
#ifndef	do	private	typedef
#include	double	protected	typeid
#line	else	public	union
#pragma	enum	register	unsigned
#undef	extern	reinterpret_cast	using
asm	false	return	virtual
auto	float	short	void
bool	for	signed	volatile
break	friend	sizeof	while
case			

APPENDIX
D

Advanced Aspects of C Operators

This appendix describes important facts about a few C operators that were omitted in earlier chapters because they were too advanced when related material was covered.

D.1 Assignment Combination Operators

All the assignment-combination operators have the same very low precedence and associate right to left. This means that a series of assignment operators will be parsed and executed right to left, no matter what operators are used. Figure D.1 demonstrates the syntax, precedence, and associativity of the arithmetic combinations.

Notes on Figure D.1. Assignment combinations.

- *Box: precedence and associativity.*

    1. This long expression shows that all the combination operators have the same precedence and that they are parsed and executed right to left.

We exercise the arithmetic assignment-combination operators. The parse tree for the last expression is shown in Figure D.2. Note that these operators all have the same precedence and they associate right to left.

```
#include <stdio.h>
void main( void )
{
    double k = 10.0;        double m = 5.0;
    double n = 64.0;        double t = -63.0;

    puts( "\n Demonstrating Assignment Combinations" );
    puts( " Assignment operators associate right to left.\n"
          " Initial values:   " );
    printf( "\t k = %.2g m = %.2g n = %.2g t = %.2g \n", k, m, n, t );

    t /= n -= m *= k += 7;
    puts( "\n Executing t /= n -= m *= k += 7 gives the values:   " );
    printf( "\t k = %.2g m = %.2g n = %.2g t = %.2g \n\n", k, m, n, t );

}
```

Figure D.1.   Assignment combinations.

2. The `+=` is parsed before the `*=` because it is on the right. The fact that `*` alone has higher precedence than `+` alone is not relevant to the combination operators.

3. The parse tree for this expression is shown in Figure D.2. Note that assignment-combination operators have two branches connected to a variable. The right branch represents the operand value used in the mathematical operation. The left branch, with the arrowhead, reflects the changing value of the variable due to the assignment action after the calculation is complete.

This is the parse tree and evaluation for the last expression in Figure D.1

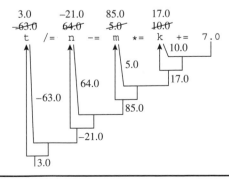

Figure D.2.   A parse tree for assignment combinations.

4. The output from this program is

```
Demonstrating Assignment Combinations
Assignment operators associate right to left.
Initial values:
        k = 10 m = 5 n = 64 t = -63

Executing t /= n -= m *= k += 7 gives the values:
        k = 17 m = 85 n = -21 t = 3
```

D.2   # More on Lazy Evaluation and Skipping

With lazy evaluation, when we skip, we skip the right operand. This isn't confusing when the right operand is only a simple variable. However, sometimes it is an expression with several operators. For example, look at the parse tree in Figure D.3. The left operand of the `||` operator is the expression `a < 10` and its right operand is `a >= 2 * b && b != 1`. The parse tree makes clear the relationship of operands to operators.

We can use parse trees to visualize the evaluation process. The stem of the tree represents the value of the entire expression. The stem of each subtree represents the value of the parts of the tree above it. To evaluate an expression, we start by writing the initial values of the variables above the expression. However, start the evaluation process *at the stem of the tree.* Starting at the top (the leaves) in C will give the wrong answer in many cases. As each operator is evaluated, write the answer on the stem under that operator. Figure D.3 illustrates the evaluation process.

The tree, as a whole, represents an assignment expression because the operator corresponding to the tree's stem is an `=`. Everything after the `=` in this assignment is a logical expression because the next operator, proceeding up the tree, is a logical operator. This is where we start considering the rules for lazy evaluation.

Skip the right operand.   Evaluation of a logical expression proceeds left to right, skipping some subexpressions along the way. We evaluate the left operand of the leftmost logical operator first. Depending on the result, we evaluate or skip the right operand of that expression. In the example, we compute `a < 10`; if that is `true`, we skip the rest of the expression, including the `&&` operator. This case is illustrated in the upper diagram in Figure D.3. The long double bars across the right branch of the OR operator are called *pruning marks*; they are used to "cut off" the part of the tree that is not evaluated and show, graphically, where skipping begins.

A natural comment at this point is, "But I thought that `&&` should be executed first because it has higher precedence." Although precedence controls the

We evaluate the expression `y = a < 10 || a >= 2 * b && b != 1` twice. Note the "pruning marks" on the tree and the curved lines around the parts of the expression that are skipped.

1. Evaluation with the values `a = 7, b =` anything: The `||` causes skipping

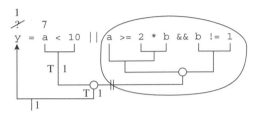

2. Evaluation with the values `a = 17, b = 20`: The `&&` causes skipping

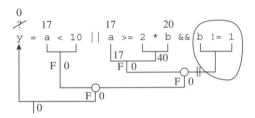

Figure D.3.   Lazy evaluation.

construction of the parse tree, precedence simply is not considered when the tree is evaluated. Because of its higher precedence, the `&&` operator "captured" the operand `a >= 2 * b`. However, logical expressions are evaluated left to right, so evaluation will start with the `||` because it is to the left of the `&&`. Only if the left operand of the `||` operation is `false`, as in the lower diagram of Figure D.3, will evaluation continue with the `&&`. In this case the left operand of the `&&` is `false`, meaning its right operand can be skipped. Graphically, evaluation starts at the stem of the logical expression and proceeds upward, doing the left side of each logical operator first and skipping the right side where possible.

The whole right operand.   When skipping happens, *all* the work on the right subtree is skipped, no matter how complicated that portion of the expression is and no matter what operators are there. In our first example, the left operand (which we evaluated) was a simple comparison but the right operand was long and complex. As soon as we found that `a < 10` was `true`, we put the answer `1` on the tree stem under the `||`, skipped *all* the work on the right side of the operator, and stored the value 1 in `y`. In Figure D.4, we also skip the rest of the

We evaluate the expression `y = a < 0 || a++ < b` for `a = -3`. Note that the increment operation in the right operand of || does not happen because the left operand is `true`.

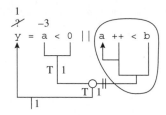

Figure D.4.   Skip the whole operand.

computation after the comparison. However, in general, we might skip only a portion of the remaining expression.

Sometimes, lazy evaluation can substantially improve the efficiency of a program. But while improving efficiency is nice, a much more important use for skipping is to avoid evaluating parts of an expression that would cause machine crashes or other kinds of trouble. For example, assume we wish to divide a number by `x`, compare the answer to a minimum value, and do an error procedure if the answer is less than the minimum. But it is possible for `x` to be 0 and that must be checked. We can avoid a division-by-0 error and do the computation and comparison in one expression by using a *guard* before the division. A guard expression consists of a test for the error-causing condition followed by the `&&` operator. The entire C expression would be

```
if (x != 0 && total / x < minimum) do_error();
```

Guarded expressions are useful in a wide variety of situations.

And nothing but the right operand.   One common fallacy about C is that, once skipping starts, everything in the expression to the right is skipped. This is simply not true; the skipping involves only the right operand of the particular operator that triggered the skip. If several logical operators are in the expression, we might evaluate branches at the beginning and end but skip a part in the middle. This is illustrated by Figure D.5. In all cases, you must look at the parse tree to see what will be skipped.

D.2.1   Evaluation Order and Side-Effect Operators

A frequent cause of confusion is the relationship between logical operators, lazy evaluation, and operators such as `++` that have side effects. When used in isolation, as they are in Figure 4.25, the increment and decrement operators are convenient

We evaluate the expression y = a < 0 || a > b && b > c || b > 10 for a = 3 and b = 17. Note that skipping affects only the right operand of the &&; the parts of the expression not on this subtree are not skipped.

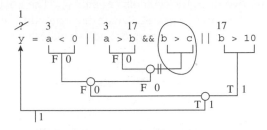

Figure D.5.   And nothing but the operand.

and relatively free of complication. When side-effect operators are used in long, complex expressions, they create the kind of complexity that fosters errors. If a side-effect operator is used in the middle of a logical expression, it may be executed sometimes but skipped at other times. If the operator is on the skipped subtree, as in Figure D.4, that operation is not performed and the value in memory is not changed. This may be useful in a program, but it also is complex and should be avoided by beginners. Just remember, the high precedence of the increment or decrement operator affects only the shape of the parse tree; it *does not* cause the increment operation to be evaluated before the logical operator.

A second problem with side-effect operators relates to the order in which the parts of an expression are evaluated. Recall that evaluation order has nothing to do with precedence order. We have stated that logical operators are executed left to right. This also is true of two other kinds of sequencing operators: the conditional operator ?...: and the comma, defined in the next section. Therefore, it may be a surprise to learn that C is permitted to evaluate most other operators right-side first or left-side first, or inconsistently, whichever is convenient for the compiler. Technically, we say that the evaluation order for nonsequencing operators is *undefined*. This flexibility in evaluation order permits an optimizing compiler to produce faster code.

However, while the undefined evaluation order usually does not cause problems, it does lead directly to one important warning: If an expression contains a side-effect operator that changes the value of a variable V, *do not use V* anywhere else in the expression. The side effect could happen either before or after the value of V is used elsewhere in the expression and the outcome is unpredictable. Writing the expression in the order we want it executed won't help; the C compiler does not have to conform to our order.

The Conditional Operator

There is only one ternary operator in C, the *conditional operator*. It has three operands and two operator symbols (`?` and `:`). The conditional operator does almost the same thing as an `if...else` with one major difference: `if` is a statement, it has no value; but `?...:` is an operator and calculates and returns a value like any other operator.

Evaluating a Conditional Operator.   We can use either a flow diagram or a parse tree to diagram the structure and meaning of a conditional operator; each kind of diagram is helpful in some ways. A flow diagram (as in Figure D.6) depicts the order in which actions happen and shows us the similarity between a conditional operator and an `if` statement, while a parse tree (Figure D.7) shows us how the value produced by the conditional operator relates to the surrounding expression.

Making a flowchart for a conditional operator is somewhat problematical since flowcharts are for statements and a conditional operator is only part of a statement. To represent the sequence of actions as we do for the `if` statement, we have to include the rest of whatever statement contains the `?...:` in the **true** and **false** boxes. Figure D.6 shows how this can be done. The condition of the `?...:` is the operand to the left of the `?`. This condition is written in the diamond-shaped box of the flowchart. The **true** clause is written between the `?` and the `:`. It is written, with the assignment operator on the left, in the **true** box. Similarly, the **false** clause is written, with another copy of the assignment operator, in the **false** box.

Looking at the flowchart, we can see that the condition of a `?...:` always is evaluated first. Then, based on the outcome, either the **true** clause or the **false** clause is evaluated and produces a result. This result then is used in the expression that surrounds the `?...:`, in this case, a `+=` statement.

Parsing a Conditional Operator.   Since `?...:` can be included in the middle of an expression, it is helpful to know how to draw a parse tree for it. We diagram

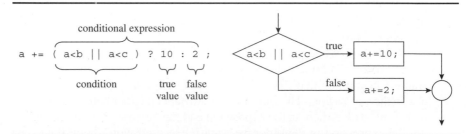

Figure D.6.   A flowchart for the conditional operator.

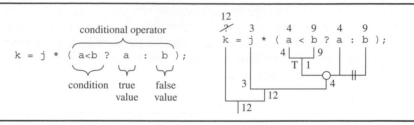

Figure D.7.   A tree for the conditional operator.

it with three upright parts (rather than two) and a stem as shown in Figure D.7. Note that ?...: has very low precedence (with precedence = 3, it falls just above assignment) so it usually can be used without putting parentheses around its operands. However, parentheses are often needed around the entire unit. This three-armed treelet works naturally into the surrounding expression. The main drawback of this kind of diagram is that it does not show the sequence of execution as well as a flowchart.

Parsing a nested set of conditional operators is not hard. First parse the higher-precedence parts of the expression. Then start at the right (since the conditional operator associates from right to left) and look for the pattern: ⟨treelet⟩ ? ⟨treelet⟩ : ⟨treelet⟩. Wherever you find three consecutive treelets separated only by a ? and a :, bracket them together and draw a stem under the ?. Even if the expression is complex and contains more than one ?, this method always works if the expression is correct. If the expression is incorrect, we will find mismatched or misnested elements.

The sequence in which the parts of a conditional expression are evaluated or skipped is critical. We convey this sequencing in a parse tree by placing a sequence-point circle under the ?. This indicates that the condition (the leftmost operand) must be evaluated first. The outcome of the condition selects either the **true** clause or the **false** clause and skips over the other. The skipping is conveyed by writing "prune marks" on either the middle branch or the rightmost branch of the parse tree, whichever is skipped. The expression on the remaining branch then is evaluated, and its value is written on the stem of the ?...: bracket and propagated to the surrounding expression. Note that, even though evaluation *starts* by calculating a **true** or a **false** value, the value of the entire conditional operator, in general, will not be **true** or **false**.

The sequence point under the ? has one other important effect. If the condition contains any postincrement operators, the increments must be done before evaluating the **true** clause or the **false** clause. Therefore, it is "safe" to use postincrement in a condition.

Finally, remember that evaluation order is not the same as precedence order. For example, suppose we are evaluating a conditional operator that prunes off a treelet containing some increment operators. Even though increment has much higher precedence than the conditional operator, the increment operations will not happen. This is why we must evaluate parse trees starting at the root, not the leaves. However, pruning does not change the parse tree—it merely skips part of it. We must not erase the parts that are skipped or try to get them out of the way by restructuring the whole diagram.

D.4 The Comma Operator

The comma operator, `,`, in C is used to write two expressions in a context that normally allows for only one. To be useful, the first of these expressions must have a side effect. For example, the following loop, which sums the first **n** values in the array named **data**, uses the comma operator to initialize two variables, the loop counter and the accumulator:

```
for (sum=0, k=n-1; k>=0; --k) sum += data[k];
```

The comma operator acts much like a semicolon with two important exceptions:

1. The program units before and after a comma must be non-**void** expressions. The units before and after a semicolon can be either statements or expressions.
2. When we write a semicolon after an expression, it ends the expression and the entire unit becomes a statement. When a comma is used instead, it does not end the expression but joins it to the expression that follows to form a larger expression.
3. The value of the right operand of the comma is propagated to the enclosing expression and may be used in further computations.

D.5 Summary

A number of nonintuitive aspects of C semantics have arisen in this appendix that are responsible for many programming errors. A programmer needs to be aware of these issues in order to use the language appropriately:

- *Use lazy evaluation.* The left operand of a logical operator always is evaluated, but the right operand is skipped whenever possible. Skipping happens when the value of the left operand is enough to determine the value of the expression.
- *Use guarded expressions.* Because of lazy evaluation, we can write compound conditionals in which the left side acts as a "guard expression" to check for and trap conditions that would cause the right side to crash. The right side is skipped if the guard expression detects a "fatal" condition.

- *Evaluation order is not the same as precedence order.* High-precedence operators are parsed first but they are not evaluated first and they may not be evaluated at all in a logical expression. Logical expressions are executed left to right with possible skipping. An operator on a part of a parse tree that is skipped will not be evaluated. Therefore, an increment operator may remain unevaluated even though it has very high precedence and the precedence of the logical operators is low.
- *Evaluation order is indeterminate.* The only operators that are guaranteed to be evaluated left to right are logical-AND, logical-OR, comma, and the conditional operator. With the other binary operators, either the left side or the right side, may be evaluated first.
- *Keep side-effect operators isolated.* If you use an increment or decrement operator on a variable, V, you should not use V anywhere else in the same expression because the order of evaluation of terms in most expressions is indeterminate. If you use V again, you cannot predict whether the value of V will be changed before or after V is incremented.
- Figure D.8 summarizes the complex aspects of the C operators with side effects and sequence points.

Group	Operators	Complication
Assignment combinations	+=, etc.	These have low precedence and strict right-to-left parsing, no matter which combination is used.
Preincrement and predecrement	++, --	If we use a side-effect operator, we don't use the same variable again in the same expression.
Postincrement and postdecrement	++, --	Remember that the postfix operators return one value for further use in the expression and leave a different value in memory. Also, don't use the same variable again in the expression.
Logical	&&, ||, !	Remember that negative integers are considered **true** values, and separate and different rules apply for precedence order and evaluation order.
	&&	Use lazy evaluation when first operand is **false**.
	||	Use lazy evaluation when first operand is **true**.
Conditional	...?...:...	The expressions both before and after the colon must produce values and those values must be the same type.
Comma	,	This is rarely used except in **for** loops.

Figure D.8.   Complications in use of side-effect operators.

APPENDIX
E

Number Representation and Conversion

In this appendix, we explore more deeply the ways in which integers and floating-point numbers are represented in computers.

E.1   Number Systems and Number Representation

Numbers are written using positional base notation; each digit in a number has a value equal to that digit times a place value, which is a power (positive or negative) of the base value. For example, the *decimal* (base 10) place values are the powers of 10. From the decimal point going left, these are $10^0 = 1$, $10^1 = 10$, $10^2 = 100$, $10^3 = 1,000$, and so forth. From the decimal point going right, these are $10^{-1} = 0.1$, $10^{-2} = 0.01$, $10^{-3} = 0.001$, $10^{-4} = 0.0001$, and so forth. Figure E.1 shows the place values for *binary* (base 2) and *hexadecimal* (base 16); the chart shows those places that are relevant for a short integer.

Just as base-10 notation (decimal) uses 10 digits to represent numbers, hexadecimal uses 16 digits. The first 10 digits are 0–9; the last six are the letters A–F. Figure E.5 shows the decimal values of the 16 hexadecimal digits; Figure E.7 shows some equivalent values in decimal and hexadecimal.

Place values for base 16 (hexadecimal) are shown on the left; base-2 (binary) place values are on the right. Each hexadecimal digit occupies the same memory space as four binary bits because $2^4 = 16$.

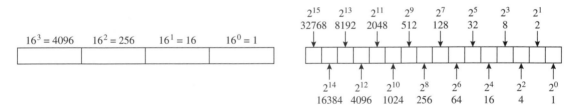

Figure E.1.   Place values.

E.2

Signed and Unsigned Integers

On paper or in a computer, all the bits in an unsigned number represent part of the number itself. Not so with a signed number: One bit must be used to represent the sign. The usual way that we represent a signed number on paper is by putting a positive or negative sign in front of a value of a given magnitude. This representation, called *sign and magnitude*, was used in early computers and still is used today for floating-point numbers. However, a different representation, called *two's complement*, is used for signed integers in most modern computers.

In this notation, the leftmost bit position has a negative place value for signed integers and a positive value for unsigned integers. All the rest of the bit positions have positive place values. Numbers with a 0 in the high-order position have the same interpretation whether they are signed or unsigned. However, a number with a 1 in the high-order position is negative when interpreted as a signed integer and a very large positive number when interpreted as unsigned. Several examples of positive and negative binary two's complement representations are shown in Figure E.2.

To negate a number in two's complement, invert (complement) all of the bits and add 1 to the result. For example, the 16-bit binary representation of $+27$ is 00000000 00011011, so we find the representation of -27 by complementing these bits, 11111111 11100100, and then adding 1: 11111111 11100101.

You can tell whether a signed two's complement number is positive or negative by looking at the high-order bit; if it is 1, the number is negative. To find the magnitude of a negative integer, complement the bits and add 1. For example, suppose we are given the binary number 11111111 11010010. It is negative because it starts with a 1 bit. To find the magnitude we complement these bits, 00000000 00101101; add 1 using binary addition, and convert to its decimal form, 00000000 00101110 = $32 + 8 + 4 + 2 = 46$. So the original number is -46.

Adding binary numbers is similar to adding decimal values, except that a carry is generated when the sum for a bit position is 2 or greater, rather than 10

The binary representations of several signed and unsigned integers follow. Several of these values turn up frequently during debugging, so it is useful to be able to recognize them.

$2^{15}=32768$	$2^{14}=16384$	$2^{13}=8192$	$2^{12}=4096$	$2^{11}=2048$	$2^{10}=1024$	$2^9=512$	$2^8=256$	$2^7=128$	$2^6=64$	$2^5=32$	$2^4=16$	$2^3=8$	$2^2=4$	$2^1=2$	$2^0=1$	Interpreted as a signed short int high-order bit = -32768	Interpreted as an unsigned short int high-order bit = 32768
0	1	1	1	1	1	1	1	1	1	1	1	1	1	1	1	32767	32767
0	0	1	0	0	1	1	1	0	0	0	1	0	0	0	0	10000	10000
0	0	0	0	0	0	0	0	0	0	0	0	0	0	0	1	1	1
0	0	0	0	0	0	0	0	0	0	0	0	0	0	0	0	0	0
1	1	1	1	1	1	1	1	1	1	1	1	1	1	1	1	-32768 + 32767 = -1	+32768 + 32767 = 65535
1	1	0	1	1	0	0	0	1	1	1	1	0	0	0	0	-32768 + 22768 = -10000	+32768 + 22768 = 55536
1	0	0	0	0	0	0	0	0	0	0	0	0	0	0	0	-32768 + 0 = -32768	+32768 + 0 = 32768
1	0	0	0	0	0	0	0	0	0	0	0	0	0	0	1	-32768 + 1 = -32767	+32768 + 1 = 32769

Figure E.2.   Two's complement representation of integers.

or greater, as with decimal numbers. The carry values are represented in binary and may carry over into more than one position as they can in decimal addition.

Wrap revisited.   Wrap happens whenever there is a carry *into* the sign bit (leftmost bit) of a signed integer. When x is the largest positive signed integer we can represent, $x + 1$ will be the smallest (farthest from 0) negative integer. To be specific, for a 2-byte model, the largest signed value is 32,767, which is represented by the bit sequence $x =$ 01111111 11111111. The value of $x + 1$ is 10000000 00000000 in binary and -32768 in base 10.

Similarly, with unsigned integers, wrap happens whenever there is a carry *out of* the leftmost bit of the integer. In this case, if x is the largest unsigned integer, $x + 1$ will be 0. To be specific, for a 2-byte model, the largest unsigned value is 65,535, which is represented by the bit sequence $x =$ 11111111 11111111. The value, in binary, of $x + 1$ is 00000000 00000000.

Wrap also can happen when any operation produces a result too large to store in the variable supposed to receive it. Unfortunately, there is no systematic way to detect wrap after it happens. Avoidance is the best policy, and that requires a combination of programmer awareness and caution when working with integers.

E.3   **Representation of Real Numbers**

A real number, N, is represented by a signed mantissa, m, multiplied by a base, b, raised to some signed exponent, x; that is,

$$N = \pm m \times b^{\pm x}$$

Inside the computer, each of the components of a real number is stored in some binary format. The IEEE (Institute for Electrical and Electronic Engineers) established a standard for floating-point representation and arithmetic that has been carefully designed to give predictable results with as much precision as possible. Most scientists doing serious numerical computations use systems that implement the IEEE standard. Figure E.3 shows the way that the number -10 is represented according to the IEEE standard for four-byte real numbers. This representation uses 32 bits divided into three fields to represent a real value. The base, $b = 2$, is not represented explicitly; it is built into the computer's floating-point hardware.

The mantissa is represented using the sign and magnitude format. The sign of the mantissa (which is also the sign of the number) is encoded in a single bit, bit 31, in a manner similar to that used for integers: A 0 for positive numbers or a 1 for negative values. The magnitude of the mantissa is separated from the sign, as indicated in Figure E.3, and occupies the right end of the number.

After every calculation, the mantissa of the result is *normalized*; that means it is returned to the form $1.XX \ldots X$, where each X represents a one or a zero. In this form, the leading bit always is 1 and is always followed by the decimal point. A number always is normalized before it is stored in a memory variable. Since all mantissas follow this rule, the 1 and the decimal point do not need to be stored explicitly; they are built into the hardware instead. Thus the 23 bits in the mantissa of an IEEE real number are used to store the 23 X bits.

In Figure E.3, the fraciton 0.25, or 0.01 in binary, is stored in the mantissa bits and the leading 1 is recreated by the hardware when the value is brought from memory into a register.

When we add or subtract real numbers on paper, the first step is to line up the decimal points of the numbers. A computer using floating-point arithmetic must start with a corresponding operation, denormalization. To add or subtract two numbers with different exponents, the bits in the mantissa of the operand with the smaller exponent must be **denormalized**: The mantissa bits are shifted rightward and the exponent is increased by 1 for each shifted bit position. The shifting process ends when the exponent equals the exponent of the larger operand. We call this number representation *floating point* because the computer hardware automatically "floats" the mantissa to the appropriate position for each addition or subtraction operation.

The number -10 in binary IEEE format for type `float`:

	sign	exponent	mantissa
$-10.0 = -1.25 \times 2^3 =$	1	1000001 0	1. 0100000 00000000 00000000
	31	30 ... 23	22 ... 0

Figure E.3.   Binary representation of reals.

The precision of a floating-point number is the number of digits that are mathematically correct. Precision directly depends on the number of bits used to store the mantissa and the amount of error that may accumulate due to round-off during computations. Typically a calculation is performed using a few additional bits beyond the lengths of the original operands. The final result then must be rounded off to return it to the length of the operands involved. The different floating-point types use different numbers of bits in the mantissa to achieve different levels of precision. Typical limits are given in Chapter 7.

The exponent is represented in bits 23 ... 30, which are between the sign and the mantissa. Each time the mantissa is shifted right or left, the exponent is adjusted to preserve the value of the number. A shift of one bit position causes the exponent to be increased or decreased by 1. In the IEEE standard real format, the exponent is stored in *excess 127 notation*. Here, the entire 8 bits are treated as a positive value, then the excess value, 127, is subtracted from the 8-bit value to determine the true exponent. In Figure E.3, $127 + 3 = 130$, which is the value stored in the eight exponent bits. While this format may be complicated to understand, it has advantages in developing hardware to do quick comparisons and calculations with real numbers.

E.4	**Base Conversion**

Binary to decimal.   We use the table of place values in Figure E.1 when converting a number from base 2 to base 10. The process is simple and intuitive: Add the place values that correspond to the one bits in the binary representation. The result is the decimal representation (see Figure E.4).

Binary to and from hexadecimal.   When a programmer must work with numbers in binary or hexadecimal, it is useful to know how to go from one representation to the other. The binary and hexadecimal representations are closely related. Since $16 = 2^4$, each hex digit corresponds to 4 bits. Base conversion from hexadecimal to binary (or vice versa) is done by simply expanding (contracting) the number using the table in Figure E.5.

$$2^{12} \quad 2^9 \quad 2^6 \quad 2^3 \ 2^0$$

$$0001 \quad 0010 \quad 0100 \quad 1001 \ = \ 2^{12} + 2^9 + 2^6 + 2^3 + 2^0$$
$$= 4096 + 512 + 64 + 8 + 1 = 4681$$

$$0111 \quad 1011 \quad 1010 \quad 0010 \ = \ 2^{14} + 2^{13} + 2^{12} + 2^{11} + 2^9 + 2^8 + 2^7 + 2^5 + 2^1$$
$$= 16384 + 8192 + 4096 + 2048 + 512 + 256 + 128 + 32 + 2 = 31{,}650$$

Figure E.4.   Converting binary numbers to decimal.

Decimal	Hexadecimal	Binary
0	0	0000
1	1	0001
2	2	0010
3	3	0011
4	4	0100
5	5	0101
6	6	0110
7	7	0111
8	8	1000
9	9	1001
10	A	1010
11	B	1011
12	C	1100
13	D	1101
14	E	1110
15	F	1111

Binary: 0001 0010 0100 1001

Hexadecimal: 1   2   4   9

Binary: 0111 1011 1010 0010

Hexadecimal: 7   B   A   2

Figure E.5. Converting between hexadecimal and binary.

Decimal to binary. It also is possible to convert a base-10 number, N, into a base-2 number, T, using only the table of place values and a calculator or pencil and paper. First, look at the table in Figure E.1 and find the largest place value that is smaller than N. Subtract this value from N and write a 1 in the corresponding position in T. Keep the remainder for the next step in the process. Moving to the right in T, write a 1 if the next place value can be subtracted (subtract it and save the remainder) or a 0 otherwise. Continue this process, reducing the remainder of N until it becomes 0, then fill in all the remaining places of T with zeros. Figure E.6 illustrates this process of repeated subtraction for both an integer and a real value.

Hexadecimal to decimal. Converting a hexadecimal number to a decimal number is analogous to the binary-to-decimal conversion. Each digit of the hexadecimal representation must be converted to its decimal value (for example, C and F must be converted to 12 and 15, respectively). Then each digit's decimal value must be multiplied by its place value and the results added. This process is illustrated in Figure E.7.

Decimal to hexadecimal. The easiest way to convert a number from base 10 to base 16 is first to convert the number to binary, then convert the result to base 16. The job also can be done by dividing the number repeatedly by 16; the remainder on each division, when converted to a hex digit, becomes the next digit of the answer, going right to left. We do not recommend this method, however, because it is difficult to do in your head and awkward to calculate remainders on most pocket calculators.

$$10,542 = 10\ 1001\ 1000\ 1110$$
$$\underline{-8,096 = 2^{13}}$$
$$2,446$$
$$\underline{-2,048 = 2^{11}}$$
$$398$$
$$\underline{-\ 256 = 2^8}$$
$$142$$
$$\underline{-\ 128 = 2^7}$$
$$14$$
$$\underline{-\ \ \ 8 = 2^3}$$
$$6$$
$$\underline{-\ \ \ 4 = 2^2}$$
$$2$$
$$\underline{-\ \ \ 2 = 2^1}$$
$$0$$

$$630.3125 = 10\ 0111\ 0110\ .\ 0101$$
$$\underline{-512.\ \ \ \ \ = 2^9}$$
$$118.3125$$
$$\underline{-\ 64.\ \ \ \ \ = 2^6}$$
$$54.3125$$
$$\underline{-\ 32.\ \ \ \ \ = 2^5}$$
$$22.3125$$
$$\underline{-\ 16.\ \ \ \ \ = 2^4}$$
$$6.3125$$
$$\underline{-\ \ 4.\ \ \ \ \ = 2^2}$$
$$2.3125$$
$$\underline{-\ \ 2.\ \ \ \ \ = 2^1}$$
$$0.3125$$
$$\underline{-\ 0.25\ \ \ = 2^{-2}}$$
$$0.0625$$
$$\underline{-\ 0.0625 = 2^{-4}}$$
$$0$$

Figure E.6.   Converting decimal numbers to binary.

```
2A3C  =  2*16³ + 10*16² + 3*16 + 12
      =  2*4096 + 10*256 + 48 + 12 = 10,812
BFD   =  11*16² + 15*16 + 13
      =  11*256 + 240 + 13 = 2,816 + 253 = 3,069
A2.D2 =  10*16¹ + 2*16⁰ + 13*16⁻¹ + 2*16⁻²
      =  160 + 2 + .8125 + 0.0078125 = 162.8203125
```

Figure E.7.   Converting hexadecimal numbers to decimal.

E.5   Self-Test Exercises

1. What base-10 number equals the two's complement binary value 11010110 ?

2. Do the following addition in binary two's complement: $01110110 + 10001001 = ?$

3. Express 00110110_2 in bases 10 and 16.

4. Express 5174_{10} in binary and hexadecimal.

5. What is the IEEE binary 4-byte floating-point representation of 10.125?

6. Use binary arithmetic to multiply 00010110_2 by 4_{10}, then express the answer in bases 16 and 10.

7. How many times would you need to divide 100110_2 by 2_{10} to get the quotient 1?

APPENDIX
F

The `tools` *Library*

T he `tools` library is a collection of definitions, designed to ease a begin-
tner's entry into C programming and to make the differences between C
implementations less bothersome to those who work in a multisystem environment.

The library consists of a header file, `tools.h`, and a source code file,
`tools.c`. Inside these files are other `#include` commands (see Figure F.1),
`#define` commands and `typedef` declarations (see Figure F.2), and definitions
of several functions. These things are described in this appendix. In addition, the
files (and all the program examples in the text) are available in electronic form
for use by purchasers of this text.

F.1   Using the `tools` Library in a Program

The right way to use a local library is to `#include "tools.h"` at the top of each
program and include `tools.c` as one code module in a multimodule project. Each
module then is compiled separately and the resulting object files linked together to
make an executable application. All modern development environments provide
some way to build and manage projects. Unlike the C language, however, these
facilities are not standardized and can be complicated to use.

Name	Library Functions, Types, and Constants Used
`stdio.h`	`printf()`, `scanf()`, `gets()`, `puts()`, and others
`stdlib.h`	`rand()`, `srand()`, `abs()`, `malloc()`, and others
`math.h`	`fabs()`, `sqrt()`, `pow()`, `exp()`, `sin()`, `cos()`, and others
`string.h`	`strcmp()`, `strcpy()`, `strlen()`, and others
`time.h`	`time_t`, `time()`, `ctime()`, and others
`ctype.h`	`toupper()`, `tolower()`, `isspace()`, `isdigit()`, `isalpha()`, and others
`limits.h`	`INT_MAX`, `LONG_MIN`, and others
`float.h`	`DOUBLE_MAX` and others
`stdarg.h`	For functions with a variable # of arguments (not covered here)
`???.h`	A system-dependent header file for screen I/O for some systems

Figure F.1.   Files included by `tools.h` **and** `tools.c`.

It also is possible (but not advisable) to use the **tools** library by including **tools.c** at the top of a program. Beginners might do this initially, while they are becoming familiar with their systems and the C language. When using the tools this way, the source code for **tools.c** and the program will be compiled as a single unit (they should be in the same file directory). This is less efficient than the multimodule approach. The examples in this book include **tools.h** rather than **tools.c**; learn how to make this work on your system as soon as possible.

Name	Purpose
NAME	Substitute your own name
Type of system	Choose one of the systems listed in Section F.2 and put the name of that system in the **#define** command on the first noncomment line of **tools.h**
CLASS	Substitute your information.
ENATURAL	2.7182818284590451
GRAVITY	9.80665
PI	3.1415927
PRN	Symbolic name for the printer stream in many systems.
`bool`	Enumerated type consisting of **false** and **true**.
`string`	Type definition, synonym for **char***
`stream`	Type definition, synonym for **FILE***

Figure F.2.   Constants and types defined in `tools.h`.

F.1.1 Organizing a Project

On any system, the project management program must be able to locate all the files that constitute the project. This could be done in many ways; the way we present here is the simplest (but not the most economical of space) and will work on all systems. As you try these techniques for the first time, remember that it is important to do the steps in order. Otherwise, files are likely to be stored in the wrong places or be connected incorrectly to each other.

Disk directories.   When you begin a new course (this one or any other) for which you will use the computer, create a directory on your disk for use with that course. In this discussion, we call the course directory `cs110`, as illustrated in Figure F.3.

Next, create a subdirectory to hold any files that accompany the course text and any given to you by the instructor. In the diagram, we call this directory `appliedc`. Copy the course files into this directory.

For each programming assignment, create another subdirectory in the course directory; all files relevant to the assignment will be stored here. Move or copy the two `tools` library files into this directory. If you will be creating a new program by modifying an old one, copy that program into your new directory also. Now you are ready to begin working on the new program.

Personalization.   The `banner()` function prints a personalized output heading. Before you can use it, you must modify the `#define` commands on the second and third noncomment lines of the file `tools.h`:

```
#define NAME    "Patience S. Goodenough"
#define CLASS   "CS 110"
```

Replace `"Patience S. Goodenough"` and `"CS 110"` by your own name and course number, in double quotes.

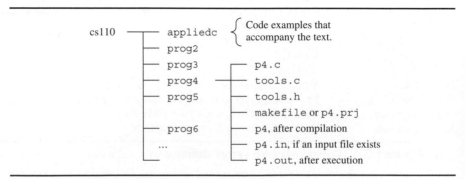

Figure F.3.   Disk directory structure.

F.1.2   Using the `tools` with Visual C++

To start a new program in Visual C++ or a similar integrated programming environment, you must first invoke (click on the icon for) the product you will use. When it begins execution, use the directory commands to navigate into the project directory.

If you are starting with an existing file, find it in the directory listing and open it. If starting from scratch, find the file menu and select the option for creating a new file. Either way, the text editor will be invoked and give you either the existing program or a blank screen to type on.

Before you go further, find the Save As option on the file menu and save the file under a new name. Choose one that is appropriate: either one like `lab4.c` or one that relates to the content of your program, like `velocity.c`. Be sure that the file name ends in `.c`, not `.cpp`. The letters after the dot determine which compiler will be used to translate your program. You want a C compiler, not a C++ compiler, which has slightly different rules and produces less helpful error comments. The first time you save a file, you must give it a name. After that, when you save it again, it will be stored under the same name.

Now you can type the new program into the editor window. Save the file frequently as you work on it. Some systems automatically will keep one backup copy of each file; this is very helpful in the event of an accident. If the system offers you a choice, make a backup.

Once you have created a source file, you can create a project. With the source file still showing in the editor window, find the project menu and select the option for a new project. In a typical system, you will be asked to supply a name for it, select the type of project to create, and designate the files that should be part of it. Note that this will be the third name for the assignment: the directory has a name, the source code file has a name that ends in `.c`, and the project must have a name. To avoid confusion, these names should be related but not identical.

The selection of a project type is highly nonstandard; select the simplest kind of project that is supported. You may need to ask the local expert what type this is. Last, you must designate the files that are parts of the project. Select `tools.c` and your own program file; say, `p4.c` as in the illustration. Do not select `tools.h` as a file to compile. When finished, close the project and the system will check the dependencies and create a project file for you.

In various systems, a project file has a name ending in `.prj` or `.mak`. To compile and link, go back to the project menu and select an option, Make or Build. (If you select Compile, it will compile but not link.) If compilation and linking are both successful, then select the Run option and begin testing the program.

F.1.3   Using the `tools` with UNIX

Every UNIX system has a makefile facility that serves the same purpose as a project facility on a Windows-based system and requires more or less the same information. Modern make facilities can be elaborate and heavily automated. The makefile presented in Figure F.4 is a "plain vanilla" version: It is simple but serves the purpose.

The simple makefile consists of pairs of lines. The first line of each pair names a target file (on the left) and lists the other files on which it depends. All these must exist and be up to date to create the target. The dependency lists are used to determine what compilation and linking steps need to be done. If the programmer gives the command to "make" a target that already exists, its creation time will be compared to the times of the files on which it depends. If the target is a newer file, no work needs to be done. If not, it will be created or re-created using the command given in the second line. This strategy is applied recursively, if one of the supporting files does not exist or is not up to date, it will be made; and so forth.

The second line of each pair is a system command that, when run, will make the target file. This line must begin with a **tab** character, denoted here by **<tab>**.

In this example, we make an executable program named **prog4**. To generate a differently named program, simply substitute another name for **prog4** throughout the file.

Notes on Figure F.4: A makefile for the tools **library.**   In this example, we use the Free Software Foundation C compiler, **gcc**. Other systems may use a different compiler.

- *First box: linking object files to make an executable application.*

  1. The target here is an executable application, **prog4**, which depends on the object files **p4.o** and **tools.o**. If one of these does not exist, or its creation time is less recent than the files on which it depends, the make facility will find the appropriate lines for that target and it will be made before proceeding to make **prog4**.
  2. The second line here is a command to make the target by linking the standard libraries with the object files listed on the right. Every

```
prog4:   p4.o tools.o
<tab>    gcc -o prog4 p4.o tools.o
```

```
p4.o:   tools.h p4.c
<tab>    gcc -c -Wall p4.c
```

```
tools.o:   tools.h tools.c
<tab>    gcc -c tools.c
```

Figure F.4.   A makefile for the tools **library.**

compiler automatically links the object files to some set of standard library routines. Error messages at this stage that refer to missing functions mean we may need to explicitly write a system library name on the end of the linking command.

- *Second box: compiling a source file to make an object file.*

  1. An object file is dependent on its C source file as well as any header files it may include. The first line here declares that **p4.o** depends on **p4.c** and **tools.h**.
  2. To generate an object file, the **-c** (compile) option is specified, followed by any other desired compiler options. The source file is named on the end of the line. The name of the **.o** file is generated from the name of the source file by replacing **.c** with **.o**.
  3. The **-Wall** compiler option indicates that all possible warnings about incorrect program syntax should be generated, even those that would not stop the translation process, such as minor mismatches of argument and parameter types.

- *Third box: a simpler compile statement.*

  1. The same format is used to compile the **tools.c** file. Because the **tools** library has been tested and debugged, there should be no errors in it. Therefore, we need not specify an option like **-Wall** to find them.
  2. There is no need to change the two lines concerning **tools** when compiling another program.

F.2   Portability Command

In professional practice, programmers avoid using nonstandardized commands as much as possible and segregate them from the rest of the program whenever they must be used. For example, the C standard does not include a function to clear the user's video screen. However, clearing the screen is a simple and essential way to make the output neat and easy to read. Therefore, many C compilers support some kind of a clear-screen command. Unfortunately, because these are not standardized, they differ from one system to the next. This makes any program that uses a compiler's local clear-screen command nonportable: It cannot be compiled and run on a different system.

Increasing ease of use while maintaining portability is one purpose of the **tools** library. It contains multiple versions of a few nonstandard functions and the code to select the correct version for the local system. The selection code is somewhat confusing but quite easy to use. The programmer does not need to understand how it works to use it effectively.

For instance, to use the **banner()** function and the other nonstandardized tools, first configure the **tools.h** file for the local system. To do this, find the **#define** command near the beginning of **tools.h** that names the operating system being used and modify that line so that it names the local system. The **tools** library contains code that supports these systems:

```
#define VISUAL      /* Use for Visual C++. */
#define BORLAND     /* Use for Borland or Turbo C or C++. */
#define UNIX        /* Use for a UNIX system. */
```

The correct code for the system will be automatically selected and included when you compile the tools. If your system is not listed here, the **tools.h** and **tools.c** files must be extended by someone who understands systems programming and your installation before you can use **clearscreen()** or other nonstandardized tools. The other functions in **tools.c** rely only on standard facilities and should work on any standard ISO C system.

F.3   Functions Declared in tools.h and Defined in tools.c

The functions in the **tools** library are listed here alphabetically. A more complete description of each is given in one of the following sections. In addition, if a tool was used in the text, the section number in which it was first used or discussed is given.

- `void banner( void )`: Sections 5.2, F.4.
- `void bye( void )`: Sections 5.2, F.4.
- `void cleanline( stream sin )`: Sections 15.5.4, F.4.1.
- `void clean_and_log( stream sin, stream sout )`: Sections 15.5.4, F.4.1.
- `void clearscreen( void )`: Section F.4.
- `void delay( int seconds )`: Sections 6.2.7, F.4.
- `int evenly( int range )`: Section F.6.
- `void fatal( string format, ... )`: Sections 5.2, F.4.1.
- `void fbanner( stream sout )`: Section F.4.
- `void hold( void )`: Section F.4.
- `char menu_c(string title, int n, const string menu[])`: Sections 13.4.5, F.7.
- `int menu_i(string title, int n, const string menu[])`: Sections 13.4.5, F.7.
- `string oclock( char hour[] )`: Sections 13.3.1, F.5.
- `double randy( void )`: Sections 14.4.3, F.6.
- `int round( double d )`: Sections 7.5.2, F.6.
- `void say( string format, ... )`: Sections 15.1.1, F.4.

- `int strequal( string s1, string s2 )`: Sections 13.3, F.7.
- `int strnequal( string s1, string s2, int n )`: Section F.7.
- `string today( char date[] )`: Sections 13.3.1, F.5.
- `void when( char date[], char hour[] )`: Sections 13.3.1, F.5.

F.4   Process and Stream Management

The `clearscreen()` **function.**   This is a system-dependent function with three different definitions (see Figure F.5). Its purpose is to clear the video screen and position the cursor at the upper left corner. The UNIX definition sends a formfeed character to the stream. On some systems, this is interpreted as a command to clear the screen; on others, it may print one character or one line of whitespace. The Visual C++ definition does nothing because there seems to be no simple way to clear the screen on this system. For Borland C, we include the Borland console I/O header file and call the `clrscr()` function in it. The Code Warrior compiler seems to work properly using the UNIX options.

The `banner()` **and** `fbanner()` **functions.**   The `banner()` function displays the programmer's personal heading on the standard output stream. It is actually implemented by a call on `fbanner()`, as shown in Figure F.6, which can be used to print the banner on any output stream. Both functions read the current date and time from the system clock and print a heading that consists of a pair of dashed lines enclosing the programmer's name, class, and the date and time at which the program was executed.

The definition of the `clearscreen()` function is system dependent.

Definition for UNIX:

```
void clearscreen( void ) { fprintf( stderr, "\f" ); }
```

Definition for Visual C++:

```
void clearscreen( void ) { }
```

Definition for Borland C:

```
#include <conio.h>
void clearscreen( void ) { clrscr(); }
```

Figure F.5.   Clearing the screen.

These functions print an output banner to **stdout** or to a selected stream:

```
void banner( void ){ fbanner( stdout ); }
/* ----------------------------------------------------------- */
void fbanner( stream sout )
{
  char date[16], time[9];
  when( date, time );
  fprintf( sout, "\n ----------------------------------------------------------" );
  fprintf( sout, "\n\t %s \n\t %s \n\t %s %s\n", NAME, CLASS, date, time );
  fprintf( sout, " ----------------------------------------------------------\n" );
}
```

Figure F.6.   The `banner()` **and** `fbanner()` **functions.**

The `hold()` **function.**   Programs that display information to the screen often produce so much output so fast that the user has no time to inspect it all. Screens full of words fly past, and only the last screenful sits still to be read. To address this problem, many programs alternate between displaying output and holding the screen. A signal from the user releases the hold and returns the program to its output phase. The simplest strategy for this, tell the user to hit Enter and call `getchar()` to receive the signal, will only work if the input stream is empty.

Unfortunately, the **stdin** stream often contains the newline character that terminated the prior line of input. If so, a single call on `getchar()` will read the pending newline character and continue without waiting. Making two calls on `getchar()` sometimes works; the first `getchar()` reads the pending newline and the second one waits for the user to hit the Enter key. However, if unread characters or extra whitespace are at the end of the previous line, this does not work either. When writing a library function, it is important that it *always* work. The closest we can come with simple code is to ask the user to enter some specific character and hit the Enter key. The program then reads characters until the designated character occurs, then reads one more to clear out the newline. We implement this strategy in `hold()` using a ' . ' that (unlike newlines and spaces) is visible and unlikely to be left over from a previous line of input.

When called, `hold()` reads characters from **stdin** until a ' . ' is encountered. During the waiting period, nothing else happens. The **while** loop that reads and inspects the input is called a *tight loop* (it has no body); all the work of the loop is done by the loop test (see Figure F.7). The **(void)** cast in the last line of `hold()` deserves some explanation. We use `hold()` to put the program into a blocked state. The user types a period and hits Enter to release it and let execution continue. In this situation, hitting Enter is important, not the input character itself, so we discard this character without storing it or using it. The **(void)** cast tells the compiler that we intend to discard the character. Without

The `while` loop has no body; all action is accomplished by the loop test. This function is called by `fatal()` and one version of `bye()`.

```
void hold( void )
{
    fputs( "\n\n\a Press . and \"Enter\" to continue", stderr );
    while (getchar() != '.');      /* tight loop finds the period */
    (void)getchar();               /* read final newline */
}
```

Figure F.7.   The `hold()` **function uses** `stderr`.

this cast, some compilers give an error warning such as `function call has no effect`, which is not true or relevant in this context.

The `delay()` **function.**   This function (first shown in Figure 6.20) suspends activity by entering a loop that reads the clock continually until the specified number of seconds has elapsed. It then returns and the program resumes processing. This function differs from `hold()` in that `delay()` waits for a specific number of seconds to pass, while `hold()` waits indefinitely for the user's response.

The `bye()` **function.**   The `bye()` function displays a closing message and, depending on the system in use, may wait for user input to be entered. On such systems, the function should not be used in programs that have no other keyboard input.

C translators normally run within an environment called a C shell. The shell is set up by each user to use a particular text editor and know where to locate the executable code for the compiler, the linker, and the system libraries. The shell uses constants to describe the physical limits of the hardware and other essentials. A programmer enters code, edits, compiles, links, and runs the program within this shell.

Some C shells (older DOS versions of Turbo and Borland C, for example) provide convenient menu-driven windowing environments. The system menu and the program's source code are displayed in one window, while the program's output shows in a different window. Only one of these windows is active and visible at any time. When the user gives the command to run the program, the source code window disappears and the output window fills the screen. As execution proceeds, prompts, input, and output appear in this window. However, when the last line of output is printed and the program terminates, the output window instantly disappears, before the user has had a chance to look at the output. This is annoying to the experienced user and greatly confusing to the beginner. It happens because the program returns control to the C shell and the shell switches the display to the window containing the main menu. In such systems, the only way to keep the output showing on the screen is to put the program into a "wait" state after the last output is displayed but before returning to the system.

In many other systems, this problem does not arise. For this reason, two versions of the **bye()** function are in the **tools** library; both versions are shown in Figure F.8. The first version of **bye()** is appropriate for systems in which there is no need to hold the output on the monitor screen. It simply prints a message and quits. The second version of **bye()** is appropriate for those systems in which the screen disappears immediately from sight unless the system is put into a wait state; so it prints a message and calls **hold()**. The correct version for your system is selected by writing a **#define** command at the top of **tools.h**, which identifies your system.

The say() **function.**   The **say()** function (see Figure F.9) effectively calls **fprintf()** to display a message on the **stderr** stream. The arguments should be a format string and a list of fields to print (just like **printf()**). This function actually calls **vfprintf(stderr, …)**, passing on the given format and output list. At the end of the output, **say()** rings the attention bell and displays a newline character (so the programmer need not include \n and \a in the message).

Error messages and user information should be displayed on **stderr** (rather than **stdout**) because **stderr** usually is directed to the user's console even when **stdout** is redirected. The **fatal()** and **say()** functions make it convenient to use **stderr**. These two functions also use one of the most advanced and obscure aspects of C, the **stdarg** facility for writing functions with variable-length parameter lists. Such functions act like **printf()**; they have one or more required parameters, followed by a series of optional parameters. One of the

---

The first version of **bye()** is used for command-line systems and windowing systems with multiple, simultaneous windows.

```
void bye( void )
{
    fputs( "\n\n Normal termination.\n", stderr );
}
```

The second version of **bye()** is used in systems that do not wait for the user to look at the output screen before returning to the editing environment.

```
void bye( void )
{
    fprintf( stderr, "\n\n Normal termination." );
    hold();
}
```

Figure F.8.   The bye() **function uses** stderr.

The **say()** function is used for displaying messages of all sorts on the **stderr** stream. The **fatal()** function is used after an error has been detected and further progress is impossible.

```
void say( string format, … )
{
    va_list vargs;               /* optional arguments */

    va_start( vargs, format );
    vfprintf( stderr, format, vargs );
    fprintf( stderr, "\a\a\n" );
}
/* ----------------------------------------------------- */
void fatal(string format, … )
{
    va_list vargs;               /* optional arguments */

    va_start( vargs, format );
    vfprintf( stderr, format, vargs );
    fprintf( stderr, "\a\a\n" );
    hold();
    exit( 1 );
}
```

Figure F.9.   The say() and fatal() functions.

required parameters must say how many optional ones should be present on any given call. Unfortunately, explaining how this facility works clearly is beyond the scope of this text. The **say()** and **fatal()** functions use this mechanism in only a simple way, and their source code is included here for those who are curious.

F.4.1 Error-Handling Functions

The fatal() function.   The **fatal()** function (see Figure F.9) provides a convenient and concise way for the programmer to handle errors when recovery is impossible. The arguments are a format and an output list, as for **say()**. First, **fatal()** calls **vfprintf()** to display the specified message on the **stderr** stream and rings a bell to attract the user's attention, just as **say()** does. Then it calls **hold()** to block the process and hold the screen. When released by user input, **fatal()** aborts the program by calling **exit(1)**. This is the standard C function used to end operation of a program gracefully in an emergency situation. It flushes all output buffers, closes all files, and returns an integer code (in this case, 1, which signifies abnormal termination) to the operating system.

This function is used for recovering from file input errors. In addition to flushing the current input line, it echoes the flushed characters to the designated output stream.

```
void clean_and_log( stream sin, stream sout )
{
    char ch;
    do {
        ch = fgetc( sin );                  /* Read next character */
        fputc( ch, sout );                  /* Echo to logging stream */
    } while (!feof( sin ) && ch != '\n');   /* Quit at first newline */
}
```

p612

Figure F.10.   The `clean_and_log()` **function.**

p623

The `cleanline()` **function.**   The `cleanline()` function (see Figure 15.12) is used to recover from an input error. It reads and discards characters from the input stream **sin** up to and including the next newline character.

The `clean_and_log()` **function.**   The `clean_and_log()` function (see Figure F.10) also is used for recovering from file input errors. Like `cleanline()`, it flushes the rest of the current input line. In addition, it echoes the flushed characters to the designated output stream, which can be **stderr** or a user-defined stream attached to a log file.

| F.5 | **Time and Date Functions** |

The standard C library provides a set of date and time functions that allow a program to read the computer's on-line clock[1] and format the information in a useable fashion. The header file for this library is **time.h**. However, the library functions are not easy to use or to understand. Three functions in **tools.c**, `today()`, `oclock()`, and `when()`, call the library functions and extract the date and time information. The `today()` function forgets about the time and extracts the date, the `oclock()` function forgets about the date and extracts the time, and `when()` returns both the date and the time. If both time and date are needed, the `when()` function is more efficient than calling the other two separately.

The `today()` **function.**   The `today()` function (see Figure F.11) reads the system clock at execution time and returns the date through the parameter list and also returns a pointer to the date as the function's return value. The date will be stored in the form **"Sun Mar 12 2000"**. The argument must be a character

---

[1] Some older, smaller computers have no permanent clock that keeps track of real time. On such a computer, the **time()** function cannot be used.

```
#include <time.h>
string today( char date[] )
{
    time_t now;                         /* Integer encoding of date and time. */
    string nowstring;                   /* Date and time in a readable form. */

    now = time( NULL );                 /* Get date and time from the system. */
    nowstring = ctime( &now );          /* Convert to string form. */
    strncpy( date, nowstring, 10 );     /* Extract day, month, date. */
    strncpy( &date[10], &nowstring[19], 5 );   /* Extract and copy year. */
    date[15] = '\0';                    /* Put null char on end. */
    return date;
}
```

Figure F.11.   The today() function: reading the system clock.

array that is 16 or more characters long; the date will be copied into this array. A pointer to the date is returned, making it convenient to use **printf()** with a **%s** format to print the date.

The oclock() function.   The o'clock() function (see Figure F.12) reads the system clock and returns the current time through the parameter list and as the function's return value. The argument should be a pointer to a character array of length 9 or more. The time will be given in the 24-hour system in the form hours:minutes:seconds, thus: **"21:35:00"**.

The when() function.   The when() function (see Figure F.13) reads the system clock and returns the current date and time through the parameter list. The arguments should be pointers to character arrays of lengths 16 and 9, respectively. The date will be given in the form **"Sun Mar 12 2000"** and the time in the form hours:minutes:seconds on the 24-hour system: **"21:35:00"**. The statements of this function are simply a merging of those in **today()** and **oclock()**.

```
#include <time.h>
string oclock( char hour[] )
{
    time_t now;                         /* Integer encoding of the date and time. */
    string nowstring;                   /* Date and time in a readable form. */

    now = time( NULL );                 /* Get date and time from the system. */
    nowstring = ctime( &now );          /* Convert to string form. */
    strncpy( hour, &nowstring[11], 8 );    /* Extract hour:minutes:seconds. */
    hour[8] = '\0';                     /* Add the string terminator. */
    return hour;
}
```

Figure F.12.   The oclock() function.

```
#include <time.h>
void when( char date[], char hour[] )
{
    time_t now;                     /* Integer encoding of date and time. */
    string nowstring;               /* Date and time in a readable form. */

    now = time( NULL );             /* Get date and time from the system. */
    nowstring = ctime( &now );      /* Convert to string form. */
    strncpy( date, nowstring, 10 );               /* Extract day, month, date. */
    strncpy( &date[10], &nowstring[19], 5 );    /* Extract and copy year. */
    date[15] = '\0';                /* Put null char on end. */
    strncpy( hour, &nowstring[11], 8 );     /* Extract hour:minutes:seconds. */
    hour[8] = '\0';                 /* Add the string terminator. */
}
```

Figure F.13.   **The** when() **function.**

F.6   Numeric Functions

p250 **The** round() **function.**   The round() function (first shown in Figure 7.20) rounds a real number to the nearest integer.

p583 **The** randy() **function.**   The randy() function (first shown in Section 14.4.3) returns a random real number, evenly distributed between the values 0.0 and 1.0. The random number generator must be initialized by calling **srand()** before the first call on **randy()**.

The evenly() **function.**   The evenly() function (see Figure F.14) takes one integer parameter, **range**, and returns a random integer evenly distributed over the values 0…(range-1). The random number generator must be initialized by calling **srand()** before the first call on **evenly()**.

```
int evenly( int range )
{
    int num;                                    /* Random value we generate.  */
    int limit;          /* Largest representable even multiple of range. */

    limit = RAND_MAX - RAND_MAX % range;
    do { num = rand(); }                        /* Keep picking a number... */
    while (num >= limit);        /* until you get a num less than limit. */
    return num % range;                         /* Scale num to target range. */
}
```

Figure F.14.   **The** evenly() **function.**

| **F.7** | **Strings and Menus** |

String comparisons.   In addition to the functions in the standard `string` library, there are two `tools` for comparing strings. These are `strequal()` and `strnequal()`. These actually are not functions; they are macros[2] defined in terms of `strcmp()` and `strncmp()` as follows:

```
#define strequal(a,b)      !strcmp(a,b)
#define strnequal(a,b,n)   !strncmp(a,b,n)
```

In `strequal()`, the two argument strings are compared letter by letter until an inequality or the end of one string occurs. The result is `true` if all pairs of characters, including the null terminators, are equal; `false`, otherwise. The use of `strequal()` was introduced in Figure 13.24.

The operation of `strnequal()` is similar, except that the comparison loop stops after **n** character pairs, if not sooner. The result is `true` if all pairs compared are equal; `false`, otherwise.

The `menu_c()` **function.**   Two menu-handling tools are defined in this library: `menu_c()` is used for alphabetic codes and `menu_i()` for numeric selections. The `menu_c()` function is simpler and is explained in Figure 13.23. It prompts for and returns a character menu choice without doing any choice validation.

The `menu_i()` **function.**   The use of `menu_i()` (see Figure F.15) was introduced in Figure 13.26; the source code now can be given and explained. This function is a little more complex than `menu_c()` because validation is possible with an integer selection as well as necessary before the selection can be used as a subscript. Moreover, more can go wrong with integer input. When we use `getchar()` or `scanf()` with a `%c` format specifier, any keystroke is acceptable input; a read error can happen but only because of a hardware malfunction. In contrast, when we use `scanf()` with a `%i` specifier, any keystroke other than a numeral or whitespace character will cause an input error, and that error must be detected and handled before progress can resume. Error detection and handling code is necessary but it is a distraction from the logic of an application. This is the kind of task better dealt with by a library function, where possible.

The `menu_i()` function consists of an outer data validation loop and an inner counting loop that displays the menu items and their numeric labels. The validation loop takes care of input error detection and recovery and also ensures that the user's selection is within the range of valid menu choices.

---

[2]The definition and use of macros is beyond the scope of this text.

This function displays a menu and reads the user's numeric menu choice. It returns to the calling program after the user enters a valid choice.

```
int menu_i( string title, int n, const string menu[] )
{
    int ok, k, choice;
    printf( "\n%s\n\n", title );

    for (;;) {                        /* Data input and validation loop */
        for (k = 0; k < n; ++k)   printf( "\t %i.    %s\n", k, menu[k] );
        printf( "\n Enter number of desired item: " );
        ok = scanf( "%i", &choice );
        if (ok == 1 && 0 <= choice && choice < n) break;
        cleanline( stdin );
        puts( "\n Illegal choice or input error; try again.\n" );
    }

    return choice;
}
```

Figure F.15.   The `menu_i()` **function.**

Notes on Figure F.15: The `menu_i()` function.

- *Outer box: Outer loop, an infinite* `for` *loop.*

  1. This is a data validation loop. It displays the menu, prompts for and reads a selection, and checks for errors.
  2. The first inner box is the counting loop. This **for** loop, like that in `menu_c()`, displays the strings from the menu array. With `menu_c()`, the alphabetic menu codes must be incorporated into the strings in the menu array. With numeric codes, however, we can use the loop counter as the code. Therefore, the **printf()** call displays **k** as the code for `menu[k]`.
  3. The next two lines prompt the user for a choice and read that choice.
  4. The second inner box is the loop exit. The **if...break** statement tests whether the user's choice is numeric and whether the number is between **0** and **n-1**. If so, control leaves the loop. If there was a read error or the user entered a number that was negative or too large, control passes to the lower part of the loop.
  5. The last part of the loop flushes anything left on the input line and prints an error comment before returning to the top of the loop to give the user another chance.

APPENDIX
G

The Standard C Environment

T his appendix contains a list of standard ISO C symbols, `#include` files, and libraries. The libraries that have been used in this text are described by listing prototypes for all functions in the library. Each function is described briefly if it was used in this text or is likely to be useful to a student in the first two years of study. Alternative and traditional functions have not been listed. Readers who need more detailed information about the libraries should consult a standard reference book or the relevant UNIX manual page.

G.1   Built-in Facilities

These symbols are macros that are identified at compile time and replaced by current information, as indicated. If included in a source file, the relevant information will be inserted into that file.

- `__DATE__` is the date on which the program was compiled.
- `__FILE__` is the name of the source file.
- `__LINE__` is the current line number in the source file.

- **`__STDC__`** is defined if the implementation conforms to the ISO C standard.
- **`__TIME__`** is the time at which the program was compiled and should remain constant throughout the compilation.

G.2 Standard Files of Constants

We list the standard **`#include`** files that define the properties of numbers on the local system.

`limits.h`. Defines the maximum and minimum values in each of the standard integer types, as implemented on the local system. The constants defined are

- Number of bits in a character: **`CHAR_BIT`**.
- Type character: **`CHAR_MAX`**, **`CHAR_MIN`**.
- Signed and unsigned characters: **`SCHAR_MAX`**, **`SCHAR_MIN`**, **`UCHAR_MAX`**.
- Signed and unsigned short integers: **`SHRT_MAX`**, **`SHRT_MIN`**, **`USHRT_MAX`**.
- Signed and unsigned integers: **`INT_MAX`**, **`INT_MIN`**, **`UINT_MAX`**.
- Signed and unsigned long integers: **`LONG_MAX`**, **`LONG_MIN`**, **`ULONG_MAX`**.

`float.h`. Defines the properties of each of the standard floating-point types, as implemented on the local system. The constants defined are

- The value of the radix: **`FLT_RADIX`**.
- Rounding mode: **`FLT_ROUNDS`**.
- Minimum x such that $1.0 + x \neq x$: **`FLT_EPSILON`**, **`DBL_EPSILON`**, **`LDBL_EPSILON`**.
- Decimal digits of precision: **`FLT_DIG`**, **`DBL_DIG`**, **`LDBL_DIG`**.
- Number of radix digits in the mantissa: **`FLT_MANT_DIG`**, **`DBL_MANT_DIG`**, **`LDBL_MANT_DIG`**.
- Minimum normalized positive number: **`FLT_MIN`**, **`DBL_MIN`**, **`LDBL_MIN`**.
- Minimum negative exponent for a normalized number: **`FLT_MIN_EXP`**, **`DBL_MIN_EXP`**, **`LDBL_MIN_EXP`**.
- Minimum power of 10 in the range of normalized numbers: **`FLT_MIN_10_EXP`**, **`DBL_MIN_10_EXP`**, **`LDBL_MIN_10_EXP`**.
- Maximum representable finite number: **`FLT_MAX`**, **`DBL_MAX`**, **`LDBL_MAX`**.
- Maximum exponent for representable finite numbers: **`FLT_MAX_EXP`**, **`DBL_MAX_EXP`**, **`LDBL_MAX_EXP`**.
- Maximum power of 10 for representable finite numbers: **`FLT_MAX_10_EXP`**, **`DBL_MAX_10_EXP`**, **`LDBL_MAX_10_EXP`**.

IEEE floating-point standard. The minimum values of the C constants that conform to the IEEE standard are listed in Figure G.1.

Name	FLT_constant value	DBL_constant value
RADIX	2	
EPSILON	1.19209290E−07F	2.2204460492503131E−16
DIG	6	15
MANT_DIG	24	53
MIN	1.17549435E−38F	2.2250738585072014E−308
MIN_EXP	−125	−1021
MIN_10_EXP	−37	−307
MAX	3.40282347E+38F	1.7976931348623157E+308
MAX_EXP	128	1024
MAX_10_EXP	38	308

Figure G.1.   Minimum values.

G.3   The Standard Libraries and `main()`

G.3.1   The Function `main()`

The `main()` function is special in two ways. First, every C program must have a function named `main()`, and that is where execution begins. A portion of a program may be compiled without a `main()` function, but linking will fail unless some other module does contain `main()`.

The other unique property of `main()` is that it has two official prototypes and is frequently used with others. The two standardized prototypes are:

- `int main( void );`
- `int main( int argc, char* argv[] );`

The `int` return value is intended to return a status code to the system and is needed for interprocess communication in complex applications. However, it is irrelevant for a simple program. In this case, nonstandard variants, such as `void main( void )`, can be used and will work properly. Having no return values works because most systems do not rely on a status code being returned, and simple programs have no meaningful status to report.

G.3.2   Characters and Conversions

Header file.   `<ctype.h>`.

Functions.

- `int isalnum( int ch );`
  Returns `true` if the value of `ch` is a digit (0–9) or an alphabetic character (A–Z or a–z). Returns `false` otherwise.

- `int isalpha( int ch );`
  Returns **true** if the value of **ch** is an alphabetic character (A–Z or a–z). Returns **false** otherwise.
- `int islower( int ch );`
  Returns **true** if the value of **ch** is a lower-case alphabetic character (a–z). Returns **false** otherwise.
- `int isupper( int ch );`
  Returns **true** if the value of **ch** is an upper-case alphabetic character (A–Z). Returns **false** otherwise.
- `int isdigit( int ch );`
  Returns **true** if the value of **ch** is a digit (0–9). Returns **false** otherwise.
- `int isxdigit( int ch );`
  Returns **true** if the value of **ch** is a hexadecimal digit (0–9, a–f, or A–F). Returns **false** otherwise.
- `int iscntrl( int ch );`
  Returns **true** if the value of **ch** is a control character (ASCII codes 0–31 and 127). Returns **false** otherwise. The complementary function for a standard ASCII implementation is `isprint()`.
- `int isprint( int ch );`
  Returns **true** if the value of **ch** is an ASCII character that is not a control character (32–126). Returns **false** otherwise.
- `int isgraph( int ch );`
  Returns **true** if the value of **ch** is a printing character other than space (33–126). Returns **false** otherwise.
- `int isspace( int ch );`
  Returns **true** if the value of **ch** is a whitespace character (horizontal tab, carriage return, newline, vertical tab, formfeed, or space). Returns **false** otherwise.
- `int ispunct( int ch );`
  Returns **true** if the value of **ch** is a printing character but not space or alphanumeric. Returns **false** otherwise.
- `int tolower( int ch );`
  If the value of **ch** is an upper-case character, returns that character converted to lower-case (a–z). Returns the letter unchanged otherwise.
- `int toupper( int ch );`
  If the value of **ch** is a lower-case character, returns that character converted to upper-case (A–Z). Returns the letter unchanged otherwise.

G.3.3 Mathematics

Header file. `<math.h>`.

Constant. `HUGE_VAL` is the largest representable floating-point value.

Trigonometric functions.   These functions all work in units of radians:

- `double sin( double );`
  `double cos( double );`
  `double tan( double );`
  These are the mathematical functions sine, cosine, and tangent.
- `double asin( double );`
  `double acos( double );`
  These functions compute the principal values of the mathematical arc sine and arc cosine functions.
- `double atan( double x );`
  `double atan2( double y, double x );`
  The `atan()` function computes the principal value of the arc tangent of `x`, while `atan2()` computes the principal value of the arc tangent of `y/x`.
- `double sinh( double );`
  `double cosh( double );`
  `double tanh( double );`
  These are the hyperbolic sine, cosine, and tangent functions.

Logarithms and powers.

- `double exp( double x );`
  Computes the exponential function, e^x, where e is the base of the natural logarithms.
- `double log( double x );`
  `double log10( double x );`
  These are the natural logarithm and base-10 logarithm of x.
- `double pow( double x, double y );`
  Computes x^y. It is an error if x is negative and y is not an exact integer or if x is 0 and y is negative or 0.
- `double sqrt( double x );`
  Computes the nonnegative square root of x. It is an error if x is negative.

Manipulating number representations.

- `double ceil( double d );`
  The smallest integral value greater than or equal to `d`.
- `double floor( double d );`
  The largest integral value less than or equal to `d`.
- `double fabs( double d );`
  The absolute value of `d`. Note: `abs()` is defined in `<stdlib.h>`.
- `double fmod( double x, double y );`
  The answer, `f`, is less than `y`, has the same sign as `x`, and `f+y*k` approximately equals `x` for some integer `k`. It may return 0 or be a run-time error if `y` is 0.

- `double frexp( double x, int* nptr );`
  Splits a nonzero x into a fractional part, f, and an exponent, n, such that $|f|$ is between 0.5 and 1.0 and $x = f \times 2^n$. The function's return value is f, and n is returned through the pointer parameter. If x is 0, both values will be 0.
- `double ldexp( double x, int n );`
  The inverse of `frexp()`; it computes and returns the value of $x \times 2^n$.
- `double modf( double x, double* nptr );`
  Splits a nonzero x into a fractional part, f, and an integer part, n, such that $|f|$ is less than 1.0 and $x = f + n$. Both f and n have the same sign as x. The function's return value is f and n is returned through the pointer parameter.

G.3.4 Input and Output

Header file. `<stdio.h>`.

Predefined streams. `stdin, stdout, stderr`.

Constants.

- `EOF` signifies an error or end-of-file during input.
- `NULL` is the zero pointer.
- `FOPEN_MAX` is the number of streams that can be open simultaneously (ISO C only).
- `FILENAME_MAX` is the maximum appropriate length for a file name (ISO C only).

Types. `FILE`, `size_t`, `fpos_t`.

Stream functions.

- `FILE* fopen( const char* filename, const char* mode );`
  `int fclose( FILE* str );`
  For opening and closing programmer-defined streams.
- `int fflush( FILE* str );`
  Sends the contents of the stream buffer to the associated device. It is defined only for output streams.
- `FILE* freopen( const char* filename, const char* mode, FILE* str );`
  Reopens the specified stream for the named file in the new mode.
- `int feof( FILE* str );`
  Returns `true` if an attempt has been made to read past the end of the stream `str`. Returns `false` otherwise.

- `int ferror( FILE* str );`
  Returns **true** if an error occurred while reading from or writing to the stream **str**.
- `void clearerr( FILE* str );`
  Resets any error or end-of-file indicators on stream **str**.
- `int rename( const char* oldname, const char* newname );`
  Renames the specified disk file.
- `int remove( char* filename );`
  Deletes the named file from the disk.

Input functions.

- `int fgetc( FILE* str );`
  `int getc( FILE* str );`
  These functions read a single character from the stream **str**.
- `int getchar( void );`
  Reads a single character from the stream **stdin**.
- `int ungetc( int ch, FILE* str );`
  Puts a single character, **ch**, back into the stream **str**.
- `char* fgets( char* ar, int n, FILE* str );`
  Reads up to **n-1** characters from the stream **str** into the array **ar**. A newline character occurring before the *n*th input character terminates the operation and is stored in the array. A null character is stored at the end of the input.
- `char* gets( char* ar );`
  Reads characters from the stream **stdin** into the array **ar** until a newline character occurs, then stores a null character at the end of the input. The newline is not stored as part of the string.
- `int fscanf( FILE* str, const char* format, ... );`
  Reads input from stream **str** under the control of the format. It stores converted values in the addresses on the variable-length output list that follows the format.
- `int scanf( const char* format, ... );`
  Same as **fscanf()** to stream **stdin**.
- `int sscanf( char* s, const char* format, ... );`
  Same as **fscanf()** except that the input characters come from the string **s** instead of from a stream.
- `size_t fread( void* ar, size_t size, size_t count,`
  `        FILE* str );`
  Reads a block of data of **size** times **count** bytes from the stream **str** into array **ar**.

Output functions.

- `int fputc( int ch, FILE* str );`
  `int putc( int ch, FILE* str );`
  These functions write `ch` to stream `str`.
- `int putchar( int ch );`
  Writes a single character, `ch`, to the stream `stdout`.
- `int fputs( const char* s, FILE* str );`
  Writes `s` to stream `str`.
- `int puts( const char* s );`
  Writes string `s` and a newline character to the stream `stdout`.
- `int fprintf( FILE* str, const char* format, ... );`
  Writes values from the variable-length output list to the stream `str` under the control of the format.
- `int printf( const char* format, ... );`
  Writes values from the variable-length output list to the stream `stdout` under the control of the format.
- `int sprintf( char* ar, const char* format, ... );`
  Writes values from the variable-length output list to the array `ar` under the control of the format.
- `size_t fwrite( const void* ar, size_t size,`
        `size_t count, FILE* str );`
  Writes a block of data of `size` times `count` bytes from the array `ar` into the stream `str`.

Advanced functions.   The following functions are beyond the scope of this text; their prototypes are listed without comment.

- `int setvbuf( FILE* str, char* buf, int bufmode,`
  `size_t size );`
- `void setbuf( FILE* str, char* buf );`
- Buffer mode constants `BUFSIZ, _IOFBF, _IOLBF, _IONBF`
- `int fseek( FILE* str, long int offset, int from );`
- `long int ftell( FILE* str );`
- `void rewind( FILE* str );`
- Seek constants `SEEK_SET, SEEK_CUR, SEEK_END`
- `int fgetpos( FILE* str, fpos_t* pos );`
- `int fsetpos( FILE* str, const fpos_t* pos );`
- `void perror( const char* s );`
- `int vfprintf( FILE* str, const char* format,`
  `va_list arg );`
- `int vprintf( const char* format, va_list arg );`

- `int vsprintf( char* ar, const char* format,`
  `va_list arg );`
- `FILE* tmpfile( void );`
- `char* tmpnam( char* buf );` and constants `L_tmpnam`, `TMP_MAX`

G.3.5 Standard Library

Header file. `<stdlib.h>`.

Constants.

- `RAND_MAX`: the largest value that can be returned by `rand()`.
- `EXIT_FAILURE`: signifies unsuccessful termination when returned by `main()` or `exit()`.
- `EXIT_SUCCESS`: signifies successful termination when returned by `main()` or `exit()`.

Typedefs. `div_t` and `ldiv_t`, ISO C only, the types returned by the functions `div()` and `ldiv()`, respectively. Both are structures with two components, `quot` and `rem`, for the quotient and remainder of an integer division.

General functions.

- `int abs( int x );`
  `long labs( long x );`
  These functions return the absolute value of `x`. Note: `fabs()`, for floating-point numbers, is defined in `<math.h>`.
- `div_t div( int n, int d );`
  `ldiv_t ldiv( long n, long d );`
  These functions perform the integer division of `n` by `d`. The quotient and remainder are returned in a structure of type `div_t` or `ldiv_t`.
- `void srand( unsigned s );`
  `int rand( void );`
  The function `srand()` is used to initialize the random-number generator and should be called before using `rand()`. Successive calls on `rand()` return pseudo-random numbers, evenly distributed over the range `0...RAND_MAX`.
- `void* bsearch( const void* key, const void* base,`
  `      size_t count, size_t size, int (*compar)`
  `      (const void* key, const void* value) );`
  Searches the array starting at `base` for an element that matches `key`. A total of `count` elements are in the array. It uses `*compar()` to determine whether two items match. See the text for explanation.

- `int qsort( void* base, size_t count, size_t size,`
      `int (*compar)(const void* e1, const void* e2) );`
   Quicksorts the elements of the array starting at **base** and continuing for
   count elements. It uses ***compar()** to compare the elements. See the
   text for explanation.

Allocation functions.

- `void* malloc( size_t size );`
   Dynamically allocates a memory area of **size** bytes and returns the ad-
   dress of the beginning of this area.
- `void* calloc( size_t count, size_t size );`
   Dynamically allocates a memory area of **count** times **size** bytes. It
   clears all the bits in this area to 0 and returns the address of the beginning
   of this area.
- `void free( void* pt );`
   Returns the dynamically allocated area ***pt** to the system for future reuse.
- `void* realloc( void* pt, size_t size );`
   Resizes the dynamically allocated area ***pt** to **size** bytes. If this is larger
   than the current size and the current allocation area cannot be extended,
   it allocates the entire **size** bytes elsewhere and copies the information
   from ***pt**.

Control functions.

- `void exit( int status );`
   Flushes all the buffers, closes all the streams, and returns the status code
   to the operating system.
- `int atexit( void (*func)( void ) );`
   ISO C only. The function **(*func)()** is called when **exit()** is called
   or when **main()** returns.

String to number conversion functions.

- `double strtod( const char* str, char** p );`
   `double atof( const char* str );`
   The function **strtod()** converts the ASCII string **str** to a number of
   type **double** and returns that number. It leaves ***p** pointing at the first
   character in **str** that was not part of the number. The function **atof()**
   does the same thing but does not return a pointer to the first unconverted
   character. The preferred function is **strtod()**; **atof()** is deprecated in
   the latest version of the standard.
- `long strtol( const char* str, char** p, int b );`
   The function **strtol()** converts the ASCII string **str** to a number of

type `long int` expressed in base `b` and returns that number. It leaves
`*p` pointing at the first character in `str` that was not part of the number.
This function is preferred over both `atoi()` and `atol()`, which are
deprecated in the latest version of the standard.

- `int atoi( const char* str );`
  `long atol( const char* str );`
  The function `atoi()` converts the ASCII string `str` to a number of type
  `int` expressed in base 10 and returns that number; `atol()` converts to
  type `long int`. The function `strtol()` is preferred over both of these,
  which are deprecated in the latest version of the standard.
- `unsigned long strtoul( const char* str, char** p,`
      `int b );`
  Converts the ASCII string `str` to a number of type `long unsigned int`
  expressed in base `b` and returns that number. It leaves `*p` pointing at the
  first character in `str` that was not part of the number.

Advanced functions.   The following functions are beyond the scope of this
text; their prototypes are listed without comment.

- `void abort( void );`
- `char* getenv( const char* name );`
- `int system( const char* command );`

G.3.6   Strings

Header file.   `<string.h>`.

String manipulation.

- `char* strcat( char* dest, const char* src );`
  Appends the string `src` to the end of the string `dest`, overwriting its null
  terminator. We assume that `dest` has space for the combined string.
- `char* strncat(char* dest, const char* src, size_t n);`
  This function is the same as `strcat()` except that it stops after copying
  `n` characters, then writes a null terminator.
- `char* strcpy( char* dest, const char* src );`
  Copies the string `src` into the array `dest`. We assume that `dest` has
  space for the string.
- `char* strncpy(char* dest, const char* src, size_t n);`
  Copies exactly `n` characters from `src` into `dest`. If fewer than `n` characters are in `src`, null characters are appended until exactly `n` have been
  written.
- `int strcmp( const char* p, const char* q );`
  Compares string `p` to string `q` and returns a negative value if `p` is lexi-

cographically less than **q**, 0 if they are equal, or a positive value if **p** is greater than **q**.

* `int strncmp(const char* p, const char* q, size_t n);`
  This function is the same as **strcmp()** but returns after comparing at most **n** characters.
* `size_t strlen( const char* s );`
  Returns the number of characters in the string **s**, excluding the null character on the end.
* `char* strchr( const char* s, int ch );`
  Searches the string **s** for the first (leftmost) occurrence of the character **ch**. Returns a pointer to that occurrence if it exists; otherwise returns **NULL**.
* `char* strrchr( const char* s, int ch );`
  Searches the string **s** for the last (rightmost) occurrence of the character **ch**. Returns a pointer to that occurrence if it exists; otherwise returns **NULL**.
* `char* strstr( const char* s, const char* sub );`
  Searches the string **s** for the first (leftmost) occurrence of the substring **sub**. Returns a pointer to the first character of that occurrence if it exists; otherwise returns **NULL**.

Memory functions.

* `void* memchr( const void* ptr, int val, size_t len );`
  Copies **val** into **len** characters starting at address **ptr**.
* `int memcmp( const void* p, const void* q, size_t n );`
  Compares the first **n** characters starting at address **p** to the first **n** characters starting at **q**. Returns a negative value if **p** is lexicographically less than **q**, 0 if they are equal, or a positive value if **p** is greater than **q**.
* `void* memcpy(void* dest, const void* src, size_t n);`
  Copies **n** characters from **src** into **dest** and returns the address **src**. This may not work correctly for overlapping memory regions but often is faster than **memmove()**.
* `void* memmove(void* dest, const void* src, size_t n);`
  Copies **n** characters from **src** into **dest** and returns the address **src**. This works correctly for overlapping memory regions.
* `void* memset( void* ptr, int val, size_t len );`
  Copies **val** into **len** characters starting at address **ptr**.

Advanced functions.   The following functions are beyond the scope of this text; their prototypes are listed without comment:

* `int strcoll( const char* s1, const char* s2 );`
* `size_t strcspn( const char* s, const char* set );`
* `char* strerror( int errnum );`

- `char* strpbrk( const char* s, const char* set );`
- `size_t strspn( const char* s, const char* set );`
- `char* strtok( char* s, const char* set );`
- `size_t strxfrm( char* d, const char* s, size_t len );`

G.3.7   Time and Date

Header file.   `<time.h>`.

Constants.   `CLOCKS_PER_SEC` is the number of clock "ticks" per second of the clock used to record process time.

Types.

- `time_t;`
  The integer type used to represent times on the local system.
- `clock_t;`
  The arithmetic type used to represent the process time on the local system.
- `struct tm;`
  A structured representation of the time containing the following fields, all of type `int`: `tm_sec` (seconds after the minute), `tm_min` (minutes after the hour), `tm_hour` (hours since midnight, 0–23), `tm_mday` (day of the month, 1–31), `tm_mon` (month since January, 0–11), `tm_year` (years since 1900), `tm_wday` (day since Sunday, 0–6), `tm_yday` (day since January 1, 0–365), `tm_isdst` (daylight savings time flag, `>0` if DST is in effect, `0` if not, `<0` if unknown).

Functions.

- `clock_t clock();`
  Returns an approximation to the processor time used by the current process, usually expressed in microseconds.
- `time_t time( time_t* tptr );`
  Reads the system clock and returns the time as an integer encoding of type `time_t`. Returns the same value through the pointer parameter.
- `char* ctime( const time_t* tptr );`
  `char* asctime( const struct tm* tptr );`
  These functions return a pointer to a string containing a printable form of the date and time: `"Sat Sep 14 13:12:27 1999\n"`. The argument to `ctime()` is a pointer to a `time_t` value such as that returned by `time()`. The argument to `asctime()` is a pointer to a structured calendar time such as that returned by `localtime()` or `gmtime()`.
- `struct tm* gmtime( const time_t* tp );`
  `struct tm* localtime( const time_t* tp );`

These functions convert a time represented as a `time_t` value to a structured representation. The `gmtime()` returns Greenwich mean time; the `localtime()` converts to local time, taking into account the time zone and Daylight Savings Time.

- `time_t mktime( struct tm* tp );`
  Converts a time from the `struct tm` representation to the integer `time_t` representation.
- `double difftime( time_t t1, time_t t2 );`
  Returns the result of `t1-t2` in seconds as a value of type `double`.
- `size_t strftime( char* s, size_t max,`
      `const char* format, const struct tm* tp );`
  `size_t wcsftime( w_char* s, size_t max,`
      `const w_char* format, const struct tm* tp );`
  The function `strftime()` formats a single date and time value specified by `tp`, storing up to `maxsize` characters into the array `s` under control of the string `format`. The function `wcsftime()` docs the same thing with wide characters.

G.3.8   Variable-Length Argument Lists

This library, known as the *vararg* facility, permits programmers to define functions with variable-length argument lists. This is an advanced feature of C and beyond the scope of this text. The list of functions is included here because this facility was used to define `say()` and `fatal()`.

Header file.   `<stdarg.h>`.

Type.   `va_list`.

Functions.   `va_start`, `va_arg`, and `va_end`.

G.4   Libraries Not Explored

Each of the remaining libraries is named and the names of functions and constants in them are listed without prototypes or explanation. This list can serve as a starting point for further exploration of C.

- *Errors*. Header file: `<errno.h>`. Constants: `EDOM` and `ERANGE`.
  Variable: `errno`.
- *Nonlocal jumps*. Header file: `<setjmp.h>`. Type: `jmpbuf`.
  Functions: `setjmp` and `longjmp`.

- *Signal handling.* Header file: `<signal.h>`. Type: `sig_atomic_t`. Constants: `SIG_DFL`, `SIG_ERR`, `SIG_IGN`, `SIGABRT`, `SIGFPE`, `SIGILL`, `SIGINT`, `SIGSEGV`, and `SIGTERM`. Functions: `signal`, `raise`.
- *Control.* Header file: `<assert.h>`. Constant: `NDEBUG`. Function: `assert`.
- *Localization.* Header file: `<locale.h>`. Constants: `LC_ALL`, `LC_TIME`, `LC_CTYPE`, `LC_MONETARY`, `LC_NUMERIC`, `LC_COLLATE`, and `NULL`. Type: `struct lconv`. Functions: `localeconv` and `setlocale`.
- *Wide-character handling.* Header file: `<wctype.h>`. Functions: `iswctype`, `towctrans`, `WEOF`, `wint_t`, `wctrans`, `wctrans_t`, `wctype`, and `wctype_t`. In addition, this library contains wide analogs of all the functions in the `ctype` library, all with a `w` as the third letter of the name: `iswupper`, `towlower`, and so on.
- *Extended multibyte to wide-character conversion.* Header file: `<wchar.h>`. Functions: `btowc`, `mbrlen`, `mbrtowc`, `mbstate_t`, `wcrtomb`, `mbsinit`, `mbsrtowcs`, `wcsrtombs`, `wcstod`, `wcstol`, `wcstoul`, and `wctob`.
- *Wide-string handling.* Header file: `<wchar.h>`. Functions: `wcscat`, `wcschr`, `wcscmp`, `wcscoll`, `wcscpy`, `wcscspn`, `wcserror`, `wcslen`, `wcsncat`, `wcsncmp`, `wcsncpy`, `wcspbrk`, `wcsrchr`, `wcsspn`, `wcsstr`, `wcstok`, `wcsxfrm`, `wmemchr`, `wmemcmp`, `wmemcpy`, `wmemmove`, and `wmemset`.
- *Wide-character input and output.* Header file: `<wchar.h>`. Functions: `fwprintf`, `fwscanf`, `wprintf`, `wscanf`, `swprintf`, `swscanf`, `vfwprintf`, `vwprintf`, `vwsprintf`, `fgetwc`, `fgetws`, `fputwc`, `fputws`, `getwc`, `getwchar`, `putwc`, `putwchar`, and `ungetwc`.

APPENDIX H

Glossary

accessible A variable is accessible everywhere it is visible.

aggregate A composite data object such as an array or a structure.

algorithm A method for solving a problem, it must be unambiguous, fully defined and effective, and terminate under all conditions.

ALU (arithmetic/logic unit) The part of a CPU that contains the instructions that actually perform addition, multiplication, and so forth.

ANSI (American National Standards Institute) An agency that sponsors and promulgates a wide variety of standards. In the field of computing, it has sponsored standards for many languages, the ASCII character code, and the RS232 communication interface.

argument An input to a function. A function call supplies an argument value for each parameter name declared in the function definition.

argument vector An ordered list of distinct values, possibly of different types, that is associated on a one-to-one basis with the ordered list of parameters for a function, serving as their initial values for a function call.

arity The number of operands required by an operator. The arity of all C operators is unary, binary, or ternary. A unary operator requires one operand, a binary operator two, and a ternary operator three.

array A contiguous, numbered set of variables of a given base type, which can be used and passed to functions as a unit.

ASCII (American Standard Code for Information Interchange) The character code built into most modern personal computers. This 7-bit encoding system contains codes for the numerals; the upper- and lower-case English alphabet; a variety of punctuation, grouping, and mathematical symbols; and a set of control characters. International ASCII is an 8-bit code that, in addition, has some graphics characters and many letters used in European alphabets but not English.

assignment The act of storing a value in the memory location of a variable.

associativity With precedence, a rule that determines the interpretation of an expression. Associativity applies to adjacent operators with equal precedence and may be right to left or left to right. This property is listed in the precedence table (Appendix B).

BAM (bit allocation map) The table used by UNIX to keep track of which disk sectors are free and which are in use. Each disk (hard or floppy) has its own BAM.

base That integer which is raised to the power represented by the exponent, to form a scale factor for the mantissa of a floating-point number. In the IEEE floating-point representation, the base is 2.

base type The type of the elements of an array or of the referent of a pointer.

binary file A file in which the data are stored in the form of as binary numbers, not as ASCII code. Often used for digital images and executable code.

binary search An iterative or recursive method for searching a sorted array efficiently. At each step, the remaining unsearched portion of the array is divided in half, and the middle element is tested. Then the search continues with whichever half contains the target value.

bit The minimal unit of information, a bit can have the value 1 or 0.

bitwise operator An operator that manipulates the bit pattern of the representation of an object, affecting its numeric or symbolic value in a nonobvious way.

block Zero or more program statements enclosed in curly brackets that function syntactically as one statement. Statements are blocked together for use with conditional and loop control structures. Any block may start with local declarations.

bool The type of a truth value in C++, this type will become part of the C standard in the future. The values of this type are `false`, represented by 0, and `true`, represented by 1.

buffer An array used to hold input until it can be fully processed or to hold output until it is fully constructed and written to its destination. Programmers often declare a character array to be used as a buffer for interactive text input.

bus The main communication line that connects the computer's CPU with the main memory, secondary memory, and I/O devices.

bus error One kind of fatal program error caused by attempting to access a memory address that does not exist or is inappropriate for the hardware.

busy wait In a program, a loop that does no useful work, but simply waits while continually testing for the occurrence of some condition. A busy-wait loop can be used to synchronize execution of a program with some external event, but is only appropriate for systems that are not time-shared.

byte A byte (equal to 8 bits) is the smallest addressable unit of memory in most computers.

C library Every C system has several library modules, each containing a group of related function definitions and each with its own header file. The most commonly used library modules are **stdio** (standard input and output routines), **math** (mathematical and trigonometric functions), and **string** (string handling functions).

cache A very fast, but small, segment of memory, a processor cache is used to store data or instructions that have been used and are likely to be needed again soon. Keeping them in a cache speeds up processing if reused. Several other kinds of caches are used at other levels in computers.

call by address A method of parameter passing. Refers to using the address of an argument (rather than a copy of its value) to initialize a function parameter. This permits the function to change the value of a variable in the caller.

call by value A method of parameter passing. Refers to using the value of an argument to initialize a function parameter. If the argument is a variable, a copy of its value is used. This brings information into the function but does not allow the function to access or change variables that belong to the caller.

call graph A chart that shows what functions are called by each function used in a program. The chart starts with **main()** at the top and the functions called by **main()** below it. In the third layer are functions called by those in the second layer, and so forth.

cast A C operator for specifying that the representation of an expression's value should be converted to a different type.

cluster The smallest amount of disk storage that can be allocated for a file, a cluster often is two or four disk sectors.

collating sequence The sequence in which the characters are arranged in the code (such as ASCII) used on the local computer.

command line A character string that is interpreted by the operating system and used to invoke some system software or a user's own program. In C, the same command line that is used to run a program can be used to deliver a small amount of control information from the user to the program.

comment Nonprogram text embedded in a program to explain its form and function to human readers. Comments are written by the programmer and are treated as whitespace by the C compiler.

compile module A file and all the files included by it compiled simultaneously by one call on the compiler.

condition A boolean expression whose value can be used in a control statement to determine program actions.

constant expression An expression that involves only constant operands, not variables.

controller The hardware circuits that control the physical operation and parts of an I/O device.

conversion Changing the representation of a value from one form to another with roughly the same meaning. Examples include converting a 2-byte integer to a 4-byte representation or converting an integer to a floating-point representation.

CPU (central processing unit) The brains of a computer, it contains the ALU, the clock, many registers, the bus interface, and circuitry that makes these parts work together.

crash An error that causes failure of the program in which it occurs. See also hang and system crash.

cursor In a text editor, a mark that shows where the next character entered will appear in the text. In a C program that uses arrays, it is a pointer that moves along an array, marking the next slot to be processed.

dangling pointer A pointer that no longer refers to a valid object. When an object is deallocated, any pointer that formerly referred to it is a dangling pointer.

data type The semantic class to which an object belongs, the data type of an object determines what functions can be applied to it. Data types in C include the integer types (`char`, `short`, `int`, `long`, `unsigned`), the floating-point types (`float`, `double`, `long double`), pointer types, and various compound types (`string`, `stream`, `struct`).

debug To find the syntactic and logical errors in a program.

declarations A declaration creates an object or a type and gives it a name and, possibly, a value. In C, declarations may occur at the beginning of any program block.

dereference To follow a pointer and access its referent.

DES (data encryption standard) A nationally accepted algorithm for encrypting files in such a way that decryption is extremely difficult and time consuming, if not impossible.

device driver A piece of software that forms the interface between the operating system and a device controller, the driver takes I/O instructions from the operating system in a standard instruction format and produces the specialized instructions required by the device controller it drives.

digital image A matrix of values representing a camera image, where each value represents the amount of light captured by the corresponding position of the camera lens.

DOS (disk operating system) The single-user operating system used on older IBM-compatible personal computers.

dynamic allocation The on-demand distribution of a block of memory from the system to a program via a memory pointer as the result of a call on a function such as `malloc()`.

enumerated type A type defined by a list of symbols and represented by C as small integer constants. For example, an enumeration that represents the seasons might be `enum SEASON{WIN, SPR, SUM, FALL}`.

epsilon test A comparison for approximate equality, used instead of `==`, when comparing real numbers that might have representational or computational error.

error recovery A process of dealing constructively with erroneous input or other processing errors so that processing can continue and an operator can later identify the nature of the error and take corrective action.

escape code A character that is written in C as a backslash followed by an ASCII code such as `\x20` or a predefined symbolic code such as `\n`. Although any character can be written as a numeric escape code, these codes are generally used only for characters with no symbolic code.

exception An unusual condition that requires some special action. Examples are end of file, numeric overflow, and hardware failure.

exponent That portion of the representation of a floating-point number that specifies the power of the base by which to multiply the mantissa.

expression A code phrase formed of operators and operands, according to the syntactic rules of the language; `3 + x * y` is an expression.

external A symbol declared as `extern` and used in one code module but defined and initialized in another code module. References to external symbols are connected by the system linker to the actual objects defined in other modules.

FAT (file allocation table) The table used by DOS to keep track of which disk sectors are free and which belong to a file. Each disk (hard or floppy) has its own FAT.

file A collection of data stored on a file device such as a disk or a tape, each file has a name and a definite length, which are entered into the file directory of the file device.

floating point A representation for real numbers. An IEEE standard floating-point number has a sign, a base-2 exponent, and a mantissa with one bit to the left of the binary point.

flow diagram A diagram of an algorithm or program that shows blocks of statements in rectangles and conditionals in diamond-shaped boxes, connected by arrows, to form loops and sequences such that there is one continuous, branching path from beginning to end. The diagram shows all possible ways for control to progress through the blocks, and the conditions under which each path may be taken.

flush When an output stream is flushed, the contents of the stream buffer are sent to their destination (the screen, the printer, or a file). When an input stream is flushed, all characters pending in the stream buffer are discarded.

format As an adjective, the layout of the input or output data; as a noun, a quoted string that describes that layout so that a `stdio` function can decipher the input data or display the output with the desired layout.

function A block of code that can be called from another part of the program. A function has zero or more parameters and may have a return value. These parts form the interface between the function and the rest of the program. A function also has a block of code and (optionally) local variables.

function call An invocation of a function. In C, this is denoted by the function name followed by parentheses enclosing an appropriate list of arguments.

garbage The contents of memory before it has been initialized by a program.

generic type A nonspecific type, a type name that refers to a group or category of types.

global A symbol defined outside all functions, usually at the top of a module. The opposite of local. A global object or function is accessible from all functions in the same program module that come after its definition.

hang A total system freeze up. The entire computer becomes unresponsive. See also crash and system crash.

header file A file of declarations (constants, types, and prototypes) used to co-ordinate the actions of one code module with others that have been written and compiled separately.

I-Node Used in the UNIX operating system to store information about a file, such as its owner, creation date, location on the disk, size, and the like. This is the information you see in a directory listing.

identifier The name a programmer declares for an object, a type, or a function.

IEEE (Institute of Electrical and Electronic Engineers) A professional society for electrical engineers, it is of interest here because of its sponsorship of a standard for floating-point computation. Appendix G.2 gives the minimum values of C constants that conform to the IEEE standard.

index column In a multicolumn table, the column that contains the key value.

indirect access A reference to a memory location through a pointer: First, the pointer is accessed to get the address stored in it; then the memory location at that address is accessed to get the value stored there.

Infinity The result of floating-point overflow, a value with an exponent of all 1 bits. It can be positive or negative and is treated specially by modern hardware.

initialize To store a value in a variable when it is created.

initializer In C, a constant expression written in a declaration that supplies an initial value for the variable being declared. Lists of values enclosed in curly brackets are used to initialize aggregate objects.

integer type A type whose machine representation is a binary integer. In C, this includes enumerated types and signed and unsigned versions of types `int`, `long int`, `short int`, and `char`.

interface A standardized set of hardware and software conventions to facilitate communication between devices; by conforming to a standard interface, equipment produced by a variety of manufacturers can be successfully connected and run together.

I/O devices (input/output devices) Input devices include keyboards, mice, trackballs, card readers, and the like. Output devices include video screens and printers. Secondary memory devices such as disks, tapes, and CD-ROMs sometimes are considered I/O devices.

ISO (International Standards Organization) The European counterpart of ANSI, the ISO adopted the 1989 ANSI standard for the C language with minor editing changes; this standard now is known as the ISO standard for C.

iteration Repetition of a sequence of statements.

justification The alignment of an output value in a specified width output field, either beginning at the left of the field with padding on the right or ending at the right with padding on the left.

k The abbreviation for kilobyte, which means 1,000 bytes, this term also is used loosely to mean 1,024 bytes.

keyword A word defined by the C standard as part of the C language grammar; for example, `while`, `return`, `struct`, or `sizeof`.

lazy evaluation A method for finding the value of an expression that involves logical operators. The left operand is evaluated first, and if it fully determines the result of the operation, evaluation of the right operand is skipped entirely.

literal A series of symbols, written as part of the program code, that represents a number (2, 0.4), a character value (`'v'`), or a string (`"fair"`). There is a way to write a literal value for every built-in type in C.

local Defined within the current function or block.

log file A file that records data about exceptional conditions or erroneous data that have been found during processing.

loop A construct for controlling iteration, it generally contains a termination condition that is checked before or after each repetition.

makefile A file, used by the "make" facility that describes how to compile and link a multimodule program. Contains dependencies, rules, and actions.

man page An on-line documentation format used in UNIX systems to describe the interface and operation of system components, including commands, library functions, system calls, and the like.

mantissa That portion of a floating-point representation that is multiplied by the base value raised to some exponent to obtain the real number value.

MAR (memory address register) The piece of a CPU that holds the address of the main memory location that is currently in use.

mask A bit vector consisting of a particular sequence of 1's and 0's necessary to cause a particular outcome when used with a specific bitwise operator, or a single flag value that indicates the validity of a particular item in an array with respect to future processing.

matrix A two-dimensional arrangement of values that normally do not have significant individual importance and that normally is processed as a whole rather than having its rows or columns processed individually.

MDR (memory data register) The piece of a CPU that holds the data read from or to be stored into the address in the MAR.

member One of the fields in a structure type definition.

memory recycling Making memory available for later reuse, thus minimizing the amount of physical memory needed by an application. The function `free()` recycles dynamically allocated memory blocks.

menu A list of options presented to a user, from which to select a service or option offered by the program being executed.

mHz (megahertz) A 1-megahertz processor has a clock speed of 1 million cycles per second.

MIDI (musical instrument digital interface) An interface that permits a computer to communicate with electronic musical instruments.

module One part of a large project or application; a source code file and its accompanying header file(s). The modules of a project are compiled separately and later linked together to form an executable program.

NaN (not a number) The error code returned by some systems as a result of floating-point overflow or underflow. It is represented by a bit pattern with an exponent of all 1 bits.

normalize To adjust the representation of a floating-point value such that the mantissa has one significant digit to the left of the decimal point by raising or lowering the exponent value appropriately to cause the alignment.

NULL A special pointer to nothing. Technically, a pointer whose value is 0.

null character The character whose ASCII code is 0 and whose symbolic form is `'\0'`. This is used to end strings and, in that context, is called a *null terminator*.

null string A string with no character except the null terminator. Its length (as measured by `strlen()`) is 0. The literal representation of the null string is a pair of adjacent double quotes.

number system A method for representing numbers. In a positional base system, a small integer is designated as the base of the system, and every integer is represented by a series of digits, where each digit is between 0 and the base − 1. C uses four bases: binary (base 2) for internal representations, and decimal (base 10), hexadecimal (base 16), and octal (base 8) for input, output, and program literals.

object code The translated version of a program, a source file is the input to a compiler; an object file is its output.

on-board Physically mounted on the same chip as the CPU.

operand A value or expression that is one object of an action performed by an operator.

operator A symbol in the C language representing an action performed on one, two, or three values (operands). Examples are `+`, `%`, `--`, and `&`.

OS (operating system) An operating system is a large, complex program that forms the interface between the user and the raw computer machinery.

overflow A hardware error condition, overflow errors can be caused by attempting to divide by 0 or to compute a number larger than the maximum representable number.

packing Storing a set of individual values in a variable large enough to contain all of them, so that the set can be passed back and forth to functions as a single unit.

padding Bits or bytes that are added to a value to lengthen it to a required standard length. Zero bits, space characters, and null characters are commonly used for padding.

parallel arrays A set of arrays with the same length that are accessed using the same subscript, used to represent a set of objects. Each array represents one property of the objects and each subscript position represents the features of one object.

parameter A variable that forms part of the interface to a function; the function definition declares the type and the local name for each parameter. When the function is called, an argument value, supplied by the call, is stored in the parameter. Inside the function, the argument value is accessed by using the parameter name.

parse To analyze the structure of an expression according to the syntactic rules of the language.

pipeline A modern machine architecture in which several instructions, simultaneously, are in different stages of execution.

pixel A picture element, or dot, used to form an image on a graphics display device. A typical monitor display has 1024×768 pixels.

pointer The address of a variable or a variable in which the address of another variable is stored.

pointer variable A variable that stores the address of another variable.

pointers with an array During sequential processing of an array or a list, three kinds of pointers are often used: A *head* pointer and a *tail* pointer are set to the beginning and end of the array and are not changed. A *scanner* or *cursor* is initialized to the beginning and moves, stepwise, to the end, pointing at each element in turn.

portable code Code that does not rely on the particular properties of one compiler or one system, and so will run correctly on many kinds of computers.

precedence A set of rules that, together with the associativity rule, determine the interpretation of an expression in C. The precedence value of every operator is listed in the precedence table (Appendix B). When two different operators are adjacent in an expression, with one operand between them, precedence determines which will be parsed first.

precision An indication of the potential accuracy of a value, often measured in terms of the maximum number of significant digits that can be stored reliably in a representation.

precondition A part of the documentation of a function that specifies conditions that must be true of the arguments to enable valid operation of the function.

preprocessor command A line, generally at the top of a program, that starts with # and gives the compiler instructions about how to compile the program or where to find essential definitions. Most programs use the commands `#include` and `#define`. However, the preprocessor recognizes many more commands.

program A sequence of commands, declarations, and statements written in a computer language and translated into machine language. Programs are used to control computers.

prompt A message displayed on the video screen that tells the user what kind of data to enter.

prototype A function declaration in the ISO form, it lists the name of the function, the type of each parameter, and the type of the result.

pseudocode An imprecise, informally defined language for expressing algorithms; generally a mixture of English and some programming language. An author or programmer often develops his or her own pseudocode.

pseudo-random numbers A series of numbers, produced by a pseudo-random number generator, that have no obvious pattern. Such numbers are used when a random choice is required.

ragged array An array of strings, it is called ragged because the strings are generally not the same length and, when diagrammed, look like a striped flag with a ragged right end.

RAM (random access memory) Any memory location in a RAM may be accessed with equal speed. Used for the main memory of modern computers.

read arm That part of a disk drive to which the read head is attached. The read arm telescopes in and out to position the head over one of the circular tracks on the disk.

read/write head The part of a disk drive that senses the data recorded on the disk surface during a "read" operation. It sends the data to the disk controller, which puts it on the bus to be sent to the CPU.

real type In C, the three representations of real numbers are the types `float`, `double`, and `long double`.

recursion A kind of repetition in which a function solves a large problem by breaking it into simpler pieces. One piece will be solved directly and the function will call itself one or more times to solve the rest.

redirection A user may redirect a predefined stream to connect to a file instead of to the keyboard or the video screen. When `stdin` is redirected, input comes from a file instead of from the keyboard. Redirecting `stdout` sends output that comes to a file instead of to the video screen.

referent The object at which a pointer points.

register A part of a computer's CPU that holds one address or one number, a processor has several registers used to bring information from memory, perform computations on it, or store it into memory. The instruction register stores the address of the next machine instruction to be executed.

representation range A bounded region of values in some representation scheme. A representation may or may not be able to represent every value in this region, depending on the inherent precision.

representational error The difference between a real number and the best representation of that number in the computer. All computer representations of irrational numbers (such as π) and repeating binary fractions (such as one-third) have representational error.

RISC (reduced instruction set computer) A recently developed machine architecture in which the computer has a small number of basic instructions that operate at a superfast pace. Doing a task like division may take many instructions.

robust code Code that handles all kinds of inputs, valid and invalid, without catastrophic failure. It does something sensible with any input and continues appropriately.

ROM (read only memory) Data are stored in ROM when it is manufactured and cannot be changed thereafter by an ordinary computer. This kind of memory is especially useful for operating-system software, since errors in user programs cannot destroy it.

row-major order A linear ordering of the elements of a 2-dimensional array in which the first row is listed from left to right, followed by the second row, and so forth. Elements of a 2-dimensional C array are laid out in memory in row-major order.

RS232 A standard serial interface, used to connect computers to modems, some printers, some mice, and other serial devices.

run-time stack A data structure that is part of the C run-time system. An activation record, or frame, is created on the stack each time a function is called and holds the arguments, local variables, and return address of the function call. The frame is destroyed when the function returns.

scope The scope of a name is the portion of the program between its creation and its deallocation. The scope of a local variable or parameter name is the function in which it is defined. The scope of a global variable or function name is all parts of the compile module that follow its definition.

SCSI (small computer systems interface) A standard interface for hard disk controllers.

search A method to find the position of a key value in the array, if it is present, given an array of values and a key value of the same type.

sector The smallest addressable unit of disk storage, one disk track has several sectors; each sector has an address and space for data.

seek On a disk device, the action of moving the read arm in or out to position it over a desired disk track.

segmentation fault One kind of fatal program error caused by attempting to access a memory address that belongs to the system or to another process.

sentinel A distinguishable data item that marks the end of a sequence of data, a sentinel must be the same data type as the rest of the data, but its value must be outside the set of meaningful data values.

servo-mechanism An electromechanical device that positions itself on command and uses feedback sensors to achieve accurate positioning.

shell The command interpreter used in a nongraphical user interface to pass commands to an operating system.

side effect A change in the value of a memory variable or the state of an I/O stream. Most operators have only direct effects, that is, they only compute a value and return it as a result. Some C operators, for example, `++` and `-=`, also have side effects and change the value of a memory variable. Overuse of side-effect operators makes a program harder to debug.

simulation Attempting to predict aspects of the behavior of a physical system by creating and evolving an approximate (mathematical) model of it. A typical example is an aircraft flight simulator.

sort To arrange the elements of an array in order, according to a specific criterion. The sorting algorithms covered in this text are selection, insertion, and quicksort.

source code The symbolic program code that a programmer has written, a file containing this code is called a *source file* and generally is created using a text editor.

stack frame That portion of the run-time stack that stores parameters, local variables, and the return address for one invocation of a function.

standard A full formal definition of the syntax and semantics of a computer language, it forms the basis of all translators for the language.

statement A statement denotes an action that must be executed at run time. Declarations, preprocessor commands, and comments are not considered to be statements in C.

static One of the storage classes in C, the opposite of dynamic. Static storage is allocated and initialized once at load time and remains available throughout execution. Static variables may be either global or local, which determines the scope of visibility.

stderr The standard error stream, defined by the C system and customarily used to display information for the operator.

stdin The standard input stream, defined by the C system.

stdout The standard output stream, defined by the C system.

storage class One property of an object. The storage class of a function, constant, or variable is specified by the object's declaration and determines its lifetime and visibility. C storage classes include **auto**, **static**, **extern**, and **register**.

stream A system data structure that allows a program to get input or produce output. Programmer-defined streams allow a program to use files. The three predefined streams are **stdin** for keyboard input and **stdout** and **stderr** for screen output.

string In source code, a string is a series of characters enclosed in quotes. In a running program, it is a pointer to an array of characters that must end in a null character. Strings have many uses, including menu data structures and formats for **scanf()** and **printf()**.

structure An object with several members whose type was declared using the keyword `struct`, with each member given a name in the type declaration. A member name is used with the dot operator or the arrow operator to access one part of a structure. The structure also can be assigned, passed to a function, or returned from a function as a unit.

stub testing A method of testing a program early in its development by writing dummy definitions, called stubs, for functions that have not yet been developed.

subscript An integer enclosed in square brackets that, when used with an array name, denotes one slot of the array.

syntax The grammatical rules of a language, the legal forms for identifiers, keywords, punctuation, and expressions are defined by the syntax of a language.

system crash A system crash is a kind of system failure in which the computer stops responding to its control devices and all running programs are lost.

test plan A set of proposed program inputs, together with the output that should result from each. As a set, the items should cause all parts of the program to be executed at least once.

testing by amputation A method of testing parts of a program early in its development by commenting out calls on functions that have not yet been written.

text editor A major piece of system software that lets a user enter lines of text into a computer file and later modify them. It is like a word processor, but simpler.

tight loop A loop containing few instructions, often to be performed a large number of times. Tightening a loop can improve the efficiency of a program.

toggle To change a bit from whatever state it is in to the other state: from 1 to 0 or from 0 to 1.

track On a disk, the circular band of sectors that can be read from one position of the disk's read arm.

truth value The result of a comparison or logical operator: `true` or `false`.

two's complement A method for representing positive and negative binary integers. Given any number N, represented in two's complement, the representation of $-N$ can be found by writing N in binary, inverting every bit, adding 1, and ignoring overflow.

type Short for data type.

type definition A declaration that names a new data type and defines a representation for that type.

undefined In a language, a construct that is part of the standard syntax but whose semantics and implementation are not fully defined. This leaves the compiler writer free to implement the syntax in a way that is convenient and fitting for the local system and hardware. The most commonly used undefined feature of C is the type `int`, which can be the same as either `long int` or `short int`.

undefined value In a program, the value of a variable that has been declared but not initialized.

underflow A hardware error condition caused by attempting to compute a floating-point number so close to 0 that it cannot be represented.

UNIX A popular operating system that can support multiple users simultaneously.

unsigned A representation for integers in which every bit is used to represent magnitude and all numbers are 0 or positive. The alternative in C is the `signed` representation, in which one bit is used to represent the sign of the number.

usage error An attempt to call a program or function with the wrong number or type of arguments.

validate To check a program input to ensure that its nature and value are such that the program can produce meaningful output from it. An invalid input might cause a serious or fatal error or meaningless output.

variable An area of computer memory that has been given a name by the program and can be used to store a value. Each variable can contain a specific type of value (such as an integer or character). The amount of memory required for a variable depends on its type and the characteristics of the local computer system.

vector A one-dimensional arrangement of values that normally do not have significant individual importance and that normally is processed as a whole.

visibility A variable is visible everywhere within its scope except where it is masked by another variable or parameter with the same name in an enclosed scope.

void The keyword used to declare that a function has no parameters or no result.

whitespace A character or series of characters that appears as space when displayed or printed. This includes an ordinary space, the newline and form feed characters, and horizontal and vertical tabs.

window system An operating system in which a graphic window interface operates on top of the command-line system and makes it easier and faster to use. In a window environment, multiple windows can be displayed on the screen, each containing a different document or type of information. The user can select one window at a time as the "active" window by clicking on it with the mouse.

word The unit of memory that can pass across the bus between the CPU and main memory at one time. Small computers usually have 2-byte words; workstations and larger computers have words that are 4 bytes or longer.

wrap The action of a counter when incremented past the maximum value it can represent. Suppose `count` is a variable that contains the largest representable unsigned integer. When 1 is added to `count`, its value will "wrap around" to 0. If `count` is a signed integer, it will wrap to the smallest negative representable integer.

APPENDIX
I

Answers to Self-Test Exercises

Chapter 1

1. Machine language, CPU, floating-point coprocessor, register, clock, bit, byte, word cache.

2. Bus, memory, ROM, RAM, bit, byte, word.

3. Bus, CD-ROM, device controller, device driver, parallel interface, serial interface.

4. Local area network, global network, gateway, firewall, server, client, hub.

5. Operating system, multiprogramming, system kernel, system libraries, memory management system, file system manager, device driver, command shell, windowing system, assembler, compiler.

6. (a) Arithmetic and logic unit, (b) binary digit, (c) central processing unit, (d) International Standards Organization, (e) American Standard Code for Information Interchange, (f) American National Standards Institute, (g) input or output, (h) operating system, (i) read only memory, (j) wide area network, (k) local area network, (l) musical instrument digital interface, (m) small computer systems interface, (n) megahertz, (o) random access memory.

Chapter 2

1. There are several reasons. He does not fully understand what is required and must ask the teacher. She does not know how to use the text editor. He does not know how to save a file or print it. She has trouble with the design or debugging stage because she is unfamiliar with program logic. He has trouble with the coding stage because he has forgotten how to spell an essential word or punctuate a program. The network is down and the student cannot dial into the lab from her dorm room. The teaching assistant is sick and not in the lab to help. Everybody just came down with the flu. The dog ate it (a good general excuse).

2. False. You need to compare the results to the test plan. It is not a good idea to turn in a program that computes garbage.

3. Explain the difference between the following:

   (a) An algorithm is a description of the steps used in solving a problem. It can be written in any language as long as the steps are clear and unambiguous. A program often implements an algorithm and is written in a language that can be translated by a compiler or interpreter into machine language.

   (b) A command is an instruction to carry out some action, and often includes the names of one or more objects to use while doing so. A declaration gives a name to an object and sometimes creates that object.

   (c) A compiler translates source code into a list of machine instructions, called *object code*, that can be stored in a file for later execution. An interpreter decodes the source code and carries out the program's actions without generating object code. Compiled code generally is faster than interpreted code.

   (d) A linking loader is a major piece of system software. It starts with object code and links it with the object code for the system libraries. The result is a load module, a program that is ready to put into the computer's memory and run.

Chapter 3

1. What is wrong with each of the following `if` statements? They are supposed to identify and print out the middle value of three `double` values: `x`, `y`, and `z`.

   (a) You can't compare three numbers by writing `(x < y < z)` or `(y < x < z)`. You must write it like this: `(x < y && y < z)`.

   (b) The curly brackets are missing. You need brackets around both pairs of lines that are indented.

   (c) Remove the semicolons after the two inner `if` statements. Do not put a semicolon between the `if (x < z)` and the dependent action, `printf("x=%g", x)`.

2. For `int` use `%i`, for `double` use `%g`.

3. The program will compile. On many systems, it will crash when you try to run it. In any case, the data being read will not go into the variable. Some compilers will give you a warning message but compile anyway.

4. The address of the variable will be printed, not its contents. Some compilers will give a warning message.

5. The rest of the program, up to the end of the next comment, will be "sucked into" the unterminated comment. If something essential (like one curly bracket) "disappears," the compiler will give an error comment when the lack is discovered. This comment may be very difficult to understand because the line number given is not the line on which the error was made.

6. The dependent clause (which should be executed only when the test is true) becomes independent and is executed unconditionally.

7. The `1==d`, two simple `if` statements. The `2==c`, two `if` statements and one `else` statement. The `3==a`, one `if` statement and one `else` statement. The `4==b`, one simple `if` statement and a following statement

8. (a) `integer` should be `int`.

   (b) Do not type a comma in a literal number.

   (c) Either change the semicolon to a comma or repeat the type name: `int count`.

   (d) The `==` should be a single `=`. The double equal sign is used for comparison, not initialization.

   (e) The `duble` should be `double`.

I.4   Chapter 4

1. (a) Change the semicolon after **d** to a comma or declare **a** separately. (b) Misspelled; `doubel` should be `double`. (c) An integer literal does not have a decimal point. (d) A constant must have an initializer. (e) Misspelled; `integer` should be `int`. (f) Although an expression is correct in an initializer, it must be a constant expression. Here, **g** is a variable, not a constant.

2.

Left operand	op	Right operand
z	*	2
z*2	/	3
	-	z
-z	+	y
z*2/3	-	-z+y
x	=	z*2/3-(-z+y)

3. (a) Parentheses are needed to subtract value of **b**, not add it. (b) Parentheses are needed to cause addition before multiplication. (c) Parentheses are optional; * is done before

+ because of precedence. (d) Parentheses are optional; associativity is left before right. (e) Parentheses make a difference; this makes sense without them but not with them.

4. (a) `d = 33`; (b) `d = 133`; (c) `d = 156`; (d) `e = -405`; (e) `d = 0`; (f) `e = -22.5`; (g) `e = 13.5`; (h) `e = 3.5`; (i) `d = 0`; (j) `d = 24`.

5. (a) `k = 35.0`; (b) `k = 1.66667`; (c) `k = 10.2`; (d) `k = 4.0`.

6. (a) The `"stdio"` should be `<stdio.h>` (two errors); (b) Delete the semicolon after `3.14159;`; (e) Add a declaration `double w;`; (f) `"Self-test Exercise/n"` should be `"Self-test Exercise\n"`; (g) Add `)` before the semicolon in `printf( "If I...late!!";`; (h) The `puts()` is correct but `printf()` is better; (i) The `scanf( %g, v )` should be `scanf( "%lg", &v )` (three errors); (j) The `w = v * Pi` should be `PI`, the other lines are correct.

7. (a) `liters = ounces / 33.81474;` (b) `circumf = 2 * PI * r;` (c) `area = b * h / 2.0;`.

8. (a) `t = x >= y && y >= z;`

(b) `x = (y + z) || v == 3 && !(z == y / v);`

Chapter 5

1. (a) `double hypot;`
       `hypot = sqrt( base*base + height*height );`

(b) `double theta;`
       `if (x!=0) theta = arctan( y / x );`

(c) `double y;`
       `y = r * cos( theta );`

2. (a) `double cube( double x );`

(b) `void three_beeps( void );`

3. (a) `double tangent( double x ) {return sin( x )/cos( x );}`

(b) `double surface( double r ) { return 4 * PI * r * r; }`

4. (a) An argument is a value sent from the caller to the function being called. A parameter is inside the function and is a place to store the argument. Within the function, the parameter name is used to refer to the argument value.

(b) A prototype tells the name of a function and the types of its parameters and return value. It ends in a semicolon. It supplies the information needed to properly compile a call on its function. A function header contains the same information, plus parameter names. The function header is followed by curly brackets enclosing the function's code.

(c) A header file contains constant definitions and prototypes. We include header files in source code files which contain code that uses the symbols or functions declared in the header file.

(d) A local library is a set of function definitions in common use in the local environment. A standard library defines the functions specified by the language standard and is supplied with every compiler.

(e) A function declaration is a prototype; it specifies the name and parameter types for the function. A function call is a command to perform the function; it must supply an argument for every parameter specified by the declaration.

(f) A function declaration is just the prototype. The definition is the whole function: header plus code block.

5. The standard specifies that the compiler will "make up" a prototype for every untyped function. Its return type always will be **int**. If your function returns **void** or **double**, the compiler will give a fatal error comment (illegal function redeclaration) when it translates the function header.

I.6　　Chapter 6

1. A series of **if...else** statements can test a series of varied and possibly complex conditions. A **switch** statement is much more limited, it makes a multiway choice on the basis of matching a value to one of a set of constant case labels. The **switch** is more efficient for situations in which it can be used at all.
   You could use a switch to compare input to the legal inputs that the program expects. You could not use a **switch** to test whether an input number was within one of several value ranges, such as 0–5 or 6–18.

2. The test in a **do...while** loop is made after executing the body on every repetition. The test in a **while** loop is made before executing the body the first time and after executing the body every time and therefore always is made one time more than the body is executed. If it always is correct to do a process once, a **do...while** loop can be used to test whether it should be repeated. A **while** loop is used to check for valid data before processing it and for most other purposes.

3. The output is **A. 10 45**. The rewritten loop is

   ```
   for (sum = k = 0; k < 10; ++k) { sum += k; }
   ```

4. The output depends on the input; the loop calculates 2^n. A sample output:

   ```
      Please enter an exponent >=0: 6
   B. 64
   ```

5.  ```
    scanf( "%i", &choice );
    switch (choice) {
      case 1: add(); break;
      case 2: modify(); break;
      case 3: delete(); break;
      default: puts( "Error; the legal choices are 1...3" );
    }
    ```

6. Linear interpolation:

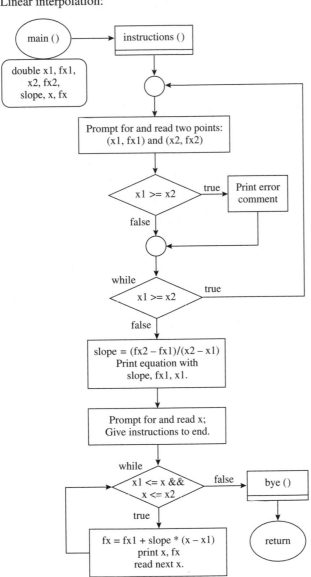
    ```

7. `if (k==2 || k==12) puts( "You lose" );`
    `else if (k==7 || k==11) puts( "You win" );`
    `else puts( "Try again" );`

8. The flowchart is followed by a trace and its output:

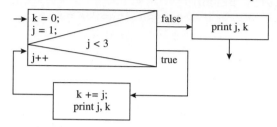

j	1	2	3
k	0	1	3
loop test	T	T	F

Output:

```
1   1
2   3
3   3
```

9. (a) This prints the numbers from 0 to 2. Corrected it is:

    `for (k=1; k<=3; ++k) printf( "k=%i", k );`

    (b) This prints the numbers 1 and 2. Correct it by continuing `while (k<=3);`.

1.7   Chapter 7

1. (a) `<time.h>` (b) `"tools.h"` (c) `<limits.h>` (d) `<stdlib.h>`
    (e) `<stdio.h>` (f) `<math.h>` (g) `"tools.h"` (h) `<math.h>`

2. (a) 33333 is `long int`; (b) 10U is `unsigned int`; (c) 32270 is `int`; (d) −20 is
    `int`; (e) 3000000000 is `long unsigned`; (f) 100L is `long int`; (g) 32,767 is not
    legal because of the comma; (h) 65432 is `long int`.

3. (a) Where the amount of storage matters (integers take less storage).

    (b) Where we need precise (not approximate) computation and comparisons.

    (c) Where integer division or `int` functions from the library will be used.

    (d) To represent a loop counter or some other object that is best modelled by integers.

4. (a) `true`; (b) `true`; (c) `false`, the remainder is discarded after `/`; (d) the result is
    5, which is interpreted as `true`.

5. (a) `k = 1`; (b) `k = 1`; (c) `f = 5.1`, with less precision; (d) `k = 9`;
    (e) `k = 11`; (f) `f = 3.25`; (g) `f = 3.0`; (h) `f = 4.0`; (i) `f = 3.0`;
    (j) `f` is set to 10.2 and is not changed after that.

6.
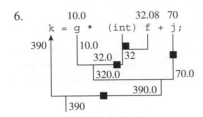

7. (a) `1.234568e+03  1234.5678??  1234.57`
   (b) `1.235e+03    1234.568   1.23e+03       1234.6`

8. (a) **k** is 33. (b) garbage, this number is too large for a **short int**. (c) garbage, **k** is not a long integer. (d) **m** is 33. (e) garbage, you need **%lg** for a **double**. (f) **d** is 109e−02 = 1.09. (g) garbage, you need **%g** for a float. (h) **x** is approximately −43.2109 but may be imprecise after the sixth digit.

I.8   Chapter 8

1. (a)
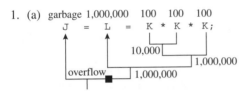

   (b) garbage   2000 2000 2000
       L = M * M * M;

   (c) garbage   2000 2000 2000
       F = M * M * M;

   (d) 8.0e9   2000 2000 2000
       F = (float) M * M * M;

2. (a) This is **INT_MAX**, which usually is either 32,767 or 2,147,483,647.

   (b) This is **UINT_MAX** and should be either 65,535 or 4,294,967,295.

   (c) When *x* equals **INT_MAX** (32,767 or 2,147,483,647).

3. ```
short int k, m=32700;
for (k=0; k<100; ++m, ++k) printf("%hi \n", m);
```

4. (a) The answer will be close to, but not exactly equal to zero. It might cause under-flow. (b) meaningful; (c) the addition will have no meaningful effect because 0.1 is insignificant in comparison to the large value; (d) will cause overflow; a **float** can handle powers only up to about 37.

5. (a) 7.523e+01; (b) 1.2e−04; (c) 9.998e−01; (d) 3.2767e+04.

6. (a) True, the integer 3 will be converted to **double** and can be represented exactly as a **double**.

(b) False, the integer will be converted to 3.0 which != 3.3.

(c) True, they are the same type and their values are different.

(d) False, when the value of **w** is stored in **j**, the fractional part is truncated.

(e) False, the less-precise **float** value is converted to **double**, but precision is not added during that conversion, so the result is not equal to the more precise **double** value.

(f) False, the difference between them is approximately 0.3.

(g) False, the difference between them is approximately 0.3, even if you make **x** less precise by shortening it.

(h) True for some values, false for others. For most possible values of **z**, the tail end of the result of the division is nonzero and gets truncated; the lost bits cannot be regained by a later multiplication. We don't get back exactly what we started with.

(i) True, this is asking whether **4.0 == 4**. The **4** is converted to **double** and represented exactly (it is a small integer).

(j) False, because 0.3 is a repeating fraction.

## I.9                                    Chapter 9

1.

| Scope | Parameters | Variables | Constants |
|-------|------------|-----------|-----------|
| global | — | | EPSILON<br>TRIES |
| main() | — | do_it_again | |
| newton() | — | k, x<br>delta_x | |
| f() | x | — | |
| fprime() | x | — | |
```

2. (a) Local names in **main()**: **x, y, ch1, ch2**;
   (b) parameters in **n_marks()**:   **n, ch**; local variable: **k**.

3. Include **<stdio.h>**:

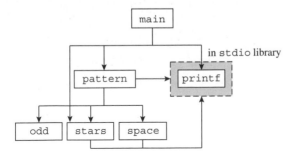

4. All the functions in Figure I.1 except **odd()** are **void** and have no return values. The
   output is

Name	Arguments	Variables	Output or Return
main()	—	k=0	
stars(max)	n=7	k=0...7	*******
return to main()		k=1	\n
stars(MAX)	n=7	k=0...7	*******
return to main()		k=2	\n
pattern(k)	p=2		
stars(1)	n=1	k=0...1	*
space(2,3)	m=2 and n=3	k=0, 2, 4	2 2
odd(MAX)	n=7		return 1
return to pattern()			" "
stars(1)	n=1	k=0...1	*
return to main()		k=3	\n
Repeat **pattern(k)** for	k=3, 4, 5		
pattern(k)	n=3		* 3 3 *\n
pattern(k)	n=4		* 4 4 *\n
pattern(k)	n=5		* 5 5 *\n
return to main()		k=6	
Repeat **stars(MAX)** for	k=6, 7		
stars(MAX)	n=7	k=0...7	*******\n
stars(MAX)	n=7	k=0...7	*******\n

Figure I.1.   Tracing calls.

```
* * * * * *
* * * * * *
*   2   2   *
*   3   3   *
*   4   4   *
* * * * * *
* * * * * *
```

5. In `cyl_vol()`, `d` and `h` are parameters, **r** is a local variable.

6. The main program and two functions are diagrammed:

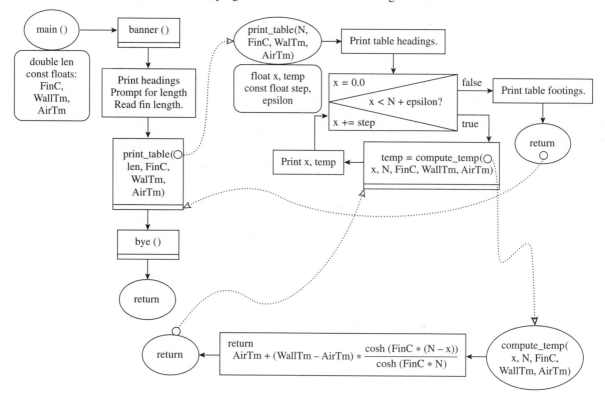

7. (a) Legal and meaningful.

   (b) Legal and meaningful; the argument is coerced to **int**.

   (c) Legal but the return value should be used.

   (d) Legal and meaningful; return value is coerced to **float**.

   (e) Illegal; returns **void**, can't be used in an assignment.

   (f) Legal, possibly an error, both arguments are coerced.

   (g) Legal and meaningful.

   (h) Illegal; function calls do not have type names in the parentheses.

(i) Legal but possibly an error; result of **triple()** is coerced to **double** and **x** is coerced to **int**.

(j) Legal and meaningful; **triple()** returns an **int** and **k** is an **int**, so **%i** is appropriate for both.

I.10   Chapter 10

1. An array of 15 short integers occupies **15*sizeof(short)** = **30** bytes. An array of three **double**s occupies **3*sizeof(double)** = **24** bytes. So the array of short integers occupies more space.

2. (a) temps

[0]	[1]	[2]	[3]	[4]	[5]

   (b) Its base type is **float**. Its length is 6. Its size is **6*sizeof(float)** = **24**.

   (c) ```
for (k=0; k<6; ++k) {
      printf("Enter value [%i]: ", k);
      scanf("%g", &temps[k]);
}
```

   (d) ```
if (temps[5] <= 32.0) printf( " freezing" );
else printf( " above freezing" );
```

3. (a) ```
float ff[5] = { 1.9, 2.5, -3.1, 17.2 }; or
float ff[5] = { 1.9, 2.5, -3.1, 17.2, 0.0 };
```

   (b) ```
int positive( float ar[], int n )
{    int k, count=0;
     for (k=0; k<n; ++k) if (ar[k]>0.0) ++count;
     return count;
}
```

   (c) ```
int positive(float ar[], int n);
```

   (d) ```
scanf( "%g", &ff[4] );
```

4. (a) Prototype: **float CHKBAL(float ibal, float checks[]);**.

   (b) Call: **end_balance=CHKBAL(start_balance, check_amounts);**.

   (c) Function header: **float CHKBAL(float ibal, float checks[])**.

5. (a) ```
12: 4096
10: 1024
 8: 256
 6: 64
 4: 16
 2: 4
```

   (b) ```
for (k = 12; k > 0; k -= 2)
      printf( "%2i: %i \n", k, ara[k] );
```

6. (a) Remove the subscript brackets: `x = fun( dub );`.

(b) There are two errors here, (i) incompatible type for argument 1 of `fill` and (ii) **void** value is not ignored as it ought to be. To correct this, add a subscript to denote an individual **double** and eliminate the assignment. The result is: `fill( dub[0] );`.

(c) This function has a return value that probably should not be ignored. Store it somewhere: `j = fix( flo[5] );`.

(d) GOOD.

(e) The first argument should be an entire array, not one array element. Eliminate the subscript on it: `x = q( dub, ary[0] );`.

7. Object diagram, trace, and output:

(a) load

10.2	5.0	30.6	10.0	51.0
[0]	[1]	[2]	[3]	[4]

(b) `j:`   0 1 2 3 4 5
`j<5:`   T T T T T F   Output:
                                  10.2   5   30.6 9.9550.95
`j<=2:` T T T F F

I.11   **Chapter 11**

1. (a) The character literal `'6'` is represented in the computer (in ASCII) as the binary integer $00110110 = 54$ in base 10. The integer literal **6** is represented in binary as $00000000\ 00000110 = 6$ in base 10.

(b) The string literal `"true"` is represented in the computer by a series of characters (four characters plus a null character). In contrast, **true** is represented by the integer 1; it is a truth value, and a constant of the enumerated type **bool**, not a word.

2. (a) A whitespace character is a character in the ASCII set that is commonly used in text files but is not visible when printed. In standard C there are six: `' '`, `\n`, `\r`, `\t`, `\v`, and `\f`.

(b) An escape code character is a character literal written in single quotes with a back-slash. There are 11 common character escape codes, the 5 whitespace characters listed previously and these: `'\0'`, `'\\'`, `'\''`, `'\"'`, `'\a'`, and `'\b'`. In addition, any character can be written by using a backslash and the ASCII character code.

3.   `1:1`   `3:3`   `5:5`

4. (a) `c = 'c'`.

(b) `c = 'b'` (it was POSTdecrement).

(c) `c = 'E'`.

(d) `k = 7`.

(e) `b = 0 (false)`.

(f) `b = 0 (false)`.

5. (a) `d = 'a'`.

   (b) `d = '6'` (`%c` reads one keystroke).

   (c) `k = 70` and `d = ' '` (`%c` does not skip leading whitespace).

   (d) Read error; only numeric input can be read with a `%i` field.

   (e) `d = 'g'`.

   (f) If the user typed the \ key, `d` would be a backslash character. If Enter was struck, `d` would be a newline.

6.
```
void er_out( error_t code )
{
    switch (code) {
        case DATA_OK:    puts( " Great!" );            break;
        case TOO_SMALL: puts( " Bigger, please." ); break;
        case TOO_BIG:    puts( " That's too big." ); break;
        default: puts( " Hey, I said positive!" );
    }
}
```

7.
```
Type a character and hit ENTER: Z
90 Z
Z
```

I.12   Chapter 12

1. (a) `fp = &y;`.

   (b) `fp = &s[1];`.

   (c) `x = *fp;`.

   (d) `*fp = y;`.

   (e) `*fp = s[3];`.

   (f) `scanf( "%g", &x );`.

   (g) `scanf( "%g", fp );` (no change).

   (h) `printf( "%g", s[1] );`.

2. (a)
```
int m=3;
int n=0;
int * ptr1 = &m;
int * ptr2 = NULL;
```

(b) ptr1 = ptr2 = &n;
   *ptr2 = 9;

3. #include "tools.h"
   void same(int in1, int in2, bool* out1)
           { *out1 = (in1 == in2); }

   void main(void)
   {
       bool answer;
       int k, degrees[6] = { 34, 29, 31, 36, 37, 33 };
       for (k=0; k<6; ++k) {
           same(degrees[k], 31, &answer);
           if (answer) printf(" Degrees[%i] is 31\n", k);
       }
   }

4. #include "tools.h"
   void freeze(int temperatures[], int* n);
   void show(int temperatures[], int n);

   void main(void)
   {
       int max = 6;
       int degrees[6] = { 34, 29, 31, 36, 37, 33 };
       freeze(degrees, &max);
       printf("\n After freeze: max = %i\n", max);
       show(degrees, 6);
   }
   /* -- */
   void freeze(int temperatures[], int* n)
   {
       int k;
       for(k = *n-1; k >= 0; --k)
       if (temperatures[k] >= 32) --(*n); /* or --*n */
   }
   /* -- */
   void show(int t[], int n)
   {
       int k;
       for(k=0; k<n; ++k) printf(" [%i] %i\t ", k, t[k]);
       puts("");
   }

   Output:
   After freeze: max = 2

```
    main

    int       max          6 5  4  3 2
    int []    degrees [0]       34
                      [1]       29
                      [2]       31
                      [3]       36
                      [4]       37
                      [5]       33

    freeze

    int []    temperatures        O
    int*      n                   O

    int       k           5 4 3 2 1 0 -1
```

5. Storage for the quadratic roots program:

Scope	Input Parameters	Output Parameters	Variables	Constants
global	—	—	—	EPS
main()	—	—	double a, b, c, r1, r2, root_type, n_roots	—
solve()	double a, b, c	double* rp1, *rp2	double d, two_a, sroot	—
iszero()	double x	—	—	—

6. Two traces of the quadratic root program:
   ```
   Output:
     Find the roots of a*x^2 + b*x + c = 0
     Enter the values of a, b, and c: 0 3 1
     The equation is   0 *x^2 + 3 *x + 1 = 0
     Linear equation -- root at -c/b = -0.333
   ```

   ```
   In main():              In solve():
          a = 0                   a = 0
          b = 3                   b = 3
          c = 1                   c = 1
         r1 = ? -.333           rp1 = &r1
         r2 = ?                 rp2 = &r2
    n_roots = ?                   d = ?
                              two_a = ?
                              sroot = ?
                              return: LINEAR
   ------------------------------------------------
   Output:
     Find the roots of a*x^2 + b*x + c = 0
     Enter the values of a, b, and c: 0 0 1.
     The equation is   0 *x^2 + 0 *x + 1 = 0
     Degenerate equation -- no roots
   ```

```
In main():              In solve():
        a = 0               a = 0
        b = 0               b = 0
        c = 1               c = 1
       r1 = ?             rp1 = &r1
       r2 = ?             rp2 = &r2
  n_roots = ?               d = ?
                         two_a = ?
                         sroot = ?
                        return: NONE
```

7. Output:

```
X = 4 Y = 3 Z = 5
```

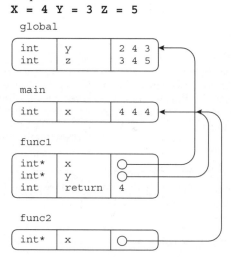

Chapter 13

1. (a) **hello?**
   groan!   save me 0h!

   (b) There are not enough bytes in **t** to hold the entire word **finished**, so the copying process will overflow the array boundary and overwrite something else.

2. (a) Variable **t** is a pointer, not a character array. It does not have enough bytes to hold a word of more than three letters. Set **t = name** first.

   (b) Variable **word** is an array, so its address is passed to **scanf()** automatically. Remove the ampersand.

   (c) Using the **s** specifier, input stops at the first whitespace. It will not read the middle and last names. Format should be **"%19[^\n]"**.

   (d) The referent of **w** is **word**, which has space for the input, but **w** already is an address, so remove the ampersand.

(e) This will work properly if the input is short enough, but it will overflow the array boundary if there are more than 19 letters before the newline. Format should be `"%19[^\n]"`.

3.
```
string message;
int v;
if (v>=1 && v<=10) message = "good";
else message = "bad";
printf( "%s", message );
```

4. (a) Initialize **t** to point at something before trying this.

   (b) This is the wrong kind of 0 constant, it should be **t = NULL**.

   (c) We can't copy a **char** array using assignment; it should be:
   `strcpy( name, word )`.

   (d) In this case, it is correct because **name** contains the null string. However, if the message in **name** is longer than nine letters, this copy operation does not put a null terminator on the copied word.

   (e) The return value from **strcmp(name, word)** is 0 if the words are equal, so the message is inappropriate. We need to say **if(!strcmp(name, word))** or **if (strcmp(name, word)==0)**.

   (f) Since **w** has been set to refer to **word**, it is correct to copy into it. However, the ampersand before **name** must be removed and some length limitation should be used because **word** is shorter than **name**.

5. (a) True, it is a pointer.

   (b) True, it was declared to be 12.

   (c) False, it is 10.

   (d) False, **w** refers to **word**, which holds a string of length 7.

   (e) True. The null string has string length 0.

   (f) False, **word** holds a string of length 7.

6. Output:
```
I love you
Yes, I do
I love you truly Drew!
```
The final configuration of message and pointers is:

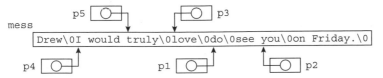

7. (a)
```
#define N 5
const string menu[N] = { "O Order", "X Cancel",
              "I Inspect", "C Complain", "G Go home" };
```

(b)
```
for( ; choice != 'g'; ) {
    choice = menu_c( "Choose next task: ", N, menu );
    switch (tolower(choice)) {
        case 'o': Order(); break;
        case 'x': Cancel(); break;
        case 'i': Inspect(); break;
        case 'c': Complain(); break;
        case 'g': break;
        default: continue;
    }
}
```

(c) Flow diagram:

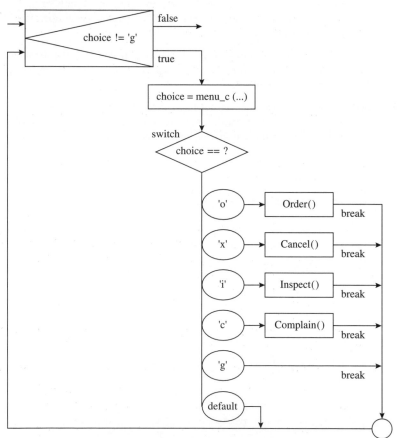

8. Enumerations and parallel arrays. The partially completed program below analyzes whether a box is big enough in each dimension to hold some equipment whose dimensions are given by the array **mindims**. A box can be impossible, too short, too skinny, too flat, or big enough. Fill in some of the missing parts as follows:

   (a) ```
const string labels[] = { "bad input","too short",
       "too narrow","too thin","just right"};
```

   (b) ```
const string dims[3] = {"length","width","height"};
```

   (c) ```
dim_type
analyze(double actual[], double const min[])
{   int k;
     dim_type code = GOOD;
     for (k=0; k<3; ++k)
         if (actual[k] < min[k]) {
             printf(" Your %s is %g; minimum is %g.\n",
                        dims[k], actual[k], min[k]);
             code = k;
         }
     return code;
}
```

   (d) ```
printf( " The box is %s.\n", labels[result]);
```

I.14
Chapter 14

1. (a) An array would be better to represent the coordinates of the points of a pentagon because no point is "special" and all are processed uniformly.

   (b) A structure would be better to represent a table of gasses and their properties. All the properties are represented by real numbers, but they have different names and different purposes.

   (c) You could use parallel arrays to represent the x, y, and z coordinates of a set of points, but it would be better to represent each point as a coherent object (an array or a structure) and make an array of those objects.

   (d) When you use one of the menu functions, the menu items need to be in a separate array and the information corresponding to each item in a parallel array. Depending on the circumstances, that might be a parallel array of structures or several parallel arrays.

2. ```
typedef struct APPT{ char lname[20]; char fname[20];
                     int hour, minute; } appt_t;
```

3. (a) ```
typedef enum DAY { SUN, MON, TUE, WED,
                   THU, FRI, SAT } day_type;
```

(b) `typedef struct TODAY { day_type dow,`
`                    int year, month, date; } today_type;`

(c) `today_type my_day = { FRI, 1999, 8, 20 };`

4. (a) `trip_t ct, vacation;` You can't use an **enum** constant as a variable name.

(b) You cannot enter an enumeration value directly. It can be read as an integer, but some compilers will give error warnings about this. Using a cast works and does not produce warning errors.
`int code; scanf( "%i", &code );`
`vacation.start = (trip_t)code;`

(c) `vacation.end = VT;` an enumeration constant is not a string.

(d) `vacation.days = 3;` vacation is a structure, not a pointer to a structure.

(e) Answer is correct.

5. A two-level structure.

(a) `typedef struct POINT { int hor, vert; } point;`

(b) `typedef struct LINE { point p1, p2; int thick; } line;`

(c) `line corners = { {0, 0}, {1599, 1199}, 15 };`

(d)
```
void get_line( line c, line* in )
{
    for (;;) {
        printf( "\n Point 1 ; "
          "Enter x %i..%i and y %i..%i: ",
          c.p1.hor, c.p2.hor, c.p1.vert, c.p2.vert );
        scanf( "%i%i", &in->p1.hor, &in->p1.vert );
        if (in->p1.hor >= c.p1.hor &&
            in->p1.hor <= c.p2.hor &&
            in->p1.vert >= c.p1.vert &&
            in->p1.vert <= c.p2.vert) break;
        puts( "\t Out of range -- try again." );
    }
    for (;;) {
        printf( " Point 2 ; "
          "Enter x %i..%i and y %i..%i: ",
          c.p1.hor, c.p2.hor, c.p1.vert, c.p2.vert );
        scanf( "%i%i", &in->p2.hor, &in->p2.vert );
        if (in->p2.hor >= c.p1.hor &&
            in->p2.hor <= c.p2.hor &&
            in->p2.vert >= c.p1.vert &&
            in->p2.vert <= c.p2.vert) break;
        puts( "\t Out of range -- try again." );
    }
    for (;;) {
        printf( " Line thickness; "
                " Enter 0..%i: ", c.thick );
```

```
        scanf( "%i", &in->thick );
        if (in->thick >= 0 && in->thick <= 15) break;
        puts( "\t Out of range -- try again." );
    }
}
```

6. A three-day trip:

0:CT	2:MA	1
2:MA	5:VT	1
5:VT	0:CT	1

<table>
<tr><td>**I.15**</td><td># Chapter 15</td></tr>
</table>

1. (a) The **scanf()** function reads only from **stdin**, while **fscanf()** can read either from **stdin** or from a user-defined stream.

   (b) The **say()** function writes its output on **stderr** while **printf()** writes on **stdout**.

   (c) The **say()** and **fatal()** functions both write to **stderr**, but **say()** returns control to the program, while **fatal()** aborts execution.

   (d) The **fgetc()** function reads a single character from a designated stream. The name **getc()** is an alternate for the same function: **fgetc()** is preferred.

2. (a) Happy tested the value of **ch** before initializing it. This would lead to trouble if the location happened to contain a newline character.

   (b) It is a minor error, but the test for **feof()** is made before the input step, not after. This should not cause trouble in this situation, but technically, it is undefined.

3. (a) **ok = 1, j = 37, k** is unchanged, and the "**.21 46**" stays in the stream.

   (b) **ok = 3, x = 24.5, y = 17, z = -0.22**.

   (c) **ok = 2, k = 37**, the **71** is read and discarded, and the **26** stays in the stream.

   (d) **ok = 1, j = 66, k** is unchanged.

   (e) **ok = 72**, which is the ASCII code for **H**.

4. (a) The name of the stream and the name of the file both indicate that an input file is being opened, but the mode is **"w"**, which is used for output files. The mode probably should be **"r"**.

   (b) The mode **"bw"** should be **"wb"**, which means "for writing binary data." The **b** is unnecessary in some systems, but harmless and appropriate for an image. However, the file name indicates an input file, and it is being opened for writing. The model should probably be **"rb"**.

   (c) You need quotes around the file name: **"data.in"**.

   (d) A pathname needs either slashes (DOS) or backslashes (UNIX) between the directory names, not periods, and the filename should have a **.out** extension.

The backslashes need to be doubled in C because backslash is a special character. The first argument should be either `"c:jones/cs110/labs.out"` or `"c:jones\\cs110\\labs.out"`.

(e) A `.c` file is a text file. It is unlikely that data should be written to it at all, and even more unlikely that it should be written in binary mode.

5. (a) `fscanf( fin, " %23[^,], %23[^,], %31[^\n]", name, title, company );` Note: The three spaces and two commas in the format are necessary to remove whitespace and commas from the input stream.

(b) `fscanf( fin, "%g%g%g", &x, &y, &z );`

(c) `fscanf( fin, "%g %c %31[^\n]", &t, &code, label );`
Note: We can omit the space before the `%c` if we are sure that the letter always follows the number without intervening whitespace.

(d) There are two good solutions: The first stores the newline at the end of the string, the second does not: `fgets( title, 23, fin );`
`fscanf( fin, " %23[^\n]", title );`

(e) `fscanf( fin, " %23[^,], %c%i", name, &code, &age );`
Note: The spaces and commas in the format are necessary for proper operation.

6. You can use `feof()` after all kinds of input statements; it works the same way and equally well after `fscanf()`, `fgets()`, `fgetc()`, and `fread()`. If the end of file condition occurs at the very beginning of the read operation, all of these functions return a recognizable code. With `fscanf()` and `fgetc()`, the code is **EOF**, but the end-of-file code from `fgets()` is **NULL** and `fread()` returns 0. Clearly, it is less complex to use `feof()` than to use the return values. In addition, an end-of-file condition can occur in the middle of an input operation with `fscanf()` and `fread()`, and, in that case, neither returns **EOF**. Finally, the value **EOF** also is used to indicate a read error by `fgetc()`.

7. In an unbuffered output stream, data go immediately to the destination (file or device) when written by the program. In a buffered stream, the data go first to a buffer and stay there until the buffer is full or the stream is flushed. Then the data go to the destination. An unbuffered input stream reads characters from the device when they are called for by the program. A buffered input stream reads a block of information into a buffer and passes it to the program on demand. Most streams are buffered because the size of the buffer can be matched to the amount of data the device is designed to transfer. A disk cannot read or write a partial sector; it must transfer data to or from a sector as a unit. The standard output stream is buffered because it minimizes the number of times that the devices must be accessed, which speeds up processing. The **stderr** stream is not buffered because it is important for user-information messages to be displayed promptly, especially those displayed before a program aborts or while it is crashing. Since data in the buffers are lost when the program has an abnormal end, a buffered stream cannot be used for emergency messages.

I.16   Chapter 16

1. On an array of six data items, `find_min()` is called five times, with `start` = 0, 1, 2, 3, 4. On each call it does `6-start-1` comparisons. Altogether the total is $5 + 4 + 3 + 2 + 1 = 15$ comparisons and five swaps.

2. In an unsorted array, you must search the entire array before you can conclude that the key item is not there. In a sorted array, you can stop searching once you find the key item or go past the position that should hold the key item. On the average, this is N/2 comparisons.

3. There are two ways to change it: Change all minima to maxima or swap the selected items to the end of the array, not the beginning. The changes needed to do the first strategy are much simpler, so we present those. In Figure 16.18, the name of the subfunction needs to be changed twice, in the prototype and in the call:

```
int find_max( float data[], int begin, int n );
where = find_max( data, start, n );
```

Also, in Figure 16.21, change the function name and one operator in the `if` statement:

```
int find_max( float data[], int begin, int n );
if (data[cursor] > data[finger]) finger=cursor;
```

4.
```
     0  1  2  3  4  5  6  7  8  9   min is  swap with
    ---------------------------------------------------
0.  77 32 86 12 14 64 99  3 43 21   slot 7  slot 0
1.   3 32 86 12 14 64 99 77 43 21   slot 3  slot 1
2.   3 12 86 32 14 64 99 77 43 21   slot 4  slot 2
3.   3 12 14 32 86 64 99 77 43 21   slot 9  slot 3
4.   3 12 14 21 86 64 99 77 43 32   slot 9  slot 4
5.   3 12 14 21 32 64 99 77 43 86   slot 8  slot 5
6.   3 12 14 21 32 43 99 77 64 86   slot 8  slot 6
7.   3 12 14 21 32 43 64 77 99 86   slot 7  itself
8.   3 12 14 21 32 43 64 77 99 86   slot 9  slot 8
9.   3 12 14 21 32 43 64 77 86 99   sorted
```

5.
```
int find_max( word_t data[], int begin, int n )
{
    int cursor;
    int finger = begin;
    for ( cursor = begin + 1; cursor<n; ++cursor) {
        if (strcmp( data[cursor], data[finger] ) > 0)
            finger = cursor;
    }
    return finger;
}
```

6.
```
bool mask = { true,true,true,false,true,true,false,true,
              true,false,true,false };
```

```
7. void flip_print( int data[], bool mask[] )
   {
       int k;
       for (k = 0; k < 12; ++k) {
           if (mask[k]) printf( "%i\n", data[k] );
           mask[k] = !mask[k];
       }
   }
```

I.17 **Chapter 17**

1. (a) Flowchart for nested **for** loop:

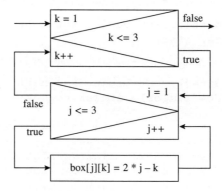

(b) Box array with initial values:

box	[0]	[1]	[2]	[3]
[0]	?	?	?	?
[1]	?	1	0	-1
[2]	?	3	2	1
[3]	?	5	4	3
[4]	?	?	?	?

(c) The 5 is in **box[3][1]**.

(d) If an **int** occupies 2 bytes, then **sizeof box = 5 * 4 * sizeof(int) = 20 * 2 = 40** bytes.
    If an **int** occupies 4 bytes, then **sizeof box = 20 * 4 = 80** bytes.

(e) Slot **[1][2]** has the lower memory address because lower subscripts have lower addresses and all of row 1 is stored before any of row 2.

(f) The **10** is stored in a location 8 or 16 bytes past the end of the array. This could cause a memory violation of one sort or another if the array is near the end of the program's own memory area.

2. Lumber array:

lumber	[0]	[1]	[2]	[3]
[0]	2.5	0	0	0
[1]	.5	2.5	0	0
[2]	1.0	1.5	2.5	0

3. Loop execution trace:

k	0	0	0	0	1	1	1	2	2	3	4
m	0	1	2	3	1	2	3	2	3	3	
output	1	2	3		4	6		9			

Output:
1 2 3
4 6
9

4. Loop execution trace.

k	0	0	0	0	1	1	1	1	2	2	2	2	3
m	0	1	2	3	0	1	2	3	0	1	2	3	
output	..1	...	..3			...	..4	...		..3	...	..9	

Output:
..1.....3
.....4...
..3.....9

5.
```
float
find_min( float data [N][N], int* row, int* col )
{
    int r, c;
    float m = data[0][0];
    for (r=0; r<N; ++r )
        for (c=0; c<N; ++c )
            if (data[r][c] < m) {
                *row = r;
                *col = c;
                m = data[r][c];
            }
    return m;
}
```

6.
```
#define  Z  3
#define  W  7
int k, m;

printf( "        " );
for (k = 0; k < Z; ++k) printf( " %2i", k );
puts( "\n  --------------" );
for (m = 0; m < W; ++m) {
    printf( " %4i:", m );
```

```
        for (k = 0; k < Z; ++k) printf( " %2i", mat[m][k] );
        putchar( '\n' );
    }
```

I.18   Chapter 18

1. (a) 2730, 4013, 61937, and 2816.

   (b) f 10 11 12 13 14 15 16 17 18 19 1a 1b 1c 1d 1e 1f 20 21 22 23

   (c) $105_{10} = 69_{16}$

   (d) $101010_2 = 2a_{16}$

   (e) $0011010110101100 = 0011\ 0101\ 1010\ 1100 = 35ac$; as a hexadecimal literal,
   0x35ac.

2. (a) The result is not negative and seems unrelated to the input.
   ```
   short and long unsigned ints: -23000 -470123
        short in hu = 42536   in hx = a628
        long in lu = 4294497173  in lx = fff8d395
   ```

   (b) The number **4294967295** is the biggest **unsigned int** that can be read and
   written on a machine with 4-byte integers. In hex it is **0xffffffff** Since **f** is
   the largest digit in hexadecimal, a string of eight **f**s is the largest number that can
   be represented.

   (c) $75_{16} = 117_{10}$

3. (a) ```
   const int xmask = 0xf0f0f0f0;
   const int vmask = 0x0f000000;
   const int emask = 0x000f0f0f;
   ```

   (b) ```
   X = input & xmask;
   V = input & vmask;
   E = input & emask;
   ```

   (c) ```
   V >>= 24;
   E <<= 8;
   ```

   (d) `result = X | V | E;`

4. ```
   typedef struct IBM704 {
        unsigned int        :5 ;
        unsigned int op     :3 ;
        unsigned int        :1 ;
        unsigned int decr :15;
        unsigned int        :5 ;
        unsigned int ix     :3 ;
        unsigned int        :1 ;
        unsigned int addr :15;
   } ibm_t;
   ```

5. Several solutions are possible; this is one.
   ```
   #define OP 0x70
   ```

```
#define DECR 0x7F
#define IDX 0x07
#define ADDR 0x7F
```

6. (a) `w = 0;`

   (b) `w = 255;`

   (c) `w = 5;`

   (d) `v = 6` and `w = (v<<3) + (v<<1) = 48+12 = 60;`

   (e)
   ```
   w = x | y & x | z<<y^mask>>x
     = ((x | (y & x)) | ((z<<y)^(c3>>x)));
     = ((x | 0) | ((16) ^ ((1100 0011) >> 1)));
     = (x | ((0001 0000) ^ (0110 0001)));
     = (1 | 0111 0001 );
     = 0111 0001 = 64+32+16+1 = 113 = 0x71
   ```

   (f) `w = 255;`

   (g) `w = 2;`

   (h) `w = 1 ^~2 = 1^(1111 1101) = (1111 1100) = 252;`

   (i) `w = 1|2| (4>>2) = 3|1 = 3;`

   (j) `w = 1&2&~4 = 1&2&(1111 1011) = 0&(1111 1011) = 0`

I.19

Chapter 19

1. (a) Misspelling; write **malloc**, not **maaloc**.

   (b) The object **darray** was not allocated by **malloc()** or **calloc()**, so it cannot be recycled by calling **free()**.

   (c) The result of **calloc()** is a pointer to a memory allocation; it must be stored somewhere. Also, it must be cast to type **(int*)** not type **(int)**.

   (d) We create enough space for five integers and store the result in a **float** pointer. The resulting type mismatch is a semantic error but it is legal C. Also, the comma should be an asterisk.

   (e) You need to store the result of **realloc()** back into **fp**.

   (f) Syntax crror; the multiply sign should be a comma:
   calloc(10, sizeof(int)).

   (g) The cast is wrong; it should be **(float*)**. More serious, though, the **malloc** was omitted.

   (h) The first parameter of **realloc()** must be a pointer to a previously allocated memory area. Also, the comma between the given parameters should be a *****:
   max*sizeof(float).

2. say

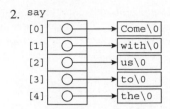

```
[0]  O  ──────→  Come\0
[1]  O  ──────→  with\0
[2]  O  ──────→  us\0
[3]  O  ──────→  to\0
[4]  O  ──────→  the\0
```

3. (a) We could do most things but less efficiently. We could emulate **realloc()** by first calling **malloc()** to get new storage, then copying the data, then calling **free()** to release the first area. However, **realloc()** allows us to shorten an allocation area very efficiently without copying the data, and we couldn't do that with only **malloc()** and **free()**.

   (b) If the language did not have **free()**, there would be no way to recycle dead memory areas. This would increase the memory requirements of many applications, make them slower, and lead to a greater likelihood of programs running out of memory altogether.

4.
```
int k;
p = malloc( 10*sizeof(int) );
for (k=0; k<10; ++k) p[k] = 0;
```

5.
```
void
swap( string data[], int m, int k )
{
    string swap = data[k];
    if (strcmp(data[m], swap) > 0 ) {
        data[k] = data[m];
        data[m] = swap;
    }
}
```

6. Two versions are given, one using subscripts, the other using pointers:
```
void
recycle( string data[], int n )
{
    int k;
    for (k=0; k<n; ++k)   free( data[k] );
    free( data );
}
/* ------------------------------------ */
void
recycle( string data[], int n )
{
    string* p=data, *pend=data+n;
    for ( ; p < pend; ++p)   free( *p );
    free( data );
}
```

7. (a) Advantages: This implementation is the most efficient with respect to both space usage and the time required to access an element. This kind of matrix also is most convenient for the programmer because it can be initialized in the declaration and accessed using two subscripts. Disadvantages: To change the size, the program must be edited and recompiled.

   (b) Advantages: This implementation is only marginally less efficient than (a) with respect to space usage, and equally efficient with respect to time. Disadvantages: The size of the matrix must be known before it can be allocated. There is no simple way to resize it. It cannot be initialized in a declaration. To access the matrix using two subscripts, the programmer must define an accessing function.

   (c) Advantages: This implementation is very flexible; the number of rows can easily be resized dynamically, and the number of columns can be increased, although at somewhat greater cost. This kind of matrix is convenient for the programmer because it can be accessed using two subscripts. Disadvantages: Some space is consumed by overhead on each separately allocated array, and the time needed to process such a matrix is substantially greater because two memory accesses are needed (rather than one) to access a matrix element.

I.20   Chapter 20

1.

21	4	13	17	24	8	15	max slot 4, swap slot 0
24	4	13	17	21	8	15	max slot 4, swap slot 1
24	21	13	17	4	8	15	max slot 3, swap slot 2
24	21	17	13	4	8	15	max slot 6, swap slot 3
24	21	17	15	4	8	13	max slot 6, swap slot 4
24	21	17	15	13	8	4	max slot 5, swap slot 5
24	21	17	15	13	8	4	sorted.

2. The = sign marks the position of **hole** at the beginning of each pass.

```
21 = 4   13   17   24     8   15    insert 4.
 4  21 = 13   17   24     8   15    insert 13.
 4  13  21 = 17   24     8   15    insert 17.
 4  13  17  21 = 24     8   15    insert 24.
 4  13  17  21   24 =   8   15    insert 8.
 4   8  13  17   21   24 = 15    insert 15.
 4   8  13  15   17   21   24 = done.
```

3. (a) OK; (b) `char* b[10];` (c) `char** p = &b[0];`
   (d) `char* q = malloc( 12 );`
   (e) `char** s = malloc( 4 * sizeof(char*) )`.

4. `float mat[N][N];`
   `float* begin = &mat[0][0];`   `/* or = mat[0]; */`
   `float* end = &mat[N-1][N-1];`
   `float* off = &mat[N-1][N];`   `/* or = mat[N]; */`

5. (a) `point_t tri[3] = {{0,0},{0,1},{1,0}};`

   (b) `point_t* tp = tri;        /* or = &tri[0]; */`

   (c) `point_t* tri_end = tri+3;  /* or = &tri[3]; */`

6. (a) `xp = &x;`
      `yp = &tri[1].y;           /* or = &(tri[1].y); */`
      `pp = &tri[2];`

   (b) `*xp = pp->x;`

   (c) `tri[1].y = 3.3;`

   (d) `printf ( " x-coord of last point = %g\n", (tp+2)->x );`

7. The output is 1 0 1 0 1 0 1 0 1

8.
```
triangle_t tri_in( void )
{
    point_t* pp = calloc( 3, sizeof(point_t) );
    point_t* scan = pp, *tri_end = pp+3;
    for ( ; scan < tri_end; ++scan) {
        printf( "Enter x and y for one corner > " );
        scanf( "%lg%lg", &scan->x, &scan->y);
    }
    return pp;
}
```

I.21   Chapter 21

1. (a) Symbols declared as **extern** can be shared by multiple code modules, while **static** symbols are private within the module that defines them.

   (b) Symbols declared as **static** are allocated and initialized once, when the program is loaded, while **auto** symbols are allocated and initialized each time control enters the scope that defines them.

   (c) Symbols at the top level, outside of all functions, are **extern** by default, while symbols defined within a function are **auto** by default.

2. (a) Searching for 5.72:
```
First call: left = 0, right = 15, mid = 7
            ( recurse / return 11 )
Next call:  left = 8, right = 15, mid = 11
            ( return 11 )
```

   (b) Searching for 2.1:
```
First call: left = 0, right = 15, mid = 7
            ( recurse / NOT_FOUND )
```

```
Next call:   left = 0, right =  6, mid = 3
             ( recurse / NOT_FOUND )
Next call:   left = 0, right =  2, mid = 1
             ( recurse / NOT_FOUND )
Next call:   left = 0, right =  0, mid = 0
             ( NOT_FOUND )
```

3. Let us refer to the three **if** statements as *a*, *b*, and *c*, respectively. Then the six possible orders are *abc*, *bac*, *cab*, *cba*, *acb*, and *bca*. Order *abc* is the given order that works properly. The other five possibilities are analyzed next. For (bac) and (bca), the function always terminates properly but it gives the wrong answer when **left==right==mid** and the key value is in that slot. For (cab) and (cba), if you put the last **if** first, with its **else**, the function does not exit normally, it keeps trying to recurse and will go on forever or until it bombs. For (acb), the function will terminate and return the correct answer if the key value is somewhere in the array, but it will become an infinite recursion if the key value is not there.

4. ```
Stack frames for sum:
First call: a->2, n=5, partial=? (recurse)
Second call: a->3, n=4, partial=? (recurse)
Third call: a->5, n=3, partial=? (recurse)
Fourth call: a->7, n=2, partial=? (recurse)
Fifth call: a->11, n=1, partial=0 (return 11+0=11)
Fourth frame: a->7, n=2, partial=11 (return 7+11=18)
Third frame: a->5, n=3, partial=18 (return 5+18=23)
Second frame: a->3, n=4, partial=23 (return 3+23=26)
First frame: a->2, n=5, partial=26 (return 2+2=28)
Return 28
```

5. We start with the values in this order: 799, 404, 175, 967, 872, 671, 572, 53, 276, 267, 387, 802, 279, 567, 726, 24, 840. The calls on **quick()** are shown in Figure I.2; each call indicates the parameters, action taken, value or values that are sorted by the call, and the return address.

6. It will work. We have to show (a) that every subarray will be examined and (b) that the partition algorithm will work on every one.

   (a) Whether we do the left side or the right side first makes no difference; the same pointers will be used to denote the subarrays in either case.

   (b) For the partition to work, we need to know that the comparisons and swaps work independently of the order in which we do them (they do, obviously) and that the partition step always ends by identifying a split point within the current subarray. This is true, if we get to the end of the function. The only problem might be looping off the end of the array. The algorithm relies on sentinel values to stop the loops; they always must be in place at both ends of the subarray we currently are sorting. The pivot value is swapped to the left end of the part of the current subarray and will stop the right-to-left scan. The value on the right end of the current subarray must be greater than the pivot value to stop the left-to-right scan. In the beginning, we put a max sentinel there; it works. On subsequent passes
```

Calls on quick()	Parameters first	last	Local variables how_ many	split	Action	Values now sorted	Return to call
1	->[0]	->[16]	17	->[4]	call 2a, 2b	276	to caller
2a	->[0]	->[3]	4	->[0]	call 3a, 3b	24	to 1, 1st
3a	->[0]	->[1]	0		no work		to 2a, 1st
3b	->[1]	->[3]	2	->[2]	call 4a, 4b	175	to 2a, 2nd
4a	->[1]	->[1]	1	->[1]	no work	53	to 3b, 1st
4b	->[3]	->[3]	1	->[3]	no work	267	to 3b, 2nd
2b	->[5]	->[16]	12	->[6]	call 5a, 5b	387	to 1, 2nd
5a	->[5]	->[5]	1		no work	279	to 2b, 1st
5b	->[7]	->[16]	10	->[13]	call 6a, 6b	802	to 4b, 2nd
6a	->[7]	->[12]	6	->[7]	call 7a, 7b	404	to 5b, 1st
7a	->[7]	->[6]	0		no work		to 6a, 1st
7b	->[8]	->[12]	5	->[10]	call 8a, 8b	671	to 6a, 2nd
8a	->[8]	->[9]	2		swap[8][9]	572, 567	to 7b, 1st
8b	->[11]	->[12]	2		no swap	726, 799	to 7b, 2nd
6b	->[14]	->[16]	3	->[16]	call 9a, 9b	967	to 5b, 2nd
9a	->[14]	->[15]	2		no swap	840, 872	to 6b, 1st
9b	->[17]	->[16]	0		no work		to 6b, 2nd

Figure I.2.   Calls on quick().

that involve the end of the array, the same max-sentinel value is still there and still works. If a left-to-right scan ends in the middle of the array, it ends at a value previously used as a pivot value. This previous pivot is greater than everything to its left, including subsequently chosen pivot values. Therefore, partition always stops and always works.

7.
```
long int
product ( int a[], int n )
{
    long int partial;

    if (n == 1)  partial = 1;
    else  partial = product( &a[1], n - 1 );
    return a[0] * partial;
}
```

I.22   Chapter 22

1. (a) Spelling error: **mysort** needs a **t**.

   (b) Usage error: The number of items to sort was omitted. The input and output files will be opened properly. Then **strtol()** will be called to convert the **-a** to a number and fail.

(c) The argument **-ad** is wrong (it does not match either **-a** or **-d**), so the program says that the sort order is undefined and aborts.

(d) The number of items to sort is negative. The program detects that it is less than 2 and aborts.

(e) Usage error: The argument count is too small. (The number of items to sort is missing.)

2. (a) Everything will work fine. As long as the sort prepares the data using the same comparison function as the search, performance will be correct.

(b) Using **sort_int_down()** for **qsort()** and **sort_int_up()** for **bsearch()** is inconsistent. The search succeeds if the key happens to be in the table slot searched first. After that, **bsearch()** always looks in the wrong half of the table and never finds what it is looking for.

(c) The same bad result as in part (b); **bsearch()** always looks up when it should look down and looks down when it should look up.

3. (a) Get the first ASCII digit and subtract **' 0 '** to get an integer **0...9**.

(b) Use this to initialize N.

(c) Get the next character, C; if it is not an ASCII digit, end this loop. Otherwise repeat these two steps:
(i) Multiply N by 10 to prepare for a new digit on the right.
(ii) Add in the new digit (C-**' 0 '**)

(d) You now have an integer equivalent of the ASCII number.

4. (a) There are two errors. First, the arguments to **sort_up()** should be type **void***, and they should be cast to type **string*** within the function. Second, **st1** and **st2** must be dereferenced before the call on **strcmp()**; they are supposed to be type **char***, not **string***.

(b) Here the arguments to **sort_up()** are the correct type, **void***, but we cast them to type **char***, which is inappropriate because they are actually type **string***. This is a semantic error, but since the arguments appear to be the correct type for **strcmp()**, there is no error comment. This causes the pointer parts of the strings to be compared, not the character arrays. A swap will happen if the second pointer refers to an array that was allocated before the referent of the first pointer. But creation-order has nothing to do with alphabetical order or the contents of the arrays.

5. (a) **Strength:** Interactive data entry lets the user actively participate in controlling the progress of the program. **Weaknesses:** Data entered interactively are ephemeral, gone as soon as they are entered unless the program makes a written record of the transactions. This method is prone to error because all human activity is prone to error. An interactive program should be written in such a way that no harm is done when invalid or ridiculous data are entered. This method is most appropriate when the amount of data is small or when the data entered might depend on answers to a previous data set, as with the root-finding programs.

(b) **Strengths:** Reading data from a file is least error prone because data in a file can be checked and validated before entering it into the program. It also is repeatable:

The same data can be used a second time. **Weaknesses:** A small error in an input file can cause a widespread program failure unless it is detected and recovery techniques are implemented. File I/O takes more programming knowledge and more effort to do well than interactive input. Reading data from a file is the only appropriate method for a large amount of data or when the data are produced by some automated process or experimental equipment.

(c) **Strengths:** Command-line arguments give the computer operator last-minute control over important aspects of program execution, such as the identity and size of input files and the amount of feedback desired. **Weaknesses:** Such communication is limited to only a few words or control codes. Also, it is difficult to run command-line programs in some integrated development environments. Command-line arguments are appropriate for very small amounts of data that relate to the control and overall operation of the program. This method commonly is used in conjunction with file input.

6. The command line must supply the following information:

(a) The name of the executable program (required), which is `lookfor`.

(b) The word to search for (required).

(c) The name of the file to be searched (required).

(d) Up to three options (case sensitivity, first or all occurrences, verbose or not).

Therefore, three to six arguments must be present in a command. The name of the command must be first; after that, the order of the other arguments is arbitrary. We choose to put the word first, the options next (in any order), and the file name last because that is common practice. We need to establish codes and default values for the three options. We choose single-letter codes, since they are easiest to decode:

(a) `-s` for case-sensitive comparisons; the default will be non-case sensitive.

(b) `-a` for all occurrences of the word; the default will be the first occurrence.

(c) `-v` for verbose output; the default will be nonverbose.

Some sample command lines are shown here:

```
lookfor gold rainbow.in
lookfor insanity -a -v papers.doc
lookfor bear -s woods.txt
```

I.23   **Chapter 23**

1. Module structure for the roots application:

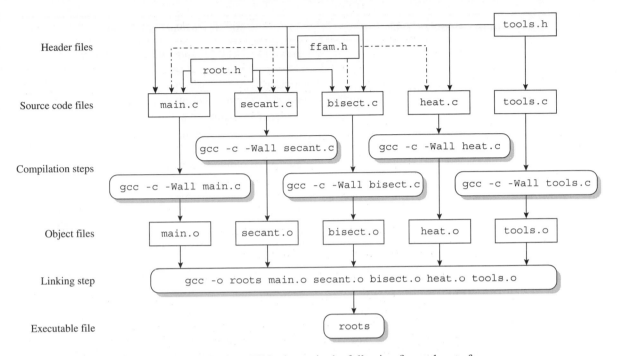

2. Call graph for the roots application. White boxes in the following figure denote functions defined for this application, light gray boxes are from the **tools** library, and dark gray are standard C library functions. The hexagon encloses a global variable, dotted arrows show the functions that use or change it. For relationships, see Figure I.3.

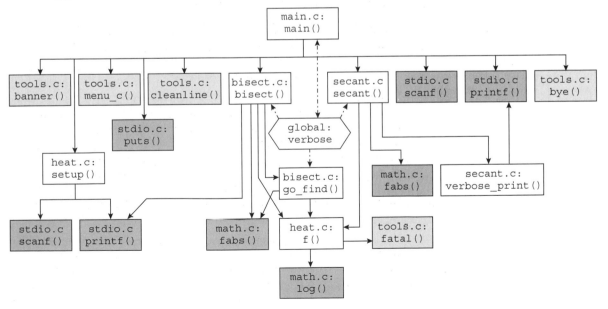

In the Module Graph	Because in the Call Graph
`main.c` includes `tools.h`	`main()` calls `banner()`, `menu_c()`, `cleanline()`, and `bye()` from the `tools` library
`main.c` includes `tools.h` which includes `stdio.h`	`main()` calls `scanf()`, `puts()`, and `printf()` from the standard I/O library.
`main.c` includes `ffam.h`	`main()` calls `setup()`, whose prototype is in `ffam.h`
`main.c` includes `root.h`	`main()` calls `bisect()` and `secant()`, whose prototypes are in `root.h`
`secant.c` and `bisect.c` include `tools.h`, which includes `stdio.h` and `math.h`	Functions in both modules call `printf()`, whose prototype is in `stdio.h` and `fabs()`, whose prototype is in `math.h`.
`secant.c` and `bisect.c` include `ffam.h`	`secant()`, `bisect()`, and `go_find()` call `f()`, whose prototype is in `ffam.h`
`heat.c` includes `tools.h`	`f()` calls `fatal()`, whose prototype is in `tools.h`.
`heat.c` includes `tools.h`, which includes `stdio.h` and `math.h`	`setup()` calls `scanf()` and `printf()` from the standard I/O library, and `f()` calls `log()` from the standard math library.
`secant.c` and `bisect.c` include `root.h`, `heat.c` includes `ffam.h`, `tools.c` includes `tools.h`	Each module includes its own header file to use any defined constants and to have properly defined prototypes of its functions.

Figure I.3.   Relationships between the module graph and the call graph.

3. (a) `main.c` should include `main.h`, `mod1.h`, and `mod2.h`.

   (b) `mod1.c` should include `main.h`, `mod1.h`, and `mod2.h`.

   (c) `mod2.c` should include `main.h` and `mod2.h`.

4. (a) `OBJ = main.o mod1.o mod2.o` instead of `OBJ = dummy.o`, and so forth.

   (b) Should be `CFLAGS = -Wall` instead of `-all`.

   (c) Add main's header file to list for the main module:
       `main.o: main.c main.h mod1.h mod2.h`.

   (d) Should be `gcc -c` ... not `-o`.

   (e) Add two header files to the list for module 1:
       `mod1.o: mod1.c mod1.h main.h mod2.h`.

   (f) Should be `gcc -c $(CFLAGS) mod1.c`, not `mod2.c`.

   (g) Add the source file of module 2 to the list:
       `mod2.o: mod2.c mod2.h main.h`.

(h) Add dollar sign: `gcc -c $(CFLAGS) mod2.h` instead of `-c (CFLAGS)` and change **mod2.h** to **mod2.c**.

(i) This line is OK, but this line and line (j) should be moved to between lines (b) and (c).

(j) The command must give the intended name of the executable application, not the name of the module it came from: `gcc -o apple $(OBJ)` instead of `-o main`.

(k) OK.

(l) The **rm** command needs to list the name of the executable application, since that is one of the files that is supposed to be deleted. No file is named main. Also, OBJ is misspelled: `rm -f $(OBJ) apple` instead of `rm -f $(OBJS) main`.

I.24   Appendix E

1. $11010110 = -00101010 = -42$

2. The sum is 11111111, which is -1.

3. $00110110_2 = 36_{16} = 2 + 4 + 16 + 32 = 54_{10}$

4. $5174_{10} = $ **0001 0100 0011 0110** in binary and $= 1436_{16}$

5. $10.125 = 8 + 2 + \frac{1}{8} = 1010.001$
   As a **float**: **0 10000010 1.0100010 00000000 00000000**

6. $010110_2 * 100_2 = 01011000_2 = 58_{16} = 88_{10}$

7. Five times.

Index

abs, 139, 285
Absolute value function, 139
Accessibility, 331–332
Accumulators, 180, 181, 998
Actions, 44, 63–64, 68
Activation records, 878–879
Active call, 882, 894–895
Actual arguments, 153
Ada, 15
Addition, 289, 303
  float and, 293–294
  with pointers, 841
Address, 47, 55
  arrays and, 383–384, 398, 537
  bytes and, 4, 5
  C and, 15
  call by; *see* Call/pass by address
  effective, 374, 376
  in machine languages, 13, 515
  memory, 449
  menus and machine, 515
  pointer as, 442, 443–445, 471
  pseudo-random numbers and, 261–264
  return, 318, 879
  shifting and masking Internet, 753–755
  subscripts and, 371f
  value parameters versus value, 559–560
Address arguments, 321, 448–449
Address operator, 471; *see also* Ampersands
Aggregate types, 366
  array versus structure as, 552, 586
  arrays as, 552; *see also* Arrays
  strings as; *see* Strings
  structures as, 552–597
Algorithms, 22–23, 26
  binary search, 471, 658f, 881, 886–896
  bisection; *see* Bisection method
  Chauvenet's, 658, 664–677
  combination operators and, 108
  conversion and, 243–246

DES encryption, 748
  encryption, 748
  errors with, 303, 690–690
  example of, 32
  for finding real roots of equation, 294–302
  Gauss's, 810; *see also* Gaussian distribution; Gaussian elimination
  insertion sort; *see* Insertion sort
  for iteration versus recursion, 881–883
  Newton's method, 294–302, 974, 978
  for number-base conversion, 742
  for pseudo-random numbers, 260–264, 271
  quicksort; *see* Quicksort
  secant, 294, 954–977, 978
  selection sort, 678, 688
  simple array, 656–697
Alignment, 235
Allocation
  cleared memory, 789–790
  dynamic memory, 698, 786–798, 827
  external storage and, 877
  mass memory, 788f
  resizing of, 787f
  on run-time stack, 875
  stack overflow and, 881
  virtual memory and, 924–925
Allocation functions, 1035
alpha, 258
Alphabetical order, 420, 421
ALU; *see* Arithmetic and logic unit (ALU)
American National Standards Institute (ANSI), 14
American Standard Code for Information Interchange (ASCII), 7–8, 410–412, 432, 434
  bit/byte representation of, 411
  chart, 985

command-line arguments and, 935
comparisons and, 421
conversion to binary data from, 709–710, 935
enumerations and, 426–427
hexadecimal notation and, 744
international, 411, 412, 432, 434, 604
printing, 415–416
streams and, 604
style and, 433
Ampersands, 47, 51, 445–448, 458, 471
  arrays and, 371, 399, 400, 690
  errors with, 83, 473, 537, 690, 863
  functions and, 837f
  in returning multiple function results, 458–459
  in skipping, 992–993
  style and, 472
Amputation, testing by, 343, 349
AND, 115, 117, 118–119, 749–750
Angle brackets, 142, 326
ANSI; *see* American National Standards Institute (ANSI)
ANSI C, 14, 555, 825, 928
ANSI prototypes, 322f
Answer codes, 427
Application directory, 955–956
Approximate representations, 283–285, 291–292, 301
Archive files, 748, 952f
Argument counts, 919
Argument vectors, 919, 920, 935
Arguments, 138, 140, 142–147, 148, 318–319
  actual, 153
  address, 321, 448–449
  array; *see* Array arguments
  call by value and, 320
  coercion and, 251, 253, 322
  command-line, 918–927, 936–937

decoding, 920–927
design and, 342, 353
in dynamic arrays, 825
function interfaces and, 317
function types and, 147
functional, 320f, 935
number of, 322
optional, 923, 925, 936
order of, 328–330, 354, 355, 936
prototypes and, 141, 251
pseudo-random numbers and, 261–264
structures and, 555, 558
style and, 354, 355
variable-length lists of, 1039
Arithmetic
  character, 421
  mixed type, 257–260, 271
  pointer, 840–842, 848, 864
  types for, 257–260, 271, 322
Arithmetic and logic unit (ALU), 3–4
Arithmetic negation, 751–752
Arithmetic operators, 4, 44, 102, 107–108, 421; *see also* Operators
  bits and, 743
  coercion and, 251
  combination, 108
  errors with, 272
  formulas and, 53–54
  generic, 240
  overflow error and, 289–292
  precedence and associativity for, 104, 991–992
Arity, 103
Array arguments, 370, 382–384, 398
  errors with, 690
  memory address and, 449
Array elements, 367
Array length, 367, 368, 399
array_min, 883
Array of structures, 555, 560–564, 585, 586

Chauvenet table as, 664–677
parallel arrays versus, 561–562, 586–587, 657
Array parameters, 382–384, 398, 471
errors with, 399, 400
in returning multiple function results, 458, 459, 471
Array slots, 367, 370, 376
arguments and, 383
and coding idioms, 861
errors with, 399, 400
memory address of, 449
Arrays, 320f, 366–408
accessing, 370–373
accessing member of one structure in, 561
accessing one structure in, 561
array of, 367, 698, 706–709, 728, 729
versus bit vectors, 748–749
bsearch and, 918
for Carnival Guessing Game, 659–663
character; see Character arrays
compound, 698
dynamic, 786–832
of dynamic strings, 794–798
errors with, 399–400, 537, 690
global, 509
masking and, 659–663, 673, 675, 688, 690
mean value of, 384–391, 398
members as, 552–554
menu, 510–517
multidimensional, 398, 710–711, 729
nonarrays versus, 690
parallel; see Parallel arrays
qsort() and, 918
in Quiz Program, 634–635
ragged, 486, 508, 509, 536, 794–798, 825
resizing, 791–792, 824
for screening out faulty data, 663–677
searching, 656–663
sentinel loops and, 189
simple algorithms for, 656–697
size of, 369–370
sorted, 658, 677–687
statistical measures and, 384–398
of strings, 486, 508–517, 536, 698, 935; see also Argument vectors
strings and, 486, 488–492, 496–497, 508–517
structures and, 552–554, 586; see also Array of structures
style and, 399, 688–690, 729
three-dimensional (3D), 711, 729

two-dimensional; see Two-dimensional arrays
Arrays and pointers, 383f, 698, 834, 835–836, 841, 846–852
data packs and, 860
in dynamic matrix, 809–823
errors with, 827, 862–863
scanners and, 846–847
semantics and, 860
sentinels and, 847–848
simulation involving, 799–809
Arrow operators, 556, 587
Arrows
in flow diagrams, 59
in function-call graph, 339
ASCII; see American Standard Code for Information Interchange (ASCII)
ask(), 637–638
Assemblers, 13
Assembly languages, 13, 14
assert.h, 1040
Assignment combinations, 990–992, 999
Assignment operators, 53, 54, 107–108, 130, 990–992
characters and, 420
comparison operators versus, 115
compilers and, 115
for/while loops and, 173
pointers and, 446–448, 835
Assignment statements, 44, 53
declarations and, 97
direct, 446–447, 839, 840, 859
expressions and, 54
in flow diagrams, 59
functions and, 320
indirect, 446, 448, 451, 839, 840, 859
side effects of, 107–108, 110
structure, 555, 556, 558, 587
syntax for string, 538
Associativity, 94, 103–104
for assignment combination operators, 990–992
parsing and, 105–107
Assumptions, binary search and, 910
Asterisks, 443, 445–448, 471; see also Stars
errors with, 473, 863
names with, 604
pointers and, 834–835, 837f
style and, 472
Attention code, 413
auto, 874, 875, 876, 908, 911
Automatic storage, 875
Automatic type coercion, 250–252
Auxiliary memory, 7

average(), 385–391, 396, 671, 677, 725, 726
Average, finding, 30–36

b_in, 605–606
b_out, 605–606
Backup, 7
BAD_INITIAL_POINTS, 964, 972, 974
badswap(), 451–453, 473
banner(), 143, 144, 147, 320, 506
modules and, 315
tools library and, 1010, 1014, 1015–1016
base, 244, 245
Base-2 notation, 742, 1000–1002
logarithm for, 266–268
Base-10 notation, 233, 235, 742, 744, 773, 1000–1002
logarithm for, 1030
Base-16 notation, 742, 773, 1000, 1004, 1005
Base case, 882, 885, 911
Base conversion, 243–246, 1004–1006
Base type, 367, 368–369, 399, 443
BASIC, 29
beep(), 150, 323
Beginner's toolbox, 44
Big-endian machine, 620f
bin_search, 887–896, 932
Binary data, 4, 12–13, 410, 742, 1000–1002
conversion from, 744, 1004
conversion to, 709–710, 744, 1005, 1006
for matrix, 709–710
for real numbers, 1002
Binary files, streams and, 604
Binary operators, 103
Binary search, 471, 658f, 881, 886–896, 909
bisect(), 462–468, 961, 966, 967
Bisection method, 294, 459–471, 954, 978
adapting, 966–969
as example of divide and conquer, 881
Bit-manipulation operators, 15, 102, 774
Bit vectors, 748–752, 772
bitfields versus, 773
errors with, 773
Bitfields, 759–771, 772, 773
bit vectors versus, 773
errors with, 774
Bitmasks, 767, 772, 773
Bits, 4, 410, 742–783
ASCII characters and, 411, 412, 432
C and, 15

on disks, 6
errors in calculating with, 773–774
int and, 230f, 230–231, 232
integers and, 1000–1005
interfaces and, 9
masking and arrays of, 659f
padding, 414f
positive and negative signs and, 745
in Skylight Controller Program, 764–771
style in calculating with, 772–773
Bitwise-logic operators, 748
Bitwise operators, 743, 748–755, 772, 773
errors with, 773
logical operators versus, 773
masking and, 749–752, 772
summary of, 772
Blocks, 46, 138
buffers and, 602–603, 643
function comment, 152–153
function layout and, 355
variables and, 95
Body, 70, 174, 178, 195, 348
bool, 428, 457, 563, 575, 670
Boolean variables and functions, 428–432
Borland C, 34, 603, 1017
Borland C++, 34
Brackets, 105, 106; see also Angle brackets; Curly brackets
in function-call graph, 339
square, 498, 925
style and, 537
subscripts in, 367, .399, 400
break statement, 68, 170, 175–177; see also if... break statement/loop
menus and, 524
nested logic and, 219
in Roots of Equation Program, 962
sequential search and, 658
switch statement and, 198, 202, 524
bsearch, 918, 931–934, 935, 936
Bubble sort, 678f
Buffers, 48, 51, 521, 602–603, 643–644
in dynamic arrays, 826
error recovery and, 622
errors with, 646
exit() and, 145f
file redirection and, 862
keyboard versus input, 414
Bugs, 21, 36
Built-in facilities, 1026–1027
Bus, 2, 8–9
Busy wait loops, 195, 286

By value, 320; *see also* Call/pass
  by value
bye(), 143, 146, 147, 526, 638,
  1017–1018
  design steps and, 341
  in Gaussian elimination, 823
  modules and, 315
  in Multiplication Table
    Program, 700
Bytes, 4–5, 95, 101, 410
  ASCII characters and, 411
  bitwise operators and, 748
  giga-, 7
  int and, 229, 230–231, 234, 273
  interfaces and, 9

C code, 20
C compiler, 12, 20, 21, 948; *see
    also* Compilers
  missing prototypes and,
    321–322
  side effects and, 995
C programming language, 14–16,
    29, 34
  advanced aspects of operators
    in, 990–999
  ANSI, 14, 555, 825, 928
  assembly language compared
    with, 13
  built-in facilities of, 1026–1027
  character types in, 411
  comparison of structures and,
    555
  defect of, 448f
  FORTRAN compared to, 15–16
  function declarations and
    definitions in older versions
    of, 321
  fundamental concepts of, 42–92
  ISO; *see* ISO C
  keyboard buffer lacking in, 414
  matrix in, versus FORTRAN
    and Pascal, 702f
  operators in, versus other
    languages, 102–103,
    108–110
  parts of speech in, 44
  popularity of, 101
  precedence of operators in, 987;
    see also Precedence
  standard, 14
  subscript checking lacking in,
    373–374, 690
C++ programming language, 16,
    34, 861
  bool in, 428f
  call by reference in, 448f
  constants in, 99f
  declarations in, 47
  exception handler in, 959f

FORTRAN and, 16
  function layout and, 355
  modules in, 313
  reference parameters in, 459f
  structures in, 562f
C shell, 1017–1018
Cache memory, 5
CAD; *see* Computer-aided design
    (CAD)
Calculations; *see also* Arithmetic
    operators; Computations
  errors with, 288–294, 303
  real variables for, 269
Call by reference, 448f
Call/pass by address, 320–321,
    448–459, 471
  errors with, 473, 587, 690
  structures and, 555, 559, 586
  style and, 472, 586
Call/pass by value, 448, 451, 459
  errors with, 587
  structures and, 555, 558, 586
  style and, 586
Callers, 142, 316, 317f, 318
Calling sequence, 319
calloc(), 787, 789–797, 824–825,
    836
Calls; *see* Function calls
Canned code, 26, 27
Carnival Guessing Game,
    659–663
Case labels, 196–198
Case sensitivity, 100
Case studies, parse tree to debug,
    123–128
cases, 196
Casting, 248–257, 271, 788
  command-line arguments and,
    936
  errors with, 272, 937
  style and, 825; *see also* Type
    casts
CD-ROM; *see* Compact disk,
    read-only memory
    (CD-ROM)
ceil(), 804
Cellular phones, 10
Central processing unit CPU,
    2–4, 7
char, 196f, 229f, 353, 424, 432
  arrays and, 367, 538; *see also*
    Character arrays
  command-line arguments and,
    924
  gets() and, 497
  input functions and, 1032
  int versus, 433
  pointers and, 443
  printing and, 415–416
  short int versus, 419–420
  signed, 411–412

stream input and, 619
  strings and, 488–492, 493, 536,
    537
  unsigned, 411–412
Character arithmetic, 421
Character arrays, 491, 500, 536
  errors with, 538, 644, 646–647
  structures and, 560
  style and, 537
Character-handling library, 140,
    1028–1029
Character literals, 412–413, 432,
    744
Characters
  ASCII; *see* American Standard
    Code for Information
    Interchange (ASCII)
  comparing, 421
  enumerations and, 410–440
  errors with, 432–433
  illegal, 621
  input with, 413–419, 434
  as integers, 410, 411, 415,
    419–420, 433
  operations on, 419–432
  output with, 413, 415–419
  representations of, 410–411
  search for, 504, 505
  as short integers, 411
  strings and, 486
  wide, 1040
Chat rooms, 9
chauv_ratio(), 666–674
Chauvenet's algorithm, 658,
    664–677
Chauvenet's criteria, 664
Chauvenet's ratio, 667–668
check_data(), 889, 891–893,
    932
Circuits, bits and, 742
Classes, 313, 849f, 874–877
clean_and_log(), 622–623,
    628, 633, 644, 1020
cleanline(), 622–623, 624, 644,
    646, 1020
Cleanup commands, 953–954
Cleared memory allocation,
    789–790
clearscreen(), 1014, 1015
Clock, 3, 194, 261, 1020–1021
close_skylight(), 769–770
Closing comments, 146
clrscr, 1015
Code management, 945–946
Code Warrior compiler, 1015
Codes, 20
  answer, 427
  attention, 413
  "bulletproof," 347
  C, 20
  canned, 26, 27

compact, 15
  design and, 348
  efficient, 910
  error, 428, 937, 965
  escape, 412–413, 432, 744
  function layout and, 355
  generic, 935–936, 937
  for idioms, 861
  libraries of; *see* Libraries
  machine, 12–13, 20
  object; *see* Object code
  pseudo-; *see* Pseudocode
  reuse of, 956
  source; *see* Source code
  status, 427, 612, 862
  success or failure, 657–658
  translation, 7–8
  writing, 23, 29–33
Coercions, 249, 250–254, 258,
    271; *see also* Type
    coercions
  arrays and, 368f
  design and, 353
  errors with, 272
  parameter, 330
  return type and, 318, 322–323
Collating sequence, 421
Columns, 348, 656–658, 701–702
Combination operators, 107–108,
    130
Comma operator, 998, 999
Command line, 919, 934–935
Command-line arguments,
    918–927
  errors with, 937
  interactive programs versus,
    936
  style and, 936–937
Command-line interpreters, 11
Command-line switch, 931, 936
Command shells, 11
Commands, 21
  compilation, 952f, 953, 1013
  preprocessor, 43, 45
Commas, 96, 97, 117f, 231, 495,
    498
  in arrays of structures, 561
  in for loop, 172
Comments, 43, 45
  closing, 146
  in designing functions, 342,
    350, 354, 355
  error; *see* Error comments
  errors with, 83
  function layout and, 355
  function stub and, 343, 354
  strings and, 488, 539
Communication, 9–10
  interfunction, 462, 464, 473
  interprocess, 959f
  module, 954–955

Compact disk, read-only memory (CD-ROM), 6
Comparison functions, 928–931, 933
  errors with, 937
  qsort() and, 927
  semantics of, 114–115
  in sorted tables, 656–657
  string, 503–505, 517–519, 538, 1023–1024
  style and, 936
  syntax for string, 538
  of two structures, 555, 562–563, 575, 587
Comparison operators, 115, 130
  assignment operators versus, 115
  coercion and, 251
  pointers and, 842
Comparisons, 102
  ALU and, 3
  of characters, 421
  floating-point; *see* Floating-point comparisons
  logical operators to test, 115–120
  meaningful, 284–285
Compilation, 20, 32, 944, 945, 946
  design and, 349
  errors in, 82–83, 354, 473
  linking and, 948–951, 977–978, 1011
  modular development and, 354, 947, 948–950
  reducing commands for, 952f
  stages of, 43
Compilation commands, 952f, 953, 1013
Compilation errors, 21
Compile only, 949–950
Compile time, 29
Compile-time errors, 14, 32–33
  arrays and, 374, 398
  ISO C and, 14
  pointer operators and, 473
Compiler options, 946, 949
Compilers, 12, 21, 27, 28, 35; *see also* C compiler
  bitfield types and, 760
  errors of, 354, 618
  format errors and, 618
  function calls and, 143
  gcc, 618f, 925f, 1012
  gnu C, 230f, 761, 948f
  indeterminate answers and, 241
  versus interpreters, 29
  libraries and, 139
  modular design and, 353, 354
  older, 235f

and operations on structures, 555
overflow errors and, 288
parameter order and, 328–329
pre-ANSI C, 555
relational operators and, 115
sizeof and, 101
syntax and layout for, 69–70
Complement operators, 750–751, 1001–1002
Components, 552–554
compose, 519, 527
Compound arrays, 698
Compound objects, 320f, 398, 555
Compound types, 366
Compression, 748
Computations, 3–4, 15; *see also* Arithmetic operators; Calculations
  algorithms for, 26; *see also* Algorithms
  associativity in, 94; *see also* Associativity
  in case study, 125–126
  declarations in, 94; *see also* Declarations
  expressions in; *see* Expressions
  for/while loops and, 173
  FORTRAN for scientific, 15–16
  integer division for, 270
  in interpolation, 213
  lazy evaluation in, 117–120
  mixing types in, 246–260
  objects in, 94; *see also* Objects
  overflow errors in; *see* Overflow
  parse trees in; *see* Parse trees/parsing
  precedence in; *see* Precedence
  problem specification and analysis and, 24–25
  of projectile distance, 257–260
  of resistance, 126–128, 254–257
  Simpson's 1/3 rule and, 205–206
  software emulation of, 271
  style and, 217, 218
  underflow errors in; *see* Underflow
  in using parse tree to debug, 125–126
  variables in, 94; *see also* Variables
compute_ temp, 347–352
Computed subscripts, 370–371
Computer, parts of, 2–18
Computer-aided design CAD, 565
Concatenation, 505–506
Concurrent processes, 959f

Conditional operator, 996–997, 999
Conditional statements, 60–70, 170, 457
  function layout and, 355
  style and, 217
Conditions, 62–70, 69, 72; *see also* Loop condition
  in **do... while** loop, 174
  in **for** loop, 171, 173
  in recursion, 882
const, 97–100, 333, 509
  menus and, 524, 537
  in Roots of Equation Program, 965
  static and, 666, 689, 876
Constant definitions, 314–316, 351, 354
Constant expressions, 198, 367, 399
Constant names, 53
Constant operands, 198
Constant seed, 261
Constants, 44, 53, 97–100
  in arrays, 690
  enumeration, 426–427, 434
  functions and, 148
  global variables and, 333–334
  in Grapefruits and Gravity Program, 55
  int and, 230
  libraries and, 142
  literal, 97–100, 233
  memory for, 34
  modules and, 945
  problem specification and analysis and, 24
  standard files of, 1027–1028
  static storage and, 875
  style and, 772
  symbolic, 97–100
  tables of, 875, 876, 910
  in **tools** library, 1009, 1031, 1034, 1038
  writing character, 412–413
continue statement, 170, 175, 177–178
  menus and, 524
  nested logic and, 219
  in Roots of Equation Program, 962
Control, transfer of, 153
Control functions, 1035
Control instructions, 21
Control patterns, if statements in, 68–69
Control statements, 44, 58, 170–226
Control units, 171, 218
Convergence tolerance, 299–300, 303

Conversion formulas, 78–79
Conversion specifiers, 49, 83, 231, 234–240, 744
  design and, 348
  errors with, 272, 646
  floating-point, 236–237
  mismatches and, 745
  printf() and, 415
  scanf() and, 414
  strings and, 493, 497–498
  style and, 272
  for unsigned values, 745
Conversions, 246–260, 271, 322–323
  base, 243–246, 1004–1006
  binary, 709–710, 744–748, 1004–1006
  command-line arguments and, 935
  decimal, 1002–1004
  design and, 353
  diagramming, 252–254
  errors in, 330, 621
  extended multibyte to wide-character, 1040
  hexadecimal, 1004, 1005
  number-base, 1000–1006, 742
  pointers and, 443
  prototypes and, 321–323
  string to number, 1035–1036
  "suspicious," 330
Conversions library, 1028–1029
Copying
  of strings, 505, 506, 517–519, 538
  of structures, 555, 556, 587
Correlation coefficient, 392–397
cos(), 258, 836
Counted/counting loops, 70–73, 179–181, 698
  application of, 202–209
  arrays and, 374–375, 378
  data validation; *see* Data validation loops; Input validation loops; Validation
  debugging printouts and, 27
  defective, 178–179
  errors with, 218–219
  increment in, 111–112
  infinite, 122, 176–179
  input-controlled, 182
  input validation, 73–75, 182
  logical operators and, 118
  in menus, 516
  Monte Carlo, 581–584
  premature exit from, 176
  query, 182–186
  relational operators and, 114
  sentinel, 182, 188–193, 194
  simple **if** statement in, 68
  summation, 179–181, 190

validation, 73–75; *see also* Data
  validation loops; Input
  validation loops; Validation
  in Voltage Ramp Program,
  120–123
Counters, 72, 180, 181
  combination operators and, 108
  increment and decrement
    operators with, 113
CPU; *see* Central processing unit
  (CPU)
Crashes, 15, 27, 646
  arrays and, 377, 690
  buffers and, 643
  division and, 271
  dynamic arrays and, 827
  error messages versus, 937
  lazy evaluation and, 993–994
  menus and, 515
  pointers and, 472, 473, 862, 863
  strings and, 538
  uninitialized sentinel and, 862
Creation, external storage and,
  877
Cruise control, 286
Cryptography, 742
  ctime(), 506–508
  ctype library, 140, 420, 421
  ctype.h, 315, 1028–1029
Curly brackets, 44, 46, 69–70
  arrays and, 368, 560
  errors with, 83, 178–179
  function layout and, 355
  nested loops and, 729
Cursors, 846–847, 850–852, 1015
cyl_vol, 326–328

Dangling pointers, 790, 826
Data, bad/faulty, 663–677, 674
Data columns, 656–657
Data encapsulation, 861
Data files; *see* Files
data_list, dynamic arrays and,
  794
Data modularity, 331–337
Data object declarations, 312,
  552–555
Data objects; *see* Objects
Data omission, 621–622
Data organization, 690
data_pack, 849, 854, 855, 861
  in binary search, 891
  command-line arguments and,
    920–921, 924
  optional arguments and, 926
  qsort() and, 931
  in quicksort, 897, 899
Data retrieval, 690
Data sets, 625
  partitioning, 902–908

sentinel loops and, 189
Data structures; *see* Structures
Data types, 101; *see also* Types
  bits and, 773
  hexadecimal literals and, 773
  library for, 139; *see also*
    Standard I/O library
  numeric, 228–279
Data validation loops, 187–188;
  see also Input validation
  loops; Validation
  bisection method and, 464
  for menus, 514–516, 517
Data values, 94–95; *see also*
  Values
Date functions; *see* Time-date
  functions
Deallocation, 875, 877
Debugging, 14, 26, 34–35, 37
  array parameters and, 459
  binary representation and, 1002
  call by address and, 472
  in case study, 123–128
  function stubs and, 343,
    353–354
  functions and, 163, 342–343,
    354
  global variables and, 317f, 336
  loops and, 218, 219
  modules and, 139, 354, 690
    945
  names and, 129
  OS-ROM and, 6
  parse tree for, 123–128
  pointers and, 840
  pseudo-random numbers and,
    261
  repeat query in, 182
  stack diagrams for, 909
  streams and, 600–601
  style and, 354
  tag names and, 585
  types and, 101
Debugging printouts, 27, 36–37,
  303; *see also* Diagnostic
  printouts
Decimal notation, 233, 235, 411,
  412, 742, 1000–1002
  conversion from, 744, 1005
  conversion to, 744–748, 1004,
    1005
  hexadecimal versus, 773
  style and, 773
Decimal places, 228, 232
Declarations, 21, 43, 46–47, 81,
  95–97, 138
  array, 367–368, 399
  bitfield, 759–760, 765–768
  call correspondence with,
    321–330
  const; *see* **const**

data object, 312
design of, 342, 347, 350
in Echo Program, 51
enum, 426–427; *see also*
  typedef
errors with, 355
extern, 877
in Fin Temperature Program,
  345, 347–348
in flow diagrams, 58
function calls and, 321–330
function layout and, 355
in functions, 148
in Grapefruits and Gravity
  Program, 55
local, 148
in Lumber Program, 563
member, 552–554
modules and, 314–316
pointer, 443–444, 446, 834–837
static, 876
for strings, 491, 492
structure, 552–555, 585
style and, 585
syntax for, 95–96, 321
two-dimensional arrays and,
  701–702, 706
Decoding, 749, 754–755, 772,
  773
  of command-line arguments,
    919–927
  style and, 936
Decrement operators, 107,
  108–114
  with pointers, 841–842
  side effects and, 994, 995, 999;
    see also Side effects
  style and, 130
  update expression and, 174
  in Voltage Ramp Program,
    120–123
decrypt(), 756–759
Decryption, 755–759
"Deep" copy, 557f
Default
  precedence, 103–104
  streams and, 599–602, 605
default, 196–199, 202, 768
Default output precision, 239
#define, 53, 55, 97–100, 333
  arrays and, 370, 372, 385
  bisection method and, 467
  bitmasks and, 772
  in calling library functions, 144
  dynamic arrays and, 794
  dynamic memory allocation
    and, 787, 823
#endif and, 947–948
  enumerated types and, 425–426
  in Gas Pressure Table, 534
  in Heat Flow Simulation, 803

hexadecimal notation and, 749
in Memo Program, 527–529
menus and, 527, 529
nested loops and, 699, 729
pointers and, 844
Simpson's 1/3 rule and, 204
in Skylight Controller Program,
  765
tools library and, 1010, 1018
two-dimensional arrays and,
  699, 729
in writing file of voltages,
  609–610
Degenerate cases, 457–458,
  467–468, 577
  recursion and, 911
Degrees of freedom, 384
delay(), 194–196, 1017
Delay loops, 194–196
Delegated work, 571
delta_x, 297–302
demo_type, 760–763
Denormalized numbers, 292–293,
  302, 1003
Dependencies, 950, 952–953, 979
Dereference operators, 446, 459,
  471, 838; *see also*
  Asterisks; Stars
  errors with, 473, 863, 937
  for structure comparison, 587
Des encryption logarithm, 748
Design, 312–364
  of arrays, 368
  computations and, 94
  debugging printouts and, 27
  of drivers, 27
  for Fin Temperature Program,
    343–352
  of functions, 342
  functions and, 139
  modular; *see* Modular design;
    Modules
  process of, 341–343
  of solutions, 26–27
Development environment, 27–29
Device controller, 763–771
Device drivers, 8–9, 11
Diagnostic printouts, 83; *see also*
  Debugging printouts
Diagnostics, library for, 1040
Diagrams; *see also* Flow
  diagrams; Function-call
  graphs; Parse trees/parsing
  of conversions, 252–254
  object, 97, 99, 100, 129
  pointer, 863
  of rectangle on xy-plane, 566
  stack, 879–880, 909
  of switch statement, 198–200
  of two structured types, 570
  variable, 97

Digital images, 719–727
Direct-access memory, 6
Direct assignment, 446–447, 839, 840, 859
Direct reference, 839, 859
Directories, 955–956, 1010
    application, 955–956
    disk, 1010
    sub-, 945, 978, 1010
Disk directories, 1010
Disks, 6, 7, 11
display_ points(), 716
Distributed computing, 10
Distribution, Gaussian, 384, 664
Divide and conquer, 881, 902–907, 909
divisible(), 428–432
Division, 240–246, 270
    application of, 254–257
    overflow error and, 289f, 303
    real and integer, 240–241, 271
    style and, 271
    type casts and, 254–257
    underflow errors and, 293
do_ it_ again, 185–186
do_ quiz(), 632–638
do statement/loop, 70
do... while statement/loop, 170, 174–175, 424
    bisection method and, 464, 470
    continue and, 177–178
    data validation loops with, 187–188
    error recovery and, 623
    in Points of a Rectangle Program, 571–575
    recursion and, 883
    in testing, 182–185
    while versus, 189
Documentation, 354
Dollar sign, 487
DOS, 11, 12, 601, 948
Dot operators, 556, 558, 587
double, 46, 52, 55, 95, 114f, 232–240, 273
    ampersand and, 449
    arrays and, 383–384
    badswap() and, 451
    bisection method, 462
    casting and, 249–252
    command-line arguments and, 935
    conversions and, 246–260, 322, 323–325
    declarations with, 96
    exp() and, 319
    float versus, 269–270
    floating-point comparisons and, 283
    in Grapefruits and Gravity Program, 57

importance of, 270
increment and decrement operators with, 109
    in interpolation, 211
    logarithms and powers, 1030
long, 52f, 233–240, 271
    manipulating number representations, 1030
    modules and, 316
    overflow error and, 291–292
PI and, 98
    pointers and, 443, 444–445, 836, 837
    in Points of a Rectangle Program, 566, 569–570, 575, 586
    in Quadratic Roots Program, 457–458
    return type and, 318
    in Roots of Equation Program, 966
    Simpson's 1/3 rule and, 205
    sizeof and, 101
    style and, 328
    in summation loop, 181
    trigonometric functions and, 1030
    two-dimensional arrays and, 706
Double inclusion, 978–979
Double root, 458
double:double functions, 147, 151–155
Drivers, 26, 27
drop(), 151–154, 185–186
"Dummy" definitions, 343
Dynamic arrays, 786–832
    pointers and, 846
    simulation with, 799–808
    sorting with, 793–794
    style and, 825–826
    2D, 809, 825, 826
Dynamic matrix, 809–823
Dynamic memory allocation, 698, 786–798, 827

E-mail, 9
Echo, 23, 50–52, 126, 598
    integer input and, 235
    in interpolation, 212
Editor; see Text editor
Effective address, 374, 376
Effective addresses, 374, 376
efndef, 978
#efndef, 947–948
Elements, 367
Emacs, 28
Embedded formatting commands, 28
Encoding, 749, 772, 773

encrypt(), 756–759
Encryption, 748, 749, 755–759
End of file; see also EOF
    detecting, 614
    errors with, 625–628, 644
Engineering, C and, 16
English language, 7, 14, 22, 59
Entry point, 318
enum, 426–427, 434, 566, 765
Enumerated types, 425–432, 432, 501, 571–575
    character data and, 410–440
    comparison of, 937
    printing, 509, 536
Enumeration constants, 426–427, 434
Enumeration specification, 426–427
EOF, 607, 645, 1031
EPS, 462, 470, 643, 964
Epsilon test, 284–285, 288, 575
Epsilon values
    Newton's method and, 295–302, 303
    in Quadratic Roots Program, 457
equal(), 571, 574, 575
Equal precedence, 104
Equal sign, 53, 96, 97, 98, 115, 445–448, 860
    qsort() and, 930
    strings and, 503, 536
"Equals" versus "gets," 72, 115
Equations, system of, 810
er_ type, 965
errno.h, 1039
Error checking, 497, 910, 937
    ISO C and, 14, 15
Error codes, 428, 937, 964
Error comments, 26, 33, 82–83, 910
    arrays and, 374, 399
    comparison operators and, 115
    missing prototypes and, 321–322
    structures and, 587
    unsafe conversion and, 248
    usage and, 925
Error correction, 31–33, 36–37, 127–128
Error detection, streams and, 617–628
Error handling, 303, 313, 1019–1020
Error messages
    crashes versus, 937
    file redirection and, 862
    tools library and, 1013
Error prompts, in menus, 513
Error recovery, 622–628
Error tolerance, 462

Errors
    with algorithms, 303, 690
    with arithmetic operators, 272
    with arrays, 368, 537, 690
    with buggers, 646
    in calculating with bits, 773–774
    calculation, 288–294
    with characters, 432–433
    with command-line arguments and, 936–937
    compilation, 82–83, 354, 473
    compile-time; see Compile-time errors
    conversion, 330, 621
    with conversion specifiers, 272
    with dynamic arrays, 826–827
    end-of-file, 625–628, 644
    expression, 103, 127
    file input, 625–628
    file management, 606–607, 644
    file processing, 620–622, 644
    with files, 646–647
    with floating-point comparisons, 303
    with formats, 272, 598, 617–620
    illegal input characters and, 621
    with initializers, 368
    input, 598
    input format, 620
    library for, 1039
    linking, 33, 83, 911, 947
    logical, 35, 36
    with menus, 515
    in modular organization, 978–979
    with nested loops, 729–730
    newline, 620–621
    with order of magnitude, 303
    overflow; see Overflow
    parameter coercion, 330
    with pointers, 443, 472–473, 861–864
    punctuation semicolons, etc., 33, 83, 178, 218; see also specific punctuation marks
    with recursion, 910–911
    round-off, 284, 343
    run-time see Run-time errors
    semantic, 491
    with sorting, 690
    spelling, 33, 83
    stream-closing, 607
    stream-opening, 606–607
    with streams, 617–628, 646–647
    with strings, 537–539
    with structures, 587
    subscript, 373–374, 377–378, 729, 730

swap functions with, 452
syntax, 142, 355–356, 491
with tables, 272
with two-dimensional arrays, 729–730
underflow, 292–293, 302
usage, 923, 925
Escape code, 412–413, 432, 744
Evaluation
lazy, 117–120, 992–997, 999
order of, 994, 995, 997
wire gauge adequacy, 198
evenly(), 1022
Exam averages, 378
Exception condition, 617–628, 959f
Excess notation, 1004
Exchange sort, 678f
Executable file, 29
Execution, 20, 21, 34–35
main() and, 45
memory during, 36
simple sequential, 58
Execution stack, 878
exit(), 145f, 600, 1019
Exit test, 177, 376
Exits
no, 178
premature, 176
two, 193
exp(), 316, 318, 319, 320, 322, 340
Experiments, pseudo-random numbers for, 264–269, 271
Exponent, 231–232, 233, 248, 1003, 1004
and orders of magnitude, 293–294
overflow errors and, 302, 303
underflow errors and, 292–293
Exponential functions, 1030
Exporting, 946, 959, 977
Expressions, 53–54, 101–107
with casts and coercions, 253–254
constant, 198
errors with, 103
finding errors in, 127
for/while loops and, 173
guarded, 994
lazy evaluation and, 992–997
logical, 992–997
long, 130
mask-and-shift, 759
selection, 554
strings and, 488
Extended multibyte to wide-character conversion, 1040
extern, 95f, 874, 877, 908, 977

in Roots of Equation Program, 959–960, 965, 966, 967
style and, 910
External function calls, 957–958
External linkage, 877
External variables, 331–332, 979

f(), 300–302, 315–316, 318, 319
assignment statements and, 320
bisection method and, 462–470
function-call graphs and, 340
in Heat Transfer Program, 461
pointers and, 462–470, 472
return type and, 318
style and, 472
f_in, 605–606, 626–627
f_log, 626–627
f_out, 605–606
fabs(), 153, 157, 284–285
Factorial function/operations, 289–292
Failure code, 657–658
Failure to converge, 297–298
false, 62–70, 114–117, 421–422
Boolean variables and, 428–432
conditional operator and, 996, 997
lazy evaluation and, 992–993, 999
masking and, 659, 661, 663, 677, 688
strings and, 504, 1023
fatal(), 154, 200, 202, 627, 1018–1019
in binary search, 892
optional arguments and, 926
parallel arrays and, 381
pseudo-random numbers and, 263
stderr and, 600, 1018–1019
tools library and, 715
in writing file of voltages, 611
Fatal error comment, 322–323
fbanner(), 1015–1016
fclose(), 604–607, 643, 645
feof(), 612, 613, 614, 617, 625, 627, 628
Chauvenet's algorithm and, 673
style and, 645
ferror(), 625, 627, 628
fetch, 8
ffam, 966
fflush(), 603, 604, 607, 644, 645
fgetc, 613–614, 644, 646
fgets(), 613–614, 644, 646–647
Field-width specification, 234, 235–240, 272, 415
design and, 348
strings and, 493, 496, 497–498
Fields, 552–554

File input, 614–615, 625–628
File management
errors with, 606–607, 644, 646–647
with modular construction, 945–948
File processing errors, 620–622, 644, 646–647
File redirection, 600–602
command-line arguments and, 936
style and, 645, 862
File system manager, 11
FILENAME_MAX, 1031
Files, 946
archive, 748, 952f
end of; *see* End of file; **EOF**
errors with, 646–647
executable, 29
header; *see* Header files
input functions for, 313, 612–614, 644
names for, 28, 646
object, 29, 945, 1012–1013
opening, 645
output functions for, 313, 607–608, 644
project, 946, 977, 978
reading data from, 614–615
source code, 30–31, 944, 946–947, 1013
streams and, 48, 643, 646
in **tools** library, 1009
writing data to, 608–612
Fin Temperature Program, 344, 350–352
find_min(), 683–684, 686, 690
find_pivot(), 811, 818–820
finite(), 300–302
Finite-difference equation, 800
Firewall, 9
Flagging, 617
float, 52f, 232–240, 273
addition and, 293–294
arrays and, 367–368
casting and, 249–252
conversions and, 246–260, 322, 323
design and, 347, 350
double versus, 269–270
dynamic arrays and, 794
floating-point comparisons and, 283–285, 288
function stub and, 347
modules and, 315, 316
overflow error and, 291–292
pointers and, 849
in Points of a Rectangle Program, 566
qsort() and, 928–929
in quicksort, 899

return type and, 318
selection sort algorithm and, 678, 679
streams and, 619
struct and, 553f
style and, 472
underflow error and, 293
y and, 319
Floating-point comparisons, 282–288, 575, 934
algorithms in, 294–302, 303
errors with, 303, 937
overflow errors with, 288–292
underflow errors with, 292–293
Floating-point coprocessor, 4
Floating-point numbers, 55, 228, 231–234, 270–271, 1003; *see also* Real numbers
conversion of, 246–260, 271
Cruise Control Program and, 285–288
and finding roots of equation, 294–302
input of, 235–236
integer division and, 254
versus integer operations, 240
lengths of, 270
literals as, 233–234
output of, 236–240
overflow errors with, 288–292
precision of, 1003; *see also* Precision
underflow errors with, 292–293
Floating-point standard, 288, 1027–1028
Floating-point type-specifier, 233; *see also* Type specifiers
Flow diagrams, 22, 57–60; *see also* Function-call graphs
for action with an alternative, 64
for asking a question, 61
for asking more than one question, 66
for conditional operator, 996
for counted sentinel loop, 191
for **do... while** loop, 175
for Grapefruit and Gravity Program, 153
for **for** loop, 172, 173, 176
for loops with **break** and **continue,** 176
for memo maker, 526
for menu loop, 526
for Monte Carlo loop, 583
for Multiplication Table Program, 700
for Quadratic Roots Program, 158
for repeating a process, 183
for summation loop, 180

for Voltage Ramp Program, 122
for **while** loop, 173
Flow of control, 142, 339
Flushing, 603, 604, 622–624
Folders, 946
fopen(), 599, 604–607, 627, 643, 1031
  command-line arguments and, 923
  errors with, 644, 646
  in Image Smoothing Program, 722
  style and, 645
  two-dimensional arrays and, 715
  in writing file of voltages, 611
FOPEN_MAX, 1031
for statement/loop, 70, 170, 171–174
  arrays and, 374, 377, 388, 399
  Chauvenet's algorithm and, 666–667
  comma operator in, 999
  continue and, 177–178
  data validation loops with, 187, 188
  errors with, 218
  in finding roots of equation, 300
  if... break statement and, 175–176, 177
  in Image Smoothing Program, 726–727
  infinite, 177, 219
  linear regression and, 395
  masking and, 663
  in menus, 514, 524, 526, 1024
  nested, 698–700, 704
  pointers and, 850
  in Prime Number Program, 431, 432
  in quicksort, 907
  in search loop, 194
  selection sort and, 683–684
  in sentinel loops, 189, 190–193, 194
  in sequential search, 688
  streams and, 617
  strings and, 501, 524
  style and, 217, 218
  in summation loop, 181
  switch and, 524
  two-dimensional arrays and, 718
Formal parameters, 318–319, 323–325
Format, of unsigned integers, 746–748
Format errors, 598, 617–620
Formats, 48–50, 51, 55
  errors with, 272
  string merging and, 487

strings and, 493, 498
Formulas, 53–54, 313
  arrays and, 399
  conversion, 78–79
  errors with, 83
  in Fin Temperature Program, 350
  names for, 272
  problem specification and analysis and, 24
  slope of line, 295–296
FORTRAN, 14, 15–16, 29, 230, 702f
FORTRAN-77, 16
fprime(), 300–302
fprintf(), 608, 644, 852, 1018
  stderr and, 600
  streams and, 617
  in writing file of voltages, 611
fputc(), 608, 644
fputs(), 608, 644
Fractions, 254
  floating-point comparisons and, 283–284
  and orders of magnitude, 294
  repeating, 239
  unsafe conversion and, 248
fread(), 606, 710, 722, 728, 1032
free(), 787, 790–794, 823, 824, 826
  errors with, 826
  in Heat Flow Simulation, 804
Free Software Foundation, 618f, 948f, 1012
fscanf(), 612–613, 616–617, 625–628, 644
  in binary search, 892
  Chauvenet's algorithm and, 673
  errors and, 646–647
  in Quiz Program, 633–638
  two-dimensional arrays and, 710f, 715
Function body, 148, 154
Function-call graphs, 312, 339–340, 353
  Chauvenet's algorithm and, 670
  for computing statistics, 670
  for Fin Temperature Program, 345, 347
  for Gaussian elimination, 811
  for Heat Flow Simulation, 801
  for Quicksort Program, 897
  for Quiz Program, 630
  for selection sort, 682
  statistics, 387
Function calls, 44, 45, 47–50, 138, 142–155; see also entries beginning Call
  active, 882, 894–895
  arrays and, 382–384
  bsearch() and, 933

declaration correspondence with, 321–330
  design of, 342, 351–352
  errors with, 83, 355–356
  in flow diagrams, 59
  header files and, 317
  initialization during, 875
  interfaces and, 317
  modules and, 313–316
  nested, 320
  pointers and, 837
  prototypes and, 313–316, 321–323
  recursive, 902; see also Recursion
  run-time stack and, 878–880
  structure comparison and, 563
  style and, 472, 644–645, 910
  syntax errors in, 142
  syntax for, 321, 326–328
Function comment blocks, 152–153
Function declarations, 314–316, 321
Function definitions, 148, 154, 163, 312, 313–316, 321
  structures and, 555
  style and, 354, 355, 472
Function headers, 148, 153, 355–356
  errors with, 163
  formal parameter names and, 323–325
  function stub and, 343, 354
  for menus, 513
  names for prototypes and, 324f
  syntax for, 321
Function parameters; see Functional parameters; Parameters
Function pointers, 836–838, 845, 860, 861
Function results, 142
Function skeleton, 341, 347, 350
Function stub, 343, 346–352, 353–354
Functional arguments, 320f, 935
Functional parameters
  pointers as, 860
  qsort() and, 931
Functions, 21, 138–139, 313
  advanced, 1033, 1036, 1037
  allocation, 1034
  arguments and, 318–319; see also Arguments
  arrays and, 370
  as "black boxes," 317, 318
  Boolean, 428–432
  character, 421–423
  characters and conversions and, 1028–1029

in characters and conversions library, 1028–1029
  communication between, 316–321
  comparison; see entries beginning Comparison
  control, 1035
  conversion, 1035–1036; see also Conversions
  designing, 342
  documentation and, 354
  of dynamic memory allocation, 787
  entry point of, 318
  errors with, 163
  exponential, 1030
  external storage and, 877
  for gas models, 332–337, 339
  general, 1034
  generic, 928, 935, 936–937
  I/O see I/O functions
  ideal purpose of, 342, 347, 350
  Input, 313, 612–614, 644
  layout of, 355
  libraries and, 139–168; see also Libraries; Library functions
  logarithm, 266–268, 1030
  memory, 1037
  modules and, 945
  for Monte Carlo simulation, 584
  names for, 129, 163, 837f, 911
  numeric, 1022
  output, 313, 607–608, 644
  as parameters, 918, 927–934
  parameters and, 318–319; see also Functional parameters; Parameters
  pointers and, 834, 835, 836–837, 842–846
  for Prime Number Program, 430
  program blocks and, 46
  programmer-defined, 313
  pseudo-random numbers and, 261–264
  purposes of, 148
  recursion by, 874–917
  returning results from, 319–321
  state of, 876
  strings, 499–502; see also Strings
  structures and, 555, 584, 586
  style and, 354, 644–645, 909
  sub-, 142
  swap, 451–453
  symmetric, 297
  time-date, 506–508, 1020–1022, 1038–1039
  in **tools** library, 1014–1015
  trigonometric, 253, 258, 1030

user-defined, 148–155
utility, 139
of variable-length argument
   lists, 1039
fwrite(), 710, 722, 726, 728, 1032
fxlow, 469, 470
fxmid, 469, 470

g(), 315–316, 320
Games, 191–192, 949–951
   guessing, 264–269, 659–663
   pseudo-random numbers for,
     264–269, 271
   quizzes, 264–269, 271,
     628–638, 645
   UNIX makefile for, 951–952
Garbage, 73, 96
   conversions and, 248, 271
   errors producing, 272
   integer input and, 235
   menus and, 515
   overflow errors and, 291, 303
   pointers and, 471, 472, 863
   "Garbage in, garbage out" GIGO,
     73
Garbage in, information out, 625
Gas models, 332–337, 339
Gas Pressure Table, 530–535
Gas Prices Computation
   Program, 76
Gateway, 9
Gaussian distribution, 384, 664
Gaussian elimination, 809–817,
   825
gcc compiler, 618f, 925f, 1012
Generic code, 935–936, 937
Generic functions, 928, 935,
   936–937
Generic types, 928, 936
Geometric progression, 24
Geometric series, 23–24, 25
get_data(), 383–384, 385–391,
   393–396, 849–851
   in binary search, 889, 891–893
   in quicksort, 899
get_names(), 796
get_quiz(), 630–638
get_rect(), 570
get_transform(), 715
getc, 614f
getchar(), 414, 417–419, 517f,
   614f, 1016
   menu_i and, 1023
   stdin and, 600
   style and, 434
getche(), 603
gets(), 497–499, 538, 613
   errors and, 646–647
   stdin and, 600
Gigabytes, 7

GIGO; *see* "Garbage in, garbage
   out" (GIGO)
Global arrays, 368f, 509, 524, 537
Global constants, 334–336
   external storage and, 877
   static storage and, 876–877
Global definitions, 354
Global network, 9
Global variables, 154, 317f, 318f,
   333–337
   eliminating, 336–339
   errors with, 356
   external storage and, 877
   pointers and, 472
   recursion and, 909
   static storage and, 875–876
   style and, 354, 472, 909, 910,
     978
Gnu C, 230f, 760, 761, 948f
go_find(), 467–471, 966–968
"Goodness of fit," 391, 392
goto statement, 170
Graphics library, 140
Graphics windowing packages,
   565
GRAVITY, 257–258
Greeting message, 55
Grouping symbols, 103, 106
Guarded expressions, 994
"Guarding," 118–119
Guessing games, 264–269,
   659–663

Hard disks, 6, 7, 8, 48
Hardware, 2–10
   bitfields and, 760
   bits and, 742, 748, 759
   C and, 15, 434
   characters and, 434
   machine language and, 12–13
   operating system and, 11, 12
   orders of magnitude and,
     293–294
   run-time errors and, 598
   sizeof and, 101
Head pointers, 846
Header files, 50–51, 142, 317,
   945, 946–947
   duplication of, 947–948,
     978–979
   errors with, 355–356
   in Heat Transfer Program,
     957–958
   #include and, 142, 321–322,
     521
   int and, 230
   modules and, 313–316, 317,
     945
   in Roots of Equation Program,
     964–966

for **tools** library, 1008
Heat conduction, 799–808
Heat transfer, 461, 956–959
Hex character literals, 743–744
Hexadecimal literals, 743–744,
   744, 773
Hexadecimal notation, 235, 411,
   415f, 743–748, 771,
   1000–1001
   conversion to/from, 1004–1005
   decimal versus, 773
   style and, 773
Hexintegar literal, 743–744
Hierarchical data structures, 566,
   585
High-level languages, 13–16, 22
High precedence, 104
hold(), 1016–1017
Hole pointers, 855–859
HORIZONTAL, 964, 972, 975
Hub, 9, 10
HUGE_VAL, 289, 300, 1029

I/O; *see* Input/output I/O
I/O conversion specifiers,
   234–235; *see also*
   Conversion specifiers
I/O formats, of numeric types,
   228, 231
I/O functions, 47–50, 416–419
   buffers and, 602–603, 643
   pointers and, 849–852
   in problem specification and
     analysis, 23–24
   streams and, 599–603
   strings and, 493–501
   unbuffered, 603
   unsigned and hexadecimal,
     744–748
I/O library; *see* Standard I/O
   library
I/O utility functions, 672–674
IC; *see* Instruction counter IC
ideal(), 334–337, 880
Identifiers, 100–101, 142–143
Idioms, 861
IEEE; *see* Institute for Electrical
   and Electronic Engineers
   (IEEE)
if statement/loop, 60–70, 170
   bool and, 457
   in calling library functions, 145
   comparison operators and, 115
   in counted sentinel loop, 193
   curly brackets and, 69–70
   errors with, 83, 218
   floating-point comparisons and,
     285
   input errors and, 598
   nested, 196

pointers and, 844–845
   in Points of a Rectangle
     Program, 575
   relational operators and, 60–70
   strings and, 489, 503
   three ways to use, 68–69
   truth values and, 432
if... break statement/loop,
   175–176
   Chauvenet's algorithm and,
     666–667
   command-line arguments and,
     926
   in counted sentinel loop,
     192–193, 194
   data validation loops with, 187,
     188
   infinite for loop and, 177, 219
   linear regression and, 395
   menus and, 1024
   in search loop, 194
   in sequential search, 688
   two-dimensional arrays and,
     718
if... continue statement/loop,
   177–178
if... else statement/loop, 62–70,
   170, 457
   conditional operator compared
     to, 996
   in counted sentinel loop, 192
   errors with, 937
   floating-point comparisons and,
     288
   increment and, 112
   in Points of a Rectangle
     Program, 577
   primary applications of, 68–69
   in Projectile Program, 257
   in Quadratic Roots Program,
     155–159
   recursion and, 882
   series of, 64–67, 69, 196
   strings and, 523
   style and, 217
   in writing file of voltages, 611
ifndef, 978
#ifndef, 947–948
Image processing, 719–727, 728
Image smoothing, 719–727, 728
Importing, 946–947, 977
in_or_out(), 570–573
In-out parameters, 449, 451, 472
in-type, 427, 566, 570–576
#include, 45, 47, 53, 334, 345,
   1027–1028
   bisection method and, 466
   in calling library functions,
     143–144, 313–316
   header files and, 142, 321–322,
     521, 946–947

in Heat Transfer Program, 957–958
in interpolation, 211
modules and, 313–316, 979
prototype placement and, 354
Simpson's 1/3 rule and, 204
static and, 876f
tools library, 1008–1009
Increment operators, 107, 108–114
continue and, 177–178
errors with, 219
parsing, 110
with pointers, 841–842, 847–848, 863
side effects and, 994, 995, 999; *see also* Side effects
style and, 130, 217
update expression and, 174
in Voltage Ramp Program, 120–123
Indentation, 69, 217, 218
Indeterminate answers, 241
Index columns, 656–658
Index values, for ASCII table, 412
Indirect assignment, 446, 448, 451, 839, 840, 859
Indirect reference, 451, 838–839, 859
Indirection, 446
Infinite loops, 219, 881
Infinite recursion, 881, 911
Infinity, 248, 288, 294, 300–302, 303
Information
arrays and, 370
design and, 342, 348, 350, 353
garbage and, 625
Initialization, 368–369, 398–399
for arrays of structures, 560
comma operator and, 998
external storage and, 877
during function call, 875
pointer; *see* Pointer initialization
string literals and, 487, 536
strings and, 489, 490, 536
structures and, 554–555, 585
style and, 217
syntax for string, 538
three-dimensional arrays and, 711
Initialization expression, 171, 172
Initialization statement, 172–173
Initializers, 58, 72, 96, 97
Input
into array, 849–851
buffering of, 602–603, 622
character, 413–419, 434
of floating-point numbers, 235–236

garbage bad, 73
illegal characters in, 621
integer, 234–235
in interpolation, 212
pointers and, 839–840, 849–851
sentinel loops and, 189
stream, 602–603, 605–606, 612–617
string, 496–499, 537, 538
unbuffered, 603
Input buffers, 414
Input-controlled loops, 182
Input devices, 2, 7–8
Input errors, 598, 646
Input files, names of, 646
Input formats, 49, 620
Input functions, 313, 612–614, 644, 1032
Input list, 612, 618
Input/output I/O, 11–12, 47–50, 1032–1034; *see also* entries beginning I/O
memory-mapped, 764
wide-character, 1040
Input parameters, 449
Input stream, 48; *see also* Standard input stream; Streams
Input validation loops, 73–75, 182; *see also* Data validation loops; Validation
interpolation and, 212–213
in Projectile Program, 257
Inputs, series of, 69
Insertion sort, 677–678, 852–862
for ascending order, 855–859
command-line arguments and, 926
quicksort and, 908, 910
search and move in, 858
steps in, 857
inside(), 579–582
Institute for Electrical and Electronic Engineers (IEEE), 55, 232, 300, 1003
floating-point standard of, 1027–1028
and orders of magnitude, 294
overflow error and, 289, 291
Instruction cache, 4
Instruction counter IC, 3
Instruction cycle, 4
Instruction register IR, 3
instructions(), 150
int, 46, 49, 95, 101, 114f, 115, 196f
advanced functions and, 1033
arrays and, 367, 369, 383–384
bsearch() and, 932, 934
casting and, 249–252, 254, 255
char versus, 419–420, 433

characters and conversions and, 1028–1029
command-line arguments and, 924, 935
fclose() and, 604
feof() and, 612
fgetc() and, 613–614
fgets() and, 613–614
fopen() and, 604
fprintf() and, 608
fputc() and, 608
fputs() and, 608
fscanf() and, 612–613
hexadecimal notation and, 746–748
input functions and, 1032
in ISO C, 147f
number conversion and, 244, 245, 249–260
output functions and, 1033
pointers and, 443
in Points of a Rectangle Program, 566
prototype errors and, 163
short versus **long,** 229–230
signed versus **unsigned,** 229, 230–231
streams and, 604, 608, 1031
struct and, 553f
in summation loop, 181
INT_MAX, 189, 229, 260
INT_MIN, 229
Integer division, 240–246, 254–257, 270
Integer literals, 228, 231, 743–744
Integer modulus, 241–246
Integer operations; *see* Addition; Division; Multiplication; Subtraction
Integer types, 228–231
Integer variables, in Echo Program, 51
Integers
abs and, 139
ALU and, 3–4
in arrays, 367
bytes and, 4
characters as short, 410, 411, 415, 419–420, 433
combination operators and, 108
comparison function for, 934, 937
comparison of, 282
conversion specifiers for, 234–235; *see also* Conversion specifiers
increment and decrement operators with, 109
index columns and, 657
operations with, 240–246

overflow errors with, 288–292, 302
pointers and, 443
in problem specification and analysis, 24–25
programming style for, 271–272
real types versus, 269
short versus **long,** 229–231
signed, 1002–1005
signed, 229–231
sizeof and, 101
style and, 536
time() and, 194
truth values of, 116–117
underflow errors and, 292
unsigned, 743–748, 1002–1005; *see also* Unsigned numbers; Unsigned values
unsigned, 229–231
Integrated development environment, 27, 28, 34, 37
Integration
by polynomial approximation, 203–204
by Simpson's 1/3 rule, 202–209
by summing rectangles, 159–162
Intel, 863
Interactive programs
command-line versus, 936
stream redirection and, 600–601
style and, 645
Interfaces, 8–9, 138, 317–318, 342, 946
bitfield types and, 759–760
C and, 15
characters and, 432
design of, 342, 347, 350
in encryption and decryption, 756–759
errors with, 978
kinds of, 9
menus as, 537
prototypes and, 141, 145
serial versus parallel, 9
in Voltage Ramp Program, 120–123
International ASCII, 411, 412, 421, 432, 434, 604
International Standards Organization (ISO), 14, 326; *see also* ISO C
Internet, 9, 753–755
Interpolation, 209–216
Interpreters
versus compilers, 29
debuggers as, 34–35

Interprocess communication, 959f
Interruption, 142
IR; *see* Instruction register (IR)
isalpha(), 421, 422
isdigit(), 421, 422
islower(), 421, 422
ISO; *see* International Standards Organization (ISO)
ISO C, 14, 15, 55, 1026
  EOF in, 607f
  function declarations, definitions, calls in, 321
  function types in, 147f
  int and, 230
  long double in, 232, 240
  mass memory allocation in, 788f
  operations on structures in, 555, 556
  parameter coercion errors and, 330
  percent sign in, 235
  sin() and **cos()** in, 258
  tools library and, 1014
isspace(), 422
isupper(), 421, 422
iszero(), 457
Iteration, 881; *see also* Loops
  for bisection method, 468
  in Heat Flow Simulation, 803–808
  recursion and, 881–883, 908, 909, 910

Java, 230
"Jump" instruction, 4

kbhit, 603
Key values, 193–194, 657–659, 687–688
Keyboard, 7, 8
  buffers and, 414, 602–603
  menus and, 510
  streams and, 48, 602–603
  unbuffered I/O and, 603
Keyboard buffer, 48, 51
Keywords, 43, 45
  list of, in C, 988–989
  variable names and, 46

LAN; *see* Local area network LAN
Language translation, 7
Languages, types of, 12–16
Laptop, 10
Laser, in CD-ROM, 6
Layout, 69–70

function, 355
two-dimensional arrays and memory, 701–702
Lazy evaluation, 117–120, 992–997, 999
Least-squares curve fitting, 209, 391–398
Length conversion, 246
Lexical order, 421
Libraries, 29, 138, 139–168, 1026
  header files for, 142, 313, 945
  linkers and, 29
  local, 133, 140–141
  math *see* Mathematics library
  standard I/O; *see* Standard I/O library
  tools library; *see* **tools** library
  using, 141–147
Library functions, 138–168
  generalized, 918
  modules and, 313–316
LIMIT, 191, 461, 467, 964, 969
limits.h, 229
Line breaks, 326; *see also* **break** statement
Linear equations, solving system of, 811–823
Linear interpolation, 209–216
Linear regression, 391–398
linear_ system, 811–823
Linkers/linking, 29, 35, 945, 948–951
  compilation and, 948–951, 977–978, 1011
  errors with, 33, 83, 911, 947
  external storage and, 877
  rule for, 952–953
  scope and, 331
Linux, 230f, 925f
Literal values, 54, 97–100, 228, 231, 434; *see also* Character literals
  constants as, 97–100, 233
  floating-point, 233–234
  hexadecimal, 743–744
  string; *see* String literals
Little-endian architecture, 620f
Load module, 29, 947
Local area network LAN, 9
Local arrays, 368f
Local constants, in arrays, 690
Local declarations, 148
Local libraries, 133, 140–142; *see also* **tools** library
Local names, 95
Local parameters, 331
Local variables, 148, 154, 331, 333–337
  errors with, 356
  run-time stack and, 878–880
  style and, 354, 910

visibility of, 331–332
locale.h, 1040
Localization, library for, 1040
Log files, 625, 646
Logarithm functions, 266–268, 1030
Logic
  bitwise, 748
  pointer, 840–842, 864
Logical-AND, 118–119; *see also* AND
Logical errors, 35, 36
  unsafe conversion and, 247
  warnings and, 143
Logical expressions, 992–997
Logical NOT, 751–752; *see also* NOT
Logical operators, 102, 115–120, 130
  ALU and, 3
  bitwise operators versus, 773
  complications with, 999
  lazy evaluation and, 992–997
  nested logic and, 218
  parse trees for, 117
  style and, 130
  truth tables for, 116–120
  in Voltage Ramp Program, 120–123
Logical-OR, 119–120; *see also* OR
long, 196f, 229–230, 231, 273
  ampersand and, 449
  command-line arguments and, 924, 935
  in decoding Internet address, 755
  hexadecimal notation and, 743, 747
  number conversion and, 244, 246, 252, 323
  overflow error and, 288
  streams and, 618
long double, 52f, 232, 233–240, 271
Long expressions, 129
Loop body, 70, 174
  design and, 348
  null empty, 178, 195
Loop condition, 881
Loop control, design and, 348
Loop counters, 72, 218, 219; *see also* Counters
  arrays and, 376–378
  comma operator and, 998
  integers for, 269, 271
  style and, 271
Loop invariant, 178f
Loop test, 70, 72, 173, 177
Loop variable, 72, 178, 182
  design and, 348

menus and, 511
  as subscript, 374
Loops, 70–75, 170–226; *see also* Iteration
  applications of, 179–196
  array algorithms and, 683–684
  arrays and, 375–378, 690
  break and, 175–177
  busy wait, 195, 286
  Cash Register Program with, 190
  character input and, 417–418, 423–425
  combination operators in, 108
  comma operator and, 998
  continue and, 175, 177–178
  counted sentinel, 190–193; *see also* Counted/counting loops
  delay, 194–196
  design of, 348
  do, 70; *see also* **do** statement/loop
  do... while; *see* **do... while** statement/loop
  errors with, 83, 218–219, 690
  exit test for, 177, 376
  and file processing errors, 621
  for; *see* **for** statement/loop
  function layout and, 355
  if; *see* **if** statement/loop
  if... break; *see* **if... break** statement/loop
  if... continue statement, 177–178
  if... else *see* **if... else** statement/loop
  infinite, 219, 646, 881
  in insertion sort, 855–859
  integer modulus and, 243
  for interactive game, 191–192
  key values for, 193–194
  for menus, 513–517, 524–527, 536, 962, 1024
  nested; *see* Nested loops
  overflow errors and, 288, 301
  pointers and, 841–842, 862
  program efficiency and, 910
  recursion versus, 881
  in Roots of Equation Program, 962–963
  scanning, 846–849
  search, 193–194
  selection sort and, 683–684
  strings and, 501
  in structure comparisons, 563
  style and, 536
  summing, 389
  validation; *see* Data validation loops; Input validation loops; Validation

Low memory, 6
Low precedence, 104, 107
Lumber Program, 563–564

Machine code/language, 4,
    12–13, 20
  compilers and, 29
  example of translating into,
    31–33
  integer operations and, 240
  menus and, 515
  programs and, 4
Macros, 504f, 1023, 1026–1027
Magnetic tapes, 7
Magnitude
  and sign, 1002
  of vector, 372–373
main(), 45–46, 95, 138, 316
  arrays and, 387, 390–391, 451
  assignment statements and, 320
  average and, 389–391
  badswap() and, 451, 453
  in binary search, 888–892
  bisection method and, 464–468
  bitfields and, 762
  in calling library functions, 145,
    147, 313–316
  Chauvenet's algorithm and,
    673–674, 676, 678–682
  command-line arguments and,
    919, 920–921, 926, 935
  design steps and, 341
  dynamic arrays and, 792
  in Fin Temperature Program,
    344–346, 351
  function-call graphs and, 339
  in Gas Pressure Table, 531,
    534–535
  in Gaussian elimination,
    812–823
  global variables and, 334–337
  in Heat Flow Simulation, 803,
    807
  in Ice Cream Program, 512–514
  for insertion sort, 852
  interpolation and, 212
  linear regression and, 394
  in Memo Program, 527–529
  menus and, 512–514, 527
  modules and, 313–316, 944
  in Monte Carlo method, 580
  optional arguments and, 926
  pointers and, 464–468, 472, 844
  in Points in a Rectangle,
    568–569
  in Quadratic Roots Program,
    458
  in query loop, 183–186
  in quicksort, 897, 899, 930
  in Quiz Program, 634

recursion and, 886, 909
  in Roots of Equation Program,
    956, 958–961, 966, 967,
    968
  run-time stack and, 879–880
  selection sort and, 678–679
  setup() and, 824
  Simpson's 1/3 rule and, 204,
    205
  in Skylight Controller Program,
    765, 768
  style and, 472, 909
  testing and, 343
Main memory, 4, 5–6
  buffers and, 48
  constants and, 34
  secondary, or direct-access
    memory, and, 6
  virtual memory and, 924f, 925
Main program, 316
  for image smoothing, 720–722
  for sorting, 681
  for 2D point transformation,
    714
Mainframes, 11
Make facility, 950–954, 978
Makefiles, 946, 950–954,
    1011–1012
  for roots, 976–977
  style and, 978
malloc(), 490f, 787–797, 806,
    824–825
  in dynamic matrix, 809, 813
  in Gaussian elimination, 813
  pointers and, 846
Mantissa, 231–232, 233, 248,
    1002–1003
  and orders of magnitude,
    293–294
  underflow errors and, 292–293
MAR; see Memory address
    register (MAR)
Masking, 659–663, 673, 675, 688
  bitwise operators and, 749–752,
    767, 772
  in encryption and decryption,
    756–759
  errors with, 690, 773
  of Internet address, 753–755
Mass memory allocation,
    788–789
math, 139
Mathematical notation, 233
Mathematical operators, 53–54
Mathematics library, 139, 140,
    1029–1031
  arrays and, 391
  fabs() and, 285
  header file for, 142
  Quadratic Roots Program and,
    155–162

trigonometry in, 253, 258
math.h, 313, 315–316,
    1029–1031
Matrix, 698, 701–704, 728
  dynamic, 809–823, 825
  errors with, 730
  reading and writing binary data
    for, 709–710
MAX, 66, 1031
MAX_ITER, 964, 975
MDR; see Memory data register
    (MDR)
mean, 387
Mean value of array, 384–391,
    398, 664
Measurements
  real variables for, 269
  of torque, 638–643
Megahertz MHz, 3
Member declarations, 552–554
Members, 552–554, 555, 556
Memo maker, 524–527
Memory, 4–7
  allocation of; see Allocation
  arrays and, 374, 375–378, 690
  auxiliary, 7
  buffers and; see Buffers;
    Streams
  bytes of; see Bytes
  C and, 15
  cache, 5
  command-line arguments and,
    924f, 925
  direct-access, 6
  dynamic allocation of,
    786–798, 827
  during execution, 36
  low, 6
  main; see Main memory
  pointers in, 445, 863f
  in Quadratic Roots Program,
    457–458
  random access RAM, 2, 5–6
  read-only ROM, 4, 6
  resizing allocation of, 787f
  at run time, 29
  secondary, 6, 7
  stack overflow and, 881
  string literals and, 489
  strings and, 491, 536, 538
  structures and, 559–560
  subscripts and, 374
  two-dimensional arrays and,
    701–702
  types of, 5
  variables and, 46, 95
  virtual, 924f, 925
Memory address, 449
Memory address register MAR,
    3, 8
Memory data register MDR, 3, 8

Memory faults, 377–378
Memory functions, 1037
Memory management system, 11
Memory-mapped I/O, 764
menu(), 513–517
menu_c(), 515–516, 524–526,
    526, 537, 1023, 1024
  in array of structures, 562
  in Roots of Equation Program,
    961
  in Skylight Controller Program,
    768
menu_i(), 515–516, 521, 532,
    535, 537, 1023–1024
  in array of structures, 562
  pointers and, 844–845
Menus, 509–517
  enhanced processing in, 659
  function pointers and, 860
  in Heat Transfer Program, 961
  for Ice Cream Program,
    510–514
  integers for, 269
  in Magic Memo Maker,
    524–527
  masking and, 659–663
  parsing and, 524–527
  pointers and, 842–846, 862
  processing, 524–527
  in Roots of Equation Program,
    962
  strings and, 517–529, 536,
    1023–1024
  style and, 537
  subscripts and, 657
Message construction, 517–524
MHz; see Megahertz (MHz)
Microcode, 4
Microsoft C, 603
Microsoft Visual C++, 34
MIDI; see Musical instrument
    digital interface (MIDI)
Minimum, finding, 883–886, 994,
    1027
Miniumum values, 1028
mod, 432
Modems, interfaces and, 9
Modifiers, 95f, 98–100
Modular design, 312–364, 571,
    944–982
  arrays and, 690
  errors in, 978–979
  monolithic versus, 354
  multimodule, 945, 948–954,
    977
  recursion and, 909
  in Roots of Equation Program,
    954–977
  style and, 909, 978
Module communication, 954–955

Module interfaces, 946; *see also*
    Interfaces
Modules, 14, 138–139, 312–316,
    353; *see also* Modular
    design
    C and, 16
    C++ and, 16
    dependencies of, 950, 952–953,
        979
    external storage and, 877
    functions and, 148
    global variables and, 331
    load, 29, 947
    scope and, 331–332
    static storage and, 876f
    streams and, 644–645
    style and, 644–645
Modulus, 241–246, 271
Modulus operator, 241–246, 270
Monte Carolo method, 578–585
Mouse, 7
    interfaces and, 9
    menus and, 510
    structures and, 566
Multidimensional arrays, 398,
    710–711, 729
Multimodule program, 945,
    948–954, 977
    structure of, 954–956
    tools library and, 1008
Multiplication, 289, 320
    deference operators versus, 473
    underflow errors and, 293
Multiplication table, 698–700
Multiprocessing system, 11
Multiprogramming systems, 11,
    12
Musical instrument digital
    interface MIDI, 9

n_ marks(), 329–330
n_ stars(), 324–325, 329
Names, 129–130
    with asterisks, 604
    for constants, 53
    errors with, 646
    for files, 28, 646
    for floating-point numbers, 272
    for formal parameters, 323–325
    for formulas, 272
    for functions, 129, 163, 837f,
        911
    local, 95
    for loop counters, 271
    with numbers, 911
    for objects, 100–101, 129, 163
    for parameters, 323–325, 353,
        355
    for prototypes and function
        headers, 324f

recursion and, 911
    for structures, 552–554, 585,
        586
    for subscripts, 688, 730
    tag, 552–554, 585
    for type declarations, 586
    for variables; *see* Variable
        names
NaN, 248, 294, 303
Negation, 751–752
Nested function calls, 320
Nested logic, 218, 219, 458
Nested loops
    for, 218, 698–701, 704, 728
    errors with, 729–730
    if, 196, 218, 457
    if... else, 217
Nested **switch** statement, 218
Network socket, 599
Networks, 9–10
Newline character, 495–499, 501,
    644, 646
    missing, 620–621
    as sentinel value, 189
    unbuffered I/O and, 603
Newton's method, 294–302, 974,
    978
NMAX, 395
no_ go, 517–524
NO_ ROOT, 427, 462–468, 964
Non-**void** functions, 324,
    326–328, 998
Nonfatal error handling, 68
Noninteractive programs, stream
    redirection and, 600–601
Nonlocal jumps, library for, 1039
Nonwhitespace, menus and, 516,
    517
Normal distribution, 384
Normalized numbers, 1003
NOT, 115, 117, 751–752
NULL, 399, 443, 444–445, 471,
    472, 1031
    calloc() and, 790
    gets() and, 497, 613
    malloc() and, 789
    streams and, 607, 627
    strings and, 504
    style and, 472, 536, 861
    two-dimensional arrays and,
        715
    in writing file of voltages, 611
Null character, 538
    errors with, 827
    escape code and, 413
    null string and, 488, 492
    as sentinel value, 189
    string merging and, 487
Null pointer, 492, 844
Null strings, 488, 492

Null terminator, 488, 491, 536,
    538, 539
Number-base conversion, 742,
    1000–1006
Number representation,
    1000–1006, 1030
Number symbol #, 98
Numbers, 282–310
    bits and, 742–783
    command-line arguments and,
        935
    conversion of ASCII to, 935,
        1035–1036
    denormalized, 292–293, 302
    discrete versus continuous in
        comparisons, 282
    encryption and decryption of,
        755–759
    masking and arrays of, 659f
    prime, 428–432
    in problem specification and
        analysis, 24–25
    random, 139
    reading and writing, 234–240
    real; *see* Floating-point
        numbers; Real numbers
    unsigned; *see* Unsigned
        integers; Unsigned
        numbers; Unsigned values
Numeric functions, 1022
Numeric types, 228–279,
    264–269
Numerical approximation, 799

Object code, 20, 874, 945
Object files, 29, 945, 1012–1013
Object-oriented languages, 16,
    849f, 861, 957f
Objects, 44, 81, 128
    addresses of, 442; *see also*
        Pointers
    compound, 320f, 398
    declarations and, 96, 128
    diagramming of, 97, 99, 100,
        129
    names for, 100–101, 129, 163
    null, 492
    simple, 835
    two-part, 502
    types for, 81, 128; *see also*
        Types
    variable number of
        varying-sized, 795–798
oclock(), 507, 1020–1021
Octal numbering system, 13
Off-board sentinel, 846, 847–848,
    861
On-board sentinel, 846, 847–848,
    861
open_ skylight(), 769–770

Operands, 103–107
    combination operators and, 108
    constant, 198
    integer, 240, 241, 252, 271
    lazy evaluation and, 992–997,
        999
    normalized numbers and, 1003
    and orders of magnitude, 294
    real, 252
    type casts and, 249–250
Operating system OS, 10–12, 946
    device drivers and, 8–9
    RAM and, 5–6
    read-only memory and, 5–6
    ROM OS-ROM, 6
Operations, 21
    on characters, 419–432
    integer, 240–246
    pointers and, 443, 445–448
    on structures, 555–585
Operators, 102–103, 129–130
    advanced aspects of C, 990–999
    arithmetic; *see* Arithmetic
        operators
    arrow, 556, 587
    assignment, 107–108
    binary, 103
    bit-manipulation, 15, 102
    bitwise; *see* Bitwise operators
    combination, 107–108,
        990–992, 999
    comma, 998, 999
    comparison, 115
    complement, 750–751
    conditional, 994–997, 999
    constant expression and, 198
    decrement; *see* Decrement
        operators
    dereference, 446, 459
    dot, 556, 558, 587
    errors with, 272, 473, 538, 587
    for/while loops and, 173
    generic, 240
    increment; *see* Increment
        operators
    logical; *see* Logical operators
    overflow error and, 289–292
    pointer; *see* Pointer operators
    postdecrement, 109–110, 999
    postfix; *see* Postfix operators
    postincrement, 109–110, 999
    precedence of, 987; *see also*
        Precedence
    predecrement, 109–110, 999
    prefix; *see* Prefix operators
    preincrement, 109–110, 999
    relational, 114–115
    shift; *see* Shift operators
    side-effect, 113, 114, 995, 999;
        see also Side effects
    style and, 861

subscripts and, 371f
tertiary, 103
unary, 103, 104–106
Optical disk storage, 6
Optional arguments, 923, 925, 936
OR, 115, 117, 750
Order of arguments, 328–330, 354, 355, 936
Order of evaluation, 995, 997
Order of magnitude, 293–294, 303
Order of parameters, 328–330, 353, 355
Order of rows, 701
OS; *see* Operating system (OS)
OS-ROM memory, 6
Output
from array, 851–852
buffering of, 603
character, 413, 415–419
of floating-point numbers, 236–240
integer, 235
interpolation and, 213
pointers and, 839–840, 849–852
run-time errors and, 598; *see also* Run-time errors
stream, 603, 606, 607–612
string, 493–496
symbolic, 509
unbuffered, 603
verbose, 967–973
Output devices, 2, 7–8
Output errors, 646
Output files, names of, 646
Output formats, 49–50
Output functions, 313, 607–608, 644, 1032
Output list, 607, 618
Output parameters, 449
Output statements, 27
Output stream, 48
Overflow, 288–292, 300–302, 353
bits and, 745
precision and, 288–292
representational errors and, 291–292, 303
stack, 881
strings and, 538

Packing, 759
Padding bits, 414f
"Paged out," 924f, 925
Parallel arrays, 378–382, 398, 511, 537, 561–562
arrays of structures versus, 561–562, 586–587, 657
errors with, 690
in menus, 511, 537

style and, 586–587
as tables, 380, 398, 561–562, 657, 690
Parallel interface, 9
Parameter coercions, 330
Parameter declarations, 142–143, 145
prototypes and, 321–323
Parameter lists, 317
Parameter order, 328–330
Parameters, 318–319, 324–325
array; *see* Array parameters
bsearch() and, 918
coercion and, 322
command-line arguments and, 936
design and, 342, 348, 350, 351, 353
errors with, 355
formal, 318–319, 323–325
function-call graphs and, 340
function layout and, 355
functions as, 918, 927–934
global variables and, 331, 334, 339–340
in Heat Flow Simulation, 803
in-out, 449, 451, 472
input, 449
names for, 323–325, 353, 355
and number of arguments, 322
order of, 328–330, 353, 355
output, 449
pointer; *see* Pointer parameters
qsort() and, 918, 931
recursion and, 909
reference, 459f
run-time stack and, 878–880
string, 499–501
structures and, 559–560
style and, 354, 355, 472, 909
by value passing and, 320
value versus address, 559–560
for variations in behavior, 324–325
Parentheses, 46, 47f, 54, 103, 130, 317
errors with, 473
function calls and, 142
function layout and, 355
parsing and, 105–107
pointers and, 473, 863
Parse trees/parsing, 94, 105–107
for assignment combination, 108, 990–992, 999
associativity and, 104–105
in case study, 123–128
for conditional operator, 996–997
of conversion, 252–253
of increment/decrement operators, 110, 114

for lazy evaluation, 992–997
for logical operators, 117, 118
menus and, 524–527
in Points of a Rectangle Program, 577
partition(), 901–903, 905–908, 910
Partitioning, 902–908, 909
Pascal, 14, 15, 230, 702f
Pass by address; *see* Call/pass by address
Pass by value; *see* Call/pass by value
Password validation, 517–524
PCs; *see* Personal computers (PCs)
Pentium, 620f
Percent sign, 49, 234–235, 414, 415; *see also* Modulus operator
binary and decimal conversion and, 744
streams and, 616, 619
strings and, 493, 497–499, 500, 537
for unsigned input and output, 744
Periods, 556; *see also* Dot operators
Peripherals, 8–9
Personal computers PCs
int and, 230
virtual memory and, 924
Personalization, 1010
PI, 54, 98, 257–258
Pivot values, 901, 903–904, 907, 908
Pivoting, 818–821
Pixels, 703, 719
Place-value notation, 244
point_type, 569–571
Pointer arithmetic and logic, 840–842, 848, 864
Pointer comparisons, 842
Pointer initialization, 443–444, 471, 472, 834–837
style and, 861
uninitialized sentinel and, 862
Pointer operators, 445–448, 471
errors with, 473
style and, 472
Pointer parameters, 317f, 338f, 449–451, 456–459, 471
command-line arguments and, 936
errors with, 473
structures and, 559–560, 587
style and, 472, 936
Pointer variables, 443, 445, 788, 834–835, 838

Pointers, 15, 370–371, 442–483, 834–873
arrays and; *see* Arrays and pointers
base type of, 443
casting values versus, 937
dangling, 790, 826
dynamic arrays and, 846
error recovery and, 622
errors with, 443, 472–473, 827, 861, 862–864, 937
as functional parameters, 860
functions and, 842–846; *see also* Function pointers
head, 846
hole, 855–859
initialization and, 443–444
mass memory allocation and, 788
menu of, 842–846
in modern computers, 863f
new ways to use, 834
NULL, 443–445
out of bounds, 862
purposes of, 442
qsort() and, 927
scanning, 846–849, 861
strings and, 486, 488–492, 496, 536, 538
struct and, 553f
structures and, 555, 556, 587
style and, 472, 861–862
subscripts versus, 848–849, 861
tail, 846
Points in a Rectangle Program, 565–578
Polynomial approximation, 203–204
Portability, 14, 101, 230, 273, 412, 1013–1014
position_labels, 768
Position variables, 657–658
Positional notation, 243
Postdecrement operators, 109–110, 999
Postfix operators, 103, 106, 110, 130, 999
prefix versus, 112–113
update expression and, 174
Postincrement operators, 109–110, 999
pow(), 391, 836, 837
Powers, 101, 1030
Precedence, 54, 83, 94, 103, 863, 987
for assignment combination operators, 990–992
of bitwise operators, 773
defaults for, 103–104
of dot operator, 558
evaluation order versus, 997

of logical operators, 117–118
parsing and, 105–107, 992, 997, 999
pointers and, 837f, 863
side effects and, 995
of subscripts, 371f
Precedence table, 103–104
Precision, 97, 228, 232, 273, 1003
conversions and, 246, 248, 259, 271, 353
correct versus, 291
double for, 270
floating-point comparisons and, 283–285, 303; *see also* Overflow; Underflow
and orders of magnitude, 293–294
Preconditions, 342, 347, 350
Predecrement operators, 109–110, 999
Predefined escape code sequence, 413
Predefined streams, 599, 643, 1031
Predefined value, 188
Prefix operators, 103, 105, 106, 110, 130
postfix versus, 112–113
update expression and, 174
Preincrement operators, 109–110, 999
Premature exit, 176
Preprocessor commands, 43, 45, 98, 313, 504f, 946
Prime numbers, 428–432
print_ answers(), 823
print_ array(), 804, 808
print_ data(), 671, 677, 849–851, 899
print_ matrix(), 815, 823
print_ stats(), 671–674
print_ table(), 345–352, 431–432, 708
print_ upper(), 501
Printers
interfaces and, 9
keyboard and, 7, 8
streams and, 48
printf(), 47, 48, 50, 138, 139, 327
in calling library functions, 145
character input and, 413, 416–417
conversion specifiers and, 238, 240, 415, 744
decimal conversion and, 744, 745
double and, 52
errors with, 618
fatal() and, 154
in Grapefruits and Gravity Program, 57

linear regression and, 396
menus and, 516, 1024
modules and, 315
nested loops and, 699–700
null character and, 488
in Numerical Integration Program, 161
parallel arrays and, 381
pointers and, 839, 840, 845, 860
in Points of a Rectangle Program, 575
puts() and, 49, 52
in Quadratic Roots Program, 457
secant method and, 973
Simpson's 1/3 rule and, 203
stdout and, 600, 603
streams and, 603
strings and, 487, 493–495, 537
in writing file of voltages, 611
Printing
of ASCII characters, 415–416
of date and time, 507–508
of enumerated types, 509, 536
of Heat Flow Simulation, 808
of memo maker, 527–529
of tables, 698–700
of Wind Speed Table, 708
Printouts, debugging; *see* Debugging printouts
Probability theory, 262
Problem solving, 881
Problem specification and analysis, 23–25
bisection method, 460
Computing Resistance Program, 254
Cruise Control Program, 286
decoding Internet address, 754
for encrypting numbers, 756
Exam Averages Program, 378
Fin Temperature Program, 344, 350–352
Finding an Average Program, 30
Gas Pressure Table, 530–535
Gas Prices Program, 76
General Root Finder Program, 955
Image Smoothing Program, 720
integration by Simpson's rule, 204
interpolation, 210–211
linear regression, 392
Measuring Torque Program twisting circular shaft, 639
Monte Carlo method and, 578–579
Points in a Rectangle Program, 566, 567

Prime Number Calculation Program, 429
Projectile Program, 258
Quiz Program random selection, 629
Roots of Quadratic Equation Program, 155, 970
secant method, 970
Skylight Controller Program, 764
sorting numbers, 679
statistics, 385
2D point transformation, 713
in using parse tree to debug, 124
Voltage Ramp Program, 120–123
Wire Gauge Adequacy Evaluation Program, 198
writing data to file, 609
Process management, 1015–1020
Process scheduler, 11
Processing windows, 703
Processor; *see* Central processing unit (CPU)
Programs, 20–40, 918–942; *see also* Software
defined, 4, 20
efficiency of, 910, 993
errors in, 82–83
example of calculations in, 54–67
example of simplest, 44–46
execution of; *see* Execution
main memory and, 5–6, 316
meaning of, 21
modular, 312–364, 571
multimodule, 945
overall structure of, 80–81, 138
parts of, 42–44
prototype of, 54–52; *see also* Prototypes
robust, 617, 625, 644, 646
simple one-module versus large, 944–945, 977
testing of; *see* Test plan; Testing
tracing operation of, 879–880
Program block, 46
Program bugs; *see* Bugs; Debugging; Logical errors
Program construction, 29–33
Program design; *see* Design
Program development, 20, 21, 343–352; *see also* Development environment
Program files, names for, 28
Program verification, 25–26; *see also* Verification
Programmer-defined functions, 313–316, 387
Programmer-defined streams, 604–606, 638–643

Programmer-defined subprograms, 341
Programmer-defined types, 312
Programming style, 82, 129–130, 327–328
arrays and, 399, 688–690
for calculating with bits, 772–773
command-line arguments and, 936–937
for dynamic arrays, 825–826
for/while loops and, 173
function calls and, 472
functions and, 163, 313, 354–355
global variables and, 335, 336
loops and, 217–218
for modular organization, 978
numeric types and, 271–272
pointers and, 472, 861–862
prototypes and, 472
for recursion, 909–910
spacing in, 146
streams and, 644–646
for strings, 536–537
structures and, 585–587
two-dimensional arrays and, 728–729
Project files, 946, 977, 978, 1011
Project management, 1010
Projectile computation, 258
Prompts, 11, 49f
in Computing Resistance Program, 255
in Grapefruits and Gravity Program, 55
in menus, 513
in Points of a Rectangle Program, 575
in Projectile Program, 257
string merging and, 487
Prototypes, 54–52, 141–142, 148, 947
of advanced functions, 1033
ANSI, 322f
arrays and, 383–384, 387
bisection method and, 462–468
coercion and, 251
design of, 342, 349, 351
errors with, 163, 355
function calls and, 142–143, 145
function interfaces and, 317
global variables and, 334–337
header files and, 142
identifiers in, 143
missing, 321–322, 354
modules and, 313–316, 945
names for function headers and, 324f

parameter type checking and, 321–323
pointers and, 450
return and, 251
style and, 354
syntax for, 321
types of, 323
void and, 323–325
Pruning marks, 118, 119, 120, 992, 993
Pseudo-random numbers, 260–269
Pseudocode, 22, 59
putchar(), 415, 416, 501, 600
puts(), 46, 47, 48, 138, 139
infinite loops and, 219
null character and, 488
printf() and, 49, 52
putchar() versus, 415
stdout and, 600, 603
strings and, 487, 493–495, 501

qsort(), 918, 927–934, 935
bsearch() and, 932, 934
style and, 936
Quadratic interpolation, 209
Quadratic Roots Program, 155–162, 454–457
Quanitities, simple, integers for, 269
Query loops, 182–186
Question marks, 97, 117f
Questions, simple, integers for, 269
quick(), 900, 902–908
Quicksort, 861, 862, 896–908, 909
possible improvements in, 908
style and, 910
quicksort(), 897–900, 901
Quiz Program, 264–269, 271, 628–638, 645
Quotation marks, 46, 83, 142, 487, 536
for character literals, 412–413, 432, 434
errors with, 539
null string and, 488
Quotient, 241, 254

R(), 334–336
Radians, 253, 258
Radix sort, 896
Ragged arrays, 486, 508, 509, 536
dynamic, 794–798, 825
RAM; see Random access memory (RAM)
rand(), 260–264, 271, 583, 634, 910

RAND_MAX, 260–261, 263, 583
Random access memory RAM, 2, 5–6
Random locations, 377–378, 398
Random numbers, 139
bits and, 742
Monte Carlo method and, 580–585
pseudo-, 260–264, 271
Random selection, 628–638
randy(), 641, 1022
read, 34
read_file(), 670, 679–681
read_file, 796
read_file(), dynamic arrays and, 794
Read-only memory ROM, 4, 6
read_point(), 714–716
read_system(), 813
Reading binary matrix data, 709–710
Reading data from files, 614–615
Reading unsigned integers, 745
Real division, 240–241, 245, 271
Real numbers, 4, 55, 228, 410; *see also* Floating-point numbers
binary representation of, 1004
conversion of, 246–260
integers versus, 269
in problem specification and analysis, 24–25
representation of, 1002–1004
Real-time clock, 194, 261
realloc(), 787, 791–792, 805, 824, 826
errors with, 827
insertion sort and, 855
Reasonableness, 643
Rebooting, 15
rect_type, 570–575
Rectangles, summing a series of, 202–209
Recursion, 658f, 874–917, 909
binary search, 471, 658f, 881, 886–896, 909
errors with, 910–911
infinite, 881, 911
iteration and, 881–883, 908, 909, 910
quicksort, 861, 862, 896–908, 909
run-time stack and, 878–880, 909
simple example of, 883–886
style and, 909–910
tail, 883, 909
Recursive descent, 883–884, 909
Redirection, 600–602, 645, 862, 936

Reference
call by, 448f
direct, 839, 859
errors with, 863
indirect, 451, 838–839, 859
pointers and, 446, 451, 861, 863
style and, 861
Reference parameters, 459f
Referents, 443, 536, 827, 835–840
register, 95f, 874, 908
Registers, 3
orders of magnitude and, 293–294
in Skylight Controller Program, 766–767
Regression, 391–398
regression(), 394–396
Relational operators, 114–115, 120–123
Remainder, 241, 270
Repeat query, 182, 184
Repeating binary fractions, 239
Repeating process, 27; *see also* Loops
do... while statement for, 174
Representation ranges, 229–230, 232
scientific notation and, 233
Representational errors, 235, 246, 247, 282–284
epsilon test and, 284–285
overflow error and, 291–292, 303
Representational properties, 270
Representations
approximate, 283–285, 291–292
character, 410–411
number, 1000–1006
of real numbers, 1002–1004
string, 486
Resistance, computing, 126–128, 254–257
Resizing arrays, 791–792, 824
Resizing memory allocation, 787f
return, 148, 154–155, 161, 318, 458–459
coercion and, 251, 322–323
functions and, 319–321
run-time stack and, 878–879
sequential search and, 658
Return address, 318, 879
return statement
in Heat Flow Simulation, 803, 807
in Points of a Rectangle Program, 574
recursion and, 882
in Roots of Equation Program, 966

Return type, 318
Return values, 353, 509
function-call graphs and, 340
function interface and, 317
for multiple function results, 454–457, 471, 472, 557
of **scanf()**, 623–624
structures and, 555, 557–560
two parameters and a, 326–328
Revision control systems, 946
rhdigit, number conversion and, 244, 245
Right justified, 493
Robust program, 617, 625, 644, 646, 936
ROM; *see* Read-only memory (ROM)
ROOT_OK, 427, 462–468, 964, 972
Roots, quadratic program, 155–162, 454–457
Roots of equation, finding, 294–302, 459–471, 954–977, 978
Rotation, 711, 712
round(), 1022
Round-off errors, 284, 293, 343
Rounding, 249–252
floating-point comparisons and, 284
truncating versus, 248, 249
Row-major order, 701
Rows, 701–702
Rules, 952–953
Run-time errors, 21, 29, 598
overflow errors and, 288
pointers and, 471
subscripts and, 374
unsafe conversion and, 248
Run-time stack, 875, 878–880, 908, 909

s_in, 605–606
s_out, 605–606
Safe conversions, 246–247, 271
say(), 600, 638, 644, 854, 898, 1018–1019, 1038
Scaling, 809, 821
scanf(), 47, 48, 49, 51, 138, 139, 319f, 321
arrays and, 367, 372–373, 374, 383–384, 400, 449, 451
binary conversion and, 744
in binary search, 889
character input and, 413–415, 417, 424
command-line arguments and, 924, 935
in Computing Resistance Program, 255

conversion specifiers and, 238, 744
double and, 48, 52, 248
errors and, 83, 537, 618, 620, 621, 646–647
floating-point input and, 235–236
in Gas Pressure Table, 534
in Grapefruits and Gravity Program, 55–57
in Heat Flow Simulation, 804
in Image Smoothing Program, 723
input format errors and, 620
interpolation and, 213
linear regression and, 394
loops and, 122, 182, 187, 188
menu_ i() and, 1023
menus and, 516
null character and, 488
password validation and, 518
pointers and, 860
stdin and, 600
string input and, 497–499, 537
string literals and, 487
string parameters and, 499–501
structures and, 558
style and, 434
using return value of, 623–624
Scanners, 846–849, 903–907
Scanning loops, 846–847, 910
Scanning pointers, 846–849, 861
Scientific notation, 231–232, 233, 235; *see also* entries beginning Base
Scope, 331–337, 353
storage class and, 908
style and, 472
Screen
clearing, 1013, 1015
keyboard and, 7, 8
streams and, 48
SCSI; *see* Small computer systems interface (SCSI)
Search key, 657–658
Search loops, 193–194, 657–658
Searching
of array data structure, 656–663
binary, 471, 658f, 881, 886–896
for character, 504, 505
of Chauvenet table, 665–667
command-line arguments and, 935
in insertion sort, 858
recursion and, 874
sequential, 657–658, 687–688, 886
for substring, 504–505
of table, 657–658
secant(), 961, 973

Secant method, 294, 954–977, 978
algorithm for, 971
problems with, 974–976
verbose output and, 972
Secondary memory, 6, 7
Seed, 260–264
Selection expressions, 554
Selection sort, 677–687, 688
quicksort versus, 910
steps in, 685–686
Semantics, 114–115, 129–130, 491
Semicolons, 46, 83, 98, 163, 218, 356
Sentinel loops, 182, 188–193
application of, 209–216
counted, 190–193, 194
Sentinels, 846–849, 861, 862
Sequence points, 117
Sequential search, 657–658, 687–688, 886
Serial interface, 9
Server-client relationship, 9
setjmp.h, 1039
setup(), 802–803, 824, 854, 855
in binary search, 887
command-line arguments and, 920–921, 930
in Heat Transfer Program, 956, 958
in quicksort, 898, 900
in Roots of Equation Program, 959
Setup function, 854–855
"Shallow" copy, 557f
Sharing resources, 9
Sharing time, 11, 27
Shift operators, 748, 752–755, 759, 773, 774
short, 196f, 229–230, 231, 273, 757
arrays and, 369
char versus, 419–420
hexadecimal notation and, 747
number conversion and, 244, 249, 252, 323
overflow error and, 288
streams and, 618, 619
Side effects, 107–108, 110, 994, 995, 999
for/while loops and, 173
increment/decrement operators and, 113, 114, 994, 999
Sign and magnitude, 1002
Signal handling, library for, 1040
signal.h, 1040
signed char, 411–412
signed int, 229, 230–231
conversion of, 247, 249–260

hexadecimal notation and, 747–748
Signed integers, 1002
signed long, 229, 230–231
Signed shift, 753
signed short, 229, 230–231
sim_ cool(), 801–804
Simple algorithms, 656–697
Simple array, 656–697
Simple calculations, 52–57
Simple list recursion, 883
Simple sequential execution, 58
Simple statements, 81
Simple structures, 835
Simple values, versus complex, 114f
simpson(), 205–209
Simpson's 1/2 rule, 202–209
simulate(), 581, 582–584
Simulation, 799–808
sin(), 253, 258, 836
Sine and cosine functions, 258
sizeof, 101, 102
arrays and, 369–370, 860
errors with, 538
malloc() and, 789, 796
strings and, 502–503, 536
Skipping, 118–120, 992–997
"Sliding downhill," 297–299
Small computer systems interface SCSI, 8
smooth_ image(), 725
Software; *see also* Programs
compatibility of, 12
device driver, 8–9, 10
reuse of, 690
solve(), 454–457, 810, 819, 821
sort_ data(), 682–684, 690, 852–857, 920–921, 930–931
sort_ down(), 930
Sorted arrays, 658, 677–687, 688–690
Sorted tables, 656–657
Sorting
bsearch(), 918, 931–934
bubble, 678f
command-line arguments and, 926–934, 935
dynamic arrays in, 793–794
errors with, 690
exchange, 678f
by finding the minimum, 684–687
insertion; *see* Insertion sort
quick; *see* Quicksort
radix, 896
recursion and, 874
by selection, 677–687, 688, 910
Source code, 20, 21, 945, 947
creating files for, 30–31

text editor and, 28
translators and, 29
Source code files, 30–31, 944, 946–947
for **tools** library, 1008, 1013
Spacing, 146, 235, 495
speed(), 706
Spline curve fitting, 209
Split point, 893, 901–907
sq_ sum(), 396–398
sqrt(), 143, 145, 147, 155, 157, 387
srand(), 261–264, 271, 323, 910
sroot, 458
Stack diagrams, 879–880, 909
Stack frames, 878–879
Stack overflow, 881
Standard C, 14, 1026–1040
Standard deviation, 384–391, 664
Standard I/O library, 45, 139
header file for, 142
streams and, 599–602
strings and, 493–501; *see also* String library
Standard input stream, 48, 51
Standard libraries, 139–140, 947, 1012, 1028–1040; *see also* Libraries
header file for, 142
quicksort in, 927
return behavior of functions in, 507f
Standard output stream, 48
Stars, 459; *see also* Asterisks
Statements, 21, 44, 46
compound, 81–82
conditional, 60–70; *see also* **if** statement/loop; **if... else** statement/loop
in Echo Program, 51–52
functions and, 148
loop; *see* Loops
parsing; *see* Parse trees/parsing
simple, 81
static, 95f, 666, 689, 874, 875–877, 908, 977
errors with, 911
in Heat Transfer Program, 957–958
in Roots of Equation Program, 964
run-time stack and, 878–879
style and, 910, 978
verbose_ print() and, 971
Static allocation area, 875
Static storage, 875–877
Static variables, 666
Statistical measures
arrays and, 384–398
Chauvenet's, 658, 664–677
least squares fit, 209, 391–398

bitfield, 759–771, 772, 773, 774
compound, 366
enumerated; *see* Enumerated types
errors in matching, 83, 143, 248, 251–252, 323; *see also* Type mismatches
of functions, 141, 147; *see also* Prototypes
generic, 928
global variables and, 333–334
mixing, 246–260
parameter declarations and, 142–143, 356
programmer-defined, 312
structured; *see* Structures
in **tools** library, 1009, 1038–1039

Unary operators, 103, 104–106, 751
Undefined evaluation order, 995
Underflow errors, 292–293, 302
Underscores, 100
Unitialized pointers, 443–444
UNIX, 11, 12, 948
C and, 14
clearscreen() and, 1015
command-line arguments and, 919f, 925
device drivers and, 8
editors in, 28
load module in, 29
local libraries and, 140
makefiles in, 950–954
stream redirection in, 601
tools library and, 1011–1013
two-dimensional arrays and, 710f
UNIX ed, 28
UNIX vi, 28
Unpacking, 758
Unsafe conversions, 246, 247–248, 271
unsigned, 196f, 229, 230–231, 771
bitfield declaration and, 760
casting and, 249–252
conversion of, 247, 249–260, 323
in decoding Internet address, 755
in encryption and decryption, 756–759
hexadecimal notation and, 743–748, 746
pseudo-random numbers and, 263
unsigned char, 411–412

Unsigned integers, 743–748, 1002
unsigned long, 229, 230–231196f
Unsigned numbers, 291, 771
Unsigned shift, 753
unsigned short, 196f, 229, 230–231
Unsigned values, conversion specifiers for, 745
Update expression, in **for** loop, 171, 173–174, 178, 219
Usage errors, 923, 925
User-defined functions, 148–155, 157–162
Utility functions, 139, 672–674, 935
Utility programs, 11

Validation; *see also* Data validation loops; Input validation loops
in Gas Prices Program, 78
if... else for, 69
logical-OR in, 119–120
in Odometer Program, 73–75
password, 517–524
pseudo-random numbers and, 263
Value, call by; *see* Call/pass by value
Values, 94–95
address parameters versus, 559–560
casting pointers versus, 937
command-line arguments and, 936
conditional operator and, 999
errors checking and, 937
initial, 368–369; *see also* Initialization
literal, 54
maximum and minimum, 1027–1028
modules and, 945
pivot, 901, 903–907, 908
return; *see* Return values
simple versus complex, 114f
types of, 46
undefined, 96–97, 248, 303
unsigned; *see* Unsigned integers; Unsigned numbers; Unsigned values
vander(), 334–337, 880
Vararg facility, 1038
Variable-length argument lists, 1038–1039
Variable names, 46, 47, 100–101, 554
arrays and, 399

in Echo Program, 51
errors with, 356
expressions and, 54
for formulas, 272
style and, 272
Variables, 44, 46–47, 95–97
accessibility of, 331–332
assignment statements and, 53
Boolean, 428–432
diagramming of, 96, 97, 99, 100, 129
external, 331–332, 979; *see also* **extern**
global; *see* Global variables
local; *see* Local variables
pointer, 443, 445, 471, 472, 834–835, 838
position, 657–658
scope of, 331
size of, 101
static, 666
storage classes of, 874–877
stream, 605
string; *see* String variables
subscript; *see* Subscripts
visibility of, 331–332
Variance, 384–391, 398, 677
variance(), 385–391, 671–672
Vectors, 748–752, 772, 919, 935
verbose, 967–973, 978
verbose_print, 971, 973
Verification, 35–37
vfprintf(), 1018, 1019
Virtual memory, 924f, 925
Visibility, 331–337, 353
automatic storage and, 875
escape code and, 412–413
external storage and, 877
static storage and, 876–877
storage class and, 908
Visual C++, 34, 1011, 1015
vmax, 120
void, 45, 317, 319, 323–325, 326, 354
arrays and, 383–384
calloc() and, 790, 824
as generic type name, 928
hold() and, 1016–1017
malloc() and, 788–789, 824
qsort() and, 929, 931, 935
void:void, 147, 148–151, 323
volatile, 95f
Voltage Ramp Program, 120–123
volume, 327

Walking on memory, 375–378
Warning messages, 143, 248, 330, 618f
hold() and, 1017
matrix and, 730

pointers and, 863
void pointer and, 788f
wchar.h, 1040
wctype.h, 1040
Web, 9–10
when(), 506–507, 1020–1022
while statement/loop, 70–75, 170; *see also* **do... while** statement/loop
comparison operators and, 115
continue and, 177–178
data validation loops with, 187–188
errors with, 83, 218
hold() and, 1016–1017
if... break statement and, 175–176
increment and, 111–112
input errors and, 598
in Numerical Integration Program, 160–161
in quicksort, 907
sentinel loops with, 189
in Skylight Controller Program, 770
for statement and, 170, 171–174
strings and, 503
style and, 217
Whitespace, 413, 432, 495, 498–499
scanf() and, 414, 417
style and, 434
Wide-character handling, 1040
Wide-character input and output, 1040
Wide-string handling, 1040
Wind Speed Calculation Program, 707–709
Windowing systems, 11, 12, 1011
graphics packages for, 565
menus in, 509–510
Windows, processing, 703
wipe(), 822
Wire Gauge Adequacy Evaluation Program, 198
Word processors, 28
Words and bytes, 4, 4f, 101
work(), 184–186, 345, 432
design steps and, 341
in Fin Temperature Program, 345
in Gas Pressure Table, 531, 532–534
testing and, 343
Work, delegated, 571
Workmaster, improving, 423–424
Workstations, 11, 101
int and, 230
virtual memory on, 924–925
World Wide Web, 9–10

Wrapping, 288, 291, 302, 1002
write_ file, 680–682, 796
Writing binary matrix data,
    709–710

Writing data to files, 608–612,
    683

Writing unsigned integers, 745

x, 320
xlow, 467–470
xmid, 469, 470
XOR, 751

xup, 467–470
y, 319, 320
z, 320
Zero test, 457